Success and Failure in Arms Control Negotiations

sipri

Stockholm International Peace Research Institute

SIPRI is an independent international institute for research into problems of peace and conflict, especially those of arms control and disarmament. It was established in 1966 to commemorate Sweden's 150 years of unbroken peace.

The Institute is financed mainly by the Swedish Parliament. The staff, the Governing Board and the Scientific Council are international.

The Governing Board and the Scientific Council are not responsible for the views expressed in the publications of the Institute.

Governing Board

Ambassador Dr Inga Thorsson, Chairman (Sweden)
Egon Bahr (Federal Republic of Germany)
Professor Francesco Calogero (Italy)
Dr Max Jakobson (Finland)
Professor Dr Karlheinz Lohs (German Democratic Republic)
Professor Emma Rothschild (United Kingdom)
Sir Brian Urquhart (United Kingdom)
The Director

Director

Dr Walther Stützle (Federal Republic of Germany)

sipri

Stockholm International Peace Research Institute
Pipers väg 28, S-171 73 Solna, Sweden
Cable: PEACERESEARCH STOCKHOLM
Telephone: 46 8/55 97 00

Success and Failure in Arms Control Negotiations

April Carter

sipri

Stockholm International Peace Research Institute

OXFORD UNIVERSITY PRESS
1989

Oxford University Press, Walton Street, Oxford OX2 6DP
Oxford New York Toronto
Delhi Bombay Calcutta Madras Karachi
Petaling Jaya Singapore Hong Kong Tokyo
Nairobi Dar es Salaam Cape Town
Melbourne Auckland
and associated companies in
Berlin Ibadan

Oxford is a trade mark of Oxford University Press

Published in the United States
by Oxford University Press, New York

© SIPRI 1989

British Library Cataloguing in Publication Data
Carter, April
  Success and failure in arms control negotiations.
  SIPRI Monographs
  1. Nuclear weapons. Arms control. International
  cooperation, history I. Title II. Stockholm
  International Peace Research Institute III. Series
  327.1'74
ISBN 0–19–829128–0

Library of Congress Cataloging in Publication Data
Carter, April
  Success and failure in arms control negotiations
  SIPRI—Stockholm International Peace Research Institute—T.p.
  Includes index.
  1. Nuclear arms control—United States. 2. Nuclear arms
  control—Soviet Union. I. Stockholm International
  Peace Research Institute. II. Title
  JX1947.7.C345   1989   327.1'74—dc20   89–8610
ISBN 0–19–829128–0

Typeset and originated by Stockholm International Peace Research Institute
Printed and bound in
Great Britain by Biddles Ltd.,
Guildford and King's Lynn

Contents

Preface

Forty years after the founding of NATO, the prospects for a fundamental change in the relations between the Soviet Union and the West, and for significant progress in arms control, appear brighter than ever before. Still, major fundamental differences remain. This survey is focused on the major arms control negotiations on nuclear and conventional weapons between the USA and the USSR which have been conducted during the last 30 years. The basic objective was to identify, and to examine critically, those factors which both promoted success and led to failure in past negotiations. This volume primarily presents a political assessment of arms control talks. Scientific, technological and strategic issues inevitably figure largely in any assessment, however, and these issues are examined with respect to their political implications for arms control negotiations. Writing this kind of survey necessitates making many political judgements. These judgements are entirely mine.

I am grateful to SIPRI for making it possible for me to use their library resources during the summer months of 1984 through 1986. I also owe a debt of gratitude to Owen Greene for helpful comments on an earlier draft of most chapters and to Jane Sharp for an overview of the entire manuscript. Don Odom has been responsible for editing the typescript and for preparing camera-ready copy. I am greatly indebted to him for his skill, enthusiasm and hard work in getting this book ready for publication. Above all, I am grateful to Frank Blackaby for his advice on the outline of the book and for detailed comments on each chapter. Any errors or misjudgements contained in the text, however, remain my sole responsibility.

Banbury, UK, June 1989   APRIL CARTER

Acronyms

ABM	anti-ballistic missile
ACDA	Arms Control and Disarmament Agency
AEC	Atomic Energy Commission
ALCM	air-launched cruise missile
ARPA	Advanced Research Projects Agency
ASAT	anti-satellite
BWC	Biological Weapons Convention
CBM	confidence-building measure
CD	Conference on Disarmament
CDE	Conference on Disarmament in Europe
CFE	Conventional Forces in Europe negotiations
CIA	Central Intelligence Agency
CFE	Conventional Armed Forces in Europe talks
CPSU	Communist Party of the Soviet Union
CSBM	confidence- and security-building measure
CSCE	Conference on Security and Cooperation in Europe
CTB	comprehensive test ban
CTBT	comprehensive test ban treaty
DDR&E	Director Defense Research and Engineering
DOD	Department of Defense
DOE	Department of Energy
ENDC	Eighteen-Nation Disarmament Committee
FBS	forward-based systems
GLCM	ground-launced cruise missile
ICBM	intercontinental ballistic missile
INF	intermediate-range nuclear forces
ISA	International Security Affairs
JCS	Joint Chiefs of Staff
MAD	mutual assured destruction
MBFR	Mutual and Balanced Force Reduction talks

MIRV	multiple independently targetable re-entry vehicle
MOD	Ministry of Defence
NATO	North Atlantic Treaty Organization
NNA	neutral and non-aligned states
NPT	Non-Proliferation Treaty
NSA	National Security Agency
NSC	National Security Council
NTM	national technical means (of verfication)
OST	Outer Space Treaty
PNE	peaceful nuclear explosion
PNET	Peaceful Nuclear Explosions Treaty
PTBT	Partial Test Ban Treaty
R&D	research and development
SALT	Strategic Arms Limitation Talks
SBT	Sea-Bed Treaty
SDI	Strategic Defense Initiative
SLBM	submarine-launched ballistic missile
SLCM	sea-launched cruise missile
SRINF	shorter-range intermediate nuclear forces
START	Strategic Arms Reduction Talks
TNDC	Ten-Nation Disarmament Committee
TNF	theatre nuclear forces
TTB	threshold test ban
TTBT	Threshold Test Ban Treaty
USAF	United States Air Force
WTO	Warsaw Treaty Organization

1. Clarifying the problem

I. Introduction

Since the end of World War II, there have been numerous negotiations to limit arms. The United Nations General Assembly and its Disarmament Commission have debated ambitious proposals for general disarmament. The Geneva Conference on Disarmament (CD), set up with 18 countries in 1962 and now composed of 40 states, has had a comprehensive test ban (CTB) for nuclear devices on its agenda since 1962 and a chemical weapons ban since 1968. Member states of the North Atlantic Treaty Organization (NATO) and the Warsaw Treaty Organization (WTO) have debated conventional force reductions since 1973 in Vienna. The USA and the USSR have also held a series of bilateral talks on curbing nuclear missiles: the most recent round opened in Geneva in 1985 with separate negotiations on Intermediate-range Nuclear Forces (INF), Strategic Arms Reductions (START) and Space Weapons. These talks resulted in one striking success—the Treaty between the USA and the USSR on the elimination of their intermediate-range and shorter-range missiles (the INF Treaty) signed in December 1987. The much more difficult issues of curbing strategic and space weapons, however, were left on the agenda for the new Bush Administration in 1989.

The degree of hostility between Moscow and Washington has influenced the likelihood of agreement. During the period of acute cold war from the late 1940s to the early 1950s, almost no progress on arms control was achieved. The first breakthrough was the 1959 Antarctic Treaty, whereby states with an interest in that region, including the USA and the USSR, agreed to reserve the Antarctic region for purely peaceful purposes. Between 1963 and 1976, there were a series of arms control agreements and treaties of varying significance, both of a bilateral (between the USA and the USSR), as well as a multilateral character.

From the mid-1970s until the mid-1980s, relations between Moscow and Washington greatly deteriorated. Despite the chill in superpower relations, the Strategic Arms Limitation Talks (SALT) process, which began in 1969 and resulted in the signing of SALT I in 1972, produced the SALT II Treaty, a second agreement to limit strategic nuclear arms. SALT II, signed in 1979 amid growing US–Soviet discord, was never ratified by the US Senate. During the subsequent five years of renewed cold war, no arms control agreements were concluded, and the idea of arms control was under attack in the USA.

Nevertheless, both the second Reagan Administration (elected at the end of 1984) and the new Gorbachev administration (which assumed power in the USSR in 1985) began to demonstrate a desire for renewed *détente* and to achieve some progress in arms control. The summit meetings at Geneva in late 1985 and at Reykjavik in October 1986 dramatized this desire.

During the Reykjavik consultations, radical proposals for nuclear disarmament were tabled by both sides, but the summit meeting broke down in recriminations. Rapid progress on an INF agreement, however, followed and eventually resulted in a triumphant Washington summit meeting in December 1987 at which the INF Treaty was signed. Although the prospects for arms control appear brighter and more promising in the later 1980s than they have for many years, the obstacles to major cuts in nuclear or conventional arms remain formidable. Despite many complex and lengthy negotiations, and despite a number of specific agreements, the result of these efforts to curb arms has been decidedly meagre to date.

II. A multifaceted global proliferation problem

The period since 1945 has witnessed a dramatic arms buildup worldwide. Global investment in conventional arms has sky-rocketed, and the arms trade to the less developed countries greatly expanded in the 1970s.[1] There are five declared nuclear weapon states: the USA, the USSR, China, Great Britain and France. Israel is known to possess nuclear weapon capability[2] and India to have conducted a nuclear explosion. The question of whether South Africa is now a nuclear weapon state has been hotly debated, and Pakistan appears to be moving rapidly towards acquiring a nuclear capacity. Several other countries could acquire nuclear weapons within a short period of time. The world stockpile of nuclear warheads—now estimated at about 50 000—is rapidly growing. In addition, there are also thousands of missiles and bombers with which to deliver these warheads to their targets.

The sheer quantity of arms, as disconcerting as it is, represents only one dimension of the problem. According to most experts, the greatest dangers are those posed by rapid technological development. In the nearly 45 years after Hiroshima and Nagasaki, a qualitative arms competition has resulted in the development of the hydrogen and neutron bombs, as well as the miniaturization of nuclear warheads. This qualitative technological competition has also resulted in the development and deployment of the intercontinental ballistic missile (ICBM), multiple independently re-targetable warheads (MIRVs) and the modern cruise missile. Missile accuracy has greatly increased. This development has encouraged the development of nuclear war-fighting scenarios and has aroused fears of a pre-emptive first strike during a crisis. Today, new technologies, designed to destroy satellites and to create a shield against ballistic missiles, are on the verge of leading to a much greater militarization of space.

Technological change is, moreover, greatly enhancing the range and destructiveness of conventional weapons, and blurring the distinction between weapons which can fire conventional and nuclear warheads. The military utility of deadly nerve gases has been enhanced by the new binary method of production (which makes them safer to handle), while recent developments in genetic engineering are increasing the military feasibility of biological warfare—the selective spreading of disease and plague. From a global perspective, therefore, it can be cogently argued that negotiations to restrain or to cut armaments have singularly failed.

III. Arms control negotiations: a record of partial success

Although the public's hopes and expectations from arms control negotiations have not been fulfilled, the talks to limit arms can claim some success. A long list of agreements, mostly dating from the 1960s and 1970s, can be cited. The important question, then, seems to be: why have *some* arms control negotiations failed? This question encourages us to focus more precisely on why agreement has proved impossible in particular negotiations; for example, why has a nuclear CTB—on the arms control agenda for 32 years—proved to be so elusive.

Although it is useful to narrow the field of enquiry, it is possible to be too focused in one's approach. Merely reaching an agreement is scarcely a sufficient criterion of success in arms control; much depends on the specific content of the agreement. Certainly, various measures for judging the success of an arms control agreement are possible: for example, whether all of the relevant parties have signed and ratified it, the duration and scope of the agreement, and whether or not it is subsequently honoured. These specific considerations, however, can be subsumed under the main criterion that is usually and quite rightly used to assess particular agreements: whether or not the long-term goal of curbing arms is promoted by it. From this standpoint, it is usually accepted that some agreements deal with issues that are militarily peripheral, although these agreements may, nevertheless, help to foreclose possible future developments. Other agreements are clearly 'cosmetic', designed mainly to give an impression of progress and goodwill when more substantive issues cannot be resolved. Still others actually do aim to impose a ban on important (or potentially important) weapon developments.

There is no consensus on the usefulness of various treaties, nor on the categories in which they should be placed. Many would accept that the 1967 Outer Space Treaty (OST) and the 1971 Sea-Bed Treaty (SBT) fall into the category of marginal agreements, banning deployments not seriously envisaged at the time. The OST forbids the placement of nuclear weapons in earth orbit or on celestial bodies (but not on missiles passing through space), whereas the SBT prohibits the placement of nuclear weapons on the floor of the seas and the oceans (but not on submarines). Even marginal agreements, however, may foreclose unforeseen military developments. The OST has gained in political significance because it precludes some of the potential elements of the US Strategic Defense Initiative (SDI) programme. For the most part, arms control advocates were bitterly critical of the 1974 Threshold Test Ban Treaty (TTBT) between the USA and the USSR, which banned underground tests with a yield over 150 kilotons, on the grounds that the Treaty does not stop most militarily significant testing and is a diversion from a CTB. The TTBT, therefore, might qualify as a cosmetic agreement. The agreement most widely considered to be a real contribution to arms control was the 1972 Anti-Ballistic Missile (ABM) Treaty between the USA and the USSR which halted the development of anti-missile systems on both sides.

IV. Arms control or disarmament?

The goal of negotiations may either be limited arms control or varying degrees of disarmament. Disarmament implies reducing arms, or banning them altogether, on the assumption that a military buildup is in itself a major source of tension and promotes the likelihood of war. A general reduction in arms was the goal of a League of Nations Conference in 1932. This theme was put back on the agenda in the proposals made by the great powers in the late 1940s and early 1950s in which total nuclear disarmament and major cuts in conventional arms were envisaged. During the height of the cold war, disarmament proposals had a purely propagandistic tone. During the thaw of the mid-1950s, however, a brief period of more serious negotiations on the possibility of disarmament occurred. After an agreement between the US and Soviet governments on broad general principles, new proposals concerning general and complete disarmament were tabled in 1962. This goal has been espoused by the United Nations General Assembly in three special sessions (1978, 1982 and 1988).

In the view of many observers, ambitious schemes for disarmament seemed to be doomed to failure. One response to the dismal negotiating record of the 1950s—the 'arms control' approach—was developed by strategic theorists in the West around 1960 at about the same time as theories of nuclear deterrence were being elaborated in detail.[3] Initially, arms control advocates sharply distinguished themselves from proponents of disarmament, because the aim of arms control was not necessarily to abolish or minimize arms, but to create a stable military balance. In some circumstances, this might necessitate an *increase,* rather than a decrease, of military forces. Indeed, the original school of arms control theorists stressed the desirability of the USA and the USSR retaining nuclear weapons so as to ensure mutual deterrence. This school of thought also held the opinion that political conflict, rather than a military buildup, was the primary cause of tension. Nevertheless, these early theorists were concerned with the avoidance of war, either by technological accident or by political miscalculation, and the prevention of destabilizing developments in nuclear weaponry.

Arms control: divergent Western and Soviet views

The initial Soviet response to the theory of arms control was hostile, partly because the theory was associated with the kind of US strategic thinking which Soviet commentators criticized and partly because of the unfortunate connotations of 'control' in the Russian language. The word 'control' in Russian implies 'inspection' or 'regulation'—the issues which most bitterly divided the USSR from the West in disarmament negotiations of the 1950s. Moreover, the USSR has remained strongly committed to the principle that the aim must be general and comprehensive disarmament, and not simply a sophisticated juggling of the military balance. To some degree, this position may represent a public propaganda stance, but it may also reflect certain differences in perception between the Soviet and the Western governments.[4]

The theoretical divergences between Western governments and the Soviet Union concerning the question of arms control did not, however, prevent Moscow from negotiating on more limited issues in the late 1950s and early 1960s. The USSR has always recognized the need to avoid accidental war—a priority enshrined in the 1963 Hot Line Agreement. Moreover, the USSR and the USA have a number of common interests related to ensuring nuclear stability; and during the 1960s, the Soviet leadership moved towards a more explicit acceptance of this goal. Even the linguistic misunderstanding of the term 'arms control' was also gradually removed.

In the West, the original sharp theoretical differences between the theories of disarmament and arms control have also been eroded. Advocates of both perspectives agree that one major aim is to save some of the vast economic resources devoted to military ends. Many prominent arms controllers, notably Robert McNamara while he was US Secretary of Defense, have espoused some form of arms race theory. Many committed supporters of arms control now believe in the need for measures which could lead incrementally to halting and reversing arms competition, and may even accept disarmament as an ultimate goal. Particularly in the USA, arms control is the politically respectable rubric covering a wide range of viewpoints concerning defence and arms limitation.

Apart from theoretical considerations, rigid distinctions between arms control and disarmament are also unsatisfactory in practice. Quite often, when it comes to negotiating agreements, it may be possible to combine both arms control and disarmament goals in one measure. A good example is one of the most important agreements reached to date: the Non-Proliferation Treaty (NPT) of 1968. From the standpoint of arms control, the stability of mutual deterrence between the two major powers might be endangered by irrational or erratic behaviour by a minor nuclear power. The prevention of nuclear weapon proliferation, therefore, has become a major preoccupation of arms controllers. From a disarmament standpoint, however, the pledge by the non-nuclear signatories to abstain from acquiring nuclear weapons greatly enhances the possibility of general nuclear disarmament in the future, however remote that goal may appear now.

Arms control and disarmament goals also overlap with respect to efforts aimed at banning particularly destructive weapons. Although the primary goal of arms control is the prevention of war, an important secondary objective is the limitation of damage should war break out. Thus, the 1972 Biological Weapons Convention (BWC), which forbids the production or stockpiling of biological and toxin weapons, may be regarded as a damage-limitation measure. The BWC, however, also resulted in the actual destruction of stocks. Therefore, the Convention has also been hailed as a significant measure of disarmament.[5]

V. Measuring success in arms control

The theoretical criticisms associated with arms control and disarmament are relevant to the main theme of this book. On the one hand, certain ideas behind arms control may help to explain why states, concerned with their military security, have always hesitated to commit themselves to comprehensive disarmament agreements. One difficult problem is how to maintain a military balance between participants throughout all stages of the disarmament process and to quell the inevitable fears of cheating. On the other hand, the case for disarmament suggests why limited arms control measures have so often failed.[6] Advocates of disarmament have argued the need to move away from purely military interpretations of security and have stressed the ineffectiveness of partial measures of arms control that only serve to channel arms competition into new areas. Therefore, limited arms control agreements do not serve to actually curb the momentum of weapon research and development. These issues are explored in more detail in later chapters.

The real purpose of arms control negotiations

Arms control and détente

The primary purpose behind arms limitation talks may not be to curb arms at all. Sometimes talks are conducted for the purpose of maintaining or promoting diplomatic relations (an important element in US–Soviet negotiations during the 1970s). Indeed, the criterion for the success of talks may sometimes have had less to do with the content of an agreement than its perceived contribution to *détente*. A good example of this may be the SALT I accords which were judged partly from this standpoint. The promotion of *détente* was perhaps the most significant contribution made by the first major arms control agreement between the USA and the USSR: the 1963 Partial Test Ban Treaty (PTBT). The PTBT has often been criticized from the standpoint of arms control; although the Treaty did reduce pollution of the atmosphere by nuclear testing, it did not reduce the *rate* of testing, which continued underground. Nevertheless, despite the fact that the PTBT did not result in any genuine check on nuclear weapon developments, it symbolized a new understanding between Moscow and

Washington, and set in motion a process which led to a series of further arms control agreements.

The relationship between arms control agreements and *détente* is controversial. A key question is whether arms control promotes *détente,* or simply is one of the by-products of improved political relations. Commentators have also queried whether arms control agreements necessarily promote *détente* at all. If one side comes to view an agreement as 'unequal', then it may become a cause of tension; to some extent, this process occurred within the United States in reaction to SALT I. Accusations of arms control treaty violations (whether or not they are valid) may also promote distrust and hostility. To reach an agreement at all, it seems that some degree of good will is required. Certainly, an agreement to limit arms cannot maintain good will if it is otherwise in short supply. Still, the mere fact of an agreement can symbolize and strengthen moves towards closer political ties. The strength of this effect may, however, be related to the actual content of an agreement and whether or not it appears to reflect a genuine commitment to arms control by the signatories.

Promoting *détente* is a goal closely linked to arms control and involves seeking mutual benefit in various forms of co-operation, even if there is also continued competition. Quite often, states enter into talks, designed ostensibly to promote mutual reductions in arms and mutual security, with the aim of gaining some quite different unilateral advantage.[7] Proposals for talks and various moves during talks may be intended to win diplomatic prestige or to embarrass an opponent. Negotiations may be designed either to reassure allies or to defuse public anxiety at home, or to be a convenient substitute for actual arms control. Failure can be blamed on the other side. In some cases, arms control talks serve to protect military programmes or commitments, such as the case of the decision by the Nixon Administration in 1973 to initiate negotiations on mutual force reductions in Europe at a time when the US Senate was threatening to cut US forces in Europe by half. During the negotiations, the Senate was dissuaded from pressing for unilateral cuts.[8]

VI. Conclusion

Thus far, our discussion has assumed that governments undertake negotiations for coherent, if sometimes cynical, purposes. The reality, however, is often more complex. Governments are not unitary actors exercising a single will to achieve completely coherent goals; bureaucracies and vested interests also compete to promote certain points of view. Indeed, some institutions and groups are likely to be more favourable to arms control than others, and others may be vehemently opposed. Therefore, a negotiating position, more often than not, is the outcome of domestic conflict or a compromise on a 'lowest common denominator' on which all parties can agree.

Reflection upon the reality of arms control suggests numerous reasons why negotiations fail. Nevertheless, a list of general reasons (elaborated in chapter 2) provides only a starting point for the analysis. To explain properly the causes of failure, as well as the possible factors promoting success, it is necessary to examine a full range of possible explanations and to consider whether (or to what degree) they apply to specific historical cases. The aim of this approach is to assess the degree of importance to be attached to different kinds of explanation.

The use of case studies may also reveal the degree to which arms control negotiations have failed at two levels: the significant omissions from specific agreements that have been reached and the negotiations which have to date ended in no agreement at all. Taken together, these two criteria almost add up to the broader concept of failure: the fact that there has been, in effect, no real restraint in the buildup of arms. The omission of multiple warhead missiles from SALT I, for example, indicates how agreements have failed to check crucial technological developments, and the failure to conclude a nuclear CTB suggests the strength of obstacles to significant arms control. Even so, individual case studies of negotiations may not fully encapsulate the key reasons for lack of success in curbing arms. Therefore, it may be relevant to ask why some issues have never been included on the arms control agenda or have only surfaced at a propaganda level. Certainly, the fundamental obstacles to arms control and disarmament must be examined within a total political and strategic context in order to be properly understood.

Most of the case studies in this book illustrate degrees of success, as well as of failure. Indeed, when one studies the record of particular negotiations, the reasons for success or failure often appear to be intertwined. Therefore, it may be illuminating to examine in more general terms some of the forces that have encouraged governments to negotiate in the first place and have promoted particular agreements. That task is reserved for the final chapter.

Notes and references

[1] For a current discussion of global military expenditure and its relationship to the debt crisis, see Deger, S., 'World military expenditure', SIPRI, *SIPRI Yearbook 1989: World Armaments and Disarmament* (Oxford University Press: Oxford, 1989), pp. 133–77.

[2] The revelations by an Israeli nuclear technician, Mordechai Vanunu, suggest that Israel possesses a nuclear arsenal of at least 100 weapons. Israel's declared policy has remained ambiguous on its nuclear weapon status. See *Sunday Times* (London), 5 and 12 Oct. 1986. See also Cohen, A. and Frankel, B., 'Israel's nuclear ambiguity', *Bulletin of the Atomic Scientists*, vol. 43, no. 2 (Mar. 1987), pp. 15–19.

[3] Two classical statements of arms control theory can be found in: Bull, H., *The Control of the Arms Race* (Weidenfeld and Nicolson: London, 1961), and Brennan, D. G. (ed.), *Arms Control and Disarmament* (Jonathan Cape: London, 1961).

[4] See, for example, Sheynin, Y., 'Disarmament or "balance of terror"?', *Survival*, vol. 3, no. 3 (Nov.–Dec. 1961); and Shulman, M.D., 'SALT: through the looking glass', eds W. H. Kincade and J. D. Porro, *Negotiating Security: An Arms Control Reader* (The Carnegie Endowment for International Peace: Washington, DC, 1979), pp. 21–22.

[5] See, for example, Sims, N. A., *Approaches to Disarmament: An Introductory Analysis* (Quaker Peace and Service: London, 1979), revised and expanded edition, p. 75.

[6] Noel Baker, P. J., *Disarmament* (Garland Publishing Inc: New York, 1972), first published 1926, pp. 7–25 and 48–65.

[7] This is what Iklé has termed 'negotiating for side-effects'. See Iklé, F. C., *How Nations Negotiate* (Harper and Row: New York, 1964), especially chapter 4.

[8] It is often argued that anxiety to ward off congressional pressure to reduce troops in Europe was a major reason for embarking on the MBFR negotiations. See, for example, Meyer, S. M., 'The changing context of MBFR', eds W. H. Kincade, N. V. Yinger and G. C. Duffy, *Approaches to East–West Arms Control* (Arms Control Association: Washington, DC, 1979).

2. A framework for analysis

I. Introduction

The general literature on arms control and disarmament reflects the changes in political perceptions, as well as shifts in academic interests. Moreover, a specific analysis of the obstacles to agreement on limiting arms also reflects these changing emphases. During the late 1950s and early 1960s, pessimism concerning the achievement of comprehensive disarmament was often combined with optimism about the prospects for more limited agreements to reduce the risk of war and to curb weapon developments. This optimism was sustained by such important agreements as the 1963 PTBT and the 1968 NPT, and by the fact that the USA and the USSR initiated SALT, the first negotiations concerned with the constraint of central strategic arsenals, in 1969. It was during the course of negotiations for the SALT II Treaty that a demonstrable shift in attitudes toward arms limitation occurred.

Primarily, criticism of the entire process of arms control negotiations came from two separate quarters. The first grouping—political, military and academic figures in the United States (whose main concern was a buildup of US and Western military strength)—criticized arms control talks for undermining and distorting US military planning, and levelled perhaps the most politically significant and most damaging criticism against SALT II and other possible agreements. These critics tended toward the view that the Soviet Union has not genuinely sought arms control, but instead has achieved a unilateral advantage through SALT.[1] There have always been committed opponents of arms control in the United States, but the lobby opposed to negotiations acquired greater political weight in the late 1970s. President Reagan's first Administration particularly reflected the influence of this lobby. Included within this grouping were those who were totally opposed to any form of arms control and others who were prepared to accept that perhaps some agreed restraints were desirable. Nevertheless, the overall aim in the late 1970s was to put the United States into a position to negotiate from military strength, if not from outright superiority.

Disillusioned arms controllers have been the other major source of criticism. Although they view the restriction of arms as both a desirable and necessary goal, many do not believe it will be achieved through the present process of negotiations. Indeed, some of them have argued that the effect of the present approach to arms control negotiations is—in practice—actually to encourage an *arms buildup*. This, they contend, directly contradicts the avowed aim of the talks.[2] The exponents of this type of criticism tend, therefore, to advocate forms of tacit unilateral restraint in weapon programmes and the implementation of unilateral initiatives. Some go further and recommend more radical forms of unilateral disarmament. This grouping includes political and academic representatives of the arms control community in the United States and in Europe, and theorists from the peace movements who became prominent in the early 1980s. It also reflects the views of many non-aligned observers impatient with the great power record on arms control. The principal characteristic of this grouping, then, is diversity; it includes both the advocates of 'arms control' in the technical sense, as well as advocates of genuine disarmament. This grouping has gained in influence since the mid-1970s.

There have been interesting shifts of emphasis in the academic literature concerning the problems related to arms limitation. During the 1950s and 1960s, the analysis tended to reflect the view that arms limitation problems stem from the nature of international relations and the perceived need to maintain military defence. At a more concrete level, commentators focused on the specific conflict between the two major powers since 1945—the United States and the Soviet Union. The differences in ideology, domestic politics, geopolitical position and military strategy between the two great powers all underlined the extreme difficulty of reaching agreement on mutually beneficial arms reductions. Political analysis was supplemented by a number of psychological commentaries which pointed to the role of fear, suspicion, over-simplification and stereotyping in perceptions of an opponent, and suggested that these were significant obstacles to arms limitation.

By the 1970s, the focus of the analysis began to shift from treating states as unitary actors (whether in the arms race or in arms control talks) to an emphasis upon the role of competing domestic institutions in policy making. This approach also stressed the irrationality that may result from the pressure of competing interests. Viewed from this perspective, the decisions to acquire arms, or the decisions concerning their limitation, are not simply rational responses to the actions or proposals of the other side, but the outcome of intricate bureaucratic manœuvring. Indeed, a number of academic commentators sought to explain some of the special difficulties involved in arms control talks through an application of this kind of analysis to the negotiating process. Another theme that received considerable scrutiny during the 1970s was that of the possible impact on arms control from the momentum of technological research and development, a process that incessantly churns out new weapons and strategic possibilities that need to be controlled—that is, if any kind of stability in the military balance between the great powers is to be achieved.[3]

Of course, this summary of analytic trends is, necessarily, over-simplified. Certainly, observers of military and arms control developments in the 1960s were aware both of domestic factors and of the significance of technological research and development in influencing government decisions. Recent commentators have, moreover, frequently pointed to problems for arms control that arise out of international politics, or to the specific nature of the conflict between the major powers and their differing approaches to strategic and arms control issues.[4] It is clear however that, over time, shifts in intellectual emphasis have occurred and have resulted in a wide range of explanations for the comparative failure of arms control talks.

The major obstacles to disarmament that arise out of interstate competition and out of mutual fear and suspicion (as well as the resistance of vested domestic interests) serve to impede negotiations for more limited arms control, although the difficulties may be less acute than for proposals concerning general disarmament. On the other hand, some of the reasons given for the failure of partial agreements to curb the arms race—for example, the momentum of weapon development and the tendency of agreements simply to channel arms competition—would not apply to total disarmament. Because complete disarmament—or even abandonment of central weapons—still appears to be a chimera, this chapter concentrates on the possible causes for the failure of more limited arms control talks.

Because the main competition in arms occurs between the United States and the Soviet Union, and because agreement between them is essential for the success of multilateral treaties (except for certain regional pacts), it is not surprising that much of the literature focuses on difficulties between these two states. Many of these problems are inherent in relations between any major powers. A number of examples can be cited from the conferences on limiting arms between the two world wars, as well as from the US–Soviet confrontation since 1945. Nevertheless, this confrontation has had features unique to it, in particular, that of an ideological conflict between the leading capitalist and leading socialist power. Therefore, the next section examines the obstacles to agreement between the USA and the USSR in some detail. Some additional barriers to negotiations, which may result when other countries (in addition to the two great powers) are involved, are considered briefly in section III. Finally, factors promoting success in arms control negotiations are examined in section IV.

The aim of this chapter, which draws on the existing literature concerning the difficulties encountered in arms control negotiations, is not only to summarize the arguments that are used, but also to set out a comprehensive set of possible explanations for the overall failure of arms control to date. Any classification of these explanations into different categories is bound to be rather arbitrary; indeed, these explanations overlap in real life. For example, perceptions of a threat to national security or prestige strengthen domestic resistance; and the conduct of negotiations reflects international tensions and domestic pressures. It is helpful, however, to distinguish between different types of explanation.

II. Obstacles to agreement between the USA and the USSR

The propaganda contest

Many of the problems in negotiations between the USA and the USSR arise from the fact (see chapter 1) that arms control talks are often vehicles for pursuing political competition between the great powers. The propaganda content is usually highest when proposals for sweeping measures of disarmament are on the table, or when the emphasis is on deep cuts in nuclear forces.[5] Still, few arms control talks are entirely free from propaganda. Even when the negotiations are sincere, Moscow and Washington tend to frame proposals with an eye to international propaganda impact or domestic consumption. This possibility is enhanced when negotiations are more or less public, but even in private talks the temptation to consider how the record will appear is always there.

Even when there is some genuine interest in achieving an agreement, the tendency to negotiate partly in order to win a propaganda advantage still retains two major drawbacks. First, policy makers may elevate the propaganda impact of a proposal above the requirement of making it potentially acceptable to the other side. Second, if a proposal smacks of propaganda, then it is reasonable to assume that the government presenting it is not really serious. The opponents of an agreement can claim that the other side is indulging in pure propaganda. Indeed, the mere *expectation* of propaganda may be enough to throw doubt on the sincerity of the other's intentions. Of course, when propaganda is actually the aim of arms control talks—whether to impress non-aligned opinion, to defuse anxiety among allies or to encourage domestic pressures on the other side—the likelihood of agreement is minimized.

The pursuit of prestige

States may seek prestige as a by-product of entering into arms limitation negotiations or from the terms of the final agreement. This is not necessarily an obstacle to serious negotiations; indeed, if the prestige of a state or an individual head of state or chief negotiator is linked to achieving a settlement, it may well serve as a positive spur to agreement. Nevertheless, considerations of prestige can also prompt governments to drag their feet over starting talks, so as not to appear too eager. They may well enter into lengthy 'talks about talks' in which issues such as the venue and the agenda become matters of 'face'. Issues of diplomatic prestige, therefore, may promote one of the greatest nemeses of arms control negotiations—delay.

The central problem for arms control that results from the search for prestige stems from the lamentable fact that, in a world of international power politics, there is a close association between prestige and armaments. The power of a state is measured partly by the size of its armed forces and so, therefore, is its prestige.[6] Some types of weapon system—for example, in the past battleships—

especially symbolize the prestige of military power. Today nuclear weapons and missiles are widely believed to confer superior status; indeed, they have become almost a badge of great power aspiration. Therefore, negotiations designed to curb arms—especially those which are status symbols—not only run up against the intractable difficulties of ensuring military security, but also raise the inevitable issues of national pride. Moreover, the negotiations may result in a shift in the balance of this military prestige from one contender for great power status to another.

Quite often, one of the effects of arms control talks is to promote a quest for parity in the arms under discussion. Although parity, at the outset, may appear to be the most equitable outcome (and therefore the easiest to justify to domestic opinion in most circumstances), the quest for parity is likely to create political, as well as strategic, problems. A state, accustomed to military superiority in a certain area, may have to accept equal status with a competitor. During the inter-war period, the Naval Treaties codified Britain's abandonment of the claim to be the world's greatest naval power and, more or less, established the United States as an equal power.[7] More recently, the SALT process has been regarded as symbolizing an analogous tilting of the balance of nuclear power away from undisputed US superiority towards a recognition of Soviet equality.

The pursuit of political advantage

States usually pursue a wide range of political goals through the process of arms control negotiations. For example, a state may seek to acquire a reputation for peace and disarmament concerns as part of an overall strategy to secure international good will. On the other hand, states may have much more specific objectives, such as the Soviet Union's concern, during the 1950s and 1960s, with the Federal Republic of Germany. In this instance, the Soviet Union first sought to prevent West German rearmament and integration into NATO, and next to ensure that the FRG would never have access to nuclear weapons. Indeed, some Western analysts have concluded that the Soviet Union has been much more interested in clear political gains than in the technicalities of arms control.[8] Certainly, there is not *necessarily* an inherent conflict between seeking political goals and accepting arms control. Nevertheless, it is often implied in this analysis of Soviet behaviour that the commitment to arms control has not been serious and, as a result, that the West has been taken for a ride.[9]

It should be noted, however, that the USA has certainly pursued its political goals as well. One of the USA's major reasons for stressing on-site verification, for example, has been to try to 'open up' the Soviet system.[10] Furthermore, during the 1950s, the United States ensured Western supremacy within the forums where arms limitation was discussed. Indeed, the Soviet Union was not conceded parity of representation until the Ten Nation Disarmament Conference was set up by the UN General Assembly in September of 1959. Maintenance of

Table 2.1. Obstacles to agreement between the USA and the USSR

Great Power Confrontation

>   The propaganda contest
>   Seeking to acquire or maintain prestige
>   Seeking political advantage
>   Political linkage
>   Political conflict
>   Alliance politics
>   Strategic goals in negotiations
>   Strategic asymmetry

Ideological conflict and perceptions

Psychological obstacles

The momentum of weapons technology

Domestic obstacles to arms control

>   Military and bureaucratic resistances in both USA and USSR
>   US political process—Presidential elections and Congress
>   Soviet political process—lack of democratic checks and secrecy

Obstacles in the negotiating process

>   Verification
>   Divergent negotiating styles
>   Bargaining theories and tactics
>   Political organizational and technical problems

Arms control talks promote the arms race

>   Bargaining chips effect
>   Military price tag
>   Parity and levelling-up
>   Channelling (also called the 'displacement effect')
>   Talks consume trust

Soviet inferiority was carried over into proposals for supranational bodies to be responsible for overseeing disarmament measures to be implemented during this period.[11] It is clear, then, that an awareness of political goals can generate distrust and undermine prospects for agreement.

The imposition of political linkage

Political linkage is now often cited as one of the chief obstacles to achieving satisfactory arms control agreements.[12] It was not, however, until President

Richard Nixon and National Security Advisor (later Secretary of State) Henry Kissinger developed the theory of 'linkage' that a coherent strategy of using arms control talks to promote US advantage in relations with the Soviet Union was articulated.[13] Political linkage can refer to two quite different things. It is important to distinguish here between linkage as a deliberate strategy and linkage as an inevitable element in international politics.

A strategy of linking progress in arms control to the general international behaviour of the negotiating partner has been especially associated with the Nixon–Kissinger policies toward the Soviet Union; but in essence, it has been pursued by other US administrations. US policies have also linked *détente* with arms control in an attempt to influence Soviet *domestic* policies, such as those concerning human rights and emigration, either through explicit linkage (as in the case of the Jackson–Vanik Amendment to the 1973 Trade Bill) or by implied linkage (such as that suggested by President Jimmy Carter's rhetoric on human rights). Although the Soviet Union has practised forms of deliberate linkage between different negotiations, and has delayed arms control talks apparently to indicate displeasure at certain US dealings with China, the USSR (perhaps surprisingly) has not adopted linkage as an avowed means of constraining US activities in the Third World. Rather than returning the policy in kind, Moscow's reaction to Washington's linkage attempts has generally been one of anger and indignation.

The second kind of linkage is not based on a specific policy but arises out of the nature of the superpower relationship; some actions by one side may make a negative response inevitable. For example, after Soviet troops entered Czechoslovakia in August 1968, President Lyndon Johnson felt obligated to cancel the inauguration of the SALT negotiations, which were due to begin in September. Although governments retain some degree of discretion in how they choose present the actions of the other side and in deciding what kind of a response is appropriate, US administrations are particularly vulnerable to pressure from public opinion. On the other hand, the Soviet Union twice chose to avoid a break-off of the SALT negotiations, despite the extreme provocation resulting from the USA's invasion of Cambodia and the mining of Haiphong harbour.[14] The linkage that arises out of the superpower relationship can be damaging for the prospects of arms control and is almost impossible to avoid altogether.

The Soviet Union, however, is not always either willing or able to ignore international incidents and crises just for the sake of arms control. Indeed, the USSR may wish to uphold its own national dignity. For example, the dispatch of a US U-2 reconnaissance plane over the Soviet Union—just before the planned summit meeting between First Secretary Nikita Khrushchev and President John Kennedy in May 1960—was perceived as a provocation.[15] The Soviet Union also must weigh its obligations to its allies against the desirability of rapprochement, or agreement, with the United States. The Soviet Union, at times, may feel vulnerable to charges of being too conciliatory.

Political conflict

The general state of the relationship between the two major world powers inevitably affects the conduct of arms control talks. Even though there is an inescapable antagonism inherent in conflicting great power ambitions, these powers may often co-operate to promote international stability and to avoid unnecessary risks of war, and may also establish quite close diplomatic and economic ties. The relationship between the USA and the USSR has been characterized by acute cold war periods of extreme hostility and minimum contact, by periods of relative closeness and *détente,* and by many gradations in between. The total political relationship between the great powers comprises elements of 'linkage', both in terms of a deliberate policy of making arms control talks dependent on other issues and in terms of a response to political crises. The relationship, however, covers the whole spectrum of contacts and conflicts between Moscow and Washington, and involves much more than linkage.

Although political conflict often generates such psychological reactions as fear and distrust, to reduce an explanation of political conflict to just these psychological factors would be an gross over-simplification. Some very real issues of power and national interest are at stake. The central point made by psychological analyses of the role of fear or suspicion is that these attitudes have become exaggerated and detached from existing political realities.

Political competition between the great powers encourages both to accept certain risks to extend their sphere of influence and to pursue policies designed to restrict or put pressure on the other side. For example, the United States has been interested in trying to play the 'China card' since the early 1970s through the promotion of co-operation with Beijing. At times, the Soviet Union may have been encouraged to reach agreement with the USA to limit the dangers of a Sino–US military combination; but in some cases, the USA's moves toward China appear to have been counter-productive for arms control.

Alliance politics

The USA and the USSR are global powers concerned with the maintenance of their existing alliances and with the extension of their spheres of influence. More often than not, bilateral arms control negotiations between the USA and the USSR have had serious implications for the allies of the great powers. In some cases, these consequences may be primarily of an ideological or political nature. In other instances, arms control negotiations may have a direct impact on alliance strategy.

As a result, an important factor in arms control talks may be the pressures and interests of important allies. For example, the United States respected French and British desires to exclude their national nuclear forces from talks on limiting nuclear arms. Further, the USA has acted to reassure European allies concerned that strategic arms limitation could lead to the 'decoupling' of US nuclear deterrence from Europe.[16] Indeed, the question of the USA's nuclear forward-based systems (FBS)—regarded as an essential component of the US nuclear guarantee to its allies world-wide—proved to be a considerable problem in the SALT negotiations. Although the Soviet Union plays a more overtly dominant role in the WTO—despite the case of maverick Romania—even the USSR has had to consider the interests of allied governments in negotiations dealing with Europe. When the China still counted as an ally (even though a troublesome one), Chinese views on peaceful coexistence and nuclear weapons were a significant factor with the Kremlin. By the late 1950s, however, the influence of Chinese views with the Soviet Union had waned. By that time, the views of the Chinese and Khrushchev had become diametrically opposed.[17]

The reverse side of great power concern with avoiding alliance cleavages (as a result of negotiations) is the suspicion that the other side is seeking to create just that sort of division. The Soviet Union is regularly suspected—and often publicly accused—of trying to drive a wedge between the United States and its NATO partners through proposals concerning forward bases or missile cuts.[18] It is difficult to discern whether Soviet proposals primarily reflect genuine strategic concern or, instead, are designed to influence politics within NATO. What makes the task especially difficult is the fact that both motives, to one degree or another, may have played a part simultaneously. With the possible exception of Romania, the United States has apparently not perceived much scope for promoting divisions in the WTO.

Strategic goals in negotiations

Arms control talks are intimately linked to strategic concerns and aims. The natural military tendency, to try to use negotiations to minimize the opponent's advantages while maximizing one's own, may be reflected in the process of negotiations. These strategic goals may be reflected in the nature of the specific proposals that are presented or—perhaps more importantly—in what is *excluded* from a final agreement.

Arms control negotiations may potentially influence an opponent's arms programme even if no agreement is reached. If the mere existence of negotiations serves to encourage a moratorium on certain developments or to discourage new weapon production, and if the talks are then drawn out, they may enable the side previously at a disadvantage to catch up. These motives have often been attributed to the Soviet Union, which has usually been somewhat behind the United States technologically in weapon development.[19] Whether talks have been used deliberately in an attempt to achieve unilateral constraint by the other side, and whether such a tactic is likely to succeed, are questions which remain open for debate. In any event, the mere belief that this is the case may serve to undermine the talks in progress, or may reduce the prospects for serious negotiations in the future.

To propose arms control measures that grant clear military advantages to one's own side is a standard tactic. This approach, however, may be counter-productive if both parties refuse to modify their own proposals significantly, or if the tactic is interpreted as a lack of interest in serious talks. This negotiating tactic has convinced many observers that genuine arms reductions are very nearly impossible. In some cases, biased original proposals may be a bargaining manœuvre that is open to amendment. However, the possibility of the proposals being misperceived in terms of a wholly cynical move (so encouraging intransigence from the other side) suggests that this approach obstructs progress.

Perhaps the most crucial question is the degree to which military commitment to certain programmes, or to the pursuit of strategic advantage, is maintained, especially in the face of what appears to be a serious prospect for agreement. A stronger commitment to unilateral measures to achieve military security, than to the attainment of mutual security through arms control, may either sabotage the chances of agreement, or may result in an agreement that fails to curb central military developments. Therefore, the failure of arms control talks, in either the narrow or the broader sense, is likely to result.

In theory, arms control negotiations can be employed as a means of attempting to discern information concerning the military programmes and deployments, or to uncover the main strategic concerns of an opponent.[20] The Soviet Union has traditionally been much more suspicious of possible 'fishing expeditions' than the United States. These misgivings have resulted from an awareness of technological inferiority, as well as from a tradition of extreme secretiveness concerning the Soviet Union's armed forces and deployments. Soviet suspicion has been especially pronounced with respect to proposals for inspection and verification of disarmament measures. Although only the Soviet Union has expressly stated the fear that inspection could be used as a guise for espionage, the US military has recently indicated some concerns on this score, especially when extensive inspection has been suggested.

Strategic asymmetry

The pursuit of formal parity through arms control negotiations almost immediately encounters the reality of the obstacle of strategic asymmetries. When geography, military tradition and technological choices have resulted in major differences in the strategic postures between opposing powers, it is convenient to seek unilateral military advantage under the guise of urging apparently equal numbers. It is also easy to confuse public opinion and to seek propaganda victories. If negotiations do become serious, then the quest for genuine military equality is made more difficult by asymmetries. There may well be a conflict between formal parity and a fair military balance.

Competing great powers have often had different military priorities and force structures. Salvador de Madariaga has observed that one of the problems of disarmament talks between Britain and France in the 1920s was that the former was traditionally a naval power, while the latter relied heavily on a standing army.[21] The differences between the USA and the USSR today, however, are even more marked.[22]

Geographically, the United States, with a close ally to the north and a long-standing sphere of influence to the south, is less vulnerable to attack than the Soviet Union. When this sense of security is threatened (such as by military bases in Cuba), Washington becomes extremely nervous. The Soviet Union, on the other hand, has a number of hostile (or potentially hostile) states on its borders. After China ceased to be an ally, this especially became the case. However, the Soviet Union, by virtue of its strategic location and its immense area, is much better positioned than the United States to fight a conventional war in Europe.

The West has always viewed the Soviet Union as having actual or potential superiority in terms of numbers of troops. The two superpowers, together with their allies, have traditionally pursued different policies with regard to the development and deployment of conventional armaments. Whereas the USSR has emphasized quantity, the West has placed more reliance on quality. Even so, the qualitative gap in weapon technologies between the two sides has narrowed. From a strategic standpoint, the WTO's and NATO's commitment to different doctrines has been reflected, to an extent, in alliance deployments. Strategic doctrines reflect Moscow's intense fear of surprise attack, on the one hand, and the political concerns of the West German Government to ensure a NATO defence of the FRG's frontier, on the other.

In addition, strategic nuclear planning has resulted in significant differences in nature of the nuclear arsenals of each side. Whereas the USA places more emphasis on bombers, the USSR stresses medium-range missiles. Beginning in the early 1960s, the USA has placed more of its nuclear warheads on submarines, while the USSR has deployed many more on land. Moreover, differences in the technology and design of missiles have complicated the problems of agreeing on what, exactly, constitutes nuclear parity.

III. Ideological conflict and ideologically influenced perceptions

Ideological conflict not only affects the policies and goals of each power, but also the perceptions and suspicions regarding each other. During the cold war of the early 1950s, the Soviet Union espoused the goal of communist victory in the inevitable war with the forces of capitalism, while the United States was committed to rolling back, or at least containing, communism by all available means. Although both countries actually pursued policies much more cautious than the official propaganda of the period indicates, as long as each portrayed the other as a militaristic power seeking global domination, the prospects for any arms limitation were virtually non-existent. After both governments gradually came to accept the need for some form of peaceful coexistence and to recognize the common danger of nuclear annihilation, there have been a series of agreements. Nevertheless, despite some improvement, the inherent confrontation between two systems with dissimilar ideologies still complicates attempts at arms control. Ideology has become superimposed on the more traditional type of competition between great powers, and has sharpened distrust concerning the intentions and good faith of the other side.

Ideological differences are also reflected in divergent economic and political systems. Soviet observers of the United States have noted the strength of anti-communist sentiment among sections of the US electorate and the political power of the military–industrial complex. As a result, the USSR has generally doubted the genuine and long-term commitment of US governments to arms limitations. On the other hand, US commentators have cited the strength of the defence sector of the Soviet economy. With regard to Western perceptions of the Soviet Union, the most important element—at least as far as arms control is concerned—has been the view that Soviet governments are secretive about military matters, that they maintain control over the information available to their people, and that there is no freedom or opportunity to expose government policies or to protest about them. As a result, many commentators in the USA and other countries in the West have believed that it would be fairly easy for the Soviet Union to cheat on an arms control agreement. They have also maintained that it would be well nigh impossible for USA to cheat, because of the much greater openness and press coverage within US society [23] This conviction has led to the perennial US insistence concerning the implementation of stringent measures of international inspection and control in order to monitor agreements, that is, unless they can be monitored by purely national means.

In the past, Soviet Union's hostility to proposals for on-site verification has been based on genuine fears stemming from recent historical experience. Soviet governments have inherited an awareness from the inter-war period, when a militarily vulnerable Soviet Union was encircled by hostile capitalist powers. Germany's 'blitzkrieg' of 1940 has remained a vivid reminder of the danger from a surprise attack. During the 1950s, US nuclear superiority fuelled Soviet fears concerning a crippling first strike. The Soviet Union, therefore, has condemned verification proposals (often quite bitterly) as a guise for Western espionage which, under certain circumstances, could provide the information required for a pre-emptive attack.[24] Soviet opposition to inspection has also been underpinned by a much longer Russian tradition for secretiveness. Although the Soviet position began to change in the 1970s and early 1980s, the dramatic conversion of the USSR to detailed on-site inspection occurred with the INF Treaty of 1987. So this issue, which has been central in any historical perspective, is now a residual problem for the USSR.

US governments have stressed the need for verification, because of the view that the Soviet Union has, in the past, failed to honour a number of its international agreements. Frequently, arms control opponents in the USA have evoked the historical record of violated international agreements. The Soviet Union's non-aggression pacts with Lithuania, Latvia and Estonia signed in the 1920s and 1930s, and broken during World War II, are often cited. Most of the examples compiled for various congressional committees, however, date from the Stalinist period. The Western conviction—that if the Soviet Union could cheat in an arms control agreement, then it *would* cheat—was particularly strong during the 1950s.[25] The relevance of past history to present arms control, however, was questionable, and both sides began to move away from historically based fears and rigid positions during the 1960s and 1970s. Nevertheless, the ghosts of the past still haunt many in powerful positions, and threaten the prospects for genuine arms control. As late as in the early 1980s, the Reagan Administration revived memories of past treaties violated by the USSR. As part of the revival of cold war attitudes, the Reagan Administration launched a barrage of public (although not very well substantiated) accusations that the Soviet Union had also violated recent arms control treaties.[26] Even after the Reagan Administration was forced to the conference table by a combination of allied pressure and US domestic opinion, US negotiators persisted in strenuously insisting on the importance of detailed verification, which they believed the Soviet Union would resist.

IV. Psychological obstacles to agreement

The preceding discussion concerning some of the obstacles to effective negotiations has illustrated the fact that problems arise not only from the actual exploitation of these factors by the great powers, but also from the mere *suspicion* of such ulterior purposes. The psychological elements in the conflict between the USA and the USSR are of considerable importance. A difficult and crucial question, then, is the point at which reasonable (although in some cases possibly mistaken) distrust ends, and wholly irrational fear and suspicion take over. A number of psychologists have argued that conflict tends to distort perceptions of the other side and that irrational elements have entered into attempts to achieve arms limitation.

Several psychological mechanisms have been identified as contributing to the tension and suspicion in arms control negotiations. They include the propensity to project on to the opponent one's own negative attitudes and motives, to stereotype the opponent and to over-simplify the perception of threats so that all of the opponent's moves appear to be offensive. Other psychological mechanisms include a bias in receiving information, so that the other side's motives are misinterpreted, and a self-image that requires the adoption of a 'tough' and unyielding stance.[27]

The extent to which these psychological elements are dominant in attitudes to arms control appears to be related to the general political climate. Fear and suspicion, as well as stereotyped and selective perceptions, have been much more acute in periods of cold war than during periods of comparative *détente*. On the other hand, the conflict of great power interests, as well as the clash of ideologies between the USSR and the USA, is likely, even under the best circumstances, to produce some tension and misperception. Further, the attitudes of some policy makers, perhaps moulded during a period of extreme confrontation, may remain relatively fixed.

Distrust, it has been strongly argued, is the root cause of armament and, therefore, makes disarmament impossible. This thesis, initially argued by de Madariaga in the 1920s, has recently been revived by Barbara Tuchman.[28] Although Tuchman does not regard distrust as an insuperable obstacle to limited arms control measures, it remains a serious problem.

V. The momentum of weapon technology

Whereas the influence of irrational psychological attitudes may vary according to the situation, the problem of the momentum of R&D in the sphere of weapon technology is ever present. Indeed, most discussions of the obstacles to arms control tend to give this factor prominence.

An analysis concerning the difficulties posed by R&D for arms control usually divides into two separate arguments. First, there is the contention that the momentum of technological development creates problems for particular negotiations. Second, it is argued that technological change tends to undermine and render obsolete agreements already achieved and, thus, to threaten the overall long-term enterprise of arms control.

Changes and improvements in technology or scientific knowledge may affect the outcome of a specific set of negotiations in a number of ways. First, strategic perceptions concerning the issues that are important may change during the talks and result in a shift in negotiating position. Second, the perceived possibilities of detection and verification may also change with similar effect. At times, these alterations in view may actually be helpful in surmounting obstacles. However, they can also serve to create new complications and to exacerbate suspicions of bad faith.

These considerations notwithstanding, two further (and perhaps more significant) problems remain. First, some weapons in early stages of development at the outset of talks may be too far advanced by the end of the negotiations to make scrapping them feasible. Second, there is the danger that decision makers do not perceive the full importance of including certain issues until it is too late.[29] These difficulties are also relevant to the second thesis: that technological change undermines the whole enterprise of achieving real arms control through limited periodic agreements.[30]

In a broader sense, new refinements in technology may promote the failure of arms control by nullifying the benefits from concluded agreements. In this instance, advances in technology may permit more effective exploitation of loopholes than was foreseen at the time. With regard to the 1963 PTBT, the scope of underground nuclear tests was not fully understood at the time. Today, the SDI research programme threatens a reinterpretation, or outright abandonment, of the 1972 ABM Treaty. Another long-term problem which arises out of technological change may be the complication of accepted arms control categories: for example, the eroding distinction between strategic and theatre weapons. In addition, new technology can also enhance verification problems. Cruise missiles illustrate both of these developments.

Technological developments can also facilitate, as well as hinder, effective arms control. Perhaps the most obvious and least controversial example is the significant improvement since the 1950s in national technical means (NTM) of verification. This has been achieved mainly through the evolution of satellite surveillance systems.

Sometimes technological momentum is treated as though it were a purely autonomous factor. Technological momentum is, however, both an outcome of political and strategic conflict between the great powers, as well as a product of domestic politics in both the USA and the USSR. These processes have resulted in a high priority on weapon R&D, as well as the allocation of vast sums for arms procurement and deployment—by both sides. Therefore, any serious attempt to control weapons research and development encounters resistance that is fuelled by the 'logic' of the strategic confrontation between the USA and the USSR, on the one hand, and the power of domestic institutional interests, on the other.

VI. Domestic obstacles to arms control

Many commentators stress the importance of the domestic obstacles which impinge on the conclusion of control agreements. In any detailed account of a negotiation, the internal political difficulties appear, at least superficially, to be quite formidable.[31] Domestic obstacles may be classified in terms of those broadly applicable to both the USA and the USSR, and those that are specific to each system.

According to a number of observers, the decision making process on arms control, in both Moscow and Washington, is weighted towards the military. In both capitals, the military establishments are influential not only because of their responsibility for national security, but also because they possess the necessary expertise. Furthermore, the views of scientists and civilians directly involved in the defence sector also serve to reinforce the influence of the armed forces. If one assumes that professional concerns (combined with vested interests in prestige and jobs) tend to make the military unenthusiastic about arms control, then the influence of these groups clearly represents an obstacle to significant agreement.[32] Although detailed case studies suggest a slightly more complex picture, the basic hypothesis remains convincing nevertheless.

A second phenomenon, common to both the United States and the Soviet Union, is a bureaucratic process of decision making. Obviously, the diversity between the political systems creates certain differences in the functioning of the respective bureaucratic processes. However, in both cases, a range of institutional interests are in involved in co-ordinating policy. Bureaucratic decision making can maximize the opportunities for opponents of arms control to obstruct and undermine negotiations, and to present the actions and proposals of the other side in the most unfavourable light.[33] However, even in the absence of a committed domestic opposition to progress in talks, the inherent nature of bureaucratic politics serves to generate long delays and the formulation of proposals that are based on internal domestic compromise, rather than on a coherent strategy of how to achieve arms control.

Many of the domestic obstacles to arms control specific to the USA arise from its particular style of democratic politics. The four-year cycle of presidential elections creates difficulties at a number of levels.[34] The election may result either in a change of course in the middle of a set of negotiations, or in the inevitable delays as a new administration tries to decide on its policy line. In addition, during the final year of an incumbency, a president is almost certainly consumed with re-election politics. The Administration's negotiating position will frequently reflect election-year considerations. In particular, the incumbent will be vulnerable to accusations of neglecting US defence needs, or of failing to be tough enough with the Soviet Union.

Perhaps even more central is the role of the Congress, which is an unusually influential legislature on foreign policy issues. The Congress retains a pivotal role concerning arms control because of the constitutional requirement that treaties must be ratified by two-thirds of the Senate.[35] Whereas the Senate's concurrence becomes crucial only after an agreement has been signed, an awareness of the problems of Senate ratification may have a powerful influence on an administration's decision making at earlier stages of negotiations. At times, congressional pressure has served actively to promote agreements. Most administrations, however, feel obliged to try to conciliate those powerful Senators who are dubious about arms control. Congress also provides a platform for military interests should they be overridden in the bureaucratic process of decision making; indeed, the Department of Defense (DOD) or the Joint Chiefs of Staff (JCS) retain the option to testify against ratification of a proposed arms control agreement.

A third hazard is the mere difficulty of keeping secrets in Washington. Although this characteristic may reflect a degree of open government it may also pose significant problems for the conduct of diplomacy. This is especially the case in negotiations that are supposed to be confidential. Regular leaks of arms control proposals to the press may result in congressional and public opposition to a possible concession before there has been a genuine opportunity to negotiate seriously.

The Soviet Union has not had these problems. On the whole, the USSR has displayed much greater continuity in its foreign policy and in its arms control negotiations. Nevertheless, the Soviet Union has experienced its own brand of leadership difficulties as illustrated by a succession of ailing general secretaries during the early 1980s. Not only can the Soviet Government insure virtually total secrecy during negotiations, the Government can also guarantee ratification of any agreement it has concluded. In fact, the obstacles facing arms control in the Soviet Union have usually been the *opposite* of those plaguing the

United States: namely, the overall lack of any direct popular or legislative pressure on the Soviet leadership either to influence the content of arms control policies, or to hold the leadership accountable for a lack of progress. Objectively, this factor reduces the likelihood that the Soviet Union will curb its military programme in the interests of arms control. The pressures for radical measures—in any society—are much more likely to come from below, than from those directly involved in government. The absence of any genuine opportunity for independent scrutiny of government action or for open protest has also presented a problem in terms of Western perceptions concerning the Soviet Union as a negotiating partner. These factors have served to strengthen Western fear that the USSR could cheat on an arms control agreement and not be detected.

VII. Obstacles in the negotiating process

Verification

Until the 1980s, one of the major difficulties in arms control negotiations has centred on the issue of verification. The USA's insistence on verification, coupled with the Soviet Union's resistance to it (based on ideological and historical considerations), became a ritualized element in arms control talks. In the 1960s and 1970s, however, some agreements, through a reliance upon rapidly improving NTM of verification, managed to circumvent the extremely sensitive issue of on-site inspection. Nevertheless, the stubborn adherence to positions either for or against on-site inspection has continued to serve, on occasion, as a tactic to avoid serious negotiations concerning substantive measures to curb arms.

Divergent negotiating styles

Frequently cited as a source of misunderstanding in arms control talks are the differences in the negotiating styles between the USA and the USSR. During the 1950s, these differences caused profound frustration to US negotiators, and these differences have still been noted as late as the 1970s. Today, simple stereotypes of Soviet negotiating behaviour can be misleading. Indeed, there have been significant changes in Soviet negotiating style,[36] especially since the accession of Mikhail Gorbachev to the top leadership posts in the Soviet Union.

The USA has traditionally stressed technical detail, both in its proposals designed to limit arms and to insure verification. As a result, the USA has given a prominent role to scientific experts during many negotiations. The Soviet Union, on the other hand, has given priority to the achievement of broadly-outlined agreements in principle, rather than in minute technical detail. This approach has its roots in pre-Revolution Russian diplomacy and is based on the assumption that detail is secondary. US negotiators, however, continue to insist that detail is vital to a proper understanding of the implications of any arms control proposal.[37] It is interesting to note that de Madariaga also observed a similar divergence in negotiating styles between the French and the empirically minded British during inter-war negotiations.[38]

The Soviet Union has displayed a greater awareness of the political implications of arms control negotiation, as opposed to the USA's emphasis upon finding technological solutions. The classic example of this gap in negotiating views occurred at the 1958 Surprise Attack Conference. Whereas the USSR apparently focused primarily on the threat of attack from the FRG, the West produced numerous technical studies of ways to prevent the danger of surprise attack.[39] On the other hand, it should be noted that Western proposals for extensive inspection of Soviet-controlled territory offered major political and strategic advantages to the West, which were not openly acknowledged.[40] Still, it would certainly be implausible to argue that the US Government has been completely unaware of political side-effects of negotiations, at least from the beginning of the SALT process. Nor is it true that the USSR has been wholly unwilling to engage in very detailed technical discussions, although it has, however, been the USA which has emphasized detail.

In the past, the Soviet Union has been reluctant to discuss detailed information concerning its own force structures or to reveal its own scientific information. On the whole, Soviet civilian diplomats have been much less well informed concerning strategic and technological issues than their US counterparts. During the course of the SALT negotiations between 1969 and 1979, however, these problems were modified to some extent. With respect to negotiating tactics, the Soviet Union has traditionally displayed a willingness to make public proposals for disarmament or other forms of arms control which were apparently designed to influence public opinion. The USSR, however, has often left the initiative concerning the presentation of detailed proposals to the United States. Thereupon, the Soviet Union would react. This tactic, of course, is designed to force the other side to disclose its hand. Even so, the Soviet Union has often taken the initiative in proposing treaty language as a basis for negotiation. More recently, the Soviet Union has displayed a willingness to initiate its own proposals with the result that the gap between US and Soviet negotiating styles has narrowed. Indeed, General Secretary Gorbachev has set the pace in proposing the arms control agenda and in offering specific solutions.

Bargaining theories and tactics

Without doubt, bargaining theories have had a major influence—from the US side—on the conduct of arms control talks. Two views have been popularized: first, that it is necessary to negotiate from a position of strength, and second, that the possession of 'bargaining chips' is essential. Although both ideas provide a rationale for an arms buildup (on the grounds that a buildup is the way to achieve arms control), the concepts are not identical. The belief in negotiation from strength is derived from the general assumption that an opponent will only negotiate seriously when faced by a powerful military threat and, therefore, has an incentive to seek mutual cuts. The idea of 'bargaining chips' is also based on the assumption that the opposing side will only negotiate in good faith if there is a real incentive to make concessions in order to remove some strategic threat. A 'bargaining chip' is however something the negotiator is in principle prepared from the beginning to abandon. 'Strength', by contrast, is a condition to be maintained.

The concept of negotiating from strength has been particularly unfortunate in the current context of US–Soviet relations, because it is often associated with US thinking regarding the best way to negotiate with the Soviet Union during the height of the cold war (as espoused by John Foster Dulles).[41] The concept also retains overtones of employing military superiority to force the Soviet Union to comply with US wishes. Therefore, the idea runs counter to the long-term determination of the Soviet Union to achieve equal status and military strength. Although the idea of negotiating from strength was not stressed in the late 1960s and early 1970s—the most productive period for arms control agreements—the concept has enjoyed a recent revival.

The view that it is necessary to pursue an arms buildup as a prelude to arms limitation negotiations (summarized by the slogan 'we arm to parley') is deeply rooted in thinking about war and peace. The idea has a certain political appeal because of its ambiguous nature. As Coral Bell has suggested, the phrase 'negotiations from strength' appeals simultaneously to a liberal and universalist belief in conducting international affairs by reasoned negotiation in pursuit of peace, as well as to a *realpolitik* view of the world that stresses the need for use of force and for national military strength.[42] Any attempt to put the idea into practice is likely to reflect a similar ambivalence and to reduce the likelihood of an arms control agreement.

From the point of view of pure logic, if both sides strive to negotiate from strength, no serious negotiation could take place. Nevertheless, the theory does assume that there are circumstances under which a position of weakness can induce negotiations. The idea of negotiating from strength relies on certain intuitive perceptions concerning the nature of bargaining: that the opponent must envisage certain advantages in negotiating an agreement and, further, that the strength of an initial bargaining position will usually determine how advantageous the outcome is to one's own side. On the other hand, if the opponent feels he is being forced to go to the conference table, or to accept a proposal, he may reject out of hand what seems to be an insulting approach. Moreover, if an opponent perceives that he is negotiating from a position of weakness, then the logical response would be to stall during the talks and to launch an all-out military effort to achieve a better bargaining position. Therefore, the theory of negotiating from strength may appear to be an attempt to secure unilateral advantage, rather than a fair and equitable outcome. As a result, the strategy is likely to be counter-productive more often than not.

The idea of bargaining chips, however, is a more limited concept. Indeed, the idea retains fewer connotations of trying to force an agreement on the other side Instead, the concept of bargaining chips implies a certain willingness to make concessions in order to reach a settlement. In practice, however, political leaders may apply the concept to propose an additional investment in arms in a fashion that comes perilously close to negotiating from strength. During the SALT talks, the concept of bargaining chips was very much in vogue with the US side. However, many experts in arms control have expressed scepticism concerning the idea, because—from the record of most negotiations—it is far from clear that the idea of bargaining chips has been used effectively. There are particular problems which result from the attempted use of weapons as bargaining chips.[43] For example, no self-respecting military establishment is likely to develop expensive, and perhaps elaborate, weapon systems simply to scrap them in an arms control agreement. If the weapons appear at all effective, then the military is very likely to insist on retaining them. Conversely, if the weapons appear ineffective, then their value as a bargaining chip is reduced; very likely, the weapons would be abandoned regardless of whether an agreement is concluded or not.

Although the application of bargaining theories may undermine the likelihood of an agreement, preconceived ideas concerning the necessary, or desired, outcome of negotiations may also create problems. The precept that a fair settlement must mean the achievement of exact parity is a source of considerable difficulty in the light of nuclear and conventional force structure asymmetries (discussed above). Nor is an objective definition of parity a simple matter, especially when such dissimilar systems, as well as strategic disparities, are being compared. Furthermore, given the inherent mutual suspicion in arms control talks that one side is attempting to obtain some strategic advantage over the other, a fair definition of parity becomes well nigh impossible to conclude. Instead, the quest for an *artificial parity* may strengthen the tendency—well demonstrated in arms talks to date—to restrict those weapons that are easiest to curb and to avoid, perhaps, the most dangerous or destabilizing weapon developments.

Political, organizational and technical problems

Many of the difficulties involved in formal arms control negotiations are linked to the domestic political obstacles (discussed above). Usually, the delegations are dispatched to negotiations to represent the main governmental agencies involved and to ensure that the interests of these agencies are not overlooked during the process of talks and concessions. As a result, negotiating teams may include important members who are doubtful about the purpose of the talks and who will actually seek to strengthen the opposition at home.

Apart from considerations of team composition, the negotiators often face considerable practical problems from the bureaucratic procedures of decision making at home. Frequently, delegations mark time while waiting for instructions; and because of the problems inherent in bureaucratic compromise, those directions that are received may either be inadequate or confusing, or both. As a result, negotiating proposals may be ill-conceived. Furthermore, decision makers at home may either shift their position arbitrarily or may instruct the withdrawal of previous offers entirely.

Many of the problems that arise out of the process of arms control negotiations are common to *any* category of formal negotiations. Nevertheless, because of the extreme sensitivity of arms control negotiations, these problems appear to loom larger than in most other talks. One major problem is the relative inflexibility of official negotiating positions which is due, at least in part, to the need to maintain both a consistent public stance and a credible bargaining reputation.[44] Inflexibility may also result from a linkage between different sets of negotiations and the subsequent necessity to maintain consistency across the board. Thus, arms control talks may reflect positions taken up on other issues: for example, the willingness to accord diplomatic recognition to certain countries, or a particular attitude towards the organization of the United Nations. Considerations of diplomatic prestige or of bargaining tactics may also serve to cause a certain intransigence in a state's bargaining position. A state may be reluctant to shift from an initial stance to a more moderate bargaining position out of the fear that such a move will encourage the other side to stall for further concessions.

Another factor—not unique to arms control, but often cited as a major problem—is the extreme complexity of some arms limitation talks. Although some analysts occasionally speculate as to whether the so-called complexity of arms control talks constitutes a genuine problem, it is widely agreed that the SALT talks (especially SALT II) did involve some extremely complex technical issues.[45] Other arms control issues—for example, a ban on chemical weapons—may also involve numerous technical problems of definition and control.

Inflexibility, reluctance to make concessions and the inherent complexity of arms control talks may all serve *simultaneously* to promote considerable delays in making progress, even if both sides are sincere about reaching an agreement. Furthermore, home-government bureaucratic processes may compound the delay. In addition, the sheer length of time required by most arms control negotiations may also become a problem; the momentum of research, development and production of weapons is not usually subject to the same kind of delays.

A number of other aspects of formal negotiations, which may prove to be important, may at least be open to improvement. For example, the forum chosen for talks, or the degree of publicity or secrecy involved, may create difficulties. In addition, the conceptual framework for the negotiations may be unsatisfactory in that it prevents proper examination of the whole set of relevant issues. Sometimes, there may also be genuine confusion or misunderstanding at a crucial point that may serve to prevent a possible breakthrough. Any number (or all) of these factors may cause serious problems for a particular set of negotiations. Still, these problems are only of secondary importance to an analysis of the central obstacles facing arms control talks in general.

VIII. Arms control talks promote the arms race

Quite a number of analysts have suggested that the process of arms control negotiations not only fails to curb the spiral of weapon development, but may also provide impetus to it.[46] Several mechanisms which could could explain this escalatory effect are present in arms control talks.

First, the theory of bargaining chips may encourage governments to ask for new weapons, or for the expansion of a programme, on the grounds that these measures are necessary to provide leverage in present or forthcoming negotiations. The belief in bargaining chips may, therefore, stimulate weapon programmes which would otherwise be pursued with less vigour. In respect to the USA, the concept of bargaining chips may serve to encourage Congress to agree to military expenditures that it otherwise might resist. Whether weapons have actually been developed primarily as bargaining chips is a question to be examined in more detail (see below), but there is ample evidence that representatives of the US Government have justified military programmes in these terms. For example, the Reagan Administration urged a reluctant Congress to endorse its new binary nerve gas programme to prevent a weakening of the USA's position in the chemical weapon talks at Geneva.[47]

The second important factor which may result in arms control talks actually serving to accelerate military programmes is the fact that military and political opponents of arms control often exact a price for accepting an agreement. Several US presidents have been obliged to make specific concessions, both to the JCS and to the more hawkish members of Congress, by promising to implement a range of military measures in areas not covered under an agreement and to give priority to major investment for these options. In addition to specifically buying off opposition, US presidents may feel a more generalized pressure to reassure opponents of arms control through the promotion of new weapons or the recommendation of higher defence budgets.

The use of the bargaining chip argument in the justification of new weapons, as well as an increased investment in arms (in order to secure acquiescence to particular agreements), are well-established features of the US political landscape. There is little evidence that the Soviet leadership views weapons as bargaining chips, unless the weapons are becoming obsolete. Nevertheless, the Soviet military may exact certain concessions as the price for accepting arms control limitations, although—because of the secrecy surrounding the Soviet political system—this process is more difficult to discern. However, even if the escalatory impact of arms control talks is registered primarily in the United States, it is still likely to be reflected in Soviet military planning and developments in due course. At a minimum, it is likely that Soviet perceptions concerning the USA's seriousness of purpose in arms control will be adversely affected.

Other ways in which arms control negotiations may actually serve to boost arms competition are equally applicable to either the USSR or the USA. For example, both sides may perceive a need for parity within a context of strategic asymmetry that may well result in 'levelling up' to the higher numbers deployed by other side. In the absence of negotiations, however, there might actually be less pressure to match the other side. This, in turn, could possibly result in lower planned deployments than might otherwise be the case.[48]

Levelling up to achieve parity is related to a more general side-effect of negotiations, which tend to focus much greater attention—both from the government and the public—upon the numbers of weapons possessed or planned to be deployed by each side. Negotiations also serve to foster anxiety concerning perceived inequalities, as well as possible future vulnerabilities.[49] Any attempt to limit arms by agreement, therefore, may actually *strengthen* military and political lobbies for more and newer weapons. This is accomplished by giving salience to oversimplified assessments of numbers and military potentialities on the other side. Moreover, the process of negotiations— by creating perceptions of bad faith, unfair negotiating tactics or deliberate delays—may serve to generate increased hostility, rather than the promotion of an intended greater good will and trust. Indeed, some commentators have even suggested that negotiations can actually undermine the conditions required to achieve arms control with the effect that the negotiations 'consume trust'.[50] Negotiations, therefore, may actually make it *harder* for governments to quietly curb military demands for increased expenditure and new weapons.

Another factor that is often cited is that arms control agreements serve to channel weapon development by diverting resources into those areas which are not controlled by treaty.[51] Because, in practice, these areas tend to comprise the latest weapon technology, the result may be to boost the qualitative arms race. Whether channelling really reflects the inherent weakness of arms control negotiations, and the special difficulty of controlling the most significant weapon systems, or whether it represents a harmful and unintended consequence of arms control agreements, is open to further examination in the case studies. If the attempt to include new technology in detailed negotiations is thwarted, then the first argument appears to be stronger. On the other hand, if weapons previously regarded as being of minor interest are boosted after an agreement (which closed off certain other developments), then the case that channelling can serve to enhance the development of weapon technology seems more plausible. In some circumstances, both conclusions might be equally applicable.

IX. Multilateral negotiations

Multilateral negotiations in which the USA and the USSR are the principal protagonists naturally reflect the numerous obstacles encountered in bilateral talks. This is the case not only with regard to negotiations between alliances, such as the Mutual and Balanced Force Reduction (MBFR) or the Conventional Forces in Europe (CFE) talks, but also with respect to negotiations in which non-aligned countries are involved. The Conference on Security and Co-operation in Europe (CSCE) which concluded the 1975 Helsinki Document, was primarily a meeting which was focused upon concerns relating to the process of *détente*. Nevertheless, the Conference did result in the agreement of a series of confidence-building measures and the convening of the Stockholm Conference on Disarmament in Europe (CDE) in the 1980s. Through its 'basket three' on human rights issues, the CSCE created a political linkage between *détente* and respect for certain political principles. Although this linkage could have been valuable, the CSCE, in practice, became less an instrument of *détente,* and more a forum for ideological conflict—with US governments stressing abuses of civil rights in the Soviet Union. In the past, multilateral arms control talks have also encountered the perennial problem of on-site verification. Although the Soviet Union accepted the need for some form of on-site verification of a ban on chemical weapons in 1983, the chemical weapon talks in Geneva were obstructed in the mid-1980s by the gap between the Soviet position and the extreme verification demands made by the Reagan Administration.

If a large number of states are involved in arms control talks, then a multiplicity of national interests is likely to complicate negotiations even further. Although the allies of the great powers often fall into line, some may express particular sensitivities which rule out certain options: for example, West German concerns strongly influence negotiations concerning both nuclear and conventional weapons in Europe. In addition, those states which aspire to great-power status may also be motivated by considerations of prestige and, therefore, be unwilling to submit to the leadership of the USA or the USSR. These states may actually prove to be particularly intractable about reaching any arms control agreements at all, as the record of both France and China since 1960 indicates. Often, non-aligned states have attempted to mediate between the USA and the USSR but have become angry and impatient with the great powers and, therefore, have created their own obstacles. Alan Neidle observes that even a rather marginal arms control measure—a ban on radiological warfare—has foundered in the Geneva 40-nation CD. When the USA and the USSR finally did submit a joint treaty for consideration, 'it was chewed up by the non-aligned with a piranha-like fury'.[52] Although this episode can be interpreted as a serious attempt by the non-aligned states to give substance to a cosmetic proposal, even genuine pressure for significant arms control may block—or threaten to disrupt—limited arms control agreements.

It is reasonable to surmise that a state's attitude toward arms control is influenced by its own sense of security. Those states that are involved in regional conflicts—and, therefore, perceive a strong military threat to their territory—tend to be more interested in an arms buildup, as opposed to agreements designed to limit arms. After its border war with China in 1962, India—which was originally one of the main proponents of nuclear disarmament—became one of the most recalcitrant states involved in the negotiations to prevent the spread of nuclear weapons through the NPT. All states, however, are likely to be influenced by a desire for military protection against attack, concerns for sovereignty and prestige, and the propaganda temptations provided by arms control negotiations.

One indication of the comparative failure of such negotiations since 1945 is that most countries have never been under pressure to consider limiting arms at the level that might affect them most directly: for example, curbs on conventional arms or the arms trade. Because of the propagandist nature of general disarmament plans tabled since 1945, limits on conventional arms have never been pursued in the serious detail that the League of Nations attempted in the years 1928–35. Therefore, much of the time the smaller states have been able to adopt a high-minded stance in relation to the lamentable failure of the great powers to curb their nuclear arsenals, without having to face up to the difficulties of arms control for themselves.

Two sets of negotiations, however, have served to raise major military and political questions for all states regardless of rank. The negotiations leading to the 1968 NPT raised fundamental questions concerning the best means of achieving security—either through nuclear deterrence or through the prevention of the the proliferation of nuclear weapons. The NPT negotiations also raised questions concerning the supposed link between nuclear weapons and prestige. The talks on chemical weapons are also of critical concern to many states. Most could acquire chemical weapons, if they so decided.

X. Factors promoting success

Despite the numerous obstacles that stand in the path of even limited arms control there are important political factors which promote some degree of restraint on arms. The multiplicity of arms control negotiations demonstrates that governments feel obliged to *look* as though they are trying to curb arms. The problem so far has been that: although the forces favouring arms control have been powerful enough to get governments to the negotiating table, they have been too weak—except in special circumstances—to pressure those governments to conclude significant agreements.

The primary impetus to arms control or disarmament may well be general awareness of the increasing destructiveness of the weapons of war. The first organized peace movements in Europe and the USA arose immediately after the Napoleonic Wars; the first governmental conference to consider disarmament

Table 2.2. Factors promoting agreement

General factors

       Increasing destructiveness of weapons
       Inhumane nature of modern weapons
       Cost of weapons

Specific factors

       Political groups lobbying for arms control
       Technological and strategic doubts about particular weapons
       Particular national economic needs
       Strategic self-interest

---

took place in 1899; and more serious attempts to negotiate arms limitations emerged from the unprecedented carnage of World War I.[53] During the aftermath of World War II, political attitudes had become unfavourable to disarmament. The 'lessons of Munich'—as well as an intensifying cold war—seemed to suggest that arms were necessary to deter and repel aggression. Nevertheless, a growing awareness concerning the horrific dangers posed by nuclear weapons—the destruction of millions, the poisoning of the environment and the deformation of any surviving generations—inspired negotiations to curb nuclear testing, to prevent the spread of nuclear weapons and to cut existing arsenals. Similar fears have promoted the 1972 BWC and the long-standing negotiations to ban chemical weapons.

An awareness of the inhumane and totally destructive nature of modern weapons of mass destruction serves to encourage a belief that the common interests and long-term security of humanity must outweigh any immediate and purely national security calculations, and the resultant self-interest in retaining such weapons. This commitment to a universal interest in disarmament measures is greatly reinforced by the enormous costs of modern weaponry, including most conventional weapons. The vast expenditure on the instruments of death and destruction can be compared to the need for resources to prevent famine, disease and crippling poverty in large parts of the world. Indeed, the connection between disarmament and development was clearly illustrated by the Brandt Report.[54]

Experience to date indicates that a belief in the horrors, dangers and wastefulness of modern weapons is a necessary, although insufficient, impetus for governments to seek disarmament or to implement genuine curbs on arms. Governments—as well as general public opinion—tend to be equally, if not more, receptive to the long-standing arguments for the need for strong military defences. This apparently schizophrenic tendency is not *necessarily* irrational—there may be real conflicts between immediate national security and an overall interest in peace and disarmament. Still, the standard postwar response to these competing conceptions of security has been to build up arms, while attending numerous conferences to curtail or eliminate them. This dual approach, which is liable to promote either conscious hypocrisy or genuine schizophrenia, seldom results in any real limit on arms.

Certain groups, however, have succeeded in maintaining a fairly consistent commitment to the goal of arms limitation. Among these groups are included certain sections within the legislature in many countries, a world-wide academic community specializing in arms control, and the peace movements. In the USA, some members of Congress, as well as a relatively active arms control lobby, have played a consistent role since the mid-1950s. In general, arms control pressure groups have become better organized and have gained in influence. In recent years, the Congress has also displayed a greater tendency to intervene in weapon expenditure and arms control negotiations, sometimes establishing direct links between the authorization of funds and progress in arms control. At times (for example, during the late 1950s and the early 1980s), popular movements against nuclear weapons have had a strong effect on governmental attitudes and have influenced, particularly, the policies of some opposition parties in Western Europe. During the 1970s, partly as a result of the SALT process, an academic group with increasing strategic expertise, understanding of the West and overall sympathy for arms control developed in the USSR.[55] Although the groups favouring curbs on arms (in both East and West) tend to have limited political clout in most circumstances, the groups do ensure that the case for arms control or disarmament is—to one degree or another—being advanced.

At times, even purely national interests or strategic realities may favour the limitation of certain weapons. For example, the great powers may possess a mutual interest in preventing smaller countries acquiring dangerous and destabilizing weapons, such as in the US–Soviet co-operation to prevent the spread of nuclear weapons. In addition, weapons with questionable combat value because they are difficult to control or are technologically vulnerable are easier to give up. Weapons hard to control are as likely to harm one's own troops, or civilians, as the other side. This category applies to biological and chemical weapons. If the technological effectiveness of a number of bombers and missiles is in doubt, then governments or legislatures are more inclined to abandon such weapons, either through unilateral decision or mutual agreement. An overall scepticism concerning the reliability of ABM defences served to generate support for the 1972 ABM Treaty.

National economic interests can also facilitate arms control. Weapon systems that involve vast expenditure—such as ABM defences—often encounter stiff opposition from cost-conscious legislators and voters. Governments that are concerned with keeping down taxes, as well as spending more on welfare or developing other sectors of their economies, may balk at spending too much on defence. Even in the USA, these countervailing economic concerns act to restrain weapon expenditures, despite the major industrial, scientific and military interests that benefit from weapon R&D, and so act to promote programmes such as SDI. From the standpoint of the centrally-planned and controlled economy of the Soviet Union, the incentive to divert funds from the military to civilian sectors is even more powerful. It is widely assumed that General Secretary Gorbachev's consistent policy since 1985, to promote arms control and to pressure the West to reciprocate, is partly due to a commitment to modernize the Soviet economy.

Finally, calculations of national strategic self-interest may reveal an advantage in adhering to certain arms control agreements, as opposed to engaging in an unrestricted race for superiority or, at least, equality. Both the US and Soviet military establishments have been persuaded to accept the SALT agreements—at least in part—on strategic grounds. For example, in the early 1980s, the JCS favoured a continued adherence to SALT II by the USA. Apparently, the JCS believed that while the USSR could rapidly multiply the number of warheads on ICBMs, the USA could not increase its warheads so easily. During the 1980s, as in the period after 1969, the Soviet Union has appeared anxious to avoid engaging in a competition for new ABM defences.

This kind of strategic reasoning, however, limits the range of possible agreements and is unlikely to favour radical cuts in weapons. This sort of perspective may moreover tempt the side which is ahead to attempt either to negotiate from strength or to develop bargaining chips. Nevertheless, at times, an enlightened strategic self-interest may actually converge with the political conviction that a common interest is to be found in limiting arms. The original theory of arms control did envisage arms control as an adjunct of national military strategy through the creation of a safer environment in which to implement a coherent nuclear deterrence posture. Nevertheless, some military doctrines are more congruent with arms control than others; for example, the deterrence theory of mutual assured destruction (MAD) was closely associated with a belief in various forms of arms control. Arms control greatly benefits from being viewed as an adjunct of national defence. The chances for the eventual success of arms control is greatly enhanced. On the other hand, arms control may also become vulnerable to shifts in strategic doctrine and weapon deployments, as well as technological advances in weaponry.

One form of arms control—the taking of steps to avoid accidental nuclear war and to control crises—meshes with strategic interests regardless of whichever doctrine is currently the fashion. The simplest measure of crisis management is the mere improvement of communications between heads of government during a crisis. The desire to avoid unintended war, by promoting a sense of security on each side, has been extended to an examination of a range of confidence-building measures, such as advance notification of military manoevres and the exchange of observers at certain exercises.

The multiplicity of national interests—either in a bilateral or multilateral setting—can favour arms control agreements as well as to hinder them. Although the allies of the great powers have often raised further obstacles, these states have also exerted pressure to promote *détente* and arms control in pursuance of their own national goals. On numerous occasions, the non-aligned states have acted as a force for arms control, either as a voting bloc at the United Nations or through a role in particular negotiations to promote technical solutions and political compromises.

XI. Conclusion

In order to explain why arms control negotiations often fail, it is not enough to recite all the possible factors involved. One must also analyse the relevance of these factors. The case studies—which are considered in subsequent chapters—examine the role of various factors in each set of negotiations and attempt to identify those obstacles which could be overcome and those which proved insuperable. The case studies also explore the factors which promote negotiations or facilitate an agreement of some kind. The validity of any ultimate conclusions, however, also depends on a broader theoretical perspective. The theoretical issues—raised briefly at the beginning of this discussion—are examined in chapter 10.

Notes and references

[1] For a fairly moderate critique of arms control for distorting US defence planning and failing to constrain the USSR, see Burt, R., 'A glass half empty', *Foreign Policy*, no. 36 (fall 1979), pp. 33–48. For a more extreme anti-Soviet critique of arms control, see Van Cleave, W. R., 'Political and negotiating asymmetries: Insult in SALT II', *Contrasting Approaches to Strategic Arms Control*, ed. R. L. Pfaltzgraff, Jr (D. C. Heath: Lexington, Mass., 1974).

[2] See Rathjens, G. W., Chayes, A. and Ruina, J. P., *Nuclear Arms Control Agreements: Process and Impact* (Carnegie Endowment for International Peace: Washington, DC, 1974). See also Gelb, L. H., 'A glass half full', *Foreign Policy*, no. 36 (fall 1979), pp. 21–32. Gelb begins his article by claiming: 'Arms control has essentially failed . . . Three decades of U.S.–Soviet negotiations to limit arms competition have done little more than to codify the arms race'.

[3] See Bertram, C., 'Arms control and technological change: elements of a new approach', *The Future of Arms Control*, Part II, ed. C. Bertram, Adelphi Paper no. 146 (International Institute of Strategic Studies: London, Summer 1978).

[4] See, for example, Shulman, M. D., 'Arms control in an international context', *Arms, Defense Policy and Arms Control*, eds F. A. Long and G. W. Rathjens (Norton: New York, 1976).

[5] Spanier, J. and Nogee, J., *The Politics of Disarmament: A Study in Soviet–American Gamesmanship* (Praeger: New York, 1962); and Myrdal, A., *The Game of Disarmament: How the United States and Russia Run the Arms Race* (Spokesman: Nottingham, 1980).

[6] de Madariaga, S., *Disarmament* (Oxford University Press: London, 1929), pp. 25–27.

[7] Bull, H., 'Strategic arms limitation: the precedent of the Washington and London naval treaties', *SALT: Problems and Prospects*, ed. M. A. Kaplan (General Learning Press: Morristown, N. J., 1973).

[8] Ranger, R., *Arms and Politics 1958–1978: Arms Control in a Changing Political Context* (Gage: Toronto, 1982).

[9] See, for example, Van Cleave (note 1). Ranger partly implies this (note 8).

[10] For example, in the 1958–63 test ban talks. See Jacobson, H. K. and Stein, E., *Diplomats, Scientists and Politicians: The United States and the Nuclear Test Ban Negotiations* (University of Michigan Press: Ann Arbor, Mich., 1966), p. 87.

[11] Equal Soviet bloc representation on the proposed control commission for a test ban treaty was not conceded by the USA until 1961.

[12] Neidle, A. F. (ed.), *Nuclear Negotiations: Reassessing Arms Control Goals in US–Soviet Relations* (University of Texas: Austin, Tex., 1982), pp. 132–33; and Sharp, J. M. O., 'Confidence building measures in SALT', *Arms Control*, vol. 3, no. 1 (May 1982), pp. 50–51.

[13] Gaddis, J. L., *Strategies of Containment* (Oxford University Press: Oxford, 1982), pp. 111–29.

[14] The USSR did not break off negotiations after the USA's invasion of Cambodia in May 1970. Nor did the USSR do so after the USA's mining of Haiphong harbour, just before the May 1972 summit meeting.

[15] Talbott, S. (ed.), *Khrushchev Remembers: Vol. 2. The Last Testament* (Penguin Books: Harmondsworth, 1977), pp. 504–24.

[16] Talbott, S., *Deadly Gambits: The Reagan Administration and the Stalemate in Nuclear Arms Control* (Pan Books: London, 1985), pp. 111–13.

[17] Although China openly attacked proposals for a test ban treaty in 1962–63, it had opposed the negotiations much earlier. See Gittings, J., *The Sino–Soviet Dispute* (Oxford University Press: Oxford, 1968).

[18] See, for example, Wolfe, T. W., 'The Soviet Union and arms control', *Arms Control for the Late Sixties*, eds J. E. Dougherty and J. F. Lehman, Jr (D. Van Nostrand: Princeton, N. J., 1967), p. 133; and Nacht, M., 'The bad, the dull and the empty', *Arms Control: The Multilateral Alternative*, ed. E. C. Luck (New York University Press: New York, 1983), p. 103.

[19] These suspicions were voiced during the test ban talks and during SALT; see subsequent chapters. These attitudes are summarized in an article by Nye, J. S., Jr, 'Restarting arms control', *Foreign Policy*, no. 47 (summer 1982), p. 100. See also Krepon, M., *Strategic Stalemate: Nuclear Weapons and Arms Control in American Politics* (Macmillan: London, 1984), p. 69.

[20] Bunn, G., 'Nuclear arms control: obstacles to agreement', *Reassessing Arms Control*, ed. D. Carlton and C. Schaerf (Macmillan: London, 1985), p. 85.

[21] See de Madariaga (note 6), p. 30.

[22] For a clear summary, see Krell, G., 'The problems and achievements of arms control', *Arms Control*, vol. 2, no. 3 (Dec. 1981), pp. 260–63.

[23] Wright, M., *Disarm and Verify: An Explanation of the Central Difficulties and National Policies* (Chatto and Windus: London, 1964), pp. 37–38.

[24] Burns, E. L. M., *A Seat at the Table: The Struggle for Disarmament* (Clarke, Irwin and Co.: Toronto, 1972), p. 130.

[25] For example, see *Soviet Treaty Violations*, Department of Defense, (Office of Armed Forces Information and Education: Washington, DC, 1962). The charge has been extended to claim that the Soviet Union has consistently broken promises and that official Marxist–Leninist theory advocates promise-breaking. See, for example, *Soviet treaty violations: a 40 year record of broken promises*, Department of Defense (Office of Armed Forces Information and Education, Washington, DC, 10 June 1959), Fact Sheet No 1. H.

[26] The US allegations of arms control violations since 1981 have ranged from technical violations of SALT and the PTBT, to more serious allegations of cheating in SALT. The most serious allegations concerned Soviet use of biological weapons in Kampuchea and Laos, chemical weapons in Afghanistan and the breaching of the 1972 Biological Weapons Convention. None of these latter allegations has been proved by independent observers, and many experts have cast doubt on the allegations concerning Kampuchea and Laos. See Perry Robinson, J., 'Chemical and biological warfare: developments in 1982', SIPRI, *World Armaments and Disarmament: SIPRI Yearbook 1983* (Taylor & Francis: London, 1983), pp. 391–423. Subsequent *SIPRI Yearbooks* have contained lists of US allegations and Soviet counter-allegations.

[27] For a recent discussion, see Laszlo, E. and Keys, D., *Disarmament: The Human Factor* (Pergamon: Oxford, 1981).

[28] Tuchman, B., 'The alternative to arms control', *Arms Control and International Security*, ed. R. Kolkowicz and N. Joeck (Westview Press: Boulder, Colo., 1984). James Wadsworth argued 20 years earlier that suspicion between the USSR and the West was the root cause of the failure of disarmament talks. See Wadsworth, J., *The Price of Peace* (Praeger: New York, 1962), especially p. 15.

[29] For a rebuttal of arguments that the arms control process cannot deal with technological developments, see Slocombe, W. B., 'Technology and future arms control', *New Technology and Western Security Policy,* Part II, Adelphi Paper no. 198, (International Institute of Strategic Studies: London, 1985), pp. 40–41. Citing the ABM Treaty, Slocombe suggests arms control negotiations can cover technological change and that when omissions of new technology do occur they are often deliberate.

[30] The broader and perhaps stronger thesis is summarized by Baker, J. C., 'Alternatives to formal negotiations', eds W. H. Kincade, N. V. Yinger and G. C. Duffy, *Approaches to Arms East–West Arms Control* (Arms Control Association: Washington, DC, 1979), p. 28. This wider claim is also refuted by Slocombe (note 29), p. 41.

[31] See, for example, Miller, S. E., 'Politics over promise: domestic impediments to arms control', *International Security,* vol. 8, no. 4 (spring 1984), pp. 67–90.

[32] Lamb, J. and Mandell, B., 'How arms control begins at home: the American and Soviet cases', *International Journal,* vol. 36, no. 3 (summer 1981), pp. 505–607.

[33] Järvenpää, P. O., 'Bureaucratic politics and arms control: the case of flexible nuclear options', in Kincade, Yinger and Duffy (note 30).

[34] A point stressed by York, H. F., 'Bilateral negotiations and the arms race', *Scientific American,* vol. 249, no. 4 (Oct. 1983), pp. 112–13.

[35] See Miller (note 31) and York (note 34) among numerous references.

[36] For a recent and balanced assessment, see Garthoff, R. F., 'Negotiating with the Russians: some lessons from SALT', *International Security,* vol. 1, no. 4 (spring 1977), pp. 5–7. A more hostile view of Soviet negotiating tactics can be found in Dean, A. H., *The Test Ban and Disarmament: The Path of Negotiation* (Harper & Row: New York, 1966), pp. 34–47. This work reflects not only Dean's own experience but also what seems to have become, during the 1950s, a precept in US circles concerning the Soviet negotiating style.

[37] See Sims, N. A., *Approaches to Disarmament: An Introductory Analysis* (Quaker Peace and Service: London, 1979), Revised and Expanded Edition, p. 108, for an analysis of the 'broad-brush treatment' favoured by Russian leaders.

[38] See de Madariaga (note 6), pp. 19–22.

[39] Luard, E., 'The background of the negotiations to date', *First Steps to Disarmament: A New Approach to the Problem of Arms Reductions,* ed. E. Luard, (Thames and Hudson: London, 1965), p. 31. For a detailed analysis, see Ranger (note 8), pp. 31–39.

[40] See Bechhoefer, G. G., 'Negotiating with the Soviet Union', ed. D. G. Brennan, *Arms Control, Disarmament and National Security,* (George Brazilier: New York, 1961), p. 280–81.

[41] Perhaps the best known statement of the need for the USA to negotiate from strength was Philip Mosely's 1951 article which drew on his experiences in negotiating with the Soviet Union between 1942 and 1949. The article has been frequently reproduced. See Mosely, P. E., 'Some Soviet techniques in negotiations', *Negotiating with the Russians,* ed. R. Dennett and J. E. Johnson (World Peace Foundation: Boston, 1951).

[42] Bell, C., *Negotiations from Strength: A Study in the Politics of Power* (Chatto & Windus: London, 1962).

[43] See Gray, R. C. and Bresler, R. J., 'Why weapons make poor bargaining chips', *Bulletin of the Atomic Scientists,* vol. 33, no. 7 (Sep. 1977). For a more in-depth discussion, see Sheehan, M. J., *Arms Control: Theory and Practice* (Basil Blackwell: Oxford, 1988).

[44] Steinberg, G. M., 'Informal arms control: restraint without ceremony', *Arms Control Today,* vol. 12, no. 6 (June 1982), pp. 87–88. See also Bunn (note 20), pp. 87–88.

[45] See, for example, Williams, P., 'What future for arms control?', *ADIU Report,* vol. 7, no. 1 (Jan.–Feb. 1985), p. 3. The significance of complexity as an obstacle is the focus of Taylor, T., 'The bankruptcy of the strategist's approach', *The Arms Race in the 1980s,* eds D. Carlton and C. Schaerf (Macmillan: London, 1982), p. 50.

[46] Perhaps the best comprehensive analysis is found in Rathjens, Chayes and Ruina (note 2), but many other analysts have used these arguments. For a sceptical analysis, see Krell (note 22).

[47] See Perry Robinson, J., *NATO Chemical Weapons Policy and Posture,* ADIU Occasional Paper, no. 4 (Armament and Disarmament Information Unit, University of Sussex: Brighton, Sep. 1986), p. 32.

[48] Gelb (note 2) p. 26, also argues that the pursuit of strict equality may create military instabilities.

[49] See Roberts, A., 'Arms control in a blind alley', *New Society,* vol. 71, no. 1159 (14 Mar. 1985), p. 396.

[50] See Bertram (note 3), p. 3.

[51] For a treatment of the 'rechannelling effect', see Williams (note 45), p. 3. This is also sometimes called the 'displacement effect'.

[52] Neidle, A. F., 'The rise and fall of multilateral arms control', *Arms Control: The Multilateral Alternative,* ed. E. C. Luck (New York University Press: New York, 1983), p. 17.

[53] Hinsley, F. H., *Power and the Pursuit of Peace: Theory and Practice in the History of Relations Between States* (Cambridge University Press: Cambridge, 1967).

[54] *North–South: A Programme for Survival,* The Report of the Independent Commission on International Development issues under the Chairmanship of Willy Brandt (Pan Books: London, 1980).

[55] Hough, J. F., 'The Soviet view of the strategic situation', *Arms Control and International Security,* eds R. Kolkowicz and N. Joeck (Westview Press: Boulder, Colo., 1984).

3. The test ban talks: 1958–63

I. Introduction

Serious consideration of the possibility of negotiating a nuclear test ban treaty can be dated from 1957, when both the Soviet Union and the West began to alter their previous views about how to approach such a ban. Specific talks between the three established nuclear powers—the USA, the USSR and the UK—commenced in 1958 with the initial goal of a nuclear CTB. Some 30 years later, this goal still has not been achieved. The talks, however, did result in the PTBT of 1963, which prohibited atmospheric, outer space and underwater nuclear tests. The important question concerning underground tests, however, was left open. In any event, following the successful conclusion of the PTBT, there was no further serious attempt by the nuclear powers to discuss a CTB for over 20 years.

The test ban talks which occurred between 1958 and 1963 are instructive for a number of reasons. Whereas previous East–West negotiations had been centred on the goal of conventional and nuclear disarmament, and had for the most part been propaganda exercises, the talks leading to the PTBT were the first negotiations to be focused on a more limited arms control objective. Indeed, an agreement appeared a real possibility. Although the cold war attitudes had partially thawed by the late 1950s, the negotiations still reflected the legacy of deep suspicion, as well as the impact of the ideological divergence between the Soviet Union and the West which was embodied in their respective approaches to arms control. At the same time, the talks also reflected the gradual movement toward a new political accommodation. During the late 1950s, the issue of nuclear testing had aroused popular concern world-wide. It is possible to trace the pressures on both the US and Soviet governments to reach an agreement. The opposition to any test ban was openly and strongly voiced within the United States, and there is evidence of opposition inside the Soviet Union. An examination of the talks leading to the PTBT and the political context in which they occurred, enables us to consider the factors that made a partial agreement possible and why a CTB failed. Therefore, the PTBT negotiations provide a good case study for exploring whether the reason for failure can be attributed to mistakes within the course of negotiations or to more fundamental obstacles.

The PTBT talks are also interesting because they were carried out in a number of different forums. Preparatory East–West negotiations concerning the technical issues of verification during 1958 gave scientists an unprecedented responsibility as chief negotiators. Tripartite talks (between the USA, USSR and UK) were held from 31 October 1958 until they effectively broke down at the end of 1961. Early in 1962, the talks were transferred to the new Eighteen-Nation Disarmament Committee (ENDC), which for the first time included eight non-aligned states. The final phase of the intensive negotiations that preceded the conclusion of the PTBT in 1963 were conducted in secrecy in Moscow between the USA, the USSR and the UK. Throughout this period, various debates and resolutions in the UN General Assembly formed an important element in the diplomacy of the test ban talks.

Progress towards a test ban was significantly affected by two international crises and by a change in US administrations. After the Soviet Union downed a US U-2 reconnaissance aircraft over Soviet territory at the beginning of May 1960 and the US subsequently accepted responsibility for the flights, the Paris summit between President Dwight Eisenhower and First Secretary Khrushchev collapsed; and the test ban talks suffered a major reverse. During the aftermath of the October 1962 Cuban missile crisis, however, both Kennedy and Khrushchev displayed a new willingness to try to reach arms control agreements. The test ban talks also reflected the impact of a change of administration in Washington when Kennedy replaced Eisenhower as President in January 1961.

Because of their importance, as well as their intrinsic interest, the various stages of the test ban negotiations have been the focus of several excellent studies. In addition, many of the participants in the talks provided their own first-hand accounts and post-mortem analysis.[1] Furthermore, the memoirs and commentaries from the US and British perspectives are supplemented by several works detailing the views of some of the non-aligned participants in the ENDC.[2] Although Soviet interpretations are less readily available, Western scholars have unearthed a good deal of material concerning policy making in the USSR under Khrushchev. Moreover, although his recollections are not always reliable, Khrushchev's memoirs are available. Therefore, a good basis for a case study of the test ban negotiations exists.

II. Summary history of the test ban talks, 1958–63

In the early 1950s, the USA and the USSR began their first thermonuclear weapon tests. As evidence mounted concerning the dangerous effects of nuclear fall-out on health, international anxiety mounted. Third World opposition to great power nuclear testing was first expressed at the 1955 Bandung Non-Aligned Conference and was voiced perennially thereafter in the forums of the United Nations. By 1957, scientists and parliamentarians, as well as overall public opinion in the United States and Western Europe, had elevated the concern over the dangers of nuclear testing into the rank of a major issue. It was in this context that the Soviet Union began to urge in 1955 that cessation of nuclear tests should be the first step to nuclear disarmament. At the same time, the USSR argued that no special controls to verify a test ban were necessary. The West, however, insisted that a nuclear test ban was only possible as part of a broader disarmament programme that was implemented with proper safeguards to prevent cheating.

During the United Nations Disarmament Sub-Committee meeting in London in 1957, both the USSR and the West modified their positions. The Soviet Union indicated a willingness to begin with a temporary moratorium on testing and to consider some form of controls. The West indicated that it might give priority to a test ban and accept a temporary moratorium on testing while a control system was established. Western delegates also introduced the idea of possible talks of a technical nature concerning how a control system might be set up. The Disarmament Sub-Committee, however, disbanded in September 1957. The USSR decided to boycott the Sub-Committee because of its dominance by Western powers. Apart from the Soviet Union, it had been composed of the USA, the UK, Canada and France. Indeed, Soviet insistence concerning balanced representation in disarmament bodies was to become one of the central issues in negotiations during the following years.

The Soviet Union was publicly committed to beginning test ban talks and, after a series of nuclear tests, announced a unilateral moratorium on further tests in March 1958. Washington was now under pressure to respond. In January 1958, the Afro–Asian Solidarity Conference in Cairo had called for an end to testing, and the US State Department proved to be sensitive to international opinion on this issue. In Washington, the Senate Foreign Relations Sub-Committee on Disarmament provided a platform for strong advocates of a test ban during Sub-Committee hearings early in 1958. Nevertheless, there remained strong opposition to a ban, especially from some nuclear scientists at weapons laboratories and from some in various quarters of the military. As a result, the Eisenhower Administration sought a compromise position. In an exchange of letters with Khrushchev, Eisenhower offered technical talks on the inspection of disarmament, which was later modified to the monitoring of a test ban. Much to the surprise of the West, the Soviet Union agreed to East–West talks on control in this context without insisting on a moratorium. After further correspondence, it was agreed that a Conference of Experts should meet in Geneva on 1 July 1958.

The Conference of Experts

At the outset of the 1958 Geneva Conference of Experts, the United States envisaged a purely technical discussion without any political commitment to negotiate a separate test ban. US scientists responsible for the negotiations were given minimal advance briefing concerning political issues and were assisted by rather junior State Department advisors. The Soviet Union, on the other hand, was fully aware of the political implications of the Conference and was determined to initiate talks about a test ban with Washington. The Soviet Union scored an almost immediate political gain: the recognition by the West of the principle of equal East–West representation at the Conference. Soviet experts were joined by colleagues from Poland and Czechoslovakia, and US scientists were assisted by British and Canadian experts.

The Soviet side received political guidance from a senior diplomat, Semyon Tsarapkin, head of the section for international organizations in the Foreign Ministry and a veteran of disarmament negotiations. The Soviet negotiators were also backed by high-ranking Polish and Czechoslovakian diplomats. Tsarapkin is usually credited with having steered the Conference toward a conclusion which would later pave the way for initiating talks concerning a test ban. The Western scientists opposed an initial Soviet attempt to get a commitment in principle to a test ban, but conceded to the Soviet view that the Conference should recommend a single system of inspection, rather than a range of possible systems. Once the focus was on one system, it was natural to choose a British proposal that compromised between Soviet and US proposals by accepting that very low-yield underground explosions could not be reliably detected or identified. The Conference's final communiqué, issued on 21 August 1958, stated that the technical equipment needed for a control system had been agreed and that a workable system to detect violation of a possible ban could be established. Despite certain qualifications in the communiqué, the Conference appeared to have laid the groundwork for future talks. The next day President Eisenhower responded by suggesting that the three nuclear powers should begin negotiations concerning a 'suspension' of tests and the establishment of an international control system.

The Conference of Experts generated considerable optimism because scientists from the USA and the USSR were able to engage in serious technical discussions and to emerge with an agreement, and because the Soviet Union seemed willing to meet Western concerns about inspection. This optimism, however, proved to be premature. During the subsequent four years of talks, most of the disputes centred around differing interpretations of the technical requirements and the political structure of a control system.

Much of the technical argument concerning the adequacy of a control system was strongly influenced by political concerns; this was the case in the debates *among* US scientists, as well as in the disagreements between US and Soviet experts. Still, there were many technical problems of a very genuine nature concerning verification which were exacerbated by the fact that scientists in 1958 had inadequate data for deciding many important issues. Furthermore, tests conducted in different environments posed multiple problems of detection and identification. Low-level nuclear explosions in the atmosphere were the easiest to detect and identify. Underwater explosions could also be detected to a fair degree of certainty, although absolute identification through the collection of radioactive debris might be more difficult. High altitude or in-space tests, for which there was a paucity of experimental data, could be very difficult to detect. Although the Conference did not recommend special technical measures for dealing with the high altitude or in-space test problem, the Conference suggested that detection should be, at least theoretically, possible. Underground nuclear explosions could be detected through the measurement of seismic waves, but the scientists disagreed concerning just how small an explosion could be detected and how reliably a nuclear explosion could be distinguished from an earthquake (especially in the case of low-yield tests). Moreover, it should be noted that at the time the Geneva Conference met, the Soviet Union had carried out no underground tests. The scientists were relying on the data produced by a single US underground test, the September 1957 'Rainier' detonation of 1.7 kilotons.

The Conference considered four key methods of detecting nuclear tests: the recording of acoustic waves, hydroacoustic waves for underwater tests, radio signals and seismic waves, and the collection of radioactive debris. The technology to implement the first three methods could be installed in a network of control posts, but the collection of debris was thought to require additional provisions for on-site inspection and for aircraft to investigate possible radioactive clouds. Soviet scientists disputed the necessity of flights, but conceded that some flights might be recommended if the aircraft of the state whose territory was being surveyed were used.

The recommendations contained in the Experts' Report concerning on-site inspections were ambiguous and stated, simply, that 'the international control organ can send an inspection group to the site' of a suspicious event. The Report recommended a total of 170–180 control posts to be located on land, on islands and on ships. Each post would be staffed by about 30 specialists. It was surmised that such a control system would have a high probability of detecting and identifying explosions down to 1 kiloton (kt) in the atmosphere below the altitude of 10 kilometres (km), and a good probability of detecting (but not always identifying) explosions at between 10 and 50 kms. There would also be a good probability of detecting explosions as small as 1 kt underwater and underground, but in most cases it would not be possible to distinguish them from earthquakes. At the level equivalent to a 5 kt explosion, however, the Report estimated that the system could identify 90 per cent of earthquakes and, furthermore, could distinguish those earthquakes from nuclear explosions. The Geneva Conference of Experts recognized that there were gaps and uncertainties in the proposed control system. Indeed, the presumed adequacy of the proposed system would soon be seriously contested.

Tripartite talks in Geneva

On 31 October 1958, test ban talks between the USA, the USSR and the UK began somewhat inauspiciously in Geneva. In August, President Eisenhower had called for a moratorium on nuclear testing to coincide with the opening of the negotiations. As a result, both the USA and the UK actually accelerated their nuclear testing programmes in order to conclude as many tests as possible before the deadline. The Soviet Union invoked the escape clause in its moratorium dating from 31 March 1958 and began a major series of tests on 30 September. In fact, the Soviet Union conducted two tests (early in November) after the Conference had already started, but then ceased. The tone of Soviet public statements was hostile. In a *Pravda* interview, Khrushchev attacked the USA for limiting its own promised moratorium to one year, for attempting to link a suspension of tests to major measures of disarmament and for placing such emphasis on a control system. In addition, the Soviet Union attempted to mobilize the UN General Assembly behind a resolution which called for an immediate end to testing and omitted any reference to international control. The head of the US delegation to the Conference told a reporter the day before it was due to start that 'it could wind up in a few weeks'.[3]

Although the negotiations were held outside the framework of the United Nations (as the Conference of Experts had been), they were, nonetheless, serviced by the UN Secretariat. The official title for the talks was 'The Conference on the Discontinuance of Nuclear Weapon Tests', which reflected a compromise between the Western emphasis on 'suspension' and the Soviet call for 'cessation' of testing. Although Ambassador James Wadsworth, the leader of the US delegation, had experience in arms control negotiations at the UN, he lacked technical expertise in the intricacies of verifying nuclear tests. Wadsworth's deputy was Robert Bacher, a physicist, who had been one of the chief negotiators during the Conference of Experts and was favourable to a test ban. In addition to senior advisors from the Departments of State and Defense, and the Atomic Energy Commission (AEC), the delegation included two congressmen. Tsarapkin headed the Soviet delegation. Tsarapkin's deputy was Evgenii K. Federov, a scientist who had led the Soviet group at the Conference of Experts. The British delegation, headed by David Ormsby Gore, was drawn from the Foreign Office and included no senior scientist.

The negotiations began with a dispute concerning the agenda, which was not surprising considering the gap that existed between the two sides. The West still emphasized the necessity of a suspension of nuclear tests as a first step toward more substantial measures of disarmament, and the USSR introduced a brief draft which proposed an indefinite test ban. The central source of disagreement between the two sides, however, was the fact that the West wanted to begin by examining the details of a control system, while the USSR suggested that the details of control could be considered in a separate document after an agreement in principle concerning a test ban had been concluded. Compared with its conciliatory tone at the Conference of Experts, the Soviet delegation appeared to be taking a tougher line. The USA's disquiet was increased by the fact that a Conference on Surprise Attack, convened at about the same time, broke up after six weeks because of total failure to agree on an agenda. The Soviet Union was aware of strong domestic opposition in the USA to any test ban and, therefore, retained its own doubts concerning US intentions.

After the Christmas recess, Soviet suspicions deepened when the US delegation submitted new technical data which were derived from US nuclear tests carried out during 1958. The new data appeared to invalidate the findings of the Conference of Experts and to require many more on-site inspections. Wadsworth wrote later that the new data 'spread a pall over the negotiations from which they never completely recovered' and that 'all the latent suspicion that had been lulled by our comparatively good progress in the negotiations blazed up more fiercely than ever'.[4] Nevertheless, both sides made concessions to get the negotiations off the ground. Before Christmas, the USSR had agreed that provisions for a control system could be part of a test ban treaty and had initiated discussion concerning the details. On 19 January 1959, the West reciprocated by announcing that it would no longer make a test ban contingent on wider disarmament measures. Furthermore, in March, the USA and the UK accepted the Soviet view that the treaty should be of indefinite duration, provided there was a right to withdraw in the event of violations.

The key issues in the negotiations were the political organization of the control system and the adequacy of technical methods of verification. Two lesser problems concerned which countries should be parties to the treaty and whether, or under what terms, 'peaceful nuclear explosions' (PNEs) could be allowed. Despite diametrically opposed views on many questions, both sides did apparently engage in serious negotiations up to May 1960 and made some effort to respond to the other side's concerns. Although the UK co-ordinated its position with the USA, Great Britain sometimes attempted to mediate between the USA and the USSR.

The West envisaged a very elaborate organization to ensure compliance with the test ban treaty, partly because it was seen as a model for inspecting wider disarmament measures, and partly because the USA and the UK suspected that the Soviet Union would cheat. The USSR, on the other hand, feared that any international control body would be dominated by the West (as the UN was at the time) and used as a pretext for political interference or espionage in the Soviet Union.

The USA proposed a conference of parties to the treaty that would periodically review the control system; a Control Commission composed of the nuclear weapon states and a few other countries which would set up the control system and decide if the treaty had been violated; and an administrator appointed by and responsible to the Commission. The administrator would have executive powers, and manage a central headquarters and regional offices which would supervise the control posts. Each of the 180 control posts would be staffed by an international team, and a permanent inspectorate to check possible violations would be based at headquarters. According to the US plan, the administrator would automatically authorize an on-site inspection according to criteria to be agreed.

The Soviet Union accepted the overall framework, but differed over the composition of the Commission and the headquarters staff. The crucial disagreements over the central organization, however, concerned the method of decision making in the Commission, the role of the administrator and the procedure for invoking on-site inspections. The USSR favoured unanimous decision making in the Commission, which would have provided the USSR, in effect, with veto power. Neither did the Soviet Union desire a specifically designated nor influential administrator. Regarding procedure, the USSR proposed that a country accused of treaty violations should put its case to the Commission before an on-site inspection was authorized.

A number of other issues also divided the USA and the USSR. For example, the Soviet Union opposed the idea of a permanent inspectorate. The staffing of control posts also reflected a deep division between the two sides. The USA urged the designation of an international team for each post in which there should be no nationals of the host country, whereas the USSR maintained that each control post should be staffed entirely by the host country, except for an observer representing the other side.

Through subsequent negotiation, the gap between the two sides narrowed somewhat. The Soviet Union clarified the issues for which it wished to reserve the right of veto in the Control Commission. The USA and the UK recognized that over certain issues, such as the revision of the treaty, a right of veto was reasonable. The West also accepted the right of a veto in the appointment of the administrator to meet Soviet apprehension about the role of a chief executive officer. The Soviet Union accepted the principle of a permanent inspectorate, and the West offered to set a quota for the number of annual inspections. Both sides exchanged various proposals concerning the composition of the Commission and the staffing of the headquarters; both were to comprise representatives of East and West, and of non-aligned states. Concessions were made on the staffing of control posts, and both sides accepted that there should be some mix of nationals of the host country and an international team.

Surprisingly, it was the issue concerning the technical data (upon which the system of detection and verification would be based) that caused the greater acrimony in the talks and *not* the specifically political differences. The Soviet Union assumed that the technical issues had been settled by the Conference of Experts. When the USA produced new data based on its own underground and high altitude tests carried out during 1958 which emphasized the difficulty of detecting tests in both environments, the USSR suspected an attempt to sabotage the progress already achieved. The Soviet Union's response was to insist on standing by the findings of the Conference of Experts. The new data on underground explosions (based on only two tests out of a series of eight that had produced adequate data) suggested that the magnitude of the Rainier detonation had been overestimated on the Richter scale and that it was actually harder to detect the first motion of a nuclear test on a seismograph than was first indicated. According to a State Department release, the Geneva system could only identify tests as low as a yield of 20 kt, instead of the 5 kt as was previously thought. The State Department maintained that the task of distinguishing tests from earthquakes was much greater than the Conference of Experts had previously surmised.[5] Although the Panel of Experts commissioned by Eisenhower to evaluate the new findings recommended some measures to improve the Geneva system, opponents of a test ban in the USA seized on the latest data to demonstrate why a verifiable ban was impossible.

The Conference of Experts, however, had not covered the issue of high-altitude tests. On this issue, the Soviet Union proved to be more receptive to further technical discussion concerning methods of detection. A Technical Working Group was duly established. The USSR insisted that the Group should report to the Conference only a week after it had started work, but in practice the deadline was extended somewhat. The gap between the scientists from the two sides was even greater than at the Conference of Experts, and the Soviet scientists ruled out use of backscatter radar on the grounds that it could be used for other purposes. On 10 July 1959, the Group reported to the Conference with a number of agreed recommendations on the use of satellites to detect high-altitude tests and of additional equipment at control posts.

A second Technical Working Group was finally constituted in November 1959 to examine the implications of the data from the 1958 US underground tests. The USA pressed for these discussions because both supporters and opponents of a test ban within the Administration hoped technical talks would strengthen their positions. As a major concession, the Soviet Union had agreed to set up the second Working Group. Nevertheless, the Soviet delegates remained deeply suspicious that the purpose of the new data was to undermine the possibility of a CTB.

The Soviet suspicions were enhanced when, in addition to producing the underground test findings, the US scientists unveiled a new theory of how to camouflage underground tests through 'decoupling'—the detonation of nuclear devices in very large cavities. The theory of decoupling emerged as a result of research authorized by Edward Teller at the Lawrence Livermore National Laboratory immediately after the Conference of Experts. In March 1959, Rand physicist Albert Latter persuasively argued for the theory in a paper which circulated within government circles and was not made public until December that year. Although decoupling had been raised at the Conference of Experts, the idea was dismissed by Hans Bethe as impractical. Latter's analysis, however, persuaded Bethe and other scientists that decoupling was at least theoretically possible, although some US scientists remained sceptical concerning the theory's feasability. When they were first confronted with the theory in the Working Group, the Soviet scientists were incredulous. Later, they conceded the hypothetical possibility of decoupling, while stressing that it had not been tried in practice. The fact that Teller and Latter were known to be enthusiasts for the US nuclear weapon programme, as well as strong opponents of a test ban, suggested that the whole purpose of introducing the theory was to prevent agreement. The Soviet scientists were also dismissive of the new seismic data, arguing that the US instruments for recording the 1958 tests were less sensitive that those proposed for the Geneva system. In any event, the second Working Group broke up in acrimony in December 1959.

The failure of the second Working Group to reach an agreement strengthened the position of the critics of a test ban in Washington. As a result, President Eisenhower adopted a compromise position concerning the contentious question of whether or not the USA should continue its moratorium on all nuclear testing. The USA had observed the moratorium since 31 October 1958, and had already extended it once until the end of 1959. Eisenhower announced on 29 December that the USA would feel free to resume testing but would give advance notice. The USSR had renewed its own moratorium in August 1959 when the USA extended its suspension of tests to the end of the year. In January 1960, the Soviet Union criticized the new US position, but reiterated that it would not resume testing until the West did so. Yet, the fiasco of the second Working Group and the USA's retreat from a formal commitment to a moratorium were less damaging to the Conference than might have been expected. Countervailing factors were that the USA, the UK and the USSR, together with nine other states, had agreed on the Antarctic Treaty on 1 December 1959; and the USA and the USSR had also agreed on the setting up of a UN Committee on the peaceful uses of outer space. In both Washington and Moscow, influential groups were anxious to keep the talks going.

One way to bypass the most intractable problems of detecting and identifying low-yield underground tests was to try for a test ban which was not comprehensive. Indeed, the West had made a number of proposals for a more limited ban before 1963. The first US offer was floated in April 1959 and proposed a ban on atmospheric tests. When the offer was presented in Geneva, however, it was expanded to cover underwater tests as well. A partial test ban was still linked to an international control system and was dismissed by a Soviet Union anxious for a CTB.

In February 1960, the USA made a more constructive offer when it proposed a phased treaty leading to a CTB. In phase one, atmospheric, underwater and outer space tests (as high as could be covered by controls) would be banned. In addition, underground tests down to the threshold where adequate control could be exercised would also be banned. The USA suggested that this threshold should apply to detonations of a seismic magnitude of 4.75 on the Richter scale. The plan included an international control system and a provision for a number of on-site inspections (about 20 visits per year to the Soviet Union) to check unidentified events. Provided detection and identification methods improved, the threshold could be lowered; meanwhile, the USA would feel free to test below the threshold.

After an initially negative response, the Soviet Union accepted the idea of a phased treaty but urged that a moratorium on tests below the threshold be written into the treaty. The USSR also discussed possible criteria for establishing what constituted a suspicious event. On 29 March 1960, Eisenhower and British Prime Minister Harold Macmillan publicly announced an offer to implement a voluntary moratorium on nuclear tests that would accompany a threshold agreement. The Soviet reply, delivered on 3 May, suggested that this offer could be acceptable, provided that the three parties could agree on the length of the moratorium.

During the period just before the planned summit meeting (set for 16 May in Paris), the prospects for a limited test ban treaty seemed promising. Although the Soviet Union had waived its claim to a veto in the Control Commission on most issues, including treaty revision, the USSR held out for a veto on budgetary matters. Both sides agreed to implement to a joint research programme to improve methods of detecting and identifying tests below the 4.75 seismic threshold and, in principle, to a quota for tests. Although there were still questions to be resolved on staffing control posts and procedures for aircraft flights, the most significant remaining problems were likely to concern the duration of a moratorium and the exact number of proposed inspection visits.

After the summit meeting was aborted by the U-2 incident, both sides continued to elaborate upon problems of detail until the end of the year. However, there was still no agreement on any issue of substance. The Eisenhower Administration was now marking time until the presidential election and was attempting to avoid any action which might create problems for a future Republican Administration. Although the USA continued to refrain from nuclear testing and to negotiate, it took no further initiatives. On 27 May 1960, the Soviet Union retreated from its earlier willingness to join in a research programme on underground tests and offered a quota of three inspections a year. The Soviet Union, however, did go through the motions of serious talks. At the UN General Assembly, however, the USSR initiated a bitter dispute concerning the role of the Secretary General.

After the Democrats won the presidential election and John F. Kennedy entered the White House in January 1961, the new Administration reviewed the test ban talks and embarked on a more activist policy of seeking an agreement. In March, the USA introduced new proposals for a revised draft treaty which was based on the phased treaty idea. These proposals included some concessions to the USSR, and proposed a moratorium of three years (the period estimated to require a research programme into detection of underground tests), offered East–West parity on the Control Commission and accepted a Soviet right of veto on the total budget. In addition, the ban was to include all high altitude tests.

The Soviet Union, however, had already decided to embark on another major series of nuclear tests, and its response to the Kennedy Administration's proposals was almost completely negative. The Soviet delegation proposed that the single administrator should be replaced by a *troika*—three executives representing Western, Eastern and non-aligned interests—thus replicating the Soviet Union's proposals on how the UN should be run. This proposal, patently unacceptable to the West, also had the effect of reinstating a Soviet veto right on every issue. The West had opposed a similar proposal by the USSR in the UN.

In June 1961, the Soviet Union indicated that it had lost interest in test ban negotiations, saying the answer lay in the implementation of general and comprehensive disarmament. On 30 August, Moscow announced a new series of nuclear tests. The USA responded with a resumption of underground tests, but President Kennedy, together with Prime Minister Harold Macmillan of Britain, offered a ban on atmospheric testing without any international controls. The USSR rejected the proposal, accused the West of hypocrisy, and pointed to the French nuclear tests in 1960 and 1961.

The autumn of 1961 ended with a flurry of activity concerning nuclear testing. The Soviet test series ended with an explosion of over 50 megatons (mt) at the end of October, and Kennedy began preparations for atmospheric tests early in November. In September, the Geneva Conference formally went into recess amid mutual accusations to await the outcome of the UN General Assembly debate on nuclear testing. The Conference resumed briefly in November but adjourned without issuing any agreed statement.

It was through the United Nations that the nuclear powers were brought together again to discuss nuclear testing in 1962. After the West had conceded the principle of equal NATO and WTO representation, the Ten-Nation Disarmament Committee (TNDC) was set up to discuss plans for general disarmament in May 1959, but folded in June 1960 during the aftermath of the U-2 affair.

The Eighteen-Nation Disarmament Committee

After the collapse of the TNDC, the UN General Assembly voted to establish the Eighteen Nation Disarmament Committee (ENDC) which would meet at Geneva in March 1962. Although the ENDC was set up following the McCloy–Zorin agreement on principles of general disarmament in September 1961, the participants—especially the non-aligned states—were primarily concerned about nuclear testing. France, the only member of the Committee opposed in principle to a test ban, boycotted all meetings.

The ENDC began its deliberations in an atmosphere of mutual hostility between the USA and USSR. In March 1962, Kennedy announced that the USA would resume testing above ground unless the Western treaty draft was signed by April. Khrushchev replied that a new US series would force the USSR to resume testing. When the ENDC convened, the USA and the UK put forward some amendments to their draft treaty by proposing the abolition of the 4.75 seismic threshold and the reversion to a CTB, but without an increase in the number of control posts or on-site inspections in the Soviet Union. The USSR rejected these proposals and argued that no international controls were required for tests in any environment.

In light of the deadlock between the nuclear powers, the eight non-aligned states took the initiative and produced a memorandum in April which sought a compromise between the Western and Soviet positions. The non-aligned proposal abandoned the vast and elaborate control system envisaged by the West, and advocated the use of national monitoring facilities instead. Swedish research indicated that national stations were already monitoring nuclear tests with a high degree of efficiency. The memorandum suggested the establishment of an international scientific commission to evaluate data and recognized the case for on-site inspection if unidentified and suspicious events took place. Although the memorandum was a promising move towards tackling problems of control and technical detection, the document was rather ambiguously phrased, partly because of differences of emphasis among the eight. The USA and the USSR almost immediately contrived their own contradictory interpretations of the memorandum, and no further progress was achieved in the ENDC before the summer recess.

In July, the USA published preliminary findings concerning its Vela research programme for the detection and identification of underground tests. These findings suggested that, on balance, the problems were not as great as previously thought.[6] Although the Vela programme findings were potentially helpful, their immediate impact was obscured by confusing and contradictory statements by US officials concerning whether or not the findings meant control posts in the USSR were no longer required. At first, the Soviet Union reacted contemptuously to yet another set of new US data and resumed atmospheric tests in July. The Soviet delegation, however, would later prove to be more receptive.

In August, the USA again took the initiative and tabled two alternative draft treaties. The first proposed a CTB, but its provisions were modified to take account of the eight-nation memorandum and the latest research findings. It also required a simplified international organization and mandated a control system based mostly on national posts. The treaty also included a quota of on-site inspections, but the number was left open. The second treaty proposed a partial test ban in the atmosphere, outer space and underwater with no international inspection. Various non-aligned states in the ENDC had urged an immediate partial ban as a possible first step. The US view was that a CTB was still preferable but that a partial ban would be a valuable advance. The USSR responded negatively to the USA's CTB proposal and insisted that a partial ban must be linked to a moratorium on underground tests. The USA had already made it clear that such a moratorium was totally unacceptable; because the Soviet Union had resumed tests in 1961, US domestic opinion was adamantly opposed to an unconditional moratorium.

Although the October 1962 Cuban missile crisis temporarily disrupted the negotiations, both sides made serious efforts to promote arms control in its aftermath. In November, a significant switch in the Soviet position concerning a test ban occurred when the Soviet delegation at Geneva hinted that the USSR would accept 'black boxes' (automatic recording stations) as a monitoring device and later named three possible sites. In December, Khrushchev wrote to Kennedy and offered to permit two or three on-site inspections a year and the location of three black boxes in the USSR. Khrushchev's correspondence, designed to promote a breakthrough, led to direct US–Soviet talks in January 1963 in which Britain was included. Still, an agreement concerning the number of inspections in the USSR proved to be impossible to conclude. In light of the new research findings, the West was willing to accept as few as eight to ten inspection visits per year; previously the West had envisaged 12 to 20. The USSR, however, would not budge from its proposal of three. Similarly, the West proposed a minimum of 10 black boxes in the USSR, but the Soviet side insisted that three were adequate.

In February 1963, the ENDC resumed its deliberations, but the discussions degenerated into a numbers game. Although the West reduced its inspection demand to seven visits per year, the Soviet Union still insisted upon no more than three. The eight non-aligned states again prepared to mediate and privately drew up proposals which envisaged four to five inspections a year over a fixed number of five or seven years. The proposals were leaked to the great powers before they were to be publicly presented, however; and the USA and the USSR, hinting that the proposals would actually hinder an agreement, pressured the other participants to bury the proposals. Sweden and India were persuaded to veto the new eight–nation compromise (which was never tabled), although Swedish Ambassador Alva Myrdal revealed its contents at a public meeting in May. The non-aligned delegations at Geneva then abandoned their efforts. By late April 1963, the Soviet delegation indicated that it was too late for compromise. Indeed, Prime Minister Khrushchev told an Italian newspaper that even the offer of two or three on-site inspections per year might be withdrawn.

The Moscow Conference

Despite the stalemate at the ENDC discussions, there was significant progress between the USA and the USSR in other areas. Technical talks concerning a 'hot line' between the two capitals to reduce the risk of accidental war were begun in April 1963 and concluded with an agreement in June. Both sides made conciliatory public gestures. After private contacts with Khrushchev, Kennedy made a major speech on 10 June in which he called for new attitudes toward peace and announced a new set of test ban negotiations to be held in Moscow. Before the talks began on 15 July, Khrushchev made it publicly clear that the USSR would not accept a CTB because of the West's insistence on on-site inspection. However, Khrushchev indicated that the Soviet Union would accept a treaty which banned atmospheric, underwater and outer space tests without demanding an underground test moratorium. Both the USA and the UK were willing to accept a partial ban, although President Kennedy wanted a final push for a CTB.

The Moscow negotiations were conducted by Soviet Foreign Minister, Andrei Gromyko, US Ambassador Averell Harriman (whom President Kennedy had entrusted with this final crucial stage) and Lord Hailsham for the UK.

Unlike the earlier stages of the test ban negotiations which had formally been private but in practice were well publicized by press conferences and official statements, the Moscow talks were held in the strictest secrecy. In Washington, President Kennedy retained close personal control over the talks and for the most part excluded the bureaucracy.

After a final brief attempt to conclude a CTB, the USA settled for a partial test ban. Discussion centred on the Western draft treaty of August 1962. The USA and the UK agreed to drop a clause allowing PNEs above ground (they were, of course, still permitted underground) in return for Soviet acceptance of easier conditions for amending the treaty.

The PTBT talks only lasted 10 days. Neither side had pressed for unacceptable conditions. The USSR urged a non-aggression pact between NATO and the WTO but recognized the impossibility of negotiating such a pact on the spot. The USSR also urged that France should be a party to the treaty, as it had done at various stages earlier in the negotiations, but abandoned this position after the USA enquired about China. By then, China had broken away publicly from the USSR and was seeking to develop its own nuclear weapons. It was agreed that the PTBT should be open to accession by all countries. All three of the original parties were listed as depository governments to obviate possible problems in the case of countries not recognized by one side or the other.

The PTBT was initialled on 25 July and formally signed on 5 August by the three foreign ministers. Although France and China denounced the Treaty as an attempt to preserve nuclear hegemony, the PTBT was widely hailed in the rest of the world. In the United States, some open dissent was voiced, but a vigorous campaign by the Administration secured Senate ratification by 80 votes to 19— twelve votes over the 67 (or two-thirds majority) which was required.

III. Was a CTB possible?

In reviewing the course of negotiations between 1958 and 1963, it is important to ask whether a CTB could have been achieved at any stage through greater political and diplomatic skill. There are two periods in which a CTB appears to have been a genuine possibility: the spring of 1960 and from December 1962 to January 1963.

By early 1960, the test ban talks had reached a stage when both sides seemed ready to settle for a phased treaty with a seismic threshold of 4.75 for underground testing combined with a moratorium on lower-yield tests. The USSR had agreed in principle to on-site inspection and to the placement of control posts in the Soviet Union; the West had recognized the case for setting a specific quota of inspections. Both sides had made concessions concerning the control organization. The broader political circumstances also looked favourable; the Antarctic Treaty had been signed in December 1959, and a summit meeting was scheduled for May 1960. Despite vocal opposition in the

USA to the Soviet Union's test ban proposal of March, the Administration in general and Eisenhower personally were more favourable to a test ban than before. Prime Minister Harold Macmillan, who had made personal efforts to promote a test ban, is on record as claiming that an agreement could have been achieved early in 1960. Indeed, Macmillan blaimed the failure to achieve an agreement on the obsession of some US scientists with 'big holes'.[7] The shooting down of the US U-2 reconnaissance aircraft, therefore, apparently destroyed the previous hopes for a test ban, although it took about three weeks for the impact of the U-2 incident to be felt in the test ban negotiations.

Nevertheless, it is highly unlikely that a quick agreement could have been reached in 1960. Major stumbling blocks remained; such issues included the number of on-site inspections and the length of a voluntary moratorium, as well as numerous tricky points concerning a control organization which was then still envisaged as being extremely elaborate.

The possibility of a breakthrough to agree a CTB appears to have been much greater in December 1962, despite the previous period of mutual hostility which resulted in part from renewed testing. The results of the latest US research, together with the role of the non-aligned states, had enabled the USA to relax its control requirements and to simplify the control procedures and organization, thus removing key areas of disagreement. The USA's August 1962 CTBT draft no longer required internationally staffed control posts in the USSR, nor aircraft flights over Soviet territory. The only genuine problem which remained was on-site inspection. In September 1962, a Pugwash Conference proposed a possible technical solution to alleviate this problem; three Soviet and three US scientists recommended the installation of unmanned monitoring stations or 'black boxes'.

The narrow brush with disaster during the Cuban missile crisis served to strengthen the personal commitment of both Kennedy and Khrushchev to arms control. The crisis also strengthened Kennedy's domestic position and made a foreign policy success more important for Khrushchev. Kennedy's perceived 'success' in handling the missile crisis had made him less vulnerable to right-wing criticism, and after two years in office, he had gained the experience and authority to fight for ratification of a test ban in the Senate. Khrushchev, on the other hand, had been weakened by his role in the missile crisis for which he was publicly attacked by China. As a result, Khrushchev needed to demonstrate to the Chinese (in addition to his domestic opponents) that his policy of peaceful coexistence and of recognizing that moderate elements existed in the US leadership could work. A test ban treaty would be a potent symbol of success. In the wake of the missile crisis, the Soviet press made the best of the USSR's retrenchment by stressing that its concessions should lead to arms control.[8]

In December 1962, Khrushchev took the initiative and reverted to the earlier position that the USSR would accept two or three inspections in addition to the placement of three black boxes. This was interpreted as a major breakthrough but the commitment to precise figures proved a serious obstacle. Khrushchev personally and the Soviet delegation at Geneva officially regarded it as a final concession. The USA, however, refused to accept such a low figure. Apparently, Khrushchev had understood that his offer would be acceptable to the West. Most non-aligned delegates at Geneva, as well as some US observers, thought that there had been a real misunderstanding in informal communications.[9] When the Geneva talks resumed, the Soviet delegation seemed genuinely bitter that the USA was still holding out for eight inspections per year. On the other hand, neither President Kennedy nor Senator Hubert Humphrey, the key supporter of a test ban in the Senate, believed that a treaty which stipulated only three annual inspections in the USSR would be ratified.[10]

In March 1963, it appeared (at least superficially) that the USA and the USSR were prevented from concluding a CTB by an inability to bridge the difference between three and seven annual inspections, and by a diplomatic misunderstanding. However, the fact that both Moscow and Washington sabotaged the attempt at a compromise by the non-aligned states indicates that prospects for a CTBT were only illusory. The last genuine opportunity to conclude a CTBT may have been during the unofficial three-power talks in January, before the domestic opponents of a test ban had marshalled their forces. Beginning in late January 1963, after an agreement began to appear likely, the opposition in the USA became more vocal. Republican congressmen began to campaign against a test ban and were joined by some Democratic senators. When the Congressional Joint Committee on Atomic Energy held hearings in March, it provided a platform to critics of the US draft treaty of August 1962.

Khrushchev had been unable to move beyond the figure of three inspections per year largely because of domestic pressures. Khrushchev told Kennedy's unofficial mediator, US journalist Norman Cousins, that he had asked the Council of Ministers to authorize an offer of three inspections a year on the understanding that it was enough and could not ask for a new figure.[11] In February 1963, Soviet Defence Minister Marshal Rodion Malinovski made a hawkish speech condemning advocates of 'pacifism' and 'abstract negation of war'.[12]

Whether one judges that a CTB might have been achieved in January 1963 depends partly on one's assessment of how far skilful political leadership can circumvent the forces resisting major arms control. In most arms control negotiations, there usually is some latitude for manœuvre. Indeed, it was the skilful exploitation of this factor which facilitated the achievement of the PTBT later in 1963. What it is much more doubtful, however, is whether either Kennedy or Khrushchev could have pushed through a successful treaty which banned all nuclear tests and involved international inspection. In May 1963, a survey of the US Senate revealed that only 57 senators would have voted to ratify a CTBT, which was 10 votes short of the two-thirds majority required. Furthermore, the survey also revealed that any reduction of the number of inspections inside the USSR below seven would probably have eroded support.[13] The JCS openly opposed the US draft treaty of August 1962.

When President Kennedy announced a new moratorium on atmospheric testing in June 1963, he did not include underground tests which were, in fact, carried out both before and after the ratification of the PTBT. These actions were apparently designed to secure military and conservative support for the Treaty. By May, Khrushchev had irrevocably retreated from a CTB and a commitment to permit inspections on Soviet territory. Undoubtedly, the opposition to a total ban, both in the USA and in the USSR, was intensified by the perceived intransigence of the other side concerning the number of yearly inspections. Nevertheless, the basis of the opposition was rooted in much more fundamental political, ideological and military causes. It is to these factors that we now turn in examining some of the obstacles to the test ban talks. Certainly, considerable the conclusion of *any* agreement faces substantial obstacles; in the case of a CTB, however, the difficulties proved to be especially intractable.

IV. The real purpose of the talks

The first question that it is necessary to answer is whether either the USA or the USSR was negotiating seriously for a test ban before the end of 1962, or whether the aim of the talks was primarily to conciliate international and domestic public opinion or to achieve some ulterior political or strategic motive. In the test ban talks, the motives of both sides were more ambiguous than in most other negotiations. At least partly, this ambiguity may have resulted from the fact that the test ban talks marked a transition from the ritualistic posturing of the earlier sessions on general and comprehensive disarmament to the conduct of serious negotiations on limited arms control in the late 1960s and early 1970s. The aims of various sections within the governing bureaucracies and political élites in both countries were even more diverse than usual and resulted in considerable confusion or deadlock in policy making at various stages.

The USA entered into the test ban talks only reluctantly. A combination of Soviet diplomacy, pressure from allies and non-aligned states such as Japan and India, and the domestic anxieties over nuclear fall-out, served to manœuvre the USA into the negotiations. Even so, it was not until early 1959 that the USA committed itself to seek the conclusion of a test ban independent of a wider agreement. At this stage, the State Department favoured negotiations to avoid being put at a diplomatic disadvantage and to explore how far the USSR would go in negotiating on a control system, although Secretary of State John Foster Dulles doubted the prospects for success. The Central Intelligence Agency (CIA) was interested in the possibility of opening up Soviet society through the implementation of an international control system.[14]

Although President Eisenhower decided in favour of talks, he remained uncertain concerning the advisability of a CTB. The USA negotiated seriously in 1959, at least in the sense of putting forward proposals, and made a number of concessions to see how far the Soviet Union might go concerning the control system and inspection issues. The Department of Defense (DOD) and the AEC, however, were adamantly opposed to a test ban, and Washington did not pursue the negotiations with much vigour or enthusiasm.[15] Only after the Soviet Union accepted the principle of a threshold treaty in March 1960 did the Eisenhower Administration indicate that it really wanted an agreement. The DOD shifted to the view that the benefits of an agreement that reduced Soviet secrecy and isolation from the rest of the world outweighed the value of further testing, and the President became enthusiastic.[16] After the U-2 incident and the summit débâcle, however, the Administration lost all apparent interest in an agreement.

The Kennedy Presidency inaugurated a rather more vigorous approach to the Geneva negotiations. Nevertheless, because the USSR did not reciprocate, the extent of Kennedy's commitment was not immediately tested. After the Soviet Union had resumed nuclear testing in September 1961, both sides seemed more anxious to conclude a major series of tests than to move towards agreement, a situation which lasted until late 1962. US motives, therefore, were very mixed, and genuine desire for a test ban predominated only for a very brief period of time from 1960 and until early 1961. Even so, the talks were not apparently deliberately conceived as a means of achieving ulterior ends.

Before September 1961, many Americans suspected the USSR of bad faith in the test ban talks. In 1958, Kissinger suggested that the Soviet Union might use a moratorium to prepare its own test programme.[17] After attending the opening of the test ban talks, Senator Albert Gore, Sr argued that the Soviet aim was to hold back the US nuclear weapons development—in particular, tactical nuclear weapons—and that the USSR would not accept a treaty with any genuine controls.[18] After the Soviet Union was the first to begin testing again in 1961 (and had clearly been planning a major new series for at least six months), the view that the Soviet aim had been to inhibit US testing while using the period of negotiations to catch up gained in plausibility. Arthur Dean (head of the US delegation by 1961) observed that the tests confirmed what the delegation had begun to suspect in the early spring of 1961: 'that the talks had been deliberately misused as a screen for test preparations'.[19]

The detailed evidence from the period, however, does not support the view that the Soviet Union was negotiating throughout in bad faith. Until May 1960, the negotiating record indicates that the USSR was at least as serious as the USA. Indeed, the USSR made a number of substantial concessions, including acceptance of the threshold concept which tipped the balance in Washington in March 1960. James Wadsworth's impression was that 'at the start, and for some considerable time thereafter, the Soviets were genuinely seeking agreement'.[20] Because Wadsworth wrote this at a time when the test ban talks appeared to have completely collapsed—largely as a result of Soviet intransigence—his assessment is of considerable interest.

It is quite likely that the Soviet decision to resume testing was definitively made after the U-2 affair. This incident together with conflicts concerning the role of the UN in the Congo resulted in worsening US–Soviet relations and greatly reduced the prospects for arms control. Moreover, because the USA did not formally renew its commitment to a moratorium after the end of 1959, the Soviet Union may have anticipated a resumption of US tests by 1961. In fact, the JCS in February 1961 pressed hard for a resumption of nuclear testing both in the atmosphere and underground, but President Kennedy decided against it.[21] In addition, the renewed testing by the Soviet Union may have been prompted in part by the rapid buildup of Minuteman and Polaris missiles by the Kennedy Administration.[22]

The USSR must have been engaged in intensive preparations for testing from about March 1961, and it was at this stage that Soviet lack of interest in immediate progress towards a test ban was most clearly reflected at Geneva. The USSR apparently did not try very hard to disguise its intentions. Although the Soviet Union was no doubt aware that a moratorium on US testing would tend to reduce the US lead if talks broke down (the Soviet Union apparently maintained its laboratory research throughout), it cannot reasonably be concluded that the main purpose was to use the talks to hold back the US weapon programme and to serve as a screen for the USSR's weapon R&D.

V. Obstacles to Agreement

Great power confrontation

The test ban talks took place at a time when the extreme cold war hostility of the early 1950s had receded but before either side had adopted a coherent policy of *détente*. Relations between Moscow and Washington fluctuated between cautious attempts to reach an understanding and bitter polemics concerning a number of issues. The test ban talks also reflected these tensions and were impeded by the political and military obstacles arising out of the great power confrontation.

Although propaganda certainly played a role in the test ban talks, proposals were apparently not made *solely* for propaganda purposes. The possible exception may have been those proposals tabled by both sides at the very end of 1961 which were clearly not meant to be taken seriously. Even when President Kennedy and Prime Minister Macmillan proposed an atmospheric ban without controls in September 1961 (in an apparent attempt to head off renewed Soviet tests), the offer was genuine, although they also intended to put the Soviet Union in the wrong.[23] The Soviet Union, on the other hand, undoubtedly did attempt to mobilize US and international opinion behind some of its moves, but this could be viewed as aiding, rather than hindering, progress.

Robert Gilpin observes that when the USSR accepted the 4.75 seismic threshold proposal in March 1960, 'the propaganda impact . . . was great'.[24] The move was also productive. However, Western suspicion that the Soviet Union was primarily engaging in propaganda, as opposed to serious negotiation, was a problem. Senator Clinton Anderson, Chairman of the Joint Committee on Atomic Energy, immediately declared that the Soviet offer of March was 'phony'.[25] In 1964, Michael Wright, a British representative at the Geneva test ban talks, examined the thesis that the Soviet record on the test ban, as well as on general and comprehensive disarmament, showed that 'Soviet policy over disarmament has been a gigantic exercise in propaganda'. Wright, however, is cautiously inclined to the view that reversals in the Soviet position may have reflected domestic conflicts.[26]

The test ban talks suffered from several kinds of political linkage. Both sides related their position in the talks to their stance in other negotiations or on other issues. The West continued to insist upon an elaborate and expensive control organization (until the non-aligned countries publicly demonstrated it to be both unnecessary and inappropriate) because of a commitment to the principles of international inspection and control in the context of the Geneva CD. The Soviet Union pursued its quest for parity in representation on international bodies within the context of discussions concerning the composition of a Control Commission. Equal representation on the Commission was an inherently reasonable requirement. The Eisenhower Administration, however— probably because of its implications for other forums—never conceded this point, although President Kennedy promptly did. The Soviet Union also linked its quarrels concerning UN budget contributions, as well as the role of the UN Secretary General, to its position on the control organization for a test ban. The West, however, stood by its own UN policies. The most damaging injection of UN issues into the test ban talks, however, was the Soviet proposal, early in 1961, for a *troika* instead of single administrator. Whether the USSR felt obliged to make this proposal in the interests of consistency or was now looking for a plausible way of blocking the talks at that stage is not entirely clear.

The negotiations were also visibly influenced by wider international events, both positively as in early 1960 and negatively as in the case of the U-2 affair. Indeed, Khrushchev chose to make a major issue of the U-2 flight. In his memoirs, Khrushchev noted that Soviet aircraft could not overfly the USA and that 'the U-2 affair was a unilateral, unprovoked demonstration of their supposed superiority and outrageous treachery'.[27] The Soviet reaction demonstrated that the USA could not dictate conditions from a position of power. Khrushchev, therefore, appears to have broken off the summit meeting and to have stopped serious negotiations in the test ban talks in an attempt to constrain US behaviour and to assert Soviet prestige and power. The U-2 affair also apparently strengthened forces in the Kremlin hostile to arms control and accommodation with the West. By the end of 1960, relations had worsened over the UN disputes. In August 1961, just before Khrushchev announced resumption of testing, the Berlin crisis erupted and complicated US–Soviet relations even further.

With regard to the test ban, both sides had problems with their allies. In 1957, the USA moved first towards giving priority to the suspension of tests. The USA found the British Government, at least initially, to be unreceptive because the UK desired to develop its own nuclear arsenal. Nevertheless, Britain had fallen into line by late 1958. Indeed, amidst strengthened popular opposition to nuclear weapons and testing, Prime Minister Macmillan by 1959 had become a committed advocate of a test ban. France, however, proved to be totally intransigent: partly because it was in the early stages of acquiring its own nuclear weapons (it did not test any until 1960), and partly because after Charles De Gaulle came to power in 1958, France had become increasingly hostile to US influence and had attempted to assert its national independence.[28] The French commitment to the testing and development of its own nuclear weapons created problems within the negotiations. The Soviet Union alleged that France could carry out tests on behalf of the USA, and a refusal by France to adhere to a test ban treaty would obviously weaken it. The Soviet Union also insisted, at various stages, that France must be a party to the treaty, although in the final Moscow negotiations the USSR conceded that this was not a realistic requirement.

The question of Chinese participation presented even more serious difficulties for the test ban negotiations. Whereas the USA could overlook France on the test ban issue, the USSR could almost certainly not ignore perhaps its most important ally of the 1950s, especially one that had become by 1963 a major threat on Soviet borders. From 1957 onward, Chinese polemics against Khrushchev's policy of peaceful coexistence greatly increased the Soviet Union's difficulties of accommodation with Washington and had served to strengthen the hand of ideological and military hardliners in the Soviet Union.[29] In 1958, Moscow withdrew its nuclear assistance to Beijing; and as both competed for leadership of the world communist movement, relations between the two states steadily worsened. Khrushchev had become vulnerable to the charge of appeasing imperialism.

The greatest obstacles to a test ban agreement, however, were strategic. During the negotiations, questions of strategic asymmetry influenced the respective attitudes of the USA and the USSR. The USA placed a strong emphasis on its nuclear arsenal as a means of protecting 'the free world' against the Soviet Union, which was perceived as having greatly superior conventional strength. Indeed, part of the case for nuclear testing was framed within this context. More specifically, NATO relied on tactical nuclear weapons based in Europe to help deter a WTO conventional attack, whereas the Soviet Union at this stage had displayed little interest in such weapons. As a result, the USA was much more concerned with continuing to carry out low-yield nuclear explosions; and the campaign against a test ban was linked to the campaign to develop a 'clean bomb' and to speculation concerning the possibility of a neutron bomb.[30] After the USA's 'Hardtack I' high-altitude tests in 1958, the US military was also anxious to experiment further to develop the possibilities of anti-missile missiles.[31]

In most aspects of nuclear weapon technology and testing, the USA was ahead of the USSR. The USA's perception of its own superiority, however, did provide some incentive to agree on a test ban in order to freeze this advantage permanently. In fact, this consideration was apparently a factor in the

Administration's March 1960 decision to try seriously for a ban.[32] Nevertheless, the fact that only the USA had embarked on a sustained programme of underground tests meant that the US military and scientists were particularly unwilling to cede the military advantage of testing underground. By August 1963, the Soviet Union had actually carried out only one experimental underground test[33] and appeared, at least up until 1963, to be less committed to keeping this option open. Although the Soviet Union retained ability to place larger warheads on missiles, the USSR undoubtedly must have recognized the USA's superiority in nuclear weapon technology at the time.[34] However, this awareness concerning the USA's lead could have influenced Soviet policy either way. On the one hand, there must have been strong military pressure to try to catch up through further testing, which may have resulted in the major Soviet test series of 1961 and 1962. On the other hand, Soviet leaders may also have calculated that a test ban would stop the USA from making further advances in warhead design and, therefore, on balance would be to the strategic advantage of the USSR. Whether or not this consideration was a factor in Soviet decision making is difficult to determine.

The greatest impediment to Soviet acceptance of Western test ban proposals, however, was the system of international controls, which included proposals for overflights and on-site inspection. At least in part, Soviet opposition to these controls was based on a sense of military weakness and vulnerability which had been manifested in Soviet bluffing concerning its military strength. Khrushchev later observed that he had been prepared to accept inspection and overflights within border regions of the USSR, but would not have allowed the West 'to send its inspectors criss-crossing around the Soviet Union'. According to Khrushchev's memoirs, to have permitted these inspections would have facilitated the discovery that 'we were in a relatively weak position, and that realization might have encouraged them [the West] to attack us'.[35] Although Khrushchev's memoirs are not always reliable on some details, the level of general anxiety he expressed was clearly significant.

Ideological and psychological obstacles

Khrushchev's remarks indicate that ideological antagonism, manifested by mutual fear and suspicion, were certainly still very acute at the time of the test ban talks. The deep distrust that existed was based primarily on simplified perceptions of 'communism' and 'capitalism', and on a cold war interpretation of history. Jacobson and Stein note that when the Geneva Conference opened on 31 October 1958, it did so in a cold war atmosphere of profound suspicion of the motives of the other side.[36]

Opponents of a test ban, such as Edward Teller, asserted that the USSR would use a test ban agreement to cheat. Indeed, Teller appeared before Senator Humphrey's Sub-Committee on Disarmament and stated categorically that 'hiding tests means organized lying and organized lying is something . . . which can be safely practised in Russia'.[37] Although most US diplomats and politicians were not quite so extreme in their views, they nevertheless did share a certain scepticism concerning Soviet motives, a general anxiety that the USSR would cheat and a belief that the closed nature of Soviet society would make it easier to evade detection.

The Soviet view of the West, shaped by a record of Western hostility to the Bolshevik government, was marked by equally deep suspicions and mistrust. James Wadsworth and Arthur Dean, the US Chief Negotiators at the test ban talks, both apparently received this impression. Wadsworth expressed his view: 'It seems to me that suspicion is ingrained in the Russian make up'; whereas Dean observed: 'The expectation of hostility, which arises from Communist theory and is reinforced by a selective reading of history, permeates every aspect of official Soviet diplomatic behaviour'.[38] Although these views may reflect somewhat stereotyped Western assumptions, the Soviet intransigence concerning on-site inspection did indicate a profound distrust of Western intentions.

In any event, the Soviet Union appeared to be gradually moving toward a recognition of diverse political interests and attitudes within the USA, and the US Government was beginning to accept that the Soviet Union could be genuinely serious in seeking arms control. Even so, a developing sense of mutual interest could still be undermined by the actions of either side. As journalist Daniel Lang noted after visiting the Conference: 'Time and again, suspicion has supplied some new snag just when matters were rolling smoothly along'.[39]

Technological momentum

Technical problems concerning the effects of nuclear tests, as well as the methods necessary to adequately detect them, played a major role in the test ban talks. Between 1958 and 1963, the degree of knowledge concerning these questions increased considerably, and the instruments available for monitoring tests improved, as well. The end result of this progress in scientific knowledge was to pave the way for the conclusion of the PTBT. As a result of technological advances, the USA had finally come to accept that tests in the atmosphere, outer space and underwater could be adequately monitored by national means. Earlier, the USA had not accepted this possibility. Nevertheless, the evolution of US scientific thinking in 1959 (with respect to the 'new data' from the 1958 tests) and the development of the theory of 'decoupling' resulted in greatly increased Soviet suspicion. In fact, the 1958 'new data' were based on very limited evidence from two underground tests. Because the conclusions would later be invalidated by a more extended US research programme, the Soviet scientists apparently had some grounds for being sceptical. Certainly, the genuine scientific uncertainties associated with detecting and identifying nuclear tests, given the extreme political sensitivity of inspection, did exacerbate the problems of agreement.

Technological developments, with respect to possible new weapons, did occur during the talks. By late 1959, the US military was anxious to resume testing in order to produce a new warhead for the solid-state Minuteman ICBM, to develop an anti-missile missile and to explore the possibility of the neutron bomb.[40] At the end of its 1961 test series, the Soviet Union revealed that it had developed an H-bomb of an explosive power of over 50 mt. Technological change was enhancing the military usefulness of underground tests and, during hearings on the PTBT, the AEC testified before the Senate Foreign Relations Committee that weapons development would go forward, 'with the exception of investigations of certain weapons effects and the complete development of complex multimegaton weapons.'[41] The JCS explained that although atmospheric testing could extend the scope of a possible anti-ballistic missile system, a US system could be developed without it.[42]

By 1963, the proved military usefulness of underground testing was a crucial factor in gaining support for the PTBT. At the same time, however, underground testing undermined the value of the Treaty as a curb to the nuclear arms race. Subsequent developments eroded this function of the Treaty even further. After the conclusion of the 1963 PTBT, the overall annual rate of underground nuclear testing did not abate. It soon became clear that more information than had been foreseen could be gained from underground testing. Further, it also became evident that it was possible to conduct underground tests of higher yields than anticipated.[43] Technological momentum, therefore, had reduced the importance of the 1963 PTBT as an arms control measure.

Domestic obstacles

Assessing attitudes to a test ban is complicated by the fact that some opponents of a CTB were more receptive at various stages to a partial ban which could be satisfactorily verified, while supporters of a CTB sometimes recognized a tactical advantage in a partial ban as a first step. Nevertheless, there was a fairly clearly defined rift between individuals and groups hostile in principle to a test ban and those who strongly inclined in favour.

In the United States, the strongest opposition to a nuclear test ban came from nuclear scientists associated with the design of nuclear weapons and from the AEC, which made the bombs and had a vested interest in promoting military, as well as peaceful, uses of nuclear energy. Edward Teller and Ernest O. Lawrence played key roles in the scientific research and politics of developing the H-bomb and, from 1957, were also ardent advocates of research into 'clean' bombs with minimal fall-out.[44] Rear Admiral Lewis Strauss, Chairman of the AEC from 1953 until July 1958, co-operated with Teller and Lawrence to ensure development of the H-bomb and was a dedicated opponent of a test ban. Strauss shared Teller's passionate anti-communism and hatred of the Soviet

Union.[45] After Strauss was replaced by John McCone at the head of the AEC, there was a change in political style, but McCone was equally as opposed to a test ban.[46] The new personnel appointed by the Kennedy Administration did not alter the basic commitment of the AEC to maintain the weapon laboratories.

Because of its proprietary interest in continued testing of nuclear weapons, the JCS displayed displeasure at testing moratoria and hostility towards a test ban. The JCS also had an advisory role on the Committee of Principals—the body with official responsibility for test ban policy under Presidents Eisenhower and Kennedy. In May 1963 , during the prelude to the Moscow talks, the JCS were formally co-opted so as to appease Congress.[47] During most of the test ban negotiations, the JCS could rely on the two sides failing to agree. Early in 1963, however, the JCS was clearly caught off guard when it appeared a test ban might be possible. The JCS initiated public attacks against the US draft treaty of August 1962 and made clear their resistance to a CTB.[48] They would have preferred to avoid even a partial ban, but were persuaded to give qualified support for ratification in return for military concessions from President Kennedy.[49] The views of civilian officials in the Department of Defense were more variable. Although the DOD was hostile to a test ban in general, the Department did support a genuine attempt at agreement in March 1960; and in 1963, DOD went along with the PTBT. By 1962, Secretary of Defense Robert McNamara was moving toward positive initiatives on arms control.

The other main source of opposition lay in sections of Congress. The Joint Committee on Atomic Energy and the Senate Committee on Armed Forces Preparedness Sub-Committee held hearings at various stages which provided a platform to test ban opponents and sceptics. According to Michael Wright, there was an overall impression that 'the Ghost of Senator McCarthy still brooded over Capitol Hill.[50] Opposition to a test ban was voiced not only by some Republican congressmen, but by a number of important Democrats, including some southern Democrats and Senator Henry Jackson. The public debate about nuclear testing also gave a platform to such defence experts as Paul Nitze and Henry Kissinger, who had opposed a total test ban during the late 1950s.[51]

Those who campaigned in favour of a test ban included some prominent nuclear scientists, as well as a number of congressmen; and test ban advocates.were granted a hearing by the Senate Foreign Relations Committee's Sub-Committee on Disarmament. The test ban also enjoyed some support from within the Administration. Harold Stassen, Special Assistant to the President on Disarmament Problems (with cabinet rank) from 1955 to 1958, paved the way for the USA to concentrate on a test ban. Stassen, however, was a controversial figure often at odds with Secretary of State Dulles, and resigned early in 1958.[52] The President's Scientific Advisory Committee, set up in 1957 as a White House agency, became the strongest advocate of a test ban within the Eisenhower Administration and was represented on the Committee of Principals.[53] The creation of the Arms Control and Disarmament Agency (ACDA) under President Kennedy provided an additional voice in favour of arms control. The decisive counterweight to military views, however, was provided by the Department of State. Although Secretary of State Dulles was renowned for his cold-war anti-Soviet rhetoric, by 1958 he was persuaded, from a foreign policy standpoint, to enter into talks focused on nuclear testing. Because the State Department is directly responsible for negotiations, it has a natural inclination to search for negotiable proposals. The CIA adopted a middle course between the the State and Defense Departments.[54]

Given the deep divisions within the Administration and in Congress concerning the desirability of a test ban, the role of the President was crucial. Eisenhower tended to avoid active intervention in policy making, although at times he seems to have tipped the balance in favour of test ban talks and concessions. Eisenhower personally displayed a certain ambivalence about the possible desirability of a ban. When the PTBT was up for ratification, he only gave it a qualified endorsement.[55] At least until the end of 1960, US policy on a test ban was often vacillating and inefficient. Although the Eisenhower Administration did engage in a serious research programme to examine the problems of detection and identification, the delegation at Geneva was often left without adequate instructions or was forced to cling to untenable positions for months at a time. Wright observed somewhat caustically that 'instructions were doled out to them from Washington much as a Victorian workhouse master might dole out the gruel'.[56] Wright also suggested that central control in Washington became even more lax when Dulles had to retire through ill health early in 1959. In any event, the divisions in Washington were reflected in the US delegation at Geneva.[57]

In contrast to Eisenhower, Kennedy pursued a more activist role in formulating test ban policy and displayed a greater personal commitment to achieve an agreement. Kennedy demonstrated this most clearly in 1963, when he took considerable care to ensure that the Moscow talks were held in total secrecy and to exercise direct personal control over them, thus bypassing the normal bureaucratic channels.[58] This procedure enabled him to present critics of any test ban with a *fait accompli*. Khrushchev's willingness to accept secrecy may have reflected his own seriousness at this stage about reaching agreement, but probably took account of Kennedy's domestic difficulties. Indeed, a Soviet diplomatic manual, published in 1968, suggests that public negotiations at this stage would have made it easier for US adversaries of a test ban to block agreement.[59]

Although resistance to a comprehensive or partial test ban was less public in the USSR, there is strong evidence that opposition existed. According to comments made by Khrushchev to Western visitors in early 1963, some of the nuclear scientists in the Soviet Union were anxious to continue testing; indeed, the scientific journal *Vestnik Akademii Nauk SSSR (Bulletin of the USSR Academy of Sciences)* failed to report the conclusion of the PTBT at all.[60] Both before and after the Treaty, Soviet military comment was distinctly cool; the military journal *Krasnaya Zvezda (Red Star)* refrained from comment for nearly a week.[61] Only three members of the Party Presidium (at the time, the name for the Politburo) joined Khrushchev at the signing ceremony for the Treaty. Indeed, some western commentators have deduced that there was strong opposition within the Politburo which was only slightly mitigated when the powerful Frol Kozlov suffered a stroke in April 1963.[62] Christer Jönsson concludes that 'the partial test ban treaty represented a compromise of sorts in the internal bargaining'.[63]

From 1958 to 1963, the overall course of the test ban talks indicates the influence of competing forces on Soviet policy making. From early 1958 until his ouster in 1964, Khrushchev was the undisputed head of the Party and the government as First Secretary and Chairman of the Council of Ministers, respectively. Still, even Khrushchev (despite his consolidation of power) was restricted by the views of powerful groupings within the élite; and both the domestic and foreign policies of the Soviet Union reflected the effects of competing pressures. The most obvious change occurred during the aftermath of the U-2 incident when Khrushchev's opponents apparently succeeded in combining to limit his power of action and to impose a harder line in foreign affairs.[64]

Policy vacillations also occurred during the periods when the Soviet Union was showing interest in a test ban. Quite often, there was also a marked gap between the tone of Soviet remarks and their actual negotiation position. For example, in a *Pravda* interview published on 29 August 1958, Khrushchev was highly critical of the USA, but concluded by accepting its proposal for the Geneva Conference.[65] Bloomfield, Clemens and Griffiths, citing the final PTBT negotiations and the agreement not to orbit nuclear weapons in space, find that from at least September 1962 until mid-1964, there was a continued gap between a hostile and propagandist tone in public negotiations and a much more conciliatory approach in private talks.[66] Public statements, of course, may also be directed to an international audience. Nevertheless, one possible explanation for such an apparently schizophrenic approach is that the public utterances were intended for a domestic audience within the Soviet Union which had become accustomed to bitter attacks on the USA and Western imperialism.

Some groups in the Soviet Union favoured a test ban. Among Soviet scientists, perhaps the most prestigious was Andrei Sakharov, the prime inventor of the Soviet H-bomb and then still part of the Soviet establishment.[67] Writers and intellectuals who favoured internal de-Stalinisation, such as Ilya Ehrenburg, also tended to support external *détente* and arms control.[68] Khrushchev could also expect support from various sections of the Party hierarchy. Nevertheless, the combination of ideological opposition and professional military resistance created very considerable constraints.

Supplementary evidence of divisions within the Kremlin concerning arms control and improved relations with the West is provided by the negotiations on a 'War Propaganda Resolution'. After brief, but intensive, negotiations at Geneva, the heads of the Soviet and US delegations were able to agree to the text of a formal resolution in May 1962. Ambassador Valerian Zorin had already checked on various aspects of the draft with Moscow, and expressed pleasure in presenting the resolution (which had been agreed) to the ENDC. A few days later, the Bulgarian delegation began to attack the resolution, and Zorin thereupon attempted to get his earlier positive comments expunged from the record. In his account of this incident, Arthur Dean concludes that Zorin had obviously lost out in a struggle in Moscow.[69]

Negotiating styles and problems in negotiations

The Geneva Conference, in particular the Conference of Experts, exemplified the theory that whereas the West is more concerned about the technical aspects of arms control, the Soviet Union is more concerned about the political implications. When it came to disputes over the 'new data' introduced in 1959, both sides took this approach to disingenuous extremes. The Soviet Union tended to use political arguments to discredit scientific findings; the USA insisted that it was dealing solely with scientific issues, although these concerns had very major implications for the amount of inspection required in the Soviet Union. The opening stages of the 'Conference on the Discontinuance of Nuclear Weapons Testing' appeared to illustrate another standard difference between the two sides: whereas the Soviet Union urged agreement on a test ban in principle before examining the details of control, the United States immediately introduced detailed proposals concerning how a control system might work. Both sides, however, were primarily interested in establishing, in principle, what the relationship should be between a nuclear test ban and an international system of controls.

Various negotiating tactics adopted by both the Soviet and US delegations also encouraged mutual impatience and distrust and the perception of the other side as either insincere, unscrupulous or unreasonable. What is not always clear, however, is whether a negotiating position was adopted for bargaining purposes in a deliberate attempt to sabotage the talks or in a response to domestic pressures. For example, the opening stand taken by the Soviet Union at the Geneva Conference in October 1958, which was a retreat from the conclusions of the Conference of Experts, could have been either the staking out of an initial maximalist position or the reflection of genuine conflicts in Moscow. There is some evidence that Khrushchev was interested in a test ban in early 1959, but many of his colleagues were not.[70] Subsequent Soviet negotiating concessions are compatible with either view. Senator Gore, who was then attached to the US delegation, immediately concluded that the Soviet Union was not serious about discussing controls.[71]

The appearance of rigidity or of deliberately stalling because there may be bargaining advantages in waiting for the other side to move (a strategy which Dean attributes to the Soviet Union), may actually reflect either domestic conflict or bureaucratic inertia.[72] Daniel Lang observed this phenomenon at work on the US side in August 1960 and lamented that 'our delegation is distressingly split'. According to Lang, in the absence of clear instructions from

Washington, the delegation contrived 'a negative makeshift unity that . . . often consisted of opposing the Soviet Union merely for the sake of opposing it, by the technique of raising new issue upon new issue'.[73]

The greatest problem apparent in the negotiations may have been the rigidity displayed by both sides concerning the issue of on-site inspection which had acquired a symbolic significance quite disproportionate to its real importance. It is difficult to believe that the security of the Soviet Union would have been jeopardized by allowing seven inspections per year instead of three. On the other hand, it can be argued that US insistence on inspection was based as much on political as on scientific requirements. Some Swedish scientists speculated as to whether, in view of the difficulties of collecting evidence of radioactive debris on site, such inspections really assisted the identification of underground tests.[74] In April 1960, similar doubts had already been raised in evidence before the US Congress, and US scientists as early as April 1958 had begun to question the likelihood of achieving real evidence from on-site inspection.[75] The position of both sides concerning the principle of international on-site inspection was largely determined by political and ideological factors stemming from their perceived historical experience. To an extent, these views were a carry-over from the disarmament propaganda of the 1940s and 1950s, and resulted from the intransigence of powerful domestic groupings on both sides. International on–site inspection was also an issue which test ban opponents could use to effect. There was less political emphasis by both sides on the issue of unmanned seismic stations in Soviet territory, although the scientific arguments in favour of these were stronger.

Negotiating rigidity in the test ban talks was also enhanced by the fact that both sides took up strong public positions early on and kept repeating them at intervals, despite some concessions on detail. The relatively public nature of the negotiations encouraged both sides to negotiate partly for the record. In principle, the tripartite Geneva talks from 1958 until 1961 were meant to be private. However, press briefings and leaks by the delegations ensured publicity, until it was finally agreed to publish monthly records of the Conference in 1960.[76] The same process occurred when the ENDC was established: an agreement to negotiate in private was promptly violated by press statements from the US, Soviet and other delegations in attendance.[77] In addition, both sides attempted to use the UN General Assembly as a platform from which to mobilize world support behind their own positions and to stigmatize the other side as being the main obstacle to progress. Certainly, there are arguments for, as well as against, negotiating in public (examined in chapter 11); and the UN debates were not entirely great power propaganda exercises. Indeed, the debates served to focus pressure upon the great powers, especially as the number of non-aligned countries represented in the UN increased. Nevertheless, the test ban talks did suffer from the unremitting glare of publicity; and progress often depended upon private mediation and communications.

Private and unofficial talks also retain certain drawbacks: negotiators may make offers they cannot deliver after the issues are finally debated by governments, and there may be more scope for misunderstanding in off-the-record discussions. A particularly important example of such an apparent misunderstanding occurred in late 1962 when Khrushchev's attempt at a breakthrough was stymied by his mistaken belief that the USA would then accept two to four on-site inspections in the USSR per year. Before Khrushchev sent his letter to President Kennedy in December, there had been two informal meetings. The first was between Jerome Wiesner, Kennedy's Special Assistant for Science and Technology, and Evgenii K. Fedorov, a Soviet test ban negotiator and personal contact through Pugwash. When they met in October Wiesner indicated that if the Soviet Union could accept a small number of inspections, then the USA would reduce the number required, which had been a minimum of 12 up to that time. Early in November, Arthur Dean, the head of the US delegation to the ENDC, met Vasily Kuznetsov, the deputy and sometimes acting head of the Soviet delegation, and said that the USA would come down to eight or ten inspections per year. In his December letter to Kennedy, Khrushchev's claimed Dean had told Kuznetsov two to four inspections were acceptable.[78] Dean, however, claims categorically that he made it clear that the USA was not offering anything lower than eight to ten, and views the Soviet interpretation as a typical example of the 'twisting technique' of Soviet diplomacy.[79]

It is difficult to see why Khrushchev would have deliberately misrepresented the position at a time when, according to the available evidence, he was apparently genuinely seeking the agreement of a test ban. Theodore Sorensen records that the Soviet delegation to the off-the-record talks from December 1962 until January 1963 left Washington 'complaining bitterly that Khrushchev had risked his political prestige within the Kremlin to get their mission approved' and would be embarrassed by its failure.[80] The source of the misunderstanding remains unclear, but may have arisen out of Wiesner's discussion with Federov.[81]

Apparently, the test ban talks did not suffer from any direct attempts either to negotiate from strength or to make use of bargaining chips. On the contrary, from 1958 to 1960, the negotiations were associated with a voluntary nuclear test moratorium by both sides. Even allowing for the burst of testing by all three nuclear powers in 1958 before the moratorium came into force and for the element of propaganda, the test suspension may still be viewed as as a useful initiative to demonstrate sincerity and good will. After the USSR resumed testing in 1961, however, the result was to discredit the concept of a moratorium concurrent with negotiations among many sectors of Western opinion. On the contrary, the renewal of testing served to confirm the worst suspicions in the minds of test ban opponents and even to alienate some previous supporters of a test ban such as Hans Bethe.[82] The USA's reactions to the Soviet test series tended to ignore the fact that the USA had ceased to be formally committed to a moratorium from the end of 1959 and, more than once, had seriously considered a renewal of testing. Instead, the USA viewed the Soviet Union's tests as clear evidence of bad faith. In 1961, the impact of the Soviet test programme may have been to increase the number of concessions Kennedy felt forced to grant to the US military establishment to secure ratification of the PTBT.

VI. Did the PTBT promote the arms race?

There are at least two grounds upon which it may be argued that the effect of the PTBT upon the military competition between the USA and USSR was counter-productive. The first argument centres around the contention that, in order to secure support for the Treaty, President Kennedy had to accelerate underground testing, and to reaffirm defence and foreign policy commitments. The second argument revolves around the allegation that the conclusion of the PTBT served to defuse public concern about nuclear weapons.

Before the Senate floor debate on ratification commenced, Kennedy made an eight-point commitment which included support for a vigorous underground testing programme, the maintenance of weapon laboratories and a strong strategic nuclear force. The eight-point plan included support for the continuation of nuclear testing for peaceful purposes and the improvement of facilities for detecting nuclear tests. Kennedy also gave assurances that the PTBT would neither inhibit the USA from using nuclear weapons, nor would it alter the status of the German Democratic Republic. Two points were designed to meet the widespread fear of Soviet cheating: a promise to ensure action if Cuba was used to bypass the PTBT and a guarantee that the USA would maintain readiness to test in all environments.[83] The average rate of US nuclear testing increased after the 1963 Treaty, but it is less clear whether or not this was a direct reaction to the Treaty.[84] Although the 'safeguards' that were demanded by the JCS provide exemplary evidence of the power exerted by the military on policy making and illustrate the mechanism whereby Presidents seeking ratification of arms control may make counter-productive concessions, it is difficult to demonstrate conclusively that the concessions actually promoted the US military programme.

The argument that the PTBT lulled public opinion and demobilized peace movements is more convincing.[85] The end atmospheric testing removed the apprehensions concerning the effects of radioactive fall-out that had caused the most widespread public alarm and had served to reduce greatly the pressure for a CTB. Indeed, the mere fact that an arms control agreement had been concluded also created a sense that the USA and USSR were acting more rationally and were, perhaps, less likely to start a world war. Because nuclear arsenals continued to grow, this impression was (at least in part) an illusion. Nevertheless the PTBT did usher in an era of substantially improved relations between Moscow and Washington, and greatly improved the prospect of further arms control.

The positive effects of the PTBT were that it symbolized and promoted a new sense of common interest between the USA and USSR after a period of 1950s cold-war hostilities which still surfaced during the test ban negotiations. The Treaty also served to defuse US paranoia concerning Soviet violation of international agreements. Indeed, it soon became evident that the USSR intended to observe the PTBT. The USA's commitment to maintain a readiness to test in all environments was soon forgotten. A belief that Moscow was finally serious about at least some forms of arms control also encouraged Washington to pursue other arms control talks. Indeed, the origins of SALT can be traced to the period immediately following the PTBT. The most enduring legacy of the PTBT, however, was that it laid the foundations for the 1968 NPT.

VII. Conclusion

Numerous obstacles to agreement blocked the test ban talks up to 1963, and it is worth asking why it was possible to achieve a treaty in that particular year. The roles played by the US and Soviet leaders may provide part of the answer: the fact that both wanted a treaty and had enough power in the summer of 1963 to push it through. However, there were wider objective factors which made a test ban desirable, such as the strength of a growing international concern about the possible dangers of atmospheric nuclear tests and a developing awareness (greatly accentuated by the Cuban missile crisis) in both the USA and USSR concerning the dangers of the nuclear arms race. In addition, both the USA and the USSR began to recognize the need for a degree of *détente* and of arms control, and to realize that they possibly shared a mutual interest in preventing the spread of nuclear weapons. Indeed, an awareness concerning the dangers of an unrestrained proliferation was indicated by some US policy makers (as well as the Soviet Union) as early as the late 1950s. Although the USA was especially concerned about China and the USSR about the FRG, both great powers perceived the existence of a general danger.[86] The other consideration, no doubt, which influenced both sides was the fact that after the test series in 1961 and 1962, neither side was at a decisive disadvantage. Furthermore, neither side felt compelled to continue testing in the atmosphere for any pressing military reasons.

On the other hand, military considerations did weigh against a CTB. This may have been especially the case with the United States which, at that stage, had more experience with underground tests and a much greater strategic interest in developing lower-yield nuclear weapons. The USA was also still attached to the concept of PNEs, a policy enshrined in its Plowshare project.

In the Soviet Union, the military establishment very likely also viewed the loophole of underground testing as a means of developing a nuclear arsenal. The most crucial obstacle to a CTB, however, seems to have centred upon the West's insistence upon an international control system and inspections, regardless of how limited in number. By April 1963, Khrushchev apparently bowed to domestic pressure in the Soviet Union on this issue. Khrushchev may also have felt that his December concession had been rebuffed and, therefore, retreated from a CTB as a matter of prestige.

Because the PTBT could be monitored by national means only, there was no need to enter into controversy about the problems of detecting underground tests and the number of inspections required to deter cheating. This proved to be a major advantage in securing the ratification of the PTBT in the USA. Up to 1963, the main obstacles to a CTB had consisted of the military advantages from continued underground testing and the reluctance of the Soviet Union to accept the number of on-site inspections that the USA insisted was required.

Notes and references

[1] The most comprehensive historical account, although it focuses mainly on the US role, is provided in Jacobson, H. K. and Stein, E., *Diplomats, Scientists and Politicians. The United States and the Nuclear Test Ban Negotiations* (University of Michigan Press: Ann Arbor, Mich., 1966). For details of the negotiations, see US Disarmament Administration of the Department of State, *Geneva Conference on the Discontinuance of Nuclear Weapon Tests: History and Analysis of Negotiations* (US Government Printing Office: Washington, DC, Oct. 1961); and US Arms Control and Disarmament Agency, *International Negotiations on Ending Nuclear Weapon Tests, September 1961–September 1962* (US Government Printing Office: Washington, DC, 1962). For the period up to 1960, see Gilpin, R., *American Scientists and Nuclear Weapons Policy* (Princeton University Press: Princeton, N.J., 1962); and Divine, R. A., *Blowing on the Wind: The Nuclear Test Ban Debate, 1954–1960* (Oxford University Press: New York, 1978).

[2] For non-aligned accounts, see Lall, A.S., *Negotiating Disarmament: The ENDC The First Two Years 1962–64* (Center for International Studies, Cornell University: Ithaca, N.Y., 1964), Cornell Research Papers in International Studies No. 11; Ahmed, M. S., *The Neutrals and the Test Ban Negotiations: An Analysis of the Non-Aligned States' Efforts between 1962–63* (Carnegie Endowment for International Peace: Washington, DC, Feb. 1967), Occasional Paper No. 4; Myrdal, A., *The Game of Disarmament: How the United States and Russia Run the Arms Race* (Spokesman: Nottingham, 1980), pp. 84–95.

[3] See Divine (note 1), p. 236.

[4] Wadsworth, J., *The Price of Peace* (Praeger: New York, 1962), p. 24.

[5] See Gilpin (note 1), p. 226. Scientific estimates varied, especially when decoupling was taken into account. The Berkner panel suggested technical means whereby the capabilities of the Geneva system could be improved to enable it to detect explosions down to 10 kilotons, and noted that adding a network of unmanned stations might cover explosions down to 1 kiloton.

[6] See Jacobson and Stein (note 1), pp. 386–88. The positive findings were that there were fewer shallow earthquakes in the USSR than previously estimated and that the sensitivity of seismographs could be greatly enhanced if they were put in deep holes. The negative finding was that the seismic waves from an underground explosion varied considerably depending on the medium in which it was conducted in.

[7] Schlesinger, A., *A Thousand Days: John F. Kennedy in the White House* (Houghton Mifflin: Boston, Mass., 1965), p. 452.

[8] Bloomfield, L., Clemens, W. C. and Griffiths, F., *Soviet Interests in Arms Control and Disarmament: The Decade Under Khrushchev 1955–64* (MIT Press: Cambridge, Mass., 1965), p. 152.

[9] See Jacobson and Stein (note 1), p. 439; and Ahmed (note 2), pp. 54–55.

[10] See Jacobson and Stein (note 1), p. 440.

[11] See Jacobson and Stein (note 1), p. 433.

[12] See Bloomfield, Clemens and Griffiths (note 8), p. 186.

[13] See Jacobson and Stein (note 1), p. 448.

[14] See Jacobson and Stein (note 1), p. 87.

[15] See Jacobson and Stein (note 1), p. 87 and p. 471.

[16] See Jacobson and Stein (note 1), p. 246.

[17] Kissinger, H. A., 'Nuclear testing and the problem of peace', *Foreign Affairs*, vol. 37, no. 1 (Oct. 1958), pp. 1–18.

[18] See Divine (note 1), p. 244.

[19] Dean, A. H., *The Test Ban and Disarmament: The Path of Negotiation* (Harper and Row: New York, 1966), p. 90.

[20] See Wadsworth (note 4), p. 73.

[21] See Jacobson and Stein (note 1), p. 277.

[22] Clemens, W. C., Jr, *The Superpowers and Arms Control: From Cold War to Independence* (D. C. Heath: Lexington, Mass., 1973), p. 8.

[23] See Jacobson and Stein (note 1), p. 282.

[24] See Gilpin (note 1), p. 248.

[25] See Gilpin (note 1), p. 249.

[26] Wright, M., *Disarm and Verify: An Explanation of the Central Difficulties and National Policies* (Chatto and Windus: London, 1964), pp. 114–17.

[27] Talbott, S. (ed.), *Khrushchev Remembers: Vol. 2 The Last Testament* (Penguin Books: Harmondsworth, 1977), p. 510.

[28] See Divine (note 1), p. 228.

[29] Linden, C. A., *Khrushchev and the Soviet Leadership 1957–1964* (Johns Hopkins Press: Baltimore, Md., 1966), pp. 175–82.

[30] See Divine (note 1), pp. 147–52 and 304–6.

[31] See Jacobson and Stein (note 1), p. 146.

[32] See Jacobson and Stein (note 1), p. 245. Allen Dulles of the CIA noted that intelligence estimates showed the USA to be ahead and that a test ban would be in US interests.

[33] SIPRI, *World Armaments and Disarmament: SIPRI Yearbook 1972* (Almqvist and Wiksell: Stockholm, 1972), p. 406. This information is based on US sources.

[34] Bloomfield, Clements and Griffiths (note 8, pp. 95–97) suggest that the USSR may have considered itself to be ahead after the 1958 tests, but also stress the Soviet incentive to stop underground tests as well to inhibit US advances in miniaturization and development of low-yield and 'cleaner' bombs.

[35] See Talbott (note 27), p. 605.

[36] See Jacobson and Stein (note 1), p. 112.

[37] See Divine (note 1), p. 191.

[38] See Wadsworth (note 4), p. 15 and Dean (note 19), p. 34.

[39] Lang, D., *An Inquiry into Enoughness: Of Bombs and Men and Staying Alive* (Secker and Warburg: London, 1966), p. 43.

[40] See Divine (note 1), p. 290.

[41] Hearings before the Committee on Foreign Relations, US Senate, 88th Congress (US Government Printing Office: Washington, DC, 1963), pp. 212–13.

[42] Note 41, pp. 272–74.

[43] SIPRI, *World Armaments and Disarmament: SIPRI Yearbook 1968/69* (Almqvist and Wiksell: Stockholm, 1969), pp. 246–47.

[44] See Divine (note 1), pp. 148–52.

[45] See Divine (note 1), p. 10.

[46] Gilpin suggests McCone was less intransigent in opposing a test ban than Strauss; Divine and Jacobson and Stein argue that there was a change in style but not in substance. See Gilpin (note 1), p. 199; Divine (note 1), p. 218; and Jacobson and Stein (note 1), p. 88.

[47] See Jacobson and Stein (note 1), p. 451.

[48] See Jacobson and Stein (note 1), p. 451.

[49] See Jacobson and Stein (note 1), p. 459. General Curtis Le May, Air Force Chief of Staff, was least enthusiastic but did not oppose ratification.

[50] See Wright (note 26), p. 123.

[51] See Divine (note 1), pp. 230 and 290.

[52] See Divine (note 1), p. 178.

[53] See Jacobson and Stein (note 1), pp. 32 and 471. The President's Scientific Advisory Council represented a range of views, but for the first time in 1957 the President had access to scientists who were not linked to the AEC or DOD. The succession of Special Advisors to the President for Science and Technology, James R. Killian and George B. Kistiakowsky (under Eisenhower), and Jerome Wiesner (under Kennedy), all favoured a test ban.

[54] See Jacobson and Stein (note 1), p. 471.

[55] See Jacobson and Stein (note 1), p. 461.

[56] See Wright (note 26), p. 120.

[57] See Lang (note 39), p. 45.

[58] See Jacobson and Stein (note 1), pp. 451–52.

[59] Kovalev, A., *Azbuka Diplomatii* [The ABC's of Diplomacy] (Moscow, 1968), p. 18, cited by Jönsson, C., *The Soviet Union and the Test Ban: A Study in Soviet Negotiating Behaviour* (Studentlitteratur: Lund, 1975), p. 201.

[60] Garthoff, D. F., 'The Soviet military and arms control', *Survival,* no. 19 (Nov.–Dec. 1977), p. 243; and Jönsson, C., 'Soviet Foreign Policy and Domestic Politics: A Case Study', *Cooperation and Conflict,* vol. 12, no. 3 (1977), p. 143.

[61] See Jönsson (note 60), pp. 143–44.

[62] See Bloomfield, Clemens and Griffiths (note 8), p. 187.

[63] See Jönsson (note 60), p. 143.

[64] Tatu, M., *Power in the Kremlin* (Collins: London, 1969), p. 122.

[65] See Divine (note 1), p. 229.

[66] See Bloomfield, Clemens and Griffiths (note 8), p. 151.

[67] See Talbott (note 27), p. 103, which recounts Sakharov's opposition to a resumption of testing in November 1958. See also York, H. F., 'Sakharov and the nuclear test ban', *Bulletin of the Atomic Scientists,* vol. 37, no. 9 (Nov. 1981), pp. 33–37.

[68] See Jönsson (note 60), p. 140. Ehrenburg supported a resolution at a conference in London in September 1961 calling on all governments engaged in nuclear testing to cease, soon after resumption of Soviet testing.

[69] See Dean (note 19), pp. 27–30.

[70] See Jönsson (note 60), pp. 136–37.

[71] See Jacobson and Stein (note 1), p. 126.

[72] See Dean (note 19), p. 45. Dean is making a general comment on Soviet tactics here.

[73] See Lang (note 39), p. 45.

[74] See Jacobson and Stein (note 1), p. 372.

[75] See Jacobson and Stein (note 1), pp. 224 and 253. Supporters of a test ban in the USA, no doubt, hesitated to press the limited value of on-site inspection because of disputes concerning the effectiveness of seismic detection and because the need for on-site inspection was part of political orthodoxy.

[76] The US Disarmament Administration of the Department of State (note 1), p. 22.

[77] See Lall (note 2), pp. 9–10.

[78] See Jacobson and Stein (note 1), pp. 425–26.

[79] See Dean (note 19), pp. 40–42 and 44.

[80] Sorensen, T. C., *Kennedy* (Hodder and Stoughton: London, 1965), p. 728.

[81] Burns, E. L. M., *A Seat at the Table: The Struggle for Disarmament* (Clarke, Irwin and Co: Toronto, 1972), p. 167. Burns notes that both Dean and Kuznetsov held to their version of the private conversation. Kuznetsov 'remarked some time later that he had "got hell" from Mr Khrushchev over the incident'. Burns adds: 'this seems to be a prime example of how a simple misunderstanding between honest representatives can wreck a promising diplomatic negotiation'. Jacobson and Stein (note 1, p. 440), observe that Western delegations denied Soviet versions of the Kuznetsov–Dean talks but not of the Federov–Wiesner talks. Sorensen (note 80, p. 728), footnotes that Kennedy thought Macmillan might have been the source of Khrushchev's confusion.

[82] See Jacobson and Stein (note 1), p. 342.

[83] See Jacobson and Stein (note 1), p. 462.

[84] See SIPRI (note 43), pp. 243–44.

[85] Boyer, P., 'From activism to apathy: America and the nuclear issue 1963–1980', *Bulletin of the Atomic Scientists,* vol. 40, no. 7 (Aug.–Sep. 1984), pp. 14–23.

[86] Advocates of a test ban in the USA pointed to the dangers of nuclear proliferation. See Divine (note 1), p. 250 and Gilpin (note 1), p. 292. Dulles and the State Department argued this connection in 1958, see Jacobson and Stein (note 1), p. 87. For Soviet views, see Bloomfield, Clemens and Griffiths (note 8), pp. 93–94.

4. Negotiating a CTB

I. Introduction

After the PTBT was signed in 1963, the great powers made no serious attempt to negotiate a CTB. The ENDC at Geneva, however, continued to debate ways in which a CTB might be implemented. In the early 1970s, there were also Senate hearings concerning the possibility of a CTB. The Nixon Administration was not particularly interested in pursuing this possibility, however, although a Threshold Test Ban Treaty (TTBT) proposed by the USSR was quickly concluded during the course of 1974. Two years later, the TTBT was formally extended to cover PNEs. The Carter Administration made a serious effort to reach an agreement concerning a CTB and initiated tripartite talks between the USA, the USSR and the UK in 1977. These talks continued to the end of 1980 and then lapsed when Ronald Reagan became President.

This chapter briefly examines the evolution of negotiations, research and debate relating to a CTB up to 1977, and in rather more detail the trilateral talks from 1977–80. The course of these talks has not been publicly documented in the amount of detail accorded to the 1958–63 test ban negotiations. This can be attributed to several reasons. First, unsuccessful negotiations usually arouse less interest. Second, the SALT negotiations commanded the major focus of attention. Third, the participants in the CTB negotiations have been hesitant to violate an agreement to avoid disclosing the details. Nevertheless, enough information has emerged concerning the content of proposals made during the talks, as well as the political pressures exerted to prevent agreement, to make an analysis of the negotiations possible. The final section of this chapter attempts to summarize developments since 1980.

II. Talks in the Geneva Committee on Disarmament

At the beginning of 1962, the negotiations for a test ban treaty were transferred to the newly created ENDC. Even though the final talks leading up to the PTBT had been held in Moscow between the three main nuclear powers in the summer of 1963, the ENDC remained the forum for continuing discussions of a comprehensive ban covering underground tests, which the PTBT had specified as a goal. In 1964, President Johnson, in a message to the opening session of the ENDC, urged the Committee to pursue a comprehensive test ban, a cut-off of production of fissile material and the prevention of proliferation. The test ban, however, did not receive high priority by the ENDC during 1964. The Committee was primarily engaged in discussing US proposals for a verified freeze on strategic nuclear delivery vehicles and for the scrapping of medium-range bombers. In addition, the Committee was also considering a Soviet proposal for reducing military budgets. By the end of 1964, the Soviet Union was threatening to leave the United Nations if penalized for not paying its contribution to the Congo peace-keeping action, and there was stalemate in the ENDC. Disarmament issues were temporarily taken up in the reconvened UN Disarmament Committee, which focused on preventing the spread of nuclear weapons. When the ENDC met again in July 1965, its primary, as well as most productive, arms control topic was that of an NPT. Although the ENDC engaged in a continuing discussion of a CTB, the problems concerning verification remained a stumbling block.[1]

In April 1969, Sweden took a major initiative to move the ENDC negotiations concerning a total test ban forward and presented a draft treaty banning underground tests. Previously, only the USA and the USSR had proposed draft treaties, and neither had done so since 1963. The Swedish draft tackled the verification issue by proposing an exchange of seismic information to make it easier to detect underground events and to identify earthquakes. It gave each party the right to make enquiries about an event and to invite inspection on its own territory. If doubt still remained about possible violation of the treaty, a party could suggest methods which might remove this suspicion. Although on-site inspection could be requested as part of the last resort procedure, the Swedish proposal did not stipulate any form of on-site inspection. Both the USA and the USSR opposed the Swedish proposal on the basis of the the verification issue. Whereas the USA asserted the need for regular on-site inspection on the grounds that other methods could not reliably detect and identify low level underground explosions, the USSR objected to the provision of on-site verification, even if such verification was by invitation.[2]

The Geneva CD—renamed the Conference of the Committee on Disarmament in 1969 and enlarged to include 26 states—continued to examine the technicalities of verification. Canada pressed for measures to ensure an exchange of seismic data. In December 1969, the UN General Assembly passed a resolution authorizing the Secretary General to seek information from governments concerning their seismic stations and their willingness to make seismic records available. Canada used information, provided by 33 countries which had seismic stations, to assess the existing international capacity to detect and identify underground explosions in 1970.[3] Canada and Sweden continued to work on improving seismic techniques and in 1972 produced a paper for the CD concerning an international experiment designed to distinguish shallow earthquakes from underground nuclear tests. Canada and Sweden, together with Japan, agreed to promote co-operation to identify underground tests by seismic means.[4] Between 1969 and 1972, the UK also presented papers concerning the technicalities of detection.

Although certain members of the CD seriously sought to promote a test ban, the great powers displayed very little interest. However, in accordance with its declared concern about verification, the USA took one initiative to test international detection capabilities. In 1968, the USA proposed offered to provide advance notice before conducting some underground explosions so as to enable other countries to check their seismic records of these events. The first nuclear test in this programme was announced in September 1969, and the USA reported the seismic data derived from this explosion to the CD . During this period, the USA's own seismic detection facilities were improving. By the end of 1970, data from the new seismic arrays in Alaska and Norway could be transmitted directly to Washington.[5]

III. Mounting pressure in the USA for a CTB

The improvement in seismic technology strengthened the position of arms control advocates in the USA who were in favour of a CTBT. In April 1968, a SIPRI conference of seismic experts concluded that it was possible, through seismic methods alone, not only to identify earthquakes (which had been true for larger earthquakes before 1963), but also to positively identify nuclear explosions. Thus, it was alleged that nuclear tests could be directly identified by seismic means and not just deduced from seismic information which simply suggested that an earthquake was unlikely. The SIPRI conference was significant because it was the first time scientists from a wide range of countries agreed that this breakthrough had occurred.[6]

Even greater political importance was attached to a meeting convened by the DOD's Advanced Research Projects Agency (ARPA) at Woods Hole, Massachusetts in July 1970. The purpose of this meeting was to examine various seismic means to distinguish earthquakes from nuclear explosions. The Woods Hole Conference concluded that progress in seismology had made it possible to distinguish between most earthquakes and nuclear explosions,[7] and that most explosions could be identified down to as low as two kilotons, if exploded in hard rock.[8]

A summary of the conclusions of the Woods Hole Conference, published by the *Washington Post*, had widespread repercussions. DOD immediately repudiated the article, claiming that it presented a much too optimistic assessment of the seismic capacity for identifying underground tests. DOD also asserted that the Woods Hole Conference report was simply a set of technical papers which represented the views of the authors and not of ARPA. When foreign embassies and individual Senators requested copies of the Woods Hole report, the technical papers were sent without the original summary. This tactic served to make the technical findings all but incomprehensible, except to those specialists schooled in the techniques. ARPA then rewrote the original summary in a form which was more pessimistic concerning the identification of underground tests. A number of the Conference participants complained that they had learned of the revised summary from the press, and some indicated that the first summary was a more accurate statement of their views. [9]

The Woods Hole report aroused the particular interest of Senator Clifford Case, who requested that the Subcommittee on Arms Control hold hearings concerning the prospects for a CTBT. The Subcommittee, chaired by Senator Edmund Muskie, convened in July 1971 and heard evidence from a range of experts. In October, a subcommittee of the Congressional Joint Committee on Atomic Energy, which had a much more hawkish reputation than the Senate Foreign Relations Committee, initiated hearings. Although these proceedings were almost certainly intended to damp down optimistic forecasts of the technical possibilities for a CTB, they actually had the opposite effect. Defence scientists were more willing than previously to argue that seismic events which registered a magnitude above 4.0 (usually estimated as equal to 1 or 2 kilotons exploded in hard rock) could be positively identified. The hearings also cast doubt on one previously suggested way for the Soviet Union to violate a test ban: to test in dry alluvium, which produces much smaller seismic signals than usual. DOD revealed that it believed that the Soviet Union probably did not have deposits of alluvium deep enough to conceal explosions over 1 or 2 kilotons, and larger explosions would result in craters detectable by satellites.[10] A third interesting aspect of the hearings was that witnesses questioned the usefulness of on-site inspections. In February 1973, Senator John Pastore, the Chairman of the Joint Committee, co-sponsored a Senate resolution which called for positive proposals concerning a CTB.[11]

During 1972 and 1973, Senate pressure mounted for a US initiative to conclude a CTBT. Further Senate Foreign Relations Committee hearings were held in May 1972 which culminated in the Senate's passage of Resolution No. 67 in February 1973. The Resolution urged a nuclear test moratorium and new US proposals for a comprehensive ban, and resulted in another round of Senate Foreign Relations Committee hearings. Senator Edward Kennedy, one of the co-sponsors of the Resolution, drew on the results of the Woods Hole Conference and other scientific evidence to argue the case for a CTB.

IV. The 1974 Threshold Test Ban Treaty

The Nixon Administration was not receptive to calls for a CTB. Describing his role as chief foreign policy architect and negotiator during this period, former Secretary of State Henry Kissinger writes dismissively about the 'staple of Soviet disarmament schemes' and observes that Soviet proposals for a CTB had been consistently rejected by US administrations of both parties.[12] One reason for opposing the Soviet proposals was that they called for a ban on testing by all countries and gave the original signatories the right to withdraw if some countries refused to sign the treaty. Because of the pressure this formula exerted on France, the USA objected. By the early 1970s, the US had also become somewhat sympathetic to Chinese nuclear sensitivities. Other US objections to a total ban on underground tests rested on the USA's traditional concern with verification and a desire for strategic advantage. Kissinger remarks that: 'The Defense Department and its scientific advisers argued persuasively that our weapons could not be improved without testing'.[13]

In February 1974, Soviet Ambassador Anatoly Dobrynin proposed a CTB which the USA rejected. After Gromyko raised the issue a second time with Nixon and received yet another US rejection, the USSR tried a different approach. During Kissinger's visit to Moscow in March 1974, the Soviet Union introduced the idea of a threshold test ban (TTB). Kissinger responded quite favourably to this suggestion, partly because the USSR was more reliant on high-yield nuclear weapons and partly because a TTB would tend to favour the USA. After brief negotiations, the TTB was formulated, not in terms of seismic magnitude (which was feared might result in disputes concerning measurement), but in terms of explosive yield which was set at 150 kt. At the June 1974 summit meeting in Moscow, however, Prime Minister Alexei Kosygin reverted to earlier arguments for a CTBT, which Nixon and Kissinger apparently did not take very seriously. In any event, the TTB issue was delegated to foreign minister level, at which the details of the Threshold Test Ban Treaty (TTBT) were agreed.[14] The TTBT was set to run initially for five years and would be automatically renewed unless either party wished to terminate it.

The decision by the USSR and the USA to conclude the TTBT represented a reversal of their previous positions. From 1971 until 1973, both states had opposed various proposals made at the Geneva CD and the UN General Assembly for limits either on the magnitude or on the number of nuclear explosions.[15] The principal reason for the Soviet Union to agree to such a ban appears to have been a desire to maintain some form of *détente*. The USA, on the other hand, perhaps viewed the TTBT in terms of military advantage and the attainment of some long-term gains with respect to arms control. Kissinger argued that the Soviet agreement to list their test sites, as well as to supply geological information concerning them, was a step forward. Above all, however, President Nixon—ensnared in the Watergate imbroglio—needed some sort of an agreement out of the 1974 summit meeting.

A rapid conclusion of the TTBT proved to be possible mainly because the limit of 150 kt was set high enough not to cause serious difficulty for the military establishments on either side. However, the limit did create immediate problems with respect to testing programmes already planned. For example, the USA had scheduled tests of higher magnitude for warheads designed for the Minuteman III and Trident programmes. The TTBT only escaped a clash with military interests because of the clause which stipulated that the treaty would not come into effect until 31 March 1976. The US Secretary of Defense stated that the delay would allow 'completion of certain developments under way'.[16] The AEC requested a supplementary allocation of $100 million to fund additional high-yield tests before the onset of the deadline.[17] During the period between the Treaty signing and 31 March 1976, the USA conducted 12 tests with yields of more than 200 kt.[18] The Soviet Union also capitalized on the Treaty's grace period and conducted high-yield tests, most likely for its SS-17, -18 and -19 missile programmes.[19] Indeed, five tests with yields of over 200 kt were conducted by the USSR.[20]

Because the military used the 21-month period to conduct high yield tests, many supporters of arms control were highly critical of the TTBT. They were even more alarmed concerning the high level of the threshold. In an article written before the details of the Treaty were known, Senator Edward Kennedy, a key proponent for a CTBT, had argued that the level of the threshold would tend to be set by arms developers, rather than arms controllers. Furthermore, there would be pressure to test up to the limit allowed.[21] The TTBT's 150-kt limit apparently proved Kennedy to be correct. Kissinger, however, claimed that the Treaty would inhibit new large warheads. Still, the scramble to test higher-yield weapons before the March 1976 deadline did imply that the 150-kt limit served to impose at least some military restrictions. Still, not all experts were convinced. George Kistiakowsky, a former scientific adviser to President Eisenhower, argued that the state of weapon technology would permit tests below 150 kt that would provide assurance that, after certain changes, warheads with a much higher yield could work.[22]

Arms control advocates had other objections to the TTBT. The US and Canadian Pugwash executive committees described it as 'the ultimate mockery' of the 1974 June Summit meeting.[23] They also pointed out that a TTBT created technical difficulties in assessing exact yield from measuring seismic magnitude.[24] Certainly, the TTBT negotiations had recognized this difficulty, but it was resolved in such a way that led to even further criticism: a separate understanding had been reached (revealed by the US press in June 1976) which permitted each side one or two minor unintended breaches of the 150-kt threshold each year.[25] Several criticisms focused on the TTBT's political implications. First, it was asserted that the Treaty would not demonstrate the great powers' willingness to scale down their own arsenals and, therefore, would not serve to strengthen the NPT. Indeed, it was argued that, to the contrary, the Treaty would only serve to exacerbate the distrust, because the 150-kt limit possessed no arms control validity and no relation to verification possibilities (both of which suggested the implementation of a much lower threshold). Further, it was contended that the TTBT might actually result in an indefinite postponement of serious talks concerning a CTBT.[26] A final objection, raised in 1974, concerned the fact that the Treaty did not address the vexatious question of PNEs. Indeed, it was not until 1976 that a treaty to regulate PNEs was concluded.

V. The Peaceful Nuclear Explosions Treaty

Because the characteristics of a PNE are indistinguishable from those of a military detonation, the PNE issue created special problems for test ban talks from the beginning. The use of nuclear explosions to create dams and canals or harbours, or to unearth natural resources such as oil and gas or metallic ores, was first promoted in the United States and launched by President Eisenhower as the Plowshares Project. At that stage, the Soviet Union had shown no apparent interest in PNEs. Nevertheless, by 1974, the USA had abandoned attempts to use nuclear explosions for possibly peaceful purposes.

A major problem with PNEs, of course, was the resultant radioactivity and the danger of contamination.[27] Indeed, there were other environmental problems. For example, the opponents of an AEC plan to conduct underground nuclear explosions in Colorado in 1973 in order to free natural gas argued that the explosions would damage oil shale. Certainly, oil shale was potentially more valuable, in energy terms, than natural gas; but there were also fears of a more general nature concerning environmental damage.[28] This 1973 AEC plan represented the last Plowshares experiment. Economic, as well as environmental considerations, led the USA to abandon PNEs. The economic advantages originally anticipated simply had not materialized. The US delegate to the Geneva Conference noted, in a discussion concerning PNEs, that the USA had not realized any commercial benefits from PNE technology.[29] Another basis for further scepticism concerning PNEs was a growing awareness concerning the proliferation dangers from allegedly peaceful nuclear explosions—a problem dramatized by the Indian explosion in 1974.[30]

It is ironic that the Soviet Union, which had been critical of the US Plowshares Program, would be strongly committed to the idea of using PNEs for major engineering projects by the 1970s. Obviously, there was a danger that a supposedly peaceful programme of nuclear explosions could be used to breach the TTBT. Therefore, during the 1974 TTBT negotiations, the USA stipulated that a PNE treaty must be negotiated before the TTB came into effect. Thus, Washington appeared to negotiate a bilateral treaty which legitimized PNEs. Nevertheless, a bonus for the USA was that the USSR, after some initial resistance, did agree in principle to some form of on-site inspection for PNEs. Because the site would obviously depend upon the nature of the project, sites could not be pre-designated, as they were under the terms of the TTBT.

The PNET set an upper limit of 150 kt for each individual explosion, but did permit a series of explosions up to a maximum of 1500 kt, provided each explosion could be measured. The parties to the Treaty were obliged to exchange detailed information concerning each explosion. Although on-site inspection was specified as a possibility for a single explosion, it was mandatory for a series with a total yield over 150 kt at which designated personnel had the right to be present and to measure each explosion. This clause was hailed as an important precedent for on-site inspection, even if it was limited to certain circumstances.[31]

Nevertheless, the PNET was still not favourably received by arms control advocates, partly because it was seen as an appendage to the unsatisfactory TTBT and partly because it was feared that it would undermine attempts to prevent proliferation. The PNET also contained an escape clause that permitted future consideration of the possibility of carrying out an individual explosion above 150 kt. In July 1976, the TTBT and PNET were submitted to the Senate for ratification, but the Senate postponed action until after the November 1976 presidential and congressional elections. During the election campaign, Jimmy Carter denounced the two treaties as inadequate and committed himself to the goal of a CTB. After he assumed the presidency, Carter did not seek ratification of the TTBT and PNET; instead, he remained committed to the achievement of a CTB. The USA's subsequent inaction concerning the ratification of the two treaties meant that the verification provisions did not come into effect. Although President Reagan eventually submitted both treaties to the Senate for ratification in January 1987, he asked the Senate to examine additional verification measures which the Soviet Union would have to accept as a condition of the treaties coming into force. In any event, renewed US–Soviet talks concerning additional verification measures failed to conclude protocols before Reagan left office in January 1989.

VI. The trilateral talks on a CTB 1977–80

By the beginning of 1977, the great powers appeared to be receptive to international plans concerning a ban on underground testing. In September 1975, the Soviet Union submitted a draft CTBT to the UN General Assembly— the first nuclear weapon state to produce such a document since 1963. The content of the draft treaty, however, was not calculated to reassure the USA concerning verification. The draft provided primarily for use of NTM, to be supplemented by voluntary co-operation over the exchange of seismic data and by consultation. Complaints of treaty violations could be submitted to the UN Security Council in which, of course, the great powers retained the right of veto. Although the Soviet recommendations concerning PNEs by nuclear weapon states were vague, the draft treaty did recognize the need for a procedure to be negotiated. The USA and the UK criticized the draft treaty for failing to deal adequately with the issues of verification and PNEs.[32] Nevertheless, the Soviet Union was prepared to make some response to the criticisms of the verification provisions contained in the draft treaty. In February 1977, the USSR produced an expanded version which provided for voluntary on-site inspection in the event of suspected violations [33]

On behalf of the new Administration, Secretary of State Cyrus Vance visited Moscow in March 1977 to discuss an arms control agenda. Both sides proposed that priority should be given to the establishment of a working group to consider a CTB. Six days after Carter's inauguration, the President urged the need for a CTB in a letter to General Secretary Leonid Brezhnev. Furthermore, Carter publicly appealed for an end to all testing. In June 1977, the USA and the USSR held preliminary joint consultations concerning a CTB and apparently acceded to a British request participate in further private negotiations.[34] Trilateral talks on a CTB began in July and opened as a formal negotiation in October.

The three countries agreed to strict secrecy concerning the details of the negotiations. Although the record of the negotiations has not officially been made public, the available evidence suggests that considerable progress was made in late 1977 and early 1978. In previous exchanges concerning a test ban, the principal issues had already been defined: namely, how to deal with PNEs, verification, and the accession of France and China. The Soviet Union insisted that a CTBT could not come into force unless all nuclear weapon states adhered to it. The USSR's concern about China was understandable—in this instance, a major and (at the time) hostile border state would have been able to continue testing. Furthermore, the USSR also feared that France might serve as a proxy for the USA's test programme. Although the USA may have had less cause for concern with regard to Chinese or French participation than the USSR, some US commentators demanded that no nuclear weapon state should remain outside a test ban.[35] Still, the Soviet Union's insistence that a CTB must be dependent on Chinese and French participation (when both Peking and Paris had refused to sign any treaty limiting their nuclear forces or test programmes) constituted an obstacle to substantial progress.

In November 1977, the Soviet Union made what was then hailed in the Western press as a significant concession. General Secretary Brezhnev announced to the Supreme Soviet that the USSR would offer a moratorium on PNEs, as a step towards meeting the US demand that such explosions must be included in any CTB. Later clarification revealed that Brezhnev's offer was for a three-year moratorium, and that the Soviet Union wished to use this period to explore means of distinguishing between PNEs and military detonations. It was proposed that a protocol covering PNEs should be attached to the treaty.[36] The Soviet Union also indicated that it would consider extending the three-year moratorium.[37] The USSR also conceded that a CTBT could be concluded without initial French and Chinese participation, but that the position should be reviewed after three years. The implication was that a longer-term or permanent treaty would depend on French and Chinese acceptance of a test ban.[38]

By March 1978, the prospects for a CTBT appeared to be quite promising. The Soviet Union had moved closer toward the USA's position concerning verification by agreeing, in principle, to permit the location of automatic seismic stations (black boxes) on its territory and to admit challenge inspections. For its part, the Western powers accepted that parties would not be bound to agree to all requests to permit an on-site inspection.[39] The Soviet Union agreed to co-operate in research concerning the possibilities of international seismic monitoring and to make five of its own stations available for calculations. In March 1978, the CD published the results of this research.[40] Also in March, the US Administration apparently decided to give the CTB negotiations equal weight with SALT II.[41]

In Washington, the possibility of concluding a CTBT received such intense scrutiny that it actually proved to be counter-productive in that it revealed the depth of the disagreement over the issue. The initial progress in the talks appears to have been due largely to the commitment of ACDA Director Paul

Warnke, who personally headed the CTB delegation, and to the strong support of President Carter. Almost from the outset, the Department of Energy (DOE) and the JCS preferred the option of a new TTB.[42] The outcome of these debates in Washington was a partial retreat from the official US negotiating position held in March 1978 when the USA favoured an indefinite treaty. Carter signed Presidential Decision Memorandum No. 38 on 20 May 1978, which authorized the US delegation to seek a five-year CTB.[43] The President, therefore, had decided against setting a threshold which would have permitted some continued testing at the cost of possibly concluding a treaty of limited duration. Although the decision to propose a five-year limit was intended to conciliate the DOE, the JCS and the DOD, the position apparently was decided without their concurrence.[44]

Further pressure from test ban critics led to yet another revision of the USA's CTBT proposals. In June, Carter decided to reduce the duration of the proposed CTB to only three years and to qualify the comprehensiveness of the ban by allowing very low-yield underground tests in the range of up to 100 pounds TNT to keep nuclear weapon scientists up-to-date and to allow for the testing of nuclear triggers.[45] This decision followed almost immediately a 90-minute briefing by the heads of the nuclear weapon laboratories at Livermore and Los Alamos. Whereas the opponents of a CTB interpreted Carter's move as a response to technical facts of which he had not previously been aware, CTBT supporters regarded the decision as bowing to the strength of political opposition.[46] In any event, congressional opposition became very vocal in 1978 when hearings were held by the Senate and House Armed Services Committees. Public statements by some congressmen indicated that a CTBT would face strong resistance.[47]

Scientific and military opposition in the United States stressed two arguments: the familiar complaint that it would be impossible to detect Soviet cheating in the case of low-level underground tests and the rather new assertion that continued testing was essential to maintain nuclear weapon reliability. The argument that nuclear warhead testing was required to ensure that the devices would not explode by mistake and would perform properly in wartime was apparently first made in 1971.[48] Nevertheless, the argument gained widespread currency after 1978. Many scientists have challenged this justification for nuclear testing and have argued that weapons in the existing stockpile could be checked without sample tests. Furthermore, before this argument was presented to President Carter, no nuclear tests were apparently conducted solely to measure stockpile reliability. The proponents of proof testing, however, argue that such tests were incorporated into development programmes; therefore, the fact that testing had not been carried out especially for evaluation purposes afterward does not prove an overall lack of necessity.[49]

In practice, CTB opponents were almost certainly more concerned about retaining the freedom to test new warhead designs for new missiles so as to ensure a counterforce capability.[50] They were also anxious to keep nuclear weapon laboratories at top efficiency. To meet these concerns, Carter cut the initial duration of the treaty to three years, allowed for very low-yield tests to continue and included a clause that the treaty could not be automatically renewed but would require further Senate ratification. Despite these concessions, domestic opposition was not conciliated and the inherent value of the proposed treaty was undermined. In October 1978, a report from the House Armed Services Committee argued that the shorter duration of the treaty did not resolve the problems inherent in a CTB but, instead, served to reduce the treaty's effectiveness as an arms control measure.[51] With considerable justification, critics could also point to the fact that such a treaty would not achieve one of its main political purposes: namely, to strengthen the non–proliferation régime by demonstrating a serious commitment on the part of the nuclear powers to limit their own arsenals.[52]

When the trilateral talks resumed in September 1978, the US delegation presented the new proposal for a three-year treaty. Apparently the negotiators were not able to specify the precise ceiling envisaged for the very low-yield tests to be exempted from the treaty. Then, at the end of October 1978, Paul Warnke resigned as Director of ACDA in a move that was intended to placate US arms control critics even further. Warnke, the chief advocate for a CTBT within the Carter Administration, was replaced temporarily by Thomas D. Davies, the Assistant Director of ACDA. The 1978 ACDA Report to Congress concerning the test ban negotiations struck an optimistic note on the progress achieved. Still, by the end of the year, informed observers were very sceptical concerning the likelihood of a CTBT. Indeed, the Soviet Union had become suspicious of US intentions.[53]

Herbert York assumed responsibility for heading the US delegation to the CTB negotiations. Although York was a former Director of the Lawrence Livermore Laboratory and DOD employee, he possessed a recognized commitment to arms control. In 1979, some progress on the verification issue was achieved. After long delays, first by the Soviet and then by the US side, a joint team of Soviet and British experts visited US seismic facilities in August. When the three delegations made a formal report to the 40-nation Geneva CD in July 1980, a number of issues concerning verification measures apparently had been agreed. The USSR, the US and the UK committed themselves to an international exchange of seismic data to be supervised by an international committee of experts. The states also agreed to accept the location tamper-proof seismic stations on their territory and the right of a party to request an on-site inspection, although this request could be refused if reason was given.[54] Much of the text of a potential treaty, then, had apparently been concluded.

Nevertheless, in 1979, both the UK and the USA were raising further obstacles in the talks. The UK objected to having as many seismic stations on its territory as the US and the USSR, while the USA was stipulated that seismographs to be located in the Soviet Union had to be made in the United States. Previously, the USA had indicated that the seismographs could be manufactured anywhere. Ambassador Andranik Petrosyants, Chairman of the Soviet State Committee on the Utilization of Atomic Energy and head of the

Soviet delegation at the time, reportedly told Herbert York angrily in private: 'You must realize that we are not some sixth rate Arab country'.[55] The USA also quibbled concerning the language of the preamble to the treaty.[56] York's own sense of frustration about his role in an Administration deeply divided on the CTB issue was indicated by a talk he gave to a conference on arms control in 1981.[57] By 1980, the trilateral talks had become another ritual negotiation.

It is hard to know how much further the Soviet Union might have been willing to go to reach a CTBT. US representatives involved in these negotiations believed the Soviet Union was serious.[58] Even Zbigniew Brzezinski, Carter's National Security Adviser who was personally not anxious to promote a CTB, wrote a memo in March 1978 which indicated that the USSR was clearly seeking accommodation on a CTB.[59] The Soviet Union's concessions regarding PNEs, certain verification issues, and the role of France and of China also indicated a desire for a CTB. The USSR had agreed that the protocol covering PNEs was to be an integral part of the treaty and that the moratorium on PNEs would last as long as the treaty, unless agreement could be reached on ways of distinguishing peaceful from military explosions after it had come into force.[60] Soviet concessions on verification included the acceptance of 10 automatic seismic stations in the USSR and the willingness, not only to accept on-site challenge inspections in principle but also to discuss the personnel and equipment to be involved.[61] Despite Soviet moves on verification, the official reports by the USA and the UK on the talks in 1979 and 1980 indicate that many technical details had yet to be agreed—particularly concerning seismic stations.[62] The implication was that the USSR was proving intransigent on detail. Ronald Mason, the chief scientific adviser to the British Ministry of Defence (MOD) at the time, confirmed that 'negotiations of the technical details proved very difficult'. Mason notes that when the talks were halted in 1980, 'the selection of sites for national seismic stations, their design, manufacture, installation and methods of transmission to the participants' had still not been settled, nor had 'many questions concerned with the functions of inspection teams'.[63]

There are several possible explanations for the Soviet Union raising difficulties concerning this kind of detail. One is that the Soviet Union was still deeply suspicious that treaty verification could be used as a guise for intelligence gathering—the explanation suggested by Mason. Another interpretation is that the Soviet negotiators had no incentive to make concessions on verification, because the other two parties backed away from serious interest in concluding a CTB. A third explanation suggests that these details could only be resolved by high–level political intervention in Moscow which was not forthcoming after Gromyko and Vance had agreed in September 1978 that the CTB talks were a lower priority than SALT II. Taken together, these explanations are not necessarily incompatible with each other.

The Soviet position concerning the duration of the treaty is of interest in attempting an assessment of Soviet attitudes to a CTB. In November 1977, US press reports indicated that the USSR in the first instance wanted a three-year treaty which would become permanent if China and France formally, or perhaps even tacitly, also agreed to adhere.[64] Assistant Secretary of Defense David E. McGiffert testified before the House Armed Services Committee in August 1978 that 'the Soviets continue to insist on the adherence of all other nuclear states before agreeing to a treaty of more than a few years'.[65] In his public reflections concerning the negotiations, York laments the fact that both the USA and USSR were very equivocal concerning what happened after the initial brief period of the treaty and observes that neither side seemed really committed to a long–term ban.[66] Still, during 1978, the Soviet position was obviously influenced by the switches in the US proposals. The public pronouncements suggest that the USA was moving closer to the Soviet Union by initially proposing a short-term treaty.[67] However, on the basis of information from Paul Warnke, Raymond Garthoff states that one of the concessions made by the USSR was to accept the principle of a treaty of indefinite duration and that the Soviet delegation wished for a treaty that was simply renewed after an initial period—not renegotiated and re–ratified.[68] The genuine willingness of the USSR to agree on an indefinite treaty and the lengths to which it would go to press for Chinese and French accession apparently were never properly tested.

VII. Obstacles to agreement

Great power confrontation

Before the PTBT was agreed in 1963, both the USA and the USSR were keenly aware of international public opinion concerning nuclear testing. They were also aware of the potential propaganda advantages that accrued from the introduction of test ban proposals. The PTBT served to defuse public concern about nuclear tests. Indeed, the possibility for a CTB regained political significance only after it had become a possible symbol of great power compliance with the spirit of the NPT during the 1970s. No doubt, the Soviet Union was aware of the propaganda advantage in publicly espousing a CTBT when the USA was apparently so clearly uninterested. Nevertheless, when serious trilateral talks began in 1977, an agreement to negotiate in strict secrecy ruled out an openly propagandist stance.

The CTBT talks of 1977–80 were low-profile negotiations in comparison with the SALT II negotiations. Therefore, the CTBT negotiations were apparently not burdened with concerns for either a search for prestige or for political advantage. Moreover, unlike SALT II, the the CTB negotiations were not a touchstone for *détente* between the USA and the USSR. Even so, the negotiations may have been affected by political linkage as reflected by the deterioration of relations between the USA and the USSR in 1978. The role of the Soviet Union in the Horn of Africa, the USA's exclusion of the USSR from negotiations in the Middle East and the USA's normalization of relations with China together represented an overall worsening of US–Soviet relations. Nevertheless, what it more probable is that the growing Soviet suspicion of the

USA's real intentions in the CTB talks was due to frequent changes in US proposals. Certainly, the fact that the negotiations failed to make genuine progress in 1979 and 1980 resulted from specific obstacles in negotiating a CTB and not from a further erosion of *détente*. York, who was in a good position to know, stated categorically that the 'opponents of the goals of the CTB were able to slow things to a standstill well before Afghanistan and Tehran' and that 'the latter were not the reasons why we didn't succeed'.[69] John Edmonds, head of the UK delegation to the talks, agrees with York's conclusion.[70]

Nevertheless, it may be worth asking whether there was any apparent linkage between the CTB and the SALT II negotiations. There is no evidence of negative linkage, because Cyrus Vance and Andrei Gromyko agreed to pursue a CTBT in March 1977 when there was acute misunderstanding over SALT II. Further, the September 1978 impasse in the CTB talks apparently did not hinder the SALT II negotiations which were then accorded agreed priority. There may have been some positive linkage in the sense of trying to achieve breakthrough on several arms control fronts at once. For example, after making substantial SALT II concessions in September and October 1977, the Soviet Union held out an olive branch in the CTB talks in November.

Alliance politics apparently did play some role in influencing the USA's attitude toward a CTB. The USA's unwillingness to pressure France encouraged French opposition to Soviet attempts to make a CTBT's permanence conditional on French and Chinese adherence.[71] In general, the NATO allies were more concerned with the outcome of the SALT II negotiations and their impact on the European nuclear balance than with the CTB talks. Still, the UK, both as a nuclear weapon and NATO member-state, retained serious interest in the CTB negotiations. Furthermore, the UK had a direct role in the tripartite talks.

Although the British Labour Government which was in power until the spring of 1979 favoured a test ban in principle, it does not appear to have played an active diplomatic role. David Owen, the UK's Foreign Secretary at the time, has claimed that Great Britain resisted a reduction of the proposed treaty's duration to only three years until the USSR reluctantly agreed.[72] In 1979, however, the British position in the trilateral talks had become positively obstructive: Britain refused to accept the same number of seismic stations on its home and overseas territory as the USA and the USSR while the Soviet Union insisted that each party should accept an equal number. This switch in British policy may be explained by the desire, on the part of Prime Minister Margaret Thatcher, to adopt a more independent position and to demonstrate the new Conservative Government's more uninhibited commitment to the maintenance of an independent nuclear force.[73] After the Thatcher Government had decided to modernize British nuclear forces through the purchase of the US Trident missiles, it also wanted to be free to conduct tests for its new Trident warhead programme. The MOD had already mobilized its political forces to resist a CTB, which it viewed as damaging both to the US and the British nuclear arsenals. Indeed, British nuclear scientists co-operated with US colleagues to block the negotiations.[74] The extent of British Government's obstruction in 1979 apparently prompted Carter's discussions with Brezhnev at the June 1979 summit concerning the possibility of a separate CTBT between only the USA and the USSR.[75]

The USA's support for a CTB was based on political, rather than strategic military, motives. Carter Administration officials mainly emphasized the need to strengthen the non–proliferation regime. By the late 1970s, even the strategic significance of a CTB had become a matter for dispute, and some CTB advocates tended to minimize the effects of a CTB. In 1981, Jack Ruina argued that: 'A test ban will not directly affect the nuclear arms race. Both the qualitative and the quantitative nuclear arms race can continue unimpeded—at least in the first order.'[76] Nevertheless, most proponents have regarded a CTBT as a key to halting nuclear competition and the beginning of a nuclear disarmament.process. Moreover, the military and scientific opponents of a CTB have taken the same view. Donald Kerr, speaking at the same symposium as Ruina, commented: 'The weapons laboratories of the United States have maintained for years that testing is an essential element of the nuclear weapon capability of the nation'.[77] The predominant military view in the USA has been that a total test ban would be a strategic disadvantage to the USA, because a ban would reduce confidence in the nuclear stockpile and inhibit development of new designs. In addition, CTB opponents in the USA have maintained that a ban, in practice, would operate to the strategic advantage of the Soviet Union.

Because of the strategic asymmetries and political differences between the USA and the USSR, some US commentators have believed that a CTBT would result in the attainment of a unilateral advantage by the Soviet Union. Therefore, it may be enlightening to ask whether or not there is any evidence that the USSR deliberately sought such an advantage either from the process of the talks or from the terms of a final treaty. Because there never was any question of a moratorium on testing in conjunction with the 1977–80 talks, the USSR could not be accused (as it had between 1958 and 1963) of trying to inhibit the USA's testing programmes through an engagement of the USA in negotiations. Both states continued to conduct nuclear tests throughout the time of the CTB negotiations. Even so, it may be relevant to note that the Soviet Union tested more nuclear weapons at this stage, than the USA. In fact, the USSR conducted more nuclear tests in 1978 than in any year since 1963.[78] One possible explanation for this record testing rate is that the Soviet military believed a CTBT was imminent and accelerated the test programme. In 1979, the number of Soviet explosions increased again, but dropped slightly the following year.[79]

The high rate of nuclear testing by the USSR from 1977 until 1980 may shed some light on the Soviet Union's strategic calculations concerning a CTBT. The high testing rate strongly suggests that the USSR perceived a military advantage in conducting further tests. Viewed from the perspective of the Soviet Union, it is doubtful whether a CTB was regarded as conferring automatically a strategic advantage to the USSR.

US commentators have suggested three reasons why Soviet Union would gain more from a CTB than the USA. The first reason revolves around the idea that the USSR would find a way to cheat. Second, some observers contend that the Soviet Union would find it easier to maintain its nuclear weapon laboratories in a state of readiness than the United States, whose nuclear scientists would be attracted elsewhere. Furthermore, because the Soviet Union relies on larger and more crudely designed warheads than the United States, the USSR's stockpile would suffer less from deterioration if proof tests were not carried out.[80] These arguments can be taken to refer primarily to the unintended effects of a treaty. If one assumes that the Soviet Union had these considerations in mind all along when negotiating a CTB, then the first two arguments are wholly implausible. Certainly, there is no evidence whatsoever that the USSR has signed an arms control treaty since 1945 with the intention of violating it. Given US verification and intelligence resources (together with the tendency of various groups in the USA to suspect Soviet cheating), it would be very imprudent to do so. Nor is it credible that Soviet attitudes toward a treaty would be influenced by hypothetical calculations about the impact of a treaty on nuclear weapon laboratories. The third argument, which relates to the difference between Soviet and US warheads, is potentially a more serious strategic factor. Nevertheless, it is improbable that the Soviet military would be so sanguine concerning the effect on their nuclear stockpile. Indeed, not all Western scientists agree that the Soviet stockpile would necessarily be less affected by a CTB than would the US stockpile.[81]

Although the USA's perceptions concerning the asymmetric effects of a test ban may have served to strengthen domestic opposition in the USA, there are no grounds to assume that the USSR viewed the conclusion of a CTBT as means for exploiting a strategic advantage.[82] On the other hand, the Soviet Union may well have viewed a CTB as a means of restricting the future advantage of the USA. Certainly, the continuation of nuclear tests has been linked to the development of new weapon technology. Therefore, if one assumes that the USA still has a technological edge, then an unrestricted test programme may tend to promote US technological and, hence, strategic superiority.[83] On the other hand, a desire to restrain unpredictable and potentially destabilizing developments in weaponry is a positive incentive for arms control—not an obstacle to its achievement.

Psychological and domestic obstacles

In 1977, the trilateral CTBT talks began in an atmosphere much more conducive to serious negotiations and to an agreement than the original test ban talks that commenced in 1958. During the interim, the USA and the USSR reached a number of arms control agreements and enjoyed a period of *détente*. Although the level of mutual distrust began to increase in 1978, and even more markedly in 1979 and 1980, this potential obstacle to agreement was not the real reason for the failure of the talks. Psychological factors, however, played an important role—not through a direct impact on the negotiations, but through the fuelling of the deep suspicions towards the Soviet Union on the part of the USA's CTB opponents.

Most accounts of the 1977–80 negotiations conclude that domestic opposition in the USA undercut any genuine possibility of an agreement. In the executive branch, the most intransigent resistance to a CTB came from the JCS, the directors of the nuclear weapon laboratories and the successor to the AEC, the DOE.[84] The JCS has consistently opposed a test ban whenever it seemed to be seriously on the political agenda. The JCS' earlier objections to a CTB and lack of enthusiasm for a partial ban are documented in chapter 3. Jack Evernden recounts how, while employed by the Department of Defense in the mid-1960s, he was asked to give technical advice on a letter from the JCS which withdrew its support for a CTB. This letter was drafted almost immediately after it became clear that seismic means existed that would permit earthquakes and nuclear tests to be distinguished down to quite low levels.[85] Several commentators suggest that the JCS played a decisive role in obstructing agreement in 1978.[86] Opposition to a CTB from the nuclear weapon laboratories has always been quite open and played a well-documented role in persuading President Carter to move to a proposal for a three-year treaty.[87] The DOE, the directing governmental body for the weapon laboratories in the USA, has also opposed a CTB. The fact that James Schlesinger, a former Secretary of Defense and Kissinger's principal opponent on SALT II, served President Carter's Secretary of Energy probably added considerable weight and vehemence to the DOE's objections.[88] Opposition from the DOD and Secretary of Defense Harold Brown appears to have been more muted.[89] The other powerful figure in the Administration who was markedly unenthusiastic about a CTB was National Security Adviser Zbigniew Brzezinski. In his memoirs, Brzezinski observes that he had thought a CTBT to be a 'non-starter', although he 'went through the motions of holding meetings, discussing options and developing negotiating positions'. Although Brzezinski does not clarify his views concerning the substance of a possible CTBT, he does indicate that he considered the ratification of both SALT II and a CTBT to be difficult.[90] As in the 1958–63 test ban negotiations, the President was very aware of the strength of opposition to a CTB in sections of Congress. The 1978 hearings by the House and Senate Armed Services Committees (see above) substantiate this point. In any event, it can be reasonably asserted that a perceived need to choose between either a ratification of SALT II or of a CTBT had encouraged the Administration to downgrade the latter set of negotiations by late 1978.[91]

The Carter Administration's divisions concerning a CTB ran even deeper than those concerning SALT II. York comments that over half the members of the inter-agency backstopping and working group that dealt handled the detail of the CTB talks and reported to the cabinet–level body ultimately responsible were opposed to conducting negotiations at all and did not, in any case, desire a CTBT. York, however, suggests that this was 'a problem peculiar to the test ban' and did not apply to the SALT II negotiations in which most participants were not against the actual negotiations.[92] Barry Blechman agrees that the CTB negotiations led to a more prolonged and 'vicious' bureaucratic struggle than that of any other issue in the Carter Administration.[93] As a result, the CTB delegation was hampered by long delays as opponents of the negotiations insisted on taking points of detail up to cabinet level.[94]

Even allowing for the involvement of different personalities, the nature of the opposition to a CTB in the USA since the late 1950s has remained remarkably consistent. The opposition has reflected the commitment of both the military and the scientific professional communities as well as an ideologically-based distrust of the Soviet Union. A similar continuity of opposition in Moscow may also be deduced. Quite a substantial amount of direct and indirect evidence exists which suggests the presence of internal political conflict concerning the negotiations conducted between 1958 and 1963. With regard to the 1977–80 talks, it is also possible to discern an appreciable amount of conflict. Whereas the changing US proposals reflected a growing internal resistance to a CTB, the negotiating record of 1977–78 is clearly indicative of the Soviet Union's desire for a treaty.

In the Soviet Union, some military resistance to a CTB seems probable and may have focused on the question of French and Chinese accession to a treaty, and the details of verification. Even so, military opposition may have been reduced by Marshal Nikolai Ogarkov's accession to the post of Chief of the General Staff in 1977. It should be remembered that Ogarkov tended to stress the deterrent rather than war-fighting role of nuclear weapons. Furthermore, Ogarkov also was anxious to develop new conventional weapon technologies as an alternative to tactical nuclear weapons.[95]

The November 1977 concessions probably reflected General Secretary Brezhnev's personal desire for progress at a time when he appeared, despite poor health, to be at the peak of his power.[96] Moreover, there were two reasons why domestic Soviet opposition to a test ban in the late 1970s would be much less intense than in the Khrushchev period. First, the Soviet Union was in a much stronger military position in terms of its nuclear arsenal and was no longer seriously behind the USA. Therefore, a CTB would not serve to enshrine nuclear inferiority. Second, there was no longer an acute ideological disagreement concerning the principle of peaceful coexistence and an accommodation with the West. Furthermore, there was little need to be concerned about doctrinal conflicts with Beijing. As a result of these factors, the resistance to a CTB by the Soviet élite may have been more muted than in the case of the political élite in the USA.

Deadlock on a CTB since 1981

The Soviet Union has continued to express an interest in CTB negotiations, so the decision whether or not to pursue them has depended on the US

Administration. Upon taking office in 1981, the Reagan Administration initially deferred any action concerning the CTB issue. In October 1981, ACDA Director Eugene Rostow told the United Nations that a CTB was a 'long-term goal', but that international conditions were not propitious for immediate action.[97] In July 1982, the Administration formally decided not to pursue the trilateral talks.

As a result of the US decision, the responsibility for promoting a test ban shifted to the 40-nation Geneva CD. In 1983 (as in 1969), Sweden took the initiative and tabled a draft treaty. The 1983 treaty was a revised version of a 1977 draft and drew on the reported conclusions of the tripartite talks as well as the latest developments in verification.[98] The USA participated in an *ad hoc* CTB working group at Geneva but disputed the group's mandate. The USA insisted that the group should only concentrate on verification issues.[99]

In 1985, nuclear testing and the possibility of a CTB again became salient political issues. The Soviet Union announced a moratorium on nuclear testing which was set to begin on 6 August 1985 and called on the USA to reciprocate. In September 1985, the NPT Review Conference again put a CTB high on the agenda of measures to be taken by the nuclear weapon states. Despite the USA's non-response, the Soviet Union, in the context of wide-ranging proposals for arms control, extended its moratorium on nuclear tests beyond the initial deadline of January 1986 and called for a CTB. General Secretary Mikhail Gorbachev noted in his speech that 'it was by no means easy for us' to decide to extend the unilateral moratorium which hinted that there was some internal opposition to the move.[100] Nevertheless, the USSR extended the moratorium to March 1986 and, furthermore, refrained from conducting any nuclear tests before the Reykjavik summit meeting which had been set for October. The Soviet Union also indicated its flexibility on the verification issue by agreeing to the requests of an unofficial group of US scientists to set up seismic instruments to study conditions at the Semipalatinsk nuclear testing site and to permit joint research with Soviet scientists.

The Reagan Administration responded to the offer of January 1986 by disputing the value of an unverified moratorium and insisted that further nuclear tests were necessary in order to modernize the USA's nuclear forces. Some observers concluded that the tests were believed to be especially important for the SDI programme.[101] In the autumn of 1985, ACDA testified to the House Foreign Affairs Committee that a CTB should be dependent upon deep cuts in nuclear arsenals and a better verification capability. However, one ACDA document even expressed the view that CTB negotiations should not take place even if verification was watertight.[102] In a reply to the USSR's March 1986 extension of its test moratorium, President Ronald Reagan repeated an earlier proposal for talks to improve verification of the TTBT and PNET on the grounds that there was doubt concerning Soviet compliance with these treaties.[103]

The Soviet Union's extension of the moratorium not only encouraged international support for a bilateral suspension of testing and further negotiations for a CTB, but also prompted domestic support within the USA. In February 1986, by a vote of 268 to 148, the US House of Representatives approved a resolution which called for the submission of the TTBT and PNET to the Senate for ratification and for renewed negotiations concerning a verifiable CTBT. Furthermore, in March 1986, 63 members of Congress wrote to the President and urged a bilateral moratorium on nuclear tests. The members argued that the USA would gain, not lose, from a strategic standpoint with the implementation of a moratorium. Because the USA was ahead in warhead design, they contended that a moratorium would prevent the USSR from achieving further progress in the yield of warheads in relation to their weight.[104]

At the Reykjavik summit meeting, General Secretary Gorbachev in an apparent concession to President Reagan appeared to relax the pressure for an immediate CTB and agreed, instead, to work with the USA towards the improvement of verification. At a bilateral US–Soviet meeting in Geneva in November 1986, however, the Soviet delegation urged the negotiation of a CTB while the US side preferred to discuss only the revision of the protocols to the TTBT and PNET which President Reagan was about to submit to the Senate for ratification. In 1987, the Soviet Union had indicated that it would not continue to observe a unilateral testing moratorium and would resume testing as soon as the USA conducted a nuclear test. Therefore, after a US test on 3 February 1987, the USSR responded by conducting a test of its own on 17 February. Gorbachev's attempt to pressure the Reagan Administration into serious CTB talks or to undertake a moratorium, therefore, appears to have failed.[105]

During 1987, both the Soviet Union and the US Congress continued to call for a negotiated test ban. Indeed, the House of Representatives proposed a testing limit of 1 kt. During the prelude to the Washington summit meeting of December 1987, however, the USSR agreed to give priority to ensuring adequate verification and the negotiation of verification protocols for the TTBT and the PNET which had been signed in the 1970s. In November 1987, bilateral talks resumed at Geneva. The US and Soviet foreign ministers publicly called for the signature of these new protocols at the Moscow summit meeting in 1988, but this goal proved to be overly optimistic. The best that could be achieved was an agreement for a Joint Verification Experiment which authorized an exchange of teams to monitor nuclear tests at the Semipalatinsk and the Nevada test sites.[106] The long-term prospects for a new test ban at a much lower threshold now appear to have improved considerably.

Among sections of Congress, the support for a CTB has been strengthened by the continued improvements in verification capabilities. By 1986, most experts believed that existing seismological stations, combined with additional ones that could be installed to monitor a treaty, could reliably detect tests down to at least 1 kt. A minimum of 25 tamper-proof seismic stations would be required in the USSR.[107] Seismic methods could be supplemented by satellite monitoring to detect activity associated with underground tests and by on–site challenge inspections. The Reagan Administration continued to emphasize strict verification out of its belief that the Soviet Union would cheat on a test ban.

Indeed, the Reagan Administration frequently accused the Soviet Union of past violations of the TTBT and other treaties. Nevertheless, by 1986, there was a good deal of evidence (for example, a number of public statements by US officials) that verification problems were no longer the main obstacle to a CTB. Instead, the central issue had become the perceived need to conduct further nuclear tests for strategic reasons, such as to test warheads for the new Trident and Midgetman missiles, and to test components for the US SDI programme.[108] Furthermore, the Soviet military was clearly anxious to resume development of its own warhead programme in the event the USA continued to test for strategic reasons.

Throughout the late 1980s, the British Government has opposed a CTB. Although Thatcher has supported the US Administration's policies in general, the UK's opposition to a CTB is motivated by two specific strategic considerations. First, the UK is dependent on Washington for the Trident missile which will become the basis for the British nuclear force in the future. It is difficult for the British Government, therefore, to act to block the US test programme for Trident. In addition, the UK needs to test its own nuclear warheads for Trident. Whereas the US Administration has become increasingly open about the strategic reasons for wanting to continue nuclear testing, official British statements continued to cite verification difficulties as an obstacle to a CTB.

VIII. Conclusion

Since 1963, one of the chief obstacles to a CTB—verification—has gradually diminished in importance. There are both technical and political reasons for this change. The technical means for reliable verification of nuclear explosions have increased considerably such that, although there remains some scope for some scientific dispute, the weight of expert opinion suggests that problems only persist at yields below 1 kt. This is a significant example of scientific and technological development assisting, not hindering, arms control. From the standpoint of political factors, the Soviet Union has recently proven to be much more willing to consider different forms of on-site inspection on its territory as demonstrated by its position in a number of arms control negotiations.[109] Although the USSR did agree to the placement of three automatic stations and up to three on-site inspections per year during the course of the 1958–63 negotiations, it did so with considerable reluctance. Furthermore, the concession appeared to have been a matter of dispute in Moscow. By the 1970s, the USSR apparently felt less vulnerable strategically and less committed ideologically to oppose all on-site verification. Still, the most dramatic shift in the Soviet Government's attitude occurred under General Secretary Gorbachev who, by 1987, was displaying unprecedented willingness to accept stringent on-site verification of arms control agreements and was challenging the West to commit itself more enthusiastically to the principle of arms control.

The other major obstacle to a CTB has been the perception by those with a professional interest in nuclear weapons that such a ban would hinder strategic plans and restrict technological development. As we have seen, this domestic opposition has been both overt and sustained in the USA, although the details of the argument have somewhat changed. In the USSR, domestic opposition clearly existed between 1958 and 1963, but has been much less evident since the late 1970s.

In both the USSR and the USA, the views of the political leaders have been decisive.The attitudes of political leaders of course depends on whether they envisage, on balance, greater security through mutual arms control or through the pursuit of national strategic superiority. Until at least the late 1980s, the Soviet leadership appears to have been inclined toward the view that there is an advantage in nuclear arms control, especially to curb the development of new arms. The Soviet leadership's fears concerning a disadvantage in the technological competition with the West and the drain on limited economic resources have been strong incentives to seek arms control. Nevertheless, there has also been evidence of strong pressure for the USSR to build up strategic power in preference to bargaining away weapons. Political leaders in the USA have vacillated between the advantages of arms control and the perceived need to keep ahead in the nuclear arms race. Of course, negotiations on missile levels may seek, simultaneously, agreed mutual restraint *and* unilateral advantage. A CTBT, however, poses a more clear-cut choice between the two objectives. No doubt, this is why US domestic opposition to CTB talks has been more intense than in the case of the SALT II negotiations.

Notes and references

[1] Burns, E. L. M., *A Seat at the Table* (Clarke, Irwin & Co: Toronto, 1972), pp. 193-206.

[2] SIPRI, *SIPRI Yearbook of World Armaments and Disarmament, 1968/69* (Almqvist & Wiksell: Stockholm, 1969), pp. 176-79.

[3] SIPRI, *SIPRI Yearbook of World Armaments and Disarmament, 1969/70* (Almqvist & Wiksell: Stockholm, 1970), pp. 208-10.

[4] SIPRI, *World Armaments and Disarmament: SIPRI Yearbook 1973* (Almqvist & Wiksell: Stockholm, 1973), p. 392.

[5] SIPRI (note 2), p. 178 and SIPRI (note 3), p. 210.

[6] SIPRI, *Seismic Methods for Monitoring Underground Explosions* (SIPRI: Stockholm, Aug. 1968).

[7] According to a summary in the *Washington Post*, 11 Apr. 1971.

[8] Dr F. A. Long, Testimony to the Arms Control Subcommittee of the Senate Foreign Relations Committee, *Prospects for Comprehensive Nuclear Test Ban Treaty,* Hearing before the Subcommittee on Arms Control, International Law and Organization of the Committee on Foreign Relations, US Senate, 92nd Congress, 1st Session (US Government Printing Office: Washington, DC, 1971), 22 and 23 July 1971, pp. 54-55.

[9] Myers, H. R., 'Comprehensive test ban treaty: grounds for objection diminish', *Science,* vol. 175, no. 4019 (21 Jan. 1972), pp. 283-84.

[10] Myers (note 9), pp. 284-86.

[11] Washington correspondent, 'New hope of comprehensive test ban', *Nature,* vol. 241, no. 5389 (9 Feb. 1973), pp. 361-62.

[12] Kissinger, H., *Years of Upheaval* (Weidenfelt & Nicolson and Michael Joseph: London, 1982), p. 1166.

[13] Kissinger (note 12), p. 1166.

[14] See Kissinger (note 11), p. 1167 and Garthoff, R. L., *Detente and Confrontation: American Soviet Relations from Nixon to Reagan* (The Brookings Institution: Washington, DC, 1985), p. 426.

[15] SIPRI, *World Armaments and Disarmament: SIPRI Yearbook 1975* (Almqvist & Wiksell: Stockholm and MIT Press: Cambridge, Mass, 1975), pp. 406-407.

[16] SIPRI (note 15), p. 409.

[17] Carter, L. J. and Gillette, R., 'Test ban: arms control groups denounce summit treaty', *Science*, vol. 185, no. 4149 (2 Aug. 1974), p. 421.

[18] SIPRI, *World Armaments and Disarmament: SIPRI Yearbook 1977* (Almqvist & Wiksell: Stockholm and MIT Press: Cambridge, Mass., 1977), p. 353.

[19] Halsted, T. A., 'Why no end to nuclear testing?, *Survival*, vol. 29, no. 2 (Mar.–Apr. 1977), p. 62.

[20] SIPRI (note 18), p. 353.

[21] Kennedy, E. M., 'Nuclear testing: time for a halt', *Arms Control Today*, vol. 4, no. 5 (May 1974), p. 2.

[22] Carter and Gillette (note 17), p. 422.

[23] Carter and Gillette (note 17), p. 421.

[24] See Kennedy (note 21), p. 2.

[25] See Halsted (note 19), p. 62.

[26] Rathjens, G. and Ruina, J., 'Commentary on the new test ban treaties' *International Security*, vol. 1, no. 3 (winter 1977), pp. 179-81; and Bolt, B. A., *Nuclear Explosions and Earthquakes: The Parted Veil* (W.H. Freeman & Co: San Francisco, Calif., (1976), p. 246.

[27] Emelyanov, V. S., 'On the peaceful use of nuclear explosions', *Nuclear Proliferation Problems*, SIPRI (Almqvist & Wiksell: Stockholm, and MIT Press: Cambridge, Mass., 1974), p. 223.

[28] Washington correspondent, 'AEC plans peaceful explosion but raises anger', *Nature*, vol. 241, no. 5391 (23 Feb. 1973), p. 494.

[29] US Arms Control and Disarmament Agency, *Documents on Disarmament 1975* (US Government Printing Office: Washington, DC, 1977), p. 243.

[30] Epstein, W., *The Last Chance: Nuclear Proliferation and Arms Control* (The Free Press: New York, 1976), p. 177. Epstein cites Fred Iklé, US ACDA Director, making statement to House of Representatives concerning the proliferation dangers of PNEs in 1974.

[31] SIPRI (note 18), p. 355.

[32] SIPRI, *World Armaments and Disarmament: SIPRI Yearbook 1976* (Almqvist & Wiksell: Stockholm and MIT Press: Cambridge, Mass., 1976), pp. 306-9.

[33] SIPRI, *World Armaments and Disarmament: SIPRI Yearbook 1978* (Taylor & Francis: London, 1978), p. 318.

[34] Edmonds, J., 'Proliferation and test bans', ed. J. O'Connor Howe *Armed Peace: The Search for World Security*, (Macmillan: London, 1984), p. 77.

[35] See Kozicharov, E., 'Congress hurdles await nuclear test ban treaty', *Aviation Week and Space Technology*, vol. 108, no. 13 (27 Mar. 1978), p. 19. He cites a Statement by the House Republican National Defence Task Force, which specified that a CTB should be universal.

[36] Shipley, D., 'Soviet offer on A-pact said less than full', *New York Times*, 14 Nov. 1977.

[37] Garthoff (note 14), p. 756.

[38] Edmonds (note 34), pp. 77-78.

[39] Garthoff (note 14), p. 757 and Edmonds (note 34), p. 78.

[40] Editorial, 'Twenty years of test ban talk', *Nature*, vol. 272, no. 5653 (6 Apr. 1978), p. 481.

[41] Kincade, W.H., 'Banning nuclear tests: cold feet in the Carter Administration', *Bulletin of the Atomic Scientists*, vol. 34, no. 11 (Nov. 1978), pp. 8-11.

[42] Clarke, D. L., *The Politics of Arms Control: The Role and Effectiveness of the US ACDA* (Free Press: New York, 1979), p. 266. Whether to seek a total ban or a threshold treaty was one of the issues in dispute in March 1978, see Kozicharov (note 35).

[43] Kincade (note 41), p. 8.

[44] Garthoff (note 14), p. 757.

[45] Hughes, P. C. and Schneider, W., Jr, 'Banning nuclear testing', ed. R. Burt *Arms Control and Defence Postures in the 1980s,* (Westview Press: Boulder, Colo., 1982) p. 22; see also Carter, J., *Keeping Faith: Memoirs of a President* (Bantam Books: New York, 1982), p. 229. Carter stresses the need (according to military leaders and Department of Energy officials) for low-level testing 'just to confirm that the triggering mechanisms on existing armaments remained functional and dependable'.

[46] Westervelt, D., 'Can cold logic replace cold feet?', *Bulletin of the Atomic Scientists,* vol. 35, no. 2 (Feb. 1979), pp. 60-62; and 'Report on a Comprehensive Test Ban by a panel of the House Armed Services Committee, October 13, 1978', US ACDA, *Documents on Disarmament 1978* (Government Printing Office: Washington, DC, 1980), p. 608.

[47] See Kozicharov (note 35).

[48] Greb. G. A. and Heckrotte, W., 'The long history: the test ban debate', *Bulletin of the Atomic Scientists,* vol. 39, no. 7 (Aug.-Sep. 1983) pp. 40-42. See also Kissinger (note 12).

[49] Owen, D. 'A total test ban', *ADIU Report,* vol. 7, no. 2 (Mar.-Apr. 1985), p. 2 claims that 'the shelf life argument was a deliberate diversion' and that 'until at least 1980 not a single US or British nuclear test had been undertaken of stockpiled weapons'. Hughes and Schneider (note 45), p. 26, put a case for proof testing.

[50] It has sometimes been argued that the reduced certainty in the effectiveness of a state's nuclear arsenals resulting from a prolonged test ban would be compatible with a second–strike deterrence theory, but not with a counterforce doctrine.

[51] See US ACDA (note 46), p. 608.

[52] See Hughes and Schneider (note 45), p. 25.

[53] See Kincade (note 41) for sceptical appraisal of the likelihood of success and Garthoff (note 13), pp. 757-78 on Soviet reactions to the USA changing positions.

[54] US ACDA, *1980 Annual Report,* 20th Annual Report of US ACDA, 97th Congress, 1st Session (Joint Committee Print, 8 Apr. 1981), pp. 74-75.

[55] Garthoff (note 14), p. 578 (footnote based on information from Herbert York).

[56] Garthoff (note 14), p. 578.

[57] York, H., 'Nuclear weapon test bans', *Arms Control in Transition: Proceedings of the Livermore Arms Control Conference,* ed. W. Heckrotte and G. C. Smith (Westview Press: Boulder, Colo., 1983), pp. 71-78.

[58] Neidle, A. F., 'Comprehensive test ban negotiations', in Neidle, A. F. (ed.), *Nuclear Negotiations: Reassessing Arms Control Goals in US Soviet Relations* (University of Austin: Texas, 1982), p. 77. This volume comprises the proceedings of a conference held on 25–26 February 1982. In this instance, Neidle himself is speaking.

[59] Brzezinski, Z., *Power and Principle: Memoirs of a Security Adviser 1977-81* (Weidenfeld and Nicholson: London, 1983), p. 188.

[60] US ACDA, *Arms Control 1978,* 18th Annual Report of ACDA, 96th Congress, 2nd Session (Joint Committee Print, 1979), p. 22.

[61] Neidle (note 58), p. 77.

[62] US ACDA (note 54), p. 73.

[63] Mason, R., 'A comprehensive test ban: essential step in arms control', *The Council for Arms Control Bulletin,* no. 25 (Mar. 1986), p. 4; Shear, J.A., 'Restraints on nuclear testing', *ADIU Report,* vol. 4, no. 5 (Sept.–Oct. 1982), pp. 2-3, confirms that serious differences remained over the treaty's scope, France and China, and details of verification.

[64] Shipley (note 36). This is confirmed by Edmonds (note 34).

[65] US ACDA (note 46), p. 499.

[66] York (note 57), p. 74.

[67] For example, the British Foreign and Commonwealth Office claimed that the USA and the UK, at the outset, sought a treaty of unlimited duration, but in the end agreed to the Soviet proposal for a three-year treaty because of their concern about stockpile reliability: *Arms Control and Disarmament,* no. 3 (Feb. 1980), p. 14. This is contradicted by former British Foreign Secretary David Owen, who writes that the Soviet Union reluctantly went along with US insistence on three years. See Owen (note 49), p. 2.

[68] Garthoff (note 14), pp. 756-57.

[69] Kissinger (note 12), p. 1166.

[70] Edmonds (note 34), pp. 79-80.

[71] Kissinger (note 12), p. 1166.

[72] Owen (note 49), p. 2. From the time Macmillan flew to Moscow and Washington to engage in diplomatic initiatives to promote a test ban during the period 1959-62, Britain's international prestige had declined further, and the Callaghan Labour Government was absorbed in economic problems and the difficulties stemming from being in a minority in Parliament.

[73] See Hughes and Schneider (note 45), p. 21 for details of the switch under Prime Minister Thatcher.

[74] Simpson, J., *The Independent Nuclear State: The United States, Britain and the Military Atom* (Macmillan: London, 1983), p. 196 and Blechman, B. M., 'The comprehensive test ban negotiations: can they be revitalized?', *Arms Control Today*, vol. 11, no. 6 (June 1981), p. 5. Both refer briefly but elusively to the British Ministry of Defence role. Owen (note 49) mentions British scientists at Aldermaston trying to undermine the CTB talks.

[75] Carter (note 45), p. 249.

[76] Heckrotte, W. and Smith. G. C. (eds), *Arms Control in Transition: Proceedings of the Livermore Arms Control Conference* (Westview Press: Boulder, Colo., 1983); contribution to discussion on nuclear test bans.

[77] Heckrotte and Smith (note 76), p. 81.

[78] SIPRI, *World Armaments and Disarmament: SIPRI Yearbook 1979* (Taylor & Francis: London, 1979), pp. 648-49 and 655. The total was 27, which included 7 believed PNEs.

[79] According to SIPRI, *World Armaments and Disarmament: SIPRI Yearbook 1981* (Taylor & Francis: London, 1981), p. 382 (there were 29 detonations in 1979 and 20 in 1980).

[80] See for example Hughes and Schneider (note 45), pp. 30-33.

[81] See Epstein, W. 'A disastrous decision', *Arms Control Today*, vol. 12, no. 8 (Sep. 1982), p. 7.

[82] Hughes and Schneider (note 44), p. 33 assert that: 'our (the USA's) technological advantage in delivery systems design . . . is dependent upon an advanced nuclear weapons design complex', and that such a design and production effort cannot be maintained without testing.

[83] A test ban treaty, unlike SALT, does not provide a great deal of latitude for attempts to write unilateral strategic advantage into the detailed terms. Views on relative strategic advantage could influence proposals on duration, but the public Soviet position was tied to France and China.

[84] Blechman (note 74), p. 5.

[85] Evernden, J. F., 'Politics, technology and the test ban', *Bulletin of the Atomic Scientists*, vol. 41, no. 3 (Mar. 1985), pp. 10-11.

[86] See for example McGeorge Bundy in Neidle (note 58), p. 78: 'I think its worth noting in passing that we didn't pursue a comprehensive test ban to completion because there was not really sufficient agreement in the Executive Branch of the United States. To put it more bluntly, there was a clear cut opposition by the Joint Chiefs of Staff'. Garthoff (note 14), p. 757 also indicates that the JCS played an important role.

[87] Garthoff (note 14), p. 757 and Edmonds (note 34), pp. 78-79.

[88] See chapter 6 for Schlesinger's role in SALT II. Garthoff (note 14), p. 759 notes Schlesinger's opposition to a CTBT. Brzezinski (note 59), p. 317 notes insightfully that when he was able to block a proposal from Vance and Warnke for negotiations concerning a cut-off of fissile material by asking for comment from Schlesinger, who, as expected, 'produced a blistering memorandum'.

[89] Garthoff (note 14), p. 757.

[90] Brzezinski (note 59), p. 172 footnote.

[91] Kincade (note 41), p. 8.

[92] York (note 57), pp. 74-76. York is ambiguous on how far these bitter divisions affected the delegation, commenting that he is 'referring primarily to the backstopping and working groups' and that the 'overseas team worked together really quite smoothly' (p. 76). However, most of the delegation members were present at the time. Zimmerman, P.D., 'Quota testing', *Foreign Policy*, no. 44 (fall 1981), p. 88 claims that the US team was divided in 1979-80 on the desirability of a CTBT.

[93] Blechman (note 74), p. 5.

[94] York (note 57), p. 75.

[95] Jacobsen, C.G., 'Soviet military expenditure', SIPRI, *World Armaments and Disarmament: SIPRI Yearbook 1986* (Oxford University Press: Oxford, 1986) pp. 269-70.

[96] For an assessment of Brezhnev's personal position within the Soviet leadership and the changes that occurred in 1977, see: Brown, A. 'Political developments: some conclusions and an interpretation' and 'political developments 1975-77', ed. A. Brown and M. Kaser *The Soviet Union since the fall of Khrushchev,* second edition, (Macmillan: London, 1978) pp. 234-49 and 305-13.

[97] Hardenbergh, C., 'News of negotiations', *Arms Control Today,* vol. 11, no. 11 (Dec. 1981), p. 7.

[98] SIPRI, *World Armaments and Disarmament: SIPRI Yearbook 1984* (Taylor & Francis: London, 1984), pp. 593-94.

[99] Hardenbergh, C., 'News of negotiations', *Arms Control Today,* vol. 12, no. 9 (Oct. 1982) p. 5, and vol. 12, no. 11 (Dec. 1982), p. 9.

[100] Garthoff, R.L., 'The Gorbachev proposal and prospects for arms control', *Arms Control Today,* vol. 16., no. 1 (Jan.-Feb. 1986), p. 4.

[101] SIPRI, *World Armaments and Disarmament: SIPRI Yearbook 1986* (Oxford University Press: Oxford, 1986), pp. 119 and 450-51.

[102] Epstein, W., 'New hope for a comprehensive test ban', *Bulletin of the Atomic Scientists,* vol. 42, no. 2 (Feb. 1986), pp. 29-30.

[103] Tower, J.D., 'News and negotiations', *Arms Control Today,* vol. 16, no. 2 (Mar. 1986), p. 14.

[104] Tower (note 103), p. 14.

[105] Hardenbergh, C. 'News of negotiations', *ADIU Report,* vol. 8, no. 6 (Nov.–Dec. 1986) p. 19 and vol. 9, no. 2 (Mar.-Apr. 1987), p. 17.

[106] Hardenbergh, C. 'News of negotiations', ADIU Report, vol. 10, no. 3 (May–June 1988), p. 19.

[107] SIPRI (note 101), p. 122.

[108] Brummer, A., 'Defence chief rules out end to US nuclear tests', *The Guardian,* 3 Mar. 1986, p. 7, and Brummer, A., '100 more nuclear tests may be needed', *The Guardian,* 23 Apr. 1986, p. 6.

[109] For example, by accepting limited IAEA inspection of civil plants in 1985 to demonstrate its commitment to the NPT in the Stockholm September 1986 Agreement on CBMs and, in principle, to the negotiations on chemical weapons.

5. SALT I: success and failure

I. Introduction

This chapter analyses the course of SALT I—the first set of negotiations between the United States and the Soviet Union to limit their strategic nuclear arsenals. The SALT negotiations provide a useful case study for a number of reasons. First, the talks encountered numerous difficulties along the way that well illustrate the obstacles that exist in any serious attempt to negotiate limits on central strategic weapons. Second, the negotiations resulted in varying degrees of success and failure. Therefore, it may be relevant to examine why it was possible to reach a satisfactory ABM Treaty (whereas the 1972 Interim Agreement was only a holding manœuvre), and to compare SALT I and SALT II. Third, the SALT process generated widespread disillusionment with arms control negotiations in general, and many of the criticisms that negotiations simply serve to channel or exacerbate the arms race are based on SALT examples. Finally, there is an unusually good literature on SALT, especially the period 1969–72, that includes accounts by several participants and extensive analysis by arms control experts. These accounts provide detailed information about events in Washington and some insights into the bureaucratic and political situation in Moscow.

II. Summary history of SALT I

Although formal negotiations did not begin until November 1969 under President Nixon, SALT I originated with the Johnson Administration. The talks—conducted over a period of two and a half years—concluded in May 1972 at the end of a triumphant summit meeting in Moscow. The SALT I accords consisted of the ABM Treaty (of unlimited duration), and the Interim Agreement on Strategic Offensive Arms. The Interim Agreement, set to run initially for five years, placed ceilings on the number of fixed ICBM launchers and the number of submarine-launched missiles that could be deployed by each side. The intention was to follow up this Agreement with a more comprehensive and lasting treaty to curb offensive nuclear arsenals. Both of the SALT I accords were to be verified by 'national technical means' (NTM) which refers to satellite reconnaissance in this case.

The willingness of the USA and the USSR to consider an agreement limiting strategic nuclear arms can be ascribed to a number of causes. One important precondition of SALT I was the development, during the early 1960s, of satellites capable of monitoring developments on the ground in sufficient detail to provide a satisfactory method of verification. Thus, it was possible to bypass the perennial stumbling block of East–West negotiations: namely, on-site verification. The use of satellites, however, was not simply a question of available technology: persuading the Soviet Union to accept this form of continuous surveillance after its vigorous protests concerning U-2 reconnaissance flights in the early 1960s required a significant change in Soviet policy.[1] This change became explicit when the Soviet delegation made it clear early on during the SALT process that national technical means of verification were envisaged.[2] In Washington, political willingness to accept the adequacy of satellite reconnaissance was encouraged after the CIA asserted that it was.[3]

During the mid-1960s, the strategic relationship between the USSR and the USA was shifting, as the former began to catch up with the latter. Indeed, by this time, the USA had clearly become more vulnerable to a nuclear attack. Therefore, the United States possessed some incentive to seek a stable nuclear balance for the future. The Soviet Union, on the other hand, had a potential interest in trying to codify approximate nuclear parity in preference to a continual striving to match a growing and improved US arsenal. Alone, the mere perception of military threat does not actively encourage arms control; rather, such perceptions are more likely to trigger a military response. In fact, this is how the USA (at least in part) did respond during the mid-1960s to a perception of a growing threat from increasingly accurate Soviet missiles. In the USA, pressure to deploy ABMs to guard either cities or missile sites increased. Further, the Soviet Union's development of an ABM system around Moscow was cited as a powerful reason for the USA to develop missiles with multiple independently targeted re-entry vehicles (MIRVs) which could penetrate ABM defences.[4]

Perhaps a more decisive factor in promoting SALT, however, was the view (shared by a powerful group within the US Administration during the mid-1960s) that arms control could serve as a means of stabilizing the nuclear balance. Two key figures in this arms control lobby were Robert McNamara and Dean Rusk.[5] In January 1967, the United States took the initiative to try to get strategic arms talks started. Initially, the Soviet Union reacted cautiously, perhaps in part because the USSR was still strongly committed to anti-missile defences. In May 1967, at the Glassboro summit meeting with President Johnson, Soviet Prime Minister Alexei Kosygin rebuffed the suggestion that the Soviet Union might halt its ABM programme. Furthermore, Kosygin declined to discuss the possibility of strategic arms talks. A year later, however, the Soviet Government was indeed prepared to consider negotiations, and Johnson announced on 1 July 1968, while signing the NPT, that strategic weapons talks would soon begin.

Finally, SALT I became possible because, during the 1960s, the relationship between the Soviet Union and the United States had moved towards a cautious *modus vivendi*. Chapter 3 illustrated how the thaw of the late 1950s allowed the nuclear test ban talks to get under way. In 1963, the conclusion of the PTBT promoted a new public sense of common interest. Indeed, the PTBT may well have paved the way for a series of gestures towards limiting arms in 1964: the conclusion of the OST in 1967 and, perhaps most significantly, the signing of the NPT in 1968. During the latter stages of negotiations for the NPT, the USA and the USSR shared an explicit common goal as pre-eminent nuclear powers: namely, the prevention of the spread of nuclear weapons. The sense of mutual great power interest, which resulted in the conclusion of the NPT, survived despite increasing US commitment to the war in Vietnam. The USA intensively bombed the North which was being armed and supported by the Soviet Union.

The degree of shared interest and understanding between the USA and the USSR has necessarily been limited by conflicting interests and ideological divergence, as well as by a heritage of deep distrust and suspicion. Therefore, diplomatic relations have been frequently disrupted by international crises, and arms control talks have been vulnerable to sudden reversals. Although the preparations for SALT survived Vietnam, after the Soviet invasion of Czechoslovakia in August 1968, Washington felt obliged to defer the talks which had been set to commence in September. As a result, a decision concerning whether or not to renew an offer for talks was left to a new president.

The incoming Nixon Administration initially began with a lesser commitment to arms control than the Johnson Administration and with a greater predisposition to build up US military strength. On the other hand, President Nixon and his National Security Adviser, Henry Kissinger, shared a theory of how to manage the superpower relationship through a combination of sanctions and incentives, and assumed that the Soviet Union badly needed to limit arms for economic reasons. Their conception of *détente* stressed political and economic co-operation but included arms control.[6] Therefore, they had a strong motive for pursuing SALT, although they were suspicious of the attitudes and goals of those who had been involved during the Johnson Administration.

President Nixon's special interest in foreign affairs, Kissinger's rapid rise to a dominant role in foreign policy, and the distrust that Nixon and Kissinger both shared concerning the government bureaucracy not only helped to shape the preparations for the talks within Washington, but also the way the negotiations were conducted. Under Johnson, the content of the SALT proposals were devised by the bureaucracy at the initiative of a group within the DOD, passed up to the JCS and finally presented to the President for approval.[7] Under Nixon, the initiative and responsibility for co-ordination lay squarely in the White House.

Two channels of negotiation were developed. The formal talks, headed by ACDA Director Gerard Smith, took place in seven sessions and alternated between Helsinki and Vienna. In these discussions, the formal texts and a great deal of complex technical detail were hammered out. The politically most significant negotiations, however, took place in secret between Henry Kissinger and Soviet Ambassador Anatoli Dobrynin in Washington, and between

Kissinger and key figures in Moscow. The Soviet Government appeared pleased to accept these dual channels and managed a rather higher degree of internal co-ordination in its negotiating stance than did the United States. The head of the Soviet delegation, Deputy Foreign Minister Vladimir Semenov, was apparently kept informed of the content of the secret 'back channel' negotiations, whereas his US counterpart was not.

By mutual assent, the content of the formal SALT negotiations was not publicized. Nevertheless, embarrassing leaks occurred periodically in Washington. The final and most difficult details of the SALT I accords were finally agreed during hectic negotiations at the 1972 Moscow Summit. President Nixon was determined to obtain full credit for SALT I, and the Soviet leadership was anxious to conclude an agreement during the Moscow meeting. Therefore, the SALT I accords were duly signed before Nixon left Moscow.

Many of the problems which arose during the SALT I negotiations concerned the precise aspects of the strategic arsenal to be controlled. Some issues provoked bitter disputes within Washington. Others tended to focus disagreement between the USA and the USSR, and presumably led to hard bargaining within the Soviet bureaucracy and the Politburo. Throughout, the preference in Washington was for a freeze on the numbers of land-based ICBM launchers and the number of tubes for submarine-launched ballistic missiles (SLBMs). This freeze could be verified by satellite reconnaissance. Most sections of the US Government, however, wanted to retain the flexibility to modernize the USA's nuclear arsenal and, therefore, to exclude MIRVs from SALT I. So, in practice, those arms control enthusiasts in Congress and the bureaucracy who did wish to include a ban on MIRVs were overruled. In April 1970, the SALT delegation was allowed to put an option banning MIRVs to the Soviet delegation The proposal included a provision (inserted by the DOD and the JCS) which made the ban conditional on the USSR's acceptance of on-site inspection. The Soviet delegation interpreted this clause as evidence that the United States was not serious. Most US commentators do not believe that the Soviet Union was interested in a MIRV ban which would have left them behind in MIRV technology at that stage. Nevertheless, Raymond Garthoff, a State Department expert on the Soviet Union who played an important role in the SALT I delegation, suggests there were signs of possible interest (see below).[8]

In any event, there were serious disagreements between the Soviet Union and the United States.[9] Whereas the USA became increasingly concerned with restricting offensive missiles (out of the fear that the Soviet Union could acquire a counterforce capability), the Soviet side primarily wanted an ABM agreement and was much less interested in any limit on offensive missiles. In particular, the Soviet Union resisted including SLBMs. Second, Washington was especially anxious concerning the counterforce capability of the large Soviet SS-9 missiles with a heavy throw-weight. The US delegation devoted a good deal of energy to setting a sub-limit on heavy missiles within the total numbers of ICBMs allowed. The US side was also concerned with defining the limits of the dimensions for the silos of existing ICBMs so that they could not be replaced by much heavier missiles. The Soviet delegation resisted both kinds of limits. The United States also wished to reach an agreement concerning how to define a 'heavy missile', whereas the Soviet Union did not. A third worry for Washington was the possibility that ICBMs might become mobile, because they could not then be reliably verified. The Soviet Union, however, did not wish to renounce this option.

One of the chief stumbling blocks in SALT I negotiations was the Soviet Union's insistence on including the USA's nuclear FBS in the discussions. Included were US bombers based in Western Europe and the Far East, and on aircraft carriers. Moscow argued that FBS should be counted as strategic weapons, because they could reach the Soviet Union. Washington, however, insisted that FBS were theatre weapons designed to offset Soviet intermediate-range missiles targeted at US allies. The US delegation also urged the problems of defining limits on intermediate-range bombers because, in principle, many types of aircraft could carry nuclear weapons. The US side contended that these aircraft could only carry out one-way missions against Soviet cities and were not able to threaten a first strike. The Soviet delegation, however, maintained that these bombers could mount a major nuclear attack against the USSR. The thrust of the Soviet argument was to claim compensation for forward-based bombers when missile ceilings were set.

Strategic bombers were not a major issue in SALT I. Early US proposals envisaged including them in the total of offensive weapons subject to ceilings and sought to specify the number of bombers allowed. Soviet counter-proposals suggested a total ceiling for all strategic weapons without specifying subtotals for bombers or missiles. Although the United States at this stage enjoyed a numerical advantage in long-range bombers, these aircraft were of an ageing subsonic variety which did not appear to cause particular concern to the Soviet Union. During the SALT I negotiations, US Air Force pressure for a new supersonic bomber did not find a very receptive audience in Washington. Nor was there any particular concern about Soviet bombers, although this was to change during SALT II. A curb on strategic bombers was omitted from the breakthrough proposals negotiated by Kissinger with Dobrynin in May 1971 mainly because of a lack of real interest from both sides

The positions of the USA and the USSR concerning the crucial issue of limiting ABM deployment were much more compatible. By 1969, the Soviet Union had totally reversed its 1967 stance on the necessity of anti-missile defences and appeared to be eager for a ban. Although the Nixon Administration proved to be more interested in ABM deployment than its predecessor, the Administration was prepared, fairly early on, to trade an ABM agreement against curbs on Soviet strategic missiles.

The details of the ABM Treaty sparked a number of quite serious disagreements. Both sides had already begun a limited ABM deployment, and neither was particularly willing to dismantle its existing ABM sites. A related problem was that the Soviet Union had already erected an ABM defence around Moscow. In March 1969, when President Nixon announced that the ABM programme would proceed, he opted for defending 12 missile sites with the new Safeguard programme. Construction of one ABM system was begun at the Minuteman base at Grand Forks, North Dakota, and a second site was under way in 1970 at the Malmstrom Air Force Base, Montana. So, the first key question for the ABM talks was whether it would be possible to achieve a total ban on ABM defence—an objective favoured by arms controllers in Washington—or whether a few sites should be allowed. If the second option was chosen, then the problem became one of how to achieve a compromise that both sides could regard as equitable. Much of the detailed manœuvring in the negotiations centred on these related issues.

There were other problems, however, that required considerable time to resolve. Washington was concerned that the Soviet anti-aircraft system based in Tallinn could possibly be upgraded to an ABM system and wanted guarantees to prevent this eventuality. The Soviet Union felt a strong need for anti-aircraft defences and resisted attempts to limit them. However, the USA insisted that controls on the nature and size of radars were necessary because radar was the key to ABM defence. It would be possible to deploy additional ABMs very quickly if one side violated or abrogated the treaty, if the right kind of radars were available. Some of the most technically complex and detailed negotiation centred on defining radar limits.

When the US negotiators pressed for inclusion of a ban on future, more sophisticated and potentially more effective ABM technologies, they raised a less contentious, but nevertheless intrinsically important question Although the ABM Treaty clearly permits research, Article V of the Treaty banned development and testing of all ABM systems or components except those that were fixed land-based.

Although the final agreements signed in Moscow in 1972 reflected the central conflicts of interest between the two sides, the most important strategic problems were deferred for later talks. Not only was a limit on MIRVs left out, so was the possibility of banning the testing and deployment of long-range cruise missiles. Although the two delegations did discuss a restriction on cruise missiles, the matter was dropped when the attempt for a comprehensive agreement was abandoned. The Soviet Union made concessions to the United States by agreeing to a sub-limit on heavy missiles within the total of ICBM launchers allowed and by accepting some definition on the limits on changes in silo dimensions. The Soviet side, however, refused until the end to define a heavy missile. The question of heavy missiles became a matter of continuing concern to Washington policy makers, who were concerned about the new Soviet SS-18 missile and wished to include it in heavy missile limits. Reluctantly, the Soviet Union agreed to set a ceiling on submarine-launched missiles and haggled until the last moment over the details: for example, which types of existing submarine would have to be scrapped if new submarines were built. Under the terms of the agreement, both sides could modernize their missiles within the agreed totals.

In the USA, the most controversial aspect of the Interim Agreement on Strategic Offensive Arms was that the USSR was granted superiority in the number of land-based and sea-based missile launchers. The USA was permitted a maximum of 1710 launchers (both ICBMs and SLBMs), while the USSR was permitted a total of 2358 of which 313 could be of the heavy ICBM variety.[10] In terms of a wider strategic equilibrium, this disparity could be justified. The United States had superiority in numbers of long-range bombers and was well ahead in MIRVing its missiles (and therefore had twice as many nuclear warheads as the Soviet Union in 1972). The USA also retained a technological edge in terms of the accuracy of its missiles. Tacitly, the USA also acknowledged the case for granting the Soviet Union some compensation for FBS. At times, Kissinger and other Administration officials cited this fact as a public *post-hoc* justification for the disparity in launchers.[11] Even so, during the talks, the United States never conceded, in principle, the Soviet case concerning FBS. The USA also made a tacit allowance for British and French nuclear forces. However, in the course of a public debate which focused almost exclusively on launcher numbers, the Administration was made to appear to have granted an unacceptable concession to the Soviet Union. During the ratification of SALT I, Senator Henry 'Scoop' Jackson, one of SALT's most powerful critics, persuaded the Senate to vote for a resolution requiring future Administrations to agree only on limits based on strict parity.

Several other features of the Interim Agreement are also significant. First, the Agreement, in effect, simply froze the existing numbers of missile silos and tubes. However, the Agreement did make allowances for the incorporation of those under construction and excluded some out-of-date submarines from the totals. Although there are certain negotiating problems involved in such a freeze—for example, agreeing on the actual numbers of submarines and SLBM tubes that exist or are being built, and clarifying the rules for modernizing and replacing missiles—a numbers freeze requires minimal military sacrifice when both sides already have extensive deployments and are not too far apart in launcher numbers. Second, the Agreement reflected Soviet reluctance to reveal details of their strategic forces. It should be noted that no figures were given for the number of ICBM launchers (although the Protocol did specify upper limits for modern submarines and SLBMs). Therefore, various US representatives were left to provide interpretations to the Congress and the press. Third, both sides insisted on appending unilateral interpretations to the Agreement, which were totally rejected by the other. Thus, the USA was able to assert its understanding of what was meant by a 'heavy missile'. The USSR, on the other hand, specified a total of US and NATO submarines to be allowed and reserved the right to exceed its own totals if NATO allies went over the Soviet-defined total. Because the Agreement was also accompanied by agreed statements and common understandings, there was considerable scope for confusion or misrepresentation. Indeed, the USSR was subsequently accused of breaching the agreement on heavy missiles, which the Soviet Union had never endorsed.[12]

Although the ABM Treaty proved to be less contentious, some US strategists were unhappy that the doctrine of mutual assured destruction had been formalized in this way.[13] Further, some sections within the US military continued to hanker for a programme to develop ABMs for missile sites.[14] Nevertheless, arms control advocates believed the Treaty to be a major achievement. At Soviet insistence, the ABM Treaty did embody strict and rather artificial parity, and permitted both sides to deploy a specified number of ABMs around their capital cities and around one missile site each. The terms of the Treaty were carefully drafted to prevent these two sites from becoming the basis for a nationwide 'heavy' ABM system. As a result, the Soviet Union was allowed to maintain its rather inefficient ABM system around Moscow (valued at least partly as a hedge against Chinese attack), and the USA retained the Grand Forks ABM site as a palliative for an Air Force anxious to maintain some form of ABM technology. Within agreed limits, modernization of each site was allowed. When the Treaty was amended in 1974, the extra site granted to each side for purposes of symmetry was discarded

During the course of the SALT I negotiations, it became clear that both sides were interested in the possibility of an agreement to reduce the risk of accidental war. Negotiations focused partly on modernizing the Hot Line set up in 1963. The chief issues concerned which satellites to use for Hot Line communications, and more general measures to prevent accidents and to notify the other side of untoward incidents involving nuclear weapons. In 1971, the Soviet Union wanted to complete these agreements independent of SALT. The United States, however, initially held out for linking them to a SALT treaty, but then acceded to Soviet wishes with a view toward easing the negotiation of other SALT issues and offsetting the negative impact of Kissinger's visit to China.[15] The conclusion of two agreements during 1971 also indicated to Congress and to the international community that something was being achieved through the prolonged bilateral talks.

In the eyes of committed supporters of arms control, the greatest failure of SALT I concerned the lack of any controls on qualitative improvements in offensive missiles. In particular, SALT I failed to place any restrictions on the development and deployment of MIRVs. This meant that a freeze on missile numbers was negated by a rapid increase in the number of warheads (and targets) per missile. Gerard Smith's attempts—with some support from within ACDA and the State Department—to include MIRVs in the negotiations were thwarted. When Nixon eventually did allow the matter to be raised, a MIRV ban was tied to conditions known to be unacceptable to Moscow. Pressure from Republican Senator Edward Brooke to slow down MIRV development, as well as from members of both Houses who supported proposals for a moratorium on MIRV testing, was ignored by the White House. Whether it might have been possible to include a ban on MIRVs in SALT I is one of the issues upon which US participants in the negotiating process subsequently disagreed.

III. Obstacles to agreement

Great power confrontation

The SALT I negotiations reflected the inevitable tensions and ambitions inherent in the great power relationship between the USA and the USSR. Although, on balance, SALT I suffered less from the pursuit of conflicting great power goals than did most other serious arms control talks, these factors did impinge on progress at various stages

Propaganda

The propaganda content of the SALT I negotiations was unusually low. In large measure, this resulted from the fact that the talks were kept confidential. Furthermore, both sides appeared to be genuinely interested in an agreement. However, there was some awareness of how proposals would appear on the public record, especially if the talks collapsed. Kissinger attempted to conciliate Congress (which was entitled to periodic confidential briefings) by making it appear as though the USA was exploring both a MIRV and a total ABM ban.[16] At Helsinki in November 1970, a Soviet official told Gerard Smith that the US proposal to ban MIRVs had never been considered more than a sop to Congress; therefore, the Soviet Government dismissed it as propaganda.[17]

The Soviet insistence concerning the inclusion of FBS in the SALT negotiations probably contained an element of propaganda and represented a continuation of the long-standing Soviet claim that US foreign bases were an unacceptable threat to the USSR. Nevertheless, Soviet opposition to FBS was based primarily on strategic and political fears. The USSR also raised the familiar proposal for a no-first-use of nuclear weapons agreement, which Smith was inclined to dismiss as a move designed for the negotiating record and to influence Congress.[18]

Political prestige

Prestige considerations may impact on arms control negotiations in at least two different ways. The first pertains to a state's gain or loss of prestige as a general outcome of negotiating. The second refers to the concern for prestige with respect to specific negotiating tactics or the tabling of proposals during the course of the talks.

Clearly, SALT represented a bid by the Soviet Union for recognition of equal status with the USA, both as a great power and as a nuclear power. The very fact that the talks were bilateral implied this status. On the Soviet side, prestige considerations served as a stimulus to serious negotiation and to seeking an agreement. Of course, any recognition of Soviet equality by the USA would imply the USA's abandonment of a claim to superiority. This realization served to stimulate potential opposition to SALT in the United States. As Michael

Nacht has commented: 'Parity is a fine idea for Americans to subscribe to as long as they enjoy superiority'.[19] The perception that parity is being reached arouses fears about imminent inferiority, and some of the US unease about the inequality of launcher numbers in SALT I could be linked to concern about a loss of US status in the eyes of the world—a possible perception that the USA was slipping.[20] These anxieties, however, did not become a real obstacle to arms control until SALT II.

Prestige worries apparently did not significantly affect the tactics of either side in approaching the SALT talks. Smith records some hard bargaining about the venue of the talks, but it did not become a major issue. The Soviet Union delayed starting negotiations (set for mid-1969), possibly because a demonstration of its eagerness to begin the SALT negotiations in January 1969 had met an initially unreceptive audience in the new Administration.[21] The delay, however, only lasted for about a month and could have been caused less by a desire to save face than by suspicions concerning US intentions.[22]

Political advantage

The Soviet drive to achieve recognized military and political parity through SALT implied not only increased great power status but also the potential political advantages accruing from that status. This may have been one reason why the Nixon Administration had initial doubts about accepting parity as a goal. Moscow's political aims were formally embodied in the Declaration of Basic Principles, which set out the necessity of peaceful coexistence between the two great powers. During the Moscow summit meeting in 1972, the USA agreed to sign the Declaration as a concession to the importance attached to it by the USSR, after requiring some changes in the Soviet draft. Official Soviet commentary concerning SALT I referred to the increased military and economic power of the USSR and a to a change in the correlation of forces in the world in favour of socialism which resulted in the SALT I accords.[23]

On the whole, the Soviet Union did not attempt to use the SALT I negotiations for extraneous political purposes. There was, however, one startling *démarche* by the Soviet delegation which aroused suspicion on the US side. At a concert, Semenov passed a note to Smith which proposed an agreement that pledged the USA and the USSR to retaliate jointly against a provocative nuclear attack by a third country. Smith viewed this move either as an attempt to isolate China or else to disrupt US relations with Britain and France.[24] Kissinger interpreted the proposal as a Soviet attempt to make collusion against China 'the real Soviet price for a Summit' and as a 'blatant embodiment of condominium'.[25] Garthoff, however, contends that the Soviet move arose quite logically out of consideration of a total ban on ABMs, which could have left each side more vulnerable to third party attacks.[26]

Political linkage

The Nixon Administration's use of political linkage to pursue political gains through the SALT negotiations was a multifaceted approach which involved several strategies. One strategy was to create deliberate links between different sets of negotiations. US leaders consciously orchestrated the four-power talks designed to regularize the position of Berlin in relation to the SALT negotiations.[27] At this stage, the USA calculated that the Soviet Union wanted a Berlin agreement to complete the *Ostpolitik* of Willy Brandt's government more than it wanted to move ahead on SALT. Linkage, therefore, served as a bargaining counter. Still, this linkage was in a context of shared interest in reaching an agreement on both issues. Henry Kissinger believed the Soviet Union was also playing this game and noted that the USSR, at one point, was delaying the SALT negotiations in order to achieve progress on Berlin.[28]

A second strategy was to relate the content of SALT to progress in other areas. Hersh claims that Kissinger used the Soviet need for grain sales in early 1972 to persuade the Soviet Government to include SLBMs in SALT.[29]

A third type of linkage was the attempt to influence Soviet actions (or to get the Soviet Union to constrain third parties) by threatening to delay or break off SALT. Early in 1969, the Administration deliberately refrained from initiating the SALT negotiations to signal to the Soviet Union that it would have to earn arms control as a part of a package. Nixon and Kissinger attempted to get the Soviet Union to urge moderation on Hanoi in the negotiations to end the war in Viet Nam and warned the Soviet Union against building a submarine base in Cuba in the autumn of 1970. In December 1971, Kissinger also threatened to cancel the planned Moscow summit meeting, if the USSR did not prevent India from invading West Pakistan.[30] So, according to this theory of political linkage, if the Soviet Union desired arms control more than the USA, then the USSR would, in cases of conflict, compromise its other political interests to achieve a SALT agreement.

The Soviet Union apparently did not attempt to influence US behaviour in other spheres by threatening to disrupt SALT, nor did the USSR use delays in the negotiations as a sign of diplomatic displeasure. After the United States invaded Cambodia in May 1970, the US delegation feared that the Soviet Union would break off talks. The Soviet delegation, however, only made a limited formal protest.[31] Despite a US bombing raid on Hanoi in mid-April 1972 (which sank one Soviet ship and damaged three others) and Nixon's authorization of the mining of Haiphong harbour in May, the Soviet leadership still decided not to cancel the planned Moscow summit meeting.[32]

The Soviet decision to continue with the summit meeting may be interpreted in terms of Moscow's own perceptions of linkage. Newhouse notes that the Bonn Parliament was in the process of deciding whether to ratify the *Ostpolitik* treaties which recognized the existing frontiers of Europe and created a new framework for relations between the FRG and the Soviet Union.[33] The Soviet leadership may have feared that cancelling the summit meeting would jeopardize ratification, especially as Chancellor Brandt was not assured of majority support. The Soviet Union was also seeking concrete gains in terms of grain imports, as well as increased trade with (and imports of Western technology from) both the USA and Western Europe. Therefore, powerful economic incentives existed for the Soviet Union to complete SALT I and to consolidate relations with Washington.[34] In this respect, political linkage may have actually served to promote arms control.

The policy of linkage as practiced by Nixon and Kissinger clearly subordinated arms control to other great power goals. This created obstacles to arms control, because it involved the risk of delay or the threat of a break-off of the negotiations. A similar policy from the Soviet side would probably have destroyed SALT I. For example, if the Soviet leadership had cancelled the May 1972 summit meeting—and reports indicate that the Politburo was sharply divided[35]—then an agreement would probably have been postponed until after the Presidential election. Further, the ratification process might then have continued into—and been overwhelmed by—the Watergate crisis.

In practice, the greatest damage to SALT I was inflicted not by deliberate linkage, but by the linkage inherent in great power relations. Despite the fact that the Johnson Administration had displayed no apparent desire to pursue linkage, the Soviet invasion of Czechoslovakia made it politically impossible for the Administration to begin the SALT negotiations in September 1968. The subsequent delay of over a year did have strategic significance. For example, the United States had moved from the testing of MIRVs in 1968 to actual production in 1969, and the Soviet Union had added 375 ICBMs and SLBMs to its nuclear arsenal.[36]

Alliance politics

The United States was aware that bilateral talks with the Soviet Union on nuclear arms might create fears in Western Europe that a Soviet–US agreement could result in some sort of condominium.[37] The Europeans might also have become alarmed by the spectre of the US nuclear force becoming decoupled if the USA lost its nuclear supremacy. In his memoirs, Kissinger notes that European governments in 1969 were keen for the USA to begin SALT, but that some ambivalence developed after the strategic implications became clear. Josef Luns, the Dutch Foreign Minister, commented that strategic nuclear parity was 'a shocking idea'.[38] The USA interpreted the Soviet insistence on taking account of nuclear FBS as an attempt to divide the USA from the European members of NATO. If this was an aim of the Soviet Union, then it was unsuccessful. NATO allies were regularly briefed during the talks and friction with European or other allies was not a significant factor in SALT I. In general, alliance politics focused on moves towards *détente* and arms control in Europe, and not on SALT.

Strategic goals in negotiations

If the process of negotiations is used to divert attention from a military build up (while encouraging restraint by the other side), then arms control talks can be used to promote strategic advantage. Some US commentators have accused the Soviet Union of pursuing these tactics in SALT I.[39] Certainly, the USSR did continue to build missile submarines, at an estimated rate of between seven and nine a year, during the SALT I negotiations. The Soviet Union suspended construction of ICBM silos for a period in 1970–71, but this move may have been preparatory to switching to a new generation of larger missiles. Furthermore, decisions were made about this time to proceed with MIRVed SS-17, SS-18 and SS-19 missiles for deployment in the later 1970s.[40] The moratorium on silo construction in 1970–71 may have also been intended as a signal of restraint to promote the negotiations, although this is a matter of dispute.[41]

Moscow may have hoped that the SALT talks would strengthen pressures within the USA for a slowing down of the US MIRV programme. Indeed, some Congressmen did urge a halt to MIRV testing and deployment in 1969 and 1970. Still, there is no evidence that the USSR was engaging in SALT for purely Machiavellian reasons. It could equally be claimed that the United States pressed ahead with its own strategic programme of MIRVing its missiles, replacing Polaris with Poseidon and developing Minuteman III, while trying simultaneously to constrain the Soviet ICBM and SLBM programmes.

In fact, it cannot be convincingly argued that either side engaged in SALT purely as a blind or as an attempt to steal a march on the other. Had this been the case, it is unlikely they would have even reached an agreement. Still, neither the USA nor the USSR ever seriously considered negotiating away its central strategic programme. So, the Interim Agreement must be viewed as a very unsatisfactory arms control measure. The commitment to unilateral strategic goals prevailed over the willingness to promote common security by genuine arms restrictions. Although Kissinger did claim that the Soviet Union agreed to cut its planned submarine missile force, he relied on rather dubious US worst-case estimates to support this assertion.[42]

In arms control talks, a standard negotiating tactic is to put forward a proposal which incorporates a unilateral strategic advantage for the side making the proposal. This may be a bargaining tactic, but can often lead to proposals being dismissed out of hand by the other side. Extremely biased proposals were put forward by both the USA and the USSR concerning MIRVs, and were duly rejected as not being serious.[43] Nevertheless, many of the proposals from both sides were accepted as a real starting point for negotiation.

During the course of arms control negotiations, it is reasonable to probe the intentions and programmes of the other side, and this process may sometimes be valuable in dispelling misunderstandings. For example, during the SALT I negotiations the US delegation was able to reassure the Soviet Union that the United States was not committed to a policy of 'launch-on-warning'.[44] The US delegation generally considered informal soundings in SALT to be useful, although the JCS representative had reservations because of the necessity to provide information. This may prompt the parties to a negotiation to fear that the talks are a guise for acquiring military intelligence. At times, the Soviet delegation did suspect a 'fishing expedition': for example, when the US delegation first raised the question of future ABM technology.[45] These suspicions, however, were not so intense as to disrupt the talks.

Strategic asymmetry

The strategic asymmetry between the USA and the USSR influenced the negotiations and the perceptions of bargaining advantage or disadvantage. The US nuclear force was concentrated more heavily on submarines than on land. The USA was well ahead with MIRVs and relied on relatively light missiles. In fact, the USA's only heavy missiles were the obsolete Titan, a land-based weapon. The Soviet Union, on the other hand, had placed the majority of its warheads on land-based ICBMs. The USSR was significantly behind with MIRVs and had developed heavy missiles capable of carrying large nuclear warheads. The United States was becoming increasingly concerned about the vulnerability of its land-based ICBMs, a fear the Soviet Union professed to be unable to understand. In the view of the USSR, a Soviet first strike against land-based missiles would clearly be suicidal given the considerable US sea-borne missile force.[46]

The asymmetry between the two sides in long-range bombers and the much more important asymmetry posed by US forward-based bombers have already been noted. The United States tended to discount the possibility that the Soviet Union felt genuinely threatened by these forward-based nuclear-armed bombers, although the Soviet delegation pointed out how nervous Washington became at the possibility of nuclear bases in Cuba [47]

Asymmetry is not necessarily always a problem in negotiations. The fact that the Soviet Union was behind the USA in its ABM technology and worried by its technological inferiority is widely interpreted as having provided the Soviet Government with an incentive to reach an ABM agreement. Still, these asymmetries did present some real problems: for example, the dispute over how to count forward-based bombers. Asymmetries also tend to confuse public debate and encourage over-simplified criticism of arms control. Public criticism of the SALT I Interim Agreement, for instance, obscured US superiority in warheads by stressing the Soviet advantage in numbers of missile launchers.

IV. Other types of difficulty

Psychological obstacles

Suspicion and distrust regarding the opponent's true motives impedes most arms control negotiations. Clearly, such factors influenced the negotiating tactics and positions adopted in SALT I. Smith suggests that US distrust of Soviet good faith in arms control resulted in the complexity of some of the early US proposals, because there was a desire to tie the Soviet Union down.[48] The anxieties of the DOD concerning verification and the possible upgrading of Soviet anti-aircraft defences led to prolonged negotiation and were fuelled by a perennial suspicion of Soviet intentions. Secretary of Defense Laird and Senator Jackson voiced their suspicions in Washington. Apart from a generalized distrust of the Soviet Union, the apparent Soviet delays during 1970 aroused doubts about Soviet motives.[49] Conversely, the Soviet Union must have distrusted many aspects of US foreign and defence policy during this period. Clearly, the Soviet Union began the SALT negotiations with grave doubts about US motives.

By the end of the first round of talks, however, the Soviet Union was convinced that the US side was serious in wanting a SALT agreement, and the doubting voices in Moscow were not powerful enough to prevent serious negotiations and the conclusion of the SALT I accords. In Washington, the general political climate also favoured arms control and *détente*, and the paranoid fears and suspicions associated with the cold war era were confined to a minority of SALT critics. According to both Smith and Garthoff, the two delegations developed a good working relationship in the negotiations, and even a degree of personal trust and friendship. Paul Nitze's account suggests good personal relations were a screen for Soviet attempts to manipulate and divide the US delegation. However, Nitze published his account of SALT after he had resigned from the delegation and would soon become one of the main opponents of SALT II.[50]

Technological momentum

SALT I is often presented as the lost opportunity to put a cap on the arms race. Two possible lines of argument have been suggested. The first is that the delays in starting and pursuing negotiations, combined with the inexorable pace of technological developments, made it impossible to ban new weapons. The second is that the negotiators did not seize the opportunity to curb weapons under development when such a curb was apparently still possible.

The change in the strategic situation between September 1968 and November 1969 provides a good illustration of the price that is sometimes exacted by the passage of time. Although this period witnessed substantial progress in the US MIRV programme, actual deployment did not begin until June 1970.[51] Over time, increased expenditures of resources and commitment by the armed services to weapons under development may also result. If tests prove a weapon is effective, then it becomes just that much harder to reverse a weapon programme.

In SALT I, a more cogent case can be made that the negotiators failed to halt various weapons that were still in an early stage. During this period, the US B-1 bomber was being designed, and the Soviet Backfire bomber was under development. At the time, the USA still had not committed itself to production and deployment of the new strategic air-, sea- or land-based cruise missiles. It was not necessarily too late to negotiate a MIRV ban, because the USA had not begun deployment when SALT I commenced. Further, the USSR had not yet tested MIRVs. Retrospectively, Henry Kissinger has expressed public regret that he did not foresee—despite the benefit of specialist advice—the full implications of MIRVs during SALT I. Instead, Kissinger, chose to ignore warnings from academic arms control specialists concerning the dangers of MIRVs.[52]

The real problem is not that technological momentum outstrips the foresight of decision makers, but that decisions are made on the basis of narrow interpretations of military need, bargaining advantage and the requirements of domestic politics.[53] All of these considerations influenced the US refusal to negotiate seriously on MIRVs. Although some sections of the US bureaucracy (in particular, ACDA) wanted to negotiate on MIRVs and had strong support in Congress, the DOD and the military were adamantly opposed.[54] The Johnson Administration's package of SALT proposals did not include MIRVs on the assumption that the JCS would never sanction a ban on them.[55] Under Nixon, the JCS made it quite clear that they regarded the MIRV programme, in which the USA was reckoned to be five years ahead, as essential. In 1970, Melvin Laird had come to share this view.[56] Therefore, the final decision rested with Nixon and Kissinger, whose inclination was to build up US military power to facilitate tough bargaining with the Soviet Union and to oppose any unilateral gestures of restraint. In fact, the Administration actually accelerated its programme for the testing and production of MIRVs in 1969. This was done in order to achieve early deployment in 1970.[57] Raymond Garthoff concludes that Nixon and Kissinger thought it was impossible in terms of domestic politics to pursue simultaneous limits on ABMs and MIRVs, which would have meant a collision course with the Pentagon and Nixon's own constituency—the political right.[58] Furthermore, Kissinger apparently did not believe that the Soviet Union was then interested in a MIRV ban.[59]

The Soviet Union was not prepared to take any initiative on MIRVs, probably because of the perception that it was in a weak position. Smith believes that the Soviet delegation was expecting a MIRV offer, but was not enthusiastic to discuss controls. Garthoff records the disappointment of a member of the Soviet delegation at the time, after it became clear that the USA's MIRV offer was not serious. Garthoff has since been told by senior Soviet officials that Moscow could have accepted a fair MIRV ban. He concludes the decision was 'finely balanced'.[60] Weiler notes that 'contrary to published accounts the USSR never specifically accepted or rejected a MIRV test ban, while continuing to advocate a ban on production and deployment'.[61] Still, the evidence of the Soviet record on SALT I (that the military refused to concede any of its missile programmes under development) does cast doubt on the likelihood that the Soviet Union would have been willing to forgo MIRVs.

Although technological momentum led to the development of the new weapon possibilities in the first place, strategic calculations and domestic intransigence by both sides were crucial in the failure to curb MIRV deployment.

Domestic obstacles

The most important question in assessing the role of bureaucratic politics associated with SALT is the extent to which the military establishments of the USA and the USSR exerted a decisive influence over the course of decisions. It is also necessary to consider the role of other sources of opposition to the talks, so as to determine whether the decision making processes led to confusion or delay.

The domestic 'negotiations' connected with SALT in Washington have been documented in detail. The roles of the DOD and the JCS are especially interesting in that they were not wholly predictable. The initiative to prepare the first package of SALT proposals occurred during 1968, after it became apparent that the Soviet Union was willing to talk. The initiative was taken by the Office of International Security Affairs (ISA) of the DOD. The ISA was then headed by Paul Warnke, and according to John Newhouse, a lot of the work was done by Morton Halperin, an academic on temporary assignment to the ISA. The ISA—together with ACDA—produced a set of draft proposals that would not be thrown out by the Pentagon and co-ordinated committees within the DOD to discuss them. After the proposals were submitted to the JCS for consideration, they were then forwarded to the President. The most interesting aspect of these proposals is that they were apparently framed almost entirely with a view to what the JCS might be prepared to accept and not to what the Soviet Union might agree. After three days of deliberation, the JCS approved the package (with only some minor qualifications) to the pleasure and astonishment of everyone else concerned. The JCS had agreed to a proposal for a freeze on ICBM and SLBM launchers, and a ban on mobile ICBMs. ABM deployment, however, was not limited. The SALT proposals received strong support from Harold Brown, the Secretary of the Air Force, and backing from Robert McNamara's replacement as Secretary of Defense, Clark Clifford.[62]

Instead of promoting SALT, the DOD became the section of the bureaucracy within the Nixon Administration most hostile to the talks. Besides Melvin Laird, who was a hawkish Secretary of Defense, a number of civilian theoreticians centred in the office of the Director of Defense Research and Engineering (DDR&E) were among the most committed critics of SALT and continually stressed verification problems.[63] DDR&E comprised the pivotal SALT unit in DOD and opposed (based on worst-case scenarios) CIA estimates of Soviet military plans on the assumption that what the USSR technically could do, it inevitably would do. The CIA, however, apparently concentrated on an estimation of what the USSR was actually doing.[64] Other DOD civilians also disagreed with the CIA about the adequacy of NTM to verify a SALT agreement.

On the other hand, the JCS, despite a general lack of enthusiasm for arms control, were prepared to go along with a freeze on missile ceilings and on ABMs. However, they drew the line at a total ban on ABMs[65] or MIRVs. In principle, the Nixon Administration sought to avoid the appearance of tailoring SALT proposals to suit the JCS. In practice, however, Nixon and Kissinger did heed the views of the JCS, and shared their distrust for CIA estimates and for ACDA. After the May 1971 breakthrough, at a tricky point in the negotiations concerning SLBM numbers, Kissinger swung the JCS behind the high levels for SLBMs proposed for the USSR on the somewhat dubious grounds that without an agreement the total would be even higher.[66] During the frantic last minute bargaining in Moscow in May 1972, the JCS threatened a revolt over the details of the SLBM agreement, but were eventually persuaded to stand by the agreement.[67] The fact that the military were more moderate than some of their civilian counterparts made the SALT accords possible, but the views of the JCS did set clear limits.

Whereas the DOD and the JCS had wielded considerable influence, the strongest advocates of arms control in the bureaucracy were correspondingly weak. ACDA has never carried much weight in Washington and has been, in effect, a junior partner of the State Department. Under Nixon, ACDA's role was even further undermined. Nixon personally disliked the Agency, possessed an exaggerated belief in its influence with Congress and tended to attribute all unauthorized leaks to it. In arms control policy making, the State Department usually plays a significant role and tends to seek negotiable agreements. As National Security Adviser, however, Kissinger took the initiative in all of the important foreign policy issues. Secretary of State William Rogers was relegated to a figurehead position. Rogers was not even informed of back channel negotiations in SALT I until the initial agreement with Dobrynin in May 1971 was publicized. Moreover, primary responsibility for the negotiations lay not with the State Department, but with the White House and the National Security Council. At the White House, Kissinger chaired the key committee for framing SALT proposals: the Verification Panel. Although the State Department and ACDA both urged a curb on MIRVs and a total ABM ban, their views were not given much weight.[68]

White House control over the policy making for SALT was intended to encourage detailed analysis of options, transcend inter-agency squabbles, ensure coherent proposals and avoid long delays. However, not all the participants were convinced that these goals were achieved. Kissinger himself became impatient concerning the amount of detail produced for discussion and records that Nixon was visibly bored by it.[69] In practice, some of the proposals were the product of inter-agency compromise, rather than coherent policy making. In his memoirs, Kissinger marvels that all the agencies agreed to propose to the Soviet Union an ABM system for each capital, at a time when the Administration was pressing Congress for ABM defences around ICBM bases and Congress was most unlikely to accept a capital defence.[70] Because of Kissinger's other foreign policy priorities, SALT policy making frequently was subject to delays; and there was a lack of control over SALT developments.[71]

With respect to the Soviet Union, there is some evidence to suggest that policy making on arms control was heavily influenced by the military and that the bureaucratic machinery was cumbersome.[72] In Moscow, the Politburo ultimately controlled the SALT process. During the final hectic negotiations in May 1972, the Politburo met several times to discuss SALT and was clearly the final arbiter throughout. Detailed proposals, however, were apparently co-ordinated by the Defense Council, the body in which some key Politburo members meet with representatives of the military. The Military Industrial Commission, which oversees the Soviet defence industry, also had a role in policy making; L. V. Smirnov, the chairman of the Commission at the time, was dramatically produced during the May summit meeting in Moscow to negotiate some of the unresolved issues directly with Kissinger.[73]

Continuous bureaucratic responsibility for SALT policy making was divided between the Foreign Ministry, which was responsible for diplomacy, and the Defence Ministry, which was apparently responsible for military and technical detail. In the Foreign Ministry, arms control specialists, the Policy Planning Division and the US Desk were involved. Gromyko, in his role as Foreign Minister, played a key role in negotiations in Moscow. Specialist academic institutes with knowledge of security issues and of the USA also fed ideas into the policy making process. Still, there appears to have been a total division between the Foreign and Defence Ministries in their SALT roles and no direct co-ordination between them. Gerard Smith was told that this gap extended to their respective computers, which 'do not always supply the same answers'.[74] The balance of power seemed to be clearly weighted towards the Ministry of Defence, where a section responsible for SALT served under the General Staff. The military experts maintained a monopoly of the relevant technical and strategic information, and—as the US delegation was startled to discover—were unwilling to discuss the details of the Soviet military programme in front of their civilian colleagues.[75] In addition, there was high-ranking military representation on the SALT delegation. During the initial stages, the top military representative was General Ogarkov.

There are indications of overt Soviet military hostility to SALT. Wolfe, citing articles by Soviet military writers in 1968 and 1969, suggests that some sections of the Soviet military were sceptical about SALT from the outset.[76] Wolfe also records that the Soviet military press highlighted the FBS issue in the spring of 1970. The reports, which coincided with strong Soviet insistence within SALT on the inclusion of FBS in offensive weapon totals, maintained that the main

FBS role was strategic attack on the USSR.[77] Raymond Garthoff suggests that the *absence* of references to SALT in military journals and in statements by most military leaders indicates reservations about the talks.[78] William Jackson, footnoting a speech by Marshal Grechko in February 1971, cites military unhappiness with the omission of forward-based US bombers from SALT I.[79] Nevertheless, given the apparent extent of military control over detail, it is reasonable to assume that military leaders (while adamantly resisting compromises on their planned programmes) assented to the substance of the accords. In fact, the Soviet General Staff seems to have responded much like the JCS.

The Soviet political hierarchy appeared to be divided over SALT I, both before and after the negotiations. Several commentators quote the text of a speech by Gromyko (printed in *Pravda* on 28 June 1968) in which he attacked 'good-for-nothing theoreticians who try to tell us . . . that disarmament is an illusion', and interpret this as a response to opposition to SALT.[80] After SALT I was concluded, a *Pravda* article in June 1972 referred to 'obstructionist actions by rightist and leftist foes of relaxation'.[81] Garthoff believes the Politburo was narrowly divided on many SALT issues in 1971 and 1972.[82] Still, it is generally agreed that SALT was aided when General Secretary Brezhnev, who was an advocate of *détente*, strengthened his personal power at the 24th CPSU Congress in March 1971 and succeeded in appointing four of his supporters to the Politburo. Brezhnev explicitly expressed support for SALT in his speech before the Congress, citing the the need 'to achieve positive results'.[83] Just before the May 1972 summit meeting, the balance of forces in favour of SALT shifted again when Pyotr Shelest, the Ukrainian Party Secretary usually identified as a strong opponent of *détente,* was ousted from his post.[84] Furthermore, by 1972, Brezhnev had assumed primary responsibility for foreign policy from Prime Minister Kosygin. Nevertheless, Brezhnev was still bound by a process of collegial decision making in the Politburo.

V. Obstacles in the negotiating process

Verification

In arms control talks prior to SALT, competing ideological attitudes had resulted in the USA's insistence upon detailed verification out of fear of Soviet cheating, and prompted the USSR to resist what appeared to be espionage and an attempt to meddle in Soviet domestic affairs. In the SALT negotiations, these attitudes did not impinge in the quite the same way, because of the mutual agreement to rely on NTM for verification. The SALT I negotiations, however, did suggest the extent to which attitudes concerning on-site inspections had become ritualized. Washington assumed that the Soviet Union would ignore a proposal which included a requirement for on-site inspection and was proved correct. In this instance, however, Soviet rejection appears to have been influenced by the USA's lack of seriousness about its own MIRV proposal, as well as by the overall unacceptability of on-site inspection to the Soviet Union.

During SALT I, one interesting fact that emerged was that the US military was just as unlikely, in practice, to accept certain kinds of detailed on-site inspection. Garthoff reveals that when the provision for such inspection was tacked onto the US MIRV proposal, no studies of what such inspection might mean and how much it would add to verifying compliance had been carried out. After an inter-agency study was belatedly conducted, some officials began to wonder whether the USA itself would really wish for on-site inspection.[85]

Negotiating styles

The divergence between US and Soviet negotiating styles, which had marked earlier arms control negotiations, manifested itself again in SALT. Whereas the Soviet Union preferred broad agreements that imposed general restraints and had political impact, the United States stressed very specific limits based on strategic calculations. The Soviet delegation sought agreement in principle before looking at the detail; the US side was more concerned with the implications of the fine print.[86] The USA would take the initiative in making a series of detailed proposals; the Soviet Union tended to react with counter-proposals. However, the Soviet delegation did prove to be prepared to table formal treaty language as a basis for the later negotiations.

Smith regarded the Soviet approach as an attempt to stake out the maximum bargaining position while retaining flexibility.[87] Kissinger took a more jaundiced view of Soviet bargaining tactics, which he regarded as tough and often unreasonable; the USSR tended to hold out on concessions until the very last minute.[88] Kissinger's view reflected his ideological hostility to the Soviet Union, but was probably influenced by the fact that he had to deal with the most intractable questions on which Moscow was least willing to compromise (such as SLBM limits). On the other hand, the US delegation obtained considerable concessions on the ABM Treaty, which the Soviet Union was anxious to conclude. Kissinger also had to negotiate with Andrei Gromyko who, with long practice in defending Soviet interests tenaciously, has never been regarded by Western diplomats as an easy negotiating opponent. Kissinger, however, did accord Gromyko a certain amount of respect.[89]

Perhaps the most significant problem for SALT I, which arose out of the traditional Soviet position in negotiations, was the refusal to disclose details concerning the Soviet Union's strategic arsenal. The USSR's insistence on military secrecy (noted above) meant that the Interim Agreement on Offensive Arms included no figures for land-based ICBMs. Further, the Agreement was thin on detail, although the Protocol did specify the maximum number of SLBMs permitted for each side. The overall lack of clarity in the Agreement concerning numbers had unfortunate effects on its reception in the United States. After Smith's refusal to reveal numbers had begun to create suspicion,

Kissinger felt compelled (the night after the Agreement had been formally signed) to brief US journalists in Moscow about the implications of the Agreement for the missile forces of the respective sides.[90] Even so, the full details of the Agreement were first publicly spelled out by SALT's chief congressional opponent, Senator Jackson, who stressed that the launcher numbers favoured the Soviet Union.[91] Although secrecy had not hampered the actual conduct of the negotiations, it did help to undermine confidence in the final Agreement and served to create a political climate in Washington less favourable to SALT II.

Bargaining tactics and delays

The USA's negotiating tactics—particularly the presentation of numerous options for the Soviet Union's consideration—have been criticized for being counter-productive. Frye suggests that this may have caused confusion in Moscow and have been interpreted as a delaying tactic. Frye also suggests that offering the Soviet Union a 'menu' from which to choose encouraged agreement on the lowest common denominator.[92] Smith notes that the USA by August 1971 had put forward six approaches in 10 months of negotiation. The Soviet delegation, however, was still waiting for a final offer on ABMs. Smith criticizes this 'quick change performance', which he judges was based not on strategic analysis but on assumptions about 'congressional support' and 'on somewhat shallow and probably incorrect notions about the utility of bargaining chips'. He also thinks that rapid switches may have served to confuse the Soviet delegation.[93]

When the USA offered, on 10 April, either a total ABM ban or one site outside each capital, the USA got itself into particular difficulties. To Washington's embarrassment, the Soviet Union promptly accepted the capital site ABM offer. The USA then began to back down and eventually withdrew the offer. Garthoff suggests that Kissinger had assumed that the Soviet Union would demand higher ABM levels and that such a reaction would help the Administration to get more funds out of Congress for the Safeguard system.[94] To some extent, these criticisms can also be levelled at the Soviet tactics. Smith notes that the Soviet delegation had also put forward different proposals for an ABM solution in rapid succession at one stage, and Garthoff comments that both sides changed their positions. Still, only the USA withdrew an offer which the other side had already accepted.[95]

The US delegation suffered from delays in awaiting instructions from Washington and from increasing distrust and friction between the delegation and the White House. According to Smith, the White House was annoyed if its instructions were queried. Kissinger refused to believe reports from the delegation about informal Soviet approaches and claimed, at one point, that the delegation 'heard what they wanted to hear' about Soviet receptivity to a US proposal for a total ABM ban.[96] The delegation itself, however, was unusually cohesive, and members avoided sending conflicting private reports back to their respective agencies in Washington. Occasionally General Allison, the JCS representative, dissented from his colleagues, but was a valued member of the delegation nonetheless.[97]

The really serious problems for the US delegation (and arguably for the handling of the whole negotiation) arose out of the dual channels. These difficulties were not due to the basic procedure of high-level consultation parallel to detailed negotiations, but the secretive way in which Nixon and Kissinger handled the back channel which often left the delegation in the dark. The delegation also felt that the high-level consultations were conducted with less precision and left gaps which they then had to fill, but this too was partly due to lack of advance consultation.[98]

The Soviet delegation was handicapped by the bureaucratic inflexibility in Moscow (outlined above) which led to a slowness in reacting to US proposals. The Soviet delegation spent its time between formal negotiating sessions engaged in intensive discussions in Moscow concerning the positions to be taken up in the next session. In December 1970, the Soviet delegation privately urged the Americans not to reject out of hand a document proposing provisions to limit the deployment of ABM systems; there had been lengthy discussions in Moscow and more details would be provided if the USA agreed to consider the proposal.[99]

During the session, the Soviet delegation usually received instructions after a Politburo meeting. Apparently, the Soviet delegation was also sufficiently high ranking to be authorized to decide some minor questions on a collegial basis.[100] Co-ordination between the Soviet delegation and Moscow in the back channel was clearly good; Semenov knew what was happening when Smith did not. Garthoff records that he sometimes found out what was going on in the back channel from his Soviet counterpart.[101]

Sometimes, the SALT delegation experienced confusion because of misunderstandings which resulted from the sheer detail of some proposals or from translations which altered the nuance of a word.[102] A more serious misunderstanding arose in the context of the provisions for the Agreement on Prevention of Accidents. The two sides had read different implications into the language used about notification of nuclear detonations.[103] Smith claims that the incident was the most extreme case of mutual incomprehension during SALT I. Because the USA finally accepted the Soviet wording, the problem was resolved. Overall, the delegations had a good working relationship, and misunderstandings could be resolved.

Bargaining chips

During SALT I, the concept of 'bargaining chips' achieved wide currency in US political debate on arms control. SALT I also witnessed the most plausible example of a bargaining chip that may have actually served to *promote* arms control talks: the US ABM programme. The Nixon Administration believed that it was the US Safeguard programme, together with the Soviet Union's fear of USA's advantage in ABM technology, that constituted the greatest incentive to Moscow to negotiate seriously on a limitation of ABMs and to consider a curb on offensive arms. Smith regarded the ABM programme as a powerful bargaining lever; at one point, Smith agreed to go before Congress and argue for further appropriations for the Safeguard system on these grounds. That the ABM programme was the chief factor in getting the Soviet Union to sign the SALT I accords is now part of the conventional wisdom. The fact that the United States was not (unlike the USSR) increasing the number of its submarines and SLBMs during the SALT negotiations has been viewed as putting the USA at a disadvantage in this aspect of the negotiations. Kissinger commented to the press that this was not 'the most brilliant bargaining position I would recommend people to find themselves in'.[104]

The role of bargaining chips in arms control negotiations is subject to dispute. To assess the role of a bargaining chip, it is necessary to distinguish between the reasons for a state to enter into arms negotiations in the first place and the means of leverage employed during negotiations. In the case of ABM, it is argued that the programme was a spur to Soviet co-operation at both levels. Therefore, it is important to clarify the role of the US ABM programme in SALT I.

According to Alton Frye, the idea that the ABM programme was a useful bargaining chip gained acceptance in 1968, when a Senate vote favouring the Sentinel system was followed by the Soviet Union's public expression of interest in talks about strategic arms. Melvin Laird and others concluded that Moscow's willingness to talk was directly connected with Washington having just launched its own ABM programme. However, Frye points out that 'quiet communication' between the two capitals had already begun to reveal that the Soviet attitude towards ABMs was changing.[105] The Soviet commentary of the period indicated that the Soviet Union's desire for an ABM treaty was influenced by the fear that, as a result of an 'illusion of invulnerability', the USA might rely more on military force in the future.[106] Undoubtedly, Moscow was also concerned about the astronomical costs of an ABM programme and the overall inefficiency of existing ABM technology. Further, Moscow must have feared that the USA would get ahead in competition for nation-wide ABM defences. If the Soviet Union was motivated to negotiate to avoid the dangers and costs of ABM deployment in the future, then so were the exponents of the ABM Treaty in Washington. It is debatable whether the Johnson Administration's commitment to the Sentinel system was a decisive factor in getting Moscow to agree to begin the SALT negotiations, although it may have been an additional spur.

When President Nixon switched to the Safeguard ABM system in 1969 and pressed for congressional funding, he emphasized the need to maintain an incentive for the Soviet Union to negotiate. In 1970, Nixon reiterated this rationale. Because the Soviet Union continued to display strong interest in an

ABM treaty, Nixon's strategy appeared to be at least superficially successful. During 1969, however, it became increasingly clear that Moscow had considerable doubts about Nixon's seriousness over SALT, perhaps as a result of the Administration's ABM programme. In fact, the Soviet Union did not begin to negotiate in earnest until the first session of talks had indicated Washington's own commitment to do so. Therefore, there is no clear evidence that continuing Soviet interest in an early ABM Treaty was dependent on the Safeguard programme. Indeed, Moscow must have been aware that congressional opposition might well have spelled the end to Safeguard.

Although the Soviet Union's reactions to the US ABM programme are important, it is equally pertinent to examine developments in Washington. One interesting question is whether President Nixon really regarded the ABM programme as a bargaining chip or as a convenient rationale to secure congressional approval. Kissinger suggests that the Administration sometimes used bargaining chip arguments in this way.[107] Bernard Brodie, moreover, has queried whether Nixon (in light of the apparently genuine enthusiasm he displayed for Safeguard) really intended to bargain it away during SALT. According to Garthoff, Nixon in 1969 set out to build the basis of a nation-wide defence.[108] Brodie suggests the ABM programme probably became a bargaining chip because of the problems of inflation.[109]

Congress was mainly responsible for persuading the Administration to use the ABM programme as a real bargaining chip. Whereas the 90th Congress voted to press ABMs on a still hesitant President, the 91st Congress, seated in January 1969 and inspired by the Vietnam disaster to a new caution concerning large military outlays, resisted pressure from the Nixon White House for ABM funding. In August 1969, the Senate vote on whether to proceed with the Safeguard programme resulted in a tie which was resolved in favour of Safeguard by Vice President Spiro Agnew's tie-breaking vote. Over the next two years, the Congress continued to resist spending money on a technologically dubious and exhorbitantly expensive system. The Administration knew that if it did not agree to an ABM Treaty, it might be forced to abandon ABMs unilaterally.[110] In the case of the ABM programme, the Congress acted to resolve the classic puzzle of the bargaining chip: a weapon good enough to be a realistic bargaining chip is too good to give away in negotiation.

The determination to press ahead with ABM deployment also caused certain specific problems during the negotiations. The USA's decision to deploy ABMs around missile sites, when the only Soviet ABM system was around its capital, created difficulties in the talks and greatly reduced the likelihood of a total ABM ban. Moreover, the Nixon Administration incurred a heavy political debt to those congressmen who supported the requests for ABM funding, most notably Senator Jackson. Pressure from Jackson prompted the White House to complicate its existing ABM proposals even further. The USA presented a third proposal early in 1971 which stipulated that the USA should have four ABM sites around ICBM bases as compared to the one site near Moscow.[111] Although this offer may have been consistent with the USA deployment programme, it was clearly unacceptable to the Soviet Union.

Apparently, the Soviet Union was strongly influenced by a recognition of the consequences of an unrestricted ABM competition. The Safeguard programme was not necessarily a further incentive. The Soviet delegation professed puzzlement at the conflict between Washington's ABM deployment plan and its proposals for strict limits. Therefore, the Safeguard programme may have served to genuinely arouse suspicion and to encourage delay in Moscow.[112] Certainly, the programme created extra complications for the talks. Most importantly, without domestic pressure to curb ABMs, the Nixon Administration might have opted for deployment in preference to a treaty or for an agreement at a much higher level of ABM deployment.

An assessment of bargaining chips in SALT I raises the question why—if the ABM programme became a bargaining chip—the MIRV programme did not? During 1968, Secretary of Defense Clark Clifford decided to proceed with MIRV tests on the grounds that if the USA demonstrated its MIRV technology, then it would be a powerful incentive for the Soviet Union to negotiate seriously concerning strategic arms limitation.[113] When the Nixon Administration's programme of testing and developing MIRVs was challenged by Senator Edward Brooke and his Senate Resolution in March 1970, President Nixon fell back on the argument that continuing MIRV tests would be a bargaining chip for SALT. Senator Brooke produced the counter-argument that the prospect for MIRV deployment might be an incentive to the Soviet Union to negotiate, but actual deployment of MIRVs would require the talks to focus upon removing, or reducing, a force already employed. This, Brooke contended, would raise the difficult question of on-site inspection. When recording this exchange, Graham Allison comments that Senator Brooke was proved right, as SALT I excluded MIRVs.[114] Nevertheless, because MIRVs comprised the heart of a five-year strategic programme, it is very questionable that MIRVs were ever regarded as negotiable, at least by most sections of the Administration. If President Nixon was really briefly prepared to consider including MIRVs seriously in the SALT negotiations, as Frye believes he was, then this option was foreclosed by the JCS and the DOD.[115] Therefore, the case of the MIRV programme is typical of most weapons publicly justified as bargaining chips; once they are developed, the military is not prepared to negotiate them away.

The concept of bargaining chips has been espoused by the West. During SALT I, Moscow did not display any disposition to negotiate away weapons it was just developing (quite the contrary in the case of new offensive missiles). The idea of developing a weapon primarily in order to bargain it away was almost certainly a concept alien to the Soviet system of weapon procurement. The concept of bargaining chips is an approach that is wasteful of resources, disruptive to coherent strategic planning and inherently disliked by the military. By the 1980s, however, the USSR had begun to view weapon deployment in bargaining terms (see chapter 7).

VI. Did SALT I promote the arms race?

Some critics of negotiations have suggested that espousing weapons as bargaining chips may actually accelerate their development. Whether or not this was a major factor during the actual SALT I negotiations (when bargaining chip arguments were used primarily to protect ABM and MIRV developments) is unclear, although MIRV development was speeded up in 1969. Still, there is evidence that at the end of SALT I, the DOD considered the idea of bargaining chips in order to push through favoured programmes in the face of congressional, as well as some White House, resistance. Smith comments that SALT was a godsend to weapon advocates and suggests that the Navy's Trident programme was accelerated by several years. Smith quotes Laird who was testifying before a House subcommittee just 10 days after SALT I was signed:

Just as the Moscow Agreement was made possible by our successful action in such programmes as Safeguard, Poseidon and Minuteman III, these future negotiations to which we are pledged can only succeed if we are equally successful in implementing such programmes as the Trident system, the B-1 bomber . . . [and] SLCM [submarine-launched cruise missiles] . . .[116]

It is interesting to note that the US defence budget for the 1973 fiscal year was the first for several years to project an increased expenditure on strategic nuclear forces, primarily the Trident program.

The JCS have often exacted a price for agreeing to arms control. Toward the end of SALT I, Kissinger cabled from the Moscow summit meeting to obtain JCS consent to a compromise concerning one aspect of Soviet SLBM limits. The JCS agreed, but appended a 'price tag' that the Administration should agree to 'the acceleration of ongoing offensive systems and improvements to existing systems'. Kissinger comments that the Administration wanted to pursue this policy in any case, so it is not clear that the 'price tag' influenced executive willingness to add to the US nuclear arsenal.[117]

Sometimes, an agreement based on symmetry is thought to result in a higher buildup than would have occurred unilaterally. This did not apply to the SALT I Offensive Arms Agreement, which effectively endorsed the unilateral strategic plans of each side and, notably, did not require exact parity in launchers. However, the Jackson Amendment to Senate ratification of SALT I ensured that parity would become an obsession in future negotiations. Formal parity did permit the installation of two ABM sites (each with different purposes) instead of one for each side. However, two years later, when Congress refused funds for an ABM defence around Washington, both sides found it easy to give up a site that existed only on paper.

Because SALT I limited launcher numbers but not MIRVs, the Agreement may be said to have had a channelling effect. It is doubtful that SALT I altered military plans in the USA, because the strong commitment to MIRVs and to the development of Trident existed before the Agreement was signed. Further, this is precisely why SALT I omitted any curbs on MIRVs. Still, SALT I does appear to have influenced Congress through a legitimization of a MIRV buildup. Kissinger notes that, up until the SALT I Agreement which allowed for modernization, congressional opposition to MIRVs was voiced.[118] A more specific channelling effect has been identified by Herbert Scoville, who suggests that the US Navy pursued a SLCM programme because it was not covered by the Interim Agreement.[119]

Whether or not SALT I had an accelerating effect on the Soviet military programme is more difficult to discern. Although bargaining-chip arguments were apparently not employed, the Soviet General Staff may well have exacted a price tag for accepting arms control. Although Garthoff is relying primarily on deduction, he suggests that this occurred with respect to the maintenance of air defences and the MIRV programme after SALT I was concluded.[120] In principle, arms control is just as likely to have a channelling effect on the Soviet (as on the US) military programme. In practice, however, it is hard to be sure that the Soviet MIRV programme—already being planned during the SALT I talks— was accelerated because of launcher limits. Jane Sharp suggests quite plausibly that the emphasis given to the intermediate-range SS-20 missiles and the Backfire bomber was partly due to their exclusion from SALT I.[121] Still, Soviet policy (even in the 1960s) had stressed a buildup of medium-range nuclear forces.

Whether or not SALT I had a direct impact on the rapid increase in MIRVs (by both sides) during the late 1970s, the Interim Agreement has been widely perceived to have had a channelling effect. At a more fundamental level, SALT I did not seem to have curbed the most important aspect of the nuclear arms race: namely, the growth in the nuclear arsenals. Therefore, among some sectors of opinion, SALT I has served to erode confidence in the efficacy of arms control.

VI. Conclusion

This chapter has illustrated some of the quite considerable difficulties which delayed the agreement, and limited the scope, of SALT I. Generally speaking, however, the circumstances attending SALT I were unusually propitious. In the wake of defeat in Vietnam, public and congressional opinion in the United States were favourable to limiting arms. In the Soviet Union, specialized international affairs institutes with a sophisticated knowledge of the USA and the West acted as a kind of arms control lobby. Partly through personal connections with the Soviet leadership, key individuals in the institutes wielded considerable influence. For example, Georgi Arbatov of the USSR's Institute of USA and Canada Studies was a close associate of General Secretary Brezhnev. Moreover, by 1971–72, both Nixon and Brezhnev were anxious for the political kudos which result from the conclusion of a major arms control agreement. Brezhnev had identified himself as a supporter of *détente* and SALT, and the conclusion of an agreement would be an important outcome of these policies.

Increasingly, President Nixon wished to shed a warmonger image and to prove his statesmanship before the 1972 Presidential Election.

Taken together, these factors still did not secure a satisfactory agreement on offensive arms. SALT I is largely considered a success because of the ABM Treaty. In this case, there was a uniquely favourable conjunction of circumstances: a new technology promising enough to create alarm about its potential (but shaky enough to undermine military commitment to it) and requiring an expenditure so vast that governments in both Washington and Moscow were cautious. Moreover, the ABM technology emerged at a time when Washington was at least partially committed to the deterrence theory of mutual assured destruction (although reformulated in terms of nuclear sufficiency by Nixon and Kissinger) and when Moscow appeared to be implicitly moving towards a similar approach.

Notes and references

[1] Steinberg, G. M., *Satellite Reconnaissance: The Role of Informal Bargaining* (Praeger: New York, 1983).

[2] Smith, G., *Doubletalk: The Story of the First Strategic Arms Limitation Talks* (Doubleday: New York, 1980), p. 101.

[3] See Smith (note 2), pp. 30–31.

[4] Newhouse, J., *Cold Dawn: The Story of SALT* (Holt, Rhinehart and Winston: New York, 1973), pp. 72–73.

[5] See Newhouse (note 4), p. 45.

[6] Gaddis, J. L., *Strategies of Containment* (Oxford University Press: Oxford, 1982), pp. 274–343 provides an account of Nixon and Kissinger' s theory of *détente* and its implementation of it.

[7] Newhouse (note 4), pp. 111–29.

[8] Garthoff, R., *Detente and Confrontation: American Soviet Relations from Nixon to Reagan* (The Brookings Institution: Washington, DC, 1985), pp. 139–40.

[9] Summary accounts of the main issues in SALT I are contained in Labrie, R. P., *SALT Hand Book: Key Documents and Issues 1972–1979* (American Enterprise Institute for Public Policy Research: Washington, DC, 1979); and Wolfe, T. W., *The SALT experience* (Ballinger: Cambridge, Mass., 1979). Much greater detail can be found in Smith (note 2), Newhouse (note 4) and Garthoff (note 8).

[10] The Agreement sought to freeze total numbers of missile launchers at existing levels of those in place or under active construction. Because the USA wished the USSR to switch some of its missiles to a sea-based second strike force, modernization provisions encouraged the substitution of SLBMs for ICBMs. When the Agreement was signed, the USSR possessed 1618 ICBMs and was judged to have 740 SLBMs on nuclear-powered submarines. The Agreement set an upper limit of 950 SLBMs on 62 submarines for the USSR and permitted it to substitute a maximum of 210 ICBMs for SLBMs. The USA had 1054 ICBMs and 656 SLBMs in May 1972. Under the Agreement, the USA could substitute 54 ageing Titan missiles for 54 new SLBMs to be deployed on 3 new Trident submarines by 1977. This would be implemented under an agreed limit of 710 US SLBMs on 44 submarines. For the text of the Agreement and clarification of figures, see Calvo-Goller, N. K. and Calvo, M. A., *The SALT Agreements: Content–Application–Verification* (Martinus Nijhoff: Dordrecht, 1987), pp. 29–39 and 348–51.

[11] Sharp, J. M. O., 'Confidence building measures on SALT', *Arms Control*, vol. 3, no. 1 (May 1982), p. 44.

[12] Hersh, S. M., *Kissinger: The Price of Power* (Faber and Faber: London, 1983), pp. 547–48 argues that Kissinger compounded misunderstanding by misinforming Congress about the status of the understanding on heavy missiles.

[13] Brennan, D. G., *National Review,* vol. 24 (23 June 1972).

[14] See Newhouse (note 4), pp. 233–37.

[15] See Smith (note 2), pp. 294–95.

[16] See Garthoff (note 8) , p. 136.

[17] See Smith (note 2), p. 176.

[18] See Smith (note 2), p. 124.

[19] Nacht, M., 'Toward an American conception of regional security', *Daedalus,* vol. 110, no. 1 (winter 1981), p. 9.

[20] See Newhouse (note 4), p. 265.

[21] See Newhouse (note 4), pp. 140 and 163.

[22] See Garthoff (note 8), p. 131.

[23] See Wolfe (note 9), p. 19.

[24] See Smith (note 2), pp. 141–43.

[25] Kissinger, H., *White House Years* (Little Brown: Boston, Mass., 1979), p. 554.

[26] See Garthoff (note 9), pp. 180–81. He refers back to an explicit statement by Semenov linking an ABM ban to the need to provide against accidental or provocative third-party attacks, made in November 1969.

[27] See Kissinger (note 25), pp. 802–3.

[28] See Kissinger (note 25), p. 814.

[29] See Hersh (note 12), pp. 531–53.

[30] See Gaddis (note 6), pp. 293–94.

[31] See Smith (note 2), pp. 136–37.

[32] Neidle, A. F. (ed.), *Nuclear Negotiations: Reassessing Arms Control Goals in US–Soviet Relations* (University of Austin: Texas, 1982), pp. 132–33.

[33] See Newhouse (note 4), pp. 243–44.

[34] The communiqué issued after the summit meeting included provisions for strengthening economic and commercial relations between the two powers. See text in *Survival,* vol. 14, no. 4 (July–Aug. 1972), pp. 191–92. Hersh (note 12), p. 534 suggests grain sales were a particularly important consideration.

[35] See Neidle (note 32), pp. 132–33.

[36] Garthoff, R., 'SALT and the Soviet Military', *Problems of Communism,* vol. 24, no. 1 (Jan.–Feb. 1975), p. 24.

[37] See Newhouse (note 4), p. 138.

[38] See Kissinger (note 25), pp. 403–5.

[39] See, for example, Van Cleave, W. R., 'Political and negotiating asymmetries in SALT', *Contrasting Approaches to Strategic Arms Control,* ed. R. L. Pfaltzgraff, Jr (D. C. Heath: Lexington, Mass, 1973).

[40] See Jackson, W. D., 'Policy assessment at the crossroads: the Soviets and SALT', *Bulletin of the Atomic Scientists,* vol. 35, no. 4 (Apr. 1979), p. 13 on missile developments. For estimates of the Soviet submarine-building programme, see Kissinger (note 25), pp. 1129–30, who says 8–9 a year. Smith (note 2), p. 79 estimates about 7 a year.

[41] Kissinger dismisses the possibility that the Soviet moratorium was a signal (note 25), pp. 811–12. Garthoff, however, contends that it was (note 36), p. 30–31.

[42] See Garthoff (note 8), pp. 161–65.

[43] See Garthoff (note 8), pp. 136–37.

[44] See Smith (note 2), p. 134.

[45] See Smith (note 2), p. 265.

[46] See Smith (note 2), p. 136.

[47] See Smith (note 2), p. 93.

[48] See Smith (note 2), p. 122.

[49] Smith (note 2), p. 197 notes that the USSR seemed to be marking time throughout 1970. Kissinger (note 25), p. 545 complains about Soviet inflexibility, and on p. 549 suggests that the USSR was trying to improve terms offered by waiting for US domestic pressures to force unilateral initiatives.

[50] Paul Nitze was a DOD representative on the SALT delegation for SALT I and the early stage of SALT II. See Nitze, P. H., 'The strategic balance between hope and scepticism', *Foreign Policy* no. 17 (winter 1974–75), pp. 141–43.

[51] Allison, G. T., 'Questions about the arms race: who's racing whom? A bureaucratic perspective', in Pfaltzgraff (note 39), p. 48.

[52] For the Kissinger statement, see Smith (note 2), p. 177. For evidence that Kissinger had plenty of academic and political advice on the implications of MIRVs, see Garthoff (note 6), p. 141 and Hersh (note 12), pp. 150–54.

[53] The importance of domestic factors is reflected in nearly all detailed accounts. See Allison (note 51) for a representative analysis of the crucial role of domestic politics.

[54] See Smith (note 2), p. 161.

[55] See Newhouse (note 4), p. 123.

[56] See Smith (note 2), p. 161.

[57] See Hersh (note 12), p. 163.

[58] See Garthoff (note 8), p. 135.

[59] See Kissinger (note 25), p. 150.

[60] See Garthoff (note 8), pp. 139–40.

[61] Weiler, L., 'The status of SALT: a perspective', *Negotiating Security: An Arms Control Reader,* ed. W. H. Kincade and J. D. Porro (Carnegie Endowment for International Peace: Washington, DC, 1979).

[62] See Newhouse (note 4), pp. 110–29.

[63] Frye, A., 'US decision making for SALT', *SALT: The Moscow Agreements and Beyond,* ed. M. Willrich and J. B. Rhinelander (Free Press: New York, 1974), p. 80.

[64] See Smith (note 2), pp. 114–15 and Newhouse (note 4), pp. 160–61.

[65] See Smith (note 2), p. 205.

[66] See Garthoff (note 8), pp. 161–65.

[67] See Kissinger (note 25), p. 1232. Hersh (note 12), p. 537 suggests that Admiral Thomas Moorer, Chairman of the JCS, was under personal pressure to co-operate with the White House because of his involvement in spying by the Navy on the White House, uncovered in December 1971.

[68] See Frye (note 63), p. 81 and Garthoff (note 8), pp. 134–36.

[69] See Kissinger (note 25), pp. 148 and 542.

[70] See Kissinger (note 25), p. 542.

[71] See Smith (note 2), pp. 109–11.

[72] For a brief accounts of the Soviet decision making process on SALT, see Shulman, M. D., 'Salt and the Soviet Union', in Willrich and Rhinelander (note 63); and Wolfe (note 9). For a more detailed account, see Payne, S. B., *The Soviet Union and SALT* (MIT Press: Cambridge, Mass, 1980). In addition Garthoff (note 8) provides a good deal of information, and Smith (note 2) and Kissinger (note 25) provide insights based on their negotiating experience.

[73] See Kissinger (note 25), p. 1234.

[74] See Smith (note 2), p. 59.

[75] See Newhouse (note 4), pp. 55–56.

[76] See Wolfe (note 9), p. 75.

[77] Wolfe, T. W., 'Soviet interests in SALT', *SALT: Implications of Arms Control for the 1980s,* ed. W. R. Kintner and R. L. Pfaltzgraff, Jr (University of Pittsburgh Press: Pittsburgh, Pa, 1973), p. 36.

[78] See Garthoff (note 36), p. 25.

[79] See Jackson (note 40), p. 12.

[80] See Deane, M. J., *Political Control of the Soviet Armed Forces* (Macdonald and Jane's: London, 1977), p. 193.

[81] See Wolfe (note 9), p. 20.

[82] See Garthoff (note 8), p, 196.

[83] See Payne (note 72), p. 75.

[84] Pyotr Shelest is generally believed to have opposed holding the Moscow summit meeting after the US mining of Haiphong harbour. Shelest was finally dismissed from the Politburo in 1973. See Gelman, H., *The Brezhnev Politburo and the Decline of Detente* (Cornell University Press: Ithaca, 1984), pp. 157–58.

[85] See Garthoff (note 8), p. 138.

[86] Garthoff, R. L., 'Negotiating with the Russians: some lessons from SALT', *International Security,* vol. 1, no. 4 (spring 1977), pp. 5–6.

[87] See Smith (note 2), p. 124.

[88] See Kissinger (note 25), pp. 545–49.

[89] Kissinger found it much easier to talk to Ambassador Dobrynin, who had a rather different role to play, but was also more attuned to US attitudes. See Talbott, S., *End Game: The Inside Story of SALT II* (Harper and Row: New York, 1979), p. 81. For Kissinger's view of Gromyko, see Kissinger (note 25), pp. 788–93.

[90] See Kissinger (note 25), p. 1244.

[91] Roberts, A., 'Arms control in a blind alley', *New Society,* vol. 71, no. 1159 (14 Mar. 1985), p. 396.

[92] See Frye (note 63), pp. 83–84.

[93] See Smith (note 2), pp. 152 and 267.

[94] See Garthoff (note 8), p. 184.

[95] See Garthoff (note 8), p. 184 and Smith (note 2), p. 267.

[96] See Smith (note 2), pp. 258–60.

[97] Later, Senator Jackson singled General Allison out as a scapegoat for SALT I and successfully prevailed on President Nixon to have the General unceremoniously sacked.

[98] The advantages and disadvantages of the back channel are covered in detail by Kissinger (note 25), Smith (note 2) and Garthoff (note 8).

[99] See Smith (note 2), p. 195.

[100] See Smith (note 2), p. 59.

[101] See Garthoff (note 8), p. 149.

[102] See Smith (note 2), p. 292.

[103] See Smith (note 2), p. 292.

[104] Cited by Labrie (note 9), p. 46.

[105] See Frye (note 63), p. 74.

[106] See Wolfe (note 9), p. 8.

[107] See Kissinger (note 25), p. 538.

[108] See Garthoff (note 8), pp. 143–45.

[109] Brodie, B., 'On the objectives of arms control', *International Security,* vol. 1, no. 1 (summer 1976), p. 35.

[110] One important factor influencing Congress was the unexpected degree of public opposition to siting ABMs in their locality. Even Senator Jackson had to bend before his constituents' hostility to ABM defences and oppose an ABM site in his home state. See Bresler, R. J., 'The tangled politics of SALT', *Arms Control,* vol. 3, no. 1 (May 1982), p. 7.

[111] See Frye (note 63), p. 88.

[112] See Garthoff (note 8), pp. 182–83.

[113] See Frye (note 63), pp. 77. Frye notes that Clark has since expressed doubts about this 'we arm to parley' line of reasoning.

[114] See Allison (note 51), p. 49.

[115] See Frye (note 63), p. 81.

[116] See Smith (note 2), p. 340.

[117] See Kissinger (note 25), p. 1240.

[118] See Kissinger (note 25), p. 538.

[119] Scoville, H., Jr, 'A different approach to arms control—reciprocal unilateral restraint', *Arms Control and Technological Innovation,* ed. D. Carlton and C. Schaerf (Croom Helm: London, 1977), p. 172.

[120] See Garthoff (note 36), p. 32.

[121] See Sharp (note 10), p. 46.

6. SALT II: the obstacles multiply

I. Introduction

The difficulties encountered in negotiating SALT II are indicated by the sheer length of time it took to conclude a Treaty: talks began in November 1972 and final agreement was reached in June 1979. The failure of the United States ever to ratify SALT II is yet another reflection of the variety of political problems besetting this Treaty.

SALT II can be divided into three main phases: the negotiations leading up to the Vladivostok Accord of November 1974, the unsuccessful attempt under President Ford to convert this preliminary agreement into a treaty before the end of 1976 and the new efforts to reach a conclusion under President Carter. Each of these phases is summarized and analysed separately in this chapter, with the aim of highlighting the chief obstacles in each phase.

The available literature concerning SALT II, especially the first two phases, is not quite as abundant as that for SALT I. Nevertheless, there is enough material available in political memoirs, political analyses and numerous articles to trace what happened and to make some judgements.

II. Prelude to the Vladivostok Accord

The new round of negotiations was bound to be difficult because the aim was to reach a permanent or long-term agreement which would include all strategic nuclear weapon systems and cover *qualitative* as well as quantitative limits. Because MIRVs were not covered by SALT I, they would, of course, be central to a subsequent agreement. Some of the key problems in the talks leading up to the Vladivostok Accord concerned how to limit MIRVs, the continuing US anxiety about the throw-weight of heavy Soviet missiles and the USA's uncertainty whether to trade off throw-weight against US superiority in numbers of warheads or against US technological advantage. During most of this initial period, the Soviet Union insisted that it was entitled to maintain a superiority in launchers in order to offset being behind the USA in MIRVs and to compensate for strategic and geographic asymmetries. The United States rejected this claim, but vacillated between seeking complete parity or some formula for achieving 'essential equivalence'. The Soviet Union still demanded that US nuclear FBS should be taken into account, and this issue arose in the preliminary drafting of a 'Statement on the Basic Principles of Negotiations on Strategic Arms

Limitation' to be agreed at a summit meeting in June 1973. Although the Statement was a diplomatic device to suggest progress while obscuring the real issues, it did commit the parties to strive for an agreement by the end of 1974. In view of the gap between the two sides, this clause was agreed with great reluctance by both Soviet Foreign Minister Gromyko and General Secretary Brezhnev.[1]

Both the USA and the USSR put forward proposals for some form of freeze on missile testing which, in principle, is essential if qualitative competition in nuclear arms is to be capped. However, both parties proposed schemes which were manifestly designed to confer a clear strategic advantage on themselves, with the result that the proposals were rejected out of hand by the other side. In May 1973, the USA suggested that there should be a freeze on testing multiple-warhead missiles and on deployment of ICBMs for the duration of the talks. At the time, the USA was already in the process of deploying some 1050 MIRVs whereas the Soviet Union had not yet begun deployment.[2] The USSR, on the other hand, had suggested in the spring of 1973 that there should be a ban on testing all new strategic systems for the period of the new agreement, while allowing modernization of existing systems. This was seen by many US officials as an attempt to curb all the new US programmes—the Trident missile, the B-1 bomber and cruise missiles—and thereby to provide a decisive advantage to the Soviet Union.[3]

Very little progress was achieved in the talks until late in 1974. In the United States, domestic politics played a major role in discouraging consistent efforts to move towards agreement. At the preliminary session in November–December 1972, the US delegation was instructed simply to sound out the other side. After re-election, Nixon purged the arms control bureaucracy by replacing top officials in the ACDA and several members of the SALT delegation.

When the SALT II negotiations resumed in March 1973, Ambassador U. Alexis Johnson led the US delegation (Gerard Smith had resigned) and Fred Iklé had assumed the top post at ACDA. In March, the USA made a formal proposal and in May (just before the June summit meeting) presented another hastily prepared offer. During the latter half of 1973, however, the USA took no initiatives. Early in 1974, the White House did attempt to come to grips with the problems, and Secretary of State Kissinger unsuccessfully attempted to move ahead by personal negotiations before the summit meeting in June 1974. During the summit meeting, both sides slightly revised their proposals and engaged in some debate concerning SALT. Still, they remained too far apart for agreement. The delays and lack of consistency on the US side were due to President Nixon's increasing preoccupation with the Watergate scandal, which had reduced his room for domestic manœuvre, and to Kissinger's frequent absorption in other foreign policy issues. Indeed, Kissinger's formal promotion to Secretary of State in August 1973 did not signify an increase in real power: rather the reverse.[4] In the absence of initiative from the top, the bureaucracy remained deadlocked. The Verification Panel meetings on SALT II were frequently acrimonious, and the delegation seldom received clear instructions.[5]

The Soviet Union's conduct of foreign policy, however, did not suffer any obvious disruption during this period. Brezhnev was in a strong position as General Secretary, and Gromyko (Foreign Minister since 1957) was promoted to the Politburo in May 1973. The Soviet SALT delegation at Geneva was still headed by Vladimir Semenov. Continuity, however, did not result in a positive Soviet approach. On the contrary, Western commentators generally agree that the Soviet position in SALT up to late 1974 was intransigent. Moscow must have had justifiable doubts about Washington's seriousness in the talks at this stage and about the ability of President Nixon to deliver an agreement. In some quarters in Moscow, Watergate was apparently suspected of being a ploy by opponents of arms control.[6] Still, Soviet policy makers almost certainly saw a strategic advantage in not rushing the talks at this stage. The Soviet Union improved its missile force and secured a diplomatic advantage in a tough bargaining position.

Despite the failure to progress with SALT, both the USA and the USSR were anxious to avoid a breakdown of arms control negotiations. During the 1973 summit meeting, an Agreement on the Prevention of Nuclear War was signed following negotiations conducted by Henry Kissinger. The Soviet Union took the initiative in promoting this agreement and, unlike the United States, undertook very thorough advance preparations. The Agreement is a statement of general principles of the kind traditionally favoured by the Soviet Union and commits both sides to avoid military confrontations and to consult immediately if there is a danger of nuclear war. The June 1974 summit meeting resulted in a more concrete step, a Protocol to the ABM Treaty limiting each side to one site each instead of two. This move became politically attractive after Congress had rejected the Administration's 1973 request for a ballistic missile defence around Washington, and the Soviet Union had concluded that there was little, if any, benefit in constructing one system around a missile base. Therefore, a more restrictive ABM agreement did not require either side to relinquish anything.

After President Ford was installed in August 1974, the SALT deadlock was soon broken. Although the delegations (which met for their fifth session in Geneva from September to November) presented no new proposals and had concentrated mainly on exploring the possibility an agreement limited to 10 years as opposed to a permanent one, Kissinger initiated back channel negotiations with Ambassador Dobrynin in October before a trip to Moscow. Raymond Garthoff concludes that the proposal taken to Moscow was a serious offer, although it somewhat favoured the USA.[7] Kissinger found the Soviet leadership to be much more responsive to his overtures, and willing to consider different possibilities. Although the Soviet Union refused to reduce its heavy ICBM total, it agreed to leave out references to FBS.

The way was then cleared for the Vladivostok summit meeting of 23–24 November 1974. In the Joint Statement which emerged after the summit meeting, the parties stipulated that a new agreement would incorporate the SALT I provisions until 1977 and would then be extended until 1985. Further, each side would be allowed equal aggregates of launchers and MIRVed missile launchers. Although a total of 2400 strategic delivery vehicles, including bombers, and 1320 MIRVed missile launchers were negotiated, the figures were not included in the final statement. The agreement banned the construction of more ICBM silos and the conversion of light missile silos for heavy missile use. Still, there remained no agreed definition of a heavy missile and no clarification of which systems would be counted in the aggregate totals. As a result, the two sides began to disagree almost immediately after the Vladivostok summit meeting concerning what they had actually agreed. The two major issues which were to plague later negotiations were: (a) whether ALCMs with a range of over 600 km were to be included in the totals, as the USSR insisted; and (b) whether the Soviet Backfire bomber was to count as a strategic weapon, as the USA insisted.

Obstacles to agreement

Great power confrontation

At least until the autumn of 1974, the SALT II negotiations appeared to be conducted primarily to maintain an appearance of negotiating, rather than with the aim of moving rapidly towards an agreement. The negotiations were conducted partly for propaganda reasons and were designed both to demonstrate to world opinion that the major nuclear weapon powers were fulfilling their obligations under the NPT and to reassure domestic interests. The signing of the Agreement on the Prevention of Nuclear War, the Protocol to the ABM Treaty and the largely cosmetic TTBT during this period serves to strengthen this impression.

Even during this phase, however, the SALT II negotiations were not *primarily* a propaganda exercise. Political leaders and sections of the bureaucracy in both capitals were still genuinely concerned to promote the SALT process. The difficulties and delays that arose in 1973–74 can be traced, in large measure, to conflicting political and strategic interests between the two powers.

Deliberate political linkage does not appear to have been a direct consideration in the framing of US SALT policy during this period. The implementation of a strategy of elaborate linkage requires the sort of top-level orchestration that was not forthcoming at this time; Nixon and Kissinger had lost their previously unchallenged control over US foreign policy. Kissinger, however, did believe that the Soviet Union was attempting to link two sets of negotiations. Brezhnev wanted to give priority to the Agreement on Prevention of Nuclear War, and Dobrynin indicated that, until this was settled, Brezhnev could not intervene to expedite SALT.[8]

The central difficulty was the changing status of *détente* which reflected a worsening of the political relationship between Moscow and Washington. After SALT I, there was an expansion of economic co-operation and trade. However, this move towards closer co-operation was partly undermined when Senator

Jackson imposed his own version of 'political linkage', by attaching an amendment to a trade bill in October 1972 which denied 'most favoured nation' status to any communist country restricting emigration. Representative Charles Vanik introduced a similar amendment in the House. Although the Soviet Union did act in April 1973 to ease emigration restrictions on Jews (imposed in the form of an exit tax the previous August), congressional leaders continued to press for more concessions in relation to trade.

The October 1973 Middle East crisis revealed the fragility of *détente*. The Soviet Union sought to intervene militarily, and the United States employed a global nuclear alert to keep Soviet troops out of the Middle East and to restrict Soviet influence. In the wake of the crisis, support both for *détente* and for arms control was waning in the USA. Kissinger observes that by the summer of 1974 SALT had become a 'whipping boy in a deeper struggle over the entire nature of US–Soviet relations'.[9] There appears to have been a hardening of the Soviet position as well after the Middle East War. While Soviet leaders continued to call for *détente*, at the same time they stressed the need to strengthen the military defence of the Soviet Union and to avoid illusions about imperialism.[10]

During this period, a major source of Soviet concern was the enunciation of the Schlesinger Doctrine in January 1974, which envisaged a US strategic counterforce capability and the possibility of limited nuclear war. Garthoff concludes that the Schlesinger Doctrine had an adverse impact on SALT. He observes that the US delegation during SALT I had assured their Soviet counterparts that the USA was not seeking counterforce capability; now the same Administration had changed course.[11] Soviet commentators interpreted the Doctrine as an attempt to move away from parity and to gain political advantage through strategic weapons.[12] Thomas Wolfe speculates that there may have been some direct impact on the Soviet willingness to make concessions in SALT as a result of the Doctrine. He notes that Dobrynin told Kissinger in March 1974 that his latest MIRV proposals would be viewed favourably in Moscow, but that Brezhnev subsequently rejected them.[13] During the June 1974 summit meeting, the Soviet leader vehemently criticized the Schlesinger Doctrine, which seemed to threaten the Soviet ICBM force. Still, the evidence that the new strategy directly impeded SALT is inconclusive. Dobrynin may have misjudged Moscow's reactions. According to Garthoff, this was not the first time Dobrynin had done so.[14] Further, Brezhnev's rejection of proposals that singled out limits on Soviet throw-weight may have stemmed primarily from a more general reluctance to accept proposals viewed as strategically one-sided.

Both the USA and the USSR entered SALT II with the aim of improving their strategic position. Immediately after SALT I was ratified, the United States accelerated its programme to develop a new generation of strategic weapons: Trident, the B-1 bomber and cruise missiles. The Soviet Union was clearly committed to MIRVing its own missiles and was developing four new land-based ICBMs.[15] Apparently, Moscow saw no advantage in moving rapidly toward the conclusion of a permanent agreement; the Interim Agreement was set to run until 1977, and the USSR was still behind in missile technology. In

March 1973, Dobrynin told Kissinger that the Soviet military wanted to wait, and Kissinger himself concluded that the USSR was not prepared to discuss MIRV limits until it had completed its MIRV testing programme.[16] In Washington, the pressure for an early agreement came from Kissinger, who wanted to deliver a SALT II treaty personally and saw dangers in allowing talks to drag on until 1977 while weapon programmes raced ahead. Still, Kissinger simultaneously endorsed a US strategic buildup.

Perhaps the greatest strategic obstacle of all in the SALT II talks was the fundamental difficulty that arises in any long-term attempt at arms limitation: the nature of the *relative* military position of both powers in the future. Wolfe points out that SALT I served largely to validate the existing position each side had reached unilaterally; SALT II was intended to define the future strategic relationship by mutual agreement.[17] Although considerations of political status, and potential advantage or loss related to future military strength, were at stake, above all there was concern about military security and possible vulnerability.

Domestic obstacles

In view of such contentious strategic issues, it is not surprising that military opposition to SALT II (or at least to anything that might appear as a concession to the other side) was more pronounced than it was during SALT I. This seems to have been the case in both Moscow and Washington. In his press conference at the 1974 Moscow summit meeting, Kissinger commented that: 'both sides have to convince their military establishments of the benefits of restraint, and this is not a thought that comes easily to military people on either side'.[18]

In the initial stages of SALT II, Soviet military resistance to concessions can be deduced from the unyielding Soviet negotiating stance. Even so, more specific evidence (including Dobrynin's comment to Kissinger previously cited) is available. During 1973–74, Soviet journals reflect a degree of controversy in the Soviet Union concerning SALT. According to Hedrick Smith, Brezhnev's MIRV proposal at the June 1974 summit meeting resulted from heeding the advice of those within the military-industrial complex.[19] Indeed, before the summit meeting the Defence Minister, Marshal Andrei Grechko, and General of the Army Alexei Yepishev, publicly called for readiness to resist imperialism, although Grechko also gave general endorsement to SALT and *détente*.[20] At the summit meeting Brezhnev was flanked by Colonel General Mikhail Kozlov, first deputy chief of the General Staff. Kissinger has revealed that he co-operated with Dobrynin to limit military presence during the later discussions of the 1974 summit meeting, because the two generals sitting beside Brezhnev kept interrupting him.[21]

It is difficult to interpret the precise nature of General Secretary Brezhnev's relationship with his generals and the Ministry of Defence. Dobrynin told Kissinger that the Ministry 'did not have much use for SALT' and that Grechko had encapsulated his Ministry's attitude to SALT by telling Dobrynin: 'If you want my personal opinion I'll give it to you; if you want my official opinion, the standard answer is no'.[22] Kissinger refused to believe that Brezhnev and the Politburo were really as bound by their own military as Dobrynin suggested. It is probable that Brezhnev often agreed with his military advisers. Furthermore, sometimes he may have found it useful, from a diplomatic standpoint, to attribute opposition to SALT proposals to them. Still, the military carried very considerable weight, especially when the Politburo was divided. Garthoff records that Soviet military leaders accepted the Vladivostok Accord with great reluctance, because it required equal aggregates with no compensation for US forward-based nuclear weapons.[23] A remark made by Gromyko's deputy to Paul Warnke in 1977 revealed that Brezhnev may have had to fight to get the Vladivostok Accord accepted. The aide noted that 'Brezhnev had to spill blood to get the Vladivostok accords'.[24]

Resistance from the military and the DOD in the United States was also pronounced during 1973–74. Senator Jackson's relentless efforts, coupled with Nixon's growing political weakness, had strengthened the opposition. With the appointment of James Schlesinger as Secretary of Defense, a powerful voice was raised against SALT. Although the previous Secretary, Melvin Laird, had not been enthusiastic about SALT, Schlesinger brought more theoretical coherence and greater political weight to bear in the battle against SALT. Soon, Schlesinger became engaged in a political feud with Kissinger.

Nixon's memoirs suggest that the Pentagon's opposition to SALT reached a climax at a National Security Council (NSC) meeting in June 1974, when Schlesinger in effect demanded that any SALT agreement should enshrine US military advantage.[25] Yet another confrontation between Kissinger and Schlesinger occurred before Kissinger's trip to Moscow in October 1974. This time the Defense Secretary argued that the USA should demand substantial reductions and a low limit on MIRVs for each side, or else pursue a major arms buildup over the next five years. Kissinger believed that the Soviet Union would only accept the higher ceilings and that the USA should seek agreement on these together with gradual limits on modernization. On this occasion, the JCS reportedly sided with Kissinger, on the grounds that his ceilings would allow them to complete their own major programmes and that Congress would not consent to a massive increase in military expenditure.[26] Yet, after the Vladivostok Accord was signed, some members of the JCS were dismayed to learn that the Soviet Union had accepted equal aggregates, despite the fact that President Ford had raised the MIRV launcher ceiling to take account of their views.[27] Ambassador Johnson particularly emphasizes the intransigence of the JCS: their single-minded insistence on deploying as many weapons as possible and opposition to any SALT agreement that might be negotiable.[28] Within the JCS, Admiral Elmo Zumwalt, the Chief of Naval Operations, took the most hard-line position. After his retirement in mid-1974, the Admiral publicly acknowledged his hostility to SALT, although Zumwalt's memoirs indicate that he had been assisting Senator Jackson for some time.[29] Mid-1974 also witnessed the departure of Paul Nitze. Fearing a weakened President would be forced into concessions to the Soviet Union, Nitze left the SALT delegation and soon became one of SALT's most forceful critics.

During this period, the bureaucratic counterweights to military pressure were also weakened. ACDA had been the most ardent (if not the most influential) advocate of radical measures in SALT. In 1973, however, a number of individuals favoured by Senator Jackson were appointed to key posts. ACDA's new director, Fred Iklé, pursued a hawkish line on SALT, while a newly created Verification Division was soon in dispute with the CIA. This Division, headed by a former official of DDR&E which had spearheaded resistance to SALT I, was—in the view of the State Department—a group of 'politically obtuse cold war ideologues'.[30] By this time, Kissinger had lost some of his personal control over the SALT process. As a result, proposals were designed to conciliate Washington's interests rather than to invoke a serious response in Moscow, and numerous bureaucratic delays thwarted the negotiations.[31]

Obstacles in the negotiating process

Washington's inability to produce a clear brief (together with long periods during which the delegation had no new instructions) created considerable frustration in Geneva, according to Ambassador Johnson.[32] More than once, Johnson considered resigning. The absence of a real negotiating position on the US side seems to have been matched by long delays in Moscow, which left the Soviet delegation to mark time.[33] Johnson was critical of Semenov's reliance on detailed official instruction even in private and informal talks, and comments on the strict control exercised by military representatives within the Soviet delegation.[34] Johnson's perceptions of the diplomatic role played by Semenov and the delegation, however, are more negative than those of his predecessor, Gerard Smith. Apart from differences in personal attitudes (which clearly bias individual assessments), Johnson's views were probably influenced by the fact that the Soviet delegation was obviously meant to stall throughout this period. Even when they appeared to take an initiative (such as in promoting a draft treaty) the Soviet delegation maintained a rigid negotiating stance.[35] One reason for the lack of progress at Geneva was that the Soviet Government had come to expect all major proposals and concessions to be made by Kissinger or the President and not by the US delegation.

One of the problems in the diplomacy for SALT II was that Kissinger, despite remaining in charge as Secretary of State, no longer had the power to pull off his highly personal style of secret negotiations in which he tried to neutralize opposition inside Washington by failing to reveal everything he had promised. Indeed, Kissinger's approach now proved to be counter-productive. In June 1974, Senator Jackson claimed that Kissinger and the Soviet leadership had stuck a 'secret deal', which allowed the Soviet to exceed the ceilings set down in the Interim Agreement. The charges were complex in detail and groundless in substance, but they gained credibility from Kissinger's tendency to agree to more than he was prepared to reveal and to withhold information.[36] Kissinger did not, for example, keep Schlesinger and the JCS fully informed during the prelude to Vladivostok. This may have been understandable in view of their tendency to block moves towards an agreement, but it certainly was not conducive to making critics of the SALT process any more confident.[37] The absence of US military advisers at the summit meeting made it more difficult to secure military support in its aftermath, when the two sides began to disagree in their interpretations of the Vladivostok Accord.

Escalating the arms race

Chapter 5 illustrated how the bargaining chip argument was used at the conclusion of SALT I to accelerate the new generation of US nuclear weapons. Although in many instances the idea of a 'bargaining chip' was invoked to justify military developments desired for straightforward strategic reasons, some public figures genuinely subscribed to it. In 1973, attempts to slow down the Trident programme were narrowly defeated in the Senate (by a vote of 49 to 47). In this instance, the bargaining chip argument probably swung a few crucial votes as it had done in the Senate debate over production of Trident in 1972.[38] In fact, Kissinger promoted a long-range cruise missile programme in 1973 explicitly because of the negotiating stance on SALT that he had adopted. In May 1973, he floated the idea that the USSR should not MIRV its heavy missiles in return for a US guarantee not to deploy ALCMs with a range over 3000 km. Kissinger, however, was also aware that the Pentagon was then reluctant to develop such a weapon. Although Brezhnev did not pursue the offer, Kissinger returned to Washington and successfully intervened to prevent the Pentagon from abandoning the long-range ALCM on budgetary grounds.[39]

At Vladivostok, the commitment to parity had the effect of setting ceilings higher than one or the other of the parties might have aimed for unilaterally. To placate the JCS, after domestic bargaining, the proposed MIRV launcher ceiling was raised to 1320. Because the first Soviet MIRVed missile test took place in mid-1973, it would obviously take the Soviet Union quite some time to reach this level, and Brezhnev had apparently indicated that he was receptive to a lower agreed ceiling. On the other hand, Soviet pressure resulted in a higher level for all delivery vehicles, than the USA wanted at the time. At Vladivostok, Brezhnev and Ford proposed 2500 and 2100, respectively, and eventually settled on 2400. Schlesinger then had a legitimate rationale to ask for more missiles, and he promptly did.[40] Kissinger had said privately in Moscow that the USA would not go above 2200 delivery vehicles in the 10-year period up to 1985, but it is not clear whether Brezhnev abandoned this requirement at Vladivostok, or whether secret assurances were given.[41]

The high ceilings set by the Vladivostok Accord proved to be counter-productive, at least in terms of public opinion in the United States. Almost in unison, both arms control advocates and its critics criticized the limits for being set too high. A dearth of information on what had been agreed at Vladivostok also gave rise to unease about the Agreement. Although both houses of Congress voted in support of the Vladivostok Accord early in 1975 (and despite endorsements from senior figures in the Administration, including Schlesinger and the Chairman of the JCS), disillusionment and distrust of SALT were beginning to set in.

Political distrust was more actively fomented by SALT opponents who had begun to publicize claims that the USSR had violated the first SALT agreements. Although problems were resolved through the SALT Standing Consultative Commission, allegations continued and illustrated how previous arms control agreements can be used to generate distrust about ongoing negotiations.

II. Failure to sign a treaty: 1974–76

The two delegations returned to Geneva early in 1975 with initial optimism about reaching an agreement. This optimism, however, proved to be premature. The US delegation insisted, contrary to the Soviet interpretation of Vladivostok, that long-range ALCMs were not included in SALT II. The Soviet delegation refused to accept the USA's claim that the Backfire bomber was a strategic system that should be included in the totals. Soviet inflexibility concerning the Backfire was strengthened by the fact that Henry Kissinger had apparently made a private agreement in Moscow to exclude the Backfire, but neither the President nor the Secretary of Defense were informed of this understanding.[42] Because Kissinger continued to be the chief SALT negotiator, he could not effectively withdraw his own concession. Further, the Soviet Union introduced an additional complication by insisting on the need to include long-range SLCMs as well in any agreement. Quite apart from these post-Vladivostok problems, the two delegations were unable to progress on the earlier questions of how to verify which missiles were MIRVed and how to define a heavy missile.[43]

When it became clear that the delegations had reached a deadlock, Kissinger and Ford engaged in a series of exploratory talks with Gromyko and Brezhnev in July 1975 to discuss various ways of resolving these problems. Although the United States put forward most of the suggestions, both sides made some concessions. In Washington, however, domestic in-fighting had undermined the apparent movement toward consensus. In September, President Ford instructed Kissinger to work together with Schlesinger to produce a new set of SALT proposals. Moscow, however, regarded a radically new US offer as a retreat from the previous US negotiating position and, in late October, rejected it out of hand.

After Cuban troops were reported in Angola in October 1975, Kissinger's planned autumn trip to Moscow was postponed. During the succeeding months, Washington attempted to resolve its internal differences. After a series of NSC meetings in which the new Secretary of Defense, Donald Rumsfeld, and the JCS held out for their terms, Kissinger went to Moscow in January 1976 in a last-ditch effort to conclude an agreement under the Ford Administration. This time, Kissinger was accompanied by a Pentagon representative and brought two proposals. The offer favoured by the Pentagon permitted the USA to retain ALCMs with a range up to 2500 km, but only if deployed on heavy bombers, which would then be counted in the MIRV launcher total. This proposal also specified that all Soviet Backfire bombers produced after October 1977 should be included in the 2400 aggregate. Sea-launched and ground-launched cruise missiles were not included, but were to be limited in range to 600 km and 2500 km respectively. As Kissinger expected, Brezhnev rejected this proposal. The second proposal suggested a reduction of the aggregate ceiling to 2300 by October 1980 and the placement of limits on SLCMs and Backfire bombers, although they would be dealt with outside the total aggregates allowed. Here, Brezhnev displayed more interest. In Washington, however, the DOD, the JCS and Iklé at ACDA all expressed grave doubts, and this second proposal fell through.

President Ford then authorized Kissinger to try again, this time offering a three-year limit only on cruise missiles and Backfire bombers until 1980. Moscow rejected this proposal, arguing that it was a step backwards from the January US position. This signalled the end of the US SALT efforts under Kissinger and Ford; the President was now entering what would become a gruelling election campaign. In September 1976 (a month after Ford had been confirmed as the Republican presidential candidate), the Soviet Union indicated that it still retained some hope of an agreement by permitting Gromyko to raise the SALT issue. By then, however, Washington had become incapable of response. Although the US and Soviet delegations continued to talk about legal and technical problems in detail throughout 1976, and produced about 50 pages of draft treaty, they still did not tackle the central problems.

Obstacles to agreement

Great power confrontation

During 1975–76, *détente* continued to erode. The USSR was beginning to exert greater power and influence, and to expand its military presence in the Third World, particularly in Africa. Secretary of Defense Schlesinger and others interpreted those developments as part of a growing Soviet military threat and cited, for example, a missile storage base in Somalia in evidence.[44] In the view of the USA, the dispatch of Cuban troops to Angola in October 1975, amounted to a surrogate Soviet intervention. Washington, therefore, felt constrained to demonstrate its displeasure by postponing Kissinger's autumn 1975 trip to Moscow. Political linkage had once again disrupted the SALT negotiations, although Garthoff suggests that Angola may have partly been a public excuse for delay necessitated by Washington's inability to reach a consensus on SALT.[45]

The economic aspect of *détente* had not fulfilled Soviet expectations. Although Congress eventually passed the Trade Bill in late 1974, it contained a requirement that it should be reviewed within 18 months, at which time Soviet policy on allowing Jewish emigration was expected to come under sharp scrutiny. Immediately after the Vladivostok summit meeting, Congress passed the Stevenson Amendment to the Export–Import Bank Bill, imposing strict limits on the amount that could be loaned to the Soviet Union and thus undermining Soviet hopes of substantial loans for Siberian energy projects.[46] In January 1975, the Soviet Union abrogated the Trade Agreement, obviously concluding that its terms were now unacceptable.[47] These developments, and a renewed spate of accusations in the summer of 1975 that the USSR was cheating on SALT I, may well have served to harden the Soviet negotiating position on SALT.

Domestic obstacles

Military opposition to SALT concessions and the resultant dispute and deadlock in Washington were a continuing major obstacle to talks. Although Kissinger's personal antagonist, Schlesinger, was dismissed by President Ford in September 1975, Schlesinger's successor as Secretary of Defense, Donald Rumsfeld, was almost as hostile to arms control. Ford, therefore, came under pressure within his own Administration to take a tough line in negotiations. Ford's SALT position was also constrained by presidential politics in 1976, when he was challenged from the right in the Republican primaries by Ronald Reagan and from Senator Jackson who was running in the Democratic primaries. In addition to presidential candidates campaigning against arms control, Nitze and Zumwalt were also launching sustained attacks on the SALT process.

Although the Soviet Union appeared to have an interest in following up on the Vladivostok Accord during the tenure of the Ford Administration, there was clear political and military resistance to making major concessions, especially with respect to Backfire bombers and cruise missiles. During this phase of the talks, the general stance of the Soviet side could be described as intransigent.

During a final interview as Secretary of State, Kissinger cited some of the obstacles which, in his view, had plagued SALT II. Kissinger blamed the failure to conclude a SALT II agreement on partly the other side, partly the election and partly internal disputes within the Administration'. Thus, Kissinger underscored the importance of domestic problems in the USA with regard to arms control during this period.[48]

Obstacles in negotiations

When the Geneva delegations resumed negotiations at Geneva early in 1975, they had a genuine basis from which to work. As a result, the negotiations proceeded in a more business-like fashion than the discussions of 1973–74. The delegations used a Joint Draft Text that incorporated both the Soviet and US drafts, and operated largely through US–Soviet working groups: one each on drafting, definitions and verification. Definitions were important, because each side had developed its own strategic vocabulary; and straightforward translation was not possible. For example, the section of a missile which carries the separate MIRV warheads into space (a 'bus' in the US terminology) required 69 words of description in the final treaty.[49]

Progress was impeded, however, because the divisions in Washington now surfaced more openly in the delegation. Lieutenant-General Edward Rowny had been appointed the new JCS representative at Geneva in early 1973 on the insistence of Senator Jackson, in preference to the original JCS nominee for the job.[50] When Rowny was assigned to the joint US–Soviet definitions group, his stance was so unyielding that the Soviet side soon refused to negotiate with him.[51] Ambassador Johnson resolved the problem by arranging for the drafting and definitions groups to merge. The delegation remained, however, hampered by the JCS' and the DOD's quibbling over the treaty language and their insistence that discussion should be re-opened on points already agreed.[52] From the Soviet side, progress was also slowed by a lack of instructions when higher-level talks were scheduled.[53] Nevertheless, a good deal of work was achieved on the details of a SALT II Treaty. The central obstacle which remained, however, was either the unwillingness or inability (or both) of Washington and Moscow to compromise on the central issues dividing them.

Bargaining chips

This second phase of SALT provided a classic illustration of how a weapon first sponsored as a bargaining chip may soon become indispensable in the eyes of the military. The USAF, not especially interested in ALCMs in 1973, was prepared to abandon work on the forerunner of the cruise missile in expectation of budgetary pressure from Congress. This, the USAF hoped, would facilitate the preservation of the expensive B-1 bomber programme. Although William Hyland notes that 'the cruise missile program was only saved by a directive from the White House [which] stopped the cancellation', the White House still viewed the weapon as a bargaining chip, 'since it seemed to have no strategic justification in its own right'.[54] Hyland's account is in agreement with Kissinger's version. The Pentagon then began to see positive advantages in the cruise missile and pressed for SLCM development in their 1975 budget. The cruise missile issue became an increasing obstacle in SALT II and subsequent strategic arms talks.

The USA also sought to apply bargaining chip theory with respect to the Soviet arsenal. After Vladivostok, the Backfire bomber suddenly became a major problem in SALT. According to Johnson, Washington had previously regarded the Backfire primarily as a medium-range bomber, and not a strategic bomber. After the JCS made it an issue, however, Kissinger agreed to permit Johnson to raise the matter at Geneva so as to 'see what we would get out of it'.[55] What apparently began (in Kissinger's view at least) as a 'bargaining chip' was, in Johnson's opinion, 'transmuted by deft Pentagon political manœuvring into a major obstacle to concluding and ratifying SALT II.'[56]

III. The final phase: 1977–79

The election of Jimmy Carter as President in 1976 ushered in a new Democratic Administration and resulted in a re-evaluation of the US position concerning SALT. The Carter Administration's initial impulse was to build on the agreements which had been achieved under President Ford and to move rapidly, as a first step, toward a treaty based on the Vladivostok Accord before engaging in more ambitious attempts to curb arms in SALT III. Kissinger had stated that an agreement should be possible in 1977, and Carter himself in 1976 had said publicly that his first aim as President would be to conclude a treaty already '90 per cent complete'.[57] Carter, however, began to have second thoughts and in great secrecy decided to try immediately for significantly lower missile levels on each side. Although he apparently was motivated by a genuine desire to promote satisfactory arms control, Carter was also strongly influenced by the arguments of Senator Jackson and other SALT critics that the USA should only reach agreement if the Vladivostok numbers were reduced. Thus, the new proposal that Secretary of State Cyrus Vance took to Moscow in late March 1977 set an upper limit of 1800 or 2000 on strategic delivery vehicles, and 1000 or 1200 on MIRV missile launchers, and banned any new ICBMs.

The Soviet leadership, aware that the SALT I Interim Agreement would expire in October 1977, was apparently eager to move forward rapidly. In January 1977, General Secretary Brezhnev made a public statement urging the need to consolidate agreement on the basis of the Vladivostok Accord, and wrote to President Carter at the beginning of February. The Carter Administration's March initiative created an extremely hostile reaction in Moscow, partly because it ran counter to Soviet views on correct diplomatic behaviour and the established procedures on SALT. The proposal jettisoned the results of several years' of hard negotiation (as well as a specific agreement) and was presented to Moscow with very little advance notice. Further, Carter had already publicly announced important elements in the proposals before Vance's departure for Moscow.

Although the March 1977 proposals did include valuable arms control elements (for example, a qualitative curb on development of new missiles), in the view of many commentators, the proposals were heavily biased in favour of the United States. The Soviet Union was required to destroy half of its heavy missiles (despite the higher total agreed at Vladivostok) and to accept a limit of 550 for MIRVed ICBMs, which happened to be the existing total of US Minuteman missiles. Because the USSR was deploying its main missile force on land, the proposal required the Soviet Union to cut its programme considerably. The USA, on the other hand, maintained its primary missile force at sea (the Soviet Union still had no sea-launched MIRVs), and the only restriction placed on SLBMs was the MIRV launcher totals. The only direct sacrifice by the USA was the future possibility of the MX missile. The proposal did exclude the Backfire if the USSR guaranteed it would not be turned into a strategic bomber, but it permitted the USA to deploy an unlimited number of cruise missiles with a range below 2500 km. ALCMs with a range over 600 km were confined to heavy bombers.[58] The only aspect of the proposal which clearly favoured the USSR was that it was still able to retain a much heavier throw-weight for its MIRVed ICBMs, which—in the view of commentators such as Nitze—was a substantial advantage.[59]

The Soviet Union categorically rejected the US proposal. Further, the Soviet leadership was not impressed by Vance's fall-back offer of an agreement to defer all contentious issues, which they considered to be a retreat from achievements attained up to that time. Vance and Carter responded to the Soviet Union's rebuff by publicly attacking Moscow with the complaint that the Soviet Union had offered no counter-proposal. Then, Foreign Minister Gromyko, who had remained silent up to that point, publicly threatened to re-open the question of US FBS. Gromyko's threat was an understandable reaction to the US demand that the Soviet Union cut its heavy missiles, because Kissinger had signed an *aide-mémoire* after the Vladivostok summit meeting recognizing that the USA would accept the Soviet heavy missile force in return for the USSR dropping the FBS question from the SALT negotiations.[60] However, Gromyko's warning, together with the uncompromising Soviet stance after the Moscow meeting, confirmed the belief of some US officials that the Soviet leadership would not accept genuine strategic cuts. Vance has since commented that 'perhaps the most serious cost' of this initial failure was that SALT opponents during the ratification debate held up the deep cuts proposal as the only acceptable standard of 'real arms control'.[61] Moscow, on the other hand, doubted if the new Administration really wanted a SALT agreement.[62] The SALT process seemed to be in danger of breaking down in a flurry of public recriminations.

Washington soon accepted the necessity of a return to the established procedures and style of SALT diplomacy. Vance reopened the back channel with Ambassador Dobrynin, and the two SALT delegations resumed detailed negotiations at Geneva. The US delegation was now led by Paul Warnke, the newly-appointed head of ACDA, who was a committed, if controversial, advocate of arms control. Warnke's deputy at Geneva was Ralph Earle. Vance was prepared to delegate much of the responsibility for the SALT negotiations to Warnke and the Geneva team, but played an important role in top-level meetings when necessary. Although President Carter's National Security

Adviser, Zbigniew Brzezinski, did not directly participate in SALT diplomacy, he was influential, nevertheless, in Washington policy making concerning arms control. Brzezinski tended to favour a tough negotiating line, as did the newly installed Secretary of Defense, Harold Brown; and both carried considerable weight with the President.

In May 1977, Vance and Gromyko met again and agreed on the outlines of a new 'three-tiered approach' as a basis for agreement. First, SALT II should be in force until 1985 and be based on the Vladivostok Accord; precise ceilings, however, would be open to further negotiation. Second, the most difficult issues, such as the cruise missile and Backfire bomber, could be covered by a three-year protocol to the treaty to provide more time to find a permanent solution. Third, the two sides would agree to a 'joint statement of principles' to govern SALT III. This formula satisfied both the Soviet Union's insistence on starting from the Vladivostok Accord and President Carter's commitment to seeking a more far-reaching arms control. The crucial problems now centred around the agreement upon the details, as Gromyko made clear in a press conference after he had accepted the three-tier approach in principle.

After the broad framework of the three-tiered approach had been agreed, US officials then engaged in a serious attempt to find a compromise formula which took account of all the disputed issues in the negotiations. The Administration had been converted to the view that the problem of the throw-weight of Soviet heavy missiles was less important than an overall constraint of MIRVs. The light, but accurate SS-19 missile (which Paul Nitze in particular was then portraying as a greater threat than the heavy SS-18) had aroused increasing concern. The Administration also reluctantly accepted that ALCMs should count as MIRVs, a point Kissinger had earlier conceded. President Carter found this decision especially difficult. Carter had opted for heavy reliance on ALCMs when he rather abruptly cancelled the expensive B-1 strategic bomber programme in June 1977. The third major problem, which had assumed increasing importance in the talks, was how to distinguish a MIRVed missile from one which was not. Because the USSR had a more complex ICBM force than the USA, the Soviet military wanted the flexibility to place MIRV warheads and single warheads on the same class of missile, and in certain cases to have MIRVed and unMIRVed missiles at the same sites. Considerable energy was expended over two sites in the Ukraine which then held a mix of MIRVed missiles and single-warhead missiles; the US military wanted to count them all as being MIRVed.[63] In general, the Pentagon asked for simple methods of counting those missiles which were MIRVed as a hedge against cheating.

The Administration's package, put together in Washington for Gromyko's planned visit in September, reflected these concerns. The USA produced a four-part proposal that suggested: (a) an initial aggregate ceiling of 2400 on delivery vehicles to be lowered to 2160 before 1985, (b) a maximum of 1320 MIRV launchers, (c) a maximum of 1200 MIRVed missile launchers and (d) a maximum of 800 MIRVed ICBMs. The purpose of the 1320 ceiling was to give the USAF 120 cruise missile-carrying bombers 'free' before they had to start being counted as MIRVed missiles. This tilted the proposal in favour of the USA, as did a clause requiring that all the missiles at the two disputed sites in the Ukraine count in the 800 MIRVed ICBM total. Still, the package dropped the heavy missile argument, included ALCMs and accepted the Vladivostok totals as a starting point. Soviet Foreign Minister Gromyko arrived in Washington ready for compromise and, after he referred the details to Moscow, accepted all elements of the proposal in principle. Gromyko, however, did suggest somewhat higher totals. The SALT II Treaty, which was eventually based on this package, contained levels that represented a compromise between the US and Soviet ceilings. The problem represented by the expiration of the Interim Agreement in October was solved by an exchange of statements which committed both parties to continued observance. The negotiations now appeared as if they were close to completion.

Why, then, after the apparent breakthrough in September 1977, did the SALT negotiations drag on for so long? The Soviet leadership assumed that by demonstrating a willingness to cut their own MIRV programme they had conceded enough to reach agreement. Indeed, Washington had hoped for a summit meeting to conclude SALT II by the end of the year.[64] Moreover, the Soviet Union made a further significant concession in October 1977, when it announced it was cancelling the solid-fuelled SS-16 missile. This had been a source of worry to the USA, which feared that the intermediate-range SS-20 could easily be converted into a mobile ICBM by the addition of the third stage of the SS-16. Although US analysts believed that the SS-16 had proved militarily unattractive, its abandonment was an unusual Soviet gesture and met the USA's concern about one verification problem.[65] President Carter reacted publicly with enthusiasm and seemed to be promising a treaty within weeks.

The remaining problems, however, represented quite substantial strategic issues for both sides: for example, the precise ceilings to be agreed and the timing of reductions, which would require the Soviet Union to dismantle some of its missiles. The restriction of new technology was even more contentious. Both parties wanted a limit to the testing and deployment of new missiles, but each side demanded one exception. The USSR insisted on a new single-warhead ICBM to replace the ageing SS-11s, while the USA insisted on the new MX missile, then intended to be mobile and therefore less vulnerable than the Minuteman force. At one point the Soviet Union did suggest a ban on both, but the USA rejected this offer as 'asymmetrical'. The MX missile caused additional difficulties when the Pentagon held out for the right to a multiple-basing mode, which meant moving missiles around between different silos. Furthermore, National Security Adviser Brzezinski and Defense Secretary Brown demanded that the Soviet Union accept this plan in advance of detailed negotiation. The Soviet side pointed to the verification difficulties entailed in such a plan. The negotiators were, furthermore, required to wrestle with the questions concerning how many MIRVed warheads to allow per missile and how to define what was meant by a 'new' missile system.

Cruise missiles continued to be a source of serious disagreement. The Soviet Union pressed for limits on ground-launched and sea-launched cruise missiles, while the United States wished to exclude them from the three-year protocol. In 1978, the Pentagon added to the cruise missile difficulties when it demanded the option to put conventional as well as nuclear warheads on cruise missiles and to exclude conventionally armed cruise missiles from SALT II. Eventually, this demand was withdrawn. Decision makers in Washington realized that the USSR, in due course, could exercise the same option and that it would be impossible to distinguish nuclear-equipped cruise missiles from those armed with conventional warheads. Problems still remained over how ALCMs should be covered in the treaty. When the DOD wanted to link restrictions on range to flight profiles, this proposal was rejected by the Soviet Union as a device to extend the range. The USSR, on the other hand, maintained that if limits were set to the number of warheads per missile, then there should also be a limit to the number of cruise missiles on a heavy bomber. The USAF, however, was then exploring the possibility of equipping a modified jumbo jet with up to 80 cruise missiles and had no intention of accepting the maximum of 20 missiles urged by the Soviet delegation. Another disagreement centred on whether the USA should be permitted to provide cruise missile technology to its NATO allies. Before the September 1977 breakthrough, the Soviet delegation had expressed their concern over this possibility and, in 1978, reverted to opposing NATO access to cruise missile technology. The US negotiators, however, felt obliged to propitiate both the Pentagon and NATO governments by keeping this option open, and eventually secured agreement to a suitably obscure text, one that sounded restrictive without really being binding.[66]

New issues besieged the SALT delegations during 1978. Not the least of their worries was that the problems surrounding verification were becoming increasingly politicized and appeared as if they might wreck the treaty. Immediately after the September 1977 meeting with Gromyko in Washington, congressional and other critics of the SALT process made sustained accusations of Soviet cheating over SALT I, which the Administration felt it had to meet by publishing materials from the SALT Standing Consultative Committee. During 1978, US military experts became alarmed that the Soviet Union was trying to prevent them from checking tests of missiles by coding the electronic signals sent from the missile back to earth: that is, by encrypting the telemetry. If a protocol preventing tests of new missiles were to be agreed, then it would be vital to ensure that both sides could verify the agreement and that neither side impeded verification. On the other hand, some encrypting could be defended on the legitimate grounds of protecting military secrets. The dividing line, then, between verifying SALT II compliance and conducting espionage was thin indeed. The negotiations concerning telemetry encryption dragged on unsatisfactorily and were not finally resolved until 1979. Encryption proved to be an issue on which the Soviet Union chose to be intransigent.

Although many new problems burdened the SALT negotiations during 1978, there was also a familiar headache for the USA: that of determining what assurances could be wrested from the Soviet Union about the Backfire bomber if it was excluded from SALT. The USA suggested production limits, refuelling restrictions and rules concerning where the Backfire bomber could be based. The Soviet delegation particularly objected to an attempt to dictate where the bomber could be based and regarded the proposal as an attempted intrusion upon Soviet sovereignty.

During this final phase, political obstacles that had nothing to do with the content of the negotiations impeded the SALT process. Relations between the USA and the USSR were deteriorating in the wake of the Soviet aid to the revolutionary government in Ethiopia and the United States' exclusion of the USSR from the main peace talks in the Middle East. In the USA, the anti-SALT lobby was becoming increasingly vociferous and influential, and the *Washington Post* reported that the Administration was going slow in the talks partly in the hope of more favourable attitudes emerging later.[67] In fact, throughout 1978, patient negotiation unravelled most of the SALT issues. Both sides were initially prepared to trade off concessions, but at the end of the year the Soviet Union held back. Moscow appeared to be angered by US moves to establish full diplomatic relations with the PRC and to hold a summit meeting with the Chinese leadership.

Early in 1979, the final details of the SALT II Treaty were finally ironed out. Compromises had been reached on cruise missiles. The USA accepted a limit on deploying ground-launched and SLCMs with a range over 600 km for the duration of the three-year protocol, and abandoned its claim to deploy conventionally armed cruise missiles outside SALT. In turn, the USSR gave up its attempt to restrict the range of ALCMs. The Backfire bomber problem was resolved when the USA ceased asking for restraints on fuelling and basing, and accepted Soviet assurances that production would be limited and that the bomber would not be upgraded to intercontinental range. At the same time, the USA reserved the right to modernize its own FB-111 bombers. Ultimate aggregates agreed under SALT II were: 2250 launchers by 1985, 1320 MIRVed systems, 1200 MIRVed missile launchers and 820 MIRVed ICBMs. Each side was allowed to introduce one new kind of ICBM.[68]

The SALT II Treaty was a document of almost impenetrable complexity for anyone not well acquainted with the issues, and there has been considerable disagreement as to whether it constituted, on balance, a worthwhile arms control agreement. The case against the Treaty revolves around the charge that it failed to curb development of new missiles and allowed a major expansion in the number of warheads on both sides. Still, without SALT II, quantitative levels would have been even higher. The Treaty required the USSR to cut back on its ICBM programme and the USA on its ALCM target. The USSR made an important concession to the USA in agreeing to a freeze on the number of warheads to be placed on existing kinds of ICBM. This 'fractionation' freeze would limit the heavy SS-18 missile to 10 warheads, the SS-19 to six and the SS-17 to four. Each missile was capable of carrying considerably more.[69] The SALT II Treaty also made some attempt at qualitative controls through limits on new missiles and on flight-tests of various kinds of missiles, and included a three-year limit on mobile ICBMs. Some progress was made concerning the problems of verifying a complex agreement, for example, by requiring bombers to have 'functionally related observable differences'. A major advance over SALT I (which represented a very significant concession by the Soviet Union) was that an agreed 'data base' was published with the Treaty. This data base set out the numbers of strategic weapons on both sides.

The main problem with the SALT II Treaty, however, was that it simply came too late. In the USA, there was growing disillusionment with the SALT process and *détente*, and the political opposition to SALT was gaining strength. When President Carter flew to the Geneva summit meeting in June 1979 to sign the Treaty, he had already exhausted most of his political capital. Indeed, Senator Jackson compared him to Neville Chamberlain flying off to meet Hitler at Munich. No one, including the Soviet leadership, had great confidence that SALT II would pass the Senate ratification process.

Obstacles to agreement

Great power confrontation

In March 1977, propaganda appeared to be the primary aim of a proposal, for the first time in the SALT process. President Carter publicized his radical new approach to arms reductions before the Soviet Union had even been able to study the proposal, let alone respond. The combination of advance publicity, the stress on deep cuts in nuclear arsenals and the one-sided nature of the proposal would almost certainly prompt the Soviet leadership to suspect a strong propaganda motive. Indeed, Secretary of Defense Brown feared this interpretation of Carter's public comments. Although Carter and Brzezinski were almost certainly not averse to outflanking the Soviet Union's own long-term propaganda position, which portrayed the USSR as the true advocate of peace, Carter's main avowed motive for going public was to appeal for popular support over the heads of his bureaucracy.[70] In any event, Brzezinski admits in his memoirs that publicizing the deep-cuts offer may have been a mistake.[71]

During this phase of the negotiations, prestige considerations probably weighed most heavily with US critics of SALT II. Although their main anxieties concerned a military imbalance, these critics were principally worried that the USA was slipping behind the Soviet Union in the great power stakes. The Soviet Union, for its part, was still sensitive about any perceived attempts to interfere in its domestic affairs and interpreted such proposals as a slur on Soviet national sovereignty. As a result, the Soviet SALT delegation strongly resisted US efforts to influence the decisions concerning the locations where Backfire bomber would be based in the USSR.[72]

Political linkage became more important during this phase of SALT II than it had been in earlier phases. One of the early difficulties was President Carter's personal commitment to a strong public stand on human rights, which reversed the tendency of the previous Nixon–Ford Administrations to play down human rights issues in the Soviet Union in the interest of *détente*. When Carter publicly announced elements of his March 1977 SALT proposals, he also stressed that Vance would raise human rights and Jewish emigration problems in Moscow. Thus, Carter gave the impression that progress in arms control was linked to human rights concessions.[73] Congressional critics of SALT tried to make this linkage explicit in July 1978. They attempted to dissuade Vance from meeting Gromyko to discuss the SALT negotiations, because the trial of Anatoli Shcharansky and other dissidents had just been announced. Although Vance refused to cancel the meeting, he did take other measures to indicate US disapproval. After the extension of Soviet military aid to the Marxist government in Ethiopia in 1978 and the intervention of Cuban troops created alarm about growing Soviet military power in the Horn of Africa, a specific policy of linkage seemed to be adopted by the US Administration. Brzezinski's reported advocacy of a delay in the SALT negotiations, in an attempt to discipline Soviet activities in the Third World, appeared to publicly threaten to impose linkages if local conflicts were exploited.[74] *Pravda* responded by accusing Brzezinski of 'blackmail'.[75] Brzezinski himself stressed the inevitability of linkage between arms control and Soviet actions, especially in relation to the ratification process, and claimed he was misunderstood.[76] Nevertheless, Brzezinski's general views on the need for reciprocity in *détente*, and for a tough US stance against Soviet intervention abroad, suggested a linkage policy.

The most important move to link the outcome of SALT to Soviet behaviour occurred after the Treaty had been signed and was proceeding through the Senate. After the Soviet Union sent troops into Afghanistan in December 1979, President Carter suggested to a willing Senate that ratification of SALT II be delayed. Although the likelihood of the Treaty being passed without wrecking amendments was already slim, this delay ensured that SALT II would never be ratified by the USA.

The USA's own actions may have provoked the Soviet leadership into what appeared to be its own form of linkage. At the end of May 1978, Gromyko visited Washington on the heels of a visit to China by Brzezinski. In China, Brzezinski had publicly attacked the Soviet Union and briefed Chinese leaders on the SALT negotiations. Gromyko made Soviet displeasure at these actions quite clear and, at the same time, denied Soviet intervention in the Horn of Africa. Secretary of State Vance noted of this period that 'our relations with the Soviets were at their lowest point for several years'.[77] The progress anticipated from the meeting between Gromyko and Carter did not occur, although Gromyko did agree to freeze the number of warheads on existing types of ICBM.

US policy towards China apparently prompted the Soviet Union to delay the SALT negotiations yet again at the end of 1978. Vance and Gromyko were scheduled to meet in Geneva in December for last-minute negotiations, and provisional plans were made for a summit meeting in mid-January 1979 for the signing of the SALT II Treaty. Then, the USA suddenly announced the establishment of full diplomatic relations with China and that Deng Xiaoping would visit the USA in 1979. Gromyko then came to Geneva and raised a totally new issue—how to deal with remotely piloted vehicles. Some observers interpreted this move as a response to the USA's playing of the 'China card'.[78] Brzezinski contests this interpretation and cites Dobrynin in support of his own view that the SALT delay was due to issues within the negotiations.[79] However, on the basis of his meeting with Gromyko, Vance is certain that the timing of the announcement on diplomatic recognition and the reference in the US–Chinese communiqué to their opposition to 'hegemony' (implying Soviet global designs in the Chinese vocabulary) did create an obstacle. In Vance's words, the US move 'stimulated visceral Soviet fears of a *de facto* US–PRC alliance'.[80]

Both sides, at one time or another, apparently pursued a policy of linkage in relation to the SALT negotiations. Moreover, the deteriorating political relationship between Moscow and Washington during 1978 and 1979 was not conducive to support for SALT II in the USA. In the autumn of 1979, suspicion of the Soviet Union was magnified when the Administration suddenly 'discovered' a Soviet brigade of 2600 troops in Cuba, although the brigade had been there for years, if not since 1962. Then, the Administration compounded its troubles by unwisely allowing Senator Frank Church to go public on the question.[81] On closer examination, the Cuba 'crisis' proved to be an artificial creation. Still, the episode further damaged the chances of SALT ratification.

Washington encountered more trouble from its West European allies during this phase of SALT II than in its earlier stages. Chancellor Helmut Schmidt of the FRG and the heads of other European governments expressed growing concern that the USA and the USSR were in the process of reaching a SALT agreement that left Western Europe vulnerable to an expanding arsenal of medium-range missiles: in particular, the new mobile and MIRVed SS-20s. These fears were voiced at a NATO Nuclear Planning Group in October 1977 and at the Foreign and Defence Ministers' meeting in December that year. In a now famous speech, Chancellor Schmidt publicly expressed the fear that SALT would establish strategic parity between the USA and the USSR (thereby resulting in a deadlock at that level), but leave the Soviet Union with overall military superiority in Europe. In Schmidt's view, this would occur unless steps were taken to remove the disparity of power.[82]

The insistence of US negotiators on limiting the Soviet Backfire bomber to a theatre role seemed to indicate US disregard for West European security. Warnke recalled a discussion with Schmidt in late 1977 in which Schmidt persuaded Warnke to admit that the Backfire was a good theatre bomber and a very poor intercontinental bomber. Schmidt then asked: 'why do you insist, in effect, that the Soviets not use the Backfire for something that it is no good for and encourage them, instead, to use all of them to attack Western Europe?'[83]

The concern of some European military planners about the SS-20s and the Backfire bomber was compounded by the willingness of the USA to consider bargaining away cruise missiles, which could become a NATO weapon. It was to appease allied fears (see above) that the USA refused to assent to the Soviet desire to impose a ban on transferring cruise missile technology and the Pentagon pressed for conventionally armed cruise missiles. Although Soviet anxiety about cruise missile transfer was almost certainly due to their traditional fear of West German access to nuclear weapons, some US commentators interpreted it as an attempt to stir up trouble in NATO.[84]

The argument that the goal of arms control was undermined by the search for strategic advantage can most plausibly be raised with respect to the March 1977 proposals. In the view of many commentators, the US proposals were strongly biased in favour of their own strategic programme. Some argue that the episode proves that the USSR puts its unilateral strategic interests much higher than satisfactory arms control, because it refused even to consider the proposals.[85] Otherwise, it can be claimed that—although both sides insisted on retaining their favoured strategic programmes (which limited the arms control value of SALT II)—neither held out for clearly unequal terms. Although the Soviet Union was still in the process of catching up with its MIRV technology, it probably regarded itself as being in a more equal position by the late 1970s. This perception may have been one reason why the Soviet Union was prepared to consider some cuts in its arsenal and a *de facto* limit on missile throw-weight through a freeze on warhead numbers. Although SALT II did manage to find formulas for dealing with the asymmetries in the strategic deployments of the two sides, it was at the cost of accepting very high overall totals.

Psychological obstacles

There was probably more suspicion and hostility generated by the actual process of negotiations during 1977–79 than at any time in SALT. This was certainly the case in March–April 1977 in the wake of President Carter's new proposals. During 1978, both sides showed signs of impatience as the negotiations dragged on. At various stages, Secretary of State Vance and President Carter expressed frustration and anger over the delays. Moreover, Gromyko was reported to be visibly angry when the USA pressed the Soviet Union to admit that a July 1978 missile test had been encrypted in a way that would not be permissible under SALT II.[86] Nevertheless, business-like relations were usually maintained within the negotiations. Extreme suspicion and hostility were manifested only by SALT opponents—such as the Committee on the Present Danger founded in 1976—who portrayed the Soviet Union as a ruthless aggressor committed to a relentless military buildup.

Technological momentum

The final phase of SALT II witnessed an increased military commitment to two types of military technology which had not been fully developed during SALT I: mobile ICBMs and cruise missiles. During the SALT I negotiations, the Soviet Union had resisted attempts to place a ban on mobile missiles. By the time of SALT II, however, the tables had turned. Now, the USA appeared to be more committed to a mobile ICBM, while the USSR pointed to verification problems. Mobile missiles, however, were not an example of unforeseen technological development, rather an instance when resistance to arms control provided a gap for military planners to exploit. From the beginning of SALT II, the USA resisted reductions on cruise missiles which had been urged by the USSR. The length of the SALT II negotiations did mean that a weapon which might have been negotiated away at the beginning was regarded as central to the US arsenal at the end. Still, military perceptions of the uses of cruise missiles and Kissinger's earlier use of the weapon as a bargaining chip played a more crucial role in the development of the missile than pure technological momentum.

During the course of SALT II, new developments in missile technology prompted the USA to re-evaluate the nature of the Soviet threat to its own land-based ICBMs. The switch in September 1977 to limits on total MIRV capability, rather than limits on heavy missiles, was, however, an advantage rather than an additional obstacle in the negotiations (despite prolonged bargaining concerning the numbers of MIRVs per missile type). In any event, the increasing US concern about the SS-19 did illustrate how a weapon development may force a switch during talks.

Domestic obstacles

Military interests on both sides demonstrated their natural professional tendency to obstruct or impede any serious attempt at arms control. On the US side, the JCS were distinctly intransigent on a number of issues. From the beginning, the JCS held out for treating the Soviet Backfire bomber in terms of its potential intercontinental capability, rather than its planned medium-range deployment. On this point, the JCS disagreed with many civilians in the DOD. Even so, the JCS eventually changed their position in 1978 and opted for the right to deploy the FB-111 in preference to restricting the Backfire bomber in the SALT negotiations.[87] The JCS also took a hard line by requiring the USSR to concede the US demand for a multiple basing mode for the MX missile and by rejecting Soviet complaints (first raised in 1973) that shelters constructed over the Malmstrom missile base in Montana impeded verification. The shelters were modified in 1977, but were not removed until 1979.[88] On the basis of his experience in SALT II discussions, even Brzezinski (who was often sympathetic to Pentagon views) marvels at the 'degree to which the military seem to prefer simply to have more and more weapons, irrespective of the strategic consequences'.[89] The new Secretary of Defense, Harold Brown, despite the role he played in launching the SALT I negotiations in 1968, took a tough line on the talks. For example, Brown backed the JCS position concerning multiple basing modes and urged the maximum range for ALCMs to be included in the SALT agenda.

The Soviet General Staff almost certainly played a role in the USSR's rejection of the March 1977 proposals. Garthoff suggests that they were becoming increasingly concerned about the USA using its forward-based nuclear weapons to circumvent parity at the intercontinental level.[90] The military would also have been closely involved in the negotiations concerning the encryption of missile tests and may have been responsible for the relatively unyielding stance taken by Soviet negotiators on this question. During Vance's October 1978 talks with Gromyko about telemetry, the head of the Soviet delegation, Vladimir Semenov, repudiated his previous understanding with Warnke, presumably because it had been overridden in Moscow.[91] On the other hand, there were indications that from the autumn of 1977 onwards that the Soviet military were being somewhat less intransigent than in the earlier stages of SALT II—or else were not allowed such a decisive say in the final policy making—or both.

Nikolai Ogarkov became Chief of the Soviet General Staff early in 1977, and is believed (by Western analysts) to have favoured a strictly deterrent role for nuclear weapons as opposed to a war-fighting role.[92] A civilian, Dimitri Ustinov, had been appointed Minister of Defence in 1976, and General Secretary Brezhnev was publicly nominated Commander-in-Chief of the armed forces in October 1977. A shift in Soviet nuclear doctrine away from an emphasis on having the capacity to win a nuclear war toward a 'military détente' was signalled by Brezhnev's January 1977 speech in Tula, USSR. Brezhnev stressed the Soviet Union's concern with avoiding a nuclear war and its willingness to reach an accommodation on SALT, and explicitly repudiated the goal of nuclear superiority and the aim of a first strike.[93] Hence, a change at the top of the Soviet General Staff seems to have coincided with some increase in civilian control over the armed forces and an extension of Brezhnev's personal influence.

In Washington, SALT policy making reflected the usual divisions both at the Cabinet level and between the bureaucracies. Vance and Warnke, together with their departments, were lined up against Brown, the DOD and the JCS. During this phase, the CIA under Stansfield Turner tended to side with the Pentagon and took a tough line on verification requirements. For example, Turner was dissatisfied with the Warnke–Semenov understanding on telemetry encryption and urged an outright ban. Turner also pressed last-minute problems concerning encryption during Vance's December 1978 SALT negotiations in Moscow.[94] After leaving his post at ACDA, Warnke publicly confirmed that SALT had been influenced by bureaucratic conflict in Washington.[95] The Geneva delegation partly reflected these conflicts; General Rowny, the JCS representative, was critical of the delegation leadership and disagreed with his colleagues on policy. Rowny left the delegation in 1979 to join the political opponents of SALT.[96] Brzezinski chaired the Special Coordination Committee set up under the NSC in January 1977 to handle the SALT negotiations.

Although Brzezinski tended to support the Pentagon, in Talbott's view, Brzezinski sometimes sought to forge a compromise between the agencies.[97] Brzezinski's own account suggests that initially he acted as a mediator between Brown and Warnke, but at various points later on he clearly sided with Brown.[98] As a Polish *émigré,* Brzezinski held an extremely hostile view of the Soviet Union; indeed, the USSR regarded him as one of their main enemies within the Administration. As Henry Kissinger's successor, he seemed to be emulous to achieve a better result in the SALT negotiations. Indeed, Brzezinski was influential in the framing of the March 1977 proposals that rejected Kissinger's Vladivostok Accord.

After Carter assumed the presidency, the initial SALT review was conducted by the bureaucracy under the guidance of the NSC staff. Partly because he felt the results were too conservative, Carter changed the organization as well as the policy related to the negotiations. Preparations for the March 1977 *démarche* were carried out in a secretive and conspiratorial manner. The relevant bureaucracies were not properly consulted about the proposals, nor were any experts on the Soviet Union except the NSC's William Hyland, who advised against them.[99] The revised proposals for the May 1977 meeting with Andrei Gromyko were also put together in an *ad hoc* and behind-the-scenes manner. This time the Pentagon, as well as the Geneva delegation, was excluded. After the negotiations had settled into a more orderly routine, policy making was the province of the NSC or its Special Coordination Committee. More detailed briefing was the responsibility of a SALT backstopping committee representing the NSC, the State Department and ACDA, the DOD and the JCS, and the CIA. Although the arrangement resulted in better consultation, it sparked the inevitable bureaucratic disagreement as well.

During this phase, the Congress was more deeply involved in SALT policy making than it had been earlier. From the outset, the Carter Administration was concerned about the prospect for Senate ratification. Senator Jackson had strongly contested Paul Warnke's nomination to ACDA. Although Warnke was confirmed in his ACDA post by a vote of 70 to 29, he was confirmed as the chief SALT negotiator only by the margin of 58 to 40. This latter vote constituted a warning to the Administration not to concede too much in the negotiations. Carter, therefore, felt compelled to listen to Jackson, and the March 1977 proposals were influenced in spirit, if not in detail, by the views of Jackson and his aide Richard Perle. During 1978, Secretary of State Vance was concerned that his soundings of pro-SALT senators indicated that many would prefer to defer ratification of a SALT Treaty until after the November 1978 mid-term congressional elections. Electoral pressures had necessitated a hard line towards the USSR and SALT.[100] However, other senators feared that opposition to SALT would become even more serious if the Treaty were delayed. The Republican Party leadership in the Senate apparently decided that it could not muster support for both the Panama Treaty and for SALT and opted, instead, to back the former and to oppose the latter.[101]

Congressmen were assigned to the SALT delegation at Geneva. A number of individual Senators became experts on certain aspects of SALT and thus served to harden the Administration's stand on several issues. Senator John Glenn, for example, familiarized himself with the intricacies of telemetry encryption, urged the delegation to insist on clarification of the issue and warned the Soviet delegation that he would vote against SALT unless this matter was settled to his satisfaction.[102] In September 1978, two congressmen specializing in the SALT issue prevailed on the Administration to raise for the first time a new and purely hypothetical issue: ballistic missiles with a 'depressed trajectory', which could possibly be used as an instrument of surprise attack.[103] Nevertheless, the role of congressmen was not wholly counter-productive. For example, a group of senators favourable to arms control persuaded the Soviet delegation of the need for an agreed data base; and as a result of briefings on SALT issues, many individual members of Congress became better informed.[104] Still, the Administration had gone to excessive lengths to propitiate the Senate without notable success.[105]

When the Treaty was sent to the Senate, the Foreign Relations Committee (a group traditionally favourable to arms control) did vote for ratification, but only by a margin of nine to six. Senator Glenn, a Committee member, argued that the USA was not then capable of monitoring SALT II.[106] The notoriously hawkish Senate Armed Services Committee voted 10 to 0 with seven abstentions against ratification. The Select Committee on Intelligence split over the issue of Treaty verification and issued a cautious report that suggested some aspects of the Treaty could be verified only with low confidence.

The Carter period amply illustrated the difficulties posed for arms control by fairly frequent changes in the presidency. Although Carter apparently had a more genuine desire for arms limitation (and a much greater capacity to understand the technical issues) than most of his predecessors, his lack of experience in Washington and in international affairs caused him to be politically inept at achieving his aims. Further, Carter has been criticized for not exercising strong enough control over his competing aides and for failing to mesh his China and SALT policies.[107] Faced with a formidable public campaign against the SALT II Treaty, the Carter Administration did not put its weight behind the Treaty until April 1979. Moreover, in a counter-productive attempt to conciliate SALT critics, the forceful and committed exponent of SALT, Paul Warnke, was replaced by Brzezinski's nominee, a former staff director for the JCS, General George M. Seignious. Later it was revealed that the General had been (until October 1978) a member of one of the committees set up to campaign *against* SALT.[108] Compounding his troubles, Carter was also unfortunate in suffering political damage from events largely beyond his control. In 1979, the toppling of the Shah of Iran and the subsequent seizure of the US Embassy overshadowed his position. Still, Carter displayed little talent for extricating himself from his troubles.

Whereas political volatility created problems in Washington, the Soviet side was marked by an almost excessive immobility. The senior Party and

Government officials tended to remain solidly in place. Western commentators had noted the increasing age of the Politburo and the 'petrification' of policy making under General Secretary Brezhnev.[109] This 'continuity' was also reflected in the Soviet SALT delegation. In 1977, the leader of the delegation, Vladimir Semenov, was nearly 70 years old; and the most senior scientific delegate, Alexander Shchukin, was almost 80. When he took over the largely symbolic state post of President in 1977, Brezhnev appeared to be at the peak of his personal power in the USSR. This accession may have served to strengthen Brezhnev's hand in trying for a conclusion to SALT II later that year. Brezhnev's health, however, had already begun to fail, and soon deteriorated even further. After China invaded Vietnam early in 1979, the US State Department feared that Brezhnev was too ill to assert himself in the Politburo and to save SALT II.[110] By the time of the June 1979 summit meeting, Brezhnev's poor health was a recognized factor of some embarrassment to the Soviet Union. Because the Soviet bureaucracy is not inherently suited to swift or innovative action, the division of responsibilities for the SALT negotiations between the Foreign and Defence Ministries meant that initiative had to come from the General Secretary or the Politburo. Kissinger commented that: 'Experience has shown that the Soviet bureaucracy may be structurally incapable of originating a creative SALT position'.[111] Lack of dynamism at the top contributed to the impression of Soviet bureaucratic rigidity and may have caused Soviet intransigence on some issues during 1978.

Obstacles within negotiations

Verification

Verification was a much more contentious issue in this stage of the SALT negotiations than it had been at any time earlier. In part, this reflected the nature of the technology that the SALT II Treaty was trying to control. There are no simple ways to verify the number of warheads on a missile or of cruise missiles in a bomber. The monitoring of new missile tests is also important in verifying whether each side is keeping to the rules concerning missile types. In addition, the US emphasis upon verification arose out of suspicion of Soviet intentions and against a background of accusations of Soviet cheating on SALT I. Therefore, verification had become an issue reflecting the ideological divisions between the two sides and, for some of those who stressed the technical difficulties, a pretext for obstructing the entire SALT process. In response, the Soviet Union began to display some of its traditional resistance to US verification demands.

Other problems

After the initial débâcle over the March 1977 proposals, the two sides resumed business-like negotiations at Geneva, as well as at higher levels. The SALT delegations established working groups to grapple with the detail of legal texts and to design informal rules for avoiding political friction, and these groups appeared to work well.[112] This time, the USA found no difficulty in co-ordinating the work at Geneva with informal back-channel soundings and high-level talks. Cyrus Vance trusted Paul Warnke and the Geneva delegation and kept them informed. Vance also seemed to be more willing to delegate than Kissinger had been. Therefore, the organization of negotiations did not create unnecessary difficulties. Vance also accorded Gromyko a degree of respect and apparently established a satisfactory negotiating relationship with his Soviet counterpart.

At this stage of the SALT II negotiations, however, three main problems arose. First, both sides tended to be inflexible simply for the sake of strengthening their bargaining position. A second problem centred upon the introduction of new issues late in the talks. The third difficulty concerned the sheer complexity of the issues to be resolved.

Although inflexibility in negotiations may stem from domestic resistance to making any concessions, it was also employed by both sides as a negotiating tactic. Initial intransigence (especially when Gromyko was conducting the talks) was a standard Soviet negotiating stance. Talbott records that Gromyko spent the first day of his September 1977 visit to Washington in stonewalling. Only after Gromyko had met the President (and the USA had threatened the collapse of the talks if he were not more accommodating) did Gromyko reveal that he had come authorized to compromise.[113] However, when Gromyko accepted the substance of the new US proposal, but suggested slightly higher ceilings, President Carter chose to be unyielding. On Brzezinski's advice, Carter refused to settle for the new Soviet ceilings. Because the USA had made a totally new proposal and a number of concessions since March, Carter's aim was to strengthen the US bargaining position.[114] As a result, it took another six months (until April 1978) to resolve the exact numbers to be allowed.[115]

The large number of new issues raised by both sides during 1978 has already been indicated. Although the Soviet Union did introduce new questions late in the negotiations, the United States was primarily responsible for making additional demands. In Washington, there was an awareness that some of the points urged by the USA had confused the talks. For example, after the Soviet side had agreed that 120 unMIRVed missile launchers (at the two Ukrainian bases where MIRVed missiles were also deployed) should count as being MIRVed, the Pentagon then insisted that a rule on how to count missile launchers should be written into the SALT text. In January 1978, the Soviet Geneva delegation conceded this point. Then, the Pentagon requested a text which specified how MIRVed missiles should be distinguished from single-warhead missiles. Warnke regarded this requirement as unreasonable and, apparently, the Soviet Union did as well. The USSR withheld agreement on this point until the very end of the negotiations.[116]

A degree of additional confusion occurred when the USA sought to avoid detailed negotiations through the tactic of making unilateral declarations, which it hoped the Soviet side would not contradict. The USA adopted this approach on the sensitive question of reserving its right to have a multiple basing mode for the MX missile. Not surprisingly, the Soviet Union chose to object explicitly, which led the USA to repeat the tactic, phrasing its position in even stronger terms. A White House staff member told Talbott that this was: 'another example of our changing signals on the Russians . . . Frankly, if the Soviets ever came to us and tried this sort of nonsense we'd never accept it. We'd scream bloody murder'.[117]

The complexity of many SALT questions, however, was genuine, and resulted in an extremely long and complicated Joint Draft Treaty, incorporating the language preferred by each side concerning disputed points. The delegations had to spend considerable time in finding a precise formula for the Treaty and in translating it between English and Russian. Even punctuation posed a problem. The definition of a MIRVed missile alone required *four pages*. One US participant in SALT is said to have commented: 'It would take seven Talmudic scholars three weeks just to get through the Joint Draft Treaty'.[118]

It is possible that genuine misunderstanding may have played some part in creating obstacles and delays. Vance suggests that the Soviet Union did not understand the USA's proposal on telemetry encryption. In Vance's view, Moscow feared that the USA would claim the right to challenge any encryption, which led to the set-back on this issue in October 1978.[119] Of course, the USSR may have been simply testing the effectiveness of taking an intransigent stand.

Accelerating the arms race

During the period 1977–79, President Carter did not consistently try to buy off the SALT opposition by increasing the defence budget. The cancellation of the B-1 bomber and the deferral of production of the neutron bomb created the impression that his Administration was not whole-heartedly committed to defence, despite Carter's endorsement of a cruise missile buildup and protection of the MX missile programme. By 1979, however, the situation had changed. A desperate Administration was now prepared to try to secure support for SALT II through concessions to the military.

William Sweet has commented that the ratification process of SALT II was almost a parody of scenarios produced by critics of arms control negotiations. The Administration announced full-scale development of the MX missile in early June. When Senators Jackson, Nunn and Tower wrote in August 1979 asking for a real increase in the budget of at least four to five per cent, Carter set up a special budget committee to consider the matter and, in the end, conceded a real increase of three per cent.[120] However, the Administration's commitment to MX missile deployment and higher defence spending was not due solely to the perceived need to propitiate key senators. There were pressures from within the Administration based on strategic arguments. Brzezinski suggests that Carter himself had become more receptive to the case for a higher defence budget. Still, Brzezinski's account makes clear that both the MX missile and the defence-spending decisions were seen as necessary requirements if Senate ratification of SALT was to be achieved.[121] With some apparent satisfaction, Brzezinski notes that: 'SALT, rather than being the vehicle of acquiescent accommodation with the Soviet Union, was becoming the catalyst for a more assertive posture.'[122]

Did the SALT II process itself promote deployment of more rather than fewer weapons? The verification problems at the two Ukrainian bases where the USSR had a mix of single-warhead and MIRVed missiles provides an interesting small-scale example of how it most probably encouraged an increase in warheads. Although the USA insisted that all the silos at these bases be counted as containing MIRVed missiles, at the time Washington believed that two-thirds were not MIRVed. Warnke, however, comments that the USSR was bound to replace the single warheads with MIRVed missiles in due course. Thus, the US over-counting could be viewed as counter-productive and as 'a self-fulfilling prophecy'.[123] Although this incident illustrates how arms control negotiations may produce ironic results, the really important consideration is, of course, the impact of the Treaty as a whole.

The SALT II Treaty carefully observed the requirements of formal parity, which are often criticized for having the unintended effect of raising arms levels higher than they might have been without any agreement. Did SALT II actually have this effect? If the SALT levels are compared with actual US and Soviet figures for missiles and bombers deployed in June 1979, then the USA was still slightly below the 1200 sub-ceiling on MIRVed ballistic missile launchers. The USSR only had 752. Although both sides were slightly over the 2250 launcher aggregate, the US numbers included obsolescent bombers, and the Soviet Union's figures included some ageing single-warhead missiles. Still, if the SALT figures are compared with projected force totals for 1985 without the Treaty, SALT II does appear to have had some constraining effect.[124] Whereas the USA had to cut back its planned ALCM deployments, the USSR was forced to curb its missile deployments. In addition, the USSR had accepted limits on the number of warheads.

Still, it is plausible that the SALT process as a whole may have done more to prompt an arms buildup than to curb it. Not only did the Agreement immediately do what three Senators favourable to arms control had feared—help 'make the world safe for MX'[125]—but the wider political and psychological impact was largely negative. In the opinion of many commentators, SALT II served to increase mutual distrust rather than to reduce it.

IV. Conclusion

SALT II was not entirely a failure. A number of reasons have been presented which substantiate SALT II's significance as a measure of arms control. Certainly, SALT II was a more serious attempt to limit strategic arms than the

SALT I Interim Agreement. Even after SALT's main critics came to power in the Reagan Administration, they nevertheless felt constrained to observe the terms of the Treaty up to 1985. Yet, a Treaty which created so much cynicism among so many advocates of arms control (as well as among its critics) can hardly be regarded as a success. What, then, were the major causes of this partial failure?

A Soviet commentator, Genrikh Trofimenko, drew the lesson that SALT was undermined by the US resistance to accepting parity with the USSR.[126] Many Western commentators would agree. Jane Sharp notes how difficult it was for Britain to accept its loss of naval superiority and to cede parity to the United States in the 1920s, and points out how much harder it is for the USA to grant parity to an ideological enemy.[127] Renouncing superiority implies a loss of prestige and of political advantage in great power competition that certainly weighed heavily with many critics of SALT. Most significant of all, however, was the fear that parity would soon give way to US military inferiority. The central claim of SALT opponents was that, as a result of the SALT process, the USA was becoming weaker than the USSR.

Trofimenko also suggested that the US political process may make arms control negotiations with Washington impossible. Western experts agree that the combination of bureaucratic in-fighting, frequent presidential elections and the requirements of Senate ratification pose very considerable obstacles to reaching a satisfactory agreement.

The Soviet Union also clearly bore some of the responsibility for the continued delays in concluding the SALT II agreement. Garthoff, who is unusually well informed about and sympathetic to the Soviet position, comments that the Soviet leadership contributed to the débâcle by holding out for the most favourable possible terms, while the Carter Administration's credibility eroded.[128] The Soviet Union's intransigence was also a product of a negotiating style that left the initiative to the USA and often delayed necessary concessions. This approach was reinforced by the Soviet military's resistance to US demands, bureaucratic inflexibility and, in later years, a lack of dynamism at the top of the Soviet political system.

Notes and references

[1] Kissinger, H. A., *Years of Upheaval* (Weidenfeld and Nicolson and Michael Joseph: London, 1982), pp. 272–73.

[2] Garthoff, R. L., *Detente and Confrontation: American Soviet Relations from Nixon to Reagan* (The Brookings Institution: Washington, DC, 1985), pp. 328–29.

[3] See Kissinger (note 1), p. 270.

[4] See Kissinger (note 1), pp. 3–4.

[5] Johnson, U. A. with McAllister, J. O., *The Right Hand of Power: The Memoirs of an American Diplomat* (Prentice Hall: Englewood Cliffs, N.J., 1984), pp. 582–83 and p. 589.

[6] See Garthoff (note 2), p. 409.

[7] Garthoff (note 2), p. 443.

[8] See Kissinger (note 1), pp. 268–69.

[9] Kissinger (note 1), p. 1169.

[10] Gelman, H., *The Brezhnev Politburo and the Decline of Detente* (Cornell University Press: Ithaca, N.Y., 1984), pp. 160–61, citing speeches by Kirilenko and Brezhnev.

[11] See Garthoff (note 2), p. 418.

[12] Wolfe, T. W., *The SALT Experience* (Ballinger: Cambridge, Mass., 1979), pp. 163–64, citing an article by Trofimenko of Sep. 1974.

[13] Wolfe (note 12), p. 169.

[14] Garthoff (note 2), p. 420.

[15] See Kissinger (note 1), p. 274.

[16] Kissinger (note 1), pp. 268 and 271.

[17] See Wolfe (note 12), p. 93.

[18] See Wolfe (note 12), p. 102.

[19] See Wolfe (note 12), p. 169.

[20] See Garthoff (note 2), p. 433.

[21] See Garthoff (note 2), pp. 429–30.

[22] See Kissinger (note 1), p. 269.

[23] See Garthoff (note 2), p. 446.

[24] Talbott, S., *Endgame: The Inside Story of SALT II* (Harper and Row: New York, 1979), p. 73.

[25] See Garthoff (note 2), p. 423.

[26] See Wolfe (note 12), p. 160.

[27] See Garthoff (note 2), p. 445.

[28] Johnson and McAllister (note 5), pp. 591, 595 and 598.

[29] See Garthoff (note 2), p. 442. But Johnson records that he found Zumwalt easier to talk to than the other chiefs.

[30] Clarke, D. L., *The Politics of Arms Control: The Role and Effectiveness of the U.S. ACDA* (Free Press: New York, 1979), p. 57.

[31] See Kissinger (note 1), pp. 271 and 1018 for examples.

[32] Johnson and McAllister (note 5), pp. 589, 599–600 and 603.

[33] See Johnson and Mc Allister (note 5), pp. 591 and 604.

[34] Johnson and McAllister (note 5), pp. 585–86.

[35] Johnson and McAllister (note 5), p. 596.

[36] See Kissinger (note 1), pp. 1143–46 and Garthoff (note 2), p. 422.

[37] See Garthoff (note 2), p. 444.

[38] Rathjens, G. W., Chayes, A. and Ruina, J. P., *Nuclear Arms Control Agreements: Process and Impact* (Carnegie Endowment for International Peace: Washington, DC, 1974), p. 19.

[39] See Kissinger (note 1), pp. 271 and 273.

[40] Scoville, H., Jr, 'A different approach to arms control—reciprocal unilateral restraint', *Arms Control and Technological Innovation,* eds D. Carlton and C. Schaerf (Croom Helm: London, 1977), p. 172.

[41] See Garthoff (note 2), p. 445.

[42] See Garthoff (note 2), pp. 448–49.

[43] See Wolfe (note 12), p. 199.

[44] See Garthoff (note 2), p. 440.

[45] Garthoff (note 2), p. 452.

[46] See Gelman (note 10), pp. 148–49.

[47] Holloway, D., 'Foreign and defence policy', *The Soviet Union Since the Fall of Khrushchev,* eds A. Brown and M. Kaser (Macmillan: London, 1978), 2nd edn, pp. 68–69.

[48] See Garthoff (note 2), p. 801.

[49] Johnson and McAllister (note 5), pp. 609–10.

[50] See Johnson and McAllister (note 5), p. 574.

[51] See Johnson and McAllister (note 5), p. 609.

[52] See Johnson and McAllister (note 5), p. 612.

[53] See Johnson and McAllister (note 5), p. 612.

[54] Hyland, W. L. 'Instructional Impediments', *Arms Control and Defense Postures in the 1980s,* ed. R. Burt (Westview Press: Boulder, Colo., 1982), p. 107.

[55] Johnson and McAllister (note 5), pp. 606–7.

[56] Johnson and McAllister (note 5), p. 614.

[57] New York Times, 4 Dec. 1976, cited by Garthoff (note 2), p. 802

[58] See Wolfe (note 12), pp. 221–22, Garthoff (note 2), p. 806, and Talbott (note 24), pp. 60–61.

[59] Senate Armed Service Committee SALT II Hearings, Part 3, p. 949. Krepon, M., *Strategic Stalemate: Nuclear Weapons and Arms Control in American Politics* (Macmillan: London, 1984), p. 90.

[60] See Talbott (note 24), p. 63.

[61] Vance, C., *Hard Choices: Critical Years in America's Foreign Policy* (Simon and Schuster: New York, 1983), p. 55.

[62] Interview with Georgi Arbatov, cited by Garthoff (note 2), p. 566.

[63] The two sites were at Derazhnya and Pervomaisk, and the problem became known on the US side as 'D-and-P'. See Talbott (note 24), pp. 111–19.

[64] See Garthoff (note 2), p. 813 on Soviet views and Talbott (note 24), p. 132 on the US hopes.

[65] See Talbott (note 24), pp. 133–35.

[66] See Talbott (note 24), pp. 149–51.

[67] Cited by Wolfe (note 12), p. 231.

[68] For a summary and analysis of the Treaty, see 'SALT II: an analysis of the agreements', SIPRI, *World Armaments and Disarmament: SIPRI Yearbook 1980* (Taylor & Francis: London, 1980), pp. 209–83.

[69] See SIPRI (note 68), pp. 217–18. The Treaty also set a limit of 14 warheads for SLBMs.

[70] See Talbott (note 24), p. 66.

[71] Brzezinski, Z., *Power and Principle: Memoirs of the National Security Adviser 1977–1981* (Weidenfeld and Nicolson: London, 1983), p. 164.

[72] See Talbott (note 24), p. 213.

[73] See Garthoff (note 2), p. 805.

[74] See Garthoff (note 2), p. 815.

[75] See Talbott (note 24), p. 147.

[76] See Brzezinski (note 71), pp. 185–86.

[77] See Vance (note 61), p. 102.

[78] See Garthoff (note 2), pp. 818–19.

[79] Brzezinski (note 71), p. 330.

[80] Vance (note 61), p. 112.

[81] This episode is examined in detail by Duffy G., 'Crisis mangling and the Cuban brigade', *International Security,* vol. 8 (summer 1983), pp. 828–48. It is summarized by Brzezinski (note 71), pp 346–53. He apparently warned the President that it might be a 'phony' issue.

[82] See Talbott (note 24), pp. 141–42.

[83] Paul Warnke, quoted in Neidle, A. F. (ed.), *Nuclear Negotiations: Reassessing Arms Control Goals in US–Soviet Relations* (University of Texas: Austin, 1982), p. 71. This book comprises the proceedings of a conference held on 25–26 Feb. 1982.

[84] See Talbott (note 24) p. 142.

[85] For example, see Lambert, B. S., 'Arms control and defense planning in Soviet strategic policy', *Arms Control and Defense Postures in the 1980s,* ed. R. Burt (Westview Press: Boulder, Colo., 1982), p. 68.

[86] See Talbott (note 24), pp. 204, 215 and 244.

[87] See Talbott (note 24), pp. 213–14.

[88] See Talbott (note 24), pp. 114–19

[89] See Brzezinski (note 71), p. 168.

[90] See Garthoff (note 2), p. 807.

[91] See Vance (note 61), p. 109.

[92] See Jacobsen, C.G. 'Soviet military expenditure', SIPRI, *Armaments and Disarmament: SIPRI Yearbook 1986* (Oxford University Press: Oxford, 1986), pp. 269–70 and Garthoff (note 2), pp. 771–80.

[93] See Garthoff (note 2), pp. 771, 783 and 802.

[94] See Vance (note 61), pp. 108 and 111–12.

95 'Diplomacy at home and abroad: Paul Warnke on negotiating SALT', *Arms Control Today*, (note 95) p. 3.

96 See Talbott (note 24), pp. 140 and 166.

97 See Talbott (note 24), p. 199.

98 See Brzezinski (note 71), pp. 158, 170, 316–17 and 325.

99 See Garthoff (note 2), pp. 804–5.

100 See Vance (note 61), p. 100.

101 Carter, J., *Keeping Faith: Memoirs of a President* (Bantam Books: New York, 1982), p. 224.

102 See Talbott (note 24), p. 198.

103 See Talbott (note 24), pp. 207–9.

104 'Arms control lessons of the Carter Administration: looking back, looking forward', *Arms Control Today*, vol. 11, no. 3 (Mar. 1981), p.1, comment by Earle.

105 Warnke comments critically on the role of some senators seeking a veto in the negotiations in *Arms Control Today* (May, 1979), p. 7.

106 George, R. Z., 'The future context of arms control', *Arms Control*, vol. 1, no. 2 (Sep. 1980), p. 134.

107 Duffy, G. 'Is the SALT era over?', *The Arms Race in the 1980s*, eds D. Carlton and C. Schaerf (MacMillan: London, 1982), pp. 114–123.

108 See Clarke (note 30), p. 231.

109 Hough, J. F. 'The Brezhnev era: The man and the system', *Problems of Communism*, vol. 25, no. 2 (Mar./Apr. 1976).

110 See Talbott (note 24), pp. 251–52.

111 See Kissinger (note 1), p. 1007.

112 Earle gave qualified support to the 'back channel' when used as it was under President Carter; see *Arms Control Today*, Mar. 1981, p. 6.

113 See Talbott (note 24), pp. 123–24.

114 See Talbott (note 24), p. 130.

115 Brzezinski saw continuing bargaining advantage in the USA being willing to wait for Soviet concessions throughout 1978. He backed Brown in resisting an attempt by Vance and Warnke to move rapidly towards an agreement in January 1978, and believed that Soviet concessions in July reflected the value of delaying tactics. See Brzezinski (note 71), pp. 170 and 326.

116 See Talbott (note 24), pp. 139–40.

117 See Talbott (note 24), pp. 174–75.

118 See Talbott (note 24), p. 94.

119 See Vance (note 61), p. 109.

120 Sweet, W. 'Building up to negotiate down?', *Bulletin of the Atomic Scientists*, vol. 35, no. 8 (Oct. 1979), pp. 9–10.

121 See Brzezinski (note 61), pp. 336–37 and 345.

122 See Brzezinski (note 61), p. 345.

123 See Neidle (note 83), p. 76.

124 'SALT II evaluated', *Arms Control Today*, vol. 9, no. 7 (July/Aug. 1979), pp. 3–4.

125 See Sweet (note 120), p. 9.

126 Cited by Garthoff (note 2), p. 825.

127 Sharp, J. M. O., 'Confidence building measures in SALT', *Arms Control*, vol. 3, no. 1 (May 1982), pp. 48–49.

128 See Garthoff (note 2), p. 801.

7. INF and START: 1981–83

I. Introduction

The missile talks that began in 1981, collapsed in late 1983 and resumed in 1985 provide a more dramatic example of early failure, and of later partial success, than either SALT I or II. When the Soviet Union walked out of the negotiations on intermediate-range missiles and allowed the talks on strategic nuclear missiles to lapse at the end of 1983, the INF and START negotiations looked like a particularly striking example of failure in arms control. Some commentators were inclined to view the collapse of the negotiations as the ultimate failure of the whole approach of seeking negotiated reductions in nuclear weapons. The discussions seemed to be textbook examples of the problems inherent in negotiations, such as the search for an artificial parity and the use of bargaining chips. Furthermore, the talks also seemed to be an example of how not to conduct a negotiation. Major proposals were apparently presented with an eye to achieving a propaganda advantage, and domestic and alliance requirements took precedence over the search for an acceptable compromise.

The negotiations that began in 1985 led to the signing of one of the most important arms control agreements reached to date—the Treaty between the USA and the USSR to eliminate their intermediate-range and shorter-range missiles (the INF Treaty) at the Washington summit in December 1987. Whether the INF Treaty was achieved despite the earlier breakdown of negotiations, or whether it was a demonstration of the soundness of Western tactics in continuing with the deployment of INF, is a controversial and important question which will be examined in chapter 8. There are good reasons for analyzing these two stages separately.

Although the negotiations that broke down in November 1983 and were resumed in March 1985 retained some continuity both in terms of format as well as initial negotiating positions, the political context in which the two phases were conducted had changed dramatically. In Moscow, Mikhail Gorbachev and an invigorated Soviet leadership soon produced new initiatives. In Washington, the second Reagan Administration had begun a process of gradual, though decisive, change towards arms control and relations with the Soviet Union. The first set of missile talks clearly reflected the new cold war tensions of the early 1980s. The second phase of the negotiations began in 1985 and took place in the context of growing *détente*. Still, it is important not to gloss over the failure of the talks that collapsed in 1983 because of the eventual success in achieving the INF Treaty. In 1983, there was general agreement that the INF and START negotiations had failed.

II. The failure of the missile talks: 1981-83

After publicly repudiating SALT, the Reagan Administration took office committed to a buildup of US military strength before seeking any genuine arms control. The Administration pressed ahead with plans to increase the US nuclear arsenal and restored, for example, the B-1 bomber programme that President Carter had cancelled. Although the Reagan Administration in time did bring itself to promise *de facto* adherence to SALT II restrictions, these constraints did not, in practice, restrain any immediate nuclear weapon developments.

The Reagan Administration, despite some internal resistance, soon found itself being drawn into further talks concerning a curb on nuclear missiles. The strongest pressure for the USA to begin INF negotiations came from Western Europe. Negotiations on 'theatre nuclear forces' (TNF) had been officially launched in the autumn of 1980 under President Carter. These discussions stemmed directly from the NATO 'dual-track' decision of December 1979 to deploy 464 ground-launched cruise missile (GLCM) launchers and 108 Pershing II missiles in Western Europe, but at the same time to engage in arms control talks on TNF. Although the deployments were primarily designed to bolster the NATO's flexible response strategy, the Alliance hoped that the weapons would strengthen the negotiation position with the USSR and would result in a reduction of Soviet SS-20's deployment in exchange for reductions in the planned deployments.[1] European political agitation against the missiles, coupled with US anxiety about NATO cohesion, constituted the main impetus for the talks that the Reagan Administration began in Geneva in November 1981 under the revised title of Intermediate-range Nuclear Forces (INF) negotiations.

Increasing congressional reluctance to endorse all of President Reagan's planned defence spending, the specific problems concerning deployment of the MX missile and the widespread public and congressional concern for some form of arms control eventually compelled the Administration to address curbing long-range missiles. The Strategic Arms Reduction Talks (START) began at the end of June 1982. The new designation was intended to signal the new US commitment to deep cuts, as opposed to the tinkering represented by SALT.

Both negotiations, however, collapsed. In late November 1983, the Soviet Union walked out of the INF talks to protest against NATO's deployment of cruise and Pershing II missiles in Western Europe, and two weeks later refused to agree upon a date for any further START session. Although the INF talks seemed for a while in 1982 to have some possibility of resulting in an agreement, START never took on the character of a serious negotiation during this period.

The conditions for arms control appeared to be singularly inauspicious during 1981. During the 1980 presidential campaign, Ronald Reagan not only had advocated a renewed US military superiority, he also espoused a simple anti-communist world view reminiscent of the early 1950s. After he took office, Reagan gave a number of speeches castigating the Soviet Union, which he denounced at one point as an 'evil empire'. Reagan also endorsed a more openly interventionist US military policy around the world. Although *détente* was arguably dead before Reagan entered the White House, Reagan's policies and rhetoric alarmed many in Europe who feared the development of a new cold war.

The new Administration expressed hostility to the whole conception of arms control as practised by its predecessors, and placed well known opponents of arms control in key positions. Eugene Rostow assumed the top post at the ACDA, and Paul Nitze was appointed to head the INF delegation in Geneva. Both Rostow and Nitze were Democrats with a long record of government service, and owed their jobs to their prominent role on the Committee on the Present Danger and for their vigour in attacking SALT II. General Rowny, who had left the SALT II delegation to campaign against the Treaty, was to head the START negotiations. Although a number of the National Security Council (NSC) staff members had also displayed hostility to arms control, the most articulate and able opponents of arms control were based in the Department of Defense. Caspar Weinberger and his deputies, Fred Iklé and, in particular, Richard Perle, were unremitting in their resistance to serious arms reduction negotiations with the Soviet Union. Only the State Department under Alexander Haig, and later under George Shultz, displayed some of its traditional interest in arms control talks.

Viewed in conjunction with the developments in Washington, the position in Moscow did not appear to be very much more promising. Although the Soviet leadership was still publicly committed to the SALT process, it had not demonstrated any interest, even rhetorically, in sudden deep cuts in strategic missile forces. However, the USSR had, in connection with SALT II, supported the general goal of eventual reductions in SALT III.[2] The Soviet leaders reacted sharply to Reagan's attacks and argued that the USA had been responsible for ending *détente* in the late 1970s. The Soviet Union naturally did not accept the US view that Soviet forces in Afghanistan were one of the main sources of renewed distrust; the USSR had become enmeshed in a guerrilla war, and a rapid withdrawal was unlikely. On another front, the Soviet Union's political and security interests were being successfully challenged by the rise of the Solidarity movement in Poland. Any direct or indirect Soviet action to crush this movement (which seemed increasingly probable during 1981) would clearly mean greater deterioration of relations with the West. In this context, even an energetic Soviet leadership would have had little leeway for promoting either *détente* or arms control. In practice, however, Brezhnev's deteriorating health created a general immobility at the top. The only issue on which Moscow had a strong incentive to be conciliatory was the prevention of the deployment of the new NATO missiles. In a last minute attempt to stave off the NATO decision on deployment, Brezhnev offered some unilateral Soviet initiatives during a speech in October 1979. In particular, he referred to a possible reduction in Soviet INF if deployment of the new NATO missiles was abandoned.[3] Nevertheless, during this stage of the talks, Western attempts to use deployment as a bargaining counter for an INF agreement proved to be double-edged. Although the Soviet Union wanted to prevent the new deployments, the USSR resisted being coerced into making major concessions.

III. The INF talks

In addition to the purely military implications, the USSR and the USA were also concerned over the political repercussions of the 1979 NATO decision. The Soviet Union apparently regarded the new missiles as a clear military threat, but US assessments of the military value of the deployments seemed to vary greatly. In Brzezinski's view, the missiles played a political role in the reassurance of the USA's NATO allies; the military rationale for the deployment was not the paramount concern. Whereas Weinberger believed deployment to be militarily essential, Perle regarded the missiles as militarily irrelevant.[4] The Soviet Union, of course, had obvious reasons for concern about the deployment of the Pershing IIs in the FRG. The missiles would be able to reach well into Soviet territory and potentially even to Moscow. Moreover, the missiles were very accurate and had a very short flight time.

Cruise missiles, on the other hand, were much slower. Although cruise missiles were intended to evade radar controls by flying close to the contours of the earth, the US military began to speculate that with improved aircraft radar the Soviet Union might be able to shoot them down. According to Paul Warnke, Soviet negotiators referred to GLCMs as 'German-launched cruise missiles'. The Soviet Union had good grounds for fearing that cruise missiles intended for use with conventional warheads would eventually be made available to West German and other NATO forces, despite the fact that the nuclear-armed cruise missiles destined for the FRG would be exclusively under US control.[5] Soviet representatives, therefore, expressed considerable concern over GLCMs, which could not be reliably intercepted, at least in any numbers.

If military concerns encouraged the USSR to enter the INF negotiations, then political anxieties prompted the USA to come to the conference table. The deployment of new missiles had been intended to placate European allies and to cement the NATO alliance. Instead, the move threatened to create extreme alarm in Europe and to split the alliance. Even the governments that had agreed to the deployments were ambivalent about the decision. A reduction of the Soviet nuclear threat to Europe by arms control was preferable to the acceptance of new missiles. By December 1979, NATO support for deployment had become a test of alliance unity and resolve. The arms control track of the NATO decision was designed to quiet European fears. After public reaction to the planned deployments resulted in a large and highly visible peace movement in Western Europe during 1980 and 1981, even right-wing governments became more concerned about negotiations. The position of the FRG was especially sensitive. Helmut Schmidt, one of the chief architects of the NATO decision, was still in power in 1981, but was being strongly opposed on the INF issue by the rank and file within his own Social Democratic Party. Early in 1981, NATO governments (in particular the FRG and Italy who were committed to accept significant numbers of the NATO missiles) urged the USA to announce a date for starting talks on the European missiles. The State Department, and Alexander Haig personally, were receptive to European anxieties, although some members of the Administration were not. Haig managed to secure President Reagan's agreement to a public US announcement at the NATO meeting in Rome in May 1981 that negotiations would begin by the end of the year. This public deadline created a commitment that enabled those in the Administration who favoured talks to override the stalling tactics of the opponents.

The Reagan Administration inherited two sets of guidelines relevant to its initial INF proposal. The first stemmed from the NATO December 1979 decision and the Integrated Decision Document that the NATO ministers had endorsed. The NATO guidelines envisaged that planned deployments might be reduced (but not cancelled) if agreement were reached with the USSR to curb its own missiles and specified that all Soviet intermediate range missiles should be covered in any ceiling. The second set of principles was hammered out during the initial talks, which commenced under President Carter, and stated that the aim should be equality of intermediate-range missiles on both sides, that equality should focus on warheads and not just launchers, and that SS-20 mobility had to be covered to prevent them being moved between the European and Asian parts of the USSR. The Reagan Administration accepted the case for focusing on missiles only (the JCS proved especially reluctant to submit the issue of aircraft to negotiations), but disagreed initially on whether to include shorter-range as well as intermediate-range missiles. The final decision, which resulted from internal manœuvring, was to propose a zero option covering intermediate-range missiles. The zero option called for the USSR to abandon all its SS-20s, together with the older SS-4s and SS-5s that the SS-20s were to replace, in return for the USA cancelling its planned GLCM and Pershing II deployments.

President Reagan achieved a short-term propaganda coup by announcing the zero option, which was simple and bold, and offered an apparently ideal solution in terms of West European public opinion. However, the proposal was totally unacceptable to the Soviet Union, which was being asked to relinquish its latest missiles (already being deployed) against US missiles which were still being tested. Later in the INF talks, a Soviet negotiator bitterly expressed the hope that, in due course, the USSR would be asked to give up 'paper missiles'.[6]

The Soviet Union strongly contested the proposition that the new US deployments were required to balance its own SS-20s, SS-4s and SS-5s. In the view of the Soviet Union, a nuclear balance in Europe already existed. The SS-20 programme was a routine modernization which could lead to replacement of the SS-4s and SS-5s, and would not change the total number of warheads. The Soviet Union reiterated its earlier proposal for a mutual moratorium on the deployment of new missiles and announced its own version of a zero option: the abolition of all medium-range bombers and missiles threatening Europe. In Bonn, Brezhnev had suggested in November 1981 that both sides could begin by making substantial reductions. The Soviet delegation at Geneva interpreted Brezhnev's comment in slightly more detail, suggesting that both sides implement reductions to a maximum of 600 medium-range systems by 1985 and 300 by 1990. Medium-range systems were defined as those with a range of 1000 km or more. As a longer-term goal, the Soviet Union proposed elimination of all shorter-range battlefield nuclear weapons in Europe.

The Geneva delegations immediately became involved in a dispute concerning the balance of forces that existed and what systems on each side should be counted. According to Soviet arithmetic, both sides had just under 1000 medium-range systems. This total included FB-111 bombers based in the USA and all US bombers based on aircraft carriers (even those not normally assigned to Europe), and excluded many Soviet tactical aircraft with an estimated range of more than 1000 km. The US delegation complained that the Soviet figures were questionable and produced estimates which were based on equally dubious assumptions. The US figures attempted to show that the Soviet Union had 3825 intermediate systems against only 560 for NATO. These estimates included all 2700 Soviet nuclear-capable tactical aircraft and excluded most comparable NATO aircraft. Furthermore, the US estimates included shorter-range Soviet missiles, but excluded the NATO Pershing 1a missiles.[7]

Clearly, both sides juggled the totals to score debating points.[8] Although there are genuine problems in assessing the combat range of aircraft (determined by altitude of flight and weight of payload) and in knowing which aircraft have dual-capable (nuclear and non-nuclear) roles, objective criteria for determining range exist, and formulas could have been devised to deal with the latter problem. Nevertheless, genuine differences remained between the two sides, both in perceptions of military threat and in views of what legitimately ought to count in assessing a balance. According to the Soviet Union, US aircraft, sea-based systems, and the British and French nuclear forces were all part of the theatre military balance.[9] The USA was especially concerned about total numbers of Soviet systems, especially SS-20s, even if they were apparently deployed in Asian areas of the USSR. In addition, because the SS-20s were triple MIRVed, there also remained the question of whether the balance should be assessed in terms of launchers or warheads.

From the Soviet standpoint, the negotiations concerned not only the balance in the European theatre, but also the Soviet Union's total strategic position. The new missiles, in particular the Pershing IIs, could be regarded as strategic missiles capable of attacking Soviet targets and carrying out the same missions as intercontinental missiles. These missiles, therefore, represented a menacing element in the USA's total strategic buildup. Throughout the SALT II negotiations, the USSR had similarly viewed the USA's forward-based bombers as belonging to the USA's strategic arsenal. The Soviet Union's emphasis on bombers in its initial INF proposal may have been influenced by an awareness that the Reagan Administration in 1981 was threatening to abandon the SALT II constraints. In addition, the spectre of unlimited US sea-based cruise missiles had both strategic and theatre implications for the Soviet Union.[10] The difficulty of distinguishing between theatre and strategic weapons is well illustrated by the 400 warheads on US Poseidon missiles assigned to a theatre nuclear role in NATO. In talks with Schmidt in mid-1980, Brezhnev insisted that these weapons would have to be counted in the theatre balance, but the Soviet delegation at Geneva excluded the Poseidon warheads, perhaps in recognition of their inclusion in START.[11] The overlap between theatre and strategic systems prompted some arms control analysts to argue that the INF and START negotiations should be merged.

Among the many disagreements between the two sides, perhaps the most enduring issue at the INF negotiations was Soviet insistence that the British and French nuclear forces must be counted in the NATO total, as part of the threat arrayed against the USSR. The USA was bound to oppose this requirement, because of the British and French insistence that their independent forces could not be included in the counting rules for the negotiations in any way. The US delegation argued that third country forces were irrelevant to a bilateral negotiation. Further, the USA maintained that these forces were indeed independent—not NATO—forces and that formal allowance for these forces (along with the USA's nuclear FBS) had already technically been made in the SALT treaties. Therefore, these forces were inappropriate for INF negotiations. According to Talbott, the US side early on maintained that the USSR was trying to count the obsolescent British Vulcan bomber as equivalent to an SS-20 missile. Nevertheless, because the UK and France were both MIRVing their missile forces, the Soviet case was in fact becoming stronger.[12]

The other key question which impinged on the legitimate interests of both sides was the setting of equal global limits on both US and Soviet missiles, and the prohibition of SS-20s being transferred between the European and Asian theatres. The USSR had a genuine concern to meet the nuclear threat posed by China and to avoid cuts which took no account of its strategic needs in other theatres. The USA had a double commitment: first, to prevent SS-20s deployed in Asian areas of the USSR from being rapidly redeployed against Europe; and second, to reassure Japan and South Korea, that the SS-20s moved out of the European theatre were not simply re-targeted against Asian countries. This problem appeared to be more amenable to compromise. The USSR, early in the negotiations, began to hint at possible concessions.

The first session of the INF negotiations before Christmas 1981 was devoted to setting out initial positions and arguing about the military balance. When the two delegations returned early in 1982, the USA presented a draft treaty. Although the treaty was largely a formalization of the zero-option proposal, as a result of bureaucratic politics in Washington, it now included two clauses clearly unacceptable to the Soviet Union. The first clause stipulated a unilateral freeze on Soviet shorter-range missiles—the SS-12s and SS-22s—and set no limits on US and West German Pershing 1as. The second provision specified that only nuclear-armed GLCMs were covered by the treaty, which permitted NATO to deploy conventionally armed GLCMs. This wording raised obvious verification problems, because a conventionally armed cruise missile is indistinguishable from a nuclear-armed one. Apparently, Richard Perle had succeeded in overriding the JCS judgement that the USA would never need to put conventional warheads on GLCMs, and had succeeded in securing Reagan's endorsement of what he assumed to be a Pentagon decision: namely, to keep the option open.[13] On Nitze's insistence, the treaty would be of indefinite duration. This was designed to prevent the Soviet Union from developing a new generation of missiles during the course of a finite agreement.

The USSR tabled a Statement of Intention in February and a draft treaty in May. Whereas both documents retained the substance of the initial Soviet proposal for phased reductions to 600 and then 300 systems, subsequent discussions of the Statement suggested possible Soviet concessions on which aircraft should be counted and the problem of transferring SS-20s within the USSR. Moreover, the draft treaty proposed an SS-20-free zone between the European and Asian parts of the USSR which would prevent rapid movement of the missiles in a crisis. The Statement envisaged a 10-year agreement, which was open to renewal. The draft treaty amended these conditions, however, to set a time-table for reductions and to allow for an indefinite duration of the agreement.[14] Informal soundings indicated that the USSR might be willing to negotiate a bilateral freeze on short-range missiles not included in the draft treaty. Nevertheless, the proposed reduction to 300 intermediate-range systems, to be made up on the NATO side almost entirely of British and French forces, was clearly not negotiable for the USA.

In order to bridge the gap between the two sides, an initiative embodying major compromises was needed. Because it was manifestly evident that no such initiative could emerge from Washington, Nitze, who was anxious for an agreement partly to prevent NATO disunity, took an individual initiative. Nitze did not consult with anyone except Rostow, his immediate superior at ACDA, and put together a package for informal behind-the-scenes negotiation. After cautious soundings between Nitze and Yuli Kvitsinsky, the two heads of delegation took what later became famous as a 'walk in the woods' on 16 July 1982 and hammered out a possible INF agreement.[15] Kvitsinsky had taken part in behind-the-scenes talks during the Berlin negotiations of 1970, and had the requisite experience and authority to take some risks on his own initiative. Nevertheless, Kvitsinsky covered himself by first clearing the procedure with Foreign Minister Gromyko. Nitze and Kvitsinsky agreed to a formula whereby the initiative (and hence the blame) could be attributed to the other side. They also agreed to submit the proposal as a total package not as a basis for further compromise and pledged strictest secrecy. The key concession from the US side was a proposal to cancel Pershing II altogether. Nitze reasoned that this was the missile Moscow was most concerned about, and therefore the Pershing II was a good bargaining counter. He also concluded that the role of the Pershing II could be fulfilled by other longer-range US missiles, while the Pershing 1a could be replaced by a modernized Pershing 1b for a battlefield role. The package also recognized that the USSR could not be expected to remove all its SS-20s, and proposed allowing 75 SS-20s in Europe against 75 cruise missile launchers with four missiles per launcher. Nitze and Kvitsinsky agreed on a freeze of SS-20s in Asian areas of the USSR at the existing level of about 90. Soviet concern over aircraft was met by establishing a ceiling of 150 medium-range bombers for both the USA and the USSR which covered such key bombers as the USA's F-111 and FB-111, and the Soviet Union's Backfire, Blinder and Badger. The agreement, however, excluded carrier-based aircraft. Although the Soviet Union acquired considerable gains from this package, including US abandonment of equal global limits for US and Soviet intermediate-range missiles, the USSR conceded some GLCM deployment, and accepted that there would be no curbs on US sea-based systems and, above all, no explicit compensation for British and French nuclear forces.

When Nitze brought the proposal back to Washington, he won some initial cautious support in the State Department. At DOD, Iklé also recognized certain advantages for the USA in the package. As information leaked into a wider circle, however, Perle was alerted and, according to later newspaper accounts (and to Talbott), took action to ensure that the package was repudiated (although Perle himself later denied this).[16] Perle's opposition was reinforced by Weinberger's doubts about giving up Pershing II and by some NSC officials' unhappiness with Nitze's unauthorized playing of a lone hand. In the end, Reagan was persuaded to reject the walk-in-the-woods package. What happened in Moscow is less clear, although Kvitsinsky told Nitze that the package had been rejected at Politburo level. The chief leverage for the package in Moscow was to have been Brezhnev's desire for a final Summit meeting. Although Nitze had hinted at the possibility of a summit in his early soundings, Moscow's own probings did not detect any strong interest in Washington for a summit. Kvitsinsky also intimated that some quarters in Moscow were glad that the Reagan Administration had rejected the package, and later indicated that the Defence Ministry had opposed any deal which permitted NATO deployment.[17] For a time, the details of the walk-in-the-woods agreement were kept secret, even from NATO governments. After Rostow was dismissed as ACDA Director in January 1983 and replaced by Kenneth Adelman, a more intransigent opponent of arms control, Rostow decided to vindicate himself and publicized both his own and Nitze's role in seeking an INF agreement.

After the resumption of the Geneva talks in the autumn of 1982, the negotiations had become more polemical. The Soviet Union no longer hinted at possible concessions. Instead, the Soviet Union threatened to walk out of the talks and to deploy further missiles, if the Pershing II and cruise missile deployments went ahead. The US delegation was instructed to stand fast with the zero option and to repeat previous arguments. Not surprisingly, there was no progress for the rest of the year. The death of Leonid Brezhnev and the accession of Yuri Andropov to the post of General Secretary, however, did result in a new proposal from the Soviet Union on 21 December 1982. In turn, Reagan felt under pressure to display a willingness to take some initiative in response. NATO governments had become increasingly insistent that the USA should at least appear as though it were negotiating seriously. As a result, Reagan endorsed a new interim solution of missile levels above zero, which was presented at Geneva in late March 1983.

Both the Andropov offer and the interim solution, however, were still more attuned to propaganda than to genuine negotiating purposes. Andropov stated that the USSR would reduce Soviet medium-range missiles in Europe to match the British and French missile arsenals, if the planned NATO missile deployments were abandoned. Later, the Soviet Union hinted that some of the total number of SS-20s might be cut and not simply redeployed in Asian areas of the USSR. This offer was not regarded as totally unreasonable by everyone in the West. In fact, Warnke had put forward a somewhat similar proposal, which gained support from the West German Social Democratic Party. Nevertheless, the Andropov offer was summarily rejected by Washington, London, Paris and the Christian Democratic government in Bonn.[18] The US Interim Proposal, principally put together by Assistant Secretary of State Richard Burt, envisaged some reduction in the NATO missile deployments in return for a cut in the total number of SS-20s to achieve the same number of warheads. No precise figures were proposed, ostensibly to preserve flexibility, but in reality because the Administration could not agree. Gromyko publicly turned down the proposal a few days after Nitze presented it at Geneva; the deployment of new US missiles, global SS-20 ceilings, and the refusal to count British and French forces had made it unacceptable to the Soviet Union.

During the last few months before the final deployment deadline, a flurry of new proposals were exchanged by both sides. In August 1983, Andropov offered to remove 81 SS-20s targeted on Europe and to destroy them, leaving 162 SS-20s to match British and French ballistic missile launchers. In September, the USA responded with a new complex proposal which mandated a reduction in the numbers of both Pershing II and GLCMs to be deployed in return for cuts in Soviet missiles. The USA retained the principle of a global ceiling, but offered a compromise recognition of the separate role of SS-20s in the Asian area by proposing to keep some of the missiles allotted to the USA under the proposal out of the European theatre. At the end of October, the Soviet Union lowered the number of SS-20s in its proposal to 140 on the basis of matching warheads, not launchers, and indicated a possible freeze on SS-20s targeted on Asia if the USA and its allies did not build up their own nuclear forces in that area. In mid-November, the Geneva delegation elaborated this proposal by adding numbers to it, which suggested a global ceiling of intermediate-range land-based missile warheads of 420 on each side, and would have necessitated a substantial cut in total Soviet SS-20 deployments.

All of these last-minute overtures were brusquely turned down by the other side. On 1 September, the Soviet Union shot down a South Korean civilian airliner over Soviet territory, and the relations between the two great powers deteriorated to an even lower point. Although Reagan responded to the Korean airliner incident with a bitter verbal attack, it is doubtful whether the action made a substantial difference in the INF negotiations. At this stage, Washington was primarily interested in ensuring that the missile deployments took place on time as a demonstration of NATO resolve and unity. The Soviet Union, on the other hand, was already committed to a break-off of negotiations once this had happened.

Throughout most of 1983, West European governments remained optimistic that some compromise agreement would be possible. After the details of the walk-in-the-woods package became public, the governments displayed considerable interest. The election victories of the West German Christian Democrats and of the British Conservatives early in 1983 ensured that the missile deployments would proceed in key countries, but even these governments would have preferred an agreement which limited the NATO deployments and reduced Soviet missiles. Nitze became increasingly worried by widespread public hostility to the deployments in Western Europe and continued to hope for some last-minute compromise. Confusing signals from Moscow suggested briefly there might be some disposition in Soviet circles to reach a last-minute agreement. Kvitsinsky hinted privately in talks with Nitze in November that the Soviet Union might come down to 120 SS-20s in Europe (a cut of about half), in return for cancellation of the NATO missile deployments. Further, Kvitsinsky indicated that the Soviet Union might possibly abandon the principle of compensation for British and French forces in the INF negotiations, while reserving the right to raise the issue in the START negotiations. The Soviet Union canvassed this idea in West European capitals, attributing it to Nitze. After West European governments began to make political use of it as the latest Soviet concession, however, Soviet Defence Minister Dmitri Ustinov publicly repudiated the idea.[19]

After the negotiations collapsed, each side published its own version of what had happened and blamed the other side. Kvitsinsky and Nitze also provided their own versions of their private negotiations and the last-minute exchanges in November 1983. In its formal report to Congress in 1984, ACDA implied that the Soviet Union had rejected the walk-in-the-woods compromise, and that Washington had been willing to continue behind-the-scenes negotiation.[20] Although it was strictly true that the Reagan Administration had not closed the formal channel, Nitze (according to Talbott's detailed account) was forbidden to pursue the package or advance any new proposals. The history of the INF negotiations had now become the subject of a propaganda conflict.

IV. The START negotiations

Although the Reagan Administration invented a new name for its strategic arms negotiations in 1981, it did not manage to produce anything resembling a policy until May 1982, when the President unveiled the outlines of a two-stage approach to negotiations in an address at Eureka College. In the first phase, the aim would be to reduce the total number of ballistic missile launchers to 850 on each side, total warheads for each to 5000 and a total of ICBM warheads to 2500. In the second phase, the problem of total missile throw-weight would be addressed. After further bureaucratic wrangling, the Eureka College speech was converted into an initial negotiating position at the end of June 1982. The main addition was that a *de facto* throw-weight limit was superimposed on phase one in the form of ceilings on heavy and medium missiles on both sides.

The Eureka plan had similarities to the zero option: it sounded clear, simple and radical. In addition, it was designed to favour US strategic programmes and force structure, whereas it would require fundamental changes in Soviet deployments. Most of the USA's ballistic missiles and warheads were sea-based; most Soviet deployments were on land. Under the terms of the proposal, the USSR would be obliged to abandon a high proportion of its ICBM force, whereas the USA could actually increase its land-based warheads from the existing total of 1650 to 2500. The Eureka proposal was also compatible with US modernization programmes: the MX missile on land and the new Trident missile at sea. Still, the total ceilings proposed would, if implemented, require a reduction of the size of the Trident submarine force planned in 1982.[21] Alexander Haig comments in his memoirs that the 2500 ICBM limit 'would require such drastic reductions in the Soviet inventory as to suggest that they were unnegotiable'.[22]

The wholly one-sided nature of the Eureka proposal, however, was not immediately apparent to those who did not understand the asymmetries in US and Soviet force structures. Among their number was included, according to his own later public testimony, President Reagan.[23] The Eureka proposal and the USA's initial negotiating position also excluded elements in the strategic arsenal where the USA was ahead: namely, strategic bombers and ALCMs. These weapons were of considerable concern to the Soviet Union and, of course, had been included in SALT II.

The delay in reaching a START decision in Washington was not due to a shortage of ideas; to the contrary, there was an excess of proposals and a number of sharp differences over what should be restricted. Throughout, Perle (with the support of General Rowny) was primarily concerned with restricting the throw-weight of Soviet missiles and thus resurrected one of the USA's central concerns from SALT I. Both Rostow and Nitze were sympathetic to this aim, but suggested that it be accomplished through a limitation on the size of individual warheads. On Burt's initiative, the State Department wanted the negotiations to focus on launchers, the unit familiar to the SALT negotiations. The others opposed a ceiling on launchers, not only because it was too similar to the SALT proposals, but for the strategic reason that they favoured both sides moving away from large land-based MIRVed missiles to smaller, mobile single-warhead missiles. The State Department responded to this suggestion by asserting that arms control should limit existing weapons. The other key group was the JCS, whose main concern was to ensure START proposals meshed with their strategic targeting plans. The JCS prefered to place the primary emphasis on the ratio of US warheads to Soviet launchers. This made the JCS a potential ally of the State Department and, after joint talks and compromises, it was a joint JCS–State Department proposal that formed the basis for the Eureka speech. Perle, however, did achieve recognition of his throw-weight concerns in phase two and in the additional restrictions on missiles incorporated in the official US negotiation position.[24] The main characteristic that all of the competing START proposals shared was that they would be totally unacceptable to the Soviet Union. The State Department's proposal did have some concern about 'negotiability', although this implied an appeasement of the Soviet Union in the first Reagan Administration. Nevertheless, making headway in the bureaucratic negotiations in Washington meant ignoring, at least initially, the likelihood of an agreement in Geneva.

When the START talks officially opened, the Soviet delegation not surprisingly made it clear that the US proposal was totally unacceptable. If the proposal had been designed as an opening move which would allow for future concessions, then its one-sidedness might not have been a long-term obstacle to negotiations. Yet the Reagan Administration, for the most part, did not wish to make concessions, nor did it have an effective mechanism for fashioning new proposals. By the beginning of 1983, however, President Reagan was under increasing congressional pressure to make some progress in the negotiations. The State Department made a brief and abortive attempt at opening up a back channel between George Shultz and Ambassador Dobrynin to seek a new initiative, but the Secretary of State had nothing new to offer. The Administration had already fallen back, as its predecessors had earlier done during the SALT negotiations, to seeking agreement on more peripheral confidence-building measures: in particular a modernization of the 'hot line'. This issue, pursued at Geneva and in separate technical talks in Moscow and Washington, survived into 1984 when all other arms control talks were at an impasse. Congress, however, proved to be unwilling to accept an updated hot line as a substitute for progress in the START negotiations. Indeed, some members of Congress, together with senior figures experienced in defence and arms control issues from earlier Administrations, collaborated with some members of the NSC staff to promote two START initiatives in 1983.

The Administration was forced to accept outside assistance in formulating policy because its MX missile programme had become a hostage in Congress to some signs of progress in arms control. The MX programme was in trouble largely because an entire series of proposals for a basing mode which would render it invulnerable to a pre-emptive strike had been discarded as either politically unacceptable or technologically faulty, and Congress was extremely resistant to authorizing funds for it. In order to woo congressional support and to overcome the bureaucratic impasse within the Administration, an independent commission was set up early in 1983 to review the MX programme and overall US strategy. The bipartisan commission was headed by Brent Scowcroft, a former aide to Henry Kissinger, and included such prominent members of previous Administrations as Kissinger, Schlesinger and Brown. This respectably conservative group produced a report which urged a limited stopgap MX deployment in hardened silos (thus leaving them still vulnerable), the development of a new generation of single-warhead ICBMs for the 1990s and a serious commitment to arms control agreements which would move both sides away from MIRVed ICBMs.

The Scowcroft Commission report provided an impetus to formulating a new position at the START negotiations in Geneva. In July 1983, the USA presented a draft treaty, which retained the 5000-warhead ceiling, but dropped the 850-launcher limit in order to encourage development of single-warhead missiles. Further, instead of insisting on reduction in specific Soviet ICBMs, the document left it open to the Soviet side to suggest an alternative approach to restricting throw-weight. Under this new proposal, the two phases which had been a source of confusion were merged into one, and an equal ceiling was proposed for bombers and ALCMs. These concessions did not, however, make the substance of the US position any more acceptable to the USSR, especially as SLCMs were totally excluded.

The final US move at Geneva took place in October 1983 and stemmed from a congressional initiative for a quite new approach labelled 'build-down'. Build-down originated in a Senate resolution sponsored by Senators Sam Nunn and William S. Cohen in February 1983, and proposed the destruction of two nuclear warheads for every new warhead deployed. After a bipartisan group of congressmen persuaded the Administration to accept it, a new negotiator was appointed to pursue the proposal at Geneva. James Woolsey, Scowcroft's deputy on the Commission with experience of SALT, was appointed member-at-large to the US delegation with responsibility for heading a joint US–Soviet working group to discuss the build-down proposal. Although the Soviet Union complained publicly that the details of build-down were obscure, the USSR was probably more confused by the politics of it. The original July draft treaty remained on the table, and Rowny, who still headed the START delegation, insisted that this was the real proposal and that the build-down concept was a gimmick to quieten Congress. Further, many members of the Administration were known to oppose the build-down proposal. The Soviet delegation refused to co-operate in the build-down working group, and so the last US initiative before the complete collapse of the talks failed.[25]

Some commentators have argued that the build-down proposal could have been the basis for serious Soviet negotiations. Not only did the concept envisage a scaling down of ballistic missile warheads to 5000 each, the build-down proposal also placed limits on new bombers and ALCMs, and proposed balancing missile throw-weight against bomber carrying capacity. Indeed, after the USSR had scrapped the idea at Geneva in October 1983, Soviet foreign affairs representatives in Moscow indicated interest to a US congressional delegation in early 1984. This approach may, however, have been designed to woo Congress and is difficult to assess.

Throughout the first stage of the START negotiations, the Soviet delegation insisted, with considerable justification, that the United States was not negotiating seriously. On the other hand, the Soviet delegation's own tactics and proposals did not indicate much willingness to go beyond the staking out of initial positions and the making of cosmetic adjustments for propaganda purposes to match various measures of US 'flexibility'. The Soviet Union appeared to be committed to treating the START negotiations as though they were SALT III and initially offered a reduction in total strategic delivery vehicles to 1800 (450 below the SALT II total). This total would be conditional on no further deployment of FBS by the USA. After Reagan's Eureka speech, Gromyko issued a public warning that the Soviet Union would counter a re-opening of the heavy-missile question by re-opening discussions on FBS. The Soviet proposal also required a total ban on the deployment of long-range cruise missiles, whether launched from the air, sea or land, but permitted research and production. This clause was blatantly one-sided in that it prevented US deployment and permitted the USSR to catch up in cruise missile technology. In the case of ALCMs, the proposal meant retreating from the SALT II agreement to permit deployment within specific constraints. This stance was probably adopted, at least partly, for bargaining purposes. In fact, when the Soviet delegation elaborated its proposal in response to the USA's new position in June 1983, the Soviet Union did relax its veto on ALCMs and SLCMs. At this point, the Soviet Union explained its proposed sub-ceilings of 11 000 ballistic missile warheads, 7000 ICBM warheads and 680 MIRVed ICBMs. Although these figures represented a concession to the US desire to move from counting launchers to counting warheads and involved a cut in the MIRVed ICBM total allowed under SALT II, the proposal still did not attempt to meet the principal US concerns.[26]

Several interpretations of Soviet negotiating behaviour are possible. One explanation is that the Soviet Union was committed throughout to close linkage between the START and INF negotiatons. Because the initial Soviet START proposal ruled out new NATO missile deployments (both in its clause requiring no further FBS deployments and in its ban on GLCM deployment), and the Soviet Union's June 1983 proposals were conditional on the NATO missile programme being abandoned, this interpretation appears convincing. Moreover, the Soviet Union put the START negotiations in limbo after the INF talks broke down. A second possible interpretation is that the Soviet General Staff were committed to their central strategic programmes whatever happened and were not prepared to tolerate more than marginal arms control constraints upon them. This view is consistent with what seems to have happened in the SALT I Interim Agreement, and may have been reflected in Soviet protests that the USA was trying to restructure Soviet forces. This interpretation could be taken in conjunction with a third explanation: that Soviet decision making was paralyzed by bureaucratic conflict or by inertia in the absence of decisive leadership from the top. Brezhnev died in November 1982, about four months after START began, and Andropov became seriously ill during 1983. The fourth possibility is that the Soviet Union was provisionally willing to negotiate in earnest, but only if the USA changed its tactics and displayed a willingness to respond.

To some extent, all four explanations may apply. The Soviet Union was plainly trying to prevent the NATO missile deployment and to increase the political costs of proceeding with it. However, Moscow appeared to be somewhat ambivalent about whether or not to cancel the START talks if deployment went ahead. At the beginning of October 1983, arms control expert Gloria Duffy was informed by Soviet officials that the START negotiations would not end because of failure in the INF talks.[27] Soviet military intransigence is likely to have been reinforced not only by the Reagan Administration's general policies and military programmes, but also by specific negotiating behaviour at the START negotiations. For example, the US side had not only resurrected the issue of throw-weight, but also was again insisting that the Backfire bomber would have to be included in any strategic bomber count. The fact that Andropov was no longer active by the autumn of 1983 (when President Reagan had been pushed by Congress into a radically new negotiating position) may have been crucial in the final collapse of the negotiations. The inability of Moscow to react constructively to the October build-down proposals must have been reinforced by the fact that the INF talks had priority and were in a critical final phase.

V. Obstacles to agreement

The INF and START negotiations overlapped in time, were closely related in subject matter and, to some extent, were politically linked. Although both negotiations clearly suffered from many of the same obstacles to agreement, there are some interesting differences between the two sets of talks which make a comparative analysis worthwhile.

Great power confrontation

There was a strong propaganda element in the way both sides treated both sets of negotiations. Both Reagan and Brezhnev had announced the substance of their negotiating positions with maximum publicity before the INF talks began at Geneva. Despite an agreement between Nitze and Kvitsinsky to keep the details of the negotiation private, the Soviet leadership replied to the main US initiatives publicly in Moscow.[28] Reagan also sought public relations advantage by making his changes of position widely known and in 1983 engaged in a public exchange of proposals with Andropov.[29] The main target for these attempts to demonstrate a willingness to negotiate seriously on INF was West European public opinion. In the case of the START negotiations, the main audience was US public opinion and Congress. As a first response to President Reagan's Eureka speech, Brezhnev attempted to woo the popularly based nuclear freeze movement with his own suggestion of an immediate freeze both on numbers of weapons and on modernization programmes.[30] Within the formal negotiations at Geneva, the emphasis from both sides was on scoring debating points rather than on engaging in substantive discussion. In the INF negotiations, however, both delegations retained some hope of real progress and apparently maintained an atmosphere of serious debate. The polemical content in the START negotiations was much higher. The propaganda surrounding both sets of negotiations reflected the fact that both sides were initially more interested in influencing wider political constituencies than in producing negotiable proposals. Still, the pursuit of public advantage was not among the most serious obstacles to success.

The issue of prestige arose most clearly in relation to missile deployment in Europe. By the autumn of 1983, US prestige and credibility within NATO was viewed as depending on getting the missiles in place on schedule. Persistent technological problems with Pershing II were overridden by the imperative of deployment. The possibility of an INF agreement inevitably took second place as deployment drew near. There was also a major prestige consideration on the Soviet side. The Soviet Union had committed itself to preventing deployment and had publicly threatened to walk out of the talks if the missiles were installed. Although most members of the Reagan Administration had apparently dismissed this threat as a bluff, the Soviet Union could not easily back down even if it had wished to do so. Moreover, the Soviet Union was not willing to be seen as negotiating under threat, and despite new proposals in 1983 as the deployment deadline approached, the likelihood of major Soviet concessions receded. Prestige considerations appear to have only marginally affected the START negotiations. Whereas Reagan was committed to pursuing the goal of deep cuts and had rejected the framework embodied in the SALT process, the Soviet Union was committed to maintaining the SALT process as far as possible. These divergent public positions may have served to make the negotiating offers of the two sides more inflexible.

Both the USA and the Soviet Union had political goals in the INF and START negotiations. Simply put, the Soviet Union aimed to stimulate domestic opposition in the USA and Western Europe to the Reagan Administration's military programme, while the US Government sought to defuse it. These aims, however, are so closely interconnected with the propaganda element in the negotiations, on the one hand, and alliance politics on the other, that the pursuance of these objectives cannot really be viewed as an additional obstacle to serious negotiation.

The potential role of political linkage in the Geneva negotiations is much more interesting. The Reagan Administration came to power strongly committed to the principle that arms control should be linked to Soviet international behaviour. Two major events which might have been expected to invoke linkage occurred during the negotiations—the imposition of martial law in Poland in December 1981, and the shooting down of the South Korean airliner in December 1983. After Solidarity had been outlawed, the Reagan Administration mounted a campaign for economic sanctions against the Soviet Union; and earlier in 1981, Secretary of Defense Weinberger had obtained partial support from the NATO Nuclear Planning Group for the principle that arms control talks should be linked to Soviet non-intervention in Poland.[31] In practice, however, the newly convened INF talks were not halted over imposition of martial law, because other political pressures had taken priority. Indirect Soviet intervention in Poland provided a reason for delays in START, but this apparent linkage appears to have served, in part, as a rationalization for the Administration's inability to take any decisions.[32] Certainly, from the standpoint of political linkage, it could be argued that Poland was more relevant to the INF negotiations. Although the Korean airliner incident did result in brief polemics within the INF negotiations, the event had no significant or lasting impact. Soviet intransigence, in response to the Congress-initiated build-down proposal at the START negotiations, could have been reinforced by anger at Reagan's denunciations, but many other explanations are possible. The airliner incident may have had such little impact, because both sets of negotiations had already reached rock bottom; and nothing could make the situation much worse. The most significant fact related to political linkage, however, is that the Reagan Administration, by 1983, had effectively abandoned it as a deliberate instrument of policy. Specific linkage was not a real obstacle in either the INF or the START negotiations.[33]

On the Soviet side, the main question about linkage is to what extent the START negotiations were totally dependent on what happened in the INF talks. When accused of this tactic by General Rowny, a Soviet Foreign Ministry representative replied that the Soviet delegation was not waiting to see progress in the INF talks, but to see when the USA became serious in the START negotiations.[34] Although the Soviet Union was disposed to impose some linkage, it does not appear to have been unalterably committed to breaking off the START negotiations at the same time as the INF talks. This may well have been a subject of dispute in Moscow. Clearly, the tendency to apply such linkage did not help the START negotiations. By the time the USA put forward its first potentially negotiable proposal—the build-down package—the NATO missile deployments were only weeks away.

Allied pressure played both a positive and negative role in the INF talks. Without strong pressure from within NATO (and the USA's concern for the unity of the alliance), the Reagan Administration might not have been brought to the conference table at all and, once there, might not have progressed from the zero option. The insistence of both Britain and France on excluding their nuclear forces from being counted in the INF talks (having earlier refused to see them explicitly counted in any way in SALT I or II) was a major obstacle in the way of a compromise agreement.[35] Richard Ullman argued that the Andropov offer to match SS-20s in the European theatre with British and French missiles could have been a basis for negotiations. According to Ullman: 'Only by regarding the British and French weapons as non existent could Western spokesmen characterize Andropov's proposed bargain as one that would leave the Soviets with 162 missiles . . . and the West with none'.[36] Although the USA's awareness of the security interests of its Asian allies and friends also impinged on the issue of global cuts in SS-20s and NATO missiles, both sides felt they had some flexibility to find ways around this problem. In the case of the START negotiations, allied influence appears to have been minimal.

With respect to the INF talks, alliance politics on both sides overlapped with strategic goals. The INF negotiations could be viewed simply as a screen for easing the politics of missile deployment. Certainly, there was a tendency in Washington to regard them in this way. For some in the Reagan Administration, deployment was a strategic objective; for others, it was a political objective. The Soviet Union, on the other hand, was clearly inclined to use the INF talks as part of a wider strategy of trying to prevent the deployment of the new missiles.[37] The Soviet Union's tactics at the INF negotiations could also be viewed as an attempt to get all US INF (including bombers) removed from Europe and as an element in a more general policy of trying to split the Alliance.[38] Although the Soviet Union may have hoped that European opposition might prevent missile deployment, by mid-1983, Moscow clearly could not rely on such an outcome. It is also plausible that the USSR regarded the INF negotiations as a forum in which to try for a reduction of USA's nuclear FBSs; the Soviet Union can scarcely have expected to secure total removal. The Soviet Union was certainly trying to influence West European attitudes in its INF negotiating tactics. What is much more questionable is whether the Soviet leadership really wanted to destabilize NATO or to remove all US military presence. The evidence from the MBFR negotiations (see Chapter 9) points to the contrary.

The early proposals put forward by both the USA and the USSR in the INF negotiations clearly demonstrated an interest in achieving unilateral strategic advantage under the guise of arms control negotiations. This emphasis ensured that the proposals were non-negotiable as they were presented, and subsequent formal changes were designed more for propaganda than as substantive concessions. There was, however, rather more indication of flexibility on the Soviet side, which by late 1983 was offering quite substantial reductions in SS-20s. The tendency to seek major cuts in Soviet forces was not merely a tactic on the US side, but inherent in the philosophy of many in the Reagan Administration. To the Reagan Administration, deep cuts in arms control terms meant primarily deep cuts in the Soviet arsenal. This view, especially evident in the START proposals, was made explicit by General Rowny, the chief START negotiator. Rowny is reported to have told Victor Karpov, his Soviet counterpart, that the USA was obliged to seek reductions in Soviet forces at the same time as it ensured modernization of its own. Karpov is said to have replied that this comment was 'revealing of the essence of the American position'[39] The initial Soviet proposals in the START negotiations were not inherently unreasonable and were based on SALT II. Although some totally one-sided requirements were tacked on, they were almost certainly designed for bargaining purposes.

Both the INF and the START negotiations amply illustrated the obstacles that arise from a search for parity in a context of strategic asymmetry. The INF disputes concerning the balance of forces involved such problems as what to count, how to weigh the different weapons against each other and the determination of the exact geographical area in which a balance was sought. Some of the difficulties revolved around the question of whether land-based SS-20s were comparable to sea-based British and French missiles, how a cruise missile could be compared with a ballistic missile and how missiles compare with bombers. Despite the fact that NATO seemed genuinely to perceive the Soviet Union as having nuclear superiority in the European theatre, this perception was expressed in terms of misleading statistics and statements. The prominence accorded to the SS-20 threat was partly a product of politics.

The Soviet Union's claim that a balance in European INF already existed was disingenuous. The USSR maintained this claim between 1979 and 1982 while it deployed increasing numbers of SS-20s. The Soviet Union's own military anxieties, however, were genuinely felt and not unreasonable. Problems about the degree of threat posed by bombers and cruise missiles (areas in which the USA was technologically superior) also plagued the START negotiations. Furthermore, the familiar SALT asymmetries of the Soviet concentration on land-based missile forces and heavier throw-weight reappeared in the START discussions and prompted the Reagan Administration to propose what amounted to a basic restructuring of Soviet forces. The Congress-initiated build-down proposal attempted to take account of all these force asymmetries through a variety of formulas which—although intended to promote parity—also served to confuse a simple idea.[40]

The problem of achieving parity is exacerbated by the fact that modernization and deployment programmes follow timetables that are usually not in harmony with negotiations. This is one reason why the USA rejected Brezhnev's proposal for a freeze at the beginning of the START negotiations. Furthermore, trading weapons already deployed against weapons still being tested is also likely to appear as an inequitable exchange, as the Soviet response to the zero option proposal in the INF negotiations made clear.

The difficulties inherent in the attainment of parity or equity in arms control are greatly exacerbated by an attempt to achieve major reductions.[41] Marginal inequalities become strategically much more significant at reduced levels of arms and, therefore, are likely to be contested more fiercely. This has been one of the elements in the case for replacing disarmament with arms control, in which a stable military balance is given a higher priority than weapon reductions. Thus, Reagan's proposals for deep cuts were likely to be difficult to negotiate even if they had been more equitable.

Ideological and psychological obstacles

The Reagan Administration's revival of the ideological conflict between the USA and the USSR was reflected both in a series of highly polemical speeches and in the dominant attitudes among key Administration officials. The Soviet Union was portrayed as a totalitarian enemy, ruthless in its intentions and committed to a policy of deceit. Any concessions, particularly in the area of arms control, constituted appeasement. These attitudes were coupled with the belief that the Soviet Union would inevitably cheat in any arms control agreement, and the Administration quickly made a major issue of ensuring compliance with past treaties and publicized allegations of violations, while reserving the right to abandon treaties that conflicted with military programmes. In practice, Reagan Administration policy was modified by normal bureaucratic processes, in particular through the role of the State Department, and was susceptible to pressure from European allies and later from the Congress, and reflected a diversity of views. Nevertheless, even after the Administration had moderated its views on abandoning SALT II and had been prompted to begin new negotiations, the USA's arms control policy was still marked by a deep ideologically based distrust of the Soviet Union. This distrust was manifested, in part, by an even greater emphasis than usual on verification. For example, with respect to the START negotiations Washington engaged in prolonged debate on how to limit the Soviet Union's missile inventories, and how to verify that there were no excess stocks by on-site inspection.[42]

The Soviet Union responded sharply to the Administration's attacks and to the allegations of Soviet cheating, and compiled its own list of alleged US violations. Despite the increase in the intensity of the rhetoric, the USSR does not appear to have abandoned its policy goals of the 1970s which sought to retain a co-operative, as well as a competitive, great power relationship with the United States and to ensure nuclear stability through arms control. Most Western commentators agree that ideology has played a decreasing role in shaping the Soviet Union's goals and perceptions in international affairs. The Soviet Union's reactions to Reaganism reflected more an expression of national pride and a long-standing tendency for Soviet defensiveness to Western criticisms than a renewed ideological purism. The new Administration's attitudes and policies clearly fostered Soviet suspicion and scepticism about the sincerity of US arms control efforts. These reactions were well founded in political reality and were shared by many in the West. Although there were other considerations in both cases, an exaggerated suspicion in Moscow probably influenced the Soviet Union's reactions to the only two serious efforts made by the US side to move towards an agreement—the Nitze *démarche* to Kvitsinsky and the Congress-inspired build-down proposal in the START negotiations. Of the two actions, suspicion probably played a more significant role in the refusal by the USSR to seriously consider the build-down offer. At the end of September 1983, a representative of the Institute of the USA and Canada Studies in Moscow informed Duffy that any further US proposals 'must be suspected of having hidden motive . . . perhaps some pre-election calculation or some domestic purpose'.[43]

Technological momentum

The most dramatic technological development, which took on major political significance in 1983, was the evolution of ABM technologies. In his speech outlining the SDI programme in March 1983, President Reagan gave political prominence to the potentialities of 'star wars' technology. Although Reagan envisaged the creation of a space-based defensive shield which could intercept all incoming missiles, the President's strategic and scientific advisers thought in terms of an ABM defence for land-based missiles such as the vulnerable MX. A programme of field testing and development of new ABM technologies would, in the view of most arms control experts, violate the terms of the 1972 ABM Treaty. In a speech to the Soviet START delegation at Geneva, General Rowny seemed to indicate that this was the Administration's intention and implied that US honouring of the ABM Treaty would be dependent on progress in START.[44]

The new US ABM programme, dubbed the Strategic Defense Initiative or SDI, had obvious implications for the START negotiations. The SDI programme threatened to fuel a further destabilizing arms race in space and to spark an intensified competition to produce enough offensive missiles so as to ensure saturation and penetration of any space-based shield. Because the Soviet Union valued the 1972 ABM Treaty, the USSR was likely to view the USA's renewed commitment to pursue ABM defences with alarm and suspicion. So, clearly the introduction of the SDI programme did not help the START negotiations, although the full extent to which the programme was an obstacle to strategic arms control did not become apparent until the USSR resumed missile negotiations at Geneva in 1985.

Evidence that the Soviet Union appeared to be developing a new solid-fuelled mobile ICBM increased the USA's anxieties during 1983. This development, if confirmed, constituted an apparent violation of the SALT II prohibition on the development of more than one new ICBM. Because the Soviet Union was ahead in development of mobile missiles (the US Midgetman missile was still in the research stage), the US military could claim increased cause for alarm concerning a 'window of vulnerability' for the USA's ICBM force and a greater incentive to develop ABM missile defences. Although many doubt that the 'window' exists (because the USSR could not destroy sea-based forces), the concept has carried considerable weight in Pentagon politics. On the other hand, evidence that the Soviet Union was also considering the development of mobile ICBMs encouraged those who thought that strategic stability would be enhanced by a shift away from a reliance upon heavy MIRVed ICBMs to the development of smaller and less vulnerable missiles. Whether or not this theory, then fashionable in sectors of Congress and the Administration, was really conducive to satisfactory arms control is debatable.

Domestic obstacles to arms control

Among Reagan Administration officials, those in charge of the DOD were especially hostile to arms control. This opposition has already been underscored and need not be reiterated here. Nevertheless, it is interesting to examine the position of the JCS, which emerged as the group most inclined to cause difficulties throughout SALT II negotiations. The members of the JCS who were in office at the time Reagan assumed the presidency were, in contrast, comparatively soft on arms control in the eyes of their new political masters. After all, this was the JCS which had testified in favour of ratifying SALT II. If Talbott's account is accurate, the views of the JCS were overridden by Perle in an extraordinarily high-handed manner. It is also worth noting that those who counted as comparative doves in the Administration—such as Alexander Haig and his deputy Richard Burt—were distinctly hawkish toward the Soviet Union and on the relationship between defence and arms control.[45]

During the first Reagan Administration, the high turnover of personnel had rather mixed results on the balance of forces in conflicts over arms control. In June 1982, Secretary of State Haig resigned in frustration and was replaced by George Shultz. Shultz gave priority to problems in the Middle East, rather than to arms control, and was inclined to defer to Weinberger on disputed issues such as the importance of throw-weight. Kenneth Adelman replaced Eugene Rostow, who was asked to resign as head of ACDA in January 1983. Many observers, both in Europe and in the US Congress, viewed Adelman as a hardline opponent of arms control. After confirmation, Adelman tended to side with Perle. The appointments of Schultz and Adelman weakened support within the Reagan Administration for serious arms control negotiations.

In addition to the changes at the State Department and ACDA, there were also switches in the NSC staff, which had more ambiguous results. Although Reagan's first Assistant for National Security, Richard Allen, was suitably antagonistic to arms control, he was not intended to play the powerful role of previous Advisers. In fact, most of Allen's energies seem to have been diverted to fending off a federal investigation into his private transactions. At the end of 1981, Allen was replaced by William Clark, a Reagan crony from California who had no experience in foreign affairs. Nevertheless, Clark attempted to give the NSC a more dominant voice in arms control policy. Clark and his deputy, Robert McFarlane, helped to undermine the walk-in-the-woods package, but apparently left Perle and Burt to contend over the direction of INF policy. McFarlane, however, did take the initiative in getting the Administration off the hook concerning the MX missile issue by promoting the Scowcroft Commission. The result was a final victory for MX deployment and a purely cosmetic shift in the Administration's negotiating position. McFarlane's initiative was also an acknowledgement that there was bureaucratic deadlock within the Reagan Administration.

Although bureaucratic conflict, often resulting in long delays in reaching any decision, has always hampered arms control policy making in Washington, the chaos generated by bureaucratic in-fighting in the Reagan Administration was exceptional. Haig comments that the failure to delineate responsibilities 'liberated a cacophony of vested interests'.[46] Perhaps the closest parallel with the Reagan Administration was with policy making as practiced under Eisenhower. Like Reagan, Eisenhower also adopted a laissez-faire attitude to his presidential role. Reagan's inability and unwillingness to understand arms control issues or to intervene in the decision making process, coupled with his failure to grant real authority to someone to act on his behalf, ensured that either no decisions were reached or, if they were, they were the result of bureaucratic compromise or manœuvre. Reagan's interest apparently focused mainly on the public relations impact that would result when he was called on to announce a proposal.[47]

As opposed to the change of personnel and attitudes in Washington, continuity prevailed in Moscow. Little evidence is available to suggest that the bureaucratic structure for dealing with arms control policy in the USSR had altered. In Jerry Hough's assessment, an important result of the SALT process for the USSR had been 'the legitimization of civilian interest in strategic questions'.[48] Soviet diplomats and foreign policy analysts had studied US theories and proposals, and helped to formulate responses. Some of their views appeared in Soviet publications. Although this development may have altered the climate of ideas within which the Soviet leadership operated, it did not effectively reduce the professional and political weight of the military in decision making. Where Soviet scholars and commentators could have the most direct political influence was on the thinking of the General Secretary. Georgi Arbatov, Director of the Institute of USA and Canada Studies in Moscow, is usually credited with having had access to Brezhnev, and earlier had also worked for Andropov. Because Andropov had used a circle of reform-minded scholars as advisers while serving in earlier political posts within the Party, there was some Western speculation that he would as General Secretary be open to liberal ideas in both domestic and international affairs.[49] Although Andropov did take certain initiatives in both internal and international spheres, his time in power was too brief to arrive at a worthwhile assessment of his policies. The Andropov period—coinciding with the prelude to the NATO missile deployments in 1983 and witnessing the destruction of the South Korean airliner— was not propitious for an arms control agreement.

With respect to the walk-in-the-woods package, Brezhnev's ill health may have reduced the likelihood of a positive response in Moscow. Kvitsinsky was apparently relying on Brezhnev to overrule the anticipated objections from Defence Minister Ustinov.[50] Even so, if Brezhnev was interested in accepting the package as part of a deal for a summit meeting, then the lack of response from Washington was probably even more crucial. It is not necessary to search for special domestic obstacles to the acceptance of the walk-in-the-woods deal in Moscow. Strong political prestige and strategic reasons existed for the Soviet Union not to concede the deployment of the new NATO missiles. In 1982, there was still a good chance that European opposition would prevent the deployments in any case.

VI. Obstacles in the negotiating process

Both the INF and START negotiations raise a number of interesting issues concerning the actual conduct of negotiations. In 1981, the Reagan Administration came to power committed to the theory of negotiation from strength. This commitment resulted in a delay of the START negotiations while the USA built up its strategic arsenal. The decision to press ahead with the NATO missile deployments could also be viewed as a means of negotiating from comparative strength and illustrated the degree to which this approach can be potentially effective, as well as its substantial drawbacks for arms control. Although the Soviet Union had an incentive to negotiate, it also had an incentive to demonstrate that it would not bow to military pressure and would not make concessions under threat. Although the various Andropov offers to match SS-20s to the levels of British and French forces can be interpreted as a success for NATO's pursuit of INF deployment, dominant governing and strategic circles in the West did not view Andropov's concessions in this way.[51] NATO's initiation of missile deployment ensured that the USSR would, at least in the short-term, withdraw from the INF negotiations. In the USA, there was also a lack of agreement as to whether deployment was essential to consolidate a stronger US position, or whether some or all of the missiles were merely bargaining chips to be traded away as part of an agreement. When the Carter Administration decided on the total of 572 missiles, Brzezinski believed that the number might be reduced through arms control bargaining.[52]

The Soviet Union's buildup of SS-20s between December 1979 and 1983 could be viewed as its own form of negotiating from strength, especially considering that the Soviet leadership, simultaneously with its own buildup, was insisting that no NATO deployments could be tolerated. The Soviet Union has not, however, openly endorsed this theory. The Soviet strategy actually appears closer to a bargaining chip approach.[53] For example, the Soviet Union is believed to have deferred dismantling some of its SS-4s and SS-5s, and to have accelerated its SS-20 deployment. Moreover, Brezhnev's 1979 offer to reduce medium-range missiles, together with Andropov's later offers to reduce SS-20s, indicates a willingness to bargain some of the missiles away. Nevertheless, the psychological and political effects of the SS-20 buildup figured prominently in the NATO's official rationale deployment and served to strengthen the case that the USSR was cynical about the INF negotiations.

One of the artificial requirements usually posed by the logic of arms control negotiations is the search for exact parity. Even if exact parity does not reflect real strategic needs or promote a stable balance, this parity is sought partly in order to make the agreement seem simple and equitable to a public audience.[54] One of the effects of the INF negotiations was to alter the purpose of the 1979

NATO decision. The Western INF negotiating position assumed that there should be parity between NATO and Soviet INF. The 1979 NATO decision, however, had deliberately avoided parity so as not to create a balance in Europe, which might be seen as decoupling US strategic forces from Europe.[55] As previously discussed, the search for exact parity accentuates the difficulty of making allowances for strategic asymmetries. The exact parity requirement, imposed on SALT negotiations after 1972 by Senator Jackson, was used by the USA in the START negotiations to produce superficial parity which actually masked great inequalities.

The conflicts over arms control policy, coupled with the inadequacy of decision making mechanisms in Washington, resulted in long delays in providing instructions for the negotiating teams. Another, less obvious, disadvantage in the first Reagan Administration was the absence of a senior figure who had presidential support to pursue behind-the-scenes soundings with Ambassador Dobrynin in Washington, or to discuss arms control with Gromyko or other Soviet leaders in Moscow. Although Kissinger's back channel created problems, it did provide a means of sounding out Soviet intentions informally and of floating ideas. Further, Kissinger's back channel could bypass the bureaucracies in both capitals. In the Carter Administration, Cyrus Vance and Paul Warnke had managed to use these channels without creating undue problems for their Geneva delegation. In the Reagan Administration, Nitze felt he had to open his own back channel talks; but, despite his personal authority and distinction, he still did not carry enough weight in Washington to implement it successfully. The existence of a back channel might also have made Moscow more willing to take the build-down proposals in the START negotiations more seriously.

The experience of the INF and START negotiations also raises interesting questions about the importance of the personalities of individual negotiators. The heads of US delegations to the negotiations examined thus far have either been high-ranking political appointees to ACDA (Smith and Warnke) or experienced US diplomats. The exception is Herbert York, who brought extensive relevant scientific experience and a genuine commitment to the CTB negotiations. Reagan took considerable pains to appoint heads of delegations who had been critical of recent US arms control policy. Until the walk-in-the-woods package was revealed, many commentators were dubious whether Nitze, in view of his attitude towards the Soviet Union, would promote a negotiable agreement.[56] However, in the case of Nitze, Reagan chose a negotiator with experience in successfully working out the detail of SALT I. Furthermore, Nitze enjoyed the respect of both the European governments and his Soviet counterparts, and possessed the personal goal of achieving an agreement he believed to be in the US interest.[57] In the appointment of General Rowny, Reagan chose an individual with a reputation for having created difficulties on the SALT II delegation and who was characterized by his lack of diplomatic skills. Rowny, who was openly disliked by his Soviet counterparts, seems to have alienated most of his own delegation and was distrusted among congressmen anxious for arms control. In 1983, Reagan was urged to remove Rowny from the START delegation in order to symbolize a commitment to progress. Reagan, however, refused to dismiss Rowny. The General provided a symbol to Reagan's right-wing constituency that the Administration had not gone soft on arms control. As a result, the build-down coalition insisted on the basically unworkable device of putting in their own negotiator alongside Rowny. The appointment of Rowny did not damage START negotiations in the sense of upsetting a serious dialogue, because, with the possible exception of the build-down initiative, there was never anything to wreck. Rowny's appointment, however, did remove the possibility of useful informal soundings or hints, or of the Geneva delegation playing a constructive role in Washington policy making. To head the START delegation, the Soviet Union had appointed Victor Karpov, a former deputy head and, from 1978, the leader of the Soviet SALT delegation. With the appointment of Karpov, the Soviet Union underscored a continuity with the previous SALT negotiations and suggested a potential willingness to take the START negotiations seriously. The appointment of Kvitsinsky as the leader of the INF delegation also indicated the importance of the INF talks to the Soviet Union.

Negotiations can be influenced both by the way they are conducted and by their frame of reference. The INF and START negotiations have been cited as illustrating the disadvantages of essentially bargaining in public. Public bargaining not only encourages propaganda moves and proposals that are formulated with misleading simplicity and embody spurious parity, but also often promotes rigidity within the negotiations.[58] However, the real problem of the INF and START negotiations was not the openness with which the talks were conducted, but the propagandistic intent of the heads of government and the basic unwillingness to make genuine concessions. Most commentators agree that the negotiations were badly handled; in addition, many argue that the negotiations might have been more fruitful if they had been merged.[59] The distinction between strategic and theatre forces—the case for separating START and INF—is by no means clear cut, as the nuclear FBS issue in the SALT negotiations amply demonstrated. In addition, technological development has created such grey area weapons as cruise missiles which may fulfil either strategic or theatre roles. It is also argued that by combining the forces it is easier to make allowances for strategic asymmetries and to design more flexible trade-offs than is the case when the focus is only on one category of forces. Those who resisted proposals to merge the two sets of negotiations feared that, in practice, the talks would become so complex that the possibility of agreement would recede even further. By running the two negotiations more or less concurrently, the main political interest became focused on the INF talks; and the lack of progress in the START negotiations can be explained, at least partly, because both sides neglected the strategic talks.[60] Nevertheless, the disadvantages of conducting negotiations in two separate forums would later become an asset when the talks resumed in 1985.

Promoting the arms race

A powerful case can be made that the end result of the first stage of INF negotiations was, in the short run, to increase the total number of nuclear weapons deployed in Europe and to enhance political tensions. Although the political pressures generated by the negotiations were closely connected with the politics of deployment, the propaganda requirements of INF encouraged oversimplification of the strategic issues in Europe, such as by equating SS-20 deployments and the new NATO missiles through the zero option. In NATO, the desire to demonstrate the political will and unity of the alliance was linked to claims that the commitment to deploy was necessary for success in the negotiations. The figure of 572 NATO missiles, set high for bargaining purposes, was translated into an essential minimum deployment failing the conclusion of an INF agreement. Although the counter-productive impact of INF would have been less strong if the negotiations had not been so closely tied to deployment, the NATO deployment would probably not have occurred without the talks. The promise of arms control negotiations had persuaded doubting European governments to authorize the new missiles. After the INF negotiations had broken down, Helmut Schmidt commented that he had hoped that the missile deployments would be unnecessary.[61] The INF talks also played a role in defusing anxious public opinion in Western Europe.

The Soviet Union's decisions on missile deployment were strongly influenced by the threat of the NATO deployments and were a means of increasing its bargaining power in the INF negotiations. While there was still some prospect of reaching a compromise in the talks, the Soviet Union is believed to have retained some of the SS-4s and SS-5s due to be dismantled, and to have continued with the rapid deployment of SS-20s.[62] When the negotiations collapsed, these missiles were in place. In addition, the Soviet Union then committed itself to deploy new shorter-range missiles in the GDR and Czechoslovakia. Thus, the immediate outcome was a higher Soviet deployment than might otherwise have been implemented, although one could argue that the Soviet military seized on a useful rationale to legitimize deployments which were already planned.

The breakdown of the INF negotiations also led to an increase in political tension and to recriminations between the two sides. The Soviet Union was bitter at the USA's refusal to postpone deployment or to seek a compromise agreement, and the West blamed the USSR for walking out of the talks. From the end of 1983 and throughout 1984, relations between the USA and USSR had deteriorated to their lowest level since the most extreme period of the cold war.

Up until 1983, the INF negotiations demonstrated how a combination of negotiating from strength and the use of bargaining chips can lead, not to an agreement to reduce weapons, but to the actual deployment of more arms. Whether this result was inevitable from the time the 1979 NATO decision was taken is less clear. Conceivably, a different US administration could have concluded an agreement that curbed SS-20 deployment and avoided the deployment of some, or all, of the NATO missiles. The military and political logic of the NATO decision, coupled with the development of the GLCMs and the Pershing II missiles, however, ensured there would be pressure to deploy at least some of them.

The START negotiations were not directly linked to any particular military programme, but the Reagan Administration did employ the familiar tactic of using the talks as a means of convincing a reluctant Congress to authorize expenditure on controversial weapons. Some Administration officials insisted on the importance of weapon modernization as a goal in and of itself, and were unwilling to consider the implementation of a bargaining chip strategy. Haig, however, argued for the modernization programme on the basis that it would provide a necessary incentive for the Soviet Union to negotiate in earnest.[63] By 1983, the case for deploying MX was based partly on the claim that it was a necessary bargaining chip in the START negotiations.[64] Talbott, pointing to the Scowcroft Commission and the build-down proposals, has argued that the Administration, by stressing the link between weapon programmes and arms control, was obliged in the end to accept congressional intervention in arms control as the price of getting its strategic programme.[65] While there is some validity to Talbott's observation, the solid achievement of the Scowcroft Commission was to legitimize a limited MX deployment and the development of the new Midgetman missile. The Commission's immediate impact on the START negotiations was a public relations shift in the US position. Although the build-down proposals were a substantive initiative, they resulted in failure nevertheless. Despite limiting total warheads, build-down set a premium on strategic modernization; whether or not build-down constituted inherently a desirable arms control measure has been the subject of dispute.[66] Throughout the START negotiations, the US side proceeded from the assumption that the talks would channel, not prevent, modernization. Therefore, the START negotiations would not serve to promote qualitative arms control.

VI. Conclusion

If we search for a central reason why the INF and START negotiations collapsed in 1983, an obvious explanation is that progress in arms control depends on a degree of *détente* between the great powers. Therefore, the steadily deteriorating relations between the USSR and the USA from the late 1970s guaranteed that the negotiations would be fruitless. The political and economic incentives to seek agreement on arms control that existed in the early 1970s were absent, and the intensification of ideological conflict and mutual suspicion created even further barriers. The high propaganda content in the proposals made by both sides and the politicization of the negotiating process reflected the hostilities of the new cold war. Nevertheless, despite the further crises in East–West relations in 1981 and 1982 which resulted from the suppression of Solidarity and the South Korean airliner incident, the negotiations do not seem to have suffered from direct linkage. To the contrary, the evidence suggests that the primary problems lay not in the international climate, but in the specific policies and attitudes of the US and Soviet governments.

Because the major change of policy occurred in Washington, a powerful case can be made that the primary responsibility for the failure of the first stage of the negotiations rested with the Reagan Administration. The Administration was unabashedly committed to building up military superiority before negotiating seriously on arms control, entered the negotiations unwillingly and displayed no genuine interest in concluding an agreement. The Administration never had a coherent or unified policy, and the opponents of arms control were strong enough to block any attempts at compromise. In general, the views of the President and his right-wing supporters in the Republican Party were in tune with those of the opponents to arms control. Thus, based on this interpretation, Moscow's intransigence may have been primarily reactive.

Although the major responsibility for the failure to achieve progress in the START negotiations can be convincingly attributed to the Reagan Administration, assessing the blame for the collapse of the first stage of the INF talks is somewhat more complicated. In this case, the Administration inherited the 1979 NATO decision with its inherent contradiction resulting from an attempt to promote new missile deployments simultaneously with negotiations to restrict missiles. Moreover, the Soviet Union clearly viewed its participation in the INF talks as part of a wider political game to prevent deployment. Because of its public statements, the Soviet Union backed into the position where it had to walk out of the negotiations once the NATO deployments began. So, the blame for the breakdown of the INF negotiations in 1983 rests partly with the USSR. Still, it is abundantly clear that Reagan's zero-option proposal was devised purely for propaganda purposes at the time; as a whole, the Administration was committed to beginning the missile deployments by the agreed date and not to concluding an INF agreement.

Whether or not the decision to press ahead with NATO's missile deployments was a disastrous illustration of how bargaining chips get converted into new arms, or whether NATO plans for such deployment were a necessary lever to promote Soviet interest in negotiations, was a hotly contested issue in 1983. Indeed, whether or not the 1987 INF Treaty was due to NATO deployments, and thus a vindication of the policy of 'arming to disarm', remains a highly debatable question (see chapter 8).

The course of the INF and START negotiations up until the collapse in 1983, however, demonstrates one positive fact: namely, the strength and continuity of the pressures that now exist for arms control. However bad one judges the management of arms control to be in the first Reagan Administration, because of opposition to arms control in principle and of bureaucratic muddle, it is remarkable that the Administration ever went to the conference table at all. It did so only because of West European and congressional pressures, together with the force of US domestic opinion. Still, the record of the first stage of the negotiations indicates that pressure from popular movements or from Congress can only persuade US Administrations to begin talks. Such pressure cannot make a reluctant Administration genuinely seek an agreement. A powerful case can be made that, during Reagan's first term, arms control negotiations served to screen, and not to restrict, an arms buildup.

Notes and references

[1] Lunn, S., 'Cruise missiles and the prospects for arms control', *ADIU Report,* vol. 3, no. 5 (Sep.–Oct. 1981), pp. 1–4 goes into some detail on INF modernization and the bases of the 1979 NATO decision.

[2] Arbatov, G., *Cold War or Detente? The Soviet Viewpoint* (Zed Books: London, 1983), p. 135 gives a brief semi-official statement of Soviet attitudes to strategic reductions.

[3] Garthoff, R. L., 'Brezhnev's opening: the INF tangle', *Foreign Policy,* no. 41 (winter 1980–81), pp. 82–83, discusses Brezhnev's speech and proposed unilateral initiative.

[4] Brzezinski, Z., *Power and Principle: Memoirs of the National Security Adviser 1977–81* (Weidenfeld and Nicolson: London, 1983), pp. 290–310, sets out his views. See also Talbott, S., Deadly Gambits: The Reagan Administration and the Stalemate in Nuclear Arms Control (Pan Books: London, 1985), pp. 178–79 on Weinberger's and Perle's views.

[5] Neidle, A. F. (ed.), *Nuclear Negotiations: Reassessing Arms Control Goals in US Soviet Relations* (University of Austin: Texas, 1982), pp. 57–58 gives Warnke's comments.

[6] Talbott (note 4), p. 159.

[7] Sharp, J. M. O., 'Four approaches to an INF agreement', *Arms Control Today,* vol. 12, no. 3 (Mar. 1982), p. 2 produces tables of US and Soviet figures based on material in the *New York Times,* 30 Nov. 1981 and on interviews in Geneva.

[8] Garthoff (note 3) analyses the Soviet view. Arbatov (note 2), p. 137 puts the Soviet case briefly.

[9] Freedman, L., 'Nuclear arms control', *The Nuclear Debate: Issues and Politics,* ed. P. Williams (Routledge and Keegan Paul: London, 1984), pp. 38–46, gives a forceful analysis of how Soviet figures, especially on aircraft, were juggled.

[10] Garthoff speaking in Neidle (note 5), pp. 44–47 gives a succinct comment on the Soviet view of the new deployments in a total strategic context.

[11] Jones, C., 'The Soviet view of INF', *Arms Control Today,* vol. 12, no 3 (Mar. 1982), p. 4.

[12] Talbott (note 4), pp. 85 and 109.

[13] Talbott (note 4), pp. 103–4.

[14] The Statement of Intention was publicized by TASS. Details of the Treaty are in Talbott (note 4), pp. 110–11.

[15] The elements of the package were widely publicized early in 1983. For an inside account see Talbott (note 4), pp. 118–30.

[16] Talbott (note 4), pp. 118–19 notes Perle's denial. Press accounts early in 1983 and Talbott assigned Perle the responsibility for having the package turned down.

[17] Talbott (note 4), pp. 148 and 186.

[18] Borawski, J., 'INF round IV', *Arms Control Today,* vol. 13, no. 2 (Mar. 1983), p. 4 notes Warnke's suggestion of 16 Sep. 1982 that all intermediate-range missiles should be counted, and the proposal for a Soviet reduction of its missiles and warheads to match approximately British and French missiles in return for cancellation of NATO deployments.

[19] Talbott (note 4), pp. 200–5 on 'the walk in the park'.

[20] US ACDA, *1983 Annual Report,* 23rd Annual Report of ACDA, 98th Congress, 2nd Session (Joint Committee Print: Washington, DC, 1984), p. 26. The Report says that the package was studied in Washington and that '[T]here was concern both about certain substantive elements' and about the Soviet Union treating it as a new offer open to further

amendment. It then adds: '[H]owever, Ambassador Nitze was authorized to continue conversations in the informal channel'. The next paragraph covers the Soviet rejection.

[21] Klinger, G. and Scoville, H., Jr, 'The politics and strategy of START ', *Arms Control Today*, vol. 12, no. 7 (July–Aug. 1982), p. 4–5.

[22] Haig, A., *Caveat: Realism, Reagan and Foreign Policy* (Weidenfeld and Nicolson: London, 1984), p. 223.

[23] See *New York Times*, 16 Oct. 1983 (excerpted in *Bulletin of the Atomic Scientists*, vol. 39, no. 10 (Dec. 1983), p. 28).

[24] Talbott (note 4), pp. 233–71.

[25] US ACDA (note 20), pp. 6–16 gives a summary of the US negotiating positions in 1983, including the role of the Scowcroft Commission. For detailed behind-the-scenes politics see Talbott, pp. 300–14, 330–42.

[26] Talbott (note 4), pp. 280–81 and 326.

[27] Duffy, G., 'Have the Soviets "written off" Arms Control?' *Arms Control Today*, vol. 13, no. 10 (Nov. 1983), pp. 8–9.

[28] Talbott (note 4), pp. 105 and 182.

[29] Talbott (note 4), pp. 181, 194 and 197–99.

[30] Survival, vol. 24, no. 5 (Sep.–Oct. 1982), pp. 229–32 gives extracts from Reagan's Eureka address and Brezhnev's freeze proposal.

[31] Talbott (note 4), p. 47.

[32] Talbott (note 4), p. 233.

[33] Krepon, M., 'SALT II: a retrospective look', *Arms Control Today*, vol. 13, no. 2 (Mar. 1983), p. 7. He notes: 'Today, the Reagan Administration is, by its own account, negotiating earnestly with the Russians in four separate forums, while events in Africa, Cuba and Afghanistan continue as before. One must now add the imposition of martial law in Poland to the list.'

[34] Talbott (note 4), p. 294.

[35] Grove, E. J., 'Allied nuclear forces complicate negotiations', *Bulletin of the Atomic Scientists*, vol. 42, no. 6 (June–July 1986), pp. 18–22.

[36] Ullman, R. H., 'Out of the Euromissile mire', *Foreign Policy*, no. 50 (spring 1983), p. 39–40.

[37] Treverton, G. F., 'Intermediate nuclear force negotiations: issues and alternatives', *Nuclear Weapons in Europe: Modernization and Limitation*, ed. O. M. McGraw and J. D. Porro (D.C. Heath: Lexington, Mass., 1983), pp. 94–95.

[38] See Freedman (note 9) for first interpretation. Haig (note 22), p. 226 sees Soviet statements after the December 1979 decisions as an attempt to use the opportunity of disturbing West European, especially West German, political stability and so of weakening NATO.

[39] Talbott (note 4), p. 280.

[40] Frye, A., 'Strategic build-down: a context for restraint', *Foreign Affairs*, vol. 62, no. 2 (winter 1983–84), pp. 293–317 gives a clear and authoritative interpretation of the build-down proposal. Freedman (note 9) complains about the complexity of the final proposal.

[41] Krepon, M., 'Reagan's approach: START off from the beginning', *Arms Control Today*, vol. 11, no. 9 (Oct. 1981), pp. 1–2 and 5 gives a good summary of the problems in the START context.

[42] Talbott (note 4), pp. 288–92.

[43] Duffy (note 27), p. 8.

[44] Talbott (note 4), p. 319. For detailed analysis of implications of SDI for the ABM Treaty, see: Stützle, W., Jasani, B. and Cowen, R., *The ABM Treaty: To Defend or Not to Defend*, SIPRI (Oxford University Press: Oxford, 1987), pp. 105–35.

[45] Haig's attitudes emerge clearly from his memoirs (note 22). See also Burt, R., 'Defense policy and arms control: defining the problem', *Arms Control and Defense Postures in the 1980s*, ed. R. Burt (Westview Press: Boulder, Colo., 1982).

[46] Haig (note 22), p. 233.

[47] Bundy, M., 'Some thought about unilateral moderation', *Arms Control and International Security*, ed. R. Kolkowicz and N. Joeck (Westview Press: Boulder, Colo., 1984), p. 16. Bundy comments: '[S]uch leadership as the President has exercised has been for the purpose of

ensuring opening positions that meet immediate political requirements. There is no sign whatever of any intent to take operational leadership in the process of negotiations'.

[48] J. F. Hough, 'The Soviet view of the strategic situation', in Kolkowicz and Joeck (note 47), p. 96.

[49] Hough (note 48) indicates this argument briefly. See also: Rush, M., Meissners, A., Brown, A. and Simes, D., 'The Andropov accession', *Problems of Communism*, vol. 32, no. 1 (Jan. – Feb. 1983).

[50] Talbott (note 4), p. 149.

[51] Ullman (note 36), p. 39.

[52] Brzezinski (note 4), p. 308. He also thought the USA might be asked by NATO to reduce the numbers.

[53] See Sabin, P., 'Should INF and START be merged? A historical perspective', *International Affairs,* vol. 60, no. 3 (summer 1984), p. 421 and Sharp, J. M. O., 'A perspective', *Bulletin of the Atomic Scientists,* vol. 39, no. 10 (Dec. 1983), pp. 12–13.

[54] Freedman, L., 'Negotiations on nuclear forces', *Bulletin of the Atomic Scientists,* vol. 39, no. 10 (Dec. 1983), p. 27 comments on 'the dead hand of parity' in arms control talks.

[55] Garthoff, R. L., 'Postmortem on INF talks', *Bulletin of the Atomic Scientists,* vol. 40, no. 10 (Dec. 1984), p. 9.

[56] See for example Bundy (note 47), p. 16. He notes: '[V]ery few disinterested observers would pick Eugene Rostow, Paul Nitze and Edward Rowny as the men most likely to work toward a sound compromise with Moscow' and adds that despite Nitze's experience he operated with a worst-case analysis of Soviet intentions.

[57] Talbott (note 4), p. 54. On contrast between Nitze and Rowny see also Krepon, M., *Strategic Stalemate: Nuclear Weapons and Arms Control in American Politics* (Macmillan: London, 1984), p. 92.

[58] Freedman (note 54), p. 26.

[59] For example Lodgaard, S., 'The dual-track decision and breakdown in Geneva', paper delivered at the seminar on *Euromissiles y Pacifismo*, Segovia, Spain, 1984 (31 May–2 June), p. 10. Sabin (note 53) looks at the case for a merger and the problems.

[60] Freedman (note 9), p. 38.

[61] Garthoff (note 55), p. 7 notes that Schmidt had recently said that he had hoped deployment would never become necessary.

[62] See Sabin (note 53) and Sharp (note 53).

[63] Talbott (note 4), pp. 275–76.

[64] Talbott (note 4), pp. 301–2.

[65] Talbott (note 4), pp. 243, 276 and 302.

[66] Paine, C., 'Breakdown on the build-down', *Bulletin of the Atomic Scientists,* vol. 39, no. 10 (Dec. 1983), pp. 4–6.

8. INF and START: 1985–89

I. Introduction

The second stage of the missile talks which began in 1985 provide a striking contrast with the negotiations that collapsed in 1983. The second set of negotiations culminated in the signing of the INF Treaty: a significant agreement which mandated the destruction of the USA's and USSR's intermediate-range nuclear missiles. The Soviet Union accepted unprecedented measures of detailed on-site inspection, and the US Senate (which had failed to ratify SALT II) ratified the Treaty in time for the Moscow summit meeting between Reagan and Gorbachev in 1988. Progress toward a START agreement, however, proved to be slower in coming, despite optimistic predictions by political leaders on both sides that a Treaty might be signed in Moscow. However, by 1988 an eventual agreement on a 50 per cent reduction in strategic nuclear forces did appear to be a realistic goal. This was certainly not the case in 1983.

The successful conclusion of the INF portion of the second set of missile talks, therefore, served to vindicate the entire process of nuclear arms control negotiations which had been questioned in 1983. The division of the negotiations into separate INF and strategic discussions provoked criticism during the first stage, but proved to make excellent political, if not strategic, sense. Although the INF and START negotiations were conducted amid a good deal of publicity, this now helped, rather than hindered, progress (especially with respect to the INF talks). This chapter will examine the evolution of the negotiations within the context of the changing political environment in which they occurred. This chapter also seeks to explain the reasons for the comparative success of these negotiations, despite the continuing obstacles to arms control.

II. Brighter prospects for an INF treaty: 1985–87

In 1984, the relations between the USA and the USSR were at their lowest level since the original cold war. The USSR walked out of the missile talks to protest against NATO's deployment of Pershing II and GLCMs. Bilateral nuclear arms control negotiations appeared to be out of the question, although the Soviet Union—alarmed by SDI—urged talks on the demilitarization of space. Domestic factors in both countries made an immediate resumption of negotiations unlikely. President Reagan faced re-election in November 1984, and the USSR, of course, chose to wait for a new Administration. In Moscow, the Chernenko interregnum resulted in few initiatives either in domestic or foreign policy.

Reagan's landslide re-election created a new political context in the USA. The new Administration began to signal a much greater interest in arms control negotiations and in securing an agreement with the Soviet Union. In January 1985, the US and Soviet Foreign Ministers met and agreed to begin talks. The USA conceded that there should be negotiations on space weapons, and the USSR agreed to the US position that START and INF should be resumed despite continued NATO missile deployment.[1] Despite these promising signs, there was still no immediate evidence of a general conversion to arms control in the second Reagan Administration. The Administration refused to consider the possibility a comprehensive test ban and pressed for high funding for the SDI programme. The Administration was determined to test new SDI technology, even at the cost of 're-interpreting' the ABM Treaty, and indicated in May 1986 that the USA would no longer observe the SALT II limits. Administration officials, in particular Defense Secretary Caspar Weinberger, continued to stress alleged Soviet violations of previous arms control treaties, and the Administration remained vehemently anti-communist and suspicious of the Soviet Union. Nevertheless, after re-election Reagan clearly wanted a place in history as a peace maker, as well as an exponent of US military power, and appeared to be genuinely alarmed about the dangers of nuclear weapons. He had also been under increasing pressure from a Democrat-controlled Congress which was unwilling to fund his ambitious military expansion and remained dubious about SDI. The State Department under George Shultz assisted in encouraging a new *détente* and promoting agreement.

Notwithstanding Reagan's apparent change of heart concerning arms control, an even more important change occurred in the Soviet Union in March 1985. The accession of Mikail Gorbachev to the top leadership post in the Soviet Union placed, for the first time in many years, the responsibility for policy making in the USSR in the hands of a relatively young and energetic leader. As General Secretary, Gorbachev rapidly demonstrated his commitment to economic and political reform at home, and the pursuit of a dynamic and innovative foreign policy abroad. Since March 1985, the Soviet Union has taken the initiative in arms control and, through a rapid succession of new proposals, forced the West to rethink its own position. Although one motive for Gorbachev's attempt to cut nuclear and conventional arms is the need to release more resources to invest in the Soviet domestic economy, Gorbachev's approach also suggests a broad commitment to disarmament and new political relations with the West.

The most dramatic and well publicized aspects of the new *détente* were the summit meetings between Gorbachev and Reagan. The first meeting at Geneva in November 1985 and the second at Reykjavik in October 1986 paved the way for progress on arms control and culminated in the signing of the INF Treaty at the Washington summit meeting in December 1987. These top-level and largely symbolic meetings, however, occurred within the context of the broader dialogue on arms control. On 12 March 1985, the two powers resumed arms control negotiations at Geneva under the title of the 'umbrella talks'. Within 10 days, however, the delegations divided into three working groups. Each group retained primary responsibility for a particular topics—intermediate-range missiles, strategic nuclear forces and space weapons. The Soviet Union ensured continuity by initially reassigning Viktor Karpov to head the START talks and Yuli Kvitsinsky to the INF negotiations. Alexei Obukov assumed responsibility for the Space Talks.[2] The USA, on the other hand, appointed a new slate of negotiators. Paul Nitze had been promoted to a special post in Washington to co-ordinate and advise on arms control policy, and General Rowny was moved to an honorific post as presidential advisor. Maynard Glitman, a career diplomat who had represented the USA at the MBFR talks, assumed responsibility for the INF negotiations, and John Tower, a former Republican Senator from Texas who had served as chairman of the Senate Armed Services Committee, replaced Rowny in the START talks. The overall head of the US delegation, who retained primary responsibility for the Space Talks, was Max Kampelman, a former Washington attorney who had led the US delegation to the Madrid CSCE in the late 1970s.[3]

The INF and START negotiations resumed with both sides initially taking up more or less the same positions as they had held in late 1983. This meant that both sides were still far from agreement. The disagreement concerning space weapons was even greater. The USSR advocated a total ban on use of force in space and a dismantling of existing anti-satellite weapons. This, together with a proposal for a moratorium on the development of new weapons, would halt the SDI programme. The USA, on the other hand, refused to consider any reduction in its SDI effort and argued the advantages of both sides acquiring defences against ballistic missiles. Whereas the USSR had made an agreement at the INF and START negotiations contingent on a space weapons ban, the USA wanted separate INF and START agreements and no general ban on space weapons. Given these very substantial differences in the negotiating positions between the two sides, the prospects for success in the negotiations seemed unlikely.

During the first two sessions between March and July, progress was indeed almost non-existent. The USSR announced a six-month suspension of its INF deployments and called for a freeze on the still far from complete NATO cruise missile deployments. Predictably, the USA refused the Soviet Union's request. During 1985, NATO was still pressuring a reluctant Government in the Netherlands to authorize the basing of cruise missiles in the country in 1988. NATO viewed the cruise missile deployments as an important bargaining counter and during the first session, both the USA and the USSR recited their set positions. When talks resumed on 30 May, the Soviet Union accused the United States of inflexibility, while President Reagan ordered his negotiators to wait for a Soviet initiative.[4] After the second session ended in July, Karpov stated that there had been no progress in the negotiations.[5]

During the third round, the USSR presented several comprehensive proposals, and the USA responded with a counter-proposal. The USA welcomed the Soviet proposal of a 50 per cent cut in strategic arsenals and the imposition of a limit of 6000 strategic nuclear warheads. This proposal was much closer to the US position, which emphasized deep cuts, than earlier Soviet offers had been. The USSR also recognized US concerns by proposing a maximum of 3600 warheads on ICBMs, although the USA wanted a lower total of 3000. The Soviet Union, however, still insisted on counting forward-based bombers, the Pershing II and GLCMs in the totals for US strategic forces. The Soviet proposals on space weapons suggested a possible concession on SDI by drawing a distinction between acceptable research on space weapons inside laboratories, and research and testing outside—which was unacceptable under terms of the ABM Treaty. The USA, however, continued to insist on unhampered research and the provision for some field testing for the SDI programme.

With respect to INF in particular, the USA and the USSR remained far apart concerning the details of their proposals. Although the Soviet Union still claimed the right to match the British and French nuclear forces, there remained, on the part of both the USA and the USSR, some potential bargaining flexibility in this area. Perhaps the most hopeful sign for a potential INF agreement was provided by Gorbachev's speech of 3 October in which he indicated that an INF agreement might be decoupled from agreements on START and on space weapons. Gorbachev also proposed talks with Britain and France concerning their nuclear weapons.[6]

The principal value of the 1985 Geneva summit meeting was that it symbolized the emergence of a new *détente*. Although the only specific agreements that were concluded as a prelude to the summit concerned such non-controversial issues as air safety over the North Pacific and closer co-operation on scientific and environmental matters, the summit meeting, nevertheless, marked a change in mood between the two sides and elicited a new sort of rhetoric from President Reagan. The two leaders committed themselves to pursue arms control negotiations vigorously, and called for an interim INF agreement.[7]

In a speech at the beginning of 1986, Gorbachev set the scene for further negotiations by proposing that all nuclear weapons should be dismantled, in three stages, by the end of the century. In the first stage, he called for a 50 per cent cut in US and Soviet strategic forces and the elimination of US and Soviet intermediate-range nuclear forces. With respect to the Geneva talks, perhaps the most important signal was the suggestion that British and French forces might be frozen in stage one. Thus, the USSR indicated that it would no longer insist on counting them in any INF agreement.[8] President Reagan, in a letter of reply sent in February, indicated that opponents of arms control had again become dominant in the Administration's policy making. In his letter, Reagan commented that most of the Gorbachev proposal was not immediately relevant and raised the issues of past Soviet non-compliance with treaties, regional problems and conventional force imbalances as obstacles to nuclear disarmament.

Reagan's letter, however, did indicate a willingness to press ahead with the conclusion of an INF agreement covering land-based missiles. The US delegation in Geneva proposed the elimination of all INF—in stages—in both Europe and elsewhere within three years. In addition, shorter-range INF (SRINF) would be frozen at existing levels of missiles. Because Soviet negotiating proposals had envisaged retaining at least some of their Asian-based SS-20s, the Soviet delegation was dismissive concerning the new US offer. This session of the Geneva negotiations, therefore, ended in deadlock.[9] Earlier, commentary in Moscow had criticized the Reagan letter for offering nothing new or positive, and Soviet officials were angry at such a belated response from the USA.[10] In the first months of 1986, the spirit of the Geneva summit meeting had dissipated on both sides.

Under circumstances of mutual hostility and recrimination, the delegations reconvened on 8 May 1986. The Soviet delegation attacked the USA for the bombing of Libya, and the US delegation responded with accusations concerning Soviet activities in Afghanistan. On 27 May, the Reagan Administration announced that the USA would cease observing the SALT II limits. Despite the generally acrimonious atmosphere, the USA did begin to develop verification requirements for an INF agreement in this session, and the USSR tabled a new START proposal before the negotiations ended in June. The new Soviet offer suggested a ceiling of 1600 strategic delivery vehicles for each side (on the basis of previous Soviet calculations, a 50 per cent cut would have left the USA slightly more but the USSR less) and a higher warhead limit of 8000. The proposal made some concessions to the USA by no longer counting forward-based systems (FBS)—although the offer stipulated that these weapons should be frozen at the current levels. The Soviet proposal abandoned a demand for a total ban on SLCMs with a range of over 600 km and permitted the deployment of submarine-launched cruise missiles. Still, the proposal excluded cruise missiles on surface ships.[11]

During the summer, both sides began to display greater flexibility with the aim of a summit meeting in December. In a July letter to General Secretary Gorbachev, President Reagan put forward a series of new proposals. Gorbachev, however, accelerated the pace of negotiations by persuading Reagan to accept an October summit meeting in Reykjavik. The summit was part of a deal to secure the release from the Soviet Union of Nicholas Daniloff, a US journalist whom the Soviet Union accused of being a spy. Western commentators observed that Reagan had been bounced into a summit meeting for which he was ill-prepared; and, indeed, Mr Gorbachev brought detailed proposals to Iceland to which the US delegation had to respond at short notice.[12]

The Reykjavik meeting came close to recommending dramatic measures of nuclear disarmament. Over a two day period, detailed bargaining resulted in provisional INF, START and space weapon agreements. On the second day, General Secretary Gorbachev agreed to a global reduction of INF to 100 missiles on each side—the Soviet missiles to be deployed in Asian areas of the USSR and the US missiles in the USA. He also offered a freeze on SRINF (defined as land-based missiles between 500 and 1000 km in range) at the January 1983 levels. Both sides clarified, in principle, the verification requirements to check such an agreement. Regarding strategic forces the two leaders accepted that there should be reductions over the next five years to 1600 delivery vehicles and 6000 warheads. The USSR excluded all FBS from this count and conceded the deployment of long-range ALCMs; the problem of SLCMs was deferred. Bombers and short-range ALCMs would count as only one delivery vehicle. President Reagan also apparently agreed to a proposal that both sides would continue to observe the ABM Treaty for a further period of 10 years and that all strategic ballistic missiles would be phased out over the same period.[13]

The Reykjavik negotiations collapsed in bitter recriminations when—despite being extended by an extra afternoon session—the USA insisted on maintaining its SDI research programme, and General Secretary Gorbachev linked all progress in missile reductions to a ban on SDI. In doing so, Gorbachev reinstated the linkage between INF and an agreement on space weapons that he had abandoned at the end of 1985. In the the course of subsequent polemics, and at a meeting of the two Foreign Ministers in Vienna in November 1985, Moscow and Washington produced differing interpretations of what had been agreed at Reykjavik. The USA denied that President Reagan had agreed to the goal of eliminating all nuclear weapons, while the USSR insisted that he had done so. There were also differences in the interpretation of what had been agreed concerning the reduction of ballistic missiles.[14]

The Reykjavik summit had widespread and revealing repercussions. Journalistic comment suggested that the goal of nuclear disarmament had general and instinctive popular appeal. Reactions in Washington, at the NATO headquarters in Brussels and in many West European capitals, however, displayed acute alarm at the prospect of significant measures of nuclear disarmament. Not only military and strategic opinion, but many politicians in the USA, expressed incredulity at the proposal to dismantle all ballistic missiles within 10 years, let alone the prospect of total nuclear disarmament. Military circles within NATO publicized grave reservations about the proposed INF agreement and ballistic missile ban, and governments in London, Paris and Bonn hastened to try to modify the terms of a possible INF agreement. Prime Minister Thatcher went to Washington to stress her opposition to a total elimination of ballistic missiles, which would press Britain to follow suit, and to assert her belief that total nuclear disarmament was an impossible and dangerous goal.[15]

Nevertheless, progress towards an INF agreement was rapid during 1987. In a speech on 28 February, Gorbachev once more severed the link between INF and a space treaty and suggested that an INF treaty could be concluded on the basis of understandings reached at Reykjavik. The US Government, which had displayed a willingness to move ahead on INF since the summit meeting, responded almost at once by proposing a draft treaty at Geneva on 4 March. This envisaged eliminating all intermediate-range missiles in Europe but retained the option of building up NATO SRINF missiles to the Soviet level.[16] With the major exception of Caspar Weinberger (who soon raised objections about verifying any SRINF settlement), the majority opinion in the Administration now favoured the conclusion of an INF agreement.[17] Many US analysts and politicians had always viewed the NATO INF deployments as politically, rather than militarily, significant; and a ban on intermediate-range missiles promised the President a dramatic success in arms control without impairing US security or favoured weapon programmes. Because Reagan was increasingly beleaguered by congressional investigations and revelations concerning the Iran–Contra scandal, a foreign policy success became correspondingly attractive. Furthermore, Gorbachev continued to demonstrate his own desire for an early agreement and offered further concessions.

III. Delays over the START negotiations

During 1987, there were no signs of similar progress toward a START agreement. Reagan's personal commitment to SDI, Weinberger's pressure for early deployment of SDI technologies by the mid-1990s, and the Administration's backing for a reinterpretation of the ABM Treaty to permit SDI testing, ruled out a space treaty acceptable to Moscow.[18] Nor was there any agreement on how to deal with anti-satellite (ASAT) weapons. The USA retreated from the Reykjavik goal of a ballistic missile ban within 10 years and proposed a draft START treaty at Geneva in May 1987 which envisaged 50 per cent cuts in strategic forces over seven years, with limits of 1600 delivery vehicles and 6000 warheads. Although the USA and the USSR still agreed on the totals, they now disagreed on the crucial question of sub-limits for ICBMs, SLBMs and bombers. Furthermore, although the USSR had hinted at some concessions on SDI research and testing, the Soviet delegation still linked START to restrictions on both.[19]

During the latter part of 1987, the energies of the two Foreign Ministers and their advisers were fully absorbed with ironing out the remaining problems on INF in time for the Washington summit meeting which was set for early December. Therefore, the START negotiations took a backseat to INF. In the euphoria surrounding the Washington summit meeting and the successful conclusion an INF Treaty, both parties promised rapid progress on START. Indeed, both Foreign Minister Shevernadze and Secretary of State Shultz continued to make some encouraging statements about the possibility of the conclusion of a START agreement by the time of the next summit meeting set for Moscow in early 1988. However, there were clear indications that no such agreement was possible in the time available. In February 1988, President Reagan said as much; and, in April, General Secretary Gorbachev complained of the USA 'marking time'.[20] The drafting and implementation of a START treaty poses problems of verification and of detail of an extremely formidable and complex nature. Despite an agreement in principle issued at the end of the Washington summit meeting, which included Soviet concessions on limiting the number of heavy missiles and their total throw-weight, numerous clauses in the Joint Draft Treaty text still had to be resolved.[21]

Significant issues were still at stake in the START negotiations in 1988, as comments both during and after the Moscow summit of 29 May to 2 June revealed. The new rules for counting ALCMs, the more intractable problem of how to verify limits on long-range SLCMs and the means to ensure that they were not carrying extra nuclear warheads had yet to be resolved. The USA favoured omitting SLCMs from a START agreement if satisfactory arrangements could not be reached concerning verification—a position which the USSR bitterly opposed. A possible ban on mobile missiles—an issue dating back to the early days of SALT I—was also again on the agenda.[22] In May 1988, the Pentagon, spurred on by the search for an invulnerable land-based missile force, reactivated plans to develop a mobile missile. The USSR was already deploying mobile SS-24s and SS-25s.[23] The problem of verifying mobile missiles, however, prompted the USA to press for a ban. The disagreement over SDI remained a major obstacle at Moscow. Soviet concern appeared to have diminished as it became clear that technological difficulties and lack of funds would abort President Reagan's more ambitious plans for a 'space shield' against missiles. Furthermore, despite the acceptance of a formula to observe the ABM Treaty for a fixed term, the USA and the USSR could not agree on what was to be permitted during this period or what would happen after the expiration of the agreement.[24] General Secretary Gorbachev reasserted the Soviet position that START depended on an agreement on weapons in space.[25]

The Moscow summit occurred soon after the USA and the USSR had reached an agreement on withdrawing military aid to the competing forces in Afghanistan, but it was marked by a high level of propaganda and clearly did not meet Gorbachev's expectations. The ratification of the INF Treaty was celebrated in Moscow, but it appeared as though little additional progress would be achieved concerning on arms control during President Reagan's remaining time in office. The Soviet Union seemed to be looking ahead to the next US Administration; and immediately after the Moscow summit, Washington played down the prospects for a START agreement under President Reagan.[26] Still, there had been a dramatic change in US–Soviet relations since 1985, and it is necessary to examine in more detail how this change, and the INF Treaty which symbolized it, came about.

IV. Prelude to the INF Treaty

The strategic context of negotiations for an INF Treaty in 1987 had changed dramatically compared to 1983. On both sides, nuclear missile deployments had changed, which served both to help, and to hinder, an INF settlement. The attitudes of the Reagan Administration and key West European governments had also shifted in such a way that not only created new possibilities, but new problems as well. In the Soviet Union, the leadership's attitude towards the conclusion of a treaty had also changed radically and in a direction much more unequivocally favourable to an agreement—at least during those times when Gorbachev appeared to be clearly in control of policy.

By 1987, NATO had implemented the initial stages of its INF deployment programme—108 Pershing II missiles were in place in FR Germany, and GLCM deployment was under way in Britain, Italy, Belgium and the FRG. Early in 1985, the Belgian Government only reluctantly fell into line and accepted its share of the missiles. After prolonged public protests and considerable doubts among the Dutch leadership, the Government committed the Netherlands in November 1985 to receive GLCMs in 1988.[27] NATO cruise missile deployment continued throughout the period of the negotiations in 1987, and by September, approximately 240 cruise missiles were in place.[28]

The Soviet Union had not significantly increased its SS-20 force targeted against Europe since 1983. By mid-1986, the Western estimate was 270 missiles (carrying 910 warheads) compared with 240 missiles reported in late 1983.[29] The USSR, however, had deployed more SRINF since 1983—thereby creating a greater imbalance in the 500 to 1000 km range than existed before—as West European opponents of INF were quick to stress. Although the Soviet Union had a strategic incentive to give up some SS-20s in return for the dismantling of Pershing IIs and GLCMs, it had no obvious strategic incentive to abandon superiority in INF missiles—which would have remained even after full NATO deployment. The Soviet Union's willingness to relinquish all SS-20s in the European theatre (and later to give them up completely) was clearly influenced by wider political considerations together with some strategic re-calculations concerning the need for INF. Later Soviet concessions on SRINF owed even more to political factors.

In 1987, the political context for negotiations had changed dramatically since 1983. Whereas in 1983 the US Administration on the whole had no desire for an agreement, most West European governments—under strong pressure from peace-movement and left-wing groups opposed to INF deployment—were anxious for an agreement and favoured the walk-in-the-woods package. In 1987, however, the positions were reversed. Now, it was President Reagan who wanted a Treaty—partly as a result of a personal ambition to secure a place in history as a peacemaker, but more concretely in response to congressional pressure, and as an escape from domestic scandal and ignominy. The British and West German Governments—alarmed about a possible weakening of the US nuclear guarantee to Europe and (after re-election of right-wing governments in 1983) less concerned about popular opposition to the missiles—raised objections. France, which like Britain was also afraid that significant moves towards nuclear disarmament in Europe would threaten its independent nuclear force—joined the British and West Germans in voicing these concerns.

The initial West European reaction to US soundings in 1986 and early in 1987 was to express a preference for retaining some INF on each side. The main line of argument centred on the problems which a zero option INF agreement would create in Europe by leaving the USSR with overwhelming superiority in SS-22s and SS-23s, while NATO's only SRINF were the 72 ageing Pershing 1a missiles. Although these missiles were strictly under West German control and, therefore, were not technically US missiles, the USA retained control of the nuclear warheads. Initially, the British Government was inclined to favour a build up of Western SRINF forces to counteract the effects of eliminating the INF missiles. The FRG, alarmed at the prospects of an INF agreement, was ambivalent about how to treat SRINF.[30] Because the USA had the responsibility for the INF negotiations, as well as the decisive voice within NATO, the political position by 1987 was favourable to an agreement compared with 1983. Although the West Europeans can try to prompt Washington to act, or can create diplomatic difficulties for the USA, Western Europe cannot, in the end, determine the outcome of the USA's negotiations with the Soviet Union.

The other, and perhaps most important change, was the fact that the Soviet Union had taken the initiative by pressuring both the USA and Western Europe to respond favourably to a rapid succession of Soviet proposals designed to address Western anxieties. Through his proposals, Gorbachev exposed the doubts and divisions within NATO, as well as the superficiality of the original zero option proposed by Reagan in 1981. Furthermore, Gorbachev demonstrated the fact that NATO deployments had not really been conceived simply to offset the SS-20s (as public relations statements suggested), but to ensure graduated nuclear response and to strengthen the coupling of US nuclear forces to Europe.[31]

Gradually, West European governments came around to accepting the Soviet proposal of a zero option on INF in Europe and a second Soviet offer (made at the end of April) to eliminate all SRINF (missiles in the 500–1000 km range), as well.[32] In May 1987, Prime Minister Thatcher decided to support the 'double-zero option'. Although Thatcher's action was almost certainly partly in deference to President Reagan's wishes, the timing suggested that the primary motive was to strengthen the position of the Conservatives in the general election called for June. The Conservatives could then claim that their earlier tough stand on NATO deployments had paid off with the prospects of major nuclear disarmament in Europe.[33] In the FRG, the Government, hampered by a split in the coalition between Chancellor Kohl's Christian Democrats and the liberal Free Democrats, took longer to fall into line with Washington. The FRG is acutely aware of the implications of various nuclear missiles if there were a war in Central Europe and, at the same time, the FRG is sensitive to the political implications of nuclear missiles in relations with the GDR and other countries in Eastern Europe. Chancellor Kohl, therefore, suggested the inclusion of Soviet missiles with a range below 500 km in any agreement. In particlular, the FRG was concerned about the 300-km range SS-1c, or 'Scud B' missiles. In mid-May, Kohl proposed that all nuclear missiles in Europe should be covered in the negotiations. However, the Chancellor was not enthusiastic about having additional SRINF (in particular the Pershing 1b conversion from the Pershing II being mooted by the Pentagon) on West German territory. Kohl's hesitations concerning an INF agreement had domestic repercussions as well, and were presented as one reason why the CDU lost two state elections in May.[34] Bonn, under pressure from Washington to reach a decision before President Reagan visited West Berlin in mid-June, resolved to back double zero early in June, but insisted on retaining the Pershing 1as.[35] The French Government, strongly opposed to an INF agreement, was concerned about the implications of such an agreement for French forces. France, however, was not part of NATO's integrated military structure, or involved in the actual NATO deployments; therefore, it could not reasonably block an agreement supported by other key countries.

SRINF, a fairly minor issue in the INF talks between 1981 and 1983, only gained great prominence when an INF agreement seemed likely. One problem with the double-zero option was whether the 72 West German Pershing 1a missiles should be included in an agreement. Whereas the Soviet Union claimed that these missiles should be included, the FRG—backed by NATO military opinion—opposed their inclusion.[36] As other obstacles were removed, it became clear that so minor an issue as the Pershing 1as would not be allowed to impede an INF treaty. In August, Chancellor Kohl resolved the entire problem by pledging to destroy the Pershing 1a missiles (after the USA had removed the warheads) when the USA and the USSR had dismantled their INF forces.[37]

The Soviet Union's desire to maintain at least 100 SS-20 warheads in its Asian areas, which had also loomed large in the 1981–83, caused much greater difficulty in the INF negotiations than the SRINF issue. Rather than permit the regional deployment of a limited number of INF missiles, the USA and its allies preferred a global zero option which eliminated all INF. The Soviet position created further difficulty over where the counterbalancing US missiles should be deployed—the USSR objected to the USA placing them in Alaska.[38] In May, Gorbachev floated an alternative solution when he offered to abandon all the Soviet Asian SS-20s in return for withdrawal of US nuclear bases in the Pacific. The USA, however, viewed this offer as a clearly unrealistic option.[39] At the end of July, he made a more definite offer to accept a global zero option on INF and, therefore, to relinquish the placement of any SS-20s in Asia. This initiative appeared to be an attempt to break the deadlock that had developed at Geneva and, at the same time, to be part of a wider Soviet strategy to reassure its Asian neighbours.[40]

Verification, the issue which has divided the USA and the USSR so often before, did not prove to be a matter of fundamental dispute between the two sides. Both parties agreed on the need for on-site inspection to verify the removal and destruction of the missiles, and to check some aspects of production. Nevertheless, specific aspects of verification did cause a variety of difficulties and delays throughout 1987, and even after the Treaty had been signed. Indeed, the Senate delayed ratification until doubts about Soviet compliance could be resolved.

Both sides appeared briefly to revert to their traditional positions on verification when in February 1987 the USSR—taking a tough line in the wake of the Reykjavik débâcle—resisted the inclusion of verification provisions in the actual treaty. A Senate Arms Control Group visiting Geneva warned the Soviet Union on 2 March that Senate ratification of an INF Treaty would depend upon adequate verification measures.[41] However, on 6 March the Soviet delegation stressed that it wanted strict inspection—including the right of Soviet inspectors to visit factories where the missiles were made. As the full implications of verification became apparent—Soviet access to privately owned plants could require special congressional legislation—some right-wing US Senators expressed dismay about the implications of verification.[42]

Gradually, the Geneva talks did elaborate a whole panoply of inspection measures. The two sides agreed on the necessity to verify the initial totals of missiles to be destroyed, a quota of spot checks to verify Treaty implementation, inspection measures to confirm the removal of missiles from bases and procedures to oversee the destruction of missiles at agreed sites. The delegations also defined the means of verifying that plants able to produce INF missiles were not doing so. This would be accomplished by 'portal' monitoring. The negotiations were tedious and protracted, not only because of their technical complexity, but because of political difficulties. The inspection of missile bases had to be arranged with the West European countries involved. The USA's insistence on checking the Votkinski plant (which produces SS-25s), because two stages of the SS-25 are very similar to the SS-20, was opposed by the Soviet Union on the grounds that this involved monitoring strategic missiles not covered, of course, under terms of the INF Treaty. A compromise was reached when the USSR was allowed to monitor the MX missile production plant at Utah, which had manufactured Pershing IIs.[43]

Last minute sources of disagreement included the timetable for destroying the missiles on each side and the question of what should be done with the nuclear warheads (the USSR preferred destruction). On the eve of the Washington summit meeting, a dispute arose concerning the adequacy of the information being supplied by both sides to support the initial data base. The Foreign Ministers met in September and again in late November, and ironed out remaining points of disagreement.

The INF Treaty delivered for signature in Washington provided the press and the public with more precise information about the missile stocks that each side would be required to dismantle over a three-year period. The USA would dismantle 429 cruise and Pershing II missiles already deployed, and a further 430 undeployed missiles. The USSR was committed to dismantling 857 deployed missiles and a further 895 in store, a total of 1752. The USA was to dismantle just under 1000 warheads, the Soviet Union over 3000. Although the missiles were to be destroyed at specified sites (100 could be fired by each side, minus warheads, to speed the process), the nuclear materials in the warheads could be reprocessed after dismantling for use in new devices. Details concerning how the missiles would be destroyed, as well as the stages of the process and the types of inspection which were mandated, were set out in two protocols. A memorandum of understanding elaborated upon the numbers, characteristics and deployment of missiles.[44]

The INF Treaty signed in Washington on 8 December 1987 was hailed as a historic measure of arms control. For the first time, the USA and the USSR had agreed to reduce their nuclear arsenals and to eliminate a category of nuclear missiles. Even more important, it was the first time the two powers had agreed on measures for detailed on-site inspection to verify disarmament. West European governments, which had resisted an INF agreement only a few months before, promptly claimed credit for the success. Despite strong right-wing opposition in the USA, the Washington political establishment as a whole appeared to welcome the Treaty.

In the Senate, however, the Treaty faced opposition. The influential Chairman of the Senate Armed Services Committee, Senator Sam Nunn, was sceptical about its value, and such right-wing Senators as Jesse Helms were vehemently opposed. There were charges that the Soviet Union had not declared all its missiles and was planning to cheat and to evade verification obligations.

Senate supporters of arms control in principle raised very different issues. They were anxious to ensure that a future Administration could not reinterpret the terms of the INF Treaty in the way that President Reagan had reinterpreted the ABM Treaty. It was clear that majority opinion in the Senate was in favour of the Treaty, which had been secured by a right-wing Republican President, and which could—with some misinterpretation of the record—be presented as a triumph for the Administration's tough line up to 1983. At the same time, the Treaty appealed to a widespread desire for cuts in the nuclear arsenals of both sides. Senator Robert Dole, a candidate for the Republican party's Presidential nomination, abandoned his opposition to the Treaty after the Washington summit meeting and proclaimed his support for it in recognition of prevailing sentiments. Therefore, the Administration was able—after further negotiations with the USSR—to clarify a number of points relating to verification, and so to persuade the Senate to hold its floor debate on the INF Treaty and to vote for ratification—all in time for the Moscow summit.[45]

With the signing and ratification of the INF Treaty, the negotiations which reconvened in 1985 had achieved a partial success. The INF Treaty was concluded only after both the US and Soviet governments had circumvented numerous obstacles along the way. In the case of START, the obstacles to agreement proved to be much more intractable.

V. Obstacles to agreement

Great power confrontation

Because the second set of missile talks occurred during an era of growing *détente* and because both parties had some genuine interest in concluding an agreement, there was less emphasis on propaganda, or jockeying for purely political advantage, than there had been in the first stage of the negotiations between 1981 and 1983. Nevertheless, Gorbachev's carefully orchestrated proposals included an element of propaganda designed to appeal to Western popular opinion. Gorbachev's embrace of the zero option for European INF effectively wrong-footed NATO, which faced considerable embarrassment if it appeared to reject its own original proposal. Gorbachev's initial zero option offer, in fact, fell considerably short of the global zero option put forward by the USA in 1981. Later, Gorbachev would accept the more encompassing zero option proposal. The Soviet Union's tactics served to encourage the USA to negotiate seriously on INF and to reduce West European opposition. Therefore, the tactics actually enhanced the overall goal of the arms control negotiations, rather than being an end in themselves or a substitute for genuine negotiations.[46]

From 1985 to 1987, the obstacles of political conflict and political linkage did not adversely affect the conduct or outcome of the negotiations to any great extent. Although Reagan kept the issue of Afghanistan and the question of human rights inside the USSR on the agenda at summit meetings, these issues did not predominate over arms control concerns, and there was no explicit linkage. Gorbachev made concessions on both issues including a token withdrawal of troops from Afghanistan in 1986 and the release of 140 political prisoners in February 1987. Moreover, there were strong indications that Moscow wanted a settlement in Afghanistan that would permit the Soviet Union to end its military intervention.[47] A dispute over the bugging of the US Embassy in Moscow was not allowed to wreck State Secretary Shultz's visit in April 1987. Although the Soviet Union did express its anger over the US bombing of Libya in 1986, the missile talks suffered only a temporary set-back from the coolness created by this episode.

When Paul Nitze toured European capitals early in 1986 (and before the USA presented its proposals at Geneva), European allied resistance to a zero-option INF agreement became clear. The USA's commitment to an agreement, and popular support for it at home, undermined the British and West German governments' tendencies (see above) to discover fresh obstacles to any new Soviet offer. However, the USA's allies and friends in the far East—in particular Japan and China—were unhappy at the prospect of some SS-20s remaining in the Asian areas of the USSR. So, the USA's proposals in early 1986 took account of their Asian allies' misgivings which were expressed to General Rowny, the US envoy.[48] At Reykjavik, however, the USA proved willing to consider proposals which left some Soviet SS-20s deployed in Asia. Furthermore, Washington appeared to be prepared to subordinate allied concerns to conclude an agreement, although the USA did attempt to find a formula to keep any residual Soviet SS-20s out of range of Japan before Gorbachev's offer to abandon them at the end of July 1987.[49]

Allied views have not been an important factor in the Space Talks or in the START negotiations. Although NATO European members were at first distinctly unenthusiastic about the Reagan's SDI programme (in part because they feared it might tend to uncouple the US nuclear deterrent from Europe), the allies were persuaded to endorse it out of deference to the dominant alliance partner, and in return for promises of a share in research and development contracts.[50] West European governments have generally favoured some reductions in the nuclear arsenals of the great powers. On the other hand, these governments have also favoured the USA's retention of sufficient forces to maintain its nuclear guarantee to Europe. Furthermore, France and Britain wish to preserve their own nuclear status. Therefore, the USA's retreat from the more radical goals of Reykjavik to a 50 per cent cut over seven years in strategic forces pleased most European governments, although it is unlikely that Prime Minister Thatcher's role in securing this retreat was as significant as she herself has claimed.

With respect to the Space Talks and the START negotiations, both the USA and the USSR sought some strategic advantage. In particular, the USA has wanted to maintain its technological advantage in space and ant-satellite weapons (ASAT) weapons, and the USSR has been anxious to curtail that advantage. At the START negotiations, both parties have engaged in the familiar game of tailoring their arms control proposals to enhance their own main programmes and to curb those of the opponent. The original START proposals presented by the USA in late 1985 included a limit of 3000 warheads on Soviet ICBMs, which was thought to reduce significantly the danger of a pre-emptive Soviet attack against US missile silos, and command and control centres.[51] The Soviet proposals were designed to curb longer-range cruise missiles—an area in which the USA was well ahead—and the USA resisted restrictions on ALCMs and SLCMs. Nevertheless, it should be pointed out that these manœuvres are not necessarily destructive of a satisfactory outcome to negotiations. That parties to arms control negotiations should try to restrict what they regard as especially dangerous and destabilizing developments on the other side is in itself reasonable. Furthermore, standard negotiating practice entails some hard bargaining. Still, there is a considerable danger that the side which thinks it is at an overall strategic advantage will prefer to retain that unilateral lead rather than agree to arms control, and that a bargaining advantage will be retained as part of the military programme. The USA's intransigence over the SDI programme—which also illustrated vividly the threat posed by new technology to arms control—amply illustrates both of these dangers.

Some Western commentators claimed that the USSR would gain a unilateral strategic advantage from an INF agreement. At first, these observers focused on the Soviet advantage in SRINF; then, after the USSR offered the double-zero option, they stressed the Soviet Union's conventional force advantage—

especially in tanks.[52] A more balanced interpretation suggests that the military problems associated with INF did not arise from the USSR seeking to exploit a strategic advantage (after all, Gorbachev did abandon significant numerical superiority both in SS-20 warheads and in SRINF); rather, the problems arose quite naturally from the previously existing strategic asymmetries between the WTO and NATO.

Psychological obstacles

The Soviet zero option concession and the double-zero offer aroused deep suspicions in NATO circles. General Bernard Rogers, the Supreme Allied Commander Europe (SACEUR), publicly expressed the fear that the Soviet Union was implementing a plan to denuclearize Europe and to make the region vulnerable to 'intimidation and blackmail'.[53] Other observers discerned a desire on the part of the Soviet Union to disrupt NATO's strategy of flexible response. The West German military reiterated its belief that the USSR was trying to divide the Alliance and to separate the USA from Europe.[54]

These assessments assume that the primary motive of any Soviet action in relation to arms control must be to achieve some strategic or political advantage over the West. The belief that the Soviet Union only makes concessions if there is a hidden catch reflects the tradition of ideological conflict and the perpetuation of ideologically-biased perceptions. The depth of the resultant distrust clearly created considerable reluctance within many military circles, and among right-wing parties and groups in Western Europe, to support an INF agreement. On this occasion, however, Western European doubts about the Soviet Union's true motive and resistance to an INF agreement were overriden by other political factors.

Domestic obstacles

In Washington, the resistance to a missile agreement was clearly less pronounced after 1985 than it had been in the first Reagan Administration. Nevertheless, there was continuing evidence of a conflict between the Pentagon and the State Department over arms control policy and a resumption of *détente*. Because the Administration, despite congressional doubts, remained united behind SDI, the main bone of contention concerned a potential INF agreement. Indeed, a really strong commitment to an INF agreement does not seem to have developed in the Reagan Administration until 1987. By that time, Reagan had already espoused radical proposals to cut nuclear arms at Reykjavik, and the arch-opponent of arms control, Richard Perle, suddenly found himself in the ironic position of having to defend the Reykjavik proposals to a sceptical West European audience. The mid-term congressional elections strengthened the Democrats in the House—where they were already dominant—and, furthermore, enabled the Democrats to take control of the Senate from the

Republicans. Therefore, it seemed quite likely that congressional pressure for arms control would increase. The embarassing Iran–Contra scandal had served to make President Reagan more anxious for an arms control success. Early in March 1987, Donald Regan was replaced as White House Chief of Staff by the moderate Howard Baker. The appointment of Baker, trusted by Congress and generally believed to favour arms control, greatly improved the chances of such a treaty being successfully shepherded through the bureaucracy. Because Richard Perle had never regarded the NATO INF deployments as strategically necessary, he appeared to be willing to give some public support to the possibility of a treaty. The chief onus for opposing an INF agreement, therefore, devolved upon Perle's boss, Weinberger. Weinberger continued to raise objections and stressed, for example, the verification problems associated with a SRINF agreement.[55] In April, a surprise intervention came from Henry Kissinger and Richard Nixon, who made a public statement warning of the dangers of an INF treaty based on the double-zero option for NATO and urged that a treaty should be linked to the conventional balance.[56] Their views offered support to the outspoken resistance of General Rogers. However, the opponents of an INF agreement now seemed to be on the defensive—both Weinberger and Rogers had been replaced before the Washington summit meeting.

Western commentators regularly suggested that Gorbachev either was facing, or would shortly face, serious resistance to his arms control policies from the USSR's military professionals and party ideologues. Sometimes these comments seemed to be wishful thinking rather than carefully reasoned analysis. Certainly, it is always convenient for Western sceptics if the obstructions are raised by Moscow. Although there were some indications that Gorbachev was being forced to respond to domestic pressures not to concede too much too soon, these examples could also be explained in terms of bargaining tactics. Soon after the Geneva summit meeting, Gorbachev made a tough–sounding speech to the Supreme Soviet in which he warned the USA against any attempt to acquire military superiority and recalled the first Reagan Administration's responsibility in promoting a new cold war.[57] Gorbachev's sudden revival of linkage between an INF agreement and an end to SDI research could have reflected a need to conciliate the Soviet military. Marshal Sergei Akhromeyev, the Chief of the Soviet General Staff who had played a prominent role at the Geneva summit, indicated general, but somewhat qualified, support for Mr Gorbachev's arms control programme in a speech to military officers on 1 March 1987. The Marshal linked a separate INF agreement to Western acceptance of Soviet inspectors at NATO missile bases and reiterated the standard Soviet position that there was no imbalance of conventional forces in Europe. Thus, the Marshal signalled Soviet military's reservations about meeting all NATO demands.[58] Some commentators believed that continued Soviet insistence on retaining some SS-20s in Asian areas reflected the military's refusal to make concessions in Asia in return for flexibility in Europe.[59] By 1987, however, Gorbachev appeared to have consolidated the support in the Politburo for both domestic and foreign policy reforms. In 1985, the veteran Foreign Minister Andrei Gromyko was replaced by Eduard Shevardnadze; and between 1985 and 1987, Gorbachev managed to replace a number of Politburo members .[60]

VI. Obstacles in the negotiating process

In the missile negotiations after 1985, the perennial and fundamental differences between the Soviet Union and the West—the Soviet penchant for military secrecy and its reluctance to accept Western demands for on-site verification—had become much less pronounced. The one area in which the Soviet Union proved to be very unwilling to make disclosure concerned its own progress in space weapons. In May 1985, General Nikolai Chervov admitted what the West had long maintained—that the USSR did have an ASAT system. Chervov, however, claimed that the system was composed of land-based missiles only—not of satellites capable of destroying other satellites—and had not been tested in space. Although the General also admitted in February 1986 that the Soviet Union was conducting space research—which included the use of lasers—Chervov denied that this research was intended for military purposes.[61]

To verify an INF agreement, the USSR proved willing to compile a comprehensive data base and to contemplate on-site inspection of a quite extensive nature. Indeed, it began to appear that the objections to intrusive on-site verification, which endangered other military secrets and challenged national sovereignty, might come from the USA and Western Europe. A diplomat in Washington was quoted as saying that: 'No one wants a bunch of Russians trooping over Greenham Common'.[62] According to some press reports, the CIA, the National Security Agency (NSA) and the FBI were urging that some US installations should be exempted from on-site inspection.[63]

The most important questions raised by the post-1985 missile talks centre on what role was played by negotiating from strength and the use of bargaining chips. Here, a sharp distinction should be drawn between claims that SDI promoted negotiations on strategic and space weapons and claims that NATO missile deployment led to an INF Treaty. Periodically, the SDI programme has been justified as a means of bringing the Soviet Union to the negotiating table. Indeed, the Soviet interest in 1984 in beginning talks on space weapons did lend some credibility to this argument.[64] However, subsequent US intransigence about pressing ahead with the research, testing and early deployment of SDI demonstrated that the programme was not negotiable under President Reagan. It was initially an obstacle to START and has continued to block progress in the Space Talks. If the Bush Administration is dissuaded from going ahead with SDI on the grounds of technological unreliability and escalating costs, or is inclined to view the dangers of an arms race in space as outweighing the advantages of the USA being ahead in space technology—or both—this situation could, quite possibly, change in the future

A more plausible case can be made that NATO's firmness in pressing ahead with the INF deployments (which resulted, in the short-run, in a breakdown of the negotiations) paid off, in the long-run, with an INF agreement which was much better than could have been envisaged previously.[65] The immediate result of NATO INF deployments, however, was not encouraging. At the end of 1983, when the USSR retaliated by deploying shorter-range SS-21s and SS-23s in the GDR and Czechoslovakia (a deployment which may have been planned independent of the NATO action), and in addition put in a number of SS-22s, the position appeared to have worsened. Moreover, when the INF talks resumed, the FRG soon insisted on the removal of SRINF in Eastern Europe as a condition for agreeing to an INF treaty. These Soviet deployments, then, appeared to be a further obstacle.[66] However, after some of the NATO missiles—including the Pershing IIs—were in place, reductions in Soviet INF in Europe made more military sense for the USSR than in 1981, when the USA was asking Moscow to give up new SS-20s against 'paper missiles'. Furthermore, it can be argued that Western 'firmness' on demanding concessions on SRINF resulted in the surprisingly radical 'double-zero' offer.

Nevertheless, military deployments and bargaining rigidity more often promote the same response on the other side, and not major concessions to abandon deployed weapons. A central question which remains is: why was the Soviet Government by 1987 willing to be so accommodating on arms control in Europe? One obvious explanation is that the SS-20s had less military value than they once did. It has often been suggested that the SS-25, first deployed in 1985–86, could replace the SS-20 as a reserve weapon.[67] However, Soviet ICBMs could always cover the same targets as SS-20s, and Western commentators have not generally assumed that the SS-20s were becoming less useful strategically. A second possible explanation is that the Soviet military may have been willing to pay the price—the removal of the SS-20s—for the compensating removal of the threat posed by the Pershing IIs.

These explanations are not, however, really satisfactory. Many US commentators believe that is was the Soviet military which spearheaded the refusal of the 'walk-in-the-woods' package which would have removed Pershing IIs on much more favourable military terms than the INF Treaty. If Gorbachev was influenced solely, or even primarily, by calculations of military advantage, then he could have used the Soviet Union's superiority in INF and SRINF to strike a much harder bargain. Instead, he chose to relinquish a position of considerable advantage to meet NATO much more than half way. This decision only becomes explicable when viewed in terms of wider political and economic considerations, and including a genuine interest in achieving measures of arms control.

The widespread tendency of Western politicians and press commentators to ascribe the success in achieving an INF agreement to NATO's perserverance in carrying out its missile deployment is, therefore, a grossly over-simplified claim. Gorbachev's strategic and political perspective undoubtedly did *not* assign primary importance to having SS-20s in Europe, and he might well have chosen to remove them in exchange for some other measures of Western disarmament. It is true, however, that the NATO deployments did make a relatively simple INF bargain possible, whereas trading SS-20s within the context of a START agreement would have been much more complex, and could have encountered still other strategic and political obstacles. An even more important point is that the NATO's newly deployed INF were the only nuclear weapons that NATO members were at all willing to include in an agreement. Britain and France refused any compromise proposal which even took account of their own missiles, and Washington has always resisted reductions or limits on its nuclear FBS. The US tendency to view INF as political bargaining counters—together with the whole context of Pershing II and cruise missile deployment—made it difficult for NATO to refuse to relinquish these missiles. As previously illustrated, however, some Western governments were very reluctant to accept the zero option (and even more reluctant concerning the double zero-option) and were manœuvred into compliance by the extent of Soviet concessions, President Reagan's desire for an agreement and their own domestic opinion.

Accelerating the arms race?

The INF Treaty constitutes the first measure of genuine nuclear disarmament to date, but there are a number of ways in which it could result in an arms *buildup*. There was ample evidence of the military pressure to compensate for abandoning NATO INF during 1987, as the talks seemed to be moving towards a successful conclusion. One response was to demand a 'price' for the loss of INF. NATO military advisors urged the Defence Ministers as early as May 1987 that there should be a compensatory buildup in conventional forces.[68] Calls were also made for NATO to modernize its battlefield nuclear weapons in Europe.[69] A second and even more significant response was to call for new deployments which would effectively circumvent the INF Treaty. There were reports that the USA might deploy bombers equipped with ALCMs in Britain and other NATO countries to substitute for the GLCMs removed, and that the case for a major SLCM deployment had been strengthened.[70] General Rogers pressed for ALCMs in Europe and for a SLCM force under the Supreme Commander's direct control to substitute for the loss of ground INF.[71] Initial Western reactions to the likelihood of a zero INF option suggested a further measure of levelling-up by bringing NATO's SRINF up to the Soviet levels. The Pentagon seemed particularly interested in this context in the deployment of a modified Pershing II as a shorter-range Pershing 1b.[72] This line of argument, however, was pre-empted by the Soviet double-zero offer.

In the wake of the signing and ratification of the INF Treaty, Gorbachev's diplomacy and disarmament initiatives have made a major NATO military build-up difficult to justify; but there has been continued pressure to strengthen and update NATO's nuclear armoury. The result of these conflicting tendencies has been that an increase in NATO conventional forces is extremely unlikely, that the US Congress has been asked to agree on funding for aircraft equipped with ALCMs to be based in Britain and that NATO remained split on the issue of modernizing its short-range land-based nuclear missiles in 1989.

An increase in NATO conventional forces as a 'price' for INF was always the least likely option. West European governments have been reluctant for budgetary and political reasons to increase investment in conventional forces and the USA now has its own budgetary and domestic political imperatives for reducing its forces in Europe. Moreover, the USSR is offering the possibility of conventional force reductions at the Conventional Forces in Europe negotiations which opened in March 1989.

It was much more probable that abolition of ground INF would have a displacement effect and that land-based missiles would be replaced by less visible ALCMs or SLCMs. The main responsibility for developing this option lies in Washington. Moreover, Britain under the Thatcher government can be relied upon to provide bases for new aircraft equipped with ALCMs. By the time of NATO's April 1989 Nuclear Planning Group meeting, however, NATO had not collectively endorsed this aspect of nuclear modernization.[73]

NATO plans to modernize its land-based short-range missile force by deploying new cruise missiles with a range of 400 km are controversial for a number of reasons. Gorbachev has offered negotiations on a 'triple zero' basis to eliminate such weapons, and public opinion is by now sensitive on proposals to increase land-based missiles. The most important factor, however, is that such missiles would have to be deployed in West Germany, where public opinion was is strongly opposed to deploying new missiles. Chancellor Kohl was therefore extremely reluctant to agree on this form of modernization.

The total outcome of the INF Treaty remains uncertain. It may, in the long term, provide a powerful argument in favour of the use of bargaining chips or negotiations from strength—politicians have already claimed the Treaty as a victory for NATO 'firmness'. In this sense, the Treaty may be used to reduce the likelihood of further arms control. On the other hand, the tremendous symbolic and political significance of a treaty to dismantle a category of nuclear weapons could strengthen belief in the possibility of further nuclear disarmament. The Treaty may serve to create a momentum for other significant agreements, promote a new atmosphere of genuine *détente* and result in less distrust between the superpowers. Certainly an agreement that entails dismantling weapons and the implementation of strict verification procedures should—provided the parties adhere to the Treaty—provide a historic foundation for future disarmament efforts.

VII. The factors promoting an INF agreement

Despite the numerous difficulties encountered during nearly three years of negotiation, the USA and the USSR signed the INF Treaty in December 1987.

Why were the two parties successful in concluding the INF Treaty, when a treaty from either the Space Talks or START negotiations proved to be so elusive? Although several possible explanations to this question have already been suggested in the detailed analysis of the negotiations, it is worthwhile to recapitulate and to underscore certain points in this section.

Perhaps the first and overriding reason that an INF Treaty proved to be possible was the startling change in arms control policy inaugurated by Gorbachev after he assumed power early in 1985. Gorbachev's sustained initiatives revived an atmosphere of *détente*, forced the West to respond to his offers on INF, and demonstrated a fundamental re-evaluation of Soviet political and strategic objectives. In particular, Gorbachev's willingness to accept much higher Soviet reductions in weapons where the USSR had superiority, as well as to negotiate detailed provisions for on-site inspection, made it difficult for the Reagan Administration and NATO to reject an INF agreement.

The second, reason was the more haphazard, but nevertheless genuine, change in the Reagan Administration's overall attitude towards *détente* and arms control. Although Reagan apparently underwent at least a partial change of heart in his attitudes to the USSR, it became even clearer during his second term, that Reagan was not in control of his Administration's policies. Nevertheless, Reagan's new interest in *détente* probably permitted George Shultz to take a more active role in promoting the INF negotiations and provided more scope to Paul Nitze (who had an advisory role on arms control) in overcoming the obstacles to arms control in Washington. The Iran–Contra scandal, together with increased congressional pressure, strengthened the supporters of an INF agreement; and even the best known opponents of arms control, such as Perle and Weinberger, either wanted to leave the Administration, or accepted the desirability of leaving, before the Treaty was concluded.

The third reason was that public opinion in the USA and Western Europe welcomed an arms control agreement. The evidence of popular support for a treaty provided an incentive to President Reagan and his aides, reduced right-wing opposition to a deal in the USA, and prompted Prime Minister Thatcher and Chancellor Kohl to be more receptive to an INF agreement. Because there was widespread awareness of the NATO deployments and the INF negotiations, it was clearly difficult to explain to electorates that an agreement which removed all SS-20s would be a mistake. In the end, the British and West German governments decided both to support the INF Treaty and to attempt to claim credit for it.

The fourth reason was that many (although by no means all) of the officials and analysts in Washington viewed NATO's INF as political symbols, rather than essential strategic deployments. Therefore, it was relatively easy to take the decision to dismantle them in order to achieve political gains both in terms of better East–West relations and in the domestic political arena in the USA—especially when offered favourable terms by Moscow. Gorbachev appears to have reached a similar conclusion about the SS-20s in relation to his own political priorities.

Fifth, the INF Treaty could be viewed as the most tangible product and most visible symbol of the era of *détente*. Gorbachev wanted *détente* so as to facilitate a reduction, eventually, in the Soviet military arsenal, a disengagement of the Soviet Union from such external military commitments as Afghanistan, and the pursuit of economic and political reconstruction inside the Soviet Union. Gorbachev also needed a major arms control agreement to strengthen his personal position within the Politburo. Beset by a scandal which threatened to wreck his presidency, Reagan wanted to achieve a diplomatic triumph and to secure a reputation as a peacemaker. The Congress, so as to justify reduced spending on arms, desired a return to friendlier relations with the Soviet Union. After the Geneva and Reykjavik summit meetings, *détente* had little substance. However, after the signing of the INF Treaty during a triumphant Washington summit, *détente* was now codified in the text of an important arms control treaty. Although the desire for *détente* was a result of new policies in Moscow and Washington, it also reflected an understanding of the requirements of great power relations which dates back to the late 1950s. European countries favoured *détente* for their own specific political and economic reasons, and even those governments who were ambivalent about the INF Treaty welcomed the more cordial relations the conclusion of the Treaty seemed to promise.

Notes and references

[1] *The Guardian*, 10 Jan. 1985, p. 19.

[2] Hardenbergh, C, 'News of negotiations', *ADIU Report*, vol. 7, no. 3 (May–June 1985), p. 12.

[3] *The Times*, 21 Jan. 1985, p. 4.

[4] Hardenbergh, C., 'News of negotiations', *ADIU Report*, vol. 7, no. 4 (July–Aug. 1985), p. 21.

[5] *The Guardian*, 17 July 1985, p. 8.

[6] Hardenbergh, C., 'News of negotiations', *ADIU Report*, vol. 7, no. 6 (Nov.–Dec. 1985), p. 21.

[7] Editorial, *The Council for Arms Control Bulletin*, no. 24 (Jan. 1986), p. 1.

[8] Hardenbergh, C., 'News of negotiations', *ADIU Report*, vol. 8, no. 1 (Jan.–Feb. 1986), pp. 20–21.

[9] Hardenbergh, C., 'News of negotiations', *ADIU Report*, vol. 8, no 2 (Mar.–Apr. 1986), pp. 20–21.

[10] *The Guardian*, 25 Feb. 1985, p. 9.

[11] Hardenbergh, C., 'News of negotiations', *ADIU Report*, vol. 8, no. 4 (July–Aug. 1986), pp. 20–21.

[12] See, e.g., *The Independent*, 13 Oct. 1986, p. 16.

[13] *The Guardian*, 14 Oct. 1986, p. 6, and Hardenbergh, C., 'News of negotiations', *ADIU Report*, vol. 8, no. 6 (Nov.–Dec. 1986), p. 20.

[14] *The Guardian*, 24 Oct. 1986, p. 8 and 7 Nov. 1986, p. 1.

[15] *The Guardian*, 18 Oct. 1986, p. 6 and 20 Oct. 1986, p. 1.

[16] Hardenbergh, C., 'News of negotiations', *ADIU Report*, vol. 9, no. 2 (Mar.–Apr. 1987), p. 18.

[17] *The Guardian*, 13 May 1987, p. 5.

[18] Hardenbergh (note 16), p. 19.

[19] *The Independent*, 9 May 1987, p. 7.

[20] *The Guardian*, 27 Feb. 1988, p. 7 and 23 Apr. 1988, p. 7.

[21] *Arms Control and Disarmament: Quarterly Review*, no. 8 (Jan. 1988), p. 22.

[22] *The Guardian*, 1 June 1988, p. 6, and *The Independent*, 3 June 1988, p. 1.

[23] *The Independent*, 20 May 1988, p. 8, and Davis, L. E., 'Prospects for strategic arms reduction', *Bulletin*, The Council for Arms Control, no. 37 (Apr. 1988), pp. 1–2.

[24] See Davis (note 23), p. 2, and *The Guardian*, 28 Mar. 1988, p. 6 on pressures on the SDI programme.

[25] *The Guardian*, 2 June 1988, p. 1.

[26] *The Independent*, 3 June 1988, p. 1.

[27] *The Guardian*, 2 Nov. 1985, p. 6.

[28] *The Guardian*, 19 Sep. 1987, p. 1.

[29] The International Institute for Strategic Studies,*The Military Balance 1986–1987* (IISS: London, 1986), p. 207 gives estimate for July 1986. The 1983 figures are based on the Soviet and US negotiating offers of late 1983, when both assumed 243 missiles targeted on Europe. See Talbott, S., *Deadly Gambits: The Reagan Administration and the Stalemate in Nuclear Arms Control* (Pan Books: London, 1985), pp. 198 and 204.

[30] *The Guardian*, 3 Mar. 1987, p. 1, and Hardenbergh (note 16), p. 18.

[31] Freedman, L., *Arms Control: Management or Reform* (Routledge and Kegan Paul: London, 1986), Chatham House Papers, no. 31, p. 41 notes in relation to Gorbachev's January 1986 zero-option offer for Europe that the USA felt obliged to respond positively. But adds: 'for many in the NATO establishment, Gorbachev's zero option confirmed their original misgivings about President Reagan's version. Cruise and Pershing were *not* intended to be simple responses to the SS-20, but reflected the special needs of the Alliance'. See also *The Guardian*, 3 Mar. 1987, p. 25 on NATO ambivalence to the Soviet offer of 28 Feb. 1987 to do a separate deal on the basis of a zero option for INF in Europe.

[32] *The Independent*, 16 Apr. 1987, p. 8.

[33] *The Guardian*, 15 May 1987, p. 1.

[34] Windsor, P., 'German attitudes to arms control negotiations', *Council for Arms Control Bulletin*, no 32 (May 1987), pp. 1–3. See also *The Guardian*, 16 May 1987, p. 1 and 20 May 1987, p. 7.

[35] *The Independent*, 2 June 1987, p. 1.

[36] *The Independent*, 29 Apr. 1987, p. 10 and 3 June 1987, p. 11.

[37] Hardenbergh, C., 'News of negotiations', *ADIU Report*, vol. 9, no. 5 (Sep.–Oct. 1987), p. 12.

[38] *The Independent*, 3 June 1987, p. 11.

[39] *The Guardian*, 21 May 1987, p. 6.

[40] *The Independent*, 24 July 1987, p. 1; and Freedman, L., 'Why this disarmament dawn is unlikely to prove false', *The Independent*, 24 July 1987, p. 18. Gorbachev's concession on the Asian SS-20s was initially tied to the Pershing 1a issue for bargaining purposes.

[41] *The Guardian*, 2 Mar. 1987, p. 7 for Soviet objections to including verification in the Treaty in early 1987; see also *The Guardian*, 3 Mar. 1987, p. 1 for Senate Group comments.

[42] *The Guardian*, 10 Mar. 1987, p. 8.

[43] Hardenbergh, C., 'News of negotiations', *ADIU Report*, vol. 9, no. 6 (Nov.–Dec. 1987), p. 20.

[44] *Independent*, 9 Dec. 1987, pp. 1 and 9; and *The Guardian*, 10 Dec. 1987, p. 13.

[45] *The Guardian*, 18 May 1988, p. 6, and *The Independent*, 25 May 1988, p. 10.

[46] See, for example, Cornwell, R., 'Gorbachev's disarming question flusters West', *The Independent*, 16 Apr. 1987, p. 8.

[47] *The Guardian*, 20 Dec. 1986, p. 1 and 11 Feb. 1987, p. 1. The most publicized symbol of Moscow's greater liberalism was the release from exile of Dr Sakharov.

[48] Hardenbergh (note 9), pp. 20–21.

[49] Freedman (note 40), p. 18.

[50] Phillips, S., 'European report', *ADIU Report*, vol. 8, no. 3 (May–June 1986), p. 10. See also *The Guardian*, 10 Oct. 1985, p. 8 and 1 Nov. 1985, p. 15.

[51] Hardenbergh (note 6), p. 21.

[52] For reactions by NATO military commanders see, e.g., *The Guardian*, 18 Oct. 1986, p. 6.

[53] *The Guardian*, 1 May 1987, p. 23.

[54] See, for example, *The Independent*, 7 May 1987, p. 8.

[55] See *The Guardian*, 21 Oct. 1986, p. 10 on Perle's position.

[56] *The Observer*, 26 Apr. 1987, p. 10 and *The Guardian*, 23 Apr. 1987, p. 21. Republican Presidential candidate Senator Robert Dole also criticized the proposed INF deal.

[57] *The Guardian*, 28 Nov. 1985, p. 32.

[58] *The Guardian*, 3 Mar. 1987, p. 8. For a more detailed assessment of military attitudes see Griffiths, F., '"New thinking" in the Kremlin', *Bulletin of the Atomic Scientists*, vol. 43, no. 3 (Apr. 1987), pp. 20–24. Griffiths comments that institutionally the military seem effectively subordinated but notes evidence of a debate in the military press about military response to Reagan's policies.

[59] *The Guardian*, 27 May 1987, p. 25.

[60] *The Guardian*, 17 Dec. 1986, p. 6. For more detailed analysis of Politburo changes and the role of the military see Mackintosh, M., 'The Soviet Union under new rulers: Gorbachev's first two years', *NATO Review*, vol . 35, no. 1 (Feb. 1987), pp. 1–10.

[61] See Hardenbergh (note 4), p. 21 and Hardenbergh (note 9), p. 21.

[62] *The Guardian*, 10 Mar. 1987, p. 8.

[63] *The Guardian*, 4 June 1987, p. 10.

[64] For example, Shultz claimed after the breakdown at Reykjavik that it was only the tough line by the USA on SDI that had brought both sides close to a strategic and INF agreement. *The Independent*, 13 Oct. 1986, p. 1.

[65] See, for example, Freedman (note 31), p. 41.

[66] *ADIU Report*, vol. 5, no. 6 (Nov.–Dec. 1983), p. 13 covers SRINF deployments. Hardenbergh (note 9), p. 21 comments on the West German concern about short-range missiles in the GDR and Czechoslovakia.

[67] See, for example, Sigal, L.V., 'INF deal faces conservative opposition', *Bulletin of the Atomic Scientists*, vol. 43, no. 4 (May 1987), p. 15.

[68] *The Guardian*, 27 May 1987, p. 6.

[69] *The Guardian*, 13 May 1987, p. 27 and 15 May 1987, p. 8.

[70] *The Guardian*, 22 Apr. 1987, p. 6 on the proposals before the NATO High Level Group.

[71] *The Guardian*, 1 May 1987, p. 23.

[72] See, for example, *The Observer*, 15 Mar. 1987, p. 15.

[73] See *The Guardian*, 20 Apr. 1989, p. 10.

9. Multilateral talks in Europe

I. Introduction

This chapter examines two sets of multilateral arms control negotiations: the Mutual and Balanced Force Reductions (MBFR) talks and the Conference on Security and Co-operation in Europe (CSCE) in Europe. Inaugurated in 1973, the MBFR negotiations on force reductions in Central Europe continued fruitlessly for over 15 years until they were replaced by a new forum, the Conventional Forces in Europe (CFE) negotiations, in January 1989. From the outset, the distance between the two sides in the MBFR negotiations was symbolized by NATO's insistence on using the word 'balanced' in official references to the talks and by the WTO's equally demonstrative refusal to do so. The CSCE, which also began in 1973, was primarily concerned with political and economic issues, and in the 1975 Helsinki Final Act, resulted in the agreement of some modest confidence-building measures (CBMs). The Stockholm Conference on Disarmament in Europe (CDE), set up in 1984 under the aegis of the CSCE, reached further agreement concerning some confidence- and security-building measures (CSBMs) in September 1986.

Although the USA and the USSR dominated both the MBFR and the CSCE negotiations, both great powers were influenced, nevertheless, by the multilateral character of the talks. In Vienna, the MBFR negotiations were based solely on the positions of two opposed alliances. The CSCE process, however, provided a forum for the expression of the views of the neutral and non-aligned (NNA) European states. The type of arms control being discussed was also very different in the two negotiations. Whereas the goal of the MBFR talks involved actual cuts in existing forces, the CSCE and CDE agreements only covered certain measures to prevent surprise attack and to foster mutual confidence. The CSCE negotiations were also more susceptible to changes in the character of *détente*; even when the focus was on technical issues, the CSCE process reflected the changes in the relations between Moscow and Washington more directly than the MBFR talks.

II. The MBFR talks

Origins

The origins of MBFR and CSCE were closely linked and can be traced to the late 1960s.[1] At the time, NATO and the Warsaw Pact had abandoned the aim of a political resettlement in Europe which might include the reunification of Germany and looked to more limited measures to promote stability in a Europe divided into armed blocs. Whereas the Soviet Union wished for a political ratification of the status quo in Europe and for increased economic co-operation through a conference on European security, the West held out for more specific military and technical measures to promote stability.

The aims of the two alliances in entering the MBFR talks, therefore were divergent and provide a possible explanation for the subsequent difficulties experienced at each stage of the negotiations. The NATO alliance had three main objectives. First, NATO wished to deflect growing domestic pressures, especially within the USA for a reduction of defence commitments. Second, NATO wished to use the talks as a vehicle for limiting what was a perceived growing WTO superiority in conventional arms. The third objective was to promote a Western arms control initiative in order to counter Soviet pressure for the convening of a conference on European security. The USSR, on the other hand, apparently accepted NATO's proposal for negotiations on force reductions primarily as a concession to secure such a conference. Although Moscow viewed the talks as a means of reducing the FRG's military potential, the Soviet Union apparently shared Washington's anxiety concerning a sudden and substantial reduction of US troops in Europe which might have proved to be militarily and politically destabilizing. After the SALT I negotiations had begun, both the USA and the USSR possessed a general interest in the maintenance of *détente*. European arms control talks, therefore, became one forum for achieving this goal. The Soviet Union, however, appears to have been motivated more strongly by this consideration.

The most direct pressure on the US Government to enter negotiations with the WTO on conventional arms reductions in Europe was a succession of congressional resolutions by Senator Mansfield calling for withdrawal of substantial numbers of US forces from Europe. In a June 1966 speech, Mansfield argued that the demands on US forces and finances imposed by the Vietnam War necessitated a cut in US commitments in Europe. In January 1967, Mansfield introduced his first resolution and reintroduced it in December 1969. By 1970–71, congressional sentiment in favour of reducing US troops in Europe mounted; and in May 1971, Mansfield introduced yet another resolution. This time, Mansfield called for a 50 percent reduction in US troops in Europe and stressed the need for budgetary and foreign currency savings. During the summer of 1973, Senator Mansfield and his supporters stepped up their campaign for troop withdrawals in both the House and the Senate. Although the domestic resistance to the levels of military spending in the West

European countries was also high, the demands by the US Congress for unilateral US cuts provided the motivation for NATO to propose force reduction talks in Europe.

NATO's first response to Mansfield's demands was to appoint the Harmel Study Group in 1967 to examine the future tasks of the Alliance. The Harmel Report, endorsed by NATO Ministers in December 1967, envisaged a role for NATO in promoting *détente*, as well as in ensuring military strength, and specifically proposed arms control measures including 'balanced force reductions'. In June 1968, NATO Ministers issued the Reykjavik Declaration which called for negotiations with the WTO on mutual balanced force reductions. The August 1968 invasion of Czechoslovakia by the Soviet Union strengthened Western fears about Soviet intentions and also had the concrete result of increasing the number of Soviet troops stationed in Central Europe. It did not, however, rule out the possibility of arms control negotiations. In December 1968, NATO renewed its call for negotiations on force reductions in Europe in response to a communiqué by Soviet and East European leaders urging a conference on European security. In May 1970, NATO followed up its December 1968 statement with the Rome Declaration which elaborated upon the requirements for satisfactory arms reduction talks.

Up to this point, the Soviet Union and the WTO had concentrated on stressing the need for a security conference which would recognize the existence of the GDR as a sovereign state and would require the recognition of the GDR's Oder-Neisse border with Poland by the FRG. Elected in 1969, Willy Brandt's Social Democratic Government abandoned claims to previous German territory in the East and began a process of *Ostpolitik* to regularize the FRG's relations with its Eastern neighbours. *Ostpolitik* also extended a *de facto* recognition to the GDR and served to normalize the position of West Berlin. Although the FRG's new attitude made it easier for NATO to accept the Soviet proposal for a security conference, the NATO meeting in December 1970 withheld an agreement to go ahead with the conference until the status of Berlin had been settled. In the meanwhile, the WTO had made some concessions to NATO's insistence on arms control talks by stating in a June 1970 communiqué that reductions in foreign forces might be discussed within the framework of the CSCE. Force reduction negotiations in Europe received another boost when General Secretary Brezhnev, in a speech to the 24th Congress of the Communist Party of the Soviet Union (CPSU) in 1971, specifically stated that he welcomed the proposal for force reductions in Central Europe.

The 24th Congress marked the consolidation of Brezhnev's political power and a strengthening of the Soviet Union's commitment to *détente* and arms control. The reference to European arms control may be viewed partly in this context. However, in a speech on 14 May 1971—a few days before a vote on the Mansfield Amendment was due in the US Senate—Brezhnev indicated a clear willingness on the part of the Soviet Union to take part in negotiations on reducing arms in Central Europe. Although Kissinger has claimed that Brezhnev's remarks were directed toward the promotion of the Berlin talks and were not addressed to the Congress, the timing of Brezhnev's remarks struck many commentators as being too significant to be merely coincidental.[2] Brezhnev appeared to be holding out a helping hand to the Nixon Administration's attempt to head off unilateral US troop withdrawals by promising that negotiated mutual reductions might be possible. Brezhnev's move implied that Moscow was as anxious as Washington to avoid major unilateral US troop reductions, presumably because it viewed the USA as a stabilizing influence in Western Europe and feared an increase in West German military power. In addition, perhaps the USSR did not want US troop withdrawals to highlight the number of Soviet troops located in Eastern Europe and to encourage demands for Soviet reciprocation.

During 1971, NATO edged closer to accepting the Soviet proposal for a CSCE. Soviet leaders confirmed their willingness to discuss arms reductions in Central Europe, but hedged on the nature of the forum for talks. The May 1972 summit meeting between President Nixon and General Secretary Brezhnev reportedly included a deal that a conference on European security would proceed in exchange for Soviet co-operation in force reduction talks. After a further visit by Kissinger to Moscow in September 1972, the Soviet Union publicly agreed to force reduction talks, separate from the CSCE, which would begin in 1973.

Preliminary manœuvres

Preparatory discussions to decide on participation, the format and the official title of the force reduction conference began in Vienna on 31 January 1973. The Soviet Union had wanted to discuss arms reductions in an all-European forum, which included the NNA states, rather than participate in a negotiation confined to the two alliances. When the preliminary talks opened in Vienna, the Soviet side had accepted a focus on military and technical questions to be hammered out between the opposed blocs, but the definition of Central Europe and the scope of participation was still in doubt. Although France, which had left NATO's integrated military command structure in 1966 and had emphasized its independence from the USA, was not prepared to take part in inter-bloc negotiations, it remained a major West European military power. If France was not to be covered in the area of proposed force reductions, then the Soviet Union wished to include Italy on the NATO side. Although NATO resisted the inclusion of Italy on the grounds that it was not involved in the military balance on the central front, NATO did want to count Hungarian forces in the calculations on reductions. Therefore, the WTO attempted to bargain the inclusion of Hungary against that of Italy. The WTO insisted that Hungary was relevant to the balance in the southern European theatre, and not to the central front. Because the USSR could not persuade France to join the talks and Italy refused to be included in the sphere of reductions, Hungary was not a direct participant in the formal negotiations that began on 30 October 1973.

The preparatory conference agreed that the direct participants in the talks (those parties whose forces would be covered by any agreed reductions) on the NATO side would be Belgium, the FRG, Luxembourg and the Netherlands, in addition to three non-continental countries with troops in the FRG: Great Britain, Canada and the USA. On the WTO side, the direct participants would be Czechoslovakia, the GDR, Poland and, of course, the Soviet Union which retained substantial forces in Central Europe. A category of special participants (those parties who could attend the talks but would not be liable to reductions) was created for other interested alliance members on each side. This category included Italy, Greece, Norway and Denmark from NATO; and Hungary, Bulgaria and Romania from the WTO. Romania preferred the CSCE forum for the talks and had wished to extend their scope to cover the Balkans. The Soviet Union, however, apparently preferred a more limited focus on Central Europe, as did NATO.

Even the title of the negotiations was a source of dispute. Whereas the West emphasized the concept of 'balanced force reductions' from the outset, the WTO rightly interpreted this to mean bigger reductions of their forces than on the NATO side and refused to include the word 'balanced' in the official title. Although the West did concede the point, it continued to to refer to 'Mutual Balanced Force Reductions talks' in its literature.[3] Genuine military concerns, however, underlay the verbal sparring and served to deadlock the talks until their conclusion in 1989.

Main issues and initial proposals

The term 'force reductions' is, in itself, an ambiguous concept and left open the possibility of very different interpretations. The preparatory conference narrowed the scope slightly, and excluded naval and amphibious forces. The conference also agreed to exclude border guards and internal security forces. Still, before the talks started officially in Vienna, there had been no clarification on whether the negotiations would cover reductions in both nuclear and conventional forces, or would be confined to cuts in conventional forces. In addition, there was room for further dispute over whether air, as well as ground forces, should be covered, whether the focus was on men or equipment, and what sort of weapons would be included. The original WTO position, put forward on 6 November 1973, called for reductions in both nuclear and conventional air and ground forces, and specified that foreign forces should withdraw as organic military units. The initial NATO proposal, which was tabled in reply, excluded nuclear weapons, called for reductions in ground forces only and focused primarily on the number of troops to be withdrawn. However, the Western proposal did specifically require that a whole Soviet tank army of five divisions should move out of Central Europe with all its equipment.[4]

The second question was whether only the great powers should withdraw their forces, or whether the cuts were to extend to the countries in Central Europe. The West was especially anxious to reduce the number of Soviet combat units in Central Europe, and put forward a phased plan that would confine phase one to Soviet and US troop withdrawals. Only after phase one had been completed would the details of further force reductions by all participants be hammered out. The WTO, however, was primarily interested in reducing West German forces. Although this desire can be traced partly to the fact that the Federal Republic was the major military power in Central Europe, perhaps an even greater motivation was the historic Soviet fear of a revanchist and strongly armed Germany. Therefore, the WTO envisaged an initial reduction of 20 000 troops on each side, drawn from all countries involved, to be followed in the next two years by percentage cuts in the forces of all participants. Percentage cuts, of course, would necessitate larger reductions (in real terms) in the West German forces, than in the smaller forces of other West European states. Although indigenous forces would be demobilized, foreign troops would be simply withdrawn. The WTO's approach, then, was designed to minimize Soviet force reductions in Central Europe.

The third disputed point was whether or not force reductions would specify the scale of reductions by individual national armed forces. The Soviet Union insisted on being specific, largely in order to pin down the size of the West German reduction, and became even more explicit concerning this issue in later proposals. NATO, on the other hand, was responsive to West German sensitivity to being singled out in arms control proposals and to attempts to restrict the FRG's sovereignty. The West, therefore, blocked the WTO's efforts to impose national quotas or to set a ceiling on remaining national forces. The original NATO proposal was deliberately vague about the second phase in order to avoid pre-determined, and precise, national force cuts. Later, NATO continued to insist on overall alliance reductions and ceilings which only specified the levels of US and Soviet withdrawals.

The strategic and political interests of both sides were, of course, influenced by geographical asymmetries. Soviet forces withdrawn to national territory could be stationed in the western area of the USSR and could be rapidly reintroduced into Central Europe in the event of war. US forces stationed at home had to be transported across the Atlantic Ocean. Initially, the WTO aimed to increase this disadvantage by requiring all foreign forces to remove their equipment upon redeployment. This proposal was designed in to undercut the USA's practice of pre-stocking arms and other equipment in the FRG.[5]

Geography, then, served to enhance the central problems for the MBFR talks, which were the conflicting strategic goals behind the proposed cuts (by both sides) and the inability (or refusal) of the two alliances to agree on the existing military position as a basis for agreeing on an end result. NATO's aim was not only to achieve mutual reductions, but to induce the WTO to accept bigger cuts in order to arrive at a position of equality. Behind NATO's approach was the conviction that the WTO had superiority, both in numbers of troops and in amounts of equipment, especially tanks. Therefore, the initial Western proposal required only 29 000 US soldiers, as opposed to an entire Soviet tank army of 68 000 men and 1700 tanks, to be withdrawn in phase one. The proposal also envisaged further mutual reductions to a common ceiling of 700 000 men in ground forces on each side. The WTO, however, stressed that each side should instead accept equal cuts which were initially formulated in terms of equal numbers and later changed to equal percentage cuts. The USSR insisted that there was already an equilibrium in Central Europe and that Western estimates were unrealistic and aimed at tilting the balance of power in favour of NATO.

After the WTO presented its own figures on the size of its forces in Central Europe in June 1976, the debate about reductions became more concrete. Because the WTO claimed to have ground forces of 805 000 men (150 000 fewer than NATO estimated), the two sides were unable to agree on a base line for equitable reductions. The size of NATO ground forces, then 791 000 strong, was not in dispute. The 'data discrepancy' in the estimation of WTO forces on the central front was a major cause of deadlock at Vienna.

The fact that NATO and WTO forces are structured differently makes it more difficult to agree upon the military balance and has been suggested as one of the reasons for the discrepancy in numbers. The WTO claims that NATO is counting as combat troops men in uniform undertaking administrative tasks that are performed by civilians in the West.[6] It can also be argued that numerical cuts which fail to take account of differences in structure and strategic doctrine may not address the genuine questions of military stability. Potentially, this line of reasoning undercuts the very concept of MBFR talks. However, the argument can also be used as a rationale for military resistance to accepting reductions that do not adequately address the other side's potential for mounting an offensive.

The final major obstacle in the MBFR negotiations was the perennial dilemma posed by the requirements of verification. The verification issue, indicated by the NATO term 'associated measures', was deferred until the Alliance was finally able to overcome its internal disagreements in 1979. NATO then proposed detailed measures for the inspection of compliance with troop reductions and the monitoring of temporary troop movements. Although the WTO was prepared to consider the implementation of advance notification procedures for manœuvres and the installation of temporary control posts, the WTO objected to permanent posts or an annual quota of ground and aerial inspections.[7]

Major developments in the MBFR talks

From the time of their opening proposals in 1973, the MBFR negotiators attacked the details of offers by the other side (all the time stressing the equitable nature of their own proposals), and made new offers and counter-offers designed both to provide genuine concessions and to maintain the appearance of progress. This section will examine a few of the key developments during the negotiations and will seek to explain the process by which the WTO and NATO managed to resolve some of the outstanding issues between them.

Whether or not nuclear weapons should have been included in the possible reductions was a fundamental and major issue for both sides in the MBFR negotiations. Indeed, both sides shifted from their initial positions on this issue and later became ensnared in a complicated dispute concerning the role of INF. After two years of deadlock, NATO made the first move and presented its 'Option III' proposal in December 1975. In 1972, NATO had designed three possible options for the MBFR negotiations, and Option III was envisaged as including nuclear weapons as a means to offset what NATO perceived as the WTO's massive offensive potential. NATO offered to cut some of its longer-range nuclear weapons in Europe in return for a major reduction in Soviet tanks. Under the terms of Option III, 1000 US nuclear warheads, 54 nuclear-capable F-4 Phantom US aircraft, 36 US Pershing 1 missile launchers and 29 000 US troops would be withdrawn.[8] One motive for this proposal was pressure from the US Congress for withdrawal of some of the 7000 US tactical nuclear warheads in Europe.[9] Another motive was the desire to give the Vienna talks some momentum by making NATO's initial unequal offer (the withdrawal of only 29 000 troops against a Soviet tank army of 63 000) more acceptable by including some aircraft and nuclear weapons to meet Soviet proposals. NATO, however, qualified this concession by presenting Option III as a once-only offer and not as a basis for general negotiations on nuclear disarmament in Europe.

The Option III proposal was gradually overtaken by events. NATO devised the plan to trade off nuclear weapons against Soviet tanks at a time when the tanks appeared to pose the major threat. In the later 1970s, however, NATO became more concerned about the modernization of the Soviet Union's European nuclear arsenal and began to debate the modernization of NATO's theatre nuclear forces. Option III carefully specified that residual limits on nuclear missiles and aircraft after the Pershing 1 and F-4 reductions would only apply to missiles of the same range and aircraft of the same type. During NATO discussions in 1978–79, however, it became clear that the Alliance felt free to introduce new longer-range missiles in the form of GLCMs and Pershing II missiles. After the December 1979 NATO decision to proceed with new INF deployment—a decision which included the replacement of 108 US Pershing 1 missiles with the new Pershing II and, as a gesture towards limiting nuclear stockpiles, the removal of 1000 older nuclear warheads from Europe—Option III ceased to be a negotiable proposal and was formally withdrawn. When the INF talks began, nuclear weapons were shifted from the MBFR talks to a separate set of negotiations.

Initially, the Soviet Union responded cautiously to Option III. The USSR was anxious to elicit information about the limits to be set on residual nuclear forces and resisted NATO's aim of 'balance' through higher WTO force reductions. In a counter-offer to Option III in 1976, the WTO envisaged equal reductions in

US F-4 aircraft and Soviet Fitter fighter-bombers, and in Pershing I and Soviet SS-1c Scud missiles. In addition, each side would remove an unspecified number of warheads. These nuclear reductions would accompany an initial reduction of US and Soviet conventional forces, and would be followed by a second phase in which the forces of all direct participants to the talks would be reduced. Two years later, the Soviet Union cancelled its offer to match US nuclear aircraft and missile cuts in the first phase. Instead, the Soviet Union envisaged that the USA would implement its Option III nuclear reductions and withdraw 7 per cent of its ground forces in return for Soviet removal of 7 per cent of its own men and equipment (including 1000 tanks) and one army headquarters. The Soviet decision to abandon its original proposal to reduce its own nuclear weapons in the first phase may have been either a response to NATO's plans for INF deployments or may have reflected its own nuclear modernization intentions.

The Soviet Union's concern about NATO's proposed deployments of cruise and Pershing II missiles resulted in Brezhnev's offer in October 1979 to reduce Soviet INF targeted on Europe, and to withdraw 20 000 Soviet troops and 1000 tanks unilaterally. The unilateral troop withdrawal began in December 1979 and was officially completed by August 1980. Although the withdrawal of Soviet troops was primarily designed to influence NATO's plans concerning nuclear modernization, the move had obvious implications for the MBFR negotiations. At first, it was not clear in Western circles whether the USSR would regard the unilateral action as a preliminary step towards further agreed force cuts or would insist on the 20 000 troops being counted when reductions were negotiated. By December 1979, however, WTO pronouncements made clear that the NATO call for the USSR to remove a further 30 000 troops was not acceptable in light of the unilateral withdrawal already under way.

The Soviet troop withdrawal served to illustrate the difficulties of verifying force reductions and the tendency for the other side to suspect the worst of apparently conciliatory gestures. NATO was able to verify that the Sixth Soviet Tank Division of about 10 000 men had left its garrisons in the GDR, but was not sure whether or not the remaining men and tanks—taken from a number of formations—had actually left. There were also doubts about what had happened to the withdrawn troops. Some suggested that they had been either been brought back in smaller units or had been sent to Hungary.[10] Given the scope for disagreement among intelligence agencies and the political manipulation of intelligence reports, NTM alone would clearly not be satisfactory for verifying complex troop reductions.

The changing positions on whether and how to include nuclear weapons in the MBFR negotiations, and the Soviet decision to unilaterally withdraw 20 000 men, were the most dramatic elements in the course of the MBFR negotiations. Both sides made concessions on force levels. In December 1979, NATO moderated its demands for a very large initial Soviet troop reduction and called for removal of 30 000 on the Soviet side against withdrawal of 13 000 US troops. By the early 1980s, the WTO appeared to have made more concessions in principle, but the reality of these concessions was questionable. The Soviet Union agreed that the first phase should consist only of great power troop withdrawals and ceased to insist that these reductions should be linked to cuts in nuclear weapons. The USSR agreed to a provision requiring some advance notification of troop movements into the defined Central area, and not to redeploy troops withdrawn near the northern and southern flanks.[11] Although the Soviet Union also agreed that troop ceilings should be collective and not nationally defined, in practice, it sought indirect ways to limit West German forces. The WTO apparently made major concession when it accepted NATO's proposed goals of a maximum of 700 000 troops in ground forces, and a combined total of 900 000 soldiers in ground and air forces on each side. In the view of the West, however, the data dispute nullified the real value of accepting common ceilings.

Some of the data discrepancies were clarified when the WTO provided more information in 1978 and 1980. This information showed that there was near agreement between the NATO and WTO estimates concerning the size of East German and Czechoslovakian forces. The fact that NATO had been counting Soviet ground forces responsible for air defence and a Polish amphibious division of 4500 men also emerged.[12] These points of clarification, however, still did not resolve the basic disagreement concerning the data. There may have been coherent reasons for the discrepancy, which the WTO has suggested may have stemmed from the administrative role of some men in uniform and from different rules for counting reservists in uniform.[13] Nevertheless, regardless of how one judges the veracity of the estimates, it is clear that both sides played politics with the figures.

For negotiating purposes, concessions on the data base logically affect the size of reductions each side should implement. Therefore, the original figures represent, in themselves, a potential bargaining position. Western intelligence estimates of WTO ground-force strength were revised upwards by 160 000 in the spring of 1972, while the data base released by the WTO in 1976 was closer to pre-1972 NATO estimates.[14] NATO offer some concessions on the data base in April 1984 by suggesting that only troops in combat and combat support units should be covered. This concession was based on the grounds that it made sense to focus on the most important troops and that the disagreements about data between the two sides were less acute at this level. The WTO, however, failed to reciprocate. Instead, a Czechoslovakian delegate initiated a new data dispute in July 1984 by raising the question of increases in NATO and WTO forces.[15]

The dispute over data is also linked to wider political and military considerations. NATO has always claimed that the WTO has conventional superiority in Europe and has buttressed this assertion by pointing to overall totals of troops and equipment—especially tanks. That the WTO has conventional superiority over NATO has been an article of faith in nearly all public NATO pronouncements. The acceptance of this dogma by the European public reduced the likelihood of individual governments being pressed to cut conventional forces and strengthened support for NATO's reliance on nuclear weapons. Until the advent of General Secretary Gorbachev, the Soviet Union was equally reluctant to admit any conventional superiority, which would undermine its claim to be a purely defensive alliance. Certainly, the Soviet Union could not declare openly that it required troops and tanks in Eastern Europe for policing purposes, as well as to deter a NATO attack.

The dispute over the data base remained a problem of a particularly intractable nature for the MBFR negotiations. In December 1985, NATO made an attempt to bypass the data base issue by proposing to postpone an agreement on the size of WTO forces until an initial withdrawal of US and Soviet troops had been completed. Then, the main area of disagreement became the extent of verification. Although the WTO draft treaty tabled in February 1986 provided some concessions on the principle of permanent checkpoints and on-site inspection, major differences remained between the two sides. The West, for example, wanted 30 on-site inspections per year, while the East claimed the right to refuse ill-founded requests for inspection. The WTO also wanted to avoid formal check-points to monitor the regular rotation of Soviet troops in the area. Differences remained too on the key question of collective versus national ceilings and whether US equipment should be withdrawn from Europe with the troops. By 1985, the proposed numbers of troops to be withdrawn had become token—5000 US troops and 11 500 Soviet troops in the Western version, and 6500 US troops and 11 500 Soviet troops in the WTO version.[16] Thus, the progress that had been achieved was at the cost of abandoning genuinely significant cuts in preference for the potential conclusion of a minimal agreement.

The future of the MBFR negotiations became, in itself, a subject for negotiation during 1986. In April, Gorbachev suggested that the talks should cover a wider agenda. In June, the WTO proposed transferring the negotiations to the forum of the CDE, which was then just finishing its phase of negotiating on CSBMs, or widening the existing MBFR forum. The WTO not only called for a new context for the talks but also urged much more radical cuts—25 per cent reductions in ground and tactical air forces by the 1990s.[17] NATO agreed to study the possibility of a new forum for talks on conventional arms, but was unable to reach internal agreement until February 1987 on exactly how to conduct the new talks. France still preferred negotiations within the CSCE context, and the USA remained strongly opposed. It was decided that the new negotiations should take place between all the members of NATO and the WTO (but without an explicit link with the CSCE), but that the new negotiations should not be treated as talks between two blocs. Informal discussion on procedures for a new negotiation on conventional arms began between NATO and WTO members in Vienna in February 1987.[18] The MBFR talks continued up to 1989, but in a purely ritualized manner. Both sides were in general agreement that the MBFR negotiations had failed to serve any useful purpose.

III. Why did the MBFR negotiations fail?

Real purpose of the talks

NATO's primary motive in promoting the MBFR negotiations was not a desire to achieve substantial cuts in conventional forces, but to maintain and improve its own forces. To the extent that the MBFR negotiations preempted congressional demands for unilateral US troop cuts during the 1970s and deflected the pressure for reduced defence spending in West European countries (in particular in Britain and the Netherlands), the talks, in fact, succeeded. Indeed, the MBFR negotiations have been celebrated as an outstanding success in the management of the NATO Alliance and of domestic opinion.[19] If the maintenance of force levels, rather than arms reductions, was NATO's first concern, then it is scarcely surprising that such little progress resulted from the MBFR talks. Coit Blacker notes that once congressional pressure for force reductions had slackened, the West had very little incentive to to try very hard for an agreement on terms the Soviet Union might accept.[20] Conversely, if the Soviet Union's main aim was to get the West to participate in the CSCE, then it had no reason to make major concessions. However, insofar as the Soviet Union viewed the negotiations as an instrument of *détente*, there was some inducement to negotiate with a degree of seriousness, at least up until the late 1970s.

Because there were a range of motives that led both sides to the conference table and because the logic of negotiations (once initiated) required some attempt to make progress, the cynical motivations ascribed to the MBFR talks do not provide a complete explanation for the failure of the negotiations. Therefore, it is worth examining the extent to which the arms control (enumerated in Chapter 2) impeded the MBFR negotiations.

Obstacles to agreement

Great Power confrontation

Because NATO proposed the talks in part to counter the Soviet Union's pressure for a CSCE forum, as well as to appear sincere on arms control questions, propaganda appears to have played a major role in the decision to initiate the MBFR negotiations. After the talks had begun, the WTO proved to be so anxious to publicize its own proposals that it broke an agreement on confidentiality. This action suggested a propaganda motive.[21] Prestige considerations also influenced the preliminary manœuvres concerning which countries should participate in the negotiations, and neither side wanted to back down on this issue. In a face-saving statement, NATO required that Hungary should be included in any future negotiations. Prestige considerations may also have impinged on the data dispute and resulted in both sides being anxious to maintain their general public positions on the nature of the European balance, and may possibly have encouraged the WTO's intransigence in refusing to accept Western interpretations.[22] Both the USA and the Soviet Union apparently concurred in the use of the MBFR negotiations as a means for maintaining US military presence and political influence in Europe. In addition, the Soviet Union may have sought indirect Western acceptance of the legitimacy of Soviet military presence in Central Europe. Whereas one of the Soviet Union's aims was to pressure NATO to impose limits on West German forces, NATO sought to resist this pressure and to maintain a united front. Unlike the SALT negotiations, however, the MBFR talks did not become a significant forum for the pursuit of political advantage in the relations between the great powers.

The explicit linkage imposed by NATO between the CSCE and the MBFR negotiations persuaded the USSR to join these talks more or less on NATO terms. As previously noted, however, this did not serve to promote subsequent progress. The fact that both sides viewed the MBFR negotiations as a means of promoting *détente*. was underscored most notably at the 1972 Moscow summit meeting when Nixon and Brezhnev agreed that negotiations on conventional forces should be conducted. Apparently, the Soviet Union also viewed the MBFR talks as a forum for maintaining a degree of *détente* with Europe after its relations with the USA had begun to deteriorate. When the Soviet Union and the USA began to move towards a renewed *détente* in late 1985, they offered conciliatory gestures in the MBFR negotiations. By 1987, however, both sides recognized that to secure serious progress in arms control in Europe and to consolidate the new period of *détente*, a new forum for the negotiations was required.

Although favourable political conditions did not result in genuine progress in the MBFR negotiations, the worsening of relations between the USA and the Soviet Union did not have a dramatic impact on the talks either. NATO's decision to deploy INF did result in the withdrawal of Option III and probably prompted the USSR to demand that its unilateral troop reductions be taken into account in any proposed cuts. However, the Reagan Administration continued the MBFR negotiations (despite doubts about arms control in principle) although, in line with its general approach, it toughened the verification provisions proposed by the West. When the USSR walked out of the INF talks and deferred the START negotiations indefinitely, it nevertheless continued to negotiate at Vienna. Blacker argues that both sides were more intransigent in the early 1980s as evidence for his thesis that there was a close link between MBFR and the state of US–Soviet relations.[23] However, this increased intransigence scarcely represented a dramatic set back in the context of failure to make any substantial progress ever since 1973.

The lack of progress in the MBFR negotiations even when relations were good can be explained by the fact that both sides were more interested in the talks as a symbol of *détente* (in addition to the other motives for the negotiations) than in reaching an agreement. The comparatively limited impact of the eclipse of *détente* upon the MBFR negotiations can be assigned to the multilateral character of the talks. The fact that the negotiations were multilateral (and of a long-standing nature) probably encouraged the Soviet

Union to continue negotiating and may have even discouraged the new Reagan Administration from pulling out. The low public profile and the fairly technical military character of the negotiations meant that the discussions could be (at least partially) more easily insulated from crises in the relationship between Moscow and Washington than highly visible arms control talks, and encouraged a non-polemical atmosphere within the talks.[24]

Alliance politics were necessarily central to the MBFR negotiations, however. Although the USA and the USSR were clearly the dominant partners of their respective alliances, both the WTO and NATO presented unified positions in the negotiations which were the outcome of internal compromise. In particular, NATO had to accommodate the FRG's sensitivities about any additional limits on its national sovereignty and any form of 'discrimination'. The need to reassure the FRG affected both the formulae on force ceilings and the proposals for verification which affected West German territory. This may explain why NATO, after having made such an issue of verification in 1973, failed to present any concrete proposals on the subject until 1979.[25] In general, differences of perception and interest, especially between European members and the USA, slowed down NATO's ability to promote the MBFR negotiations. Before the USA could put forward Option III (in an attempt to move the MBFR talks forward), it first had to overcome Allied resistance . In the FRG, the Christian Democrats and their right-wing partner, the Christian Socialist Union (both then in opposition) publicly opposed Option III when it was proposed at the end of 1975.[26] For their part, the West Europeans expressed annoyance at the US Administration's willingness to leak NATO proposals to the press in order to handle domestic opposition in Congress. Although the MBFR negotiations can be viewed as a 'success' within the context of Alliance politics (because NATO managed to uphold its public appearance of unity) alliance politics rendered timely and effective concessions inherently difficult.

The most important obstacle to progress in the MBFR negotiations was the fact that both sides were pursuing incompatible strategic goals. While NATO sought to gain the WTO's acceptance of disproportionate reductions in order to achieve NATO's conception of balance, the WTO was determined to press for equal reductions and the ratification of what the Soviet Union insisted was already an approximate balance. Assymetries in force structure, types and numbers of weapons deployed, in military doctrine and in the distance of the two great powers from the Central European theatre complicated the possibility of an agreement on what, exactly, would constitute a fair trade-off even further.

Ideologically biased perceptions do not seem to have had much influence on the course of the MBFR negotiations. The talks, however, did reflect, more or less, the ritualized suspicion between the two alliances as indicated by NATO's insistence of verification as a bar to cheating and the Soviet Union's fear that NATO would use verification procedures to gather intelligence. Perhaps the most notable example of NATO's endemic suspicion of Soviet actions during the MBFR negotiations was the belief that the unilateral withdrawal of Soviet troops was a trick. The Soviet Union, on the other hand, was motivated by deep and abiding suspicion of the FRG.

The momentum of weapon development and deployment did impinge on the MBFR negotiations. NATO initially devised Option III in 1972. By the time it was finally proposed in December 1975, many defence experts had concluded that it made less sense (by then) to trade NATO nuclear weapons against a WTO tank army. NATO had assumed Western superiority in tactical and theatre nuclear weapons. By 1975, however, the Alliance feared that its weapons were becoming more vulnerable to surprise attack and that the effectiveness of its bombers was being reduced by improvements in Soviet anti-aircraft defences. Indeed, NATO had already begun to discuss modernizing its theatre nuclear forces by the end of 1974. The subsequent Soviet deployment of SS-20s and the development of the Backfire bomber greatly increased Western apprehension and so contributed to the 1979 NATO decision to deploy cruise and Pershing II missiles. This decision overtook the MBFR negotiations and led eventually to the INF negotiations in 1981.

Both sides consciously tailored their proposals so as to allow weapon modernization and to ensure that the weapons that might be bargained away were of minimum military value. NATO devised Option III so as to permit the introduction of new missiles and aircraft. The 54 F-4 aircraft which NATO offered to abandon were believed to be less effective because of the development of Soviet anti-aircraft defences.[27] The Soviet counter-offer to Option III proposed the withdrawal of 54 Fitter fighter-bombers without specifying the exact model. NATO suspected that the Soviet Union intended to withdraw the older Fitter A model, which was then being gradually replaced by the newer Fitter Cs, modernized to cover a longer range and to carry a heavier payload.[28]

The domestic manœuvres in decision making on the MBFR negotiations have not been documented in much detail because the talks were not sufficiently interesting to prompt such accounts. It is reasonable to assume, however, that the military (on both sides) had an even greater influence than usual on the conduct of technical talks which concerned central front forces. Because there were no strong military incentives for either side to make serious concessions in order to achieve an agreement, the role of the military would have been conducive to negotiations of a cautious and intransigent nature.

Obstacles within the negotiating process

The MBFR discussions illustrated some of the standard differences in the general approach to negotiations between the two sides. The West's insistence on discussing military and technical issues in MBFR, as a price for joining the CSCE, demonstrated a typical contrast with the USSR's primary interest in political issues.[29] The MBFR negotiations also illustrated such familiar divergences of approach as the West's demands for strict verification and the

Soviet Union's reluctance to accept detailed inspection measures or to disclose military data.

The conduct of bargaining during the MBFR talks demonstrated that the side in the weaker position is not necessarily the more flexible in negotiations. Instead, the weaker side simply be more intransigent. Because of NATO's belief that it was at a considerable conventional military disadvantage, the Alliance entered the MBFR negotiations with the determination to achieve parity in any agreement. The Soviet Union, however, proved just as unwilling to relinquish whatever advantage it may have had at the outset. The MBFR talks suggest that the real issue in a negotiation is not whether one side has a military edge (which is almost certainly the case in most arms control talks) but whether both sides see real gains in an agreement, and can and will make the needed concessions. In the case of the MBFR negotiations each side wanted most what the other was least willing to grant: namely, the substantial withdrawal of Soviet troops from Central Europe and major reductions in West German forces.

The MBFR talks raised interesting questions about the organization of arms control talks: the degree of publicity, the scope, the decision making machinery and the forum for arms control negotiations the organization of arms control talks. Because the MBFR talks had a fairly low political profile (unlike the nuclear arms negotiations), this resulted in little domestic opposition—the exception being the significant resistance within the FRG to the Option III proposal. On the other hand, after congressional pressure to repatriate US troops had subsided, the MBFR negotiations did not attract the necessary support of groups committed to arms control. Little political impetus or public agitation in favour of particular measures resulted. Winkler comments on the contrast between the 'political storm' that greeted apparent US delay over starting missile talks after the NATO deployment decision and the 'dead silence' that greeted the dropping of Option III.[30] The MBFR negotiations fell between two stools. On the one hand, the talks were too politicized to achieve complete confidentiality and to focus on manageable technical arrangements. On the other hand, after the talks were well under way, there was no political interest on either side in reaching a broader agreement.

Some commentators have argued that the geographical scope of the talks was too narrow and that the definition of Central Europe tended to underscore the problems resulting from geographical asymmetry. Another obvious problem stemmed from the combination of the weapons and forces to be included. As long as NATO used nuclear weapons to offset WTO's conventional forces, a concentration only on conventional weapons was arguably artificial. Yet, to combine questions of nuclear and conventional forces in the same negotiations would necessarily add to the already considerable complexity of concluding an agreement on what, exactly, constituted equitable reductions.

Decision making in the MBFR negotiations had to be co-ordinated by the military alliances. NATO formulated policy through the NATO Council, the Senior Level Political Committee and a co-ordinating group located in Vienna. The most obvious problem with alliance decision making machinery (at least on the NATO side) was that it proved to be even slower than national bureaucracies in developing new positions. NATO also found it easier to agree on purely technical approaches than on the wider security issues which politically divided the Alliance. In addition, NATO's cumbersome decision making process resulted less flexibility and scope for compromise.[31] Excluding NNA European states from the MBFR negotiations meant there was no possibility for the introduction of independent proposals and perspectives in order to mediate a confrontation between the two blocs. Still, third parties can sometimes obstruct progress by being too radical in their demands. Furthermore, a smaller forum may serve to facilitate detailed technical discussions. France's refusal to join the MBFR talks represented the greatest problem arising out of the make-up of the membership of the negotiations. Because the Soviet Union was well aware of the numerically substantial French forces just outside the defined Central area, France's absence made a realistic trading off of conventional forces much more difficult to achieve. In addition, the FRG could not grant concessions in the negotiations that might upset France. Therefore, the inclusion of France in the new conventional arms talks, which began in 1989, and the wider geographical scope entailed, is an improvement over the format of the MBFR negotiations.

IV. Did the MBFR negotiations promote a military buildup?

Bargaining chip arguments were used to persuade the US Congress that unilateral troop withdrawals would jettison the possibility of mutual force reductions by removing 'the one incentive that compels the Soviet Union towards these negotiations'.[32] The MBFR negotiations, therefore, were designed to ensure the maintenance of US force levels in Europe. Quite likely, the negotiations also resulted in a delay of the withdrawal of some of the 7000 US tactical nuclear weapons in Europe. Jane Sharp quotes former US Secretary of Defense James Schlesinger as telling the Senate Foreign Relations Committee that 'there are diplomatic reasons associated with the size of that stockpile'.[33] In addition, Gregory Treverton concludes that the inclusion of F-4s in NATO's Option III resulted in the aircraft being retained in Europe for a longer period of time 'than made military sense, because NATO did not want to gut its offer to reduce them'.[34] Therefore, there appears to be considerable evidence that the MBFR negotiations actually served to prevent reductions and to prolong the deployment of obsolescent weapons. Still, NATO apparently did not introduce new weapons simply to use as bargaining chips in the MBFR talks. Although Sharp suggests that the Soviet Union may have moved 1000 T-62 tanks into the GDR as a bargaining chip, she notes that it is difficult to discriminate between strategic and diplomatic motives for this kind of measure.[35]

As a result of prompting a much closer scrutiny of WTO forces and a more alarmist assessment of the potential threat, the MBFR negotiations appear to have encouraged greater military investments by NATO The intention to negotiate on force reductions led to a re-evaluation of WTO force levels, and to new concerns about NATO's efficiency and progress in weapon standardization. This point is stressed by Jane Sharp, who views it as an undesirable by-product of MBFR, and by Stephen Meyer, who regards it as a 'fringe-benefit'.[36] The WTO also enhanced its war-fighting capability during the 1970s, but it is not clear whether the improvements were a direct result of MBFR calculations, a response to NATO moves or part of a modernization process quite independent of the talks.

Although the MBFR talks were not important enough to play a major role in 'consuming trust', the negotiations did result in a closer scrutiny by NATO of WTO force levels and strategies, and may well have served to increase the West's distrust of the Soviet Union. The negotiations may also have influenced the wider public perceptions of the military balance in Europe. Treverton suggests that the focus on numbers in the negotiations seems to have 'reinforced the common misperception of NATO's hopeless inferiority on the central front'.[37]

The focus on force levels may have also had a channelling (or displacement) effect by prompting NATO to concentrate on improving the combat strength and the efficiency of existing forces so as to minimize possible future constraints caused by reductions of force totals. Nevertheless, NATO forces are also constrained by independent political, economic and demographic factors. After NATO perceived a greater threat from the WTO, the MBFR talks were not the only reason for maximizing the efficiency of existing forces.

The MBFR talks, then, appear to have played some role in the promotion of NATO's anxieties about Soviet conventional strength and in the a consequent efforts to improve and modernize NATO forces. The major effect of the negotiations, however, was the prevention of unilateral NATO withdrawals and defence cuts that might otherwise have taken place.

V. Limited success for arms control in the CSCE

Whereas the MBFR talks achieved no results after 15 years of negotiation, both the CSCE Final Act of 1975 (Helsinki Accords) and the Stockholm CDE which met between 1984 and 1986 produced some agreement on arms control.

The CSCE began at Helsinki in July 1973, after the four occupying powers had reached an agreement regularizing the position of Berlin and guaranteeing access to the city. Although an agreement on Berlin had been a Western precondition for holding the CSCE, the USSR, in turn, had made a Berlin settlement contingent upon West German ratification of treaties with Poland and the USSR which recognized the existing frontiers. In 1972, the FRG extended *de facto* recognition to the GDR and opened the way for other Western countries to initiate normal diplomatic relations with the GDR.

The Soviet Union, therefore, had achieved many of its political goals in Europe before the Helsinki Conference was convened. But Moscow still wanted a general recognition of the political and territorial status quo in Eastern Europe, and was anxious to promote trade with the West, to acquire credits and to gain access to Western technology. The Soviet Union also had an interest in fostering closer political ties with individual West European countries, in discouraging West European military integration and in reducing US influence—provided the USA was not precipitated into a rapid and destabilizing withdrawal of its forces. The Soviet Union, therefore, had a strong incentive to make some concessions to the West in advance of, as well as during, the Conference.

The West had also achieved most of its key objectives before the CSCE convened. These goals included a separate MBFR negotiation, the Berlin agreement, and US and Canadian participation at Helsinki. With the participation of the USA and Canada in the CSCE, the USSR recognized the right of these two countries to have a role in Europe. During the preliminary negotiations on the agenda (before the formal Conference began), the West sought to ensure a discussion of greater freedom of information, an increased cultural exchange between the two halves of Europe and, especially, a focus on issues concerning human rights. In addition, the West proposed specific—although limited—measures to promote security in Europe.

Thirty-five countries, including the entire NATO and WTO memberships, were represented at Helsinki. France and Romania, two states with relatively independent foreign policies, as well as the NNA states of Europe participated. Only Albania was missing. During the course of negotiations, the issues were separated into three 'baskets'—human rights, economic and technical co-operation, and security. The CSCE's contribution to arms control was the agreement of several CBMs such as the notification of ground-force military manœuvres involving 25 000 or more troops that took place in any European country or adjacent air and sea space, and the exchange of military observers to be present at the excercises. The advance notification of smaller-scale military exercises was voluntary.

The Soviet Union proposed the creation of a permanent organ responsible for promoting security and co-operation in Europe. The West, however, feared that such an organization would be used to try to divide NATO, to intervene in the affairs of individual states (in particular, the FRG) and to promote Soviet interests. The West, however, did agree to hold periodic review conferences, which were intended to review the implementation of the Final Act and to build on what had been achieved. The first follow-up meeting took place in Belgrade from 1977–78 and the second in Madrid from 1980–83. Both conferences reflected the deterioration in US–Soviet relations. At Belgrade, the USA pursued President Carter's policy of emphasizing human rights, which resulted in mutual polemics, and no progress was made on implementing further concrete measures. The atmosphere at Madrid was even worse—the conference took place after the Soviet Union's invasion of Afghanistan, and the new Reagan Administration, which took office in January 1981, was even more hostile to the Soviet Union than the Carter Administration had been. The imposition of martial law in Poland in the winter of 1981 resulted in a lengthy adjournment during 1982, and the Madrid talks almost collapsed altogether.

The only positive outcome of the Madrid conference was the establishment of the CDE in Stockholm. As early as 1978, the French Government first proposed that such a disarmament conference should be convened on the grounds that France had always believed in discussing arms control in an all-European context. In fact, the Government was responding to domestic pressure to adopt a more positive line on arms control, and President Giscard d'Estaing wanted an arms control platform in order to counter Socialist proposals in the 1978 elections.[38] However, the Carter Administration proved to be cautious about convening a new disarmament conference, and feared that such a conference might conflict with MBFR and would not link human rights to security. The forthcoming US presidential election, and the challenge from Ronald Reagan, may well have dissuaded Carter from supporting the CDE idea in 1980. However, Carter's lack of commitment to the idea made it easier for Reagan to go along with it.[39] Other Western countries were not initially enthusiastic about the CDE proposal either, but did have some interest in extending CSBMs. By 1983, a CDE was viewed as one possible way to move forward and out of the Madrid impasse.

During the Madrid negotiations, the participants were agreed to two of France's criteria for convening a CDE—first, the meeting should be held within the CSCE framework and second, the discussions should be in two stages. The first stage would focus on the agreement of CSBMs, and the second stage would concentrate on disarmament. In this way, it was hoped that the first stage would pave the way for the second. The main problem was the geographical area the new CSBMs should cover. Whereas the Helsinki measures only extended 250 km into the Soviet Union, the French proposed a zone stretching from the Atlantic to the Urals. The Soviet Union responded to the French suggestion by requiring that CSBMs should cover an area of the Atlantic comparable to the proposed area of the Soviet Union. However, the West (which did not want the WTO monitoring reinforcement operations) resisted the inclusion of naval exercises unless they were integral to manœuvres on land.[40] In the end, it was agreed to extend 'the whole of Europe' as far as the Urals, but to only cover air and sea operations if they were related to land operations.[41] Nevertheless, the Soviet Union sought to extend the CDE mandate to independent air and sea activities.

The CDE convened in Stockholm in January 1984 with a mandate to examine CSBMs which would be politically binding, militarily significant and adequately verifiable. The Conference was required to report back to the next CSCE review conference (set for November 1986) which would then consider the results of the first phase. In 1984, the CDE made little headway, and the lack of success reflected the cold war atmosphere between East and West the year after the deployment of cruise and Pershing II missiles in Europe. Whereas the NATO Allies put forward detailed technical proposals to promote greater openness about military activity on both sides and stressed the need for verification, the WTO presented proposals for wide-ranging measures such as a treaty on non-use of force, a declaration of no-first-use of nuclear weapons, the establishment of nuclear and chemical weapon-free zones in Europe and the reductions of military budgets.[42]

At the beginning of 1985, the USA and the Soviet Union resumed nuclear negotiations at Geneva, and there were signs of greater seriousness of purpose at Stockholm. Two working groups each with a clear agenda and a timetable were set up at CDE. The first group focused on the notification and observation of military exercises; the other group examined possible confidence-building measures of a political nature and the setting of limits on military forces. Despite these hopeful developments, considerable disagreement still existed between East and West by the end of 1985. Further efforts to improve negotiating procedures, such as the addition of informal sessions at the end of working group meetings and the appointment of NNA co-ordinators to drafting groups, did not resolve the central issues when the CDE adjourned in March 1986.[43]

How did the Stockholm Conference manage to reach an agreement by the time it concluded in September 1986? One important reason was that the parties did not want to conclude the session without any agreement. The looming deadline served to focus the energies and creativity of the negotiators, and to encourage concessions. In fact, many key issues were settled during the final week of negotiations. When the negotiators stopped the clock on 19 September (the formal deadline), only two more days were required in order to hammer out the details before unveiling the agreed document. A second and related reason was the fact that the CDE was part of the wider process of the CSCE which—despite the disappointments since 1975—governments did not want to fail. In particular, the USA (having been more intransigent than its NATO Allies at the CSCE review conferences) did not want to be responsible for failure at the CDE. Perhaps the most important reason, however, was the transformation of relations between the USSR and the USA by the autumn of 1986, with a second summit meeting in prospect. The Stockholm Conference happened to end at a time when a favourable outcome (in the form of the first arms control agreement since 1979) could be used to build up to more major advances at Reykjavik in October.

The Stockholm Agreement did extend the scope of advance notification of military movements and the rights of observers, and introduced the principle of on-site inspection. The participants committed themselves to providing advance notice of land exercises involving 13 000 or more troops and of amphibious landings or parachute drops with 3000 or more troops. In addition, the Agreement stipulated the notification of transfers of over 13 000 troops into the specified area. The parties also agreed to exchange calendars of planned military activities for each year. The Stockholm Agreement required the presence of observers for exercises involving over 17 000 men, and for amphibious and parachute exercises with over 5000 men, and elaborated a detailed code of conduct to ensure that the observers would have reasonable freedom to view the exercises. Each participant accepted a quota of up to three inspections a year to check compliance with the stipulation that inspection should not be by a military ally and that each inspection should be carried out by a different state. The figure of three inspections represented a compromise between the Eastern proposal of one or two, and the Western suggestion of six per year. Compromise was also reached on the problem of whose aircraft should be used for inspection teams. The USSR wanted host aircraft in order to avoid the possibility that foreign aircraft might attempt to conduct espionage, but NATO feared that host aircraft might limit the freedom of inspectors. It was agreed to accept host aircraft for aerial inspection, but to give inspection teams the right to direct flight routes and to bring their own equipment.[44] As a concession to the Soviet Union's original position, the text of the Stockholm Document reiterated a commitment to non-use of force in the settling of disputes between CSCE members.

There were a number of gaps in the Stockholm proposals, with respect to maximizing security against surprise attack and the enhancement of mutual confidence. For example, there were no constraints on the type of military activity, the frequency or duration of military exercises, or on the numbers of men involved. The West had resisted all such limitations. However, it was agreed that exercises involving over 75 000 troops should be notified two years in advance (instead of one) and that the failure to provide such notice would necessitate the cancellation of the exercise. The placement of forces on alert status would not require advance notice—only when the alert was actually implemented. The alert notification provision applied regardless of the number of troops involved, and observers were mandatory only for alerts lasting more than 72 hours. One major omission was the exclusion, at the insistence of the NNA states, of the advance notification requirement for mobilization preparation. Another omission, which the Stockholm Agreement carried over from the MBFR negotiations, was the lack of an agreed data base on the forces already within the specified area.[45] Nevertheless, the Stockholm Conference was an advance over the Helsinki Accords and provided a breakthrough on the issue of on-site inspection.

VI. Agreement in CSCE and CDE but not in MBFR: why?

For a number of obvious reasons, agreement at the CSCE and the CDE proved to be easier to achieve than at the MBFR negotiations. First, at both Helsinki and Stockholm there were political inducements to come to an agreement. At Helsinki, both sides made some political and economic gains. The Soviet Union and Eastern Europe achieved the acceptance of the status quo and the prospect of economic co-operation; the USA and Western Europe achieved the agreement of a human rights declaration and the prospect of useful trade through the consolidation of *détente*. A security package of fairly token CBMs complemented these more substantial gains. At Stockholm, the agreement served as a means of maintaining CSCE and of reviving arms control between the USA and the USSR. Second, the content of the agreement was relatively uncontroversial, especially in the West. Neither side had to relinquish a single weapon and the agreements bypassed the central problem of whether to ratify or alter the existing ratio of conventional forces. Third, both sides had a strong common interest in measures which reduced the likelihood of surprise attack and generally served to reduce tension. Thus, CSBMs are a form of arms control in which common advantage is obvious, and the individual risks and sacrifice limited.

In addition, the CDE was able to build on the relative success of the Helsinki CBMs. The record of compliance with the Helsinki rules by both the WTO and NATO is quite good, despite the fact that some states have have provided more complete information than others, and that the USA and the USSR have disputed whether or not some Soviet activities fell within the Helsinki limits. Nevertheless, states have generally proved willing to provide the 21-days' advance notice required for major manœuvres, and there have been some exchanges of observers. NATO, however, invited observers to a larger proportion of its exercises than either the WTO, or the NNA states.[46]

Although both the USA and the Soviet Union had political incentives to reach an agreement at Stockholm, the Soviet Union made greater concessions. The final agreement (which was much closer to NATO proposals than to the broader-ranging Soviet proposals) focused on NATO concerns to reduce the danger of surprise attack and to promote confidence through an increase of information concerning military exercises. The final agreement also met the West's insistence upon adequate verification, and on this point, the USSR made significant concessions. The Soviet willingness to co-operate at Stockholm reflected its long-standing commitment to the CSCE process and its desire to establish the Soviet Union as a major partner in a context of a specifically European *détente*. In addition, the Stockholm agreement converged nicely with General Secretary Gorbachev's strategy of seeking to consolidate a new *détente* with Washington, and of manœuvring President Reagan into serious arms control negotiations and agreements. The Stockholm Conference, therefore, provided a vehicle to promote an INF Treaty and leverage for a space agreement which would serve to prevent the continuation of the SDI programme.

West European allies of the USA had their own interests in a Stockholm agreement. The new cold war of the early 1980s had been an unwelcome development, and even the right-wing governments in the FRG and the UK attempted to maintain some degree of *détente* within Europe, and had resisted the abrogation of economic ties with Eastern Europe and the Soviet Union. At Stockholm, NATO members maintained strict Alliance unity (as they had done at Vienna) and permitted the USA to take the lead in framing the Western position. When the USSR accepted the main points of the NATO position, the USA's European allies would certainly have exerted pressure for an agreement on these terms if conflicts in Washington had seemed likely to prevent it at the last minute.[47] In any event, the timing for the Stockholm Document was exceptionally favourable, and the agreement did not encounter any obvious last minute resistance from the USA.

One of the most interesting questions is whether the NNA states played a constructive role in the CSCE and the CDE. These states certainly were important in promoting the CSCE process as a whole. Finland hosted the original Conference and helped to smooth the preliminary negotiations, and Switzerland devised the scheme of grouping proposals into baskets.

At Madrid, the NNA states early on helped to prevent a total breakdown, and prepared a text for the negotiations when they resumed after an adjournment in November 1982. The final document from the Madrid Conference was based on a draft proposed by the NNA states. These states, however, have varying foreign policy interests and differing political systems , and do not always act as a single group. Malta, playing the role of maverick in the review conferences, created problems at Belgrade by its demands that the CSCE include the Mediterranean in its discussions. Malta very nearly very nearly sabotaged the Madrid Conference by holding out, until the very last minute, for a CSCE-organized forum on Mediterranean security.[48]

The NNA states, however, also performed a useful role as mediators in the CDE. For example, in 1984 Sweden, Switzerland and Yugoslavia prepared a proposal that attempted to strike a compromise between the divergent positions of East and West. Although the NNA states (on the whole) do retain a genuine commitment to arms control, these countries also have specific security concerns which can complicate the conclusion of an agreement even further. For example, some of the NNA states resisted the proposals which required the disclosure of the location of major military formations. NNA states also opposed extending CSBMs to mobilization preparations (noted above).

On the whole, the role of the NNA states has been more central in the promotion and maintenance of the CSCE process at the various conferences, rather than in specifically promoting arms control. The NNA states' contribution at Madrid was greater than at Stockholm, and there are two possible reasons for this contrast. First, the European NNA states retain a strong interest in promoting *détente*, which reduces the likelihood of a serious conflict in Europe, allows greater political flexibility and creates economic opportunities. During a period of *détente*, there is less likelihood that either of the great powers will pressure those countries that have chosen independent foreign and security policy lines. From the perspective of the NNA states, specific military measures (even CBMs) can be viewed as a possible threat to military security—a central concern of those countries who have to rely on their own defensive strength. Second, negotiations on military issues encourage the two alliances to negotiate as blocs and promote the predominance of the two great powers; the non-aligned group is in a minority position. Thus, the conduct of negotiations in an all-European forum differs significantly from those negotiations—such as the Geneva Conference on Disarmament—in which the non-aligned countries are in a majority.

There are possible advantages, as well as disadvantages, from linking arms control talks to the CSCE process. The CSCE process proved to be much more susceptible to swings in the character of US–Soviet relations than the MBFR and some other arms negotiations. Despite European interest in maintaining some measure of *détente*, the main conferences at Belgrade and Madrid (as well as the early part for the Stockholm Conference) reflected the deterioration of relations between the USA and the USSR. Negotiations linked to the CSCE, then, appear to be more highly politicized than other discussions. Whereas the Soviet Union and the European states all retain a strong interest in the maintenance of a European *détente*, the USA, which is not a European power and can negotiate bilateral economic arrangements with the USSR, has a much weaker incentive to promote the CSCE process. Therefore, the USA is less likely to make concessions in this forum. In the early stages at Stockholm, the USA proved to be less than enthusiastic about concluding an agreement.

Limiting the Stockholm Conference to the period between the two CSCE review conferences had both advantages and drawbacks. The requirement to meet a deadline is one way to reduce the tendency for the negotiating parties to lapse into fossilized and increasingly irrelevant negotiating positions, as in the case of the MBFR talks. The imposition of a deadline may be particularly important for those negotiations which do not attract much continuous media interest or notice from the general public, as was the case with the Stockholm Conference. An awareness of a deadline is likely to stimulate journalistic interest as the deadline draws near. A deadline also serves to concentrate the efforts of delegations and their domestic bureaucracies, and the responsible political figures. All of these advantages were manifest at Stockholm. On the negative side, an imposed deadline may foster a tendency to hold back serious concessions and hard bargaining until the end, as the Stockholm Conference also illustrated. The imposition of a deadline, or other strict timetable, may be a better formula for limited arms control talks, than for those negotiations attempting more radical cuts in arms. Such deadlines could result in purely cosmetic agreements, although this was certainly not the case with the Stockholm Conference.

VII. Epilogue: from MBFR to CFE

The third CSCE review conference, which began in November 1986, ended in January 1989 with the agreement to launch a new set of negotiations on conventional arms control in Europe—the Conventional Forces in Europe (CFE) talks. The CFE negotiations, which began on 6 March 1989, included the 23 member states of the WTO and NATO, but excluded any participation by the NNA states. The mandate of the CFE negotiations covers all land-based conventional forces from the Atlantic to the Urals. Aircraft were included in the formal mandate; but when the negotiations opened, NATO initially proposed to focus solely on tanks, artillery and armoured vehicles. Although sea-based forces, on NATO insistence, were excluded from the mandate, Soviet Foreign Minister Shevardnadze stressed that naval forces could be used to conduct a surprise attack. Nuclear and chemical weapons are not on the agenda of the CFE negotiations. With respect to tactical nuclear weapons, the Soviet Union has called for parallel negotiations with the CFE talks. A central aim of the CFE negotiations is the elimination of the capability to launch surprise attacks, and large-scale offensive actions. Principles of verification, including on-site inspection and detailed exchange of data, have been agreed. The talks are being held in closed plenary session, supplemented by working groups on the model of the Stockholm negotiations. The 23 countries will negotiate autonomously, but report back to the CSCE.

One factor promoting a constructive atmosphere in the new forum is the very good record of almost all states in complying with the provisions of the 1986 Stockholm agreement. During the third CSCE review conference, the 35 states agreed to convene a CDE–II to discuss further CSBMs. The CDE–II discussions are being conducted in parallel with the CFE negotiations.

Notes and references

[1] Keliher, J.G., *The Negotiations on Mutual and Balanced Force Reductions: The Search for Arms Control in Europe* (Pergamon Press: New York, 1982) gives the most detailed account of the origins and earlier part of the MBFR talks, but breaks off in 1980.

[2] Blacker, C. D., 'Negotiating security: the MBFR experience', *Arms Control*, vol. 7, no. 3 (Dec. 1986), p. 218.

[3] See Keliher (note 1), p. 41. The official title agreed was 'Mutual Reduction of Forces and Armaments and Associated Measures in Central Europe'. WTO references were often to Mutual Force Reductions.

[4] Ruehl, L., *MBFR: Lessons and Problems* (IISS: London, summer 1982) Adelphi Paper no. 176, pp. 12–15.

[5] See Keliher (note 1), p. 62.

[6] Keliher (note 1), p. 121 cites a Soviet letter to *The Times* on 19 Dec. 1974.

[7] Dean, J., 'Ten years of negotiating security in Europe', *Arms Control Today*, vol. 12, no. 8 (Sep. 1982), p. 2.

[8] See Ruehl (note 4), pp. 9 and 16.

[9] See Keliher (note 1), p. 99.

[10] See Ruehl (note 4), pp. 25–26.

[11] Sharp, J., 'Arms control strategies', *Soviet Strategy Toward Western Europe*, eds E. Moreton and G. Segal (Allen and Unwin: London, 1984), p. 257.

[12] Sharp (note 11), pp. 255–56; Ruehl (note 4), p. 23.

[13] Keliher (note 1), p. 127.

[14] Sharp (note 11), pp. 253 and 255.

[15] Hardenbergh, C., 'News of negotiations', *ADIU Report*, vol. 6, no. 3 (May–June 1984), p. 16 and vol. 6, no. 5 (Sep.–Oct.), p. 11.

[16] Hardenbergh, C., 'News of negotiations', *ADIU Report*, vol. 8, no. 1 (Jan.–Feb. 1986), p. 20 and vol. 8, no. 2 (Mar.–Apr. 1986), p. 19.

[17] Hardenbergh, C., 'News of negotiations', *ADIU Report*, vol. 8, no. 4 (July–Aug. 1986), p. 20.

[18] Hardenbergh, C., 'News of negotiations', *ADIU Report*, vol. 9. no. 2 (Mar.–Apr. 1987), p. 17.

[19] Meyer, S.M., 'The changing context of MBFR', *Approaches to East West Arms Control,* eds W. H. Kincade, N. V. Yinger and G. C. Duffy (Arms Control Association: Washington, D. C., 1979), pp. 74–85.

[20] Blacker (note 2), p. 233.

[21] See Keliher (note 1), pp. 54–55 and 68.

[22] See Sharp (note 11), p. 258.

[23] Blacker (note 2), pp. 230–31.

[24] Dean (note 7), p. 3 notes that when he was chief US negotiator from 1978–81 the tone of MBFR was 'largely non-polemical'.

[25] Keliher (note 1), p. 135.

[26] Keliher (note 1) p. 100.

[27] Ruehl (note 4), p. 16.

[28] Keliher (note 1), pp. 101–102.

[29] Ranger, R., 'MBFR: political or technical arms control?', *World Today,* vol. 30, no. 1 (Oct. 1974), p. 411 argues that this contrast extended to the content of the talks. The West was pursuing technical measures to reduce WTO ability to launch a surprise attack, whereas the Soviet Union was looking to symbolic cuts and recognition of the status quo in Europe.

[30] Winkler, T. H., *Arms Control and the Politics of European Security* (IISS: London, autumn 1982), Adelphi Paper no. 177, p. 30.

[31] Winkler (note 30), pp. 26–27.

[32] Keliher (note 1), p. 28 quoting the record of Senate proceedings in 1971.

[33] Sharp, J. M. O., 'MBFR as arms control?' *Negotiating Security: An Arms Control Reader,* eds W. H. Kincade and J. D. Porro (The Carnegie Endowment for International Peace: Washington, D. C. 1979), p. 224.

[34] Treverton, G. F., 'Intermediate force negotiations: Issues and alternatives', *Nuclear Weapons in Europe,* eds O. M. McGraw and J. D. Porro (D. C. Heath and Co: Lexington, Mass., 1983), p. 98.

[35] Sharp (note 33), p. 223–24.

[36] Sharp (note 33), p. 223 and Meyer (note 19), pp. 78–79.

[37] Treverton (note 34), p. 98.

[38] Chernoff, F., 'Negotiating security and disarmament in Europe', *International Affairs,* vol. 60, no. 3 (summer 1984), pp. 429–37.

[39] Chernoff (note 38), p. 436.

[40] Chernoff (note 38).

[41] Foreign and Commonwealth Office, 'Developments in the negotiations', *Arms Control and Disarmament Newsletter,* no. 19–20 (Jan.–June 1984), p. 32.

[42] Barton, D., 'The Conference on Confidence-and Security-Building Measures in Europe', SIPRI, *World Armaments and Disarmament: SIPRI Yearbook 1984* (Taylor and Francis: London, 1984) pp. 560–64.

[43] Brief information about the CDE during 1985 is given in the *Arms Control and Disarmament Newsletter,* nos. 23, 24 and 26 (1985); and *Arms Control and Disarmament Quarterly Review,* no. 1 (Apr. 1986).

[44] Hardenberg, C., 'News of negotiations', *ADIU Report,* vol. 8, no. 6 (Nov.–Dec. 1986), p. 19.

[45] Borawski, J., 'The Stockholm CDE: risks and opportunities', *Council for Arms Control Bulletin,* no. 29 (Nov. 1986), p. 5.

[46] Goetz, B.A., *Security in Europe: A Crisis of Confidence* (Praeger: New York, 1984), pp. 79–90, and Barton (note 42), p. 558.

[47] I am indebted to Frank Blackaby for this and several other points about the Stockholm Conference.

[48] Winkler (note 30), p. 32.

10. Arms control failure: why?

I. Introduction

There are two explanations as to why arms control negotiations fail. The first focuses on the negotiating process itself and suggests that negotiations exacerbate the difficulties inherent in trying to curb arms. The other explanation emphasizes the fundamental obstacles to arms control arising out of the nature of the arms race, rather than the mechanisms of negotiation. These explanations are not mutually exclusive. Certainly, these two approaches can overlap. Some view the problems created by negotiations as being superimposed upon the problems created by the arms race. Those who stress the role of international or domestic forces in the arms race recognize how these forces operate within the negotiating framework. Nevertheless, both explanations emphasize different primary causes for failure and suggest different remedies, such as finding an alternative to negotiated arms control, or devising ways to strengthen forces favouring arms control within the negotiating process.

This chapter examines the main variations on each type of explanation both in the light of the historical evidence, and also in relation to broader theoretical questions about the nature of the arms race and the purposes of arms control negotiations. An important issue that needs further discussion at this point concerns the difference between arms control and disarmament, and whether the goals of arms control formulated in the early 1960s still seem realistic in the late 1980s or whether the dominant conception of arms control constitutes part of the problem.

II. Problems inherent in the negotiating process

Arms control talks act as a screen for the arms race

It is quite often argued, especially within peace movement circles, that the real effect of arms control talks is not to limit the arms race, but to act as a screen for it. In this view, negotiations are a convenient device for lulling domestic and international public opinion, averting pressure for defence cuts and employing in a propaganda war with an opponent. Negotiations are not designed to curb arms. However, there are two possible versions of this theory. The first emphasizes that negotiations are a deliberate device adopted by élites to protect what they see as necessary military programmes. The second suggests that the real effect of negotiations is to legitimize an arms race, although this may be an unintended, rather than a desired, outcome.

Quite often, governments enter talks partly in response to public anxieties and pressure. Still, it does not necessarily follow that, as a general rule, the main purpose is to protect defence and to avoid arms limitation. The available evidence does not support the view that government arms control policies are so thoroughly Machiavellian. The MBFR talks provide the classic example of US Government and NATO officials launching talks to prevent troop and budget cuts. Even in the case of MBFR, however, there were other motives; indeed, if the exercise had been totally cynical, it might have been less successful with Congress.

The other possible example of a US administration entering talks to preserve its arms programme concerns the decision to enter the INF and START negotiations conducted between 1981 and 1983. In the case of INF, the Reagan Administration was pressured by allied NATO governments to negotiate; in the case of START, the Administration was responding to Congressional pressure. Moreover, the INF negotiations may have helped to secure the planned NATO missile deployments. It is also likely that START played a role in safeguarding the MX missile programme. The Reagan Administration, however, was too divided to have a coherent policy; and many prominent officials were opposed, in principle, to arms control talks and were afraid of being forced into concessions at the conference table. So the INF and START negotiations were not deliberately designed to screen weapon deployment.

The case of the INF and START negotiations fits better into the thesis that whatever the explicit (and usually mixed) motives of the participants, the overall result of talks is to reassure popular and legislative opinion and to protect major arms programmes. The essence of this position is that negotiations help disguise the dangers of the arms race by giving the false impression of control, that the talks serve to divert popular anxieties and prevent pressure for real cuts, and that the agreements reached do not really curb the buildup of arms.

Negotiations and formal arms control treaties may create a false sense of public reassurance—as in the case of the significant reduction in public concern about nuclear weapons after the 1963 Partial Test Ban Treaty. Still, there are no grounds for thinking that negotiations automatically deflect public alarm. Much of the time the general public knows very little, if anything, about the substance of the talks under way. Degrees of public alarm are usually linked to particular weapon deployments, which catch the public imagination, and to wider political factors. For example, doubts about US military spending in the early 1970s were largely due to disillusionment over Vietnam. US citizens were quite unexpectedly confronted with the prospect of ABMs in their neighbourhood. It is also possible to argue the opposite case, that negotiations and conferences may be a focus for public agitation: for example, the UN Conference on Disarmament in 1982. On the other hand, the test ban, SALT and START negotiations have triggered congressional pressure to go even further to secure arms control. Government negotiations and arms control treaties do bestow some legitimacy on wider public demands for arms cuts. The existence of treaties like the ABM Treaty does serve to strengthen domestic resistance to new developments such as the SDI. Hence, although some negotiations or agreements have diverted pressure for direct cuts in arms, others have encouraged calls for unilateral restraint.

A powerful case can be presented that existing arms control treaties have not imposed any real curbs on the buildup of arms. Agreements have been reached to ban weapons that do not exist or are not on any immediate military agenda, such as in the case of the Outer Space and Sea-Bed treaties. Other agreements have restricted those weapons that seem either to be militarily or technologically unreliable, such as the treaties on biological weapons and ABM defences in the early 1970s. At best, treaties may commit countries not to acquire weapons they do not yet have, or seriously expect to acquire (the case for most signatories of the NPT). Agreements that do tackle existing weapons of real military importance often impose only marginal curbs at very high levels: for example, SALT I and II. Agreements that appear to limit weapon development, in reality fail to do so, such as in the case of the test ban treaties to date. Even the INF Treaty, which actually involves dismantling weapons in place, has more political than strategic significance.

Nevertheless, even these inadequate treaties have resulted in some restrictions on the development of new weapons and their proliferation. Moreover, existing treaties can potentially be strengthened and can pave the way for further agreements. The existence of legally binding documents does have some impact on domestic decision making and helps to create an international framework for an arms control régime. Even highly unsatisfactory negotiations, such as the INF Talks between 1981 and 1983, may create a basis for more serious talks and agreement later, as the Soviet renewal of the zero option on intermediate-range missiles in 1987 and the conclusion of the INF Treaty that year indicated. However fragile and fragmentary the network of arms control agreements, and however misleading some of the negotiations, whether the world would be a safer place without them remains an extremely debatable question.

Arms control talks accelerate the arms race

The view that arms control talks serve to camouflage the arms race may merge into the even stronger argument that negotiations positively accelerate arms development. Although this theory might imply that existing treaties are valueless, it could concede some marginal significance to agreements achieved while still maintaining that, on balance, the negotiating and ratification process is counter-productive. The key points in this argument (examined in chapter 2) can be summarized as follows: negotiations tend to promote arms development (*a*) because weapons are justified as bargaining chips, (*b*) because of the military price exacted by domestic establishments for accepting treaties, (c) because of the levelling up encouraged by seeking parity, (d) because negotiations create an obsession with numbers on the other side and (e) because they frequently consume, rather than create, trust. Finally, it is often argued that negotiations and treaties simply channel the arms race. A subsidiary claim is that particular agreements actually legitimize weapon modernization. We can assess this argument by looking at each specific means whereby negotiations may promote an arms buildup and then make a more general judgement.

Perhaps the most cogent claim is that political use of bargaining chip arguments encourages the acquisition of new weapons or accelerates production. However, we need to distinguish between the widespread use of this rationale by US administrations to influence Congress and the possibility that weapons have been produced solely or primarily for use as bargaining chips. Numerous examples of the first tactic can be cited. At times, administration officials may have genuinely believed that pressing ahead with weapons would help arms control talks. In general, the bargaining chip argument was used to justify weapons being procured for independent strategic reasons. The real question then is whether or not the argument actually influenced Congress. Defense secretaries and other officials obviously believed that it would, and some evidence is noted that, in 1972 and 1973, it persuaded a few wavering congressmen to support the Trident programme. Bargaining-chip arguments, therefore, appear to have strengthened the case for accelerating production or deployment at various times. On the other hand, sections of Congress have often used the fact of negotiations as a reason for urging unilateral restraint, as in the cases of nuclear testing and MIRV deployment.

Whether weapons have been acquired primarily as bargaining chips remains much more doubtful. The only well documented example is the case of the long-range ALCM programme in 1973. In this instance, Henry Kissinger urged the retention of ALCMs at a time when the US Air Force was willing for budgetary and tactical reasons to give it up in order to preserve the B-1 bomber programme. Kissinger's actions appear to have accelerated ALCM development, although it is arguable that the strategic and economic attractions of the advanced cruise missile technology would have ensured that the USAF reverted to ALCMs later.[1] The accuracy of the cruise missile, its capability to evade interception by flying low, the possibility of launching it from a variety of aircraft or ships, and the comparative cheapness of mass-production all served to make cruise missiles militarily and politically attractive. The Soviet Union was also in the process of developing somewhat less sophisticated air-and sea-launched cruise missiles. The Soviet programme was cited as a reason for US cruise missile development in 1976.[2] Although forces endemic in the arms race can be cited as major causes of the US cruise missile programme, Kissinger's intervention may well have spurred development and production; and, in doing so, the problems within the SALT II negotiations became intensified.

Bargaining chip considerations may influence weapon deployments in a third respect. This concerns the tendency of governments to keep obsolescent weapons in place largely for bargaining purposes. Both the USSR and the USA have apparently done this on various occasions. The SALT I negotiations over land-based heavy missiles encouraged the USA to maintain its ageing Titan missile force longer than it might otherwise have done, so as to counter heavy Soviet ICBMs in the negotiations. During the INF Talks, the Soviet Union appeared to maintain its SS-4 and SS-5 missiles as a bargaining counter.[3] From a strategic point of view, the continued deployment of obsolescent weapons for a few more years is probably not very threatening. Nevertheless, the presence of these extra weapons can, of course, potentially be used to foster public alarm about 'overwhelming numbers' on the other side. If the MBFR talks encouraged the Soviet Union to retain old tanks in Eastern Europe (although military tradition and the use of such tanks for policing may be the main explanation for this practice), then this tactic has enabled Western governments to exaggerate Soviet conventional strength. On the other hand, Gert Krell has suggested that keeping older weapons in place may sometimes help forestall pressure for new replacements.[4] Given the drive towards modernization (the SS-4s and SS-5s did not prevent rapid deployment of SS-20s) this possibility seems fairly remote.

US administrations have paid a military price to ensure ratification of arms control treaties. This fact is well documented in relation to the PTBT, SALT I and SALT II. In the latter two cases, however, administration officials have argued that they favoured these military developments anyway. The reason for paying a 'price' is of course to conciliate the JCS and their hard-line Senate allies, who are generally committed to pressing for higher defence budgets and new weapons whether a treaty is in the offing or not. The procedural requirements of ratification obviously strengthens the hand of these interests. The tendency of administrations to recognize the necessity to 'buy support' through the defence budget, however, is clearly counter-productive.

The SALT process provided three major examples of how the requirement of parity can lead to levelling up rather than down. Artificial parity required each side to have two comparable ABM complexes. As a result, the 1972 Treaty empowered the USA to deploy ABMs around Washington and the Soviet Union to do so around a missile base. Neither side implemented this option; and two years later, the Treaty was formally revised to allow for only one ABM system each. In practice, no levelling up took place. The second example did lead to a case of levelling up. US decision makers decided during the negotiations for SALT II to equip the new MX missile with 10 warheads (although strategic requirements might have suggested fewer) to match the SS-18.[5] This action, however, was an indirect result of SALT. An emphasis on the dangers posed by the SS-18 could have well led to the same result. The third example is the most significant. At Vladivostok, mutual negotiations, combined with domestic bargaining, resulted in higher numbers of launchers and MIRVed warheads combined, than unilateral programmes then envisaged. These negotiations, therefore, served to encourage a military buildup. Moreover, the Vladivostok ceilings had a strong influence on the final SALT II totals. The SALT II ceilings for strategic forces by 1985 did, however, require some restrictions on the programmes projected by each side in 1979. Still, it could be argued that, without the focus on matching numbers fostered by SALT ever since 1972, purely unilateral strategic planning might have been more modest. This hypothesis is necessarily unprovable, but appears at face value to be more dubious in this context. President Carter's unilateral decision to cancel production of the B-1 bomber caused considerable unease. Even without SALT, advocates of strong defence in the USA would probably have looked anxiously at Soviet missile deployments. On the Soviet side, available evidence suggests that, at least up to 1977, Soviet military determination to carry out planned programmes was a major reason for Soviet intransigence in SALT. Thus, an overall assessment of the levelling up argument with respect to SALT does not seem very strong.

The idea that arms control talks increase concern about numbers of weapons on the other side seems to have some basis in fact. The MBFR preparations appear to have increased NATO anxiety about the size, strategy and potential of WTO forces. The SALT process also served to generate an obsession inside the USA with the number of Soviet strategic weapons. What is more doubtful is whether SALT had the same effect inside the Soviet Union. The Soviet Union had a long experience of being behind the USA at the strategic nuclear level and was clearly committed during the 1970s to catch up. For the Soviet Union, SALT I was a promising means of formalizing a new strategic equality, based on rough parity, and SALT II of maintaining parity.

The question which remains then is: have arms control talks consumed trust? During the 1960s, the various negotiations crowned by the NPT appeared to have the opposite effect, making it possible for Moscow and Washington to tackle the sensitive issue of central strategic arms, despite the increasing intensity of US involvement in the Vietnam War and Soviet occupation of Czechoslovakia in 1968. A persuasive case could be made, however, that after the strategic arms talks were under way the overall effect of SALT was to heighten tension. Given the wider strategic and political context of the late 1970s, however, it seems certain that *détente* would have been eroded anyway. SALT became a focus for US critics of Soviet actions and for proponents of a tougher line with the USSR. SALT may have served to make US fears more acute, but it was not the primary cause.

The tendency to use allegations of arms control violations to whip up anti-Soviet sentiment was manifested by the late 1970s and was widely employed by the Reagan Administration. The more extreme claims have usually been made by those opposing arms control in principle in order to discredit it. Nevertheless, the effect may well have been to promote a more general distrust of Soviet motives and actions among the US public. The allegations of treaty violations, however, were only part of a much wider attack on the Soviet Union by those ideologically committed to view the Soviet Union as an 'evil empire'.

The most important argument is that arms control treaties only channel rather than restrain the arms race, so that limits on numbers may promote greater emphasis on the more destabilizing technological improvements. This charge has been levelled against SALT.[6] There are three possible ways in which SALT may have had a channelling effect. First, it may have promoted the development of MIRVs. Still, it is argued in the analysis of SALT I that MIRVs were deliberately omitted from the Agreement rather than as a consequence of that omission. Second, an emphasis on the number of warheads per missile and increasing missile accuracy has been associated with re-channelling.[7] However, although the 1972 Agreement only limited launchers, it was clear after 1974 that there would be some warhead limit. SALT did not provide a major rationale for maximizing warheads per missile. Both the increased ability to place more warheads on each missile and growing missile accuracy can more plausibly be viewed as the outcome of technological momentum and a commitment to 'modernization'. Both were also prompted by the requirements of counterforce strategy, which requires multiple nuclear warheads and considerable missile accuracy to destroy missiles on the other side. The Soviet emphasis on heavy missiles, with a consequent high throw-weight and a potential for multiple warheads, pre-dated SALT. That the USA invested heavily in cruise missiles in the later 1970s because the main focus of SALT was on limiting ballistic missiles is a better case. Although cruise missile development was already likely for strategic, technological and economic reasons, the SALT framework probably did accelerate cruise missile production and strengthen the case for it in domestic debates. SALT, however, was not the only factor encouraging cruise missile production under President Carter. His decision to halt the B-1 bomber programme also strengthened the arguments for ALCMs on existing aircraft.

SALT did help to legitimize missile modernization by allowing MIRV development in SALT I and providing for MX in SALT II. Henry Kissinger noted that Congress ceased to oppose MIRVs after the 1972 Agreement, although it is not clear whether SALT I made MIRVs 'legitimate' or simply signalled that it was too late to stop both sides from going ahead. SALT II, however, did not effectively prevent subsequent questioning of the MX programme by Congress, largely because of the failure to find a convincing basing mode. Nevertheless, the Scowcroft Commission did push through a compromise on MX basing in the context of pressing for greater efforts in START and, in a sense, legitimized the MX anew.

The overall claim that arms control negotiations can be used to speed up military programmes and to exacerbate tension is a powerful one. Not all of the individual examples which are sometimes cited are, however, convincing. It is not clear that negotiations always and necessarily have this effect, or that when they do, they are always the decisive factor. It is even less clear that, on balance, arms competition and political tension would be reduced if there were no arms control talks and agreements.

There is a strong case for challenging some of the orthodox approaches to arms control negotiations and resisting attempts to use them for ulterior purposes, but not for abandoning the quest for arms control agreements altogether. The problems that arise out of the negotiating process are a reflection of the fundamental forces fuelling arms competition, and are not created primarily by the actual negotiations.

Arms control and the arms race

The obstacles to arms control obviously spring from the dynamics of the original arms race. These obstacles, however, do not appear to be identical to the forces behind the buildup of arms. For example, the economic interests often identified as performing an important role in the arms race are not visibly involved in obstructing arms control. Furthermore, the difficulties for arms control posed by the US Constitution, or by the bureaucracy of the Soviet Union, are not directly connected to the strategic confrontation between the two powers. The interests of the defence industries are indirectly represented in the USA through the DOD and Congress. The House and Senate Armed Services Committees, which tend to back new weapon programmes and to oppose arms control agreements, are largely populated by congressmen from districts reliant on defence industries. Moreover, arms control treaties to date have not had major implication for the arms industry. So arms control negotiations have not stimulated significant opposition from economic interests. Arthur Dean observed that representatives of states with large defence industries expressed their reservations to President Kennedy about the US 1962 proposals for general and complete disarmament, which would have had widespread economic repercussions if agreed.[8] The state-run Soviet economy, of course, permits less accommodation of vested economic interests, but these interests may be represented nonetheless through the bureaucracy. The SALT I summit meeting revealed the important role in arms control decision making played by Leonid V. Smirnov, the chairman of the USSR's Military Industrial Commission at the time. Furthermore, although the domestic political framework of arms control policy making exists independently of the military confrontation, it is largely due to this confrontation that the military establishment exercises such a major influence and commands such vast resources in both countries. So, in general terms, the forces that perpetuate the arms race are those that obstruct arms control.

If this is really the case, then the primary obstacles to arms control might be deduced from deciding which is the most plausible model of the main causes of the arms race. First, we need to consider briefly the implications of a theory of the arms race. The concept of an 'arms race' implies that the weapons themselves are a source of fear and tension, and generate more weapons, so that the original political conflict is magnified and perhaps perpetuated by the arsenals that have been built up. The logical response is to restrict weapon development and to consider arms cuts. Those who believe a particular political conflict is deep seated and irreconcilable, reject the idea of an arms race. In their view, the only prudent response is to arm against the enemy. Hence, some right-wing Republicans and some conservative Democrats in the USA have been convinced that the Soviet Union is bent on world domination and that US military strength is essential to contain Soviet aggression. This view excludes any interpretation of what has happened since 1945 in terms of an arms race and logically also excludes the possibility of real arms control agreements. If those who believe in an inevitable conflict between capitalism and Soviet communism (or Russian imperialism) predominate in policy making in either or both countries, then arms control is impossible. This was the case until the late 1950s, when cold war views strongly influenced both Washington and Moscow, and during the early 1980s when cold-war attitudes shaped government decisions in Washington.

The concept of an arms race in terms of an 'action–reaction' model of weapon development has also been challenged by a number of analysts in the USA. They have argued that this model is an inaccurate description of the military relationship between the USA and the USSR.[9] It is true that the two sides pursue somewhat different military strategies, and operate with divergent technological skills and imperatives, so there is not a simple one-to-one matching of weaponry. Moreover, the time required for research and development, and the independent momentum of military programmes, precludes a simplified action–reaction model of the arms race. Nevertheless, the general tendency for the USA and the USSR to pursue major programmes of military research in order to anticipate developments by the other side, as well as the tendency to try to match major weapon developments and to compensate for perceived inferiorities, does indicate an interlocking of two military processes most aptly described as an arms race.

There are two schools of thought on how the arms race is sustained. One approach emphasizes the military and political competition between the two great powers. The other suggests that arms development is not really a response to the requirements of superpower antagonism, but is a product of the irrational processes in which military, industrial, scientific and bureaucratic vested interests are committed to maintaining military investment and the promotion of specific weapon systems. The obstacle represented by the momentum of modern technology is compatible with both views—either as an additional force propelling US–Soviet competition, or as an important factor in the interlocking power struggles of domestic military establishments. Psychological stimuli can also be related to both models. International conflict encourages fear and hatred of the 'enemy' and may promote irrational stereotypes. Furthermore, those with a vested interest in the arms race may manipulate information and orchestrate propaganda to foster fear and suspicion of the official enemy.

The two approaches reflect alternative views about the primary obstacles to arms control: those obstacles arising from the competition for political and strategic advantage between the USA and the USSR (which tend to pervert or disrupt the pursuit of genuine arms restrictions), and the obstacles stemming from domestic politics. Therefore, it is relevant to first consider which model is more convincing as an explanation of the arms race and, second, to consider which explanation seems more congruent with the available evidence on arms control negotiations.

The more traditional view that the arms race is primarily the outgrowth of great power competition and the logic of strategic confrontation is more convincing than the claim that it is an artefact of domestic forces. The security fears which have shaped the military programmes of both sides are genuine, underpinned by historical experience of surprise attack and strengthened by evidence of great power ambitions. These fears are also perpetuated by strategic deployments and programmes by each side. It is within this context—great power conflict, and evidence of the military capability of the opponent—that governments must make decisions and military interests must argue their case. The legitimacy and the power of military establishments derives to a large extent from perceptions of an objective threat and a need for military defences. Even if a branch of the armed forces or a weapon laboratory is promoting its own interests, it has to produce a rationale for a new weapon based on strategic logic, and based on evidence of the capability or intentions of the other side. Moreover, the fact that vested domestic interests are in competition with each other for resources means that they can be, and sometimes are, overridden by a president or the Congress in the USA, and by government or party bodies in the USSR.

This should not imply that domestic politics has no role in promoting the arms race. The armed services in the USA clearly are in competition for prestigious and expensive weaponry and may invent strategic rationales to justify it. Centres for research in defence issues lobby for various projects and churn out a stream of new possibilities. Major companies also see the prospect for handsome profits in an economic sphere notoriously lacking in close accountability for costs. US presidential elections may provide additional impetus for an arms buildup: for example, after campaigning on the 'missile gap', President Kennedy felt compelled to make rapid decisions to strengthen strategic nuclear forces.[10] Whether or not there is a strictly military-industrial complex in the Soviet Union has been debated, but the high priority given to military research and development, and the evidence of the power of vested military interests and of an increasing tendency for scientific research to churn out new technological possibilities, do strongly suggest that domestic factors play a part in Soviet arms acquisition.[11] Therefore, domestic interests in both countries do tend to multiply arms and to impart an element of irrationality into the process of acquiring weapons. Vested interests may also play on extreme fears and suspicions, and may serve to promote additional alarm on the other side. Domestic politics inside both the USA and the Soviet Union have a significant role in accelerating the arms race, but it is a secondary role which is dependent on the wider international conflict between the two powers. There is a good deal of evidence that Soviet arms acquisition, in particular, has been motivated primarily by a need to catch up with the USA.

Do the case studies of arms control negotiations confirm the view that international factors are more important than domestic obstacles in delaying or preventing agreements; or can it be argued that, in the process of trying to limit the arms race, the domestic problems are predominant? Whereas the arms race proceeds through unilateral action by each side, negotiating and ratifying an arms control agreement requires co-operation between the two governments over a period of time. Arms control negotiations can therefore be delayed or undermined by domestic crises and changes of government, as was demonstrated during SALT II. A lack of efficient political direction from the top leaves talks hostage to vested military interests and bureaucratic bungling. This seemed to be true to some extent in both Washington and Moscow between 1981 and 1983. Furthermore, the record of arms control negotiations is littered with well documented examples of defence scientists, military representatives and civilians associated with defence departments finding ways to obstruct or prevent particular agreements, as illustrated for the test ban and the various missile talks. It is tempting to conclude (as some have) that the domestic 'negotiations' on each side are more crucial for the outcome than the formal negotiations between the great powers.

The impression that domestic conflicts and political events are paramount, however, may be misleading. Both negotiators and journalists tend to stress the domestic battles over policy, which may seem to be more important or more interesting than lengthy formal negotiations concerning detail at the conference table. Moreover, a focus on the policy making for arms control means that international factors are refracted through the views of individuals or institutions. Therefore, decisions about political linkage may revolve around the National Security Adviser and the Secretary of State. The fears about verification are voiced by the CIA or by groups in the DOD (or even ACDA), whereas the central issues of security, and the strategic implications of particular proposals, are the primary domain of the JCS and the DOD. Although we cannot fill in the detail so clearly, the same process appears to be at work in Moscow. Individuals and groups who erect obstacles to arms control are not acting merely to protect their own political or institutional interests—although this bias often influences their attitudes. They also represent what are deemed to be objective political and security interests of the state.

Even if the extent to which domestic debates and disputes are related to the political and military competition between the USA and the Soviet Union is ignored, the accounts of particular negotiations make clear the importance of such factors as international crises, relations with third powers and allies, concepts of strategic advantage and the problems posed by strategic asymmetry. It is hard to generalize about the impact of international crises or the role of other powers, because their importance has varied; and there is room for dispute about such questions as the impact of US–Chinese negotiations on Moscow in SALT I and SALT II. Still, there is little doubt that the chances of US ratification of SALT II were significantly affected by the decline of *détente* and the dispatch of Soviet forces into Afghanistan. So international politics seem to be at least as important as domestic politics in disrupting arms control, and both can, on balance, be favourable or unfavourable to arms control. On the other hand, the tendency of governments to rely on military strength and to resist giving up strategic programmes already under way—however great the objective advantages of agreeing mutual limits—is a constant factor in negotiations.

It may, therefore, be more profitable to abandon the conceptual framework which contrasts international and domestic politics, and to make an alternative distinction between the political context of negotiations (both international and domestic) and the central problems of military security. One argument for this approach is that international and domestic politics are intertwined. Although the relations between and within alliances on the world stage, on the one hand, and the institutional network of domestic politics, on the other, can be distinguished, the role of political leaderships in the great powers has had a crucial effect on how Moscow and Washington view each other. For example, First Secretary Khrushchev's succession to Stalin was critical in ending the cold war; and the first Reagan Administration did a great deal to ensure the final demise of the previous *détente*. Another reason for considering the security issues in arms control separately from the political context in which they are debated is that there is an element of contingency in both international and internal politics, whereas security concerns tend to be continuous. Of course political developments impinge on security, and perceptions of security are often conflicting. Nevertheless, arms control negotiations raise basic security problems which may alter in detail, but not in essence, over time and which apply in variable political contexts. For example, it is possible to make some comparisons between the inter-war negotiations and those held today. Fundamental changes in the domestic politics of the USA or the Soviet Union, and in the relationship between them, could, of course, moderate or even end direct military competition. Even then, however, security concerns would not automatically disappear.

Therefore, the most basic reason why arms control negotiations fail is, perhaps, the most obvious reason: both sides normally feel more secure if they believe they have the military strength to deter attack and to win a war if it does break out. This infers the tendency to prefer superiority over parity, and to fear that parity may effectively lead to inferiority. It also means that there are considerable difficulties in agreeing what does constitute parity, given the strategic asymmetries that exist. Furthermore, an anxiety about being caught at a military disadvantage prompts governments to try to insure against being vulnerable if an arms control agreement breaks down or if other parties to an agreement cheat. Thus, it is particularly difficult to ban weapon research. In addition, verification remains an intrinsically important element in arms control negotiations.

II. Central reasons why arms control negotiations fail

Problems in the pursuit of parity

It is tempting to view military superiority for one's own side as a means not only of gaining political and strategic advantage in great power competition, but also of most effectively deterring a major war. Arms control theory, however, conceptualizes the quest for military superiority as being dangerously destabilizing, because such superiority promotes fear of pre-emptive attack, and fuels an arms race as the other side strives to catch up. Arms control, on the other hand, requires a stable military balance based on approximate parity and at a nuclear level has stressed deterrence based on mutual vulnerability. Even if the principle of parity is accepted—and it is seen how reluctantly it was ceded by the USA, the previously superior power, during SALT—there is room for considerable disagreement about what constitutes present and future parity. The outcome of SALT I could be viewed as superiority for the USA if MIRVed warheads were the criterion, or as inferiority if the emphasis was solely on launchers.

Strategic perceptions are coloured by deep-seated fears that the other side will implement worst-case scenarios. A case in point was the USA's belief that the USSR was likely in the future to place the maximum possible number of warheads on its land-based missiles. Perceptions also tend to include politically motivated blindspots, such as in NATO's ability to overlook the existence of British and French nuclear forces in the INF talks, or to eliminate French conventional forces based within France from the balance of conventional forces on the Central European front. In addition, one of the main difficulties in seeking to achieve and maintain parity arises from the reality of strategic asymmetry, which has dogged talks designed to reduce nuclear or conventional arms.

The asymmetries between the USA and the Soviet Union are numerous. Such a list would include asymmetries in weapon technology, priorities and deployment, together with such areas as force structures, geographic considerations in relation to theatres of war, the nature of the respective alliances and the strategic threat from third parties to alliance security. The Soviet Union stressed high-yield nuclear warheads when the USA was concerned about miniaturization at the time of the early test ban talks. The Soviet Union has also given priority to large missiles with a heavy throw-weight, while the USA has laid more stress on lighter but highly accurate missiles. This key difference was a source of much difficulty throughout SALT. The Soviet Union's tendency to keep large reserves of tanks, whereas NATO does not, was a central issue in the MBFR talks and greatly strengthened Western perceptions of WTO conventional superiority. Deployment of nuclear weapons has been a crucial problem in missile talks. In both the SALT and START negotiations the Soviet Union's reliance upon land-based ICBMs, compared with US reliance on sea-launched missiles, created opportunities for biased proposals. The Soviet Union was concerned with the USA's nuclear FBS in SALT, while the Soviet buildup of its intermediate missile force in Europe served to heighten West European fears and to help promote the NATO 1979 deployment decision. There are numerous differences in force structure between NATO and the WTO which complicate reductions in the levels of conventional arms and troops. These differences refer to such factors as the composition of WTO and NATO military units, the disparity in the balance of professional troops and conscripts, and the particular roles assigned to uniformed troops and civilians attached to the military on the respective sides. The Soviet Union has an inherent advantage in the European theatre by virtue of its large population and ability to mobilize and deploy reserves quickly, whereas the USA has to cross the Atlantic. Nevertheless, the Soviet Union arguably has a less reliable alliance, given East European disaffection with the Soviet role in their countries, has vulnerable borders and has faced a serious potential threat from China. One of the long-running problems in the INF talks was the Soviet desire for SS-20 missiles in its Asian areas.

The problems of defining and agreeing on parity, therefore, are acute. However, the fear that apparent parity will lead to inferiority is less great when agreement is reached at high levels of arms. When deep cuts are envisaged, a marginal advantage may have much greater strategic significance. If the aim is a total ban, then the possibility that the other side will secretly retain even quite small numbers of weapons (especially of highly destructive weapons) is a cause for serious alarm. The fear for national security, therefore, underlies the emphasis on exact parity, as it does the desire to ensure verification of agreed cuts.

Verification

Verification is important to all arms control agreements, and provides reassurance that the other side is honouring them. The more radical the proposed curb on arms, the more important verification becomes. Therefore, it is not surprising that verification was central to the earlier test ban talks, when the actual possibilities were still so uncertain. Verification has been one major stumbling block in the otherwise quite promising negotiations to ban all chemical weapons.

Earlier chapters have stressed the problems posed by verification as a crucial issue in the past between the Soviet Union and the West. During the 1950s, verification loomed as an insuperable obstacle to any agreement. The West insisted on on-site inspection and the Soviet Union, on the whole, refused to accept it, although the Soviet Union indicated some willingness to compromise in relation to the nuclear test ban talks. During this period, verification was not only objectively a central problem, but both sides adopted extremely rigid and unyielding positions concerning it. Verification also symbolized the depth of the ideological divisions and the fear and distrust on both sides. The agreements reached during the 1960s bypassed the question of on-site inspection, except for IAEA checks on non-military nuclear plants under the terms of the NPT. In the 1970s, reliance was placed primarily on NTM verification. The question of on-site inspection, however, still posed major difficulties when a CTB was on the agenda. More generally, US opponents of arms control have attempted to block certain measures by imposing verification requirements so strict that they were sure that the Soviet Union would reject them. For example, verification conditions were attached to the US offer of a MIRV ban. Even though in the 1980s the Soviet Union has shown itself much more willing to accept on-site monitoring and challenge inspections, especially under the leadership of General Secretary Gorbachev, deep-rooted doubts and suspicions about inspections still influenced the attitudes of many Soviet policy makers. In the USA, sceptics about arms control have continued to use extreme verification demands as a means of blocking progress in talks. Ironically, as soon as extensive on-site inspection inside the USA has become a real possibility, as under the INF agreement, vocal opposition to it has surfaced among those concerned about military and industrial secrecy, and those who are unenthusiastic about arms control agreement.

Quite apart from the specific ideological and ritualistic element in Soviet–US exchanges on verification in the 1950s and, to a lesser extent, into the 1980s, the need for verification is intrinsic to arms cuts and other forms of arms limitation. It is also, necessarily, a problem. The concern for one's national security requires strict verification procedures to prevent others from cheating on an agreement. On the other hand, intrusive forms of verification may threaten one's own military (or in some cases economic) secrets and, therefore, may be opposed as a form of espionage. On-site inspection by international teams of inspectors may also pose a challenge to national sovereignty. Development of increasingly sophisticated ways of checking on deployments of arms or nuclear explosions allowed for arms control treaties that bypassed the problem of on-site verification. If verification is limited to NTM, then the scope of possible arms control is also limited.

Even if on-site verification is accepted, it cannot provide a total guarantee against cheating. Therefore, it does not wholly resolve the security fears inherent in arms control agreement. Governments must accept that verification can only ensure that breaches of an agreement are liable to detection. So, verification serves as a deterrent to cheating. Governments may also have to accept that information gained from verification could be turned to military use by others in the future. Any agreement to cut or to ban arms necessitates the taking of some risk to avoid the greater danger of uncontrolled arms competition.

Technological momentum

Technological momentum is a central and frequently destabilizing feature of the arms race, churning out new possibilities for weapons and often undermining an existing military balance. The technological momentum is promoted, not only by the dynamics of great power conflict and by vested domestic interests, but is also a product of modern societies, which rely heavily (for both economic and cultural reasons) on general technological 'progress'. Destabilizing developments with military implications may be created by civilian research, or be the culmination of a number of separate steps which are then linked up, as in the case of MIRVs.[12] Therefore, it should not be surprising that technological change is often cited as the central obstacle to arms control, especially when new developments may threaten to overturn existing treaties. For example, advances in genetic engineering creating new possibilities for controlled spreading of disease are seen as a threat to the Biological Weapons Convention.

Arms control agreements to date have singularly failed to curb the technological drive to produce new and improved weapons as the discussion about channelling has already underscored. The 1963 PTBT failed to limit new developments in nuclear warheads as techniques of underground testing improved. SALT I and SALT II most notably failed to prevent MIRVs, mobile ICBMs, or new bombers such as the B-1 and the Backfire. The treaties also permitted advances in missile accuracy and actually served to speed up the development of cruise missile technology. The MBFR talks concentrated on numbers of troops and tanks, and totally ignored developments in conventional weaponry, such as higher explosive yields and use of precision-guided missiles, which are capable of transforming the battlefield. Pressure from within NATO to produce and to deploy new binary nerve gas weapons conflicts with progress at the negotiating table towards a chemical weapons ban.

Without doubt, the importance of the momentum of weapons technology poses severe dangers for the achievement of arms control. What is more debatable is precisely where the problem of controlling the technological momentum lies. The failure to include relevant technology in agreements is not primarily due to lack of foresight. The potential dangers of MIRVs, for example, were elaborated by US arms controllers as early as 1964.[13] Mobile ICBMs, bombers and cruise missiles were raised early on in the SALT negotiations by both sides. The central problem is that military establishments are not willing to relinquish new weapon technology that appears to be effective. Furthermore, technological developments are the primary sphere of military competition. Neither the USA nor the Soviet Union wanted to give up its plans for mobile ICBMs. The Soviet Union refused in SALT I and the USA in SALT II. The USA was not prepared to give up its advantage in cruise missile technology during SALT II. Apart from the military imperative to pursue promising new technology, bargaining-chip theory, changing strategic programmes and doctrines, and pressures for an early agreement without too many complexities all play a part. For example, Henry Kissinger tried for a simple interim SALT agreement in May 1971; and a number of issues on the negotiating table, including a possible ceiling on bombers, were abandoned.

It is not, however, inherently impossible to include new technology in an agreement. The 1972 ABM Treaty did grapple with the importance of restricting the deployment of new technologies. Still, the Treaty could not prevent research. The Reagan Administration's commitment to its SDI programme meant that it exerted pressure to gain acceptance of a right to test SDI components within the terms of the Treaty. The reliability of this technology is still controversial and the value of SDI even more so. However, the lure of new technologies, the possibility of great military advantage, President Reagan's personal attachment to the SDI idea, and the influence of vested scientific and economic interests, all converge to threaten the ABM Treaty.

Thus, the momentum of new technological and scientific discoveries, which constantly presents new possibilities to the military, poses a threat to arms control. The major problem, however, is created by the political and strategic institutions which shape the direction of much research and insist on the development of new weapons. Basic military perceptions of national security which assume it is essential to maintain a technological edge over the other side, provide justification for the strategic use of new technologies.

Bargaining tactics

The security concerns which obstruct arms control have a direct bearing on the other major problem in negotiations: the standard approach to bargaining in arms control talks. Because governments seek some unilateral strategic gain in most arms control negotiations, they may either envisage the enshrinement of a permanent advantage in an agreement or may enter talks to persuade the other side to scale down to a position of equality. There is probably a rather greater incentive to talk if negotiations appear to remove a military threat more effectively or more cheaply than an attempt to match the threat. This belief underlies the basic argument for 'negotiating from strength' to influence the other side. Because both strategic and bargaining logic suggest that the superior side should retain its advantage in the final settlement, the chances of an agreement satisfactory to both sides are slim. During the MBFR talks, the West had no success persuading the Soviet Union to give up what the West insists is a superiority in conventional forces—one of the main Western goals in the negotiations. Because of his wider political view of the importance of arms cuts, Mikhail Gorbachev appears much more willing to sacrifice military advantage.

The theory of negotiating from strength, or at least negotiating from a position where the other side has a substantial military incentive to make concessions, has obvious dangers. It logically encourages an arms buildup in advance of, or during, negotiations which can be justified by this bargaining theory. It can also appear as an attempt to substitute the language of force for the language of reasoned assessment of common interest and to bully the other side into major concessions. Therefore, emphasis on this approach encourages an arms build-up and political hostility, which is confirmed by the historical record since 1945. The theory of negotiations from strength has been most favoured in Washington in the 1950s and early 1980s, when there was no real desire for arms control.

The belief in bargaining chips has, however, played an important role in most recent arms control talks. Although this approach is somewhat more conciliatory (by implying the willingness to give up a particular weapon in the interests of arms control), the belief that creating a military threat is the best way to achieve an agreement remains counter-productive. The use of bargaining chips to promote the arms race has been discussed. The problem here concerns the fact that a reliance on military incentives focuses only on one aspect in interstate relations to the exclusion of other equally or more important factors. Enduring arms control arrangements rely heavily on perceptions of mutual security and common interest, and on political or economic goals taking precedence over strategic confrontation. Theories of bargaining chips, as well as of negotiations from strength, tend to discount these wider considerations and so serve to downgrade their importance. Distorted perceptions of the effectiveness of bargaining chips encourage future policies based on similar calculations.

The question that remains then is: have bargaining chips ever worked? Two important examples have been examined in the context of the previous case studies above. The first concerns US superiority in ABM technology as a lever to achieve SALT I. The second revolves around NATO's 1979 decision to deploy cruise missiles, and more especially Pershing II missiles, as a lever to get the Soviet Union seriously to consider negotiating away its SS-20s. Both examples are plausible to an extent. The Soviet Union was concerned about US ABM potential and its strategic implications in 1969 and about Pershing II missiles after 1979. Nevertheless, it is extremely simplistic to assume that Western military leverage was crucial in either case. SALT I became possible to a large extent because many US policy makers and congressmen had come to believe that arms control was important in reducing the danger of nuclear war, and because Moscow was moving towards the same view. Both sides also had a strong incentive to conclude SALT I in order to promote their own versions of *détente*. In 1987, the major reasons why the INF Treaty became a reality was that President Reagan and most of his advisers (despite their earlier hostility to arms control) had come to want an arms control agreement for domestic political reasons. Mikhail Gorbachev, a new and dynamic Soviet leader, had political and economic reasons for favouring arms agreements. In addition, both leaders gave the impression that they had come to believe in the need for radical cuts in nuclear weapons.

Bargaining concepts which favour negotiations from strength and bargaining chips frequently confuse two separate ideas. The first idea is the assumption that the other side will only respond to a clear military threat. The second implies that, because of the nature of bargaining, both sides must have something to offer (and something to gain) from a deal. A narrow conception of 'negotiations from strength' tends to overlook the reciprocal nature of bargaining in the desire to achieve unilateral advantage. In principle, a weapon which is a bargaining chip meets bargaining requirements. In practice, however, the party which holds this apparent trump card may be tempted to keep it after all. That is, unless the actor is constrained by domestic pressure, as in the case of President Nixon's decision to negotiate away all but token ABM defences. Instead of relying on specific bargaining chips, the framework of negotiations can be widened to bargain different weapon systems or military advantages against each other (as it happened in SALT I and II to some extent). It is interesting to note that, from this standpoint, asymmetries may sometimes help, not hinder. Even more importantly, military factors can be bargained against political or economic gains. This may have happened in SALT I. The conventional wisdom in the USA is that Soviet desire for an ABM Treaty gave the USA leverage for an agreement on offensive arms. Hersh, however, makes the claim (with some plausibility) that the Soviet leadership finally agreed to include SLBMs in SALT I to acquire much needed US grain.[14]

Furthermore, simple models of bargaining which assume it pays to extract a high price from the other side before making key concessions (such as refraining from deploying weapons) may clash with other requirements for successful arms control. These requirements include the need for a degree of mutual trust and goodwill, a belief in the seriousness of the other side, and a genuine willingness to curb arms. This question is explored in slightly more detail in the next chapter, within the context of examining the case for unilateral initiatives to promote arms control.

Arms control and disarmament

It has been argued that governments' central concern with military security, their preference for having a strategic advantage and an overriding desire to avoid being at a significant military disadvantage are basic obstacles to arms limitation. These reasons, however, are of the kind adduced by the original arms control theorists to demonstrate why total disarmament is impossible. In the early 1960s, arms control theorists assumed that the great powers would continue to maintain nuclear arsenals and that all states would keep substantial conventional forces. They also assumed that faced with the threat of mutual destruction, especially in the event of a nuclear war, the USA and the USSR would see a common interest in securing a stable military balance. Stability depended partly on preventing war by accident and avoiding pre-emption or misunderstanding in a crisis. It also depended on ensuring, whether by tacit restraint or formal agreement, that each side could deter attack and that neither side could gain an immediate advantage if war broke out. Maintaining such a balance might mean having high levels of arms, but it did imply avoiding a constant and destabilizing quest for unilateral superiority.

Since the 1960s, the record of arms control talks confirms that nuclear weapon powers and nuclear alliances are responsive to the need to avoid war by accident or miscalculation. The first bilateral arms control agreement between the USA and the USSR established the hot line in 1963. The 1971 and 1973 agreements on avoiding accidental war were signed when progress in the SALT negotiations eluded the negotiators. Further, the improvement of communications during crises was also discussed by Moscow and Washington after all other nuclear talks had been suspended in 1984. The 1972 agreement to avoid incidents on the high seas was also reviewed successfully in Moscow in May 1984. Although it has refused to participate in any other nuclear arms control talks, France was willing to sign an agreement on avoiding accidental war with the USSR in 1976. In addition, NATO and the WTO have managed to agree on mutual confidence-building measures in 1975 and 1986, even though they have not reached any conclusions on actual weapons limits.

The willingness of either side to settle for a stable military balance defined either in terms of rough numerical equality or in terms of ending technological competition is much less evident. The only agreement designed to prevent use of destabilizing technology was the 1972 ABM Treaty, which was made possible by an unusually favourable conjunction of circumstances (see chapter 5). Further, the ABM Treaty was also facilitated by the fact that some influential policy makers (although not Nixon or Kissinger) accepted the main tenets of 1960s arms control theory and the associated belief in a deterrence theory based on mutual assured destruction (MAD). The continued strategic competition between the USA and the USSR has not only prevented US–Soviet arms control agreements, but has been destructive of the prospects for maintaining multilateral restraints as well. The argument that the NPT was designed to safeguard the hegemony of the two dominant nuclear powers has been reinforced by failure of the USA and the USSR to make any serious effort to curb their own nuclear arsenals.

Arms control theory was designed to influence political and military establishments, and it stresses military caution and military calculations. In the 1960s and early 1970s, arms control theory had a real influence in Washington and enabled advocates of arms control to have some voice within orthodox political circles. Yet the theory's very realism (which resulted in some initial success) has also been a source of weakness. If the predominant emphasis is on military calculations of security, then the case for restraint and for mutual arms limitation may often seem weaker than the case for more and better arms. The 'realism' of arms control within a context of pursuing great power political and military competition is easily trumped by the even greater realism of *realpolitik*.

In practice, arms control has been undermined by the logic and momentum of the arms competition in which the great powers have become enmeshed. The failure of arms control agreements to halt the development and deployment of new weapons illustrates the difficulty of imposing effective restraint on this competition. Moreover, government policy making in this context tends automatically to exclude radical measures of arms limitation. Thus, measures which might impose curbs on new technology, such as a ban on missile testing, have not even figured seriously on the arms control agenda. Progress in arms reduction requires new modes of thinking about security and arms limitation.

Significant controls on weapon development are most likely when there is widespread disillusionment with military strength and great power politics based on military force. The influence of the anti-Vietnam War feeling on the public and Congress with respect to attitudes to military spending and ABMs provides a case in point. Radical curbs on the nuclear arms race, such as a total nuclear test ban treaty or a ban on missile tests, require a radical vision of a nuclear weapon-free world and a political challenge to long established orthodoxies in Washington and Moscow. This vision and impetus is unlikely to come from within governmental bureaucracies. It can be provided by popular movements from below and, occasionally, by political leaders who are impelled by a genuine desire to move away from the danger of nuclear war and to elevate this common goal above the quest for strategic advantage.

Notes and references

[1] Krell, G., 'The problems and achievements of arms control', *Arms Control*, vol. 2, no. 3 (Dec. 1981), p. 269.

[2] Nalewajak, R. A., 'The realities of arms control: the cruise missile case', *Arms Control and Technological Innovation*, ed. D. Carlton and C. Schaerf (Croom Helm: London, 1977), pp. 232–46.

[3] Sharp, J. M. O., 'Confidence building measures and SALT', *Arms Control*, vol. 3, no. 1 (May, 1982), p. 49.

[4] Krell (note 1), p. 268.

[5] Talbott, S., *Endgame: The Inside Story of SALT II* (Harper and Row: New York, 1979), p. 180.

[6] See Kissinger, H., *White House Years* (Little Brown: Boston, 1979), p. 538.

[7] See Sharp (note 3), p. 46.

[8] Dean, A. H., *The Test Ban and Disarmament: The Path of Negotiation* (Harper and Row: New York, 1966), p. 26.

[9] See *e.g.*, Wohlstetter, A., 'Rivals but no race', *Foreign Policy*, no. 15 (summer 1974) and 'Is there a strategic arms race?', *Foreign Policy*, no. 16 (fall 1974); Warnke, P., 'Apes on a treadmill', *Foreign Policy*, no. 18 (spring 1975) is an answer to Wohlstetter.

[10] Allison, G. T. and Morris, F. A., 'Armaments and arms control: explaining the determinants of military weapons', *Arms, Defense Policy and Arms Control*, ed. F. A. Long and G. W. Rathjens (Norton: New York, 1976), pp. 99–129.

[11] Holloway, D., *The Soviet Union and the Arms Race* (Yale University Press: New Haven, 1983), pp. 131-60.

[12] York, H. F., 'The origins of MIRV', *The Dynamics of the Arms Race*, eds D. Carlton and C. Schaerf (Croom Helm: London, 1975), pp. 23-33.

[13] See York (note 12), p. 34.

[14] Hersh, S. M., *Kissinger: The Price of Power* (Faber and Faber: London, 1983), p. 534.

11. Arms control success: how?

I. Introduction

The prospects for negotiated arms control suddenly became much more promising in 1987 than they have been for a long time with the INF Treaty signed in Washington at the end of the year. General Secretary Gorbachev's speech to the UN General Assembly in December 1988, announcing that the Soviet Union would reduce its armed forces unilaterally by 500 000 men, held out the prospect for progress in conventional force reductions. Although there are good reasons to hope that the INF Treaty, which will involve dismantling a whole category of nuclear weapons already in place, will create a momentum for further arms control, some scepticism is still in order. The outlook for negotiated arms control looked bright in 1963 and 1972, but high hopes were later disappointed. The INF Treaty alone cannot curb the central nuclear arms competition or overcome the built-in obstacles to a ban on nuclear testing and other radical measures of nuclear arms control. Indeed, many in military and political circles in the West have cautioned against moving too fast or too far towards arms limitation for its own sake.

It is therefore relevant to discuss the political conditions for past partial successes, as well as the prospects for the future, and to examine whether negotiations could either be better managed or their content altered. Major and controversial questions about bargaining and the possible role of unilateral measures as a prelude or complement to negotiated arms control also require further consideration. This chapter examines these issues briefly but does not claim to produce definitive answers.

This chapter focuses on the choices governments make about arms control tactics, both with respect to overall foreign policy objectives and specific negotiation strategies. Although heads of government are constrained by many political and institutional forces, they do retain the power to choose at least some key ministers and officials, to reorganize parts of the bureaucracy and to promote certain policies. Both the US president and the Soviet general secretary can have considerable impact on the progress of arms control, although they may be blocked by domestic opposition or by the actions and negotiating tactics of the other side.

Two major factors serve to exert pressure on governments to negotiate seriously on arms control and to restrict strategic programmes. First, economic resources and government funds (in both East and West) are limited. Second, public pressure, either for a ban on particular weapons or for general progress in arms control, may be brought to bear on governments. Because both factors are examined in chapter 2, it is only necessary to recapitulate here. Economic constraints in the Soviet Union, as a result of a centrally-planned and weaker economy, provide a more direct and unambiguous incentive to limit arms than in the USA. Still, the extent of expenditure on the US military budget has been a source of major concern in the USA. During the Reagan era, congressional activists have sought to restrict some strategic research and production, and to prompt the START negotiations.[1] So far, public opinion has had less impact on governments in the Soviet Union, although conflicting groups within the CPSU have attempted to mobilize wider support. US administrations can manipulate, but not control, public opinion and are responsible to electorates. The US Congress is even more attuned to the opinion polls than the executive branch. General opinion measured by polls, however, is volatile, and there have been long periods when US and other Western publics have been ignorant of (and indifferent to) arms control negotiations. In the USA, consistent pressure for arms control has been exerted only by specialized groups, academic researchers and a number of congressmen. Nevertheless, movements which mobilized the public did directly influence the test ban talks up to 1963 and the INF negotiations during the 1980s.

II. Political conditions for success

The prospects for progress in arms control depend to a considerable extent on the international and domestic political context. As noted in chapter 10, these contexts tend to vary, often unpredictably. Negotiations can be undermined by deteriorating great power relations or derailed by international and domestic crises. Conversely, a desire to improve or consolidate US–Soviet relations, together with linkage between arms control and other political or economic goals that depend upon *détente*, can serve to enhance the possibility of success. Given the weight of defence interests in both governments, the possibility of agreement depends partly on the strength of countervailing forces favouring *détente* and arms control at a particular time, and on the role of the president and the general secretary. If both leaders have a strong domestic incentive to seek an agreement, are ideologically predisposed to favour *détente* or arms control, and can exert effective control over their own bureaucracies and political associates, then success is more likely. Ideally, all of these conditions should apply simultaneously, but agreements have been reached when only some of them have been present.

Negotiations for the PTBT became possible because of the thaw in the cold war by the end of the 1950s. The U-2 incident, the Berlin crisis and the dispute over the UN's role in the Congo all subsequently sharpened political conflict, but did not totally destroy the awareness of mutual interests. The Cuba crisis resulted in a renewed desire for arms control and *détente* at the highest levels in both Moscow and Washington. Khrushchev was anxious (even if somewhat erratically) to promote peaceful coexistence; and Kennedy, after launching a major arms buildup early in his presidency, later became more committed to arms control. After the total break with China early in 1963, Khrushchev acquired more latitude to pursue a test ban. Khrushchev's hand was further strengthened by the death of a key antagonist in the Secretariat. Still, Khrushchev's position after Cuba was relatively weak, and he needed a test ban agreement to enhance his personal prestige. In the USA, Kennedy's domestic standing had increased after the Cuba crisis, and his experience in dealing with Congress was growing. Kennedy, however, remained acutely aware of bureaucratic and congressional resistance to an agreement. Both leaders had to muster considerable diplomatic skill to achieve the PTBT which required them to pay a price to the hardliners in their respective governments: Khrushchev by accepting a hard anti-imperialist line in much Soviet propaganda, and Kennedy by promising the Senate both military investments and continued vigilance concerning Soviet intentions.

The 1972 SALT I agreements reflected a desire for political and economic gains from *détente* by both the USA and the Soviet Union, despite conflicts over the Vietnam War. The achievement of SALT I reflected the strength of the anti-militarist mood among much of Congress and the US public, and the Soviet wish to avoid an extremely expensive and destabilizing development of extensive anti-ballistic missile (ABM) defences. Although Brezhnev seems to have favoured limited arms control, Nixon was not committed to arms control for its own sake, indeed rather the opposite. Nixon agreed with Kissinger that arms control could be an instrument for managing superpower relationships. Nixon needed to project an image of peacemaker and statesman before the 1972 elections. Both Brezhnev and Nixon, however, were in fairly strong positions domestically: Brezhnev through his consolidation of power in 1971, and Nixon through his ability to carry most Republican and Democratic opinion with him in seeking arms control (although he owed political debts to his right-wing constituency). Most of the political conditions for success, therefore, were present when SALT I was signed and ratified. Nevertheless, both sides made concessions to their respective military establishments both during the course of, and after, the negotiation of the agreements.

During the later stages of SALT II, few of the political conditions for success existed. The Treaty was finally signed in 1979, despite growing US–Soviet discord and distrust (with the consequent lack of broad-based support for arms control within the USA), and despite Brezhnev's failing health and Carter's lack of influence with Congress. Both Carter and Brezhnev needed a summit meeting and a SALT agreement: both leaders had declared a personal commitment to arms control and both needed to bolster weakened leadership positions. To a considerable extent, the Treaty was the result of the long-term momentum of the SALT process, which had encompassed four US Presidents and had created pressure for some formal agreement. This momentum existed despite the growing chorus of voices raised in criticism of SALT I and of SALT

II proposals. However, international crises and the further decrease in Carter's prestige and influence prevented Senate ratification. Indeed, the stage was being set for a total repudiation of SALT by the political right in the USA.

Despite military intransigence which impeded more far-reaching arms control, the PTBT and the SALT I and II agreements reflected the willingness of both governments to make concessions in various areas to secure an accord. During 1986 and 1987, the moves towards an INF treaty were almost entirely the result of a concerted policy of initiatives and concessions by the Soviet Union. This momentum was possible because of General Secretary Gorbachev's strong personal commitment to arms control as a means both of reducing international insecurity and of releasing resources for internal economic development. Gorbachev was also in the process of consolidating his domestic base and of attaining a growing ascendancy over the Soviet military. To a degree, Gorbachev's success in overriding the military's opposition can be measured by the extent of his concessions to achieve the INF Treaty. In Washington, President Reagan had never had any real control over his subordinates who were competing with each other for control over the direction of policy. In the wake of the Iran–Contra affair, however, Reagan was losing popular support. He needed to salvage the reputation of his presidency and apparently wanted to end his career as a peacemaker rather than as a cold warrior. Reagan's personal desire for a treaty strengthened the position of Secretary Shultz and Chief of Staff Baker against the Pentagon. The Democratic-controlled Congress had been pressing for progress in arms control and indicated that an INF agreement would find support. Still, because of his earlier anti-communist and militarist stance, Reagan needed (like Nixon before him) to appease right-wing supporters both in and out of Congress. After the foreign ministers' meeting ended in Washington on 18 September 1987 with the formal announcement that an INF treaty had been essentially agreed, the Administration duly announced the acceleration of the SDI programme's test schedule.

In terms of Soviet foreign policy goals and domestic politics, the prospects for future progress in arms control seem better than ever before. A great deal, however, could go wrong. If reforms inside the Soviet Union create dangerous unrest, Gorbachev might lose some of his personal power. The same can be said if the pace of change in Eastern Europe threatens communist party control, creating a backlash in Moscow and the possibility of a military intervention. The most immediate problem, however, is that Gorbachev's willingness or ability to make arms control concessions must be limited by the extent of US reciprocation. The inauguration of the new Bush Administration introduced the inevitable delay and uncertainty about future US policies that follows any succession. The Bush Administration inherits both Reagan's prior arms buildup and the momentum for arms control created by the INF Agreement. It also inherits a massive budget deficit. This combination of factors may prove to be unusually propitious for arms control.

The strength of vested interests in armaments programmes, however (together with a strong anti-communist sentiment) makes a significant arms control agreement difficult to achieve and ratify in the USA. Indeed, this volume has illustrated the difficulty created by the 'objective' concerns for military security in moving from a limited conception of arms control as an aid to international stability to those measures which are also steps towards genuine disarmament. Nevertheless, Western arms control supporters now have an unprecedented opportunity to encourage a response to a new Soviet flexibility. In the longer term, a re-evaluation of Soviet domestic and foreign policy goals may make it realistic to think in more radical terms about defence.

Skilful management of negotiations is particularly important when *détente* is tenuous and domestic support for arms control is finely balanced. The course of the initial set of test ban talks illustrates how crises or misunderstandings can disrupt potential progress, and the events during the spring and summer of 1963 demonstrate the value of careful conduct of the final diplomatic soundings and negotiations. Nevertheless, even when the political omens are favourable, the conduct of negotiations can either pave the way to an agreement or can create delays, misunderstandings and additional problems. The actual content of negotiations, however, is even more important. Together with the bargaining stance adopted, the substance of the talks is crucial to the likelihood of genuine success. The next section will examine these questions.

III. Management of arms control negotiations

The negotiators

The membership of arms control delegations can influence the final outcome of the negotiations. Given the tight control usually exercised over negotiating teams by the home governments, the composition of the delegations may matter most in terms of influencing the acceptability of an agreement at home. The political weight and diplomatic skill of the leader of a delegation is one signal of the importance attached to a particular negotiation. Clearly, a senior and more experienced leader has a greater chance both of acquiring the necessary support at home for proposed compromises and of persuading his opposite number. The appointment of a genuinely intransigent or inept chief negotiator is unlikely, unless the government is uninterested in an agreement. Although many observers criticized General Rowny's role in the START negotiations, his appointment symbolized President Reagan's determination, at that stage, to be tough with the Soviet Union. There is a tendency to take the most controversial issues out of the hands of delegations and to try to resolve them at a higher level. Still, delegations are responsible for the important technical detail and the actual text, and may take the initiative on incorporating key issues. Hence, although Kissinger took a hand in shaping the SALT I Interim Agreement, the two SALT delegations were responsible for resolving the detail of the ABM Treaty including (on the US delegations' initiative) restrictions on new ABM technologies. Although there was a greater mutuality of interest in the ABM Treaty than in the Interim Agreement, a number of tricky technical problems nevertheless remained: for example, which radar systems would be allowed. It was on issues such as this that negotiating skill still counted.

The 1958 Conference of Experts, which paved the way for the first test ban talks, highlighted the role of scientists as negotiators. Critics of the Western delegation viewed the scientists' appointment as a classic example of how individuals lacking proper diplomatic and legal guidance could be manœuvred into a political decision disguised as a technical assessment. Although much of the criticism came from test ban opponents, there was some force in it. The Conference of Experts set the terms for much of the future debate and made it more difficult to update discussions concerning verification possibilities and problems. Within the context of a broader negotiation, the role of scientists on working groups would prove to be much less problematic.

The extent to which the military should be represented on negotiating teams is a contentious question. Undoubtedly, there is a need for military expertise in most arms control talks, but this could be provided by briefings and by military advisers. Furthermore, diplomats can master the technical issues relevant to a negotiation. The main reason why the military and defence departments are often directly represented on negotiating terms is to ensure them a central voice in negotiations in order to protect defence interests. In the SALT negotiations, the strong military representation on Soviet delegations reflected the dominant position of the military in arms control policy making and its exclusive claim to military information, a position which has changed somewhat in the 1980s. The US military representatives on SALT delegations, however, found themselves in an unenviable position. General Allison, who served on the SALT I delegation, was denounced as being too willing to compromise and was made a scapegoat for critics of the Interim Agreement. On the other hand, General Rowny incurred the dislike and distrust of delegation colleagues for being too obviously the Pentagon's man and an opponent of SALT II.

Some advantages, however, do result from military professionals communicating directly on various problems. Under normal circumstances, direct military representation should serve to convince bureaucrats and politicians that an agreement will not damage national security. There may even be a case for granting military representatives a major role in some talks. The 1972 Agreement between the USA and the Soviet Union on the prevention of incidents on and over the high seas was negotiated by two teams on which high-ranking naval officers predominated.[2] The delegations shared a mutual interest in avoiding incidents which could lead to war, and the Agreement was concluded with little publicity and no political controversy. Nevertheless, the Agreement did not affect the size of the navies or even the use of 'gun boat diplomacy'. Delegations which were predominantly military would be much less likely to agree to genuine arms reductions.

The conduct of the SALT negotiations gave rise to a good deal of debate about the advantages and disadvantages of conducting talks simultaneously through more than one channel. The disadvantages are that higher-level talks may undermine a negotiating position of the official delegations and create confusion over technicalities, or may relegate the delegations to a function of marking time. All of these charges have been made against Kissinger's practice of taking the SALT process into his own hands at various intervals. Still, it can be easier to break a deadlock in negotiations at the level of foreign minister and to carry the resulting compromise through the domestic bureaucracies. During the later stages of the NPT negotiations, the US delegation apparently engaged the US Secretary of State directly in the proposed resolution of one disputed clause and invoked his support for another.[3] Both before and after Kissinger became the official Secretary of State, he had established the practice of high-level consultations in nuclear arms control negotiations. This has since become standard practice. As chapter 6 illustrates, if the delegations are kept informed about the higher-level talks, many of the problems of the sort that Kissinger created disappear. After Haig, the lack of active involvement by the Secretary of State was a problem during the first stage of the INF negotiations. Shultz, as a newly appointed Secretary of State with other foreign policy priorities, refrained from engaging in any serious diplomacy to back the 'walk-in-the-woods' compromise or to attempt a similar *démarche*. Since 1985, however, Shultz apparently engaged himself quite actively in the search for some success in the missile negotiations. Further, he seems to have played an important role in negotiating the INF Treaty.

Domestic organization behind negotiations

The US secretary of state can negotiate with somewhat greater freedom than a delegation and can try to ensure that foreign policy interests predominate over purely military concerns. The secretary also has some possibility of persuading the president to support a particular line. These considerations also apply to the role of Soviet foreign minister in relation to the general secretary. Certainly, both the foreign minister and the secretary of state can be constrained by strict instructions from above, and their individual power is largely dependent on the internal politics of their respective governments. Of course, secretaries of state may, at times, be overshadowed by the influence of a national security adviser or a secretary of defense. Because of his long experience and expertise, Andrei Gromyko's influence gradually increased; and in 1973, he was appointed to a seat in the Politburo.

To a great extent, delegations to negotiations are the prisoners of their domestic bureaucracies as illustrated by the negotiations on the test ban, SALT I and II, and the first round of INF. Therefore, the speed and efficiency of negotiations depends largely on the background of research and the mechanisms for decision making in each capital. One problem may be the lack of adequate advance preparations for negotiations. This was certainly the case with respect to the early stages of the test ban talks when the USA had not seriously expected to be engaged in such negotiations. An awareness of the necessity of bureaucratic back up for arms control negotiations was one of the principal motives for setting up ACDA in 1961. Nevertheless, the main reason for long delays in dispatching new instructions to negotiating delegations has been the problems resulting from deadlock between competing agencies and personalities at the top, and the unwillingness or inability of the president to ensure a decision. The Soviet bureaucracy often seems to have been similarly at a standstill, unless the Politburo intervened to make a decision.

The efficiency of policy making also depends to a considerable degree on the mechanisms for co-ordinating arms control positions and the key personalities involved. In the USA, both factors may vary with each administration, although some form of inter-agency consultation is always required. Still, the prospects for positive initiatives on arms control are better if an institutional voice favourable to arms agreements can be ensured a permanent say in policy deliberations. The State Department is usually predisposed to favour some arms control agreements and, once negotiations are under way, the diplomats involved have some personal stake in a successful outcome. Otherwise, the agencies involved are usually doubtful or actively hostile to arms control proposals. Of course, there have been occasions when arms control sympathizers could be found in the DOD (for example in the late 1960s); and the JCS was persuaded to countenance SALT. The appointment of a special assistant for science and technology to the president in the late 1950s (mentioned in Chapter 3) placed, for the first time, an authoritative official close to the president who could explain the case for a test ban in technical terms. Furthermore, President Kennedy's scientific adviser was also influential in the test ban debates in Washington. When Congress authorized the creation of ACDA, the Agency was intended not only to provide expertise on arms control, but to represent arms control interests in successive administrations.

Given the nature of Washington politics, ACDA has encountered considerable obstacles.[4] Although ACDA has always been a junior partner to the State Department, low status has not been the principal problem. The real difficulty is that ACDA, because of its very nature, immediately became suspect in the eyes of the political right as an organization soft on the Soviet Union and ready to negotiate away US weapons. The times that ACDA and its director have made a strong case for US military restraint in support of arms control agreements (as under Gerard Smith between 1969 and 1972, and under Paul Warnke between 1977 and 1979), they have been the target of opponents of arms control in the Senate and elsewhere. Right-wing presidents also tend to distrust ACDA—Nixon was extremely suspicious of the Agency throughout his first Administration—and may attempt to staff it with hardline opponents of arms control. This occurred under Nixon after 1972, and in 1981 under Reagan who, in addition, presided over the partial dismantling of ACDA.[5] Nevertheless, ACDA's continued existence still serves to assist a president who wants to strengthen the position of arms control supporters in policy making. For example, ACDA has a role in relation to Congress in providing arms control impact statements about weapon proposals, which is an attempt to link arms control to defence decisions.[6] Upgrading the status, resources and role of ACDA would be one way for a new Administration to signal a desire to move ahead with further arms control measures.

Public or secret negotiations?

One much-debated question about the conduct of negotiations is whether they should be open or secret. Traditional diplomatic attitudes tend to favour keeping the content of talks secret, on the grounds that the absence of publicity makes it easier to explore a range of possibilities without attracting premature opposition and avoids ignorant or prejudiced pressure on negotiators. Because shifts in position do not have to be publicly justified, negotiators have a freer hand to make concessions and reach a compromise. The more public the talks, the more likely both sides are to take up fixed positions or to make apparent concessions primarily for propaganda purposes. The first test ban talks illustrated how opponents of an agreement could seize on loopholes in verification or perceived disadvantages in proposals. The first stage of the INF and START negotiations (between 1981 and 1983) are often cited as an example of the drawbacks of publicly announcing negotiating proposals and counter-proposals. By contrast, in the SALT I negotiations both sides took pains to maintain confidentiality, although some leaks did occur. The record of SALT I suggests another reason for secrecy: the Soviet Union viewed the USA's willingness to avoid disclosures as a test of its seriousness of purpose in the negotiations.

Nevertheless, on balance, the arguments for a considerable degree of openness are more convincing. Secret talks do not necessarily prevent opposition from developing. Secrecy may actually encourage selective leaks from within the bureaucracy with the aim of damaging the negotiations. Secret negotiations also permit distorted speculation. Moreover, secrecy may actually enhance suspicion, especially in the case of the USA with its emphasis upon open politics. Kissinger's secretive style of negotiating engendered a good deal of suspicion about the outcome, and about possible hidden clauses or promises in SALT I. Furthermore, Soviet unwillingness to have missile numbers publicized added to the impression that the USA had struck a questionable deal. Confidential talks do not entirely prevent propaganda considerations affecting proposals as the case of the SALT I negotiations illustrate. The deliberate use of talks for propaganda purposes is primarily a political decision and not the product of openness concerning the main developments. Although Nitze and Kvitsinsky agreed to maintain confidentiality during the first round of the INF negotiations at Geneva, President Reagan chose to give maximum publicity to his zero option offer. Both Brezhnev and his successor, Andropov, similarly addressed proposals to Western public opinion. Moreover, in an era of mass communications, maintaining secrecy about negotiations for any length of time is extremely difficult even in bilateral talks. It is even harder in multilateral negotiations. The nature of the US political system makes secrecy especially hard to sustain. Immediately after negotiations end, the main protagonists will probably rush into print if there is any public interest; and leaks to the press are a part of bureaucratic politics. The Soviet Union, because of changes in Soviet politics since the early 1970s, now appears to be less committed to secrecy for serious arms control talks. Gorbachev is apparently satisfied to pursue the missile talks with a fair degree of publicity. This openness has not precluded serious negotiations; on the contrary, it has enabled Gorbachev to ensure that the West responds to his concessions. The final reason for openness is the one indicated at the beginning of this discussion: namely, Western arms control advocates can mobilize support for particular measures or press generally for an agreement. Furthermore, the public at large has information for making a judgement.

Low-key talks which attract little publicity may be possible (and, moreover, quite desirable) if the issues involved are mainly technical and are not highly controversial. In this instance, a lack of information is less likely to promote distrust. There is no need for strong shows of public support to conclude an agreement. The negotiations are shielded from possible attack and are insulated from international crises more easily than talks with a high public profile. The 1972 Agreement on the prevention of incidents on and over the high seas might be placed into this category, as well as some of the measures designed to avoid accidental war.

Relatively open talks may also be supplemented by formal, but confidential, negotiations. The most interesting example is the concluding session of the PTBT negotiation held in strict secrecy in Moscow. The degree of secrecy was exceptional (President Kennedy kept the details from most of his own bureaucracy) and was only possible for a short period of time. Because the Moscow talks were the culmination of prolonged, fairly open negotiations, and the technical issues had already been resolved, secrecy does not seem to have created additional suspicion. Nevertheless, President Kennedy believed secrecy to be necessary because of the extent of domestic opposition to a test ban, and because speed and good timing (at this particular stage of US–Soviet relations) were essential. Hence, the Moscow PTBT talks could be seen as an exception to the general rule that at least a degree of openness about arms control talks tends to help, rather than hinder, agreement.

Formal negotiations are usually supplemented by informal sessions between heads of delegations and other members. Such informality, of course, implies discretion. Obviously, there are advantages in off-the-record soundings of the other side's position and the exploration of possible solutions to a particular problem. However, two possible disadvantages remain. First, in the absence of formal and agreed minutes, there is scope for genuine or pretended misunderstanding. The classic example is the Soviet belief that the USA would settle for only three yearly on-site inspections in the verification of a CTB. Khrushchev ascribed this understanding to an informal session between delegation leaders Dean and Kuznetsov. Second, because such talks take the participants beyond their official position, there is a possibility that either side may tentatively offer more than his government will subsequently accept. This, of course, could lead to misunderstanding and distrust between the states involved or within the home government. Although the need for informal attempts at compromise are greatest when relations between the two sides are poor and domestic bureaucracies are intransigent or unable to agree, the chances for the success of informal diplomacy are correspondingly remote. Nitze's and Kvitsinky's 'walk in the woods' is an obvious, if extreme, example both of the need for informal proposals, as well as their pitfalls. Similar advantages and drawbacks apply to informal soundings between government officials or individuals close to government, such as Kissinger's habit of dropping in on Ambassador Dobrynin and 'thinking aloud'. The more authoritative the participants in an informal discussion, the greater the chance of formalizing an informal offer. Nitze carried insufficient weight in Washington. Initially, Kissinger could dominate the policy making process, but gradually he lost the confidence of many of his political associates.

Forums for arms control

The forum selected for arms control talks automatically defines both the number of formal participants and the resultant political balance. Therefore, the question concerning the nature of a proper forum became a major issue in the 1950s and early 1960s. During this time, the Soviet Union was still struggling to establish the right to equal representation with the Western bloc, and the growing group of non-aligned nations were claiming a voice. The United Nations was the forum chosen for early disarmament talks, but serious attempts at arms control clearly required a smaller number of participants. Initially, this requirement was met by establishing a UN Sub-Committee on Disarmament. The test ban talks that began in 1958, however, evolved outside the UN framework, although the negotiations were still serviced by the UN Secretariat. At the wish of the great powers, the Eighteen Nation Disarmament Committee (ENDC), set up in Geneva in 1962 and now comprising 40 members, also remains outside the UN framework. Nevertheless, the Committee reports to the UN General Assembly and takes account of Assembly resolutions. The UN Disarmament Commission, which became inactive in 1965 and includes all UN members, was revived after the UN General Assembly Special Session on Disarmament in 1978. Despite this activity, the overall role of the UN in arms control has been downgraded since the early 1960s. During the first test ban talks, both the USA and the Soviet Union were responsive to UN General Assembly resolutions on testing and attempted to engineer support for their own positions. Since then, however, the major powers have tended to dismiss Assembly resolutions as unimportant. Furthermore, it can be argued that debates in the Assembly or in the Disarmament Commission are likely to be high in propaganda content and low in substance. Although the UN Special Sessions, which were used in an attempt to mobilize public opinion, put the issue of general and complete disarmament briefly on the public agenda, this forum appears to be the least promising for the negotiation of serious agreements.

Since the 1960s, certain conventions have developed about the form of most arms control negotiations. Although the test ban talks between 1958 and 1962, in 1963 and between 1977 and 1980 were trilateral (the USA, the Soviet Union and the UK), the USA and the Soviet Union have generally conducted negotiations concerning their nuclear arsenals on a bilateral basis. The multilateral Geneva CD has had a wide-ranging agenda and has been responsible for the NPT, the BWC and the Sea-Bed Treaty. Chemical and radiological weapons are covered by the Geneva CD, which has also continued since 1962 to be concerned about a nuclear test ban and devotes some of its time to conventional weapons and military budgets. The USA and the Soviet Union tend to hold bilateral consultations on issues before the CD (for example, on chemical weapons) with the aim of resolving the chief differences between them and agreeing on proposals to present to the Conference. President Carter launched bilateral talks on a wide range of arms control issues, including the arms trade. These negotiations were not particularly fruitful and lapsed when Reagan entered the White House in 1981.

The bilateral nature of the negotiations on arms control symbolize the military superiority and political dominance of the USA and the Soviet Union in relation to other states. It also gives rise to a suspicion that the great powers are interested, primarily, in consolidating their own military advantage or in imposing solutions on the rest of the world. Bilateral talks, however, do permit a degree of confidentiality on sensitive issues in the event that either side demands it. Despite the ups and downs of the SALT process, the bilateral nature of the discussions helped to create a common understanding of strategic issues and political interests, and to establish negotiating conventions which are conducive to possible agreements, provided other circumstances are favourable. When the USA and the Soviet Union remove issues from before the CD and enter into purely bilateral talks, they can be criticized for excluding valuable advice and pressure and reducing the importance of the Geneva forum. However, because divisions between the great powers often create the main obstacles to arms control, there is some logic in a bilateral attempt to resolve some of the major points of disagreement.

The USA and the Soviet Union certainly have a major responsibility for creating a climate conducive to arms control. However, it may be illuminating to reverse the focus and examine the role of third parties in promoting agreements. The first round of test ban talks up to 1963 suggested that there were some advantages in the presence of a third country which was seriously interested in reaching an agreement. Britain was far from an independent third party and, in fact, closely co-ordinated its position with the USA throughout the negotiations. During this period, however, the British Government still enjoyed vestiges of great power status and managed to bring pressure to bear upon Washington at various points, engaged in some diplomacy in Moscow, and attempted to promote certain compromises. Nevertheless, in the final intensive talks in Moscow the British representative, Lord Hailsham, deliberately took a back seat to avoid creating delays or complications. Between 1977–80, Britain again took part in trilateral test ban talks, but for much of the period its contribution seems to have been low key. Britain's international status had declined, and the Labour Government (although quite favourable to a test ban) was not under domestic pressure concerning arms control and had more pressing economic preoccupations. After Thatcher came to power in 1979, Britain became more obstructive. At one point, Carter and Brezhnev considered completing an agreement withouι the UK. So although a third party to talks can play some mediatory role, it can also serve to augment difficulties. France was so opposed to a test ban that it refused even to enter the talks. Indeed, if France had entered the negotiations while remaining hostile, the problems in the talks could have been greatly increased.

Although the record of the test ban talks at the Geneva CD after 1962 suggests that the non-aligned states can assist the negotiations, these states are more likely to have an impact if they propose technical solutions (for example, on verification) than if they try to exert direct political pressure on Moscow and Washington. Sweden was able to demonstrate how the existing network of national seismographic stations could possibly monitor a test ban and, thereby, to influence the West to modify its proposed verification system. The eight non-aligned countries were not able to build on their first joint attempt in 1962 to promote a compromise basis for the conclusion of a CTBT, partly because of disagreements within the group. Early in 1963, a further attempt to press a compromise on the number of on-site inspections was aborted by pressure from the great powers to prevent it being tabled. Subsequently, non-aligned states and some alliance members (such as Canada) continued to press for a test ban, but the great powers simply ignored the issue for a long period (see chapter 4).

The Geneva CD, however, remains a valuable forum, as the list of agreements it has produced suggests. Long and patient exploration of the implications, technical issues and the formulation of the specific clauses of an agreement provide the groundwork for possible major success if the USA and the Soviet Union can resolve key disputes. The Geneva Conference has made considerable progress towards the achievement of a chemical weapons ban. The Conference not only provides a forum for non-aligned states, but also permits alliance members to take independent initiatives. It is interesting that Britain, which gave up its own chemical weapons in 1957 (although it retained a research programme), has been more independent of the USA and has played a more positive diplomatic role in promoting a chemical weapons agreement than it has over a test ban.

The forum for negotiations on measures of conventional and nuclear arms control in Europe has been less clearly defined. The debates concerning participation in the MBFR talks and the discussion which led to the inauguration of CFE negotiations illustrate this point. The decision to replace MBFR by a negotiation between all members of NATO and the WTO should facilitate a more sensible count of the forces on each side than in the previous, rather arbitrary, definition of the central front. The inclusion of such countries as France, however, suggests that talks may be less disciplined and less effectively bipolar than during MBFR. Indeed, divergent allied interests may cause even greater difficulties. A loose linkage to the CSCE process which requires periodic reports appears unlikely to make a significant difference. However, the negotiations on confidence-building measures within the CSCE framework should (based on past evidence) have a good chance of success, unless there is a dramatic reversal of the new *détente*.

An interesting and still unresolved question concerns which forum will be selected to debate battlefield nuclear weapons in Europe in the future. For a time, the MBFR negotiations included limited proposals for reductions of nuclear warheads and delivery vehicles. The Soviet Union pressed for the inclusion of nuclear weapons in these negotiations, and NATO briefly offered to trade nuclear weapons against WTO tanks and men. Nevertheless, both the Soviet Union and the USA have preferred to limit serious talks on their nuclear weapons to bipolar discussions. The INF talks have already covered missiles between 500 and 5000 km in range, and Gorbachev has suggested proceeding to a 'triple zero', eliminating all land-based nuclear missiles in Europe. The NATO military and the European right will probably resist any further moves to denuclearize NATO in the interest of maintaining the strategy of flexible response, but Western public opinion, especially in the FRG, appears to be favourable to further measures of nuclear disarmament in Europe. Because many missiles and bombers, of course, can be armed with either nuclear or conventional warheads, there is a good case for linking battlefield nuclear weapons to the new European negotiations. The USA and the Soviet Union could possibly engage in separate consultations, as they have done with respect to the Geneva CD. Although British and French nuclear weapons could pose even greater problems than they have with respect to the INF Treaty, Britain and France might agree, as a minimum, only to deploy shorter-range weapons within their own territory. Then, nuclear weapon reductions could be linked to withdrawal of US and Soviet forces.

IV. Substance of arms control negotiations

The actual content of arms control talks, of course, is even more important than the forum in determining the likelihood of success. Some proposals will serve to arouse security fears; other proposals may appear to be fairly innocuous to all but the most ideologically committed opponents of arms control. There is a fundamental dilemma here, because the more limited or even token the measures involved are, the greater the chances of agreement. Because the prospect of giving up major weapons often maximizes alarm about national security (and provokes greater fear and suspicion of the other side than had previously existed), it has been suggested that the best arms control strategy would be to initiate a process of continuous negotiation and graduated agreements, each involving a small step.[7] There are, of course, considerable difficulties with this approach. Measures to prevent accidental war are inherently useful and have, at times, helped to pave the way for more far-reaching agreements. For example, the hot line preceded the 1963 Test Ban, and the agreements on avoiding accidental war and naval incidents were reached both before and simultaneously with SALT I. Furthermore, the 1986 Stockholm Agreement assisted progress on an INF treaty. Nevertheless, cosmetic agreements are often viewed as a barrier to more significant arms control. These agreements may spark considerable domestic hostility and, if proposed in a multilateral forum, may arouse suspicion and resistance among states seeking substantial progress. There is no evidence that the 1974 TTBT helped towards a CTB. Furthermore, SALT II (intended to pave the way for SALT III) was attacked by the left, as well as the right, for failing to achieve proper cuts in nuclear arsenals. The SALT example also suggests the difficulty of achieving and maintaining an arms control process which is based on agreed assumptions when US Administrations change every four years. Still, the most conclusive objection to a strategy of attempting arms control through small steps is that this approach would singularly fail to check the momentum of arms competition. If arms control is to succeed (in the broad sense of restricting the arms race), then it is necessary to eliminate whole categories of weapons and to stop technological developments.

It is only after the Soviet Union, under Gorbachev, seized upon Reagan's rhetoric about deep cuts that significant reductions in nuclear weapons have begun to appear at all possible. During the SALT era, the Soviet Union was too concerned with achieving and maintaining parity to want lower levels of missiles. The USA, on the other hand, was too anxious about Soviet throw-weight and potential advantage to contemplate major reductions in its own arsenal. US proposals for deep reductions, including Carter's abortive 1977 offer, cut most deeply into Soviet land-based ICBMs. After Reykjavik, however, both Moscow and Washington have agreed in principle to 50 per cent cuts in long-range missiles. A START agreement under these terms would, of course, be more significant from a military standpoint than the INF Treaty. Indeed, many viewed the NATO missiles removed under the INF Treaty as being primarily political symbols. Because of a START agreement's real strategic consequences, such a treaty will be all the more difficult to achieve.

Nevertheless, a START agreement appears to be possible in the near future, provided there are no major changes in either Soviet or US arms control policy. Although much more ambitious than SALT in proposing a 50 per cent reduction in warheads, the START negotiations do not undermine the principle of a strategic triad (nuclear devices deployed on land-, sea- and air-launched missiles) and permits the modernization of systems by both sides. The real crux will be the content of further missile talks after a START treaty, which could involve much more contentious measures, both by resurrecting the issue of the British, French and Chinese nuclear forces, and by requiring even greater strategic sacrifices by the USA and the Soviet Union. If arms control means the removal of whole classes of weapons, then deep cuts and the rethinking of deterrence strategy may begin to merge into measures of real disarmament. However, it is for this very reason that radical reductions are likely to be opposed, not only by those who fear the military or political implications of reducing military power, but by advocates of the original theory of arms control. This theory maintains that the aim of arms control is not the illusion of peace through disarmament, but peace through military stability and nuclear deterrence. The theory also inclines towards the view that stability may mean quite high (rather than low) levels of arms.

If arms control is to be effective in its original limited aim of promoting stability (and more especially if it is to merge into disarmament), then it must control new technologies. This volume has emphasized that the control of new technologies is often the most difficult problem of all in arms control negotiations. SALT I failed to control MIRVs, and SALT II did not prevent (and, indeed, helped to promote) the deployment of cruise missiles. Still, new technological possibilities have been curbed by agreement in certain circumstances. The ban on orbiting weapons of mass destruction was relatively easy because, despite some genuine military interest, such a development was not seriously being considered. After governments have invested heavily in development and testing of a new technology, the armed services have usually become committed to its use. Vested economic interests are at stake in future production and halting a program becomes much more difficult. Given serious doubts about technological effectiveness and the strategic rationale for going ahead (and prospects of very high government costs), then arms control may still be possible, as the 1972 ABM Treaty demonstrated. Assessments of technological and strategic merits are often mixed, so political attitudes within government and a wider public may be decisive. In the early 1970s, Congress was very sceptical about ABMs, and the Soviet Union was anxious for a ban. The circumstances surrounding the USA's SDI programme are somewhat similar, and the Soviet Union now seems even more anxious than in 1969 to curb new ABM and anti-satellite technologies. Therefore, with a new US Administration, there may be some hope for a space agreement. The fact that most experts and many congressmen believe that the terms of the 1972 ABM Treaty would be violated by the testing of SDI components has served to strengthen domestic resistance in the USA to the SDI programme. Whether the SDI programme, as well as Soviet research and development associated with anti-satellite weapons, can be halted in favour of a comprehensive treaty will be a major test for future arms control.

Progress on achieving deep cuts in nuclear arsenals and in preventing new technological developments is likely to depend upon both sides accepting a strategic doctrine which does not put a premium on increasing missile accuracy, and the efficacy of missiles and warheads for first-strike or war-fighting purposes. Instead, the parties must be prepared to rely on a concept of nuclear sufficiency for deterrent purposes. This approach is compatible with the acceptance of a CTB and the possibility of a future ban on long-range missile testing, and would emphasize the implementation of an adequate minimum deterrent. Under these conditions, the approach would also be compatible with abandoning the search for exact parity (with all of the attendant problems of achieving parity between asymmetrical systems) and the temptations to level up, rather than down. A stress on nuclear sufficiency for deterrence would also imply first abandoning those missiles which appear to be best suited to counterforce (and hence a potential first-strike) strategy, either because of their own vulnerability or because of their potential for fast and highly accurate strikes against opposing weapons.[8] These concepts evolved out of early arms control theory and the linked doctrine of MAD, which later US governments abandoned. A strategy which leaves the civilian population vulnerable to annihilation is not likely to be acceptable, either psychologically or politically, as a permanent solution to the dangers of nuclear war. Under these conditions, no pattern of nuclear weapon deployment would be immune from quite cogent strategic objections. However, as an interim stage in the search for nuclear disarmament, the idea of nuclear sufficiency for basic deterrence is probably the best available strategy. Certainly, it is infinitely preferable to the dangerous illusion of a technological solution through ballistic missile defences, which would fuel a further nuclear arms race.

The flaws in SALT encouraged those interested in arms control to seek some alternative to the often counter-productive emphasis on exact numerical equivalence. Christoph Bertram suggested that a more useful focus might be on weapons 'missions', which could serve as a means of addressing the problem of technological developments creating new instabilities.[9] To illustrate, Bertram cites the 1972 ABM Treaty as an example of successful arms control. In this case, the Treaty served to restrict existing and future ballistic missile defence projects. Although the problems of definition might be greater, this idea would apply to the restriction of counterforce capacity in favour of a second-strike deterrent force.

An emphasis on 'missions' (as opposed to exact parity in numbers) and on maximizing deterrence to an attack (rather than stressing offensive capability) possibly could be transferred to the talks on conventional forces in Europe. This distinction between offensive and defensive weapons was incorporated in the League of Nations debates about disarmament (which gave priority to 'qualitative' over 'quantitative' arms cuts), and has been incorporated in a broader theory of 'defensive' or 'non-offensive' defence by individuals and groups in Western Europe during the 1980s. Non-offensive defence tends to minimize reliance on long-range bombers and missiles, major warships and heavy tanks. It emphasizes a commitment to an in-depth defence of territory, anti-tank and anti-aircraft missiles, and a mass mobilization of territorial forces in an emergency (rather than to the maintenance of a large standing army). Variations on this strategy have already been adopted by the European NNA states. These countries have strong political incentives to avoid any appearance of military threat or provocation. Strategic and economic pressures also suggest a high emphasis on purely defensive strategy and deployments, and effective use of civilians with some military training who are able to handle fairly simple weapons.[10]

It is harder to transfer concepts of non-offensive defence to two heavily armed military alliances, which incorporate two great powers, and now rely heavily on nuclear weapons. Nevertheless, it is still possible to envisage a phasing out of battlefield nuclear weapons, major reductions in offensively oriented aircraft, tanks and heavy artillery, and explicit changes in military doctrine and strategy which would shift both alliances away from the threat of pre-emptive attacks deep into the opponent's territory towards a commitment to respond only to an unequivocal assault.[11] The deployment of weapons is also important in constructing such a strategy. A withdrawal of major offensive weapons from an agreed zone on either side of the East German border would be one step towards implementing a non-offensive defence. The argument for focusing arms control around the idea of non-offensive defence is based on two ideas. First, such a defence would be conducive to strategic stability and, thereby, greatly reduce the danger of unintended war. Secondly, the strategy would also promote political confidence, and provide a basis for substantial arms cuts and force withdrawals, without provoking a sense of extreme insecurity. The idea is currently relevant to European arms control, because it is no longer confined to unofficial circles in the West. Gorbachev addressed this concept in his speech to the Moscow Peace Forum in February 1987, incorporated it into the WTO communiqué in May, and announced in December 1988 a decision to implement unilateral reductions of those Soviet forces in Europe that are most suited to a rapid offensive. It is not clear how far the Soviet military are prepared to reverse their established commitment to pre-emptive defence in Central Europe, but some Soviet defence and arms control specialists have become interested in how to translate earlier Soviet declarations of peaceful intent into weapon deployment and strategy. NATO should welcome the discussion of these possibilities.

Negotiating tactics and unilateral measures

The content of arms control talks is closely linked to the style of negotiating adopted and to total bargaining positions. The standard approach has been to table proposals that appear to be superficially equitable, but in practice serve to enshrine maximum unilateral advantage. This strategy could be likened to that of a used car salesman who initially asks a price that is much too high, on the assumption that mutual bargaining will bring the price down. This approach can work only if both parties understand the rules of haggling and if the potential customer wants to buy in the first place. In arms control, the desire for a deal is often questionable, the commitment to come out of a deal at an advantage is more deeply-rooted and the rules are rather less clearly defined. As noted in chapter 2, a wholly unreasonable initial offer may prejudice the chances of an eventual agreement or may lead to damaging delays. Moreover, the costs of a failed arms control negotiation are often very high, unlike a single transaction in business.

In order to move away from this model of negotiating, a number of commentators have suggested a strategy based on a quite different example. When children cut a cake, they may ensure fair shares by one cutting it and the other choosing the first slice. This creates a strong incentive to cut it up fairly. To apply this analogy to the pursuit of arms control, if each side divided its arsenal into sections or components to be progressively eliminated, and permitted the other side to choose which should go first, much of the detailed argument about equivalence in an arms reduction might be avoided.[13] In an alternative conceptualization, each party would assign a value to each of its nuclear weapons and the other would choose which weapons should be abandoned at a mutually agreed value.[14] Viewed even from an abstract perspective, the 'cake strategy' appears to be unrealistic. Unlike children who simply want to eat the cake, arms control negotiators may possess multiple and complex goals, and may only want to 'eat the cake' if they can be assured, in advance, of a larger 'slice'. To implement the 'cake strategy', then, the arms control negotiators would necessarily have to begin by agreeing on the nature and size of the 'cake', and the rules for defining the 'slices' (the numerical values). This strategy could create considerable alarm among domestic opponents of major arms control concessions, and complicate both domestic and bilateral negotiations. S.H. Salter, who has proposed the assigning of mathematical values to weapons on the other side, notes that a major obstacle would be getting agreement among the armed forces on one side. Salter suggests that very small percentage cuts might serve to reduce the military's anxiety. Still, if the approach of asking the other side to choose was adopted rather more informally earlier in the negotiations, then the strategy might serve to clarify those issues of particular concern to each side. If the strategy was implemented in a reasonably favourable political context, then it also might be useful in defining what to include in a negotiation and what each side might choose as priority. Asking the other side to nominate weapons or weapon deployments it would most like to eliminate could mesh with the strategy of using arms control to promote purely defensive strategies at both nuclear and conventional levels.

More flexible negotiating tactics would only be possible, however, in those cases in which the general attitude toward bargaining had ceased to require negotiations from strength or the use of bargaining chips as a means of achieving maximum concessions. It has been shown that these bargaining tactics tend to be counter-productive, because they may well *reduce* the chances of immediate agreement and serve to promote a further arms buildup. The alternative is to exercise restraint upon military programmes as a prelude or complement to negotiations. Unilateral action to limit arms serves to indicate seriousness of purpose (deeds speaks louder than words) and to encourage either reciprocal acts or serious negotiation. A unilateral initiative to delay or to limit a weapon programme may be designed primarily as a public political gesture, to prevent an arms development from rendering an agreement on key weapons impossible or as a prelude to later agreement. Some forms of unilateral restraint may be an alternative or a complement to specific agreements.

Although arms controllers have often recommended public unilateral initiatives, the success of such gestures has, until recently, been mixed. One problem is that a unilateral gesture is often interpreted as pure propaganda and critics doubt if it has any military significance. When Brezhnev announced the withdrawal of 20 000 men and 1000 tanks, many observers in the West questioned if these withdrawals had actually taken place. Moratoriums on nuclear testing have frequently been viewed as nothing more than the period required to prepare for a new series of tests. Military resistance to any real restraint makes this kind of moratorium difficult to maintain, and when one side breaks a mutual moratorium, bitterness and suspicion may be intensified. Although the mutual cessation of testing during the 1958-63 test ban talks may have initially helped the negotiations, the Soviet resumption of testing in 1961 greatly increased Western distrust of the Soviet Union (despite the fact that the USA had, since the end of 1959, kept open the option of renewing its own tests). Although Gorbachev's unilateral test moratorium from 1985 to early 1987 had a favourable impact on sections of Western opinion, including many in the US Congress, the action still did not move the US, British or French governments. There is, however, one much-cited example of a unilateral testing moratorium which apparently led to an agreement—President Kennedy's suspension of atmospheric nuclear tests (he was bound by domestic pressures to continue testing underground) during the prelude to the confidential trilateral Moscow talks which resulted in the 1963 PTBT. Still, even this moratorium only had an effect because of the total diplomatic context in which it occurred. In this case, both Kennedy and Khrushchev were committed to the promotion of new political and economic understandings, and the rapid conclusion of a test ban agreement.

In a context of mutual arms competition and deep suspicion, there is no reason why a single unilateral gesture should have any genuine political effect. Limits on arms, whether token or substantial, only make sense as part of a coherent political strategy to promote arms control and *détente*. Charles Osgood, an early theorist of unilateral initiatives, made this point very clearly. Osgood recommended a strategy of graduated initiatives, which were graded to avoid undue military risk, pursued consistently to encourage reciprocation, and combined with limits on arms within a much wider range of diplomatic, economic and cultural initiatives.[15] President Kennedy's policy of preparing the way for the Moscow talks has been cited as an example of how Osgood's strategy can work.[16] Gorbachev's nuclear testing moratorium gained in credibility as an attempt to start new CTB talks, because it was part of a series of bold diplomatic initiatives on arms control and served to reinforce an impression of seriousness. The moratorium may have had indirect value in helping to get the USA to negotiate in earnest on INF by making it harder for the West to refuse to respond on any front.

Unilateral initiatives to limit arms are likely to have maximum impact if they have real military significance, if they contribute to a coherently articulated defence and arms control strategy, and if they are part of a wider foreign policy promoting *détente* and co-operation. On 7 December 1988, Mikhail Gorbachev, standing before the UN General Assembly, met each of these criteria in a speech in which he promised to reduce Soviet armed forces unilaterally by 500 000 men, and to withdraw 50 000 men and 5 000 tanks from Eastern Europe. This remarkable offer exemplified Gorbachev's proclaimed belief in 'defensive sufficiency' and in the need for the side with superiority in particular weapons to make greater reductions. It also complemented his record of making major concessions to reach an INF treaty, and fitted into a policy of *détente* which has included withdrawing troops from Afghanistan and substantial concessions on human rights. As a result, the immediate response to Gorbachev's unilateral initiative in the West was very favourable, despite some caveats about the Soviet Union's continuing conventional superiority even after these cuts. The offer also opened the way to productive talks on conventional force cuts in Europe. Although this example suggests that the concept of public unilateral initiatives is inherently valid, past Soviet or US governments have too often undertaken initiatives only half-heartedly, ineptly or for purely propagandistic reasons.

General unilateral restraint on new strategic developments could play a considerable role in promoting arms control, but unfortunately such restraint is hard to achieve. Some members of Congress and the US arms control community argued vigorously for unilateral US restraint on testing and deployment of MIRVs in the hope of including a ban on MIRV technology in SALT I. Nixon and Kissinger, however, were more interested in using arms control as a lever against Moscow than in actual arms control results. Moreover, they were contemptuous of the idea of unilateral initiatives, and placed greater faith in bargaining chips and an arms buildup during talks.

US governments, however, have built successfully on unilateral promises of restraint to achieve arms curbs. In late 1962, Washington publicly offered to refrain from orbiting weapons of mass destruction in space unless it was prompted to do so by the Soviet Union. Initially, Moscow refused to reciprocate, but after some quiet diplomacy in which it was understood that no on-site verification would be required, joined with the US Government in making a joint statement to the UN in 1963. These informal commitments received UN backing and led to the conclusion of the Outer Space Treaty in 1967.[17] It is indeed ironic that Nixon was responsible for one the most radical acts of unilateral disarmament ever undertaken by a great power. In November 1969, the USA decided to renounce the use of biological warfare and to destroy its stocks of biological weapons. The USA's commitment provided an impetus for British efforts at Geneva to promote negotiations on biological weapons (separately from chemical weapons) and led to the 1972 BWC which banned weapon production.[18] The BWC, however, was flawed by the absence of any verification procedures and received little attention. Clearly, the BWC was made possible because the military at that stage did not regard such weapons as usable on any serious scale. Nevertheless, the US action was an interesting and underpublicized example of unilateralism which led to an agreement.

Besides the great powers, other states have made a major contribution in promoting arms control through unilateral restraint. Canada (in 1945), and Sweden and Switzerland (in 1958) publicly announced a commitment not to acquire nuclear weapons and, thereby, set an important example to other developed states with a nuclear capacity. Canada emerged from World War II as a major power and could have decided to pursue the status of a nuclear weapon state. Sweden and Switzerland felt obliged to examine the military case for acquiring nuclear weapons to strengthen their armed neutrality. In both cases, widespread public debate led to the conclusion that the military advantages were questionable, and that there was a strong political and moral case for not becoming a nuclear weapon state.[19] Canada and Sweden also played an important part in the early diplomacy that promoted serious negotiations on a NPT.

Not all unilateral restraint or arms curbs, however, necessarily lead to a formal agreement. There are strong arguments for exercising some forms of restraint on the grounds that they conduce to stability even if the other side does not reciprocate. For example, this may involve the avoidance of unnecessarily provocative deployments which could provoke military and diplomatic incidents. The original arms control literature noted that, even in the 1950s, both sides exercised some tacit restraint, for example, by establishing bomber routes and by not jamming military communications.[20] Modest forms of restraint can be justified in purely military terms, as well as creating a better environment for more ambitious arms control. When relations between the great powers are bad, public promises of restraint or negotiations may be politically impossible or counter-productive, and tacit measures more effective.

Because of the complex and time consuming nature of so many issues in negotiations, a case for a more radical and open adoption of military restraint as a supplement to specific talks can be made. For example, NATO and the WTO might, while talking about a zone to be established in Central Europe and limits on major offensive weapons, embark on a review of strategic doctrine and begin to implement some aspects of a non-offensive defence strategy. This might include, for example, a shift in resources to greater reliance on territorial defence.

IV. Conclusion

The detailed management of negotiations is the province of governments. However, decisions concerning the context of talks, and the attitudes toward appropriate positions, are influenced by a much wider political debate. This debate, which is channelled to the general public through the mass media, is conducted by such diverse groupings as opposing political parties, legislators and former government officials, and popular protest groups. This wider opinion, of course, cannot secure direct results. By its very nature, public opinion is a diverse (and often diffuse) phenomenon. Nevertheless, strong sentiments in favour of arms control do have an effect. Widespread concern over nuclear testing did serve to encourage the conclusion of the 1963 PTBT. Although the US Congress and opposition parties can have much greater leverage on government policies on arms control, these institutions, in turn, are also responsive to public opinion and the probable views of voters.

The role of arms control and strategic experts, and academics, is an important element within the political process. These individuals may attempt to influence government policy directly, or may advise and lobby parliamentarians, or promote their views through the media. These individuals can also play a less partisan role, which involves elucidating and exploring new possibilities, and ensuring an international exchange of ideas. Although scientists have consulted across East-West boundaries as early as the 1950s, there is now an increasing awareness of the reality of an international arms control community which embraces Moscow, as well as Washington. There are common perspectives, if not always common interests. Therefore, the views of this international arms control grouping will continue to have some influence on the future thinking and action of governments on a number of arms control and disarmament fronts. Facing an uncertain future, it is important to keep asking why so many arms control negotiations have failed and to review, in the light of contemporary ideas, how future negotiations might have a greater prospect of success. This book is one contribution to the debate.

Notes and references

[1] Isaacs, J., 'Bold steps, tentative results: Congress steps into the arms control vacuum', *Arms Control Today,* vol. 14, no. 7 (Sep. 1984), pp. 2–3.

[2] See Lynn-Jones, S. M., 'A quiet success for arms control: preventing incidents at sea', *International Security,* vol. 9, no. 4 (spring 1985), pp. 154–84.

[3] See Bunn, G., 'Nuclear arms control: obstacles to agreement', *Reassessing Arms Control,* eds D. Carlton and C. Schaef (Macmillan: London, 1985), p. 89.

[4] See Clarke, D. L., *The Politics of Arms Control: The Role and Effectiveness of the US ACDA* (Free Press: New York, 1979).

[5] See Weiler, L. 'The ACDA scandal: a critical agency becomes a basket case', *Arms Control Today,* vol. 13, no. 6 (July 1983), pp. 1–3 and 7.

[6] See Lall, B. G., 'Arms Control Impact Statements: a new approach to slowing the arms race', *Negotiating Security: An Arms Control Reader,* ed. W. H. Kincade and J. D. Porro (the Carnegie Endowment for International Peace: Washington, DC, 1979), pp. 233–37.

[7] See for example Singer, J. D., 'Negotiations, initiatives and arms reduction', *Bulletin of Peace Proposals,* vol. 15, no. 4 (1984).

[8] Given the developments in missile technology since the 1960s, these distinctions are harder to make. Broadly speaking, however, land-based missiles are still more vulnerable and somewhat more accurate than sea-based missiles. The problem with the elimination of land-based ICBMs is first, of course, the fact that the Soviet Union has much more of its missile

force on land. However, given Gorbachev's own espousal of the concept of sufficiency and of the side with superiority in particular weapons cutting down, together with his emphasis on purely defensive defence, there is more scope for flexibility than in the past.

⁹ Bertram, C., 'Arms control and technological change: elements of a new approach', *Future of Arms Control: Part II,* ed. C. Bertram (IISS: London, 1978), Adelphi Paper no. 146, p. 17–18.

¹⁰ See for example Roberts, A., *Nations in Arms: the Theory and Practice of Territorial Defence* (Chatto and Windus: London, 1976).

¹¹ These ideas have been explored in some detail by unofficial groups in Western Europe, in particular FR Germany and Britain. For example, see: *Bulletin of the Atomic Scientists,* vol. 44, no. 7 (Sep. 1988), pp. 12–54.; and *Bulletin of Peace Proposals,* vol. 15, no. 1 (1984).

¹² For Soviet interest in non-offensive defence see: Steel, J., 'The new weapon in the Soviet defence vocabulary', *The Guardian,* 5 Aug. 1987, p. 25. For a more substantial analysis see 'Gorbachev and Soviet military power', *The Washington Quarterly,* vol. 11, no. 3 (Summer 1988). This issue contains a series of articles by specialists on the Soviet Union.

¹³ Calogero, F., 'A novel approach to arms control negotiations?', *Proceedings of the 27th Pugwash Conference,* Munich, Aug. 1977, pp. 1–10.

¹⁴ Salter, S., 'Some ideas to help stop world war' (Institute for Social Inventions: London, 1984).

¹⁵ Osgood, C., *An Alternative to War or Surrender* (University of Illinois Press: Urbana, Ill., 1962).

¹⁶ Etzioni, A., 'The Kennedy experiment', *Western Political Science Quarterly,* vol. 20 (1967).

¹⁷ Garthoff, R. L. 'Banning the bomb in outer space', *International Security,* vol. 5, no. 3 (winter 1980–81), pp. 26–31.

¹⁸ Geneva International Peace Research Institute (GIPRI), 'Unilateral disarmament measures', *Transnational Perspectives,* vol. 10, no. 2 (1984), pp. 20–21.

¹⁹ See Roberts (note 10) for Swedish and Swiss decisions.

²⁰ See Schelling, T. C., 'Reciprocal measures for arms stabilization', *Daedalus,* vol. 89, no. 4 (fall 1960), pp. 900–1.

Index

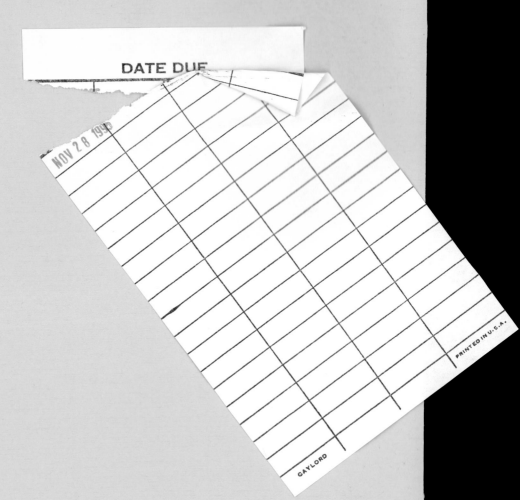

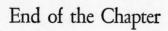

End of the Chapter

END OF
THE CHAPTER

➤➤✕◀◀

by John Galsworthy

CHARLES SCRIBNER'S SONS
New York

MAID IN WAITING

Copyright 1931 John Galsworthy; renewal copyright © 1959
R. H. Sauter

FLOWERING WILDERNESS

Copyright 1932 Charles Scribner's Sons; renewal copyright
© 1960 R. H. Sauter and A. J. P. Sellar.
Copyright 1932 John Galsworthy; renewal copyright © 1960
R. H. Sauter and A. J. P. Sellar.

ONE MORE RIVER

Copyright 1933 Charles Scribner's Sons; renewal copyright
© 1961

Contents

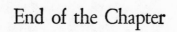

End of the Chapter

BOOK I

MAID IN WAITING

TO
FRANK GALSWORTHY

CHAPTER 1

THE BISHOP OF PORTHMINSTER was sinking fast; they had sent for his four nephews, his two nieces and their one husband. It was not thought that he would last the night.

He who had been 'Cuffs' Cherrell (for so the name Charwell is pronounced) to his cronies at Harrow and Cambridge in the sixties, the Reverend Cuthbert Cherrell in his two London parishes, Canon Cherrell in the days of his efflorescence as a preacher, and Cuthbert Porthminster for the last eighteen years, had never married. For eighty-two years he had lived and for fifty-five, having been ordained rather late, had represented God upon certain portions of the earth. This and the control of his normal instincts since the age of twenty-six had given to his face a repressed dignity which the approach of death did not disturb. He awaited it almost quizzically, judging from the twist of his eyebrow and the tone in which he said so faintly to his nurse:

"You will get a good sleep to-morrow, nurse. I shall be punctual, no robes to put on."

The best wearer of robes in the whole episcopacy, the most distinguished in face and figure, maintaining to the end the dandyism which had procured him the nickname 'Cuffs,' lay quite still, his grey hair brushed and his face like ivory. He had been a bishop so long that no one knew now what he thought about death, or indeed about anything, except the prayer book, any change in which he had deprecated with determination. In one never remarkable for expressing his feelings the ceremony of life had overlaid the natural reticence, as embroidery and jewels will disguise the foundation stuff of vestment.

He lay in a room with mullion windows, an ascetic room in a sixteenth century house, close to the Cathedral, whose scent of age was tempered but imperfectly by the September air coming in. Some zinnias in an old vase on the window-sill made the only splash of colour, and it was noticed by the nurse that his eyes scarcely left it, except to close from time to time. About six o'clock they informed him that all the family of his long-dead elder brother had arrived.

"Ah! See that they are comfortable. I should like to see Adrian."

When an hour later he opened his eyes again, they fell on his nephew Adrian seated at the foot of the bed. For some minutes he contemplated

I

the lean and wrinkled brownness of a thin bearded face, topped with grizzling hair, with a sort of faint astonishment, as though finding his nephew older than he had expected. Then, with lifted eyebrows and the same just quizzical tone in his faint voice, he said:

"My dear Adrian! Good of you! Would you mind coming closer? Ah! I haven't much strength, but what I have I wanted you to have the benefit of; or perhaps, as you may think, the reverse. I must speak to the point or not at all. You are not a Churchman, so what I have to say I will put in the words of a man of the world which once I was myself, perhaps have always been. I have heard that you have an affection, or may I say infatuation for a lady who is not in a position to marry you—is that so?"

The face of his nephew, kindly and wrinkled, was gentle with an expression of concern.

"It is, Uncle Cuthbert. I am sorry if it troubles you."

"A mutual affection?"

His nephew shrugged.

"My dear Adrian, the world has changed in its judgments since my young days, but there is still a halo around marriage. That, however, is a matter for your conscience and is not my point. Give me a little water."

When he had drunk from the glass held out, he went on more feebly:

"Since your father died I have been somewhat *in loco parentis* to you all, and the chief repository, I suppose, of such traditions as attach to our name. I wanted to say to you that our name goes back very far and very honourably. A certain inherited sense of duty is all that is left to old families now; what is sometimes excused to a young man is not excused to those of mature age and a certain position like your own. I should be sorry to be leaving this life knowing that our name was likely to be taken in vain by the Press, or bandied about. Forgive me for intruding on your privacy, and let me now say good-bye to you all. It will be less painful if you will give the others my blessing for what it is worth—very little, I'm afraid. Good-bye, my dear Adrian, good-bye!"

The voice dropped to a whisper. The speaker closed his eyes, and Adrian, after standing a minute looking down at the carved waxen face, stole, tall and a little stooping, to the door, opened it gently and was gone.

The nurse came back. The Bishop's lips moved and his eyebrows twitched now and then, but he spoke only once:

"I shall be glad if you will kindly see that my neck is straight, and my teeth in place. Forgive these details, but I do not wish to offend the sight . . ."

Adrian went down to the long panelled room where the family was waiting.

"Sinking. He sent his blessing to you all."

Sir Conway cleared his throat. Hilary pressed Adrian's arm. Lionel went to the window. Emily Mont took out a tiny handkerchief and passed her other hand into Sir Lawrence's. Wilmet alone spoke:

"How does he look, Adrian?"

"Like the ghost of a warrior on his shield."

Again Sir Conway cleared his throat.

"Fine old boy!" said Sir Lawrence, softly.

"Ah!" said Adrian.

They remained, silently sitting and standing in the compulsory discomfort of a house where death is visiting. Tea was brought in, but, as if by tacit agreement, no one touched it. And, suddenly, the bell tolled. The seven in that room looked up. At one blank spot in the air their glances met and crossed, as though fixed on something there and yet not there.

A voice from the doorway said:

"Now please, if you wish to see him."

Sir Conway, the eldest, followed the bishop's chaplain; the others followed Sir Conway.

In his narrow bed jutting from the centre of the wall opposite the mullion windows, the bishop lay, white and straight and narrow, with just the added dignity of death. He graced his last state even more than he had graced existence. None of those present, not even his chaplain, who made the eighth spectator, knew whether Cuthbert Porthminster had really had faith, except in that temporal dignity of the Church which he had so faithfully served. They looked at him now with all the different feelings death produces in varying temperaments, and with only one feeling in common, æsthetic pleasure at the sight of such memorable dignity.

Conway—General Sir Conway Cherrell—had seen much death. He stood with his hands crossed before him, as if once more at Sandhurst in the old-time attitude of 'stand at ease.' His face was thin-templed and ascetic, for a soldier's; the darkened furrowed cheeks ran from wide cheekbones to the point of a firm chin, the dark eyes were steady, the nose and lips thin; he wore a little close grizzly dark moustache—his face was perhaps the stillest of the eight faces, the face of the taller Adrian beside him, the least still. Sir Lawrence Mont had his arm through that of Emily his wife, the expression on his thin twisting countenance was as of one saying: "A very beautiful performance—don't cry, my dear."

The faces of Hilary and Lionel, one on each side of Wilmet, a seamed face and a smooth face, both long and thin and decisive, wore a sort of sorry scepticism, as if expecting those eyes to open. Wilmet had flushed deep pink; her lips were pursed. She was a tall thin woman. The chaplain stood with bent head, moving his lips as though telling over internal beads. They stayed thus perhaps three minutes, then as it were with a single indrawn breath, filed to the door. They went each to the room assigned.

They met again at dinner, thinking and speaking once more in terms of life. Uncle Cuthbert, except as a family figure-head, had never been very near to any one of them. The question whether he was to be buried with his fathers at Condaford or here in the cathedral, was debated. Probably his Will would decide. All but the General and Lionel, who were the executors, returned to London the same evening.

The two brothers having read through the Will, which was short, for there was nothing much to leave, sat on in the library, silent, till the General said;

"I want to consult you, Lionel. It's about my boy, Hubert. Did you read that attack made on him in the House before it rose?"

Lionel, sparing of words, and now on the eve of a Judgeship, nodded.

"I saw there was a question asked, but I don't know Hubert's version of the affair."

"I can give it you. The whole thing is damnable. The boy's got a temper, of course, but he's straight as a die. What he says you can rely on. And all I can say is that if I'd been in his place, I should probably have done the same."

Lionel nodded. "Go ahead."

"Well, as you know, he went straight from Harrow into the War, and had one year in the R.A.F. under age, got wounded, went back and stayed on in the army after the war. He was out in Mespot, then went on to Egypt and India. He got malaria badly, and last October had a year's sick leave given him, which will be up on October first. He was recommended for a long voyage. He got leave for it and went out through the Panama Canal to Lima. There he met that American professor, Hallorsen, who came over here some time ago and gave some lectures, it appears, about some queer remains in Bolivia; he was going to take an expedition there. This expedition was just starting when Hubert got to Lima, and Hallorsen wanted a transport officer. Hubert was fit enough after his voyage and jumped at the chance. He can't bear idleness. Hallorsen took him on; that was in December last. After a bit Hallorsen left him in charge of his base camp with a lot of half-caste Indian mule men. Hubert was the only white man, and he got fever badly. Some of those half-caste Indian fellows are devils, according to his account; no sense of discipline and perfect brutes with animals. Hubert got wrong with them—he's a hot-tempered chap, as I told you, and, as it happens, particularly fond of animals. The half-castes got more and more out of hand, till finally one of them whom he'd had to have flogged for ill-treating mules and who was stirring up mutiny, attacked him with a knife. Luckily Hubert had his revolver handy and shot him dead. And on that the whole blessed lot of them, except three, cleared out, taking the mules with them. Mind you, he'd been left there alone for nearly three months without support or news of any kind from Hallorsen. Well, he hung on somehow, half dead, with his remaining men. At last Hallorsen came back, and instead of try-ing to understand his difficulties, pitched into him. Hubert wouldn't stand for it; gave him as good as he got, and left. He came straight home, and is down with us at Condaford. He's lost the fever, luckily, but he's pretty well worn out, even now. And now that fellow Hallorsen has attacked him in his book; practically thrown the blame of failure on him, implies

4

he was tyrannical and no good at handling men, calls him a hot-tempered aristocrat—all that bunkum that goes down these days. Well, some Service member got hold of this and asked that question about it in Parliament. One expects Socialists to make themselves unpleasant, but when it comes to a Service member alluding to conduct unbecoming to a British officer, it's another matter altogether. Hallorsen's in the States. There's nobody to bring an action against: besides, Hubert could get no witnesses. It looks to me as if the thing has cut right across his career."

Lionel Cherrell's long face lengthened.

"Has he tried Headquarters?"

"Yes, he went up on Wednesday. They were chilly. Any popular gup about high-handedness scares them nowadays. I daresay they'd come round if no more were said, but how's that possible? He's been publicly criticised in that book, and practically accused in Parliament of violent conduct unbecoming to an officer and gentleman. He can't sit down under that; and yet—what can he do?"

Lionel drew deeply at his pipe.

"D'you know," he said, "I think he'd better take no notice."

The General clenched his fist. "Damn it, Lionel, I don't see that!"

"But he admits the shooting and the flogging. The public has no imagination, Con—they'll never see his side of the thing. All they'll swallow is that on a civilian expedition he shot one man and flogged others. You can't expect them to understand the conditions or the pressure there was."

"Then you seriously advise him to take it lying down?"

"As a man, no; as a man of the world, yes."

"Good Lord! What's England coming to? I wonder what old Uncle Cuffs would have said? He thought a lot of our name."

"So do I. But how is Hubert to get even with them?"

The General was silent for a little while and then said:

"This charge is a slur on the Service, and yet his hands seem tied. If he handed in his Commission he could stand up to it, but his whole heart's in the Army. It's a bad business. By the way, Lawrence has been talking to me about Adrian. Diana Ferse was Diana Montjoy, wasn't she?"

"Yes, second cousin to Lawrence—very pretty woman, Con. Ever see her?"

"As a girl, yes. What's her position now, then?"

"Married widow—two children, and a husband in a Mental Home."

"That's lively. Incurable?"

Lionel nodded. "They say so. But of course, you never know."

"Good Lord!"

"That's just about it. She's poor and Adrian's poorer; it's a very old affection on Adrian's part, dates from before her marriage. If he does anything foolish, he'll lose his curatorship."

"Go off with her, you mean? Why, he must be fifty!"

"No fool like an— She's an attractive creature. Those Montjoys are celebrated for their charm. Would he listen to you, Con?"

5

The General shook his head.

"More likely to Hilary."

"Poor old Adrian—one of the best men on earth. I'll talk to Hilary, but his hands are always full."

The General rose, "I'm going to bed. We don't smell of age at the Grange, like this place—though the Grange is older."

"Too much original wood here. Good-night, old man."

The brothers shook hands, and, grasping each a candle, sought their rooms.

CHAPTER 2

CONDAFORD GRANGE had passed from the de Campforts (whence its name) into possession of the Cherrells in 1217, when their name was spelt Kerwell and still at times Keroual, as the spirit moved the scribe. The story of its passing was romantic, for the Kerwell who got it by marrying a de Campfort had got the de Campfort by rescuing her from a wild boar. He had been a landless wight whose father, a Frenchman from Guienne, had come to England after Richard's crusade; and she had been the heiress of the landed de Campforts. The boar was incorporated on the family 'shield,' and some doubted whether the boar on the shield did not give rise to the story, rather than the story to the boar. In any case parts of the house were certified by expert masons to go back to the twelfth century. It had undoubtedly been moated; but under Queen Anne a restorative Cherrell, convinced of the millennium perhaps, and possibly inconvenienced by insects, had drained off the water, and there was now little sign that a moat had ever been.

The late Sir Conway, elder brother of the bishop, knighted in 1901 on his appointment to Spain, had been in the diplomatic service. He had therefore let the place down badly. He had died in 1904, at his post, and the letting-down process had been continued by his eldest son, the present Sir Conway, who, continually on Service, had enjoyed only spasmodic chances of living at Condaford till after the Great War. Now that he did live there, the knowledge that folk of his blood had been encamped there practically since the Conquest had spurred him to do his best to put it in order, so that it was by now unpretentiously trim without and comfortable within, and he was almost too poor to live in it. The estate contained too much covert to be profitable, and, though unencumbered, brought in but a few hundreds a year of net revenue. The pension of a General and the slender income of his wife (by birth the Honourable Elizabeth Frensham) enabled the General to incur a very small amount of supertax, to keep two hunters, and live quietly on the extreme edge of his means. His wife was one of those Englishwomen who seem to count for little, but for that very reason count for a good deal. She was unobtrusive, gentle, and always busy. In a word, she was background; and her pale face, reposeful, sensitive, a little timid, was a continual reminder that culture depends but slightly on wealth or intellect. Her husband and

7

her three children had implicit confidence in her coherent sympathy. They were all of more vivid nature, more strongly coloured, and she was a relief.

She had not accompanied the General to Porthminster and was therefore awaiting his return. The furniture was about to come out of chintz, and she was standing in the tea room wondering whether that chintz would last another season, when a Scotch terrier came in, followed by her eldest daughter Elizabeth—better known as 'Dinny.' Dinny was slight and rather tall; she had hair the colour of chestnuts, an imperfect nose, a Botticellian mouth, eyes cornflower blue and widely set, and a look of a flower on a long stalk that might easily be broken off, but never was. Her expression suggested that she went through life trying not to see it as a joke. She was, in fact, like one of those natural wells, or springs, whence one cannot procure water without bubbles: 'Dinny's bubble and squeak,' her uncle Sir Lawrence Mont called it. She was by now twenty-four.

"Mother, do we have to go into black edging for Uncle Cuffs?"

"I don't think so, Dinny; or very slight."

"Is he to be planted here?"

"I expect in the cathedral, but Father will know."

"Tea, darling? Scaramouch, up you come, and don't bob your nose into the Gentleman's Relish."

"Dinny, I'm so worried about Hubert."

"So am I, dear; he isn't Hubert at all, he's like a sketch of himself by Thom the painter, all on one side. He ought never to have gone on that ghastly expedition, Mother. There's a limit to hitting it off with Americans, and Hubert reaches it sooner than almost anybody I know. He never could get on with them. Besides, I don't believe civilians ever ought to have soldiers with them."

"Why, Dinny?"

"Well, soldiers have the static mind. They know God from Mammon. Haven't you noticed it, dear?"

Lady Cherrell had. She smiled timidly, and asked:

"Where is Hubert? Father will be home directly."

"He went out with Don, to get a leash of partridges for dinner. Ten to one he'll forget to shoot them, and anyway they'll be too fresh. He's in that state of mind into which it has pleased God to call him; except that for God read the devil. He broods over that business, Mother. Only one thing would do him good, and that's to fall in love. Can't we find the perfect girl for him? Shall I ring for tea?"

"Yes, dear. And this room wants fresh flowers."

"I'll get them. Come along, Scaramouch!"

Passing out into September sunshine, Dinny noted a green woodpecker on the lower lawn, and thought: 'If seven birds with seven beaks should peck for half a term, do you suppose the lady thought that they could find a worm?' It *was* dry! All the same the zinnias were gorgeous this year; and she proceeded to pick some. They ran the gamut in her hand from deepest red through pink to lemon-yellow—handsome blossoms, but not endearing. 'Pity,' she thought, 'we can't go to some bed of modern maids and pick one for Hubert.' She seldom showed her feelings, but she had two deep feelings not for show—one for her brother, the other for Condaford, and they were radically entwined. All the coherence of her life belonged to Condaford; she had a passion for the place which no one would have suspected from her way of talking of it, and she had a deep and jealous desire to bind her only brother to the same devotion. After all, she had been born there while it was shabby and run-down, and had survived into the period of renovation. To Hubert it had only been a holiday and leave-time perch. Dinny, though the last person in the world to talk of her roots, or to take them seriously in public, had a private faith in the Cherrells, their belongings and their works, which nothing could shake. Every Condaford beast, bird and tree, even the flowers she was plucking, were a part of her, just as were the simple folk around in their thatched cottages, and the Early-English church, where she attended without belief to speak of, and the grey Condaford dawns which she seldom saw, the moonlit, owl-haunted nights, the long sunlight over the stubble, and the scents and the sounds and the feel of the air. When she was away from home she never said she was homesick, but she was; when she was at home she never said she revelled in it, but she did. If Condaford should pass from the Cherrells, she would not moan, but would feel like a plant pulled up by its roots. Her father had for it the indifferent affection of a man whose active life had been passed elsewhere; her mother the acquiescence of one who had always done her duty by what had kept her nose to the grindstone and was not exactly hers; her sister treated it with the matter-of-fact tolerance of one who would rather be somewhere more exciting; and Hubert—what had Hubert? She really did not know. With her hands full of zinnias and her neck warm from the lingering sunshine, she returned to the drawing-room.

Her mother was standing by the tea table.

"The train's late," she said. "I do wish Clare wouldn't drive so fast."

"I don't see the connection, darling." But she did. Mother was always fidgety when Father was behind time.

"Mother, I'm all for Hubert sending his version to the papers."

"We shall see what your Father says—he'll have talked to your Uncle Lionel."

"I hear the car now," said Dinny.

The General was followed into the room by his younger daughter. Clare was the most vivid member of the family. She had dark fine shingled hair and a pale expressive face, of which the lips were slightly brightened. The eyes were brown, with a straight and eager glance, the brow low and very white. Her expression was old for a girl of twenty, being calm and yet adventurous. She had an excellent figure and walked with an air.

"This poor dear has had no lunch, Mother," she said.

"Horrible cross-country journey, Liz. Whiskey-and-soda and a biscuit's all I've had since breakfast."

"You shall have an egg-nogg, darling," said Dinny, and left the room. Clare followed her.

The General kissed his wife. "The old boy looked very fine, my dear, though, except for Adrian, we only saw him after. I shall have to go back for the funeral. It'll be a swell affair, I expect. Great figure—Uncle Cuffs. I spoke to Lionel about Hubert; he doesn't see what can be done. But I've been thinking."

"Yes, Con?"

"The whole point is whether or not the Authorities are going to take any notice of that attack in the House. They might ask him to send in his commission. That'd be fatal. Sooner than that he'd better hand it in himself. He's due for his medical on October the first. Can we pull any strings without his knowing?—the boy's proud. I can go and see Topsham and you could get at Follanby, couldn't you?"

Lady Cherrell made wry her face.

"I know," said the General, "it's rotten; but the real chance would be Saxenden, only I don't know how to get at him."

"Dinny might suggest something."

"Dinny? Well, I suppose she *has* more brains than any of us, except you, my dear."

"I," said Lady Cherrell, "have no brains at all."

"Bosh! Oh! Here she is."

Dinny advanced, bearing a frothy liquor in a glass.

"Dinny, I was saying to your mother that we want to get into touch with Lord Saxenden about Hubert's position. Can you suggest any way?"

"Through a country neighbour, Dad. Has he any?"

"His place marches with Wilfred Bentworth's."

"There it is, then. Uncle Hilary or Uncle Lawrence."

"How?"

"Wilfred Bentworth is Chairman of Uncle Hilary's Slum Conversion Committee. A little judicious nepotism, dear."

"Um! Hilary and Lawrence were both at Porthminster—wish I'd thought of that."

"Shall I talk to them for you, Father?"

"By George, if you would, Dinny! I hate pushing our affairs."

"Yes, dear. It's a woman's job, isn't it?"

The General looked at his daughter dubiously—he never quite knew when she was serious.

"Here's Hubert," said Dinny, quickly.

CHAPTER 3

HUBERT CHERRELL, followed by a spaniel dog and carrying a gun, was crossing the old grey flagstones of the terrace. Rather over middle height, lean and erect, with a head not very large and a face weathered and seamed for so young a man, he wore a little darkish moustache cut just to the edge of his lips, which were thin and sensitive, and hair with already a touch of grey at the sides. His browned cheeks were thin too, but with rather high cheekbones, and his eyes hazel, quick and glancing, set rather wide apart over a straight thin nose under gabled eyebrows. He was, in fact, a younger edition of his father. A man of action, forced into a state of thought, is unhappy until he can get out of it; and, ever since his late leader had launched that attack on his conduct, he had chafed, conscious of having acted rightly, or rather, in accordance with necessity. And he chafed the more because his training and his disposition forbade him giving tongue. A soldier by choice, not accident, he saw his soldiering imperilled, his name as an officer, and even as a gentleman, aspersed, and no way of hitting back at those who had aspersed it. His head seemed to him to be in Chancery for anyone to punch, most galling of experiences to anyone of high spirit. He came in through the French window, leaving dog and gun outside, aware that he was being talked about. He was now constantly interrupting discussions on his position, for in this family the troubles of one were the troubles of all. Having taken a cup of tea from his mother, he remarked that birds were getting wild already, covert was so sparse, and there was silence.

"Well, I'm going to look at my letters," said the General, and went out followed by his wife.

Left alone with her brother, Dinny hardened her heart, and said:

"Something must be done, Hubert."

"Don't worry, old girl; it's rotten, but there's nothing one can do."

"Why don't you write your own account of what happened, from your diary? I could type it, and Michael will find you a publisher, he knows all those sort of people. We simply can't sit down under this."

"I loathe the idea of trotting my private feelings into the open, and it means that or nothing."

Dinny wrinkled her brows.

"I loathe letting that Yank put his failure on to you. You owe it to the British Army, Hubert."

"Bad as that? I went as a civilian."

"Why not publish your diary as it is?"

"That'd be worse. You haven't seen it."

"We could expurgate, and embroider, and all that. You see, Dad feels this."

"Perhaps you'd better read the thing. It's full of 'miserable Starkey.' When one's alone like that, one lets oneself go."

"You can cut out what you like."

"It's no end good of you, Dinny."

Dinny stroked his sleeve.

"What sort of man is this Hallorsen?"

"To be just, he has lots of qualities: hard as nails, plenty of pluck, and no nerves; but it's Hallorsen first with him all the time. It's not in him to fail, and when he does, someone else has to stand the racket. According to him, he failed for want of transport: and I was his transport officer. But if he'd left the Angel Gabriel as he left me, he'd have done no better. He just miscalculated, and won't admit it. You'll find it all in my diary."

"Have you seen this?" She held up a newspaper cutting, and read:

" 'We understand that action will be taken by Captain Charwell, D.S.O., to vindicate his honour in face of the statements made in Professor Hallorsen's book on his Bolivian Expedition, the failure of which he attributed to Captain Charwell's failure to support him at the critical moment.' Someone's trying to get a dog-fight out of it, you see."

"Where was that?"

"In the *Evening Sun*."

"Action!" said Hubert bitterly; "what action? I've nothing but my word, he took care of that when he left me alone with all those dagoes."

"It's the diary then, or nothing."

"I'll get you the damned thing. . . ."

That night Dinny sat at her window reading 'the damned thing.' A full moon rode between the elm trees and there was silence as of the grave. Just one sheep-bell tinkled from a fold on the rise; just one magnolia flower bloomed close to her window. All seemed unearthly, and now and then she stopped reading to gaze at the unreality. So had some ten thousand full moons ridden since her forbears received this patch of ground; the changeless security of so old a home heightened the lonely discomfort, the tribulation in the pages she was reading. Stark notes about stark things—one white man among a crew of half-caste savages, one animal-lover among half-starved animals and such men as knew not compassion. And with that cold and settled loveliness out there to look upon, she read and grew hot and miserable.

* * *

"The lousy brute Castro has been digging his infernal knife into the mules again. The poor brutes are thin as rails, and haven't half their strength. Warned him for the last time. If he does it again, he'll get the lash . . . Had fever."

"Castro got it good and strong this morning—a dozen; we'll see if that will stop him. Can't get on with these brutes, they don't seem human. Oh! for a day on a horse at Condaford and forget these swamps and poor ghastly skeletons of mules . . ."

"Had to flog another of these brutes—their treatment of the mules is simply devilish, blast them! . . . Fever again . . ."

"Hell and Tommy to pay—had mutiny this morning. They laid for me. Luckily Manuel had warned me—he's a good boy. As it was, Castro had his knife through my gizzard. Got my left arm badly. Shot him with my own hand. Now perhaps they'll toe the mark. Nothing from Hallorsen. How much longer does he expect me to hold on in this dump of hell? My arm is giving me proper gee-up." . . .

"The lid is on at last, those devils stampeded the mules in the dark while I was asleep, and cleared out. Manuel and two other boys are all that's left. We trailed them a long way—came on the carcases of two mules, that's all; the beggars have dispersed and you might as well look for a star in the Milky Way. Got back to camp dead beat. . . . Whether we shall ever get out of this alive, goodness knows. My arm very painful, hope it doesn't mean blood-poisoning . . ."

"Meant to trek to-day as best we could. Set up a pile of stones and left despatch for Hallorsen, telling him the whole story in case he ever does send back for me; then changed my mind. I shall stick out here till he comes or till we're dead, which is on the whole more likely . . ."

And so on through a tale of struggle to the end. Dinny laid down the dim and yellowed record and leaned her elbow on the sill. The silence and the coldness of the light out there had chilled her spirit. She no longer felt in fighting mood. Hubert was right. Why show one's naked soul, one's sore finger, to the public? No! Better anything than that. Private strings— yes, they should be pulled; and she would pull them for all she was worth.

CHAPTER 4

ADRIAN CHERRELL was one of those confirmed countrymen who live in towns. His job confined him to London where he presided over a collection of anthropological remains. He was poring over a maxilla from New Guinea, which had been accorded a very fine reception in the Press, and had just said to himself: 'The thing's a phlizz. Just a low type of Homo Sapiens,' when his janitor announced:

"Young lady to see you, sir—Miss Cherrell, I think."

"Ask her in, James"; and he thought: 'If that's Dinny, where did I put my wits?'

"Oh! Dinny! Canrobert says that this maxilla is pre-Trinil. Mokley says Paulo-post-Piltdown; and Eldon P. Burbank says propter Rhodesian. I say Sapiens; observe that molar."

"I do, Uncle Adrian."

"Too human altogether. That man had toothache. Toothache was probably the result of artistic development. Altamiran art and Cromagnon cavities are found together. Homo Sapiens, this chap."

"No toothache without wisdom—how cheery! I've come up to see Uncle Hilary and Uncle Lawrence, but I thought if I had lunch with you first, I should feel stronger."

"We shall," said Adrian, "therefore go to the Bulgarian café."

"Why?"

"Because for the moment we shall get good food there. It's the latest propaganda restaurant, my dear, so we are probably safe at a moderate price. Do you want to powder your nose?"

"Yes."

"In here, then."

While she was gone Adrian stood and stroked his goatee and wondered exactly what he could order for eighteen and sixpence; for, being a public servant without private means, he rarely had more than a pound in his pocket.

"What," said Dinny, when they were seated before an omelette Bulgarienne, "do you know about Professor Hallorsen, Uncle Adrian?"

"The man who set out to discover the sources of civilisation in Bolivia?"

"Yes; and took Hubert with him."

"Ah! But left him behind, I gather?"

14

"Did you ever meet him?"

"I did. I met him in 1920, climbing the 'Little Sinner' in the Dolomites."

"Did you like him?"

"No."

"Why?"

"Well, he was so aggressively young, he beat me to the top, and—he reminded me of baseball. Did you ever see baseball played?"

"No."

"I saw it once in Washington. You insult your opponent so as to shake his nerve. You call him doughboy and attaboy, and President Wilson and Old Man Ribber, and things like that, just when he's going to hit the ball. It's ritual. The point is to win at any cost."

"Don't you believe in winning at any cost?"

"Nobody says they do, Dinny."

"And we all try when it comes to the point?"

"I have known it occur, even with politicians, Dinny."

"Would you try to win at any cost, Uncle?"

"Probably."

"You wouldn't. I should."

"You are very kind, my dear; but why this local disparagement?"

"Because I feel as bloodthirsty as a mosquito about Hubert's case. I spent last night reading his diary."

"Woman," said Adrian, slowly, "has not yet lost her divine irresponsibility."

"Do you think we're in danger of losing it?"

"No, because whatever your sex may say, you never will annihilate man's innate sense of leading you about."

"What is the best way to annihilate a man like Hallorsen, Uncle Adrian?"

"Apart from a club, ridicule."

"His notion about Bolivian civilisation was absurd, I suppose?"

"Wholly. There are, we know, some curious and unexplained stone monsters up there, but his theory, if I understand it, won't wash at all. Only, my dear, Hubert would appear to be involved in it."

"Not scientifically; he just went as transport officer." And Dinny levelled a smile at her Uncle's eyes. "It wouldn't do any harm, would it, to hold up a stunt like that to ridicule? You could do it so beautifully, Uncle."

"Serpent!"

"But isn't it the duty of serious scientists to ridicule stunts?"

"If Hallorsen were an Englishman—perhaps; but his being an American brings in other considerations."

"Why? I thought Science paid no regard to frontiers."

"In theory. In practice we close the other eye. Americans are very touchy. You remember a certain recent attitude towards Evolution; if we had let out our shout of laughter over that, there might almost have been a war."

"But most Americans laughed at it too."

"Yes, but they won't stand for outsiders laughing at their kith and kin. Have some of this soufflé Sofia?"

They ate in silence, each studying sympathetically the other's face. Dinny was thinking: 'I love his wrinkles, and it's a nice little beard for a beard.' Adrian was thinking: 'I'm glad her nose turns up a little. I have very engaging nieces and nephews.' At last she said:

"Well, Uncle Adrian, will you try and think of any way of strafing that man for the scurvy way he's treated Hubert?"

"Where is he?"

"Hubert says in the States."

"Have you considered, my dear, that nepotism is undesirable?"

"So is injustice, Uncle; and blood is thicker than water."

"And this wine," said Adrian, with a grimace, "is thicker than either. What are you going to see Hilary about?"

"I want to scrounge an introduction to Lord Saxenden."

"Why?"

"Father says he's important."

"So you are out to 'pull strings,' as they say?"

Dinny nodded.

"No sensitive and honest person can pull strings successfully, Dinny."

Her eyebrows twitched and her teeth, very white and even, appeared in a broad smile.

"But I'm neither, dear."

"We shall see. In the meantime these cigarettes are really tip-top propaganda. Have one?"

Dinny took a cigarette, and with a long puff, said:

"You saw great-Uncle 'Cuffs,' didn't you, Uncle Adrian?"

"Yes. A dignified departure. He died in amber, as you might say. Wasted on the Church; he was the perfect diplomat, was Uncle 'Cuffs.'"

"I only saw him twice. But do you mean to say that *he* couldn't get what he wanted, without loss of dignity, by pulling strings?"

"It wasn't exactly pulling strings with him, my dear; it was suavity and power of personality."

"Manners?"

"Manner—the Grand; it about died with him."

"Well, Uncle, I must be going; wish me dishonesty and a thick skin."

"And I," said Adrian, "will return to the jawbone of the New Guinean with which I hope to smite my learned brethren. If I can help Hubert in any decent way, I will. At all events I'll think about it. Give him my love, and good-bye, my dear!"

They parted, and Adrian went back to his museum. Regaining his position above the maxilla, he thought of a very different jawbone. Having reached an age when the blood of spare men with moderate habits has an even-tempered flow, his 'infatuation' with Diana Ferse, dating back to years before her fatal marriage, had a certain quality of altruism. He desired her happiness before his own. In his almost continual thoughts about her the consideration 'What's best for her?' was ever foremost. He had done without her for so long, that importunity (never in his character) was out of the question where she was concerned. But her face, oval and dark-eyed, delicious in lip and nose, and a little sad in repose, constantly blurred the outlines of maxillæ, thigh-bones, and the other interesting phenomena of his job. She and her two children lived in a small Chelsea house on the income of a husband who for four years had been a patient in a private Mental Home, and was never expected to recover his equilibrium. She was nearly forty, and had been through dreadful times before Ferse had definitely toppled over the edge. Of the old school in thought and manner, and trained to a coherent view of human history, Adrian accepted life with half-humorous fatalism. He was not of the reforming type, and the position of his lady love did not inspire him with a desire for the scalp of marriage. He wanted her to be happy, but did not see how in the existing circumstances he could make her so. She had at least peace and the sufficient income of him who had been smitten by Fate. Moreover, Adrian had something of the superstitious regard felt by primitive men for those afflicted with this particular form of misfortune. Ferse had been a decent fellow till the taint began to wear through the coatings of health and education and his conduct for the two years before his eclipse was only too liberally explained by that eclipse. He was one of God's afflicted; and his helplessness demanded of one the utmost scrupulosity. Adrian turned from the maxilla and took down a built-up cast of Pithecanthropus, that curious being from Trinil, Java, who for so long has divided opinion as to whether he shall be called man-ape or ape-man. What a distance from him to that modern English skull over the mantlepiece! Ransack the authorities as one might, one never received an answer to the question: Where was the cradle of Homo Sapiens, the nest where he had developed from Trinil, Piltdown, Neanderthal man, or from some other undiscovered collateral of those creatures? If Adrian had a passion, indeed, except for Diana Ferse, it was a burning desire to fix that breeding spot. They were toying now with the idea of descent from Neanderthal man, but he felt it wouldn't do. When specialisation had reached a stage so definite as that disclosed by those brutish specimens, it did not swerve to type so different. As well expect development of red-deer from elk! He turned to that huge globe whereon were marked all discoveries of moment concerning the origin of modern Man, annotated in his own neat handwriting with notes on geological changes, time and climate. Where—where to look? It was a detective problem, soluble only in the French fashion by instinctive appreciation of the inherently probable locality, ratified by research at the selected spot—the greatest detective problem in the world. The foothills of the Himalayas, the Fayoum, or somewhere now submerged beneath the sea? If, indeed, it were under the sea, then it would never be established to certainty. Academic—the whole thing? Not quite, for with it was conjoined the question of man's essence, the real primitive nature of the human being, on which social philosophy might and should be founded—a question nicely revived of late: Whether, indeed, man was fundamentally decent and peaceful, as examination into the lives of animals and some so-called savage peoples seemed to suggest, or fundamentally aggressive and restless, as that lugubrious record, History, seemed to assert? Find the breeding nest of Homo Sapiens, and there would emerge perhaps some evidence to decide whether he was devil-angel or angel-devil. To one with Adrian's instincts there was great attraction in this revived thesis of the inherent gentleness of man, but his habit of mind refused to subscribe easily or wholesale to any kind of thesis. Even gentle beasts and birds lived by the law of self-preservation, so did primitive man; the devilries of sophisticated man began naturally with the extension of his activities and the increase of his competitions—in other words, with the ramifications of self-preservation induced by so-called civilised life. The uncomplicated existence of uncivilised man might well afford less chance to the instinct of self-preservation to be sinister in its manifestations, but you could hardly argue anything from that. Better to accept modern man as he was and try to curb his opportunities for mischief. Nor would it do to bank too much on the natural gentleness of primitive peoples. Only last night he had read of an elephant hunt in Central Africa, wherein the primitive negroes, men and women, who were beating for the white hunters, had fallen upon the carcases of the slain elephants, torn them limb from limb, flesh from flesh, eaten it all dripping and raw, then vanished into the woods, couple by couple, to complete their orgy. After all, there was something in civilisation! But at this moment his janitor announced:

"A Professor 'Allorsen to see you, sir. He wants to look at the Peruvian skulls."

"Hallorsen!" said Adrian, startled. "Are you sure? I thought he was in America, James."

"'Allorsen was the name, sir; tall gentleman, speaks like an American. Here's his card."

"H'm! I'll see him, James." And he thought: 'Shade of Dinny! What am I going to say?'

The very tall and very good-looking man who entered seemed about thirty-eight years old. His clean-shaven face was full of health, his eyes full of light, his dark hair had a fleck or two of premature grey in it. A breeze seemed to come in with him. He spoke at once:

"Mr. Curator?"

Adrian bowed.

"Why! Surely we've met; up a mountain, wasn't it?"

"Yes," said Adrian.

"Well, well! My name's Hallorsen—Bolivian expedition. I'm told your

Peruvian skulls are bully. I brought my little Bolivian lot along; thought I'd like to compare them with your Peruvians right here. There's such a lot of bunk written about skulls by people who haven't seen the originals."

"Very true, Professor. I shall be delighted to see your Bolivians. By the way, you never knew my name, I think. This is it."

Adrian handed him a card. Hallorsen took it.

"Gee! Are you related to the Captain Charwell who's got his knife into me?"

"His uncle. But I was under the impression that it was your knife that was into him."

"Well, he let me down."

"I understand he thinks you let him down."

"See here, Mr. Charwell——"

"We pronounce the name Cherrell, if you don't mind."

"Cherrell—yes, I remember now. But if you hire a man to do a job, Mr. Curator, and that job's too much for him, and because it's too much for him you get left, what do you do—pass him a gold medal?"

"You find out, I think, whether the job you hired him to do was humanly possible, before you take out your knife, anyway."

"That's up to the man who takes the job. And what was it? Just to keep a tight rein on a few dagoes."

"I don't know very much about it, but I understand he had charge of the transport animals as well."

"He surely did; and let the whole thing slip out of his hand. Well, I don't expect you to side against your nephew. But can I see your Peruvians?"

"Certainly."

"That's nice of you."

During the mutual inspection which followed Adrian frequently glanced at the magnificent specimen of Homo Sapiens who stood beside him. A man so overflowing with health and life he had seldom seen. Natural enough that any check should gall him. Sheer vitality would prevent him from seeing the other side of things. Like his nation, matters must move his way, because there was no other way that seemed possible to his superabundance.

'After all,' he thought, 'he can't help being God's own specimen—Homo transatlanticus superbus'; and he said slyly: "So the sun is going to travel West to East in future, Professor?"

Hallorsen smiled, and his smile had an exuberant sweetness.

"Well, Mr. Curator, we're agreed, I guess, that civilisation started with agriculture. If we can show that we raised Indian corn on the American continent way back, maybe thousands of years before the old Nile civilisation of barley and wheat, why shouldn't the stream be the other way?"

"And can you?"

"Why, we have twenty to twenty-five types of Indian corn. Hrdlicka claims that some twenty thousand years was necessary to differentiate them. That puts us way ahead as the parents of agriculture, anyway."

"But alas! no type of Indian corn existed in the old world till after the discovery of America."

"No, sir; nor did any old-world type cereal exist in America till after that. Now, if the old-world culture seeped its way across the Pacific, why didn't it bring along its cereals?"

"But that doesn't make America the light-bringer to the rest of the world, does it?"

"Maybe not; if not, she just developed her own old civilisations out of her own discovery of cereals; and they were the first."

"Are you an Atlantean, Professor?"

"I sometimes toy with the idea, Mr. Curator."

"Well, well! May I ask if you are quite happy about your attack on my nephew?"

"Why, I certainly had a sore head when I wrote it. Your nephew and I didn't click."

"That, I should think, might make you all the more doubtful as to whether you were just."

"If I withdrew my criticism, I wouldn't be saying what I really thought."

"You are convinced that you had no hand in your failure to reach your objective?"

The frown on the giant's brow had a puzzled quality, and Adrian thought: 'An honest man, anyway.'

"I don't see what you're getting at," said Hallorsen, slowly.

"You chose my nephew, I believe?"

"Yes, out of twenty others."

"Precisely. You chose the wrong man, then?"

"I surely did."

"Bad judgment?"

Hallorsen laughed.

"That's very acute, Mr. Curator. But I'm not the man to advertise my own failings."

"What you wanted," said Adrian, dryly, "was a man without the bowels of compassion; well, I admit, you didn't get him."

Hallorsen flushed.

"We shan't agree about this, sir. I'll just take my little lot of skulls away. And I thank you for your courtesy."

A few minutes later he was gone.

Adrian was left to tangled meditation. The fellow was better than he had remembered. Physically a splendid specimen, mentally not to be despised, spiritually—well, typical of a new world where each immediate objective was the most important thing on earth till it was attained, and attainment more important than the methods of attainment employed.

'Pity,' he thought, 'if there's going to be a dog-fight. Still, the fellow's in the wrong; one ought to be more charitable than to attack like that in public print. Too much ego in friend Hallorsen.' So thinking, he put the maxilla into a drawer.

CHAPTER 5

DINNY PURSUED her way towards St. Augustine's-in-the-Meads. On that fine day the poverty of the district she was entering seemed to her country-nurtured eyes intensely cheerless. She was the more surprised by the hilarity of the children playing in the streets. Asking one of them the way to the Vicarage, she was escorted by five. They did not leave her when she rang the bell, and she was forced to conclude that they were actuated by motives not entirely connected with altruism. They attempted, indeed, to go in with her, and only left when she gave them each a penny. She was ushered into a pleasant room which looked as though it would be glad if someone had the time to enter it some day, and was contemplating a reproduction of the Castelfranco Francesca, when a voice said:

"Dinny!" and she saw her Aunt May. Mrs. Hilary Cherrell had her usual air of surmounting the need for being in three places at once; she looked leisurely, detached, and pleased—not unnaturally, for she liked her niece.

"Up for shopping, dear?"

"No, Aunt May, I've come to win an introduction off Uncle Hilary."

"Your Uncle's in the Police Court."

A bubble rose to Dinny's surface.

"Why, what's he done, Aunt May?"

Mrs. Hilary smiled.

"Nothing at present, but I won't answer for him if the magistrate isn't sensible. One of our young women has been charged with accosting."

"Not Uncle Hilary?"

"No, dear, hardly that. Your uncle is a witness to her character."

"And is there really a character to witness to, Aunt May?"

"Well, that's the point. Hilary says so; but I'm not so sure."

"Men are very trustful. I've never been in a Police Court. I should love to go and catch Uncle there."

"Well, I'm going in that direction. We might go together as far as the Court."

Five minutes later they issued, and proceeded by way of streets ever more arresting to the eyes of Dinny, accustomed only to the picturesque poverty of the countryside.

22

"I never quite realised before," she said, suddenly, "that London was such a bad dream."

"From which there is no awakening. That's the chilling part of it. Why on earth with all this unemployment, don't they organise a national Slum Clearance Scheme? It would pay for itself within twenty years. Politicians are marvels of energy and principle when they're out of office, but when they get in, they simply run behind the machine."

"They're not women, you see, Auntie."

"Are you chaffing, Dinny?"

"Oh! no. Women haven't the sense of difficulty that men have; women's difficulties are physical and real, men's difficulties are mental and formal, they always say: 'It'll never do!' Women never say that. They act, and find out whether it will do or not."

Mrs. Hilary was silent a moment.

"I suppose women *are* more actual; they have a fresher eye, and less sense of responsibility."

"I wouldn't be a man for anything."

"That's refreshing; but on the whole they get a better time, my dear, even now."

"They think so, but I doubt it. Men are awfully like ostriches, it seems to me. They can refuse to see what they don't want to, better than we can; but I don't think that's an advantage."

"If you lived in the Meads, Dinny, you might."

"If I lived in the Meads, dear, I should die."

Mrs. Hilary contemplated her niece by marriage. Certainly she looked a little transparent and as if she could be snapped off, but she also had a look of 'breeding,' as if her flesh were dominated by her spirit. She might be unexpectedly durable, and impermeable by outside things.

"I'm not so sure, Dinny; yours is a toughened breed. But for that your uncle would have been dead long ago. Well! Here's the Police Court. I'm sorry I can't spare time to come in. But everybody will be nice to you. It's a very human place, if somewhat indelicate. Be a little careful about your next-door neighbours."

Dinny raised an eyebrow: "Lousy, Aunt May?"

"Well, I wouldn't go so far as to say not. Come back to tea, if you can."

She was gone.

The exchange and mart of human indelicacy was crowded, for with the infallible flair of the Public for anything dramatic, the case in which Hilary was a witness to character had caught on, since it involved the integrity of the Police. Its second remand was in progress when Dinny took the last remaining fifteen square inches of standing room. Her neighbours on the right reminded her of the nursery rhyme: 'The butcher, the baker, the candlestick-maker.' Her neighbour on the left was a tall policeman. Many women were among the throng at the back of the Court. The air was close and smelled of clothes. Dinny looked at the magistrate, ascetic and as if pickled, and wondered why he did not have incense fuming on his desk. Her eyes passed on to the figure in the dock, a girl of about her own age and height, neatly dressed, with good features except that her mouth was perhaps more sensuous than was fortunate for one in her position. Dinny estimated that her hair was probably fair. She stood very still, with a slight fixed flush on her pale cheeks, and a frightened restlessness in her eyes. Her name appeared to be Millicent Pole. Dinny gathered that she was alleged by a police constable to have accosted two men in the Euston Road, neither of whom had appeared to give evidence. In the witness-box a young man who resembled a tobacconist was testifying that he had seen the girl pass twice or three times—had noticed her specially as a 'nice bit'; she had seemed worried, as if looking for something.

For somebody, did he mean?

That or the other, how should he know? No, she wasn't looking on the pavement; no, she didn't stoop; she passed *him*, anyway, without a look. Had he spoken to her? No fear! Doing? Oh, he was just outside his shop for a breath of air after closing. Did he see her speak to anyone? No, he didn't, but he wasn't there long.

"The Reverend Hilary Charwell."

Dinny saw her uncle rise from a bench and step up under the canopy of the witness box. He looked active and unclerical, and her eyes rested with pleasure on his long firm face, so wrinkled and humorous.

"Your name is Hilary Charwell?"

"Cherrell, if you don't mind."

"Quite. And you are the incumbent of St. Augustine's-in-the-Meads?"

Hilary bowed.

"For how long?"

"Thirteen years."

"You are acquainted with the defendant?"

"Since she was a child."

"Tell us, please, Mr. Cherrell, what you know of her?"

Dinny saw her uncle turn more definitely to the magistrate.

"Her father and mother, sir, were people for whom I had every respect; they brought up their children well. He was a shoemaker—poor, of course; we're all poor in my parish. I might almost say they died of poverty five and six years ago, and their two daughters have been more or less under my eye since. They work at Petter and Poplin's. I've never heard anything against Millicent here. So far as I know she's a good honest girl."

"I take it, Mr. Cherrell, your opportunities of judging of her are not very great?"

"Well, I visit the house in which she lodges with her sister. If you saw it, sir, you would agree that it requires some self-respect to deal as well as they do with the conditions there."

"Is she a member of your congregation?"

A smile came on her uncle's lips, and was reflected on the magistrate's.

"Hardly, sir. Their Sundays are too precious to young people nowadays. But Millicent is one of the girls who goes for her holidays to our Rest House near Dorking. They are always very good girls down there. My niece by marriage, Mrs. Michael Mont, who runs the house, has reported well of her. Shall I read what she says?

"'DEAR UNCLE HILARY,

"'You ask about Millicent Pole. She has been down three times, and the matron reports that she is a nice girl and not at all flighty. My own impression of her is the same.'"

"Then it comes to this, Mr. Cherrell: in your view a mistake has been made in this case?"

"Yes, sir; I am convinced of it."

The girl in the dock put her handkerchief to her eyes. And Dinny felt, suddenly, indignant at the extreme wretchedness of her position. To stand there before all those people, even if she had done as they said! And why shouldn't a girl ask a man for his companionship? He wasn't obliged to give it.

The tall policeman stirred, looked down at her, as if scenting unorthodoxy, and cleared his throat.

"Thank you, Mr. Cherrell."

Hilary stepped out of the witness box and in doing so caught sight of his niece and waved a finger. Dinny became aware that the case was over, the magistrate making up his mind. He sat perfectly silent, pressing his fingertips together and staring at the girl, who had finished mopping her eyes and was staring back at him. Dinny held her breath. On the next minute—a life, perhaps, hung in the balance! The tall policeman changed his feet. Was his sympathy with his fellow in the force, or with that girl? All the little noises in the Court had ceased, the only sound was the scratching of a pen. The magistrate held his fingertips apart and spoke:

"I am not satisfied that this case has been made out. The defendant will be dismissed. You may go."

The girl made a little choking sound. To her right the candlestick-maker uttered a hoarse: "'Ear! 'ear!"

"'Ush!" said the tall policeman. Dinny saw her uncle walking out beside the girl; he smiled as he passed.

"Wait for me, Dinny—shan't be two minutes!"

Slipping out behind the tall policeman, Dinny waited in the lobby. The nature of things around gave her the shuddery feeling one had turning up the light in a kitchen at night; the scent of Condy's Fluid assailed her nostrils; she moved nearer to the outer door. A police sergeant said:

"Anything I can do for you, Miss?"

"Thank you, I'm waiting for my uncle; he's just coming."

"The reverend gentleman?"

Dinny nodded.

"Ah! He's a good man, is the Vicar. That girl got off?"

"Yes."

"Well! Mistakes will 'appen. Here he is, Miss."

Hilary came up and put his arm through Dinny's.

"Ah! Sergeant," he said, "how's the Missis?"

"Prime, Sir. So you pulled her out of it?"

"Yes," said Hilary; "and I want a pipe. Come along, Dinny." And, nodding to the sergeant, he led her into the air.

"What brought *you* into this galley, Dinny?"

"I came after you, Uncle. Aunt May brought me. Did that girl really not do it?"

"Ask me another. But to convict her was the surest way to send her to hell. She's behind with her rent, and her sister's ill. Hold on a minute while I light up." He emitted a cloud of smoke and resumed her arm. "What do you want of me, my dear?"

"An introduction to Lord Saxenden."

"Snubby Bantham? Why?"

"Because of Hubert."

"Oh! Going to vamp him?"

"If you'll bring us together."

"I was at Harrow with Snubby, he was only a baronet then—I haven't seen him since."

"But you've got Wilfred Bentworth in your pocket, Uncle, and their estates march."

"Well, I daresay Bentworth will give me a note to him for you."

"That's not what I want. I want to meet him socially."

"Um! Yes, you can hardly vamp him without. What's the point, exactly?"

"Hubert's future. We want to get at the fountain-head before worse befalls."

"I see. But look here, Dinny, Lawrence is your man. He has Bentworth going to them at Lippinghall on Tuesday next week, for partridge driving. You could go too."

"I thought of Uncle Lawrence, but I couldn't miss the chance of seeing you, Uncle."

"My dear," said Hilary, "attractive nymphs mustn't say things like that. They go to the head. Well, here we are! Come in and have tea."

In the drawing-room of the Vicarage Dinny was startled to see again her Uncle Adrian. He was sitting in a corner with his long legs drawn in, surrounded by two young women who looked like teachers. He waved his spoon, and presently came over to her.

"After we parted, Dinny, who should appear but the man of wrath himself, to see my Peruvians."

"Not Hallorsen?"

Adrian held out a card: 'Professor Edward Hallorsen,' and in pencil, 'Piedmont Hotel.'

"He's a much more personable bloke than I thought when I met him husky and bearded in the Dolomites; and I should say he's no bad chap if taken the right way. And what I was going to say to you was: Why not take him the right way?"

"You haven't read Hubert's diary, Uncle."

"I should like to."

"You probably will. It may be published."

Adrian whistled faintly.

"Perpend, my dear. Dog-fighting is excellent for all except the dogs."

"Hallorsen's had his innings. It's Hubert's turn to bat."

"Well, Dinny—no harm in having a look at the bowling before he goes in. Let me arrange a little dinner. Diana Ferse will have us at her house, and you can stay the night with her for it. So what about Monday?"

Dinny wrinkled her rather tip-tilted nose. If, as she intended, she went to Lippinghall next week, Monday *would* be handy. It might, after all, be as well to see this American before declaring war on him.

"All right, Uncle, and thank you very much. If you're going West may I come with you? I want to see Aunt Emily and Uncle Lawrence. Mount Street's on your way home."

"Right! When you've had your fill, we'll start."

"I'm quite full," said Dinny, and got up.

CHAPTER 6

HER LUCK HELD, and she flushed her third Uncle contemplating his own house in Mount Street, as if he were about to make an offer for it.

"Ah! Dinny, come along; your Aunt's moulting, and she'll be glad to see you. I miss old Forsyte," he added in the hall. "I was just considering what I ought to ask for this house if we let it next season. You didn't know old Forsyte—Fleur's father: he was a character."

"What is the matter with Aunt Em, Uncle Lawrence?"

"Nothing, my dear. I think the sight of poor old Uncle 'Cuffs' has made her dwell on the future. Ever dwell on the future, Dinny? It's a dismal period, after a certain age."

He opened a door.

"My dear, here's Dinny."

Emily, Lady Mont, was standing in her panelled drawing-room flicking a feather brush over a bit of Famille Verte, with her parakeet perched on her shoulder. She lowered the brush, advanced with a faraway look in her eyes, said "Mind, Polly," and kissed her niece. The parakeet transferred itself to Dinny's shoulder and bent its head round enquiringly to look in her face.

"He's such a dear," said Lady Mont; "you won't mind if he tweaks your ear? I'm so glad you came, Dinny; I've been so thinking of funerals. Do tell me your idea about the hereafter."

"Is there one, Auntie?"

"Dinny! That's so depressing."

"Perhaps those who want one have it."

"You're like Michael. He's so mental. Where did you pick Dinny up, Lawrence?"

"In the street."

"That sounds improper. How is your father, Dinny? I hope he isn't any the worse for that dreadful house at Porthminster. It did so smell of preserved mice."

"We're all very worried about Hubert, Aunt Em."

"Ah! Hubert, yes. You know, I think he made a mistake to flog those men. Shootin' them one can quite understand, but floggin' is so physical and like the old Duke."

28

"Don't you feel inclined to flog carters when they lash overloaded horses up-hill, Auntie?"

"Yes, I do. Was that what they were doin'?"

"Practically, only worse. They used to twist the mules' tails and stick their knives into them, and generally play hell with the poor brutes."

"Did they? I'm so glad he flogged them; though I've never liked mules ever since we went up the Gemmi. Do you remember, Lawrence?"

Sir Lawrence nodded. On his face was the look, affectionate but quizzical, which Dinny always connected with Aunt Em.

"Why, Auntie?"

"They rolled on me; not they exactly, but the one I was ridin'. They tell me it's the only time a mule has ever rolled on anybody—surefooted."

"Dreadful taste, Auntie!"

"Yes; and most unpleasant—so internal. Do you think Hubert would like to come and shoot partridge at Lippinghall next week?"

"I don't think you could get Hubert to go anywhere just now. He's got a terrible hump. But if you have a cubby-hole left for me, could I come?"

"Of course. There'll be plenty of room. Let's see: just Charlie Muskham and his new wife, Mr. Bentworth and Hen, Michael and Fleur, and Diana Ferse, and perhaps Adrian because he doesn't shoot, and your Aunt Wilmet. Oh! ah! And Lord Saxenden."

"What!" cried Dinny.

"Why? Isn't he respectable?"

"But, Auntie—that's perfect! He's my objective."

"What a dreadful word; I never heard it called that before. Besides, there's a Lady Saxenden, on her back somewhere."

"No, no, Aunt Em. I want to get at him about Hubert. Father says he's the nod."

"Dinny, you and Michael use the oddest expressions. What nod?"

Sir Lawrence broke the petrified silence he usually observed in the presence of his wife.

"Dinny means, my dear, that Saxenden is a big noise behind the scenes in military matters."

"What is he like, Uncle Lawrence?"

"Snubby? I've known him many years—quite a lad."

"This is very agitatin'," said Lady Mont, resuming the parakeet.

"Dear Auntie, I'm quite safe."

"But is Lord—er—Snubby? I've always tried to keep Lippin'hall respectable. I'm very doubtful about Adrian as it is, but"—she placed the parakeet on the mantelpiece—"he's my favourite brother. For a favourite brother one does things."

"One does," said Dinny.

"That'll be all right, Em," put in Sir Lawrence. "I'll watch over Dinny and Diana, and you can watch over Adrian and Snubby."

"Your uncle gets more frivolous every year, Dinny; he tells me the most dreadful stories." She stood still alongside Sir Lawrence and he put his hand through her arm.

Dinny thought: 'The Red King and the White Queen.'

"Well, good-bye, Dinny," said her Aunt, suddenly; "I have to go to bed. My Swedish masseuse is takin' me off three times a week. I really am reducin'." Her eyes roved over Dinny: "I wonder if she could put you on a bit!"

"I'm fatter than I look, Auntie."

"So am I—it's distressin'. If your uncle wasn't a hop-pole I shouldn't mind so much." She inclined her cheek, and Dinny gave it a smacking kiss.

"What a nice kiss!" said Lady Mont. "I haven't had a kiss like that for years. People do peck so! Come, Polly!" and with the parakeet upon her shoulder, she swayed away.

"Aunt Em looks awfully well."

"She is, my dear. It's her mania—getting stout; she fights it tooth and nail. We live on the most variegated cookery. It's better at Lippinghall, because Augustine leads us by the nose, and she's as French as she was thirty-five years ago when we brought her back from our honeymoon. Cooks like a bird, still. Fortunately nothing makes me fat."

"Aunt Em isn't fat."

"N-no."

"And she carries herself beautifully. We don't carry ourselves like that."

"Carriage went out with Edward," said Sir Lawrence; "it was succeeded by the lope. All you young women lope as if you were about to spring on to something and make a get-away. I've been trying to foresee what will come next. Logically it should be the bound, but it may quite well revert and be the languish."

"What sort of man is Lord Saxenden, really, Uncle Lawrence?"

"One of those who won the war by never having his opinion taken. You know the sort of thing: 'Went down for week-end to Cooquers. The Capers were there, and Gwen Blandish; she was in force and had much to say about the Polish front. I had more. Talked with Capers; he thinks the Boche have had enough. I disagreed with him; he is very down on Lord T. Arthur Prose came over on Sunday; he estimates that the Russians now have two million rifles but no bullets. The war, he says, will be over by January. He is appalled by our losses. If he only knew what I know! Lady Thripp was there with her son, who has lost his left foot. She is most engaging; promised to go and see her hospital and tell her how to run it. Very pleasant dinner on Sunday—everybody in great form; we played at comfits. Alick came in after; he says we lost forty thousand men in the last attack, but the French lost more. I expressed the opinion that it was very serious. No one took it.'"

Dinny laughed. "Were there such people?"

"Were there not, my dear! Most valuable fellows; what we should have done without them—the way they kept their ends up and their courage and their conversation—the thing had to be seen to be believed. And almost all of them won the war. Saxenden was especially responsible. He had an active job all the time."

"What job?"

"Being in the know. He was probably more in the know than anybody else on earth, judging by what he says. Remarkable constitution, too, and lets you see it: great yachtsman."

"I shall look forward to him."

"Snubby," sighed her uncle, "is one of those persons at whom it is better to look back. Would you like to stay the night, Dinny, or are you going home?"

"Oh, I must go back to-night. My train's at eight from Paddington."

"In that case I'll lope you across the Park, give you a snack at Paddington, and put you into the train."

"Oh! don't bother about me, Uncle Lawrence."

"Let you cross the Park without me, and miss the chance of being arrested for walking with a young female! Never! We might even sit, and try our luck. You're just the type that gets the aged into trouble. There's something Botticellian about you, Dinny. Come along."

It was seven o'clock of the September evening when they debouched into Hyde Park, and, passing under the plane trees, walked on its withered grass.

"Too early," said Sir Lawrence, "owing to Daylight Saving. Indecorum isn't billed till eight. I doubt if it will be any use to sit, Dinny. Can you tell a disguised copper when you see him? It's very necessary. The bowler hat—for fear of being hit on the head too suddenly; they always fall off in books; tendency to look as if he weren't a copper; touch of efficiency about the mouth—they complete their teeth in the force; eyes a trifle on the ground when they're not on you; the main man dwelling a little on both feet, and looking as if he had been measured for something. Boots of course—proverbial."

Dinny gurgled.

"I tell you what we might do, Uncle Lawrence. Stage an accost. There'll be a policeman at the Paddington Gate? I'll loiter a little, and accost you as you come up. What ought I to say?"

Sir Lawrence wrinkled up an eyebrow.

"So far as I can recollect, something like: 'How do, ducky? Your night out?'"

"I'll go on, then, and let that off on you under the policeman's nose."

"He'd see through it, Dinny."

"You're trying to back out."

"Well, no one has taken a proposition of mine seriously for so long. Besides, 'Life is real, life is earnest, and the end is not the gaol'!"

"I'm disappointed in you, Uncle."

"I'm used to that, my dear. Wait till you're grave and reverend, and see how continually you will disappoint youth."

31

"But think: we could have whole columns of the newspapers devoted to us for days. 'Paddington Gate accosting incident: Alleged Uncle.' Don't you hanker to be an alleged uncle and supersede the affairs of Europe? Don't you even want to get the Police into trouble? Uncle, it's pusillanimous."

"*Soit!*" said Sir Lawrence: "One uncle in the Police Court per day is enough. You're more dangerous than I thought, Dinny."

"But, really, why should those girls be arrested? That all belongs to the past, when women *were* under-dogs."

"I am entirely of your way of thinking, Dinny, but the Nonconformist conscience is still with us, and the Police must have something to do. Without adding to unemployment it's impossible to reduce their numbers. And an idle police force is dangerous to crooks."

"Do be serious, Uncle!"

"Not that, my dear! Whatever else life holds for us—not that! But I do foresee the age when we shall all be free to accost each other, limited only by common civility. Instead of the present Vulgate, there will be revised versions for men and women. 'Madam, will you walk?' 'Sir, do you desire my company?' It will be an age not perhaps of gold, but at least of glitter. This is Paddington Gate. Could you have had the heart to spoof that noble-looking copper? Come along, let's cross."

"Your Aunt," he resumed, as they entered Paddington Station, "won't rise again, so I'll dine with you in the buffet. We'll have a spot of the 'boy,' and for the rest, if I know our railway stations, oxtail soup, white fish, roast beef, greens, browned potatoes, and plum tart—all good, if somewhat English."

"Uncle Lawrence," said Dinny, when they had reached the roast beef, "what do *you* think of Americans?"

"No patriotic man, Dinny, speaks the truth, the whole truth, and nothing but the truth, on that subject. Americans, however, like Englishmen, may be divided into two classes—Americans and Americans. In other words, some are nice and some are nasty."

"Why don't we get on better with them?"

"That's an easy one. The nasty English don't get on better with them because they have more money than we have. The nice English don't get on as well as they ought with them, because Americans are so responsive and the tone of the American voice is not pleasing to the English ear. Or take it the other way round. The nasty Americans don't get on well with the English because the tone of the English voice is unpleasing to them. The nice Americans don't get on as well with us as they should, because we're so unresponsive and sniffy."

"Don't you think they want to have things their own way too much?"

"So do we. It isn't that. It's manner, my dear, that divides us, manner and language."

"How?"

"Having what used to be the same language is undoubtedly a snare.

We must hope for such a development of the American lingo as will necessitate our both learning each other's."

"But we always talk about the link of a common tongue."

"Why this curiosity about Americans?"

"I'm to meet Professor Hallorsen on Monday."

"The Bolivian bloke. A word of advice then, Dinny: Let him be in the right, and he'll feed out of your hand. Put him in the wrong, and you'll not feed out of his."

"Oh! I mean to keep my temper."

"Keep your left up, and don't rush in. Now, if you've finished, my dear, we ought to go; it's five minutes to eight."

He put her into her carriage and supplied her with an evening paper. As the train moved out, he added:

"Give him the Botticellian eye, Dinny. Give him the Botticellian eye!"

CHAPTER 7

ADRIAN BROODED over Chelsea as he approached it on Monday evening. It was not what it used to be. Even in late Victorian days he remembered its inhabitants as somewhat troglodytic—persons inclined to duck their heads, with here and there a high light or historian. Charwomen, artists hoping to pay their rent, writers living on four-and-sevenpence a day, ladies prepared to shed their clothes at a shilling an hour, couples maturing for the Divorce Court, people who liked a draught, together with the worshippers of Turner, Carlyle, Rossetti, and Whistler; some publicans, not a few sinners, and the usual sprinkling of those who eat mutton four times a week. Behind a river façade hardening into the palatial, respectability had gradually thickened, till it was now lapping the incurable King's Road and emerging even there in bastions of Art and Fashion.

Diana's house was in Oakley Street. He could remember it as having no individuality whatever, and inhabited by a family of strict mutton-eaters; but in the six years of Diana's residence it had become one of the charming nests of London. He had known all the pretty Montjoy sisters scattered over Society, but of them all Diana was the youngest, the prettiest, most tasteful, and wittiest—one of those women who, without money to speak of or impeachment of virtue, contrive that all about them shall be elegant to the point of exciting jealousy. From her two children and her Collie dog (almost the only one left in London), from her harpsichord, four-poster, Bristol glass, and the stuff on her chairs and floors, taste always seemed to him to radiate and give comfort to the beholder. She, too, gave comfort, with her still perfect figure, dark eyes clear and quick, oval face, ivory complexion, and little crisp trick of speech. All the Montjoy sisters had that trick, it came from their mother, of Highland stock, and had undoubtedly in the course of thirty years made a considerable effect on the accent of Society, converting it from the g-dropping yaw-yaw of the 'nineties into a rather charming r- and l-pinching dialect. When he considered why Diana, with her scant income and her husband in a Mental Home, was received everywhere in Society, Adrian was accustomed to take the image of a Bactrian camel. That animal's two humps were like the two sections of Society (with the big S) joined by a bridge, seldom used after the first crossing. The Montjoys, a very old landed family in Dumfriesshire innumerably allied in the past with the nobility,

34

had something of an hereditary perch on the foremost hump—a somewhat dull position from which there was very little view, because of the camel's head—and Diana was often invited to great houses where the chief works were hunting, shooting, hospitals, Court functions, and giving debutantes a chance. As Adrian well knew, she seldom went. She was far more constantly seated on the second hump, with its wide and stimulating view over the camel's tail. Ah! They were a queer collection on that back hump! Many, like Diana herself, crossed from the first hump by the bridge, others came up the camel's tail, a few were dropped from Heaven, or—as people sometimes called it—America. To qualify for that back hump Adrian, who had never qualified, knew that you needed a certain liveliness on several fronts; either, a first-rate memory so that anything you read or listened to could be retailed with ready accuracy; or, a natural spring of wit. If you had neither of these you might appear on the hump once, but never again. Personality, of course, you must have, though without real eccentricity; but it must not be personality which hid its light under a bushel. Eminence in some branch of activity was desirable, but not a *sine quâ non*. Breeding again was welcome, but not if it made you dull. Beauty was a passport, but it had to be allied with animation. Money was desirable, but money alone wouldn't get you a seat. Adrian had noted that knowledge of Art, if vocal, was of greater value than the power to produce it; and directive ability acceptable if it were not too silent or too dry. Then, again, some people seemed to get there out of an aptitude for the 'coulisses,' and for having a finger in every pie. But first and last the great thing was to be able to talk. Innumerable strings were pulled from this back hump, but whether they guided the camel's progress at all he was never sure, however much those who pulled them thought so. Diana, he knew, had so safe a seat among this heterogeneous group, given to constant meals, that she might have fed without expense from Christmas to Christmas, nor need ever have passed a week-end in Oakley Street. And he was the more grateful in that she so constantly sacrificed all that to be with her children and himself. The war had broken out just after her marriage with Ronald Ferse, and Sheila and Ronald had not been born till after his return from it. They were now seven and six, and, as Adrian was always careful to tell her, 'regular little Montjoys.' They certainly had her looks and animation. But he alone knew that the shadow on her face in repose was due more to the fear that she ought not to have had them, than to anything else in her situation. He, too, alone knew that the strain of living with one unbalanced as Ferse had become had so killed sex impulse in her that she had lived these four years of practical widowhood without any urge towards love. He believed she had for himself a real affection, but he knew that so far it stopped short of passion.

He arrived half an hour before dinner time, and went up to the schoolroom at the top of the house, to see the children. They were receiving bedtime rusks and milk from their French governess, welcomed him with acclamation and clamoured for him to go on with the story he was telling them. The French governess, who knew what to expect, withdrew. Adrian sat down opposite the two small sparkling faces, and began where he had left off: "So the man who had charge of the canoes was a tremendous fellow, brown all over, who had been selected for his strength, because of the white unicorns which infested that coast."

"Boo! Uncle Adrian—unicorns are imaginative."

"Not in those days, Sheila."

"Then what's become of them?"

"There is only about one left, and he lives where white men cannot go, because of the 'Bu-bu' fly."

"What is the 'Bu-bu' fly?"

"The 'Bu-bu' fly, Ronald, is remarkable for settling in the calf of the leg and founding a family there."

"Oh!"

"Unicorns—as I said before I was interrupted—which infested that coast. His name was Mattagor, and this was his way with unicorns. After luring them down to the beach with crinibobs——"

"What are crinibobs?"

"They look like strawberries and taste like carrots—crinibobs—he would steal up behind them——"

"If he was in front of them with the crinibobs, how could he steal up behind them?"

"He used to thread the crinibobs through a string made out of fibre, and hang them in a row between two charm trees. As soon as the unicorns were nibbling, he would emerge from the bush where he would be hiding, and, making no noise with his bare feet, tie their tails together two by two."

"But they would feel their tails being tied!"

"No, Sheila; white unicorns don't feel with their tails. Then he would retire to the bush, and click his tongue against his teeth, and the unicorns would dash forward in wild confusion."

"Did their tails ever come out?"

"Never. That was the great thing, because he was very fond of animals."

"I expect the unicorns never came again?"

"Wrong, Ronny. Their love of crinibobs was too great."

"Did he ever ride on them?"

"Yes; sometimes he would leap lightly on to two of their backs and ride off into the jungle with one foot on each back, laughing drily to himself. So under his charge, as you may imagine, the canoes were safe. It was not the wet season, so that the landsharks would not be so numerous, and the expedition was about to start when——"

"When what, Uncle Adrian? It's only Mummy."

"Go on, Adrian."

But Adrian remained silent, with his eyes fixed on the advancing vision. Then, averting from it his eyes and fixing them on Sheila, he proceeded:

"I must now pause to tell you why the moon was so important. They could not start the expedition till the half-moon was seen advancing towards them through the charm trees."

"Why not?"

"That is what I am going to tell you. In those days people, and especially this tribe of Phwatabhoys, paid a great deal of attention to what was beautiful—things like Mummy, or Christmas carols, or little new potatoes, had a great effect on them. And before they did anything they had to have an omen."

"What is an omen?"

"You know what an amen is—it comes at the end: well, an omen comes at the beginning, to bring luck. And the omen had to be beautiful. Now the half-moon was considered to be the most beautiful thing in the dry season, so they had to wait till it came advancing to them through the charm trees, as you saw Mummy just now walking towards us through the door."

"But the moon hasn't got feet."

"No; she floats. And one fine evening she came floating, like nothing else on earth, so lovely and so slim, and with such expression in her eyes that they all knew their expedition was bound to be successful; and they abased themselves before her, saying: 'Omen! if thou wilt be with us, then shall we pass over the wilderness of the waters and the sands with thee in our eyes, and be happy in the happiness that comes with thee for ever and ever. Amen!' And when they had put it like that, they got into the canoes. Phwatabhoy by Phwatabhoy and Phwatanymph by Phwatanymph, till they were all in. And the half-moon stayed there at the edge of the charm trees and blessed them with her eyes. But one man stopped behind. He was an old Phwatabhoy who wished for the half-moon so much that he forgot everything, and started crawling towards her, hoping to touch her feet."

"But she hadn't feet!"

"He thought she had, for to him she was like a woman made of silver and ivory. And he crawled in and out of the charm trees, but never could he quite reach her, because she was the half-moon."

Adrian paused, and there was for a moment no sound; then he said: "To be continued in our next," and went out. Diana joined him in the hall.

"Adrian, you are corrupting the children. Don't you know that fables and fairy-tales are no longer to be allowed to interfere with their interest in machines? After you'd gone Ronald said: 'Does Uncle Adrian really believe you are the half-moon, Mummy?'"

"And you answered?"

"Diplomatically. But they're as sharp as squirrels."

"Well! Sing me 'Waterboy' before Dinny and her swain come."

And while she sat and sang, Adrian gazed and worshipped. Her voice was good and she sang well that strange and haunting song. The last 'Waterboy' had barely died away when the maid announced:

"Miss Cherrell. Professor Hallorsen."

Dinny came in with her head held high, and Adrian augured but poorly from the expression of her eyes. He had seen schoolboys look like that when they were going to 'roast' a new-comer. After her came Hallorsen, immensely tall in that small drawing room, his eyes swimming with health. He bowed low when presented to Dinny. "Your daughter, I presume, Mr. Curator?"

"No, my niece; a sister of Captain Hubert Cherrell."

"Is that so? I am honoured to make your acquaintance, Ma'am."

Adrian, noting that their eyes, having crossed, seemed to find it difficult to disengage, said:

"How are you liking the Piedmont, Professor?"

"The cooking's fine, but there are too many of us Americans."

"Perching just now like the swallows?"

"Ah! In a fortnight we'll all have flitted."

Dinny had come brimful of Anglo-femininity, and the contrast between Hallorsen's overpowering health and Hubert's haggard looks had at once sharpened the edge of her temper. She sat down beside that embodiment of the conquering male with the full intention of planting every dart she could in his epidermis. He was, however, at once engaged in conversation by Diana, and she had not finished her soup (clear, with a prune in it) before, stealing a look round at him, she revised her plan. After all, he was a stranger and a guest, and she was supposed to be a lady; there were other ways of killing a cat besides hanging it. She would not plant darts, she would 'charm him with smiles and soap'; that would be more considerate towards Diana and her uncle, and more effective warfare in the long run. With a cunning worthy of her cause, she waited till he was in deep water over British politics, which he seemed to regard as serious manifestations of human activity; then, turning on him the Botticellian eye, she said:

"We should treat American politics just as seriously, Professor. But surely they're not serious, are they?"

"I believe you are right, Miss Cherrell. There's just one rule for politicians all over the world: Don't say in Power what you say in Opposition; if you do, you only have to carry out what the other fellows have found impossible. The only real difference, I judge, between Parties is that one Party sits in the National 'Bus, and the other Party strap-hangs."

"In Russia, what's left of the other Party lies under the seat, doesn't it?"

"So it does in Italy," said Diana.

"And what about Spain?" added Adrian.

Hallorsen uttered his infectious laugh. "Dictatorships aren't politics. They're jokes."

"*No* jokes, Professor."

"*Bad* jokes, Professor."

"How do you *mean*—jokes, Professor?"

38

"Bluff. Just one long assumption that human nature's on the mark the Dictator makes for it. The moment his bluff's called—why! Wump!"

"But," said Diana, "suppose a majority of the people approve of their dictator, isn't that democracy, or government by consent of the governed?"

"I would say no, Mrs. Ferse, unless he was confirmed by majority every year."

"Dictators get things done," said Adrian.

"At a price, Mr. Curator. But look at Diaz in Mexico. For twenty years he made it the Garden of Eden, but see what it's been ever since he went. You can't get out of a people for keeps what isn't yet in them."

"The fault," replied Adrian, "in our political system and in yours, Professor, is that a whole lot of reforms latent in the common-sense of the people don't get a chance of being carried out because our short term politicians won't give a lead, for fear of losing the power they haven't got."

"Aunt May," Dinny murmured, "was saying: Why not cure Unemployment by a National Slum Clearance effort, and kill the two birds with one stone?"

"My! But that's a mighty fine idea!" said Hallorsen, turning on her the full of his brimming face.

"Vested interests," said Diana, "slum landlordism and the building trades are too strong for that."

Adrian added: "And there's the cash required."

"Why! that's all easy. Your Parliament could take what powers they need for a big national thing like that; and what's wrong with a Loan, anyway?—the money would come back; it's not like a Loan for war, all shot away in powder. What do you pay in doles?"

No one could answer him.

"I judge the saving would pay the interest on a pretty big Loan."

"It just, in fact," said Dinny, sweetly, "needs simple faith. That's where you Americans beat us, Professor Hallorsen."

A look slid over the American's face as though he were saying: 'Cats!'

"Well, we certainly had a pieful of simple faith when we came over to fight in France. But we ate the lot. It'll be the home fires we keep burning next time."

"Was your faith so simple even last time?"

"I fear it was, Miss Cherrell. Not one in twenty of us ever believed the Germans could get a cinch on us away over there."

"I sit rebuked, Professor."

"Why! Not at all! You judge America by Europe."

"There was Belgium, Professor," said Diana; "even we had some simple faith at the start."

"Pardon me, but did the case of Belgium really move you, Ma'am?"

Adrian was drawing circles with a fork; he looked up.

"Speaking for oneself, yes. I don't suppose it made any difference to the Army people, Navy people, big business people, or even to a large section of Society, political and otherwise. They all knew that if war came we were practically committed to France. But to simple folk like myself and some two-thirds of the population not in the know, to the working classes, in fact, generally, it made all the difference. It was like seeing What's-his-name—the Man Mountain—advancing on the smallest Fly-weight in the ring, who was standing firm and squaring up like a man."

"Mighty well put, Mr. Curator."

Dinny flushed. Was there generosity in this man? Then, as if conscious of treachery to Hubert, she said acidly:

"I've read that the sight even ruffled Roosevelt."

"It ruffled quite a few of us, Miss Cherrell; but we're a long way off over there, and things have to be near before they stir the imagination."

"Yes, and after all, as you said just now, you did come in at the end."

Hallorsen looked fixedly at her ingenuous face, bowed and was silent.

But when, at the end of that peculiar evening, he was saying good-night, he added:

"I fear you've gotten a grouch against me, Miss Cherrell."

Dinny smiled, without reply.

"All the same, I hope I may meet you again."

"Oh! But why?"

"Well, I kind of have the feeling that I might change the view you have of me."

"I am very fond of my brother, Professor Hallorsen."

"I still think I've more against your brother than he has against me."

"I hope you may be right before long."

"That sounds like trouble."

Dinny tilted her head.

She went up to bed, biting her lip with vexation. She had neither charmed nor assailed the enemy; and instead of clean-cut animosity, she had confused feelings about him.

His inches gave him a disconcerting domination. 'He's like those creatures in hairy trousers on the films,' she thought, 'carrying off the semi-distressed cow-girls—looks at one as if he thought one was on his pillion.' Primitive Force in swallow-tails and a white waistcoat! A strong but not a silent man.

Her room looked over the street, and from her window she could see the plane trees on the Embankment, the river, and the wide expanse of starry night.

"Perhaps," she said to herself, aloud, "you won't leave England so soon as you thought."

"Can I come in?"

She turned to see Diana in the doorway.

"Well, Dinny, what think you of our friend the enemy?"

"Tom Mix, mixed with the Giant that Jack killed."

"Adrian likes him."

"Uncle Adrian lives too much with bones. The sight of red blood goes to his head."

"Yes; this is the sort of 'he-man' women are supposed to fall for. But you behaved well, Dinny, though your eyes looked very green at first."

"They feel greener now I've let him go without a scratch."

"Never mind! You'll have other chances. Adrian's got him asked to Lippinghall to-morrow."

"What!"

"You've only to embroil him with Saxenden there, and Hubert's trick is done. Adrian didn't tell you, for fear your joy might show itself. The Professor wants to sample British 'hunting.' The poor man doesn't in the least realise that he's walking into a lioness's den. Your Aunt Em will be delicious with him."

"Hallorsen!" murmured Dinny: "He must have Scandinavian blood."

"He says his mother was old New England, but married out of the direct succession. Wyoming's his State. Delightful word, Wyoming."

" 'The great open spaces.' What is there about the expression 'he-man' which infuriates me, Diana?"

"Well, it's like being in a room with a burst of sun-flowers. But 'he-men' aren't confined to the great open spaces; you'll find Saxenden one."

"Really!"

"Yes. Good-night, my dear. And may no 'he-men' come to you in dreams!"

When Dinny had disrobed, she again took out the diary and re-read a passage she had turned down. It ran thus: "Feel very low to-night— as if all my sap had run out. Can only keep my pecker up by thinking of Condaford. Wonder what old Foxham would say if he could see me doctoring the mules! The stuff I've invented for their colic would raise hair on a billiard ball, but it stops the thing all right. God was in luck when He planned the inside of a mule. Dreamed last night I was standing at the end of the home spinney with pheasants coming over in a stream, and for the life of me I couldn't pull my trigger; ghastly sort of paralysis. Keep thinking of old Haddon and his: 'Go it, Master Bertie. Stick your 'eels in and take 'old of 'is 'ead!' Good old Haddon! He was a character. The rain's stopped. Dry—first time for ten days. And the stars are out.

'A ship, an isle, a sickle moon,
With few but with how splendid stars.'

If only I could sleep! . . ."

CHAPTER 8

THAT ESSENTIAL private irregularity, room by room, which differentiates the old English from every other variety of country house, was patent at Lippinghall Manor. People went into rooms as if they meant to stay there, and while there inhaled an atmosphere and fitted into garniture different from those in any of the other rooms; nor did they feel that they must leave the room as they found it, if indeed they knew how that was. Fine old furniture stood in careless partnership with fill-up stuff acquired for the purposes of use or ease. Portraits of ancestors, dark or yellow, confronted Dutch or French landscapes still more yellow or dark, with here and there delightful old prints, and miniatures not without charm. In two rooms at least were beautiful old fireplaces, defiled by the comfort of a fender which could be sat on. Staircases appeared unexpectedly in the dark. The position of a bedroom was learned with difficulty and soon forgotten. In it would be, perhaps, a priceless old chestnut wood wardrobe and a four-poster bed of an excellent period; a window-seat with cushions, and some French prints. To it would be conjoined a small room with narrow bed; and bathroom that might or might not need a stroll, but would have salts in it. One of the Monts had been an Admiral; queer old charts, therefore, with dragons lashing the seas, lurked in odd corners of the corridors; one of the Monts, Sir Lawrence's grandfather, seventh baronet, had been a racing man, and the anatomy of the thoroughbred horse, and jockey of his period (1860–1883) could be studied on the walls. The sixth baronet, who, being in politics, had lived longer than the rest, had left imprints of the earlier Victorian period, his wife and daughters in crinolines, himself in whiskers. The outside of the house was Carolean, tempered here and there by Georgian, and even Victorian fragments where the sixth baronet had given way to his feeling for improvement. The only thing definitely modern was the plumbing.

When Dinny came down to breakfast on the Wednesday morning—the shoot being timed to start at ten—three of the ladies and all the men except Hallorsen were already sitting or wandering to the side tables. She slipped into a chair next to Lord Saxenden, who rose slightly with the word:

"Morning!"

"Dinny," called Michael from a sideboard, "coffee, cocoatina or ginger beer?"

"Coffee and a kipper, Michael."

"There are no kippers."

Lord Saxenden looked up: "No kippers?" he muttered, and resumed his sausage.

"Haddock?" said Michael.

"No, thank you."

"Anything for you, Aunt Wilmet?"

"Kedgeree."

"There is no kedgeree. Kidneys, bacon, scrambled eggs, haddock, ham, cold partridge pie."

Lord Saxenden rose. "Ah! Ham!" and went over to the side table.

"Well, Dinny?"

"Just some jam, please, Michael."

"Goose-gog, strawberry, black currant, marmalade."

"Gooseberry."

Lord Saxenden resumed his seat with a plate of ham, and began reading a letter as he ate. She did not quite know what to make of his face, because she could not see his eyes, and his mouth was so full. But she seemed to gather why he had been nicknamed 'Snubby.' He was red, had a light moustache and hair, both going grey, and a square seat at table. Suddenly he turned to her and said:

"Excuse my reading this. It's from my wife. She's on her back, you know."

"I'm so sorry."

"Horrible business! Poor thing!"

He put the letter in his pocket, filled his mouth with ham, and looked at Dinny. She saw that his eyes were blue, and that his eyebrows, darker than his hair, looked like clumps of fish-hooks. His eyes goggled a little, as though he were saying: "I'm a lad—I'm a lad." But at this moment she noticed Hallorsen coming in. He stood uncertain, then, seeing her, came to the empty seat on her side.

"Miss Cherrell," he said, with a bow, "can I sit right here?"

"Of course: the food is all over there, if you're thinking of any."

"Who's that fellow?" said Lord Saxenden, as Hallorsen went foraging: "He's an American."

"Professor Hallorsen."

"Oh! Ah! Wrote a book on Bolivia? What!"

"Yes."

"Good-looking chap."

"A he-man."

He looked round at her with surprise.

"Try this ham. I used to know an uncle of yours at Harrow, I think."

"Uncle Hilary?" said Dinny. "He told me."

43

"I once laid him three strawberry mashes to two on myself in a race down the Hill steps to the Gym."

"Did you win, Lord Saxenden?"

"No; and I never paid your uncle."

"Why not?"

"He sprained his ankle and I put my knee out. He hopped to the Gym door; but I couldn't move. We were both laid up till the end of term, and then I left." Lord Saxenden chuckled. "So I still owe him three strawberry mashes."

"I thought we had 'some' breakfast in America, but it's nil to this," said Hallorsen, sitting down.

"Do you know Lord Saxenden?"

"Lord Saxenden," repeated Hallorsen with a bow.

"How de do? You haven't got our partridge in America, have you?"

"Why, no, I believe not. I am looking forward to hunting that bird. This is mighty fine coffee, Miss Cherrell."

"Yes," said Dinny. "Aunt Em prides herself on her coffee."

Lord Saxenden squared his seat. "Try this ham. I haven't read your book."

"Let me send it you; I'll be proud to have you read it."

Lord Saxenden ate on.

"Yes, you ought to read it, Lord Saxenden," said Dinny; "and I'll send you another book that bears on the same subject."

Lord Saxenden glared.

"Charming of you both," he said. "Is that strawberry jam?" and he reached for it.

"Miss Cherrell," said Hallorsen, in a low voice, "I'd like to have you go through my book and mark the passages you think are prejudicial to your brother. I wrote that book when I had a pretty sore head."

"I'm afraid that I don't see what good that would do now."

"So I could get them cut out, if you wish, for the second edition."

"That's very good of you," said Dinny, icily, "but the harm is done, Professor."

Hallorsen said, still lower: "I'm just terribly sorry to have hurt you."

A sensation, perhaps only to be summed up in the words: 'You are—are you!' flushed Dinny from top to toe with anger, triumph, calculation, humour.

"It's my brother you've hurt."

"Maybe that could be mended if we could get together about it."

"I wonder." And Dinny rose.

Hallorsen stood up too, and bowed as she passed.

'Terribly polite,' she thought.

She spent her morning with the diary in a part of the garden so sunk within yew hedges that it formed a perfect refuge. The sun was warm there, and the humming of the bees over zinnias, pentstemons, hollyhocks, asters, Michaelmas daisies, was very soothing. In that so sheltered garden

44

the dislike of casting Hubert's intimate feelings to the world's opinion came on her again. Not that the diary whined; but it revealed the hurts of mind and body with the sharpness of a record meant for no eye but the recorder's. The sound of shots kept floating to her; and presently, leaning her elbows on the top of the yew hedge, she looked out over the fields towards where they were shooting.

A voice said:

"There you are!"

Her aunt, in a straw hat so broad that it covered her to the very edges of her shoulders, was standing below with two gardeners behind her.

"I'm coming round to you, Dinny; Boswell, you and Johnson can go now. We'll look at the Portulaca this afternoon." And she gazed up from under the tilted and enormous halo of her hat. "It's Majorcan," she said, "so shelterin'."

"Boswell and Johnson, Auntie!"

"We had Boswell, and your uncle would look till we found Johnson. He makes them go about together. Do you believe in Doctor Johnson, Dinny?"

"I think he used the word 'Sir' too much."

"Fleur's got my gardenin' scissors. What's that, Dinny?"

"Hubert's diary."

"Depressin'?"

"Yes."

"I've been lookin' at Professor Hallorsen—he wants takin' in."

"Begin with his cheek, Aunt Em."

"I hope they'll shoot some hares," said Lady Mont; "hare soup is such a stand-by. Wilmet and Henrietta Bentworth have agreed to differ already."

"What about?"

"Well, I couldn't be bothered, but I think it was about the P.M., or was it Portulaca?—they differ about everything. Hen's always been about Court, you know."

"Is that fatal?"

"She's a nice woman. I'm fond of Hen, but she does cluck. What are you doin' with that diary?"

"I'm going to show it to Michael and ask his advice."

"Don't take it," said Lady Mont; "he's a dear boy, but don't take it; he knows a lot of funny people—publishers and that."

"That's why I'm asking him."

"Ask Fleur, she has a head. Have you got this zinnia at Condaford? D'you know, Dinny, I think Adrian's goin' potty."

"Aunt Em!"

"He moons so; and I don't believe there's anywhere you could stick a pin into him. Of course I mustn't say it to you, but I think he ought to have her."

"So do I, Auntie."

"Well, he won't."

"Or she won't."

"They neither of them will; so how it's to be managed I don't know. She's forty."

"How old is Uncle Adrian?"

"He's the baby, all but Lionel. I'm fifty-nine," said Lady Mont decisively. "I know I'm fifty-nine, and your father is sixty; your grandmother must have been in a great tear at that time, she kept on havin' us. What do *you* think about this question of havin' children?"

Dinny swallowed a bubble and said:

"Well, for married people, perhaps, in moderation."

"Fleur's going to have another in March; it's a bad month—careless! When are you goin' to get married, Dinny?"

"When my young affections are engaged, not before."

"That's very prudent. But not an American."

Dinny flushed, smiled dangerously and said:

"Why on earth should I marry an American?"

"You never know," said Lady Mont, twisting off a faded aster; "it depends on what there is about. When I married Lawrence, he was so about!"

"And still is, Aunt Em; wonderful, isn't it?"

"Don't be sharp!"

And Lady Mont seemed to go into a dream, so that her hat looked more enormous than ever.

"Talking of marriage, Aunt Em, I wish I knew of a girl for Hubert. He does so want distracting."

"Your uncle," said Lady Mont, "would say distract him with a dancer."

"Perhaps Uncle Hilary knows one that he could highly recommend."

"You're naughty, Dinny. I always thought you were naughty. But let me think: there *was* a girl; no, she married."

"Perhaps she's divorced by now."

"No. I think she's divorcin' him, but it takes time. Charmin' little creature."

"I'm sure. Do think again, Auntie."

"These bees," replied her aunt, "belong to Boswell. They're Italian. Lawrence says they're Fascists."

"Black shirts and no after-thoughts. They certainly seem very active bees."

"Yes; they fly a lot and sting you at once if you annoy them. Bees are nice to me."

"You've got one on your hat, dear. Shall I take it off?"

"Stop!" said Lady Mont, tilting her hat back, with her mouth slightly open: "I've thought of one."

"One what?"

"Jean Tasburgh, the daughter of our Rector here—very good family. No money, of course."

"None at all?"

46

Lady Mont shook her head, and the hat wobbled. "No Jean ever has money. She's pretty. Rather like a leopardess."

"Could I look her over, Auntie? I know fairly well what Hubert wouldn't like."

"I'll ask her to dinner. They feed badly. We married a Tasburgh once. I think it was under James, so she'll be a cousin, but terribly removed. There's a son, too; in the Navy, all there, you know, and no moustache. I believe he's stayin' at the Rectory on furlough."

"Furlough, Aunt Em."

"I knew that word was wrong. Take that bee off my hat, there's a dear." Dinny took the small bee off the large hat with her handkerchief, and put it to her ear.

"I still like to hear them buzz," she said.

"I'll ask him too," answered her aunt; "his name's Alan, a nice fellow." And she looked at Dinny's hair. "Medlar-coloured, I call it. I think he's got prospects, but I don't know what they are. Blown up in the war."

"He came down again whole, I hope, Auntie?"

"Yes; they gave him something or other for it. He says it's very stuffy in the Navy now. All angles, you know, and wheels, and smells. You must ask him."

"About the girl, Aunt Em, how do you mean, a leopardess?"

"Well, she looks at you, and you expect to see a cub comin' round the corner. Her mother's dead. She runs the parish."

"Would she run Hubert?"

"No; she'd run anybody who tried to run him."

"That might do. Can I take a note for you to the Rectory?"

"I'll send Boswell and Johnson," Lady Mont looked at her wrist. "No, they'll have gone to dinner. I always set my watch by them. We'll go ourselves, Dinny; it's only quarter of a mile. Does my hat matter?"

"On the contrary, dear."

"Very well, then; we can get out this way," and moving to the far end of the yew-treed garden, they descended some steps into a long grassy avenue, and, passing through a wicket gate, had soon arrived at the Rectory. Dinny stood in its creepered porch, behind her aunt's hat. The door stood open, and a dim panelled hallway with a scent of pot-pourri and old wood, conveyed a kind of invitation. A female voice from within called:

"A—lan!"

A male voice answered: "Hal—lo!"

"D'you mind cold lunch?"

"There's no bell," said Lady Mont; "we'd better clap." They clapped in unison.

"What the deuce?" A young man in grey flannels had appeared in a doorway. He had a broad brown face, dark hair, and grey eyes, deep and direct.

"Oh!" he said. "Lady Mont . . . Hi! Jean!" Then, meeting Dinny's eyes round the edge of the hat, he smiled as they do in the Navy.

"Alan, can you and Jean dine to-night? Dinny, this is Alan Tasburgh. D'you like my hat?"

"It's a topper, Lady Mont."

A girl, made all of a piece and moving as if on steel springs, was coming towards them. She wore a fawn-coloured sleeveless jumper and skirt, and her arms and cheeks were fully as brown. Dinny saw what her aunt meant. The face, broad across the cheek-bones, tapered to the chin, the eyes were greenish grey and sunk right in under long black lashes; they looked straight out with a light in them; the nose was fine, the brow low and broad, the shingled hair dark brown. 'I wonder!' thought Dinny. Then, as the girl smiled, a little thrill went through her.

"This is Jean," said her aunt: "my niece, Dinny Cherrell."

A slim brown hand clasped Dinny's firmly.

"Where's your father?" continued Lady Mont.

"Dad's away at some parsonical Conference. I wanted him to take me, but he wouldn't."

"Then I expect he's in London really, doin' theatres."

Dinny saw the girl flash a look at her aunt, decide that it was Lady Mont, and smile. The young man laughed.

"So you'll both come to dinner? Eight-fifteen. Dinny, we must go back to lunch. Swallows!" added Lady Mont round the brim of her hat, and passed out through the porch.

"There's a house-party," said Dinny to the young man's elevated eyebrows. "She means tails and white tie."

"Oh! Ah! Best bib and tucker, Jean."

The two stood in the porchway arm in arm. 'Very attractive!' Dinny thought.

"Well?" said her aunt, in the grass avenue again.

"Yes, I quite saw the cub. She's beautiful, I think. But I should keep her on a lead."

"There's Boswell and Johnson!" exclaimed Lady Mont, as if they were in the singular. "Gracious! It must be past two, then!"

CHAPTER 9

SOME TIME AFTER LUNCH, for which Dinny and her aunt were late, Adrian and the four younger ladies, armed with such shooting sticks as had been left by the 'guns,' proceeded down a farm lane towards where the main 'drive' of the afternoon would debouch. Adrian walked with Diana and Cicely Muskham, and ahead of them Dinny walked with Fleur. These cousins by marriage had not met for nearly a year, and had in any case but slender knowledge of each other. Dinny studied the head which her aunt had recommended to her. It was round and firm and well carried under a small hat. The pretty face wore a rather hard but, she decided, very capable expression. The trim figure was as beautifully tailored as if it had belonged to an American.

Dinny felt that she would at least get common-sense from a source so neat.

"I heard your testimonial read in the Police Court, Fleur."

"Oh! that. It was what Hilary wanted, of course. I really don't know anything about those girls. They simply don't let one. Some people, of course, can worm themselves into anybody's confidence. I can't, and I certainly don't want to. Do you find the country girls about you any easier?"

"Round us they've all had to do with our family so long that one knows pretty well all there is to know before they do themselves."

Fleur scrutinised her.

"Yes, I daresay you've got the knack, Dinny. You'll make a wonderful ancestress; but I don't quite know who ought to paint you. It's time someone came along with the Early Italian touch. The pre-Rafaelites hadn't got it a bit; their pictures lacked music and humour. *You'll* have to be done with both."

"Do tell me," said Dinny, disconcerted, "was Michael in the House when those questions were asked about Hubert?"

"Yes; he came home very angry."

"Good!"

"He thought of bringing the thing up again, but it was the day but one before they rose. Besides, what does the House matter? It's about the last thing people pay attention to nowadays."

"My father, I'm afraid, paid terrific attention to those questions."

49

"Yes, the last generation. But the only thing Parliament does that really gets the Public now, is the Budget. And no wonder; it all comes back to money."

"Do you say that to Michael?"

"I don't have to. Parliament now is just a taxing machine."

"Surely it still makes laws?"

"Yes, my dear; but always after the event; it consolidates what has become public practice, or at least public feeling. It never initiates. How can it? That's not a democratic function. If you want proof, look at the state of the country! It's the last thing Parliament bothers about."

"Who does initiate, then?"

"Whence doth the wind blow? Well, the draughts begin in the coulisses. Great places, the coulisses! Whom do you want to stand with when we get to the guns?"

"Lord Saxenden."

Fleur gazed at her: "Not for his *beaux yeux*, and not for his *beau titre*. Why, then?"

"Because I've got to get at him about Hubert, and I haven't much time."

"I see. Well, I'll give you a warning, my dear. Don't take Saxenden at his face value. He's an astute old fox, and not so old either. And if there is one thing he enjoys more than another, it's his quid pro quo. Have you got a quid for him? He'll want cash down."

Dinny grimaced.

"I shall do what I can. Uncle Lawrence has already given me some pointers."

"'Have a care; she's fooling thee,'" hummed Fleur. "Well, I shall go to Michael; it makes him shoot better, and he wants it, poor dear. The Squire and Bart will be glad to do without us. Cicely, of course, will go to Charles; she's still honey-moonish. That leaves Diana for the American."

"And I hope," said Dinny, "she'll put him off his shots."

"I should say nothing would. I forgot Adrian; he'll have to sit on his stick and think about bones and Diana. Here we are. See? Through this gate. There's Saxenden, they've given him the warm corner. Go round by that stile and come on him from behind. Michael will be jammed away at the end, he always gets the worst stand."

She parted from Dinny and went on down the lane. Conscious that she had not asked Fleur what she had wanted to, Dinny crossed to the stile, and climbing over, stalked Lord Saxenden warily from the other side. The peer was moving from one hedge to the other in the corner of the field to which he had been assigned. Beside a tall stick, to a cleft in which was attached a white card with a number on it, stood a young keeper holding two guns, and at his feet a retriever dog was lying with his tongue out. The fields of roots and stubble on the far side of the lane rose rather steeply, and it was evident to Dinny—something of an expert—that birds driven off them would come high and fast. 'Unless,' she thought, 'there's fresh cover just behind,' and she turned to look. There was not. She was in a very large grass field and the nearest roots were three hundred yards away at least. 'I wonder,' she thought, 'if he shoots better or worse with a woman watching. Shouldn't think he had any nerves.' Turning again, she saw that he had noticed her.

"Do you mind me, Lord Saxenden? I'll be very quiet."

The peer plucked at his cap, which had special peaks before and behind. "Well, well!" he said. "H'm!"

"That sounds as if you did. Shall I go?"

"No, no! That's all right. Can't touch a feather today, anyway. You'll bring me luck."

Dinny seated herself on her stick alongside the retriever, and began playing with its ears.

"That American chap has wiped my eye three times."

"What bad taste!"

"He shoots at the most impossible birds, but, dash it, he hits 'em. All the birds I miss he gets on the horizon. Got the style of a poacher; lets everything go by, then gets a right and left about seventy yards behind him. Says he can't see them when they sit on his foresight."

"That's funny," said Dinny, with a little burst of justice.

"Don't believe he's missed to-day," added Lord Saxenden, resentfully. "I asked him why he shot so darned well, and he said: 'Why! I'm used to shooting for the pot, where I can't afford to miss.'"

"The beat's beginning, my lord," said the younger keeper's voice.

The retriever began to pant slightly. Lord Saxenden grasped a gun; the keeper held the other ready.

"Covey to the left, my lord," Dinny heard a creaky whirring, and saw eight birds stringing towards the lane. Bang-bang . . . bang—bang!

"God bless my soul!" said Lord Saxenden: "What the deuce——!"

Dinny saw the same eight birds swoop over the hedge at the other end of the grass field.

The retriever uttered a little choked sound, panting horribly.

"The light," she said, "must be terribly puzzling!"

"It's not the light," said Lord Saxenden, "it's the liver!"

"Three birds coming straight, my lord."

Bang! . . . Bang-bang! A bird jerked, crumpled, turned over and pitched four yards behind her. Something caught Dinny by the throat. That anything so alive should be so dead! Often as she had seen birds shot, she had never before had that feeling. The other two birds were crossing the far hedge; she watched them vanish, with a faint sigh. The retriever, with the dead bird in his mouth, came up to the keeper, who took it from him. Sitting on his haunches, the dog continued to gaze at the bird, with his tongue out. Dinny saw the tongue drip, and closed her eyes.

Lord Saxenden said something inaudibly.

Lord Saxenden said the same word more inaudibly, and opening her eyes, Dinny saw him put up his gun.

"Hen pheasant, my lord!" warned the young keeper.

A hen pheasant passed over at a most reasonable height, as if aware that her time was not yet.

"H'm!" said Lord Saxenden, resting the butt on his bent knee.

"Covey to the right; too far, my lord!"

Several shots rang out, and beyond the hedge Dinny saw two birds only flying on, one of which was dropping feathers.

"That's a dead bird," said the keeper, and Dinny saw him shade his eyes, watching its flight. "Down!" he said; the dog panted, and looked up at him.

Shots rang out to the left.

"Damn!" said Lord Saxenden, "nothing comes my way."

"Hare, my lord!" said the keeper, sharply. "Along the hedge!"

Lord Saxenden wheeled and raised his gun.

"Oh, no!" said Dinny, but her words were drowned by the report. The hare, struck behind, stopped short, then wriggled forward, crying pitifully.

"Fetch it, boy!" said the keeper.

Dinny put her hands over her ears and shut her eyes.

"Blast!" muttered Lord Saxenden. "Tailored!" Through her eyelids Dinny felt his frosty stare. When she opened her eyes the hare was lying dead beside the bird. It looked incredibly soft. Suddenly she rose, meaning to go, but sat down again. Until the beat was over she could go nowhere without interfering with the range of the shots. She closed her eyes again; and the shooting went on.

"That's the lot, my lord."

Lord Saxenden was handing over his gun, and three more birds lay beside the hare.

Rather ashamed of her new sensations, she rose, closed her shooting stick, and moved towards the stile. Regardless of the old convention, she crossed it and waited for him.

"Sorry I tailored that hare," he said. "But I've been seeing spots all day. Do you ever see spots?"

"No. Stars once in a way. A hare's crying is dreadful, isn't it?"

"I agree—never liked it."

"Once when we were having a picnic I saw a hare sitting up behind us like a dog—and the sun through its ears all pink. I've always liked hares since."

"They're not a sporting shot," admitted Lord Saxenden; "personally I prefer 'em roast to jugged."

Dinny stole a glance at him. He looked red and fairly satisfied.

'Now's my chance,' she thought.

"Do you ever tell Americans that they won the war, Lord Saxenden?"

He stared frostily.

"Why should I?"

"But they did, didn't they?"

"Does that Professor chap say so?"

"I've never heard him, but I feel sure he thinks so."

52

Again Dinny saw that sharp look come on his face. "What do you know about him?"

"My brother went on his expedition."

"Your brother? Ah!" It was just as if he had said to himself out loud: 'This young woman wants something out of me.'

Dinny felt suddenly that she was on very thin ice.

"If you read Professor Hallorsen's book," she said, "I hope you will also read my brother's diary."

"I never read anything," said Lord Saxenden; "haven't time. But I remember now. Bolivia—he shot a man, didn't he, and lost the transport?"

"He had to shoot the man to save his own life, and he had to flog two for continual cruelty to the mules; then all but three men deserted, stampeding the mules. He was the only white man there, with a lot of Indian half-castes."

And to his frosty shrewd eyes she raised her own suddenly, remembering Sir Lawrence's: 'Give him the Botticellian eye, Dinny!'

"Might I read you a little of his diary?"

"Well, if there's time."

"When?"

"To-night? I have to go up after shooting to-morrow."

"Any time that suits you," she said, hardily.

"There won't be a chance before dinner. I've got some letters that must go."

"I can stay up till any hour." She saw him give her a quick, all-over glance.

"We'll see," he said, abruptly. And at this minute they were joined by the others.

Escaping the last drive, Dinny walked home by herself. Her sense of humour was tickled, but she was in a quandary. She judged shrewdly that the diary would not produce the desired effect unless Lord Saxenden felt that he was going to get something out of listening to it; and she was perceiving more clearly than ever before how difficult it was to give anything without parting from it. A fluster of wood-pigeons rose from some stooks on her left and crossed over to the wood by the river; the light was growing level, and evening sounds fluttered in the crisper air. The gold of sinking sunlight lay on the stubbles; the leaves, hardly turned as yet, were just promising colour, and away down there the blue line of the river glinted through its bordering trees. In the air was the damp, slightly pungent scent of early autumn with wood smoke drifting already from cottage chimneys. A lovely hour, a lovely evening!

What passages from the diary should she read? Her mind faltered. She could see Saxenden's face again when he said: "Your brother? Ah!" Could see the hard direct calculating insensitive character behind it. She remembered Sir Lawrence's words: "Were there not, my dear? . . . Most valuable fellows!" She had just been reading the memoirs of a man, who, all through the war, had thought in moves and numbers, and, after one preliminary gasp, had given up thinking of the sufferings behind those movements and those numbers: in his will to win the war, he seemed to have made it his business never to think of its human side, and, she was sure, could never have visualised that side if he *had* thought of it. Valuable fellow! She had heard Hubert talk, with a curling lip, of 'armchair strategists'—who had enjoyed the war, excited by the interest of combining movements and numbers and of knowing this and that before someone else did, and by the importance they had gained therefrom. Valuable fellows! In another book she had lately read, she remembered a passage about the kind of men who directed what was called progress: sat in Banks, City offices, Governmental departments, combining movements and numbers, not bothered by flesh and blood, except their own; men who started this enterprise and that, drawing them up on sheets of paper, and saying to these and those: 'Do this, and see you dam' well do it properly.' Men, silk-hatted or plus-foured, who guided the machine of tropic enterprise, of mineral getting, of great shops, of railway building, of concessions here and there and everywhere. Valuable fellows! Cheery, healthy, well-fed, indomitable fellows with frosty eyes. Always dining, always in the know, careless of the cost in human feelings and human life. 'And yet,' she thought, 'they really must be valuable, or how should we have rubber or coal, or pearls or railways or the Stock Exchange, or wars and win them!' She thought of Hallorsen; he at least worked and suffered for his ideas, led his own charges; did not sit at home, knowing things, eating ham, tailoring hares, and ordering the movements of others. She turned into the Manor grounds and paused on the croquet lawn. Aunt Wilmet and Lady Henrietta appeared to be agreeing to differ. They appealed to her:

"Is that right, Dinny?"

"No. When the balls touch you just go on playing, but you mustn't move Lady Henrietta's ball, Auntie, in hitting your own."

"I said so," said Lady Henrietta.

"Of course you said so, Hen. Nice position I'm in. Well, I shall just agree to differ and go on," and Aunt Wilmet hit her ball through a hoop, moving her opponent's several inches in so doing.

"Isn't she an unscrupulous woman?" murmured Lady Henrietta, plaintively, and Dinny saw at once the great practical advantages inherent in 'agreeing to differ.'

"You're like the Iron Duke, Auntie," she said, "except that you don't use the word 'damn' quite so often."

"She does," said Lady Henrietta; "her language is appalling."

"Go on, Hen!" said Aunt Wilmet in a flattering voice.

Dinny left them and retired towards the house.

When she was dressed she went to Fleur's room.

Her aunt's maid was passing a minute mowing-machine over the back of Fleur's neck, while Michael, in the doorway of his dressing-room, had his fingers on the tips of his white tie.

Fleur turned.

"Hallo, Dinny! Come in, and sit down. That'll do, thank you, Powers. Now, Michael."

The maid faded out and Michael advanced to have a twist given to the ends of his tie.

"There!" said Fleur; and looking at Dinny, added: "Have you come about Saxenden?"

"Yes. I'm to read him bits of Hubert's diary to-night. The question is: Where will be suitable to my youth and——"

"Not innocence, Dinny; you'll never be innocent, will she, Michael?"

Michael grinned. "Never innocent but always virtuous. You were a most sophisticated little angel as a kid, Dinny; looked as if you were wondering why you hadn't wings. Wistful is the word."

"I expect I was wondering why you'd pulled them off."

"You ought to have worn trouserettes and chased butter-flies, like the two little Gainsborough girls in the National Gallery."

"Cease these amenities," said Fleur; "the gong's gone. You can have my little sitting-room next door, and, if you knock, Michael can come round with a boot, as if it were rats."

"Perfect," said Dinny; "but I expect he'll behave like a lamb, really."

"You never can tell," said Michael; "he's a bit of a goat."

"That's the room," said Fleur, as they passed out. *"Cabinet particulier. Good luck! . . ."*

CHAPTER 10

SEATED BETWEEN Hallorsen and young Tasburgh, Dinny had a slanting view of her Aunt and Lord Saxenden at the head of the table, with Jean Tasburgh round the corner on his right. "She was a 'leopardess' oh! so fair!" The tawnied skin, oblique face, and wonderful eyes of the young woman fascinated her. They appeared also to fascinate Lord Saxenden, whose visage was redder and more genial than Dinny had seen it yet. His attentions to Jean, indeed, were throwing Lady Mont to the clipped tongue of Wilfred Bentworth. For 'the Squire,' though a far more distinguished personality, too distinguished to accept a peerage, was in accordance with the table of precedence, seated on her left. Next to him again Fleur was engaging Hallorsen; so that Dinny herself was exposed to the broadside of young Tasburgh. He talked easily, directly, frankly, like a man not yet calloused by female society, and manifested what Dinny described to herself as 'transparent admiration'; yet twice at least she went into what he described as a 'near-dream,' her head turned high, and motionless, towards his sister.

"Ah!" he said. "What do you think of her?"

"Fascinating."

"I'll tell her that, she won't turn a hair. The earth's most matter-of-fact young woman. She seems to be vamping her neighbour all right. Who is he?"

"Lord Saxenden."

"Oh! And who's the John Bull at the corner on our side?"

"Wilfred Bentworth, 'the Squire,' they call him."

"And next to you—talking to Mrs. Michael?"

"That's Professor Hallorsen from America."

"He's a fine-looking chap."

"So everybody says," said Dinny, drily.

"Don't you think so?"

"Men oughtn't to be so good-looking."

"Delighted to hear you say that."

"Why?"

"It means that the ugly have a look in."

"Oh! Do you often go trawling?"

"You know, I'm terribly glad I've met you at last."

"At last? You'd never even heard of me this morning."

"No. But that doesn't prevent you from being my ideal."

"Goodness! Is this the way they have in the Navy?"

"Yes. The first thing they teach us is to make up our minds quickly."

"Mr. Tasburgh——"

"Alan."

"I begin to understand the wife in every port."

"I," said young Tasburgh, seriously, "haven't a single one. And you're the first I've ever wanted."

"Oo! Or is it: Coo!"

"Fact! You see, the Navy is very strenuous. When we see what we want, we have to go for it at once. We get so few chances."

Dinny laughed. "How old are you?"

"Twenty-eight."

"Then you weren't at Zeebrugge?"

"I was."

"I see. It's become a habit to lay yourself alongside."

"And get blown up for it."

Her eyes rested on him kindly.

"I am now going to talk to my enemy."

"Enemy? Can I do anything about that?"

"His demise would be of no service to me, till he's done what I want."

"Sorry for that; he looks to me dangerous."

"Mrs. Charles is lying in wait for you," murmured Dinny, and she turned to Hallorsen, who said deferentially: "Miss Cherrell," as if she had arrived from the moon.

"I hear you shot amazingly, Professor."

"Why! I'm not accustomed to birds asking for it as they do here. I'll maybe get used to that in time. But all this is quite an experience for me."

"Everything in the garden lovely?"

"It certainly is. To be in the same house with you is a privilege I feel very deeply, Miss Cherrell."

" 'Cannon to right of me, cannon to left of me?' " thought Dinny.

"And have you," she asked, suddenly, "been thinking what amend you can make to my brother?"

Hallorsen lowered his voice.

"I have a great admiration for you, Miss Cherrell, and I will do what you tell me. If you wish, I will write to your papers and withdraw the remarks in my book."

"And what would you want for that, Professor Hallorsen?"

"Why, surely, nothing but your goodwill."

"My brother has given me his diary to publish."

"If that will be a relief to you—go to it."

"I wonder if you two ever began to understand each other."

"I judge we never did."

"And yet you were only four white men, weren't you? May I ask exactly what annoyed you in my brother?"

"You'd have it up against me if I were to tell you."

"Oh! no, I *can* be fair."

"Well, first of all, I found he'd made up his mind about too many things, and he wouldn't change it. There we were in a country none of us knew any thing about, amongst Indians and people that were only half civilised; but the captain wanted everything done as you might in England: he wanted rules, and he wanted 'em kept. Why, I judge he would have dressed for dinner if we'd have let him."

"I think you should remember," said Dinny, taken aback, "that we English have found formality pay all over the world. We succeed in all sorts of wild out of the world places because we stay English. Reading his diary, I think my brother failed from not being stolid enough."

"Well, he is not your John Bull type," he nodded towards the end of the table, "like Lord Saxenden and Mr. Bentworth there; maybe I'd have understood him better if he were. No, he's mighty high-strung and very tight held-in; his emotions kind of eat him up from within. He's like a race-horse in a hansom cab. Yours is an old family, I should judge, Miss Cherrell."

"Not yet in its dotage."

She saw his eyes leave her, rest on Adrian across the table, move on to her Aunt Wilmet, and thence to Lady Mont.

"I would like to talk to your uncle the Curator about old families," he said.

"What else was there in my brother that you didn't like?"

"Well, he gave me the feeling that I was a great husky."

Dinny raised her brows a little.

"There we were," went on Hallorsen, "in the hell of a country—pardon me!—a country of raw metal. Well, I was raw metal myself, out to meet and beat raw metal; and he just wouldn't be."

"Perhaps couldn't be. Don't you think what was really wrong was your being American and his being English? Confess, Professor, that you don't like us English."

Hallorsen laughed.

"I like *you* terribly."

"Thank you, but every rule——"

"Well," his face hardened, "I just don't like the assumption of a superiority that I don't believe in."

"Have we a monopoly of that? What about the French?"

"If I were an orang-outang, Miss Cherrell, I wouldn't care a hoot whether a chimpanzee thought himself superior."

"I see; too far removed. But, forgive me, Professor, what about yourselves? Are you not the chosen people? And don't you frequently say so? Would you exchange with any other people in the world?"

"I certainly would not."

"But isn't that an assumption of a superiority that *we* don't believe in?"

He laughed. "You have me there; but we haven't touched rock-bottom in this matter. There's a snob in every man. We're a new people; we haven't gotten your roots and your old things; we haven't gotten your habit of taking ourselves for granted; we're too multiple and various and too much in the making. We have a lot of things that you could envy us besides our dollars and our bathrooms."

"What ought we to envy you? I should very much like it made clear to me."

"Well, Miss Cherrell, we know that we have qualities and energy and faith and opportunities that you just ought to envy; and when you don't do it, we feel we've no use for that kind of gone-dead, bone-superior attitude. It's like a man of sixty looking down his nose at a youth of thirty; and there's no such God-darned—pardon me! mistake as that."

Dinny sat looking at him, silent and impressed.

"Where," Hallorsen went on, "you British irritate us is that you've lost the spirit of enquiry; or if you've still gotten it, you have a dandy way of hiding it up. I judge there are many ways in which we irritate you. But we irritate your epidermis and you irritate our nerve centres. That's about all there is to it, Miss Cherrell."

"I see," said Dinny; "that's terribly interesting and I daresay quite true. My aunt's getting up, so I must remove my epidermis and leave your nerve centres to quiet down." She rose, and over her shoulder smiled back at him.

Young Tasburgh was at the door. At him too she smiled, and murmured: "Talk to my friend the enemy; he's worth it."

In the drawing-room she sought out the 'leopardess,' but converse between them suffered from the inhibition of a mutual admiration which neither wished to show. Jean Tasburgh was just twenty-one, but she impressed Dinny as older than herself. Her knowledge of things and people seemed precise and decided, if not profound; her mind was made up on all the subjects they touched on; she would be a marvellous person—Dinny thought—in a crisis, or if driven to the wall; would be loyal to her own side, but want to rule whatever roost she was in. But alongside her hard efficiency Dinny could well perceive a strange, almost feline fascination that would go to any man's head, if she chose that it should. Hubert would succumb to her at once! And at that conclusion his sister was the more doubtful whether she wished him to. Here was the very girl to afford the swift distraction she was seeking for her brother. But was he strong enough and alive enough for the distractor? Suppose he fell in love with her and she would have none of him! Or suppose he fell in love with her, and she had all of him! And then—money! If Hubert received no appointment, or lost his commission what would they live on? He had only three hundred a year without his pay, and the girl presumably nothing. The situation was perverse. If Hubert could plunge again into soldiering, he would not need distraction. If he continued to be shelved, he would need distraction but could not afford it. And yet—was not this exactly the sort

59

of girl who would carve out a career somehow for the man she married? So they talked of Italian pictures.

"By the way," said Jean, suddenly, "Lord Saxenden says you want him to do something for you."

"Oh!"

"What is it? Because I'll make him."

Dinny smiled.

"How?"

Jean gave her a look from under her lashes.

"It'll be quite easy. What is it you want from him?"

"I want my brother back in his regiment, or, better—some post for him. He's under a cloud owing to that Bolivian expedition with Professor Hallorsen."

"The big man? Is that why you had him down here?"

Dinny had a feeling that she would soon have no clothes on.

"If you want frankness, yes."

"He's rather fine to look at."

"So your brother said."

"Alan's the most generous person in the world. He's taken a toss over you."

"So he was telling me."

"He's an ingenuous child. But, seriously, shall I go for Lord Saxenden?"

"Why should you worry?"

"I like to put my fingers into pies. Give me a free hand, and I'll bring you that appointment on a charger."

"I am credibly informed," said Dinny, "that Lord Saxenden is a tough proposition."

Jean stretched herself.

"Is your brother Hubert like you?"

"Not a scrap; he's dark, and brown-eyed."

"You know our families intermarried a long way back. Are you interested in breeding? I breed Airedales, and I don't believe much in either the tail male or the tail female theories. Prepotency can be down through either male or female, and at any point of the pedigree."

"Perhaps, but except for not being covered with yellow varnish, my father and my brother are both very like the earliest portrait we have of a male ancestor."

"Well, we've got a Fitzherbert woman who married a Tasburgh in 1547, and she's the spit of me except for the ruff: she's even got my hands." And the girl spread out to Dinny two long brown hands, crisping them slightly as she did so.

"A strain," she went on, "may crop out after generations that have seemed free from it. It's awfully interesting. I should like to see your brother, if she's so unlike you."

Dinny smiled.

"I'll get him to drive over from Condaford and fetch me. You may not think him worth your wiles."

And at this moment the men came in.

"They do so look," murmured Dinny, "as if they were saying: 'Do I want to sit next to a female, and if so, why?' Men are funny after dinner."

Sir Lawrence's voice broke the hush:

"Saxenden, you and the Squire for Bridge?"

At those words Aunt Wilmet and Lady Henrietta rose automatically from the sofa where they had been having a quiet difference, and passed towards where they would continue the motion for the rest of the evening; they were followed closely by Lord Saxenden and the Squire.

Jean Tasburgh grimaced: "Can't you just see Bridge growing on people like a fungus?"

"Another table?" said Sir Lawrence: "Adrian? No. Professor?"

"Why, I think not, Sir Lawrence."

"Fleur, you and I then against Em and Charles. Come along, let's get it over."

"You can't see it growing on Uncle Lawrence," murmured Dinny. "Oh! Professor! Do you know Miss Tasburgh?"

Hallorsen bowed.

"It's an amazing night," said young Tasburgh on her other side: "Couldn't we go out?"

"Michael," said Jean, rising, "we're going out."

The night had been justly described. The foliage of holmoaks and elms clung on the dark air unstirring; stars were diamond bright, and there was no dew; the flowers had colour only when peered into; and sounds were lonely—the hooting of an owl from away towards the river, the passing drone of a chafer's flight. The air was quite warm, and through the cut cypresses the lighted house stared vaguely. Dinny and the sailor strolled in front.

"This is the sort of night," he said, "when you can see the Scheme a bit. My old Governor is a dear old boy, but his Services are enough to kill all belief. Have you any left?"

"In God, do you mean?" said Dinny: "Ye-es, without knowing anything about it."

"Don't *you* find it impossible to think of God except in the open and alone?"

"I *have* been emotionalised in church."

"You want something beyond emotion, I think; you want to grasp infinite invention going on in infinite stillness. Perpetual motion and perpetual quiet at the same time. That American seems a decent chap."

"Did you talk about cousinly love?"

"I kept that for you. One of our great-great-great-great-grandfathers was the same, under Anne; we've got his portrait, terrible, in a wig. So we're cousins—the love follows."

"Does it? Blood cuts both ways. It certainly makes every difference glare out."

"Thinking of Americans?"

Dinny nodded.

"All the same," said the sailor, "there isn't a question in my mind that in a scrap I'd rather have an American with me than any other kind of foreigner. I should say we all felt that in the Fleet."

"Isn't that just because of language being the same?"

"No. It's some sort of grain and view of things in common."

"But surely that can only apply to British-stock Americans?"

"That still the American who counts, especially if you lump in the Dutch and Scandinavian-stock Americans, like this fellow Hallorsen. We're very much that stock ourselves."

"Why not German-Americans, then?"

"To some extent. But look at the shape of the German head. By and large, the Germans are Central or Eastern Europeans."

"You ought to be talking to my Uncle Adrian."

"Is that the tall man with the goatee? I like his face."

"He's a dear," said Dinny: "We've lost the others and I can feel dew."

"Just one moment. I was perfectly serious in what I said at dinner. You *are* my ideal, and I hope you'll let me pursue it."

Dinny curtsied.

"Young Sir, you are very flattering. 'But—' she went on with a slight blush—'I would point out that you have a noble profession—'"

"Are you never serious?"

"Seldom, when the dew is falling."

He seized her hand.

"Well, you will be one day; and I shall be the cause of it."

Slightly returning the pressure of his hand, Dinny disengaged hers, and walked on.

"Pleached alley—can you stand that expression? It seems to give joy to so many people."

"Fair cousin," said young Tasburgh, "I shall be thinking of you day and night. Don't trouble to answer."

And he held open a French window.

Cicely Muskham was at the piano, and Michael standing behind her. Dinny went up to him.

"If I go to Fleur's sitting-room now, could you show Lord Saxenden where it is, Michael? If he doesn't come by twelve, I shall go to bed. I must sort out the bits I want to read to him."

"All right, Dinny. I'll leave him on the door-mat. Good luck!"

Fetching the diary, Dinny threw open the window of the little sitting-room and sat down to make her selections. It was half-past-ten, and not a sound disturbed her. She selected six fairly long passages which seemed to illustrate the impossible nature of her brother's task. Then, lighting a cigarette, she waited, leaning out. The night was neither more nor less 'amazing' than it had been, but her own mood was deeper. Perpetual motion in perpetual quiet? If that, indeed, were God, He was not of much immediate use to mortals; but, why should He be? When Saxenden tailored the hare and it had cried, had God heard and quivered? When her hand was pressed, had He seen and smiled? When Hubert in the Bolivian wilds had lain fever-stricken, listening to the cry of the loon, had He sent an angel with quinine? When that star up there went out billions of years hence, and hung cold and lightless, would He note it on his shirt-cuff? The million million leaves and blades of grass down there that made the texture of the deeper darkness, the million million stars that gave the light by which she saw that darkness, all—all the result of perpetual motion in endless quiet, all part of God. And she herself, and the smoke of her cigarette; the jasmine under her nose, whose colour was invisible, and the movement of her brain, deciding that it was not yellow; that dog barking so far away that the sound was as a thread by which the woof of silence could be grasped; all—all endowed with the purpose remote, endless, pervading, incomprehensible, of God!

She shivered and withdrew her head. Sitting down in an arm-chair, with the diary in her lap, she gazed round the room. Fleur's taste had remodelled it; there was fine colour in the carpet, the light was softly shaded and fell pleasantly on her sea-green frock and hands resting on the diary. The long day had tired her. She lay back tilting up her face, looking drowsily at the frieze of baked China Cupids with which some former Lady Mont had caused the room to be encircled. Fat funny little creatures they seemed to her—thus tied by rosy chains to the perpetual examination of each other's behinds from stated distances. Chase of the rosy hours, of the rosy—! Dinny's eyelids drooped, her lips opened, she slept. And the discreet light visiting her face and hair and neck revealed their negligence in slumber, their impudent daintiness, as of the fair Italians, so very English, whom Botticelli painted. A tendril of short ripe hair had come apart, a smile strayed off and on to the parted lips; eyelashes, a little darker than the hair, winked flutteringly on cheeks which seemed to have a sort of transparence; and in the passing of her dreams, the nose twitched and quivered as if mocking at its slight tiptilt. Up-lifted thus, the face looked as if but a twist were needed to pluck it from its white stalk of neck. . . .

With a start her head came to the erect. He who had been 'Snubby Bantham' was standing in the middle of the room, regarding her with a hard blue unwinking stare.

"Sorry," he said; "sorry! You were having a nice snooze."

"I was dreaming of mince pies," said Dinny. "It's terribly good of you to come at whatever time of night it is."

"Seven bells. You won't be long, I suppose. D'you mind if I smoke a pipe?"

He sat down on a sofa opposite to her and began to fill his pipe. He had the look of a man who meant her to get it over, and was going to reserve judgment when she had. She better understood at that moment the conduct of public affairs. 'Of course,' she thought, 'he's giving his quo and he doesn't see his quid. That's the result of Jean!' And whether she felt gratitude to the 'leopardess' for having deflected his interest, or whether a sort of jealousy, neither she nor any other woman would have told. Her heart was beating, however, and in a quick, matter-of-fact voice she began. She read through three of the passages before she looked at him again. His face, but for the lips sucking at his pipe, might have been made of a well-coloured wood. His eyes still regarded her in a curious and now slightly hostile way, as if he were thinking: 'This young woman is trying to make me feel something. It's very late.'

With an increasing hatred of her task Dinny hurried on. The fourth passage was—except for the last—the most harrowing, at least to herself; and her voice quivered a little as she finished it.

"Bit thick that," said Lord Saxenden; "mules have no feelings, you know—most extraordinary brutes."

Dinny's temper rose; she would not look at him again. And she read on. This time she lost herself in that tortured recital, thus put into sound for the first time. She finished, breathless, quivering all over with the effort of keeping her voice controlled. Lord Saxenden's chin was resting on his hand. He was asleep.

She stood looking at him, as he not long before had looked at her. For the moment she was on the point of jerking his hand from under his chin. Her sense of humour saved her, and gazing at him rather as Venus gazes at Mars in Botticelli's picture, she took a sheet of note-paper from Fleur's bureau, wrote the words: 'So sorry I exhausted you. Good-night,' and laid it with infinite precaution on his knee. Rolling up the diary, she stole to the door, opened it and looked back; faint sounds, that would soon be snoring, were coming from him. 'Appeal to his feelings and he sleeps,' she thought: 'That's exactly how he must have won the war.' And, turning, she found herself staring up at Professor Hallorsen.

CHAPTER 11

When dinny saw Hallorsen's eyes fixed, over her head, on the sleeping peer, she swallowed a gasp. What was he imagining of her, stealing thus at midnight away from a man of title in a little private room? His eyes, now looking into hers, were extremely grave. And, terrified lest he should say: "Pardon me!" and rouse the sleeper, she clutched the diary, put her finger to her lips, murmured: "Don't wake the baby!" and glided down the passage.

In her room she laughed her fill, then sat up and reviewed her sensations. Given the reputation of the titled in democratic countries, Hallorsen probably thought the worst. But she did him some rather remarkable justice. Whatever he thought of her would not go beyond him. Whatever he was—he was a *big* dog. She could imagine him at breakfast to-morrow, saying gravely: "Miss Cherrell, I am delighted to see you looking so well." And, saddened by her conduct of Hubert's affairs, she got into bed. She slept badly, awoke tired and pale, and had her breakfast upstairs.

During country house parties one day is very like another. The men put on the same kind of variegated tie and the same plus fours, eat the same breakfast, tap the same barometer, smoke the same pipes and kill the same birds. The dogs wag the same tails, lurk in the same unexpected spots, utter the same agonized yelps, and chase the same pigeons on the same lawns. The ladies have the same breakfast in bed or not, put the same salts in the same bath, straggle in the same garden, say of the same friends with the same spice of animosity, "I'm frightfully fond of them, of course"; pore over the same rock borders with the same passion for portulaca; play the same croquet or tennis with the same rumours, or match the same antiques; differ with the same agreement, and agree with the same difference. The servants have the same way of not being visible, except at the same stated moments. And the house has the same smell of pot-pourri, flowers, tobacco, books, and sofa cushions.

Dinny wrote a letter to her brother in which she said nothing of Hallorsen, Saxenden, or the Tasburghs, but discoursed in lively fashion of Aunt Em, Boswell and Johnson, Uncle Adrian, Lady Henrietta, and asked him to come over for her in the car. In the afternoon the Tasburghs came in for tennis, and not until the shooting was over did she see either Lord Saxenden or the American. But he who had been 'Snubby Bantham' gave her so long and so peculiar a stare from the corner where he was having tea, that she knew he had not forgiven her. Careful not to notice, she was at heart dismayed. So far she seemed to have done Hubert nothing but harm. 'I'll let Jean loose on him,' she thought, and went out to find 'the leopardess.' On her way she came on Hallorsen, and hastily deciding to regain her ground with him, said:

"If you had come up a little earlier last night, Professor Hallorsen, you could have heard me read some of my brother's diary to Lord Saxenden. It might have done you more good than it did him."

Hallorsen's face cleared.

"Why," he said, "I've been wondering what soporific you had administered to that poor lord."

"I was preparing him for your book. You *are* giving him a copy?"

"I judge not, Miss Cherrell; I am not that interested in his health. He may lie awake for me. I have very little use for any man that could listen to you and go to sleep on it. What does he do in life, this lord?"

"What does he do? Well, he is what I think you call a Big Noise. I don't quite know where he makes it, but my father says he is a man who counts. I hope you have been wiping his eye again to-day, Professor, because the more you wipe his eye the better chance my brother has of recovering the position he lost by going on your expedition."

"Is that so? Do personal feelings decide these things over here?"

"Don't they over there?"

"Why—yes! But I thought the old countries had too much tradition for that."

"Oh! we wouldn't *admit* the influence of personal feelings, of course."

Hallorsen smiled.

"Isn't that just wonderful? All the world is kin. You would enjoy America, Miss Cherrell; I would like the chance to show it you some day."

He had spoken as if America were an antique that he had in his trunk; and she did not quite know how to take a remark which might have no significance or an absurdly great one. Then by his face she saw that he meant it to have the absurdly great one; and, revealing her teeth, answered:

"Thank you, but you are still my enemy."

Hallorsen put out his hand, but she had drawn back.

"Miss Cherrell, I am going to do all I can to remove the unpleasant impression you have of me. I am your very humble servant, and I hope some day to have a chance to be something else to you."

He looked terribly tall, handsome, and healthy, and she resented it.

"Let us not take anything too seriously, Professor; it leads to trouble. Forgive me now, I have to find Miss Tasburgh."

With that she skimmed away. Ridiculous! Touching! Flattering! Odious! It was all crazy! Whatever one did would be all criss-crossed and tangled, to trust to luck was best, after all!

Jean Tasburgh, who had just finished a single with Cicely Muskham, was removing a fillet from her hair.

"Come along to tea," said Dinny; "Lord Saxenden is pining for you."

At the door of the room where tea was being served, however, she herself was detached by Sir Lawrence, who, saying he had seen nothing of her yet, invited her to his study to look at his miniatures.

"My record of national characteristics, Dinny; all women, you see: French, German, Italian, Dutch, American, Spanish, Russian; and I should immensely like one of you, Dinny. Would you sit to a young man?"

"I?"

"You."

"But why?"

"Because," said Sir Lawrence, scrutinising her through his monocle, "you contain the answer to the riddle of the English lady, and I collect the essential difference between national cultures."

"That sounds terribly exciting."

"Look at this one. Here's French culture in excelsis; quick intelligence, wit, industry, decision, intellectual but not emotional æstheticism, no humour, conventional sentiment but no other, a having tendency—mark the eye; a sense of form, no originality, very clear but limited mental vision—nothing dreamy about her; quick but controlled blood. All of a piece, with very distinct edges. Now here's an American of rare type, tip-top cultured variety. Notice chiefly a look as if she had an invisible bit in her mouth and knew it; in her eyes is a battery she'll make use of but only with propriety. She'll be very well preserved to the end of her days. Good taste, a lot of knowledge, not much learning. See this German! Emotionally more uncontrolled, and less sense of form than either of those others, but has a conscience, is a hard worker, great sense of duty, not much taste, some rather unhandy humour. If she doesn't take care she'll get fat. Plenty of sentiment, plenty of good sound sense too. More capacious in every way. She isn't perhaps a very good specimen. I can't get one. Here's my prize Italian. She's interesting. Beautifully varnished, with something feral, or let's say—natural, behind. Has a mask on, prettily shaped, prettily worn, liable to fall off. Knows her own mind, perhaps too well, gets her own way if she can, and if she can't, gets somebody else's. Poetic only in connection with her senses. Strong feelings, domestic and otherwise. Clear-eyed towards danger, plenty of courage but easily unnerved. Fine taste, subject to bad lapses. No liking for Nature, here. Intellectually decisive, but not industrious or enquiring. And here," said Sir Lawrence, suddenly confronting Dinny, "I shall have my prize English specimen. Do you want to hear about her?"

"Help!"

"Oh! I'll be quite impersonal. Here we have a self-consciousness, developed and controlled to the point when it becomes unself-consciousness. To this lady Self is the unforgivable intruder. We observe a sense of humour, not devoid of wit, which informs and somewhat sterilises all else. We are impressed by what I may call a look not so much of domestic as of public or social service, not to be found in our other types. We discover a sort of transparency, as if air and dew had got into the system. We decide that *pre*cision is lacking, precision of learning, action, thought, judgment, but that *de*cision is very present. The senses are not highly developed; the æsthetic emotions are excited more readily by natural than by artificial objects. There is not the capacity of the German; the clarity of the French woman; the duality or colour of the Italian; the disciplined neatness of the American; but there is a peculiar something—for which, my dear, I will leave you to discover the word—that makes me very anxious to have you in my collection of cultures."

"But I am not in the least cultured, Uncle Lawrence."

"I use the infernal word for want of a better, and by it I don't mean learning. I mean the stamp left by blood plus bringing-up, the two taken strictly together. If that French woman had had your bringing-up, she yet wouldn't have had your stamp, Dinny; nor would you with her bringing-up have had her stamp. Now look at this pre-war Russian; more fluid and more fluent than any of the others. I found her in the Caledonian Market. That woman must have wanted to go deep into everything, and never wanted to stay there long. I'll wager she ran through life at a great pace, and, if alive, is still running; and it's taking much less out of her than it would take out of you. The face gives you the feeling that she's experienced more emotions, and been less exhausted by them than any of the others. Here's my Spaniard; perhaps the most interesting of the lot. That's woman brought up apart from man; I suspect she's getting rare. There's a sweetness here, a touch of the convent; not much curiosity, not much energy, a lot of pride, very little conceit; might be devastating in her affections, don't you think, and rather difficult to talk to? Well, Dinny, will you sit to my young man?"

"If you really want me to, of course."

"I do. This is my hobby. I'll arrange it. He can come down to you at Condaford. I must get back now and see 'Snubby' off. Have you proposed to him yet?"

"I read him to sleep last night with Hubert's diary. He dislikes me intensely. I daren't ask him anything. Is he really 'a big noise,' Uncle Lawrence?"

Sir Lawrence nodded mysteriously. "Snubby," he said, "is the ideal public man. He has practically no feelers, and his feelings are always connected with Snubby. You can't keep a man like him down; he will always be there or thereabouts. India-rubber. Well, well, the State needs him. If we were all thin-skinned, who would sit in the seats of the mighty? They are hard, Dinny, and full of brass tacks. So you've wasted your time?"

"I think I've tied a second string to my bow."

"Excellent. Hallorsen's off too. I like that chap. Very American, but sound wood."

He left her, and, unwilling to encounter again either the india-rubber or the sound wood, Dinny went up to her room.

Next morning by ten o'clock, with the rapidity peculiar to the break-up of house-parties, Fleur and Michael were bearing Adrian and Diana off to Town in their car; the Muskhams had departed by train, and the Squire and Lady Henrietta were motoring across country to their Northampton-shire abode; Aunt Wilmet and Dinny alone were left, but the Tasburghs were coming to lunch and bringing their father.

"He's amiable, Dinny," said Lady Mont: "Old School, very courtly, says 'Nevah,' 'Evah,' like that. It's a pity they've no money. Jean is strikin', don't you think?"

"She scares me a little, Aunt Em; knows her own mind so completely."

"Match-makin'," replied her aunt, "is rather amusin'. I haven't done any for a long time. I wonder what Con and your mother will say to me. I shall wake up o' nights."

"First catch your Hubert, Auntie."

"I was always fond of Hubert; he has the family face—you haven't, Dinny, I don't know where you get your colourin'—and he looks so well on a horse. Where does he get his breeches?"

"I don't believe he's had a new pair since the war, Auntie."

"And he wears nice long waistcoats. Those short waistcoats straight across are so abbreviatin'. I shall send him out with Jean to see the rock borders. There's nothin' like portulaca for bringin' people together. Ah! There's Boswell-and-Johnson—I must catch him."

Hubert arrived soon after noon, and almost the first thing he said was:

"I've changed my mind about having my diary published, Dinny. Ex-hibiting one's sore finger is too revolting."

Thankful that as yet she had taken no steps, she answered meekly: "Very well, dear."

"I've been thinking: If they're not going to employ me here, I might get attached to a Soudan regiment; or I believe they're short of men for the Indian Police. I shall be jolly glad to get out of the country again. Who's here?"

"Only Uncle Lawrence, Aunt Em, and Aunt Wilmet. The Rector and his family are coming to lunch—the Tasburghs, they're distant cousins."

"Oh!" said Hubert, glumly.

She watched the advent of the Tasburghs almost maliciously. Hubert and young Tasburgh at once discovered mutual service in Mesopotamia and the Persian Gulf. They were talking about it when Hubert became conscious of Jean. Dinny saw him give her a long look, enquiring and detached, as of a man watching a new kind of bird; saw him avert his eyes, speak and laugh, then gaze back at her.

Her aunt's voice said: "Hubert looks thin."

69

The Rector spread his hands, as if to draw attention to his present courtly bulk. "Dear Lady, at his age I was thinnah."

"So was I," said Lady Mont; "thin as you, Dinny."

"We gathah unearned increments, ah-ha! Look at Jean—lithe is the word; in forty years—but perhaps the young of to-day will nevah grow fat. They do slimming—ah-ha!"

At lunch the Rector faced Sir Lawrence across the shortened table, and the two elder ladies sat one on each side of him. Alan faced Hubert and Dinny faced Jean.

"For what we are about to receive the Lord make us truly thankful."

"Rum thing—grace!" said young Tasburgh in Dinny's ear. "Benediction on murder, um?"

"There'll be hare," said Dinny, "and I saw it killed. It cried."

"I'd as soon eat dog as hare."

Dinny gave him a grateful look.

"Will you and your sister come and see us at Condaford?"

"Give me a chance!"

"When do you go back to your ship?"

"I've got a month."

"I suppose you are devoted to your profession?"

"Yes," he said simply. "It's bred in the bone, we've always had a sailor in the family."

"And we've always had a soldier."

"Your brother's deathly keen. I'm awfully glad to have met him."

"No, Blore," said Dinny to the butler, "cold partridge, please. Mr. Tasburgh too will eat something cold."

"Beef, Sir; lamb, partridge."

"Partridge, thank you."

"I've seen a hare wash its ears," added Dinny.

"When you look like that," said young Tasburgh, "I simply——"

"Like what?"

"As if you weren't there, you know."

"Thank you."

"Dinny," said Sir Lawrence, "who was it said the world was an oyster? I say it's a clam. What's your view?"

"I don't know the clam, Uncle Lawrence."

"You're fortunate. That travesty of the self-respecting bivalve is the only tangible proof of American idealism. They've put it on a pedestal, and go so far as to eat it. When the Americans renounce the clam, they will have become realists and joined the League of Nations. We shall be dead."

But Dinny was watching Hubert's face. The brooding look was gone; his eyes seemed glued to Jean's deep luring eyes. She uttered a sigh.

"Quite right," said Sir Lawrence, "it will be a pity not to live to see the Americans abandon the clam, and embrace the League of Nations. For, after all," he continued, pursing up his left eye, "it *was* founded by an

American and is about the only sensible product of our time. It remains, however, the pet aversion of another American called Monroe who died in 1831, and is never alluded to without a scoff by people like 'Snubby.'

> " 'A scoff, a sneer, a kick or two,
> 'With few, but how splendid jeers'—

D'you know that thing by Elroy Flecker?"

"Yes," said Dinny, startled, "it's in Hubert's diary; I read it out to Lord Saxenden. It was just then he went to sleep."

"He would. But don't forget, Dinny, that Snubby's a deuced clever fellow, and knows his world to a T. It may be a world you wouldn't be seen dead in, but it's the world where ten million more-or-less-young men were recently seen dead. I wonder," concluded Sir Lawrence, more thoughtfully, "when I have been so well fed at my own table as these last days; something has come over your aunt."

Organising after lunch a game of croquet between herself and Alan Tasburgh against his father and Aunt Wilmet, Dinny watched the departure of Jean and her brother towards the rock borders. They stretched from the sunken garden down to an old orchard, beyond which rose a swell of meadow-land.

'*They* won't stop at the portulaca,' she thought.

Two games, indeed, were over before she saw them again coming from a different direction, deep in talk. 'This,' she thought, hitting the Rector's ball with all her force, 'is about the quickest thing ever known.'

"God bless me!" murmured the smitten clergyman, and Aunt Wilmet, straight as a grenadier, uttered a loud: "Damn it, Dinny, you're impossible! . . ."

Later, beside her brother in the open car, she was silent, making up her mind, as it were, to second place. Though what she had hoped for had come to pass, she was depressed. She had been first with Hubert until now. She needed all her philosophy watching the smile coming and going on his lips.

"Well, what do you think of our cousins?"

"He's a good chap. I thought he seemed rather gone on you."

"Did you now? When would you like them to come over?"

"Any time."

"Next week?"

"Yes."

Seeing that he did not mean to be drawn, she lapsed into savouring the day's slowly sinking light and beauty. The high land, Wantage, and Faringdon way, was glamoured by level sunlight; and Wittenham Clumps bastioned-up the rise ahead. Rounding to the right, they came on the bridge. In the middle of it she touched his arm:

"That stretch up there is where we saw the kingfishers, Hubert; d'you remember?"

Halted, they gazed up the quiet river, deserted and fit for the bright birds. Falling light sprinkled it through willows on the southern bank. The quietest river, it seemed, in the world, most subdued to the moods of men, flowing with an even clear stream among bright fields and those drooping shapely trees; having, as it were, a bland intensity of being, a presence of its own, gracious and apart.

"Three thousand years ago," said Hubert suddenly, "this old river used to be like those I've seen in the wilds, an unshaped flow of water in matted jungle."

He drove on. They had their backs to the sunlight now, and it was like driving into what had been painted for them.

And so they sped on, while into the sky crept the sunset glow, and the cleaned-up fields darkened a little, and gathered loneliness under the evening flight of birds.

At the door of Condaford Grange Dinny got out, humming: "'She was a shepherdess oh! so fair,'" and looking into her brother's face. He was, however, busy with the car and did not appear to see the connection.

CHAPTER 12

THE OUTLINE of a young Englishman of the inarticulate variety is difficult to grasp. The vocal variety is easily enough apprehended. Its manners and habits bulk large to the eye and have but little importance in the national life. Vociferous, critical, ingenious, knowing and advertising only its own kind, it forms an iridescence shimmering over the surface of the bog, and disguising the peat below. It constantly and brilliantly expresses almost nothing; while those whose lives are spent in the application of trained energy remain invisible, but none the less solid; for feelings continually voiced cease to be feelings, and feelings never voiced deepen with their dumbness. Hubert did not look solid, nor was he stolid; even those normal aids to the outline of the inarticulate were absent. Trained, sensitive, and no fool, he was capable of passing quiet judgment on people and events that would have surprised the vocal, but, except to himself, he never passed it. Till quite recently, indeed, he had lacked time and opportunity; but seeing him in a smoking-room, at a dinner-table, or wherever the expressive scintillate, you would know at once that neither time nor opportunity was going to make him vociferous. Going into the war, so early, as a professional, he had missed the expanding influences of the 'Varsity and London. Eight years in Mesopotamia, Egypt and India, a year of illness and the Hallorsen expedition, had given him a remote, drawn, rather embittered look. He was of the temperament that, in idleness, eats its heart out. With dog and gun or on a horse, he found it bearable, but only just; and without those adventitious aids he wilted. Three days after the return to Condaford he came to Dinny on the terrace, with the 'Times' in his hand.

"Look at this!"

Dinny read:

"SIR,—

"You will pardon me, I trust, this intrusion on your space. It has come to my knowledge that certain passages in my book, 'Bolivia and Its Secrets,' published last July, have grievously annoyed my second-in-command, Captain Hubert Charwell, D.S.O., who had charge of the transport of the expedition. On re-reading these passages I certainly believe that in the vexation caused me by the partial failure of the expedition, and owing to the over-strained state in which I returned from the adventure, I have passed undue criticism on Captain Charwell's conduct; and I wish, pending the issue of the second and amended edition which I trust will not be long delayed, to take this opportunity of publicly withdrawing in your great journal the gravamen of my written words. It is my duty and pleasure to express to Captain Charwell and the British Army of which he is a member, my sincere apology, and my regret for any pain I may have caused him.

"Sir, Your obedient servant,
"Edward Hallorsen (Professor).

"Piedmont Hotel,
        "London."

"Very handsome!" said Dinny, trembling a little.

"Hallorsen in London! What the devil does he mean by this all of a sudden?"

She began pulling yellowed leaves out of an Agapanthus. The danger of doing things for other people was being disclosed to her.

"It almost looks like repentance, dear."

"That fellow repent? Not he! There's something behind it."

"Yes, I am."

"You!"

Dinny quailed behind her smile.

"I met Hallorsen at Diana's in London; he was at Lippinghall, too. So I—er—got at him."

Hubert's sallowed face went red.

"You asked—you begged——?"

"Oh! no!"

"What then?"

"He seemed to take rather a fancy to me. It's odd, but I couldn't help it, Hubert."

"He's done this to curry favour with you?"

"You put it like a man and a brother."

"Dinny!"

Dinny flushed too, angry now behind her smile.

"I didn't lead him on. He took this highly unreasonable fancy, in spite of plenty of cold water. But, if you ask me, Hubert, he has quite a decent side to him."

"You would naturally think so," said Hubert, coldly. His face had resumed its sallow hue and was even a little ashened.

Dinny caught impulsively at his sleeve.

"Don't be silly, dear! If he chooses to make a public apology for any reason, even such a bad one, isn't it all to the good?"

"Not when my own sister comes into it. In this thing I'm like—I'm like a——" he puts his hands to his head: "I'm in Chancery. Anyone can punch my head, and I can't move."

Dinny's coolness had come back to her.

"You needn't be afraid that I shall compromise you. This letter is very good news; it takes the wind out of the whole thing. In face of this apology, who can say anything?"

But Hubert, leaving the paper in her hand, went back into the house.

Dinny had practically no 'small' pride. Her sense of humour prevented her from attaching value to her own performances. She felt that she ought to have provided against this contingency, though she did not see how.

Hubert's resentment was natural enough. If Hallorsen's apology had been dictated by conviction, it would have soothed him; arising from a desire to please his sister, it was only the more galling; and he clearly abhorred the Professor's fancy for her. Still, there was the letter—an open and direct admission of false criticism, which changed the whole position! At once she began to consider what use could be made of it. Should she send it to Lord Saxenden? Having meddled so far, she decided that she would, and went in to write the covering letter.

'Condaford Grange.
Sept. 21.

'Dear Lord Saxenden,—

'I am venturing to send you the enclosed cutting from to-day's 'Times,' for I feel it excuses me to some extent for my effrontery the other evening. I really ought not to have bored you at the end of a long day with those passages of my brother's diary. It was unpardonable, and I don't wonder that you sought refuge. But the enclosed will show you the injustice from which my brother has suffered; and I hope you will forgive me.

'Sincerely yours,
'Elizabeth Charwell.'

Enclosing the cutting, she looked up Lord Saxenden in 'Who's Who,' and addressed the envelope to his London abode, marking it 'Personal.'

A little later, trying to find Hubert, she was told that he had taken the car and gone up to London. . . .

Hubert drove fast. Dinny's explanation of the letter had disturbed him greatly. He covered the fifty odd miles in a little under two hours and reached the Piedmont Hotel at one o'clock. Since he had parted from Hallorsen nearly six months ago, no word had passed between them. He sent his card in and waited in the hall with no precise knowledge of what he wanted to say. When the American's tall figure approached behind the buttoned boy, a cold stillness possessed his every limb.

"Captain Cherrell," said Hallorsen, and held out his hand.

With a horror of 'scenes' deeper than his more natural self, Hubert took it, but without pressure in his fingers.

"I saw you were here, from the 'Times.' Is there anywhere we could go and talk for a few minutes?"

Hallorsen led towards an alcove. "Bring some cocktails," he said to a waiter.

"Not for me, thank you. But may I smoke?"

"I trust this is the pipe of peace, Captain."

"I don't know. An apology that does not come from conviction means less than nothing to me."

"Who says it doesn't come from conviction?"

"My sister."

"Your sister, Captain Cherrell, is a very rare and charming young lady, and I would not wish to contradict her."

"Do you mind my speaking plainly?"

"Why, surely no!"

"Then I would much rather have had no apology from you than know I owed it to any feeling of yours for one of my family."

"Well," said Hallorsen, after a pause, "I can't write to the 'Times' and say I was in error when I made that apology. I judge they wouldn't stand for that. I had a sore head when I wrote that book. I told your sister so, and I tell you so now. I lost all sense of charity, and I have come to regret it."

"I don't want charity. I want justice. Did I or did I not let you down?"

"Why, there's no question but that your failure to hold that pack together did in fact finish my chance."

"I admit that. Did I fail you from my fault, or from yours in giving me an impossible job?"

For a full minute the two men stood with their eyes on each other, and without a word. Then Hallorsen again held out his hand.

"Put it there," he said; "my fault."

Hubert's hand went out impulsively, but stopped half way.

"One moment. Do you say that because it would please my sister?"

"No, Sir; I mean it."

Hubert took his hand.

"That's great," said Hallorsen. "We didn't get on, Captain; but since I've stayed in one of your old homes here, I think I've grasped the reason why. I expected from you what you class Englishmen seemingly will never give—that's the frank expression of your feelings. I judge one has to translate you, and I just couldn't do it, so we went on in the dark about each other. And that's the way to get raw."

"I don't know why, but we got raw all right."

"Well, I wish it could come all over again."

Hubert shivered. "I don't."

"Now, Captain, will you lunch with me, and tell me how I can serve you? I will do anything you say to wipe out my mistake."

For a moment Hubert did not speak, his face was unmoved, but his hands shook a little.

"That's all right," he said. "It's nothing."

And they moved towards the grill-room.

CHAPTER 13

IF ONE THING is more certain than another—which is extremely doubtful —it is that nothing connected with a Public Department will run as a private individual expects.

A more experienced and less simply faithful sister than Dinny would have let sleeping dogs lie. But she had as yet no experience of the fact that the usual effect of letters to those in high places is the precise opposite of what was intended by the sender. Arousing his *amour propre,* which in the case of public men should be avoided, it caused Lord Saxenden to look no further into the matter. Did that young woman suppose for a moment that he didn't see how this American chap was feeding out of her hand? In accordance, indeed, with the irony latent in human affairs, Hallorsen's withdrawal of the charge had promoted in the authorities a more suspicious and judgmatic attitude and Hubert received, two days before his year of leave was up, an intimation to the effect that it was extended indefinitely and he was to go on half-pay, pending an enquiry into the matter raised in the House of Commons by Major Motley, M.P. A letter from that military civilian had appeared in reply to Hallorsen's asking whether he was to assume that the shooting and floggings mentioned in his book had not really taken place, and if so, what explanation could this American gentleman afford of such an amazing discrepancy? This, in turn, had elicited from Hallorsen the answer that the facts were as stated in his book, but that his deductions from them had been erroneous, and that Captain Charwell had been perfectly justified in his actions.

On receiving intimation that his leave was extended, Hubert went up to the War Office. He obtained no comfort, beyond the non-official saying of an acquaintance that the Bolivian Authorities were 'butting in.' This news created little less than consternation at Condaford. None of the four young people, indeed, for the Tasburghs were still there, and Clare away in Scotland, appreciated the report at its full value, for none of them had as yet much knowledge of the extent to which officialdom can go when it starts out to do its duty; but to the General it had so sinister a significance that he went up to stay at his Club.

After tea that day in the billiard room, Jean Tasburgh, chalking her cue, said quietly:

"What does that Bolivian news mean, Hubert?"

"It may mean anything. I shot a Bolivian, you know."

"But he tried to kill you first."

"He did."

She leaned her cue against the table; her hands brown, slim, and strong, gripped the cushion; suddenly she went up to him and put her hand through his arm. "Kiss me," she said; "I am going to belong to you."

"Jean!"

"No, Hubert; no chivalry and that sort of nonsense. You shan't have all this beastliness alone. I'm going to share it. Kiss me."

The kiss was given. It was long, and soothing to them both; but, when it was over, he said:

"Jean, it's quite impossible, until things dry straight."

"Of course they'll dry straight, but I want to help dry them. Let's be married quickly, Hubert. Father can spare me a hundred a year; what can you manage?"

"I've three hundred a year of my own, and half pay, which may be cut off."

"That's four hundred a year certain; people have married on lots less, and that's only for the moment. Of course we can be married. Where?"

Hubert stood breathless.

"When the war was on," said Jean, "people married at once; they didn't wait because the man was going to be killed. Kiss me again."

And Hubert stood more breathless than ever, with her arms round his neck. It was so that Dinny found them.

Without moving her arms, Jean said:

"We're going to be married, Dinny. Where do you think best? A Registry Office? Banns take so much time."

Dinny gasped.

"I didn't think you'd propose quite so soon, Jean."

"I had to. Hubert is full of stuffy chivalry. Dad won't like a Registry Office; why not a special licence?"

Hubert's hands on her shoulders held her away from him.

"Be serious, Jean."

"I am. With a special licence, nobody need know till it's over. So nobody will mind."

"Well," said Dinny, quietly, "I believe you're right. When a thing has to be, it had better be quickly. I daresay Uncle Hilary would tie you up."

Hubert dropped his hands. "You're both cracked."

"Polite!" said Jean. "Men are absurd. They want a thing, and when it's offered they carry on like old women. Who is Uncle Hilary?"

"Vicar of St. Augustine's-in-the-Meads; he has no sense of propriety to speak of."

"Good! You go up to-morrow, Hubert, and get the licence. We'll come after you. Where can we stay, Dinny?"

"Diana would have us, I think."

"That settles it. We'll have to go round by Lippinghall, for me to get some clothes, and see Dad. I can cut his hair while I'm talking to him; there won't be any trouble. Alan can come too; we shall want a best man. Dinny, you talk to Hubert." Left alone with her brother, Dinny said:

"She's a wonderful girl, Hubert, and far from cracked, really. It's breathless, but terribly good sense. She's always been poor, so it won't make any difference to her in that way."

"It isn't that. It's the feeling of something hanging over me, that'll hang over her too."

"It'll hang over her worse, if you don't. I really should, dear boy. Father won't mind. He likes her, and he'd rather you married a girl of breeding and spirit, than any amount of money."

"It doesn't seem decent—a special licence," muttered Hubert.

"It's romantic, and people won't have a chance to discuss whether you ought to or not; when it's done they'll accept it, as they always do."

"What about Mother?"

"I'll tell Mother, if you like. I'm sure she won't really mind—you're not being fashionable, marrying a chorus girl or anything of that sort. She admires Jean. So do Aunt Em and Uncle Lawrence."

Hubert's face cleared.

"I'll do it. It's too wonderful. After all, I've nothing to be ashamed of."

He walked up to Dinny, kissed her almost violently, and hurried out. Dinny stayed in the billiard room practising the spot stroke. Behind her matter-of-fact attitude, she was extremely stirred. The embrace she had surprised had been so passionate; the girl was so strange a mixture of feeling and control, of lava and of steel, so masterful and yet so amusingly young. It might be a risk; but Hubert was already a different man because of it. All the same she was fully conscious of inconsistency; for to herself such a sensational departure would not be possible. The giving of her heart would be no rushing affair. As her old Scotch nurse used to say: "Miss Dinny aye knows on hoo many toes a pussy-cat goes." She was not proud of that 'sense of humour not devoid of wit which informed and somewhat sterilised all else.' Indeed, she envied Jean her colourful decision, Alan his direct conviction, Hallorsen his robust adventurousness. But she had her compensations, and, with a smile breaking her lips apart, went to find her mother.

Lady Cherrell was in her sanctum next to her bedroom, making muslin bags for the leaves of the scented verbena which grew against the house.

"Darling," said Dinny, "prepare for slight concussion. You remember my saying I wished we could find the perfect girl for Hubert. Well, she's found; Jean has just proposed to him."

"Dinny!"

"They're going to be married offhand by special licence."

"But——"

"Exactly, darling. So we go up to-morrow, and Jean and I stay with Diana till it's over. Hubert will tell Father."

"But, Dinny, really——!"

Dinny came through the barrage of muslin, knelt down and put her arm round her mother.

"I feel exactly like you," she said, "only different, because after all I didn't produce him; but, Mother darling, it is all right. Jean is a marvellous creature, and Hubert's head over ears. It's done him a lot of good already, and she'll see to it that he goes ahead, you know."

"But, Dinny—money?"

"They're not expecting Dad to do anything. They'll just be able to manage and they needn't have children, you know, till later."

"I suppose not. It's terribly sudden. Why a special licence?"

"Intuition," and, with a squeeze of her mother's slender body, she added: "Jean has them. Hubert's position *is* awkward, Mother."

"Yes; I'm scared about it, and I know your father is, though he's not said much."

This was as far as either of them would go in disclosure of their uneasiness, and they went into committee on the question of a perch for the adventuring couple.

"But why shouldn't they live here until things are settled?" said Lady Cherrell.

"They'll find it more exciting if they have to do their own washing up. The great thing is to keep Hubert's mind active just now."

Lady Cherrell sighed. Correspondence, gardening, giving household orders, and sitting on village committees were certainly not exciting, and Condaford would be even less exciting if, like the young, one had none of these distractions.

"Things *are* quiet here," she admitted.

"And thank God for it," murmured Dinny; "but I feel Hubert wants the strenuous life just now, and he'll get it with Jean in London. They might take a workman's flat. It can't be for long, you know. So, Mother dear, you'll not seem to know anything about it this evening, and we shall all know you do. That'll be so restful for everybody." And, kissing the rueful smile on her mother's face, she went away.

Next morning the conspirators were early afoot, Hubert looking, so Jean put it, as though he were 'riding at a bullfinch'; Dinny resolutely whimsical. Alan had the handy air of a best man in embryo; Jean alone appeared unmoved. They set forth in the Tasburghs' brown roadster, dropping Hubert at the station and proceeding towards Lippinghall. Jean drove. The other two sat behind.

"Dinny," said young Tasburgh, "couldn't *we* have a special licence, too?"

"Reduction on taking a quantity. Behave yourself. You will go to sea and forget all about me in a month."

"Do I look like that?"

Dinny regarded his brown face.

"Well, in spots."

"Do be serious!"

"I can't; I keep seeing Jean snipping a lock and saying: 'Now Dad, bless me or I'll tonsure you!' and the Rector answering 'I—er—nevah——!' and Jean snipping another lock and saying: 'That's all right then, and I must have a hundred a year or off go your eyebrows!'"

"Jean's a holy terror. Promise me anyway, Dinny, not to marry anyone else?"

"But suppose I met someone I liked terribly, would you wish to blight my young life?"

"Yes."

"Not so do they answer on the 'screen.'"

"You'd make a saint swear."

"But not a naval lieutenant. Which reminds me: Those texts at the head of the fourth column of the 'Times.' It struck me this morning what a splendid secret code could be made out of 'The Song of Solomon,' or that Psalm about the Leviathan. 'My beloved is like a young roe' might mean 'Eight German battleships in Dover harbour. Come quickly.' 'And there is that Leviathan that takes his pastime therein' could be 'Tirpitz in command,' and so on. No one could possibly decipher it unless they had a copy of the code."

"I'm going to speed," said Jean, looking back. The speedometer rose rapidly: Forty—forty-five—fifty—fifty-five——! The sailor's hand slipped under Dinny's arm.

"This can't last, the car will bust. But it's a tempting bit of road."

Dinny sat with a fixed smile; she hated being driven really fast, and, when Jean had dropped again to her normal thirty-five, said plaintively:

"Jean, I have a nineteenth century inside."

At Folwell she leaned forward again: "I don't want them to see me at Lippinghall. Please go straight to the Rectory and hide me somewhere while you deal with your parent."

Refuged in the dining-room opposite the portrait of which Jean had spoken, Dinny studied it curiously. Underneath were the words: "1553, Catherine Tastburgh, née Fitzherbert, ætate 35; wife of Sir Walter Tastburgh."

Above the ruff encircling the long neck, that time-yellowed face might truly have been Jean fifteen years hence, the same tapering from the broad cheekbones to the chin, the same long dark-lashed luring eyes; even the hands, crossed on the stomacher, were the very spit of Jean's. What had been the history of that strange prototype; did they know it, and would it be repeated by her descendant?

"Awfully like Jean, isn't she?" said young Tasburgh: "She was a corker, from all accounts; they say she staged her own funeral, and got out of the country when Elizabeth set about the Catholics in the fifteen sixties. D'you know that was the fate of anyone who celebrated Mass just then? Ripping up was a mere incident in it. The Christian religion!

What oh! That lady had a hand in most pies, I fancy. I bet she speeded when she could."

"Any news from the front?"

"Jean went into the study with an old 'Times,' a towel, and a pair of scissors. The rest is silence."

"Isn't there anywhere from which we can see them when they come out?"

"We could sit on the stairs. They wouldn't notice us, there, unless they happen to go up."

They went out and sat in a dark corner of the stairway, whence through the bannisters they could see the study door. With some of the thrill of childhood Dinny watched for it to open. Suddenly Jean came forth, with a sheet of newspaper folded as a receptacle in one hand, and in the other a pair of scissors. They heard her say:

"Remember, dear, you're not to go out without a hat to-day."

An inarticulate answer was shut off by the closing of the door. Dinny rose above the bannisters: "Well?"

"It's all right. He's a bit grumpy—doesn't know who'll cut his hair and that; thinks a special licence a waste of money; but he's going to give me the hundred a year. I left him filling his pipe." She stood still, looking into the sheet of newspaper: "There was an awful lot to come away. We'll have lunch in a minute, Dinny, and then be off again."

The Rector's manner at lunch was still courtly, and Dinny observed him with admiring attention. Here was a widower well on in years, about to be deprived of his only daughter, who did everything about the house and parish, even to the cutting of his hair, yet he was apparently unmoved. Not a murmur escaped his lips. Was it breeding, benevolence, or unholy relief? She could not be sure; and her heart quailed a little. Hubert would soon be in his shoes. She stared at Jean. Little doubt but that she could stage her own funeral, if not other people's; still there would be nothing ungraceful or raucous about her dominations; no vulgar domesticity in the way she stirred her pies. If only she and Hubert had enough sense of humour!

After lunch the Rector took her apart.

"My deah Dinny—if I may call you that—how do you feel about it? And how does your Mothah feel?"

"We both feel it's a little bit like 'The Owl and the Pussycat went to sea!'"

"'In a beautiful pea-green boat.' Yes, indeed, but not 'with plenty of money' I feah. Still," he added, dreamily, "Jean is a good girl; very—ah—capable. I am glad our families are to be—er—reunited. I shall miss her, but one must not be—ah—selfish."

"'What we lose on the swings we gain on the roundabouts,'" murmured Dinny.

The Rector's blue eyes twinkled.

"Ah!" he said, "yes, indeed; the rough with the smooth. Jean refuses to let me give her away. Here is her birth certificate in case of—ah—questions. She is of age."

He produced a long yellowed slip. "Deah me!" he added, sincerely: "Deah me!"

Dinny continued to feel doubtful whether she was sorry for him; and, directly after, they resumed their journey.

CHAPTER 14

DROPPING ALAN TASBURGH at his Club, the two girls headed the car for Chelsea. Dinny had sent no telegram, trusting to luck. On reaching the house in Oakley Street she got out and rang the bell. An elderly maid, with a frightened expression on her face, opened the door.

"Mrs. Ferse in?"

"No, Miss; Captain Ferse."

"Captain Ferse?"

The maid, looking to right and left, spoke in a low and hurried voice.

"Yes, Miss; we're dreadfully put about, we don't know what to do. Captain Ferse came in sudden at lunch time, and we never knew nothing of it, beforehand. The Mistress was out. There's been a telegram for her, but Captain Ferse took it; and someone's been on the 'phone for her twice but wouldn't give a message." Dinny sought for words in which to discover the worst.

"How—how does he seem?"

"Well, Miss, I couldn't say. He never said nothing but 'Where's your mistress?' He *looks* all right, but not having heard anything, we're afraid; the children are in and we don't know where the Mistress is."

"Wait a minute," and Dinny went back to the car.

"What's the matter?" asked Jean, getting out.

The two girls stood consulting on the pavement, while from the doorway the maid watched them.

"I ought to get hold of Uncle Adrian," said Dinny. "There are the children."

"You do that, and I'll go in and wait for you. That maid looks scared."

"I believe he used to be violent, Jean; he may have escaped, you know."

"Take the car. I shall be all right." Dinny squeezed her hand.

"I'll take a taxi; then you'll have the car if you want to get away."

"Right! Tell the maid who I am, and then buzz off. It's four o'clock."

Dinny looked up at the house; and, suddenly, saw a face in the window of the dining-room. Though she had only twice seen Ferse, she recognised him at once. His face was not to be forgotten, it gave the impression of fire behind bars: A cut, hard face with a tooth-brush moustache, broad cheek-bones, strong-growing dark slightly-grizzled hair, and those steel-bright flickering eyes. They stared out at her now with a kind of dancing intensity that was painful, and she looked away.

"Don't look up! He's in there!" she said to Jean: "But for his eyes he looks quite normal—well-dressed and that. Let's both go, Jean, or both stay."

"No; I shall be quite all right; you go," and she went into the house.

Dinny hurried away. This sudden reappearance of one whom all had assumed to be hopelessly unhinged, was staggering. Ignorant of the circumstances of Ferse's incarceration, ignorant of everything except that he had given Diana a terrible time before his break-down, she thought of Adrian as the only person likely to know enough. It was a long anxious drive. She found her uncle on the point of leaving the Museum, and told him hurriedly, while he stood looking at her with horror.

"Do you know where Diana is?" she finished.

"She was dining to-night with Fleur and Michael. I was going too, but till then I don't know. Let's get on back to Oakley Street. This is a thunderbolt."

They got into the cab.

"Couldn't you telephone to that Mental Home, Uncle?"

"Without seeing Diana, I daren't. You say he looked normal?"

"Yes. Only his eyes—but they always were like that, I remember."

Adrian put his hands up to his head. "It's too horrible! My poor girl!"

Dinny's heart began to ache—as much for him as for Diana.

"Horrible too," said Adrian, "to be feeling like this because that poor devil has come back. Ah, me! This is a bad business, Dinny; a bad business." Dinny squeezed his arm.

"What is the law about it, Uncle?"

"God knows! He never was certified. Diana wouldn't have that. They took him as a private patient."

"But surely he couldn't come away just when he liked, without any notice being given?"

"Who knows what's happened? He may be as crazy as ever and have got away in a flash of sanity. But whatever we do," and Dinny felt moved by the expression on his face, "we must think of him as well as of ourselves. We mustn't make it harder for him. Poor Ferse! Talk about trouble, Dinny—illness, poverty, vice, crime—none of them can touch mental derangement for sheer tragedy to all concerned."

"Uncle," said Dinny, "the night?"

Adrian groaned. "That we must save her from somehow."

At the end of Oakley Street they dismissed the cab and walked to the door. . . .

On going in Jean had said to the maid: "I'm Miss Tasburgh. Miss Dinny has gone for Mr. Cherrell. Drawing-room upstairs? I'll wait there. Has he seen the children?"

"No, Miss. He's only been here half an hour. The children are up in the schoolroom with Mam'selle."

"Then I shall be between them," said Jean. "Take me up."

"Shall I wait with you, Miss?"

"No. Keep a look out for Mrs. Ferse and tell her at once."

The maid gazed at her admiringly and left her in the drawing-room. Setting the door ajar Jean stood listening. There was no sound. And she began to move silently up and down from door to window. If she saw Diana approaching she meant to run down to her; if Ferse came up she meant to go out to him. Her heart beat a little faster than usual, but she felt no real nervousness. She had been patrolling thus for a quarter of an hour when she heard a sound behind her, and, turning, saw Ferse just within the room.

"Oh!" she said: "I'm waiting for Mrs. Ferse; are you Captain Ferse?"

The figure bowed. "And you?"

"Jean Tasburgh. I'm afraid you wouldn't know me."

"Who was that with you?"

"Dinny Cherrell."

"Where has she gone?"

"To see one of her uncles, I believe."

Ferse uttered a queer sound—not quite a laugh.

"Adrian?"

"I think so."

He stood turning those bright flickering eyes on the pretty room.

"Prettier than ever," he said, "I've been away some time. Do you know my wife?"

"I met her staying at Lady Mont's."

"Lippinghall? Is Diana well?"

The words came out with a sort of hungry harshness.

"Yes. Quite."

"And beautiful?"

"Very."

"Thank you."

Looking at him from under her long lashes Jean could see nothing in him from top to toe that gave the impression of derangement. He looked what he was—a soldier in mufti, very neat and self-contained, all—all but those eyes.

"I haven't seen my wife for four years," he said, "I shall want to see her alone."

Jean moved towards the door.

"I'll go," she said.

"No!" The word came out with startling suddenness: "Stay there!" And he blocked the doorway.

"Why?"

"I wish to be the first to tell her that I'm back."

"Naturally."

"Stay there, then!"

Jean moved back to the window. "Just as you like," she said. There was a silence.

"Have you heard about me?" he asked, suddenly.

"Very little. I know you haven't been well."

He came from the door. "Do you see anything the matter with me?" Jean looked up, her eyes held his till they went flickering away.

"Nothing. You look very fit."

"I am. Sit down, won't you?"

"Thank you." Jean sat down.

"That's right," he said. "Keep your eyes on me."

Jean looked at her feet. Again Ferse uttered that travesty of a laugh.

"You've never been mentally sick, I take it. If you had you'd know that everybody keeps their eyes on you; and you keep your eyes on everybody. I must go down now. *Au revoir!*"

He turned quickly and went out, shutting the door. Jean continued to sit quite still, expecting him to open it again. She had a feeling of having been worsted, and a curious tingling all over, as if she had been too close to a fire. He did not open the door again, and she got up to do so herself. It was locked. She stood looking at it. Ring the bell? Hammer on it and attract the maid? She decided to do neither, but went to the window and stood watching the street. Dinny would be back soon and she could call to her. Very coolly she reviewed the scene she had been through. He had locked her in because he meant no one to interfere before he saw his wife —suspicious of everyone—very natural! A dim sense of what is meant to be looked on as deranged penetrated her young hard intelligence. Poor man! She wondered if she could get out of the window without being noticed, and, deciding that she couldn't, continued to stand watching the end of the street for the appearance of relief. And, suddenly, without anything to cause it, a shiver ran through her, the aftermath of that encounter. His eyes! It must be terrible to be his wife. She threw the window wider, and leaned out. . . .

CHAPTER 15

The sight of Jean at the window stayed Dinny and her uncle on the door-step.

"I'm locked in the drawing-room," said Jean, quietly; "you might let me out."

Adrian took his niece to the car.

"Stay here, Dinny. I'll send her out to you. We mustn't make a show of this."

"Take care, Uncle! I feel as if you were Daniel going into——"

With a wan smile Adrian rang the bell. Ferse himself opened the door.

"Ah! Cherrell? Come in."

Adrian held out his hand; but it was not taken.

"I can hardly expect a welcome," said Ferse.

"My dear fellow!"

"No, I can hardly expect a welcome, but I'm going to see Diana. Don't try and prevent me, Cherrell—you or anyone."

"Of course not! Do you mind if I fetch young Jean Tasburgh? Dinny is waiting for her in the car."

"I locked her in," said Ferse, sombrely. "Here's the key. Send her away."

He went into the dining-room.

Jean was standing just inside the door.

"Go out to Dinny," said Adrian, "and take her away. I'll manage. No trouble I hope?"

"Only being locked in."

"Tell Dinny," said Adrian, "that Hilary is almost sure to be able to put you both up; if you go on there now I shall know where you are if I want you. You have pluck, young lady."

"Oh, not specially!" said Jean: "Good-bye!" and ran downstairs. Adrian heard the front door close and went slowly down to the dining-room. Ferse was at the window watching the girls start the car. He turned round sharply. The movement was that of a man used to being spied on. There was little change in him, less thin, less haggard, and his hair greyer—that was all. His dress as neat as ever, his manner composed; his eyes—but then—his eyes!

"Yes," said Ferse, uncannily, "you can't help pitying me, but you'd like to see me dead. Who wouldn't? A fellow has no business to go off

88

his chump. But I'm sane enough now, Cherrell, don't make any mistake."

Sane? Yes, he seemed sane. But what strain could he stand?

Ferse spoke again: "You all thought I was gone for good. About three months ago I began to mend. As soon as I realised that—I kept dark. Those who look after us"—he spoke with concentrated bitterness—"must be so certain of our sanity that if it were left to them we should never be sane again. It's to their interest, you see." And his eyes, burning into Adrian's, seemed to add: 'And to yours, and to hers?' "So I kept dark. I had the will-power to keep dark in that place for three months, in my right mind. It's only this last week or so that I've shown them I'm responsible. They want much more than a week before they'll write home about it. I didn't want them writing home. I wanted to come straight here and show myself as I am. I didn't want Diana or anybody warned. And I wanted to make sure of myself, and I have."

"Terrible!" said Adrian below his breath.

Ferse's eyes seemed to burn into him again.

"You used to be in love with my wife, Cherrell; you still are. Well?"

"We are just as we were," said Adrian, "friends."

"You'd say that anyway."

"Perhaps. But there is no more to say, except that I'm bound to think of her first, as I always have."

"That's why you're here, then?"

"Gracious, Man! Haven't you realised the shock it will be to her? Perhaps you can't remember the life you led her before you went in there? But do you think she's forgotten? Wouldn't it be fairer to her and to yourself if you came to my room, say, at the Museum, and saw her there for the first time?"

"No; I'll see her here in my own house."

"This is where she went through hell, Ferse. You may have been right to keep dark, as you call it, so far as the doctors are concerned, but you're certainly not right to spring your recovery on her like this."

Ferse made a violent gesture.

"You want her kept from me."

Adrian bowed his head.

"That may be," he said, gently. "But look here, Ferse, you're just as well able to gauge this situation as myself. Put yourself in her place. Imagine her coming in, as she may at any minute, seeing you without warning, knowing nothing of your recovery, needing time to believe in it—with all her memories of you as you were. What chance are you giving yourself?"

Ferse groaned. "What chance shall I be given, if I don't take any chance I can? Do you think I trust anyone now? Try it—try four years of it, and see!" and his eyes went swiftly round: "Try being watched, try being treated like a dangerous child. I've looked on at my own treatment, as a perfectly sane man, for the last three months. If my own wife can't take me for what I am—clothed and in my right mind, who will or can?"

Adrian went up to him.

"Gently!" he said: "That's where you're wrong. Only *she* knew you at the worst. It should be more difficult for her than for anyone."

Ferse covered his face.

Adrian waited, grey with anxiety; but when Ferse uncovered his face again he could not bear the look on it, and turned his eyes away.

"Talk of loneliness!" said Ferse. "Go off your chump, Cherrell, then you'll know what it means to be lonely for the rest of your days."

Adrian put a hand on his shoulder.

"Look here, my dear fellow, I've got a spare room at my digs, come and put up with me till we get things straightened out." Sudden suspicion grinned from Ferse's face, an intense searching look came into his eyes; it softened as if with gratitude, grew bitter, softened again.

"You were always a white man, Cherrell; but no, thanks—I couldn't. I must be here. Foxes have holes, and I've still got this."

Adrian sighed.

"Very well; then we must wait for her. Have you seen the children?"

"No. Do they remember me?"

"I don't think so."

"Do they know I'm alive?"

"Yes. They know that you're away, ill."

"Not——?" Ferse touched his forehead.

"No. Shall we go up to them?"

Ferse shook his head, and at that moment through the window Adrian saw Diana coming. He moved quietly towards the door. What was he to do or say? His hand was on the knob when Ferse pushed by him into the hall. Diana had come in with her latchkey. Adrian could see her face grow deadly pale below the casque of her close hat. She recoiled against the wall.

"It's all right, Diana," he said quickly, and held open the dining-room door. She came from the wall, passed them both into the room, and Ferse followed.

"If you want to consult me I shall be here," said Adrian, and closed the door. . . .

Husband and wife stood breathing as if they had run a hundred yards instead of walking three.

"Diana!" said Ferse: "Diana!"

It seemed as if she couldn't speak, and his voice rose:

"I'm all right. Don't you believe me?"

She bent her head, and still didn't speak.

"Not a word to throw to a dog?"

"It's—it's the shock."

"I have come back sane, I have been sane for three months now."

"I am so glad, so glad."

"My God! You're as beautiful as ever."

And suddenly he gripped her, pressed her hard against him, and began

90

kissing her hungrily. When he let her go, she sank breathless into a chair, gazing at him with an expression of such terror that he put his hands over his face.

"Ronald—I couldn't—I couldn't let it be as it was before. I couldn't—I couldn't!"

He dropped on his knees at her feet. "I didn't mean to be violent. Forgive me!"

And then, from sheer exhaustion of the power of feeling, both rose and moved apart.

"We had better talk it over quietly," said Ferse.

"Yes."

"Am I not to live here?"

"It's your house. You must do whatever's best for you."

He uttered the sound that was so like a laugh.

"It would be best for me if you and everyone would treat me exactly as if nothing had happened to me."

Diana was silent. She was silent so long that again he made that sound.

"Don't!" she said. "I will try. But I must—I must have a separate room."

Ferse bowed. Suddenly his eyes darted at her. "Are you in love with Cherrell?"

"No."

"With anyone?"

"No."

"Scared then?"

"Yes."

"I see. Naturally. Well, it's not for God's playthings to make terms. We take what we can get. Will you wire for them to send my things from that place? That will save any fuss they might want to make. I came away without saying good-bye. There is probably something owing too."

"Of course. I will see to all that."

"Can we let Cherrell go now?"

"I will tell him."

"Let me!"

"No, Ronald, I will," and she moved resolutely past him.

Adrian was leaning against the wall opposite the door. He looked up at her and tried to smile; he had divined the upshot.

"He is to stay here, but apart. My dear, thank you so much for all. Will you see to that Home for me? I will let you know everything. I'll take him up to the children now. Good-bye!" He kissed her hand and went out.

CHAPTER 16

HUBERT CHERRELL stood outside his father's club in Pall Mall, a senior affair of which he was not yet a member. He was feeling concerned, for he had a respect for his father somewhat odd in days when fathers were commonly treated as younger brethren, or alluded to as 'that old man.' Nervously therefore he entered an edifice wherein more people had held more firmly to the prides and prejudices of a lifetime than possibly anywhere else on earth. There was little, however, either of pride or prejudice about the denizens of the room into which he was now shown. A short alert man with a pale face and a tooth-brush moustache was biting the end of a pen, and trying to compose a letter to the 'Times' on the condition of Iraq; a modest-looking little Brigadier General with a bald forehead and grey moustache was discussing with a tall modest-looking Lieutenant Colonel the flora of the island of Cyprus; a man of square build, square cheekbones and lion-like eyes, was sitting in the window as still as if he had just buried an aunt and were thinking whether or not he would try and swim the Channel next year; and Sir Conway himself was reading Whitaker's Almanac.

"Hallo, Hubert! This room's too small. Come into the hall." Hubert had the instant feeling not only that he wanted to say something to his father, but that his father wanted to say something to him. They sat down in a recess.

"What's brought you up?"

"I want to get married, Sir."

"Married?"

"To Jean Tasburgh."

"Oh!"

"We thought of getting a special licence and having no fuss."

The General shook his head. "She's a fine girl, and I'm glad you feel like that, but the fact is your position's queer, Hubert. I've just been hearing."

Hubert noticed suddenly how worn-looking was his father's face. "That fellow you shot. They're pressing for your extradition on a charge of murder."

"What?"

"It's a monstrous business, and I can't believe they'll go on with it in the face of what you say about his going for you—luckily you've still got his scar on your arm; but it seems there's the deuce of a fuss in the Bolivian papers; and those half-castes are sticking together about it."

"I must see Hallorsen at once."

"The authorities won't be in a hurry, I expect."

After this, the two sat silent in the big hall, staring in front of them with very much the same expression on their faces. At the back of both their minds the fear of this development had lurked, but neither had ever permitted it to take definite shape; and its wretchedness was therefore the more potent. To the General it was even more searing than to Hubert. The idea that his only son could be haled half across the world on a charge of murder was as horrible as a nightmare.

"No good to let it prey on our minds, Hubert," he said, at last; "if there's any sense in the country at all we'll get this stopped. I was trying to think of someone who knows how to get at people. I'm helpless in these matters—some fellows seem to know everybody and exactly how to work them. I think we'd better go to Lawrence Mont; he knows Saxenden anyway, and probably the people at the Foreign Office. It was Topsham who told me, but he can do nothing. Let's walk, shall we? Do us good."

Much touched by the way his father was identifying himself with his trouble, Hubert squeezed his arm, and they left the Club. In Piccadilly the General said, with a transparent effort: "I don't much like all these changes."

"Well, Sir, except for Devonshire House, I don't believe I notice them."

"No, it's queer; the spirit of Piccadilly is stronger than the street itself, you can't destroy its atmosphere. You never see a top hat now, and yet it doesn't seem to make any difference. I felt the same walking down Piccadilly after the war as I did as a youngster back from India. One just had the feeling of having got there at last."

"Yes; you get a queer sort of homesickness for it. I did in Mespot and Bolivia. If one closed one's eyes the whole thing would start up."

"Core of English life," began the General, and stopped, as if surprised at having delivered a summary.

"Even the Americans feel it," remarked Hubert, as they turned into Half-Moon Street. "Hallorsen was saying to me they had nothing like it over there; 'no focus for their national influence' was the way he put it."

"And yet they *have* influence," said the General.

"No doubt about that, Sir, but can you define it? Is it their speed that gives it them?"

"Where does their speed get them? Everywhere in general; nowhere in particular. No, it's their money, I think."

"Well, I've noticed about Americans, and it's where most people go wrong, that they care very little for money as money. They like to get it fast; but they'd rather lose it fast than get it slow."

"Queer thing having no core," said the General.

"The country's too big, Sir. But they have a sort of core, all the same —pride of country."

The General nodded.

"Queer little old streets these. I remember walking with my Dad from Curzon Street to the St. James' Club in '82—day I first went to Harrow— hardly a stick changed." And so, concerned in talk that touched not on the feelings within them, they reached Mount Street.

"There's your Aunt Em, don't tell her."

A few paces in front of them Lady Mont was, as it were, swimming home. They overtook her some hundred yards from the door.

"Con," she said, "you're lookin' thin."

"My dear girl, I never was anything else."

"No. Hubert, there was somethin' I wanted to ask you. Oh! I know! But Dinny said you hadn't had any breeches since the war. How do you like Jean? Rather attractive?"

"Yes, Aunt Em."

"She wasn't expelled."

"Why should she have been?"

"Oh! well, you never know. She's never terrorised me. D'you want Lawrence? It's Voltaire now and Dean Swift. So unnecessary—they've been awfully done; but he likes doin' them because they bite. About those mules, Hubert?"

"What about them?"

"I never can remember if the donkey is the sire or the dam."

"The donkey is the sire and the dam a mare, Aunt Em."

"Yes, and they don't have children—such a blessin'. Where's Dinny?"

"She's in town, somewhere."

"She ought to marry."

"Why?" said the General.

"Well, there she is! Hen was saying she'd make a good lady-in-waitin'— unselfish. That's the danger." And, taking a latchkey out of her bag, Lady Mont applied it to the door.

"I can't get Lawrence to drink tea, would you like some?"

"No, thank you, Em."

"You'll find them stewin' in the library." She kissed her brother and her nephew, and swam towards the stairs. "Puzzlin'," they heard her say as they entered the library. They found Sir Lawrence surrounded by the works of Voltaire and Swift, for he was engaged on an imaginary dialogue between those two serious men. He listened gravely to the General's tale.

"I saw," he said, when his brother-in-law had finished, "that Hallorsen had repented him of the evil—that will be Dinny. I think we'd better see him—not here, there's no cook, Em's still slimming—but we can all dine at the Coffee House." And he took up the telephone.

Professor Hallorsen was expected in at five and should at once be given the message.

"This seems to be more of an F.O. business than a Police matter," went on Sir Lawrence: "Let's go over and see old Shropshire. He must have known your father well, Con; and his nephew, Bobbie Ferrar, is about as fixed a star as there is at the F.O. Old Shropshire's always in!"

Arrived at Shropshire House Sir Lawrence said:

"Can we see the Marquess, Pommett?"

"I rather think he's having his lesson, Sir Lawrence."

"Lesson—in what?"

"Heinstein, is it, Sir Lawrence?"

"Then the blind is leading the blind, and it will be well to save him. The moment there's a chance, Pommett, let us in."

"Yes, Sir Lawrence."

"Eighty-four and learning Einstein. Who said the aristocracy was decadent? I should like to see the bloke who's teaching it, though; he must have singular powers of persuasion—there are no flies on old Shropshire."

At this moment a man of ascetic aspect with a cold deep eye and not much hair, entered, took hat and umbrella from a chair, and went out.

"Behold the man!" said Sir Lawrence. "I wonder what he charges? Einstein is like the electron or the vitamin—inapprehensible; it's as clear a case of money under false pretences as I've ever come across. Come along."

The Marquess of Shropshire was walking up and down his study, nodding his quick and sanguine grey-bearded head as if to himself.

"Ah! young Mont," he said, "did you meet that man—if he offers to teach you Einstein, don't let him. He can no more explain space bounded yet infinite, than I can."

"But even Einstein can't, Marquess."

"I am not old enough," said the Marquess, "for anything but the exact sciences. I told him not to come again. Whom have I the pleasure of seeing?"

"My brother-in-law General Sir Conway Cherrell, and his son Captain Hubert Cherrell, D.S.O. You'll remember Conway's father, Marquess—he was Ambassador at Madrid."

"Yes, yes, dear me, yes! I know your brother Hilary, too; a live wire. Sit down! Sit down, young man! Is it anything to do with electricity?"

"Not wholly, Marquess; more a matter of extradition."

"Indeed!" The Marquess, raising his foot to the seat of a chair, leaned his elbow on his knee and his bearded chin on his hand. And, while the General was explaining, he continued to stand in this attitude, gazing at Hubert, who was sitting with compressed lips, and lowered eyes. When the General had finished the Marquess said:

"D.S.O., I think your uncle said. In the war?"

"Yes, Sir."

"I shall do what I can. Could I see that scar?"

Hubert drew up his left sleeve, unlinked his shirt cuff and exposed an arm up which a long glancing scar stretched almost from wrist to elbow.

The Marquess whistled softly through teeth still his own. "Narrow escape that, young man."

"Yes, Sir. I put up my arm just as he struck."

"And then?"

"Jumped back and shot him as he came on again. Then I fainted."

"This man was flogged for ill-treating his mules, you say?"

"Continually ill-treating them."

"Continually?" repeated the Marquess. "Some think the meat-trade and Zoological Society continually ill-treat animals but I never heard of their being flogged. Tastes differ. Now, let me see, what can I do? Is Bobbie in town, young Mont?"

"Yes, Marquess. I saw him at the Coffee House yesterday."

"I will get him to breakfast. If I remember he does not allow his children to keep rabbits, and has a dog that bites everybody. That should be to the good. A man who is fond of animals would always like to flog a man who isn't. Before you go, young Mont, will you tell me what you think of this?" And replacing his foot on the ground, the Marquess went to the corner, took up a canvas that was leaning against the wall, and brought it to the light. It represented with a moderate degree of certainty a young woman without clothes.

"By Steinvitch," said the Marquess, "she could corrupt no morals, could she—if hung?"

Sir Lawrence screwed in his monocle: "The oblong school. This comes of living with women of a certain shape, Marquess. No, she couldn't corrupt morals, but she might spoil digestions—flesh sea-green, hair tomato, style blobby. Did you buy her?"

"Hardly," said the Marquess; "she is worth a good deal of money, I am told. You—you wouldn't take her away, I suppose?"

"For you, Sir, I would do most things, but not that; no," repeated Sir Lawrence, moving backwards, "not that."

"I was afraid of it," said the Marquess, "and yet I am told that she has a certain dynamic force. Well, that is that! I liked your father, General," he said, more earnestly, "and if the word of his grandson is not to be taken against that of half-caste muleteers, we shall have reached a stage of altruism in this country so complete that I do not think we can survive. I will let you know what my nephew says. Good-bye, General; good-bye, my dear young man—that is a very nasty scar. Good-bye, young Mont— you are incorrigible."

On the stairs Sir Lawrence looked at his watch. "So far," he said, "the matter has taken twenty minutes—say twenty-five from door to door. They can't do it at that pace in America—and we very nearly had an oblong young woman thrown in. Now for the Coffee House, and Hallorsen." And they turned their faces towards St. James's Street. "This street," he said, "is the Mecca of Western man, as the Rue de la Paix is the Mecca of Western woman." And he regarded his companions whimsically. What good specimens they were of a product at once the envy and mock of every other country! All over the British Empire men made more or less in their image were doing the work and playing the games of the

British world. The sun never set on the type; history had looked on it and decided that it would survive. Satire darted at its joints, and rebounded from an unseen armour. 'It walks quietly down the days of Time,' he thought, 'the streets and places of the world, without manner to speak of, without parade of learning, strength, or anything, endowed with the conviction, invisible, impermeable, of being IT.'

"Yes," he said on the doorstep of 'The Coffee House,' "I look on this as the plumb centre of the universe. Others may claim the North Pole, Rome, Montmartre—I claim the Coffee House, oldest Club in the world, and I suppose, by plumbing standards, the worst. Shall we wash, or postpone it to a more joyful opportunity? Agreed. Let's sit down here, then, and await the apostle of plumbing. I take him for a hustler. Pity we can't arrange a match between him and the Marquess. I'd back the old boy."

"Here he is," said Hubert.

The American looked very big coming into the low hall of the oldest Club in the world.

"Sir Lawrence Mont," he said. "Ah! Captain! General Sir Conway Cherrell? Proud to meet you, General. And what can I do for you, gentlemen?"

He listened to Sir Lawrence's recital with a deepening gravity. "Isn't that too bad? I can't take this sitting. I'm going right along now to see the Bolivian Minister. And, Captain, I've kept the address of your boy Manuel, I'll cable our Consul at La Paz to get a statement from him right away, confirming your story. Who ever heard of such darned foolishness? Forgive me, gentlemen, but I'll have no peace till I've set the wires going." And with a circular movement of his head he was gone. The three Englishmen sat down again.

"Old Shropshire must look to his heels," Sir Lawrence said.

"So that's Hallorsen," said the General. "Fine-looking chap."

Hubert said nothing. He was moved.

CHAPTER 17

UNEASY AND SILENT the two girls drove towards St. Augustine's-in-the-Meads.

"I don't know which I'm most sorry for," said Dinny, suddenly: "I never thought about insanity before. People either make a joke of it or hide it away. But it seems to me more pitiful than anything in the world; especially when it's partial like this."

Jean turned on her a surprised look—Dinny with the mask of humour off was new.

"Which way now?"

"Up here; we have to cross the Euston Road. Personally, I don't believe Aunt May can put us up. She's sure to have people learning to slum. Well, if she can't, we'll telephone to Fleur. I wish I'd thought of that before."

Her prediction was verified—the Vicarage was full, her aunt out, her uncle at home.

"While we're here, we'd better find out whether Uncle Hilary will do you in," whispered Dinny.

Hilary was spending the first free hour of three days in his shirt sleeves, carving the model of a Viking ship. For the production of obsolete ships in miniature was the favourite recreation now of one who had no longer leisure or muscle for mountain climbing. The fact that they took more time to complete than anything else, and that he had perhaps less time than anybody else to give to their completion had not yet weighed with him. After shaking hands with Jean, he excused himself for proceeding with his job.

"Uncle Hilary," began Dinny, abruptly, "Jean is going to marry Hubert, and they want it to be by special licence; so we've come to ask if you would marry them."

Hilary halted his gouging instrument, narrowed his eyes till they were just shrewd slits, and said:

"Afraid of changing your minds?"

"Not at all," said Jean.

Hilary regarded her attentively. In three words and one look she had made it clear to him that she was a young woman of character.

"I've met your father," he said, "he always takes plenty of time."

"Dad is perfectly docile about this."

98

"That's true," said Dinny; "I've seen him."

"And *your* father, my dear?"

"He *will* be."

"If he is," said Hilary, again gouging at the stern of his ship, "I'll do it. No point in delay if you really know your minds." He turned to Jean. "You ought to be good at mountains, the season's over, or I'd recommend that to you for your honeymoon. But why not a trawler in the North Sea?"

"Uncle Hilary," said Dinny, "refused a Deanship. He is noted for his asceticism."

"The hat ropes did it, Dinny, and let me tell you, that the grapes have been sour ever since. I cannot think why I declined a life of some ease with time to model all the ships in the world, the run of the newspapers, and the charms of an increasing stomach. Your Aunt never ceases to throw them in my teeth. When I think of what Uncle Cuffs did with his dignity, and how he looked when he came to the end, I see my wasted life roll out behind me, and visions of falling down when they take me out of the shafts. How strenuous is your father, Miss Tasburgh?"

"Oh, he just marks time," said Jean; "but that's the country."

"Not entirely! To mark time and to think you're not—there never was a more universal title than 'The Man who was.'"

"Unless," said Dinny, "it's 'The Man who never was.' Oh! Uncle, Captain Ferse suddenly turned up to-day at Diana's."

Hilary's face became very grave.

"Ferse! That's either most terrible, or most merciful. Does your Uncle Adrian know?"

"Yes; I fetched him. He's there now with Captain Ferse. Diana wasn't in."

"Did you see Ferse?"

"*I* went in and had a talk with him," said Jean; "he seemed perfectly sane except that he locked me in."

Hilary continued to stand very still.

"We'll say good-bye now, Uncle; we're going to Michael's."

"Good-bye; and thank you very much, Mr. Cherrell."

"Yes," said Hilary, absently, "we must hope for the best."

The two girls, mounting the car, set out for Westminster.

"He evidently expects the worst," said Jean.

"Not difficult, when both alternatives are so horrible."

"Thank you!"

"No, no!" murmured Dinny: "I wasn't thinking of you." And she thought how remarkably Jean could keep to a track when she was on it!

Outside Michael's house in Westminster they encountered Adrian, who had telephoned to Hilary and been informed of their changed destination. Having ascertained that Fleur could put the girls up, he left them; but Dinny, smitten by the look on his face, ran after him. He was walking towards the river, and she joined him at the corner of the Square.

"Would you rather be alone, Uncle?"

"I'm glad of *you*, Dinny. Come along."

They went at a good pace westward along the Embankment, Dinny slipping her hand within his arm. She did not talk, however, leaving him to begin if he wished.

"You know I've been down to that Home several times," he said, presently, "to see how things were with Ferse, and make sure they were treating him properly. It serves me right for not having been these last months. But I always dreaded it. I've been talking to them now on the 'phone. They wanted to come up, but I've told them not to. What good can it do? They admit he's been quite normal for the last two weeks. In such cases it seems they wait a month at least before reporting. Ferse himself says he's been normal for three months."

"What sort of place is it?"

"A largish country house—only about ten patients; each has his own rooms and his own attendant. It's as good a place, I suppose, as you could find. But it always gave me the horrors with its spikey wall round the grounds, and general air of something hidden away. Either I'm oversensitive, Dinny, or this particular affliction does seem to me too dreadful."

Dinny squeezed his arm. "So it does to me. How did he get away?"

"He'd been so normal that they weren't at all on their guard—he seems to have said he was going to lie down, and slipped out during lunch time. He must have noticed that some tradesman came at a certain time every day, for he slid out when the lodge-keeper was taking in parcels; he walked to the station and took the first train. It's only twenty miles. He'll have been in town before they found out he was gone. I'm going down there to-morrow."

"Poor Uncle!" said Dinny, softly.

"Well, my dear, so things go in this life. But to be torn between two horrors is not my dream."

"Was it in his family?"

Adrian nodded. "His grandfather died raving. But for the war it might never have developed in Ferse, but you can't tell. Hereditary madness? Is it fair? No, Dinny, I'm not a believer in divine mercy in any form that we humans can understand, or in any way that we would exercise it ourselves. An all-embracing creativity and power of design without beginning and without end—obviously. But—tie it to our apron-strings we can't. Think of a mad-house! One simply daren't. And see what the fact one daren't means for those poor creatures. The sensitive recoil and that leaves them mainly to the insensitive, and God help them!"

"According to you, God won't."

"God is the helping of man by man, somebody once said; at all events that's all the working version we can make of Him."

"And the Devil?"

"The harming of man by man, only I'd throw in animals."

"Pure Shelley, Uncle."

"Might be a lot worse. But I become a wicked Uncle, corrupting the orthodoxy of Youth."

"You can't corrupt what is not, dear. Here's Oakley Street. Would you like me to go and ask Diana if she wants anything?"

"Wouldn't I? I'll wait for you at this corner, Dinny; and thank you ever so."

Dinny walked swiftly, looking neither to right nor left, and rang the bell. The same maid answered it.

"I don't want to come in, but could you find out for me quietly from Mrs. Ferse whether she's all right, or whether she wants anything? And will you tell her that I'm at Mrs. Michael Mont's, and am ready to come at any moment, and to stay if she'd like me."

While the maid was gone upstairs she strained her ears, but no sound reached them till the maid came back.

"Mrs. Ferse says, Miss, to thank you very heartily, and to say she won't fail to send for you if she needs you. She's all right at present, Miss; but, oh dear! we *are* put about, hoping for the best. And she sends her love, Miss; and Mr. Cherrell's not to worry."

"Thank you," said Dinny: "Give her our love and say there we are—all ready."

Then, swiftly, looking neither to left nor right, she returned to Adrian. The message repeated, they walked on.

"Hanging in the wind," said Adrian, "is there anything more dreadful? And how long—oh, Lord! How long? But as she says, we mustn't worry," and he uttered an unhappy little laugh. It began to grow dusk, and in that comfortless light, neither day, nor night, the ragged ends of the streets and bridges seemed bleak and unmeaning. Twilight passed, and with the lamps form began again and contours softened.

"Dinny, my dear," said Adrian, "I'm not fit to walk with; we'd better get back."

"Come and dine at Michael's then, Uncle—do!"

Adrian shook his head.

"Skeletons should not be at feasts. I don't know how to abide myself, as your Nurse used to say, I'm sure."

"She did not; she was Scotch. Is Ferse a Scottish name?"

"May have been originally. But Ferse came from West Sussex, somewhere in the Downs—an old family."

"Do you think old families are queer?"

"I don't see why. When there's a case of queerness in an old family, it's conspicuous of course, instead of just passing without notice. Old families are not inbred like village-folk." By instinct for what might distract him, Dinny went on:

"Do you think age in families has any points to it at all, Uncle?"

"What is age? All families are equally old, in one sense. But if you're thinking of quality due to mating for generations within a certain caste, well, I don't know—there's certainly 'good breeding' in the sense that you'd apply it to dogs or horses, but you can get that in any favourable physical circumstances—in the dales, by the sea; wherever conditions are good. Sound stock breeds sound stock—that's obvious. I know villages in the very North of Italy where there isn't a person of rank, and yet not one without beauty and a look of breeding. But when you come to breeding from people with genius or those exceptional qualities which bring men to the front, I'm very doubtful whether you don't get distortion rather than symmetry. Families with military or naval origin and tradition have the best chance, perhaps—good physique and not too much brain; but Science and the Law and Business are very distorting. No! where I think 'old' families may have a pull is in the more definite sense of direction their children get in growing up, a set tradition, a set objective; also perhaps to a better chance in the marriage market; and in most cases to more country life, and more encouragement to taking their own line and more practice in taking it. What's talked of as 'breeding' in humans is an attribute of mind rather than of body. What one thinks and feels is mainly due to tradition, habit and education. But I'm boring you, my dear."

"No, no, Uncle; I'm terribly interested. You believe then in the passing on of an attitude to life rather than in blood."

"Yes, but the two are very mixed."

"And do you think 'oldness' is going out and soon nothing will be handed on?"

"I wonder. Tradition is extraordinarily strong, and in this country there's a lot of machinery to keep it alive. You see, there are such a tremendous lot of directive jobs to be done; and the people most fit for such jobs are those who, as children, have had most practice in taking their own line, been taught not to gas about themselves, and to do things because it's their duty. It's they, for instance, who run the Services, and they'll go on running them, I expect. But privilege is only justified nowadays by running till you drop."

"A good many," said Dinny, "seem to drop first, and then do the running. Well, here we are again, at Fleur's. Now do come in, Uncle! If Diana did want anything you'd be on the spot."

"Very well, my dear, and bless you—you got me on a subject I often think about. Serpent!"

CHAPTER 18

By PERTINACIOUS USE of the telephone, Jean had discovered Hubert at 'The Coffee House' and learned his news. She passed Dinny and Adrian as they were coming in.

"Whither away?"

"Shan't be long," said Jean, and walked round the corner.

Her knowledge of London was small, and she hailed the first cab. Arriving in Eaton Square before a mansion of large and dreary appearance, she dismissed the cab and rang the bell.

"Lord Saxenden in Town?"

"Yes, my lady, but he's not in."

"When will he be in?"

"His lordship will be in to dinner, but——"

"Then I'll wait."

"Excuse me—my lady——"

"Not my lady," said Jean, handing him a card; "but he'll see me, all the same."

The man struggled a moment, received a look straight between the eyes, and said:

"Will you come in here, my—Miss?"

Jean went. The little room was barren except for gilt-edged chairs of the Empire period, a chandelier, and two marble-topped console tables.

"Please give him my card the moment he comes in."

The man seemed to rally.

"His Lordship will be pressed for time, Miss."

"Not more than I am, don't worry about that." And on a gilt-edged chair she sat down. The man withdrew. With her eyes now on the darkening Square, now on a marble and gilt clock, she sat slim, trim, vigorous, interlacing the long fingers of browned hands from which she had removed her gloves. The man came in again, and drew the curtains.

"You wouldn't," he said, "like to leave a message, Miss, or write a note?"

"Thank you, no."

He stood a moment, looking at her as if debating whether she was armed.

"Miss Tasburgh?" he said.

"Tas*borough*," answered Jean. "Lord Saxenden knows me," and raised her eyes.

"Quite so, Miss," said the man, hastily, and again withdrew.

The clock's hands crept on to seven before she heard voices in the hall. A moment later the door was opened and Lord Saxenden came in with her card in his hand, and a face on which his past, present, and future seemed to agree.

"Pleasure!" he said: "A pleasure."

Jean raised her eyes, and the thought went through her: 'Purring stock-fish.' She extended her hand.

"It's terribly nice of you to see me."

"Not at all."

"I wanted to tell you of my engagement to Hubert Cherrell—you remember his sister at the Monts. Have you heard of this absurd request for his extradition? It's too silly for words—the shooting was in pure self-defence—he's got a most terrible scar he could show you at any time."

Lord Saxenden murmured something inaudible. His eyes had become somewhat frosted.

"So you see, I wanted to ask you to put a stop to it. I know you have the power."

"Power? Not a bit—none at all."

Jean smiled.

"Of course you have the power. Everybody knows that. This means such a lot to me."

"But you weren't engaged, were you, the other night?"

"No."

"Very sudden!"

"Aren't all engagements sudden?" She could not perhaps realise the impact of her news on a man over fifty who had entered the room with at all events vague hopes of having made an impression on Youth; but she did realise that she was not all that he had thought her, and that he was not all that she had thought him. A wary and polite look had come over his face.

'More hard-boiled than I imagined,' was her reflexion. And changing her tone, she said coldly: "After all, Captain Cherrell is a D.S.O. and one of you. Englishmen don't let each other down, do they? Especially when they've been to the same school."

This remarkably astute utterance, at that disillusioned moment, impressed him who had been 'Snubby Bantham.'

"Oh!" he said: "Was he there, too?"

"Yes. And you know what a time he had on that expedition. Dinny read you some of his diary."

The colour deepened in his face, and he said with sudden exasperation: "You young ladies seem to think I've nothing to do but meddle in things that don't concern me. Extradition is a legal job."

Jean looked up through her lashes, and the unhappy peer moved as if to duck his head.

"What can I do?" he said, gruffly. "They wouldn't listen to me."

"Try," said Jean. "Some men are always listened to."

Lord Saxenden's eyes bulged slightly.

"You say he's got a scar. Where?"

Jean pushed up the sleeve on her left arm.

"From here to here. He shot as the man came on again."

"H'm!"

Looking intently at the arm, he repeated that profound remark and there was silence, till Jean said suddenly: "Would *you* like to be extradited, Lord Saxenden?"

He made an impatient movement.

"But this is an official matter, young lady."

Jean looked at him again.

"Is it really true that no influence is ever brought to bear on anybody about anything?"

He laughed.

"Come and lunch with me at the Piedmont Grill the day after tomorrow —no, the day after that, and I'll let you know if I've been able to do anything."

Jean knew well when to stop; never in parish meetings did she talk on. She held out her hand: "Thank you ever so. One-thirty?"

Lord Saxenden gave her an astonished nod. This young woman had a directness which appealed to one whose life was passed among matters conspicuous for the lack of it.

"Good-bye!" she said.

"Good-bye, Miss Tasburgh; congratulations."

"Thank you. That will depend on you, won't it?" And before he could answer she was through the door. She walked back, her mind not in a whirl. She thought clearly and quickly, with a natural distrust of leaving things to others. She must see Hubert that very night; and, on getting in, she went at once to the telephone again and rang up 'The Coffee House.'

"Is that you, Hubert? Jean speaking."

"Yes, darling."

"Come here after dinner. I must see you."

"About nine?"

"Yes. My love to you. That's all." And she cut off.

She stood for a moment before going up to dress, as if to endorse that simile of 'leopardess.' She looked, indeed, like Youth stalking its own future—lithe, intent, not to be deviated, in Fleur's finished and stylistic drawing-room as much at home and yet as foreign to its atmosphere as a cat might be.

Dinner, when any of the diners have cause for really serious anxiety and the others know of it, is conspicuous for avoidance of all but quick-fire conversation. Nobody touched on the Ferse topic, and Adrian left as soon as he had drunk his coffee. Dinny saw him out.

"Good-night, Uncle dear. I shall sleep with my emergency suitcase; one can always get a taxi here at a moment's notice. Promise me not to worry."

Adrian smiled, but he looked haggard. Jean met her coming from the door and told her the fresh news of Hubert. Her first feeling, of complete dismay, was succeeded by burning indignation.

"What utter ruffianism!"

"Yes," said Jean. "Hubert's coming in a minute or two, and I want him to myself."

"Take him up to Michael's study, then. I'll go and tell Michael. Parliament ought to know; only," she added, "it's not sitting. It only seems to sit when it oughtn't to."

Jean waited in the hall to let Hubert in. When he had gone up with her to that room whose walls were covered with the graven witticisms of the last three generations, she put him into Michael's most comfortable chair, and sat down on his knee. Thus, with her arm round his neck, and her lips more or less to his, she stayed for some minutes.

"That'll do," she said, rising, and lighting cigarettes. "This extradition business isn't going to come to anything, Hubert."

"But suppose it does."

"It won't. But if it does—all the more reason for our being married at once."

"My darling girl, I can't possibly."

"You must. You don't suppose that if you *were extradited*—which is absurd—I shouldn't go too. Of course I should, and by the same boat—married or not."

Hubert looked at her.

"You're a marvel," he said, "but——"

"Oh! yes, I know. Your father, and your chivalry, and your desire to make me unhappy for my own good, and all that. I've seen your Uncle Hilary. He's ready to do it; he's a padre and a man of real experience. Now, look here—we'll tell him of this development, and if he'll still do it, we'll be done. We'll go to him together to-morrow morning."

"But——"

"But! Surely you can trust him; he strikes me as a real person."

"He is," said Hubert; "no one more so."

"Very well then; that's settled. Now you can kiss me again." And she resumed her position on his knee. So, but for her acute sense of hearing, they would have been surprised. She was, however, examining the White Monkey on the wall, and Hubert was taking out his cigarette case, when Dinny opened the door.

"This monkey is frightfully good," said Jean. "We're going to be married, Dinny, in spite of this new nonsense—that is, if your Uncle Hilary still will. You can come with us to him again to-morrow morning, if you like."

Dinny looked at Hubert, who had risen.

"She's hopeless," he said: "I can't do anything with her."

"And you can't do anything without her. Imagine! He thought that if the worst came to the worst and he was sent out to be tried, that I shouldn't be going too. Men really are terribly like babies. Well, Dinny?"

"I'm glad."

"It depends on Uncle Hilary," said Hubert; "you understand that, Jean."

"Yes. He's in touch with real life, and what he says shall go. Come for us at ten to-morrow. Turn your back, Dinny. I'll give him one kiss, and then he must be off."

Dinny turned her back.

"Now," said Jean. They went down; and soon after, the girls went up to bed. Their rooms were next each other, and furnished with all Fleur's taste. They talked a little, embraced and parted. Dinny dawdled over her undressing.

The quiet Square, inhabited for the most part by Members of Parliament away on holiday, had few lights in the windows of its houses; no wind stirred the dark branches of the trees; through her open window came air that had no night sweetness; and rumbling noises of the Town kept alive in her the tingling sensations of that long day.

'I couldn't live with Jean,' she thought, 'but,' she added with the greater justice, 'Hubert could. He needs that sort of thing.' And she smiled wryly, mocking her sense of having been supplanted. Once in bed she lay, thinking of Adrian's fear and dismay, of Diana, and that poor wretch, her husband—longing for her—shut off from everyone. In the darkness she seemed to see his eyes flickering, burning and intense; the eyes of a being that yearned to be at home, at rest, and could not be. She drew the bedclothes up to her own eyes, and over and over, for comfort, repeated to herself the nursery rhyme:

> "Mary, Mary, quite contrary,
> How does your garden grow?
> Silver bells and cockle shells
> And pretty girls all of a row!"

CHAPTER 19

IF YOU HAD examined Hilary Cherrell, Vicar of St. Augustine's-in-the-Meads in the privacy that lies behind all appearance, all spoken words, even all human gesture, you would have found that he did not really believe his faithful activity was leading anywhere. But to 'serve' was bred into his blood and bone, as they serve, that is, who lead and direct. As a setter dog, untrained, taken for a walk, will instantly begin to range, as a Dalmatian dog, taken out riding, will follow from the first under the heels of the horse, so was it bred into Hilary, coming of families who, for generations had manned the Services, to wear himself out, leading, directing and doing things for the people round him, without conviction that in his leadership or ministrations he was more than marking the time of his own duty. In an age when doubt obscured everything and the temptation to sneer at caste and tradition was irresistible, he illustrated an 'order' bred to go on doing its job, not because it saw benefit to others, not because it sighted advantage to self, but because to turn tail on the job was equivalent to desertion. Hilary never dreamed of justifying his 'order' or explaining the servitude to which his father the diplomat, his uncle the Bishop, his brothers the soldier, the 'curator,' and the judge (for Lionel had just been appointed) were, in their different ways, committed. He thought of them and himself as just 'plugging along.' Besides, each of his activities had some specious advantage which he could point to, but which, in his heart, he suspected of being graven on paper rather than on stone.

He had dealt with a manifold correspondence when, at nine-thirty on the morning after the reappearance of Ferse, Adrian entered his somewhat threadbare study. Among Adrian's numerous male friends Hilary alone understood and appreciated his brother's feelings and position. There were but two years between them in age, they had been fast chums as boys; were both mountaineers, accustomed in prewar days to each other's company in awkward ascents and descents still more awkward; had both been to the war, Hilary as Padre in France, Adrian, who spoke Arabic, on liaison work in the East; and they had very different temperaments, always an advantage to abiding comradeship. There was no need of spiritual discovery between them, and they went at once into Committee of Ways and Means.

"Any news this morning?" asked Hilary.

"Dinny reports all quiet; but sooner or later the strain of being in the same house is bound to break down his control. For the moment the feeling of being home and free may be enough; but I don't give that more than a week. I'm going down to the Home, but they'll know no more than we."

"Forgive me, old man, but normal life with her would be best."

Adrian's face quivered.

"It's beyond human power, Hilary. There's something about such a relationship too cruel for words. It shouldn't be asked of a woman."

"Unless the poor fellow's going to stay sane."

"The decision's not for you, or me, or him—it's for her; it's more than anyone ought to have to bear. Don't forget what she went through before he went into the Home. He ought to be got out of the house, Hilary."

"It would be simpler if she took asylum."

"Who would give it her, except myself, and that would send him over the edge again for a certainty."

"If she could put up with the conditions here, we could take her," said Hilary.

"But the children?"

"We could squeeze them in. But to leave him alone and idle wouldn't help him to stay sane. Could he do any work?"

"I don't suppose he could. Four years of that would rot any man. And who'd give him a job? If I could get him to come to me!"

"Dinny and that other young woman said that he looks and talks all right."

"In a way he does. Those people down there may have some suggestion."

Hilary took his brother's arm.

"Old boy, it's ghastly for you. But ten to one it won't be so bad as we think. I'll talk to May, and if, after you've seen those people, you think asylum here is the best thing for Diana—offer it."

Adrian pressed the hand within his arm.

"I'll get off now and catch my train."

Left to himself Hilary stood frowning. He had seen in his time so much of the inscrutability of Providence, that he had given up classing it as benevolent even in his sermons. On the other hand he had seen many people by sheer tenacity defeat many misfortunes, and many other people, defeated by their misfortunes, live well enough on them afterwards; he was convinced therefore, that misery was overrated, and that what was lost was usually won. The thing was to keep going and not worry. At this moment he received his second visitor, the girl Millicent Pole, who, though acquitted, had lost her job at Petter and Poplin's; notoriety not being dispelled by legal innocence.

She came, by appointment, in a neat blue dress, and all her money, as it were, in her stockings, and stood waiting to be catechised.

"Well, Millie, how's your sister?"

"She went back yesterday, Mr. Cherrell."

"Was she fit to go?"

"I don't think so, but she said if she didn't, she'd likely lose her job, too."

"I don't see that."

"She said that if she stayed away any longer they'd think we was in *that* together."

"Well, and what about *you*? Would you like to go into the country?"

"Oh, no."

Hilary contemplated her. A pretty girl, with a pretty figure and ankles, and an easy-going mouth; it looked to him, frankly, as if she ought to be married.

"Got a young man, Millie?"

The girl smiled.

"Not very special, Sir."

"Not special enough to get married?"

"He don't want to, so far as I can see."

"Do you?"

"I'm not in a hurry."

"Well, have you any views?"

"I'd like—well, I'd like to be a mannykin?"

"I daresay. Have Petters given you a reference?"

"Yes, and they said they were sorry I had to go; but being so much in the papers the other girls——"

"Yes. Now Millie, you got yourself into that scrape, you know. I stood up for you because you were hard pressed, but I'm not blind. You've got to promise me that you won't do that again; it's the first step to blue ruin."

The girl made just the answer he expected—none.

"I'm going to turn you over to my wife now. Consult with her, and if you can't get a job like your old one, we might give you some quick training, and get you a post as a waitress. How would that suit you?"

"I wouldn't mind that."

She gave him a look half-shy, half-smiling; and Hilary thought: 'Faces like that ought to be endowed by the State; there's no other way to keep them safe.'

"Shake hands, Millie, and remember what I said. Your mother and father were friends of mine, and you're going to remain a credit to them."

"Yes, Mr. Cherrell."

'You bet!' thought Hilary, and led her into the dining-room opposite, where his wife was working a typing machine. Back in his study he pulled out a drawer of his bureau and prepared to wrestle with accounts, for if there were a place where money was of more importance than in this slum centre of a Christendom whose religion scorns money, Hilary had yet to meet with it.

'The lilies of the field,' he thought, 'toil not, neither do they spin, but they beg all right. How the deuce am I going to get enough to keep the

Institute going over the year?' The problem had not been solved when the maid said:

"Captain and Miss Cherrell, and Miss Tasburgh."

'Phew!' he thought: 'They don't let grass grow.'

He had not seen his nephew since his return from the Hallorsen Expedition, and was struck by the darkened and aged look of his face.

"Congratulations, old man," he said. "I heard something of your aspiration, yesterday."

"Uncle," said Dinny, "prepare for the rôle of Solomon."

"Solomon's reputation for wisdom, my irreverent niece, is perhaps the thinnest in history. Consider the number of his wives. Well?"

"Uncle Hilary," said Hubert: "I've had news that a warrant may be issued for my extradition, over that muleteer I shot. Jean wants the marriage at once in spite of that——"

"Because of that," put in Jean.

"I say it's too chancey altogether; and not fair to her. But we agreed to put it to you, and abide by your judgment."

"Thank you," murmured Hilary; "and why to me?"

"Because," said Dinny, "you have to make more decisions-while-they-wait than anybody, except police magistrates."

Hilary grimaced. "With your knowledge of Scripture, Dinny, you might have remembered the camel and the last straw. However——!" And he looked from Jean to Hubert and back again.

"Nothing can possibly be gained by waiting," said Jean; "because if they took him I should go out too, anyway."

"You would?"

"Of course."

"Could you prevent that, Hubert?"

"No, I don't suppose I could."

"Am I dealing, young people, with a case of love at first sight?" Neither of them answered, but Dinny said:

"Very much so; I could see it from the croquet lawn at Lippinghall."

Hilary nodded. "Well, that's not against you; it happened to me and I've never regretted it. Is your extradition really likely, Hubert?"

"No," said Jean.

"Hubert?"

"I don't know; Father's worried, but various people are doing their best. I've got this scar, you know," and he drew up his sleeve.

Hilary nodded. "That's a mercy."

Hubert grinned. "It wasn't at the time, in that climate, I can tell you."

"Have you got the licence?"

"Not yet."

"Get it, then. I'll turn you off."

"Really?"

"Yes, I may be wrong, but I don't think so."

"You aren't." And Jean seized his hand. "Will tomorrow at two o'clock be all right for you, Mr. Cherrell?"

"Let me look at my book." He looked at it and nodded.

"Splendid!" cried Jean. "Now Hubert, you and I will go and get it."

"I'm frightfully obliged to you, Uncle," said Hubert; "if you really think it's not rotten of me."

"My dear boy," said Hilary, "when you take up with a young woman like Jean here, you must expect this sort of thing. *Au revoir,* and God bless you both!"

When they had gone out, he turned to Dinny: "I'm much touched, Dinny. That was a charming compliment. Who thought of it?"

"Jean."

"Then she's either a very good or a very bad judge of character. I wonder which. That was quick work. It was ten five when you came in, it's now ten fourteen; I don't know when I've disposed of two lives in a shorter time. There's nothing wrong about the Tasburghs, is there?"

"No, they seem rather sudden, that's all."

"On the whole," said Hilary, "I like them sudden. It generally means sand."

"The Zeebrugge touch."

"Ah! Yes, there's a sailor brother, isn't there?"

Dinny's eyelids fluttered.

"Has he laid himself alongside yet?"

"Several times."

"And?"

"*I'm* not sudden, Uncle."

"Backer and filler?"

"Especially backer."

Hilary smiled affectionately at his favourite niece: "Blue eye true eye. I'll marry you off yet, Dinny. Excuse me now, I have to see a man who's in trouble with the hire-purchase system. He's got in and he can't get out—goes swimming about like a dog in a pond with a high bank. By the way, the girl you saw in Court the other day is in there with your Aunt. Like another look at her? She is, I fear, what we call an insoluble problem, which being interpreted means a bit of human nature. Have a shot at solving her."

"I should love to, but she wouldn't."

"I don't know that. As young woman to young woman you might get quite a lot of change out of her, and most of it bad, I shouldn't wonder. That," he added, "is cynical. Cynicism's a relief."

"It must be, Uncle."

"It's where the Roman Catholics have a pull over us. Well, good-bye, my dear. See you to-morrow at the execution."

Locking up his accounts, Hilary followed her into the hall; opening the door of the dining-room, he said: "My Love, here's Dinny! I'll be back to lunch," and went out, hatless.

CHAPTER 20

TOWARDS SOUTH SQUARE, where Fleur was to be asked to give another reference; the girls left the Vicarage together.

"I'm afraid," said Dinny, overcoming her shyness, "that I should want to take it out of somebody, if I were you. I can't see why you should have lost your place." She could see the girl scrutinising her askance, as if trying to make up her mind whether or no to say what was in it.

"I got meself talked about," she said, at last.

"Yes, I happened to come into the Court the day you were acquitted. I thought it brutal to make you stand there."

"I reely did speak to a man," said the girl, surprisingly, "I wouldn't tell Mr. Cherrell, but I did. I was just fed-up with wanting money. D'you think it was bad of me?"

"Well, personally, I should have to want more than money before I did it."

"You never have wanted money—not reely."

"I suppose you're right, although I've never had much."

"It's better than stealin'," said the girl, grimly: "after all, what is it? You can forget about it. At least, that's what I thought. Nobody thinks the worse of a man or does anything to him for it. But you won't tell Mrs. Mont what I'm telling you?"

"Of course not. Had things been going very badly?"

"Shockin'. Me and my sister make just enough when we're in full work. But she was ill five weeks, and on the top of that I lost my purse one day, with thirty bob in it. That wasn't my fault, anyway."

"Wretched luck."

"Rotten! If I'd been a reel one d'you think they'd have spotted me—it was just my being green. I bet girls in high life have no trouble that way when they're hard up."

"Well," said Dinny, "I suppose there are girls not above helping out their incomes in all sorts of ways. All the same, I think that kind of thing ought only to go with affection; but I expect I'm old-fashioned."

The girl turned another long and this time almost admiring look on her.

"You're a lady, Miss. I must say I should like to be one myself, but what you're born you stay."

Dinny wriggled. "Oh! Bother that word! The best ladies I've known are old cottage women in the country."

"Reely?"

"Yes. And I think some of the girls in London shops are the equal of anyone."

"Well, there is some awful nice girls, I must say. My sister is much better than me. She'd never 'ave done a thing like that. Your uncle said something I shall remember, but I can't never depend on myself. I'm one to like pleasure if I can get it; and why not?"

"The point is rather: What is pleasure? A casual man can't possibly be pleasure. He'd be the very opposite."

The girl nodded.

"That's true enough. But when you're bein' chivied about for want of money you're willin' to put up with things you wouldn't otherwise. You take my word for that."

It was Dinny's turn to nod.

"My uncle's a nice man, don't you think?"

"He's a gentleman—never comes religion over you. And he'll always put his hand in his pocket, if there's anything there."

"That's not often, I should think," said Dinny; "my family is pretty poor."

"It isn't money makes the gentleman."

Dinny heard the remark without enthusiasm; she seemed, indeed, to have heard it before. "We'd better take a 'bus now," she said.

The day was sunny, and they got on the top. "D'you like this new Regent Street?" asked Dinny.

"Oh yes! I think it's fine."

"Didn't you like the old street better?"

"No. It was so dull and yellow, and all the same."

"But unlike any other street, and the regularity suited the curve."

The girl seemed to perceive that a question of taste was concerned; she hesitated, then said assertively:

"It's much brighter now, I think. Things seem to move more—not so formal-like."

"Ah!"

"I do like the top of a 'bus," continued the girl; "you can see such a lot. Life does go on, don't it?"

In the girl's cockney-fied voice, those words hit Dinny a sort of blow. What was her own life but a cut and dried affair? What risks or adventures did it contain? Life for people who depended on their jobs was vastly more adventurous. Her own job so far had been to have no job. And, thinking of Jean, she said: "I'm afraid I live a very hum-drum life. I always seem to be waiting for things."

The girl again stole a sideway look.

"Why, you must have lots of fun, pretty like you are!"

"Pretty? My nose turns up."

"Ah! but you've got style. Style's everything. I always think you may have looks, but it's style that gets you there."

"I'd rather have looks."

"Oh! no. Anyone can be a good-looker."

"But not many are," and with a glance at the girl's profile Dinny added: "You're lucky, yourself."

The girl bridled.

"I told Mr. Cherrell I'd like to be a mannykin, but he didn't seem to fall for it."

"I'm afraid I think that of all inane pursuits that's the worst. Dressing up for a lot of disgruntled women!"

"Someone's got to do it," said the girl, defiantly; "I like wearing clothes meself. But you need interest to get a thing like that. Perhaps Mrs. Mont'll speak for me. My! Wouldn't you make a mannykin, with your style, Miss, and slim."

Dinny laughed. The 'bus had halted at the Westminster end of Whitehall.

"We get off here. Ever been in Westminster Abbey?"

"No."

"Perhaps you'd like a look before they pull it down and put up flats or a Cinema."

"Are they reely goin' to?"

"I fancy it's only in the back of their minds so far. At present they talk about restoring it."

"It's a big place," said the girl, but under the walls a silence fell on her, which remained unbroken when they passed within. Dinny watched her, as with chin uplifted she contemplated the statue to Chatham and its neighbour.

"Who's the old beaver with no clothes on?"

"Neptune. He's a symbol. Britannia rules the waves, you know."

"Oh!" and they moved on till the full proportions of the old Museum were better disclosed.

"My! Isn't it full of things?"

"It is rather an Old Curiosity Shop. They've got all English history here, you know."

"It's awful dark. The pillars look dirty, don't they?"

"Shall we just have a look at the Poets' Corner?" said Dinny.

"What's that?"

"Where they bury great writers."

"Because they wrote rhymes?" said the girl. "Isn't that funny?"

Dinny did not answer. She knew some of the rhymes and was uncertain. Having scrutinised a number of effigies and names which had for her a certain limited interest, and for the girl apparently none, they moved slowly down the aisle to where between two red wreaths lay the black and gold tablet to the Unknown Warrior.

"I wonder whether 'e knows," said the girl, "but I shouldn't think 'e cares, anyway; nobody knows 'is name, so 'e gets nothin' out of it."

"No. It's we who get something out of it," said Dinny, feeling the sensation in her throat with which the world rewards the Unknown Warrior.

Out in the street again the girl asked suddenly:

"Are you religious, Miss?"

"In a sort of way, I think," said Dinny, doubtingly.

"I never was taught any—Dad and Mother liked Mr. Cherrell, but they thought it was a mistake; my Dad was a Socialist, you see, and he used to say religion was part of the capitalist system. Of course we don't go to Church, in our class. We haven't time, for one thing. You've got to keep so still in Church, too. I must say I like more movement. And then, if there's a God, why is he called He? It puts me against Him, I know. Callin' God He gets girls treated as they are, I think. Since my case I've thought about that a good deal after what the Court missionary said. A he can't get on with creation without a she, anyway."

Dinny stared.

"You should have said that to my uncle. It's quite a thought."

"They say women are the equal of men now," the girl went on, "but they aren't, you know. There wasn't a girl at my place that wasn't scared of the boss. Where the money is, there's the power. And all the magistrates and judges and clergy are he's, and all the generals. They've got the whip, you see, and yet they can't do nothin' without us; and if I was Woman as a whole, I'd show 'em."

Dinny was silent. This girl was bitter from her experience, no doubt, but there was truth behind what she was saying. The Creator was bisexual, or the whole process would have ended at the start. In that was a primal equality, which she had never before quite realised. If the girl had been of her own order she would have answered, but it was impossible to be unreserved with her; and feeling herself snobbish, she fell back on irony.

"Some rebel!—as the Americans would say!"

"Of course I'm a rebel," said the girl, "after that."

"Well, here we are at Mrs. Mont's. I've got one or two things to see to, so I'll leave you with her. I hope we shall meet again." She held out her hand, the girl took it and said simply: "I've enjoyed it."

"So have I. Good luck!"

Leaving her in the hall, Dinny walked towards Oakley Street, and her mood was that of one who has failed to go as far as she has wished. She had touched on the uncharted, and recoiled. Her thoughts and feelings were like the twittering of Spring birds who have not yet shaped out their songs. That girl had roused in her some queer desire to be at grips with Life, without supplying the slightest notion of how to do it. It would be a relief even to be in love. How nice to know one's mind, as Jean and Hubert seemed at once to have known it; as Hallorsen and Alan Tasburgh had declared they knew it. Existence seemed like a Shadow Show rather than Reality. And, greatly dissatisfied, she leaned her elbows on the river parapet, above the tide that was flowing up. Religious? In a sort of way. But what way? A passage in Hubert's diary came back to her. "Anyone who believes he's going to Heaven has a pull on chaps like me. He's got a pension dangled." Was religion belief in reward? If so, it seemed vulgar. Belief in goodness for the sake of goodness, because goodness was beautiful, like a perfect flower, a starry night, a lovely tune! Uncle Hilary did a difficult job well for the sake of doing it well. Was he religious? She must ask him. A voice at her side said:

"Dinny!"

She turned with a start, to see Alan Tasburgh standing there with a broad grin on his face.

"I went to Oakley Street to ask for you and Jean; they told me you were at the Monts. I was on my way there, and here you are, stupendous luck!"

"I was wondering," said Dinny, "whether I'm religious."

"How queer! So was I!"

"D'you mean whether *you* were or whether *I* was?"

"As a matter of fact I look on us as one person."

"Do you? Well, is one religious?"

"At a pinch."

"Did you hear the news at Oakley Street?"

"No."

"Captain Ferse is back there."

"Cripes!"

"Precisely what everybody is saying! Did you see Diana?"

"No; only the maid—seemed a bit flustered. Is the poor chap still cracked?"

"No; but it's awful for Diana."

"She ought to be got away."

"I'm going to stay there," said Dinny, suddenly, "if she'll have me."

"I don't like the idea of that."

"I daresay not; but I'm going to."

"Why? You don't know her so very well."

"I'm sick of scrimshanking."

Young Tasburgh stared.

"I don't understand."

"The sheltered life has not come your way. I want to begin to earn my corn."

"Then marry me."

"Really, Alan, I never met anyone with so few ideas."

"Better to have good ideas than many."

Dinny walked on. "I'm going to Oakley Street now."

They went along in silence till young Tasburgh said gravely:

"What's biting you, my very dear?"

"My own nature; it doesn't seem able to make trouble enough for me."

"I could do that for you perfectly."

"I am serious, Alan."

"That's good. Until you are serious you will never marry me. But why do you want to be bitten?"

Dinny shrugged. "I seem to have an attack of Longfellow: 'Life is real, life is earnest'; I suppose you can't realise that being a daughter in the country doesn't amount to very much."

"I won't say what I was going to say."

"Oh, do!"

"That's easily cured. Become a mother in a town."

"This is where they used to blush," sighed Dinny. "I don't want to turn everything into a joke, but it seems I do."

Young Tasburgh slipped his hand through her arm.

"If you can turn being the wife of a sailor into a joke, you will be the first."

Dinny smiled. "I'm not going to marry anyone, till it hurts not to. I know myself well enough for that."

"All right, Dinny; I won't worry you."

They moved on in silence; at the corner of Oakley Street she stopped.

"Now, Alan, don't come any further."

"I shall turn up at the Monts this evening and discover what's happened to you. And if you want anything done—mind, anything—about Ferse, you've only to 'phone me at the Club. Here's the number." He pencilled it on a card and handed it to her.

"Shall you be at Jean's wedding to-morrow?"

"Sure thing! I give her away. I only wish——"

"Good-bye!" said Dinny.

CHAPTER 21

SHE HAD PARTED from the young man lightly, but she stood on the door-step with nerves taut as fiddlestrings. Never having come into contact with mental trouble, her thought of it was the more scaring. The same elderly maid admitted her. Mrs. Ferse was with Captain Ferse, and would Miss Cherrell come up to the drawing-room? Where Jean had been locked in Dinny waited some time. Sheila came in, said: "Hallo! Are you waiting for Muvver?" and went out again. When Diana did appear her face wore an expression as if she were trying to collect the evidence of her own feelings.

"Forgive me, my dear, I was going through papers. I'm trying my best to treat him as if nothing had happened." Dinny went up to her and stood stroking her arm.

"But it can't last, Dinny; it won't last. I can see it won't last."

"Let me come and stay. You can put it that it was arranged before."

"But Dinny, it may be rather horrible. I don't know what to do with him. He dreads going out, or meeting people. And yet he won't hear of going away where nobody knows; and he won't see a doctor, or take any advice. He won't see anyone."

"He'll see me, and that'll accustom him. I expect it's only the first few days. Shall I go off now and get my things?"

"If you *are* going to be an angel, do!"

"I'll let Uncle Adrian know before I come back; he went down to the Home this morning."

Diana crossed to the window and stood there with her back to Dinny. Suddenly she turned:

"I've made up my mind, Dinny: I won't let him down in any way. If there's anything I can do to give him a chance, I'm going to do it."

"Bless you!" said Dinny. "I'll help!" And, not trusting either Diana or herself further, she went out and down the stairs. Outside, in passing the dining-room window, she was again conscious of a face with eyes burn-ing alive, watching her go by. A feeling of tragic unfairness was with her all the way back to South Square.

Fleur said at lunch:

"It's no good fashing yourself till something happens, Dinny. It's lucky that Adrian's been such a saint. But this is a very good instance of how little the Law can help. Suppose Diana could have got free, it wouldn't have prevented Ferse coming straight back to her, or her feeling about him as she does. The Law can't touch the human side of anything. Is Diana in love with Adrian?"

"I don't think so."

"Are you sure?"

"No, I'm not. I find it difficult enough to know what goes on inside myself."

"Which reminds me that your American rang up. He wants to call."

"Well, he can. But I shall be at Oakley Street."

Fleur gave her a shrewd look.

"Am I to back the sailor, then?"

"No. Put your money on Old Maid."

"My dear! Unthinkable."

"I don't see what one gains by marriage."

Fleur answered with a little hard smile.

"We can't stand still, you know, Dinny. At least, we don't; it's too dull."

"You're modern, Fleur; I'm mediæval."

"Well, you *are* rather early Italian in face. But the early Italians never escaped. Entertain no flattering hopes. Sooner or later you'll be fed up with yourself, and then!"

Dinny looked at her, startled by this flash of discernment in her disillusioned cousin-in-law.

"What have *you* gained, Fleur?"

"I at least am the complete woman, my dear," Fleur answered, drily.

"Children, you mean?"

"They are possible without marriage, or so I am told, but improbable. For you, Dinny, impossible; you're controlled by an ancestral complex, really old families have an inherited tendency towards legitimacy. Without it they can't be really old, you see."

Dinny wrinkled her forehead.

"I never thought of it before, but I *should* strongly object to having an illegitimate child. By the way, did you give that girl a reference?"

"Yes. I don't see at all why she shouldn't be a mannequin. She's narrow enough. I give the boyish figure another year, at least. After that, mark my words, skirts will lengthen, and we shall go in for curves again."

"Rather degrading, isn't it?"

"How?"

"Chopping and changing shape and hair and all that."

"Good for trade. We consent to be in the hands of men in order that they may be in ours. Philosophy of vamping."

"That girl won't have much chance of keeping straight as a mannequin, will she?"

"More, I should say. She might even marry. But I always refuse to worry about my neighbour's morals. I suppose you have to keep up the pretence at Condaford, having been there since the Conquest. By the way, has your father made provision against Death Duties?"

"He's not old, Fleur."

"No, but people do die. Has he got anything besides the estate?"

"Only his pension."

"Is there plenty of timber?"

"I loathe the idea of cutting down trees. Two hundred years of shape and energy all gone in half an hour. It's revolting."

"My dear, there's generally nothing else for it, except selling, and clearing out."

"We shall manage somehow," said Dinny, shortly; "we'd never let Condaford go."

"Don't forget Jean."

Dinny sat up very straight.

"She'd never, either. The Tasburghs are just as old as we are."

"Admitted; but that's a young woman of infinite variety and go. She'll never vegetate."

"Condaford is not vegetation."

"Don't get ruffled, Dinny; I'm only thinking for the best. I don't want to see you outed, any more than I want Kit to lose Lippinghall. Michael is thoroughly unsound. He says that if he's one of the country's roots he's sorry for the country, which is silly of course. No one," added Fleur, with a sudden queer depth, "will ever know from me what pure gold Michael is." Then, seeming to notice Dinny's surprised eyes, she added: "So, I can wash out the American?"

"You can. Three thousand miles between me and Condaford—no, Ma'am!"

"Then I think you should put the poor brute out of his misery, for he confided to me that you were what he called his 'ideal.'"

"Not that again!" cried Dinny.

"Yes, indeed; and he further said that he was crazy about you."

"That means nothing."

"From a man who goes to the ends of the earth to discover the roots of civilisation it probably does. Most people would go to the ends of the earth to avoid discovering them."

"The moment this thing of Hubert's is over," said Dinny, "I will put an end to him."

"I think you'll have to take the veil to do it. You'll look very nice in the veil, Dinny, walking down the village aisle with the sailor, in a feudal atmosphere, to a German tune. May I be there to see!"

"I'm not going to marry anyone."

"Well, in the meantime shall we ring up Adrian?"

From Adrian's rooms came the message that he was expected back at four o'clock. He was asked to come on to South Square, and Dinny went up to put her things together. Coming down again at half past three, she saw on the coat 'sarcophagus' a hat whose brim she seemed to recognise. She was slinking back towards the stairs when a voice said:

"Why! This is fine! I was scared I'd missed you."

Dinny gave him her hand, and together they entered Fleur's 'parlour'; where, among the Louis Quinze furniture, he seemed absurdly male.

"I wanted to tell you, Miss Cherrell, what I've done about your brother. I've fixed it for our Consul in La Paz to get that boy Manuel to cable his sworn testimony that the Captain was attacked with a knife. If your folk here are anyway sensible, that should clear him. This fool game's got to stop if I have to go back to Bolivia myself."

"Thank you ever so, Professor."

"Why! There's nothing I wouldn't do for your brother, now. I've come to like him as if he were my own."

Those ominous words had a large simplicity, a generous warmth, which caused her to feel small and thin.

"You aren't looking at all well," he said, suddenly. "If there's anything worrying you, tell me and I'll fix it."

Dinny told him of Ferse's return.

"That lovely lady! Too bad! But maybe she's fond of him, so it'll be a relief to her mind after a time."

"I am going to stay with her."

"That's bully of you! Is this Captain Ferse dangerous?"

"We don't know yet."

He put his hand into a hip pocket and brought out a tiny automatic.

"Put that in your bag. It's the smallest made. I bought it for this country, seeing you don't go about with guns here."

Dinny laughed.

"Thank you, Professor, but it would only go off in the wrong place. And, even if there were danger, it wouldn't be fair."

"That's so! It didn't occur to me, but that's so. A man afflicted that way has every consideration due to him. But I don't like to think of you going into danger."

Remembering Fleur's exhortation, Dinny said hardily:

"Why not?"

"Because you are very precious to me."

"That's frightfully nice of you; but I think you ought to know, Professor, that I'm not in the market."

"Surely every woman's in the market till she marries."

"Some think that's when she begins to be."

"Well," said Hallorsen gravely, "I've no use for adultery myself. I want a straight deal in sex as in everything else."

"I hope you will get it."

He drew himself up. "And I want it from you. I have the honour to ask you to become Mrs. Hallorsen, and please don't say 'No' right away."

"If you want a straight deal, Professor, I must."

She saw his blue eyes film as if with pain, and felt sorry. He came a little closer, looking as it seemed to her, enormous, and she gave a shiver.

"Is it my nationality?"

"I don't know what it is."

"Or the grouch you had against me over your brother?"

"I don't know."

"Can't I hope?"

"No. I am flattered, and grateful, believe me. But no."

"Pardon me! Is there another man?"

Dinny shook her head.

Hallorsen stood very still; his face wore a puzzled expression, then cleared suddenly.

"I judge," he said, "I haven't done enough for you. I'll have to serve a bit."

"I'm not worth service. It's simply that I don't feel like that towards you."

"I have clean hands and a clean heart."

"I'm sure you have; I admire you, Professor, but I should never love you."

Hallorsen drew back again to his original distance, as if distrusting his impulses. He gave her a grave bow. He looked really splendid standing there, full of simple dignity. There was a long silence, then he said:

"Well, I judge there's no use crying over spilt milk. Command me in any way. I am your very faithful servant." And, turning round, he went out.

Dinny heard the front door close with a slight choke in her throat. She felt pain at having caused him pain, but relief too, the relief one feels when something very large, simple, primitive—the sea, a thunderstorm, a bull—is no longer imminent. In front of one of Fleur's mirrors she stood despitefully, as though she had just discovered the over-refinement of her nerves. How could that great handsome, healthy creature care for one so spindly and rarefied as she looked reflected there? He could snap her off with his hands. Was that why she recoiled? The great open spaces of which he seemed a part, with his height, strength, colour, and the boom of his voice! Funny, silly perhaps—but a very real recoil! She belonged where she belonged—not to such as them, to such as him. About such juxtapositions there was even something comic. She was still standing there with a wry smile when Adrian was ushered in.

She turned to him impulsively. Sallow and worn and lined, subtle, gentle, harassed, no greater contrast could have appeared, nor any that could have better soothed her jangled nerves. Kissing him, she said:

"I waited to see you before going to stay at Diana's!"

"You *are* going, Dinny?"

"Yes. I don't believe you've had lunch or tea or anything," and she rang the bell. "Coaker, Mr. Adrian would like—"

"A brandy and soda, Coaker, thank you!"

"Now, Uncle?" she said, when he had drunk it.

"I'm afraid, Dinny, one can't set much store by what they say down there. According to them Ferse ought to go back. But why he should, so long as he acts sanely, I don't know. They queer the idea of his recovery, but they can bring nothing abnormal against him for some weeks past. I got hold of his personal attendant and questioned him. He seems a decent chap, and he thinks Ferse at the moment is as sane as himself. But— and the whole trouble lies there—he says he was like this once before for three weeks, and suddenly lapsed again. If anything really upsets him— opposition or what not—he thinks Ferse will be just as bad again as ever, perhaps worse. It's a really terrible position."

"When he's in mania is he violent?"

"Yes; a kind of gloomy violence, more against himself than anyone else."

"They're not going to do anything to get him back?"

"They can't. He went there voluntarily; I told you he hasn't been certified. How is Diana?"

"She looks tired, but lovely. She says she is going to do everything she can to give him a chance."

Adrian nodded.

"That's like her; she has wonderful pluck. And so have you, my dear. It's a great comfort to know you'll be with her. Hilary is ready to take Diana and the children if she'd go, but she won't, you say."

"Not at present, I'm sure."

Adrian sighed.

"Well, we must chance it."

"Oh! Uncle," said Dinny. "I *am* so sorry for you."

"My dear, what happens to the fifth wheel doesn't matter so long as the car runs. Don't let me keep you. You can get at me any time either at the Museum or my rooms. Good-bye and bless you! My love to her, and tell her all I've told you."

Dinny kissed him again, and soon after in a cab set forth with her things to Oakley Street.

CHAPTER 22

BOBBIE FERRAR had one of those faces which look on tempests and are never shaken; in other words, he was an ideal permanent official—so permanent that one could not conceive of the Foreign Office functioning without him. Secretaries of State might come, might go, Bobbie Ferrar remained, bland, inscrutable, and with lovely teeth. Nobody knew whether there was anything in him except an incalculable number of secrets. Of an age which refused to declare itself, short and square, with a deep soft voice, he had an appearance of complete detachment. In a dark suit with a little light line, and wearing a flower, he existed in a large ante-room wherein was almost nothing except those who came to see the Foreign Minister and instead saw Bobbie Ferrar. In fact the perfect buffer. His weakness was criminology. No murder trial of importance ever took place without the appearance, if only for half-an-hour, of Bobbie Ferrar in a seat more or less kept for him. And he preserved the records of all those trials in a specially bound edition. Perhaps the greatest testimony to his character, whatever that might be, lay in the fact that no one ever threw his acquaintanceship with nearly everybody up against him. People came to Bobbie Ferrar, not he to them. Yet why? What had he ever done that he should be 'Bobbie' Ferrar to all and sundry? Not even 'the honourable,' merely the son of a courtesy lord, affable, unfathomable, always about, he was unquestionably a last word. Without him, his flower, and his faint grin, Whitehall would have been shorn of something that made it almost human. He had been there since before the war, from which he had been retrieved just in time, some said, to prevent the whole place from losing its character, just in time, too, to stand, as it were, between England and herself. She could not become the shrill edgy hurried harridan the war had tried to make her, while his square, leisurely, be-flowered, inscrutable figure passed daily up and down between those pale considerable buildings.

He was turning over a Bulb Catalogue, on the morning of Hubert's wedding day, when the card of Sir Lawrence Mont was brought to him, followed by its owner, who said at once:

"You know what I've come about, Bobbie?"

"Completely," said Bobbie Ferrar, his eyes round, his head thrown back, his voice deep.

"Has the Marquess seen you?"

"I had breakfast with him yesterday. Isn't he amazing?"

"Our finest old boy," said Sir Lawrence. "What are you going to do about it? Old Sir Conway Cherrell was the best Ambassador to Spain you ever turned out of the shop, and this is his grandson."

"Has he really got a scar?" asked Bobbie Ferrar, through a faint grin.

"Of course he has."

"Did he really get it over that?"

"Sceptical image! Of course he did."

"Amazing!"

"Why?"

Bobbie Ferrar showed his teeth. "Who can prove it?"

"Hallorsen is getting evidence."

"It's not in our department, you know."

"No? But you can get at the Home Secretary."

"Um!" said Bobbie Ferrar, deeply.

"You can see the Bolivians about it, anyway."

"Um!" said Bobbie Ferrar still more deeply, and handed him the catalogue. "Do you know this new tulip? Complete, isn't it?"

"Now, look you, Bobbie," said Sir Lawrence, "this is my nephew; emphatically a 'good egg,' as you say, and it won't do! See!"

"The age is democratic," said Bobbie Ferrar cryptically; "it came up in the House, didn't it—flogging?"

"We can pull out the national stop if there's any more fuss there. Hallorsen has taken back his criticism. Well, I'll leave it to you; you won't commit yourself if I stay here all the morning. But you'll do your best because it really is a scandalous charge."

"Completely," said Bobbie Ferrar. "Would you like to see the Croydon murder trial? It's amazing. I've got two seats; I offered one to my Uncle. But he won't go to any trial until they bring in electrocution."

"Did the fellow do it?"

Bobbie Ferrar nodded.

"The evidence is very shaky," he added.

"Well, good-bye, Bobbie; I rely on you."

Bobbie Ferrar grinned faintly, and held out his hand.

"Good-bye," he said, through his teeth.

Sir Lawrence went westward to the Coffee House where the porter handed him a telegram: "Am marrying Jean Tasburgh two o'clock today St. Augustine's-in-the-Meads delighted to see you and Aunt Em Hubert."

Passing into the coffee room, Sir Lawrence said to the Chief Steward: "Butts, I am about to see a nephew turned off. Fortify me quickly."

Twenty minutes later he was on his way to St. Augustine's, in a cab. He arrived a few minutes before two o'clock and met Dinny going up the steps.

"You look pale and interesting, Dinny."

"I *am* pale and interesting, Uncle Lawrence."

"This proceeding appears to be somewhat sudden."

"That's Jean. I'm feeling terribly responsible. I found her for him, you see."

They entered the church and moved up to the front pews. Apart from the General, Lady Cherrell, Mrs. Hilary and Hubert there was no one except two sightseers and a verger. Someone's fingers were wandering on the organ. Sir Lawrence and Dinny took a pew to themselves.

"I'm not sorry Em isn't here," he whispered; "she still gives way. When you marry, Dinny, have 'No tears by request' on your invitation cards. What is it produces moisture at weddings? Even bailiffs weep."

"It's the veil," said Dinny; "nobody will cry to-day because there is none. Look! Fleur and Michael!"

Sir Lawrence turned his monocle on them as they came up the aisle. "Eight years since we saw them married. Take it all round, they haven't done so badly."

"No," whispered Dinny; "Fleur told me yesterday that Michael was pure gold."

"Did she? That's good. There have been times, Dinny, when I've had my doubts."

"Not about Michael."

"No, no; he's a first-rate fellow. But Fleur has fluttered their dove-cote once or twice; since her father's death, however, she's been exemplary. Here they come!"

The organ had broken into annunciation. Alan Tasburgh with Jean on his arm was coming up the aisle. Dinny admired his square and steady look. As for Jean, she seemed the very image of colour and vitality. Hubert, standing, hands behind him, as if at ease, turned as she came up, and Dinny saw his face, lined and dark, brighten as if the sun had shone on it. A chokey feeling gripped her throat. Then she saw that Hilary in his surplice had come quietly and was standing on the step.

'I do like Uncle Hilary,' she thought.

Hilary had begun to speak.

Contrary to her habit in church, Dinny listened. She waited for the word 'obey'—it did not come; she waited for the sexual allusions—they were omitted. Now Hilary was asking for the ring. Now it was on. Now he was praying. Now it was the Lord's Prayer, and they were going to the vestry. How strangely short!

She rose from her knees.

"Amazingly complete," whispered Sir Lawrence, "as Bobbie Ferrar would say. Where are they going after?"

"To the theatre. Jean wants to stay in Town. She's found a workman's flat."

"Calm before the storm. I wish that affair of Hubert's were over, Dinny."

They were coming back from the vestry now, and the organ had begun to play the Mendelssohn march. Looking at those two passing down the aisle Dinny had feelings of elation and of loss, of jealousy and of satisfaction. Then, seeing that Alan looked as if he, too, had feelings, she moved out of her pew to join Fleur and Michael; but, catching sight of Adrian near the entrance, went to him instead.

"What news, Dinny?"

"All right so far, Uncle. I am going straight back now."

With the popular instinct for experiencing emotion at second-hand a little crowd of Hilary's parishioners had gathered outside, and a squeaky cheer rose from them, as Jean and Hubert got into the brown roadster, and drove away.

"Come in this cab with me, Uncle," said Dinny.

"Does Ferse seem to mind your being there?" asked Adrian, in the cab.

"He's quite polite, just silent; his eyes are always on Diana. I'm terribly sorry for him."

Adrian nodded. "And she?"

"Wonderful; as if nothing were out of the ordinary. He won't go out, though; just stays in the dining-room—watches from there all the time."

"The world must seem to him a conspiracy. If he remains sane long enough he'll lose that feeling."

"Need he ever become insane again? Surely there are cases of complete recovery?"

"So far as I can gather, my dear, his case is not likely to be one of them. Heredity is against him, and temperament."

"I could have liked him, it's such a daring face; but his eyes *are* frightening."

"Have you seen him with the children?"

"Not yet; but they speak quite nicely and naturally about him; so he hasn't scared them, you see."

"At the Home they talked jargon to me about complexes, obsessions, repressions, dissociation—all that sort of thing, but I gathered that his case is one where fits of great gloom alternate with fits of great excitement. Lately, both have grown so much milder that he has become practically normal. What has to be watched for is the recrudescence of one or of the other. He always had a streak of revolt in him; he was up against the leadership in the war, up against democracy after the war. He'll almost certainly get up against something now he's back. If he does it will ungear him again in no time. If there's any weapon in the house, Dinny, it ought to be removed."

"I'll tell Diana."

The cab turned into the Kings Road.

"I suppose I'd better not come to the house," said Adrian, sadly.

Dinny got out, too. She stood a moment watching him, tall and rather stooping, walk away, then turned down Oakley Street, and let herself in. Ferse was in the dining-room doorway.

"Come in here," he said; "I want a talk."

In that panelled room, painted a greenish-gold, lunch had been cleared away, and on the narrow refectory table were a newspaper, a tobacco jar, and several books. Ferse drew up a chair for her and stood with his back to a fire which simulated flames. He was not looking at her, so she was able to study him as she had not yet had the chance of doing. His handsome face was uncomfortable, stiff jaw, and crisp grizzled hair set off those thirsty burning steel-blue eyes. Even his attitude, square and a-kimbo, with head thrust forward, set off those eyes. Dinny leaned back, scared and faintly smiling. He turned to her and said:

"What are people saying about me?"

"I've not heard anything: I've only been to my brother's wedding."

"Your brother Hubert? Whom has he married?"

"A girl called Jean Tasburgh. You saw her the day before yesterday."

"Oh! Ah! I locked her in."

"Yes, why?"

"She looked dangerous to me. I consented to go into that place, you know. I wasn't put there."

"Oh! I know; I knew you were there of your own accord."

"It wasn't such a bad place, but—well! How do I look?"

Dinny said softly: "You see, I never saw you before, except at a distance, but I think you look very well."

"I am well. I kept my muscles up. The fellow that looked after me saw to that."

"Did you read much?"

"Lately—yes. What do they think about me?"

At the reception of this question Dinny looked up into his face.

"How can they think about you without having seen you?"

"You mean I ought to see people?"

"I don't know anything about it, Captain Ferse. But I don't see why not. You're seeing me."

"I like *you*."

Dinny put out her hand.

"Don't say you're sorry for me," Ferse said, quickly.

"Why should I? You're perfectly all right, I'm sure."

He covered his eyes with his hand.

"I am, but how long shall I be?"

"Why not always?"

Ferse turned to the fire.

Dinny said, timidly: "If you don't worry, nothing will happen again."

Ferse spun round to her. "Have you seen much of my children?"

"Not very much."

"Any likeness to me in them?"

"No; they take after Diana."

"Thank God for that! What does Diana think about me?" This time his eyes searched hers, and Dinny realised that on her answer everything —yes, everything might depend.

"Diana is just glad."

He shook his head violently. "Not possible."

"The truth is often not possible."

"She doesn't hate me?"

"Why should she?"

"Your Uncle Adrian—what's between them? Don't just say: Nothing."

"My uncle worships her," said Dinny, quietly, "that's why they are just friends."

"Just friends?"

"Just friends."

"That's all you know, I suppose."

"I know for certain."

Ferse sighed. "You're a good sort. What would you do if you were me?"

Again Dinny felt her ruthless responsibility.

"I think I should do what Diana wanted."

"What is that?"

"I don't know. I don't think she does yet."

Ferse strode to the window and back.

"I've got to do something for poor devils like myself."

"Oh!" said Dinny, dismayed.

"I've had luck. Most people like me would have been certified, and stuck away against their will. If I'd been poor we couldn't have afforded that place. To be there was bad enough, but it was miles better than the usual run of places. I used to make my man talk. He'd seen two or three of them."

He stood silent, and Dinny thought of her uncle's words: "He'll get up against something, and that will ungear him again in no time."

Ferse went on suddenly: "If you had any other kind of job possible, would *you* take on the care of the insane? Not you, nor anyone with nerves or sensibility. A saint might, here and there, but there aren't saints enough to go round by a long chalk. No! To look after us you've got to shed the bowels of compassion, you must be made of iron, you must have a hide like leather, and no nerves. With nerves you'd be worse than the thick-skinned because you'd be jumpy, and that falls on us. It's an impasse? My God! Haven't I thought about it? And—money. No one with money ought to be sent to one of those places. Never, never! Give him his prison at home somehow—somewhere. If I hadn't known that I could come away at any time—if I hadn't hung on to that knowledge even at my worst, I wouldn't be here now—I'd be raving. God! I'd be raving! Money! And how many have money? Perhaps five in a hundred. And the other ninety-five poor devils are stuck away, willy-nilly, stuck away! I don't care how scientific, how good those places may be, as asylums go—they mean death in life. They must. People outside think we're as good as dead already—so who cares? Behind all the pretence of scientific treatment that's what they really feel. We're obscene—no longer human—the old idea of madness clings, Miss Cherrell; we're a disgrace, we've failed. Hide us away, put us underground. Do it humanely—twentieth century! Humanely! Try! You can't! Cover it all up with varnish then—varnish—that's all it is. What else can it be? Take my word for that. Take my man's word for it. He knew."

Dinny was listening, without movement. Suddenly Ferse laughed. "But we're not dead; that's the misfortune, we're not dead. If only we were! All those poor brutes—not dead—as capable of suffering in their own way as anyone else—more capable. Don't I know? And what's the remedy?" He put his hands to his head.

"To find a remedy," said Dinny, softly, "wouldn't it be wonderful?"

He stared at her.

"Thicken the varnish—that's all we do, all we shall do."

"Then why worry yourself?" sprang to Dinny's lips, but she held the words back.

"Perhaps," she said, "you will find the remedy, only that will need patience and calm."

Ferse laughed.

"You must be bored to death." And he turned away to the window.

Dinny slipped quietly out.

CHAPTER 23

In that resort of those who know—the Piedmont Grill—the knowing were in various stages of repletion, bending towards each other as if in food they had found the link between their souls. They sat, two by two, and here and there four by five, and here and there a hermit, moody or observant over a cigar, and between the tables moved trippingly the lean and nimble waiters with faces unlike their own, because they were harassed by their memories. Lord Saxenden and Jean, in a corner at the near end, had already consumed a lobster, drunk half a bottle of hock, and talked of nothing in particular, before she raised her eyes slowly from an empty claw and said:

"Well, Lord Saxenden?"

His blue stare goggled slightly at that thick-lashed glance.

"Good lobster?" he said.

"Amazing."

"I always come here when I want to be well fed. Is that partridge coming, waiter?"

"Yes, milord."

"Well, hurry with it. Try this hock, Miss Tasburgh; you're not drinking."

Jean raised her greenish glass. "I became Mrs. Hubert Cherrell yesterday. It's in the paper."

Lord Saxenden's cheeks expanded slightly with the thought: 'Now, how does that affect me? Is this young lady more amusing single or more amusing married?'

"You don't waste time," he said, his eyes exploring her, as though seeking confirmation of her changed condition. "If I'd known, I shouldn't have had the cheek to ask you to lunch without him."

"Thank you," said Jean, "he's coming along presently." And, through her lashes, she looked at him draining his glass thoughtfully.

"Have you any news for me?"

"I've seen Walter."

"Walter?"

"The Home Secretary."

"How terribly nice of you!"

132

"It was. Can't bear the fellow. Got a head like an egg, except for his hair."

"What did he say?"

"Young lady, nobody in any official department ever *says* anything. He always 'thinks it over.' Administration has to be like that."

"But of course he'll pay attention to what *you* said. What *did* you say?"

Lord Saxenden's iced eyes seemed to answer: 'Really, you know, really!' But Jean smiled; and the eyes thawed gradually.

"You're the most direct young woman I've ever come across. As a matter of fact I said: 'Stop it, Walter.'"

"How splendid!"

"He didn't like it. He's a 'just beast.'"

"Could I see him?"

Lord Saxenden began to laugh. He laughed like a man who has come across the priceless.

Jean waited for him to finish, and said:

"Then I shall."

The partridge filled the ensuing gap.

"Look here!" said Lord Saxenden, suddenly: "If you really mean that, there's one man who might wangle you an interview—Bobbie Ferrar. He used to be with Walter when he was Foreign Secretary. I'll give you a chit to Bobbie. Have a sweet?"

"No, thank you. But I *should* like some coffee, please. There's Hubert!"

Just free of the revolving cage, which formed the door, was Hubert, evidently in search of his wife.

"Bring him over here!"

Jean looked intently at her husband. His face cleared, and he came towards them.

"You've got the eye all right," murmured Lord Saxenden, rising. "How de do? You've married a remarkable wife. Have some coffee? The brandy's good, here." And taking out a card he wrote on it in a hand both neat and clear:

"Robert Ferrar, Esq., F.O., Whitehall. Dear Bobbie, do see my young friend Mrs. Hubert Charwell and get her an interview with Walter if at all possible. Saxenden."

Then, handing it to Jean, he asked the waiter for his bill.

"Hubert," said Jean, "show Lord Saxenden your scar," and, undoing the link of his cuff, she pushed up his sleeve. That livid streak stared queer and sinister above the tablecloth.

"H'm!" said Lord Saxenden: "useful wipe, that."

Hubert wriggled his arm back under cover. "She still takes liberties," he said.

Lord Saxenden paid his bill and handed Hubert a cigar.

"Forgive me if I run off now. Stay and finish your coffee. Good-bye and good luck to you both!" And, shaking their hands, he threaded his way out among the tables. The two young people gazed after him.

"Such delicacy," said Hubert, "is not his known weakness, I believe. Well, Jean?"

Jean looked up.

"What does F.O. mean?"

"Foreign Office, my country girl."

"Finish your brandy, and we'll go and see this man."

But in the courtyard a voice behind them said:

"Why! Captain! Miss Tasburgh!"

"My wife, Professor."

Hallorsen seized their hands.

"Isn't that just wonderful? I've a cablegram in my pocket, Captain, that's as good as a wedding present."

Over Hubert's shoulder, Jean read out: " 'Exonerating statement sworn by Manuel mailed stop American Consulate La Paz.' That's splendid, Professor. Will you come with us and see a man at the Foreign Office about this?"

"Surely. I don't want any grass to grow. Let's take an automobile."

Opposite to them in the cab he radiated surprised benevolence.

"You were mighty quick off the mark, Captain."

"That was Jean."

"Yes," said Hallorsen, as if she were not present, "when I met her at Lippinghall I thought she could move. Is your sister pleased?"

"Is she, Jean?"

"Rather!"

"A wonderful young lady. There's something good in low buildings. This Whitehall of yours makes me feel fine. The more sun and stars you can see from a street the more moral sense there is to the people. Were you married in a stovepipe hat, Captain?"

"No; just as I am now."

"I'm sorry about that. They seem to me so cunning; like carrying a lost cause about on your head. I believe you are of an old family, too, Mrs. Cherrell. Your habit over here of families that serve their country from father to son is inspiring, Captain."

"I hadn't thought about that."

"I had a talk with your brother, Ma'am, at Lippinghall, he informed me you'd had a sailor in your family for centuries. And I'm told that in yours, Captain, there's always been a soldier. I believe in heredity. Is this the Foreign Office?" He looked at his watch. "I'm just wondering whether that guy will be in? I've a kind of impression they do most of their business over food. We should do well to go and look at the ducks in the Park till three o'clock."

"I'll leave this card for him," said Jean.

She rejoined them quickly. "He's expected in at any minute."

"That'll be half an hour," said Hallorsen. "There's one duck here I'd like your opinion of, Captain."

Crossing the wide road to the water they were nearly run down by the sudden convergence of two cars embarrassed by unwonted space. Hubert clutched Jean convulsively. He had gone livid under his tan. The cars cleared away to right and left. Hallorsen, who had taken Jean's other arm, said with an exaggeration of his drawl:

"That just about took our paint off."

Jean said nothing.

"I sometimes wonder," continued Hallorsen, as they reached the ducks, "whether we get our money's worth out of speed. What do you say, Captain?"

Hubert shrugged. "The hours lost in going by car instead of by train are just about as many as the hours saved, anyway."

"That is so," said Hallorsen. "But flying's a real saver of time."

"Better wait for the full bill before we boast about flying."

"You're right, Captain. We're surely headed for hell. The next war will mean a pretty thin time for those who take part in it. Suppose France and Italy came to blows, there'd be no Rome, no Paris, no Florence, no Venice, no Lyons, no Milan, no Marseilles within a fortnight. They'd just be poisoned deserts. And the ships and armies maybe wouldn't have fired a shot."

"Yes. And all governments know it. I'm a soldier, but I can't see why they go on spending hundreds of millions on soldiers and sailors who'll probably never be used. You can't run armies and navies when the nerve centres have been destroyed. How long could France and Italy function if their big towns were gassed? England or Germany certainly couldn't function a week."

"Your Uncle the Curator was saying to me that at the rate Man was going he would soon be back in the fish state."

"How?"

"Why! Surely! Reversing the process of evolution—fishes, reptiles, birds, mammals. We're becoming birds again, and the result of that will soon be that we shall creep and crawl, and end up in the sea when land's uninhabitable."

"Why can't we all bar the air for war?"

"How can we bar the air?" said Jean. "Countries never trust each other. Besides, America and Russia are outside the League of Nations."

"We Americans would agree. But maybe not our Senate."

"That Senate of yours," muttered Hubert, "seems to be a pretty hard proposition."

"Why! It's like your House of Lords before a whip was taken to it in 1910. That's the duck," and Hallorsen pointed to a peculiar bird. Hubert stared at it.

"I've shot that chap in India. It's a—I've forgotten the name. We can get it from one of these boards—I shall remember if I see."

"No!" said Jean; "it's a quarter past three. He must be in by now." And, without allocating the duck, they returned to the Foreign Office.

Bobbie Ferrar's handshake was renowned. It pulled his adversary's hand up and left it there. When Jean had restored her hand, she came at once to the point. "You know about this extradition business, Mr. Ferrar?"

Bobbie Ferrar nodded.

"This is Professor Hallorsen, who was head of the expedition. Would you like to see the scar my husband has?"

"Very much," murmured Bobbie Ferrar, through his teeth.

"Show him, Hubert."

Unhappily Hubert bared his arm again.

"Amazing!" said Bobbie Ferrar: "I told Walter."

"You've seen him?"

"Sir Lawrence asked me to."

"What did Wal—the Home Secretary say?"

"Nothing. He'd seen Snubby; he doesn't like Snubby, so he's issued the order to Bow Street."

"Oh! Does that mean there will be a warrant?"

Bobbie Ferrar nodded, examining his nails.

The two young people stared at each other.

Hallorsen said, gravely:

"Can no one stop this gang?"

Bobbie Ferrar shook his head, his eyes looked very round.

Hubert rose.

"I'm sorry that I let anyone bother himself in the matter. Come along, Jean!" and with a slight bow he turned and went out. Jean followed him.

Hallorsen and Bobbie Ferrar were left confronted.

"I don't understand this country," said Hallorsen. "What ought to have been done?"

"Nothing," answered Bobbie Ferrar. "When it comes before the magistrate, bring all the evidence you can."

"We surely will. Mr. Ferrar, I am glad to have met you!"

Bobbie Ferrar grinned. His eyes looked even rounder.

CHAPTER 24

IN THE DUE COURSE of justice, Hubert was brought up at Bow Street on a warrant issued by one of its magistrates. Attending, in common with other members of the family, Dinny sat through the proceedings in a state of passive protest. The sworn evidence of six Bolivian muleteers, testifying to the shooting and to its being unprovoked; Hubert's countering statement, the exhibition of his scar, his record, and the evidence of Hallorsen, formed the material on which the magistrate was invited to come to his decision. He came to it. 'Remanded' till the arrival of the defendant's supporting evidence. That principle of British law, 'A prisoner is presumed innocent till he is proved guilty,' so constantly refuted by its practice, was then debated in regard to bail, and Dinny held her breath. The idea of Hubert, just married, being presumed innocent in a cell, while his evidence crossed the Atlantic, was unbearable. The considerable bail offered by Sir Conway and Sir Lawrence, however, was finally accepted, and with a sigh of relief she walked out, her head held high. Sir Lawrence joined her outside.

"It's lucky," he said, "that Hubert looks so unaccustomed to lying."

"I suppose," murmured Dinny, "this will be in the papers."

"On that, my nymph, you may bet the buttoned boots you haven't got."

"How will it affect Hubert's career?"

"I think it will be good for him. The House of Commons questions were damaging. But 'British Officer *versus* Bolivian Half-Castes,' will rally the prejudice we all have for our kith and kin."

"I'm more sorry for Dad than for anybody. His hair is distinctly greyer since this began."

"There's nothing dishonourable about it, Dinny."

Dinny's head tilted up.

"No, indeed!"

"You remind me of a two-year-old, Dinny—one of those whipcordy chestnuts that kick up their heels in the paddock, get left at the post, and come in first after all. Here's your American bearing down on us. Shall we wait for him? He gave very useful evidence."

Dinny shrugged her shoulders, and almost instantly Hallorsen's voice said:

"Miss Cherrell!"

Dinny turned.

"Thank you very much, Professor, for what you said."

"I wish I could have lied for you, but I had no occasion. How is that sick gentleman?"

"All right so far."

"I am glad to hear that. I have been worried thinking of you."

"What you said, Professor," put in Sir Lawrence, "about not being seen dead with any of those muleteers hit the magistrate plumb centre."

"To be seen alive with them was bad enough. I've an automobile here, can I take you and Miss Cherrell anywhere?"

"You might take us to the borders of civilisation, if you're going West."

"Well, Professor," continued Sir Lawrence, when they were seated, "what do you think of London? Is it the most barbarous or the most civilised town on earth?"

"I just love it," said Hallorsen, without ever taking his eyes off Dinny.

"I don't," murmured Dinny; "I hate the contrasts and the smell of petrol."

"Well, a stranger can't tell why he loves London, unless it's the variety and the way you've gotten freedom and order all mixed up; or maybe it's because it's so different from our towns over there. New York is more wonderful and more exciting, but not so homey."

"New York," said Sir Lawrence, "is like strychnine. It perks you up until it lays you out."

"I certainly couldn't live in New York. The West for me."

"The great open spaces," murmured Dinny.

"Why yes, Miss Cherrell; you would love them."

Dinny smiled wanly. "No one can be pulled up by the roots, Professor."

"Ah!" said Sir Lawrence, "my son once took up the question of Emigration in Parliament. He found that people's roots were so strong that he had to drop it like a hot potato."

"Is that so?" said Hallorsen. "When I look at your town folk, undersized and pale and kind of disillusioned, I can't help wondering what roots they can have."

"The townier the type, the more stubborn its roots—no open spaces for them; the streets, fried fish, and the pictures. Would you put me down here, Professor? Dinny, where are you bound for?"

"Oakley Street."

Hallorsen stopped the car and Sir Lawrence got out.

"Miss Cherrell, may I have the great pleasure of taking you as far as Oakley Street?"

Dinny bowed.

Seated thus side by side with him in the closed car, she wondered uneasily what use he would make of his opportunity. Presently, without looking at her, he said:

"As soon as your brother is fixed up I shall be sailing. I'm going to take an expedition to New Mexico. I shall always count it a privilege to have known you, Miss Cherrell."

His ungloved hands were gripping each other between his knees; and the sight moved her.

"I am very sorry for misjudging you at first, Professor, just as my brother did."

"It was natural. I shall be glad to think I have your good will when all's been said and done."

Dinny put out her hand impulsively.

"You have."

He took the hand with gravity, raised it to his lips, and returned it to her gently. Dinny felt extremely unhappy. She said, timidly: "You've made me think quite differently about Americans, Professor."

Hallorsen smiled.

"That is something, anyway."

"I'm afraid I was very crude in my ideas. You see, I haven't really known any."

"That is the little trouble between us; we don't really know each other. We get on each other's nerves, with little things, and there it ends. But I shall always remember you as the smile on the face of this country."

"That," said Dinny, "is very pretty, and I wish it were true."

"If I could have a picture of you, I should treasure it."

"Of course you shall! I don't know if I have a decent one, but I'll send you the best."

"I thank you. I think if you will allow me I will get out here; I am just not too sure of myself. The car will take you on." He tapped on the glass and spoke to the chauffeur.

"Good-bye!" he said, and took her hand again, looked at it rather long, pressed it hard, and slid his long frame through the doorway.

"Good-bye!" murmured Dinny, sitting back, with rather a chokey feeling in her throat.

Five minutes later the car pulled up before Diana's house, and, very subdued, she went in.

Diana, whom she had not seen that morning, opened the door of her room as she was passing.

"Come in here, Dinny." Her voice was stealthy, and a little shudder went through Dinny. They sat down side by side on the four-poster bed, and Diana spoke low and hurriedly:

"He came in here last night and insisted on staying. I didn't dare refuse. There's a change; I have a feeling that it's the beginning of the end, again. His self control is weakening, all round. I think I ought to send the children somewhere. Would Hilary take them?"

"I'm sure he would; or Mother would certainly."

"Perhaps that would be better."

"Don't you think you ought to go, yourself?"

Diana sighed and shook her head.

"That would only precipitate things. Could you take the children down for me?"

"Of course. But do you really think he——?"

"Yes. I'm sure he's working up again. I know the signs so well. Haven't you noticed, Dinny, he's been drinking more each evening? It's all of a piece."

"If he'd get over his horror of going out."

"I don't believe that would help. Here at all events we know what there is to know, and the worst at once if it comes. I dread something happening with strangers, and our hands being forced."

Dinny squeezed her arm.

"When would you like the children taken down?"

"As soon as possible. I can't say anything to him. You must just go off as quietly as you can. Mademoiselle can go down separately, if your mother will have her too."

"I shall come back at once, of course."

"Dinny, it isn't fair on you. I've got the maids. It's really too bad to bother you with my troubles."

"But of course I shall come back. I'll borrow Fleur's car. Will he mind the children going?"

"Only if he connects it with our feeling about his state. I can say it's an old invitation."

"Diana," said Dinny, suddenly, "have you any love for him left?"

"Love? No!"

"Just pity?"

Diana shook her head.

"I can't explain; it's the past and a feeling that if I desert him I help the fates against him. That's a horrible thought!"

"I understand. I'm so sorry for you both, and for Uncle Adrian."

Diana smoothed her face with her hands, as if wiping off the marks of trouble.

"I don't know what's coming, but it's no good going to meet it. As to you, my dear, don't for God's sake let me spoil your time."

"That's all right. I'm wanting something to take me out of myself. Spinsters, you know, should be well shaken before being taken."

"Ah! When *are* you going to be taken, Dinny?"

"I have just rejected the great open spaces, and I feel a beast."

"Between the great open spaces and the deep sea—are you?"

"And likely to remain so. The love of a good man—and all that, seems to leave me frost-bitten."

"Wait! Your hair is the wrong colour for the cloister."

"I'll have it dyed and sail in my true colours. Icebergs are sea-green."

"As I said before—wait!"

"I will," said Dinny. . . .

* * *

Fleur herself drove the South Square car to the door two days later. The children and some luggage were placed in it without incident, and they started.

That somewhat hectic drive, for the children were little used to cars, to Dinny was pure relief. She had not realised how much the tragic atmosphere of Oakley Street was on her nerves; and yet it was but ten days since she had come up from Condaford. The colours of 'the fall' were deepening already on the trees. The day had the soft and sober glow of fine October; the air, as the country deepened and grew remote, had again its beloved tang; wood smoke rose from cottage chimneys, and rooks from the bared fields.

They arrived in time for lunch, and, leaving the children with Mademoiselle, who had come down by train, Dinny went forth with the dogs alone. She stopped at an old cottage high above the sunken road. The door opened straight into the living room, where an old woman was sitting by a thin fire of wood.

"Oh! Miss Dinny," she said, "I am that glad. I haven't seen you not all this month."

"No, Betty; I've been away. How are you?"

The little old woman, for she was of pocket size, crossed her hands solemnly on her middle.

"My stummick's bad again. I 'aven't nothin' else the matter—the doctor says I'm wonderful. Just my stummick. 'E says I ought to eat more; and I've such an appetite, Miss Dinny. But I can't eat 'ardly nothin' without I'm sick, and that's the truth."

"Dear Betty, I'm so sorry. Tummies are a dreadful nuisance. Tummies and teeth. I can't think why we have them. If you haven't teeth you can't digest; and if you have teeth you can't digest either."

The old lady cackled thinly.

"'E du say I ought to 'ave the rest of my teeth out, but I don't like to part with 'em, Miss Dinny. Father 'e's got none, and 'e can bit an apple, 'e can. But at my age I can't expect to live to 'arden up like that."

"But you could have some lovely false ones, Betty."

"Oh! I don't want to 'ave no false teeth—so pretenshus. You wouldn't never wear false teeth, would you, Miss Dinny?"

"Of course I would, Betty. Nearly all the best people have them nowadays."

"You will 'ave your joke. No, I shouldn't like it. I'd as soon wear a wig. But my 'air's as thick as ever. I'm wonderful for my age. I've got a lot to be thankful for; it's only my stummick, an' that's like as if there was somethin' there."

Dinny saw the pain and darkness in her eyes.

"How is Benjamin, Betty?"

The eyes changed, became amused and yet judgmatic, as if she were considering a child.

"Oh! Father's all right, Miss; 'e never 'as anything the matter except 'is rheumatiz; 'e's out now doin' a bit o' diggin'."

"And how's Goldie?" said Dinny, looking lugubriously at a goldfinch in a cage. She hated to see birds in cages, but had never been able to bring herself to say so to these old people with their small bright imprisoned pet. Besides, didn't they say that if you released a tame goldfinch, it would soon be pecked to death?

"Oh!" said the old lady, "'e thinks 'e's someone since you give him that bigger cage." Her eyes brightened. "Fancy the Captain married, Miss Dinny, and that dreadful case against him an' all—whatever are they thinkin' about? I never 'eard of such a thing in all my life. One of the Cherrells to be put in Court like that. It's out of all knowledge."

"It is, Betty."

"I'm told she's a fine young lady. And where'll they be goin' to live?"

"Nobody knows yet; we have to wait for this case to be over. Perhaps down here, or perhaps he'll get a post abroad. They'll be very poor, of course."

"Dreadful; it never was like that in old days. The way they put upon the gentry now—oh, dear! I remember your great-grandfather, Miss Dinny, drivin' four-in-hand when I was a little bit of a thing. Such a nice old gentleman—curtly, as you might say."

Such references to the gentry never ceased to make Dinny feel uneasy, only too well aware that this old lady had been one of eight children brought up by a farm worker whose wages had been eleven shillings a week, and that she and her husband now existed on their Old Age pensions, after bringing up a family of seven.

"Well, Betty dear, what *can* you digest, so that I can tell cook?"

"Thank you kindly, Miss Dinny; a nice bit of lean pork do seem to lie quiet sometimes." Again her eyes grew dark and troubled. "I 'ave such dreadful pain; really sometimes I feel I'd be glad to go 'ome."

"Oh! no, Betty dear. With a little proper feeding I know you're going to feel better."

The old lady smiled below her eyes.

"I'm wonderful for my age, so it'd never do to complain. And when are the bells goin' to ring for you, Miss Dinny?"

"Don't mention them, Betty. They won't ring of their own accord—that's certain."

"Ah! People don't marry young, and 'ave the families they did in my young days. My old Aunt 'ad eighteen an' reared eleven."

"There doesn't seem room or work for them now, does there?"

"Aye! The country's changed."

"Less down here than in most places, thank goodness." And Dinny's eyes wandered over the room where these two old people had spent some fifty years of life; from brick floor to raftered ceiling it was scrupulously clean and had a look of homely habit.

"Well, Betty, I must go. I'm staying in London just now with a friend, and have to get back there this evening. I'll tell cook to send some little things that'll be better for you than pork even. Don't get up!"

But the little old woman was on her feet, her eyes looking out from her very soul.

"I am that glad to 'ave seen you, Miss Dinny. God bless you! And I do 'ope the Captain won't 'ave any trouble with those dreadful people."

"Good-bye, Betty dear, and remember me to Benjamin"; and pressing the old lady's hand Dinny went out to where the dogs were waiting for her on the flagged pathway. As always after such visits she felt humble and inclined to cry. Roots! That was what she missed in London, what she would miss in the 'great open spaces.' She walked to the bottom of a narrow straggling beechwood, and entered it through a tattered gate that she did not even have to open. She mounted over the damp beech mast which smelled sweetly as of husks; to the left a grey-blue sky was rifted by the turning beeches, and to her right stretched fallow ground where a squatting hare turned and raced for the hedgerow; a pheasant rose squawking before one of the dogs and rocketed over the wood. She emerged from the trees at the top, and stood looking down at the house, long and stone-coloured, broken by magnolias and the trees on the lawn; smoke was rising from two chimneys, and the fantails speckled with white one gable. She breathed deeply, and for full ten minutes stood there, like a watered plant drawing up the food of its vitality. The scent was of leaves and turned earth and of rain not far away; the last time she had stood there had been at the end of May, and she had inhaled that scent of summer which is at once a memory and a promise, an aching and a draught of delight. . . .

After an early tea she started back, in the now closed car, sitting beside Fleur.

"I must say," said that shrewd young woman, "Condaford is the most peaceful place I was ever in. I should die of it, Dinny. The rurality of Lippinghall is nothing thereto."

"Old and mouldering, um?"

"Well, I always tell Michael that your side of his family is one of the least expressed and most interesting phenomena left in England. You're wholly unvocal, utterly out of the limelight. Too unsensational for the novelists, and yet you're there, and go on being there, and I don't quite know how. Every mortal thing's against you, from Death Duties down to gramophones. But you persist generally at the ends of the earth, doing things that nobody knows or cares anything about. Most of your sort haven't even got Condafords now to come home and die in; and yet you still have roots, and a sense of duty. I've got neither, you know, I suppose that comes of being half French. My father's family—the Forsytes—may have roots, but they haven't a sense of duty—not in the same way; or perhaps it's a sense of service that I mean. I admire it, you know, Dinny, but it bores me stiff. It's making you go and blight your young life over this Ferse business. Duty's a disease, Dinny; an admirable disease."

"What do you think I ought to do about it?"

"Have your instincts out. I can't imagine anything more ageing than what you're doing now. As for Diana, she's of the same sort—the Montjoys have a kind of Condaford up in Dumfriesshire—I admire her for sticking to Ferse, but I think it's quite crazy of her. It can only end one way, and that'll be the more unpleasant the longer it's put off."

"Yes; I feel she's riding for a bad fall, but I hope I should do the same."

"I know I shouldn't," said Fleur, cheerfully.

"I don't believe that anybody knows what they'll do about anything until it comes to the point."

"The thing is never to let anything come to a point."

Fleur spoke with a tang in her voice, and Dinny saw her lips harden. She always found Fleur attractive, because mystifying.

"You haven't seen Ferse," she said, "and without seeing him you can't appreciate how pathetic he is."

"That's sentiment, my dear. I'm not sentimental."

"I'm sure you've had a past, Fleur; and you can't have had that without being sentimental."

Fleur gave her a quick look, and trod on the accelerator.

"Time I turned on my lights," she said.

For the rest of the journey she talked on Art, Letters and other unimportant themes. It was nearly eight o'clock when she dropped Dinny at Oakley Street.

Diana was in, already dressed for dinner.

"Dinny," she said, "he's out."

CHAPTER 25

PORTENTOUS—those simple words!

"After you'd gone this morning he was in a great state—seemed to think we were all in a conspiracy to keep things from him."

"As we were," murmured Dinny.

"Mademoiselle's going upset him again. Soon after, I heard the front door bang—he hasn't been back since. I didn't tell you, but last night was dreadful. Suppose he doesn't come back?"

"Oh! Diana, I wish he wouldn't."

"But where has he gone? What can he do? Whom can he go to? O God! It's awful!"

Dinny looked at her in silent distress.

"Sorry, Dinny! You must be tired and hungry. We won't wait dinner."

In Ferse's 'lair,' that charming room panelled in green shot with a golden look, they sat through an anxious meal. The shaded light fell pleasantly on their bare necks and arms, on the fruit, the flowers, the silver; and until the maid was gone they spoke of indifferent things.

"Has he a key?" asked Dinny.

"Yes."

"Shall I ring up Uncle Adrian?"

"What can he do? If Ronald does come in, it will be more dangerous if Adrian is here."

"Alan Tasburgh told me he would come any time if anyone was wanted."

"No, let's keep it to ourselves to-night. To-morrow we can see."

Dinny nodded. She was scared, and more scared of showing it, for she was there to strengthen Diana by keeping cool and steady.

"Come upstairs and sing to me," she said, at last.

Up in the drawing-room Diana sang 'The Sprig of Thyme,' 'Waley, Waley,' 'The Bens of Jura,' 'Mowing the Barley,' 'The Castle of Dromore,' and the beauty of the room, of the songs of the singer, brought to Dinny a sense of unreality. She had gone into a drowsy dream, when, suddenly, Diana stopped.

"I heard the front door."

Dinny got up and stood beside the piano.

"Go on, don't say anything, don't show anything."

145

Diana began again to play, and sing the Irish song 'Must I go bound and you go free.' Then the door was opened, and, in a mirror at the end of the room, Dinny saw Ferse come in and stand listening.

"Sing on," she whispered.

> " 'Must I go bound, and you go free?
> Must I love a lass that couldn't love me?
> Oh! was I taught so poor a wit
> As love a lass would break my heart.' "

And Ferse stood there listening. He looked like a man excessively tired or overcome with drink; his hair was disordered and his lips drawn back so that his teeth showed. Then he moved. He seemed trying to make no noise. He passed round to a sofa on the far side and sank down on it. Diana stopped singing. Dinny, whose hand was on her shoulder, felt her trembling with the effort to control her voice.

"Have you had dinner, Ronald?"

Ferse did not answer, staring across the room with that queer and ghostly grin.

"Play on," whispered Dinny.

Diana played the Red Sarafan; she played the fine simple tune over and over, as if making hypnotic passes towards that mute figure. When, at last, she stopped, there followed the strangest silence. Then Dinny's nerve snapped and she said, almost sharply:

"Is it raining, Captain Ferse?"

Ferse passed his hand down his trouser, and nodded.

"Hadn't you better go up and change then, Ronald?"

He put his elbows on his knees, and rested his head on his hands.

"You must be tired, dear; won't you go to bed? Shall I bring you something up?"

And still he did not move. The grin had faded off his lips; his eyes were closed. He looked like a man suddenly asleep, as some overdriven beast of burden might drop off between the shafts.

"Shut the piano," whispered Dinny; "let's go up."

Diana closed the piano without noise and rose. With their arms linked they waited, but he did not stir.

"Is he really asleep?" whispered Dinny.

Ferse started up. "Sleep! I'm for it. I'm for it again. And I won't stand it. By God! I won't stand it!"

He stood a moment transfigured with a sort of fury; then, seeing them shrink, sank back on the sofa and buried his face in his hands. Impulsively Diana moved towards him.

Ferse looked up. His eyes were wild.

"Don't!" he growled out. "Leave me alone! Go away!"

At the door Diana turned and said:

"Ronald, won't you see someone? Just to make you sleep—just for that."

Ferse sprang up again. "I'll see no one. Go away!"

They shrank out of the room, and up in Dinny's bedroom stood with their arms round each other, quivering.

"Have the maids gone to bed?"

"They always go early, unless one of them is out."

"I think I ought to go down and telephone, Diana."

"No, Dinny, I will. Only to whom?"

That was, indeed, the question. They debated it in whispers. Diana thought her doctor; Dinny thought Adrian or Michael should be asked to go round to the doctor and bring him.

"Was it like this before the last attack?"

"No. He didn't know then what was before him. I felt he might kill himself, Dinny."

"Has he a weapon?"

"I gave his Service revolver to Adrian to keep for me."

"Razors?"

"Only safety ones; and there's nothing poisonous in the house."

Dinny moved to the door.

"I *must* go and telephone."

"Dinny, I can't have you——"

"He wouldn't touch *me*. It's you that are in danger. Lock the door while I'm gone."

And before Diana could stop her, she slid out. The lights still burned, and she stood a moment. Her room was on the second floor, facing the street. Diana's bedroom and that of Ferse were on the drawing-room floor below. She must pass them to reach the hall and the little study where the telephone was kept. No sound came up. Diana had opened the door again and was standing there; and, conscious that at any moment she might slip past her and go down, Dinny ran forward and began descending the stairs. They creaked and she stopped to take off her shoes. Holding them in her hand she crept on past the drawing-room door. No sound came thence; and she sped down to the hall. She noticed Ferse's hat and coat thrown across a chair, and passing into the study, closed the door behind her. She stood a moment to recover breath, then, turning on the light, took up the directory. She found Adrian's number and was stretching out her hand for the receiver when her wrist was seized, and with a gasp she turned to face Ferse. He twisted her round and stood pointing to the shoes still in her hand.

"Going to give me away," he said, and, still holding her, took a knife out of his side pocket. Back, at the full length of her arm, Dinny looked him in the face. Somehow she was not so scared as she had been; her chief feeling was a sort of shame at having her shoes in her hand.

"That's a silly, Captain Ferse," she said, icily. "You know we'd neither of us do you any harm."

Ferse flung her hand from him, opened the knife, and with a violent effort severed the telephone wire. The receiver dropped on the floor. He closed the knife and put it back into his pocket. Dinny had the impression that with action he had become less unbalanced.

"Put on your shoes," he said.

She did so.

"Understand me, I'm not going to be interfered with, or messed about. I shall do what I like with myself."

Dinny remained silent. Her heart was beating furiously, and she did not want her voice to betray it.

"Did you hear?"

"Yes. No one wants to interfere with you, or do anything you don't like. We only want your good."

"I know that good," said Ferse. "No more of that for me." He went across to the window, tore a curtain aside, and looked out. "It's raining like hell," he said, then turned and stood looking at her. His face began to twitch, his hands to clench. He moved his head from side to side. Suddenly he shouted: "Get out of this room, quick! Get out, get out!"

As swiftly as she could without running Dinny slid to the door, closed it behind her and flew upstairs. Diana was still standing in the bedroom doorway. Dinny pushed her in, locked the door, and sank down breathless.

"He came out after me," she gasped, "and cut the wire. He's got a knife; I'm afraid there's mania coming on. Will that door hold if he tries to break it down? Shall we put the bed against it?"

"If we do we should never sleep."

"We shall never sleep, anyway," and she began dragging at the bed. They moved it square against the door.

"Do the maids lock their doors?"

"They have, since he's been back."

Dinny sighed in relief. The idea of going out again to warn them made her shudder. She sat on the bed looking at Diana, who was standing by the window.

"What are you thinking of, Diana?"

"I was thinking what I should be feeling if the children were still here."

"Yes, thank heaven, they're not."

Diana came back to the bed and took Dinny's hand. Grip and answering grip tightened till they were almost painful.

"Is there nothing we can do, Dinny?"

"Perhaps he'll sleep, and be much better in the morning. Now there's danger I don't feel half so sorry for him."

Diana said stonily: "I'm past feeling. I wonder if he knows yet that I'm not in my own room? Perhaps I ought to go down and face it."

"You shan't!" And taking the key from the lock Dinny thrust it into the top of her stocking: its cold hardness rallied her nerves.

"Now," she said, "we'll lie down with our feet to the door. It's no good getting worn out for nothing."

A sort of apathy had come over both of them, and they lay a long time thus, close together under the eiderdown, neither of them sleeping, neither of them quite awake. Dinny had dozed off at last when a stealthy sound awakened her. She looked at Diana. She was asleep, really asleep, dead asleep. A streak of light from outside showed at the top of the door, which fitted loosely. Leaning on her elbow she strained her ears. The handle of the door was turned, and softly shaken. There was a gentle knocking.

"Yes," said Dinny, very low, "what is it?"

"Diana," said Ferse's voice, but quite subdued: "I want her."

Dinny crouched forward close to the keyhole.

"Diana's not well," she said. "She's asleep now, don't disturb her."

There was silence. And then to her horror she heard a long moaning sigh; a sound so miserable, and as it were so final that she was on the point of taking out the key. The sight of Diana's face, white and worn, stopped her. No good! Whatever that sound meant—no good! And crouching back on the bed, she listened. No more sound! Diana slept on, but Dinny could not get to sleep again. 'If he kills himself,' she thought, 'shall I be to blame?' Would that not be best for everyone, for Diana and his children, for himself? But that long sighing moan went on echoing through her nerves. Poor man, poor man! She felt nothing now but a dreadful sore pity, a sort of resentment at the inexorability of Nature that did such things to human creatures. Accept the mysterious ways of Providence? Who could? Insensate and cruel! Beside the worn-out sleeper she lay, quivering. What had they done that they ought not to have done? Could they have helped him more than they had tried to? What could they do when morning came? Diana stirred. Was she going to wake? But she just turned and sank back into her heavy slumber. And slowly a drowsy feeling stole on Dinny herself and she slept.

A knocking on the door awakened her. It was daylight. Diana was still sleeping. She looked at her wrist watch. Eight o'clock. She was being called.

"All right, Mary!" she answered, softly: "Mrs. Ferse is here."

Diana sat up, her eyes on Dinny's half-clothed figure.

"What is it?"

"It's all right, Diana. Eight o'clock! We'd better get up and put the bed back. You've had a real good sleep. The maids are up."

They put on wrappers, and pulled the bed into place. Dinny took the key from its queer hiding nook, and unlocked the door.

"No good craning at it. Let's go down!"

They stood a moment at the top of the stairs listening, and then descended. Diana's room was untouched. The maid had evidently been in and pulled aside the curtains. They stood at the door that led from it to Ferse's room. No sound came from there. They went out to the other door. Still no sound!

"We'd better go down," whispered Dinny. "What shall you say to Mary?"

"Nothing. She'll understand."

The dining room and study doors were open. The telephone receiver still lay severed on the floor; there was no other sign of last night's terrors.

Suddenly, Dinny said: "Diana, his hat and coat are gone. They were on that chair."

Diana went into the dining room and rang the bell. The elderly maid, coming from the basement stairs, had a scared and anxious look.

"Have you seen Captain Ferse's hat and coat this morning, Mary?"

"No, Ma'am."

"What time did you come down?"

"Seven o'clock."

"You haven't been to his room?"

"Not yet, Ma'am."

"I was not well last night; I slept upstairs with Miss Dinny."

They all three went upstairs.

"Knock on his door."

The maid knocked. Dinny and Diana stood close by. There was no answer.

"Knock again, Mary; louder."

Again and again the maid knocked. No answer. Diana put her aside and turned the handle. The door came open. Ferse was not there. The room was in disorder, as if someone had tramped and wrestled in it. The water bottle was empty, and tobacco ash was strewn about. The bed had been lain on, but not slept in. There was no sign of packing or of anything having been taken from the drawers. The three women looked at each other. Then Diana said:

"Get breakfast quick, Mary. We must go out."

"Yes, Ma'am—I saw the telephone."

"Hide that up, and get it mended; and don't tell the others anything. Just say: 'He's away for a night or two.' Make things here look like that. We'll dress quickly, Dinny."

The maid went downstairs again.

Dinny said: "Has he any money?"

"I don't know. I can see if his cheque book has gone."

She ran down again, and Dinny waited. Diana came back into the hall.

"No; it's on the bureau in the dining room. Quick, Dinny, dress!"

That meant . . . What did it mean? A strange conflict of hopes and fears raged within Dinny. She flew upstairs.

CHAPTER 26

OVER A HASTY BREAKFAST they consulted. To whom should they go?

"Not to the police," said Dinny.

"No, indeed."

"I think we should go to Uncle Adrian first."

They sent the maid for a taxi, and set out for Adrian's rooms. It was not quite nine o'clock. They found him over tea and one of those fishes which cover the more ground when eaten, and explain the miracle of the seven baskets full.

Seeming to have grown greyer in these few days, he listened to them, filling his pipe, and at last said:

"You must leave it to me now. Dinny, can you take Diana down to Condaford?"

"Of course."

"Before you go, could you get young Alan Tasburgh to go down to that Home and ask if Ferse is there, without letting them know that he's gone off on his own? Here's the address."

Dinny nodded.

Adrian raised Diana's hand to his lips.

"My dear, you look worn out. Don't worry; just rest down there with the children. We'll keep in touch with you."

"Will there be publicity, Adrian?"

"Not if we can prevent it. I shall consult Hilary; we'll try everything first. Do you know how much money he had?"

"The last cheque cashed was for five pounds two days ago, but all yesterday he was out."

"How was he dressed?"

"Blue overcoat, blue suit, bowler hat."

"And you don't know where he went yesterday?"

"No. Until yesterday he was never out at all."

"Does he still belong to any Club?"

"No."

"Has any old friend been told of his return?"

"No."

"And he took no cheque book? How soon can you get hold of that young man, Dinny?"

"Now, if I could telephone, Uncle; he's sleeping at his Club."

"Try, then."

Dinny went out to the telephone. She soon reported that Alan would go down at once, and let Adrian know. He would ask as an old friend, with no knowledge that Ferse had ever left. He would beg them to let him know if Ferse came back, so that he might come and see him.

"Good," said Adrian; "you have a head, my child. And now go off and look after Diana. Give me your number at Condaford."

Having jotted it down, he saw them back into their cab.

"Uncle Adrian is the best man in the world," said Dinny.

"No one should know that better than I, Dinny."

Back in Oakley Street, they went upstairs to pack. Dinny was afraid that at the last minute Diana might refuse to go. But she had given her word to Adrian, and they were soon on the way to the station. They spent a very silent hour and a half on the journey, leaning back in their corners, tired out. Dinny, indeed, was only now realising the strain she had been through. And yet, what had it amounted to? No violence, no attack, not even a great scene. How uncannily disturbing was insanity! What fear it inspired; what nerve-racking emotions! Now that she was free from chance of contact with Ferse he again seemed to her just pitiful. She pictured him wandering and distraught, with nowhere to lay his head and no one to take him by the hand; on the edge, perhaps already over that edge! The worst tragedies were always connected with fear. Criminality, leprosy, insanity, anything that inspired fear in other people—the victims of such were hopelessly alone in a frightened world. Since last night she understood far better Ferse's outburst about the vicious circle in which insanity moved. She knew now that her own nerves were not strong enough, her own skin not thick enough, to bear contact with the insane; she understood the terrible treatment of the insane in old days. It was like the way dogs had, of setting on an hysterical dog, their own nerves jolted beyond bearing. The contempt lavished on the imbecile, the cruelty and contempt had been defensive—defensive revenge on something which outraged the nerves. All the more pitiable, all the more horrible to think about. And, while the train bore her nearer to her peaceful home, she was more and more torn between the wish to shut away all thought of the unhappy outcast and feelings of pity for him. She looked across at Diana lying back in the corner opposite with closed eyes. What must she be feeling, bound to Ferse by memory, by law, by children of whom he was the father? The face under the close casque hat had the chiselling of prolonged trial—fine-lined and rather hard. By the faint movement of the lips she was not asleep. 'What keeps her going?' thought Dinny. 'She's not religious; she doesn't believe much in anything. If I were she I should throw everything up and rush to the ends of the earth —or should I?' Was there perhaps something inside one, some sense of what was due to oneself, that kept one unyielding and unbroken?

There was nothing to meet them at the station, so leaving their things, they set forth for the Grange on foot, taking a path across the fields.

"I wonder," said Dinny, suddenly, "how little excitement one could do with in these days? Should I be happy if I lived down here all my time, like the old cottage folk? Clare is never happy here. She has to be on the go all the time. There *is* a kind of jack-in-the-box inside one."

"I've never seen it popping out of you, Dinny."

"I wish I'd been older during the war. I was only fourteen when it stopped."

"You were lucky."

"I don't know. You must have had a terribly exciting time, Diana."

"I was your present age when the war began."

"Married?"

"Just."

"I suppose he was right through it?"

"Yes."

"What was the cause?"

"An aggravation, perhaps."

"Uncle Adrian spoke of heredity."

"Yes."

Dinny pointed to a thatched cottage.

"In that cottage an old pet couple of mine have lived fifty years. Could you do that, Diana?"

"I could now; I want peace, Dinny."

They reached the house in silence. A message had come through from Adrian: Ferse was not back at the Home: but he and Hilary believed they were on the right track.

After seeing the children Diana went to her bedroom to lie down, and Dinny to her Mother's sitting-room.

"Mother, I must say it to someone—I am praying for his death."

"Dinny!"

"For his own sake, for Diana's, for the children's, for everybody's; even my own."

"Of course, if it's hopeless——"

"Hopeless or not, I don't care. It's too dreadful. Providence is a washout, Mother."

"My dear!"

"It's too remote. I suppose there is an eternal Plan—but we're like gnats for all the care it has for us as individuals."

"You want a good sleep, darling."

"Yes. But that won't make any difference."

"Don't encourage such feelings, Dinny; they affect one's character."

"I don't see the connection between beliefs and character. I'm not going to behave any worse because I cease to believe in Providence or an after life."

"Surely, Dinny——"

"No; I'm going to behave *better*; if I'm decent it's because decency's the decent thing; and not because I'm going to get anything by it."

"But why is decency the decent thing, Dinny, if there's no God?"

"O subtle and dear mother, I didn't say there wasn't God. I only said his Plan was too remote. Can't you hear God saying: 'By the way, is that ball the Earth still rolling?' And an angel answering: 'Oh! Yes, Sir, quite nicely.' 'Let's see, it must be fungused over by now. Wasn't there some particularly bugsy little parasite——'"

"Dinny!"

"'Oh! Yes, Sir, you mean man!' 'Quite! I remember we called it that.'"

"Dinny, how dreadful!"

"Now, Mother, if I'm decent, it will be because decency is devised by humans for the benefit of humans; just as beauty is devised by humans for the delight of humans. Am I looking awful, darling? I feel as if I had no eyes. I think I'll go and lie down. I don't know why I've got so worked up about this, Mother. I think it must be looking at his face." And with suspicious swiftness Dinny turned and went away.

CHAPTER 27

Ferse's disappearance was a holiday to the feelings of one who had suffered greatly since his return. That he had engaged to end that holiday by finding him was not enough to spoil Adrian's relief. Almost with zest he set out for Hilary's in a taxi, applying his wits to the problem. Fear of publicity cut him off from those normal and direct resorts—Police, Radio, and Press. Such agencies would bring on Ferse too fierce a light. And in considering what means were left he felt as when confronted with a crossword puzzle, many of which he had solved in his time, like other men of noted intellect. From Dinny's account he could not tell within several hours at what time Ferse had gone out, and the longer he left enquiry in the neighbourhood of the house, the less chance one would have of stumbling on anyone who had seen him. Should he, then, stop the cab and go back to Chelsea? In holding on towards the Meads, he yielded to instinct rather than to reason. To turn to Hilary was second nature with him—and, surely, in such a task two heads were better than one! He reached the Vicarage without forming any plan save that of enquiring vaguely along the Embankment and the King's Road. It was not yet half past nine, and Hilary was still at his correspondence. On hearing the news, he called his wife into the study.

"Let's think for three minutes," he said, "and pool the result."

The three stood in a triangle before the fire, the two men smoking, and the woman sniffing at an October rose.

"Well?" said Hilary, at last: "Any light, May?"

"Only," said Mrs. Hilary, wrinkling her forehead, "if the poor man was as Dinny describes, you can't leave out the hospitals. I could telephone to the three or four where there was most chance of his having been taken in, if he's made an accident for himself. It's so early still, they can hardly have had anybody in."

"Very sweet of you, my dear; and we can trust your wits to keep his name out of it."

Mrs. Hilary went out.

"Adrian?"

"I've got a hunch, but I'd rather hear you first."

"Well," said Hilary, "two things occur to me: It's obvious we must find out from the Police if anyone's been taken from the river. The other contingency, and I think it's the more likely, is drink."

"But he couldn't get a drink so early."

"Hotels. He had money."

"I agree, we must try them, unless you think my idea any good."

"Well?"

"I've been trying to put myself in poor Ferse's shoes. I think, Hilary, if I had a doom over me, I might run for Condaford; not the place itself, perhaps, but round about, where we haunted as boys; where I'd been, in fact, before Fate got hold of me at all. A wounded animal goes home."

Hilary nodded.

"Where *was* his home?"

"West Sussex—just under the Downs to the north. Petworth was the station."

"Oh! I know that country. Before the war May and I used to stay a lot at Bignor and walk. We could have a shot at Victoria station, and see if anyone like him has taken train. But I think I'll try the Police about the river first. I can say a parishioner is missing. What height is Ferse?"

"About five feet ten, square, broad head and cheek-bones, strong jaw, darkish hair, steel-blue eyes, a blue suit and overcoat."

"Right!" said Hilary: "I'll get on to them as soon as May is through."

Left to himself before the fire, Adrian brooded. A reader of detective novels, he knew that he was following the French, inductive method of a psychological shot in the blue, Hilary and May following the English model of narrowing the issue by elimination—excellent, but was there time for excellence? One vanished in London as a needle vanishes in hay; and they were so handicapped by the need for avoiding publicity. He waited in anxiety for Hilary's report. Curiously ironical that he—*he*—should dread to hear of poor Ferse being found drowned or run over, and Diana free!

From Hilary's table he took up an A.B.C. There had been a train to Petworth at 8.50, another went at 9.56. A near thing! And he waited again, his eyes on the door. Useless to hurry Hilary, a past-master in saving time.

"Well?" he said when the door was opened.

Hilary shook his head.

"No go! Neither hospitals nor Police. No one received or heard of anywhere."

"Then," said Adrian, "let's try Victoria—there's a train in twenty minutes. Can you come right away?"

Hilary glanced at his table. "I oughtn't to, but I will. There's something unholy in the way a search gets hold of you. Hold on, old man, I'll tell May and nick my hat. You might look for a taxi. Go St. Pancras way and wait for me."

Adrian strode along looking for a taxi. He found one issuing from the

Euston Road, turned it round, and stood waiting. Soon Hilary's thin dark figure came hurrying into view.

"Not in the training I was," he said, and got in.

Adrian leaned through the window.

"Victoria, quick as you can!"

Hilary's hand slipped through his arm.

"I haven't had a jaunt with you, old man, since we went up the Carmarthen Van in that fog the year after the war. Remember?"

Adrian had taken out his watch.

"We just shan't do it, I'm afraid. The traffic's awful." And they sat, silent, jerked back and forth by the spasmodic efforts of the taxi.

"I'll never forget," said Adrian, suddenly, "in France once, passing a '*maison d'aliénés*,' as they call it—a great place back from the railway with a long iron grille in front. There was a poor devil standing upright with his arms raised and his legs apart, clutching at the grille, like an Orang outang. What's death compared with that? Good clean earth, and sky over you. I wish now they'd found him in the river."

"They may still; this is a bit of a wild-goose chase."

"Three minutes more," muttered Adrian; "we shan't do it."

But as if animated by its national character the taxi gathered unnatural speed, and the traffic seemed to melt before it. They pulled up at the station with a jerk.

"You ask at the first class, I'll go for the third," said Hilary as they ran. "A parson gets more show."

"No," said Adrian; "if he's gone, he'll have gone first class; *you* ask there. If there's any doubt—*his eyes.*"

He watched Hilary's lean face thrust into the opening and quickly drawn back.

"He *has!*" he said; "this train. Petworth! Rush!"

The brothers ran, but as they reached the barrier the train began to move. Adrian would have run on, but Hilary grabbed his arm.

"Steady, old man, we shall never get in; he'll only see us, and that'll spill it."

They walked back to the entrance with their heads down.

"That was an amazing shot of yours, old boy," said Hilary: "What time does that train get down?"

"Twelve twenty-three."

"Then we can do it in a car. Have you any money?"

Adrain felt in his pockets. "Only eight and six," he said ruefully.

"I've got just eleven bob. Awkward! I know! We'll take a cab to young Fleur's: if her car's not out, she'd let us have it, and she or Michael would drive us. We must both be free of the car at the other end."

Adrian nodded, rather dazed at the success of his induction.

At South Square Michael was out, but Fleur in. Adrian, who did not know her so well as Hilary, was surprised by the quickness with which she grasped the situation and produced the car. Within ten minutes, indeed, they were on the road with Fleur at the wheel.

"I shall go through Dorking and Pulborough," she said, leaning back. "I can speed all the way after Dorking on that road. But, Uncle Hilary, what are you going to do if you get him?"

At that simple but necessary question the brothers looked at each other. Fleur seemed to feel their indecision through the back of her head, for she stopped with a jerk in front of an imperilled dog, and, turning, said:

"Would you like to think it over before we start?"

Gazing from her short clear-cut face, the very spit of hard, calm, confident youth, to his brother's long, shrewd face, wrinkled, and worn by the experiences of others and yet not hard, Adrian left it to Hilary to answer.

"Let's get on," said Hilary; "it's a case of making the best of what turns up."

"When we pass a post-office," added Adrian, "please stop. I want to send a wire to Dinny."

Fleur nodded. "There's one in the King's Road, I must fill up, too, somewhere."

And the car slid on among the traffic.

"What shall I say in the wire?" asked Adrian. "Anything about Petworth?"

Hilary shook his head.

"Just that we think we're on the right track."

When they had sent the wire there were only two hours left before the train arrived.

"It's fifty miles to Pulborough," said Fleur, "and I suppose about five on. I wonder if I can risk my petrol. I'll see at Dorking." From that moment on she was lost to them, though the car was a closed saloon, giving all her attention to her driving.

The two brothers sat silent with their eyes on the clock and speedometer.

"I don't often go joy-riding," said Hilary, softly: "What are you thinking of, old man?"

"Of what on earth we're going to do."

"If I were to think of that beforehand, in my job, I should be dead in a month. In a slum parish one lives, as in a jungle, surrounded by wild cats; one grows a sort of instinct and has to trust to it."

"Oh!" said Adrian, "I live among the dead, and get no practise."

"Our niece drives well," said Hilary in a low voice. "Look at her neck. Isn't that capability personified?"

The neck, white, round and shingled, was held beautifully erect and gave a remarkable impression of quick close control of the body by the brain.

For several miles after that they drove in silence.

"Box Hill," said Hilary: "a thing once happened to me hereabouts I've never told you and never forgotten, it shows how awfully near the edge of mania we live." He sunk his voice and went on: "Remember that jolly parson Durcott we used to know? When I was at Beaker's before I went to Harrow, he was a master there; he took me for a walk one Sunday over Box Hill. Coming back in the train we were alone. We were ragging a little, when all of a sudden he seemed to go into a sort of frenzy, his eyes all greedy and wild. I hadn't the least notion what he was after and was awfully scared. Then, suddenly, he seemed to get hold of himself again. Right out of the blue! Repressed sex, of course—regular mania for the moment—pretty horrible. A very nice fellow, too. There are forces, Adrian."

"Daemonic. And when they break the shell for good . . . Poor Ferse!"

Fleur's voice came back to them.

"She's beginning to go a bit wonky; I must fill up, Uncle Hilary. There's a station close here."

"Right-o!"

The car drew up before the filling station.

"It's always slow work to Dorking," said Fleur, stretching: "we can get along now. Only thirty-two miles, and a good hour still. Have you thought?"

"No," said Hilary, "we've avoided it like poison."

Fleur's eyes, whose whites were so clear, flashed on him one of those direct glances, which so convinced people of her intelligence.

"Are you going to take him back in this? I wouldn't, if I were you." And, taking out her case, she repaired her lips slightly, and powdered her short straight nose.

Adrian watched her with a sort of awe. Youth, up to date, did not come very much his way. Not her few words, but the implications in them impressed him. What she meant was crudely this: Let him dree his weird —you can do nothing. Was she right? Were he and Hilary just pandering to the human instinct for interference; attempting to lay a blasphemous hand on Nature? And yet for Diana's sake they must know what Ferse did, what he was going to do. For Ferse's sake they must see, at least, that he did not fall into the wrong hands. On his brother's face was a faint smile. He at least, thought Adrian, knew youth, had a brood of his own, and could tell how far the clear hard philosophy of youth would carry.

They started again, trailing through the traffic of Dorking's long and busy street.

"Clear at last," said Fleur, turning her head, "if you really want to catch him, you shall;" and she opened out to full speed. For the next quarter of an hour they flew along, past yellowing spinneys, fields and bits of furzy common dotted with geese and old horses, past village greens and village streets, and all the other evidences of a country life trying to retain its soul. And then the car, which had been travelling very smoothly, began to grate and bump.

"Tire gone!" said Fleur, turning her head: "That's torn it." She brought the car to a standstill, and they all got out. The off hind tire was right down.

"Pipe to!" said Hilary, taking his coat off. "Jack her up, Adrian. I'll get the spare wheel off."

Fleur's head was lost in the tool-box, but her voice was heard saying: "Too many cooks, better let me!"

Adrian's knowledge of cars was nil, his attitude to machinery helpless; he stood willingly aside, and watched them with admiration. They were cool, quick, efficient, but something was wrong with the jack.

"Always like that," said Fleur, "when you're in a hurry."

Twenty minutes was lost before they were again in motion.

"I can't possibly do it now," she said, "but you'll be able to pick up his tracks easily, if you really want to. The station's right out beyond the town."

Through Billingshurst and Pulborough and over Stopham bridge, they travelled at full speed.

"Better go for Petworth itself," said Hilary, "if he's heading back for the town, we shall meet him."

"Am I to stop if we meet him?"

"No, carry straight on past and then turn."

But they passed through Petworth and on for the mile and a half to the station without meeting him.

"The train's been in a good twenty minutes," said Adrian, "let's ask."

A porter had taken the ticket of a gentleman in a blue overcoat and black hat. No! He had no luggage. He had gone off, towards the Downs. How long ago? Half an hour, maybe.

Regaining the car hastily they made towards the Downs.

"I remember," said Hilary, "a little further on there's a turn to Sutton. The point will be whether he's taken that or gone on up. There are some houses there somewhere. We'll ask, they may have seen him."

Just beyond the turning was a little post-office, and a postman was cycling towards it from the Sutton road.

Fleur pulled the car to a walk alongside.

"Have you seen a gentleman in a blue coat and bowler hat making towards Sutton?"

"No, Miss, 'aven't passed a soul."

"Thank you. Shall I carry on for the Down, Uncle Hilary?"

Hilary consulted his watch.

"If I remember, it's a mile about to the top of the Down close to Duncton Beacon. We've come a mile and a half from the station; and he had, say, twenty-five minutes' start, so by the time we get to the top we should have about caught him. From the top we shall see the road ahead and be able to make sure. If we don't come on him, it'll mean he's taken to the Down—but which way?"

Adrian said under his breath: "Homewards."

"To the East?" said Hilary. "On then, Fleur, not too fast."

Fleur headed the car up the Downs road.

"Feel in my coat, you'll find three apples," she said. "I caught them up."

"What a head!" said Hilary. "But you'll want them yourself."

"No. I'm slimming. You can leave me one."

The brothers, munching each an apple, kept their eyes fixed on the woods on either side of the car.

"Too thick," said Hilary; "he'll be carrying on to the open. If you sight him, Fleur, stop dead."

But they did not sight him, and, mounting slower and slower, reached the top. To their right was the round beech tree clump of Duncton, to the left the open Down; no figure was on the road in front.

"Not ahead," said Hilary. "We've got to decide, old man."

"Take my advice, and let me drive you home, Uncle Hilary."

"Shall we, Adrian?"

Adrian shook his head.

"I shall go on."

"All right, I'm with you."

"Look!" said Fleur suddenly, and pointed.

Some fifty yards in, along a rough track leaving the road to the left, lay a dark object.

"It's a coat, I think."

Adrain jumped out and ran towards it. He returned with a blue overcoat over his arm.

"No doubt now," he said. "Either he was sitting there and left it by mistake, or he tired of carrying it. It's a bad sign whichever it was. Come along, Hilary!"

He dropped the coat in the car.

"What orders for me, Uncle Hilary?"

"You've been a brick, my dear. Would you be still more of a brick and wait here another hour? If we're not back by then, go down and keep close along under the Downs slowly by way of Sutton Bignor and West Burton, then if there's no sign of us anywhere along that way, take the main road through Pulborough back to London. If you've any money to spare, you might lend us some."

Fleur took out her bag.

"Three pounds. Shall I give you two?"

"Gratefully received," said Hilary. "Adrian and I never have any money. We're the poorest family in England, I do believe. Good-bye, my dear, and thank you! Now, old man!"

CHAPTER 28

WAVING THEIR HANDS to where Fleur stood by her car with the remaining apple raised to her lips, the two brothers took the track on to the Down.

"You lead," said Hilary; "you've got the best eyes, and your clothes are less conspicuous. If you sight him, we'll consult."

They came almost at once on a long stretch of high wire fence running across the Down.

"It ends there to the left," said Adrian; "we'll go round it above the woods, the lower we keep the better."

They kept round it on the hillside over grass rougher and more uneven, falling into a climber's loping stride as if once more they were off on some long and difficult ascent. The doubt whether they would catch up with Ferse, what they could do if they did, and the knowledge that it might be a maniac with whom they had to deal, brought to both their faces a look that soldiers have, and sailors, and men climbing mountains, of out-staring what was before them.

They had crossed an old and shallow chalk working and were mounting the few feet to the level on its far side, when Adrian dropped back and pulled Hilary down.

"He's there," he whispered; "about seventy yards ahead!"

"See you?"

"No. He looks wild. His hat's gone, and he's gesticulating. What shall we do?"

"Put your head up through that bush."

Adrian knelt, watching. Ferse had ceased to gesticulate, he was standing with arms crossed and his bare head bent. His back was to Adrian, and, but for that still, square, wrapped-in attitude, there was nothing to judge from. He suddenly uncrossed his arms, shook his head from side to side and began to walk rapidly on. Adrian waited till he had disappeared among the bushes on the slope, and beckoned Hilary to follow.

"We mustn't let him get too far ahead," muttered Hilary, "or we shan't know whether he's taken to the wood."

"He'll keep to the open, he wants air, poor devil. Look out!" He pulled Hilary down again. The ground had suddenly begun to dip. It sloped right down to a grassy hollow, and halfway down the slope they could see Ferse plainly. He was walking slowly, clearly unconscious of pursuit.

Every now and then his hands would go up to his bare head, as if to clear away something that entangled it.

"God!" murmured Adrian: "I hate to see him."

Hilary nodded.

They lay watching. Part of the weald was visible, rich with colour on that sunny autumn day. The grass, after heavy morning dew, was scented still; the sky of the dim spiritual blue that runs almost to white above the chalky Downs. And the day was silent well-nigh to breathlessness. The brothers waited without speaking.

Ferse had reached the level at the bottom; they could see him dejectedly moving across a rough field towards a spinney. A pheasant rose just in front of him; they saw him start, as if wakened from a dream, and stand watching its rising flight.

"I expect he knows every foot round here," said Adrian: "he was a keen sportsman." And just then Ferse threw up his hands as if they held a gun. There was something oddly reassuring in that action.

"Now," said Hilary, as Ferse disappeared in the spinney, "run!" They dashed down the hill, and hurried along over rough ground.

"Suppose," gasped Adrian, "that he's stopped in the spinney."

"Risk it! Gently now, till we can see the rise."

About a hundred yards beyond the spinney, Ferse was plodding slowly up the hill.

"All right so far," murmured Hilary, "we must wait till that rise flattens out and we lose sight of him. This is a queer business, old boy, for you and me. And at the end of it, as Fleur said: What?"

"We *must know*," said Adrian.

"We're just losing him now. Let's give him five minutes. I'll time it."

That five minutes seemed interminable. A jay squawked from the wooded hillside, a rabbit stole out and squatted in front of them; faint shiverings of air passed through the spinney.

"Now!" said Hilary. They rose, and breasted the grass rise at a good pace. "If he comes back on his tracks, here——"

"The sooner it's face to face the better," said Adrian, "but if he sees us following he'll run, and we shall lose him."

"Go slow, old man. It's beginning to flatten."

Cautiously they topped the rise. The Down now dipped a little to where a chalky track ran above a beechwood to their left. There was no sign of Ferse.

"Either he's gone into the wood or he's through that next thicket, and on the rise again. We'd better hurry and make sure."

They ran along the track between deep banks, and were turning into the brush, when the sound of a voice not twenty yards ahead jerked them to a standstill. They dropped back behind the bank and lay breathless. Somewhere in the thicket Ferse was muttering to himself. They could hear no words, but the voice gave them both a miserable feeling.

"Poor chap!" whispered Hilary: "shall we go on, and try to comfort him?"

"Listen!"

There was the sound as of a branch cracking underfoot, a muttered oath, and then with appalling suddenness a huntsman's scream. It had a quality that froze the blood. Adrian said:

"Pretty ghastly! But he's broken covert."

Cautiously they moved into the thicket; Ferse was running for the Down that rose from the end of it.

"He didn't see us, did he?"

"No, or he'd be looking back. Wait till we lose sight of him again."

"This is poor work," said Hilary, suddenly, "but I agree with you it's got to be done. That was a horrible sound! But we must know exactly what we're going to do, old man."

"I was thinking," said Adrian, "if we could induce him to come back to Chelsea, we'd keep Diana and the children away, dismiss the maids, and get him special attendants. I'd stay there with him till it was properly fixed. It seems to me that his own house is the only chance."

"I don't believe he'll come of his free will."

"In that case, God knows! I won't have a hand in caging him."

"What if he tries to kill himself?"

"That's up to you, Hilary."

Hilary was silent.

"Don't bet on my cloth," he said, suddenly; "a slum parson is pretty hard-boiled."

Adrian gripped his hand. "He's out of sight now."

"Come on, then!"

They crossed the level at a sharp pace and began mounting the rise. Up there the character of the ground changed, the hill was covered sparsely by hawthorn bushes, and yew trees, and bramble, with here and there a young beech. It gave a good cover, and they moved more freely.

"We're coming to the cross roads above Bignor," murmured Hilary. "He might take the track down from there. We could easily lose him!"

They ran, but suddenly stood still behind a yew tree.

"He's not going down," said Hilary: "Look!"

On the grassy open rise beyond the cross tracks, where a signpost stood, Ferse was running towards the north side of the hill.

"A second track goes down there, I remember."

"It's all chance, but we can't stop now."

Ferse had ceased to run, he was walking slowly with stooped head up the rise. They watched him from behind their yew tree till he vanished over the hill's shoulder.

"Now!" said Hilary.

It was a full half mile, and both of them were over fifty.

"Not too fast, old man," panted Hilary; "we mustn't bust our bellows."

They kept to a dogged jog, reached the shoulder, over which Ferse had vanished, and found a grass track trailing down.

"Sowly does it now," gasped Hilary.

Here too the hillside was dotted with bushes and young trees, and they made good use of them till they came to a shallow chalk pit.

"Let's lie up here a minute, and get our wind. He's not going off the Down or we'd have seen him. Listen!"

From below them came a chanting sound. Adrian raised his head above the pit side and looked over. A little way down by the side of the track lay Ferse on his back. The words of the song he was droning out came up quite clearly:

> "Must I go bound, and you go free?
> Must I love a lass that couldn't love me?
> Was e'er I taught so poor a wit
> As love a lass, would break my heart."

He ceased and lay perfectly still; then, to Adrian's horror, his face became distorted; he flung his fists up in the air, cried out: "I won't—I won't be mad!" and rolled over on his face.

Adrian dropped back.

"It's terrible! I must go down and speak to him."

"We'll both go—round by the track—slow—don't startle him."

They took the track which wound round the chalk pit. Ferse was no longer there.

"Quietly on, old son," said Hilary.

They walked on in a curious calm, as if they had abandoned the chase.

"Who can believe in God?" said Adrian.

A wry smile contorted Hilary's long face.

"In God I believe, but not a merciful one as we understand the word. On this hillside, I remember, they trap. Hundreds of rabbits suffer the tortures of the damned. We used to let them out and knock them on the head. If my beliefs were known, I should be unfrocked. That wouldn't help. My job's a concrete one. Look! A fox!"

They stood a moment watching his low fulvous body steal across the track.

"Marvellous beast, a fox! Great places for wild life, these wooded chines; so steep, you can't disturb them—pigeons, jays, woodpeckers, rabbits, foxes, hares, pheasants—every mortal thing."

The track had begun to drop, and Hilary pointed.

Ahead, beyond the dip into the chine they could see Ferse walking along a wire fence.

They watched till he vanished then reappeared on the side of the hill, having rounded the corner of the fence.

"What now?"

"He can't see us from there. To speak to him, we must somehow get near before we try, otherwise he'll just run."

They crossed the dip and went up along and round the corner of the fence under cover of the hawthorns. On the uneven hillside Ferse had again vanished.

"This is wired for sheep," said Hilary. "Look! they're all over the hill —Southdowns."

They reached a top. There was no sign of him.

They kept along the wire, and reaching the crest of the next rise, stood looking. Away to the left the hill dropped steeply into another chine; in front of them was open grass dipping to a wood. On their right was still the wire fencing and rough pasture. Suddenly Adrian gripped his brother's arm. Not seventy yards away on the other side of the wire Ferse was lying face to the grass, with sheep grazing close to him. The brothers crawled to the shelter of a bush. From there, unseen, they could see him quite well, and they watched him in silence. He lay so still that the sheep were paying him no attention. Round-bodied, short-legged, snub-nosed, of a greyish white, and with the essential cosiness of the Southdown breed, they grazed on, undisturbed.

"Is he asleep, d'you think?"

Adrian shook his head. "Peaceful, though."

There was something in his attitude that went straight to the heart; something that recalled a small boy hiding his head in his mother's lap; it was as if the feel of the grass beneath his body, his face, his outstretched hands, were bringing him comfort; as if he were groping his way back into the quiet security of Mother Earth. While he lay like that it was impossible to disturb him.

The sun, in the west, fell on their backs, and Adrian turned his face to receive it on his cheek. All the nature-lover and country man in him responded to that warmth, to the scent of the grass, the song of the larks, the blue of the sky; and he noticed that Hilary too had turned his face to the sun. It was so still that, but for the larks' song and the muffled sound of the sheep cropping, one might have said Nature was dumb. No voice of man or beast, no whirr of traffic came up from the weald.

"Three o'clock. Have a nap, old man," he whispered to Hilary; "I'll watch."

Ferse seemed asleep now. Surely his brain would rest from its disorder here. If there were healing in air, in form, in colour, it was upon this green cool hill for a thousand years and more undwelt on and freed from the restlessness of men. The men of old, indeed, had lived up there; but since then nothing had touched it but the winds and the shadows of the clouds. And to-day there was no wind, no cloud to throw soft and moving darkness on the grass.

So profound a pity for the poor devil, lying there as if he would never move again, stirred Adrian, that he could not think of himself, nor even feel for Diana. Ferse, so lying, awakened in him a sensation quite impersonal, the deep herding kinship men have for each other in the face of Fortune's strokes which seem to them unfair. Yes! He was sleeping now, grasping at the earth for refuge; to grasp for eternal refuge in the earth was all that was left him. And for those two quiet hours of watching that prostrate figure among the sheep, Adrian was filled not with futile rebellion and bitterness but with a strange unhappy wonder. The old Greek dramatists had understood the tragic plaything which the gods make of man; such understanding had been overlaid by the Christian doctrine of a merciful God. Merciful—No! Hilary was right! Faced by Ferse's fate—what would one do? What—while the gleam of sanity remained? When a man's life was so spun that no longer he could do his job, be no more to his fellows than a poor distraught and frightening devil, the hour of eternal rest in quiet earth had surely come. Hilary had seemed to think so too; yet he was not sure what his brother would do if it came to the point. His job was with the living, a man who died was lost to him, so much chance of service gone! And Adrian felt a sort of thankfulness that his own job was with the dead, classifying the bones of men—the only part of men that did not suffer, and endured, age on age, to afford evidence of a marvellous animal. So he lay, and watched, plucking blade after blade of grass and rubbing the sweetness of them out between his palms.

The sun wore on due west, till it was almost level with his eyes; the sheep had ceased cropping and were moving slowly together over the hill, as if waiting to be folded. Rabbits had stolen out and were nibbling the grass; and the larks, one by one, had dropped from the sky. A chill was creeping on the air; the trees down in weald had darkened and solidified; and the whitening sky seemed waiting for the sunset glow. The grass too had lost its scent; there was no dew as yet.

Adrian shivered. In ten minutes now the sun would be off the hill, and then it would be cold. When Ferse awoke, would he be better or worse? They must risk it. He touched Hilary, who lay with his knees drawn up, still sleeping. He woke instantly.

"Hallo, old man!"

"Hssh! He's still asleep. What are we to do when he wakes? Shall we go up to him now and wait for it?"

Hilary jerked his brother's sleeve. Ferse was on his feet. From behind their bush they could see him wildly looking round, as some animal warned of danger might stand gazing before he takes to flight. It was clear that he could not see them, but that he had heard or sensed some presence. He began walking towards the wire, crawled through and stood upright, turned towards the reddening sun balanced now like a fiery globe on the far wooded hill. With the glow from it on his face, bareheaded and so still that he might have been dead on his feet, he stood till the sun vanished.

"Now," whispered Hilary, and stood up. Adrian saw Ferse come suddenly to life, fling out his arm with a wild defiance, and turn to run.

Hilary said, aghast: "He's desperate. There's a chalk pit just above the main road. Come on, old man, come on!"

They ran, but stiffened as they were, had no chance with Ferse, who gained with every stride. He ran like a maniac flinging his arms out, and they could hear him shout. Hilary gasped out:

"Stop! He's not going for that pit after all. It's away to the right. He's making for the wood down there. Better let him think we've given up."

They watched him running down the slope, and lost him as, still running, he entered the wood.

"Now!" said Hilary.

They laboured on down to the wood and entered it as near to the point of his disappearance as they could. It was of beech and except at the edge there was no undergrowth. They stopped to listen, but there was no sound. The light in there was already dim, but the wood was narrow and they were soon at its far edge. Below they could see some cottages and farm buildings.

"Let's get down to the road."

They hurried on, came suddenly to the edge of a high chalk pit, and stopped aghast.

"I didn't know of this," said Hilary. "Go that way and I'll go this along the edge."

Adrian went upwards till he reached the top. Below, at the bottom some sixty steep feet down, he could see a dark thing lying. Whatever it was, it did not move, and no sound came up. Was this the end then, a headlong dive into the half dark? A choking sensation seized him by the throat, and for a moment he stood unable to call out or move. Then hastily he ran along the edge till he came to where Hilary was standing.

"Well?"

Adrian pointed back into the pit. They went on along the edge through undergrowth till they could scramble down, and make their way over the grassed floor of the old pit to the farther corner below the highest point.

The dark thing was Ferse. Adrian knelt and raised his head. His neck was broken; he was dead.

Whether he had dived deliberately to that end, or in his mad rush fallen over, they could not tell. Neither of them spoke, but Hilary put his hand on his brother's shoulder.

At last he said: "There's a cart shed a little way along the road, but perhaps we ought not to move him. Stay with him, while I go to the village and 'phone? It's a matter for the police, I suppose."

Adrian nodded, still on his knees beside the broken figure.

"There's a post office quite near, I shan't be long." Hilary hurried away.

Alone in the silent darkening pit Adrian sat cross-legged, with the dead man's head resting against him. He had closed the eyes and covered the face with his handkerchief. In the wood above birds rustled and chirped, on their way to bed. The dew had begun to fall, and into the blue twilight the ground mist of autumn was creeping. Shape was all softened, but the tall chalk pit face still showed white. Though not fifty yards from a road on which cars were passing, this spot where Ferse had leapt to his rest seemed to Adrian desolate, remote, and full of ghostliness. Though he knew that he ought to be thankful for Ferse, for Diana, for himself, he could feel nothing but that profound pity for a fellow man so tortured and broken in his prime—profound pity, and a sort of creeping identification with the mystery of Nature enwrapping the dead man and this his resting-place.

A voice roused him from that strange coma. An old whiskered countryman was standing there with a glass in his hand.

"So there been an accident, I year," he was saying; "a parson gentleman sent me with this. 'Tis brandy, Sir." He handed the glass to Adrian. "Did 'e fall over yere, or what?"

"Yes, he fell over."

"I allus said as they should put a fence up there. The gentleman said I was to tell you as the doctor and the police was comin'."

"Thank you," said Adrian, handing back the emptied glass.

"There be a nice cosy car shed a little ways along the road, maybe we could carry 'im along there."

"We mustn't move him till they come."

"Ah!" said the old countryman: "I've read as there was a law about that, in case as 'twas murder or sooicide." He peered down. "He do look quiet, don't 'e? D'e know 'oo 'e is, Sir?"

"Yes. A Captain Ferse. He came from round here."

"What, one of the Ferses o' Burton Rise? Why, I worked there as a boy; born in that parish I were." He peered closer: "This'd never be Mr. Ronald, would it?"

Adrian nodded.

"Yeou don' say! There's none of 'em there neow. His grandfather died mad, so 'e did. Yeou don' say! Mr. Ronald! I knew 'im as a young lad." He stooped to look at the face in the last of the light, then stood, moving his whiskered head mournfully from side to side. To him—Adrian could see —it made all the difference that here was no 'foreigner.'

The sudden sputtering of a motor cycle broke the stillness; it came with gleaming headlight down the cart track into the pit, and two figures got off. A young man and a girl. They came gingerly towards the group disclosed by the beam from the headlight, and stood, peering down.

"We heard there's been an accident."

"Ah!" said the old countryman.

"Can we do anything?"

"No, thank you," said Adrian; "the doctor and the police are coming. We must just wait."

He could see the young man open his mouth as if to ask more, close it without speaking, and put his arm round the girl, then, like the old countryman, they stood silent with their eyes fixed on the figure with the broken neck lying against Adrian's knee. The cycle's engine, still running, throbbed in the silence, and its light made even more ghostly the old pit and the little group of the living around the dead.

CHAPTER 29

At CONDAFORD, the telegram came just before dinner. It ran: 'Poor F dead Fell down chalk pit here Removed to Chichester Adrian and I going with him Inquest will be there. Hilary.'

Dinny was in her room when it was brought to her, and she sat down on her bed with that feeling of constriction in the chest which comes when relief and sorrow struggle together for expression. Here was what she had prayed for, and all she could think of was the last sound she had heard him utter, and the look on his face, when he was standing in the doorway listening to Diana singing. She said to the maid who had brought in the telegram:

"Amy, find Scaramouch."

When the Scotch terrier came with his bright eyes and his air of knowing that he was of value, she clasped him so tight that he became uneasy. With that warm and stiffly hairy body in her arms, she regained the power of feeling; relief covered the background of her being, but pity forced tears into her eyes. It was a curious state, and beyond the comprehension of her dog. He licked her nose and wriggled till she set him down. She finished dressing hurriedly and went to her mother's room.

Lady Cherrell, dressed for dinner, was moving between open wardrobe and open chest of drawers, considering what she could best part with for the approaching jumble sale which must keep the village nursing fund going over the year's end. Dinny put the telegram into her hand without a word. Having read it, she said quietly:

"That's what you prayed for, dear."

"Does it mean suicide?"

"I think so."

"Ought I to tell Diana now, or wait till she's had a night's sleep?"

"Now, I think. I will, if you like."

"No, no, darling. It's up to me. She'll like dinner upstairs, I expect. To-morrow, I suppose, we shall have to go to Chichester."

"This is all very dreadful for you, Dinny."

"It's good for me." She took back the telegram and went out.

Diana was with the children, who were giving as long as possible to the process of going to bed, not having reached the age when to do such a thing has become desirable. Dinny beckoned her out into her own room, and, once more without a word, handed over the telegram. Though she had been so close to Diana these last days, there were sixteen years between them, and she made no consoling gesture as she might have to one of her own age. She had, indeed, a feeling of never quite knowing how Diana would take things. She took this stonily. It might have been no news at all. Her beautiful face, fine and worn as that on a coin, expressed nothing. Her eyes fixed on Dinny's, remained dry and clear. All she said was: "I won't come down. To-morrow—Chichester?"

Checking all impulse, Dinny nodded and went out. Alone with her mother after dinner, she said:

"I wish I had Diana's self-control."

"Self-control like hers is the result of all she's been through."

"There's the Vere de Vere touch about it, too."

"That's no bad thing, Dinny."

"What will this inquest mean?"

"She'll need all her self-control there, I'm afraid."

"Mother, shall I have to give evidence?"

"You were the last person who spoke to him so far as is known, weren't you?"

"Yes. Must I speak of his coming to the door last night?"

"I suppose you ought to tell everything you know, if you're asked."

A flush stained Dinny's cheeks.

"I don't think I will. I never even told Diana that. And I don't see what it has to do with outsiders."

"No, I don't see either; but we're not supposed to exercise our own judgments as to that."

"Well, I shall; I'm not going to pander to people's beastly curiosity, and give Diana pain."

"Suppose one of the maids heard him?"

"They can't prove that *I* did."

Lady Cherrell smiled. "I wish your father were here."

"You are not to tell Dad what I told you, Mother. I can't have the male conscience fussing around; the female's is bad enough, but one has it in hand."

"Very well."

"I shan't have the faintest scruple," said Dinny, fresh from her recollection of London Police Courts, "about keeping a thing dark, if I can safely. What do they want an inquest for, anyway? He's dead. It's just morbidity."

"I oughtn't to aid and abet you, Dinny."

"Yes, you ought, Mother. You know you agree at heart."

Lady Cherrell said no more. She did. . . .

The General and Alan Tasburgh came down next morning by the first train, and half an hour later they all started in the open car; Alan driving, the General beside him, and in the back seat Lady Cherrell, Dinny and Diana wedged together. It was a long and gloomy drive. Leaning back with her nose just visible above her fur, Dinny pondered. It was dawning on her gradually that she was in some sort the hub of the approaching inquest. She it was to whom Ferse had opened his heart; she who had taken the children away; she who had gone down in the night to telephone; she who had heard what she did not mean to tell; and, lastly but much the most importantly, it must be she who had called in Adrian and Hilary. Only behind her, their niece, who had caused Diana to turn to them for assistance when Ferse vanished, could Adrian's friendship for Diana be masked. Like everybody else, Dinny read, and even enjoyed, the troubles and scandals of others, retailed in the papers; like everybody else, she revolted against the papers having anything that could be made into scandal to retail about her family or her friends. If it came out crudely that her uncle had been applied to as an old and intimate friend of Diana's, he and she would be asked all sorts of questions, leading to all sorts of suspicions in the sex-ridden minds of the Public. Her roused imagination roamed freely. If Adrian's long and close friendship with Diana became known, what would there be to prevent the Public from suspecting even that her uncle had pushed Ferse over the edge of that chalk pit, unless, of course, Hilary were with him—for as yet they knew no details. Her mind, in fact, began running before the hounds. A lurid explanation of anything was so much more acceptable than a dull and true one! And there hardened within her an almost vicious determination to cheat the Public of the thrills it would be seeking.

Adrian met them in the hall of the hotel at Chichester, and she took her chance to say: "Uncle, can I speak to you and Uncle Hilary privately?"

"Hilary had to go back to Town, my dear, but he'll be down the last thing this evening; we can have a talk then. The inquest's to-morrow."

With that she had to be content.

When he had finished his story, determined that Adrian should not take Diana to see Ferse, she said: "If you'll tell us where to go, Uncle, I'll go with Diana."

Adrian nodded. He had understood.

When they reached the mortuary, Diana went in alone, and Dinny waited in a corridor which smelled of disinfectant and looked out on to a back street. A fly, disenchanted by the approach of winter, was crawling dejectedly up the pane. Gazing out into that colourless back alley, under a sky drained of all warmth and light, she felt very miserable. Life seemed exceptionally bleak, and heavy with sinister issues. This inquest, Hubert's impending fate—no light or sweetness anywhere! Not even the thought of Alan's palpable devotion gave her comfort.

She turned to see Diana again beside her, and, suddenly forgetting her own woe, threw an arm round her and kissed her cold cheek. They went back to the hotel without speaking, except for Diana's: "He looked marvellously calm."

She went early to her room after dinner, and sat there with a book, waiting for her uncles. It was ten o'clock before Hilary's cab drew up, and a few minutes later they came. She noted how shadowy and worn they both looked; but there was something reassuring in their faces. They were the sort who ran till they dropped, anyway. They both kissed her with unexpected warmth, and sat down sideways, one on each side of her bed. Dinny stood between them at the foot and addressed Hilary.

"It's about Uncle Adrian, Uncle. I've been thinking. This inquest is going to be horrid if we don't take care."

"It is, Dinny. I came down with a couple of journalists who didn't suspect my connection. They've got hold of the mental home, and are all agog. I've a great respect for journalists, they do their job very thoroughly."

Dinny addressed Adrian.

"You won't mind my talking freely, will you, Uncle?"

Adrian smiled. "No, Dinny. You're a loyal baggage; go ahead!"

"It seems to me, then," she went on, plaiting her fingers on the bed-rail, "that the chief point is to keep Uncle Adrian's friendship for Diana out of it, and I thought that the asking of you two to find him ought to be put entirely on to me. You see, I was the last person known to speak to him, when he cut the telephone wire, you know, so, when I'm called, I could get it into their minds that you were entirely my suggestion, as a couple of Uncles who were clever and good at crossword puzzles. Otherwise, why did we go to Uncle Adrian? Because he was *such a friend*, and then you'd get at once all that they may think that means, especially when they hear that Captain Ferse was away four years."

There was silence before Hilary said:

"She's wise, old boy. Four years' friendship with a beautiful woman in a husband's absence means only one thing with a jury, and many things with the Public."

Adrian nodded. "But I don't see how the fact that I've known them both so long can be concealed."

"First impressions," said Dinny, eagerly, "will be everything. I can say that Diana suggested going to her doctor and Michael, but that I overruled her, knowing that you were marvellous at tracing things out because of your job, and could get at Uncle Hilary, who was so good at human nature. If we *start* them right, I don't believe the mere fact that you knew both of them would matter. It seems to me awfully important that I should be called as early as possible."

"It's putting a lot on you, my dear."

"Oh! no. If I'm not called before you and Uncle Hilary, will you both say that it was I who came and asked you, and I can rub it in afterwards?"

"After the doctor and the police, Diana will be the first witness."

"Yes, but I can speak to her, so that we shall all be saying the same thing."

Hilary smiled. "I don't see why not, it's very white lying. I can put in that I've known them as long as you, Adrian. We both met Diana first at that picnic Lawrence gave near the Land's End when she was a flapper, and we both met Ferse at her wedding. Family friendship, um?"

"My visits to the Mental Home will come out," said Adrian, "the Doctor's been summoned as witness."

"Oh! well," said Dinny, "you went there as his friend, and specially interested in mental derangement. After all, you're supposed to be scientific, Uncle."

Both smiled, and Hilary said: "All right, Dinny, we'll speak to the Sergeant, he's a very decent chap, and get you called early, if possible." He went to the door.

"Good-night, little serpent," said Adrian.

"Good-night, dear Uncle; you look terribly tired. Have you got a hot water bottle?"

Adrian shook his head. "I've nothing but a tooth-brush which I bought to-day."

Dinny hauled her bottle out of her bed, and forced it on him. "Shall I speak to Diana, then, about what we've been saying?"

"If you will, Dinny."

"After to-morrow the sun will shine."

"Will it?" said Adrian.

As the door closed, Dinny sighed. Would it? Diana seemed as if dead to feeling. And—there was Hubert's business!

CHAPTER 30

THE REFLECTIONS of Adrian and his niece, when together they entered the Coroner's Court on the following day, might have been pooled as follows:

A coroner's inquest was like roast beef and Yorkshire pudding on Sundays, devised for other times. When Sunday afternoons were devoted to games, murders infrequent, and suicides no longer buried at cross-roads, neither custom had its initial wisdom. In the old days, Justice and its emissaries were regarded as the foes of mankind, so it was natural to interpose a civilian arbiter between death and the Law. In an age in which one called the police 'a splendid force' was there not something unnatural in supposing them incapable of judging when it was necessary for them to take action? Their incompetence, therefore, could not well be considered the reason for the preservation of these rites. The cause was, surely, in one's dread of being deprived of knowledge. Every reader of a newspaper felt that the more he or she heard about what was doubtful, sensational, and unsavoury, the better for his or her soul. One knew that, without coroners' inquests, there would often be no published enquiry at all into sensational death; and never two enquiries. If, then, in place of no enquiry one could always have one enquiry, and in place of one enquiry sometimes have two enquiries, how much pleasanter! The dislike which one had for being nosey disappeared the moment one got into a crowd. The nosier one could be in a crowd the happier one felt. And the oftener one could find room in a Coroner's Court, the greater the thankfulness to Heaven. "Praise God from whom all blessings flow" could never go up more fervently than from the hearts of such as had been privileged to find seats at an enquiry about death. For an enquiry about death nearly always meant the torture of the living, and than that was anything more calculated to give pleasure?

The fact that the Court was full confirmed these reflections, and they passed into a little room to wait, Adrian saying: "You go in fifth wicket down, Dinny, both Hilary and I are taken before you. If we keep out of Court till we're wanted they can't say we copied each other."

They sat very silent in the little bare room. The police, the doctor, Diana and Hilary had all to be examined first.

"It's like the ten little nigger boys," murmured Dinny. Her eyes were fixed on a calendar on the wall opposite; she could not read it, but it seemed necessary.

"See, my dear," said Adrian, and drew a little bottle from his breast pocket, "take a sip or two of this—not more—it's fifty-fifty sal volatile and water; it'll steady you no end. Be careful!"

Dinny took a little gulp. It burned her throat, but not too badly.

"You too, Uncle."

Adrian also took a cautious gulp.

"No finer dope," he said, "before going in to bat, or anything like that."

And they again sat silent, assimilating the fumes. Presently Adrian said:

"If spirits survive, as I don't believe, what is poor Ferse thinking of this farce? We're still barbarians. There's a story of Maupassant's about a Suicide Club that provided a pleasant form of death to those who felt they had to go. I don't believe in suicide for the sane, except in very rare cases. We've got to stick things out; but for the insane, or those threatened with it, I wish we had that Club, Dinny. Has that stuff steadied you?"

Dinny nodded.

"It'll last pretty well an hour." He got up. "My turn, I see. Good-bye, my dear, good luck! Stick in a 'Sir,' to the Coroner, now and then."

Watching him straighten himself as he passed through the door, Dinny felt a sort of inspiration. Uncle Adrian was the man she admired most of any she had ever seen. And she sent up a little illogical prayer for him. Certainly that stuff had steadied her; the sinking, fluttering feeling she had been having was all gone. She took out her pocket mirror and powder-puff. She could go to the stake, anyway, with a nose that did not shine.

Another quarter of an hour, however, passed before she was called, and she spent it, with her eyes still fixed on that calendar, thinking of Condaford and recalling all her pleasantest times there. The old days of its unrestored state, when she was very small, hayfield days, and picnics in the woods; pulling lavender, riding on the retriever, promotion to the pony when Hubert was at school; days of pure delight in a new, fixed home, for, though she had been born there, she had been nomadic till she was four—at Aldershot, and Gibraltar. She remembered with special pleasure winding the golden silk of the cocoons of her silk-worms, how they made her think of creeping, crawling elephants, and how peculiar had been their smell.

"Elizabeth Charwell."

Nuisance to have a name that everyone pronounced wrong as a matter of course! And she rose, murmuring to herself:

> "One little nigger, walking all alone,
> Up came a coroner, and then there was none."

Someone took charge of her on her entry, and, taking her across the Court, placed her in a sort of pen. It was fortunate that she had been in such places lately, for it all felt rather familiar, and even faintly comic.

The jury in front of her looked as it were disused, the coroner had a funny importance. Down there, not far to her left, were the other little niggers; and, behind them, stretching to the blank wall, dozens and dozens and dozens of faces in rows, as of sardines set up on their tails in a huge sardine box. Then aware that she was being addressed, she concentrated on the coroner's face.

"Your name is Elizabeth Cherrell. You are the daughter, I believe, of Lieutenant-General Sir Conway Cherrell, K.C.B., C.M.G., and Lady Cherrell?"

Dinny bowed. 'I believe he likes me for that,' she thought.

"And you live with them at Condaford Grange in Oxfordshire?"

"Yes."

"I believe, Miss Cherrell, that you were staying with Captain and Mrs. Ferse up to the morning on which Captain Ferse left his house?"

"I was."

"Are you a close friend of theirs?"

"Of Mrs. Ferse. I had seen Captain Ferse only once, I think, before his return."

"Ah! his return. Were you staying with Mrs. Ferse when he returned?"

"I had come up to stay with her on that very afternoon."

"The afternoon of his return from the Mental Home?"

"Yes. I actually went to stay at their house the following day."

"And were you there until Captain Ferse left his house?"

"I was."

"During that time what was his demeanour?"

At this question for the first time Dinny realised the full disadvantage of not knowing what has been said already. It almost looked as if she must say what she really knew and felt.

"He seemed to me quite normal, except that he would not go out or see anybody. He looked quite healthy, only his eyes made one feel unhappy."

"How do you mean exactly?"

"They—they looked like a fire behind bars, they seemed to flicker."

And, at those words, she noticed that the jury for a moment looked a trifle less disused.

"He would not go out, you say? Was that during the whole time you were there?"

"No; he went out on the day before he left his home. He was out all that day, I believe."

"You believe? Were you not there?"

"No; that morning I took the two children down to my mother's at Condaford Grange, and returned in the evening just before dinner. Captain Ferse was not in then."

"What made you take the children down?"

"Mrs. Ferse asked me to. She had noticed some change in Captain Ferse, and she thought the children would be better away."

"Could you say that you had noticed a change?"

177

"Yes. I thought he seemed more restless, and, perhaps, suspicious; and he was drinking more at dinner."

"Nothing very striking?"

"No. I——"

"Yes, Miss Cherrell?"

"I was going to say something that I don't know of my own knowledge."

"Something that Mrs. Ferse had told you?"

"Yes."

"Well, you needn't tell us that."

"Thank you, Sir."

"Coming back to when you returned from taking the children to your home, Captain Ferse was not in, you say; was Mrs. Ferse in?"

"Yes, she was dressed for dinner. I dressed quickly and we dined alone together. We were very anxious about him."

"And then?"

"After dinner we went up to the drawing room, and to distract her I made Mrs. Ferse sing, she was so nervous and anxious. After a little we heard the front door, and Captain Ferse came in and sat down."

"Did he say anything?"

"No."

"How was he looking?"

"Dreadful, I thought. Very strange and strained, as if under the power of some terrible thought."

"Yes?"

"Mrs. Ferse asked him if he had had dinner, and if he would like to go to bed; and if he would see a doctor; but he wouldn't speak—he sat with his eyes closed, almost as if he might be asleep, until at last I whispered: 'Is he asleep, d'you think?' Then suddenly he cried out: 'Sleep! I'm for it again, and I won't stand it. By God! I won't stand it.'"

When she had repeated those words of Ferse, Dinny understood better than hitherto what is meant by the expression 'sensation in Court'; in some mysterious way she had supplied what had been lacking to the conviction carried by the witnesses who had preceded her. Whether she had been wise in this, she was utterly unable to decide; and her eyes sought Adrian's face. He gave her an almost imperceptible nod.

"Yes, Miss Cherrell?"

"Mrs. Ferse went towards him, and he cried out: 'Leave me alone. Go away!' I think she said: 'Ronald, won't you see someone just to give you something to make you sleep?' but he sprang up and cried out violently: 'Go away! I'll see no one—no one!'"

"Yes, Miss Cherrell, what then?"

"We were frightened. We went up to my room and consulted, and I said we ought to telephone."

"To whom?"

"To Mrs. Ferse's doctor. She wanted to go, but I prevented her and ran down. The telephone was in the little study on the ground floor, and

I was just getting the number when I felt my hand seized, and there was Captain Ferse behind me. He cut the wire with a knife. Then he stood holding my arm, and I said: 'That's silly, Captain Ferse; you know we wouldn't hurt you.' He let me go, and put his knife away, and told me to put on my shoes, because I had them in my other hand."

"You mean you had taken them off?"

"Yes, to run down quietly. I put them on. He said: 'I'm not going to be messed about. I shall do what I like with myself.' I said: 'You know we only want your good.' And he said: 'I know that good—no more of that for me.' And then he looked out of the window and said: 'It's raining like hell,' and turned to me and cried: 'Get out of this room, quick. Get out!' and I flew back upstairs again."

Dinny paused and took a long breath. This second living through those moments was making her heart beat. She closed her eyes.

"Yes, Miss Cherrell, what then?"

She opened her eyes. There was the coroner still, and there the jury with their mouths a little open, as it seemed.

"I told Mrs. Ferse. We didn't know what to do or what was coming—we didn't see what we could do, and I suggested that we should drag the bed against the door and try to sleep."

"And did you?"

"Yes; but we were awake a long time. Mrs. Ferse was so exhausted that she did sleep at last, and I think I did towards morning. Anyway the maid woke me by knocking."

"Did you hear nothing further of Captain Ferse during the night?"

The old school-boy saying 'If you tell a lie, tell a good 'un,' shot through her mind, and she said firmly: "No, nothing."

"What time was it when you were called?"

"Eight o'clock. I woke Mrs. Ferse and we went down at once. Captain Ferse's dressing-room was in disorder, and he seemed to have lain upon the bed; but he was nowhere in the house; and his hat and overcoat were gone from the chair where he had thrown them down in the hall."

"What did you do then?"

"We consulted, and Mrs. Ferse wanted to go to her doctor and to her cousin and mine, Mr. Michael Mont, the Member of Parliament; but I thought if I could get my uncles they would be better able to trace Captain Ferse; so I persuaded her to come with me to my Uncle Adrian and ask him to get my Uncle Hilary and see if they could find Captain Ferse. I knew they were both very clever men and very tactful," Dinny saw the coroner bow slightly towards her uncles, and hurried on, "and they were old family friends; I thought if they couldn't manage to find him without publicity, nobody could. So we went to my Uncle Adrian, and he agreed to get my Uncle Hilary to help him and try; then I took Mrs. Ferse down with me to the children at Condaford, and that's all I know, Sir."

The coroner bowed quite low towards her and said: "Thank you, Miss Cherrell. You have given your evidence admirably." The jury moved uneasily as if trying to bow, too, and Dinny, with an effort, stepped down from the pen and took her seat beside Hilary, who put his hand on hers. She sat very still, and then was conscious that a tear, as it were the last of the sal volatile, was moving slowly down her cheek. Listening dully to what followed, the evidence of the Doctor in charge of the Mental Home, and the coroner's address, then waiting dumbly for the jury's verdict, she suffered from the feeling that in her loyalty to the living she had been disloyal to the dead. It was a horrid sensation, that: of having borne evidence of mania against one who could not defend or explain himself; and it was with a fearful interest that she watched the jury file back into their seats, and the foreman stand up in answer to the demand for their verdict.

"We find that the deceased died from falling down a chalk pit."

"That," said the coroner, "is death from misadventure."

"We wish to express our sympathy with the widow."

Dinny almost clapped her hands. So! They had given him the benefit of the doubt—those disused men! And with a sudden, almost personal, warmth she tilted her head up and smiled at them.

CHAPTER 31

WHEN SHE HAD COME to from smiling, Dinny perceived that her uncle was looking at her quizzically.

"Can we go now, Uncle Hilary?"

"It would be as well, Dinny, before you've quite vamped the foreman."

Outside, in the damp October air, for the day was English autumn personified, she said:

"Let's go for a little breather, Uncle, and get the smell of that Court out of us."

They turned down towards the distant sea, walking at a good pace.

"I'm frightfully anxious to know what went before me, Uncle; did I say anything contradictory?"

"No. It came out at once in Diana's evidence that Ferse had come back from the Home, and the coroner treated her tenderly. It was lucky they called me before Adrian, so that his evidence was only a repetition of mine, and he was no way conspicuous. I feel quite sorry for the journalists. Juries avoid suicide and unsound mind when they can, and, after all, we don't know what happened to poor Ferse at that last minute. He may quite easily have run on over the edge, it was pretty blind there and the light was failing."

"Do you really think that, Uncle?"

Hilary shook his head. "No, Dinny. I think he meant to do it all along, and that was the nearest place to his old home. And, though I say it that shouldn't, thank God he did, and is at rest."

"Yes, oh! yes! What will happen to Diana and Uncle Adrian, now?"

Hilary filled his pipe and stopped to light it. "Well, my dear, I've given Adrian some advice. I don't know whether he'll take it, but you might back it up if you get a chance. He's waited all these years. He'd better wait another."

"Uncle, I agree terribly."

"Oh!" said Hilary, surprised.

"Yes. Diana is simply not fit to think even of him. She ought to be left to herself and the children."

"I'm wondering," said Hilary, "whether one couldn't wangle some 'bones' expedition that would take him out of England for a year."

"Hallorsen!" said Dinny, clasping her hands: "He's going again. And he loves Uncle Adrian."

"Good! But would he take him?"

"If *I* asked him," said Dinny, simply.

Hilary again gave her a quizzical look. "What a dangerous young woman you are! I daresay the Trustees would give Adrian leave. I can set old Shropshire and Lawrence on to it. We must go back now, Dinny. I've got to catch a train. It's distressing, because this air smells good; but the Meads are pining for me."

Dinny slipped her hand through his arm.

"I do admire you, Uncle Hilary."

Hilary stared. "I doubt if I follow you, my dear."

"Oh! you know what I mean: you've got all the old 'I serve' tradition, and that kind of thing; and yet you're so frightfully up-to-date, and tolerant, and free-thinking."

"H'm!" said Hilary, emitting a cloud of smoke.

"I'm sure you believe in birth control?"

"Well," said Hilary, "the position there is ironical for us parsons. It used to be considered unpatriotic to believe in limiting our population. But now that flying and poison gas have made food for powder unnecessary, and unemployment is rampant, I'm afraid there's no question but that it's unpatriotic *not* to believe in limiting our population. As for our Christian principles; being patriots, we didn't apply the Christian principle 'Thou shalt not kill' during the war; so, being patriots, we can't logically apply the Christian principle 'Thou shalt not limit' now. Birth control is essential for the slums anyway."

"And you don't believe in hell."

"I do, they've got it."

"You support games on Sundays, don't you?" Hilary nodded. "And sun bathing with nothing on?"

"I might, if there were any sun."

"And pyjamas and smoking for women."

"Not stinkers; emphatically not stinkers."

"I call that undemocratic."

"I can't help it, Dinny. Sniff." And he puffed some smoke at her.

Dinny sniffed. "There's latakia in that, it does smell good; but women can't smoke pipes. I suppose we all have a blind spot somewhere, and yours is: 'No stinkers.' Apart from that you're amazingly modern, Uncle. When I was in that Court looking at all those people, it seemed to me that yours was the only really modern face."

"It's a Cathedral town, my dear."

"Well, I think the amount of modernity is awfully overestimated."

"You don't live in London, Dinny. All the same, you're right in a way. Frankness about things is not change. The difference between the days of my youth and to-day is only the difference of expression. We had doubts, we had curiosity, we had desires; but we didn't express them. Now they do. I see a lot of young 'Varsity men—they come and work in the Meads, you know. Well, from their cradles they've been brought up to say whatever comes into their heads, and just don't they? We didn't, you know; but the same things came into our heads. That's all the difference. That and cars."

"Then I'm still old fashioned. I'm not a bit good at expressing things."

"That's your sense of humour, Dinny. It acts as a restraint, and keeps you self-conscious. Few young people nowadays seem to have much sense of humour; they often have wit—it isn't the same thing. Our young writers, and painters and musicians, could they carry on as they do if they could see a joke against themselves? Because that's the real test of humour."

"I'll think that over."

"Yes, but don't lose your sense of humour, Dinny. It's the scent to the rose. Are you going back to Condaford now?"

"I expect so, Hubert's remand won't be till after that mail boat comes in; and that's not for ten days yet."

"Well, give my love to Condaford. I don't suppose I'll ever have days again quite so good as when we were children there."

"That's what I was thinking, Uncle, when I was waiting to be the last little nigger boy."

"You're a bit young for that conclusion, Dinny. Wait till you're in love."

"I am."

"What, in love?"

"No, in waiting."

"Fearsome process, being in love," said Hilary. "Still, I never regretted it."

Dinny gazed at him sideways, and her teeth showed.

"What if you took it again, Uncle?"

"Ah! there," said Hilary, knocking his pipe out on a pillar box, "I'm definitely out of it. In my profession we can't run to it. Besides, I've never really got over my first attack."

"No," said Dinny, with compunction, "Aunt May's such a duck."

"You've said a mouthful. Here's the station. Good-bye, and bless you! I sent my bag down this morning." He waved his hand and was gone.

On reaching the hotel Dinny sought Adrian. He was not in, and, rather disconsolate, she wandered out again into the Cathedral. She was just about to sit down and take its restful beauty in, when she saw her Uncle standing against a column with his eyes fixed on the rose window. Going up she slid her arm through his. He squeezed it, but said nothing.

"Fond of glass, Uncle?"

"Terribly fond of good glass, Dinny. Ever see York Minster?"

Dinny shook her head; then, conscious that nothing she could say would lead up to what she wanted to say, she asked directly: "What are you going to do now, Uncle dear?"

"Have you been talking to Hilary?"

"Yes."

"He wants me to keep away for a year."

"So do I."

"It's a long time, Dinny; I'm getting on."

"Would you go on Professor Hallorsen's expedition if he wanted you?"

"He wouldn't want me."

"Yes, he would."

"I could only go if I were certain that Diana wished it."

"She would never say so, but I'm quite sure she wants complete rest for a long time."

"When you worship the sun," said Adrian, very low, "it is hard to go where the sun never shines."

Dinny squeezed his arm. "I know; but you'd have it to look forward to. And it's a nice healthy expedition this time, only to New Mexico. You'd come back very young, with hair all down the outsides of your legs. They do in the films. You'd be irresistible, Uncle; and I do want you to be irresistible. All that's wanted is to let the tumult and the shouting die."

"And my job?"

"Oh! that can be wangled all right. If Diana doesn't have to think of anything for a year, she'll be a different creature, and you will seem like the promised land. I do feel I know what I'm talking about."

"You're an endearing little serpent," said Adrian, with his shadowy smile.

"Diana is pretty badly wounded."

"I sometimes think it's a mortal wound, Dinny."

"No, no!"

"Why should she think of me again, if I once go away?"

"Because women are like that."

"What do you know about women, at your age? I went away long ago, and she thought of Ferse. I fancy I'm made of the wrong stuff."

"If you are, New Mexico's the very place. You'll come back a 'he-man.' Think of that! I promise to watch over her, and the children will keep you to the fore. They're always talking of you. And I'll see that they go on doing it."

"It's certainly curious," said Adrian, impersonally, "but I feel she's further from me now than when Ferse was alive."

"For the moment, and it'll be a long moment. But I know it'll dry straight in the long run. Really, Uncle."

Adrian was silent a long time. Then he said:

"I'll go, Dinny, if Hallorsen will take me."

"He shall. Bend down, Uncle. I *must* kiss you."

Adrian bent down. The kiss lighted on his nose. A verger coughed. . . .

The return to Condaford was made by car that afternoon in precisely the same order, young Tasburgh driving. He had been extremely tactful during these twenty-four hours, had not proposed at all, and Dinny was proportionately grateful. If Diana wanted peace, so did she. Alan left that same evening, Diana and the children the following day, and Clare

184

came back from her long stay in Scotland, so that none but her own family were at the Grange. Yet had she no peace. For now that the preoccupation with poor Ferse was gone, she was oppressed and worried by the thought of Hubert. Extraordinary what power of disturbance was in that overhanging issue! He and Jean wrote cheerfully from the East Coast. According to themselves they were not worrying. Dinny was. And she knew that her mother, and even more her father, were. Clare was more angry than worried, and the effect of anger on her was to stimulate her energy, so that she went out 'cubbing' with her father; and in the afternoons would disappear with the car to neighbouring houses, where she would often stay till after dinner. The festive member of the family, she was always in great request. Dinny had her anxiety to herself. She had written to Hallorsen about her uncle, sending him the promised photograph, which depicted her in her presentation frock of two years back, when she and Clare had been economically presented together. Hallorsen answered promptly: "The picture is just too lovely. Nothing will please me more than to take your uncle, I am getting in touch with him right away": he signed himself "Always your devoted servant."

She read the letter gratefully, but without a tremor, and called herself a hard-hearted beast. Her mind thus set at rest about Adrian, for she knew his year of leave could be safely left to Hilary, she thought all the time of Hubert with a growing presentiment of evil. She tried to persuade herself that this came from having nothing particular to do, from the reaction after Ferse, and the habit of nerves into which he had thrown her; but such excuses were unconvincing. If they did not believe Hubert sufficiently here to refuse his extradition, what chance would he have out there? She spent surreptitious minutes staring at the map of Bolivia, as if its conformation could give her insight into the psychology of its people. She had never loved Condaford more passionately than during these uneasy days. The place was entailed, and if Hubert were sent out there and condemned, or died in prison, or was murdered by one of those muleteers, and if Jean had no son, it would pass away to Hilary's eldest boy—a cousin she had barely seen, a boy at school; in the family, yes, but as good as lost. With Hubert's fate was wrapped up the fate of her beloved home. And, though astonished that she could think of herself at all, when it meant so terribly much more to Hubert, she never quite lost the thought.

One morning she got Clare to run her over to Lippinghall. Dinny hated driving, and not without reason, for her peculiar way of seeing the humours of what she was passing had often nearly brought her to grief. They arrived at lunch time. Lady Mont was just sitting down, and greeted them with:

"My dears, but how provokin'! Unless you can eat carrots—your Uncle's away—so purifyin'. Blore, see if Augustine has a cooked bird somewhere. Oh! and, Blore, ask her to make those nice pancakes with jam, that I can't eat."

"Oh! but, Aunt Em, nothing that you can't eat, please."

"I can't eat anythin' just now. Your Uncle's fattin', so I'm slimmin'. And, Blore, cheese ramequins, and a nice wine—and coffee."

"But this is awful, Aunt Em."

"Grapes, Blore. And those cigarettes up in Mr. Michael's room. Your Uncle doesn't smoke them, and I smoke gaspers, so we run low. And Blore."

"Yes, my lady?"

"Cocktails, Blore."

"Aunt Em, we never drink cocktails."

"You do; I've seen you. Clare, you're lookin' thin; are you slimmin' too?"

"No. I've been in Scotland, Aunt Em."

"Followin' the guns, and fishin'. Now run about the house. I'll wait for you."

When they were running about the house, Clare said to Dinny:

"Where on earth did Aunt Em learn to drop her g's?"

"Father told me once that she was at a school where an undropped 'g' was worse than a dropped 'h.' They were bringin' in a county fashion then, huntin' people, you know. Isn't she a dear?"

Clare nodded, slightly brightening her lips.

Re-entering the dining room, they heard Lady Mont say:

"James's trousers, Blore."

"Yes, my lady."

"They look as if they were comin' down. Can somethin' be done about it?"

"Yes, my lady."

"Here you are! Your Aunt Wilmet's gone to stay with Hen, Dinny. They'll be differin' all over the place. You've got a cold bird each. Dinny, what have you been doin' with Alan? He's lookin' so interestin', and his leave's up to-morrow."

"I've not been doing anything with him, Aunt Em."

"That's it, then. No. Give me my carrots, Blore. Aren't you goin' to marry him? I know he has prospects in Chancery—somewhere—Wiltshire is it? He comes and puts his head in my hand about you."

Under Clare's gaze Dinny sat with fork suspended.

"If you don't take care, he'll be gettin' transferred to China and marryin' a purser's daughter. They say Hong Kong's full of them. Oh! And my portulaca's dead, Dinny. Boswell and Johnson went and watered it with liquid manure. They've no sense of smell. D'you know what they did once?"

"No, Aunt Em."

"Had hay fever all over my pedigree rabbit—sneezin' about the hutch, and the poor thing died. I gave them notice, but they didn't go. They don't, you know. Your Uncle pets them. Are you to wed, Clare?"

"To 'wed'! Aunt Em!"

"I think it's rather sweet, the uneducated papers use it. But are you?"

"Of course not."

"Why? Haven't you the time? I don't like carrots really—so depressin'. But your Uncle's gettin' to a time of life—I have to be careful. I don't know why men have a time of life. By rights he ought to be over it."

"He is, Aunt Em. Uncle Lawrence is sixty-nine; didn't you know?"

"Well, he's never shown any signs yet. Blore!"

"Yes, my lady."

"Go away!"

"Yes, my lady."

"There are some things," said Lady Mont, as the door closed, "that you can't talk about before Blore—birth control, and your Uncle, and that. Poor Pussy!"

She rose, went to the window, and dropped a cat into a flower bed.

"How perfectly sweet Blore is with her!" murmured Dinny.

"They stray," she said, as she came back, "at forty-five, and they stray at sixty-five, and I don't know when after that. I never strayed. But I'm thinkin' of it with the Rector."

"Is he very lonely now, Auntie?"

"No," said Lady Mont, "he's enjoyin' himself. He comes up here a lot."

"It would be delicious if you could work up a scandal."

"Dinny!"

"Uncle Lawrence would love it."

Lady Mont seemed to go into a sort of coma.

"Where's Blore?" she said: "I want one of those pancakes after all."

"You sent him away."

"Oh! yes."

"Shall I tread on the gas, Aunt Em?" said Clare; "it's under my chair."

"I had it put there for your Uncle. He's been readin' me Gulliver's Travels, Dinny. The man was coarse, you know."

"Not so coarse as Rabelais, or even as Voltaire."

"Do you read coarse books?"

"Oh! well, those are classics."

"They say there was a book—Achilles, or something; your Uncle bought it in Paris; and they took it away from him at Dover. Have you read that?"

"No," said Dinny.

"I have," said Clare.

"From what your Uncle tells me, you oughtn't to."

"Oh! one reads anything now, Auntie, it never makes any difference."

Lady Mont looked from one niece to the other.

"Well," she said, cryptically, "there's the Bible. Blore!"

"Yes, my lady."

"Coffee in the hall on the tiger. And put a sniff on the fire, Blore. My Vichy."

When she had drunk her glass of Vichy they all rose.

"Marvellous!" whispered Clare in Dinny's ear.

"What are you doin' about Hubert?" said Lady Mont, in front of the hall fire.

"Sweating in our shoes, Auntie."

"I told Wilmet to speak to Hen. She sees Royalty, you know. Then there's flyin'. Couldn't he fly somewhere?"

"Uncle Lawrence went bail for him."

"He wouldn't mind. We could do without James, he's got adenoids; and we could have one man instead of Boswell and Johnson."

"Hubert would mind, though."

"I'm fond of Hubert," said Lady Mont: "and bein' married—it's too soon. Here's the sniff."

Blore, bearing coffee and cigarettes, was followed by James bearing a cedar log; and a religious silence ensued while Lady Mont made coffee.

"Sugar, Dinny?"

"Two spoonfuls, please."

"Three for me. I know it's fattenin'. Clare?"

"One, please."

The girls sipped, and Clare sighed out:

"Amazing!"

"Yes. Why is your coffee so much better than anybody else's, Aunt Em?"

"I agree," said her aunt. "About that poor man, Dinny: I was so relieved that he didn't bite either of you after all. Adrian will get her now. Such a comfort."

"Not for some time, Aunt Em: Uncle Adrian's going to America."

"But why?"

"We all thought it best. Even he did."

"When he goes to Heaven," said Lady Mont, "someone will have to go with him, or he won't get in."

"Surely he'll have a seat reserved!"

"You never know. The Rector was preachin' on that last Sunday."

"Does he preach well?"

"Well, cosy."

"I expect Jean wrote his sermons."

"Yes, they used to have more zip. Where did I get that word, Dinny?"

"From Michael, I expect."

"He always caught everythin'. The Rector said we were to deny ourselves; he came here to lunch."

"And had a whacking good feed."

"Yes."

"What does he weigh, Aunt Em?"

"Without his clothes—I don't know."

"But with?"

"Oh! quite a lot. He's goin' to write a book."

"What about?"

"The Tasburghs. There was that one that was buried, and lived in France afterwards, only she was a Fitzherbert by birth. Then there was the one that fought the battle of—not Spaghetti—the other word, Augustine gives it us sometimes."

"Navarino? But did he?"

"Yes, but they said he didn't. The Rector's goin' to put that right. Then there was the Tasburgh that got beheaded, and forgot to put it down anywhere. The Rector's nosed that out."

"In what reign?"

"I never can be bothered with reigns, Dinny. Edward the Sixth—or Fourth, was it? He was a red rose. Then there was the one that married into us. Roland his name was—or was it? But he did somethin' strikin'—and they took away his land. Recusancy—what is that?"

"It means he was a Catholic, Auntie, in a Protestant reign."

"They burnt his house first. He's in Mercurius Rusticus, or some book. The Rector says he was greatly beloved. They burnt his house twice, I think, and then robbed it—or was it the other way? It had a moat. And there's a list of what they took."

"How entrancing!"

"Jam, and silver, and chickens, and linen, and I think his umbrella, or something funny."

"When was all this, Auntie?"

"In the Civil War. He was a Royalist. Now I remember his name wasn't Roland, and she was Elizabeth after you, Dinny. History repeatin' itself."

Dinny looked at the log.

"Then there was the last Admiral—under William the Fourth—he died drunk, not William. The Rector says he didn't, so he's writin' to prove it. He says he caught cold and took rum for it; and it didn't click—where did I get *that* word?"

"I sometimes use it, Auntie."

"Yes. So there's quite a lot, you see, besides all the dull ones, right away back to Edward the Confessor or somebody. He's tryin' to make out they're older than we are. So unreasonable."

"My Aunt!" murmured Clare. "Who would read a book like that?"

"I shouldn't think so. But he'll simply love snobbin' into it; and it'll keep him awake. Here's Alan! Clare, you haven't seen where my portulaca was. Shall we take a turn?"

"Aunt Em, you're shameless," said Dinny in her ear; "and it's no good."

"'If at first you don't succeed'—d'you remember every mornin' when we were little? Wait till I get my hat, Clare."

They passed away.

"So your leave's up, Alan?" said Dinny, alone with the young man. "Where shall you be?"

"Portsmouth."

"Is that nice?"

"Might be worse. Dinny, I want to talk to you about Hubert. If things go wrong at the Court next time, what's going to happen?"

All 'bubble and squeak' left Dinny, she sank down on a fireside cushion, and gazed up with troubled eyes.

"I've been enquiring," said young Tasburgh, "they leave it two or three weeks for the Home Secretary to go into, and then if he confirms, cart them off as soon as they can. From Southampton it would be, I expect."

"You don't really think it will come to that, do you?"

He said gloomily: "I don't know. Suppose a Bolivian had killed somebody, here, and gone back, we should want him rather badly, shouldn't we, and put the screw on to get him?"

"But it's fantastic!"

The young man looked at her with an extremely resolute compassion.

"We'll hope for the best; but if it goes wrong something's got to be done about it. I'm not going to stand for it, nor is Jean."

"But what could be done?"

Young Tasburgh walked round the hall looking at the doors; then, leaning above her, he said:

"Hubert can fly, and I've been up every day since Chichester. Jean and I are working the thing out—in case."

Dinny caught his hand.

"My dear boy, that's crazy!"

"No crazier than thousands of things done in the war."

"But it would ruin your career."

"Blast my career! Look on and see you and Jean miserable for years, perhaps, and a man like Hubert broken rottenly like that—what d'you think?"

Dinny squeezed his hand convulsively and let it go.

"It can't, it shan't come to that. Besides, how could you get Hubert? He'd be under arrest."

"I don't know, but I shall know all right if and when the time comes. What's certain is that if they once get him over there, he'll have a damned thin chance."

"Have you spoken to Hubert?"

"No. It's all perfectly vague as yet."

"I'm sure he wouldn't consent."

"Jean will see to that."

Dinny shook her head. "You don't know Hubert; he would never let you."

Alan grinned, and she suddenly recognised that in him there was something formidably determined.

"Does Professor Hallorsen know?"

"No, and he won't, unless it's absolutely necessary. But he's a good egg, I admit."

She smiled faintly. "Yes, he's a good egg; but an out-size."

"Dinny, you're not gone on him, are you?"

"No, my dear."

"Well, thank God for that! You see," he went on, "they're not likely to treat Hubert as an ordinary criminal. That will make things easier perhaps."

Dinny gazed at him, thrilled to her very marrow. Somehow that last remark convinced her of the reality of his purpose. "I'm beginning to understand Zeebrugge. But——"

"No buts, and buck up! That boat arrives the day after to-morrow, and then the case will be on again. I shall see you in Court, Dinny. I must go now—got my daily flight. I just thought I'd like you to know that if the worst comes to worst, we aren't going to take it lying down. Give my love to Lady Mont; shan't be seeing her again. Good-bye, and bless you!" And, kissing her hand, he was out of the hall before she could speak.

Dinny sat on beside the cedar log, very still, and strangely moved. The idea of defiance had not before occurred to her, mainly perhaps because she had never really believed that Hubert would be committed for trial. She did not really believe it now, and that made this 'crazy' idea the more thrilling; for it has often been noticed that the less actual a risk, the more thrilling it seems. And to the thrill was joined a warmer feeling for Alan. The fact that he had not even proposed added to the conviction that he was in dead earnest. And on that tiger-skin, which had provided very little thrill to the eighth baronet, who from an elephant had shot its owner while it was trying to avoid notice, Dinny sat, warming her body in the glow from the cedar log, and her spirit in the sense of being closer to the fires of life than she had ever yet been. Her Uncle's old black and white spaniel dog, Quince, who in his master's absences, which were frequent, took little interest in human beings, came slowly across the hall and, lying down four-square, put his head on his forepaws and looked up at her with eyes that showed red rims beneath them. "It may be all that, and it may not," he seemed to say. The log hissed faintly, and a grandfather clock on the far side of the hall struck three with its special slowness.

CHAPTER 32

OVER ANY IMPENDING ISSUE, whether test match, ultimatum, the Cambridgeshire, or the hanging of a man, excitement beats up in the last few hours, and the feeling of suspense in the Cherrell family became painful when the day of Hubert's remand was reached. As some Highland clan of old, without summons issued, assembled when one of its number was threatened, so were Hubert's relatives collected in the Police Court. Except Lionel, who was in session, and his and Hilary's children, who were at school, they were all there. It might have been a wedding or a funeral, but for the grimness of their faces, and the sense of unmerited persecution at the back of every mind. Dinny and Clare sat between their father and mother, with Jean, Alan, Hallorsen and Adrian next them; just behind them were Hilary and his wife, Fleur and Michael and Aunt Wilmet; behind them again sat Sir Lawrence and Lady Mont, and in the extreme rear the Rector formed the spear tail of an inverted phalanx.

Coming in with his lawyer, Hubert gave them a clansman's smile.

Now that she was actually in Court, Dinny felt almost apathetic. Her brother was innocent of all save self-defence. If they committed him, he would still be innocent. And, after she had answered Hubert's smile, her attention was given to Jean's face. If ever the girl looked like a leopardess, it was now; her strange, deep-set eyes kept sliding from her 'cub' to him who threatened to deprive her of it.

The evidence from the first hearing having been read over, the new evidence—Manuel's affidavit—was produced by Hubert's lawyer. But then Dinny's apathy gave way, for this affidavit was countered by the prosecution with another, sworn by four muleteers, to the effect that Manuel had not been present at the shooting.

That was a moment of real horror.

Four half-castes against one!

Dinny saw a disconcerted look flit across the Magistrate's face.

"Who procured this second affidavit, Mr. Buttall?"

"The lawyer in charge of the case in La Paz, Your Honour. It became known to him that the boy Manuel was being asked to give evidence."

"I see. What do you say now on the question of the scar shown us by the accused?"

"Beyond the accused's own statement there is no evidence whatever before you, Sir, or before me, as to how or when that scar was inflicted."

"That is so. You are not suggesting that this scar could have been inflicted by the dead man after he was shot?"

"If Castro, having drawn a knife, had fallen forward after he was shot, it is conceivable, I suppose."

"Not likely, I think, Mr. Buttall."

"No. But my evidence, of course, is that the shooting was deliberate, cold-blooded, and at a distance of some yards. I know nothing of Castro's having drawn a knife."

"It comes to this, then: Either your six witnesses are lying, or the accused and the boy Manuel are."

"That would appear to be the position, Your Honour. It is for you to judge whether the sworn words of six citizens are to be taken, or the sworn words of two."

Dinny saw the Magistrate wriggle.

"I am perfectly aware of that, Mr. Buttall. What do you say, Captain Cherrell, to this affidavit that has been put in as to the absence of the boy Manuel?"

Dinny's eyes leaped to her brother's face. It was impassive, even slightly ironic.

"Nothing, Sir. I don't know where Manuel was. I was too occupied in saving my life. All I know is that he came up to me almost immediately afterwards."

"Almost? How long afterwards?"

"I really don't know, Sir—perhaps a minute. I was trying to stop the bleeding; I fainted just as he came."

During the speeches of the two lawyers which followed, Dinny's apathy returned. It fled again during the five minutes of silence which succeeded them. In all the Court the Magistrate alone seemed occupied; and it was as if he would never be done. Through her lowered lashes she could see him consulting this paper, consulting that; he had a red face, a long nose, a pointed chin, and eyes which she liked whenever she could see them. Instinctively she knew that he was not at ease. At last he spoke.

"In this case," he said, "I have to ask myself not whether a crime has been committed, or whether the accused has committed it; I have only to ask myself whether the evidence brought before me is such as to satisfy me that the alleged crime is an extraditable offence, and that the foreign warrant is duly authenticated, and that such evidence has been produced as would in this country justify me in committing the accused to take his trial." He paused a moment and then added: "There is no question but that the crime alleged is an extraditable offence, and that the foreign warrant is duly authenticated." He paused again, and in the dead silence Dinny heard a long sigh, as if from a spirit, so lonely and disembodied was the sound. The Magistrate's eyes passed to Hubert's face, and he resumed:

"I have come to the conclusion reluctantly that it is my duty on the evidence adduced to commit the accused to prison to await surrender to the foreign State on a warrant from the Secretary of State, if he sees fit to issue it. I have heard the accused's evidence to the effect that he had an antecedent justification removing the act complained of from the category of crime, supported by the affidavit of a witness which is contradicted by the affidavit of four others. I have no means of judging between the conflicting evidence of these two affidavits except in so far that it is in the proportion of four to one, and I must therefore dismiss it from my mind. In face of the sworn testimony of six witnesses that the shooting was deliberate, I do not think that the unsupported word of the accused to the contrary would justify me in the case of an offence committed in this country in refusing to commit for trial; and I am therefore unable to accept it as justification for a refusal to commit for trial in respect of an offence committed in another country. I make no hesitation in confessing my reluctance to come to this conclusion, but I consider that I have no other course open to me. The question, I repeat, is not whether the accused is guilty or innocent, it is a question of whether or not there should be a trial. I am not able to take on myself the responsibility of saying that there should not. The final word in cases of this nature rests with the Secretary of State, who issues the surrender warrant. I commit you, therefore, to prison to await the issue of such a warrant. You will not be surrendered until after fifteen days, and you have the right to apply for a writ of *habeas corpus* in regard to the lawfulness of your custody. I have not the power to grant you any further bail; but it may be that you may secure it, if you so desire, by application to the King's Bench Division."

Dinny's horrified eyes saw Hubert, standing very straight, make the Magistrate a little bow, and leave the dock, walking slowly and without a look back. Behind him his lawyer, too, passed out of Court.

She herself sat as if stunned, and her only impression of those next minutes was the sight of Jean's stony face, and of Alan's brown hands gripping each other on the handle of his stick.

She came to herself conscious that tears were stealing down her mother's face, and that her father was standing up.

"Come!" he said: "Let's get out of here!"

At that moment she was more sorry for her father than for any other of them all. Since this thing began he had said so little and had felt so much. It was ghastly for him! Dinny understood very well his simple feelings. To him, in the refusal of Hubert's word, an insult had been flung not merely in his son's face, and his own as Hubert's father, but in the face of what they stood for and believed in; in the face of all soldiers and all gentlemen! Whatever happened now, he would never quite get over this. Between justice and what was just, what inexorable incompatibility! Were there men more honourable than her father and her brother, or than that Magistrate, perhaps? Following him out into that dishevelled backwater of life and traffic, Bow Street, she noted that they were all there except Jean, Alan and Hallorsen. Sir Lawrence said:

"We must just 'take cabs and go about!' Better come to Mount Street and consult what we can each best do."

When half an hour later they assembled in Aunt Em's drawing-room, those three were still absent.

"What's happened to them?" asked Sir Lawrence.

"I expect they went after Hubert's lawyer," answered Dinny; but she knew better. Some desperate plan was being hatched, and she brought but a distracted mind to council.

In Sir Lawrence's opinion Bobbie Ferrar was still their man. If he could do nothing with 'Walter,' nothing could be done. He proposed to go again to him and to the Marquess.

The General said nothing. He stood a little apart, staring at one of his brother-in-law's pictures, evidently without seeing it. Dinny realised that he did not join in because he could not. She wondered of what he was thinking. Of when he was young like his son, just married; of long field days under burning sun among the sands and stones of India and South Africa; of longer days of administrative routine; of strenuous poring over maps with his eyes on the clock and his ear to the telephone; of his wounds and his son's long sickness; of two lives given to service and this strange reward at the end?

She herself stood close to Fleur, with the instinctive feeling that from that clear, quick brain might come a suggestion of real value.

"The Squire carries weight with the Government; I might go to Bentworth," she heard Hilary say, and the Rector add:

"Ah! I knew him at Eton, I'll come with you."

She heard her Aunt Wilmet's gruff: "I'll go to Hen again about Royalty." And Michael's:

"In a fortnight the House will be sitting"; and Fleur's impatient:

"No good, Michael. The Press is no use either. I've got a hunch."

'Ah!' she thought, and moved closer.

"We haven't gone deep enough. What's at the back of it? Why should the Bolivian Government care about a half-caste Indian? It's not the actual shooting, it's the slur on their country. Floggings and shootings by foreigners! What's wanted is something done to the Bolivian Minister that will make him tell 'Walter' that they don't really care."

"We can't kidnap him," muttered Michael; "it's not done in the best circles."

A faint smile came on Dinny's lips; she was not so sure.

"I'll see," said Fleur, as if to herself. "Dinny, you must come to us. They'll get no further here." And her eyes roved swiftly over the nine elders. "I shall go to Uncle Lionel and Alison. He won't dare move, being a new judge, but she will, and she knows all the Legation people. Will you come, Dinny?"

"I ought to be with mother and father."

"They'll be here, Em's just asked them. Well, if you stay here too, come round as much as you can; you might help."

Dinny nodded, relieved at staying in town; for the thought of Conda-ford during this suspense oppressed her.

"We'll go now," said Fleur, "and I'll get on to Alison at once."

Michael lingered to squeeze Dinny's arm.

"Buck up, Dinny! We'll get him out of it somehow. If only it wasn't 'Walter'! He's the worst kind of egg. To fancy yourself 'just' is simply to addle."

When all except her own people had gone, Dinny went up to her father. He was still standing before a picture, but not the same one. Slipping her hand under his arm, she said:

"It's going to be all right, Dad dear. You could see the Magistrate was really sorry. He hadn't the power, but the Home Secretary must have."

"I was thinking," said the General, "what the people of this country would do if we didn't sweat and risk our lives for them." He spoke without bitterness, or even emphasis: "I was thinking why we should go on doing our jobs, if our words aren't to be believed. I was wondering where that Magistrate would be—oh! I dare say he's all right according to his lights—if boys like Hubert hadn't gone off before their time. I was wondering why we've chosen lives that have landed me on the verge of bankruptcy, and Hubert in this mess, when we might have been snug and comfortable in the City or the Law. Isn't a man's whole career to weigh a snap when a thing like this happens? I feel the insult to the Service, Dinny."

She watched the convulsive movement of his thin brown hands, clasped as if he were standing at ease, and her whole heart went out to him, though she could perfectly well see the unreason of the exemption he was claiming. "It is easier for Heaven and Earth to pass than for one tittle of the Law to fail." Wasn't that the text she had just read in what she had suggested might be made into a secret naval code?

"Well," he said, "I must go out now with Lawrence. See to your mother, Dinny, her head's bad."

When she had darkened her mother's bedroom, applied the usual remedies, and left her to try and sleep, she went downstairs again. Clare had gone out, and the drawing-room, just now so full, seemed deserted. She passed down its length and opened the piano. A voice said:

"No, Polly, you must go to bed, I feel too sad"; and she became aware of her Aunt in the alcove at the end placing her parakeet in its cage.

"Can we be sad together, Aunt Em?"

Lady Mont turned round.

"Put your cheek against mine, Dinny."

Dinny did so. The cheek was pink and round and smooth and gave her a sense of relaxation.

"From the first I knew what he would say," said Lady Mont, "his nose was so long. In ten years' time it'll touch his chin. Why they allow them, I don't know. You can do nothing with a man like that. Let's cry, Dinny. You sit there, and I'll sit here."

"Do you cry high or low, Aunt Em?"

"Either. You begin. A man who can't take a responsibility. I could have taken that responsibility perfectly, Dinny. Why didn't he just say to Hubert 'Go and sin no more'?"

"But Hubert hasn't sinned."

"It makes it all the worse. Payin' attention to foreigners! The other day I was sittin' in the window at Lippin'hall, and there were three starlin's on the terrace, and I sneezed twice. D'you think they paid any attention? Where is Bolivia?"

"In South America, Aunt Em."

"I never could learn geography. My maps were the worst ever made at my school, Dinny. Once they asked me where Livin'stone kissed Stanley, and I answered: 'Niagara Falls.' And it wasn't."

"You were only a continent wrong there, Auntie."

"Yes. I've never seen anybody laugh as my school-mistress laughed when I said that. Excessive—she was fat. I thought Hubert lookin' thin."

"He's always thin, but he's looking much less 'tucked up' since his marriage."

"Jean's fatter, that's natural. You ought, Dinny, you know."

"You never used to be so keen on people getting married, Auntie."

"What happened on the tiger the other day?"

"I can't possibly tell you that, Aunt Em."

"It must have been pretty bad, then."

"Or do you mean good?"

"You're laughin' at me."

"Did you ever know me disrespectful, Auntie?"

"Yes. I perfectly well remember you writin' a poem about me:

> 'I do not care for Auntie Em,
> She says I cannot sew or hem,
> Does she? Well! I can sew a dem
> Sight better than my Auntie Em.'

I kept it. I thought it showed character."

"Was I such a little demon?"

"Yes. There's no way, is there, of shortenin' dogs?" And she pointed to the golden retriever lying on a rug. "Bonzo's middle is really too long."

"I told you that, Aunt Em, when he was a puppy."

"Yes, but I didn't notice it till he began to scratch for rabbits. He can't get over the hole, properly. It makes him look so weak. Well! If we're not goin' to cry, Dinny, what shall we do?"

"Laugh?" murmured Dinny.

CHAPTER 33

HER FATHER and Sir Lawrence not coming back to dinner, and her mother remaining in bed, Dinny dined alone with her aunt, for Clare was staying with friends.

"Aunt Em," she said, when they had finished, "do you mind if I go round to Michael's? Fleur has had a hunch."

"Why?" said Lady Mont: "It's too early for that—not till March."

"You're thinking of the hump, Auntie. A 'hunch' means an idea."

"Then why didn't she say so?" And, with that simple dismissal of the more fashionable forms of speech, Lady Mont rang the bell.

"Blore, a taxi for Miss Dinny. And, Blore, when Sir Lawrence comes in, let me know; I'm goin' to have a hot bath, and wash my hair."

"Yes, my lady."

"Do you wash your hair when you're sad, Dinny?"

Driving through the misty dark evening to South Square, Dinny experienced melancholy beyond all she had felt yet. The thought of Hubert actually in a prison cell, torn from a wife not more than three weeks married, facing separation that might be permanent, and a fate that would not bear thinking of; and all because they were too scrupulous to stretch a point and take his word, caused fear and rage to bank up in her spirit, as unspent heat before a storm.

She found Fleur and her Aunt Lady Alison discussing ways and means. The Bolivian Minister, it appeared, was away convalescing after an illness, and a subordinate was in charge. This in Lady Alison's opinion made it more difficult, for he would probably not take any responsibility. She would, however, arrange a luncheon to which Fleur and Michael should be bidden, and Dinny, too, if she wished; but Dinny shook her head, she had lost faith in her power of manipulating public men.

"If you and Fleur can't manage it, Aunt Alison, I certainly can't. But Jean is singularly attractive when she likes."

"Jean telephoned just now, Dinny. If you came in tonight, would you go round and see her at their flat; otherwise she was writing to you."

Dinny stood up. "I'll go at once."

She hurried through the mist along the Embankment and turned down towards the block of workmen's flats where Jean had found her lodgment. At the corner boys were crying the more sanguinary tidings of the day;

she bought a paper to see if Hubert's case was mentioned, and opened it beneath a lamp. Yes! There it was! "British officer committed. Extradition on shooting charge." How little attention she would have given to that, if it had not concerned her! This, that was agony to her and hers, was to the Public just a little pleasurable excitement. The misfortunes of others were a distraction; and the papers made their living out of it! The man who had sold the paper to her had a thin face, dirty clothes, and was lame; and, throwing a libationary drop out of her bitter cup, she gave him back the paper and a shilling. His eyes widened in a puzzled stare, his mouth remained a little open. Had she backed the winner—that one?

Dinny went up the bricked stairs. The flat was on the second floor. Outside its door a grown black cat was spinning round after its own tail. It flew round six times on the same spot, then sat down, lifted one of its back legs high into the air, and licked it.

Jean herself opened the door. She was evidently in the throes of packing, having a pair of combinations over her arm. Dinny kissed her and looked round. She had not been here before. The doors of the small sitting room, bedroom, kitchen and bath room were open; the walls were distempered apple green, the floors covered with dark green linoleum. For furniture there was a double bed, and some suit-cases in the bedroom, two arm-chairs and a small table in the sitting room; a kitchen table and some bath salts in a glass jar; no rugs, no pictures, no books, but some printed linen curtains to the windows and a hanging cupboard along one whole side of the bedroom, from which Jean had been taking the clothes piled on the bed. A scent of coffee and lavender bags distinguished the atmosphere from that on the stairs.

Jean put down the combinations.

"Have some coffee, Dinny? I've just made it."

She poured out two cups, sweetened them, handed Dinny one and a paper packet of cigarettes, then pointed to one of the arm-chairs and sat down in the other.

"You got my message, then? I'm glad you've come—saves my making up a parcel. I hate making parcels, don't you?"

Her coolness and unharassed expression seemed to Dinny miraculous.

"Have you seen Hubert since?"

"Yes. He's fairly comfortable. It's not a bad cell, he says, and they've given him books and writing paper. He can have food in, too; but he's not allowed to smoke. Someone ought to move about that. According to English law Hubert's still as innocent as the Home Secretary; there's no law to prevent the Home Secretary smoking, is there? I shan't be seeing him again, but you'll be going, Dinny—so give him my special love, and take him some cigarettes in case they let him."

Dinny stared at her.

"What are you going to do, then?"

"Well, I wanted to see you about that. This is all strictly for your ear only. Promise to lie absolutely doggo, Dinny, or I shan't say anything."

Dinny said, resolutely: "Cross my heart—as they say. Go on."

"I'm going to Brussels to-morrow. Alan went to-day; he's got extension of leave for urgent family affairs. We're simply going to prepare for the worst, that's all. I'm to learn flying in double quick time. If I go up three times a day, three weeks will be quite enough. Our lawyer has guaranteed us three weeks, at least. Of course, he knows nothing. Nobody is to know anything, except you. I want you to do something for me." She reached forward and took out of her vanity bag a tissue-papered packet.

"I've got to have five hundred pounds. We can get a good second-hand machine over there for very little, they say, but we shall want all the rest. Now, look here, Dinny, this is an old family thing. It's worth a lot. I want you to pop it for five hundred; if you can't get as much as that by popping, you'll have to sell it. Pop, or sell, in your name, and change the English notes into Belgian money and send it to me registered to the G.P.O. Brussels. You ought to be able to send me the money within three days." She undid the paper, and disclosed an old-fashioned but very beautiful emerald pendant.

"Oh!"

"Yes," said Jean, "it really is good. You can afford to take a high line. Somebody will give you five hundred on it, I'm sure. Emeralds are up."

"But why don't you 'pop' it yourself before you go?"

Jean shook her head.

"No, nothing whatever that awakens suspicion. It doesn't matter what you do, Dinny, because you're not going to break the law. We possibly are, but we're not going to be copped."

"I think," said Dinny, "you ought to tell me more."

Again Jean shook her head.

"Not necessary, and not possible; we don't know enough yet ourselves. But make your mind easy, they're not going to get away with Hubert. You'll take this, then?" And she wrapped up the pendant.

Dinny took the little packet, and, having brought no bag, slipped it down her dress. She leaned forward and said earnestly:

"Promise you won't do anything, Jean, till everything else has failed."

Jean nodded. "Nothing till the very last minute. It wouldn't be good enough."

Dinny grasped her hand. "I oughtn't to have let you in for this, Jean; it was I who brought the young things together, you know."

"My dear, I'd never have forgiven you if you hadn't. I'm in love."

"But it's so ghastly for you."

Jean looked into the distance so that Dinny could almost feel the cub coming round the corner.

"No! I like to think it's up to me to pull him out of it. I've never felt so alive as I feel now."

"Is there much risk for Alan?"

"Not if we work things properly. We've several schemes, according as things shape."

Dinny sighed.

"I hope to God they'll none of them be necessary."

"So do I, but it's impossible to leave things to chance, with a 'just beast' like 'Walter.'"

"Well, good-bye, Jean, and good luck!"

They kissed, and Dinny went down into the street with the emerald pendant weighing like lead on her heart. It was drizzling now and she took a cab back to Mount Street. Her father and Sir Lawrence had just come in. Their news was inconsiderable. Hubert, it seemed, did not wish for bail again. 'Jean,' thought Dinny, 'has to do with that.' The Home Secretary was in Scotland and would not be back till Parliament sat, in about a fortnight's time. The warrant could not be issued till after that. In expert opinion they had three weeks at least in which to move heaven and earth. Ah! but it was easier for heaven and earth to pass than for one tittle of the Law to fail. And yet was it quite nonsense when people talked of 'interest' and 'influence' and 'wangling' and 'getting things through'? Was there not some talismanic way of which they were all ignorant?

Her father kissed her and went dejectedly up to bed and Dinny was left alone with Sir Lawrence. Even he was in heavy mood.

"No bubble and squeak in the pair of us," he said. "I sometimes think, Dinny, that the Law is overrated. It's really a rough and ready system, with about as much accuracy in adjusting penalty to performance as there is to a doctor's diagnosis of a patient he sees for the first time; and yet for some mysterious reason we give it the sanctity of the Holy Grail and treat its dicta as if they were the broadcastings of God. If ever there was a case where a Home Secretary might let himself go and be human, this is one. And yet I don't see him doing it. I don't, Dinny, and Bobbie Ferrar doesn't. It seems that some wrongly-inspired idiot, not long ago, called Walter 'the very spirit of integrity,' and Bobbie says that instead of turning up his stomach, it went to his head, and he hasn't reprieved anybody since. I've been wondering whether I couldn't write to the 'Times' and say: 'This pose of inexorable incorruptibility in certain quarters is more dangerous to justice than the methods of Chicago.' Chicago ought to fetch him. He's been there, I believe. It's an awful thing for a man to cease to be human."

"Is he married?"

"Not even that, now," said Sir Lawrence.

"But some men don't even begin to be human, do they?"

"That's not so bad; you know where you are, and can take a fire-shovel to them. No, it's the blokes who get swelled heads that make the trouble. By the way, I told my young man that you would sit for your miniature."

"Oh! Uncle, I simply couldn't sit with Hubert on my mind!"

"No, no! Of course not! But something must turn up." He looked at her shrewdly and added: "By the way, Dinny, young Jean?"

Dinny lifted a wide and simple gaze:

"What about her?"

"She doesn't look to me too easy to bite."

"No, but what can she do, poor dear?"

"I wonder," said Sir Lawrence, raising one eyebrow, "I just wonder. 'They're dear little innocent things, they are, they're angels without any wings, they are.' That's 'Punch' before your time, Dinny. And it will continue to be 'Punch' after your time, except that wings are growing on you all so fast."

Dinny, still looking at him innocently, thought: 'He's rather uncanny, Uncle Lawrence!' And soon after she went up to bed.

To go to bed with one's whole soul in a state of upheaval! And yet how many other upheaved souls lay, cheek to pillow, unsleeping! The room seemed full of the world's unreasoning misery. If one were talented, one would get up and relieve oneself in a poem about Azrael, or something! Alas! It was not so easy as all that. One lay, and was sore—sore and anxious and angry. She could remember still how she had felt, being thirteen, when Hubert, not quite eighteen, had gone off to the war. That had been horrid, but this was much worse; and she wondered why. Then he might have been killed at any minute; now he was safer than anybody who was not in prison. He would be preserved meticulously even while they sent him across the world and put him up for trial in a country not his own, before some judge of alien blood. He was safe enough for some months yet. Why, then, did this seem so much worse than all the risks through which he had passed since he first went soldiering, even than that long, bad time on the Hallorsen expedition? Why? If not that those old risks and hardships had been endured of his free will; while the present trouble was imposed on him. He was being held down, deprived of the two great boons of human existence, independence and private life, boons to secure which human beings in communities had directed all their efforts for thousands of years, until—until they went Bolshy! Boons to every human being, but especially to people like themselves, brought up under no kind of whip except that of their own consciences. And she lay there as if she were lying in his cell, gazing into his future, longing for Jean, hating the locked-in feeling, cramped and miserable, and bitter. For what had he done, what in God's name had he done that any other man of sensibility and spirit would not do!

The mutter of the traffic from Park Lane formed a sort of ground base to her rebellious misery. She became so restless that she could not lie in bed, and, putting on her dressing gown, stole noiselessly about her room till she was chilled by the late October air coming through the opened window. Perhaps there was something in being married, after all; you had a chest to snuggle against and if need be weep on; you had an ear to pour complaint into; and lips that would make the mooing sounds of sympathy. But worse than being single during this time of trial was being inactive. She envied those who, like her father and Sir Lawrence, were at least taking cabs and going about; greatly she envied Jean and Alan. Whatever they were up to, was better than being up to nothing, like herself!

She took out the emerald pendant and looked at it. That at least was something to do on the morrow, and she pictured herself with this in her hand forcing large sums of money out of some flinty person with a tendency towards the art of lending.

Placing the pendant beneath her pillow, as though its proximity were an insurance against her sense of helplessness, she fell asleep at last.

Next morning she was down early. It had occurred to her that she could perhaps pawn the pendant, get the money, and take it to Jean before she left. And she decided to consult the butler, Blore. After all, she had known him since she was five; he was an institution and had never divulged any of the iniquities she had confided to him in her childhood.

She went up to him, therefore, when he appeared with her Aunt's special coffee machine.

"Blore."

"Yes, Miss Dinny."

"Will you be frightfully nice and tell me, *in confidence*, who is supposed to be the best pawnbroker in London?"

Surprised but impassive—for, after all, anybody might have to 'pop' anything in these days—the butler placed the coffee machine at the head of the table and stood reflecting.

"Well, Miss Dinny, of course there's Attenborough's but I'm told the best people go to a man called Frewen in South Molton Street. I can get you the number from the telephone book. They say he's reliable and very fair."

"Splendid, Blore! It's just a little matter."

"Quite so, Miss."

"Oh! And, Blore, would you—should I give my own name?"

"No, Miss Dinny; if I might suggest: give my wife's name and this address. Then if there has to be any communication, I could get it to you by telephone, and no one the wiser."

"Oh! that's a great relief. But wouldn't Mrs. Blore mind?"

"Oh! no, Miss, only too glad to oblige you. I could do the matter for you if you wish."

"Thank you, Blore, but I'm afraid I must do it myself."

The butler caressed his chin and regarded her; his eye seemed to Dinny benevolent but faintly quizzical.

"Well, Miss, if I may say so, a little nonchalance goes a long way even with the best of them. There are others if he doesn't offer value."

"Thank you frightfully, Blore; I'll let you know if he doesn't. Would half past nine be too early?"

"From what I hear, Miss, that is the best hour; you get him fresh and hearty."

"Dear Blore!"

"I'm told he's an understanding gent, who can tell a lady when he sees one. He won't confuse you with some of those Tottie madams."

Dinny laid her finger to her lips.

"Cross your heart, Blore."

"Oh! absolutely, Miss. After Mr. Michael you were always my favourite."

"And so were you, Blore." She took up the 'Times' as her father entered, and Blore withdrew.

"Sleep well, Dad?"

The General nodded.

"And Mother's head?"

"Better. She's coming down. We've decided that it's no use to worry, Dinny."

"No, darling, it isn't, of course. D'you think we could begin breakfast?"

"Em won't be down, and Lawrence has his at eight. You make the coffee."

Dinny, who shared her Aunt's passion for good coffee, went reverentially to work.

"What about Jean?" asked the General, suddenly: "Is she coming to us?"

Dinny did not raise her eyes.

"I don't think so, Dad; she'll be too restless; I expect she'll just make out by herself. I should want to, if I were her."

"I daresay, poor girl. She's got pluck, anyway. I'm glad Hubert married a girl of spirit. Those Tasburghs have got their hearts in the right place. I remember an uncle of hers in India—daring chap, a Ghoorka regiment, they swore by him. Let me see, where was he killed?"

Dinny bent lower over the coffee.

It was barely half past nine when she went out with the pendant in her vanity bag, and her best hat on. At half past nine precisely she was going up to the first floor above a shop in South Molton Street. Within a large room, at a mahogany table, were two seated gentlemen, who might have seemed to her like high-class bookmakers if she had known what such were like. She looked at them anxiously, seeking for signs of heartiness. They appeared, at least, to be fresh, and one of them came towards her.

Dinny passed an invisible tongue over her lips.

"I'm told that you are so good as to lend money on valuable jewellery?"

"Quite, Madam." He was grey, and rather bald, and rather red, with light eyes, and he stood regarding her through a pair of pince-nez which he held in his hand. Placing them on his nose, he drew a chair up to the table, made a motion with one hand, and resumed his seat. Dinny sat down.

"I want rather a lot, five hundred," and she smiled: "It was an heirloom, quite nice."

Both the seated gentlemen bowed slightly.

"And I want it at once, because I have to make a payment. Here it is!" And out of her bag she drew the pendant, unwrapped it and pushed it forward on the table. Then, remembering the needed touch of nonchalance, she leaned back and crossed her knees.

Both of them looked at the pendant for a full minute without movement or speech. Then the second gentleman opened a drawer and took out a magnifying glass. While he was examining the pendant, Dinny was conscious that the first gentleman was examining herself. That—she supposed—was the way they divided labour. Which would they decide was the more genuine piece? She felt rather breathless, but kept her eyebrows slightly raised and her eyelids half closed.

"Your own property, Madam?" said the first gentleman.

Remembering once more the old proverb, Dinny uttered an emphatic: "Yes."

The second gentleman lowered his glass, and seemed to weigh the pendant in his hand.

"Very nice," he said. "Old-fashioned, but very nice. And for how long would you want the money?"

Dinny, who had no idea, said boldly: "Six months; but I suppose I could redeem it before?"

"Oh! yes. Five hundred, did you say?"

"Please."

"If you are satisfied, Mr. Bondy," said the second gentleman, "I am."

Dinny raised her eyes to Mr. Bondy's face. Was he going to say, 'No, she's just told me a lie'? Instead, he pushed his underlip up over his upper lip, bowed to her and said:

"Quite!"

'I wonder,' she thought, 'if they always believe what they hear, or never? I suppose it's the same thing, really—*they* get the pendant and it's I who have to trust them—or, rather, it's Jean.'

The second gentleman now swept up the pendant, and producing a book, began to write in it. Mr. Bondy, on the other hand, went towards a safe.

"Did you wish for notes, Madam?"

"Please."

The second gentleman, who had a moustache and white spats, and whose eyes goggled slightly, passed her the book.

"Your name and address, Madam."

As she wrote: 'Mrs. Blore' and her aunt's number in Mount Street, the word 'Help!' came into her mind, and she cramped her left hand so as to hide what should have been the ringed finger. Her gloves fitted dreadfully well and there was no desirable circular protuberance.

"Should you require the article, we shall want £550 on the 29th of April next. After that, unless we hear from you, it will be for sale."

"Yes, of course. But if I redeem it before?"

"Then the amount will be according. The interest is at 20 per cent, so in a month, say, from now, we should only require £508 6s. 8d."

"I see."

The first gentleman detached a slip of paper and gave it to her. "That is the receipt."

"Could the pendant be redeemed on payment by anyone with this receipt, in case I can't come myself?"

"Yes, Madam."

Dinny placed the receipt in her vanity bag, together with as much of her left hand as would go in, and listened to Mr. Bondy counting notes on the table. He counted beautifully; the notes, too, made a fine crackle, and seemed to be new. She took them with her right hand, inserted them into the bag, and still holding it with her concealed left hand, arose.

"Thank you very much."

"Not at all, Madam, the pleasure is ours. Delighted to be of service. Good-bye!"

Dinny bowed, and made slowly for the door. There, from under her lashes she distinctly saw the first gentleman close one eye.

She went down the stairs rather dreamily, shutting her bag.

'I wonder if they think I'm going to have a baby,' she thought; 'or it may be only the Cambridgeshire.' Anyway she had the money, and it was just a quarter to ten. Thomas Cook's would change it, perhaps, or at least tell her where to get Belgian money.

It took an hour and visits to several places before she had most of it in Belgian money, and she was hot when she passed the barrier at Victoria with a platform ticket. She moved slowly down the train, looking into each carriage. She had gone about two-thirds down when a voice behind her called:

"Dinny!" And, looking round, she saw Jean in the doorway of a second-class compartment.

"Oh! there you are, Jean! I've had such a rush. Is my nose shiny?"

"You never look hot, Dinny."

"Well! I've done it; here's the result, five hundred. Nearly all in Belgian."

"Splendid!"

"And the receipt. Anyone can get it on this. The interest's at 20 per cent calculated from day to day, but after April 28th, unless redeemed, it'll be for sale."

"You keep that, Dinny." Jean lowered her voice. "If we have to do things, it will mean we shan't be on hand. There are several places that have no treaties with Bolivia, and that's where we shall be till things have been put straight somehow."

"Oh!" said Dinny, blankly, "I could have got more. They lapped it up."

"Never mind! I must get in. G.P.O. Brussels. Good-bye! Give my dear love to Hubert and tell him all's well." She flung her arms round Dinny, gave her a hug, and sprang back into the train. It moved off almost at once, and Dinny stood waving to that brilliant browned face turned back towards her.

CHAPTER 34

THIS ACTIVE and successful opening to her day had the most acute drawbacks, for it meant that she was now the more loose-ended.

The absence of the Home Secretary and the Bolivian Minister seemed likely to hold up all activity even if she could have been of use in those directions, which was improbable. Nothing for it but to wait, eating one's heart out! She spent the rest of the morning wandering about, looking at shop windows, looking at the people who looked at shop windows. She lunched off poached eggs at an A.B.C. and went into a cinema, with a vague idea that whatever Jean and Alan were preparing would seem more natural if she could see something of the sort on the screen. She had no luck. In the film she saw were no aeroplanes, no open spaces, no detectives, no escaping from justice whatever; it was the starkest record of a French gentleman, not quite in his first youth, going into wrong bedrooms for an hour and more on end, without anyone actually losing her virtue. Dinny could not help enjoying it—he was a dear, and perhaps the most accomplished liar she had ever watched.

After this warmth and comfort, she set her face again towards Mount Street.

She found that her mother and father had taken the afternoon train back to Condaford, and this plunged her into uncertainty. Ought she to go back, too, and 'be a daughter' to them? Or ought she to remain 'on the spot' in case anything turned up for her to do?

She went up to her room undecided, and began half-heartedly to pack. Pulling open a drawer, she came on Hubert's diary, which still accompanied her. Turning the pages idly, she lighted on a passage which seemed to her unfamiliar, having nothing to do with his hardships:

"Here's a sentence in a book I'm reading: 'We belong, of course, to a generation that's seen through things, seen how futile everything is, and had the courage to accept futility, and say to ourselves: There's nothing for it but to enjoy ourselves as best we can.' Well, I suppose that's my generation, the one that's seen the war and its aftermath; and, of course, it *is* the attitude of quite a crowd; but when you come to think of it, it might have been said by any rather unthinking person in any generation; certainly might have been said by the last generation after religion had got the knock that Darwin gave it. For what does it come to? Suppose you admit having seen through religion and marriage and treaties, and commercial honesty and freedom and ideals of every kind, seen that there's nothing absolute about them, that they lead of themselves to no definite reward, either in this world or a next which doesn't exist perhaps, and that the only thing absolute is pleasure and that you mean to have it—are you any farther towards getting pleasure? No! you're a long way farther off. If everybody's creed is consciously and crudely 'grab a good time at all costs,' everybody is going to grab it at the expense of everybody else, and the devil will take the hind-most, and that'll be nearly everybody, especially the sort of slackers who naturally hold that creed, so that *they*, most certainly, aren't going to get a good time. All those things they've so cleverly seen through are only rules of the road devised by men throughout the ages to keep people within bounds, so that we may all have a reasonable chance of getting a good time, instead of the good time going only to the violent, callous, dangerous and able few. All our institutions, religion, marriage, treaties, the law, and the rest, are simply forms of consideration for others necessary to secure consideration for self. Without them we should be a society of feeble motor bandits and streetwalkers in slavery to a few super crooks. You can't, therefore, disbelieve in consideration for others without making an idiot of yourself and spoiling your own chances of a good time. The funny thing is that no matter how we all talk, we recognize that perfectly. People who prate like the fellow in that book don't act up to their creed when it comes to the point. Even a motor bandit doesn't turn King's evidence. In fact, this new philosophy of 'having the courage to accept futility and grab a good time,' is simply a shallow bit of thinking; all the same, it seemed quite plausible when I read it."

Dinny dropped the page as if it had stung her, and stood with a transfigured look on her face. Not the words she had been reading caused this change—she was hardly conscious of what they were. No! She had got an inspiration, and she could not think why she had not had it before! She ran downstairs to the telephone and rang up Fleur's house.

"Yes?" came Fleur's voice.

"I want Michael, Fleur; is he in?"

"Yes. Michael—Dinny."

"Michael? Could you by any chance come round at once? It's about Hubert's diary. I've had a 'hunch,' but I'd rather not discuss it on the 'phone. Or could I come to you?—You *can* come? Good! Fleur too, if she likes; or, if not, bring her wits."

Ten minutes later Michael arrived alone. Something in the quality of Dinny's voice seemed to have infected him, for he wore an air of businesslike excitement. She took him into the alcove and sat down with him on a sofa under the parakeet's cage.

"Michael dear, it came to me suddenly: if we could get Hubert's diary—about 15,000 words—printed at once, ready for publication, with a good title like 'Betrayed'—or something—"

"'Deserted,'" said Michael.

"Yes, 'Deserted,' and it could be shown to the Home Secretary as about to come out with a fighting preface, it might stop him from issuing the warrant. With that title and preface and a shove from the Press, it would make a real sensation; and be very nasty for him. We could get the preface to pitch it strong about desertion of one's kith and kin, and pusillanimity and truckling to the foreigner and all that. The Press would surely take it up on those lines."

Michael ruffled his hair.

"It *is* a hunch, Dinny; but there are several points: first, how to do it without making it blackmailish. If we can't avoid that, then it's no go. If Walter sniffs blackmail, he can't possibly rise."

"But the whole point is to make him feel that if he issues the warrant he's going to regret it."

"My child," said Michael, blowing smoke at the parakeet, "it's got to be much more subtle than that. You don't know public men. The thing is to make them do of their own accord out of high motives what is for their own good. We must get Walter to do this from a low motive, and feel it to be a high one. That's indispensable."

"Won't it do if he says it's a high one? I mean need he feel it?"

"He must, at least by daylight. What he feels at three in the morning doesn't matter. He's no fool, you know. I believe," and Michael rumpled his hair again, "that the only man who can work it after all is Bobbie Ferrar. He knows Walter upside down."

"Is he a nice man? Would he?"

"Bobbie's a sphinx, but he's a perfectly good sphinx. And he's in the know all round. He's a sort of receiving station, hears everything naturally, so that we shouldn't have to appear directly in any way."

"Isn't the first thing, Michael, to get the diary printed, so that it looks ready to come out on the nail?"

"Yes, but the preface is the hub."

"How?"

"What we want is that Walter should read the printed diary, and come to the conclusion from it that to issue the warrant will be damned hard luck on Hubert—as, of course, it will. In other words, we want to sop his private mind. After that, what I see Walter saying to himself is this: 'Yes, hard luck on young Cherrell, hard luck, but the Magistrate committed him, and the Bolivians are pressing, and he belongs to the classes; one must be careful not to give an impression of favouring privilege—'"

"I think that's so unfair," interrupted Dinny, hotly. "Why should it be made harder for people just because they happen not to be Tom, Dick and Harry? I call it cowardly."

"Ah! Dinny, but we are cowardly in that sort of way. But as Walter was saying when you broke out: 'One must not lightly stretch points. The little Countries look to us to treat them with special consideration.'"

"But why?" began Dinny again: "That seems—"

Michael held up his hand.

"I know, Dinny, I know. And this seems to me the psychological moment when Bobbie, out of the blue as it were, might say: 'By the way, there's to be a preface. Someone showed it me. It takes the line that England is always being generous and just at the expense of her own subjects. It's pretty hot stuff, Sir. The Press will love it. That lay: We can't stand by our own people, is always popular. And you know'—Bobbie would continue—'it has often seemed to me, Sir, that a strong man, like you, ought perhaps to do something about this impression that we can't stand by our own people. It oughtn't to be true, perhaps it isn't true, but it exists and very strongly; and you, Sir, perhaps better than anyone, could redress the balance there. This particular case wouldn't afford a bad chance at all of restoring confidence on that point. In itself it would be right, I think'—Bobbie would say—'not to issue a warrant, because that scar, you know, was genuine, the shooting really *was* an act of self-defence; and it would certainly do the country good to feel that it could rely again on the authorities not to let our own people down.' And there he would leave it. And Walter would feel, not that he was avoiding attack, but that he was boldly going to do what was good for the Country—indispensable, that, Dinny, in the case of public men." And Michael rolled his eyes. "You see," he went on, "Walter is quite up to realising, without admitting it, that the preface won't appear if he doesn't issue the warrant. And I daresay he'll be frank with himself in the middle of the night; but if in his 6 P.M. mind he feels he's doing the courageous thing in not issuing the warrant, then what he feels in his 3 A.M. mind won't matter. See?"

"You put it marvellously, Michael. But won't he have to read the preface?"

"I hope not, but I think it ought to be in Bobbie's pocket, in case he has to fortify his line of approach. There are no flies on Bobbie, you know."

"But will Mr. Ferrar care enough to do all this?"

"Yes," said Michael, "on the whole, yes. My Dad once did him a good turn, and old Shropshire's his uncle."

"And who could write that preface?"

"I believe I could get old Blythe. They're still afraid of him in our party, and when he likes he can make livers creep all right."

Dinny clasped her hands.

"Do you think he will like?"

"It depends on the diary."

"Then I think he will."

"May I read it before I turn it over to the printers?"

"Of course! Only, Michael, Hubert doesn't want the diary to come out."

"Well, that's O.K. If it works with Walter and he doesn't issue the warrant, it won't be necessary; and if it doesn't work, it won't be necessary either, because the 'fat will be in the fire,' as old Forsyte used to say."

"Will the cost of printing be much?"

"A few pounds—say twenty."

"I can manage that," said Dinny; and her mind flew to the two gentlemen, for she was habitually hard up.

"Oh! that'll be all right, don't worry!"

"It's my hunch, Michael, and I should like to pay for it. You've no idea how horrible it is to sit and do nothing, with Hubert in this danger! I have the feeling that if he's once given up, he won't have a dog's chance."

"It's ill prophesying," said Michael, "where public men are concerned. People underrate them. They're a lot more complicated than they're supposed to be, and perhaps better principled; they're certainly a lot shrewder. All the same, I believe this will click, if we can work old Blythe and Bobbie Ferrar properly. I'll go for Blythe, and set Bart on to Bobbie. In the meantime this shall be printed," and he took up the diary. "Good-bye, Dinny dear, and don't worry more than you can help."

Dinny kissed him, and he went.

That evening about ten he rang her up.

"I've read it, Dinny. Walter must be pretty hard-boiled if it doesn't fetch him. He won't go to sleep over it, anyway, like the other bloke; he's a conscientious card, whatever else he is. After all this is a sort of reprieve case, and he's bound to recognise its seriousness. Once in his hands, he's got to go through with this diary, and it's moving stuff, apart from the light on the incident itself. So buck up!"

Dinny said: "Bless you!" fervently; and went to bed lighter at heart than she had been for two days.

CHAPTER 35

In the slow long days, and they seemed many, which followed, Dinny remained at Mount Street, to be in command of any situation that might arise. Her chief difficulty lay in keeping people ignorant of Jean's machinations. She seemed to succeed with all except Sir Lawrence, who, raising his eyebrow, said cryptically:

"*Pour une gaillarde, c'est une gaillarde!*"

And, at Dinny's limpid glance, added: "Quite the Botticellian virgin! Would you like to meet Bobbie Ferrar? We're lunching together underground at Dumourieux's in Drury Lane, mainly on mushrooms."

Dinny had been building so on Bobbie Ferrar that the sight of him gave her a shock, he had so complete an air of caring for none of those things. With his carnation, bass drawl, broad bland face, and slight drop of the underjaw, he did not inspire her.

"Have you a passion for mushrooms, Miss Cherrell?" he said.

"Not French mushrooms."

"No?"

"Bobbie," said Sir Lawrence, looking from one to the other, "no one would take you for one of the deepest cards in Europe. You are going to tell us that you won't guarantee to call Walter a strong man, when you talk about the preface?"

Several of Bobbie Ferrar's even teeth became visible.

"I have no influence with Walter."

"Then who has?"

"No one. Except—"

"Yes?"

"Walter."

Before she could check herself, Dinny had said:

"You do understand, Mr. Ferrar, that this is practically death for my brother and frightful for all of us?"

Bobbie Ferrar looked at her flushed face without speaking. He seemed, indeed, to admit or promise nothing all through that lunch, but when they got up and Sir Lawrence was paying his bill, he said to her:

"Miss Cherrell, when I go to see Walter about this, would you like to go with me? I could arrange for you to be in the background."

"I should like it terribly."

"Between ourselves, then. I'll let you know."

Dinny clasped her hands and smiled at him.

"Rum chap!" said Sir Lawrence, as they walked away: "Lots of heart, really. Simply can't bear people being hanged. Goes to all the murder trials. Hates prisons like poison. You'd never think it."

"No," said Dinny, dreamily.

"Bobbie," continued Sir Lawrence, "is capable of being Private Secretary to a Cheka, without their ever suspecting that he's itching to boil them in oil the whole time. He's unique. The diary's in print, Dinny, and old Blythe's writing that preface. Walter will be back on Thursday. Have you seen Hubert yet?"

"No, but I'm to go with Dad to-morrow."

"I've refrained from pumping you, but those young Tasburghs are up to something, aren't they? I happen to know young Tasburgh isn't with his ship."

"Not?"

"Perfect innocence!" murmured Sir Lawrence. "Well, my dear, neither nods nor winks are necessary; but I hope to goodness they won't strike before peaceful measures have been exhausted."

"Oh! surely they wouldn't!"

"They're the kind of young person who still make one believe in history. Has it ever struck you, Dinny, that history is nothing but the story of how people have taken things into their own hands, and got themselves or others into and out of trouble over it? They can cook at that place, can't they? I shall take your aunt there some day when she's thin enough."

And Dinny perceived that the dangers of cross-examination were over.

Her father called for her and they set out for the prison the following afternoon of a windy day charged with the rough melancholy of November. The sight of the building made her feel like a dog about to howl. The Governor, who was an army man, received them with great courtesy and the special deference of one to another of higher rank in his own profession. He made no secret of his sympathy with them over Hubert's position, and gave them more than the time limit allowed by the regulations.

Hubert came in smiling. Dinny felt that if she had been alone he might have shown some of his real feelings; but that in front of his father he was determined to treat the whole thing as just a bad joke. The General, who had been grim and silent all the way there, became at once matter-of-fact and as if ironically amused. Dinny could not help thinking how almost absurdly alike, allowing for age, they were in looks and in manner. There was that in both of them which would never quite grow up, or rather which had grown up in early youth and would never again budge. Neither, from beginning to end of that half-hour, touched on feeling. The whole interview was a great strain, and so far as intimate talk was concerned, might never have taken place. According to Hubert, everything in his life there was perfectly all right, and he wasn't worrying at all; according to the General, it was only a matter of days now, and the coverts were waiting to be shot. He had a good deal to say about India, and the unrest on the frontier. Only when they were shaking hands at the end did their faces change at all, and then only to the simple gravity of a very straight look into each other's eyes. Dinny followed with a hand-clasp and a kiss behind her father's back.

"Jean?" asked Hubert, very low.

"Quite all right, sent her dear love. Nothing to worry about, she says."

The quiver of his lips hardened into a little smile, he squeezed her hand, and turned away.

In the gateway the doorkeeper and two warders saluted them respect-fully. They got into their cab, and not one word did they say the whole way home. The thing was a nightmare from which they would awaken some day, perhaps.

Practically the only comfort of those days of waiting was derived by Dinny from Aunt Em, whose inherent incoherence continually diverted thoughts from logical direction. The antiseptic value, indeed, of incoher-ence became increasingly apparent as day by day anxiety increased. Her aunt was genuinely worried by Hubert's position, but her mind was too plural to dwell on it to the point of actual suffering. On the fifth of No-vember she called Dinny to the drawing-room window to look at some boys dragging a guy down a Mount Street desolate in wind and lamp-light.

"The rector's workin' on that," she said; "there was a Tasburgh who wasn't hanged, or beheaded, or whatever they did with them, and he's tryin' to prove that he ought to have been; he sold some plate or somethin' to buy the gunpowder, and his sister married Catesby, or one of the others. Your father and I and Wilmet, Dinny, used to make a guy of our gover-ness; she had very large feet, Robbins. Children are so unfeelin'. Did you?"

"Did I what, Aunt Em?"

"Make guys?"

"No."

"We used to go out singin' carols, too, with our faces blacked. Wilmet was the corker. Such a tall child, with legs that went down straight like sticks wide apart from the beginning, you know—angels have them. It's all rather gone out. I do think there ought to be somethin' done about it. Gibbets, too. We had one. We hung a kitten from it. We drowned it first—not we—the staff."

"Horrible, Aunt Em!"

"Yes; but not really. Your father brought us up as Red Indians. It was nice for him, then he could do things to us and we couldn't cry. Did Hubert?"

"Oh! no. Hubert only brought himself up as a Red Indian."

"That was your mother; she's a gentle creature, Dinny. Our mother was a Hungerford. You must have noticed."

"I don't remember Grandmother."

"She died before you were born. That was Spain. The germs there are

214

extra special. So did your grandfather. I was thirty-five. He had very good manners. They did, you know, then. Only sixty. Claret and piquet, and a funny little beard thing. You've seen them, Dinny?"

"Imperials?"

"Yes, diplomatic. They wear them now when they write those articles on foreign affairs. I like goats myself, though they butt you rather."

"Their smell, Aunt Em!"

"Penetratin'. Has Jean written to you lately?"

In Dinny's bag was a letter just received. "No," she said. The habit was growing on her.

"This hidin' away is weak-minded. Still, it *was* her honeymoon."

Her Aunt had evidently not been made a recipient of Sir Lawrence's suspicions.

Upstairs she read the letter again before tearing it up.

"Poste restante, Brussels.

"DEAR DINNY

"All goes on for the best here and I'm enjoying it quite a lot. They say I take to it like a duck to water. There's nothing much to choose now between Alan and me, except that I have the better hands. Thanks awfully for your letters. Terribly glad of the diary stunt, I think it may quite possibly work the oracle. Still we can't afford not to be ready for the worst. You don't say whether Fleur's having any luck. By the way, could you get me a Turkish conversation book, the pronouncing kind? I expect your Uncle Adrian could tell you where to get it. I can't lay hands on one here. Alan sends you his love. Same from me. Keep us informed by wire if necessary.

"Your aff^te

"JEAN."

A Turkish conversation book! This first indication of how their minds were working set Dinny's working too. She remembered Hubert having told her that he had saved the life of a Turkish officer at the end of the war, and had kept up with him ever since. So Turkey was to be the asylum, if——! But the whole plan was desperate. Surely it would not, must not come to that! But she went down to the Museum the next morning.

Adrian, whom she had not seen since Hubert's committal, received her with his usual quiet alacrity, and she was sorely tempted to confide in him. Jean must know that to ask his advice about a Turkish conversation book would surely stimulate his curiosity. She restrained herself, however, and said:

"Uncle, you haven't a Turkish conversation book? Hubert thought he'd like to kill time in prison brushing up his Turkish."

Adrian regarded her, and closed one eye.

"He hasn't any Turkish to brush. But here you are——" And fishing a small book from a shelf, he added: "Serpent!"

Dinny smiled.

"Deception," he continued, "is wasted on me, Dinny, I am in whatever know there is."

"Tell me, Uncle!"

"You see," said Adrian, "Hallorsen is in it."

"Oh!"

"And I, whose movements are dependent on Hallorsen's, have had to put two and two together. They make five, Dinny, and I sincerely trust the addition won't be needed. But Hallorsen's a fine chap."

"I know that," said Dinny, ruefully. "Uncle, do tell me exactly what's in the wind."

Adrian shook his head.

"They obviously can't tell themselves till they hear how Hubert is to be exported. All I know is that Hallorsen's Bolivians are going back to Bolivia instead of to the States, and that a very queer padded, well-ventilated case is being made to hold them."

"You mean his Bolivian bones?"

"Or possibly replicas. They're being made, too."

Thrilled, Dinny stood gazing at him.

"And," added Adrian, "the replicas are being made by a man who believes he is repeating Siberians, and not for Hallorsen, and they've been very carefully weighed—one hundred and fifty-two pounds, perilously near the weight of a man. How much is Hubert?"

"About eleven stone."

"Exactly."

"Go on, Uncle."

"Having got so far, Dinny, I'll give you my theory, for what it's worth. Hallorsen and his case full of replicas will travel by the ship that Hubert travels by. At any port of call in Spain or Portugal, Hallorsen will get off with his case, containing Hubert. He will contrive to have extracted and dropped the replicas overboard. The real bones will be waiting there for him, and he will fill up when Hubert has been switched off to a plane: that's where Jean and Alan come in. They'll fly to, well—Turkey, judging from your request just now. I was wondering where before you came. Hallorsen will pop his genuine bones into the case to satisfy the authorities, and Hubert's disappearance will be put down to a jump overboard— the splash of the replicas, I shouldn't wonder—or anyway will remain mysterious. It looks to me pretty forlorn."

"But suppose there's no port of call?"

"They're pretty certain to stop somewhere; but, if not, they'll have some alternative, which will happen on the way down to the ship. Or possibly they may elect to try the case dodge on the arrival in South America. That would really be safest, I think, though it lets out the flying."

"But why is Professor Hallorsen going to run such a risk?"

"*You* ask me that, Dinny?"

"It's too much—I—I don't want him to."

216

"Well, my dear, he also has the feeling, I know, that he got Hubert into this, and must get him out. And you must remember that he belongs to a nation that is nothing if not energetic and believes in taking the law into its own hands. But he's the last man to trade on a service. Besides, it's a three-legged race he's running with young Tasburgh, who's just as deep in it, so you're no worse off."

"But I don't want to owe anything to either of them. It simply mustn't come to that. Besides, there's Hubert—do you think he'll ever consent?"

Adrian said gravely:

"I think he has consented, Dinny; otherwise he'd have asked for bail. Probably he'll be in charge of Bolivians and won't feel he's breaking English law. I fancy they've convinced him between them that they won't run much risk. No doubt he feels fed up with the whole thing and ready for anything. Don't forget that he's really being very unjustly treated, and is just married."

"Yes," said Dinny, in a hushed voice. "And you, Uncle? How are things?"

Adrian's answer was no less quiet:

"Your advice was right; and I'm fixed up to go, subject to this business."

CHAPTER 36

THE FEELING that such things did not happen persisted with Dinny even after her interview with Adrian; she had too often read of them in books. And yet, there was history, and there were the Sunday papers! Thought of the Sunday papers calmed her curiously and fortified her resolution to keep Hubert's affair out of them. But she conscientiously posted to Jean the Turkish primer, and took to poring over maps in Sir Lawrence's study when he was out. She also studied the sailing dates of the South American lines.

Two days later Sir Lawrence announced at dinner that 'Walter' was back; but after a holiday it would no doubt take him some time to reach a little thing like Hubert's.

"A little thing!" cried Dinny: "merely his life and our happiness."

"My dear, people's lives and happiness are the daily business of a Home Secretary."

"It must be an awful post. I should hate it."

"That," said Sir Lawrence, "is where your difference from a public man comes in, Dinny. What a public man hates is *not* dealing with the lives and happiness of his fellow-beings. Is our bluff ready, in case he comes early to Hubert?"

"The diary's printed—I've passed the proof; and the preface is written. I haven't seen that, but Michael says it's a 'corker.'"

"Good! Mr. Blythe's corkers give no mean pause. Bobbie will let us know when Walter reaches the case."

"What is Bobbie?" asked Lady Mont.

"An institution, my dear."

"Blore, remind me to write about that sheep-dog puppy."

"Yes, my lady."

"When their faces are mostly white they have a kind of divine madness, have you noticed, Dinny? They're all called Bobbie."

"Anything less divinely mad than our Bobbie—eh, Dinny?"

"Does he always do what he says he will, Uncle?"

"Yes; you may bet on Bobbie."

"I do want to see some sheep-dog trials," said Lady Mont: "Clever creatures. People say they know exactly what sheep not to bite; and so thin, really. All hair and intelligence. Hen has two. About your hair, Dinny?"

"Yes, Aunt Em?"

"Did you keep what you cut off?"

"I did."

"Well, don't let it go out of the family; you may want it. They say we're goin' to be old-fashioned again. Ancient but modern, you know."

Sir Lawrence cocked his eye. "Have you ever been anything else, Dinny? That's why I want you to sit. Permanence of the type."

"What type?" said Lady Mont. "Don't be a type, Dinny; they're so dull. There was a man said Michael was a type; I never could see it."

"Why don't you get Aunt Em to sit instead, Uncle? She's younger than I am any day, aren't you, Auntie?"

"Don't be disrespectful. Blore, my Vichy."

"Uncle, how old is Bobbie?"

"No one really knows. Rising sixty, perhaps. Some day, I suppose, his date will be discovered; but they'll have to cut a section and tell it from his rings. You're not thinking of marrying him, are you, Dinny? By the way, Walter's a widower. Quaker blood somewhere, converted Liberal —inflammable stuff."

"Dinny takes a lot of wooin'," said Lady Mont.

"Can I get down, Aunt Em? I want to go to Michael's."

"Tell her I'm comin' to see Kit to-morrow mornin'. I've got him a new game called Parliament—they're animals divided into Parties; they all squeak and roar differently, and behave in the wrong places. The Prime Minister's a zebra, and the Chancellor of the Exchequer's a tiger —striped. Blore, a taxi for Miss Dinny."

Michael was at the House, but Fleur was in. She reported that Mr. Blythe's preface had already been sent to Bobbie Ferrar. As for the Bolivians—the Minister was not back, but the Attaché in charge had promised to have an informal talk with Bobbie. He had been so polite that Fleur was unable to say what was in his mind. She doubted if there was anything.

Dinny returned on as many tenterhooks as ever. It all seemed to hinge on Bobbie Ferrar, and he 'rising' sixty, so used to everything that he must surely have lost all persuasive flame. But perhaps that was for the best. Emotional appeal might be wrong. Coolness, calculation, the power of hinting at unpleasant consequences, of subtly suggesting advantage, might be what was wanted. She felt, indeed, completely at sea as to what really moved the mind of Authority. Michael, Fleur, Sir Lawrence had spoken from time to time as if they knew, and yet she felt that none of them were really wiser than herself. It all seemed to balance on the knife-edge of mood and temper. She went to bed and had practically no sleep.

One more day like that, and then, as a sailor, whose ship has been in the doldrums, wakes to movement under him, so felt Dinny when at breakfast she opened an unstamped envelope with "Foreign Office" imprinted on it.

"DEAR MISS CHERRELL,—

"I handed your brother's diary to the Home Secretary yesterday afternoon. He promised to read it last night, and I am to see him to-day at six o'clock. If you will come to the Foreign Office at ten minutes to six, we might go round together.

"Sincerely yours,

"R. FERRAR."

So! A whole day to get through first! By now 'Walter' must have the diary; had perhaps already made up his mind on the case! With the receipt of the formal note, a feeling of being in conspiracy and pledged to secrecy had come to her. Instinctively she said nothing of it; instinctively wanted to get away from everybody till all was over. This must be like waiting for an operation. She walked out into a fine morning, and wondered where on earth she should go; thought of the National Gallery, and decided that pictures required too much mind given to them; thought of Westminster Abbey and the girl Millicent Pole. Fleur had got her a post as mannequin at Frivolle's. Why not go there, look at the winter models, and perhaps see that girl again? Rather hateful being shown dresses if you were not going to buy, giving all that trouble for nothing. But if only Hubert were released she would 'go off the deep end' and buy a real dress, though it took all her next allowance. Hardening her heart, therefore, she turned in the direction of Bond Street, forded that narrow drifting river, came to Frivolle's, and went in.

"Yes, Madam"; and she was shown up, and seated on a chair. She sat there with her head a little on one side, smiling and saying pleasant things to the saleswoman; for she remembered one day in a big shop an assistant saying: "You've no idea, Moddam, what a difference it makes to us when a customer smiles and takes a little interest. We get so many difficult ladies and—oh! well——" The models were very 'late,' very expensive, and mostly, she thought, very unbecoming, in spite of the constant assurance: "This frock would just suit you, Madam, with your figure and colouring."

Not sure whether to ask after her would harm or benefit the girl Millicent Pole, she selected two dresses for parade. A very thin girl, haughty, with a neat little head and large shoulder blades came wearing the first, a creation in black and white; she languished across with a hand on where one hip should have been, and her head turned as if looking for the other, confirming Dinny in the aversion she already had for the dress. Then, in the second dress, of sea green and silver, the one that she really liked except for its price, came Millicent Pole. With professional negligence she took no glance at the client, as who should say: "What do you think! If you lived in underclothes all day—and had so many husbands to avoid!" Then, in turning, she caught Dinny's smile, answered it with a sudden startled brightness, and moved across again, languid as ever. Dinny got up, and going over to that figure now standing very still, took a fold of the skirt between finger and thumb, as if to feel its quality.

"Nice to see you again."

The girl's loose flower-like mouth smiled very sweetly. 'She's marvellous!' thought Dinny.

"I know Miss Pole," she said to the saleswoman. "That dress looks awfully nice on her."

"Oh! but, Madam, it's your style completely. Miss Pole has a little too much line for it. Let me slip it on you."

Not sure that she had been complimented, Dinny said:

"I shan't be able to decide to-day; I'm not sure I can afford it."

"That is quite all right, Madam. Miss Pole, just come in here and slip it off, and we'll slip it on Madam."

In there the girl slipped it off. 'Even more marvellous,' thought Dinny: 'Wish I looked as nice as that in undies,' and suffered her own dress to be removed.

"Madam is beautifully slim," said the saleswoman.

"Thin as a rail!"

"Oh, no, Madam is well covered."

"I think she's just right!" The girl spoke with a sort of eagerness. "Madam has style."

The saleswoman fastened the hook.

"Perfect," she said. "A little fullness here, perhaps; we can put that right."

"Rather a lot of my skin," murmured Dinny.

"Oh! But so becoming, with a skin like Madam's."

"Would you let me see Miss Pole in that other frock—the black and white?"

This she said, knowing that the girl could not be sent to fetch it in her underclothes.

"Certainly; I'll get it at once. Attend to Madam, Miss Pole."

Left to themselves, the two girls stood smiling at each other.

"How do you like it now you've got it, Millie?"

"Well, it isn't all I thought, Miss."

"Empty?"

"I expect nothing's what you think it. Might be a lot worse, of course."

"It was you I came in to see."

"Did you reely? But I hope you'll have the dress, Miss—suits you a treat. You look lovely in it."

"They'll be putting you in the sales department, Millie, if you don't look out."

"Oh! I wouldn't go there. It's nothing but a lot of soft sawder."

"Where do I unhook?"

"Here. It's very economic—only one. And you can do it for yourself, with a wriggle. I read about your brother, Miss. I do think that's a shame."

"Yes," said Dinny, and stood stony in her underclothes. Suddenly she stretched out her hand and gripped the girl's. "Good luck, Millie!"

"And good luck to you, Miss!"

They had just unclasped hands when the saleswoman came back.

"I'm so sorry to have bothered you," smiled Dinny, "but I've quite made up my mind to have this one, if I can afford it. The price is appalling."

"Do you think so, Madam? It's a Paris model. I'll see if I can get Mr. Better to do what he can for *you*—it's *your* frock. Miss Pole, find Mr. Better for me, will you?"

The girl, now in the black and white creation, went out.

Dinny, who had resumed her dress, said:

"Do your mannequins stay long with you?"

"Well, no; in and out of dresses all day, it's rather a restless occupation."

"What becomes of them?"

"In one way or another they get married."

How discreet! And soon after, Mr. Better—a slim man with grey hair and perfect manners—having said he would reduce the price 'for Madam' to what still seemed appalling, Dinny went out into the pale November sunlight saying she would decide to-morrow. Six hours to kill. She walked North-East towards the Meads, trying to soothe her own anxiety by thinking that everyone she passed, no matter how they looked, had anxieties of their own. Seven million people, in one way or another all anxious. Some of them seemed so, and some did not. She gazed at her own face in a shop window, and decided that she was one of those who did not; and yet how horrid she felt! The human face was a mask, indeed! She came to Oxford Street and halted on the edge of the pavement, waiting to cross. Close to her was the bony white-nosed head of a van horse. She began stroking its neck, wishing she had a lump of sugar. The horse paid no attention, nor did its driver. Why should they? From year's end to year's end they passed and halted, halted and passed through this maelstrom, slowly, ploddingly, without hope of release, till they both fell down and were cleared away. A policeman reversed the direction of his white sleeves, the driver jerked his reins, and the van moved on, followed by a long line of motor vehicles. The policeman again reversed his sleeves and Dinny crossed, walked on to Tottenham Court Road, and once more stood waiting. What a seething and intricate pattern of creatures, and their cars, moving to what end, fulfilling what secret purpose? To what did it all amount? A meal, a smoke, a glimpse of so-called life in some picture palace, a bed at the end of the day. A million jobs faithfully and unfaithfully pursued, that they might eat, and dream a little, and sleep, and begin again. The inexorability of life caught her by the throat as she stood there, so that she gave a little gasp, and a stout man said:

"Beg pardon, did I tread on your foot, Miss?"

As she was smiling her 'No,' a policeman reversed his white sleeves, and she crossed. She came to Gower Street, and walked rapidly up its singular desolation. 'One more ribber, one more ribber to cross,' and she was in the Meads, that network of mean streets, gutters, and child life. At the Vicarage both her Uncle and Aunt for once were in, and about to lunch. Dinny sat down, too. She did not shrink from discussing the coming 'operation' with them. They lived so in the middle of operations. Hilary said:

"Old Tasburgh and I got Bentworth to speak to the Home Secretary, and I had this note from 'the Squire' last night. 'All Walter would say was that he should treat the case strictly on its merits without reference to what he called your nephew's status—what a word! I always said the fellow ought to have stayed Liberal.'"

"I wish he *would* treat it on its merits!" cried Dinny; "then Hubert would be safe. I do hate that truckling to what they call Democracy! He'd give a cabman the benefit of the doubt."

"It's the reaction from the old times, Dinny, and gone too far, as reaction always does. When I was a boy there was still truth in the accusation of privilege. Now, it's the other way on; station in life is a handicap before the Law. But nothing's harder than to steer in the middle of the stream—you want to be fair, and you can't."

"I was wondering, Uncle, as I came along. What was the use of you and Hubert and Dad and Uncle Adrian, and tons of others doing their jobs faithfully—apart from bread and butter, I mean?"

"Ask your Aunt," said Hilary.

"Aunt May, what *is* the use?"

"I don't know, Dinny. I was bred up to believe there was a use in it, so I go on believing. If you married and had a family, you probably wouldn't ask the question."

"I knew Aunt May would get out of answering. Now, Uncle?"

"Well, Dinny, I don't know either. As she says, we do what we're used to doing; that's about it."

"In his diary Hubert says that consideration for others is really consideration for ourselves. Is that true?"

"Rather a crude way of putting it. I should prefer to say that we're all so interdependent that in order to look after oneself one's got to look after others no less."

"But is one worth looking after?"

"You mean: is life worth while at all?"

"Yes."

"After five hundred thousand years (Adrian says a million at least) of human life, the population of the world is very considerably larger than it has ever been yet. Well, then! Considering all the miseries and struggles of mankind, would human life, self-conscious as it is, have persisted if it wasn't worth while to be alive?"

"I suppose not," mused Dinny; "I think in London one loses the sense of proportion."

At this moment a maid came in.

"Mr. Cameron to see you, Sir."

"Show him in, Lucy. He'll help you regain it, Dinny. A walking proof of the unquenchable love of life, had every malady under the sun, including black-water, been in three wars, two earthquakes, had all kinds of jobs in all parts of the world, is out of one now, and has heart disease."

Mr. Cameron entered; a short spare man getting on for fifty, with bright Celtic grey eyes, dark grizzled hair, and a slightly hooked nose. One of his hands was bound up, as if he had sprained a thumb.

"Hallo, Cameron," said Hilary, rising. "In the wars again?"

"Well, Vicar, where I live, the way some of those fellows treat horses is dreadful. I had a fight yesterday. Flogging a willing horse, overloaded, poor old feller—never can stand that."

"I hope you gave him beans!"

Mr. Cameron's eyes twinkled.

"Well, I tapped his claret, and sprained my thumb. But I called to tell you, Sir, that I've got a job on the Vestry. It's not much, but it'll keep me going."

"Splendid! Look here, Cameron, I'm awfully sorry, but Mrs. Cherrell and I have to go to a Meeting now. Stay and have a cup of coffee and talk to my niece. Tell her about Brazil."

Mr. Cameron looked at Dinny. He had a charming smile.

The next hour went quickly and did her good. Mr. Cameron had a fine flow. He gave her practically his life story, from boyhood in Australia, and enlistment at sixteen for the South African war, to his experiences since the Great War. Every kind of insect and germ had lodged in him in his time; he had handled horses, Chinamen, Kaffirs, and Brazilians, broken collar-bone and leg, been gassed and shell-shocked, but there was —he carefully explained—nothing wrong with him now but "a touch of this heart disease." His face had a kind of inner light, and his speech betrayed no consciousness that he was out of the common. He was, at the moment, the best antidote Dinny could have taken, and she prolonged him to his limit. When he had gone she herself went away into the medley of the streets with a fresh eye. It was now half-past three, and she had two hours and a half still to put away. She walked towards the Regent's Park. Few leaves were left upon the trees, and there was a savour in the air from bonfires of them burning; through their bluish drift she passed, thinking of Mr. Cameron, and resisting melancholy. What a life to have lived! And what a zest at the end of it! From beside the Long Water in the last of the pale sunlight, she came out into Marylebone, and bethought herself that before she went to the Foreign Office she must go where she could titivate. She chose Harridge's and went in. It was half-past four. The stalls were thronged; she wandered among them, bought a new powder-puff, had some tea, made herself tidy, and emerged. Still a good half hour, and she walked again, though by now she was tired. At a quarter to six precisely she gave her card to a commissionaire at the Foreign Office, and was shown into a waiting-room. It was lacking in mirrors, and taking out her case she looked at herself in its little powder-flecked round of glass. She seemed plain to herself and wished that she didn't; though, after all, she was not going to see 'Walter'—only to sit in the background, and wait again. Always waiting!

"Miss Cherrell!"

There was Bobbie Ferrar in the doorway. He looked just as usual. But of course he didn't care. Why should he?

He tapped his breast pocket. "I've got the preface. Shall we trot?" And he proceeded to talk of the Chingford murder. Had she been following it? She had not. It was a clear case—completely! And he added, suddenly:

"The Bolivian won't take the responsibility, Miss Cherrell."

"Oh!"

"Never mind." And his face broadened.

'His teeth *are* real,' thought Dinny, 'I can see some gold filling.'

They reached the Home Office and went in. Up some wide stairs, down a corridor, into a large and empty room, with a fire at the end, their guide took them. Bobbie Ferrar drew a chair up to the table.

"'The Graphic' or this?" and he took from his side pocket a small volume.

"Both, please," said Dinny, wanly. He placed them before her. 'This' was a little flat red edition of some War Poems.

"It's a first," said Bobbie Ferrar; "I picked it up after lunch."

"Yes," said Dinny, and sat down.

An inner door was opened, and a head put in.

"Mr. Ferrar, the Home Secretary will see you."

Bobbie Ferrar turned on her a look, muttered between his teeth: "Cheer up!" and moved squarely away.

In that great waiting-room never in her life had she felt so alone, so glad to be alone, or so dreaded the end of loneliness. She opened the little volume and read:

> "He eyed a neat framed notice there
> Above the fireplace hung to show
> Disabled heroes where to go
> For arms and legs, with scale of price,
> And words of dignified advice
> How officers could get them free.
> Elbow or shoulder, hip or knee.
> Two arms, two legs, though all were lost,
> They'd be restored him free of cost.
>
> Then a girl guide looked in and said . . ."

The fire crackled suddenly and spat out a spark. Dinny saw it die on the hearthrug, with regret. She read more poems, but did not take them in, and, closing the little book, opened 'The Graphic.' Having turned its pages from end to end she could not have mentioned the subject of any single picture. The sinking feeling beneath her heart absorbed every ob-

ject she looked upon. She wondered if it were worse to wait for an operation on oneself or on someone loved; and decided that the latter must be
worse. Hours seemed to have passed; how long had he really been gone?
Only half-past six! Pushing her chair back, she got up. On the walls were
the effigies of Victorian statesmen, and she roamed from one to the other;
but they might all have been the same statesman, with his whiskers at different stages of development. She went back to her seat, drew her chair
close in to the table, rested her elbows on it, and her chin on her hands,
drawing a little comfort from that cramped posture. Thank Heaven! Hubert didn't know his fate was being decided, and was not going through
this awful waiting. She thought of Jean and Alan, and with all her heart
hoped that they were ready for the worst. For with each minute the worst
seemed more and more certain. A sort of numbness began creeping over
her. He would never come back—never, never! And she hoped he
wouldn't, bringing the death-warrant. At last she laid her arms flat on the
table, and rested her forehead on them. How long she had stayed in that
curious torpor she knew not, before the sound of a throat being cleared
roused her, and she started back.

Not Bobbie Ferrar, but a tall man with a reddish, clean-shaven face
and silver hair brushed in a cockscomb on his forehead, was standing
before the fire with his legs slightly apart and his hands under his coat-
tails; he was staring at her with very wide-opened light grey eyes, and
his lips were just apart as if he were about to emit a remark. Dinny was
too startled to rise, and she sat staring back at him.

"Miss Cherrell! Don't get up." He lifted a restraining hand from beneath a coat-tail. Dinny stayed seated—only too glad to, for she had begun to tremble violently.

"Ferrar tells me that you edited your brother's diary?"

Dinny bowed her head. Take deep breaths!

"As printed, is it in its original condition?"

"Yes."

"Exactly?"

"Yes. I haven't altered or left out a thing."

Staring at his face she could see nothing but the round brightness of
the eyes and the slight superior prominence of the lower lip. It was almost
like staring at God. She shivered at the queerness of the thought and her
lips formed a little desperate smile.

"I have a question to ask you, Miss Cherrell."

Dinny uttered a little sighing: "Yes."

"How much of this diary was written since your brother came back?"
She stared; then the implication in the question stung her.

"None! Oh, none! It was all written out there at the time." And she
rose to her feet.

"May I ask how you know that?"

"My brother——" Only then did she realise that throughout she had
nothing but Hubert's word—"my brother told me so."

"His word is gospel to you?"

She retained enough sense of humour not to 'draw herself up,' but her head tilted.

"Gospel. My brother is a soldier and——"

She stopped short, and, watching that superior lower lip, hated herself for using that cliché.

"No doubt, no doubt! But you realise, of course, the importance of the point?"

"There is the original——" stammered Dinny. Oh! Why hadn't she brought it! "It shows clearly—I mean, it's all messy and stained. You can see it at any time. Shall——?"

He again put out a restraining hand.

"Never mind that. Very devoted to your brother, Miss Cherrell?"

Dinny's lips quivered.

"Absolutely. We all are."

"He's just married, I hear?"

"Yes, just married."

"Your brother wounded in the war?"

"Yes. He had a bullet through his left leg."

"Neither arm touched?"

Again that sting!

"No!" The little word came out like a shot fired. And they stood looking at each other half a minute—a minute; words of appeal, of resentment, incoherent words were surging to her lips, but she kept them closed; she put her hand over them. He nodded.

"Thank you, Miss Cherrell. Thank you." His head went a little to one side; he turned, and rather as if carrying that head on a charger, walked to the inner door. When he had passed through, Dinny covered her face with her hands. What had she done? Antagonised him? She ran her hands down over her face, over her body, and stood with them clenched at her sides, staring at the door through which he had passed, quivering from head to foot. A minute passed. The door was opened again, and Bobbie Ferrar came in. She saw his teeth. He nodded, shut the door, and said:

"It's all right."

Dinny spun round to the window. Dark had fallen, and, if it hadn't, she couldn't have seen. All right! All right! She dashed her knuckles across her eyes, turned round, and held out both hands, without seeing where to hold them.

They were not taken, but his voice said:

"I'm very happy."

"I thought I'd spoiled it."

She saw his eyes then, round as a puppy dog's.

"If he hadn't made up his mind already he wouldn't have seen you, Miss Cherrell. He's not as case-hardened as all that. As a matter of fact, he'd seen the Magistrate about it at lunch time—that helped a lot."

'Then I had all that agony for nothing,' thought Dinny.

"Did he have to see the preface, Mr. Ferrar?"

"No, and just as well—it might have worked the other way. We really owe it to the Magistrate. But you made a good impression on him. He said you were transparent."

"Oh!"

Bobbie Ferrar took the little red book from the table, looked at it lovingly, and placed it in his pocket. "Shall we go?"

In Whitehall Dinny took a breath so deep that the whole November dusk seemed to pass into her with the sensation of a long, and desperately wanted drink.

"A Post Office!" she said. "He couldn't change his mind, could he?"

"I have his word. Your brother will be released tonight."

"Oh! Mr. Ferrar!" Tears suddenly came out of her eyes. She turned away to hide them, and when she turned back to him, he was not there.

CHAPTER 37

WHEN FROM that Post Office she had despatched telegrams to her father and Jean, and telephoned to Fleur, to Adrian and Hilary, she took a taxi to Mount Street, and opened the door of her Uncle's study. Sir Lawrence, before the fire with a book he was not reading, looked up.

"What's your news, Dinny?"

"Saved!"

"Thanks to you!"

"Bobbie Ferrar says, thanks to the Magistrate. I nearly wrecked it, Uncle."

"Ring the bell!" Dinny rang.

"Blore, tell Lady Mont I want her."

"Good news, Blore; Mr. Hubert's free."

"Thank you, Miss; I was laying six to four on it."

"What can we do to relieve our feelings, Dinny?"

"I must go to Condaford, Uncle."

"Not till after dinner. You shall go drunk. What about Hubert? Anybody going to meet him?"

"Uncle Adrian said I'd better not, and he would go. Hubert will make for the flat, of course, and wait for Jean."

Sir Lawrence gave her a whimsical glance.

"Where will she be flying from?"

"Brussels."

"So that was the centre of operations! The closing down of that enterprise gives me almost as much satisfaction, Dinny, as Hubert's release. You can't get away with that sort of thing, nowadays."

"I think they might have," said Dinny, for with the removal of the need for it, the idea of escape seemed to have become less fantastic. "Aunt Em! What a nice wrapper!"

"I was dressin'. Blore's won four pounds. Dinny, kiss me. Give your Uncle one, too. You kiss very nicely—there's body in it. If I drink champagne, I shall be ill to-morrow."

"But need you, Auntie?"

"Yes. Dinny, promise me to kiss that young man."

"Do you get a commission on kissing, Aunt Em?"

"Don't tell me he wasn't goin' to cut Hubert out of prison, or something. The Rector said he flew in with a beard one day, and took a spirit level and two books on Portugal. They always go to Portugal. The Rector'll be so relieved; he was gettin' thin about it. So I think you ought to kiss him."

"A kiss means nothing nowadays, Auntie. I nearly kissed Bobbie Ferrar; only he saw it coming."

"Dinny can't be bothered to do all this kissing," said Sir Lawrence; "she's got to sit to my miniature painter. The young man will be at Condaford to-morrow, Dinny."

"Your Uncle's got a bee, Dinny, collectin' the Lady. There aren't any, you know. It's extinct. We're all females now."

By the only late evening train Dinny embarked for Condaford. They had plied her with wine at dinner, and she sat in sleepy elation, grateful for everything—the motion, and the moon-ridden darkness flying past the windows. Her exhilaration kept breaking out in smiles. Hubert free! Condaford safe! Her father and mother at ease once more! Jean happy! Alan no longer threatened with disgrace! Her fellow-passengers, for she was travelling third-class, looked at her with the frank, or furtive wonderment that so many smiles will induce in the minds of any taxpayers. Was she tipsy, weak-minded, or merely in love? Perhaps all three. And she looked back at them with a benevolent compassion because they were obviously not half-seas-over with happiness. The hour and a half seemed short, and she got out on to the dimly lighted platform, less sleepy, but as elated as when she had got into the train. She had forgotten to add in her telegram that she was coming, so she had to leave her things and walk. She took the main road; it was longer, but she wanted to swing along and breathe home air to the full. In the night, as always, things looked unfamiliar, and she seemed to pass houses, hedges, trees that she had never known. The road dipped through a wood. A car came with its headlights glaring luridly, and in that glare she saw a weasel slink across just in time—queer little low beast, snakily humping its long back. She stopped a moment on the bridge over their narrow twisting little river. That bridge was hundreds of years old, nearly as old as the oldest parts of the Grange, and still very strong. Just beyond it was their gate, and when the river flooded, in very wet years, it crept up the meadow almost to the shrubbery where the moat had once been. Dinny pushed through the gate and walked on the grass edging of the drive between the rhododendrons. She came to the front of the house, which was really its back—long, low, unlighted. They did not expect her, and it was getting on for midnight; and the idea came to her to steal round and see it all grey and ghostly, tree-and-creeper-covered in the moonlight. Past the yew trees, throwing short shadows under the raised garden, she came round on to the lawn, and stood breathing deeply, and turning her head this way and that, so as to miss nothing that she had grown up with. The moon flicked a ghostly radiance on to the windows, and shiny leaves of the magnolias; and secrets lurked all over the old stone face. Lovely! Only one window was lighted, that of her father's study. It seemed strange that they had gone to bed already, with relief so bubbling in them. She stole from the lawn on to the terrace and stood looking in through the curtains not quite drawn. The General was at his desk with a lot of papers spread before him, sitting with his hands between his knees, and his head bent. She could see the hollow below his temple, the hair above it, much greyer of late, the set mouth, the almost beaten look on the face. The whole attitude was that of a man in patient silence, preparing to accept disaster. Up in Mount Street she had been reading of the American Civil War, and she thought that just so, but for his lack of beard, might some old Southern General have looked, the night before Lee's surrender. And, suddenly, it came to her that by an evil chance they had not yet received her telegram. She tapped on the pane. Her father raised his head. His face was ashen grey in the moonlight, and it was evident that he mistook her apparition for confirmation of the worst; he opened the window. Dinny leaned in, and put her hands on his shoulders.

"Dad! Haven't you had my wire? It's all right, Hubert's free."

The General's hands shot up and grasped her wrists, colour came into his face, his lips relaxed, he looked suddenly ten years younger.

"Is it—is it certain, Dinny?"

Dinny nodded. She was smiling, but tears stood in her eyes.

"My God! That's news! Come in! I must go up and tell your Mother!" He was out of the room before she was in it.

In this room, which had resisted her mother's and her own attempts to introduce æstheticism, and retained an office-like barrenness, Dinny stood staring at this and at that evidence of Art's defeat, with the smile that was becoming chronic. Dad with his papers, his military books, his ancient photographs, his relics of India and South Africa, and the old-style picture of his favourite charger; his map of the estate; his skin of the leopard that had mauled him, and the two fox masks—happy again! Bless him!

She had the feeling that her mother and he would rather be left alone to rejoice, and slipped upstairs to Clare's room. That vivid member of the family was asleep with one pyjama-d arm outside the sheet and her cheek resting on the back of the hand. Dinny looked amiably at the dark shingled head and went out again. No good spoiling beauty sleep! She stood at her opened bedroom window, gazing between the nearly bare elm-trees, at the moonlit rise of fields and the wood beyond. She stood and tried hard not to believe in God. It seemed mean and petty to have more belief in God when things were going well than when they were instinct with tragedy; just as it seemed mean and petty to pray to God when you wanted something badly, and not pray when you didn't. But after all God was Eternal Mind that you couldn't understand; God was not a loving Father that you could. The less she thought about all that the better. She was home like a ship after a storm; it was enough! She swayed, standing there, and realised that she was nearly asleep. Her bed was not made ready; but getting out an old, thick dressing-gown, she slipped off shoes, dress, and corset belt, put on the gown and curled up under the eider-down. In two minutes, still with that smile on her lips, she was sleeping. . . .

A telegram from Hubert, received at breakfast next morning, said that he and Jean would be down in time for dinner.

"'The Young Squire Returns!'" murmured Dinny. "'Brings Bride!' Thank goodness it'll be after dark, and we can kill the fatted calf in private. Is the fatted calf ready, Dad?"

"I've got two bottles of your great-grandfather's Chambertin 1865 left. We'll have that, and the old brandy."

"Hubert likes woodcock best, if there are any to be had, Mother, and pancakes. And how about the inland oyster? He loves oysters."

"I'll see, Dinny."

"And mushrooms," added Clare.

"You'll have to scour the country, I'm afraid, Mother."

Lady Cherrell smiled, she looked quite young.

"It's 'a mild hunting day,'" said the General: "What about it, Clare? The meet's at Wyvell's Cross, eleven."

"Rather!"

Returning from the stables after seeing her father and Clare depart, Dinny and the dogs lingered. The relief from that long waiting, the feeling of nothing to worry about, was so delicious that she did not resent the singular similarity in the present state of Hubert's career to the state which had given her so much chagrin two months back. He was in precisely the same position, only worse, because married; and yet she felt as blithe as a 'sandboy.' It proved that Einstein was right, and everything relative!

She was singing 'The Lincolnshire Poacher' on her way to the raised garden when the sound of a motor-cycle on the drive caused her to turn. Someone in the guise of a cyclist waved his hand, and shooting the cycle into a rhododendron bush came towards her, removing his hood.

Alan, of course! And she experienced at once the sensation of one about to be asked in marriage. Nothing—she felt—could prevent him this morning, for he had not even succeeded in doing the dangerous and heroic thing which might have made the asking for reward too obvious.

'But perhaps,' she thought, 'he still has a beard—that might stop him.' Alas! He had only a jaw rather paler than the rest of his brown face.

He came up holding out both hands and she gave him hers. Thus grappled, they stood looking at each other.

"Well," said Dinny, at last, "tell your tale. You've been frightening us out of our wits, young man."

"Let's go and sit down up there, Dinny."

"Very well. Mind Scaramouch, he's under your foot, and the foot large."

"Not so very. Dinny, you look——"

"No," said Dinny; "rather worn than otherwise. I know all about the Professor and the special case for his Bolivian bones, and the projected substitution of Hubert on the ship."

"What!"

"We're not half-wits, Alan. What was *your* special lay, beard and all? We can't sit on this seat without something between us and the stone."

"I couldn't be the something?"

"Certainly not. Put your overall there. Now!"

"Well," he said, looking with disfavour at his boot, "if you really want to know. There's nothing certain, of course, because it all depended on the way they were going to export Hubert. We had to have alternatives. If there was a port of call, Spanish or Portuguese, we *were* going to use the box trick. Hallorsen was to be on the ship, and Jean and I at the port with a machine and the real bones. Jean was to be the pilot when we got him—she's a natural flier; and they were to make for Turkey."

"Yes," said Dinny; "we guessed all that."

"How?"

"Never mind. What about the alternative?"

"If there was no port of call it wasn't going to be easy; we'd thought of a faked telegram to the chaps in charge of Hubert when the train arrived at Southampton or whatever the port was, telling them to take him to the Police Station and await further instructions. On the way there Hallorsen on a cycle would have bumped into the taxi on one side, and I should have bumped in on the other; and Hubert was to slip out into my car and be nipped off to where the machine was ready."

"Mm!" said Dinny. "Very nice on the screen; but are they so confiding in real life?"

"Well, we really hadn't got that worked out. We were betting on the other."

"Has all that money gone?"

"No; only about two hundred, and we can re-sell the machine." Dinny heaved a long sigh, and her eyes rested on him.

"Well," she said, "if you ask me, you're jolly well out of it."

He grinned. "I suppose so; especially as if it had come off I couldn't very well have bothered you. Dinny, I've got to rejoin to-day. Won't you——?"

Dinny said softly: "Absence makes the heart grow fonder, Alan. When you come back next time, I really will see."

"May I have one kiss?"

"Yes." She tilted her cheek towards him.

'Now,' she thought, 'is when they kiss you masterfully full on the lips. He hasn't! He must almost respect me!' And she got up.

"Come along, dear boy; and thank you ever so for all you luckily didn't have to do. I really will try and become less virginal."

He looked at her ruefully, as though repenting of his self-control, then smiled at her smile. And soon the splutter of his motor-cycle faded into the faintly sighing silence of the day.

Still with the smile on her lips Dinny went back to the house. He was a dear! But really one must have time! Such a lot of repenting at leisure could be done even in these days!

After their slight and early lunch Lady Cherrell departed in the Ford driven by the groom in search of the fatted calf. Dinny was preparing to hunt the garden for whatever flowers November might yield when a card was brought to her:

"Mr. Neil Wintney,
Ferdinand Studios,
Orchard Street,
Chelsea."

'Help!' she thought; 'Uncle Lawrence's young man!' "Where is he, Amy?"

"In the hall, Miss."

"Ask him into the drawing-room; I'll be there in a minute."

Divested of her gardening gloves and basket, she looked at her nose in her little powdery mirror; then, entering the drawing-room through the French window, saw with surprise the 'young man' sitting up good in a chair with some apparatus by his side. He had thick white hair, and an eye-glass on a black ribbon; and when he stood she realised that he must be at least sixty. He said:

"Miss Cherrell? Your Uncle, Sir Lawrence Mont, has commissioned me to do a miniature of you."

"I know," said Dinny; "only I thought——" She did not finish. After all, Uncle Lawrence liked his little joke, or possibly this was his idea of youth.

The 'young man' had screwed his monocle into a comely red cheek, and through it a full blue eye scrutinised her eagerly. He put his head on one side and said: "If we can get the outline, and you have some photographs, I shan't give you much trouble. What you have on—that flax-blue—is admirable for colour; background of sky—through that window—yes, not too blue—an English white in it. While the light's good, can we——?" And, talking all the time, he proceeded to make his preparations.

"Sir Lawrence's idea," he said, "is the English lady; culture deep but not apparent. Turn a little sideways. Thank you—the nose——"

"Yes," said Dinny; "hopeless."

"Oh! no, no! Charming. Sir Lawrence, I understand, wants you for his collection of types. I've done two for him. Would you look down? No! Now full at me! Ah! The teeth—admirable!"

"All mine, so far."

"That smile is just right, Miss Cherrell; it gives us the sense of spoof we want; not too much spoof, but just spoof enough."

"You don't want me to hold a smile with exactly three ounces of spoof in it?"

"No, no, my dear young lady; we shall chance on it. Now suppose you turn three-quarters. Ah! Now I get the line of the hair; the colour of it admirable."

"Not too much ginger, but just ginger enough?"

The 'young man' was silent. He had begun with singular concentration to draw and to write little notes on the margin of the paper.

Dinny, with crinkled eyebrows, did not like to move. He paused and smiled at her with a sort of winey sweetness.

"Yes, yes, yes," he said. "I see, I see."

What did he see? The nervousness of the victim seized her suddenly, and she pressed her open hands together.

"Raise the hands, Miss Cherrell. No! Too Madonnaish. We must think of the devil in the hair. The eyes to me, full."

"Glad?" asked Dinny.

"Not too glad; just—— Yes, an English eye; candid but reserved. Now the turn of the neck. Ah! A leetle tilt. Ye——es. Almost staglike; almost— a touch of the—not startled—no, of the aloof."

He again began to draw and write with a sort of remoteness, as if he were a long way off.

And Dinny thought: 'If Uncle Lawrence wants self-consciousness he'll get it all right.'

The 'young man' stopped and stood back, his head very much on one side, so that all his attention seemed to come out of his eyeglass.

"The expression," he muttered.

"I expect," said Dinny, "you want an unemployed look."

"Naughty!" said the 'young man': "Deeper. Could I play that piano for a minute?"

"Of course. But I'm afraid it's not been played on lately."

"It will serve." He sat down, opened the piano, blew on the keys, and began playing. He played strongly, softly, well. Dinny stood in the curve of the piano, listening, and speedily entranced. It was obviously Bach, but she did not know what. An endearing, cool, and lovely tune, coming over and over and over, monotonous, yet moving as only Bach could be.

"What is it?"

"A Chorale of Bach, set by a pianist." And the 'young man' nodded his eyeglass towards the keys.

"Glorious! Your ears on heaven and your feet in flowery fields," murmured Dinny.

The 'young man' closed the piano and stood up.

"That's what I want, that's what I want, young lady!"

"Oh!" said Dinny. "Is that all?"

BOOK II

FLOWERING WILDERNESS

TO
HERMON OULD

CHAPTER 1

SHORTLY AFTER the appearance of the Budget in 1930, the eighth wonder
of the world might have been observed in the neighbourhood of Victoria
Station—three English people, of wholly different type, engaged in contemplating simultaneously a London statue. They had come separately,
and stood a little apart from each other in the south-west corner of the
open space clear of the trees, where the drifting late afternoon light of
spring was not in their eyes. One of these three was a young woman of
about twenty-six, one a youngish man of perhaps thirty-four, and one a
man of between fifty and sixty. The young woman, slender and far from
stupid-looking, had her head tilted slightly upward to one side, and a faint
smile on her parted lips. The younger man, who wore a blue overcoat
with a belt girt tightly round his thin middle, as if he felt the spring wind
chilly, was sallow from sunburn; and the rather disdainful look of his
mouth was being curiously contradicted by eyes fixed on the statue with
real intensity of feeling. The elder man, very tall, in a brown suit and
brown buckskin shoes, lounged, with his hands in his trousers pockets,
and his long, weathered, good-looking face masked in a sort of shrewd
scepticism.

In the meantime the statue, which was that of Marshal Foch on his
horse, stood high up among those trees, stiller than any of them.

The youngish man spoke suddenly.

"He delivered us."

The effect of this breach of form on the others was diverse; the elder
man's eyebrows went slightly up, and he moved forward as if to examine
the horse's legs. The young woman turned and looked frankly at the
speaker, and instantly her face became surprised.

"Aren't you Wilfrid Desert?"

The youngish man bowed.

"Then," said the young woman, "we've met. At Fleur Mont's wedding.
You were best man, if you remember, the first I'd seen. I was only sixteen.
You wouldn't remember me—Dinny Cherrell, baptised Elizabeth. They
ran me in for bridesmaid at the last minute."

The youngish man's mouth lost its disdain.

"I remember your hair perfectly."

"Nobody ever remembers me by anything else."

"Wrong! I remember thinking you'd sat to Botticelli. You're still sitting, I see."

Dinny was thinking: 'His eyes were the first to flutter me. And they really are beautiful.'

The said eyes had been turned again upon the statue.

"He *did* deliver us," said Desert.

"You were there, of course."

"Flying, and fed up to the teeth."

"Do you like the statue?"

"The horse."

"Yes," murmured Dinny, "it *is* a horse, not just a prancing barrel, with teeth, nostrils and an arch."

"The whole thing's workmanlike, like Foch himself."

Dinny wrinkled her brow.

"I like the way it stands up quietly among those trees."

"How is Michael? You're a cousin of his, if I remember."

"Michael's all right. Still in the House; he has a seat he simply can't lose."

"And Fleur?"

"Flourishing. Did you know she had a daughter last year?"

"Fleur? H'm! That makes two, doesn't it?"

"Yes; they call this one Catherine."

"I haven't been home since 1927. Gosh! It's a long time since that wedding."

"You look," said Dinny, contemplating the sallow darkness of his face, "as if you had been in the sun."

"When I'm not in the sun I'm not alive."

"Michael once told me you lived in the East."

"Well, I wander about there." His face seemed to darken still more and he gave a little shiver. "Beastly cold the English spring!"

"And do you still write poetry?"

"Oh! you know of that weakness?"

"I've read them all. I like the last volume best."

He grinned: "Thank you for stroking me the right way; poets, you know, like it. Who's that tall man? I seem to know his face."

The tall man, who had moved to the other side of the statue, was coming back.

"Somehow," murmured Dinny, "I connect him with that wedding too."

The tall man came up to them.

"The hocks aren't all that," he said.

Dinny smiled.

"I always feel so thankful I haven't got hocks. We were just trying to decide whether we knew you. Weren't you at Michael Mont's wedding some years ago?"

"I was. And who are you, young lady?"

"We all met there. I'm his first cousin on his mother's side, Dinny Cherrell. Mr. Desert was his best man."

The tall man nodded.

"Oh! Ah! My name's Jack Muskham, I'm a first cousin of his father's." He turned to Desert. "You admired Foch, it seems."

"I did."

Dinny was surprised at the morose look that had come on his face.

"Well," said Muskham, "he was a soldier all right; and there weren't too many about. But I came here to see the horse."

"It is, of course, the important part," murmured Dinny.

The tall man gave her his sceptical smile.

"One thing we have to thank Foch for, he never left us in the lurch."

Desert suddenly faced round:

"Any particular reason for that remark?"

Muskham shrugged his shoulders, raised his hat to Dinny, and lounged away.

When he had gone there was a silence as over deep waters.

"Which way were you going?" said Dinny, at last.

"Any way that you are."

"I thank you kindly, Sir. Would an aunt in Mount Street serve as a direction?"

"Admirably."

"You must remember her, Michael's mother; she's a darling, the world's perfect mistress of the ellipse—talks in stepping stones so that you have to jump to follow her."

They crossed the road and set out up Grosvenor Place on the Buckingham Palace side.

"I suppose you find England changed every time you come home, if you'll forgive me for making conversation?"

"Changed enough."

"Don't you 'love your native land,' as the saying is?"

"She inspires me with a sort of horror."

"Are you by any chance one of those people who wish to be thought worse than they are?"

"Not possible. Ask Michael."

"Michael is incapable of slander."

"Michael and all angels are outside the count of reality."

"No," said Dinny, "Michael is very real, and very English."

"That is his contradictory trouble."

"Why do you run England down? It's been done before."

"I never run her down except to English people."

"That's something. But why to me?"

Desert laughed.

"Because you seem to be what I should like to feel that England is."

"Flattered and fair, but neither fat nor forty."

"What I object to is England's belief that she is still 'the goods.'"

"And isn't she, really?"

"Yes," said Desert, surprisingly, "but she had no reason to think so."
Dinny thought:

> 'You're perverse, brother Wilfrid, the young woman said,
> And your tongue is exceedingly wry;
> You do not look well when you stand on your head,
> Why will you continually try?'

She remarked, more simply:

"If England is still 'the goods,' has no reason to think so and yet does,
she would seem to have intuition, anyway. Was it by intuition, that you
disliked Mr. Muskham?" Then, looking at his face, she thought: 'I'm
dropping a brick.'

"Why should I dislike him? He's just the usual insensitive type of hunting, racing man who bores me stiff."

'That wasn't the reason,' thought Dinny, still regarding him. A strange
face! Unhappy from deep inward disharmony, as though a good angel
and a bad were forever seeking to fire each other out; but his eyes sent the
same thrill through her, as when at sixteen, with her hair still long, she
had stood near him at Fleur's wedding.

"And do you really like wandering about in the East?"

"The curse of Esau is on me."

'Some day,' she thought, 'I'll make him tell me why. Only probably I
shall never see him again.' And a little chill ran down her back.

"I wonder if you know my Uncle Adrian. He was in the East during
the war. He presides over bones at the Museum. You probably know Diana
Ferse, anyway. He married her last year."

"I know nobody to speak of."

"Our point of contact, then, is only Michael."

"I don't believe in contacts through other people. Where do you live,
Miss Cherrell?"

Dinny smiled.

"A short biographical note seems to be indicated. Since the umteenth
century, my family has been 'seated' at Condaford Grange in Oxfordshire; my father is a retired General. I am one of two daughters, and my
only brother is a married soldier just coming back from the Soudan on
leave."

"Oh!" said Desert, and again his face had that morose look.

"I am twenty-six, unmarried but with no children as yet. My hobby
seems to be attending to other people's business. I don't know why I have
it. When in Town I stay at Lady Mont's in Mount Street. With a simple
upbringing I have expensive instincts and no means of gratifying them.
I believe I can see a joke. Now you?"

Desert smiled and shook his head.

"Shall I?" said Dinny. "You are the second son of Lord Mullyon; you
had too much war; you write poetry; you have nomadic instincts and are

your own enemy; the last item has the only news value. Here we are in Mount Street; do come in and see Aunt Em."

"Thank you—no. But will you lunch with me tomorrow and go to a matinee?"

"I will. Where?"

"Dumourieux's, one-thirty."

They exchanged hand-grips and parted, but as Dinny went into her aunt's house she was tingling all over, and she stood still outside the drawing-room to smile at the sensation.

CHAPTER 2

THE SMILE FADED off her lips under the fire of noises coming through the closed door.

'My goodness!' she thought: 'Aunt Em's birthday "pawty," and I'd forgotten.'

Some one playing the piano stopped, there was a rush, a scuffle of chairs on the floor, two or three squeals, silence, and the piano-playing began again.

'Musical chairs!' she thought, and opened the door quietly. She who had been Diana Ferse was sitting at the piano. To eight assorted chairs facing alternatively east and west, were clinging one large and eight small beings in bright paper hats, of whom seven were just rising to their feet and two still sitting on one chair. Dinny saw from left to right: Ronald Ferse; a small Chinese boy; Aunt Alison's youngest, little Anne; Uncle Hilary's youngest, Tony; Celia and Dingo (children of Michael's married sister Celia Moriston); Sheila Ferse; and on the single chair Uncle Adrian and Kit Mont. She was further conscious of Aunt Em panting slightly against the fireplace in a large headpiece of purple paper, and of Fleur pulling a chair from Ronald's end of the row.

"Kit, get up! You were out."

Kit sat firm and Adrian rose.

"All right, old man, you're up against your equals now. Fire away!"

"Keep your hands off the backs," cried Fleur. "Wu Fing, you mustn't sit till the music stops. Dingo, don't stick at the end chair like that."

The music stopped. Scurry, hustle, squeals, and the smallest figure, little Anne, was left standing.

"All right, darling," said Dinny, "come here and beat this drum. Stop when the music stops, that's right. Now again. Watch Auntie Di!"

Again, and again, and again, till Sheila and Dingo and Kit only were left.

'I back Kit,' thought Dinny.

Sheila out! Off with a chair! Dingo, so Scottish-looking, and Kit so bright-haired, having lost his paper cap, were left padding round and round the last chair. Both were down; both up and on again, Diana carefully averting her eyes, Fleur standing back now with a little smile; Aunt

244

Em's face very pink. The music stopped, Dingo was down again; and Kit left standing, his face flushed and frowning.

"Kit," said Fleur's voice: "Play the game!"

Kit's head was thrown up and he rammed his hands into his pockets.

'Good for Fleur!' thought Dinny.

A voice behind her said:

"Your aunt's purple passion for the young, Dinny, leads us into strange riots. What about a spot of quiet in my study?"

Dinny looked round at Sir Lawrence Mont's thin, dry, twisting face, whose little moustache had gone quite white, while his hair was still only sprinkled.

"I haven't done my bit, Uncle Lawrence."

"Time you learned not to. Let the heathen rage. Come down and have a quiet Christian talk."

Subduing her instinct for service with the thought: 'I *should* like to talk about Wilfrid Desert!' Dinny went.

"What are you working on now, Uncle Lawrence?"

"Resting for the minute and reading the Memoirs of Harriette Wilson —a remarkable young woman, Dinny. In the days of the Regency there were no reputations in high life to destroy; but she did her best. If you don't know about her, I may tell you that she believed in love and had a great many lovers, only one of whom she loved."

"And yet she believed in love?"

"Well, she was a kind-hearted baggage, and the others loved her. All the difference in the world between her and Ninon de l'Enclos, who loved them all; both vivid creatures. A duologue between those two on 'virtue'? It's to be thought of. Sit down!"

"While I was looking at Foch's statue this afternoon, Uncle Lawrence, I met a cousin of yours, Mr. Muskham."

"Jack?"

"Yes."

"Last of the dandies. All the difference in the world, Dinny, between the 'buck,' the 'dandy,' the 'swell,' the 'masher,' the 'blood,' the 'nut,' and what's the last variety called—I never know? There's been a steady decrescendo. By his age Jack belongs to the 'masher' period, but his cut was always pure dandy—a dyed in the wool Whyte Melville type. How did he strike you?"

"Oh! Well! Horses, piquet and imperturbability."

"Take your hat off, my dear. I like to see your hair."

Dinny removed her hat.

"I met some one else there, too; Michael's best man."

"What! Young Desert? He back again?" And Sir Lawrence's loose eyebrow mounted.

A slight colour had stained Dinny's cheeks.

"Yes," she said.

"Queer bird, Dinny."

Within her rose a feeling rather different from any she had ever experienced. She could not have described it, but it reminded her of a piece of porcelain she had given to her father on his birthday, two weeks ago; a little china group, beautifully modelled, of a vixen and four fox cubs tucked in under her. The look on the vixen's face, soft yet watchful, so completely expressed her own feeling at this moment.

"Why queer?"

"Tales out of school, Dinny. Still to *you*. There's no doubt in my mind that that young man made up to Fleur a year or two after her marriage. That's what started him as a rolling stone."

Was that, then, what he had meant when he mentioned Esau? No! By the look of his face when he spoke of Fleur, she did not think so.

"But that was ages ago," she said.

"Oh, yes! Ancient story; but one's heard other things. Clubs are the mother of all uncharitableness."

The softness of Dinny's feeling diminished, the watchfulness increased.

"What other things?"

Sir Lawrence shook his head.

"I rather like the young man; and not even to you, Dinny, do I repeat what I really know nothing of. Let a man live an unusual life, and there's no limit to what people invent about him." He looked at her rather suddenly; but Dinny's eyes were limpid.

"Who's the little Chinese boy upstairs?"

"Son of a former Mandarin, who left his family here because of the ructions out there—quaint little image. A likable people, the Chinese. When does Hubert arrive?"

"Next week. They're flying from Italy. Jean flies a lot, you know."

"What's become of her brother?" And again he looked at Dinny.

"Alan? He's out on the China station."

"Your aunt never ceases to bemoan your not clicking there."

"Dear Uncle, almost anything to oblige Aunt Em; but feeling like a sister to him, the prayer-book was against me."

"I don't want you to marry," said Sir Lawrence, "and go out to some Barbary or other."

Through Dinny flashed the thought: 'Uncle Lawrence is uncanny,' and her eyes became more limpid than ever.

"This confounded officialism," he continued, "seems to absorb all our kith and kin. My two daughters, Celia in China, Flora in India; your brother Hubert in the Soudan; your sister Clare off as soon as she's spliced —Jerry Corven's been given a post in Ceylon. I hear Charlie Muskham's got attached to Government House, Cape Town; Hilary's eldest boy's going into the Indian Civil, and his youngest into the Navy. Dash it all, Dinny, you and Jack Muskham seem to be the only pelicans in my wilderness. Of course there's Michael."

"Do you see much of Mr. Muskham, then, Uncle?"

"Quite a lot at 'Burton's,' and he comes to me at 'The Coffee House';

we play piquet—we're the only two left. That's in the illegitimate season—from now on I shall hardly see him till after the Cambridgeshire."

"Is he a terribly good judge of a horse?"

"Yes. Of anything else, Dinny—no. They seldom are. The horse is an animal that seems to close the pores of the spirit. He makes you too watchful. You don't only have to watch him, but everybody connected with him. How was young Desert looking?"

"Oh!" said Dinny, almost taken aback: "A sort of dark yellow."

"That's the glare of the sand. He's a kind of Bedouin, you know. His father's a recluse, so it's a bit in his blood. The best thing I know about him is that Michael likes him, in spite of that business."

"His poetry?" said Dinny.

"Disharmonic stuff, he destroys with one hand what he gives with the other."

"Perhaps he's never found his home. His eyes are rather beautiful, don't you think?"

"It's his mouth I remember best, sensitive and bitter."

"One's eyes are what one is, one's mouth what one becomes."

"That and the stomach."

"He hasn't any," said Dinny, "I noticed."

"The handful of dates and cup of coffee habit. Not that the Arabs drink coffee—green tea is their weakness, with mint in it. Oh! God! Here's your aunt. When I said 'God!' I was referring to the tea with mint, not to her."

Lady Mont had removed her paper headdress and recovered her breath.

"Darling," said Dinny, "I *did* forget your birthday, and I haven't got anything for you."

"Then give me a kiss, Dinny. I always say your kisses are the best. Where have you sprung from?"

"I came up to shop for Clare at the Stores."

"Have you got your night things with you?"

"No."

"That doesn't matter. You can have one of mine. Do you still wear nightgowns?"

"Yes," said Dinny.

"Good girl! I don't like pyjamas for women—your uncle doesn't either. It's below the waist, you know. You can't get over it—you try to, but you can't. Michael and Fleur will be stayin' on to dinner."

"Thank you, Aunt Em; I do want to stay up. I couldn't get half the things Clare needs to-day."

"I don't like Clare marryin' before you, Dinny."

"But she naturally would, Auntie."

"Fiddle! Clare's brilliant—they don't as a rule. I married at twenty-one."

"You see, dear!"

"You're laughin' at me. I was only brilliant once. You remember, Lawrence—about that elephant—I wanted it to sit, and it would kneel. All their legs bend one way, Dinny, and I said it wouldn't follow its bent."

"Aunt Em! Except for that one occasion you're easily the most brilliant woman I know. Women are so much too consecutive."

"Your nose is a comfort, Dinny, I get so tired of beaks, your Aunt Wilmet's, and Hen Bentworth's, and my own."

"Yours is only faintly aquiline, darling."

"I was terrified of its gettin' worse, as a child. I used to stand with the tip pressed up against a wardrobe."

"I've tried that too, Auntie, only the other way."

"Once while I was doin' it your father was lyin' concealed on the top, like a leopard, you know, and he hopped over me and bit through his lip. He bled all down my neck."

"How nasty!"

"Yes. Lawrence, what are you thinkin' about?"

"I was thinking that Dinny has probably had no lunch. Have you, Dinny?"

"I was going to have it to-morrow, Uncle."

"There you are!" said Lady Mont. "Ring for Blore. You'll never have enough body until you're married."

"Let's get Clare over first, Aunt Em."

"St. George's. I suppose Hilary's doin' them?"

"Of course!"

"I shall cry."

"Why, exactly, do you cry at weddings, Auntie?"

"She'll look like an angel; and the man'll be in black tails and a toothbrush moustache, and not feelin' what she thinks he is. It's saddenin'."

"But perhaps he's feeling more. I'm sure Michael was about Fleur, or Adrian when he married Diana."

"Adrian's fifty-three and he's got a beard. Besides, he's Adrian."

"I admit that makes a difference. But I think we ought rather to cry over the man. The woman's having the hour of her life and the man's waistcoat is almost certain to be too tight."

"Lawrence's wasn't. He was always a threadpaper, and I was as slim as you, Dinny."

"You must have looked lovely in a veil, Aunt Em. Didn't she, Uncle?" The whimsically wistful look on both those mature faces stopped her, and she added: "Where did you first meet?"

"Out huntin', Dinny. I was in a ditch, and your uncle didn't like it, he came and pulled me out."

"I think that's ideal."

"Too much mud. We didn't speak to each other all the rest of the day."

"Then what brought you together?"

"One thing and another. I was stayin' with Hen's people, the Corderoys, and your uncle called to see some puppies. What are you catechisin' me for?"

"I only just wanted to know how it was done in those days."

"Go and find out for yourself how it's done in these days."

"Uncle Lawrence doesn't want to get rid of me."

"All men are selfish, except Michael and Adrian."

"Besides, I should hate to make you cry."

"Blore, a cocktail and a sandwich for Miss Dinny, she's had no lunch. And, Blore, Mr. and Mrs. Adrian, and Mr. and Mrs. Michael to dinner. And, Blore, tell Laura to put one of my nightgowns and the other things in the blue spare room. Miss Dinny'll stay the night. Those children!" And, swaying slightly, Lady Mont preceded her butler through the doorway.

"What a darling, Uncle!"

"I've never denied it, Dinny."

"I always feel better after her. Was she ever out of temper?"

"She can begin to be, but she always goes on to something else before she's finished."

"What saving grace!" . . .

At dinner that evening, Dinny listened for any allusion by her uncle to Wilfrid Desert's return. There was none.

After dinner, she seated herself by Fleur in her habitual, slightly mystified, admiration of this cousin by marriage, whose pretty poise was so assured, whose face and figure so beautifully turned out, whose clear eyes were so seeing, whose knowledge of self was so disillusioned, and whose attitude to Michael seemed at once that of one looking up and looking down.

'If I ever married,' thought Dinny, 'I could never be like that to him. I would have to look him straight in the face as one sinner to another.'

"Do you remember your wedding, Fleur?" she said.

"I do, my dear. A distressing ceremony!"

"I saw your best man to-day."

The clear white round Fleur's eyes widened.

"Wilfrid? How did you remember him?"

"I was only sixteen, and he fluttered my young nerves."

"That is, of course, the function of a best man. Well, and how was he?"

"Very dark and dissolvent."

Fleur laughed. "He always was."

Looking at her, Dinny decided to press on.

"Yes. Uncle Lawrence told me he tried to carry dissolution rather far."

Fleur looked surprised. "I didn't know Bart ever noticed that."

"Uncle Lawrence," said Dinny, "is a bit uncanny."

"Wilfrid," murmured Fleur, with a little reminiscent smile, "really behaved quite well. He went East like a lamb."

"But surely that hasn't kept him East ever since?"

"No more than measles keeps you permanently to your room. Oh! no, he likes it. He's probably got a harem."

"No," said Dinny, "he's fastidious, or I should be surprised."

"Quite right, my dear; and one for my cheap cynicism. Wilfrid's the queerest sort of person, and rather a dear. Michael loved him. But," she said, suddenly looking at Dinny, "he's impossible to be in love with—disharmony personified. I studied him pretty closely at one time—had to, you know. He's elusive, passionate, and a bundle of nerves; soft-hearted and bitter. And search me for anything he believes in."

"Except," queried Dinny, "beauty, perhaps; and truth if he could find it?"

Fleur made the unexpected answer, "Well, my dear, we all believe in those, when they're about. The trouble is they aren't, unless—unless they lie in oneself, perhaps. And if you happen to be disharmonic, what chance have you of that? Where did you see him?"

"Staring at Foch."

"Ah! I seem to remember he rather idolised Foch. Poor Wilfrid, he hasn't much chance. Shell-shock, poetry, and his breeding—a father who's turned his back on life; a mother who was half an Italian, and ran off with another. Not restful. His eyes were his best point, they made you sorry for him and they're beautiful—rather a fatal combination. Did the young nerves flutter again?" She looked rather more broadly into Dinny's face.

"No, but I wondered if yours would still if I mentioned him."

"Mine? My child, I'm nearly thirty. I have two children, and"—her face darkened—"I have been inoculated. If I ever told any one about *that*, Dinny, I might tell you, but there are things one doesn't tell."

Up in her room, somewhat incommoded by the amplitude of Aunt Em's nightgown, Dinny stared into a fire lighted against protest. She felt that what she was feeling was absurd—a queer eagerness, at once shy and bold, the sensations, as it were, of direct action impending. And why? She had reseen a man who ten years before had made her feel silly; from all accounts a most unsatisfactory man. Taking a looking-glass, she scrutinised her face above the embroidery on the too ample gown. She saw what might have satisfied but did not.

'One gets tired of it,' she thought, 'always the same Botticellian artifact,

> 'The nose that's snub,
> The eyes of blue!
> 'Ware self, you red-haired nymph,
> And shun the image that is you!'

He was so accustomed to the East, to dark eyes through veils, languishing; to curves enticingly disguised; to sex, mystery, teeth like pearls—*vide* houri! Dinny showed her own teeth to the glass. There she was on safe ground—the best teeth in her family. Nor was her hair really red—more what Miss Braddon used to call auburn! Nice word! Pity it had gone out. With all that embroidery it was no good examining herself below the Victorian washing line. Remember that to-morrow before her bath! For what she was about to examine might the Lord make her truly thankful! Putting down the glass with a little sigh, she got into bed.

CHAPTER 3

WILFRID DESERT still maintained his chambers in Cork Street. They were, in fact, paid for by Lord Mullyon, who used them on the rare occasions when he emerged from rural retreat. It was not saying much that the secluded peer had more in common with his second than with his eldest son, who was in Parliament. It gave him, however, no particular pain to encounter Wilfrid; but as a rule the chambers were occupied only by Stack, who had been Wilfrid's batman in the war, and had for him one of those sphinxlike habits which wear better than expressed devotions. When Wilfrid returned at a moment or two's notice, his rooms were ever exactly as he left them, neither more nor less dusty and unaired; the same clothes hung on the same clothes stretchers; and the same nicely cooked steak and mushrooms appeased his first appetite. The ancestral 'junk,' fringed and dotted by Eastern whims brought home, gave to the large sitting-room the same castled air of immutable possession. And the divan before the log fire received Wilfrid as if he had never left it. He lay there the morning after his encounter with Dinny, wondering why he could only get really good coffee when Stack made it. The East was the home of coffee, but Turkish coffee was a rite, a toy; and, like all rites and toys, served but to titillate the soul. This was his third day in London after two years; and in those two last years he had been through a good deal more than he would ever care to speak of, or even wish to remember; including one experience which still divided him against himself, however much he affected to discredit its importance. In other words, he had come back with a skeleton in his cupboard. He had brought back, too, enough poems for a fourth slender volume. He lay there, debating whether the longest of these poems could be included. It was the outcome of that experience; in his view the best poem he had ever written—a pity it should not be published, but—! And the 'but' was so considerable that he had many times been on the point of tearing the thing up, obliterating all trace of it, as he would have wished to blot remembrance from his mind. Again, but—! The poem expressed his defence for allowing what he hoped no one knew had happened to him. To tear it up would be parting with his defence. For he could never again adequately render his sensations in that past dilemma. He would be parting with his best protection from his own conscience, too; and perhaps with the only means of laying a ghost.

251

For he sometimes thought that unless he proclaimed to the world what had happened to him, he would never again feel quite in possession of his soul.

Reading it through, he thought: 'It's a damned sight better and deeper than Lyall's confounded poem.' And without any obvious connection he began to think of the girl he had met the day before. Curious that he had remembered her at Michael's wedding, a transparent slip of a young thing like a Botticelli Venus, Angel, or Madonna—so little difference between them—a charming young creature, then. Yes, and a charming young woman now, of real quality, with a sense of humour, and an understanding mind. Dinny Cherrell! Charwell they spelled it, he remembered. He wouldn't mind showing her his poems; he would trust her reactions.

Partly because he was thinking of her, and partly because he took a taxi, he was late for lunch, and met Dinny on the doorstep of Dumourieux's just as she was about to go away.

There is perhaps no better test of woman's character than to keep her waiting for lunch in a public place. Dinny greeted him with a smile.

"I thought you'd probably forgotten."

"It was the traffic. How can philosophers talk of time being space or space time? It's disproved whenever two people lunch together. I allowed ten minutes for under a mile from Cork Street, and here I am ten minutes late. Terribly sorry!"

"My father says you must add ten per cent to all timing since taxis took the place of hansoms. Do you remember the hansom?"

"Rather!"

"I never was in London till they were over."

"If you know this place, lead on! I was told of it but I've not yet been here."

"It's underground. The cooking's French."

Divested of their coats, they proceeded to an end table.

"Very little for me, please," said Dinny. "Say cold chicken, a salad and some coffee."

"Anything the matter?"

"Only a spare habit."

"I see. We'll both have it. No wine?"

"No, thanks. Is eating little a good sign, do you think?"

"Not if done on principle."

"You don't like things done on principle?"

"I distrust the people who do them—self-righteous."

"I think that's too sweeping. You are rather sweeping, aren't you?"

"I was thinking of the sort of people who don't eat because it's sensual. That's not your reason, is it?"

"Oh! no," said Dinny, "I only dislike feeling full. And very little makes me feel that. I don't know very much about them so far, but I think the senses are good things."

"The only things, probably."

"Is that why you write poetry?"

Desert grinned.

"I should think *you* might write verse, too."

"Only rhymes."

"The place for poetry is a desert. Ever seen one?"

"No. I should like to." And, having said that, she sat in slight surprise, remembering her negative reaction to the American professor and his great open spaces. But no greater contrast was possible than between Hallorsen and this dark, disharmonic young man, who sat staring at her with those eyes of his till she had again that thrill down her spine. Crumbling her roll, she said: "I saw Michael and Fleur last night at dinner."

"Oh!" his lips curled: "I made a fool of myself over Fleur once. Perfect, isn't she—in her way?"

"Yes," and her eyes added: 'Don't run her down!'

"Marvellous equipment and control."

"I don't think you know her," said Dinny, "and I'm sure I don't."

He leaned forward. "You seem to me a loyal sort of person. Where did you pick that up?"

"Our family motto is the word 'Leal.' That ought to have cured me, oughtn't it?"

"I don't know," he said abruptly, "whether I understand what loyalty is. Loyalty to what? To whom? Nothing's fixed in this world; everything's relative. Loyalty's the mark of the static mind, or else just a superstition, and anyway the negation of curiosity."

"There *are* things worth being loyal to, surely. Cold chicken, for instance, or one's religion."

He looked at her so strangely that Dinny was almost scared.

"Religion? Have you one?"

"Well, roughly, I suppose."

"What? Can you swallow the dogmas of any religious creed? Do you believe one legend more true than another? Can you suppose one set of beliefs about the Unknowable has more value than the rest? Religion! You've got a sense of humour. Does it leave you at the word?"

"No; only religion, I suppose, may be just a sense of an all-pervading spirit, and the ethical creed that seems best to serve it."

"H'm! A pretty far cry from what's generally meant, and even then how do you know what best serves an all-pervading spirit?"

"I take that on trust."

"There's where we differ. Look!" he said, and it seemed to her that excitement had crept into his voice: "What's the use of our reasoning powers, our mental faculties? I take each problem as it comes, I do the sum, I return the answer, and so I act. I act according to a reasoned estimate of what is best."

"For whom?"

"For myself and the world at large."

"Which first?"

"It's the same thing."

"Always? I wonder. And, anyway, that means doing so long a sum every time that I can't think how you ever get to acting. And surely ethical rules are just the result of countless decisions on those same problems made by people in the past, so why not take them for granted?"

"None of those decisions were made by people of my temperament or in my circumstances."

"No, I see that. You follow what they call case law, then. But how English!"

"Sorry!" said Desert, abruptly: "I'm boring you. Have a sweet?"

Dinny put her elbows on the table and, leaning her chin on her hands, looked at him earnestly.

"You weren't boring me. On the contrary, you're interesting me frightfully. Only I suppose that women act much more instinctively; I suppose that really means they accept themselves as more like each other than men do, and are more ready to trust their instinctive sense of general experience."

"That *has* been women's way; whether it will be much longer, I don't know."

"I think it will," said Dinny. "I don't believe we shall ever much care for sums. I *will* have a sweet, please. Stewed prunes, I think."

Desert stared at her, and began to laugh.

"You're wonderful. We'll both have them. Is your family a very formal one?"

"Not exactly formal, but they do believe in tradition and the past."

"And do you?"

"I don't know. I definitely like old things, and old places, and old people. I like anything that's stamped like a coin. I like to feel one has roots. I was always fond of history. All the same one can't help laughing. There's something very comic about the way we're all tied—like a hen by a chalk mark to its beak."

Desert stretched out his hand and she put hers into it.

"Shake hands on that saving grace."

"Some day," said Dinny, "you're going to tell me something. But at the moment what play are we going to?"

"Is there anything by a man called Shakespeare?"

With some difficulty they discovered that a work by the world's greatest dramatist was being given in a theatre beyond the pale of the river. They went to it, and, when the show was over, Desert said, hesitating: "I wonder if you would come and have tea at my rooms?"

Dinny smiled and nodded, and from that moment was conscious of a difference in his manner. It was at once more intimate yet more respectful, as if he had said to himself: 'This is my equal.'

That hour of tea, brought by Stack, a man with strange understanding eyes and something monk-like in his look, seemed to her quite perfect. It was like no other hour she had ever spent, and at the end of it she knew she was in love. The tiny seed planted ten years before had flowered. This was such a marvel, so peculiar to one who at twenty-six had begun to think she would never be in love, that every now and then she drew in her breath and looked wonderingly at his face. Why on earth did she feel like this? It was absurd! And it was going to be painful, because he wasn't going to love her. Why should he? And if he wasn't, she mustn't show, and how was she to help showing?

"When am I going to see you again?" he said, when she stood up to go.

"Do you want to?"

"Extraordinarily."

"But why?"

"Why not? You're the first lady I've spoken to for ten years. I'm not at all sure you're not the first lady I've ever spoken to."

"If we are going to see each other again, you mustn't laugh at me."

"Laugh at you! One couldn't. So when?"

"Well! At present I'm sleeping in a foreign nightgown at Mount Street. By rights I ought to be at Condaford. But my sister's going to be married in town next week, and my brother's coming back from Egypt on Monday, so perhaps I'll send for things and stay up. Where would you like to see me?"

"Will you come for a drive to-morrow? I haven't been to Richmond or Hampton Court for years."

"I've never been."

"All right! I'll pick you up in front of Foch at two o'clock, wet or fine."

"I will be pleased to come, young Sir."

"Splendid!" And, suddenly bending, he raised her hand and put his lips to it.

"Highly courteous," said Dinny. "Good-bye!"

CHAPTER 4

PREOCCUPIED WITH this stupendous secret, Dinny's first instinct was for solitude, but she was booked for dinner with the Adrian Cherrells. On her uncle's marriage with Diana Ferse the house of painful memories in Oakley Street had been given up, and they were economically installed in one of those spacious Bloomsbury squares now successfully regaining the gentility lost in the eighteen-thirties and forties. The locality had been chosen for its proximity to Adrian's "bones," for at his age he regarded as important every minute saved for the society of his wife. The robust virility, which Dinny had predicted would accrue to her uncle from a year spent in the presence of Professor Hallorsen and New Mexico, was represented by a somewhat deeper shade of brown in his creased cheeks, and a more frequent smile on his long face. It was a lasting pleasure to Dinny to think that she had given him the right advice, and that he had taken it. Diana, too, was fast regaining the sparkle which, before her marriage with poor Ferse, had made her a member of 'Society.' But the hopeless nature of Adrian's occupation, and the extra time he needed from her, had precluded her from any return to that sacred ring. She inclined more and more, in fact, to be a wife and mother. And this seemed natural to one with Dinny's partiality for her uncle. On her way there she debated whether or not to say what she had been doing. Having little liking for shifts and subterfuge, she decided to be frank. 'Besides,' she thought, 'a maiden in love always likes to talk about the object of her affections.' Again, if not to have a confidant became too wearing, Uncle Adrian was the obvious choice; partly because he knew at first hand something of the East, but chiefly because he was Uncle Adrian.

The first topics at dinner, however, were naturally Clare's marriage and Hubert's return. Dinny was somewhat exercised over her sister's choice. Sir Gerald (Jerry) Corven was forty, active and middle-sized, with a daring face. She recognised that he had great charm, and her fear was, rather, that he had too much. He was high in the Colonial service, one of those men who—people instinctively said—would go far. She wondered also whether Clare was not too like him, daring and brilliant, a bit of a gambler, and, of course, seventeen years younger. Diana, who had known him well, said:

"The seventeen years' difference is the best thing about it. Jerry wants steadying. If he can be a father to her as well, it may work. He's had infinite experiences. I'm glad it's Ceylon."

"Why?"

"He won't meet his past."

"Has he an awful lot of past?"

"My dear, he's very much in love at the moment; but with men like Jerry you never know; all that charm, and so much essential liking for thin ice."

"Marriage doth make cowards of us all," murmured Adrian.

"It won't have that effect on Jerry Corven; he takes to risk as a goldfish takes to mosquito larvæ. Is Clare very smitten, Dinny?"

"Yes, but Clare loves thin ice, too."

"And yet," said Adrian, "I shouldn't call either of them really modern. They've both got brains and like using them."

"That's quite true, Uncle. Clare gets all she can out of life, but she believes in life terribly. She might become another Hester Stanhope."

"Good for you, Dinny! But to be that she'd have to get rid of Gerald Corven first. And if I read Clare, I think she might have scruples."

Dinny regarded her uncle with wide eyes.

"Do you say that because you know Clare, or because you're a Cherrell, Uncle?"

"I think because she's a Cherrell, my dear."

"Scruples," murmured Dinny, "I don't believe Aunt Em has them. Yet she's as much of a Cherrell as any of us."

"Em," said Adrian, "reminds me of nothing so much as a find of bones that won't join up. You can't say of what she's the skeleton. Scruples are emphatically coordinate."

"No! Adrian," murmured Diana, "not bones at dinner. When does Hubert arrive? I'm really anxious to see him and young Jean. After eighteen months of bliss in the Soudan which will be top dog?"

"Jean, surely."

Dinny shook her head. "I don't think so, Uncle."

"That's your sisterly pride."

"No, Hubert's got more continuity. Jean rushes at things and must handle them at once, but Hubert steers the course, I'm pretty sure. Uncle, where is a place called Darfur? And how do you spell it?"

"With an 'r' or without. It's west of the Soudan; much of it is desert and pretty inaccessible, I believe. Why?"

"I was lunching to-day with Mr. Desert, Michael's best man, you remember, and he mentioned it."

"Has he been there?"

"I think he's been everywhere in the Near East."

"I know his brother," said Diana, "Charles Desert, one of the most provocative of the younger politicians. He'll almost certainly be Minister of Education in the next Tory Government. That'll put the finishing touch to Lord Mullyon's retirement. I've never met Wilfrid. Is he nice?"

"Well," said Dinny, with what she believed to be detachment, "I only met him yesterday. He seems rather like a mince pie, you take a spoonful and hope. If you can eat the whole, you have a happy year."

"I should like to meet the young man," said Adrian. "He did good things in the war, and I know his verse."

"Really, Uncle? I could arrange it; so far we are in daily communication."

"Oh!" said Adrian, and looked at her. "I'd like to discuss the Hittite type with him. I suppose you know that what we are accustomed to regard as the most definitely Jewish characteristics are pure Hittite according to ancient Hittite drawings?"

"But weren't they all the same stock, really?"

"By no means, Dinny. The Israelites were Arabs. What the Hittites were we have yet to discover. The modern Jew in this country and in Germany is probably more Hittite than Semite."

"Do you know Mr. Jack Muskham, Uncle?"

"Only by repute. He's a cousin of Lawrence's and an authority on blood-stock. I believe he advocates a re-introduction of Arab blood into our race-horses. There's something in it if you could get the very best strain. Has young Desert been to Nejd? You can still only get it there, I believe."

"I don't know. Where is Nejd?"

"Centre of Arabia. But Muskham will never get his idea adopted, there's no tighter mind than the pukka racing man's. He's a pretty pure specimen himself, I believe, except for this hobby."

"Jack Muskham," said Diana, "was once romantically in love with one of my sisters; it's made him a misogynist."

"H'm! That's a bit cryptic!"

"He's rather fine-looking, I think," said Dinny.

"Wears clothes wonderfully and has a reputation for hating everything modern. I haven't met him for years, but I used to know him rather well. Why, Dinny?"

"I just happened to see him the other day and wondered."

"Talking of Hittites," said Diana, "I've often thought those very old Cornish families, like the Deserts, have a streak of Phœnician in them. Look at Lord Mullyon. There's a queer type!"

"Fanciful, my love. You'd be more likely to find that streak in the simple folk. The Deserts must have married into non-Cornish stock for hundreds of years. The higher you go in the social scale, the less chance of preserving a primitive strain."

"*Are* they a very old family?" said Dinny.

"Hoary and pretty queer. But you know my views about old families, Dinny, so I won't enlarge."

Dinny nodded. She remembered very well that nerve-racked walk along Chelsea Embankment just after Ferse returned. And she looked affectionately into his face. It *was* nice to think that he had come into his own at last . . .

When she got back to Mount Street that night her uncle and aunt had gone up, but the butler was seated in the hall. He rose as she entered.

"I didn't know you had a key, Miss."

"I'm terribly sorry, Blore, you were having such a nice snooze."

"I was, Miss Dinny. After a certain age, as you'll find out, one gets a liking for dropping off at improper moments. Now Sir Lawrence, he's not a good sleeper, but, give you my word, if I go into his study almost any time when he's at work, I'll find him opening his eyes. And my Lady, she can do her eight hours, but I've known her to drop off when someone's talking to her, especially the old Rector at Lippinghall, Mr. Tasburgh—a courtly old gentleman, but he has that effect. Even Mr. Michael—but then he's in Parliament, and they get the 'abit. Still, I do think, Miss, whether it was the war, or people not having any hope of anything, and running about so, that there's a tendency, as the saying is, towards sleep. Well, it does you good. Give you my word, Miss; I was dead to the world before I had that forty winks, and now I could talk to you for hours."

"That would be lovely, Blore. Only I find, so far, that I'm sleepiest at bed time."

"Wait till you're married, Miss. Only I do hope you won't be doing that yet awhile. I said to Mrs. Blore last night: 'If Miss Dinny gets taken off, it'll be the life and soul of the party gone!' I've never seen much of Miss Clare, so that leaves me cold; but I heard my Lady yesterday telling you to go and find out for yourself how it was done, and, as I said to Mrs. Blore, 'Miss Dinny's like a daughter of the house, and'—well—you know my sentiments, Miss."

"Dear Blore! I'm afraid I must go up now, I've had rather a tiring day."

"Quite, Miss. Pleasant dreams!"

"Good-night!"

Pleasant dreams! Perhaps the dreams might be, but would reality? What uncharted country was she now entering with just a star to guide! And was it a fixed star, or some flaring comet? At least five men had wanted to marry her, all of whom she had felt she could sum up, so that a marriage would have been no great risk. And now she only wanted to marry one, but there he was, an absolutely uncertain quantity except that he could rouse in her a feeling she had never had before. Life was perverse. You dipped your finger in a lucky bag, and brought out—what? To-morrow she would walk with him. They would see trees and grass together; scenery and gardens, pictures, perhaps; the river, and fruit blossom. She would know at least how his spirit and her own agreed about many things she cared for. And yet, if she found they didn't agree, would it make any difference to her feeling? It would not.

'I understand now,' she thought, 'why we call lovers dotty. All I care about is that he should feel what I feel, and be dotty too. And of course he won't—why should he?'

CHAPTER 5

THE DRIVE to Richmond Park, over Ham Common and Kingston Bridge to Hampton Court, and back through Twickenham and Kew, was remarkable for alternation between silence and volubility. Dinny was, as it were, the observer, and left to Wilfrid all the piloting. Her feelings made her shy, and it was apparent that he was only able to expand if left to his free will—the last person in the world to be drawn out. They duly lost themselves in the maze at Hampton Court, where, as Dinny said:

"Only spiders who can spin threads out of themselves, or ghosts who can tails unfold, would have a chance."

On the way back they got out at Kensington Gardens, dismissed the hired car, and walked to the tea kiosk. Over the pale beverage he asked her suddenly whether she would mind reading his new poems in manuscript.

"Mind? I should love it."

"I want candid opinion."

"You will get it," said Dinny. "When can I have them?"

"I'll bring them round to Mount Street and drop them in your letter box after dinner."

"Won't you come in this time?"

He shook his head.

When he left her at Stanhope Gate, he said abruptly:

"It's been a simply lovely afternoon. Thank you!"

"It is for me to thank you."

"You! You've got more friends than quills upon the fretful porpentine. It's I who am the pelican."

"Adieu, pelican!"

"Adieu, flowering wilderness!"

The words seemed musical all the way down Mount Street.

A fat unstamped envelope was brought in about half past nine with the last post. Dinny took it from Blore, and slipping it under the "Bridge of San Luis Rey," went on listening to her aunt.

"When I was a girl I squeezed my own waist, Dinny. We suffered for a principle: They say it's comin' in again. I shan't do it, so hot and worryin'; but you'll have to."

"Not I."

"When the waist has settled down there'll be a lot of squeezin'."

"The really tight waist will never come in again, Auntie."

"And hats. In 1900 we were like eggstands with explodin' eggs in them. Cauliflowers and hydrangeas, and birds of a feather, enormous. They stuck out. The Parks were comparatively pure. Sea-green suits you, Dinny; you ought to be married in it."

"I think I'll go up, Aunt Em. I'm rather tired."

"That's eatin' so little."

"I eat enormously. Good-night, dear."

Without undressing she sat down to the poems, nervously anxious to like them, for she knew that he would see through any falsity. To her relief they had the tone she remembered in his other volumes, but were less bitter and more concerned with beauty. When she had finished the main sheaf, she came on a much longer poem entitled "The Leopard," wrapped round in a blank sheet of paper. Was it so wrapped to keep her from reading it; why, then, had he enclosed it? She decided that he had been doubtful, and wanted her verdict. Below the title was written the line:

"Can the leopard change its spots?"

It was the story of a young monk, secretly without faith, sent on a proselytising expedition. Seized by infidels, and confronted with the choice between death and recantation, he recants and accepts the religion of his captors. The poem was seared with passages of such deep feeling that they hurt her. It had a depth and fervour which took her breath away; it was a pæan in praise of contempt for convention faced with the stark reality of the joy in living, yet with a haunting moan of betrayal running through it. It swayed her this way and that; and she put it down with a feeling almost of reverence for one who could so express such a deep and tangled spiritual conflict. With that reverence was mingled a compassion for the stress he must have endured before he could have written this, and a feeling, akin to that which mothers feel, of yearning to protect him from his disharmonies and violence.

They had arranged to meet the following day at the National Gallery, and she went there before time, taking the poems with her. He came on her in front of Gentile Bellini's "Mathematician." They stood for some time looking at it without a word.

"Truth, quality, and decorative effect. Have you read my stuff?"

"Yes. Come and sit down, I've got them here."

They sat down, and she gave him the envelope.

"Well?" he said; and she saw his lips quivering.

"Terribly good, I think."

"Really?"

"Even truly. One, of course, is much the finest."

"Which?"

Dinny's smile said: "You ask that?"

"The Leopard?"

"Yes. It hurts me, here."

"Shall I throw it out?"

By intuition she realised that on her answer he would act, and said feebly: "You wouldn't pay attention to what I said, would you?"

"What you say shall go."

"Then of course you can't throw it out. It's the finest thing you've done."

"Inshallah."

"What made you doubt?"

"It's a naked thing."

"Yes," said Dinny, "naked—but beautiful. When a thing's naked it must be beautiful."

"Hardly the fashionable belief."

"Surely a civilised being naturally covers deformities and sores. There's nothing fine in being a savage that I can see, even in art."

"You run the risk of excommunication. Ugliness is a sacred cult, now."

"Reaction from the chocolate box," murmured Dinny.

"Ah! Whoever invented those lids sinned against the holy ghost, he offended the little ones."

"Artists are children, you mean?"

"Well, aren't they? or would they carry on as they do?"

"Yes, they do seem to love toys. What gave you the idea for that poem?" His face again had that look of deep waters stirred, as when Muskham had spoken to them under the Foch statue.

"Tell you some day, perhaps. Shall we go on round?"

When they parted, he said: "To-morrow's Sunday. I shall be seeing you?"

"If you will."

"What about the Zoo?"

"No, not the Zoo. I hate cages."

"Quite right. The Dutch garden near Kensington Palace?"

"Yes."

And that made the fifth consecutive day of meeting.

For Dinny it was like a spell of good weather, when every night you go to sleep hoping it will last, and every morning wake up and rub your eyes seeing that it has.

Each day she responded to his: "Shall I see you tomorrow?" with an "If you will"; each day she concealed from everybody with care whom she was seeing, and how, and when; and it all seemed to her so unlike herself, that she would think: 'Who is this young woman, who goes out stealthily like this, and meets a young man, and comes back feeling as if she had been treading on air? Is it some kind of a long dream I'm having?' Only, in dreams one didn't eat cold chicken and drink tea.

The moment most illuminative of her state of mind was that when Hubert and Jean walked into the hall at Mount Street, where they were to stay till after Clare's wedding. This first sight for eighteen months of her beloved brother should surely have caused her to feel tremulous. But she greeted him, steady as a rock even to the power of cool appraisement.

He seemed extremely well, brown, and less thin, but more commonplace. She tried to think that was because he was now safe and married and restored to soldiering, but she knew that comparison with Wilfrid had to do with it. She seemed to know suddenly that in Hubert there had never been capacity for any deep spiritual conflict; he was of the type she knew so well, seeing the trodden path and without real question following. Besides, Jean made all the difference! One could never again be to him, or he to her, as before his marriage. Jean was brilliantly alive and glowing. They had come the whole way from Khartoum to Croydon by air with four stops. Dinny was troubled by the inattention which underlay her seeming absorption in their account of life out there, till a mention of Darfur made her prick her ears. Darfur was where something had happened to Wilfrid. There were still followers of the Mahdi there, she gathered. The personality of Jerry Corven was discussed. Hubert was enthusiastic about 'a job of work' he had done. Jean filled out the gap. The wife of a Deputy Commissioner had gone off her head about him. It was said that Jerry Corven had behaved badly.

"Well, well!" said Sir Lawrence, "Jerry's a privateer, and women ought not to go off their heads about him."

"Yes," said Jean. "It's silly to blame men nowadays."

"In old days," murmured Lady Mont, "men did the advancin' and women were blamed; now women do it and the men are blamed."

The extraordinary consecutiveness of the speech struck with a silencing effect on every tongue, until she added: "I once saw two camels, d'you remember, Lawrence, so pretty."

Jean looked rather horrified, and Dinny smiled.

Hubert came back to the line. "I don't know," he said; "he's marrying our sister."

"Clare'll give and take," said Lady Mont. "It's only when their noses are curved. The Rector," she added to Jean, "says there's a Tasburgh nose. You haven't got it. It crinkles. Your brother Alan had it a little." And she looked at Dinny. "In China, too. I said he'd marry a purser's daughter."

"Good God, Aunt Em, he hasn't!" cried Jean.

"No. Very nice girls, I'm sure. Not like clergymen's."

"Thank you!"

"I mean the sort you find in the Park. They call themselves that when they want company. I thought everybody knew."

"Jean was rectory bred, Aunt Em," said Hubert.

"But she's been married to you two years. Who was it said: 'And they shall multiply exceedin'ly'?"

"Moses," hazarded Dinny.

"And why not?"

Her eyes rested on Jean, who flushed. Sir Lawrence remarked quickly: "I hope Hilary will be as short with Clare as he was with you and Jean, Hubert. That was a record."

"Hilary preaches beautifully," said Lady Mont. "At Edward's death he preached on 'Solomon in all his glory.' It was touchin'. And when we shot Casement, you remember—so stupid of us!—on the beam and the mote. We had it in our eye."

"If I could love a sermon," said Dinny, "it would be Uncle Hilary's."

"Yes," said Lady Mont, "he could borrow more barley-sugar than any little boy I ever knew, and look like an angel. Your Aunt Wilmet and I used to hold him upside down—like puppies, you know—hopin', but we never got it back."

"You must have been a lovely family, Aunt Em."

"Tryin'. Our father that was not in Heaven took care not to see us much. Our mother couldn't help it—poor dear! We had no sense of duty."

"And now you all have so much; isn't it queer?"

"Have I a sense of duty, Lawrence?"

"Emphatically not, Em."

"I thought so."

"But wouldn't you say as a whole, Uncle Lawrence, that the Cherrells have too much sense of duty?"

"How can they have *too* much?" said Jean.

Sir Lawrence fixed his monocle.

"I scent heresy, Dinny."

"Surely duty's narrowing, Uncle? Father and Uncle Lionel and Uncle Hilary, and even Uncle Adrian, always think first of what they ought to do. They despise their own wants. Very fine, of course, but rather dull."

Sir Lawrence dropped his eyeglasses.

"Your family, Dinny," he said, "perfectly illustrate the mandarin. They hold the Empire together. Public schools, Osborne, Sandhurst; oh! ah! and much more. From generation to generation it begins in the home. Mother's milk with them. Service to Church and State—very interesting, very admirable."

"Especially when they've kept on top, by means of it," murmured Dinny.

"Shucks!" said Hubert: "As if any one thought of that in the Services!"

"You don't think of it because you don't have to; but you would fast enough if you did have to."

"Somewhat cryptic, Dinny," put in Sir Lawrence; "you mean if anything threatened them, they'd think: 'We simply mustn't be removed, we're It.'"

"But are they It, Uncle?"

"With whom have you been associating, my dear?"

"Oh! no one. One must think sometimes."

"Too depressin'," said Lady Mont. "The Russian revolution, and all that."

Dinny was conscious that Hubert was regarding her as if thinking: 'What's come to Dinny?'

"If one wants to take out a lynchpin," he said, "one always can, but the wheel comes off."

"Well put, Hubert," said Sir Lawrence; "it's a mistake to think one can replace type or create it quickly. The sahib's born, not made, that is, if you take the atmosphere of homes as part of birth."

"No," said Lady Mont, "I won't."

"What, Aunt Em?"

"Drink champagne on Wednesday, nasty bubbly stuff!"

"Must we have it at all, dear?"

"I'm afraid of Blore. He's so used. I might tell him, but it'd be there."

"Have you heard of Hallorsen lately, Dinny?" asked Hubert, suddenly.

"Not since Uncle Adrian came back. I believe he's in Central America."

"He *was* large," said Lady Mont. "Hilary's two girls, Sheila, Celia, and little Anne, five—I'm glad you're not to be, Dinny. It's superstition, of course."

Dinny leaned back and the light fell on her throat.

"To be a bridesmaid once is quite enough, Aunt Em . . ."

When next morning she met Wilfrid at the Wallace pictures, she said: "Would you by any chance like to be at Clare's wedding to-morrow?"

"No hat and no black tails; I gave them to Stack."

"I remember how you looked, perfectly. You had a grey cravat and a gardenia."

"And you had on sea-green."

"Eau-de-nil. I'd like you to have seen my family, though, they'll all be there; and we could have discussed them afterwards."

"I'll turn up among the 'also ran'; and keep out of sight."

'Not from me,' thought Dinny. So she would not have to go a whole day without seeing him!

With every meeting he seemed less, as it were, divided against himself; and sometimes would look at her so intently that her heart would beat. When she looked at him, which was seldom, except when he wasn't aware, she was very careful to keep her gaze limpid. How fortunate that one always had that pull over men, knew when they were looking at one, and was able to look at them without their knowing!

When they parted this time, he said: "Come down to Richmond again on Thursday. I'll pick you up at Foch—two o'clock as before."

And she said: "Yes."

CHAPTER 6

CLARE CHERRELL's wedding, in Hanover Square, was "fashionable" and would occupy with a list of names a quarter of a column in the traditional prints. As Dinny said:

"So delightful for them!"

With her father and mother Clare came to Mount Street from Condaford over night. Busy with her younger sister to the last, and feeling an emotion humorously disguised, Dinny arrived with Lady Cherrell at the Church not long before the bride. She lingered to speak to an old retainer at the bottom of the aisle, and caught sight of Wilfrid. He was on the bride's side, far back, gazing at her. She gave him a swift smile, then passed up the aisle to join her mother in the left front pew. Michael whispered as she went by:

"People have rolled up, haven't they?"

They had. Clare was well known and popular, Jerry Corven even better known, if not so popular. Dinny looked round at the "audience," one could never credit a wedding with the word congregation. Irregular and with a good deal of character, their faces refused generalisation. They looked like people with convictions and views of their own. The men conformed to no particular type, having none of that depressing sameness which used to characterise the German officer caste. With herself and her mother in the front pew were Hubert and Jean, Uncle Lawrence and Aunt Em; in the pew behind sat Adrian with Diana, Mrs. Hilary and Lady Alison. Dinny caught sight of Jack Muskham at the end of two or three rows back, tall, well-dressed, rather bored-looking. He nodded to her, and she thought 'Odd, his remembering me!'

On the Corven side of the aisle were people of quite as much diversity of face and figure. Except Jack Muskham, the bridegroom and his best man, hardly a man gave the impression of being well-dressed, or of having thought about his clothes. But from their faces Dinny received the impression that they were all safe in the acceptance of a certain creed. Not one gave her the same feeling that Wilfrid's face brought of spiritual struggle and disharmony, of dreaming, suffering and discovery. 'I'm fanciful,' she thought. And her eyes came to rest on Adrian, who was just behind her. He was smiling quietly above that goatee beard of his, which lengthened his thin brown visage. 'He has a dear face,' she thought, 'not conceited, like the men who wear those pointed beards as a rule. He always will be the nicest man in the world.' And she whispered: "Fine collection of bones here, Uncle."

"I should like your skeleton, Dinny."

"I mean to be burned and scattered. H'ssh!"

The choir was coming in, followed by the officiating priests. Jerry Corven turned. Those lips smiling like a cat's beneath that thin cut moustache, those hardwood features and daring searching eyes! Dinny thought with sudden dismay: 'How could Clare! But after all I'd think the same of any face but one, just now. I'm going potty.' Then Clare came swaying up the aisle on her father's arm! 'Looking a treat! Bless her!' A gush of emotion caught Dinny by the throat, and she slipped her hand into her mother's. Poor mother! She was awfully pale! Really the whole thing was stupid! People *would* make it long and trying and emotional. Thank goodness Dad's old black tailcoat really looked quite decent—she had taken out the stains with ammonia; and he stood as she had seen him when reviewing troops. If Uncle Hilary happened to have a button wrong, Dad would notice it. Only there wouldn't be any buttons. She longed fervently to be beside Wilfrid away at the back. He would have nice unorthodox thoughts; and they would soothe each other with private smiles.

Now the bridesmaids! Hilary's two girls, her cousins Monica and Joan, slender and keen, little Celia Morison, fair as a seraph (if that was female), Sheila Ferse, dark and brilliant; and toddley little Anne—a perfect dumpling!

Once on her knees, Dinny quieted down. She remembered how they used to kneel, night-gowned against their beds, when Clare was a tiny of three and she herself a 'big girl' of six. She used to hang on to the bed-edge by the chin so as to save the knees; and how ducky Clare had looked when she held her hands up like the child in the Reynolds picture! 'That man!' thought Dinny: 'will hurt her! I know he will!' Her thoughts turned again to Michael's wedding all those ten years ago. There she had stood, not three yards from where she was kneeling now, alongside a girl she didn't know—some relative of Fleur's. And her eyes, taking in this and that with the fluttered eagerness of youth, had lighted on Wilfrid standing sideways, keeping watch on Michael! Poor Michael! He had seemed rather daft that day, from excessive triumph! She could remember quite distinctly thinking: 'Michael and his lost angel!' There had been in Wilfrid's face something which suggested that he had been cast out of happiness, a scornful and yet yearning look. That was only two years after the Armistice, and she knew now what utter disillusionment and sense of wreckage he had suffered after the war. He had been talking to her freely the last two days; had even dwelt with humorous contempt on his infatuation for Fleur eighteen months after that marriage which had sent him flying off to the East. Dinny, but ten when the war broke out, remembered it chiefly as meaning that mother had been anxious about father, had knitted all the time, and been a sort of sock depot; that everybody hated the Germans; that she had been forbidden sweets because they were made with saccharine, and finally the excitement and grief when Hubert went off to the war, and letters from him didn't often come. From Wilfrid these last few days she had gathered more clearly and poignantly than ever yet what the war had meant to some who, like Michael and himself, had been in the thick of it for years. With his gift of expression he had made her feel the tearing away of roots, and the hopeless change of values, and the growth of profound mistrust of all that age and tradition had decreed and sanctified. He had got over the war now, he said. He might think so, but there were in him still torn odds and ends of nerves not yet mended up. She never saw him without wanting to pass a cool hand over his forehead.

The ring was on now, the fateful words said, the exhortations over, they were going to the vestry. Her mother and Hubert followed. Dinny sat motionless, her eyes fixed on the East window. Marriage! What an impossible state, except—with a single being.

A voice in her ear said:

"Lend me your hanky, Dinny. Mine's soakin', and your uncle's is blue."

Dinny passed her a scrap of lawn, and surreptitiously powdered her own nose.

"Be done at Condaford, Dinny," continued her aunt. "All these people —so fatiguin', rememberin' who they aren't. That was his mother, wasn't it? She isn't dead, then."

Dinny was thinking: 'Shall I get another look at Wilfrid?'

"When I was married everybody kissed me," whispered her aunt, "so promiscuous. I knew a girl who married to get kissed by his best man. Aggie Tellusson. I wonder. They're comin' back!"

Yes! How well Dinny knew that bride's smile! How could Clare feel it, not married to Wilfrid! She fell in behind her father and mother, alongside Hubert who whispered: "Buck up, old girl, it might be a lot worse!" Divided from him by a secret that absorbed her utterly, Dinny squeezed his arm. And, even as she did so, saw Wilfrid, with his arms folded, looking at her. Again she gave him a swift smile, and then all was hurly-burly, till she was back at Mount Street and Aunt Em saying to her, just within the drawing-room door:

"Stand by me, Dinny, and pinch me in time."

Then came the entry of the guests and her aunt's running commentary.

"It *is* his mother—Kippered. Here's Hen Bentworth! . . . Hen, Wilmet's here, she's got a bone to pick . . . How d'you do? Yes, isn't it—so tirin' . . . How d'you do? The ring was so well done, don't you think? Conjurers! . . . Dinny, who's this? . . . How do you do? Lovely! No; Cherrell. Not as it's spelled, you know—so awkward . . . The presents are over there by the man with the boots, tryin' not to. Silly, I think! But they will . . . How d'you do? You *are* Jack Muskham? Lawrence dreamed the other night you were goin' to burst . . . Dinny, get me Fleur, too, she knows everybody."

Dinny went in search of Fleur and found her talking to the bridegroom.

As they went back to the door Fleur said: "I saw Wilfrid Desert in the church. How did he come there?"

Really Fleur was too sharp for anything!

"Here you are!" said Lady Mont. "Which of these three comin' is the duchess? The scraggy one. Ah! . . . How d'you do? Yes, charmin'. Such a bore, weddin's! Fleur, take the duchess to have some presents . . . How d'you do? No, my brother Hilary. He does it well, don't you think? Lawrence says he keeps his eye on the ball. Do have an ice, they're downstairs . . . Dinny, is this one after the presents, d'you think?—Oh! How d'you do, Lord Beevenham? My sister-in-law ought to be doin' this. She ratted. Jerry's in there . . . Dinny, who was it said: 'The drink, the drink!' Hamlet? He said such a lot. Not Hamlet? . . . Oh! How d'you do? . . . How d'you do? . . . How d'you do, or don't you? Such a crush! . . . Dinny, your hanky!"

"I've put some powder on it, Auntie."

"There! Have I streaked? . . . How d'you do? Isn't it silly, the whole thing? As if they wanted anybody but themselves, you know . . . Oh! Here's Adrian! Your tie's on one side, dear. Dinny, put it right. How d'you do? Yes, they are. I don't like flowers at funerals—poor things, lyin' there, and dyin' . . . How's your dear dog? You haven't one? Quite! . . . Dinny, you ought to have pinched me . . . How d'you do? How d'you do? I was tellin' my niece she ought to pinch me. Do you get faces right? No. How nice! How d'you do? How d'you do? How d'you do? . . . That's three! Dinny, who's the throw-back just comin'? Oh! . . . How d'you do? So you got here? I thought you were in China . . . Dinny, remind me to ask your uncle if it was China. He gave me such a dirty look. Could I give the rest a miss? Who is it's always sayin' that? Tell Blore 'the drink,' Dinny. Here's a covey! . . . How d'you do? . . . How de do? . . . How do? . . . Do! . . . Do! . . . How? . . . So sweet! . . . Dinny, I want to say: Blast!"

On her errand to Blore Dinny passed Jean talking to Michael, and wondered how any one so vivid and brown had patience to stand about in this crowd. Having found Blore, she came back. Michael's queer face, which she thought grew pleasanter every year, as if from the deepening impress of good feeling, looked strained and unhappy.

"I don't believe it, Jean," she heard him say.

"Well," said Jean, "the bazaars do buzz with rumour. Still, without fire of some sort there's never smoke."

"Oh yes, there is—plenty. He's back in England, anyway. Fleur saw him in the church to-day. I shall ask him."

"I wouldn't," said Jean: "if it's true he'll probably tell you, and if it isn't, it'll only worry him for nothing."

So! They were talking of Wilfrid. How find out why without appearing to take interest? And suddenly she thought: 'Even if I could, I wouldn't. Anything that matters he must tell me himself. I won't hear it from anyone else.' But she felt disturbed, for instinct was always warning her of something heavy and strange on his mind.

When that long holocaust of sincerity was over and the bride had gone, she subsided into a chair in her uncle's study, the only room which showed no signs of trouble. Her father and mother had started back to Condaford, surprised that she wasn't coming too. It was not like her to cling to London when the tulips were out at home, the lilacs coming on, the apple blossoms thickening every day. But the thought of not seeing Wilfrid daily had become a positive pain.

'I *have* got it badly,' she thought, 'worse than I ever believed was possible. Whatever is going to happen to me?'

She was lying back with her eyes closed when her uncle's voice said:

"Ah! Dinny, how pleasant after those hosts of Midian! The mandarin in full feather! Did you know a quarter of them? Why do people go to weddings? A registry office, or under the stars, there's no other way of preserving decency. Your poor aunt has gone to bed. There's a lot to be said for Mohammedanism, except that it's the fashion now to limit it to one wife and she not in Purdah. By the way, there's a story going round that young Desert's become a Moslem. Did he say anything to you about it?"

Dinny raised her startled head.

"I've only twice known it happen to fellows in the East, and they were Frenchmen, and wanted harems."

"Money's the only essential for that, Uncle."

"Dinny, you're getting cynical. Men like to have the sanction of religion. But that wouldn't be Desert's reason; a fastidious creature, if I remember."

"Does religion matter, Uncle, so long as people don't interfere with each other?"

"Well, some Moslems' notions of woman's rights are a little primitive. He's liable to wall her up if she's unfaithful. There was a sheikh when I was in Marrakesh—gruesome."

Dinny shuddered.

"From time immemorial," went on Sir Lawrence, "religion has been guilty of the most horrifying deeds that have happened on this earth. I wonder if young Desert has taken up with it to get him access to Mecca. I shouldn't think he believes anything. But you never know—it's a queer family."

Dinny thought: 'I can't and won't talk about him.'

"What proportion of people in these days do you think really have religion, Uncle?"

"In northern countries? Very difficult to say. In this country ten to fifteen per cent of the adults, perhaps. In France and southern countries, where there's a peasantry, more, at least on the surface."

"What about the people who came this afternoon?"

"Most of them would be shocked if you said they weren't Christians,

271

and most of them would be still more shocked if you asked them to give half their goods to the poor—and that only makes them Sadducees, was it?"

"Are you a Christian, Uncle?"

"No, my dear; if anything a Confucian, who, as you know, was simply an ethical philosopher. Most of our caste in this country, if they only knew it, are Confucian rather than Christian. Belief in ancestors, and tradition, respect for parents, honesty, moderation of conduct, kind treatment of animals and dependents, absence of self-obtrusion, and stoicism in face of pain and death."

"What more," murmured Dinny, wrinkling her nose, "does one want except the love of beauty?"

"Beauty? That's a matter of temperament."

"But doesn't it divide people more than anything?"

"Yes, but willy nilly. You can't make yourself love a sunset."

" 'You are wise, Uncle Lawrence, the young niece said.' I shall go for a walk and shake the wedding cake down."

"And I shall stay here, Dinny, and sleep the champagne off."

Dinny walked and walked. It seemed an odd thing to be doing alone. But the flowers in the Park were pleasing, and the waters of the Serpentine shone and were still, and the chestnut trees were coming alight. And she let herself go on her mood, and her mood was of love.

CHAPTER 7

LOOKING BACK on that second afternoon in Richmond Park, Dinny never knew whether she had betrayed herself before he said so abruptly:

"If you believe in it, Dinny, will you marry me?"

It had so taken her breath away that she sat growing paler and paler, then colour came to her face with a rush.

"You're like the East. One loves it at first sight, or not at all, and one never knows it any better."

Dinny shook her head: "Oh! I am not mysterious."

"I should never get to the end of you; no more than of one of those figures over the staircase in the Louvre. Please answer me, Dinny."

She put her hand in his, nodded, and said: "That must be a record."

At once his lips were on her, and when they left her lips she fainted.

This was without exception the most singular action of her life so far, and, coming to almost at once, she said so.

"It's the sweetest thing you could have done."

If she had thought his face strange before, what was it now? The lips, generally contemptuous, were parted and quivering, the eyes, fixed on her, glowed; he put up his hand and thrust back his hair, so that she noticed for the first time a scar at the top of his forehead. Sun, moon, stars, and all the works of God, stood still, while they were looking each into the other's face.

At last she said:

"The whole thing is most irregular. There's been no courtship; not even a seduction."

He laughed and put his arm around her. Dinny whispered:

"'Thus the two young people sat wrapped in their beatitude.' My poor mother!"

"Is she a nice woman?"

"A darling. Luckily she's fond of father."

"What is your father like?"

"The nicest General I know."

"Mine is a hermit. You won't have to realise him. My brother is an ass. My mother ran away when I was three, and I have no sisters. It's going to be hard for you, with a nomadic unsatisfactory brute like me."

"'Where thou goest, I go.' We seem to be visible to that old gentleman over there. He'll write to the papers about the awful sights to be seen in Richmond Park."

"Never mind!"

"I don't. There's only one first hour. And I was beginning to think I should never have it."

"Never been in love?"

She shook her head.

"How wonderful! When shall it be, Dinny?"

"Don't you think our families ought first to know?"

"I suppose so. They won't want you to marry me."

"Certainly you are my social superior, young Sir."

"One can't be superior to a family that goes back to the twelfth century. We only go back to the fourteenth. A wanderer and a writer of bitter verse. They'll know I shall want to cart you off to the East. Besides I only have fifteen hundred a year, and practically no expectations."

"Fifteen hundred a year! Father may be able to spare me two—he's doing it for Clare."

"Well, thank God there'll be no obstacle from your fortune."

Dinny turned to him, and there was a touching confidence in her eyes.

"Wilfrid, I heard something about your having turned Moslem. That wouldn't matter to me."

"It would matter to them."

His face had become drawn and dark. She clasped his hand tight in both of hers.

"Was that poem 'The Leopard' about yourself?"

He tried to draw his hand away.

"Was it?"

"Yes. Out in Darfur. I recanted to some fanatical Arabs to save my skin. Now you can chuck me." Exerting all her strength, Dinny pulled his hand to her heart.

"What you did or didn't do is nothing. You are you!" To her dismay and yet relief, he fell on his knees and buried his face in her lap.

"Darling!" she said. Protective tenderness almost annulled the wilder sweeter feeling in her.

"Does any one know of that but me?"

"It's known in the bazaars that I've turned Moslem, but it's supposed of my free will."

"I know there are things you would die for, Wilfrid, and that's enough. Kiss me!"

The afternoon drew on while they sat there. The shadows of the oak trees splayed up to their log; the crisp edge of the sunlight receded over the young fern; some deer passed moving slowly towards water. The sky of a clear bright blue, with white promising clouds, began to have the evening look; a sappy scent of fern fronds and horse chestnut bloom crept in slow whiffs; and dew began to fall. The sane and heavy air, the grass so green, the blue distance, the branching, ungraceful solidity of the oak trees, made a trysting hour English as lovers ever loved in.

"I shall break into cockney if we sit here much longer," said Dinny, at last; "besides, dear heart, 'fast falls the dewy eve.'" . . .

Late that evening in the drawing room at Mount Street her aunt said suddenly:

"Lawrence, look at Dinny! Dinny, you're in love."

"You take me flat aback, Aunt Em. I am."

"Whom with?"

"Wilfrid Desert."

"I used to tell Michael that young man would get into trouble. Does he love you too?"

"He is good enough to say so."

"Oh! dear. I *will* have some lemonade. Which of you proposed?"

"As a fact, he did."

"His brother has no issue, they say."

"For heaven's sake, Aunt Em!"

"Why not? Kiss me!"

But Dinny was regarding her uncle across her aunt's shoulder. He had said nothing.

Later, he stopped her as she was following out.

"Are your eyes open, Dinny?"

"Yes, this is the ninth day."

"I won't come the heavy uncle; but you know the drawbacks?"

"His religion; Fleur; the East? What else?"

Sir Lawrence shrugged his thin shoulders.

"That business with Fleur sticks in my gizzard, as old Forsyte would have said. One who could do that to the man he has led to the altar, can't have much sense of loyalty."

Colour rose in her cheeks.

"Don't be angry, my dear, we're all too fond of you."

"He's been quite frank about everything, Uncle."

Sir Lawrence sighed.

"Then there's no more to be said, I suppose. But I beg you to look forward before it's irrevocable. 'There's a species of china which it's almost impossible to mend. And I think you're made of it."

Dinny smiled, and went up to her room, and instantly she began to look back.

The difficulty of imagining the physical intoxication of love was gone. To open one's soul to another seemed no longer possible. Love stories she had read, love affairs she had watched, all seemed savourless compared with her own. And she had only known him nine days, except for that glimpse ten years ago! Had she had what was called a complex all this time? Or was love always sudden like this? A wild flower seeding on a wild wind?

Long she sat half-dressed, her hands clasped between her knees, her head drooping, steeped in the narcotic of remembrance, and with a strange feeling that all the lovers of the world were sitting within her on that bed bought at Pullbred's in the Tottenham Court Road.

CHAPTER 8

CONDAFORD RESENTED this business of love, and, with a fine rain, was sorrowing for the loss of its two daughters.

Dinny found her father and mother elaborately making no bones over the loss of Clare, and only hoped they would continue the motion in her own case. Feeling, as she said, 'Very towny,' she prepared for the ordeal of disclosure by waterproofing herself and going for a tramp. Hubert and Jean were expected in time for dinner, and she wished to kill all her birds with one stone. The rain on her face, the sappy fragrance, the call of the cuckoos, and that state of tree when each has leaves in different stage of opening, freshened her body but brought a little ache to her heart. Entering a covert, she walked along a ride. The trees were beech and hazel with here and there an English yew, the soil being chalky. A woodpecker's constant tap was the only sound, for the rain was not yet heavy enough for leaf dripping to have started. Since babyhood she had been abroad but three times—to Italy, to Paris, to the Pyrenees, and had always come home more in love with England and Condaford than ever. Henceforth her path would lie, she knew not where; there would no doubt be sand, fig trees, figures by wells, flat roofs, voices calling the Muezzin, eyes looking through veils. But surely, Wilfrid would feel the charm of Condaford and not mind if they spent time there now and then. His father lived in a show place, half shut up and never shown, which gave everyone the blues. And that, apart from London and Eton, was all he seemed to know of England, for he had been four years away in the war and eight years away in the East.

'For me to discover England to him,' she thought; 'for him to discover the East to me.'

A gale of last November had brought down some beech trees. Looking at their wide flat roots exposed, Dinny remembered Fleur saying that timber selling was the only way to meet death duties. But Dad was only sixty-two! Jean's cheeks the night of their arrival, when Aunt Em quoted the 'multiply exceedingly.' A child coming! Surely a son. Jean was the sort to have sons. Another generation of Cherrells in direct line! If Wilfrid and she had a child! What then? One could not wander about with babes. A tremor of insecurity went through her. The future how uncharted! A squirrel crossed close to her still figure, and scampered up a trunk. Smiling, she watched it, lithe, red, bushy-tailed. Thank God Wilfrid cared for animals! 'When to God's fondouk the donkeys are taken.' Condaford, its bird life, woods and streams, mullions, magnolias, fantails, pastures green, surely he would like it! But her father and mother, Hubert and Jean; would he like them? Would they like him? They would not— too unshackled, too fitful, and too bitter; all that was best in him he hid away, as if ashamed of it; and his yearning for beauty, they would not understand! And his change of religion, even though they would not know what he had told her, would seem to them strange and disconcerting! Condaford Grange had neither butler nor electric light, and Dinny chose the moment when the maids had set decanters and dessert on the polished chestnut wood, lit by candles.

"Sorry to be personal," she said, quite suddenly; "but I'm engaged."

No one answered. Each of those four was accustomed to say and think —not always the same thing—that Dinny was the ideal person to marry, so none was happier for the thought that she was going to be married. Then Jean said:

"To whom, Dinny?"

"Wilfrid Desert, the second son of Lord Mullyon—he was Michael's best man."

"Oh! but——!"

Dinny was looking hard at the other three. Her father's face was impassive, as was natural, for he did not know the young man from Adam; her mother's gentle features wore a fluttered and enquiring look; Hubert's an air as if he were biting back vexation.

Then Lady Cherrell said: "But, Dinny, when did you meet him?"

"Only ten days ago, but I've seen him every day since. I'm afraid it's a first sight case like yours, Hubert. We remembered each other from Michael's wedding."

Hubert looked at his plate. "You know he's become a Moslem," he said: "or so they say in Khartoum."

Dinny nodded.

"What!" said the General.

"That's the story, Sir."

"Why?"

"I don't know, I've never seen him. He's been a lot about in the East."

On the point of saying: 'One might just as well be Moslem as Christian, if one's not a believer,' Dinny stopped. It was scarcely a testimonial to character.

"I can't understand a man changing his religion," said the General, bluntly.

"There doesn't seem to be much enthusiasm," murmured Dinny.

"My dear, how can there be when we don't know him?"

"No, of course, Mother. May I ask him down? He *can* support a wife; and Aunt Em says his brother has no issue."

"Dinny!" said the General.

"I'm not serious, darling."

"What is serious," said Hubert, "is that he seems to be a sort of Bedouin —always wandering about."

"Two can wander about, Hubert."

"You always said you hate to be away from Condaford."

"I remember when you said you couldn't see anything in marriage, Hubert. And I'm sure both you and Father said that at one time, Mother. Have any of you said it since?"

"Cat, Dinny!"

With those simple words Jean closed the scene.

But at bed time in her mother's room, Dinny said:

"May I ask Wilfrid down then?"

"Of course, when you like. We shall be only too anxious to see him."

"I know it's a shock, Mother, coming so soon after Clare; still, you did expect me to go some time."

Lady Cherrell sighed: "I suppose so."

"I forgot to say that he's a poet, a real one."

"A poet?" repeated her mother, as if this had put the finishing touch to her disquiet.

"There are quite a lot in Westminster Abbey. But don't worry, *he'll* never be."

"Difference in religion is serious, Dinny, especially when it comes to children."

"Why, Mother? No child has any religion worth speaking of till it's grown up, and then it can choose for itself. Besides, by the time my children, if I have any, are grown up, the question will be academic."

"Dinny!"

"It's nearly so even now, except in ultra-religious circles. Ordinary people's religion becomes more and more just ethical."

"I don't know enough about it to say, and I don't think you do."

"Mother, dear, stroke my head."

"Oh! Dinny, I do hope you've chosen wisely."

"Darling, it chose me."

That she perceived was not the way to reassure her mother, but as she did not know one, she took her good-night kiss and went away.

In her room she sat down and wrote:

"Condaford Grange: Friday:

"DARLING,

"This is positively and absolutely my first love letter, so you see I don't know how to express myself. I think I will just say 'I love you' and leave it at that. I have spread the good tiding. It has, of course, left them guessing, and anxious to see you here as soon as possible. When will you come? Once you are here the whole thing will seem to me less like a very real and very lovely dream. This is quite a simple place. Whether we should live in style if we could, I can't say. But three maids, a groom chauffeur, and two gardners are all our staff. I believe you will like my mother, and I don't believe you will get on very well with my father or brother, though I expect his wife Jean will tickle your poetic fancy, she's such a vivid creature. Condaford itself I'm sure you'll love. It has the real 'old' feeling. We can go riding; and I want to walk and talk with you and show you my pet nooks and corners. I hope the sun will shine, as you love it so much. For me almost any sort of day does down here; and absolutely any will do if I can be with you. The room you will have is away by itself and supernaturally quiet; you go up to it by five twisty steps, and it's called the priest's room because Anthony Charwell, brother of the Gilbert who owned Condaford under Elizabeth, was walled up there, and fed from a basket let down nightly to his window. He was a conspicuous Catholic priest and Gilbert was a Protestant, but he put his brother first, as any decent body would. When he'd been there three months they took the wall down one night, and got him across country all the way south to the Beaulieu river and 'aboard the lugger.' The wall was put up again to save appearances; and only done away with by my great-grandfather, who was the last of us to have any money to speak of. It seemed to prey on his nerves, so he got rid of it. They still speak of him in the village, probably because he drove four-in-hand. There's a bath room at the bottom of the twisty steps. The window was enlarged, of course, and the view's jolly from it, especially now, at lilac and apple blossom time. My own room, if it interests you to know, is somewhat cloistral and narrow, but it looks straight over the lawns to the hill-rise and the woods beyond. I've had it ever since I was seven, and I wouldn't change for anything, until you're making me

'brooches and toys for my delight
Of birds' song at morning and starshine at night.'

I almost think that little 'Stevenson' is my favourite poem; so you see, in spite of my homing tendency, I must have a streak of the wanderer in me. Dad, by the way, has a great feeling for Nature, likes beasts and birds and trees. I think most soldiers do—it's rather odd. But, of course, their love is on the precise and knowledgeable rather than the aesthetic side. Any dreaminess they incline to look on as 'a bit barmy.' I have been wondering whether to put my copies of your poems under their noses. On the whole I don't think; they might take you too seriously. There is always something about a person more ingratiating than his writings. I don't expect to sleep much to-night, for this is the first day that I haven't seen you since the world began. Good-night, my dear, be blessed and take my kiss.

YOUR DINNY.

"P.S. I have looked you out the photo where I approximate most of the angels, or rather where my nose turns up least—to send to-morrow. In the meantime here are two snaps. And when, Sir, do I get some of you?

D."

And that was the end of this to her far from perfect day.

CHAPTER 9

SIR LAWRENCE MONT, recently elected to Burton's Club, whereon he had resigned from the Aeroplane, retaining besides only 'Snooks' (so-called), The Coffee House and The Parthenæum, was accustomed to remark that, allowing himself another ten years of life, it would cost him twelve shillings and sixpence every time he went into any of them.

He entered Burton's, however, on the afternoon after Dinny had told him of her engagement, took up a list of the members, and turned to D. 'Hon. Wilfrid Desert.' Quite natural, seeing the Club's pretension to the monopoly of travellers. "Does Mr. Desert ever come in here?" he said to the porter.

"Yes, Sir Lawrence, he's been in this last week; before that I don't remember him for years."

"Usually abroad. When does he come in as a rule?"

"For dinner, mostly, Sir Lawrence."

"I see: Is Mr. Muskham in?"

The porter shook his head. "Newmarket to-day, Sir Lawrence."

"Oh! Ah! How on earth you remember everything!"

"Matter of 'abit, Sir Lawrence."

"Wish I had it." Hanging up his hat, he stood for a moment before the tape in the hall. Unemployment and taxation going up all the time, and more money to spend on cars and sports than ever. A pretty little problem! He then sought the Library as the room where he was least likely to see anybody; and the first body he saw was that of Jack Muskham talking in a voice, hushed to the level of the locality, to a thin dark little man in the corner.

'That,' thought Sir Lawrence, cryptically, 'explains to me why I never find a lost collar-stud. My friend the porter was so certain Jack would be at Newmarket, that he took him for some one else when he came in.'

Reaching down a volume of Burton's "Arabian Nights," he rang for tea. He was attending to neither when the two in the corner rose and came up to him.

"Don't get up, Lawrence," said Jack Muskham with some languor; "Telfourd Yule, my cousin Sir Lawrence Mont."

"I've read thrillers of yours, Mr. Yule," said Sir Lawrence, and thought: 'Queer-looking little cuss!'

The thin, dark, smallish man, with a face rather like a monkey's, grinned. "Truth whips fiction out of the field," he said.

"Yule," said Jack Muskham, with his air of superiority to space and time, "has been out in Arabia, going into the question of how to cork-screw a really pure-strain Arab mare or two out of them for use here. It's always baffled us, you know. Stallions, yes! mares never. It's the same now at Nejd as when Palgrave wrote. Still we think we've got a rise. The owner of the best strain wants an aeroplane, and if we throw in a billiard table, we believe he'll part with at least one daughter of the sun."

"Good God!" said Sir Lawrence: "By what base means. We're all Jesuits, Jack!"

"Yule has seen some queer things out there. By the way, there's one I want to talk about. May we sit down?"

He stretched his long body out in a long chair, and the dark little man perched himself on another, with his black twinkling eyes fixed on Sir Lawrence, who had come to uneasy attention without knowing why.

"When," said Jack Muskham, "Yule here was in the Arabian desert, he heard a vague yarn among some Bedouins about an Englishman having been held up somewhere by Arabs and forced to become a Moslem. He had rather a row with them, saying no Englishman would do that. But when he was back in Egypt he went flying into the Libyan desert, met another lot of Bedouins coming from the south, and came on precisely the same yarn, only more detailed, because they said it happened in Darfur, and they even had the man's name—Desert. Then, when he was up in Khartoum, Yule found it was common talk that young Desert had changed his religion. Naturally he put two and two together. But there's all the difference in the world, of course, between voluntarily swapping religions and doing it at the pistol's point. An Englishman who does that lets down the lot of us."

Sir Lawrence, who during this recital had tried every motion for his monocle with which he was acquainted, dropped it and said: "But my dear Jack, if a man is rash enough to become a Mohammedan in a Moham-medan country, do you suppose for a minute that gossip won't say he was forced to?"

Yule, who had wriggled on to the very edge of his chair, said:

"I thought that; but the second account was extremely positive. Even to the month and the name of the Sheikh who forced the recantation; and I found that Mr. Desert had in fact returned from Darfur soon after the month mentioned. There may be nothing in it; but whether there is or not, I needn't tell you that an undenied story of that kind grows by telling and does a lot of harm, not only to the man himself, but to our prestige. There seems to me a sort of obligation on one to let Mr. Desert know what the Bedawi are spreading about him."

"Well, he's over here," said Sir Lawrence, gravely.

"I know," said Jack Muskham, "I saw him the other day, and he's a member of this Club."

Through Sir Lawrence were passing waves of infinite dismay. What a sequel to Dinny's ill-starred announcement. To his ironic, detached personality, capricious in its likings, Dinny was precious. She embroidered in a queer way his plain-washed feelings about women; as a young man he might even have been in love with her, instead of being merely her uncle by marriage. During this silence he was fully conscious that both the other two were thoroughly uncomfortable. And the knowledge of their disquiet deepened the significance of the matter in an odd way.

At last he said: "Desert was my boy's best man. I'd like to talk to Michael about it, Jack. Mr. Yule will say nothing further at present, I hope."

"Not on your life," said Yule. "I hope to God there's nothing in it. I like his verse."

"And you, Jack?"

"I don't care for the look of him; but I'd refuse to believe that of an Englishman till it was plainer than the nose on my face, which is saying a good bit. You and I must be getting on, Yule, if we're to catch that train to Royston."

This speech of Jack Muskham's further disturbed Sir Lawrence, left alone in his chair. It seemed so entirely to preclude leniency of judgment among the 'pukka sahibs' if the worst were true.

At last he rose, found a small volume, sat down again and turned its pages. The volume was Sir Alfred Lyall's "Verses Written in India," and he looked for the poem called: "Theology in Extremis."

He read it through, restored the volume, and stood rubbing his chin. Written, of course, some forty years ago, and yet doubtful if its sentiments were changed by an iota! There was that story of the Corporal in the Buffs who, brought before a Chinese General and told to 'kow-tow' or die, said: 'We don't do that sort of thing in the Buffs,' and died. Yes! That was the standard even to-day, among people of any caste or with any tradition. The war had thrown up innumerable instances. Could young Desert really have betrayed the traditions? It seemed improbable. And yet, in spite of his excellent war record, might there be a streak of yellow in him? Or was it, rather, that at times a flow of revolting bitterness carried him on to complete cynicism, so that he flouted almost for the joy of flouting?

With a strong mental effort Sir Lawrence tried to place himself in a like dilemma. Not being a believer, his success was limited to the thought: 'I should immensely dislike being dictated to in such a matter.' Aware that this was inadequate, he went down to the hall, shut himself up in a box and rang up Michael's house. Then, feeling that if he lingered in the Club he might run into Desert himself, he took a cab to South Square.

Michael had just come in from the house; they met in the hall; and, with the instinct that Fleur, however acute, was not a fit person to share this particular consultation, Sir Lawrence demanded to be taken to his son's study. He commenced by announcing Dinny's engagement, which

Michael heard with as strange a mixture of gratification and disquietude as could be seen on human visage.

"What a little cat, keeping it so dark!" he said. "Fleur did say something about her being too limpid just now; but I never thought—One's got so used to Dinny being single. To Wilfrid too? Well, I hope the old son has exhausted the East."

"There's this question of his religion," said Sir Lawrence gravely.

"I don't know that that much matters, Dinny's not fervent. But I never thought Wilfrid cared enough to change his. It rather staggered me."

"There's a story."

When his father had finished, Michael's ears stood out and his face looked haggard.

"You know him better than any one," Sir Lawrence concluded: "What do you think?"

"I hate to say it, but it might be true. It might even be natural for *him*; but no one would ever understand why. This is pretty ghastly, Dad, with Dinny involved."

"Before we fash ourselves, my dear, we must find out if it's true. Could you go to him?"

"In old days—easily."

Sir Lawrence nodded: "Yes, I know all about that, but it's a long time ago."

Michael smiled faintly. "I never knew whether you spotted that, but I rather thought so. I've seen very little of Wilfrid since he went East. Still, I could—" He stopped, and added: "If it *is* true, he must have told Dinny. He couldn't ask her to marry him with that untold."

Sir Lawrence shrugged. "If yellow in one way, why not in the other?"

"Wilfrid is one of the most perverse, complex, unintelligible natures one could come across. To judge him by ordinary standards is a washout. But if he *has* told Dinny, she'll never tell us."

And they stared at each other.

"Mind you," said Michael, "there's a streak of the heroic in him. It comes out in the wrong places. That's why he's a poet."

Sir Lawrence began twisting at an eyebrow, always a sign that he had reached decision.

"The thing's got to be faced; it's not in human nature for a sleeping dog like that to be allowed to lie. I don't care about young Desert——"

"I do," said Michael.

"It's Dinny I'm thinking of."

"So am I. But there again, Dad, Dinny will do what she will do, and you needn't think we can deflect her."

"It's one of the most unpleasant things," said Sir Lawrence, slowly, "that I've ever come across. Well, my boy, are you going to see him, or shall I?"

"I'll do it," said Michael, and sighed.

"Will he tell you the truth?"

"Yes. Won't you stay to dinner?"

Sir Lawrence shook his head.

"Daren't face Fleur with this on my mind. Needless to say, no one ought to know until you've seen him, not even she."

"No. Dinny still with you?"

"She's gone back to Condaford."

"Her people!" and Michael whistled.

Her people! The thought remained with him all through a dinner during which Fleur discussed the future of Kit. She was in favour of his going to Harrow because Michael and his father had been at Winchester. He was down for both and the matter had not yet been decided.

"All your mother's people," she said, "were at Harrow. Winchester seems to me so superior and dry. And they never get any notoriety. If you hadn't been at Winchester, you'd have been an under secretary by now."

"D'you want Kit to have notoriety?"

"Yes, the nice sort, of course, like your Uncle Hilary. You know, Michael, Bart's a dear, but I prefer the Cherrell side of your family."

"Well, I was wondering," said Michael, "whether the Cherrells weren't too straight-necked and servicey for anything."

"Yes, they're that, but they've got a quirk in them, and they look like gentlemen."

"I believe," said Michael, "that you really want Kit to go to Harrow because they play at Lord's."

Fleur straightened her own neck.

"Well, I do. I should have chosen Eton, only it's so obvious, and I hate light blue."

"Well," said Michael, "I'm prejudiced in favour of my own school, so the choice is up to you. A school that produced Uncle Adrian will do for me, anyway."

"No school produced your Uncle Adrian, dear," said Fleur; "he's palæolithic. The Cherrells are the oldest strain in Kit's make-up, anyway, and I should like to breed to it, as Mr. Jack Muskham would say. Which reminds me that when I saw him at Clare's wedding he wanted us to come down and see his stud farm at Royston. I should like to. He's like an advertisement for shooting capes—divine shoes and marvellous control of his facial muscles."

Michael nodded.

"Jack's an example of so much stamp on the coin, that there's hardly any coin behind it."

"Don't you believe it, my dear. There's plenty of metal at the back."

"The pukka sahib," said Michael. "I never can make up my mind whether that article is to the good or to the bad. The Cherrells are the best type of it, because there's no manner to them as there is to Jack; but even with them I always have the feeling of too much in heaven and earth that isn't dreamed of in their philosophy."

"We can't all have divine sympathy, Michael."

Michael looked at her fixedly. He decided against malicious intent and went on: "I never know where understanding and tolerance ought to end."

"That's where men are inferior to us. We wait for the mark to fix itself; we trust our nerves. Men don't, poor things. Luckily you've a streak of woman in you, Michael. Give me a kiss. Mind Coaker, he's very sudden. It's decided, then: Kit goes to Harrow."

"If there's a Harrow to go to by the time he's of age."

"Don't be foolish. No constellations are more fixed than the public schools. Look at the way they flourished on the war."

"They won't flourish on the next war."

"There mustn't be one then."

"Under pukka sahibism it couldn't be avoided."

"My dear, you don't suppose that keeping our word and all that was not just varnish. We simply feared German preponderance."

Michael rumpled his hair.

"It was a good instance, anyway, of what I said about there being more things in heaven and earth than are dreamed of by the pukka sahib; yes, and of many situations that he's not adequate to handle."

Fleur yawned.

"We badly want a new dinner service, Michael."

CHAPTER 10

AFTER DINNER Michael set forth, without saying where he was going. Since the death of his father-in-law, and the disclosure then made to him about Fleur and Jon Forsyte, his relations with her had been the same with a slight but deep difference. He was no longer a tied but a free agent in his own house. Not a word had ever been spoken between them on a matter now nearly four years old, nor had there been in his mind any doubt about her since; the infidelity was scotched and buried. But, though outwardly the same, he was inwardly emancipated, and she knew it. In this matter of Wilfrid, for instance, his father's warning had not been needed. He would not have told her of it anyway. Not because he did not trust her discretion—he could always trust that—but because he secretly felt that in a matter such as this he would not get any real help from her.

'Wilfrid's in love,' he thought, 'so he ought to be in by ten, unless he's got an attack of verse; but even then you can't write poetry in this traffic, or in a club, the atmosphere stops the flow.' He crossed Pall Mall and threaded the maze of narrow streets dedicated to unattached manhood until he came to Piccadilly, quiet before its storm of after-theatre traffic. Passing up a side street devoted to those male ministering angels—tailors, bookmakers, and moneylenders—he rounded into Cork Street. It was ten o'clock exactly when he paused before the well-remembered house. Opposite was the gallery where he had first met Fleur, and he stood for a moment almost dizzy from past feelings. For three years, before Wilfrid's queer infatuation for Fleur had broken it all up, he had been Wilfrid's fidus Achates. 'Regular David and Jonathan stunt,' he thought, and all his old feelings came welling up as he ascended the stairs.

The monastic visage of the henchman Stack relaxed at sight of him.

"Mr. Mont? Pleasure to see you, Sir."

"And how are you, Stack?"

"A little older, Sir; otherwise in fine shape, thank you. Mr. Desert *is* in."

Michael resigned his hat, and entered.

Wilfrid, lying on the divan in a dark dressing-gown, sat up.

"Hallo! I'm not going to say 'This is great!'"

"How are you, Wilfrid?"

"I'm not going to say 'fine'; anything else you like. Stack! Drinks."

"Congratulations, old man!"

"I met her first at your wedding, you know."

"Ten years ago, nearly. She hasn't the hair she had then. You've plucked the flower of our family, Wilfrid; we're all in love with Dinny."

"I won't talk about her, but I think the more."

"Any verse, old man?"

"Yes, a booklet going in to-morrow, same publisher. Remember the first?"

"Don't I? My only scoop."

"This is better. There's one that *is* a poem."

Stack re-entered with a tray.

"Help yourself, Michael."

Michael poured out a little brandy and diluted it but slightly. Then with a cigarette he sat down.

"When's it to be?"

"Registry office, as soon as possible."

"Oh! And then?"

"Dinny wants to show me England. While there's any sun, I suppose we shall hang around."

"Going back to Syria?"

Desert wriggled on his cushions.

"I don't know; further afield, perhaps—she'll say."

Michael looked at his feet, beside which on the Persian rug some cigarette ash had fallen.

"Old man," he said.

"Well?"

"D'you know a bird called Telfourd Yule?"

"His name—writer of sorts."

"He's just come back from Arabia and the Soudan; he brought a yarn with him." Without raising his eyes, he was conscious that Wilfrid was sitting upright.

"It concerns you; and it's queer and damaging. He thinks you ought to know."

"Well?"

Michael uttered an involuntary sigh.

"Shortly: The Bedouin are saying that your conversion to Islam was at the pistol's point. He was told the yarn in Arabia, and again in the Libyan desert, with the name of the Sheikh, and the place in Darfur, and the Englishman's name." And, still without looking up, he knew that Wilfrid's eyes were fixed on him, and that there was sweat on his forehead.

"Well?"

"He wanted you to know, so he told my Dad at the Club this afternoon, and Bart told me. I said I'd see you about it. Forgive me."

Then, in the silence, Michael raised his eyes. What a strange, beautiful, tortured, compelling face!

"Nothing to forgive, it's true."

"My dear old man!" The words burst from Michael, but no others would follow.

Desert got up, went to a drawer and took out a manuscript.

"Here, read this!"

During the twenty minutes while Michael was reading the poem, there was not a sound, except from the sheets being turned. Michael put them down at last.

"Magnificent!"

"Yes, but you'd never have done it."

"I haven't an idea what I should have done."

"Oh! yes, you have. You'd never have let sophistication and God knows what stifle your first instinct as I did. My first instinct was to say: 'Shoot and be damned,' and I wish to God I had kept to it, then I shouldn't be here. The queer thing is: If he'd threatened torture, I'd have stood out. Yet I'd much rather be killed than tortured."

"Torture's caddish."

"He wasn't a cad. Fanatics aren't. If he had bullied me I'd have sent him to hell. But he didn't—he didn't want to shoot me a bit; he begged me not to make him—stood there with the pistol and begged me. His brother's a friend of mine. By God! Fanaticism's a rum thing! He stood there ready to loose off, begging me." Desert laughed. "Damned human. I can see his eyes now. He was under a vow. He suffered right enough. I never saw a man so relieved."

"There's nothing of that in the poem," said Michael.

"Being sorry for your executioner is hardly an excuse. I'm not proud of sentimentalism, especially when it saves your life. Besides, I don't know if that was the reason. Religion if you haven't got it is a fake. To walk out into everlasting dark for the sake of a fake. If I must die I want a reality to die for."

"You don't think," said Michael miserably, "that you'd be justified in denying the thing?"

"I'll deny nothing. If it comes out, I'll stand by it."

"Does Dinny know?"

"Yes. She's read the poem. I didn't mean to tell her, but I did. She behaved as people don't. Marvellous."

"Yes. I'm not sure that you oughtn't to deny it for her sake."

"No, but I ought to give her up."

"She would have something to say about that. If Dinny's in love, it's over head and ears, Wilfrid."

"Same here!"

Overcome by the bleakness of the situation, Michael got up and helped himself to more brandy.

"Exactly!" said Desert, following him with his eyes: "Imagine if the press gets hold of it!" and he laughed again.

"I gather," said Michael, with a spurt of cheerfulness, "that it was only in the desert both times that Yule heard the story."

"What's in the desert to-day is in the bazaars to-morrow. It's no use, I shall have to face the music."

Michael put a hand on his shoulder. "Count on me, anyway. I suppose the bold way is the only way. But I feel all you're up against."

"Yellow. Labelled: 'Yellow'—might give any show away. And they'll be right."

"Rot!" said Michael.

Wilfrid went on without heeding: "And yet my whole soul revolts against dying for a gesture that I don't believe in. Legends and super-stitions—I hate the lot. I'd sooner die to give them a death-blow than to keep them alive. If a man tried to force me to torture an animal, to hang another man, to violate a woman, of course I'd die rather than do it. But why the hell should I die to gratify those whom I despise for believing outworn creeds that have been responsible for more misery in the world than any other mortal thing? Why? Eh?"

Michael had recoiled before the passion in this outburst, and was stand-ing miserable and glum.

"Symbol," he muttered.

"Symbol! For conduct that's worth standing for, honesty, humanity, courage, I hope I'd stand; I went through the war, anyway; but why should I stand for what I look on as dead wood?"

"It simply mustn't come out," said Michael violently; "I loathe the idea of a lot of swabs looking down their noses at you."

Wilfrid shrugged. "I look down my nose at myself, I assure you. Never stifle your instinct, Michael. It gets back on you."

"But what are you going to *do*?"

"What does it matter what I do? Things will be as they will be. Nobody will understand, or side with me if they did understand. Why should they? I don't even side with myself."

"I think a lot of people might now-a-days."

"The sort I wouldn't be seen dead with. No, I'm outcast."

"And Dinny?"

"I'll settle that with her."

Michael took up his hat.

"If there's anything I can do, count on me. Good-night, old man!"

"Good-night, and thanks!"

Michael was out of the street before any thinking power returned to him. Wilfrid had been caught, as it were, in a snare! One could see how his rebellious contempt for convention and its types had blinded him to the normal view. But one could not dissociate this or that from the general image of an Englishman; betrayal of one feature would be looked on as betrayal of the whole. As for that queer touch of compassion for his would-be executioner, who would see that who didn't know Wilfrid? The affair was bitter and tragic. The 'yellow' label would be stuck on indis-criminately for all eyes to see.

'Of course,' thought Michael, 'he'll have his supporters—the advanced

crowd, and Bolshies generally, and that'll make him feel worse than ever.'
Nothing was more galling than to be backed up by people you didn't understand, and who didn't understand you. And how was support like that going to help Dinny, more detached from it even than Wilfrid? The whole thing was——!

And with that blunt reflection he crossed Bond Street and went down Hay Hill into Berkeley Square. If he did not see his father before he went home, he would not sleep.

At Mount Street his mother and father were receiving a special pale negus, warranted to cause slumber, from the hands of Blore.

"Catherine?" said Lady Mont: "Measles?"

"No. Mother; I want to have a talk with Dad."

"About that young man—changin' his religion. He always gave me a pain—defyin' the lightnin', and that."

Michael stared. "It *is* about Wilfrid."

"Em," said Sir Lawrence, "this is dead private. Well, Michael?"

"The story's true, he doesn't and won't deny it. And Dinny knows."

"What story?" asked Lady Mont.

"He recanted to some fanatical Arabs on pain of death."

"What a bore!"

Michael thought swiftly: 'My God! If only everyone would take that view!'

"D'you mean, then," said Sir Lawrence, gravely, "that I've got to tell Yule there's no defence?"

Michael nodded.

"But if so, dear boy, it won't stop there."

"No, but he's reckless."

"The lightnin'," said Lady Mont, suddenly.

"Exactly, Mother. He's written a poem on it, and a jolly good one it is. He's sending it in a new volume to his publisher to-morrow. But, Dad, at any rate, get Yule and Jack Muskham to keep their mouths shut. After all, what business is it of theirs?"

Sir Lawrence shrugged the thin shoulders which at seventy-two were beginning to suggest age.

"There are two questions, Michael, and so far as I can see they're quite separate. The first is how to muzzle club gossip. The second concerns Dinny and her people. You say Dinny knows; but her people don't, except ourselves, and as she didn't tell us she won't tell them. Now that's not fair. And it's not wise," he went on, without waiting for an answer, "because this thing's dead certain to come out later, and they'd never forgive Desert for marrying her without letting them know. I wouldn't myself, it's too serious."

"It *is* agitatin'," murmured Lady Mont: "Ask Adrian."

"Better Hilary," said Sir Lawrence.

Michael broke in: "That second question, Dad, seems to me entirely up to Dinny. She must be told that the story's in the wind, then either she or Wilfrid will let her people know."

"If only she'd let him drop her. Surely he can't want to go on with it, with this story going about?"

"I don't see Dinny droppin' him," murmured Lady Mont. "She's been too long pickin' him up. Love's young dream."

"Wilfrid said he knew he ought to give her up. Oh! damn!"

"Come back to question one, then, Michael. I can try, but I'm very doubtful, especially if this poem is coming out. What is it, a justification?"

"Or explanation."

"Bitter and rebellious, like his early stuff?"

Michael nodded.

"Well, they might keep quiet out of charity, but they'll never stomach that sort of attitude, if I know Jack Muskham. He hates the bravado of modern scepticism like poison."

"We can't tell what's going to happen in any direction, but it seems to me we ought all to play hard for delay."

"Hope the Hermit," murmured Lady Mont. "Good-night, dear boy; I'm going up. Mind the dog—he's not been out."

"Well, I'll do what I can," said Sir Lawrence.

Michael received his mother's kiss, wrung his father's hand, and went.

He walked home, uneasy and sore at heart, for this concerned two people of whom he was very fond, and he could see no issue that was not full of suffering to both. And continually there came back to him the thought: 'What should I have done in Wilfrid's place?' And he concluded, as he walked, that no man could tell what he would do if he were in the shoes of another man. And so, in the spring wind of a night not devoid of beauty, he came to South Square and let himself in.

CHAPTER 11

WILFRID SAT in his rooms with two letters before him, one that he had just written to Dinny, and one that he had just received from her. He stared at the snapshots, and tried to think clearly, and since he had been trying to think clearly ever since Michael's visit of the previous evening, he was the less successful. Why had he chosen this particular moment to fall really in love, to feel that he had found the one person with whom he could bear to think of permanent companionship? He had never intended to marry, he had never supposed he would feel towards women anything but a transient urge that soon died in satisfaction. Even at the height of his infatuation with Fleur he had never supposed it would last. On the whole he was profoundly sceptical about women, as about religion, patriotism, or the qualities popularly attributed to the Englishman. He had thought himself armoured in scepticism, but in his armour was a point so weak that he had just received a fatal thrust. With bitter amusement he perceived that the profound loneliness, left by that experience in Darfur, had started in him an involuntary craving for spiritual companionship of which Dinny had, as involuntarily, availed herself. The thing that should have kept them apart had brought them together.

After Michael had left he spent half the night going over and over it, and always coming back to the crude thought that, when all was said and done, he would be set down as a coward. And yet, but for Dinny, would even that matter? What did he care for society and its opinion? What did he care for England and the English? Even if they had prestige, was it deserved, any more than the prestige of any other country? The war had shown all countries and their inhabitants to be pretty much alike, capable of the same heroisms, basenesses, endurance, and absurdities. The war had shown mob feeling in every country to be equally narrow, void of discrimination, and generally contemptible. He was a wanderer by nature, and even if England and the nearer East were closed to him, the world was wide, the sun shone in many places, the stars wheeled over one, books could be read, women had beauty, flowers scent, tobacco its flavour, music its moving power, coffee its fragrance, horses and dogs and birds were the same seductive creatures, and thought and feeling brought an urge to rhythmic expression, almost wherever one went. Save for Dinny he could strike his tent and move out, and let tongues wag behind him! And now he couldn't! Or could he? Was he not, indeed, in honour bound to? How could he saddle her with a mate at whom fingers were pointed? If she had inspired him with flaming desire, it would have been much simpler, they could have had their fling and parted, and no one the worse. But he had a very different feeling for her. She was like a well of sweet water met with in a desert; a flower with a scent coming up among the dry vegetation of the wilderness. She gave him the reverent longing that some tunes and pictures inspire; roused the same ache of pleasure as the scent of new-mown grass. She was a cool refreshment to a spirit sun-dried, wind-dried and dark. Was he to give her up because of this damned business?

In the morning when he woke the same confused struggle of feeling had gone on. He had spent the afternoon writing her a letter, and had barely finished it when her first love letter came. And he sat now with the two before him.

'I can't send this,' he thought suddenly, 'it goes over and over and gets nowhere. Rotten!' He tore it up, and read her letter a third time.

'Impossible!' he thought; 'to go down there! God and the King and the rest of it. Impossible!' And seizing a piece of paper, he wrote:

> "Cork Street. Saturday.
> "Bless you for your letter. Come up here to lunch Monday. We must talk. Wilfrid."

Having sent Stack out with this missive, he felt a little more at peace.

Dinny did not receive this note till Monday morning, there being naturally no Sunday post at Condaford. The last two days had been spent by her in avoiding any mention of Wilfrid, listening to Hubert and Jean's account of their life in the Soudan; walking and inspecting the state of trees with her father, copying his income tax return, and going to church with him and her mother. The tacit silence about her engagement was very characteristic of a family whose members were mutually devoted and accustomed to spare each other's feelings; it was all the more ominous.

After reading Wilfrid's note she said to herself blankly: 'For a love letter it's not a love letter.' And she said to her mother:

"Wilfrid's shy of coming, dear. I must go up and talk to him. If I can, I will bring him down with me. If I can't, I'll try and arrange for you to see him at Mount Street. He's lived in the desert so much that seeing people is a real strain."

Lady Cherrell's answer was a sigh, but it meant more to Dinny than words; she took her mother's hand and said: "Cheer up, Mother dear. It's something that I'm happy, isn't it?"

"That would be everything, Dinny."

Dinny was too conscious of implications in the 'would be' to answer.

She walked to the station, reached London at noon, and set out for Cork Street across the Park. The day was fine, the sun shone; spring was established to the full, with lilac and with tulips, young green of plane tree leaves, songs of birds and the freshness of the grass. But though she looked in tune, she suffered from presentiment. Why she should feel so, going to a private lunch with her lover, she could not have explained. There could be but few people in all the great town at such an hour of day with prospect before them so closely joyful; but Dinny was not deceived: all was not well—she knew it. Being before her time, she stopped at Mount Street to titivate. According to Blore, Sir Lawrence was out, but his lady in. Dinny sent up the message that she might be back to tea.

Passing the pleasant smell at the corner of Burlington Street, she had that peculiar feeling, experienced by all at times, of having once been someone else, which accounts for so much belief in the transmigration of souls.

'It only means,' she thought, 'something I've forgotten. I never really was the French washerwoman of Marie Antoinette. Oh! here's the turning!' And her heart began to beat.

She was nearly breathless when Stack opened the door to her. "Lunch will be ready in five minutes, Miss." His eyes, dark, prominent above his jutting nose, and yet reflective, and the curly benevolence of his lips, always gave her the impression that he was confessing her before she had anything to confess. He opened the inner door, shut it behind her, and she was in Wilfrid's arms. That was a complete refutation of presentiment; the longest and most satisfactory moment of the sort she had yet experienced. So long that she was afraid he would not let her go in time. At last she said, gently:

"Lunch has already been in a minute, darling, according to Stack."

"Stack has tact."

Not until after lunch, when they were alone once more with coffee, did discomfiture come with the suddenness of a thunderclap in a clear sky.

"That business has come out, Dinny."

What! That? *That!* She mastered the rush of her dismay.

"How?"

"A man called Telfourd Yule has brought the story back with him. They talk of it among the tribes. It'll be in the bazaars by now, in the London Clubs to-morrow. I shall be in Coventry in a few weeks' time. Nothing can stop a thing like that."

Without a word Dinny got up, pressed his head against her shoulder, then sat down beside him on the divan.

"I'm afraid you don't understand," he said, gently.

"That this makes any difference? No, I don't. The only difference could have been when you told me yourself. That made none. How can this, then?"

"How can I marry you?"

"That sort of thing is only in books, Wilfrid. *We* won't have linkéd misery long drawn out."

"False heroics are not in my line either; but I don't think you see yet."

"I do. Now you can stand up straight again, and those who can't understand—well, they don't matter."

"Then don't your people matter?"

"Yes, they matter."

"But you don't suppose for a minute that they'll understand?"

"I shall make them."

"My poor dear!"

It struck her, ominously, how quiet and gentle he was being. He went on:

"I don't know your people, but if they're the sort you've described—charm ye never so wisely, they won't rise. My dear, they can't, it's against their root convictions."

"They're fond of me."

"That will make it all the more impossible for them to see you tied to me."

Dinny drew away a little and sat with her chin on her hands. Then, without looking at him, she said:

"Do you want to get rid of me, Wilfrid?"

"Dinny!"

"Yes, but do you?"

He drew her into his arms. Presently she said, quietly:

"I see. Then if you don't, you must leave this to me. And anyway it's no good to meet trouble. It isn't known yet in London. We'll wait until it is. I know you won't marry me till then, so I *must* wait. After that it will be a clear issue, but you mustn't be heroic then, Wilfrid, because it'll hurt me too much—too much." She clutched him suddenly; and he stayed silent.

With her cheek to his she said, quietly:

"Do you want me to be everything to you before you marry me; if so, I can."

"Dinny!"

"Very forward, isn't it?"

"No! But we'll wait. You make me feel too reverent."

She sighed. "Perhaps it's best."

Presently she said: "Will you leave it to me to tell my people everything or not?"

"I will leave anything to you."

"And if I want you to meet any one of them, will you?"

Wilfrid nodded.

"I won't ask you to come to Condaford—yet. That's all settled then. Now tell me exactly how you heard about this."

When he had finished, she said reflectively:

"Michael and Uncle Lawrence. That will make it easier. Now, darling, I'm going. It'll be good for Stack, and I want to think. I can only think when I'm insulated from you."

"Angel."

She took his head between her hands. "Don't be tragic, and I won't either. Could we go joy-riding on Thursday? Good! Foch at noon! I'm not an angel, I'm your love."

She went dizzily down the stairs, now that she was alone, terribly conscious of the ordeal before them. She turned suddenly towards Oxford Street. 'I'll go and see Uncle Adrian,' she thought.

Adrian's thoughts at his Museum had been troubled of late by the claim of the Gobi desert to be the cradle of Homo Sapiens. The idea had been patented and put on the market, and it bid fair to have its day. He was reflecting on the changeability of anthropological fashions, when Dinny was announced.

"Ah! Dinny! I've been in the Gobi desert all the afternoon, and was just thinking of a nice cup of 'hot' tea. What do you say?"

"China tea always gives me an 'ick feeling, Uncle."

"We don't go in for so-called luxuries. My duenna here makes good old Dover tea with leaves in it, and we have the homely bun."

"Perfect! I came to tell you that I've given my young heart."

Adrian stared.

"It's really rather a terrible tale, so can I take off my hat?"

"My dear," said Adrian, "take off anything. Have tea first. Here it is."

While she was having tea Adrian regarded her with a rueful smile, caught, as it were, between his moustache and goatee. Since the tragic Ferse affair she had been more than ever his idea of a niece; and he perceived that she was really troubled.

Lying back in the only easy chair, with her knees crossed and the tips of her fingers pressed together, she looked, he thought, ethereal, as if she might suddenly float, and his eyes rested with comfort on the cap of her chestnut hair. But his face grew perceptibly longer while she was telling him her tale, leaving nothing out. She stopped at last and added:

"Uncle, please don't look like that!"

"Was I?"

"Yes."

"Well, Dinny, is it surprising?"

"I want your 'reaction,' as they call it, to what he did." And she looked straight into his eyes.

"My personal reaction? Without knowing him—judgment reserved."

"If you wouldn't mind, you shall know him."

Adrian nodded, and she said:

"Tell me the worst. What will the others who don't know him think and do?"

"What was your own reaction, Dinny?"

"I knew him."

"Only a week."

"And ten years."

"Oh! don't tell me that a glimpse and three words at a wedding——"

"The grain of mustard-seed, dear. Besides, I'd read the poem, and knew

298

from that all his feelings. He isn't a believer, it must have seemed to him like some monstrous practical joke."

"Yes, yes, I've read his verse—scepticism and love of beauty. His type blooms after long national efforts, when the individual's been at a discount, and the State has exacted everything. Ego crops out and wants to kick the State and all its shibboleths. I understand all that. But— You've never been out of England, Dinny."

"Only Italy, Paris and the Pyrenees."

"They don't count. You've never been where England has to have certain prestige. For Englishmen in such parts of the world it's all for one and one for all."

"I don't think he realised that at the time, Uncle."

Adrian looked at her, and shook his head.

"I still don't," said Dinny. "And thank God he didn't, or I should never have known him. Ought one to sacrifice oneself for false values?"

"That's not the point, my dear. In the East, where religion still means everything, you can't exaggerate the importance attached to a change of faith. Nothing could so damage the Oriental's idea of the Englishman as a recantation at the pistol's point. The question before him was: Do I care enough for what is thought of my country and my people to die sooner than lower that conception? Forgive me, Dinny, but that was, brutally, the issue."

She was silent for a minute and then said:

"I'm perfectly sure Wilfrid would have died sooner than do lots of things that would have lowered that conception; but he simply couldn't admit that the Eastern conception of an Englishman ought to rest on whether he's a Christian or not."

"That's special pleading; he not only renounced Christianity, he accepted Islam—one set of superstitions for another."

"But, can't you see, Uncle, the whole thing was a monstrous jest to him?"

"No, my dear, I don't think I can."

Dinny leaned back, and he thought how exhausted she looked.

"Well, if *you* can't, no one else will. I mean no one of our sort, and that's what I wanted to know."

A bad ache started in Adrian's midriff. "Dinny, there are ten days of this behind you, and the rest of your life before you; you told me he'd give you up—for which I respect him. Now, doesn't it need a wrench, if not for your sake—for his?"

Dinny smiled.

"Uncle, you're so renowned for dropping your best pals when they're in a mess. And you know so little about love! You only waited eighteen years. Aren't you rather funny?"

"Admitted," said Adrian. "I suppose the word 'Uncle' came over me. If I knew that Desert was likely to be as faithful as you, I should say: 'Go to it and be damned in your own ways, bless you!'"

"Then you must see him."

"Yes; but I've seen people seem so unalterably in love that they were divorced within a year. I knew a man so completely satisfied by his honeymoon, that he took a mistress two months later."

"We," murmured Dinny, "are not of that devouring breed. Seeing so many people on the screen examining each other's teeth, has spiritualised me, I know."

"Who has heard of this development?"

"Michael and Uncle Lawrence, possibly Aunt Em. I don't know whether to tell them at Condaford."

"Let me talk to Hilary. He'll have another point of view; and it won't be orthodox."

"Oh! Yes, I don't mind Uncle Hilary." And she rose. "May I bring Wilfrid to see you, then?"

Adrian nodded; and, when she had gone, stood again in front of a map of Mongolia, where the Gobi desert seemed to bloom like a rose in comparison with the wilderness across which his favourite niece was moving.

CHAPTER 12

DINNY STAYED on at Mount Street for dinner to see Sir Lawrence.

She was in his study when he came in, and said at once:

"Uncle Lawrence, Aunt Em knows what you and Michael know, doesn't she?"

"She does, Dinny. Why?"

"She's been so discreet. I've told Uncle Adrian, he seems to think Wilfrid has lowered English prestige in the East. Just what is this English prestige? I thought we were looked on as a race of successful hypocrites. And in India as arrogant bullies."

Sir Lawrence wriggled.

"You're confusing national with individual reputation. The things are totally distinct. The individual Englishman in the East is looked up to as a man who isn't to be rattled, who keeps his word, and sticks by his own breed."

Dinny flushed. The implication was not lost on her.

"In the East," Sir Lawrence went on: "the Englishman, or rather the Briton, because as often as not he's a Scot or a Welshman or a North Irishman, is generally isolated: traveller, archæologist, soldier, official, civilian, planter, doctor, engineer, or missionary, he's almost always head man of a small separate show; he maintains himself against the odds on the strength of the Englishman's reputation. If a single Englishman is found wanting, down goes the stock of all those other isolated Englishmen. People know that and recognise its importance. That's what you're up against, and it's no use underestimating. You can't expect Orientals, to whom religion means something, to understand that to some of us it means nothing. An Englishman to them is a believing Christian, and if he recants, he's understood as recanting his most precious belief."

Dinny said drily: "In fact, then, Wilfrid has no case in the eyes of our world."

"In the eyes of the world that runs the Empire, I'm afraid—none, Dinny. Could it be otherwise? Unless there were complete mutual confidence between these isolated beings that none of them will submit to dictation, take a dare, or let the others down, the thing wouldn't work at all. Now would it?"

"I never thought about it."

"Well, you can take it from me. Michael has explained to me how Desert's mind worked; and from the point of view of a disbeliever like myself, there's a lot to be said. I should intensely dislike being wiped out over such an issue. But it wasn't the real issue; and if you say: 'He didn't see that,' then I'm afraid my answer is he didn't because he has too much spiritual pride. And that won't help him as a defence, because spiritual pride is anathema to the Services, and indeed to the world generally. It's the quality, you remember, that got Lucifer into trouble."

Dinny, who had listened with her eyes fixed on her uncle's twisting features, said:

"It's extraordinary the things one can do without."

Sir Lawrence screwed in a puzzled eyeglass.

"Have you caught the jumping habit from your aunt?"

"If one can't have the world's approval, one can do without it."

" 'The world well lost for love,' sounds gallant, Dinny, but it's been tried out and found wanting. Sacrifice on one side is the worst foundation for partnership, because the other side comes to resent it."

"I don't expect more happiness than most people get."

"That's not as much as I want for you, Dinny."

"Dinner!" said Lady Mont, in the doorway: "Have you a vacuum, Dinny? They use those cleaners," she went on, as they went towards the dining room, "for horses now."

"Why not for human beings," murmured Dinny; "and clear out their fears and superstitions? Uncle wouldn't approve."

"You've been talkin', then. Blore, go away!"

When he had gone, she added: "I'm thinkin' of your father, Dinny."

"So am I."

"I used to get over him. But daughters. Still, he must."

"Em!" said Sir Lawrence, warningly, as Blore came back.

"Well," said Lady Mont, "beliefs and that—too fatiguin'. I never liked christenin's—so unfeelin' to the baby; and puttin' it upon other people; only they don't bother, except for cups and Bibles. Why do they put fern-leaves on cups? Or is that archery? Uncle Cuffs won a cup at archery when he was a curate. They used. Well, it's all very agitatin'."

"Aunt Em," said Dinny, "all I hope and want is that no one will agitate himself over me and my small affair. If people won't agitate we can be happy."

"So wise! Lawrence, tell Michael that. Blore! Give Miss Dinny some sherry."

Dinny, putting her lips to the sherry, looked across at her aunt's face. It was comforting—its slightly raised eyebrows, dropped lids, curved nose, and as if slightly powdered hair, so well held above its comely neck, shoulders and bust.

In the taxi for Paddington she had so close a vision of Wilfrid alone, with this hanging over him, that she very nearly leaned out to say: "Cork Street." But that would be to 'fuss' indeed! The cab turned into Praed

Street. All the worry in the world seemed to come from the conflict of love against love. If only her people didn't love her, and she them, how simple things would be!

A porter was saying: "Any luggage, Miss?"

"None, thank you." As a little girl she had always meant to marry a porter—they were so nice! That was before her music master came from Oxford. He had gone off to the war when she was ten. She bought a magazine and took her seat in the train. But she was very tired and lay back in her corner of the third-class carriage; railway travelling was a severe tax on her always slender purse. With head tilted, she went to sleep.

When she alighted from the train there was a nearly full moon, and the night was blowy and sweet-smelling. She would have to walk. It was light enough to take the short cut, and she climbed the first stile into the field path. She thought of the night, nearly two years ago, when she came back by this train with the news of Hubert's release, and found her father sitting up, grey and worn, in his study, and how years had seemed to drop off him when she told him the good news. And now she had news that must grieve him. It was her father she really dreaded facing. Her mother, yes! Mother, though gentle, was stubborn; but women had not the same hard and fast convictions about what was not 'done' as men. Hubert? In the old days she would have minded him most. Curious how lost he was to her! Hubert would be dreadfully upset. He was rigid in his views of what was 'the game.' Well! she could 'bear' his disapproval. But Father! It seemed so unfair to him, after his forty years of hard service!

A brown owl floated from the hedge over to some stacks. These moony nights were owl-nights and there would be screams of captured victims so dreadful in the night time. Yet who could help liking owls, their blunt soft floating flight, their measured stirring calls? The next stile led her on to their own land. There was a linhay in this field where her father's old charger sheltered at night. Was it Plutarch or Pliny who had said: 'For my part I would not sell even an old ox who had laboured for me.' Nice man! Now that the sound of the train had died away it was very quiet, only the brushing of a little wind on the young leaves, and the stamp of old Kismet's foot in the linhay. She crossed a second field and came to the narrow tree-trunk bridge. The night's sweetness was like the feelings always within her now. She crossed the plank and slipped in among the apple trees. They seemed to live brightly between her and the moving, moonlit, wind-brushed sky. They seemed to breathe, almost to be singing in praise at the unfolding of their blossoms. They were lighted in a thousand shapes of whitened branches, and all beautiful, as if some one had made each with a rapt and moonstruck pleasure and brightened it with starshine. And this had been done in here each spring for a hundred years and more. The whole world seemed miraculous on a night like this, but always the yearly miracle of the apple blooming was to Dinny most moving of all. The many miracles of England thronged her memory, while she stood among the old trunks inhaling the lichen-bark-dusted air. Upland grass with larks singing; the stilly drip in golden coverts when sun came after rain; gorse on wind-blown commons; horses turning and turning at the end of the long mole-coloured furrows; river waters now bright, now green-tinged beneath the willows; thatch and its wood smoke; swathed hay meadows, tawnied cornfields; the blueish distances beyond; and the ever-changing sky—all these were as jewels in her mind, but the chief was this white magic of the spring. She became conscious that the long grass was drenched and her shoes and stockings wet through; there was light enough to see in that grass the stars of jonquil, grape hyacinth and the pale cast-out tulips; there would be polyanthus, too, blue-bells and cowslips—a few. She slipped on upward, cleared the trees and stood a moment to look back at the whiteness of the whole. 'It might have dropped from the moon,' she thought: 'My best stockings, too!'

Across the low-walled fruit garden and lawn she came to the terrace. Past eleven! Only her father's study window lighted on the ground floor! How like that other night!

'Shan't tell him,' she thought, and tapped on it.

He let her in.

"Hallo, Dinny, you didn't stop the night at Mount Street, then?"

"No, Dad, there's a limit to my powers of borrowing nightgowns."

"Sit down and have some tea. I was just going to make some."

"Darling, I came through the orchard and I'm wet to the knees."

"Take off your stockings; here's an old pair of slippers."

Dinny slipped off the stockings and sat contemplating her legs in the lamplight, while the General lit the etna. He liked to do things for himself. She watched him bending over the tea things, and thought how trim he still was, and how quick and precise his movements. His browned hands, with little dark hairs on them, had long clever fingers. He stood up, motionless, watching the flame.

"Wants a new wick," he said. "There's going to be bad trouble in India, I'm afraid."

"India seems to be getting almost more trouble than it's worth to us."

The General turned his face with its high but small cheek-bones; his eyes rested on her, and his thin lips beneath the close little grey moustache smiled.

"That often happens with trusts, Dinny. You've got very nice legs."

"So I ought, dear, considering you and mother."

"Mine are all right for a boot—stringy. Did you ask Mr. Desert down?"

"No, not to-day."

The General put his hands into his side pockets. He had taken off his dinner jacket and was wearing an old snuff-coloured shooting coat; Dinny noticed that the cuffs were slightly frayed, and one leather button missing. His dark, high-shaped eyebrows contracted till there were three ridges right in the centre of his forehead; he said gently:

"I don't understand that change of religion, you know, Dinny. Milk or lemon?"

"Lemon, please."

She was thinking: 'Now is the moment, after all. Courage!'

"Two lumps?"

"Three with lemon, Dad."

The General took up the tongs. He dropped three lumps into the cup, then a slice of lemon, put back the tongs, and bent down to the kettle.

"Boiling," he said, and filled up the cup; he put a covered spoonful of tea into it, withdrew the spoon and handed the cup to his daughter.

Dinny sat stirring the thin golden liquid. She took a sip, rested the cup on her lap, and turned her face up to him.

"I can explain it, Dad," and thought: 'It will only make him understand even less.'

The General filled his own cup, and sat down. Dinny clutched her spoon.

"You see, when Wilfrid was far out in Darfur he ran into a nest of fanatical Arabs, remaining from the Mahdi times. The chief of them had him brought into his tent and offered him his life if he would embrace Islam."

She saw her father make a little convulsive movement, so that some of the tea was spilled into his saucer. He raised the cup and poured it back. Dinny went on:

"Wilfrid is like most of us nowadays about belief, only a great deal more so. It isn't that he doesn't believe in Christianity, he actually hates any set forms of religion, he thinks they divide mankind and do more harm and bring more suffering than anything else. And then, you know—or you would if you'd read his poetry, Dad—the war left him very bitter about the way lives are thrown away, simply spilled out like water at the orders of people who don't know what they're about."

Again the General made that slight convulsive movement.

"Yes, Dad, but I've heard Hubert talk in much the same way about that. Anyway it has left Wilfrid with a horror of wasting life, and the deepest distrust of all shibboleths and beliefs. He only had about five minutes to decide in. It wasn't cowardice, it was just bitter scorn that men can waste each other's lives for beliefs that to him seem equally futile. And he just shrugged and accepted. Having accepted he had to keep his word and go through the forms. Of course, you don't know him, so I suppose it's useless." She sighed and drank thirstily.

The General had put his own cup down; he rose, filled a pipe, lighted it and stood by the hearth. His face was lined and dark and grave. At last he said:

"I'm out of my depth. Is the religion of one's fathers for hundreds of years to go for nothing, then? Is all that has made us the proudest people in the world to be chucked away at the bidding of an Arab? Have men like the Lawrences, John Nicholson, Chamberlayne, Sandeman, a thousand others, who spent and gave their lives to build up an idea of the English as brave men and true, to be knocked into a cocked hat by every Englishman who's threatened with a pistol?"

Dinny's cup clattered on its saucer.

"Yes, but if not by every Englishman, Dinny, why by one? Why by this one?"

Quivering all over, Dinny did not answer. Neither Adrian nor Sir Lawrence had made her feel like this—for the first time she had been reached and moved by the other side. Some age-long string had been pulled within her, or she was infected by the emotion of one whom she had always admired and loved and whom she had hardly ever seen stirred to eloquence. She could not speak.

"I don't know if I'm a religious man," the General went on, "the faith of my fathers is enough for me"—and he made a gesture, as if adding, 'I leave myself aside'—"but Dinny, I could not take dictation of that sort; I could not, and I cannot understand how he could have."

Dinny said, quietly: "I won't try to make you, Dad; let's take it that you can't. Most people have done something in their lives that other people could not understand if it were known. The difference here is that this thing of Wilfrid's *is* known."

"You mean the threat is known—the reason for the——?"

Dinny nodded.

"How?"

"A Mr. Yule brought the story back from Egypt; Uncle Lawrence thinks it can't be scotched. I want you to know the worst." She gathered her wet stockings and shoes in her hand. "Would you mind telling Mother and Hubert for me, Dad?" And she stood up.

The General drew deeply at his pipe, which emitted a gurgling sound.

"Your pipe wants cleaning, dear. I'll do it to-morrow."

"He'll be a pariah," burst from the General, "he'll be a pariah! Dinny, Dinny!"

No two words could have moved and disarmed her more. At one stroke they shifted his opposition from the personal to the altruistic.

She bit her lip and said:

"Dad, I shall pipe my eye if I stay down here with you. And my feet are very cold. Good-night, darling!"

She turned and went quickly to the door, whence she saw him standing like a horse that had just been harnessed.

She went up to her room and sat on her bed, rubbing her cold feet one against the other. It was done! Now she had only to confront the feeling that would henceforth surround her like a wall over which she must climb to the fulfilment of her love. And what surprised her most while she rubbed and rubbed, was knowing that her father's words had drawn from her a secret endorsement which had not made the slightest inroad on her feeling for Wilfrid. Was love, then, quite detached from judgment? Was the old image of a blind God true? Was it even true that defects in the loved one made him the dearer? That seemed borne out, at all events, by the dislike one had for the too good people in books; one's revolt against the heroic figure; one's impatience at the sight of virtue rewarded.

'Is it,' she thought, 'that my family's standard is higher than mine; or is it simply that I want him close to me, and don't care what he is or does so long as he comes?' And she had a strange and sudden feeling of knowing Wilfrid to the very core, with all his faults and shortcomings, and with a something that redeemed and made up for them, and would keep her love alive, for in that, in that only, was an element mysterious to her. And she thought with a rueful smile: 'All evil I know by instinct; it's goodness, truth, beauty, that keep me guessing!' And almost too tired to undress, she got into bed.

CHAPTER 13

'The briery,' Jack Muskham's residence at Royston, was old-fashioned and low, unpretentious without, comfortable within. It was lined with the effigies of race-horses and sporting prints. Only in one room, seldom used, was any sign of a previous existence. 'Here,' as an American newspaper man put it, when he came to interview the 'last of the dandies' on the subject of bloodstock, 'here were evidences of this aristocrat's early life in our glorious Southland. Here we sensed his adventurous existence in the wide open spaces of New Mexico, Arizona and Sonora, when as a very young man this dude of dudes rounded cattle, and rode the bucking bronco with our boys out there. Here were specimens of Navaho rugs and silver work; the plaited horsehair from El Paso; the great cowboy hats; and a set of Mexican harness dripping with silver. I questioned my host about this phase of his career. "Oh! that," he said, in his Britisher's drawl, "I guess"—yes, he said guess—"I had five years cowpunchin' when I was a youngster. You see, I had only one thought—horses, and my father thought that might be better for me than ridin' steeplechases here, don't you know."

'"Can I put a date to that?" I asked this long lean patrician with the watchful eyes, and the languid manner.

'"Why, yes," he answered, "I left Eton College in '96, and went straight out to Tommy Delahay's ranch in Texas. I came back in 1901, and except for the war I've been breedin' bloodstock ever since, don't you know."

'"And in the war?" I queried.

'"Oh!" he answered; and I seemed to sense that I was intruding on him: "The usual thing. Yeomanry, cavalry, trenches, and that. The last two years I was in charge of remounts for my division. You see," he added and a smile played about his well-regulated features, "horses come natural to me."

'"Tell me, Mr. Muskham," I asked: "Did you enjoy your life over with us out there?"

'"Enjoy?" he said: "Rather, don't you know."'

The interview, when reproduced in a Western paper was baptised with the heading:

"British Dandy Enjoyed
Life In Southland Says"

The stud farm was fully a mile from Royston Village, and at precisely a quarter to ten every day, when not away at races, bloodstock sales, or what not, Jack Muskham mounted his potter pony and ambled off to what the journalists had termed his 'equine nursery.' He was accustomed to point to this potter pony as an example of what horses become if never spoken to in but a gentle voice. She was an intelligent little three-year-old, three-quarter-bred, with a fine mouse-coloured coat over which someone seemed to have thrown a bottle of ink and then imperfectly removed the splashes. Beyond a slightly ragged crescent on her forehead, she had no white at all; her mane was hogged, and her long tail banged just below her hocks. Her eyes were quiet and bright, and—for a horse—her teeth were pearly. She moved with a daisy-clipping action, quickly recovering from any stumble. Ridden with a single loose rein applied to her neck, her mouth was never touched. She was but fourteen-two, and Jack Muskham's legs, he using long stirrup leathers, came down very far. Riding her, as he said, was like sitting in a very easy chair. Besides himself, only one boy, chosen for the quietness of his voice, hands, nerves and temper, was allowed to handle her.

Dismounting from this animal at the gate of the quadrangular yard which formed the stables, Jack Muskham would enter, smoking one of his special cigarettes in a short amber holder, and be joined on the central grass by his stud groom. They would then go round the boxes together— where the foals would be with their mothers, and the yearlings boxed two by two—and have this and that one out to be led round the tan track which adjoined the boxes round the yard. After this inspection, they would pass under the archway opposite the entrance, and go to the paddocks to see the mares, foals and yearlings at grass. Discipline in his 'equine nursery' was perfect; to all seeming his employees were as quiet, as clean, as well-behaved as the horses they had charge of. From the moment of his entrance to the moment when he emerged and remounted his potter pony, his talk would be of horses—sparing and to the point. And, daily, there were so many little things to see and say, that he was rarely back at the house till one o'clock. He never discussed breeding on its scientific side with his stud groom, in spite of that functionary's considerable knowledge, because, to Jack Muskham, the subject was as much a matter of high politics as the foreign relations of his country are to a secretary for foreign affairs. His mating decisions were made in privacy, following the conclusions of close study welded to what he would have termed his 'flair,' and others might have called his prejudices. Stars might come loose, Prime Ministers be knighted, Archdukes restored, towns swallowed up by earthquakes, together with all other forms of catastrophe, so long as Jack Muskham could blend St. Simon on Speculum with the right dashes of Hampton and Bend Or; or, in accordance with a more original theory of his own, could get old Herod through Le Sancy at the extreme top and extreme bottom of a pedigree which had Carbine and Barcaldine blood in between. He was, in fact, an idealist. To breed the perfect horse was his ideal, as little realistic, perhaps, as the ideals of other men, and far more absorbing—in his view. Not that he ever mentioned it—one did not use such a word! Nor did he bet, so that he was never deflected in his judgments by earthly desires. Tall, in his cigar-brown overcoat specially lined with camel's hair, and his fawn-coloured buckskin shoes and fawn-coloured face, he was probably the most familiar figure at Newmarket; nor was there any member of the Jockey Club, with the exception of three, whose dicta were more respected. He was in fact an outstanding example of the eminence in his walk of life that can be attained by a man who serves a single end with complete and silent fidelity. In truth, behind this ideal of the perfect horse lay the shape of his own soul. Jack Muskham was a formalist, one of the few survivors in a form-shattering age; and that his formalism had pitched on the horse for its conspicuous expression was due in part to the completeness with which the race-horse was tied to the stud book, in part to the essential symmetry of that animal, and in part to the refuge the cult of it afforded from the whirr, untidiness, glare, blare, unending scepticism and intrusive blatancy of what he termed "this mongrel age."

In 'the Briery' two men did all the work, except scrubbing, for which a woman came in daily. But for that, there was no sign in all the house that women existed in this world. It was monastic as a club which has not succumbed to female service, and as much more comfortable, as it was smaller. The rooms were low, and two wide staircases reached the only upper floor, where the rooms were lower still. The books, apart from endless volumes relating to the race-horse, were either works of travel or of history, or detective novels; other fiction, with its scepticism, slangy diction, descriptions, sentiment, and sensation was absent, if an exception be made of complete sets of Surtees, Whyte Melville and Thackeray.

As, in the pursuit by men of their ideals, there is almost always some saving element of irony, so in the case of Jack Muskham. He, whose aim in life was the production of the perfect thoroughbred, was actually engaged in an attempt to cast the thoroughbred, as hitherto conceived, from muzzle to crupper, on the scrap-heap, and substitute for it an animal with a cross of blood not as yet in the Stud Book!

Unconscious of this discrepancy, he was seated at lunch with Telfourd Yule, still discussing the transportation of Arab mares, when Sir Lawrence Mont was announced.

"Lunch, Lawrence?"

"I have lunched, Jack. But coffee would be the very thing; also some brandy."

"Then let's go into the other room."

"You have here," said Sir Lawrence, "what I never thought to see again, the bachelor's box of my youth. Jack is very remarkable, Mr. Yule. A man who can afford to date in these days is a genius. Do I see 'Surtees' and 'Whyte Melville' entire? Mr. Yule, what did Mr. Waffles say in 'Soapy

Sponge's Sporting Tour,' when they were holding Caingey up by the heels to let the water run out of his boots?"

Yule's humorous mug spread, but he spoke not.

"Exactly!" said Sir Lawrence: "No one knows now-a-days. He said: 'Why, Caingey, old boy, you look like a boiled porpoise with parsley sauce.' Ah! and what did Mr. Sawyer answer in 'Market Harboro,' when the Honourable Crasher drove at the turnpike gate, saying: 'It's open, I think'?"

Yule's face expanded further, and he was still more silent.

"Dear, dear! Jack?"

"He said: 'I think not.'"

"Good! And was it? No!" Sir Lawrence sank into a chair. "Well! Have you arranged to steal that mare? Fine! And when you get her over?"

"I shall put her to the most suitable sire standing. I shall mate the result again with the most suitable sire or mare I can find. Then I shall match the result privately against the best of our own of the same age. If I'm proved right I ought to be able to get her entered in the Stud Book. I'm trying to get three mares by the way."

"How old are you, Jack?"

"Rising fifty-three."

"I'm sorry. This is good coffee."

After that the three sat silent, awaiting the real purpose of this visit.

"I've come, Mr. Yule," said Sir Lawrence, suddenly, "about that affair of young Desert's."

"Not true, I hope?"

"Unfortunately, yes. He makes no bones about it." And turning his monocle on Jack Muskham's face, he saw there exactly what he had expected.

"A man," said Muskham, slowly, "ought to keep his form better than that, even if he *is* a poet."

"We won't go into the rights and wrongs, Jack. Let it go at what you say. All the same," and Sir Lawrence's manner acquired strange gravity, "I want you two to keep mum. If it comes out, it can't be helped, but I beg that you'll neither of you say anything."

"I don't like the look of the fellow," said Muskham, shortly.

"That applies to at least nine-tenths of the people we see about; the reason is not adequate."

"He's one of those bitter sceptical young moderns, with no real knowledge, and no reverence for anything."

"I know you hold a brief for the past, Jack, but don't bring it into this."

"Why not?"

"Well, I didn't want to mention it, but he's engaged to my favourite niece, Dinny Cherrell."

"That nice girl?"

"Yes. We none of us like it, except my boy Michael, who still swears

311

by Desert. But Dinny has got her teeth into it, and I don't think anything will budge her."

"She can't be allowed to marry a man who's bound for Coventry the moment this comes out."

"The more he's taboo, the closer she'll stick to him."

"I like *that*," said Muskham. "What do you say, Yule?"

"It's no affair of mine. If Sir Lawrence wants me to say nothing, I shall say nothing."

"Of course it's no affair of ours; all the same, if making it known would stop your niece, I'd do it. I call it a damned shame!"

"It would have just the opposite effect, Jack. Mr. Yule, you know a lot about the Press. Suppose this story leaks into the Press as it well may; what then?"

Yule's eyes snapped.

"First they'll tell it vaguely of a certain English traveller; then they'll find out whether it's denied by Desert; then they'll tell it of him, with a good many details wrong, but not so wrong as all that. If he admits it, he can't object. The Press is pretty fair, and damned inaccurate."

Sir Lawrence nodded. "If I knew anyone going in for journalism, I should say: 'Be strictly accurate, and you will be unique.' I have not read any absolutely accurate personal paragraphs in the papers since the war."

"That's their point," said Yule, "they get a double shot—first the inaccurate report and then the correction."

"I loathe the Press," said Muskham. "I had an American Pressman here. There he sat, and short of kicking him out—I don't know what on earth he made of me."

"Yes, you date, Jack. To you Marconi and Edison are the world's two greatest malefactors. Is it agreed, then, about young Desert?"

"Yes," said Yule; and Muskham nodded.

Sir Lawrence passed swiftly from the subject.

"Nice country about here. Are you staying long, Mr. Yule?"

"I go back to Town this afternoon."

"Let me take you."

"Willingly."

Half an hour later they had started.

"My cousin Jack," said Sir Lawrence, "ought to be left to the nation. In Washington there's a museum with groups of the early Americans under glass smoking the communal pipe, holding tomahawks over each other, and that sort of thing. One might have Jack—" Sir Lawrence paused: "That's the trouble! How could one have Jack preserved? It's so difficult to perpetuate the unemphatic. You can catch anything that jumps around; but when there's no attitude except a watchful languor—And yet a man with a God of his own."

" 'Form,' and Muskham is its prophet."

"He might, of course," murmured Sir Lawrence, "be preserved in the act of fighting a duel. That's perhaps the only human activity formal enough."

"'Form's' doomed," said Yule.

"H'm! Nothing so hard to kill as the sense of shape. For what *is* life but the sense of shape, Mr. Yule? Reduce everything to dead similarity, and still shape will 'out.'"

"Yes," said Yule, "but form is shape brought to perfection point and standardised; and perfection bores our bright young things."

"That nice expression. But do they exist outside books, Mr. Yule?"

"Don't they! And yawn-making—as they'd call it! I'd sooner attend City dinners for the rest of my life than spend a week-end in the company of those bright young things."

"I doubt," said Sir Lawrence, "whether I've come across them."

"You should thank God. They never stop talking day or night, not even in their couplings."

"You don't seem to like them."

"Well," said Yule, looking like a gargoyle, "they can't stand me any more than I can stand them. A boring little crowd, but, luckily, of no importance."

"I hope," said Sir Lawrence, "that Jack is not making the mistake of thinking young Desert is one."

"Muskham's never met a bright young thing. No; what gets his goat about Desert is the look of his face. It's a deuced strange face."

"Lost angel," said Sir Lawrence: "'Spiritual pride, my buck!' Something fine about it."

Yule nodded. "I don't mind it myself; and his verse is good. But all revolt's anathema to Muskham. He likes mentality clipped, with its mane plaited, stepping delicately to the snaffle."

"I don't know," murmured Sir Lawrence, "I think those two might like each other, if they could shoot each other first. Queer people we English!"

CHAPTER 14

WHEN ABOUT THE SAME TIME that afternoon Adrian entered his brother's parish and traversed the mean street leading to the Vicarage of St. Augustine's-in-the-Meads, English people were being almost too well illustrated six doors round the corner.

An ambulance stood in front of a house without a future, and all who had something better to do were watching it. Adrian made one of the party. From the miserable edifice two men and a nurse were bearing the stretched-out body of a child, followed by a wailing, middle-aged, red-faced woman, and a growling, white-faced man with a drooping moustache.

"What's up?" said Adrian to a policeman.

"The child's got to have an operation. You'd think she was goin' to be murdered, instead of havin' the best that care can give her. That's the Vicar. If he can't quiet 'em, no one can."

Adrian saw his brother come out of the house and join the white-faced man. The growling ceased, but the woman's wails increased. The child was ensconced by now in the ambulance, and the mother made an unwieldy rush at the door.

"Where's their sense?" said the policeman stepping forward.

Adrian saw Hilary put his hand on the woman's shoulder. She turned as if to deliver a wide-mouthed imprecation, but a mere whimper issued. Hilary put his arm through hers, and drew her quietly into the house. The ambulance drove away. Adrian moved up to the white-faced man and offered him a cigarette. He took it with a "Thanks, Mister," and followed his wife.

All was over. The little crowd had gone. The policeman stood there alone.

"The Vicar's a wonder," he said.

"My brother," said Adrian.

The policeman looked at him more respectfully.

"A rare card, Sir, the Vicar."

"I quite agree. Was that child very bad?"

"Won't live the day out, unless they operate. Seems as if they'd saved it up to make a close run. Just an accident the Vicar happening on it. Some people'd rather die than go into 'ospitals, let alone their children."

"Independence," said Adrian. "I understand the feeling."

"Well, if you put it that way, Sir, so do I. Still they've got a wretched home in there, and everything of the best in the 'ospital."

" 'Be it ever so humble—'" quoted Adrian.

"That's right. And in my opinion it's responsible for these slums. Very slummy round these parts, but try and move the people, and don't they let you know! The Vicar does good work, reconditionin' the 'ouses, as they call it. If you want him, I'll go tell him."

"Oh! I'll wait."

"You'd be surprised," said the policeman, "the things people'll put up with sooner than be messed about. And you can call it what you like: Socialism, Communism, Government by the people for the people, all comes to that in the end, messin' you about. Here! You move on! No hawkin' in this street!"

A man with a barrow who had looked as if he had been going to cry 'Winkles!' altered the shape of his mouth.

Adrian, stirred by the confusion of the policeman's philosophy, waited in hopes of more, but at this moment Hilary emerged and came towards them.

"It won't be their fault if she lives," he said, and answering the policeman's salute, added: "Are those petunias coming up, Bell?"

"They are, Sir; my wife thinks no end of 'em."

"Splendid! Look here! You'll pass the hospital on your way home, you might ask about that child for me; and ring me if the news is bad."

"I will, Vicar; pleased to do it."

"Thanks, Bell. Now, old man, let's go in and have some tea."

Mrs. Hilary being at a meeting, the brothers had tea by themselves.

"I've come about Dinny," said Adrian, and unfolded her story.

Hilary lighted a pipe. "That saying," he said at last: " 'Judge not that ye be not judged,' is extraordinarily comforting, until you've got to do something about it. After that it appears to amount to less than nothing; all action is based on judgments, tacit or not. Is Dinny very much in love?"

Adrian nodded. Hilary drew deeply at his pipe.

"I don't like it a little bit, then. I've always wanted a clear sky for Dinny; and this looks to me like a sirocco. I suppose no amount of putting it to her from other people's points of view is any good?"

"I should say none."

"Is there anything you want me to do?"

Adrian shook his head. "I only wanted your reaction."

"Just sorrow that Dinny's going to have a bad time. As to that recantation, my cloth rises on me, but whether it rises because I'm a parson, or a public-school Englishman, I don't know. I suspect the older Adam."

"If Dinny means to stick to this," said Adrian, "one must stick to her. I always feel that if a thing one hates has to happen to a person one loves, one can only help by swallowing the idea of it whole. I shall try to like him, and see his point of view."

315

"He probably hasn't one," said Hilary. "*Au fond,* you know, like 'Lord Jim,' he just jumped; and he almost certainly knows it at heart."

"The more tragic for them both; and the more necessary to stand by."

Hilary nodded.

"Poor old Con will be badly hit. It gives such a chance to people to play the Pharisee. I can see the skirts being drawn aside."

"Perhaps," said Adrian, "modern scepticism will just shrug its shoulders and say: 'Another little superstition gone west!' "

Hilary shook his head.

"Human nature, in the large, will take the view that he kow-towed to save his life. However sceptical people are now-a-days about religion, patriotism, the Empire, the word gentleman and all that, they still don't like cowardice—to put it crudely. I don't mean to say that a lot of them aren't cowards, but they still don't like it in other people; and if they can safely show their dislike, they will."

"Perhaps the thing won't come out."

"Bound to one way or another; and, for young Desert, the sooner the better. Give him a chance to captain his soul again. Poor little Dinny! This'll test her sense of humour. Oh! dear me! I feel older. What does Michael say?"

"Haven't seen him since."

"Do Lawrence and Em know?"

"Probably."

"Otherwise it's to be kept dark, eh?"

"Yes. Well, I must be getting on."

"I," said Hilary, "shall carve my feelings into my Roman galley; I shall get half an hour at it, unless that child has collapsed."

Adrian strode on to Bloomsbury. And while he went he tried to put himself in the place of one threatened with sudden extinction. No future life, no chance of seeing again those he loved; no promise, assured or even vague, of future conscious experience analogous to that of this life!

'It's the sudden personal emergency coming out of the blue,' he thought, 'with no eyes on you, that's the acid test. Who among us knows how he'll come through it?'

His brothers, the soldier and the priest, would accept extinction as a matter of simple duty; even his brother the judge, though he would want to argue the point, and might convert his executioner. 'But I?' he thought. 'How rotten to die like that for a belief I haven't got, in a remote corner of the earth, without even the satisfaction of knowing that my death was going to benefit anybody, or would ever be known!' Without professional or official prestige to preserve, faced by such an issue, requiring immediate decision, one would have no time to weigh and balance; would be thrown back on instinct. One's temperament would decide. And if it were like young Desert's, judging from his verse; if he were accustomed to being in opposition to his fellows, or at least out of touch with them; scornful of convention and matter-of-fact English bull-doggedness; secretly, perhaps, more in sympathy with Arabs than with his own countrymen, would he not almost infallibly decide as Desert had? 'God knows how I should have acted,' thought Adrian, 'but I understand, and in a way I sympathise. Anyway, I'm with Dinny in this, and I'll see her through; as she saw me through that Ferse business.' And having reached a conclusion, he felt better. . . .

But Hilary carved away at his Roman galley. Those classical studies he had so neglected had led up to his becoming a parson, and he could no longer understand why. What sort of young man could he have been to think he was fit for it? Why had he not taken to forestry, become a cowboy, or done almost anything that kept him out of doors instead of in the slummy heart of a dim city? Was he or was he not based on revelation? And, if not, on what was he based? Planing away at an after deck such as that whence those early plumbers, the Romans, had caused so many foreigners to perspire freely, he thought 'I serve an idea, with a superstructure which doesn't bear examination.' Still, the good of mankind was worth working for! A doctor did it in the midst of humbug and ceremony. A statesman, though he knew that democracy, which made him a statesman, was ignorance personified. One used forms in which one didn't believe, and even exhorted others to believe in them. Life was a practical matter of compromise. 'We're all Jesuits,' he thought, 'using doubtful means to good ends. I should have had to die for my cloth, as a soldier dies for his. But that's neither here nor there!'

The telephone bell rang, and a voice said:

"The Vicar! . . . Yes, Sir! . . . That girl. Too far gone to operate. So if you'd come, Sir."

Hilary put down the receiver, snatched his hat and ran out of the house. Of all his many duties the deathbed was least to his taste, and, when he alighted from the taxi before the hospital, the lined mask of his face concealed real dread. Such a child! And nothing to be done except patter a few prayers and hold her hand. Criminal the way her parents had let it run on till it was too late. But to imprison them for it would be to imprison the whole British race, which never took steps to interfere with its independence, till the last minute, and that too late!

"This way, Sir," said a nurse.

In the whiteness and order of a small preliminary room Hilary saw the little figure, white covered, collapsed and with a deathly face. He sat down beside it, groping for words with which to warm the child's last minutes.

'Shan't pray,' he thought, 'she's too young.'

The child's eyes, struggling out of their morphined immobility, flitted with terror round the room, and fixed themselves, horror-stricken, first on the white figure of the nurse, then the doctor in his overalls. Hilary raised his hand.

"D'you mind," he said, "leaving her with me a moment?"

They passed into an adjoining room.

"Loo!" said Hilary, softly.

Recalled by his voice from their terrified wandering, the child's eyes rested on a smile.

"Isn't this a nice clean place? Loo! What d'you like best in all the world?"

The answer came almost inaudibly from the white puckered lips: "Pictures."

"That's exactly what you're going to have, every day—twice a day. Think of that. Shut your eyes and have a nice sleep, and when you wake the pictures will begin. Shut your eyes! And I'll tell you a story. Nothing's going to happen to you. See! I'm here."

He thought she had closed her eyes, but pain gripped her suddenly again; she began whimpering and then screamed.

"God!" murmured Hilary: "Another touch, doctor, quick!"

The doctor injected morphia.

"Leave us alone again."

The doctor slipped away, and the child's eyes came slowly back to Hilary's smile. He laid his fingers on her small emaciated hand.

"Now, Loo, listen!

'The Walrus and the Carpenter were walking hand in hand,
They wept like anything to see such quantities of sand.
"If seven maids with seven brooms could sweep for half a year,
Do you suppose," the Walrus said, "that they could get it clear?"
"I doubt it," said the Carpenter, and shed a bitter tear!'"

On and on went Hilary, reciting "The Mad Hatter's Tea-Party." And, while he murmured, the child's eyes closed, the small hand lost warmth.

He felt the cold penetrating his own hand and thought: 'Now, God, if you are—give her pictures!'

CHAPTER 15

WHEN DINNY opened her eyes on the morning after she had told her father, she could not remember what her trouble was. Realisation caused her to sit up with a feeling of terror. Suppose Wilfrid ran away from it all, back to the East or further! He well might and think he was doing it for her sake.

'I can't wait till Thursday,' she thought: 'I must go up. If only I had money, in case—!' She rummaged out her trinkets and took hasty stock of them. The two gentlemen of South Molton Street! In the matter of Jean's emerald pendant they had behaved beautifully. She made a little parcel of her pledgeable ornaments, reserving the two or three she normally wore. There were none of much value, and to get a hundred pounds on them, she felt, would strain the benevolence of South Molton Street.

At breakfast they all behaved as if nothing had happened. So, then, they all knew the worst!

'Playing the angel!' she thought.

When her father announced that he was going up to Town, she said she would come with him.

He looked at her, rather like a monkey questioning man's right not to be one too. Why had she never before noticed that his brown eyes could have that flickering mournfulness?

"Very well," he said.

"Shall I drive you?" asked Jean.

"Thankfully accepted," murmured Dinny.

Nobody said a word on the subject occupying all their thoughts.

In the open car she sat beside her father. The may-blossom, rather late, was at its brightest, and its scent qualified the frequent drifts of petrol fume. The sky had the high brooding grey of rain withheld. Their road passed over the Chilterns, through Hampden, Great Missenden, Chalfont and Chorley Wood; land so English that no one, suddenly awakened, could at any moment of the drive have believed he was in any other country. It was a drive Dinny never tired of; but to-day the spring green and brightness of the may and apple bloom, the windings and divings through old villages, could not deflect her attention from the impassive figure by whom she sat. She knew instinctively that he was going to try and see Wilfrid, and, if so—she was, too. But when he talked it was of India.

And when she talked it was of birds. And Jean drove furiously and never looked behind her. Not till they were in the Finchley Road did the General say:

"Where d'you want to be set down, Dinny?"

"Mount Street."

"You're staying up, then?"

"Yes, till Friday."

"We'll drop you and I'll go on to my Club. You'll drive me back this evening, Jean?"

Jean nodded without turning and slid between two vermilion-coloured 'buses, so that two drivers simultaneously used a qualitative word.

Dinny was in a ferment of thought. Dared she telephone Stack to ring her up when her father came? If so, she could time her visit to the minute. Dinny was of those who at once establish liaison with 'staff.' She could not help herself to a potato without unconsciously conveying to the profferer that she was interested in his personality. She always said 'Thank you,' and rarely passed from the presence without having made some remark which betrayed common humanity. She had only seen Stack three times, but she knew he felt that she was a human being, even if she did not come from Barnstaple. She mentally reviewed his no longer youthful figure, his monastic face, black-haired and large-nosed, with eyes full of expression, his curly mouth at once judgmatic and benevolent. He moved upright and almost at a trot. She had seen him look at her as if saying to himself: 'If this is to be our fate, could I do with it? I could.' He was, she felt, permanently devoted to Wilfrid. She determined to risk it. When they drove away from her at Mount Street, she thought: 'I hope I shall never be a father!'

"Can I telephone, Blore?"

"Certainly, Miss."

She gave Wilfrid's number.

"Is that Stack? Miss Cherrell speaking . . . Would you do me a little favour? My father is going to see Mr. Desert to-day, General Sir Conway Cherrell; I don't know at what time, but I want to come myself while he's there . . . Could you ring me up here as soon as he arrives, then? I'll wait in . . . Thank you so very much . . . Is Mr. Desert well? . . . Don't tell him or my father, please, that I'm coming. Thank you ever so!"

'Now,' she thought, 'unless I've misread Dad! There's a picture gallery opposite, I shall be able to see him leave from the window of it.'

No call came before lunch, which she had with her aunt.

"Your Uncle has seen Jack Muskham," said Lady Mont, in the middle of lunch; "Royston, you know; and he brought back the other one, just like a monkey—they won't say anything. But Michael says he mustn't, Dinny."

"Mustn't what, Aunt Em?"

"Publish that poem."

"Oh! but he will."

"Why? Is it good?"

"The best he has ever written."

"So unnecessary."

"Wilfrid isn't ashamed, Aunt Em."

"Such a bore for you, I do think. I suppose one of those companionable marriages wouldn't do, would it?"

"I'm surprised at you, dear."

"Until death—it's a long time—and so much in between. Still, there's our name. And things get about so. I should hate you to get into the papers, Dinny."

"Not more than I should myself, Auntie."

"Fleur got into the papers, libellin'."

"I remember."

"What's that thing that comes back and hits you by mistake?"

"A boomerang?"

"I knew it was Australian. Why do they have an accent like that?"

"Really I don't know, darling."

"And marsupials? Blore, Miss Dinny's glass."

"No more, thank you, Aunt Em. And may I get down?"

"Let's both get down"; and, getting up, Lady Mont regarded her niece with her head on one side: "Deep breathin' and carrots to cool the blood. Why gulfstream, Dinny? What gulf is that?"

"Mexico, dear."

"The eels come from there, I was readin'. Are you goin' out?"

"I'm waiting for a 'phone call."

"When they say tr-r-roubled, it hurts my teeth. Nice girls, I'm sure. Coffee?"

"Yes, *please!*"

"It does. One comes together like a puddin' after it."

Dinny thought: 'Aunt Em always sees more than one thinks.'

"Bein' in love," continued Lady Mont, "is worse in the country—there's the cuckoo. They don't have it in America, somebody said. Perhaps they don't fall in love there. Your Uncle'll know. He came back with a story about a poppa at Nooport. For that you *must* fall in love. At least, it used to be so. I feel other people's insides," continued her Aunt, uncannily: "Where's your father gone?"

"To his Club."

"Did you tell him, Dinny?"

"Yes."

"You're his favourite."

"Oh! no, Clare."

"Fiddle!"

"Did the course of your love run smooth, Aunt Em?"

"I had a good figure," replied her aunt; "too much perhaps; we had then. Lawrence was my first."

"Really?"

321

"Except for choir-boys and our groom, and a soldier or two. There was a little Captain with a black moustache. Inconsiderate, when one's fourteen."

"I suppose your 'wooing' was very decorous?"

"No; your Uncle was passionate. Ninety-one. There'd been no rain for thirty years."

"No such rain?"

"No! No rain at all—I forget where. There's the telephone!"

Dinny reached the 'phone just in front of the butler.

"It'll be for me, Blore, thank you."

She took up the receiver with a shaking hand.

"Yes? . . . I see . . . thank you, Stack . . . thank you very much . . . Will you get me a taxi, Blore?"

She directed the taxi to the gallery opposite Wilfrid's rooms, bought a catalogue, and went upstairs to the window. Here, under pretext of minutely examining Number 33, called 'Rhythm,' a misnomer so far as she could see, she kept watch of the door opposite. Her father could not already have left Wilfrid, for it was only seven minutes from the telephone call. Very soon, however, she saw him issuing from the door, and watched him down the street. His head was bent and he shook it once or twice; she could not see his face, but she could picture its expression.

'Gnawing his moustache,' she thought; 'poor Dad!'

The moment he rounded the corner she ran down, slipped across the street and up the first flight. Outside Wilfrid's door she stood with her hand raised to the bell. Then she rang.

"Am I too late, Stack?"

"The General's just gone, Miss."

"Oh! May I see Mr. Desert? Don't announce me."

"No, Miss," said Stack. Had she ever seen eyes more full of understanding?

Taking a deep breath, she opened the door. Wilfrid was standing at the hearth with his head bent down on his folded arms. She stole silently up, waiting for him to realise her presence.

Suddenly he threw his head up, and saw her.

"Darling!" said Dinny, "so sorry for startling you!" And she tilted her head, with lips a little parted and throat exposed, watching the struggle on his face.

He succumbed and kissed her.

"Dinny, your father——"

"I know. I saw him go. 'Mr. Desert, I believe! My daughter has told me of an engagement, and—er—your position. I—er—have come about that. You have—er—considered what will happen when your—er—escapade out there becomes—er—known. My daughter is of age, she can please herself, but we are all extremely fond of her, and I think you will agree that in the face of such an—er—scandal it would be wholly wrong on your part —er—to consider yourself engaged to her at present.'"

322

"Almost exact."

"And you answered?"

"I'd think it over. He's perfectly right."

"He is perfectly wrong. I have told you before. 'Love is not love which alters when it alteration finds.' Michael thinks you ought not to publish 'The Leopard'."

"I must. I want it off my chest. When I'm not with you I'm hardly sane."

"I know! But, darling, those two are not going to say anything; need it ever come out? Things that don't come out quickly often don't come out at all. Why go to meet trouble?"

"It isn't that. It's some damned fear in me that I *was* yellow. I want the whole thing out. Then, yellow or not, I can hold my head up. Don't you see, Dinny?"

She did see. The look on his face was enough. 'It's my business,' she thought, 'to feel as he does, whatever I think; only so I can help; perhaps only so I can keep him.'

"I understand, perfectly, Michael's wrong. We'll face the music, and our heads shall be 'bloody but unbowed.' But we won't be 'captains of our souls,' whatever happens."

And, having got him to smile, she drew him down beside her. After that long close silence, she opened her eyes with the slow look all women know how to give.

"To-morrow is Thursday, Wilfrid. Will you mind if we drop in on Uncle Adrian on the way home? He's on our side. And about our engagement, we can say we aren't engaged, and *be* all the same. Good-bye, my love!"

Down in the vestibule by the front door as she was opening it, Stack's voice said:

"Excuse me, Miss."

"Yes?"

"I've been with Mr. Desert a long time, and I've been thinking. You're engaged to him, if I don't mistake, Miss?"

"Yes and no, Stack. I hope to marry him, however."

"Quite, Miss. And a good thing, too, if you'll excuse me. Mr. Desert is a sudden gentleman, and I was thinking if we were in leeaison, as you might say, it'd be for his good."

"I quite agree; that's why I rang you up this morning."

"I've seen many young ladies in my time, but never one I'd rather he married, Miss, which is why I've taken the liberty."

Dinny held out her hand. 'I'm terribly glad you did; it's just what I wanted; because things are difficult, and going to be more so, I'm afraid.'

Having polished his hand, Stack took hers, and they exchanged a rather convulsive squeeze.

"I know there's something on his mind," he said. "That's not my business. But I have known him to take very sudden decisions. And if you were to give me your telephone numbers, Miss, I might be of service to you both."

Dinny wrote them down. "This is the town one at my uncle's, Sir Lawrence Mont's, in Mount Street; and this is my country one at Condaford Grange in Oxfordshire. One or the other is almost sure to find me. And thank you ever so. It takes a load off my mind."

"And off mine, Miss. Mr. Desert has every call on me. And I want the best for him. He's not everybody's money, but he's mine."

"And mine, Stack."

"I won't bandy compliments, Miss, but he'll be a lucky one, if you'll excuse me."

Dinny smiled. "No, I shall be the lucky one. Good-bye, and thank you again."

She went away, treading, so to speak, on Cork Street. She had an ally in the lion's mouth; a spy in the friend's camp; a faithful traitor! Thus mixing her metaphors she scurried back to her aunt's house. Her father would almost certainly go there before returning to Condaford.

Seeing his unmistakable old 'bowler' in the hall, she took the precaution of removing her own hat before going to the drawing room. He was talking to her aunt, and they stopped as she came in. Every one would always stop now, as she came in! Looking at them with quiet directness she sat down.

The General's eyes met hers.

"I've been to see Mr. Desert, Dinny."

"I know, dear. He is thinking it over. We shall wait till every one knows, anyway."

The General moved uneasily.

"And if it is any satisfaction to you, we are not formally engaged."

The General gave her a slight bow, and Dinny turned to her aunt, who was fanning a pink face with a piece of lilac-coloured blotting paper.

There was a silence, then the General said:

"When are you going to Lippinghall, Em?"

"Next week," replied Lady Mont, "or is it the week after? Lawrence knows. I'm showin' two gardeners at the Chelsea Flower Show. Boswell and Johnson, Dinny."

"Oh! Are they still with you?"

"More so. Con, you ought to grow pestifera—no, that's not the name —that hairy anemone thing."

"Pulsatilla, Auntie."

"Charmin' flowers. They want lime."

"We're short of lime at Condaford," said the General, "as you ought to know, Em."

"Our azaleas were a dream this year, Aunt Em."

Lady Mont put down the blotting paper.

"I've been tellin' your father, Dinny."

"Thank you, dear."

"That it's no good fussin' you."

Dinny, watching her father's glum face, said: "Do you know that nice shop in Bond Street, Auntie, where they make animals? I got a lovely little Vixen and her cubs there to make Dad like foxes better."

"Huntin'," said Lady Mont, and sighed: "When they get up chimneys, it's rather touchin'."

"Even Dad doesn't like digging out, or stopping earths, do you, Dad?"

"N-no!" said the General, "on the whole, no!"

"Bloodin' children, too," said Lady Mont; "I saw you blooded, Con."

"Messy job, and quite unnecessary! Only the old raw-hide school go in for it now."

"He looked so nasty, Dinny."

"Yes, you haven't got the face for it, Dad. It wants one of those snub-nosed, red-haired, freckled boys, that like killing for the sake of killing."

The General rose.

"I must be going back to the Club. Jean picks me up there. When shall we see you, Dinny? Your mother—" and he stopped.

"Aunt Em's keeping me till Saturday."

The General nodded. He suffered his sister's and daughter's kiss with a face that seemed to say, 'Yes—but——'

From the window Dinny watched his figure moving down the street, and her heart twitched.

"Your father!" said her aunt's voice behind her: "All this is very wearin'!"

"I think it's very dear of Dad not to have mentioned the fact that I'm dependent on him."

"Con *is* a dear," said Lady Mont; "he said the young man was respectful. Who was it said: 'Garoo—garoo'?"

"Lewis Carroll."

"That's what I feel."

Dinny turned from the window.

"Auntie! I don't feel the same being at all as I did two weeks ago. I'm utterly changed. Then I didn't seem to have any desires; now I'm all one desire, and I don't seem to care whether I'm decent or not. Don't say Epsom salts!"

Lady Mont patted her arm.

"'Honour thy father and thy mother,'" she said; "but then there was 'Forsake all and follow me'—you can't tell."

"I can," said Dinny. "Do you know what I'm hoping now? That everything will come out to-morrow. If it did, we could be married at once."

"Let's have some tea, Dinny. Blore, tea! Indian and strong!"

CHAPTER 16

DINNY TOOK her lover to Adrian's door at the Museum the next day, and left him there. Looking round at his tall, hatless, girt-in figure, she saw him give a violent shiver. But he smiled, and even at that distance she felt the beauty of his eyes.

Adrian, already warned, received the young man with what he stigmatised to himself as 'morbid curiosity,' and placed him at once in mental apposition to Dinny. A curiously diverse couple they would make! Yet, with a perception not perhaps unconnected with the custody of skeletons, he had a feeling that his niece was not physically in error. This was a figure that could well stand or lie beside her. Its stringy grace and bony gallantry accorded with her style and slenderness; and the darkened face, with its drawn and bitter lines, had eyes which even Adrian, who had all the public-school-man's impatience of male film stars, could see would be attractive to the female gender. Bones broke the ice to some degree; and over the identity of a supposed Hittite in moderate preservation they became almost cordial. Places and people they had both seen in strange conditions were a further incentive to human feeling. But not till he had taken up his hat to go, did Wilfrid say suddenly:

"Well, Mr. Cherrell, what would *you* do?"

Adrian, who was locking up, halted and considered his questioner with narrowed eyes.

"I'm a poor hand at advice, but Dinny is a precious baggage——"

"She is."

Adrian bent and shut the door of a cabinet.

"This morning," he said, "I watched a solitary ant in my bath-room, trying to make its way and find out about things. I'm sorry to say I dropped some ashes from my pipe on it to see what it would do. Providence all over—always dropping ashes from its pipe on us to observe the result. I've been in several minds, but I've come to the conclusion that if you're really in love with Dinny—" The convulsive movement of Wilfrid's body ended in the tight clenching of his hands on his hat—"as I see you are, and as I know her to be with you, then stand fast and work your way with her through the ashes. She'd rather be in the cart with you than in a Pullman with the rest of us. I believe," and Adrian's face was illuminated by earnestness, "that she is one of those of whom it is not yet written, 'and they

326

twain shall be one *spirit.*'" The young man's face quivered. 'Genuine!'
he thought.

"So think first of her, but not in the 'I love you so that nothing will
induce me to marry you' fashion. Do what she wants—when she wants
it—she's not unreasonable. And I don't believe honestly that you'll either
of you regret it."

Desert took a step towards him, and Adrian could set that he was intensely moved. But he mastered all expression, save a little jerky smile,
made a movement of one hand, turned, and went out.

Adrian continued to shut the doors of cupboards that contained bones.
'That,' he was thinking, 'is the most difficult, and in some ways the most
beautiful face I've seen. The spirit walks upon its waters and is often
nearly drowned. I wonder if that advice was criminal, because for some
reason or other I believe he's going to take it.' And he returned to the reading of a geographic magazine which Wilfrid's visit had interrupted. It
contained a spirited account of an Indian tribe on the Amazon which
had succeeded, even without the aid of American engineers at capitalistic
salaries, in perfecting the Communistic ideal. None of them, apparently,
owned anything. Their whole lives, including the processes of nature,
were passed in the public eye. They wore no clothes, they had no laws;
their only punishment, something in connection with red ants, was inflicted for the only offence, that of keeping anything to themselves. They
lived on the cassava root variegated with monkey, and were the ideal
community!

'A wonderful instance,' thought Adrian, 'of how the life of man runs
in cycles. For the last twenty thousand years we've been trying, as we
thought, to improve on the form of existence practised by these Indians,
only to find it re-introduced as the perfect form of life.'

He sat for a time with a smile biting deep into the folds of his mouth.
Doctrinaires, extremists! That Arab who put a pistol to young Desert's
head was a symbol of the most mischievous trait in human nature! Ideas
and creeds, what were they but half truths, only useful in so far as they
helped to keep life balanced. The geographical magazine slipped off his
knee.

He stopped on the way home in the garden of his square to feel the
sun on his cheek and listen to a blackbird. He had all he wanted in life;
the woman he loved, fair health, a fair salary—seven hundred a year and
the prospect of a pension—two adorable children, not his own, so that
he was free from the misgivings of more normal parents; an absorbing
job, a love of nature, and another thirty years, perhaps, before him. 'If
at this moment,' he thought, 'someone put a pistol to my head and said:
"Adrian Cherrell, renounce Christianity or out go your brains!" should
I say with Clive in India: "Shoot me and be damned!"' And he could not
answer. The blackbird continued to sing, the young leaves to twitter in
the breeze, the sun to warm his cheek, and life to be desirable in the quiet
of that one-time fashionable square. . . .

Dinny, when she left those two on the verge of acquaintanceship, had paused, in two minds and then gone north to St. Augustine's-in-the-Meads. Her instinct was to sap the opposition of the outlying portions of her family, so as to isolate the defences of her immediate people. She moved towards the heart of practical Christianity with certain rather fearful exhilaration.

Her Aunt May was in the act of dispensing tea to two young ex-Collegians, before their departure to a club where they superintended the skittles, chess, draughts and ping-pong of the neighbourhood.

"If you want Hilary, Dinny, he had two committees, but they might collapse because he's almost the whole of both."

"You and Uncle know about me, I suppose?"

Mrs. Hilary nodded. She was looking very fresh in a sprigged dress.

"Would you mind telling me what Uncle feels about it?"

"I'd rather leave that to him, Dinny. We neither of us remember Mr. Desert very well."

"People who don't know him well will always misjudge him. But neither you nor Uncle care what other people think." She said this with a guileless expression which by no means deceived Mrs. Hilary, accustomed to Women's Institutes.

"We're neither of us very orthodox, as you know, Dinny, but we do both of us believe very deeply in what Christianity stands for, and it's no good pretending we don't."

Dinny thought a moment.

"Is that more than gentleness and courage and self-sacrifice, and must one be a Christian to have those?"

"I'd rather not talk about it. I should be sorry to say anything that would put me in a position different from Hilary's."

"Auntie, how model of you!"

Mrs. Hilary smiled. And Dinny knew that judgment in this quarter was definitely reserved.

She waited, talking of other things, till Hilary came in. He was looking pale and worried. Her aunt gave him tea, passed a hand over his forehead, and went out.

Hilary drank off his tea and filled his pipe with a knot of tobacco screwed up in a circular paper.

"Why Corporations, Dinny? Why not three doctors, three engineers, three architects, an adding machine, and a man of imagination to work it and keep them straight?"

"Are you in trouble, Uncle?"

"Yes, gutting houses on an overdraft is ageing enough, without corporational red tape."

Looking at his worn but smiling face, Dinny thought: 'I can't bother him with my little affairs.' "You and Aunt May couldn't spare time, I suppose, to come to the Chelsea Flower Show on Tuesday?"

"My goodness," said Hilary, sticking one end of a match into the centre of the knob and lighting it with the other end, "how I would love to stand in a tent and smell azaleas!"

"We thought of going at one o'clock, so as to avoid the worst of the crush. Aunt Em would send for you."

"Can't promise, so don't send. If we're not at the main entrance at one you'll know that Providence has intervened. And now, what about you? Adrian has told me."

"I don't want to bother you, Uncle."

Hilary's shrewd blue eyes almost disappeared. He expelled a cloud of smoke.

"Nothing that concerns you will bother me, my dear, except in so far as it's going to hurt you. I suppose you *must*, Dinny?"

"Yes, I must."

Hilary sighed.

"In that case it remains to make the best of it. But the world loves the martyrdom of others. I'm afraid he'll have a bad Press, as they say."

"I'm sure he will."

"I can only just remember him, as a rather tall scornful young man in a buff waistcoat. Has he lost the scorn?"

Dinny smiled.

"It's not the side I see much of at present."

"I sincerely trust," said Hilary, "that he has not what they call devouring passions."

"Not so far as I have observed."

"I mean, Dinny, that once that type has eaten its cake, it shows all the old Adam with a special virulence. Do you get me?"

"Yes. But I believe it's a 'marriage of true minds' with us."

"Then, my dear, God's speed. Only, when people begin to throw bricks, don't resent it. You're doing this with your eyes open, and you'll have no right to. Harder to bear than having your own toe trodden on, is seeing one you love batted over the head. So catch hold of yourself hard at the start, and go on catching hold, or you'll make it worse for him. If I'm not wrong, Dinny, you can get very hot about things."

"I'll try not to. When Wilfrid's book of poems comes out, I want you to read 'The Leopard,' it gives his state of mind about the whole thing."

"Oh!" said Hilary, blankly. "Justification? That's a mistake."

"That's what Michael says. I don't know whether it is or not; I think in the end—not. Anyway it's coming out."

"There beginneth a real dog-fight. 'Turn the other cheek' and 'too proud to fight' would have been better left unsaid. All the same, it's asking for trouble, and that's all about it."

"I can't help it, Uncle."

"I realise that, Dinny; it's when I think of the number of things you won't be able to help that I feel so blue. And what about Condaford? Is it going to cut you off from that?"

"People do come round, except in novels; and even there they have to in the end, or else die; so that the heroine may be happy. Will you say a word for us to Father if you see him, Uncle?"

"No, Dinny. An elder brother never forgets how superior he was to you when he was big and you were not."

Dinny rose.

"Well, Uncle; thank you ever so for not believing in damnation, and even more for not saying so. I shall remember all you've said. Tuesday, one o'clock at the main entrance; and don't forget to eat something first, it's a very tiring business, flower-show people always seem so plain."

When she had gone Hilary refilled his pipe.

'"And even more for not saying so!"' he repeated in thought. 'That young woman can be caustic. I wonder how often I say things I don't mean in the course of my professional duties.' And seeing his wife in the doorway, he added:

"May, would you say I was a humbug—professionally?"

"Yes, dear. How could it be otherwise?"

"The forms a parson uses aren't broad enough to cover the variations of human nature? But I don't see how they could be. Would you like to go to the Chelsea Flower Show on Tuesday?"

Mrs. Hilary, thinking: 'Dinny might have asked *me*,' replied cheerfully: "Very much."

"Let's try and arrange so that we can get there at one o'clock."

"Did you talk to her about her affair?"

"Yes."

"Is she immovable?"

"Quite."

Mrs. Hilary sighed. "It's an awful pity. Do you think a man could ever live that down?"

"Twenty years ago I should have said 'No.' Now I'm not sure. It seems a queer thing to say, but it's not the really religious people who'll matter."

"Why?"

"Because they won't come across them. It's the army and Empire people, and Englishmen overseas, whom they will come across continually. The hub of unforgiveness is in her own family to start with. It's the yellow label. The gum they use putting that on is worse than the patent brand of any hotel that wants to advertise itself."

"I wonder," said Mrs. Hilary, "what the children would say about it."

"Queer that we don't know."

"We know less about our children than any of their friends do. Were we like that to our elders, I wonder?"

"My elders looked on us as biological specimens; they had us at an angle, and knew quite a lot about us. We've tried to put ourselves on a level with our youngsters, elder brother and sister business, and we don't know a thing. We've missed the one knowledge, and haven't got the other. A bit humiliating, but they're a decent crowd. It's not the young people I'm afraid of in Dinny's business, it's those who've had experience of the value of English prestige, and they'll be justified; and those who like to think he's done a thing they wouldn't have done themselves—and they won't be justified a bit."

"I think Dinny's over-estimating her strength, Hilary."

"No woman really in love could do otherwise. To find out whether she is or not will be her job. Well, she won't rust."

"You speak as if you rather liked it."

"The milk is spilled, and it's no good worrying. Let's get down to the wording of that new appeal. There's going to be a bad trade slump. Just our luck! All the people who've got money will be sticking to it."

"I wish people wouldn't be less extravagant when times are bad. It only means less work still. The shopkeepers are moaning about that already."

Hilary reached for a notebook and began writing. His wife looked over his shoulder presently and read:

"To all whom it may concern:

"And whom does it not concern that there should be in our midst thousands of people so destitute from birth to death of the bare necessities of life, that they don't know what real cleanliness, real health, real fresh air, real good food is?"

"One real will cover the lot, dear."

CHAPTER 17

Arriving at the Chelsea Flower Show, Lady Mont said thoughtfully: "I'm meetin' Boswell and Johnson at the calceolarias, Dinny. What a crowd!"

"Yes, and all plain. Do they come because they're yearning for beauty they haven't got?"

"I can't get Boswell and Johnson to yearn. There's Hilary! He's had that suit ten years. Take this and run for tickets, or he'll try and pay."

With a five pound note Dinny slid towards the wicket, avoiding her uncle's eyes. She secured four tickets, and turned smiling.

"I saw you being a serpent," he said: "Where are we going first? Azaleas. I like to be thoroughly sensual at a flower show."

Lady Mont's deliberate presence caused a little swirl in the traffic, while her eyes from under slightly drooped lids took in the appearance of the people selected, as it were, to show off flowers.

The tent they entered was warm with humanity and perfume, though the day was damp and cool. The ingenious beauty of each group of blossoms was being digested by variegated types of human beings linked only by that mysterious air of kinship which comes from attachment to the same pursuit. This was the great army of flower-raisers—growers of primulas in pots, of nasturtiums, gladioli and flags in back London gardens, of stocks, hollyhocks and sweet williams in little provincial plots; the gardeners of larger grounds; the owners of hothouses and places where experiments are made—but not many of these, for they had already passed through or would come later. All moved with a prying air, as if marking down their own next ventures; and alongside the nurserymen would stop and engage as if making bets. And the subdued murmur of voices, cockneyfied, countrified, cultivated, all commenting on flowers, formed a hum like that of bees, if not as pleasing. This subdued expression of a national passion, walled-in by canvas, together with the scent of the flowers, exercised on Dinny a hypnotic effect, so that she moved from one brilliant planted posy to another, silent and with her slightly upturned nose twitching delicately.

Her aunt's voice roused her:

"There they are!" she said, pointing with her chin.

Dinny saw two men standing so still that she wondered if they had forgotten why they had come. One had a reddish moustache and sad cow-like eyes; the other looked like a bird with a game wing; their clothes were stiff with Sundays. They were not talking nor looking at the flowers, but as if placed there by Providence without instructions.

"Which is Boswell, Auntie?"

"No moustache," said Lady Mont; "Johnson has the green hat. He's deaf. So like them."

She moved towards them, and Dinny heard her say:

"Ah!"

The two gardeners rubbed their hands on the sides of their trousered legs, but did not speak.

"Enjoyin' it?" she heard her aunt say. Their lips moved, but no sound came forth that she could catch. The one she had called Boswell lifted his cap and scratched his head. Her aunt was pointing now at the calceolarias, and suddenly the one in the green hat began to speak. He spoke so that, as Dinny could see, not even her aunt could hear a word, but his speech went on and on and seemed to afford him considerable satisfaction. Every now and then she heard her aunt say: "Ah!" But Johnson went on. He stopped suddenly, her aunt said: "Ah!" again, and came back to her.

"What was he saying?" asked Dinny.

"No," said Lady Mont, "not a word. You can't. But it's good for him." She waved her hand to the two gardeners, who were again standing without sign of life, and led the way.

They passed into the rose tent now, and Dinny looked at her watch. She had appointed to meet Wilfrid at the entrance of it.

She cast a hurried look back. There he was! She noted that Hilary was following his nose, Aunt May following Hilary, Aunt Em talking to a nurseryman. Screened by a prodigious group of 'K. of Ks.' she skimmed over to the entrance, and, with her hands in Wilfrid's, forgot entirely where she was.

"Are you feeling strong, darling? Aunt Em is here, and my Uncle Hilary and his wife. I should so like them to know you, because they all count in our equation."

He seemed to her at that moment like a highly-strung horse asked to face something it has not faced before.

"If you wish, Dinny."

They found Lady Mont involved with the representatives of 'Plant-em's Nurseries.'

"That one—south aspect and chalk. The nemesias don't. It's cross-country—they do dry so. The phloxes came dead. At least they said so: you can't tell. Oh! Here's my niece! Dinny. This is Mr. Plantem. He often sends. Oh! . . . ah! Mr. Desert! How d'you do? I remember you holdin' Michael's arms up at his weddin'." She had placed her hand in Wilfrid's and seemingly forgotten it, the while her eyes from under their raised brows searched his face with a sort of mild surprise.

"Uncle Hilary," said Dinny.

"Yes," said Lady Mont, coming to herself. "Hilary, May—Mr. Desert."

Hilary, of course, was entirely his usual self, but Aunt May looked as if she were greeting a dean. And almost at once Dinny was tacitly abandoned to her lover.

"What do you think of Uncle Hilary?"

"He looks like a man to go to in trouble."

"He is. He knows by instinct how not to run his head against brick walls, and yet he's always in action. I suppose that comes of living in a slum. He agrees with Michael that to publish 'The Leopard' is a mistake."

"Running my head against a brick wall, um?"

"Yes."

"The die, as they say, is cast. Sorry if you're sorry, Dinny."

Dinny's hand sought his. "No. Let's sail under our proper colours— only, for my sake, Wilfrid, try to take what's coming quietly, and so will I. Shall we hide behind this firework of fuchsias and slip off? They'll expect it."

Once outside the tent they moved towards the Embankment exit, past the rock gardens, each with its builder standing in the damp before it, as though saying: 'Look on this, and employ me!'

"Making nice things and having to cadge round to get people to notice them!" said Dinny.

"Where shall we go, Dinny?"

"Battersea Park?"

"Across this bridge, then."

"You were a darling to let me introduce them, but you did so look like a horse trying to back through its collar. I wanted to stroke your neck."

"I've got out of the habit of people."

"I'm glad you're not dependent on people."

"The worst mixer in the world. But you, I should have thought——"

"I only want you; I think I must have a nature like a dog's. Without you, now, I should just be lost."

The twitch of his mouth was better than an answer.

"Ever seen the Lost Dog's Home? It's over there, in the corner."

"No. Lost dogs are dreadful to think about. Perhaps one ought to, though. Yes, let's!"

The establishment had its usual hospitalised appearance of all being for the best considering that it was the worst. There was a certain amount of barking and of enquiry on the faces of a certain amount of dogs. Tails wagged as they approached. Such dogs as were of any breed looked quieter and sadder than the dogs that were of no breed, and those in the majority. A black spaniel was sitting in a corner of the wired enclosure, with head dropped between long ears. They went round to him.

"How on earth," said Dinny, "can a dog as nice as that stay unclaimed? He *is* sad!"

Wilfrid put his fingers through the wire. The dog looked up. They saw a little red under his eyes, and a wisp of hair loose and silky on his forehead. He raised himself slowly from off his haunches, and they could

334

see him pant very slightly as though some calculation or struggle were going on in him.

"Come on, old boy!"

The dog came slowly, all black, four-square on his feathered legs. He had every sign of breeding, making him more mysterious than ever. He stood almost within reach; his shortened tail fluttered feebly, then came to a droop again, precisely as if he had said: 'I neglect no chance, but you are not.'

"Well, old fellow," said Wilfrid.

Dinny bent down. "Give me a kiss."

The dog looked up at them. His tail moved once, and again dropped.

"Not a good mixer, either," said Wilfrid.

"He's too sad for words." She bent lower and this time got her hand through the wire. "Come, darling!" The dog sniffed her glove. Again his tail fluttered feebly; a pink tongue showed for a moment as though to make certain of his lips. With a supreme effort Dinny's fingers reached his muzzle smooth as silk.

"He's awfully well bred, Wilfrid."

"Stolen, I expect, and then got away. Probably from some country kennel."

"I believe I could hang dog thieves."

The dog's dark brown eyes had the remains of moisture in their corners. They looked back at Dinny, with a sort of suspended animation, as if saying: 'You are not my past, and I don't know if there is a future.'

She looked up. "Oh! Wilfrid!"

He nodded and left her with the dog. She stayed stooped on her heels, slowly scratching behind the dog's ears, till Wilfrid, followed by a man with a chain and collar, came back.

"I've got him," he said; "he reached his time limit yesterday, but they were keeping him another week because of his looks."

Dinny turned her back, moisture was oozing from her eyes. She mopped them hastily, and heard the man say:

"I'll put this on, Sir, before he comes out, or he might leg it; he's never taken to the place."

Dinny turned round.

"If the owner turns up we'll give him back at once."

"Not much chance of that, Miss. In my opinion that's the dog of some one who's died. He slipped his collar, probably, and went out to find him, got lost, and no one's cared enough to send here and see. Nice dog, too. You've got a bargain. I'm glad. I didn't like to think of that dog being put away; young dog, too."

He put the collar on, led the dog out to them, and transferred the chain to Wilfrid, who handed him a card.

"In case the owner turns up. Come on, Dinny; let's walk him a bit. Walk, boy!"

The nameless dog, hearing the sweetest word in his vocabulary, moved forward to the limit of the chain.

"That theory's probably right," said Wilfrid, "and I hope it is. We shall like this chap."

Once on a grass they tried to get through to the dog's inner consciousness. He received their attention patiently, without response, his tail drooped and his eyes, suspending judgment.

"We'd better get him home," said Wilfrid. "Stay here, and I'll bring up a cab."

He wiped a chair with his handkerchief, transferred the chain to her and swung away.

Dinny sat watching the dog. He had followed Wilfrid to the limit of the chain, and then seated himself in the attitude in which they had first seen him.

What did dogs feel? They certainly put one and one together; loved, disliked, suffered, yearned, sulked, and enjoyed like human beings; but they had a very small vocabulary and so—no ideas! Still, anything must be better than living in a wire enclosure with a lot of dogs less sensitive than yourself!

The dog came back to her side, but kept his head turned in the direction Wilfrid had taken, and began to whine.

A taxi drew up. The dog stopped whining, and began to pant.

"Master's coming!" The dog gave a tug at the chain.

Wilfrid had reached him. Through the slackened chain she could feel the disillusionment; then it tightened and the wagging of the tail came fluttering down the links, as the dog sniffed at the turnups of Wilfrid's trousers.

In the cab the dog sat on the floor with his chin hanging over Wilfrid's shoe. In Piccadilly he grew restless and ended with his chin on Dinny's knee. Between Wilfrid and the dog the drive was an emotional medley for her, and she took a deep breath as she got out.

"Wonder what Stack will say," said Wilfrid. "A spaniel in Cork Street is no catch."

The dog took the stairs with composure.

"House trained," said Dinny, thankfully.

In the sitting room the dog applied his nose to the carpet. Having decided that the legs of all the furniture were uninteresting and the place bereft of his own kind, he leaned his nose on the divan and looked out of the corners of his eyes.

"Up!" said Dinny. The dog jumped on to the divan.

"Jove! He does smell!" said Wilfrid.

"Let's give him a bath. While you're filling it, I'll look him over."

She held the dog, who would have followed Wilfrid, and began parting his hair. She found several yellow fleas, but no other breed.

"Yes, you do smell, darling."

The dog turned his head and licked her nose.

"The bath's ready, Dinny!"

"Only dog fleas."

"If you're going to help, Dinny, take off your dress and put on that bath gown. You'll spoil it."

Behind his back, Dinny slipped off her frock and put on the blue bath gown, half hoping he would turn, and respecting him because he didn't. She rolled up the sleeves and stood beside him. Poised over the bath, the dog protruded a long tongue.

"He's not going to be sick, is he, Dinny?"

"No; they always do that. Gently, Wilfrid, don't let him splash—that frightens them. Now!"

Lowered into the bath, the dog, after a scramble, stood still with his head drooped, concentrated on keeping foothold of the slippery surface.

"This is hair shampoo, better than nothing. I'll hold him. You do the rubbing in."

Pouring some of the shampoo on the centre of that polished black back, Dinny heaped water up the dog's sides and began to rub. This first domestic incident with Wilfrid was pure joy, involving no mean personal contact with him as well as with the dog. She straightened up at last.

"Phew! My back! Sluice him and let the water out. I'll hold him."

Wilfrid sluiced, the dog behaving as if not too sorry for his fleas. He shook himself vigorously, and they both jumped back.

"Don't let him out," cried Dinny, "we must dry him in the bath."

"All right. Put your hands round his neck and hold him still."

Wrapped in a huge towel, the dog lifted his face to her; its expression was drooping and forlorn.

"Poor boy, soon over now, and you'll smell lovely."

The dog shook himself.

Wilfrid withdrew the towel. "Hold him a minute. I'll get an old blanket; we'll make him curl up till he's dry."

Alone with the dog, who was now trying to get out of the bath, Dinny held him with his forepaws over the edge, and worked away at the accumulations of sorrow about his eyes.

"There! That's better!"

They carried the almost inanimate dog to the divan, wrapped in an old Guard's blanket.

"What shall we call him, Dinny?"

"Let's try him with a few names, we may hit on his real one."

He answered to none. "Well," said Dinny, "let's call him 'Foch.' But for Foch we should never have met."

CHAPTER 18

FEELINGS AT CONDAFORD, after the General's return, were vexed and uneasy. Dinny had said she would be back on Saturday, but it was now Wednesday and she was still in London. Her saying: "We are not formally engaged" had given little comfort, since the General had added: "That was soft sawder." Pressed by Lady Cherrell as to what exactly had taken place between him and Wilfrid, he was laconic.

"He hardly said a word, Liz. Polite and all that, and I must say he doesn't look like a fellow who'd quit. His record's very good. The thing's inexplicable."

"Have you read any of his verse, Con?"

"No. Where is it?"

"Dinny has them somewhere. Very bitter. So many writers seem to be like that. But I could put up with anything if I thought Dinny would be happy."

"Dinny says he's actually going to publish a poem about that business. He must be a vain chap."

"Poets almost always are."

"I don't know who can move Dinny. Hubert says he's lost touch with her. To begin married life under a cloud like that!"

"I sometimes think," murmured Lady Cherrell, "that living here, as we do, we don't know what will cause clouds and what won't."

"There can't be a question," said the General, with finality, "among people who count."

"Who does count, nowadays?"

The General was silent. Then he said shrewdly:

"England's still aristocratic underneath. All that keeps us going comes from the top. Service and tradition still rules the roost. The socialists can talk as they like."

Lady Cherrell looked up astonished at this flow.

"Well," she said, "what are we to do about Dinny?"

The General shrugged.

"Wait till things come to a crisis of some sort. Cut-you-off-with-a-shilling is out of date; besides, we're too fond of her. You'll speak to her, Liz, when you get a chance, of course. . . ."

Between Hubert and Jean discussion of the matter took a rather different line.

"I wish to God, Jean, Dinny had taken to your brother."

"Alan's got over it. I had a letter from him yesterday. He's at Singapore now. There's probably somebody out there. I only hope it isn't a married woman. There are so few girls in the East."

"I don't think he'd go for a married woman. Possibly a native; they say Malay girls are often pretty."

Jean grimaced.

"A Malay girl instead of Dinny!"

Presently she murmured: "I'd like to see this Mr. Desert. I think I could give him an idea, Hubert, of what'll be thought of him if he carries Dinny into this mess."

"You must be careful with Dinny."

"If I can have the car I'll go up to-morrow and talk it over with Fleur. She must know him quite well, he was their best man."

"I'd choose Michael of the two; but for God's sake take care, old girl."

Jean, who was accustomed to carry out her ideas, slid away next day before the world was up, and was at South Square, Westminster, by ten o'clock. Michael, it appeared, was down in his constituency.

"The safer his seat," said Fleur, "the more he thinks he has to see of them. It's the gratitude complex. What can I do for you?"

Jean slid her long-lashed eyes round from the Fragonard, which she had been contemplating as though it were too French, and Fleur almost jumped. Really, she *was* like a 'leopardess'!

"It's about Dinny and her young man, Fleur. I suppose you know what happened to him out there?"

Fleur nodded.

"Then can't something be done?"

Fleur's face became watchful. She was twenty-nine, Jean twenty-three, but it was no use coming the elder matron!

"I haven't seen anything of Wilfrid for a long time."

"Somebody's got to tell him pretty sharply what'll be thought of him if he lugs Dinny into this mess."

"I'm by no means sure there'll be a mess; even if his poem comes out. People like the Ajax touch."

"You've not been in the East."

"Yes, I have; I've been round the world."

"That's not the same thing at all."

"My dear," said Fleur, "excuse my saying so, but the Cherrells are about thirty years behind the times."

"I'm not a Cherrell."

"No, you're a Tasburgh, and, if anything, that's a little worse. Country rectories, cavalry, navy, Indian civil—how much d'you suppose all that counts nowadays?"

"It counts with those who belong to it; and he belongs to it, and Dinny belongs to it."

"No one who's really in love belongs anywhere," said Fleur. "Did you care two straws when you married Hubert with a murder charge hanging over his head?"

"That's different. He'd done nothing to be ashamed of."

Fleur smiled.

"True to type. Would it surprise you, as they say in the Courts, if I told you that there isn't one in twenty people about town who'd do otherwise than yawn if you asked them to condemn Wilfrid for what he did? And there isn't one in forty who won't forget all about it in a fortnight."

"I don't believe you," said Jean, flatly.

"You don't know modern Society, my dear."

"It's modern Society," said Jean, even more flatly, "that doesn't count."

"Well, I don't know that it does much; but then what does?"

"Where does he live?"

Fleur laughed.

"In Cork Street, opposite the Gallery. You're not thinking of bearding him, are you?"

"I don't know."

"Wilfrid can bite."

"Well," said Jean, "thanks. I must be going."

Fleur looked at her with admiration. The girl had flushed, and that pink in her brown cheeks made her look more vivid than ever.

"Well, good-bye, my dear; and do come and tell me about it, I know you've the pluck of the devil."

"I don't know that I'm going at all," said Jean. "Good-bye!"

She drove, rather angry, past the House of Commons. Her temperament believed so much in action, that Fleur's worldly wisdom had merely irritated her. Still, it was not so easy as she had thought to go to Wilfrid Desert and say: 'Stand and deliver me back my sister-in-law.' She drove, however, to Pall Mall, parked her car near the Parthenæum, and walked up to Piccadilly. People who saw her, especially men, looked back, because of the admirable grace of her limbs and the colour and light in her face. She had no idea where Cork Street was, except that it was near Bond Street. And, when she reached it, she walked up and down before locating the Gallery. 'That must be the door, opposite,' she thought. She was standing uncertainly in front of a door without a name, when a man with a dog on a lead came up the stairs and stood beside her.

"Yes, Miss?"

"I am Mrs. Hubert Cherrell. Does Mr. Desert live here?"

"Yes, Ma'am; but whether you can see him I don't know. Here, Foch, good dog! If you'll wait a minute I'll find out."

A minute later Jean, swallowing resolutely, was in the presence. 'After all,' she was thinking, 'he can't be worse than a parish meeting when you want money from it.'

Wilfrid was standing at the window, with his eyebrows raised.

"I'm Dinny's sister-in-law," said Jean. "I beg your pardon for coming, but I wanted to see you."

Wilfrid bowed.

"Come here, Foch."

The spaniel, who was sniffing round Jean's skirt, did not respond until he was called again. He licked Wilfrid's hand and sat down behind him. Jean had flushed.

"It's frightful cheek on my part, but I thought you wouldn't mind. We've just come back from the Soudan."

Wilfrid's face remained ironic, and irony always upset her. Not quite stammering, she continued:

"Dinny has never been in the East."

Again Wilfrid bowed. The affair was not going like a parish meeting. "Won't you sit down?" he said.

"Oh! thank you, no; I shan't be a minute. You see, what I wanted to say was that Dinny can't possibly realise what certain things mean out there."

"D'you know, that's what occurred to me."

"Oh!"

A minute of silence followed, while the flush on her face and the smile on Wilfrid's deepened. Then he said:

"Thank you for coming. Anything else?"

"Er—no! Good-bye!"

All the way down stairs she felt shorter than she had ever felt in her life. And the first man she passed in the street jumped, her eyes passed through him like a magnetic shock. He had once been touched by an electric eel in Brazil, and preferred the sensation. Yet, curiously, while she retraced her steps towards her car, though worsted, she bore no grudge. Even more singularly, she had lost most of her feeling that Dinny was in danger.

Regaining her car, she had a slight altercation with a policeman and took the road for Condaford. Driving to the danger of the public all the way, she was home by lunch. All she said of her adventure was that she had been for a long drive. Only, in the four-poster of the chief spare room, did she say to Hubert:

"I've been up and seen him. D'you know, Hubert, I really believe Dinny will be all right. He's got charm."

"What on earth," said Hubert, turning on his elbow, "has that to do with it?"

"A lot," said Jean. "Give me a kiss, and don't argue . . ."

When his strange young visitor had gone, Wilfrid flung himself on the divan and stared at the ceiling. He felt like a general who has won a 'victory'—the more embarrassed. Having lived for thirty-five years, owing to a variety of circumstances, in a condition of marked egoism, he was unaccustomed to the feeling which Dinny from the first had roused within him. The old-fashioned word 'worship' was hardly admissible, but no other adequately replaced it. When with her his sensations were so restful and refreshing, that when not with her he felt like one who had taken off his soul and hung it up. Alongside this new beatitude was a growing sense that his own happiness would not be complete unless hers was too. She was always telling him that she was only happy in his presence. But that was absurd, he could never replace all the interests and affections of her life before the statue of Foch had made them acquainted. And, if not, for what was he letting her in? The young woman, with the eyes, who had just gone, had stood there before him like an incarnation of this question. Though he had routed her, she had left the query printed on the air.

The spaniel, seeing the incorporeal more clearly even than his master, was resting a long nose on his knee. Even this dog he owed to Dinny. He had got out of the habit of people. With this business hanging over him, he was quite cut off. If he married Dinny, he took her with him into isolation. Was it fair?

But, having appointed to meet her in half an hour, he rang the bell.

"I'm going out now, Stack."

"Very good, Sir."

Leading the dog, he made his way to the Park. Opposite the cavalry memorial he sat down to wait for her, debating whether he should tell her of his visitor. And just then he saw her coming.

She was walking quickly from Park Lane, and had not yet seen him. She seemed to skim, straight and—as those blasted novelists called it—'willowy'! She had a look of spring, and was smiling as if something pleasant had just happened to her. This glimpse of her, all unaware of him, soothed Wilfrid. If she could look so pleased and carefree, surely he need not worry. She halted by the bronze horse which she had dubbed 'the jibbing barrel,' evidently looking for him. She turned her head so prettily this way and that, but her face had become a little anxious. He stood up. She waved her hand, and came quickly across the drive.

"Been sitting to Botticelli, Dinny?"

"No—to a pawnbroker. If you ever want one I recommend Frewens of South Molton Street."

"*You*, at a pawnbroker's?"

"Yes, darling. I've got more money of my own on me than I ever had in my life."

"What do you want it for?"

Dinny bent and stroked the dog.

"Since I knew you I've grasped the real importance of money."

"And what's that?"

"Not to be divided from you by the absence of it. The great open spaces are what we want now. Take Foch off the lead, Wilfrid; he'll follow, I'm sure."

CHAPTER 19

IN A CENTRE of literature such as London, where books come out by the half-dozen almost every day, the advent of a slender volume of poems is commonly of little moment. But circumstances combined to make the appearance of 'The Leopard and other Poems' a 'literary event.' It was Wilfrid's first production for four years. He was a lonely figure, marked out by the rarity of literary talent among the old aristocracy, by the bitter lively quality of his earlier poems, by his Eastern sojourn and isolation from literary circles, and finally by the report that he had embraced Islam. Someone, on the appearance of his third volume four years ago, had dubbed him 'a sucking Byron'; the phrase had caught the ear. Finally, he had a publisher who understood the art of what he called 'putting it over.' During the few weeks since he received Wilfrid's manuscript, he had been engaged in lunching, dining, and telling people to look out for 'The Leopard,' the most sensation-making poem since 'The Hound of Heaven.' To the query "Why?" he replied in nods and becks and wreathèd smiles. Was it true that young Desert had become a Mussulman? Oh! Yes. Was he in London? Oh! yes, but, of course, the shyest and rarest bird of the literary flock.

He who was Compson Grice Ltd. had from the first perceived that in 'The Leopard' he had a winner—people would not enjoy it, but they would talk about it. He had only to start the snowball rolling down the slope, and when moved by real conviction, no one could do this better than he. Three days before the book came out he met Telfourd Yule by a sort of accidental prescience.

"Hallo, Yule, back from Araby?"

"As you see."

"I say, I've got a most amazing book of poems coming out on Monday. 'The Leopard,' by Wilfrid Desert. Like a copy? The first poem's a corker."

"Oh!"

"Takes the wind clean out of that poem in Alfred Lyall's 'Verses written in India,' about the man who died sooner than change his faith. Remember?"

"What's the truth about Desert taking to Islam?"

"Ask him."

"That poem's so personal in feeling—it might be about himself."

"Indeed?"

And Compson Grice thought, suddenly: 'If it were! What a stunt!'

"Do you know him, Yule?"

"No."

"You must read the thing; I couldn't put it down."

"Ah!"

"But would a man publish such a thing about his own experience?"

"Can't say."

And, still more suddenly, Compson Grice thought: 'If it were, I could sell a hundred thousand!'

He returned to his office, thinking: 'Yule was deuced close. I believe I was right, and he knows it. He's only just back; everything's known in the Bazaars, they say. Now, let's see, where am I?'

Published at five shillings, on a large sale there would be a clear profit of sixpence a copy. A hundred thousand copies would be two thousand five hundred pounds, and about the same in royalties to Desert! By George! But, of course, loyalty to client first! And there came to him one of those inspirations which so often come to loyal people who see money ahead.

'I must draw his attention to the risk of people saying that it's his own case. I'd better do it the day after publication. In the meantime I'll put a second big edition in hand.'

On the day before publication, a prominent critic, Mark Hanna, who rang a weekly bell in the "Carillon," informed him that he had gone all out for the poem. A younger man, well known for a certain buccaneering spirit, said no word, but wrote a criticism. Both critiques appeared on the day of publication. Compson Grice cut them out and took them with him to the 'Jessamine' restaurant, where he had bidden Wilfrid to lunch.

They met at the entrance and passed to a little table at the far end. The room was crowded with people who knew everybody in the literary, dramatic and artistic world. And Compson Grice waited, with the experience of one who had entertained many authors, until a bottle of Mouton Rothschild 1870 had been drunk to its dregs. Then, producing from his pocket the two reviews, he placed that of Mark Hanna before his guest, with the words: "Have you seen this; it's rather good?"

Wilfrid read it.

The reviewer had indeed gone 'all out.' It was almost all confined to 'The Leopard,' which it praised as the most intimate revelation of the human soul in verse since Shelley.

"Bunk! Shelley doesn't reveal except in his lyrics."

"Ah! Well," said Compson Grice, "they have to work-in Shelley."

The review acclaimed the poem as "tearing away the last shreds of the hypocritical veil which throughout our literature has shrouded the muse in relation to religion." It concluded with these words: "This poem, indeed, in its unflinching record of a soul tortured by cruel dilemma, is the most amazing piece of imaginative psychology which has come our way in the twentieth century."

Watching his guest lay down the cutting, Compson Grice said, softly: "Pretty good! It's the personal fervour of the thing that gets them."

Wilfrid gave his queer shiver.

"Got a cigar cutter?"

Compson Grice pushed one forward with the other review.

"I think you ought to read this in the 'Daily Phase.'"

The review was headed: 'Defiance: Bolshevism and the Empire.'

Wilfrid took it up.

"Geoffrey Coltham?" he said: "Who's he?"

The review began with some fairly accurate personal details of the poet's antecedents, early work and life, ending with the mention of his conversion to Islam. Then, after some favourable remarks about the other poems, it fastened on 'The Leopard,' sprang as it were, at the creature's throat, and shook it as a bulldog might. Then, quoting these lines:

> 'Into foul ditch each dogma leads.
> Cursed be superstitious creeds,
> In every driven mind the weeds!
> There's but one liquor for the sane—
> Drink deep! Let scepticism reign
> And its astringence clear the brain!'

it went on with calculated brutality:

'The thin disguise assumed by the narrative covers a personal disruptive bitterness, which one is tempted to connect with the wounded and overwhelming pride of one who has failed himself and the British world. Whether Mr. Desert intended in this poem to reveal his own experience and feelings in connection with his conversion to Islam—a faith, by the way, of which, judging from the poor and bitter lines quoted above, he is totally unworthy—we cannot of course say, but we advise him to come into the open and let us know. Since we have a poet in our midst, who, with all his undoubted thrust, drives at our entrails, cuts deep into our religion and our prestige, we have the right to know whether or not he is a renegade.'

"That, I think," said Compson Grice, quietly, "is libellous."

Wilfrid looked up at him, so that he said afterwards: "I never knew Desert had such eyes."

"I *am* a renegade. I took conversion at the pistol's point, and you can let everybody know it."

Smothering the words: 'Thank God!' Compson Grice reached out his hand. But Wilfrid had leaned back and veiled his face in the smoke of his cigar. His publisher moved forward on to the edge of his chair.

"You mean that you want me to send a letter to the 'Daily Phase' to say that 'The Leopard' is practically your own experience?"

"Yes."

"My dear fellow, I think it's wonderful of you. That is courage, if you like."

The smile on Wilfrid's face caused Compson Grice to sit back, and swallow the words:

"The effect on the sales will be marvellous." He substituted: "It will strengthen your position enormously. But I wish we could get back on that fellow."

"Let him stew!"

"Quite!" said Compson Grice. He was by no means anxious to be embroiled, and have all his authors slated in the important 'Daily Phase.'

Wilfrid rose. "Thanks very much. I must be going."

Compson Grice watched him leave, his head held high and his step slow. 'Poor devil!' he thought: 'It *is* a scoop!'

Back in his office, he spent some time finding a line in Coltham's review which he could isolate from its context and use as advertisement. He finally extracted this: "Daily Phase: 'No poem in recent years has had such power' "—(the remaining words of the sentence he omitted because they were 'to cut the ground from under the feet of all we stand for'). He then composed a letter to the Editor. He was writing—he said—at the request of Mr. Desert, who far from needing any challenge to come into the open, was only too anxious that everyone should know that 'The Leopard' was indeed founded on his personal experience. For his own part—he went on—he considered that this frank avowal was a more striking instance of courage than could be met with in a long day's march. He was proud to have been privileged to publish a poem which in psychological content, quality of workmanship and direct human interest, was by far the most striking of this generation.

He signed himself "Your obedient servant, Compson Grice." He then increased the size of the order for the second edition, directed that the words "First edition exhausted, second large impression," should be ready for use immediately, and went to his Club to play Bridge.

His Club was the Polyglot, and in the hall he ran on Michael. The hair of his erstwhile colleague in the publishing world was ruffled, the ears stood out from his head, and he spoke at once:

"Grice, what are you doing about that young brute Coltham?"

Compson Grice smiled blandly and replied:

"Don't worry! I showed the review to Desert, and he told me to draw its sting by complete avowal."

"Good God!"

"Why? Didn't you know?"

"Yes, I knew, but——"

These words were balm to the ears of Compson Grice, who had been visited by misgivings as to the truth of Wilfrid's admission. Would a man really publish that poem if it were his own case; could he really want it known? But this was conclusive: Mont had been Desert's discoverer and closest friend.

346

"So I've written to the 'Phase' and dealt with it."

"Did Wilfrid tell you to do that?"

"He did."

"To publish that poem was crazy. 'Quem deus—'" He suddenly caught sight of the expression on Compson Grice's face: "Yes," he added, bitterly, "you think you've got a scoop!"

Compson Grice said coldly:

"Whether it will do us harm or good, remains to be seen."

"Bosh!" said Michael: "Everybody will read the thing now, blast them! Have you seen Wilfrid to-day?"

"He lunched with me."

"How's he looking?"

Tempted to say 'Like Asrael!' Compson Grice substituted: "Oh! all right —quite calm."

"Calm as hell! Look here, Grice! If you don't stand by him and help him all you can through this, I'll never speak to you again."

"My dear fellow," said Compson Grice, with some dignity, "what do you suppose?" And straightening his waistcoat, he passed into the card room.

Michael, muttering: "Cold-blooded fish!" hurried in the direction of Cork Street. 'I wonder if the old chap would like to see me,' he thought.

But at the very mouth of the street he recoiled and made for Mount Street instead. He was informed that both his father and mother were out, but that Miss Dinny had come up that morning from Condaford.

"All right, Blore. If she's in I'll find her."

He went up and opened the drawing-room door quietly. In the alcove under the cage of her aunt's parakeet, Dinny was sitting perfectly still and upright, like a little girl at a lesson, with her hands crossed on her lap and her eyes fixed on space. She did not see him till his hand was on her shoulder.

"Penny!"

"How does one learn not to commit murder, Michael?"

"Ah! Poisonous young brute! Have your people seen 'The Phase'?"

Dinny nodded.

"What was the reaction?"

"Silence, pinched lips."

Michael nodded.

"Poor dear! So you came up?"

"Yes, I'm going to the theatre with Wilfrid."

"Give him my love, and tell him that if he wants to see me I'll come at any moment. Oh! and, Dinny, try to make him feel that we admire him for spilling the milk."

Dinny looked up, and he was moved by the expression on her face.

"It wasn't all pride that made him, Michael. There's something egging him on, and I'm afraid of it. Deep down he isn't sure that it wasn't just cowardice that made him renounce. I know he can't get that thought out of his mind. He feels he's got to prove, not to others so much as to himself, that he isn't a coward. Oh! I know he isn't. But so long as he hasn't proved it to himself and everybody, I don't know what he might do."

Michael nodded. From his one interview with Wilfrid he had formed something of the same impression.

"Did you know that he's told his publisher to make a public admission?"

"Oh!" said Dinny blankly: "What then?"

Michael shrugged.

"Michael, will anyone grasp the situation Wilfrid was in?"

"The imaginative type is rare. I don't pretend I can grasp it. Can you?"

"Only because it happened to Wilfrid."

Michael grasped her arm.

"I'm glad you've got the old-fashioned complaint, Dinny, not just this modern 'physiological urge.'"

CHAPTER 20

WHILE DINNY was dressing her Aunt came to her room.

"Your Uncle read me that article, Dinny. I wonder!"

"What do you wonder, Aunt Em?"

"Coltham—but he died."

"This one will probably die, too."

"Where do you get your boned bodies, Dinny? So restful."

"Harridge's."

"Your Uncle says he ought to resign from his Club."

"Wilfrid doesn't care two straws about his Club; he probably hasn't been in a dozen times. But I don't think he'll resign."

"Better make him."

"I should never dream of 'making' him do anything."

"So awkward when they use black balls."

"Auntie, dear, could I come to the glass?"

Lady Mont crossed the room and took up the slim volume from the bedside table.

"'The Leopard!' But he did change them, Dinny."

"He did not, Auntie, he had no spots to change."

"Baptism and that."

"If baptism really meant anything, it would be an outrage on children till they knew what it was about."

"Dinny!"

"I mean it. One doesn't commit people to things entirely without their consent, it isn't decent. By the time Wilfrid could think at all he had no religion."

"It wasn't the givin' up, then, it was the takin' on."

"He knows that."

"Well," said Lady Mont, turning toward the door, "I think it served that Arab right; so intrudin'! Do you want a latch-key? Ask Blore."

Dinny finished dressing quickly and ran downstairs. Blore was in the dining-room.

"Aunt Em says I may have a key, Blore, and I want a taxi, please."

Having telephoned to the cab-stand and produced a key, the butler said: "What with her ladyship speaking her thoughts out loud, Miss, I'm obliged to know, and I was saying to Sir Lawrence this morning: 'If Miss

Dinny could take him off just now, on a tour of the Scotch Highlands where they don't see the papers, it would save a lot of vexation.' In these days, Miss, as you'll have noticed, one thing comes on the top of another, and people haven't the memories they had. You'll excuse my mentioning it."

Dinny took the key.

"Thank you ever so, Blore. Nothing I'd like better; only I'm afraid he wouldn't think it proper."

"In these days a young *lady* can do anything, Miss, so long as she does it properly."

"Men still have to be careful, Blore."

"Well, Miss, of course, relatives are difficult; but it could be arranged."

"I think we shall have to face the music."

The butler shook his head.

"In my belief, whoever said that first is responsible for a lot of unnecessary unpleasantness. Here's your taxi, Miss."

In the taxi she sat a little forward, getting the air from both windows on her cheeks, which needed cooling. Even the anger and vexation left by that review were lost in this sweeter effervescence. At the corner of Piccadilly she read a newspaper poster: "Derby horses arrive." The Derby to-morrow! How utterly she had lost count of events. The restaurant chosen for their dinner was Blafard's in Soho, and her progress was impeded by the traffic of a town on the verge of national holiday. At the door, with the spaniel held on a leash, stood Stack. He handed her a note: "Mr. Desert sent me with this, Miss. I brought the dog for a walk."

Dinny opened the note with a sensation of physical sickness.

"Dinny Darling,

Forgive my failing you to-night. I've been in a torture of doubt all day. The fact is, until I know where I stand with the world over this business, I have an overwhelming feeling that I must not commit you to anything; and a public jaunt like this is just what I ought to avoid for you. I suppose you saw 'The Daily Phase'—that is the beginning of the racket. I must go through this next week on my own, and measure up where I am. I won't run off, and we can write. You'll understand. The dog is a boon, and I owe him to you. Good-bye for a little, my dear love.
                                        Your devoted

                                                      W.D."

It was all she could do not to put her hand on her heart under the driver's eyes. Thus to be shut away in the heat of the battle was what, she knew now, she had been dreading all along. With an effort she controlled her lips, said: "Wait a minute!" and turned to Stack.

"I'll take you and Foch back."

"Thank you, Miss."

She bent down to the dog. Panic was at work within her breast! The dog! He was a link between them!

"Put him into the cab, Stack."

On the way she said quietly:

"Is Mr. Desert in?"

"No, Miss, he went out when he gave me the note."

"Is he all right?"

"A little worried, I think, Miss. I must say I'd like to teach manners to that gentleman in 'The Daily Phase'."

"Oh! you saw that?"

"I did; it oughtn't to be allowed is what I say."

"Free speech," said Dinny. And the dog pressed his chin against her knee. "Is Foch good?"

"No trouble at all, Miss. A gentleman, that dog, aren't you, boy?"

The dog continued to press his chin on Dinny's knee; and the feel of it was comforting.

When the cab stopped in Cork Street, she took a pencil from her bag, tore off the empty sheet of Wilfrid's note, and wrote:

"DARLING,

As you will. But by these presents know: I am yours for ever and ever. Nothing can or shall divide me from you, unless you stop loving

Your devoted

DINNY.

You won't do that, will you? Oh! don't!"

Licking what was left of the gum on the envelope, she put her half sheet in and held it till it stuck. Giving it to Stack, she kissed the dog's head and said to the driver: "The Park end of Mount Street, please. Good-night, Stack!"

"Good-night, Miss!"

The eyes and mouth of the motionless henchman seemed to her so full of understanding, that she turned her face away. And that was the end of the jaunt she had been so looking forward to.

From the top of Mount Street she crossed into the Park and sat on the seat where she had sat with him before, oblivious of the fact that she was unattached, without a hat, in evening dress, and that it was past eight o'clock. She sat with the collar of her cloak turned up to her chestnut-coloured hair, trying to see his point of view. She saw it very well. Pride! She had enough herself to understand. Not to involve others in one's troubles was elementary. The fonder one was, the less would one wish to involve them. Curiously ironical how love divided people just when they most needed each other! And no way out, so far as she could see. The strains of the Guards' band began to reach her faintly. They were playing —Faust?—no—Carmen! Wilfrid's favourite opera! She got up and walked over the grass towards the sound. What crowds of people! She took a chair some way off and sat down again, close to some rhododendrons. The Habañera! What a shiver its first notes always gave one! How wild, sudden, strange and inescapable was love! '*L'amour est enfant de Bohème*' . . . ! The rhododendrons were late this year. That deep rosy one! They had it at Condaford. Where was he—oh! where was he at this moment! Why could not love pierce veils, so that in spirit she might walk beside him, slip a hand into his! A spirit hand was better than nothing! And Dinny suddenly realised loneliness as only true lovers do when they think of life without the loved one. As flowers wilt on their stalks, so would she wilt—if she were cut away from him. "See things through alone!" How long would he want to? Forever? At the thought she started up; and a stroller, who thought the movement meant for him, stood still and looked at her. Her face corrected his impression and he moved on. She had two hours to kill before she could go in; she could not let them know that her evening had come to grief. The band was finishing off Carmen with the Toreador's song. A blot on the opera, its most popular tune! No, not a blot, for it was meant, of course, to blare above the desolation of that tragic end, as the world blared around the passion of lovers. The world was a heedless and a heartless stage for lives to strut across, or in dark corners join and cling together . . . How odd that clapping sounded in the open! She looked at her wrist watch. Half past nine! An hour yet before it would be really dark. But there was a coolness now, a scent of grass and leaves; the rhododendrons were slowly losing colour, the birds had finished with song. People passed and passed her; she saw nothing funny about them, and they seemed to see nothing funny about her. And Dinny thought: 'Nothing seems funny any more, and I haven't had any dinner.' A coffee stall? Too early, perhaps, but there must be heaps of places where she could get something, still! No dinner, almost no lunch, no tea—a condition appropriate to the lovesick! She began to move towards Knightsbridge, walking fast, by instinct rather than experience, for this was the first time she had ever wandered alone about London at such an hour. Reaching the gate without adventure, she crossed and went down Sloane Street. She felt much better moving, and chalked up in her mind the thought: 'For love-sickness, walking!' In this straight street there was practically nobody to notice her. The carefully closed and blinded houses seemed to confirm, each with its tall formal narrow face, the indifference of the regimented world to the longings of street walkers such as she. At the corner of the King's Road a woman was standing.

"Could you tell me," said Dinny, "of any place close by where I could get something to eat?"

The woman addressed, she now saw, had a short face with high cheekbones on which, and round the eyes, was a good deal of make-up. Her lips were good-natured, a little thick; her nose, too, rather thick; her eyes had the look which comes of having to be now stony and now luring, as if they had lost touch with her soul. Her dress was dark and fitted her curves, and she wore a large string of artificial pearls. Dinny could not help thinking she had seen people in Society not unlike her.

"There's a nice little place on the left."

"Would you care to come and have something with me?" said Dinny, moved by impulse.

"Why! I would," said the woman. "Fact is, I came out without anything. It's nice to have company, too." She turned up the King's Road and Dinny turned alongside. It passed through her mind that if she met someone it would be quaint; but for all that she felt better.

'For God's sake,' she thought, 'be natural and don't ask questions.'

The woman led her into a little restaurant, or rather public house, for it had a bar. There was no one in the eating room, which had a separate entrance, and they sat down at a small table with a cruet-stand, a hand-bell, a bottle of Worcester sauce, and in a vase some failing pyrethrums which had never been fresh. There was a slight smell of vinegar.

"I *could* do with a cigarette," said the woman.

Dinny had none in her bag. She tinkled the bell.

"Any particular sort?"

"Gaspers."

A waitress appeared, looked at the woman, looked at Dinny, and said: "Yes?"

"A packet of Players, please. A large coffee for me, strong and fresh, and some cake or buns, or anything. What will you have?"

The woman looked at Dinny, as though measuring her capacity, looked at the waitress, and said, hesitating: "Well, to tell the truth, I'm hungry. Cold beef and a bottle of stout?"

"Vegetables?" said Dinny: "A salad?"

"Well, a salad, thank you."

"Good! And pickled walnuts? Will you get it as quickly as you can, please?"

The waitress passed her tongue over her lips, nodded, and went away.

"I say," said the woman, suddenly, "it's awful nice of you, you know."

"It was so friendly of you to come. I should have felt a bit lost without you."

"*She* can't make it out," said the woman, nodding her head towards the vanished waitress. "To tell you the truth, nor can I."

"Why? We're both hungry."

"No doubt about that," said the woman, "you're going to see me eat. I'm glad you ordered pickled walnuts, I never can resist a pickled onion, and it don't do."

"I might have thought of cocktails," murmured Dinny, "but perhaps they don't make them here."

"A sherry and bitters wouldn't be amiss. I'll get 'em." The woman rose and disappeared into the bar.

Dinny took the chance to powder her nose. She also dived her hand down to the pocket in her 'boned body' where the spoils of South Molton

Street were stored, and extracted a five-pound note. She was feeling a sort of sad excitement.

The woman came back with two glasses. "I told 'em to charge it to our bill. The liquor's good here."

Dinny raised her glass and sipped. The woman tossed hers off at a draught.

"I wanted that. Fancy a country where you couldn't get a drink!"

"But they can, of course, and do."

"You bet. But they say some of the liquor's awful."

Dinny saw that her gaze was travelling up and down her cloak and dress with insatiable curiosity.

"Pardon me," said the woman, suddenly: "You got a date?"

"No, I'm going home after this."

The woman sighed. "Wish she'd bring those blinkin' cigarettes."

The waitress reappeared with a bottle of stout and the cigarettes. Staring at Dinny's hair, she opened the bottle.

"Cool!" said the woman, taking a long draw at her 'Gasper,' "I wanted that."

"I'll bring you the other things in a minute," said the waitress.

"I haven't seen you on the stage, have I?" said the woman.

"No, I'm not on the stage."

The advent of food broke the ensuing hush. The coffee was better than Dinny hoped and very hot. She had drunk most of it and eaten a large piece of plum cake before the woman, putting a pickled walnut in her mouth, spoke again.

"D'you live in London?"

"No. In Oxfordshire."

"Well, I like the country, too; but I never see it now. I was brought up near Maidstone—pretty round there." She heaved a sigh with a flavouring of stout. "They say the Communists in Russia have done away with vice—isn't that a scream? An American journalist told me. Well! I never knew a budget make such a difference before," she continued, expelling smoke as if liberating her soul: "Dreadful lot of unemployment."

"It does seem to affect everybody."

"Affects me, I know," and she stared, stonily. "I suppose you're shocked at that."

"It takes a lot to shock people nowadays, don't you find?"

"Well, I don't mix as a rule with bishops."

Dinny laughed.

"All the same," said the woman defiantly, "I came across a parson who talked the best sense to me I ever heard; of course I couldn't follow it."

"I'll make you a bet," said Dinny, "that I know his name. Cherrell?"

"In once," said the woman, and her eyes grew round.

"He's my uncle."

"Cool! Well, well! It's a funny world! And not so large. Nice man he was," she added.

"Still is."

"One of the best."

Dinny, who had been waiting for those inevitable words, thought: 'This is where they used to do the "My erring sister" stunt.'

The woman uttered a sigh of repletion.

"I've enjoyed that," she said, and rose. "Thank you ever so. I must be getting on now, or I'll be late for business."

Dinny tinkled the bell. The waitress appeared with suspicious promptitude.

"The bill, please, and can you get me that changed?"

The waitress took the note with a certain caution.

"I'll just go and fix myself," said the woman; "see you in a minute." She passed through a door.

Dinny drank up the remains of her coffee. She was trying to realise what it must be like to live like that. The waitress came back with the change, received her tip, said "Thank you, Miss," and went. Dinny resumed the process of realisation.

"Well," said the woman's voice behind her, "I don't suppose I'll ever see you again. But I'd like to say I think you're a jolly good sort."

Dinny looked up at her.

"When you said you'd come out without anything, did you mean you hadn't anything to come out with?"

"Sure thing," said the woman.

"Then would you mind taking this change. It's horrid to have no money in London."

The woman bit her lips, and Dinny could see that they were trembling.

"I wouldn't like to take your money," she said, "after you've been so kind."

"Oh! bosh! Please!" And catching her hand, she pressed the money into it. To her horror, the woman uttered a loud sniff. She was preparing to make a run for the door, when the woman said:

"D'you know what I'm going to do? I'm going home to have a sleep. My God, I am! I'm going home to have a sleep."

Dinny hurried back to Sloane Street. Walking past the tall blinded houses, she recognised with gratitude that her love-sickness was much better. If she did not walk too fast, she would not be too soon at Mount Street. It was dark now, and in spite of the haze of city light, the sky was alive with stars. She did not enter the Park again, but walked along its outside railings. It seemed an immense time since she had parted from Stack and the dog in Cork Street. Traffic was thickening as she rounded into Park Lane. To-morrow all these vehicles would be draining out to Epsom Downs; the Town would be seeming almost empty. And, with a sickening sensation, it came to her how empty it would always feel without Wilfrid to see or look forward to.

She came to the gate by the 'jibbing barrel,' and suddenly, as though all that evening had been a dream, she saw Wilfrid standing beside it.

She choked and ran forward. He put out his arms and caught her to him.

The moment could hardly be prolonged, for cars and pedestrians were passing in and out; so arm-in-arm they moved towards Mount Street. Dinny just clung to him, and he seemed equally wordless; but the thought that he had come there to be near her was infinitely comforting.

They escorted each other back and forth past the house, like some footman and housemaid for a quarter of an hour off duty. Class and country, custom and creed, all were forgotten. And, perhaps, no two people in all its seven millions were in those few minutes more moved and at one in the whole of London.

At last the comic instinct woke.

"We can't see each other home all night, darling. So one kiss—and yet—one kiss—and yet—one kiss!"

She ran up the steps, and turned the key.

CHAPTER 21

WILFRID's MOOD when he left his publisher at 'The Jessamine' was angry and confused. Without penetrating to the depths of Compson Grice's mental anatomy, he felt that he had been manipulated; and the whole of that restless afternoon he wandered, swung between relief at having burnt his boats, and resentment at the irrevocable. Thus preoccupied, he did not really feel the shock his note would be to Dinny, and only when, returning to his rooms, he received her answer, did his heart go out to her, and with it himself to where she had fortuitously found him. In the few minutes while they paraded Mount Street silent and half-embraced, she had managed to pass into him her feeling that it was not one but two against the world. Why keep away and make her more unhappy than he need? And he sent her a note by Stack next morning asking her to go 'joy-riding.' He had forgotten the Derby, and their car was involved almost at once in a stream of vehicles.

"I've never seen the Derby," said Dinny. "Could we go?"

There was the more reason why they should go because there was no reasonable chance of not.

Dinny was astonished at the general sobriety. No drinking and no streamers, no donkey-carts, false noses, badinage. Not a four-in-hand visible, not a coster nor a Kate; nothing but a wedged and moving stream of motor 'buses and cars mostly shut.

When, at last, they had 'parked' on the Down, eaten their sandwiches and moved into the crowd, they turned instinctively toward the chance of seeing a horse.

Frith's "Derby Day" seemed no longer true, if it ever was. In that picture people seemed to have lives and to be living them, in this crowd everybody seemed trying to get somewhere else.

In the paddock, which at first sight still seemed all people and no horses, Wilfrid said suddenly:

"This is foolish, Dinny, we're certain to be seen."

"And if we are? Look, there's a horse!"

Quite a number of horses, indeed, were being led round in a ring. Dinny moved quickly towards them.

"They all look beautiful to me," she said in a hushed voice, "and just as good one as the other—except this one; I don't like his back."

357

Wilfrid consulted his card. "That's the favourite."

"I still don't. D'you see what I mean? It comes to a point too near the tail, and then droops."

"I agree, but horses run in all shapes."

"I'll back the horse you fancy, Wilfrid."

"Give me time, then."

The people to her left and right kept on saying the horse's names as they passed. She had a place on the rail with Wilfrid standing close behind her.

"He's a pig of a horse," said the man on her left, "I'll never back the brute again."

She took a glance at the speaker. He was broad and about five feet six, with a roll of fat on his neck, a bowler hat, and a cigar in his mouth. The horse's fate seemed to her less dreadful.

A lady sitting on a shooting-stick to her right, said:

"They ought to clear the course for the horses going out. That lost me my money two years ago."

Wilfrid's hand rested on her shoulder.

"I like that one," he said, "Blenheim. Let's go and put our money on."

They went to where people were standing in little queues before a row of what looked like pigeon-holes.

"Stand here," he said. "I'll lay my egg and come back to you."

Dinny stood watching.

"How d'you do, Miss Cherrell?" A tall man in a grey top hat with a very long case of field-glasses slung round him, had halted before her. "We met at the Foch statue and your sister's wedding—remember?"

"Oh! yes. Mr. Muskham." Her heart was hurrying, and she restrained herself from looking towards Wilfrid.

"Any news of your sister?"

"Yes, we heard from Egypt. They must have had it terribly hot in the Red Sea."

"Have you backed anything?"

"Not yet."

"I shouldn't touch the favourite—he won't stay."

"We thought of Blenheim."

"Well, nice horse, and handy for the turns. But there's one more fancied in his stable. I take it you're a neophyte. I'll give you two tips, Miss Cherrell. Look for one or both of two things in a horse: leverage behind, and personality—not looks, just personality."

"Leverage behind? Do you mean higher behind than in front?"

Jack Muskham smiled. "That's about it. If you see that in a horse, especially where it has to come up a hill, back it."

"But personality? Do you mean putting his head up and looking over the tops of people into the distance? I saw one horse do that."

"By jove, I should like you as a pupil! That's just about what I do mean."

"But I don't know which horse it was," said Dinny.

"That's awkward." And then she saw the interested benevolence on his face stiffen. He lifted his hat and turned away. Wilfrid's voice behind her said:

"Well, you've got a tenner on."

"Let's go to the Stand and see the race."

With his hand within her arm, she tried to forget the sudden stiffening of Jack Muskham's face. The crowd's multiple entreaty that she should have her 'fortune told' did its best to distract her, and she arrived at the Stand in a mood of indifference to all but Wilfrid and the horses. They found standing room close to the bookmakers near the rails.

"Green and chocolate—I can remember that. Pistache is my favourite chocolate filling. What shall I win if I do win, darling!"

"Listen!"

They isolated the words "Eighteen to one Blenheim?"

"A hundred and eighty!" said Dinny. "Splendid!"

"Well, it means that he's not fancied by the stable; they've got another running. Here they come! Two with chocolate and green. The second of them is ours."

The parade, enchanting to all except, possibly, the horses, gave her the chance to see the brown horse they had backed adorning its perched rider.

"How d'you like him, Dinny?"

"I love them nearly all. How can people tell which is the best by looking at them?"

"They can't."

The horses were turning now and cantering past the Stand.

"Would you say Blenheim is higher behind than in front?" murmured Dinny.

"No. Very nice action. Why?"

But she only pressed his arm and gave a little shiver.

Neither of them having glasses, all was obscure to them when the race began. A man just behind kept saying: "The favourite's leadin'! The favourite's leadin'!"

As the horses came round Tattenham Corner, the same man burbled: "The Pasha—the Pasha'll win—no, the favourite—the favourite wins!—no, he don't—Iliad—Iliad wins."

Dinny felt Wilfrid's hand grip her arm.

"Ours," he said, "on the side—look!"

Dinny saw a horse on the far side in pink and brown, and nearer her the chocolate and green. It was ahead, it was ahead. They had won!

Amidst the silence and discomfiture those two stood smiling at each other. It seemed an omen!

"I'll take you to the car, draw your money, and we'll be off."

He insisted on her taking all the money, and she ensconced it with her own wealth, so much more insurance against any sudden decision to deprive her of himself.

They drove again into Richmond Park on the way home, and sat a long time among the young bracken, listening to the cuckoos, very happy, in the sunny, peaceful, whispering afternoon.

They dined together in a Kensington restaurant, and he left her finally at the top of Mount Street.

That night she slept unvisited by doubts or dreams, and went down to breakfast with clear eyes and a flush of sunburn on her cheeks. Her uncle was reading 'The Daily Phase.' He put it down and said:

"When you've had your coffee, Dinny, you might glance at this. There is something about publishers," he added, "which makes one doubt sometimes whether they are men and brothers. And there is something about editors which makes it certain sometimes that they are not."

Dinny read Compson Grice's letter, printed under the headlines:

"MR. DESERT'S APOSTASY
OUR CHALLENGE TAKEN UP.
A CONFESSION."

Two stanzas from Sir Alfred Lyall's poem 'Theology in extremis' followed:

> "Why? Am I bidding for glory's roll?
> I shall be murdered and clean forgot;
> Is it a bargain to save my soul?
> God, whom I trust in, bargains not.
> Yet for the honour of English race
> May I not live or endure disgrace . . .

> "I must be gone to the crowd untold
> Of men by the Cause which they served unknown,
> Who moulder in myriad graves of old;
> Never a story and never a stone
> Tells of the martyrs who die like me,
> Just for the pride of the old countree."

And the pink of sunburn gave way to a flood of crimson.

"Yes," murmured Sir Lawrence, watching her, " 'the fat is in the fire,' Dinny, as old Forsyte would have said. Still I was talking to a man last night who thought that nowadays nothing makes an indelible mark. Cheating at cards, boning necklaces—you go abroad for two years and it's all forgotten. As for sex abnormality, according to him it's no longer abnormal. So we must cheer up!"

Dinny said passionately: "What I resent is that any worm will have the power to say what he pleases."

Sir Lawrence nodded: "The greater the worm, the greater the power. But it's not the worms we need bother about; it's the people with 'pride of English race,' and there are still a few about."

"Uncle, is there any way in which Wilfrid can show publicly that he's not a coward?"

"He did well in the war."

"Who remembers the war?"

"Perhaps," muttered Sir Lawrence, "we could throw a bomb at his car in Piccadilly, so that he could look at it over the side and light a cigarette. I can't think of anything more helpful."

"I saw Mr. Muskham yesterday."

"Then you were at the Derby?" He took a very little cigar from his pocket. "Jack takes the view that you are being victimised."

"Oh! Why can't people leave one alone?"

"Attractive nymphs are never left alone. Jack's a misogynist."

Dinny gave a desperate laugh.

"I suppose one's troubles *are* funny."

She got up and went to the window. It seemed to her that all the world was barking, like dogs at a cornered cat, and yet there was nothing in Mount Street but a van from the Express Dairy.

CHAPTER 22

JACK MUSKHAM occupied a bedroom at 'Burton's' Club when racing kept him overnight in town. Having read an account of the Derby in 'The Daily Phase,' he turned the paper idly. The other features in 'that rag' were commonly of little interest to him. Its editing shocked his formalism, its news jarred his taste, its politics offended him by being so like his own. But his perusal was not perfunctory enough to prevent him from seeing the headline 'Mr. Desert's Apostasy.' Reading the half column that followed it, he pushed the paper away and said: "That fellow must be stopped."

Glorying in his yellow streak, was he, and taking that nice girl with him to Coventry! Hadn't even the decency to avoid being seen with her in public on the very day he was confessing himself as yellow as that rag!

In an age when tolerations and condonations seemed almost a disease, Jack Muskham knew and registered his own mind. He had disliked young Desert at first sight. The fellow's name suited him! And to think that this nice girl, who, without any training, had made those shrewd remarks about the race-horse, was to have her life ruined by this yellow-livered young braggart! It was too much! If it hadn't been for Lawrence, indeed, he would have done something about it before now. But there his mind stammered. What? . . . Here was the fellow publicly confessing his disgrace! An old dodge, that—taking the sting out of criticism! Making a virtue of necessity! Parading his desertion! That cock shouldn't fight, if he had his way! But once more his mind stammered . . . No outsider could interfere. And yet, unless there was some outward and visible sign condemning the fellow's conduct, it would look as if nobody cared.

'By George!' he thought, 'I'll raise the matter. This Club, at least, can sit up and take notice. We don't want rats in "Burton's"!'

He brought the matter up in Committee meeting that very afternoon, and was astonished almost to consternation by the apathy with which it was received. Of the seven members present—'the Squire,' Wilfred Bentworth, being in the Chair—four seemed to think it was a matter between young Desert and his conscience, and besides it looked like being a newspaper stunt. Times had changed since Lyall wrote that peom. One went so far as to say he didn't want to be bothered, he hadn't read 'The Leopard,' he didn't know Desert, and he hated 'The Daily Phase.'

362

"So do I," said Jack Muskham, "but here's the poem." He had sent out for it and spent an hour after lunch reading it. "Let me read you a bit. It's poisonous."

"For heaven's sake no, Jack."

The fifth member, who had so far said nothing, supposed that if Muskham pressed it, they must all read the thing.

"I do press it."

'The Squire,' hitherto square and silent, remarked: "The secretary will get copies and send them round to the Committee. Better send them, too, a copy of to-day's 'Daily Phase.' We'll discuss it at meeting next Friday. Now about this claret?" And they moved to consideration of important matters.

It has been noticed that when a newspaper of a certain type lights on an incident which enables it at once to exhibit virtue, and beat the drum of its policy, it will exploit that incident, within the limits of the law of libel, without regard to the susceptibilities of individuals. Secured by the confession in Compson Grice's letter, 'The Daily Phase' made the most of opportunity, and in the eight days intervening before the next Committee gave the Committee men little chance of professing ignorance or indifference. Everybody, indeed, was reading and talking about 'The Leopard,' and, on the morning of the adjourned meeting, 'The Daily Phase' had a long allusive column on the extreme importance of British behaviour in the East. It had also a large-type advertisement. " 'The Leopard and other poems' by Wilfrid Desert: published by Compson Grice: 400,000 copies sold: Third Large Impression ready."

A debate on the ostracism of a fellow-being will bring almost any man to a Committee meeting; and the attendance included some never before known to come.

A motion had been framed by Jack Muskham:

"That the Honourable Wilfrid Desert be requested, under Rule 23, to resign his membership of Burton's Club, because of conduct unbecoming to a member."

He opened the discussion in these words:

"You've all had copies of Desert's poem 'The Leopard' and 'The Daily Phase' of yesterday week. There's no doubt about the thing. Desert has publicly owned to having ratted from his religion at the pistol's point, and I say he's no longer fit to be a member of this Club. It was founded in memory of a very great traveller who'd have dared Hell itself. We don't want people here who don't act up to British traditions, and make a song about it into the bargain."

There was a short silence, and then the fifth member of the Committee at the previous meeting remarked:

"It's a deuced fine poem, all the same."

A well-known K.C., who had once travelled in Turkey, added:

"Oughtn't he to have been asked to attend?"

"Why?" asked Jack Muskham. "He can't say more than he has said in that poem, or in that letter of his publisher."

The fourth member of the Committee at the previous meeting muttered: "I don't like paying attention to 'The Daily Phase.' We're not politicians."

"We can't help his having chosen that particular rag," said Jack Muskham.

"Very distasteful," continued the fourth member, "diving into matters of conscience. Are we all prepared to say we wouldn't have done the same?"

There was a sound as of feet shuffling, and a wrinkled expert on the early civilisations of Ceylon, murmured: "To my mind, Desert is on the carpet—not for apostasy, but for the song he's made about it. Decency should have kept him quiet. Advertising his book! It's in a third edition, and everybody reading it. Making money out of it seems to me the limit."

"I don't suppose," said the fourth member, "that he thought of that. It's the accident of the sensation."

"He could have withdrawn the book."

"Depends on his contract. Besides, that would look like running from the storm he's roused. As a matter of fact, I think it's rather fine to have made an open confession."

"Theatrical!" murmured the K.C.

"If this," said Jack Muskham, "were one of the Service Clubs, they wouldn't think twice about it."

An author of 'Mexico Revisited' said drily:

"But it is not."

"I don't know if you can judge poets like other people," mused the fifth member.

"In matters of ordinary conduct," said the expert on the civilisation of Ceylon, "why not?"

A little man at the end of the table opposite the Chairman remarked, "The D-d-daily Ph-Phase!" as if releasing a small spasm of wind.

"Everybody's talking about the thing," said the K.C.

"My young people," put in a man who had not yet spoken, "scoff. They say: 'What does it matter what he did?' They talk about hypocrisy, laugh at Lyall's poem, and say it's good for the Empire to have some wind let out of it."

"Exactly!" said Jack Muskham: "That's the modern jargon. All standards gone by the board. Are we going to stand for that?"

"Anybody here know young Desert?" asked the fifth member.

"To nod to," replied Jack Muskham.

Nobody else acknowledged acquaintanceship.

A very dark man with deep lively eyes, said suddenly:

"All I can say is I trust the story has not got about in Afghanistan; I'm going there next month."

"Why?" said the fourth member.

"Merely because it will add to the contempt with which I shall be regarded anyway."

Coming from a well-known traveller, this remark made more impression than anything said so far. Two members, who, with the Chairman, had not yet spoken, said simultaneously: "Quiet!"

"I don't like condemning a man unheard," said the K.C.

"What about that, 'Squire'?" asked the fourth member.

The Chairman, who was smoking a pipe, took it from his mouth.

"Anybody anything more to say?"

"Yes," said the author of 'Mexico Revisited'; "let's put it on his conduct in publishing that poem."

"You can't," growled Jack Muskham; "the whole thing's of a piece. The point is simply: Is he fit to be a member here or not? I ask the Chairman to put that to the meeting."

But the 'Squire' continued to smoke his pipe. His experience of Committees told him that the time was not yet. Separate or 'knot' discussions would now set in. They led nowhere, but ministered to a general sense that the subject was having justice done to it.

Jack Muskham sat silent, his long face impassive and his long legs stretched out.

"Well?" said the member who had revisited Mexico, at last.

The 'Squire' tapped out his pipe.

"I think," he said, "that Mr. Desert should be asked to give us his reasons for publishing that poem."

"Hear, hear!" said the K.C.

"Quiet!" said the two members who had said it before.

"I agree," said the authority on Ceylon.

"Anybody against that?" said the 'Squire.'

"I don't see the use of it," muttered Jack Muskham. "He ratted, and he's confessed it."

No one else objecting, the 'Squire' continued:

"The secretary will ask him to see us and explain. There's no other business, gentlemen."

In spite of the general understanding that the matter was 'sub judice,' these proceedings were confided to Sir Lawrence before the day was out by three members of the Committee, including Jack Muskham. He took the knowledge out with him to dinner at South Street.

Since the publication of the poems and Compson Grice's letter, Michael and Fleur had talked of little else, forced to by the comments and questioning of practically every acquaintance. They differed radically. Michael, originally averse from publication of the poem, now that it was out, stoutly defended the honesty and courage of Wilfrid's avowal. Fleur could not forgive what she called the 'stupidity of the whole thing.' If he had only kept quiet and not indulged his conscience or his pride, the matter would have blown over, leaving practically no mark. It was, she said, unfair to Dinny, and unnecessary so far as Wilfrid himself was concerned; but of course he had always been like that. She had not forgotten the uncompromising way in which eight years ago he had asked her to become his mistress, and the still more uncompromising way in which he had fled from her when she had not complied. When Sir Lawrence told them of the meeting at 'Burton's' she said simply:

"Well, what could he expect?"

Michael muttered:

"Why is Jack Muskham so bitter?"

"Some dogs attack each other at sight. Others come to it more meditatively. This appears to be a case of both. I should say Dinny is the bone."

Fleur laughed.

"Jack Muskham and Dinny!"

"Sub-consciously, my dear. The workings of a misogynist's mind are not for us to pry into, except in Vienna. They can tell you everything there; even to the origin of hiccoughs."

"I doubt if Wilfrid will go before the Committee," said Michael, gloomily.

"Of course he won't, Michael."

"Then what will happen?"

"Almost certainly he'll be expelled under rule whatever it is."

Michael shrugged. "He won't care. What's a Club more or less?"

"No," said Fleur; "but at present the thing is in flux—people just talk about it; but expulsion from his Club will be definite condemnation. It's just what's wanted to make opinion line up against him."

"And *for* him."

"Oh! for him, yes; but we know what that amounts to—the disgruntled."

"That's all beside the point," said Michael, gruffly. "I know what he's feeling. His first instinct was to defy that Arab, and he bitterly regrets that he went back on it."

Sir Lawrence nodded.

"Dinny asked me if there was anything he could do to show publicly that he wasn't a coward. You'd think there might be, but it's not easy. People object to be put into positions of extreme danger in order that their rescuers may get into the papers. Van horses seldom run away in Piccadilly. He might throw some one off Westminster Bridge, and jump in after him; but that would merely be murder and suicide. Curious that, with all the heroism there is about, it should be so difficult to be deliberately heroic."

"He ought to face the Committee," said Michael; "and I hope he will. There's something he told me. It sounds silly; but knowing Wilfrid, one can see it made all the difference."

Fleur had planted her elbows on the polished table and her chin on her hands. So, leaning forward, she looked like the girl contemplating a china image in her father's picture by Alfred Stevens.

"Well?" she said. "What is it?"

366

"He says he was sorry for his executioner."

Neither his wife nor his father moved, except for a slight raising of the eyebrows. He went on, defiantly:

"Of course, it sounds absurd, but he said the fellow begged him not to make him shoot—he was under a vow to convert the infidel."

"To mention that to the Committee," Sir Lawrence said slowly, "would be telling it to the marines."

"He's not likely to," said Fleur, "he'd rather die than be laughed at."

"Exactly! I only mention it to show that the whole thing's not so simple as it appears to the pukka sahib."

"When," murmured Sir Lawrence, in a detached voice, "have I heard anything so nicely ironical? But all this is not helping Dinny."

"I think I'll go and see him again," said Michael.

"The simplest thing," said Fleur, "is for him to resign at once."

And with that common-sense conclusion the discussion closed.

CHAPTER 23

THOSE WHO LOVE, when the object of their love is in trouble, must keep sympathy to themselves and yet show it. Dinny did not find this easy. She watched, lynx-eyed, for any chance to assuage her lover's bitterness of soul. But though they continued to meet daily, he gave her none. Except for the expression of his face when he was off guard, he might have been quite untouched by tragedy. Throughout that fortnight after the Derby she came to his rooms, and they went joy-riding accompanied by the spaniel 'Foch'; and he never mentioned that of which all more or less literary and official London was talking. Through Sir Lawrence, however, she heard that he had been asked to meet the Committee of Burton's Club, and had answered by resignation. And, through Michael, who had been to see him again, she heard that he knew of Jack Muskham's part in the affair. Since he so rigidly refused to open out to her, she, at great cost, tried to surpass him in obliviousness of purgatory. His face often made her ache, but she kept that ache out of her own face. And all the time she was in bitter doubt whether she was right to refrain from trying to break through to him. It was a long and terrible lesson in the truth that not even real love can reach and anoint deep spiritual sores. The other half of her trouble, the unending quiet pressure of her family's sorrowful alarm, caused her an irritation of which she was ashamed.

And then occurred an incident, which, however unpleasant and alarming at the moment, was almost a relief because it broke up that silence.

They had been to the Tate Gallery and, walking home, had just come up to the steps leading to Carlton Terrace. Dinny was still talking about the Pre-Raphaelites, and saw nothing till Wilfrid's changed expression made her look for the cause. There was Jack Muskham, with a blank face, formally lifting a tall hat as if to some one who was not there, and a short dark man removing a grey felt covering, in unison. They passed, and she heard Muskham say:

"That I consider the limit."

Instinctively her hand went out to grasp Wilfrid's arm, but too late. He had spun round in his tracks. She saw him, three yards away, tap Muskham on the shoulder, and the two face each other, with the little man looking up at them like a terrier at two large dogs about to fight. She heard Wilfrid say in a low voice:

"What a coward and cad you are!"

There followed an endless silence, while her eyes flitted from Wilfrid's convulsed face to Muskham's, rigid and menacing, and the terrier man's black eyes snapping up at them. She heard him say: "Come on, Jack!" Saw a tremor pass through the length of Muskham's figure, his hands clench, his lips move:

"You heard that, Yule?"

The little man's hand pushed under his arm, pulled at him; the tall figure turned; the two moved away; and Wilfrid was back at her side.

"Coward and cad!" he muttered: "Coward and cad! Thank God I've told him!" He threw up his head, took a gulp of air, and said: "That's better! Sorry, Dinny."

In Dinny feeling was too churned up for speech. The moment had been so savagely primitive; and she had the horrid fear that it could not end there; an intuition, too, that she was the cause, the hidden reason of Muskham's virulence. She remembered Sir Lawrence's words: "Jack thinks you are being victimised." What if she were! What business was it of that long, lounging man who hated women! Absurd. She heard Wilfrid muttering:

"The limit! He might know what one feels!"

"But, darling, if we all knew what other people felt, we should be angels. He's only a member of the Jockey Club."

"He's done his best to get me outed, and he couldn't even refrain from *that*."

"It's I who ought to be angry, not you. It's I who force you to go about with me. Only you see I like it so. But, darling, I don't shrink in the wash. What *is* the use of my being your love if you won't let yourself go with me?"

"Why should I worry you with what can't be cured?"

"I exist to be worried by you. *Please* worry me!"

"Oh! Dinny, you're an angel!"

"I repeat it is not so. I really have blood in my veins."

"It's like ear-ache; you shake your head, and shake your head, and it's no good. I thought publishing 'The Leopard' would free me, but it hasn't. Am I 'yellow,' Dinny—am I?"

"If you were yellow I should not have loved you."

"Oh! I don't know. Women can love anything."

"Proverbially we admire courage before all. I'm going to be brutal. Has doubt of your courage anything to do with your ache? Isn't it just due to feeling that other people doubt?"

He gave a little unhappy laugh. "I don't know; I only know it's there."

Dinny looked up at him.

"Oh! darling, don't ache! I do so hate it for you."

They stood for a moment looking deeply at each other, and a vendor of matches, without the money to indulge in spiritual trouble, said:

"Box o' lights, Sir?"

Though she had been closer to Wilfrid that afternoon than perhaps ever before, Dinny returned to Mount Street oppressed by fears. She could not get the look on Muskham's face out of her head, nor the sound of his: "You heard that, Yule?"

It was silly! Out of such explosive encounters nothing but legal remedies came nowadays; and of all people she had ever seen, she could least connect Jack Muskham with the Law. She noticed a hat in the hall, and heard voices, as she passed her uncle's study. She had barely taken off her own hat, when he sent for her. He was talking to the little terrier man, perched astride of a chair, as if riding a race.

"Dinny, Mr. Telfourd Yule; my niece Dinny Cherrell."

The little man bowed over her hand.

"Yule has been telling me," said Sir Lawrence, "of that encounter. He's not easy in his mind."

"Neither am I," said Dinny.

"I'm sure Jack didn't mean those words to be heard, Miss Cherrell."

"I don't agree, I think he did."

Yule shrugged. The expression on his face was rueful, and Dinny liked his comical ugliness.

"Well, he certainly didn't mean *you* to hear them."

"He ought to have, then. Mr. Desert would prefer not to be seen with me in public. It's I who make him."

"I came to your uncle because when Jack won't talk about a thing, it's serious. I've known him a long time."

Dinny stood silent. The flush on her cheeks had dwindled to two red spots. And the two men stared at her, thinking, perhaps, that with her cornflower-blue eyes, slenderness, and that hair, she looked unsuited to the matter in hand. She said quietly: "What can I do, Uncle Lawrence?"

"I don't see, my dear, what anyone can do at the moment. Mr. Yule says that he left Jack going back to Royston. I thought possibly I might take you down to see him to-morrow. He's a queer fellow; if he didn't date so, I shouldn't worry. Such things blow over, as a rule."

Dinny controlled a sudden disposition to tremble.

"What do you mean by 'date'?"

Sir Lawrence looked at Yule and said: "We don't want to seem absurd. There's been no duel fought between Englishmen, so far as I know, for seventy or eighty years; but Jack is a survival. We don't quite know what to think. Horse-play is not in his line; neither is a law court. And yet we can't see him taking no further notice."

"I suppose," said Dinny with spirit, "he won't see, on reflection, that he's more to blame than Wilfrid?"

"No," said Yule, "he won't. Believe me, Miss Cherrell, I am deeply sorry about the whole business."

Dinny bowed. "I think it was nice of you to come, thank you!"

"I suppose," said Sir Lawrence, doubtfully, "you couldn't get Desert to send him an apology?"

'So that,' she thought, 'is what they wanted me for.' "No, Uncle, I couldn't—I couldn't even ask him. I'm quite sure he wouldn't."

"I see," said Sir Lawrence, glumly.

Bowing to Yule, Dinny turned towards the door. In the hall she seemed to be seeing through the wall behind her the renewed shrugging of their shoulders, the ruefulness on their glum faces, and she went up to her room. Apology! Thinking of Wilfrid's badgered, tortured face, the very idea of it offended her. Stricken to the quick already on the score of personal courage, it was the last thing he would dream of. She wandered unhappily in her room, then took out his photograph. The face she loved looked back at her with the sceptical indifference of an effigy. Wilful, sudden, proud, self-centred, deeply dual; but cruel, no, and cowardly—*no!*

'Oh! my darling!' she thought, and put it away.

She went to her window and leaned out. A beautiful evening—the Friday of Ascot week, the first of those two weeks when in England fine weather is almost certain! On Wednesday there had been a deluge, but to-day had the feel of real high summer. Down below a taxi drew up—her uncle and aunt were going out to dinner. There they came, with Blore putting them in and standing to look after them. Now the 'staff' would turn on the wireless. Yes! Here it came! She opened her door. Grand opera! Rigoletto! The twittering of those tarnished melodies came up to her, in all the bravura of an age which knew better than this, it seemed, how to express the emotions of wayward hearts.

The gong! She did not want to go down and eat, but she must, or Blore and Augustine would be upset. She washed hastily, compromised with her dress, and went down.

But while she ate she grew more restless, as if sitting still and attending to a single function were sharpening the edge of her anxiety. A duel! Fantastic, in these days! And yet—Uncle Lawrence was uncanny, and Wilfrid in just the mood to do anything to show himself unafraid. Were duels illegal in France! Thank heaven she had all that money. No! It was absurd! People had called each other names with impunity for nearly a century. No good to fuss; to-morrow she would go with Uncle Lawrence and see that man. It was all, in some strange way, on her account. What would one of her own people do if called a coward and a cad—her father, her brother, Uncle Adrian? What *could* they do? Horsewhips, fists, law courts—all such hopeless, coarse, ugly remedies! And she felt for the first time Wilfrid had been wrong to use such words. Ah! But was he not entitled to hit back? Yes, indeed! She could see again his head jerked up and hear his: 'Ah! That's better!'

Swallowing down her coffee, she got up and sought the drawing room. On the sofa was her aunt's embroidery thrown down, and she gazed at it with a feeble interest. An intricate old French design needing many coloured wools—grey rabbits looking archly over their shoulders at long, curious, yellow dogs seated on yellow haunches, with red eyes, and tongues hanging out; leaves and flowers, too, and here and there a bird, all set in a background of brown wool. Tens of thousands of stitches, which, when finished, would lie under glass on a little table, and last till they were all dead and no one knew who had worked it. *Tout lasse, tout passe!* The strains of Rigoletto still came floating from the basement. Really Augustine must have drama in her soul, to be listening to a whole opera.

"*Donna e mobile!*"

Dinny took up her book, the 'Memoirs of Harriette Wilson'; a tome in which no one kept any faith to speak of except the authoress, and she only in her own estimation; a loose, bright, engaging, conceited minx, with a good heart and one real romance among a peck of love affairs.

"*Donna e mobile!*" It came mocking up the stairs, fine and free, as if the tenor had reached his Mecca. *Mobile!* No! That was more true of men than of women! Women did not change, except in America, where nothing had roots, they said. One loved—one lost, perhaps! She sat with closed eyes till the last notes of that last act died away, then went up to bed. She passed a night broken by dreams, and was awakened by a voice saying:

"Someone on the telephone for you, Miss Dinny."

"For me? Why! What time is it?"

"Half-past seven, Miss."

She sat up startled.

"Who is it?"

"No name, Miss; but he wants to speak to you special."

With the thought 'Wilfrid!' she jumped up, put on a dressing-gown and slippers, and ran down.

"Yes. Who is it?"

"Stack, Miss. I'm sorry to disturb you so early, but I thought it best. Mr. Desert, Miss, went to bed as usual last night, but this morning the dog was whining in his room, and I went in, and I see he's not been in bed at all. He must have gone out very early, because I've been about since half-past six. I shouldn't have disturbed you, Miss, only I didn't like the look of him last night. . . . Can you hear me, Miss?"

"Yes. Has he taken any clothes or anything?"

"No, Miss."

"Did anybody come to see him last night?"

"No, Miss. But a letter came by hand about half-past nine. I noticed him distraught, Miss, when I brought the whisky in. Perhaps it's nothing, but being so sudden, I . . . Can you hear me, Miss?"

"Yes. I'll dress at once and come round. Stack, can you get me a taxi, or, better, a car, by the time I'm there?"

"I'll get a car, Miss."

"Is there any service to the Continent he could have caught?"

"Nothing before nine o'clock."

"I'll be round as quick as I can."

"Yes, Miss. Don't you worry, Miss; he might be wanting exercise or something."

Dinny replaced the receiver and flew upstairs.

CHAPTER 24

WILFRID'S TAXI-CAB, whose tank he had caused to be filled to the brim, ground slowly up Haverstock Hill towards the Spaniards Road. He looked at his watch. Forty miles to Royston—even in this growler he would be there by nine! He took out a letter and read it through once more.

> "Liverpool Street Station.
> Friday.

"SIR,

"You will agree that the matter of this afternoon cannot rest there. Since the Law denies one decent satisfaction, I give you due notice that I shall horsewhip you publicly whenever and wherever I first find you unprotected by the presence of a lady.

> Yours faithfully,
>
> J. MUSKHAM.

"The Briery, Royston."

'Whenever and wherever I first find you unprotected by the presence of a lady!' That would be sooner than the swine thought! A pity the fellow was so much older than himself.

The cab had reached the top now, and was speeding along the lonely Spaniards Road. In the early glistening morning the view was worth a poet's notice, but Wilfrid lay back in the cab, unseeing, consumed by his thoughts. Something to hit at. This chap, at any rate, should no longer sneer at him! He had no plan except to be publicly on hand at the first possible moment after reading those words: "Unprotected by the presence of a lady!" Taken as sheltering behind a petticoat! Pity it was not a real duel! The duels of literature jig-sawed in his brain—Bel Ami, Bazarov, Dr. Slammer, Sir Lucius O'Trigger, D'Artagnan, Sir Toby, Winkle—all those creatures of fancy who had endeared the duel to readers. Duels and runs on banks, those two jewels in the crown of drama—gone! Well, he had shaved—with cold water!—and dressed with as much care as if he were not going to a vulgar brawl. The dandified Jack Muskham and a scene of low violence! Very amusing! The cab ground and whirred its way on through the thin early traffic of market and milk carts; Wilfrid sat drowsing after his almost sleepless night. Barnet he passed, and Hatfield, and the confines of Welwyn Garden City, then Knebworth, and the long villages of Stevenage, Gravely and Baldock. Houses and trees seemed touched by unreality in the fine haze. Postmen, and maids on doorsteps, boys riding farm horses, and now and then an early cyclist, alone inhabited the outdoor world. And, with that wry smile on his lips and his eyes half closed, he lay back, his feet pressed against the seat opposite. He had not to stage the scene, nor open the brawl. He had but to deliver himself, as it were registered, so that he could not be missed.

The cab slowed up.

"We're gettin' near Royston, Governor; where d'you want to go?"

"Pull up at the Inn."

The cab resumed its progress. The morning light hardened. All, now, was positive, away to the round, high-lying clumps of beeches. On the slope to his right he saw a string of sheeted race-horses moving slowly back from exercise. The cab entered a long village street, and near its end stopped at an hotel. Wilfrid got out.

"Garage your cab. I'll want you to take me back."

"Right, Governor."

He went in and asked for breakfast. Just nine o'clock! While eating he enquired of the waiter where the Briery was.

"It's the long 'ouse back on the right, Sir; but if you want Mr. Muskham, you've only to stand in the street outside 'ere. 'E'll be passing on his pony at five past ten; you can set your watch by him going to his stud farm when there's no racing."

"Thank you, that will save me trouble."

At five minutes before ten, smoking a cigarette, he took his position at the hotel gate. Girt-in, and with that smile, he stood motionless, and through his mind passed and repassed the scene between Tom Sawyer and the boy in the too-good clothes, walking round each other with an elaborate ritual of insults before the whirlwind of their encounter. There would be no ritual to-day! 'If I can lay him out,' he thought, 'I will!' His hands, concealed in the pockets of his jacket, kept turning into fists; otherwise he stood, still as the gatepost against which he leaned, his face veiled in the thin fume rising from his cigarette. He noticed with satisfaction his cabman talking to another chauffeur outside the yard, a man up the street opposite cleaning windows, and a butcher's cart. Muskham could not pretend this was not a public occasion. If they had neither of them boxed since schooldays, the thing would be a crude mix-up; all the more chance of hurting or being hurt! The sun topped some trees on the far side and shone on his face. He moved a pace or two to get the full of it. The sun—all good in life came from the sun. And suddenly he thought of Dinny. The sun to her was not what it was to him. Was he in a dream— was she real? Or, rather, were she and all this English business some rude interval of waking? God knew! He stirred and looked at his watch: Three minutes past ten, and there, sure enough, as the waiter had said, coming up the street was a rider, unconcerned, sedate, with a long easy seat on a small well-bred animal. Closer and closer, unaware! Then the rider's eyes came round, there was a movement of his chin. He raised a hand to his hat, checked the pony, wheeled it and cantered back.

'Hm!' thought Wilfrid: 'Gone for his whip!' And from the stump of his cigarette he lighted another. A voice behind him said:

"What'd I tell you, Sir? That's Mr. Muskham."

"He seems to have forgotten something."

"Ah!" said the waiter, "he's regular as a rule. They say at the stud he's a Turk for order. Here he comes again; not lost much time, 'as 'e?"

He was coming at a canter. About thirty yards away he reined up and got off. Wilfrid heard him say to the pony, "Stand, Betty!" His heart began to beat, his hands in his pockets were clenched fast; he still leaned against the gate. The waiter had withdrawn, but with the tail of his eye Wilfrid could see him at the hotel door, waiting as if to watch over the interview he had fostered. His cabman was still engaged in the endless conversation of those who drive cars; the shopman still cleaning his windows; the butcher's man rejoining his cart. Muskham came deliberately, a cut and thrust whip in his hand.

'Now!' thought Wilfrid.

Within three yards Muskham stopped. "Are you ready?"

Wilfrid took out his hands, let the cigarette drop from his lips, and nodded. Raising the whip, the long figure sprang. One blow fell, then Wilfrid closed. He closed so utterly that the whip was useless and Muskham dropped it. They swayed back clinched together against the gate, as if struck by the same idea, unclinched and raised their fists. In a moment it was clear that neither was any longer expert. They drove at each other without science, but with a sort of fury, length and weight on one side, youth and agility on the other. Amidst the scrambling concussions of this wild encounter, Wilfrid was conscious of a little crowd collecting —they had become a street show! Their combat was so breathless, furious and silent, that its nature seemed to infect that gathering, and from it came nothing but a muttering. Both were soon cut on the mouth and bleeding, both were soon winded and half dazed. In sheer breathlessness they clinched again and stood swaying, striving to get a grip of each other's throats.

"Go it, Mr. Muskham!" cried a voice.

As if encouraged, Wilfrid wrenched himself free and sprang; Muskham's fist thumped into his chest as he came on, but his outstretched hands closed round his enemy's neck. There was a long stagger, and then both went crashing on the ground. There, again as if moved by the same thought, they unclinched and scrambled up. For a moment they stood panting, glaring at each other for an opening. For a second each looked round him. Wilfrid saw Muskham's blood-stained face change and become rigid, his hands drop, and hide in his pockets; saw him turn away.

And suddenly he realised why. Standing up in an open car, across the street, was Dinny, with one hand covering her lips and the other shading her eyes.

Wilfrid turned as abruptly and went into the hotel.

CHAPTER 25

WHILE DINNY DRESSED and skimmed along the nearly empty streets, she had been thinking hard. That letter brought last night by hand surely meant that Muskham was the cause of Wilfrid's early sortie. Since he had slipped like a needle into a bundle of hay, her only chance was to work from the other end. No need to wait for her uncle to see Jack Muskham. She could see him alone just as well, perhaps better. It was eight o'clock when she reached Cork Street, and she at once said: "Has Mr. Desert a revolver, Stack?"

"Yes, Miss."

"Has he taken it?"

"No."

"I ask because he had a quarrel yesterday."

Stack passed his hand over his unshaven chin. "Don't know where you're going, Miss, but would you like me to come with you?"

"I think it would be better if you'd go and make sure he isn't taking a boat train."

"Certainly, Miss. I'll take the dog, and do that."

"Is that car outside for me?"

"Yes, Miss. Would you like it opened?"

"I would; the more air, the better."

The henchman nodded, his eyes and nose seeming to Dinny unusually large and intelligent.

"If I run across Mr. Desert first, where shall I get in touch with you, Miss?"

"I'll call at Royston post-office for any telegram. I'm going to see a Mr. Muskham there. The quarrel was with him."

"Have you had anything to eat, Miss? Let me get you a cup of tea."

"I've had one, thank you." It saved time to say what was not true.

That drive, on an unknown road, seemed interminable to her, haunted by her uncle's words: "If Jack didn't date so, I shouldn't worry. . . . He's a survival." Suppose that, even now, in some enclosure—Richmond Park, Caen Wood, where not—they were playing the old-fashioned pranks of honour! She conjured up the scene—Jack Muskham, tall, deliberate; Wilfrid, girt-in, defiant, trees around them, wood-pigeons calling, their hands slowly rising to the level—! Yes, but who would give the word? And pistols!

People do not go about with dueling pistols nowadays. If that had been suggested, Wilfrid would surely have taken his revolver! What should she say if, indeed, she found Muskham at home? "Please don't mind being called a cad and coward! They are really almost words of endearment." Wilfrid must never know that she had tried to mediate. It would but wound his pride still further. Wounded pride. Was there any older, deeper, more obstinate cause of human trouble, or any more natural and excusable! The consciousness of having failed oneself! Overmastered by the attraction that knows neither reason nor law, she loved Wilfrid none the less for having failed himself; but she was not blind to that failure. Ever since her father's words "by any Englishman who's threatened with a pistol" had touched some nerve in the background of her being, she had realised that she was divided by her love from her instinctive sense of what was due from Englishmen.

The driver stopped to examine a back tire. From the hedge a drift of elder-flower scent made her close her eyes. Those flat, white, scented blossoms! The driver remounted and started the car with a jerk. Was life always going to drag her away from love? Was she never to rest drugged and happy in its arms?

'Morbid!' she thought: 'I ought to be keying my pitch to the Jockey Club.'

Royston began, and she said: "Stop at the post-office, please."

"Right, lady!"

There was no telegram for her, and she asked for Muskham's house. The post-mistress looked at the clock.

"Nearly opposite, Miss; but if you want Mr. Muskham, I saw him pass riding just now. He'll be going to his stud farm—that'll be through the town and off to the right."

Dinny resumed her seat, and they drove slowly on.

Afterwards she did not know whether her instinct or the driver's stopped the car. For when he turned round and said: "Appears like a bit of a mix-up, Miss," she was already standing, to see over the heads of that ring of people in the road. She saw only too well the strained, blood-streaked faces, the rain of blows, the breathless swaying struggle. She had opened the door, but with the sudden thought: 'He'd never forgive me!' banged it to again, and stood, with one hand shading her eyes, the other covering her lips, conscious that the driver, too, was standing.

"Something like a scrap!" she heard him say, admiringly.

How strange and wild Wilfrid looked! With only fists they could not kill each other! And mixed with her alarm was a sort of exultation. He had come down to seek battle! Yet every blow seemed falling on her flesh, each clutch and struggling movement seemed her own.

"Not a bloody bobby!" said the driver, carried away: "Go it! I back the young 'un."

Dinny saw them fall apart, then Wilfrid rushing with outstretched hands; she heard the thump of Muskham's fist on his chest, saw them clinch, stagger, and fall; then rise and stand gasping, glaring. She saw Muskham catch sight of her, then Wilfrid; saw them turn away; and all was over. The driver said: "Now, that was a pity!" Dinny sank down on the car seat, and said quietly:

"Drive on, please!"

Away! Just away! Enough that they had seen her—more than enough, perhaps!

"Drive on a little, then turn and go back to Town." They wouldn't begin again!

"Neither of 'em much good with 'is 'ands, Miss, but a proper spirit."

Dinny nodded. Her hand was still over her mouth, for her lips were trembling. The driver looked at her.

"You're a bit pale, Miss—too much blood! Why not stop somewhere and 'ave a drop o' brandy?"

"Not here," said Dinny; "the next village."

"Baldock. Right-o!" And he put the car to speed.

The crowd had disappeared as they passed the hotel. Two dogs, a man cleaning windows, and a policeman, were the only signs of life.

At Baldock she had some breakfast. Conscious that she ought to feel relieved, now that the explosion had occurred, she was surprised by the foreboding which oppressed her. Would he not resent her having come as if to shield him? Her accidental presence had stopped the fight, and she had seen them disfigured, blood-stained, devoid of their dignities. She decided to tell no one where she had been, or what she had seen— not even Stack, or her uncle.

Such precautions are of small avail in a country so civilised. An able, if not too accurate, description of the "Encounter at Royston between Mr. John Muskham, cousin of Sir Charles Muskham, Bart., the well-known breeder of bloodstock, and the Hon. Wilfrid Desert, second son of Lord Mullyon, author of 'The Leopard' which has recently caused such a sensation," appeared in that day's last edition of the 'Evening Sun,' under the heading "Fisticuffs in High Quarters." It was written with spirit and imagination, and ended thus: "It is believed that the origin of the quarrel may be sought in the action which it is whispered was taken by Mr. Muskham over Mr. Desert's membership of Burton's Club. It seems that Mr. Muskham took exception to Mr. Desert continuing a member after his public acknowledgement that 'The Leopard' was founded on his own experience. The affair, no doubt, was very high-spirited, if not likely to improve the plain man's conception of a dignified aristocracy."

This was laid before Dinny at dinner time by her uncle without comment. It caused her to sit rigid, till his voice said: "Were you there, Dinny?"

'Uncanny, as usual,' she thought; but though by now habituated to the manipulation of truth, she was not yet capable of the lie direct, and she nodded.

"What's that?" said Lady Mont.

Dinny pushed the paper over to her aunt, who read, screwing up her eyes, for she had long sight.

"Which won, Dinny?"

"Neither. They just stopped."

"Where is Royston?"

"In Cambridgeshire."

"Why?"

Neither Dinny nor Sir Lawrence knew.

"He didn't take you on a pillion, Dinny?"

"No, dear. I just happened to drive up."

"Religion is very inflamin'," murmured Lady Mont.

"It is," said Dinny, bitterly.

"Did the sight of you stop them?" said Sir Lawrence.

"Yes."

"I don't like that. It would have been better if a bobby or a knockout blow——"

"I didn't want them to see me."

"Have you seen him since?"

Dinny shook her head.

"Men are vain," said her aunt.

That closed the conversation.

Stack telephoned after dinner that Wilfrid had returned; but instinct told her to make no attempt to see him.

After a restless night she took the morning train to Condaford. It was Sunday and they were all at church. She seemed strangely divided from her family. Condaford smelled the same, looked the same; and the same people did the same things, yet all was different! Even the Scottish terrier and the spaniels sniffed her with doubting nostrils, as if uncertain whether she belonged to them any more.

'And do I?' she thought. 'The scent is not there when the heart is away!'

Jean was the first to appear, Lady Cherrell having stayed to Communion, the General to count the offertory, and Hubert to inspect the village cricket pitch. She found Dinny sitting by an old sundial in front of a bed of delphiniums. Having kissed her sister-in-law, she stood and looked at her quite a minute, before saying: "Take a pull, my dear, or you'll be going into a decline, whatever that is."

"I only want my lunch," said Dinny.

"Same here. I thought my Dad's sermons were a trial even after I'd censored them; but your man here!"

"Yes, one *can* 'put him down.'"

Again Jean paused, and her eyes searched Dinny's face.

"Dinny, I'm all for you. Get married at once, and go off with him."

Dinny smiled.

"There are two parties to every marriage."

381

"Is that paragraph in this morning's paper true, about a fight at Royston?"

"Probably not."

"I mean was there one?"

"Yes."

"Who began it?"

"Probably I did. There's no other woman in the case."

"Dinny, you're very changed."

"No longer sweet and disinterested."

"Very well!" said Jean. "If you want to play the lovelorn female, play it!"

Dinny caught her skirt. Jean knelt down and put her arms round her.

"You were a brick to me when I was up against it. Cry down my back, if you like."

Dinny laughed.

"What are my father and Hubert saying now?"

"Your father says nothing and looks glum. Hubert either says: 'Something must be done,' or: 'It's the limit.'"

"Not that it matters," said Dinny suddenly, "I'm past all that."

"You mean you're not sure what *he'll* do? But, of course, he must do what you want."

Again Dinny laughed.

"You're afraid," said Jean, with startling comprehension, "that he might run off and leave you?" And she subsided on to her hams the better to look up into Dinny's face. "And, of course, he might. He looks proud. You know I went to see him?"

"Oh?"

"Yes; he got over me. I couldn't say a word. Great charm, Dinny."

"Did Hubert send you?"

"No. On my own. I was going to let him know what would be thought of him if he married you, but I couldn't. I should have imagined he'd have told you about it. But I suppose he knew it would worry you."

"I don't know," said Dinny; and did not. It seemed to her at that moment that she knew very little.

Jean sat silently pulling an early dandelion to pieces.

"If I were you," she said, at last, "I'd vamp him. If you'd once belonged to him, he couldn't leave you."

Dinny got up: "Let's go round the gardens and see what's out."

CHAPTER 26

SINCE DINNY said no further word on the subject occupying every mind, no word was said by anyone; and for this she was truly thankful. She spent the next three days trying to hide the fact that she was very unhappy. No letter had come from Wilfrid, no message from Stack; surely if anything had happened, *he* would have let her know. On the fourth day, feeling that she could bear the suspense no longer, she telephoned to Fleur, and asked if she might come up to them.

The expressions of her father's and her mother's faces when she said she was going, affected her as do the eyes and tails of dogs whom one must leave. How much more potent was the pressure put by silent disturbance than by nagging!

Panic assailed her in the train. Had her instinct to wait for Wilfrid to make the first move been wrong? Ought she to have gone straight to him? And on reaching London she told her driver: "Cork Street."

But he was out, and Stack did not know when he would be in. The henchman's demeanour seemed to her strangely different, as if he had retreated to a fence and were sitting on it. Was Mr. Desert well? Yes. And the dog? Yes, the dog was well. Dinny drove away disconsolate. At South Square again no one was in; it seemed as if the world were in conspiracy to make her feel deserted. She had forgotten Wimbledon, the Horse Show, and other activities of the time of year. All such demonstrations of interest in life were, indeed, so far from her present mood that she could not conceive people taking part in them.

She sat down in her bedroom to write to Wilfrid. There was no longer any reason for silence, for Stack would tell him she had called.

She wrote:

"South Square, Westminster.
"Ever since Saturday I've been tortured by the doubt whether to write, or wait for you to write to me. Darling, I never meant to interfere in any way. I had come down to see Mr. Muskham and tell him that it's I only who was responsible for what he so absurdly called the limit. I never expected you to be there. I didn't really much hope even to find him. Please let me see you.

Your unhappy
DINNY."

She went out herself to post it. On the way back she came on Kit, with his governess, the dog, and the two youngest of her Aunt Alison's children. They seemed entirely happy; she was ashamed not to seem so too, so they all went together to Kit's schoolroom to have tea. Before it was over Michael came in. Dinny, who had seldom seen him with his little son, was fascinated by the easy excellence of their relationship. It was, perhaps, a little difficult to tell which was the elder, though a certain difference in size and the refusal of a second helping of strawberry jam, seemed to favour Michael. That hour, in fact, brought her the nearest approach to happiness she had known since she left Wilfrid five days ago. After it was over she went with Michael to his study.

"Anything wrong, Dinny?"

Wilfrid's best friend, and the easiest person in the world to confide in, and she did not know what to say! And then, suddenly she began to talk, sitting in his armchair, her elbows on her knees, her chin in her hands, staring not at him, but at her future. And Michael sat on the window-sill, his face now rueful, now whimsical, making little soothing sounds. Nothing would matter, she said, neither public opinion, the Press, nor even her family, if only there were not in Wilfrid himself this deep bitter unease, this basic doubt of his own conduct, this permanent itch to prove to others and, above all, to himself, that he was not 'yellow.' Now that she had given way, it poured out of her, all that bottled-up feeling that she was walking on a marsh, where at any moment she might sink in some deep, unlooked-for hole thinly covered by specious surface. She ceased and lay back in the chair exhausted.

"But, Dinny," said Michael, gently, "isn't he really fond of you?"

"I don't know, Michael; I thought so—I don't know. Why should he be? I'm an ordinary person, he's not."

"We all seem ordinary to ourselves. I don't want to flatter you, but you seem to me less ordinary than Wilfrid."

"Oh! no!"

"Poets," said Michael, gloomily, "give a lot of trouble. What are we going to do about it?"

That evening after dinner he went forth ostensibly to the House, and in fact to Cork Street.

Wilfrid was not in, so he asked Stack's permission to wait. Sitting on the divan in that unconventional, dimly-lighted room, he twitted himself for having come. To imply that he came from Dinny would be worse than useless. Besides, he hadn't. No! He had come to discover, if he could, whether Wilfrid really was in love with her. If not, then—well, then the sooner she was out of her misery the better. It might half break her heart, but that was better than pursuing a substance which wasn't there. He knew, or thought he knew, that Wilfrid was the last person to endure a one-sided relationship. The worst of all disasters for Dinny would be to join herself to him under a misconception of his feelings for her. On a little table close to the divan, with the whiskey, were the night's letters—

only two, one of them, he could see, from Dinny herself. The door was opened slightly and a dog came in. After sniffing at Michael's trousers, it lay down with its head on its paws and its eyes fixed on the door. He spoke to it, but it took no notice—the right sort of dog. 'I'll give him till eleven,' thought Michael. And almost immediately Wilfrid came. He had a bruise on one cheek and some plaster on his chin. The dog fluttered round his legs.

"Well, old man," said Michael, "that must have been a hearty scrap."

"It was. Whiskey?"

"No, thanks."

He watched Wilfrid take up the letters and turn his back to open them.

'I ought to have known he'd do that,' thought Michael; 'there goes my chance He's bound to pretend to be in love with her!'

Before turning round again Wilfrid made himself a drink and finished it. Then, facing Michael, he said: "Well?"

Disconcerted by the abruptness of that word, and by the knowledge that he had come to pump his friend, Michael did not answer.

"What d'you want to know?"

Michael said abruptly: "Whether you're in love with Dinny."

Wilfrid laughed. "Really, Michael!"

"I know. But things can't go on like this. Damn it! Wilfrid, you ought to think of her."

"I am." He said it with a face so withdrawn and unhappy, that Michael thought: 'He means that.'

"Then for God's sake," he said, "show it! Don't let her eat her heart out like this!"

Wilfrid had turned to the window. Without looking round he said: "You've never had occasion to try and prove yourself the opposite of yellow. Well, don't! You won't find the chance. It comes when you don't want it, not when you do."

"Naturally! But, my dear fellow, that's not Dinny's fault."

"Her misfortune."

"Well, then?"

Wilfrid wheeled round.

"Oh! damn you, Michael! Go away! No one can interfere in this. It's much too intimate."

Michael rose and clutched his hat. Wilfrid had said exactly what he himself had really been thinking ever since he came.

"You're quite right," he said, humbly. "Good-night, old man! That's a nice dog."

"I'm sorry," said Wilfrid; "you meant well, but you can't help. No one can. Good-night!"

Michael got out, and all the way downstairs he looked for the tail between his legs.

When he reached home Dinny had gone up, but Fleur was waiting down for him. He had not meant to speak of his visit, but, after looking at him keenly, she said:

"You haven't been to the House, Michael. You've been to see Wilfrid."

Michael nodded.

"Well?"

"No go!"

"I could have told you that. If you come across a man and woman quarrelling in the street, what do you do?"

"Pass by the other side, if you can get there in time."

"Well?"

"They're *not* quarrelling."

"No, but they've got a special world no one else can enter."

"That's what Wilfrid said."

"Naturally."

Michael stared. Yes, of course. She had once had her special world, and not with—him!

"It was stupid of me. But I *am* stupid."

"No, not stupid; well-intentioned. Are you going up?"

"Yes."

As he went upstairs he had the peculiar feeling that it was she who wanted to go to bed with him rather than he with her. And yet, once in bed, that would all change, for of such was the nature of man!

Dinny, in her room above theirs, through her open window could hear the faint murmur of their voices, and, bowing her face on her hands, gave way to a feeling of despair. The stars in their courses fought against her! External opposition one could cut through or get round; but this deep spiritual unease in the loved one's soul, that—ah! that—one could not reach; and the unreachable could not be pushed away, cut through, or circumvented. She looked up at the stars that fought against her. Did the ancients really believe that or was it just with them, as with her, a manner of speaking? Did those bright wheeling jewels on the indigo velvet of all space really concern themselves with little men, the lives and loves of human insects, who, born from an embrace, met and clung and died and became dust? Those candescent worlds, circled by little offsplit planets—were their names taken in vain, or were they really in their motions and their relative positions the writing on the wall for men to read?

No! That was only human self-importance! To his small wheel man bound the Universe. Swing low, sweet chariots! But they didn't! Man swung with them—in space. . . .

CHAPTER 27

Two DAYS LATER the Cherrell family met in conclave because of a sudden summons received by Hubert to rejoin his regiment in the Soudan. He wished to have something decided about Dinny before he left. The four Cherrell brothers, Sir Lawrence, Michael and himself, gathered, therefore, in Adrian's room at the Museum after Mr. Justice Charwell's Court had risen. They all knew that the meeting might be futile, because, as even Governments find, to decide is useless if decision cannot be carried out.

Michael, Adrian and the General, who had been in personal touch with Wilfrid, were the least vocal. Sir Lawrence and the Judge the most vocal; Hubert and Hilary were now vocal and now dumb.

Starting from the premise which nobody denied, that the thing was a bad business, two schools of thought declared themselves—Adrian, Michael and to some extent Hilary, believed there was nothing to be done but wait and see; the rest thought there was much to be done, but what— they could not say.

Michael, who had never seen his four uncles so close together before, was struck by the resemblance in the shape and colouring of their faces, except that the eyes of Hilary and Lionel were blue and grey, and of the General and Adrian brown and hazel. They all, notably, lacked gesture, and had a lean activity of figure. In Hubert these characteristics were accentuated by youth, and his hazel eyes at times looked almost grey.

"If only," Michael heard his father say, "you could injunct her, Lionel?" and Adrian's impatient:

"We must let Dinny alone; trying to control her is absurd. She's got a warm heart, an unselfish nature, and plenty of sense." Then Hubert's retort:

"We know all that, Uncle, but the thing will be such a disaster for her we must do what we can."

"Well, what *can* you do?"

'Exactly!' thought Michael, and said: "Just now she doesn't know how she stands."

"You couldn't get her to go out with you to the Soudan, Hubert?" said the Judge.

"I've lost all touch with her."

"If someone wanted her badly—" began the General and did not finish.

"Even then," murmured Adrian, "only if she were quite sure Desert didn't want her more."

Hilary took out his pipe. "Has anyone tried Desert?"

"I have," said the General.

"And I, twice," muttered Michael.

"I suppose," said Hubert gloomily, "I could have a shot."

"Not, my dear fellow," put in Sir Lawrence, "unless you can be quite certain of keeping your temper."

"I never can be certain of that."

"Then don't!"

"Would *you* go, Dad!" asked Michael.

"I?"

"He used to respect you."

"Not even a blood relation!"

"You might take a chance, Lawrence," said Hilary.

"But why?"

"None of the rest of us can, for one reason or another."

"Why shouldn't *you?*"

"In a way I agree with Adrian, it's best to leave it all alone."

"What exactly is the objection to Dinny's marrying him?" asked Adrian. The General turned to him abruptly.

"She'd be marked out for life."

"So was that fellow who stuck to his wife when she was convicted. Everybody respected him the more."

"There's no such sharp hell," said the Judge, "as seeing fingers pointed at your life's partner."

"Dinny would learn not to notice them."

"Forgive me, but you're missing the point," muttered Michael. "The point is Wilfrid's own feeling. If he remains bitter about himself, and marries her—that'll be hell for her, if you like. And the fonder she is of him, the worse it'll be."

"You're right, Michael," said Sir Lawrence, unexpectedly. "I'd think it well worth while to go, if I could make him see that."

Michael sighed.

"Whichever way it goes, it's hell for poor Dinny."

"'Joy cometh in the morning,'" murmured Hilary through a cloud of smoke.

"Do you believe that, Uncle Hilary?"

"Not too much."

"Dinny's twenty-six. This is her first love. If it goes wrong—what then?"

"Marriage."

"With somebody else?"

Hilary nodded.

"Lively!"

"Life is lively."

"Well, Lawrence?" asked the General, sharply: "You'll go?"

Sir Lawrence studied him for a moment, and then replied: "Yes."

"Thank you!"

It was not clear to any of them what purpose would be served, but it was a decision of sorts, and at least could be carried out.

Wilfrid had lost most of his bruise and discarded the plaster on his chin when Sir Lawrence, encountering him on the stairs at Cork Street that same late afternoon, said:

"D'you mind if I walk a little way with you?"

"Not at all, Sir."

"Any particular direction?"

Wilfrid shrugged, and they walked side by side, till at last Sir Lawrence said:

"Nothing's worse than not knowing where you're going!"

"You're right."

"Then why go, especially if in doing so you take someone with you? Forgive my putting things crudely, but, except for Dinny, would you be caring a hang about all this business? What other ties have you got here?"

"None. I don't want to discuss things. If you'll forgive me, I'll branch off."

Sir Lawrence stopped. "Just one moment, and then I'll do the branching. Have you realised that a man who has a quarrel with himself is not fit to live with until he's got over it? That's all I wanted to say; but it's a good deal. Think it over!" And, raising his hat, Sir Lawrence turned on his heel. By George! He was well out of that! What an uncomfortable young man! And, after all, one had said all one had come to say! He walked towards Mount Street, reflecting on the limitations imposed by tradition. But for tradition, would Wilfrid mind being thought 'yellow'? Would Dinny's family care? Would Lyall have written his confounded poem? Would not the Corporal in the Buffs have kow-towed? Was a single one of the Cherrells, met in conclave, a real believing Christian? Not even Hilary—he would bet his boots! Yet not one of them could stomach this recantation. Not religion, but the refusal to take the 'dare'! That was the rub to them. The imputation of cowardice, or at least of not caring for the good name of one's country. Well! About a million British had died for that good name in the war; had they all died for a futility? Desert himself had nearly died for it, and got the M. C., or D. S. O., or something! All very contradictory! People cared for their country in a crowd, it seemed, but not in a desert; in France but not in Darfur.

He heard hurrying footsteps, and, turning around, saw Desert behind him. Sir Lawrence had almost a shock looking at his face, dry, dark, with quivering lips and deep suffering eyes.

"You were quite right," he said, "I thought I'd let you know. You can tell her family I'm going away."

At this complete success of his mission Sir Lawrence experienced dismay.

"Be careful!" he said: "You might do her a great injury."

"I shall do her that, anyway. Thank you for speaking to me. You've made me see. Good-bye!" He turned and was gone.

Sir Lawrence stood looking after him, impressed by his look of suffering. He turned in at his front door doubtful whether he had not made bad worse. While he was putting down his hat and stick, Lady Mont came down the stairs.

"I'm so bored, Lawrence. What have you been doin'?"

"Seeing young Desert; and it seems, I've made him feel that until he can live on good terms with himself, he won't be fit to live with at all."

"That's wicked."

"How?"

"He'll go away. I always knew he'd go away. You must tell Dinny at once what you've done." And she went to the telephone.

"Is that you, Fleur? . . . Oh! Dinny. . . . This is Aunt Em! . . . Yes. . . . Can you come round here? . . . Why not? . . . That's not a reason. . . . But you must! Lawrence wants to speak to you . . . At once? Yes. He's done a very stupid thing. . . . What? . . . No! . . . He wants to explain. In ten minutes . . . very well."

'My God!' thought Sir Lawrence. He had, suddenly, realised that to deaden feeling on any subject one only needed to sit in conclave. Whenever the Government got into trouble, they appointed a Commission. Whenever a man did something wrong, he went into consultation with solicitor and counsel. If he, himself, hadn't been sitting in conclave, would he ever have gone to see Desert and put the fat into the fire like this? The conclave had dulled his feelings. He had gone to Wilfrid as some juryman comes in to return his verdict after sitting on a case for days. And now he had to put himself right with Dinny, and how the deuce would he do that? He went into his study, conscious that his wife was following.

"Lawrence, you must tell her exactly what you've done, and how he took it. Otherwise it may be too late. And I shall stay until you've done it."

"Considering, Em, that you don't know what I said, or what he said, that seems superfluous."

"No," said Lady Mont, "nothing is, when a man's done wrong."

"I was charged to go and see him by your family."

"You ought to have had more sense. If you treat poets like innkeepers, they blow up."

"On the contrary, he thanked me."

"That's worse. I shall have Dinny's taxi kept at the door."

"Em," said Sir Lawrence, "when you want to make your will, let me know."

"Why?"

"Because of getting you consecutive before you start."

"Anything I have," said Lady Mont, "is to go to Michael, to be kept for Catherine. And if I'm dead when Kit goes to Harrow, he's to have my grandfather's 'stirrup-cup' that's in the armoire in my sitting-room at Lippin'hall. But he's not to take it to school with him, or they'll melt it, or drink boiled peppermints out of it, or something. Is that clear?"

"Perfectly."

"Then," said Lady Mont, "get ready and begin at once when Dinny comes."

"Quite!" said Sir Lawrence, meekly. "But how the deuce am I to put it to Dinny?"

"Just put it, and don't invent as you go along."

Sir Lawrence played a tune with his fingers on the window-pane. His wife stared at the ceiling. They were like that when Dinny came.

"Keep Miss Dinny's taxi, Blore."

At the sight of his niece Sir Lawrence perceived that he had, indeed, lost touch with feeling. Her face, under its chestnut-coloured hair, was sharpened and pallored, and there was a look in her eyes that he did not like.

"Begin," said Lady Mont.

Sir Lawrence raised one high thin shoulder as if in protection.

"My dear, your brother has been recalled, and I was asked whether I would go and see young Desert. I went. I told him that if he had a quarrel with himself he would not be fit to live with till he'd made it up. He said nothing and turned off. Afterwards he came up behind me in this street, and said that I was right. Would I tell your family that he was going away. He looked very queer and troubled. I said: 'Be careful! You might do her a great injury.' 'I shall do her that, anyway,' he said. And he went off. That was about twenty minutes ago."

Dinny looked from one to the other, covered her lips with her hand, and went out.

A moment later they heard her cab move off.

CHAPTER 28

EXCEPT FOR RECEIVING a little note in answer to her letter, which relieved her not at all, Dinny had spent these last two days in distress of mind. When Sir Lawrence made his communication, she felt as if all depended on whether she could get to Cork Street before Wilfrid was back there, and, in her taxi, she sat with hands screwed tight together in her lap, and eyes fixed on the driver's back, a back indeed so broad that it was not easy to fix them elsewhere. Useless to think of what she was going to say—she must say whatever came into her head when she saw him. His face would give her a lead. She realised that if he once got away from England, it would be as if she had never seen him. She stopped the cab in Burlington Street and walked swiftly to his door. If he had come straight home, he must be in! In these last two days she had realised that Stack had perceived some change in Wilfrid, and was conforming to it, and when he opened the door, she said:

"You mustn't put me off, Stack, I must see Mr. Desert." And, slipping past, she opened the door of the sitting-room. Wilfrid was pacing up and down.

"Dinny!"

She felt that if she said the wrong thing, it might be, then and there, the end; and she only smiled. He put his hands over his eyes; and, while he stood thus blinded, she stole up and threw her arms round his neck.

Was Jean right? Ought she to——?

Then, through the opened door Foch came in. He slid the velvet of his muzzle under her hand, and she sank on her knees to kiss him. When she looked up, Wilfrid had turned away. Instantly she scrambled up, and stood, as it were, lost. She did not know of what, if of anything, she thought, not even whether she was feeling. All seemed to go blank within her. He had thrown the window open and was leaning there holding his hands to his head. Was he going to throw himself out? She made a violent effort to control her nerves, and said very gently: "Wilfrid!" He turned and looked at her, and she thought: 'My God! He hates me!' Then his expression changed and became the one she knew; and she was aware once more of how at sea one is with wounded pride—so multiple and violent, and changing in its moods!

"Well?" she said: "What do you wish me to do?"

"I don't know. The whole thing is mad. I ought to have buried myself in Siam by now."

"Would you like me to stay here, to-night?"

"Yes! No! I don't know."

"Wilfrid, why take it so hard? It's as if love were nothing to you. Is it nothing?"

For answer he took out Jack Muskham's letter.

"Read this!"

She read it. "I see. It was doubly unfortunate that I came down."

He threw himself down again on the divan, and sat there looking up at her.

'If I do go,' thought Dinny, 'I shall only begin tearing to get back again.' And she said: "What are you doing for dinner?"

"Stack's got something, I believe."

"Would there be enough for me?"

"Too much, if you feel as I do."

She rang the bell.

"I'm staying to dinner, Stack. I only want about a pin's head of food."

When he had gone, craving a moment in which to recover her balance, she said: "May I have a wash, Wilfrid?"

While she was drying her face and hands, she took hold of herself with all her might, and then as suddenly relaxed. Whatever she decided would be wrong, would be painful, perhaps impossible. Let it go!

When she came back to the sitting-room he was not there. The door into his bedroom was open, but the room was empty. Dinny rushed to the window. He was not in the street. Stack's voice said:

"Excuse me, Miss: Mr. Desert was called out. He told me to say he would write. Dinner will be ready in a minute."

Dinny went straight up to him.

"Your first impression of me was the right one, Stack; not your second. I am going now. Mr. Desert need have no fear of me. Tell him that, please."

"Miss," said Stack, steadily, "I told you he was very sudden; but this is the most sudden thing I've ever known him do. I'm sorry, Miss. But I'm afraid it's a case of cutting your losses. If I can be of service to you, I will."

"If he leaves England," said Dinny, steadily, "I should like to have Foch."

"If I know Mr. Desert, Miss, he means to go. I've seen it coming on him ever since he had that letter the night before you came round in the early morning."

"Well," said Dinny, "shake hands, and remember what I said."

They exchanged a hand-grip, and, still unnaturally steady, she went out and down the stairs. She walked fast, giddy and strange in her head, and nothing but the word: So! recurring in her mind. All that she had felt, all that she had meant to feel, compressed into that word of two letters. In her life she had never felt so withdrawn and tearless, so indifferent as to where she went, what she did, or whom she saw. The world might well be without end, for its end had come. She did not believe that he had designed this way of breaking from her. He had not enough insight into her for that. But, in fact, no way could have been more perfect, more complete. Drag after a man! Impossible! She did not even have to form that thought, it was instinctive.

She walked, and walked, for three hours, about the London streets, and turned at last towards Westminster with the feeling that if she didn't she would drop. When she went in at South Square, she summoned all that was left in her to a spurt of gaiety; but, when she had gone up to her room, Fleur said:

"Something very wrong, Michael."

"Poor Dinny! What the hell has he done now?"

Going to the window, Fleur drew aside the curtain. It was not yet quite dark. Except for two cats, a taxi to the right, and a man on the pavement examining a small bunch of keys, there was nothing to be seen.

"Shall I go up and see if she'll talk?"

"No. If Dinny wants us, she'll let us know. If it's as you think, she'll want no one. She's proud as the devil when her back's to the wall."

"I hate pride," said Fleur; and, closing the curtain, she went towards the door. "It comes when you don't want it, and does you down. If you want a career, don't have pride." She went out.

'I don't know,' thought Michael, 'if I have pride, but I haven't got a career.' He followed slowly upstairs, and for some little time stood in the doorway of his dressing-room. But no sound came from upstairs.

Dinny, indeed, was lying on her bed, face down. So this was the end! Why had the force called love exalted and tortured her, then thrown her, used and exhausted, quivering, longing, wounded, startled, to eat her heart out in silence and grief? Love and pride, and the greater of these is pride! So the saying seemed to go within her, and to be squeezed into her pillow. Her love against his pride! Her love against her own pride! And the victory with pride! Wasteful and bitter! Of all that evening only one moment now seemed to her real: when he had turned from the window, and she had thought: 'He hates me!' Of course, he hated her standing like the figure of his wounded self-esteem; the one thing that prevented him from crying out: 'God damn you all! Good-bye!'

Well, now he could cry it and go! And she—suffer, suffer—and slowly get over it. No! Lie on it, keep it down, keep it silent, press it into her pillows. Make little of it, make nothing of it, while inside her, it swelled and ravaged her. The expression of instinct is not so clear as that; but behind all formless throbbing there is meaning; and that was the meaning within Dinny's silent and half smothered struggle on her bed. How could she have acted differently? Not her fault that Muskham had sent the letter with that phrase about the protection of a woman. Not her fault that she had rushed down to Royston! What had she done wrong? The whole thing arbitrary, gratuitous! Perhaps love in its courses was always so! It seemed to her that the night ticked while she lay there; the rusty ticking of an old clock. Was it the night, or her own life, abandoned and lying on its face?

CHAPTER 29

WILFRID HAD OBEYED impulse when he ran down into Cork Street. Ever since the sudden breaking off of that fierce undignified scuffle at Royston, and the sight of Dinny standing in the car covering her eyes with a hand, his feelings towards her had been terribly confused. Now at the sudden sight, sound, scent of her, warmth had rushed up in him and spent itself in kisses; but the moment she had left him his insane feeling had returned and hurled him down into a London where at least one could walk and meet no one. He went south and became involved with a queue of people trying to get into 'His Majesty's.' He stood among them thinking: 'As well in here as anywhere.' But, just as his turn came, he broke away, and branched off eastward; passed through Covent Garden, desolate and smelling of garbage, and came out into Ludgate Hill. Hereabouts he was reminded by scent of fish that he had eaten nothing since breakfast. And going into a restaurant, he drank a cocktail and ate some hors d'œuvres. Asking for a sheet of paper and envelope, he wrote:

"I had to go. If I had stayed, you and I would have been one. I don't know what I'm going to do—I may finish in the river to-night, or go abroad, or come back to you. Whatever I do, forgive, and believe that I have loved you. Wilfrid."

He addressed the envelope and thrust it into his pocket. But he did not post it. He could never express what he was thinking or feeling. Again he walked east. Through the City zone, deserted as if it had been mustard-gassed, he was soon in the cheerier Whitechapel Road. He walked, trying to tire himself out and stop the whirling of his thoughts. He moved northwards now, and towards eleven was nearing Chingford. All was moonlit and still when he passed the hotel and went on towards the Forest. One car, a belated cyclist, a couple or two, and three tramps, were all he met before he struck off the road in among the trees. Daylight was gone, and the moon was silvering the leaves and branches. Thoroughly exhausted, he lay down on the beech mast. The night was an unwritten poem—the gleam and drip of light like the play of an incoherent mind, fluttering, slipping in and out of reality; never at rest; never the firm silver of true metal; blemished and gone like a dream. Up there were the stars he had travelled by times without number, the Wain, and all the others that seemed meaningless, if not nameless, in this town world.

He turned over and lay on his face, pressing his forehead to the ground. And suddenly he heard the drone of a flying machine. But through the heavily-leafed boughs he could see no gliding, sky-scurrying shape. Some night-flier to Holland; some English airman picking out the lighted shape of London, or practising flight between Hendon and an East Coast base. After flying in the war he had never wished to fly again. The very sound of it brought back still that sick, fed-up feeling from which the Armistice had delivered him. The drone passed on and away. A faint rumbling murmur came from London, but here the night was still and warm, with only a frog croaking, a bird cheeping feebly once, two owls hooting against each other. He turned again on to his face, and fell into an uneasy sleep.

When he woke light was just rifting the clear darkness. A heavy dew had fallen; he felt stiff and chilled, but his mind was clear. He got up and swung his arms, lighted a cigarette and drew the smoke deep in. He sat with his arms clasped round his knees, smoking his cigarette to its end without ever moving it from his lips, and spitting out the stub with its long ash just before it burned his mouth. Suddenly he began to shiver! He got up to walk back to the road. Stiff and sore, he made poor going. It was full dawn by the time he reached the road, and then, knowing that he ought to go towards London, he went in the opposite direction. He plodded on, and every now and then shivered violently. At last he sat down and, bowed over his knees, fell into a sort of coma. A voice saying: "Hi" roused him. A fresh-faced young man in a small car had halted alongside.

"Anything wrong?"

"Nothing," muttered Wilfrid.

"You appear to be in poor shape, all the same. D'you know what time it is?"

"No."

"Get in here, and I'll run you to the hotel at Chingford. Got any money?"

Wilfrid looked at him grimly and laughed.

"Yes."

"Don't be touchy! What you want is a sleep and some strong coffee! Come on!"

Wilfrid got up. He could hardly stand. He lay back in the little car, huddled beside the young man, who said: "Now we shan't be long."

In ten minutes, which to a blurred and shivering consciousness might have been five hours, they were in front of the hotel.

"I know the 'boots' here," said the young man, "I'll put you in charge of him. What's your name?"

"Hell!" muttered Wilfrid.

"Hi! George: I found this gentleman on the road. He seems to have gone a bit wonky. Put him into some decent bedroom. Heat him up a good hot bottle, and get him into bed with it. Brew him some strong coffee, and see that he drinks it."

The "boots" grinned. "That all?"

"No; take his temperature, and send for a doctor. Look here, Sir," the young man turned to Wilfrid, "I recommend this chap. He can polish boots with the best. Just let him do for you, and don't worry. I must get on. It's six o'clock." He waited a moment, watching Wilfrid stagger into the hotel on the boots' arm, then sped away.

The "boots" assisted Wilfrid to a room. "Can you undress, Governor?"

"Yes," muttered Wilfrid.

"Then I'll go and get you that bottle and the coffee. Don't be afraid, we don't have damp beds 'ere. Were you out all night?"

Wilfrid sat on the bed and did not answer.

"'Ere!" said the "boots": "Give us your sleeves!" He pulled Wilfrid's coat off, then his waistcoat and trousers. "You've got a proper chill, it seems to me. Your under-things are all damp. Can you stand?"

Wilfrid shook his head.

The "boots" stripped the sheets off the bed, pulled Wilfrid's shirt over his head; then with a struggle wrenched off vest and drawers, and wrapped him in a blanket.

"Now, Governor, a good pull and a pull altogether." He forced Wilfrid's head on to the pillow, heaved his legs on to the bed, and covered him with two more blankets.

"You lie there, I won't be gone ten minutes."

Wilfrid lay, shivering so that his thoughts would not join up, nor his lips make consecutive sounds owing to the violent chattering of his teeth. He became conscious of a chambermaid, then of voices.

"His teeth'll break it. Isn't there another place?"

"I'll try under his arm."

A thermometer was pressed under his arm and held there.

"You haven't got yellow fever, have you, Sir?"

Wilfrid shook his head.

"Can you raise yourself, Governor, and drink this?"

Robust arms raised him, and he drank.

"One 'undred and four."

"Gawd! 'Ere, pop this bottle to his feet, I'll phone the Doc."

Wilfrid could see the maid watching him, as if wondering what sort of fever she was going to catch.

"Malaria," he said, suddenly. "Give me a cigarette! In my waistcoat."

The maid put a cigarette between his lips and lit it. Wilfrid took a long pull.

"A-gain!" he said.

Again she put it between his lips, and again he took a pull.

"They say there's mosquitoes in the forest. Did you find any last night, Sir?"

"In the sys-system."

Shivering a little less now, he watched her moving about the room, collecting his clothes, drawing the curtains so that they shaded the bed. Then she approached him, and he smiled up at her.

"Another nice drop of hot coffee?"

He shook his head, closed his eyes again, and shivered deep into the bed, conscious that she was still watching him and then again of voices.

"Can't find a name, but he's some sort of nob. There's money and this letter in his coat. The doctor'll be here in five minutes."

"Well, I'll wait till then, but I've got my work to do."

"Same 'ere. Tell the Missus when you call her."

He saw the maid stand looking at him with a sort of awe. A stranger, and a nob, with a curious disease, interesting to a simple mind. Of his face pressed into the pillow, she couldn't see much—one dark cheek, one ear, some hair, the screwed-up eye under the brow. He felt her touch his brow timidly with a finger. Burning hot, of course!

"Would you like your friends written to, Sir?"

He shook his head.

"The doctor'll be here in a minute."

"I'll be like this two days—nothing to be done—quinine—orange juice—" Seized by a violent fit of shivering, he was silent. He saw the doctor come in; and the maid, still leaning against the chest of drawers biting her little finger. She took it from her mouth and he heard her say:

"Shall I stay, Sir?"

"Yes, you can stay."

The doctor's fingers closed on his pulse, raised his eyelid, pushed his lips apart.

"Well, Sir? Had much of this?"

Wilfrid nodded.

"All right! You'll stay where you are, and shove in quinine, and that's all I can do for you. Pretty sharp bout."

Wilfrid nodded.

"There are no cards on you. What's your name?"

Wilfrid shook his head.

"All right! Don't worry! Take this."

CHAPTER 30

STEPPING FROM an omnibus, Dinny walked into the large of Wimbledon Common. After a nearly sleepless night, she had slipped out, leaving a note to say she would be away all day. She hurried over the grass into a birch grove, and lay down. The high moving clouds, the sunlight striking in and out of the birch tree branches, the water wagtails, the little dry patches of sand, and that stout wood-pigeon, undismayed by her motionless figure, brought her neither peace nor the inclination to think of nature. She lay on her back, quivering and dry-eyed, wondering for whose inscrutable delight she was thus suffering. The stricken do not look for outside help, they seek within. To go about exuding tragedy was abhorrent to her. She would not do that! But the sweetness of the wind, the moving clouds, the rustle of the breeze, the sound of children's voices, brought no hint of how she was to disguise herself and face life afresh. The isolation in which she had been ever since the meeting with Wilfrid under Foch's statue, now showed nakedly. All her eggs had been in one basket, and the basket had fallen. She dug with her fingers at the sandy earth; and a dog, seeing a hole, came up and sniffed it. She had begun to live, and now she was dead. "No flowers by request!"

So sharp had been her realisation of finality yesterday evening, that she did not even consider the possibility of tying up the broken thread. If he had pride, so had she! Not the same sort, but as deep in her marrow. No one had any real need of her! Why not go away? She had nearly three hundred pounds. The notion gave her neither exhilaration nor any real relief; but it would save her from making herself a nuisance to those who would expect her to be her old cheerful self. She thought of the hours she had spent with Wilfrid in places like this. So sharp was her memory, that she had to cover her lips to prevent anguish welling out of them. Until she met him she had never felt alone. And now—she *was* alone! Chill, terrifying, endless! Remembering how she had found swift motion good for heartache, she got up and crossed the road where the Sunday stream of cars was already flowing out of town. Uncle Hilary had once exhorted her not to lose her sense of humour. But had she ever had one? At the end of Barnes Common she climbed on to a 'bus and went back to London. She must have something to eat, or she would be fainting. She got down near Kensington Gardens and went into an hotel.

After lunch she sat some time in the Gardens, and then walked to Mount Street. No one was in, and she sank down on the sofa in the drawing-room. Thoroughly exhausted, she fell asleep. Her aunt's entrance woke her, and sitting up, she said:

"You can all be happy about me, Aunt Em. It's finished."

Lady Mont stared at her niece sitting there with a ghostly little smile, and two tears, starting not quite together, ran down her cheeks.

"I didn't know you cried at funerals, too, Aunt Em."

She got up, went over to her aunt, and with her handkerchief removed the marks the tears had made.

"There!"

Lady Mont got up. "I *must* howl," she said, "I simply must." And she swayed rapidly out of the room.

Dinny sat on, that ghost of a smile still on her face. Blore brought in the tea things, and she talked to him of Wimbledon, and his wife. He did not seem to know which of the two was in worse shape, but, as he was going out, he turned and said:

"And if I might suggest, Miss Dinny, a little sea air for you."

"Yes, Blore, I was thinking of it."

"I'm glad, Miss; one overdoes it at this time of year."

He, too, seemed to know that her course was run. And, feeling suddenly that she could not go on thus attending her own funeral, she stole to the door, listened for sounds, then slipped down the stairs and away.

But she was so physically exhausted that she could scarcely drag herself as far as St. James's Park. There she sat down by the water. People, sunbeams and ducks, shading leaves, spiky reeds, and this sirocco within her! A tall man walking from the Whitehall end, made a little convulsive movement, as if to put his hand to his hat, corrected it at sight of her face, and lounged on. Realising what her face must be expressing, she got up, and trailing on to Westminster Abbey, went in and sat down in a pew. There, bent forward, with her face resting on her arms, she stayed quite half an hour. She had not prayed, but she had rested, and the expression on her face had changed. She felt more fit to face people, and not show so much.

It was past six, and she went on to South Square. Getting unseen to her room, she had a long hot bath, put on a dinner frock, and resolutely went down. Only Fleur and Michael were there, and neither of them asked her any questions. It was clear to her that they knew. She got through the evening somehow. When she was going up, both of them kissed her, and Fleur said:

"I've told them to put you a hot water bottle; stuck against your back, it helps you to sleep. Good-night, bless you!"

Again Dinny had the feeling that Fleur had once suffered as she was suffering now. She slept better than she could have hoped.

With her early tea she received a letter with the heading of an hotel at Chingford.

"Madam,

"The enclosed letter addressed to you was found in the pocket of a gentleman who is lying here with a very sharp attack of malaria. I am posting it on to you, and am

Truly yours,

Roger Queal, M.D."

She read the letter . . . "Whatever I do, forgive, and believe that I have loved you. Wilfrid." And he was ill! All the impulses which sprang up she instantly thrust back. Not a second time would she rush in where angels feared to tread! But hurrying down, she telephoned to Stack the news that he was lying at the Chingford hotel with an attack of malaria.

"He'll want his pyjamas and his razors, then, Miss. I'll take 'em down to him."

Forcing back the words: "Give him my love," she said: "He knows where I am if there is anything I can do."

The blacker bitterness of her mood was gone; yet she was as cut off from him as ever! Unless he came or sent for her, she could make no move; and deep down she seemed to know that he would neither come nor send. No! He would strike his tent and flit away from where he had felt so much.

Towards noon Hubert came to say good-bye. It was, at once, clear to her that he, too, knew. He was coming back for the rest of his leave in October, he said. Jean was to stay at Condaford till after her child was born in November. She had been ordered to be out of the summer heat. He seemed to Dinny that morning like the old Hubert again. He dwelt on the advantage of being born at Condaford. And endeavouring to be sprightly, she said:

"Quaint to find you talking like that, Hubert. You never used to care about Condaford."

"It makes a difference to have an heir."

"Oh! It'll be an heir, will it?"

"Yes, we've made up our minds to a boy."

"And will there be a Condaford by the time he comes into it?"

Hubert shrugged. "We'll have a try at keeping it. Things don't last unless you set yourself to keep them."

"And not always then," murmured Dinny.

CHAPTER 31

WILFRID'S WORDS: "You can tell her family I'm going away," and Dinny's: "It's finished," had travelled, if not like wildfire, throughout the Cherrell family. There was no rejoicing as over a sinner that repenteth. All were too sorry for her, with a sorrow nigh unto dismay. Each wanted to show sympathy, none knew how. Sympathy smelling of sympathy was worse than none. Three days passed during which not one member of the family succeeded in expressing anything. Then Adrian had a brain-wave: He would ask her to eat something with him, though why food should be regarded as consolatory neither he nor anyone else has ever known. He appointed a café which had perhaps more repute than merit.

Since Dinny was not of those young women who make the ravages of life into an excuse for French-varnishing their surfaces, he had every opportunity to note her pallor. He forbore to comment. Indeed, he found it difficult to talk at all, for he knew that though, when enthralled by women, men remain devoted to their mental mainsprings, women, less bodily enthralled, stay mentally wrapped up in the men they love. He began, however, to tell her how someone had tried to 'sell him a pup.'

"He wanted five hundred pounds, Dinny, for a Cromagnon skull found in Suffolk. The whole thing looked extraordinary genuine. But I happened to see the County archæologist. 'Oh!' he said: 'he's been trying to palm that off on you, has he? That's the well-known "pup." He's dug it up at least three times. The man ought to be in gaol. He keeps it in a cupboard and every five or six years digs a hole, puts it in, takes it out, and tries to sell it. It possibly *is* a Cromagnon skull, but he picked it up in France, about twenty years ago. It would be unique, of course, as a British product.' Thereon I went off to have another look at where it was found last time. And it was plain enough, when you already knew it, that he'd put the thing in. There's something about antiques that saps morale."

"What sort of man was he, Uncle?"

"An enthusiastic-looking chap, rather like my hairdresser."

Dinny laughed. "You ought to do something, or he *will* sell it next time."

"The depression's against him, my dear. Bones and first editions are extraordinarily sensitive. He'll have to live a good ten years to get anything like a price."

"Do many people try to palm things off on you?"

"Some succeed, Dinny. I regret that 'pup,' though; it was a lovely skull. There aren't many as good now-a-days."

"We English certainly are getting uglier."

"Don't you believe it. Put the people we meet in drawing rooms and shops into cassock and cowls, armour and jerkins, and you'll have just the faces of the fourteenth and fifteenth centuries."

"But we do despise beauty, Uncle. We connect it with softness and immorality."

"Well, it makes people happy to despise what they haven't got. We're only about the fourth—no, the fifth—plainest people in Europe. But take away the Celtic infusions, and I admit we'd be the first."

Dinny looked round the café. Her survey added nothing to her conclusions, partly because she took but little in, and partly because the lunchers were nearly all Jews or Americans.

Adrian watched her with an ache. She looked so bone-listless.

"Hubert's gone, then?" he said.

"Yes."

"And what are you going to do, my dear?"

Dinny sat looking at her plate. Suddenly she raised her head and said: "I think I shall go abroad, Uncle."

Adrian's hand went to his goatee.

"I see," he said, at last. "Money?"

"I have enough."

"Where?"

"Anywhere."

"By yourself?"

Dinny nodded.

"The drawback to going away," murmured Adrian, "is the having to come back."

"There doesn't seem to be anything much for me to do just now. So I think I'll cheer people up by not seeing them for a bit."

Adrian debated within himself.

"Well, my dear, only you can decide what's best for you. But if you felt like a long travel, it strikes me that Clare might be glad to see you in Ceylon."

Seeing by the surprised movement of her hands that the idea was new to her, he went on:

"I have a feeling that she may not be finding life very easy."

Her eyes met his.

"That's what I thought at the wedding, Uncle; I didn't like his face."

"You have a special gift for helping others, Dinny; and whatever's wrong about Christianity, it's not the saying 'To give is more blessed than to receive.'"

"Even the Son of Man liked his little joke, Uncle."

Adrian looked at her hard, and said:

"Well, if you do go to Ceylon, mind you eat your mangoes over a basin."

He parted from her a little later and, too much out of mood to go back to work, went to the Horse Show instead.

CHAPTER 32

AT SOUTH SQUARE 'The Daily Phase' was among those journals which
politicians take lest they should miss reading correctly the temperature of
Fleet Street. Michael pushed it over to Fleur at breakfast.

During the six days since her arrival neither of them had said a word
to Dinny on the subject of Wilfrid. It was she who now said: "May I see
that?"

Fleur handed her the paper. She read, gave a little shudder, and went
on with her breakfast. Kit broke the ensuing hush by stating Hobbs'
average. Did Aunt Dinny think he was as great as W. G. Grace?

"I never saw either of them, Kit."

"Didn't you see W. G.?"

"I think he died before I was born."

Kit scrutinised her doubtfully.

"Oh!"

"He died in 1915," said Michael: "You'd have been eleven."

"But haven't you really seen Hobbs, Auntie?"

"No."

"I've seen him three times. I'm practising his hook to leg. 'The Daily
Phase' says Bradman is the best batsman in the world now. Do you think
he's better than Hobbs?"

"Better news than Hobbs."

Kit stared.

"What is news?"

"What newspapers are for."

"Do they make it up?"

"Not always."

"What news were you reading just now?"

"Nothing that would interest you."

"How do you know?"

"Kit, don't worry!" said Fleur.

"May I have an egg?"

"Yes."

The hush began again, till Kit stopped his eggspoon in mid-air and
isolated a finger:

"Look! The nail's blacker than it was yesterday. Will it come off, Auntie?"

"How did you do that?"

"Pinched it in a drawer. I didn't cry."

"Don't boast, Kit."

Kit gave his mother a clear upward look and resumed his egg.

Half an hour later, when Michael was just settling down to his correspondence, Dinny came into his study.

"Busy, Michael?"

"No, my dear."

"That paper! Why can't they leave him alone?"

"You see the 'Leopard' is selling like hot cakes. Dinny, how does it stand now?"

"I know he's been having malaria, but I don't even know where or how he is."

Michael looked at her face masked in its desperate little smile, and said, hesitatingly:

"Would you like me to find out?"

"Not for me, Michael. If he wants me, he knows where I am."

"I'll see Compson Grice. I'm not lucky with Wilfrid myself."

When she was gone he sat staring at the letters he had not begun to answer, half dismayed, half angered. Poor dear Dinny! What a shame! He pushed the letters aside, and went out.

Compson Grice's office was near Covent Garden, which, for some reason still to be discovered, attracts literature. When Michael reached it, about noon, that young publisher was sitting in the only well-furnished room in the building, with a newspaper cutting in his hand and a smile on his lips. He rose and said: "Hallo, Mont! Seen this in 'The Phase'?"

"Yes."

"I sent it round to Desert, and he wrote that at the top and sent it back. Neat, eh!"

Michael read in Wilfrid's writing:

> "Whene'er the lord who rules his roosts
> Says: 'Bite!' he bites, says 'Boost!' he boosts."

"He's in town, then?"

"Was half an hour ago."

"Have you seen him at all?"

"Not since the book came out."

Michael looked shrewdly at that comely fattish face. "Satisfied with the sales?"

"We're in the forty-first thousand, and going strong."

"I suppose you don't know whether Wilfrid is going back to the East?"

"Haven't the least little idea."

"He must be pretty sick with the whole thing."

Compson Grice shrugged.

"How many poets have ever made a thousand pounds out of a hundred pages of verse?"

"Small price for a soul, Grice."

"It'll be two thousand before we've done."

"I always thought it a mistake to print 'The Leopard.' Since he did it I've defended it, but it was a fatal thing to do."

"I don't agree."

"Obviously. It's done you proud."

"You can sneer," said Grice, with some feeling, "but he wouldn't have sent it to me if he hadn't wished it to come out. I am not my brother's keeper. The mere fact that it turns out a scoop is nothing to the point."

Michael sighed.

"I suppose not; but this is no joke for him. It's his whole life."

"Again, I don't agree. That happened when he recanted to save himself being shot. This is expiation, and damned good business into the bargain. His name is known to thousands who'd never have heard of it."

"Yes," said Michael, brooding, "there is that, certainly. Give me persecution to keep a name alive. Grice, will you do something for me? Make an excuse to find out what Wilfrid's intentions are. I've put my foot into it with him, and can't go myself, but I specially want to know."

"H'm!" said Grice. "He bites."

Michael grinned. "He won't bite his benefactor. I'm serious. Will you?"

"I'll try. By the way, there's that book by a French Canadian I've just published. Top-hole! I'll send you a copy—your wife will like it." 'And,' he added to himself, 'talk about it.' He smoothed back his sleek dark hair, and extended his hand. Michael shook it with a little more warmth than he really felt, and went away.

'After all,' he thought, 'what is it to Grice except business? Wilfrid's nothing to him! In these days we have to take what the gods send.' And he fell to considering what was really making the Public buy a book not concerned with sex, memoirs, or murders. The Empire? The prestige of the English? He did not believe it. No! What was making them buy it was that fundamental interest which attached to the question how far a person might go to save his life without losing what was called his soul. In other words the book was being sold by that little thing—believed in some quarters to be dead—called Conscience. A problem posed to each reader's conscience, that he could not answer easily; and the fact that it had actually happened to the author brought it home to the reader that some awful alternative might at any moment be presented to himself. And what would he do then, poor thing? And Michael felt one of those sudden bursts of consideration and even respect for the Public which often came over him and so affected his more intelligent friends that they alluded to him as 'Poor Michael!'

So meditating, he reached his room at the House of Commons and had settled down to the consideration of a private bill to preserve certain natural beauties, when a card was brought to him.

"General Sir Conway Cherrell.

"Can you see me?"

Pencilling: "Delighted, Sir!" he handed the card back to the attendant, and got up. Of all his uncles he knew Dinny's father least, and he waited with some trepidation.

The General came in, saying:

"Regular rabbit warren this, Michael."

He had the confirmed neatness of his profession, but his face looked worn and worried.

"Luckily, we don't breed here, Uncle Con."

The General emitted a short laugh.

"No, there's that. I hope I'm not interrupting you. It's about Dinny. She's still with you?"

"Yes, Sir."

The General hesitated, and then, crossing his hands on his stick, said firmly:

"You're Desert's best friend, aren't you?"

"Was. What I am now, I really don't know."

"Is Desert still in town?"

"Yes; he's been having a bout of malaria, I believe."

"Dinny still seeing him?"

"No, Sir."

Again the General hesitated, and again seemed to firm himself by gripping his stick.

"Her mother and I, you know, only want what's best for her. We want her happiness, the rest doesn't matter. What do you think?"

"I really don't believe it matters what any of us think."

The General frowned.

"How do you mean?"

"It's just between those two."

"I understood that he was going away."

"He said so to my father, but he hasn't gone. His publisher told me just now that he was still at his rooms this morning."

"How is Dinny?"

"Very low in her mind. But she keeps her end up."

"He ought to do something."

"What, Sir?"

"It's not fair to Dinny. He ought either to marry her, or go right away."

"Would you find it easy, in his place, to make up your mind?"

"Perhaps not."

Michael made a restless tour of his little room.

"I think the whole thing is way below any question of just yes or no. It's a case of wounded pride, and where you've got that, the other emotions don't run straight. You ought to know that, Sir. You must have had similar cases, when fellows have been court-martialled."

The word seemed to strike the general with the force of a revelation. He stared at his nephew and did not answer.

"Wilfrid," said Michael, "is being court-martialled, and it isn't a short sharp business like a real court-martial—it's a desperate long drawn out affair, with no end to it that I can grasp."

"I see," said the General, quietly: "But he should never have let Dinny in for it."

Michael smiled. "Does love ever do what's correct?"

"That's the modern view, anyway."

"According to report, the ancient one, too."

The General went to the window and stood looking out.

"I don't like to go and see Dinny," he said, without turning round, "it seems like worrying her. Her mother feels the same. And there's nothing we can do."

His voice, troubled not for himself, touched Michael.

"I believe," he said, "that in some way it'll be all over very soon. And whichever way will be better for them and all of us than this."

The General turned round.

"Let's hope so. I wanted to ask you to keep in touch with us, and not let Dinny do anything without letting us know. It's very hard waiting down there. I won't keep you now; and thank you, it's been a relief. Good-bye, Michael!"

He grasped his nephew's hand, squeezed it firmly, and was gone.

Michael thought: 'Hanging in the wind! There's nothing worse. Poor old boy!'

CHAPTER 33

COMPSON GRICE, who had no mean disposition and a certain liking for Michael, went out to lunch mindful of his promise. A believer in the power of meals to solve difficulties, he would normally have issued an invitation and obtained his information over the second or third glass of really old brandy. But he was afraid of Wilfrid. Discussing his simple *sole meunière* and half bottle of Chablis, he decided on a letter. He wrote it in the Club's little green-panelled writing room, with a cup of coffee by his side and a cigar in his mouth.

> "The Hotch Potch Club.
> Friday.

"DEAR DESERT,

"In view of the remarkable success of 'The Leopard' and the probability of further large sales, I feel that I ought to know definitely what you would like me to do with the royalty cheques when they fall due. Perhaps you would be so good as to tell me whether you contemplate going back to the East, and, if so, when; and at the same time let me have an address to which I can remit with safety. Possibly you would prefer that I should simply pay your royalties into your bank, whatever that is, and take their receipt. Hitherto our financial transactions have been somewhat lean, but 'The Leopard' will certainly have—indeed is already having—an influence on the sales of your two previous books; and it will be advisable that you should keep me in touch with your whereabouts in future. Shall you be in Town much longer? I am always delighted to see you, if you care to look in.

"With hearty congratulations and best wishes,

> I am sincerely yours,
> COMPSON GRICE."

This letter, in his elegant and upright hand, he addressed to Cork Street, and sent at once by the Club messenger. The remains of his recess he spent sounding in his rather whispering voice the praises of his French Canadian product, and then took a taxi back to Covent Garden. A clerk met him in the lobby.

"Mr. Desert is waiting up in your room, Sir."

"Good!" said Compson Grice, subduing a tremor and thinking: 'Quick work!'

Wilfrid was standing at a window which commanded a slanting view of Covent Garden market; and Grice was shocked when he turned round —the face was so dark and wasted and had such a bitter look: the hand, too, had an unpleasant dry heat in the feel of it.

"So you got my letter?" he said.

"Thanks. Here's the address of my bank. Better pay all cheques into it and take their receipt."

"You don't look too fearfully well. Are you off again?"

"Probably. Well, good-bye, Grice. Thanks for all you've done."

Compson Grice said, with real feeling: "I'm terribly sorry it's hit you so hard."

Wilfrid shrugged and turned to the door.

When he was gone his publisher stood twisting the bank's address in his hands. Suddenly he said out loud: "I don't like his looks; I absolutely don't!" And he went to the telephone. . . .

Wilfrid walked north, he had another visit to pay. He reached the Museum just as Adrian was having his cup of 'Dover' tea and bun.

"Good!" said Adrian, rising. "I'm glad to see you. There's a spare cup. Do sit down."

He had experienced the same shock as Grice at the look on Desert's face and the feel of his hand.

Wilfrid took a sip of tea. "May I smoke?" He lighted a cigarette, and sat, hunched in his chair. Adrian waited for him to speak.

"Sorry to butt in on you like this," said Wilfrid, at last, "but I'm going back into the blue. I wanted to know which would hurt Dinny least— just to clear out, or to write."

Adrian lived through a wretched and bleak minute.

"You mean that if you see her you can't trust yourself."

Desert gave a shivering shrug.

"It's not that exactly. It sounds brutal, but I'm so fed up that I don't feel anything. If I saw her—I might wound her. She's been an angel. I don't suppose you can understand what's happened in me. I can't myself. I only know that I want to get away from everything and everybody."

Adrian nodded.

"I was told you'd been ill—you don't think that accounts for your present feeling? For God's sake don't make a mistake in your feelings now."

Wilfrid smiled.

"I'm used to malaria. It's not that. You'll laugh, but I feel like bleeding to death inside. I want to get to where nothing and nobody reminds me. And Dinny reminds me more than anyone."

"I see," said Adrian, gravely. And he was silent, passing his hand over his bearded chin. Then he got up and began to walk about.

"Do you think it's fair to Dinny or yourself not to try what seeing her might do?"

"Yes," said Desert, almost with violence. "I tell you, I should hurt her."

"You'll hurt her any way; her eggs are all in one basket. And look here, Desert! You published that poem deliberately. I always understood you did so as a form of expiation, even though you had asked Dinny to marry you. I'm not such a fool as to want you to go on with Dinny if your feelings have really changed; but are you sure they have?"

"My feelings haven't changed. I simply have none. Being a pariah dog has killed them."

"D'you realise what you're saying?"

"Perfectly. I knew I was a pariah from the moment I recanted, and whether people knew it or not didn't matter. All the same—it *has* mattered."

"I see," said Adrian again, and came to a standstill. "I suppose that's natural."

"Whether it is to others, I don't know; it is to me. I am out of the herd, and I'll stay there. I don't complain. I side against myself." He spoke with desperate energy.

Adrian said, very gently: "Then you just want to know how to hurt Dinny least? I can't tell you: I wish I could. I gave you the wrong advice when you came before. Advice is no good, anyway. We have to wrestle things out for ourselves."

Desert stood up. "Ironical, isn't it? I was driven to Dinny by my loneliness. I'm driven away from her by it. Well, good-bye, Sir; I don't suppose I shall ever see you again. And thanks for trying to help me."

"I wish to God I could."

Wilfrid smiled the sudden smile that gave him his charm.

"I'll try what one more walk will do. I may see some writing on the wall. Anyway you'll know I didn't want to hurt her more than I could help. Good-bye!"

Adrian's tea was cold and his bun uneaten. He pushed them away. He felt as if he had failed Dinny, and yet for the life of him could not see what he could have done. That young man looked very queer! 'Bleeding to death inside!' Gruesome phrase! And true, judging by his face! Fibre sensitive as his, and a consuming pride! "Going back into the blue." To roam about in the East—a sort of Wandering Jew; become one of those mysterious Englishmen found in out-of-the-way places, with no origins that they would speak of, and no future but their present. He filled a pipe and tried his best to feel that, after all, in the long run Dinny would be happier unmarried to Desert. And he did not succeed. There was only one flowering of real love in a woman's life, and this was hers. He had no doubt on that point. She would make shift—oh yes; but she would have missed 'the singing and the gold.' And, grabbing his battered hat, he went out. He strode along in the direction of Hyde Park; then, yielding to a whim, diverged towards Mount Street.

413

When Blore announced him his sister was putting the last red stitches in the tongue of one of the dogs in her French tapestry. She held it up.

"It ought to drip. He's looking at that bunny. Would blue drips be right?"

"Grey, on that background, Em."

Lady Mont considered her brother sitting in a small chair with his long legs hunched up.

"You look like a war correspondent—camp stools, and no time to shave. I do want Dinny to be married, Adrian. She's twenty-six. All that about bein' yellow. They could go to Corsica."

Adrian smiled. Em was so right, and yet so wrong!

"Con was here to-day," resumed his sister. "He'd been seein' Michael. Nobody knows anythin'. And Dinny just goes walks with Kit and Dandy, and nurses Catherine, and sits readin' books without turnin' the page."

Adrian debated whether to tell her of Desert's visit to him.

"And Con says," went on Lady Mont, "that he can't make two ends meet this year—Clare's weddin' and the Budget, and Jean expectin'—he'll have to cut down some trees, and sell the horses. We're hard up, too. It's lucky Fleur's got so much. Money is such a bore. What do you think?"

Adrian gave a start.

"Well, no one expects a good thing now-a-days, but one wants enough to live on."

"It's havin' dependents. Boswell's got a sister that can only walk with one leg; and Johnson's wife's got cancer—poor thing! And everybody's got somebody. Dinny says at Condaford her mother does everythin' in the village. So how it's to go on, I don't know. Lawrence doesn't save a penny."

"We're falling between two stools, Em; and one fine day we shall reach the floor with a bump."

"I suppose we shall live in almshouses." Lady Mont lifted her work up to the light. "No, I shan't make it drip. Or else go to Kenya; they say there's somethin' that pays there."

"What I hate," said Adrian, with sudden energy, "is the thought of Mr. Tom Noddy or somebody buying Condaford and using it for week-end cocktail parties."

"I should go and be a banshee in the woods. There couldn't be Condaford without a Cherrell."

"There dashed well could, Em. There's a confounded process called evolution; and England is its home."

Lady Mont sighed, and, getting up, swayed over to her parakeet.

"Polly! You and I'll go and live in an almshouse."

CHAPTER 34

WHEN COMPSON GRICE telephoned to Michael, or rather to Fleur, for Michael was not in, he sounded embarrassed.

"Is there any message I can give him, Mr. Grice?"

"Your husband asked me to find out Desert's movements. Well, Desert's just been in to see me, and practically said he was off again; but—er—I didn't like his looks, and his hand was like a man in fever."

"He's been having malaria."

"Ah! By the way, I'm sending you a book I'm sure you'll like, it's by that French Canadian."

"Thank you, very much. I'll tell Michael when he comes in."

And Fleur stood thinking. Ought she to pass this on to Dinny? Without consulting Michael she did not like to, and he, tied tightly to the House just now, might not even be in to dinner. How like Wilfrid to keep one on tenterhooks! She always felt that she knew him better than either Dinny or Michael. They were convinced of a vein of pure gold in him. She, for whom he had once had such a passion, could only assess that vein at nine carats. 'That, I suppose,' she thought rather bitterly, 'is because my nature is lower than theirs.' People assessed others according to their own natures, didn't they? Still it was difficult to give high value to one whose mistress she had not become, and who had then fled into the blue. There was always extravagance in Michael's likings; in Dinny —well, Dinny she did not really understand.

And so she went back to the letters she was writing. They were important, for she was rallying the best and brightest people to meet some high-caste Indian ladies who were over for the Conference. She had nearly finished them when she was called to the telephone by Michael, asking if there were any message from Compson Grice. Having given him what news there was, she went on:

"Are you coming in to dinner? . . . Good! I dread dining alone with Dinny; she's so marvellously cheerful, it gives me the creeps. Not worry other people and all that, of course; but if she showed her feelings more it would worry us less. . . . Uncle Con! . . . It's rather funny, all the family seem to want now the exact opposite of what they wanted at first. I suppose that's the result of watching her suffer. . . . Yes, she went in the car to sail Kit's boat on the Round Pond; they sent Dandy and the boat back in the car, and are walking home. . . . All right, dear boy. Eight o'clock; don't be late if you can help it. . . . Oh! here *are* Kit and Dinny. Good-bye!"

Kit had come into the room. His face was brown, his eyes blue, his sweater the same colour as his eyes, his shorts darker blue; his green stockings were gartered below his bare knees, and his brown shoes had brogues; he wore no cap on his bright head.

"Auntie Dinny has gone to lie down. She had to sit on the grass. She says she'll be all right soon. D'you think she's going to have measles? Of course, I've had them, Mummy, so when she's insulated I can still see her. We saw a man who frightened her."

"What sort of man?"

"He didn't come near; a tall sort of man; he had his hat in his hand, and when he saw us, he almost ran."

"How do you know he saw you?"

"Oh! he went like that, and scooted."

"Was that in the Park?"

"Yes."

"Which?"

"The Green Park."

"Was he thin, and dark in the face?"

"Yes; do you know him too, Mummy?"

"Why 'too,' Kit? Did Auntie Dinny know him?"

"I think so; she said: 'Oh!' like that, and put her hand here. And then she looked after him; and then she sat down on the grass. I fanned her with her scarf. I love Auntie Dinny. Has she a husband?"

"No."

When he had gone up, Fleur debated. Dinny must have realised that Kit would describe everything. She decided only to send up a message and some sal volatile.

The answer came back: "I shall be all right by dinner."

But at dinner time a further message came to say she still felt rather faint: might she just go to bed and have a long night?

Thus it was that Michael and Fleur sat down alone.

"It was Wilfrid, of course."

Michael nodded.

"I wish to God he'd go. It's so wretched—the whole thing! D'you remember that passage in Turgenev, where Litvinov watches the train smoke curling away over the fields?"

"No. Why?"

"All Dinny's tissue is going up in smoke."

"Yes," said Fleur between tight lips. "But the fire will burn out."

"And leave——?"

"Oh! She'll be recognisable."

Michael looked hard at the partner of his board. She was regarding the morsel of fish on her fork. With a little set smile on her lips she raised

416

it to her mouth and began champing, as if chewing the cud of experience. Recognisable! Yes, *she* was as pretty as ever, though more firmly moulded, as if preparing for the revival of shape. He turned his eyes away, for he still squirmed when he thought of that business four years ago, of which he had known so little, suspected so much, and talked not at all. Smoke! Did all human passion burn away and drift in a blue film over the fields, obscure for a moment the sight of the sun, and the shapes of the crops and the trees, then fade into air and leave the clear hard day; and no difference anywhere? Not quite! For smoke was burnt tissue, and where fire had raged there was alteration. Of the Dinny he had known from a small child up, the outline would be changed—hardened, sharpened, refined, withered? And he said:

"I must be back at the House at nine, the Chancellor's speaking. Why one should listen to him, I don't know, but one does."

"Why you should listen to anyone will always be a mystery. Did you ever know any speaker in the House change anyone's opinion?"

"No," said Michael, with a wry smile, "but one lives in hopes. We sit day after day talking of some blessed measure, and then take a vote, with the same result as if we'd taken it at the end of the first two speeches. And that's gone on for hundreds of years."

"So filial!" said Fleur. "Kit thinks Dinny is going to have measles. He's asking, too, if she has a husband. . . . Coaker, bring the coffee, please. Mr. Mont has to go."

When he had kissed her and gone, Fleur went up to the nurseries. Catherine was the soundest of sleepers, and it was pleasant to watch her, a pretty child with hair that would probably be like her own and eyes so hesitating between grey and hazel that they gave promise of becoming ice-green. One small hand was crumpled against her cheek, and she breathed lightly as a flower. Nodding to the nurse, Fleur pushed open the door into the other nursery. To wake Kit was dangerous. He would demand biscuits, and, very likely, milk, want light conversation and ask her to read to him. But in spite of the door's faint creaking he did not wake. His bright head was thrust determinedly into the pillow from under which the butt of a pistol protruded. It was hot, and he had thrown back the clothes, so that, by the glimmer of the night-light his blue-pyjamaed figure was disclosed to the knees. His skin was brown and healthy and he had a Forsyte's chin. Fleur moved up and stood quite close. He looked 'such a duck,' thus determinedly asleep in face of the opposition put up by his quickening imagination. With feathered finger-tips she gripped the sheet, pulled it up, and gingerly let it down over him; then stood back with her hands on her hips, and one eyebrow raised. He was at the best age in life, and would be for another two years until he went to school. No sex to bother him as yet! Everybody kind to him; everything an adventure out of books. Books! Michael's old books, her own, the few written since fit for children. He was at the wonderful age! She looked swiftly round the twilit room. His gun and sword lay ready on a chair! One supported disarmament, and armed children to the teeth! His other toys, mostly mechanised, would be in the schoolroom. No, there on the window-sill was the boat he had sailed with Dinny, its sail still set; and there on a cushion in the corner was 'the silver dog,' aware of her but too lazy to get up. She could see the slim feather of his tail cocked and waving gently at her. And afraid lest she might disturb this admirable peace, she blew a kiss to both of them and stole back through the door. Nodding again to the nurse, she inspected Catherine's eyelashes, and went out. Down the stairs she tip-toed to the floor on which was Dinny's room above her own. Was it unfeeling not to look in and ask if there were anything she wanted? She moved closer to the door. Only half-past nine! She could not be asleep. Probably she would not sleep at all. It was hateful to think of her lying there silent and unhappy. Perhaps to talk would be a comfort, would take her mind off! She was raising her hand to knock when a sound came forth, smothered, yet unmistakable—the gasping sobs of one crying into her pillow. Fleur stood as if turned to stone. A noise she had not heard since she herself had made it nearly four years ago! It turned her sick with the force of memory—a horrible, but a sacred sound. Not for worlds would she go in! She covered her ears, drew back, and fled downstairs. For further protection from the searing sound she turned on the portable wireless. It gave forth from the second act of "Madame Butterfly." She turned it off, and sat down again at her bureau. She wrote rapidly a kind of formula: "Such a pleasure it, etc.—meet those very charming Indian ladies who, etc.—Yours, etc., Fleur Mont." Over and over and over, and the sound of that sobbing in her ears! It was stuffy to-night! She drew the curtains aside and threw the window wider to let in what air there was. A hostile thing, life, full of silent menace and small annoyances. If you went towards and grasped life with both hands, it yielded, perhaps, then drew back to deal some ugly stroke. Half past ten! What were they jabbering about now in Parliament? Some twopenny-ha'-penny tax. She closed the window and drew the curtains again, stamped her letters, and stood looking round the room before turning out and going up. And, suddenly, came a memory—of Wilfrid's face outside, close to the glass of the window, on the night he fled from her to the East. If it were there now; if, for a second time in his strange life, he came like a disembodied spirit to that window, seeking now not her but Dinny? She switched off the light and groped her way to the window, cautiously drew the curtains apart a very little, and peered out. Impatiently, she dropped the curtain and went upstairs. Standing before her long mirror, she listened a moment, and then carefully did not. How like life, that! One shut eyes and ears to all that was painful—if one could. And who could blame? Plenty, to which one could shut neither eyes nor ears, seeped in even through closed lids and cotton-wool. She was just getting into bed when Michael came. She told him of the sobbing, and he in turn stood listening; but nothing penetrated the room's solid roofing. He went into his dressing-room and came back presently in a dressing-gown she had given him, blue, with embroidered cuffs and collar, and began to walk up and down.

"Come to bed," said Fleur; "you can't help by doing that."

They talked a little in bed. It was Michael who fell asleep. Fleur lay wakeful. Big Ben struck twelve. The Town murmured on, but the house was very still. A little crack now and then, as though some board were settling down after the day's pressure of feet; the snuffle, not loud, of Michael's breathing—such, and the whispering, as it were, of her own thoughts, were its only noises. From the room above not a sound. She began to think of where they should go in the long vacation. Scotland had been spoken of, and Cornwall; she herself wanted the Riviera for a month at least. To come back brown all over; she had never been properly sunbrowned yet! With Mademoiselle and Nanny the children would be safe! What was that? A door closing. Surely the creaking of stairs! She touched Michael.

"Yes?"

"Listen!"

Again that faint creaking.

"It began above," whispered Fleur; "I think you ought to see."

He got out of bed, put on his dressing-gown and slippers, and, opening the door quietly, looked out. Nothing on the landing, but the sound of someone moving in the hall! He slipped down the stairs.

There was a dim figure by the front door, and he said gently:

"Is that you, Dinny?"

"Yes."

Michael moved forward. Her figure left the door, and he came on her sitting on the coat 'sarcophagus.' He could just see that her hand was raised holding a scarf over her head and face.

"Is there anything I can get you?"

"No. I wanted some air."

Michael checked his impulse to turn the light up. He moved forward, and in the darkness stroked her arm.

"I didn't think you'd hear," she said. "I'm sorry."

Dared he speak of her trouble? Would she hate him for it, or be grateful?

"My dear," he said, "anything that'll do you good."

"It's silly. I'll go up again."

Michael put his arm round her; he could feel that she was fully dressed. After a moment she relaxed against him, still holding the scarf so that it veiled her face and head. He rocked her gently—the least little movement side to side. Her body slipped till her head rested against his shoulder. Michael ceased to rock, ceased almost to breathe. As long as she would, let her rest there!

WHEN WILFRID left Adrian's room at the Museum, he had no plan or direction in his mind, and walked along like a man in one of those dreams where the theme is repeated over and over, and the only end is awakening. He went down the Kingsway to the Embankment, came to Westminster Bridge, turned on to it, and stood leaning over the parapet. A jump and he would be out of it. The tide was running down—English water escaping to the seas, nevermore to come back, glad to go! Escape! Escape from all those who made him think of himself. To be rid of this perpetual self-questioning and self-consciousness! To end this damned mawkish indecision, this puling concern as to whether one would hurt her too much! But of course one would not hurt her too much! She would cry and get over it. Sentiment had betrayed him once! Not again! By God! Not again!

He stood there a long time, leaning on the parapet, watching the bright water and the craft creeping by; and every now and then a passing cockney would stand beside him, as if convinced that he must be seeing something of sensational interest. And he was! He was seeing his own life finally 'in the blue,' unmoored, careering like the Flying Dutchman on far waters to the far ends of the world. But at least without need for bravado, kow-towing, appeal or pretence, under his own flag, and that not at half mast.

"I've 'eard," said a voice, "that lookin' at the water long enough will make 'em jump sometimes."

Wilfrid shuddered, and walked away. God! How raw and jagged one had got! He walked off the Bridge past the end of Whitehall into St. James's Park, skirted the long water up to the geraniums and the large stone males, females and fruits in front of the Palace, passed into the Green Park and threw himself down on the dry grass. He lay there, perhaps an hour, on his back with his hand over his eyes, grateful for the sun soaking into him. When he got up he felt dizzy, and had to stand some minutes to get his balance before moving towards Hyde Park Corner. He had gone but a little way when he started and swerved off to the right. Coming towards him, nearer the riding track, were a young woman and a little boy. Dinny! He had seen her gasp, her hand go to her heart. And he had swerved and walked away. It was brutal, horrible, but it was final. So a man, who had thrust a dagger home, would feel. Brutal, hor-

rible, but final! No more indecision! Nothing now but to get away as quick
as ever he could! He turned towards his rooms, striding along as if possessed, his lips drawn back in such a smile as a man has in a dentist's chair.
He had stricken down the only woman who had ever seemed to him worth
marrying, the only woman for whom he had felt what was worthy to be
called real love. Well! Better strike her down like that than kill her by
living with her! He was as Esau, and as Ishmael, not fit for a daughter
of Israel. And a messenger boy turned and stared after him—the pace at
which he walked was so foreign to the youth's habitual feelings. He
crossed Piccadilly with no concern whatever for its traffic, and plunged
into the narrow mouth of Bond Street. It suddenly struck him that he
would never see Scott's hats again. The shop had just been shut, but those
hats rested in rows, super-conventional hats, tropical hats, ladies' hats,
and specimens of the newest Trilby or Homburg, or whatever they called
it now. He strode on, rounded the scent of Atkinson's, and came to his
own door. There he had to sit down at the foot of the stairs before he could
find strength to climb. The spasmodic energy which had followed the
shock of seeing her had ebbed out in utter lassitude. He was just beginning to mount when Stack and the dog came down. It rushed at his legs
and stood against him, reaching its head up. Wilfrid crumpled its ears.
To leave it once more without a master!

"I'm off early to-morrow, Stack. To Siam. I probably shan't be coming
back."

"Not at all, Sir?"

"Not at all."

"Would you like me to come too, Sir?"

Wilfrid put his hand on the henchman's shoulder.

"Jolly good of you, Stack; but you'd be bored to death."

"Excuse me, Sir, but you're hardly fit to travel alone at present."

"Perhaps not, but I'm going to."

The henchman bent his eyes on Wilfrid's face. It was a grave intent
gaze, as if he were committing that face finally to heart.

"I've been with you a long time, Sir."

"You have, Stack; and nobody could have been nicer to me. I've made
provision in case anything happens to me. You'd prefer to go on here,
I expect, keeping the rooms for when my father wants them."

"I should be sorry to leave here, if I can't come with you. Are you sure
about that, Sir?"

Wilfrid nodded. "Quite sure, Stack. What about Foch?"

Stack hesitated, then said with a rush: "I think I ought to tell you, Sir,
that when Miss Cherrell was here last—the night you went off to Epping
—she said that if you was to go away at any time, she would be glad to
have the dog. He's fond of her, Sir."

Wilfrid's face became a mask.

"Take him his run," he said, and went on up the stairs.

His mind was once again in turmoil. Murder! But it was done! One did not bring a corpse to life with longing or remorse. The dog, if she wanted him, was hers, of course! Why did women cling to memories, when all they should wish should be to forget? He sat down at his bureau and wrote:

"I am going away for good. Foch comes to you with this. He is yours if you care to have him. I am only fit to be alone. Forgive me if you can, and forget me. Wilfrid."

He addressed it, and sat on the bureau slowly turning his head and looking round the room. Under three months since the day he had come back. He felt as if he had lived a lifetime. Dinny over there at the hearth, after her father had been! Dinny on the divan looking up at him! Dinny here, Dinny there! Her smile, her eyes, her hair! Dinny, and that memory in the Arab tent, pulling at each other, wrestling for him. Why had he had not seen the end from the beginning? He might have known himself! He took a sheet of paper and wrote:—

"MY DEAR FATHER,

"England doesn't seem to agree with me, and I am starting to-morrow for Siam. My bank will have my address from time to time. Stack will keep things going here as usual, so that the rooms will be ready whenever you want them. I hope you'll take care of yourself. I'll try and send you a coin for your collection now and then. Good-bye.

Yours affectionately,

WILFRID."

His father would read it and say: "Dear me! Very sudden! Queer fellow!" And that was about all that anyone would think or say—except——!

He took another sheet of paper and wrote to his bank; then lay down, exhausted, on the divan.

Stack must pack, he hadn't the strength. Luckily his passport was in order, that curious document which rendered one independent of one's kind; that password to whatever loneliness one wanted. The room was very still, for at this hour of lull before dinner traffic began there was hardly any noise from the streets. The stuff which he took after attacks of malaria had opium in it, and a dreamy feeling came over him. He drew a long breath, and relaxed. To his half-drugged senses scents kept coming —the scent of camel's dung, of coffee roasting, carpets, spices and humanity in the *Suks*, the sharp unscented air of the desert, and the fœtid reek of some river village; and sounds—the whine of beggars, a camel's coughing grunts, the cry of the jackal, Muezzin call, padding of donkeys' feet, tapping of the silversmiths, the creaking and moaning of water being drawn. And before his half-closed eyes visions came floating; a sort of long dream picture of the East as he had known it. Now it would be another East, further and more strange! . . . He slipped into a real dream. . . .

CHAPTER 36

SEEING HIM TURN AWAY from her in the Green Park, Dinny had known for certain it was all over. The sight of his ravaged face had moved her to the depths. If only he could be happy again, she could put up with it. For since the evening he left her in his rooms, she had been steeling herself, never really believing in anything but this. She slept little and had breakfast upstairs. A message was brought her about ten o'clock that a man with a dog was waiting to see her.

She finished dressing quickly, put on her hat, and went down. It could only be Stack.

The henchman was standing beside the 'sarcophagus,' holding Foch on a lead. His face, full of understanding as ever, was lined and pale, as if he had been up all night.

"Mr. Desert sent this, Miss." He held out a note.

Dinny opened the door of the drawing room.

"Come in here, please, Stack. Let's sit down."

He sat down and let go of the lead. The dog went to her, and put his nose on her knee. Dinny read the note.

"Mr. Desert says that I may have Foch."

Stack bent his gaze on his boots. "He's gone, Miss. Went by the early service to Paris and Marseilles."

She could see the moisture in the folds of his cheeks. He gave a loud sniff, and angrily brushed his hand over his face.

"I've been with him fourteen years, Miss. It was bound to hit me. He talks of not coming back."

"Where has he gone?"

"Siam."

"A long way," said Dinny, with a smile. "The great thing is that he should be happy again."

"That is so, Miss. I don't know if you'd care to hear about the dog's food. He has a dry biscuit about nine, and shin of beef or sheep's head, cooked, with crumbled hound-meal, between six and seven, and nothing else. A good quiet dog, he is, perfect gentleman in the house. He'll sleep in your bedroom, if you like."

"Do you stay where you are, Stack?"

"Yes, Miss. The rooms are his lordship's. As I told you, Mr. Desert is sudden; but I think he means what he says. He never was happy in England."

"I'm sure he means what he says. Is there anything I can do for you, Stack?"

The henchman shook his head, his eyes rested on Dinny's face and she knew he was debating whether he dared offer sympathy. She stood up.

"I think I'll take Foch a walk and get him used to me."

"Yes, Miss. I don't let him off the lead except in the Parks. If there's anything you want to know about him any time, you have the number."

Dinny put out her hand.

"Well, good-bye, Stack, and best wishes."

"The same to you, Miss, I'm sure." His eyes had something more than understanding in them, and the grip of his hand a spasmodic strength. Dinny continued to smile till he was gone and the door closed, then sat down on the sofa with her hands over her eyes. The dog, who had followed Stack to the door, whined once, and came back to her. She uncovered her eyes, took Wilfrid's note from her lap and tore it up.

"Well, Foch," she said, "what shall we do? Nice walk?"

The tail moved; he again whined slightly.

"Come along, then, boy."

She felt steady, but as if a spring had broken. With the dog on the lead she walked towards Victoria Station, and stopped before the statue. The leaves had thickened round it, and that was all the change. Man and horse, remote, active, and contained—'workmanlike'! A long time she stood there, her face raised, dry-eyed, thin and drawn; and the dog sat patiently beside her.

Then, with a shrug, she turned away and led him rapidly towards the Park. When she had walked some time, she went to Mount Street and asked for Sir Lawrence. He was in his study.

"Well, my dear," he said, "that looks a nice dog, is he yours?"

"Yes. Uncle Lawrence, will you do something for me?"

"Surely."

"Wilfrid has gone. He went this morning. He is not coming back. Would you be so very kind as to let my people know, and Michael and Aunt Em, and Uncle Adrian. I don't want ever to have to speak of it."

Sir Lawrence inclined his head, took her hand and put it to his lips. "There was something I wanted to show you, Dinny." He took from his table a little statuette of Voltaire. "I picked that up two days ago. Isn't he a delightful old cynic? Why the French should be so much pleasanter as cynics than other peoples is mysterious, except that cynicism, to be tolerable, must have grace and wit; apart from those, it's just bad manners. An English cynic is a man with a general grievance. A German cynic is a sort of wild boar. A Scandinavian cynic is a pestilence. An American jumps around too much to make a cynic, and a Russian's state of mind is not constant enough. You might get a perfectly good cynic in Austria, perhaps, or northern China—possibly it's a question of latitude."

Dinny smiled.

"Give my love to Aunt Em, please. I'm going home this afternoon."

"God bless you, my dear," said Sir Lawrence. "Come here, or to Lippinghall, whenever you want; we love having you." And he kissed her forehead.

When she had gone, he went to the telephone, and then sought his wife.

"Em, poor Dinny has just been here. She looks like a smiling ghost. It's all over. Desert went off for good this morning. She doesn't want ever to speak of it. Can you remember that?"

Lady Mont, who was arranging some flowers in a Chinese ginger jar, dropped them and turned round.

"Oh! dear!" she said: "Kiss me, Lawrence!"

They stood for a moment embraced. Poor Em! Her heart was soft as butter! She said into his shoulder: "Your collar's all covered with hairs. You *will* brush your hair after you've put your coat on. Turn, I'll pick them off."

Sir Lawrence turned.

"I've telephoned to Condaford and Michael and Adrian. Remember, Em! The thing is as if it never was."

"Of course I shall remember. Why did she come to you?"

Sir Lawrence shrugged. "She's got a new dog, a black spaniel."

"Very faithful, but they get fat. There! Did they say anything on the telephone?"

"Only: 'Oh!' and 'I see,' and 'Of course.'"

"Lawrence, I want to cry; come back presently, and take me somewhere."

Sir Lawrence patted her shoulders and went out quickly. He, too, felt peculiar. Back in his study, he sat in thought. Desert's flight was the only possible solution! Of all those affected by this incident, he had the clearest and most just insight into Wilfrid. True, probably, that the fellow had a vein of gold in him which his general nature did its best to hide. But to live with? Not on your life! Yellow? Of course he wasn't that! The thing was not plain-sailing, as Jack Muskham and the pukka sahibs supposed, with their superstition that black was not white, and so on. No, no! Young Desert had been snared in a most peculiar way. Given his perverse nature, its revolts, humanitarianism and want of belief, given his way of hob-nobbing with the Arabs, his case was as different from that of the ordinary Englishman as chalk from cheese. But, whatever his case, he was not a man to live with! Poor Dinny was well out of that! What pranks Fate played! Why should her choice have fallen there? If you came to that, why anything where love was concerned? It knew no laws, not even those of common sense. Some element in her had flown straight to its kindred element in him, disregarding all that was not kindred, and all outside circumstance. She might never get again the chance of that particular 'nick,' as Jack Muskham would call it. But—good God!—marriage was a life-long business; yes, even in these days, no passing joke! For marriage you wanted all the luck and all the give and take that you could get. Not much give and take about Desert—restless, disharmonic, and a poet! And proud—with that inner self-depreciative pride which never let up on a man! A liaison, one of those leaping companionships young people went in for now—possibly; but that didn't fit Dinny; even Desert must have felt so. In her the physical without the spiritual seemed out of place. She was a lady, yes, a lady. And if people did not know what that meant in these days, all the worse for them!

'Where,' he thought, 'can I take poor Em at this time in the morning? The Zoo she doesn't like; I'm sick of the Wallace. Madame Tussaud's! Gaiety will break through. Madame Tussaud's!'

AT CONDAFORD Jean went straight from the telephone to find her mother-in-law, and repeated Sir Lawrence's words with her usual decision. The gentle rather timid expression on Lady Cherrell's face changed to a startled concern.

"Oh!"

"Shall I tell Father?"

"Please, dear."

Alone again with her accounts, Lady Cherrell sat thinking. The only one of the family, except Hubert, who had never seen Wilfrid Desert, she had tried to keep an open mind, and had no definite opposition on her conscience. She felt now only a troubled sympathy. What could one do? And, as is customary in the case of another's bereavement, she could only think of flowers.

She slipped out into the garden, and went to the rose beds, which, flanked by tall yew hedges, clustered round the old sundial. She plucked a basket full of the best blossoms, took them up to Dinny's narrow and conventual bedroom, and disposed them in bowls by the bedside and on the window-sill. Then, opening the door and mullioned window wide, she rang for the room to be dusted and the bed made. The Medici prints on the walls she carefully set exactly straight, and said:

"I've dusted the pictures, Annie. Keep the window and door open. I want it all to smell sweet. Can you do the room now?"

"Yes, m'lady."

"Then I think you'd better, I don't know what time Miss Dinny will be here."

Back with her accounts, she could not settle to them, and, pushing them into a drawer, went to find her husband. He, too, was seated before bills and papers without sign of animation. She went up to him and pressed his head against her.

"Jean's told you, Con?"

"Yes. It's the only thing, of course; but I hate Dinny to be sad."

They were silent till Lady Cherrell said:

"I'd tell Dinny about our being so hard up. It would take her mind off."

The General ruffled his hair. "I shall be three hundred down on the year. I might get a couple of hundred for the horses, the rest must come

427

out of trees. I don't know which I dislike more. Do you think she could suggest something?"

"No, but she would worry and that would prevent her toubling so much over the other thing."

"I see. Well, Jean or you tell her, then. I don't like to. It looks like hinting that I want to reduce her allowance. It's a pittance as it is. Make it plain there's no question of that. Travel would have been the thing for her, but where's the money to come from?"

Lady Cherrell did not know, and the conversation lapsed.

Into that old house, which for so many centuries human hopes, fears, births, deaths, and all the medley of everyday emotions had stamped with a look of wary age, had come an uneasiness which showed in every word and action, even of the servants. What attitude to adopt? How to show sympathy, and yet not show it? How to welcome, and yet make it clear that welcome did not carry rejoicing? Even Jean was infected. She brushed and combed the dogs, and insisted on taking the car to the station for every afternoon train.

Dinny came by the third. Leading Foch, she stepped out of the carriage almost into Jean's arms.

"Hallo, my dear," said Jean, "here you are! New dog?"

"Yes; a darling."

"What have you got?"

"Only those things. It's no use looking for a porter, they're always trundling bicycles."

"I'll get them out."

"Indeed, you won't! Hold Foch!"

When, carrying her suitcase and dressing-bag, she reached the car, Dinny said:

"Would you mind if I walk up by the fields, Jean? It's good for Foch; and the train was stuffy; I should like a sniff of the hay."

"Yes, there's some down still. I'll take these along, and have fresh tea ready."

She left Dinny standing with a smile on her face. And all the way to the Grange she thought of that smile, and swore under her breath. . . .

Entering the field path, Dinny let Foch off his lead. By the way he rushed to the hedgerow, she realised how he had missed all this. A country dog! For a moment his busy joy took up her attention; then the sore and bitter aching came back again. She called him and walked on. In the first of their own fields the hay was still lying out, and she flung herself down. When she once got home she must watch every word and look, must smile and smile, and show nothing. She wanted desperately these few minutes of abandonment. She didn't cry, but pressed herself against the hay-covered earth, and the sun burned her neck. She turned on her back and gazed up at the blue. She framed no thoughts, dissolved in aching for what was lost and could never be found now. And the hum of summer beat drowsily above her from the wings of insects drunk on heat and honey. She crossed her arms on her chest to compress the pain within her. If she could die, there, now, in full summer with its hum and the singing of the larks; die and ache no more! So she lay motionless, until the dog came and licked her cheek. And, ashamed, she got up and stood brushing the hayseeds and stalks from her dress and stockings.

Past old Kismet in the next field she came to the thread of stream and crossed it into the disenchanted orchard, smelling of nettles and old trees; then on, to the garden and the flagstones of the terrace. One magnolia flower was out, but she dared not stop and sniff, lest its lemon-honey scent should upset her again; and, coming to the French window, she looked in.

Her mother was sitting with the look on her face that Dinny called 'waiting for Father.' Her father was standing with the look on his face that she called 'waiting for Mother.' Jean seemed expecting her cub to come round the corner.

'And I'm the cub,' thought Dinny, and stepped over the threshold, saying:

"Well, Mother darling, can I have some tea? . . ."

That evening after good-night had been said, she came down again, and went to her father's study. He was at his bureau, poring, with a pencil, over something he had written. She stole up, and read over his shoulder:

"Hunters for sale: Bay gelding, fifteen three, rising ten, sound, good-looking, plenty of bone, fine jumper. Mare: Blue roan: fifteen one, rising nine, very clever, carries lady, show jumper, sound wind and limb. Apply Owner: Condaford Grange, Oxon."

"M'm!" he said, and crossed out the 'wind and limb.'

Dinny reached down and took the paper.

The General started and looked around.

"No," she said. And tore the sheet.

"Here! You mustn't do that. It took me——"

"No, Dad, you can't sell the horses, you'd be lost."

"But I *must* sell the horses, Dinny."

"I know. Mother told me. But it isn't necessary. I happen to have quite a lot." She put the notes she had been carrying so long on his bureau.

The General stood up.

"Impossible!" he said: "Very good of you, Dinny, but quite impossible!"

"You mustn't refuse me, Dad. Let me do something for Condaford. I've no use for it, and it happens to be just the three hundred Mother says you want."

"No use for it? Nonsense, my dear! Why! With that you could have a good long travel!"

"I don't want a good long travel. I want to stay at home and help you both."

The General looked hard into her face.

"I should be ashamed to take it," he said. "It's my own fault that I've got behind."

"Dad! You never spend anything on yourself."

"Well, I don't know how it is—one little thing and another, it piles up."

"You and I will go into it. There must be things we could do without."

"The worst is having no capital. Something comes along and I have to meet it out of income; insurance is heavy, and with rates and taxes always going up, income gets smaller all the time."

"I know; it must be awful. Couldn't one breed something?"

"Costs money to start. Of course we could do perfectly well in London or Cheltenham, or abroad. It's keeping the place up, and the people dependent on it."

"Leave Condaford! Oh! no! Besides, who would take it? In spite of all you've done, we're not up to date, Dad."

"We're certainly not."

"We could never put 'this desirable residence' without blushing unseen. People won't pay for other people's ancestors."

The General stared before him.

"I do frankly wish, Dinny, the thing wasn't such a trust. I hate bothering about money, screwing here and screwing there, and always having to look forward to see if you can make do. But, as you say, to sell's unthinkable. And who'd rent it? It wouldn't make a boys' school, or a country club, or an asylum. Those seem the only fates before country houses now-a-days. Your Uncle Lionel's the only one of us who's got any money —I wonder if he'd like to take it on for his week-ends."

"No, Dad! No! Let's stick to it. I'm sure we can do it, somehow. Let me do the screwing and that. In the meantime you *must* take this. Then we shall start fair."

"Dinny, I——"

"To please me, dear."

The General drew her to him, and kissed her forehead.

"That business of yours," he muttered into her hair: "My God, I wish——"

She drew back.

"I'm going out for a few minutes now, just to wander round. It's so nice and warm."

And winding a scarf over her head, she was gone through the opened window.

The last dregs of the long daylight had drained down beyond the rim, but warmth abided, for no air stirred, and no dew fell—a still, dry, dark night, with swarming stars. From the moment she stepped out Dinny was lost in it. But the old house shrouded in its creepers lived for her eyes, a dim presence with four still-lighted windows. She stood under an elm tree leaning against its trunk, with her arms stretched back, and her hands clasping it behind her. Night was a friend—no eye to see, no ear to listen. She stared into it, unmoving, drawing comfort from the solidity and breadth behind her. Moths flew by almost touching her face. Insentient nature, warm, incurious, busy even in the darkness. Millions of little creatures burrowed and asleep, hundreds floating or creeping about, billions of blades of grass and flowers straightening up ever so slowly in the comparative coolness of the night. Nature! Pitiless and indifferent even to the only creatures who crowned and petted her with pretty words! Threads broke and hearts broke, or whatever really happened to the silly things—nature twitched no lip, heaved no sigh! One twitch of nature's lip would have been more to her than all human sympathy. If, as in the 'Birth of Venus,' breezes could puff at her, waves like doves lap to her feet, bees fly round her seeking honey! If for one moment in this darkness she could feel at one with the starshine, the smell of earth, the twitter of that bat, the touch of a moth's wing on her nose!

With her chin tilted up, and all her body taut against the tree trunk, she stood breathless from the darkness and the silence and the stars. Ears of a weasel, nose of a fox to hear and scent out what was stirring! In the tree above her head a bird chirped once. The drone of the last train, still far away, began, swelled, resolved itself into the sound of wheels and the sound of steam, stopped, then began again and faded out in a far drumming. All hushed once more! Where she stood the moat had been, filled in so long that this great elm tree had grown. Slow, the lives of trees, and one long fight with the winds; slow and tenacious like the life of her family clinging to this spot.

'I *will* not think of him,' she thought, 'I *will* not think of him!' As a child that refuses to remember what has hurt it, so would she be! And, instantly, his face formed in the darkness—his eyes, and his lips. She turned round to the trunk, and leaned her forehead on its roughness. But his face came between. Recoiling, she walked away; over the grass swiftly and without noise, invisible as a spirit. Up and down she walked, and the wheeling soothed her.

'Well,' she thought, 'I have had my hour. It can't be helped. I must go in.'

She stood for a moment looking up at the stars, so far, so many, bright and cold. And with a faint smile she thought:

'I wonder which is my lucky star!'

BOOK III

ONE MORE RIVER

TO
RUDOLF and VIOLA SAUTER

CHAPTER 1

CLARE, who for seventeen months had been the wife of Sir Gerald Corven of the Colonial Service, stood on the boat deck of an Orient liner in the river Thames, waiting for it to dock. It was ten o'clock of a mild day in October, but she wore a thick tweed coat, for the voyage had been hot. She looked pale, indeed a little sallow, but her clear brown eyes were fixed eagerly on the land and her slightly touched-up lips were parted, so that her face had the vividness to which it was accustomed. She stood alone, until a voice said:

"Oh! *here* you are!" and a young man appearing from behind a boat stood beside her. Without turning, she said:

"Absolutely perfect day. It ought to be lovely at home."

"I thought you'd be staying in Town for a night at least; and we could have had a dinner and theatre. Won't you?"

"My dear young man, I shall be met."

"Perfectly damnable, things coming to an end."

"Often more damnable, things beginning."

He gave her a long look, and said suddenly:

"Clare, you realise, of course, that I love you?"

She nodded. "Yes."

"But you don't love me?"

"Wholly without prejudice."

"I wish—I wish you could catch fire for a moment."

"I am a respectable married woman, Tony."

"Coming back to England, because——"

"Of the climate of Ceylon."

He kicked at the rail. "Just as it's getting perfect. I've not said anything, but I know that your—that Corven——"

Clare lifted her eyebrows, and he was silent; then both looked at the shore, becoming momentarily more and more a consideration.

When two young people have been nearly three weeks together on board a ship, they do not know each other half as well as they think they do. In the abiding inanity of a life when everything has stopped except the engines, the water slipping along the ship's sides, and the curving of the sun in the sky, their daily chair-to-chair intimacy gathers a queer momentum and a sort of lazy warmth. They know that they are getting talked about, and do not care. After all, they cannot get off the ship, and there is nothing else to do. They dance together, and the sway of the ship, however slight, favours the closeness of their contacts. After ten days or so they settle down to a life together, more continuous than that of marriage, except that they still spend their nights apart. And then, all of a sudden, the ship stops, and they stop, and there is a feeling, at least on one side, perhaps on both, that stock-taking has been left till too late. A hurried vexed excitement, not unpleasurable because suspended animation is at an end, invades their faculties; they are faced with the real equation of land animals who have been at sea.

Clare broke the silence.

"You've never told me why you're called Tony when your name is James."

"That *is* why. I *wish* you'd be serious, Clare; we haven't much time before the darned ship docks. I simply can't bear the thought of not seeing you every day."

Clare gave him a swift look, and withdrew her eyes to the shore again. 'How clean!' she was thinking. He had, indeed, a clean oval-shaped brown face, determined, but liable to good humour, with dark grey eyes inclined to narrow with his thoughts, and darkish hair, and he was thin and active.

He took hold of a button of her coat.

"You haven't said a word about yourself out there, but you aren't happy, I know."

"I dislike people who talk about their private lives."

"Look!" he put a card into her hand: "That club always finds me."

She read:

MR. JAMES BERNARD CROOM,
The Coffee House,
St. James' Street.

"Isn't The Coffee House very out of date?"

"Yes, but it's still rather 'the thing.' My Dad put me down when I was born."

"I have an uncle by marriage who belongs—Sir Lawrence Mont, tall and twisty and thin; you'll know him by a tortoise-shell-rimmed eye-glass."

"I'll look out for him."

"What are you going to do with yourself in England?"

"Hunt a job. That's more than one man's work, it seems."

"What sort of job?"

"Anything except school-mastering and selling things on commission."

"But does anybody ever get anything else nowadays?"

"No. It's a bad lookout. What I'd like would be an estate agency, or something to do with horses."

"Estates and horses are both dying out."

"I know one or two racing men rather well. But I expect I shall end as a chauffeur. Where are you going to stay?"

"With my people. At first, anyway. If you still want to see me when you've been home a week, 'Condaford Grange, Oxfordshire,' will find me."

"Why did I ever meet you?" said the young man with sudden gloom.
"Thank you."

"Oh! you know what I mean! God! she's casting anchor. Here's the tender! Oh! Clare!"

"Sir?"

"Hasn't it meant anything to you?"

Clare looked at him steadily before answering.

"Yes. But I don't know if it will ever mean any more. If it doesn't, thank you for helping me over a bad three weeks."

The young man stood silent, as only those can be silent whose feelings are raging for expression. . . .

The beginnings and endings of all human undertakings are untidy; the building of a house, the writing of a novel, the demolition of a bridge, and eminently, the finish of a voyage. Clare landed from the tender in the usual hurly-burly, and still attended by young Croom, came to rest in the arms of her sister.

"Dinny! How sweet of you to face this bally-hooley! My sister, Dinny Cherrell—Tony Croom. I shall be all right now, Tony. Go and look after your own things."

"I've got Fleur's car," said Dinny. "What about your trunks?"

"They're booked through to Condaford."

"Then we can go straight off."

The young man, going with them to the car, said 'Good-bye' with a jauntiness which deceived no one; and the car slid away from the dock.

Side by side the sisters looked at each other, a long and affectionate scrutiny; and their hands lay, squeezed together, on the rug.

"Well, ducky!" said Dinny, at last. "Lovely to see you! Am I wrong to read between the lines?"

"No. I'm not going back to him, Dinny."

"No, never, non?"

"No, never, non!"

"Oh! dear! Poor darling!"

"I won't go into it, but it became impossible." Clare was silent, then added suddenly, with a toss back of her head: "Quite impossible!"

"Did he consent to your coming?"

Clare shook her head. "I slipped off. He was away. I wirelessed him, and wrote from Suez."

There was another silence. Then Dinny squeezed her hand and said: "I was always afraid of it."

"The worst of it is I haven't a penny. Is there anything in hats now, Dinny?"

"'All British' hats—I wonder."

"Or, perhaps, I could breed dogs—bull terriers; what d'you think?"

"I don't at present. We'll enquire."

"How are things at Condaford?"

"We rub on. Jean has gone out to Hubert again, but the baby's there —just a year old now. Cuthbert Conway Cherrell. I suppose we shall call him 'Cuffs.' He's rather a duck."

"Thank God, I haven't that complication. Certain things have their advantages." Her face had the hardness of a face on a coin.

"Have you had any word from him?"

"No, but I shall, when he realises that I mean it."

"Was there another woman?"

Clare shrugged.

Again Dinny's hand closed on hers.

"I'm not going to make a song of my affairs, Dinny."

"Is he likely to come home about it?"

"I don't know. I won't see him if he does."

"But, darling, you'll be hopelessly hung up."

"Oh! Don't let's bother about me. How have you been?" And she looked critically at her sister. "You look more Botticellian than ever."

"I've become an adept at skimping. Also I've gone in for bees."

"Do they pay?"

"Not at present. But on a ton of honey we could make about seventy pounds."

"How much honey did you have this year?"

"About two hundredweight."

"Are there any horses still?"

"Yes, we've saved the horses, so far. I've got a scheme for a Condaford Grange bakery. The home farm is growing wheat at double what we sell it at. I want to mill and bake our own and supply the neighbourhood. The old mill could be set going for a few pounds, and there's a building for the bakery. It wants about three hundred to start it. We've nearly decided to cut enough timber."

"The local traders will rage furiously."

"They will."

"Can it really pay?"

"At a ton of wheat to the acre—*vide* Whitaker—we reckon thirty acres of our wheat, plus as much Canadian to make good light bread, would bring us in more than eight hundred and fifty pounds, less say, five hundred, cost of milling and baking. It would mean baking one hundred and sixty two-pound loaves a day and selling about fifty-six thousand loaves a year. We should need to supply eighty households, but that's only the village, more or less. And we'd make the best and brightest bread."

"Three hundred and fifty a year profit," said Clare. "I wonder."

"So do I," said Dinny. "Experience doesn't tell me that every estimate of profit should be halved, because I haven't had any, but I suspect it. But even half would just tip the beam the right way for us, and we could extend operations gradually. We could plough a lot of grass in time."

"It's a scheme," said Clare, "but would the village back you?"

"So far as I've sounded them—yes."

"You'd want somebody to run it."

"M'yes. It would have to be someone who didn't mind what he did. Of course he'd have the future, if it went."

"I wonder," said Clare, again, and wrinkled her brows.

"Who," asked Dinny, suddenly, "was that young man?"

"Tony Croom? Oh! He was on a tea plantation, but they closed down." And she looked her sister full in the face.

"Pleasant?"

"Yes, rather a dear. *He* wants a job, by the way."

"So do about three million others."

"Including me."

"You haven't come back to a very cheery England, darling."

"I gather we fell off the gold standard or something while I was in the Red Sea. What is the gold standard?"

"It's what you want to be on when you're off, and to be off when you're on."

"I see."

"The trouble, apparently, is that our exports and carrying trade profits and interests from investments abroad don't any longer pay for our imports; so we're living beyond our income. Michael says anybody could have seen that coming; but we thought 'it would be all right on the night.' And it isn't. Hence the National Government and the election."

"Can they do anything if they remain in?"

"Michael says 'yes'; but he's notably hopeful. Uncle Lawrence says they can put a drag on panic, prevent money going out of the country, keep the pound fairly steady, and stop profiteering; but that nothing under a wide and definite reconstruction that will take twenty years will do the trick; and during that time we shall all be poorer. Unfortunately no Government, he says, can prevent us liking play better than work, hoarding to pay these awful taxes, or preferring the present to the future. He also says that if we think people will work as they did in the war to save the country, we're wrong; because instead of being one people against an outside enemy, we're two peoples against the inside enemy of ourselves, with quite opposite views as to how our salvation is to come."

"Does he think the socialists have a cure?"

"No; he says they've forgotten that no one will give them food if they can neither produce it nor pay for it. He says that communism or free trade socialism only has a chance in a country which feeds itself. You see, I've been learning it up. They all use the word Nemesis a good deal."

"Phew! Where are we going now, Dinny?"

"I thought you'd like lunch at Fleur's, afterwards we can take the three-fifty to Condaford."

Then there was silence, during which each thought seriously about the other, and neither was happy. For Clare was feeling in her elder sister the subtle change which follows in one whose springs have been broken and mended to go on with. And Dinny was thinking: 'Poor child! Now we've both been in the wars. What will she do? And how can I help her?'

CHAPTER 2

"WHAT A NICE LUNCH!" said Clare, eating the sugar at the bottom of her coffee cup: "The first meal on shore is lovely! When you get on board a ship and read the first menu, you think: 'My goodness! What an enchanting lot of things!' and then you come down to cold ham at nearly every meal. Do you know that stealing disappointment?"

"Don't I?" said Fleur. "The curries used to be good, though."

"Not on the return voyage. I never want to see a curry again. How's the Round Table Conference going?"

"Plodding on. Is Ceylon interested in India?"

"Not very. Is Michael?"

"We both are."

Clare's brows went up with delightful suddenness.

"But you can't know anything about it."

"I *was* in India, you know, and at one time I saw a lot of Indian students."

"Oh! yes, students. That's the trouble. They're so advanced and the people are so backward."

"If Clare's to see Kit and Kat before we start," said Dinny, "we ought to go up, Fleur."

The visit to the nurseries over, the sisters resumed their seats in the car.

"Fleur always strikes me," said Clare, "as knowing so exactly what she wants."

"She gets it, as a rule; but there've been exceptions. I've always doubted whether she really wanted Michael."

"D'you mean a love affair went wrong?"

Dinny nodded. Clare looked out of the window.

"Well, she's not remarkable in that."

Her sister did not answer.

"Trains," Dinny said, in their empty third-class compartment, "always have great open spaces now."

"I rather dread seeing Mother and Dad, Dinny, having made such an almighty bloomer. I really must get something to do."

"Yes, you won't be happy at Condaford for long."

"It isn't that. I want to prove that I'm not the complete idiot. I wonder if I could run an hotel. English hotels are still pretty backward."

"Good idea. It's strenuous and you'd see lots of people."

"Is that caustic?"

"No, darling, just common sense; you never liked being buried."

"How does one go to work to get such a thing?"

"You have me there. But now's the time if ever; nobody's going to be able to travel. But I'm afraid there's a technical side to managing hotels that has to be learned. Your title might help."

"I shouldn't use his name. I should call myself Mrs. Clare."

"I see. Are you sure it wouldn't be wise to tell me more about things?"

Clare sat silent for a little, then said suddenly: "He's a sadist."

Looking at her flushed face, Dinny said: "I've never understood exactly what that means."

"Seeking sensation and getting more sensation when you hurt the person you get it from. A wife is most convenient."

"Oh! darling!"

"There was a lot first; my riding whip was only the last straw."

"You don't mean——!" cried Dinny, horrified.

"Oh! yes."

Dinny came over to her side and put her arms round her.

"But, Clare, you must get free."

"And how? My word against his. Besides, who would make a show of beastliness? You're the only person I could ever even speak to of it."

Dinny got up and let down the window. Her face was as flushed as her sister's. She heard Clare say dully:

"I came away the first moment I could: It's none of it fit for publication. You see, ordinary passion palls after a bit, and it's a hot climate."

"Oh! heaven!" said Dinny, and sat down again opposite.

"My own fault. I always knew it was thin ice, and I've popped through, that's all."

"But, darling, at twenty-four you simply can't stay married and not married."

"I don't see why not; *mariage manquè* is very steadying to the blood. All I'm worrying about is getting a job. I'm not going to be a drag on Dad. Is his head above water, Dinny?"

"Not quite. We were breaking even, but this last taxation will just duck us. The trouble is how to get on without reducing staff. Every one is in the same boat. I always feel that we and the village are one. We've got to sink or swim together, and somehow or other we're going to swim. Hence my bakery scheme."

"If I haven't got another job, could I do the delivering? I suppose we've still got the old car."

"Darling, you can help any way you like. But it all has to be started. That'll take till after Christmas. In the meantime there's the election."

"Who is our candidate?"

"His name is Dornford—a new man, quite decent."

"Will he want canvassers?"

442

"Rather!"

"All right. That'll be something to do for a start. Is this National Government any use?"

"They talk of 'completing their work'; but at present they don't tell us how."

"I suppose they'll quarrel among themselves the moment a constructive scheme is put up to them. It's all beyond me. But I can go round saying 'Vote for Dornford.' How's Aunt Em?"

"She's coming to stay to-morrow. She suddenly wrote that she hadn't seen the baby; says she's feeling romantic—wants to have the priest's room, and will I see that 'no one bothers to do her up behind, and that.' She's exactly the same."

"I often thought about her," said Clare. "Extraordinarily restful."

After that there was a long silence, Dinny thinking about Clare, and Clare thinking about herself. Presently she grew tired of that and looked across at her sister. Had Dinny really got over that affair of hers with Wilfrid Desert of which Hubert had written with such concern when it was on, and such relief when it was off? She had asked that her affair should never be spoken of, Hubert had said, but that was over a year ago. Could one venture, or would she curl up like a hedgehog? 'Poor Dinny!' she thought: 'I'm twenty-four, so she's twenty-seven!' And she sat very still looking at her sister's profile. It was charming, the more so for that slight tip-tilt of the nose which gave to the face a touch of adventurousness. Her eyes were as pretty as ever—that cornflower blue wore well; and their fringing was unexpectedly dark with such chestnut hair. Still the face was thinner, and had lost what Uncle Lawrence used to call its 'bubble and squeak.' 'I should fall in love with her if I were a man,' thought Clare, 'she's *good*. But it's rather a sad face, now, except when she's talking.' And Clare drooped her lids, spying through her lashes: No! one could not ask! The face she spied on had a sort of hard-won privacy that it would be unpardonable to disturb.

"Darling," said Dinny, "would you like your old room? I'm afraid the fantails have multiplied exceedingly—they coo a lot just under it."

"I shan't mind that."

"And what do you do about breakfast? Will you have it in your room?"

"My dear, don't bother about me in any way. If anybody does, I shall feel dreadful. England again on a day like this! Grass is really lovely stuff, and the elm trees, and that blue look!"

"Just one thing, Clare. Would you like me to tell Dad and Mother, or would you rather I said nothing?"

Clare's lips tightened.

"I suppose they'll have to know that I'm not going back."

"Yes; and something of the reason."

"Just general impossibility, then."

Dinny nodded. "I don't want them to think you in the wrong. We'll let other people think that you're home for your health."

"Aunt Em?" said Clare.

"I'll see to her. She'll be absorbed in the baby, anyway. Here we are very nearly."

Condaford Church came into view, and the little group of houses mostly thatched which formed the nucleus of that scattered parish. The home-farm buildings could be seen, but not the Grange, for situate on the lowly level dear to ancestors, it was wrapped from the sight in trees.

Clare, flattening her nose against the window, said:

"It gives you a thrill. Are you as fond of home as ever, Dinny?"

"Fonder."

"It's funny. I love it, but I can't live in it."

"Very English—hence America and the Dominions. Take your dressing-case, and I'll take the suit-case."

The drive up through the lanes, where the elms were flecked by little golden patches of turned leaves, was short and sweet in the lowered sunlight, and ended with the usual rush of dogs from the dark hall.

"This one's new," said Clare, of the black spaniel sniffing at her stockings.

"Yes, Foch. Scaramouch and he have signed the Kellogg Pact, so they don't observe it. I'm a sort of Manchuria." And Dinny threw open the drawing-room door.

"Here she is, Mother."

Advancing towards her mother, who stood smiling, pale and tremulous, Clare felt choky for the first time. To have to come back like this and disturb their peace!

"Well, Mother darling," she said, "here's your bad penny! You look just the same, bless you!"

Emerging from that warm embrace, Lady Charwell looked at her daughter shyly, and said:

"Dad's in his study."

"I'll fetch him," said Dinny.

In that barren abode which still had its military and austere air, the General was fidgeting with a gadget he had designed to save time in the putting on of riding boots and breeches.

"Well?" he said.

"She's all right, dear, but it *is* a split, and I'm afraid complete."

"That's bad!" said the General, frowning.

Dinny took his lapels in her hands.

"It's not her fault. But I wouldn't ask her any questions, Dad. Let's take it that she's just on a visit; and make it as nice for her as we can."

"What's the fellow been doing?"

"Oh! his nature. I knew there was a streak of cruelty in him."

"How d'you mean—knew it, Dinny?"

"The way he smiled—his lips."

The General uttered a sound of intense discomfort.

"Come along!" he said: "Tell me later."

444

With Clare he was perhaps rather elaborately genial and open, asking no questions except about the Red Sea and the scenery of Ceylon, his knowledge of which was confined to its spicy off-shore scent, and a stroll in the Cinnamon Gardens at Colombo. Clare, still emotional from the meeting with her mother, was grateful for his reticence. She escaped rather quickly to her room where her bags had already been unpacked.

At its dormer window she stood listening to the coo-rooing of the fantails and the sudden flutter and flip-flap of their wings climbing the air from the yew-hedged garden. The sun, very low, was still shining through an elm tree. There was no wind, and her nerves sucked up repose in that pigeon-haunted stillness, scented so differently from Ceylon. Native air, deliciously sane, fresh and homespun with a faint tang of burning leaves. She could see the threading blue smoke from where the gardeners had lighted a small bonfire in the orchard. And almost at once she lit a cigarette. The whole of Clare was in that simple action. She could never quite rest and be still, must always move on to that fuller savouring which for such natures ever recedes. A fantail on the gutter of the sloped stone roof watched her with a soft dark little eye, preening itself slightly. Beautifully white it was, and had a pride of body; so too had that small round mulberry tree which had dropped a ring of leaves, with their unders uppermost, spangling the grass. The last of the sunlight was stirring in what yellowish green foliage was left, so that the tree had an enchanted look. Seventeen months since she had stood at this window and looked down over that mulberry tree at the fields and the rising coverts! Seventeen months of foreign skies and trees, foreign scents and sounds and waters. All new, and rather exciting, tantalising, unsatisfying. No rest! Certainly none in the white house with the wide verandah she had occupied at Kandy. At first she had enjoyed, then she had wondered if she enjoyed, then she had known she was not enjoying, lastly she had hated it. And now it was all over and she was back! She flipped the ash off her cigarette and stretched herself; and the fantail rose with a fluster.

CHAPTER 3

DINNY WAS 'SEEING TO' Aunt Em. It was no mean process. With ordinary people one had question and answer and the thing was over. But with Lady Mont words were not consecutive like that. She stood with a verbena sachet in her hand, sniffing, while Dinny unpacked for her.

"This is delicious, Dinny. Clare looks rather yellow. It isn't a baby, is it?"

"No, dear."

"Pity! When we were in Ceylon every one was havin' babies. The baby elephants—so enticin'! In this room—we always played a game of feedin' the Catholic priest with a basket from the roof. Your father used to be on the roof, and I was the priest. There was never anythin' worth eatin' in the basket. Your Aunt Wilmet was stationed in a tree to call 'Cooee' in case of Protestants."

" 'Cooee' was a bit premature, Aunt Em. Australia wasn't discovered under Elizabeth."

"No. Lawrence says the Protestants at that time were devils. So were the Catholics. So were the Mohammedans."

Dinny winced and veiled her face with a corset belt.

"Where shall I put these undies?"

"So long as I see where. Don't stoop too much! They were all devils then. Animals were treated terribly. Did Clare enjoy Ceylon?"

Dinny stood up with an armful of underthings.

"Not much."

"Why not? Liver?"

"Auntie, you won't say anything except to Uncle Lawrence and Michael, if I tell you? There's been a split."

Lady Mont buried her nose in the verbena bag.

"Oh!" she said: "His mother looked it. D'you believe in 'like mother like son'?"

"Not too much."

"I always thought seventeen years' difference too much, Dinny. Lawrence says people say: 'Oh! Jerry Corven!' and then don't say. So, what was it?"

Dinny bent over a drawer and arranged the things.

"I can't go into it, but he seems to be quite a beast."

Lady Mont tipped the bag into the drawer, murmuring: "Poor, dear Clare!"

"So, Auntie, she's just to be home for her health."

Lady Mont put her nose into a bowl of flowers. "Boswell and Johnson call them 'God-eat-yers.' They don't smell. What disease could Clare have —nerves?"

"Climate, Auntie."

"So many Anglo-Indians go back and back, Dinny."

"I know, but for the present. Something's bound to happen. So not even to Fleur, please."

"Fleur will know whether I tell her or not. She's like that. Has Clare a young man?"

"Oh! no!" And Dinny lifted a puce-coloured wrapper, recalling the expression of the young man when he was saying good-bye.

"On board ship," murmured her aunt, dubiously.

Dinny changed the subject.

"Is Uncle Lawrence very political just now?"

"Yes, so borin'. Things always sound so when you talk about them. Is your candidate here safe, like Michael?"

"He's new, but he'll get in."

"Married?"

"No."

Lady Mont inclined her head slightly to one side and scrutinised her niece from under half-drooped lids.

Dinny took the last thing out of the trunk. It was a pot of anti-phlogistine.

"That's not British, Auntie."

"For the chest. Delia puts it in. I've had it, years. Have you talked to your candidate in private?"

"I have."

"How old is he?"

"Rather under forty, I should say."

"Does he do anything besides?"

"He's a K.C."

"What's his name?"

"Dornford."

"There were Dornfords when I was a girl. Where was that? Ah! Algeciras! He was a Colonel at Gibraltar."

"That would be his father, I expect."

"Then he hasn't any money."

"Only what he makes at the Bar."

"But they don't—under forty."

"He does, I think."

"Energetic?"

"Very."

"Fair?"

"No, darkish. He won the Bar point-to-point this year. Now, darling, will you have a fire at once, or last till dressing time?"

"Last. I want to see the baby."

"All right, he ought to be just in from his pram. Your bathroom's at the foot of these stairs, and I'll wait for you in the nursery."

The nursery was the same mullion-windowed, low-pitched room as that wherein Dinny and Aunt Em herself had received their first impressions of that jigsaw puzzle called life: and in it the baby was practising his totter. Whether he would be a Charwell or a Tasburgh when he grew up seemed as yet uncertain. His nurse, his aunt, and his great-aunt stood, in triangular admiration, for him to fall alternatively into their outstretched hands.

"He doesn't crow," said Dinny.

"He does in the morning, Miss."

"Down he goes!" said Lady Mont.

"Don't cry, darling!"

"He never cries, Miss."

"That's Jean. Clare and I cried a lot till we were about seven."

"I cried till I was fifteen," said Lady Mont, "and I began again when I was forty-five. Did you cry, Nurse?"

"We were too large a family, my Lady. There wasn't room like."

"Nanny had a lovely mother—five sisters as good as gold."

The nurse's fresh cheeks grew fresher; she drooped her chin, smiling, shy as a little girl.

"Take care of bow legs!" said Lady Mont: "That's enough totterin'."

The nurse, retrieving the still persistent baby, placed him in his cot, whence he frowned solemnly at Dinny, who said:

"Mother's devoted to him. She thinks he'll be like Hubert."

Lady Mont made the sound supposed to attract babies.

"When does Jean come home again?"

"Not till Hubert's next long leave."

Lady Mont's gaze rested on her niece.

"The rector says Alan has another year on the China station."

Dinny, dangling a bead chain over the baby, paid no attention. Never since the summer evening last year, when she came back home after Wilfrid's flight, had she made or suffered any allusion to her feelings. No one, perhaps not even she herself, knew whether she was heart-whole once more. It was, indeed, as if she had no heart. So long, so earnestly, had she resisted its aching, that it had slunk away into the shadows of her inmost being, where even she could hardly feel it beating.

"What would you like to do now, Auntie? He has to go to sleep."

"Take me round the garden."

They went down and out on to the terrace.

"Oh!" said Dinny, with dismay, "Glover has gone and beaten the leaves off the little mulberry. They were so lovely, shivering on the tree and coming off in a ring on the grass. Really gardeners have no sense of beauty."

448

"They don't like sweepin'. Where's the cedar I planted when I was five?"

They came on it round the corner of an old wall, a spreading youngster of nearly sixty with flattening boughs gilded by the level sunlight.

"I should like to be buried under it, Dinny. Only I suppose they won't. There'll be something stuffy."

"I mean to be burnt and scattered. Look at them ploughing in that field. I do love horses moving slowly against a skyline of trees."

" 'The lowin' kine,' " said Lady Mont, irrelevantly.

A faint clink came from a sheepfold to the east.

"Listen, Auntie!"

Lady Mont thrust her arm within her niece's.

"I've often thought," she said, "that I should like to be a goat."

"Not in England, tied to a stake and grazing in a mangy little circle."

"No, with a bell on a mountain. A he goat, I think, so as not to be milked."

"Come and see our new cutting bed, Auntie. There's nothing now, of course, but dahlias, godetias, chrysanthemums, Michaelmas daisies, and a few pentstemons and cosmias."

"Dinny," said Lady Mont, from among the dahlias, "about Clare? They say divorce is very easy now."

"Until you try for it, I expect."

"There's desertion and that."

"But you have to *be* deserted."

"Well, you said he made her."

"It's not the same thing, dear."

"Lawyers are so fussy about the law. There was that magistrate with the long nose in Hubert's extradition."

"Oh! but he turned out quite human."

"How was that?"

"Telling the Home Secretary that Hubert was speaking the truth."

"A dreadful business," murmured Lady Mont, "but nice to remember."

"It had a happy ending," said Dinny quickly.

Lady Mont stood, ruefully regarding her.

And Dinny, staring at the flowers, said suddenly:

"Aunt Em, somehow there must be a happy ending for Clare."

CHAPTER 4

THE CUSTOM known as canvassing, more peculiar even than its name, was in full blast round Condaford. Every villager had been invited to observe how appropriate it would be if they voted for Dornford, and how equally appropriate it would be if they voted for Stringer. They had been exhorted publicly and vociferously, by ladies in cars, by ladies out of cars, and in the privacy of their homes by voices speaking out of trumpets. By newspaper and by leaflet they had been urged to perceive that they alone could save the country. They had been asked to vote early, and only just not asked to vote often. To their attention had been brought the startling dilemma that whichever way they voted the country would be saved. They had been exhorted by people who knew everything, it seemed, except how it would be saved. Neither the candidates nor their ladies, neither the mysterious disembodied voices, nor the still more incorporeal print, had made the faintest attempt to tell them that. It was better not; for in the first place, no one knew. And, in the second place, why mention the particular when the general would serve? Why draw attention, even, to the fact that the general is made up of the particular; or to the political certainty that promise is never performance? Better, far better, to make large, loose assertion, abuse the other side, and call the electors the sanest and soundest body of people in the world.

Dinny was not canvassing. She was 'no good at it,' she said; and, perhaps, secretly she perceived the peculiarity of the custom. Clare, if she noticed any irony about the business, was too anxious to be doing something to abstain. She was greatly helped by the way everybody took it. They had always been 'canvassed,' and they always would be. It was a harmless enough diversion to their ears, rather like the buzzing of gnats that did not bite. As to their votes, they would record them for quite other reasons—because their fathers had voted this or that before them, because of something connected with their occupation, because of their landlords, their churches, or their trades unions; because they wanted a change while not expecting anything much from it; and not a few because of their common sense.

Clare, dreading questions, pattered as little as possible and came quickly to their babies or their health. She generally ended by asking what time they would like to be fetched. Noting the hour in a little book, she would come out not much wiser. Being a Charwell—that is to say, no 'foreigner' —she was taken as a matter of course; and though not, like Dinny, personally known to them all, she was part of an institution, Condaford without Charwells being still almost inconceivable.

She was driving back from this dutiful pastime towards the Grange about four o'clock on the Saturday before the election, when a voice from an overtaking two-seater called her name, and she saw young Tony Croom.

"What on earth are you doing here, Tony?"

"I couldn't go any longer without a glimpse of you."

"But, my dear boy, to come down here is too terribly pointed."

"I know, but I've seen you."

"You weren't going to call, were you?"

"If I didn't see you otherwise. Clare, you look so lovely."

"That, if true, is not a reason for queering my pitch at home."

"The last thing I want to do; but I've got to see you now and then, otherwise I shall go batty."

His face was so earnest and his voice so moved, that Clare felt for the first time stirred in that hackneyed region, the heart.

"That's bad," she said; "because I've got to find my feet, and I can't have complications."

"Let me kiss you just once. Then I should go back happy."

Still more stirred, Clare thrust forward her cheek.

"Well, quick!" she said.

He glued his lips to her cheek, but when he tried to reach her lips, she drew back.

"No. Now, Tony, you must go. If you're to see me, it must be in Town. But what is the good of seeing me? It'll only make us unhappy."

"Bless you for that 'us.'"

Clare's brown eyes smiled; their colour was like that of a glass of Malaga wine held up to the light.

"Have you found a job?"

"There are none."

"It'll be better when the election's over. *I'm* thinking of trying to get with a milliner."

"You!"

"I must do something. My people here are as hard pressed as everybody else. Now, Tony, you said you'd go."

"Promise to let me know the first day you come up."

Clare nodded, and re-started her engine. As the car slid forward gently, she turned her face and gave him another smile.

He continued to stand with his hands to his head till the car rounded a bend and she was gone.

Turning the car into the stable yard, she was thinking 'poor boy!' and feeling the better for it. Whatever her position in the eyes of the Law, or according to morality, a young and pretty woman breathes more easily when inhaling the incense of devotion. She may have strict intentions, but she has also a sense of what is due to her, and a dislike of waste. Clare looked the prettier and felt the happier all that evening. But the night was ridden by the moon; nearly full, it soared up in front of her window, discouraging sleep. She got up and parted the curtains. Huddling into her fur coat, she stood at the window. There was evidently a frost, and a ground mist stretched like fleece over the fields. The tall elms, ragged-edged, seemed to be sailing slowly along over the white vapour. The earth out there was unknown by her, as if it had dropped from that moon. She shivered. It might be beautiful but it was cold, uncanny; a frozen glamour. She thought of the nights in the Red Sea, when she lay with bedclothes thrown off, and the very moon seemed hot. On board that ship people had 'talked' about her and Tony—she had seen many signs of it, and hadn't cared. Why should she? He had not even kissed her all those days. Not even the evening he came to her stateroom and she had shown him photographs, and they had talked. A nice boy, modest and a gentleman! And if he was in love, now, she couldn't help it—she hadn't tried to 'vamp' him. As to what would happen, life always tripped one up, it seemed, whatever one did! Things must take care of themselves. To make resolutions, plans, lay down what was called 'a line of conduct,' was not the slightest use! She had tried that with Jerry. She shivered, then laughed, then went rigid with a sort of fury. No! If Tony expected her to rush into his arms, he was very much mistaken. Sensual love! She knew it inside out. No, thank you! As that moonlight, now, she was cold! Impossible to speak of it even to her mother, whatever she and Dad might be thinking.

Dinny must have told them something; for they had been most awfully decent. But even Dinny didn't know. Nobody should ever know! If only she had money, it wouldn't matter. 'Ruined life,' of course, and all that, was just old-fashioned tosh. Life could always be amusing if one made it so. She was not going to skulk and mope. Far from that! But money she must somehow make. She shivered even in her fur coat. The moonlight seemed to creep into one's bones. These old houses—no central heating, because they couldn't afford to put it in! The moment the election was over she would go up to London and scout round. Fleur might know of something. If there was no future in hats, one might get a political secretaryship. She could type, she knew French well, people could read her handwriting. She could drive a car with anybody, or school a horse. She knew all about country-house life, manners, and precedence. There must be lots of Members who wanted somebody like her, who could tell them how to dress, and how to decline this and that without anybody minding, and generally do their crossword puzzles for them. She'd had quite a lot of experience with dogs, and some with flowers, especially the arrangement of them in bowls and vases. And if it were a question of knowing anything about politics, she could soon mug that up. So, in that illusory cold moonshine, Clare could not see how they could fail to need her. With a salary and her own two hundred a year, she could get along quite well! The moon, behind an elm tree now, no longer had its devastating impersonality, but rather an air of bright intrigue, peeping through those still thick boughs with a conspiring eye. She hugged herself, danced a few steps to warm her feet, and slipped back into her bed. . . .

Young Croom, in his borrowed two-seater, had returned to Town at an unobtrusive sixty miles an hour. His first kiss on Clare's cold but glowing cheek had given him slight delirium. It was an immense step forward. He was not a vicious young man. That Clare was married was to him no advantage. But whether, if she had not been married, his feelings towards her would have been of quite the same brand, was a question he left unexamined. The subtle difference which creeps into the charm of a woman who has known physical love, and the sting which the knowledge of that implants in a man's senses—such is food for a psychologist rather than for a straightforward young man really in love for the first time. He wanted her, as his wife if possible; if that were not possible, in any other way that was. He had been in Ceylon three years, hard-worked, seeing few white women, and none that he had cared for. His passion had, hitherto, been for polo, and his meeting with Clare had come just as he had lost both job and polo. Clare filled for him a yawning gap. As with Clare, so with him in the matter of money, only more so.

He had some two hundred pounds saved and would then be 'bang up against it' unless he got a job. Having returned the two-seater to his friend's garage, he considered where he could dine most cheaply, and decided on his club. He was practically living there, except for a bedroom in Ryder Street, where he slept and breakfasted on tea and boiled eggs. A simple room it was, on the ground floor, with a bed and a dress cupboard, looking out on the tall back of another building, the sort of room that his father, coming on the Town in the 'nineties, had slept and breakfasted in for half the money.

On Saturday nights The Coffee House was deserted save for a certain number of 'old buffers' accustomed to week-ending in St. James' Street. Young Croom ordered the three-course dinner and ate it to the last crumb. He drank Bass, and went down to the smoking room for a pipe. About to sink into an armchair, he noticed standing before the fire a tallish thin man with twisting dark eyebrows and a little white moustache, who was examining him through a tortoise-shell-rimmed monocle. Acting on the impulse of a lover craving connection with his lady, he said:

"Excuse me, Sir, but aren't you Sir Lawrence Mont?"

"That has been my lifelong conviction."

Young Croom smiled.

"Then, Sir, I met your niece, Lady Corven, coming home from Ceylon. She said you were a member here. My name's Croom."

"Ah!" said Sir Lawrence, dropping his eyeglass: "I probably knew your father—he was always here, before the war."

"Yes, he put me down at birth. I believe I'm about the youngest in the club."

Sir Lawrence nodded. "So you met Clare. How was she?"

"All right, I think, Sir."

"Let's sit down and talk about Ceylon. Cigar?"

"Thank you, Sir, I have my pipe."

"Coffee, anyway? Waiter, two coffees. My wife is down at Condaford staying with Clare's people. An attractive young woman."

Noting those dark eyes, rather like a snipe's, fixed on him, young Croom regretted his impulse. He had gone red, but he said bravely:

"Yes, Sir, I thought her delightful."

"Do you know Corven?"

"No," said young Croom, shortly.

"Clever fellow. Did you like Ceylon?"

"Oh! yes. But it's given me up."

"Not going back?"

"Afraid not."

"It's a long time since I was there. India has rather smothered it. Been in India?"

"No, Sir."

"Difficult to know how far the people of India really want to cut the painter. Seventy per cent peasants! Peasants want stable conditions and a quiet life. I remember in Egypt before the war there was a strong nationalist agitation, but the *fellaheen* were all for Kitchener and stable British rule. We took Kitchener away and gave them unstable conditions in the war and so they went on the other tack. What were you doing in Ceylon?"

"Running a tea plantation. But they took up economy, amalgamated three plantations, and I wasn't wanted any more. Do you think there's going to be a recovery, Sir? I can't understand economics."

"Nobody can. There are dozens of causes of the present state of things, and people are always trying to tie it to one. Take England: There's the knock-out of Russian trade, the comparative independence of European countries, the great shrinkage of Indian and Chinese trade; the higher standard of British living since the war; the increase of national expenditure from two hundred odd millions to eight hundred millions, which means nearly six hundred millions a year less to employ labour with. When they talk of over-production being the cause, it certainly doesn't apply to us. We haven't produced so little for a long time past. Then there's dumping, and shocking bad organisation, and bad marketing of what little food we produce. And there's our habit of thinking it'll be 'all right on the night,' and general spoiled-child attitude. Well, those are all special English causes, except that the too high standard of living and the spoiled-child attitude are American too."

"And the other American causes, Sir?"

"The Americans certainly have over-produced, and over-speculated.

And they've been living so high that they've mortgaged their future—instalment system and all that. Then they're sitting on gold, and gold doesn't hatch out. And, more than all, they don't realise yet that the money they lent to Europe during the war was practically money they'd made out of the war. When they agree to general cancellation of debts they'll be agreeing to general recovery, including their own."

"But will they ever agree?"

"You never know what the Americans will do, they're looser jointed than we of the old world. They're capable of the big thing, even in their own interests. Are you out of a job?"

"Very much so."

"What's your record?"

"I was at Wellington and at Cambridge for two years. Then this tea thing came along, and I took it like a bird."

"What age are you?"

"Twenty-six."

"Any notion of what you want to do?"

Young Croom sat forward.

"Really, Sir, I'd have a shot at anything. But I'm pretty good with horses. I thought possibly I might get into a training stable; or with a breeder; or get a riding mastership."

"Quite an idea. It's queer about the horse—he's coming in as he goes out. I'll talk to my cousin Jack Muskham—he breeds bloodstock. And he's got a bee in his bonnet about the reintroduction of Arab blood into the English thoroughbred. In fact, he's got some Arab mares coming over. Just possibly he might want some one."

Young Croom flushed and smiled.

"That would be frightfully kind of you, Sir. It sounds ideal. I've had Arab polo ponies."

"Well," murmured Sir Lawrence, thoughtfully, "I don't know that anything excites my sympathy more than a man who really wants a job and can't find one. We must get this election over first, though. Unless the socialists are routed horse-breeders will have to turn their stock into potted meat. Imagine having the dam of a Derby winner between brown bread and butter for your tea—real 'Gentleman's Relish'!"

He got up.

"I'll say good-night, now. My cigar will just last me home."

Young Croom rose too, and remained standing till that spare and active figure had vanished.

'Frightfully nice old boy!' he thought, and in the depths of his armchair he resigned himself to hope and to Clare's face wreathed by the fumes of his pipe.

CHAPTER 5

On that cold and misty evening, which all the newspapers had agreed was to 'make history,' the Charwells sat in the drawing room at Conda-ford round the portable wireless, a present from Fleur. Would the voice breathe o'er Eden, or would it be the striking of Fate's clock? Not one of those five but was solemnly convinced that the future of Great Britain hung in the balance; convinced, too, that their conviction was detached from class or party. Patriotism divorced from thought of vested interest governed, as they supposed, their mood. And if they made a mistake in so thinking, quite a number of other Britons were making it too. Across Dinny's mind, indeed, did flit the thought: 'Does any one know what will save the country and what won't?' But, even by her, time and tide, in-calculably rolling, swaying and moulding the lives of nations, was un-gauged. Newspapers and politicians had done their work and stamped the moment for her as a turning point. In a sea-green dress, she sat, close to the 'present from Fleur,' waiting to turn it on at ten o'clock, and regu-late its stridency. Aunt Em was working at a new piece of French tapestry, her slight aquilinity emphasised by tortoise-shell spectacles. The General nervously turned and re-turned *The Times* and kept taking out his watch. Lady Charwell sat still and a little forward, like a child in Sunday School before she has become convinced that she is going to be bored. And Clare lay on the sofa, with the dog Foch on her feet.

"Time, Dinny," said the General; "turn the thing on."

Dinny fingered a screw, and 'the thing' burst into music. " 'Rings on our fingers and bells on our toes,' " she murmured, " 'We have got music wherever we goes.' "

The music stopped, and the voice spoke:

"This is the first election result: Hornsey . . . Conservative, no change."

The General added: "H'm!" and the music began again.

Aunt Em, looking at the portable, said: "Coax it, Dinny. That burrin'!"

"It always has that, Auntie."

"Blore does something to ours with a penny. Where is Hornsey—Isle of Wight?"

"Middlesex, darling."

"Oh! yes! I was thinkin' of Southsea. There he goes again."

"These are some more election results . . . Conservative, gain from

456

Labour . . . Conservative, no change . . . Conservative, gain from Labour."

The General added: "Ha!" and the music began again.

"What nice large majorities!" said Lady Mont: "Gratifyin'!"

Clare got off the sofa and squatted on a footstool against her mother's knees. The General had dropped *The Times*. The 'voice' spoke again:

". . . Liberal National, gain from Labour . . . Conservative, no change . . . Conservative, gain from Labour."

Again and again the music spurted up and died away; and the voice spoke.

Clare's face grew more and more vivid, and above her Lady Charwell's pale and gentle face wore one long smile. From time to time the General said: "By George!" and "This is something like!"

And Dinny thought: 'Poor Labour!'

On and on and on the voice breathed o'er Eden.

"Crushin'," said Lady Mont: "I'm gettin' sleepy."

"Go to bed, Auntie. I'll put a slip under your door when I come up."

Lady Charwell, too, got up. When they were gone, Clare went back to the sofa and seemed to fall asleep. The General sat on, hypnotised by the chant of victory. Dinny, with knees crossed and eyes closed, was thinking: 'Will it really make a difference; and, if it does, shall I care? Where is *he*? Listening as we are? Where? Where?' Not so often now, but quite often enough, that sense of groping for Wilfrid returned to her. In all these sixteen months since he left her she had found no means of hearing of him. For all she knew he might be dead. Once—only once—she had broken her resolve never to speak of her disaster, and had asked Michael. Compson Grice, his publisher, had, it seemed, received a letter from him written in Bangkok, which said he was well and had begun to write. That was nine months ago. The veil, so little lifted, had dropped again. Heartache —well, she was used to it.

"Dad, it's two o'clock. It'll be like this all the time now. Clare's asleep."

"I'm not," said Clare.

"You ought to be. I'll let Foch out for his run, and we'll all go up."

The General rose.

"Enough's as good as a feast. I suppose we'd better."

Dinny opened the French window and watched the dog Foch trotting out in semblance of enthusiasm. It was cold, with a ground mist, and she shut the window. If she didn't he would neglect his ritual and with more than the semblance of enthusiasm trot in again. Having kissed her father and Clare, she turned out the lights and waited in the hall. The wood fire had almost died. She stood with her foot on the stone hearth, thinking. Clare had spoken of trying to get a secretaryship to some new Member of Parliament. Judging by the returns that were coming in, there would be plenty of them. Why not to their own new Member? He had dined with them, and she had sat next him. A nice man, well read, not bigoted. He even sympathised with Labour, but did not think they knew their way about as yet. In fact he was rather notably what the drunken youth in the play called: 'a Tory Socialist.' He had opened out to her and been very frank and pleasant. An attractive man, with his crisp dark hair, brown complexion, little dark moustache and rather high soft voice; a good sort, energetic and upright-looking. But probably he already had a secretary. However, if Clare was in earnest, one could ask. She crossed the hall to the garden door. There was a seat in the porch outside, and under it Foch would be crouched, waiting to be let in. Sure enough, he emerged, fluttering his tail, and padded towards the dogs' communal water-bowl. How cold and silent! Nothing on the road; even the owls quiet; the garden and the fields frozen, moonlit, still, away up to that long line of covert! England silvered and indifferent to her fate, disbelieving in the Voice o'er Eden; old and permanent and beautiful, even though the pound had gone off gold. Dinny gazed at the unfeverish night. Men and their policies—how little they mattered, how soon they passed, a dissolving dew on the crystal immensity of God's toy! How queer—the passionate intensity of one's heart, and the incalculable cold callousness of Time and Space! To join, to reconcile? . . .

She shivered and shut the door.

At breakfast the next morning she said to Clare:

"Shall we strike while the iron's hot, and go and see Mr. Dornford?"

"Why?"

"In case he wants a secretary, now he's in."

"Oh! Is he in?"

"Very much so." Dinny read the figures. The usual rather formidable Liberal opposition had been replaced by a mere five thousand Labour votes.

"The word 'national' is winning this election," said Clare. "Where I went canvassing in the town they were all Liberals. I just used the word 'national,' and they fell."

Hearing that the new Member would be at his headquarters all the morning, the sisters started about eleven o'clock. There was so much coming and going round the doors that they did not like to enter.

"I do hate asking for things," said Clare.

Dinny, who hated it quite as much, answered:

"Wait here and I'll just go in and congratulate him. I might have a chance of putting in a word. He's seen you, of course."

"Oh! yes, he's seen me all right."

Eustace Dornford, K.C., new Member elect, was sitting in a room that seemed all open doors, running his eye over the lists his agent was putting on the table before him. From one of those doors Dinny could see his riding boots under the table, and his bowler hat, gloves and riding whip upon it. Now that she was nearly in the presence it seemed impossible to intrude at such a moment, and she was just slipping away when he looked up.

"Excuse me a moment, Minns. Miss Cherrell!"

She stopped and turned. He was smiling and looking pleased.

"Anything I can do for you?"

She put out her hand.

"I'm awfully glad you've won. My sister and I just wanted to congratulate you."

He squeezed her hand, and Dinny thought: 'Oh! dear! this is the last moment to ask him,' but she said:

"It's perfectly splendid, there's never been such a majority here."

"And never will be again. That's my luck. Where's your sister?"

"In the car."

"I'd like to thank her for canvassing."

"Oh!" said Dinny, "she enjoyed it;" and suddenly feeling that it was now or never, added: "She's at a loose end, you know, badly wants something to do. Mr. Dornford, you don't think—this is too bad—but I suppose she wouldn't be of any use to you as a secretary, would she? There, it's out. She does know the county pretty well; she can type, and speak French, and German a little, if that's any use." It had come with a rush, and she stood looking at him ruefully. But his eager expression had not changed.

"Let's go and see her," he said.

Dinny thought: 'Gracious! I hope he hasn't fallen in love with her!' and she glanced at him sidelong. Still smiling, his face looked shrewd now. Clare was standing beside the car. 'I wish,' thought Dinny, 'I had her coolness.' Then she stood still and watched. All this triumphal business, these people coming and going, those two talking so readily and quickly; the clear and sparkling morning! He came back to her.

"Thank you most awfully, Miss Cherrell. It'll do admirably. I did want some one, and your sister is very modest."

"I thought you'd never forgive me for asking at such a moment."

"Always delighted for you to ask anything at any moment. I must go back now, but I'll hope to see you again very soon."

Gazing after him as he re-entered the building, she thought: 'He has very nicely cut riding breeches!' And she got into the car.

"Dinny," said Clare, with a laugh, "he's in love with you."

"What!"

"I asked for two hundred, and he made it two hundred and fifty at once. How did you do it in one evening?"

"I didn't. It's you he's in love with, I'm afraid."

"No, no, my dear. I have eyes, and I know it's you; just as you knew that Tony Croom was in love with me."

"I could see that."

"And I could see this."

Dinny said quietly: "That's absurd. When do you begin?"

"He's going back to Town to-day. He lives in the Temple—Harcourt Buildings. I shall go up this afternoon, and start in the day after to-morrow."

"Where shall you live?"

"I think I shall take an unfurnished room or a small studio, and decorate and furnish it gradually myself. It'll be fun."

"Aunt Em is going back this afternoon. She would put you up till you find it."

"Well," said Clare, pondering, "perhaps."

Just before they reached home Dinny said:

"What about Ceylon, Clare? Have you thought any more?"

"What's the good of thinking? I suppose he'll do something, but I don't know what, and I don't care."

"Haven't you had a letter?"

"No."

"Well, darling, be careful."

Clare shrugged: "Oh! I'll be careful."

"Could he get leave if he wanted?"

"I expect so."

"You'll keep in touch with me, won't you?"

Clare leaned sideways from the wheel and gave her cheek a kiss.

CHAPTER 6

THREE DAYS after their meeting at The Coffee House, young Croom received a letter from Sir Lawrence Mont, saying that his cousin Muskham was not expecting the Arab mares till the spring. In the meantime he would make a note of Mr. Croom and a point of seeing him soon. Did Mr. Croom know any vernacular Arabic?

'No,' thought young Croom, 'but I know Stapylton.'

Stapylton, of the Lancers, who had been his senior at Wellington, was home from India on leave. A noted polo player, he would be sure to know the horse jargon of the East; but, having broken his thighbone schooling a steeple-chaser, he would keep; the business of finding an immediate 'job of work' would not. Young Croom continued his researches. Everyone said: 'Wait till the election's over!'

On the morning after the election, therefore, he issued from Ryder Street with the greater expectation, and, on the evening after, returned to The Coffee House with the less, thinking: 'I might just as well have gone to Newmarket and seen the Cambridgeshire.'

The porter handed him a note, and his heart began to thump. Seeking a corner, he read:

"DEAR TONY,

"I have got the job of secretary to our new Member, Eustace Dornford, who's a K.C., in the Temple. So I've come up to Town. Till I find a tent of my own, I shall be at my Aunt Lady Mont's in Mount Street. I hope you've been as lucky. I promised to let you know when I came up; but, I adjure you to sense and not sensibility, and to due regard for pride and prejudice.

Your shipmate and well-wisher,
CLARE CORVEN."

'The darling!' he thought: 'What luck!' He read the note again, placed it beneath the cigarette case in his lefthand waistcoat pocket, and went into the smoking room. There, on a sheet of paper stamped with the Club's immemorial design, he poured out an ingenuous heart:

"DARLING CLARE,

"Your note has perked me up no end. That you will be in Town is mag-

nificent news. Your uncle has been very kind to me and I shall simply
have to call and thank him. So do look out for me about six o'clock to-
morrow. I spend all my time hunting a job, and am beginning to realise
what it means to poor devils to be turned down day after day. When my
pouch is empty, and that's not far away, it'll be even worse for me. No
dole for this child, unfortunately. I hope the pundit you're going to take
in hand is a decent sort. I always think of M.P.s as a bit on the wooden
side. And somehow I can't see you among Bills and petitions and letters
about public-house licences and so forth. However, I think you're splendid
to want to be independent. What a thumping majority! If they can't do
things with that behind them, they can't do things at all. It's quite impossible for me not to be in love with you, you know, and to long to be
with you all day and all night, too. But I'm going to be as good as I can,
because the very last thing is to cause you uneasiness of any sort. I think
of you all the time, even when I'm searching the marble countenance of
some fish-faced blighter to see if my piteous tale is weakening his judgment. The fact is I love you terribly. To-morrow, Thursday, about six!

"Good-night, dear and lovely one,

YOUR TONY."

Having looked up Sir Lawrence's number in Mount Street, he addressed the note, licked the envelope with passion, and went out to post
it himself. Then, suddenly, he did not feel inclined to return to The Coffee House. The place had a grudge against his state of mind. Clubs were
so damned male, and their whole attitude to women so after-dinnerish—
half contempt, half lechery! Funk-holes they were, anyway, full of comfort, secured against women, immune from writs; and men all had the
same armchair look once they got inside. The Coffee House, too, about
the oldest of all clubs, was stuffed with regular buffers, men you couldn't
imagine outside a club. 'No!' he thought; 'I'll have a chop somewhere, and
go to that thing at Drury Lane.'

He got a seat rather far back in the upper boxes, but his sight being
very good, he saw quite well. He was soon absorbed. He had been out
of England long enough to have some sentiment about her. This pictorial
pageant of her history for the last thirty years moved him more than he
would have confessed to any one sitting beside him. Boer War, death of
the Queen, sinking of the "Titanic," Great War, Armistice, health to 1931
—if any one asked him afterwards, he would probably say: 'Marvellous!
but gave me the "pip" rather!' While sitting there it seemed more than the
'pip'; the heartache of a lover, who wants happiness with his mistress and
cannot reach it; the feeling of one who tries to stand upright and firm
and is forever being swayed this way and that. The last words rang in
his ears as he went out: 'Greatness and dignity and peace.' Moving and
damned ironical! He took a cigarette from his case and lighted it. The
night was dry and he walked, threading his way through the streams of
traffic, with the melancholy howling of street-singers in his ears. Skysigns

and garbage! People rolling home in their cars, and homeless night-birds! 'Greatness, and dignity, and peace!'

'I must absolutely have a drink,' he thought. The Club seemed possible again now, even inviting, and he made towards it. ' "Farewell, Piccadilly! Good-bye, Leicester Square!" ' Marvellous that scene, where those Tommies marched up in a spiral through the dark mist, whistling; while in the lighted front of the stage three painted girls rattled out: ' "We don't want to lose you, but we think you ought to go." ' And from the boxes on the stage at the sides people looked down and clapped! The whole thing there! The gaiety on those girls' painted faces getting more and more put-on and heartbreaking! He must go again with Clare! Would it move her? And, suddenly, he perceived that he didn't know. What did one know about any one, even the woman one loved? His cigarette was scorching his lip and he spat out the butt. That scene with the honeymooning couple leaning over the side of the "Titanic," everything before them, and nothing before them but the cold deep sea. Did that couple know anything except that they desired each other? Life was damned queer, when you thought about it! He turned up The Coffee House steps, feeling as if he had lived long since he went down them. . . .

It was just six o'clock when he rang the bell at Mount Street on the following day.

A butler, with slightly raised eyebrows, opened the door.

"Is Sir Lawrence Mont at home?"

"No, Sir. Lady Mont is in, Sir."

"I'm afraid I don't know Lady Mont. I wonder if I could see Lady Corven for a moment?"

One of the butler's eyebrows rose still higher. 'Ah!' he seemed to be thinking.

"If you'll give me your name, Sir."

Young Croom produced a card.

" 'Mr. James Bernard Croom,' " chanted the butler.

"Mr. Tony Croom, tell her, please."

"Quite! If you'll wait here a moment. Oh! here is Lady Corven."

A voice from the stairs said:

"Tony? What punctuality! Come up and meet my aunt."

She was leaning over the stair-rail, and the butler had disappeared.

"Put your hat down. How can you go about without a coat? I shiver all the time."

Young Croom came close below her.

"Darling!" he murmured.

She placed one finger to her lips, then stretched it down to him, so that he could reach it with his own.

"Come along!" She had opened a door when he reached the top, and was saying: "This is a shipmate, Aunt Em. He's come to see Uncle Lawrence. Mr. Croom, my aunt, Lady Mont."

Young Croom was aware of a presence slightly swaying towards him. A voice said: "Ah! Ships! Of course! How d'you do?"

Young Croom, aware that he had been 'placed,' saw Clare regarding him with a slightly mocking smile. If only they could be alone five minutes, he would kiss that smile off her face! He would——!

"Tell me about Ceylon, Mr. Craven."

"Croom, Auntie. Tony Croom. Better call him Tony. It isn't his name, but everybody does."

"Tony! Always heroes. I don't know why."

"This Tony is quite ordinary."

"Ceylon. Did you know her there, Mr.—Tony?"

"No. We only met on the ship."

"Ah! Lawrence and I used to sleep on deck. That was in the 'naughty nineties.' The river here used to be full of punts, I remember."

"It still is, Aunt Em."

Young Croom had a sudden vision of Clare and himself in a punt up a quiet backwater. He roused himself and said:

"I went to 'Cavalcade' last night. Great!"

"Ah!" said Lady Mont: "That reminds me." She left the room.

Young Croom sprang up.

"Tony! Behave!"

"But surely that's what she went for!"

"Aunt Em is extraordinarily kind, and I'm not going to abuse her kindness."

"But, Clare, you don't know what——"

"Yes I do. Sit down again."

Young Croom obeyed.

"Now listen, Tony! I've had enough physiology to last me a long time. If you and I are going to be pals, it's got to be platonic."

"Oh, God!" said young Croom.

"But it's got to; or else—we simply aren't going to see each other."

Young Croom sat very still with his eyes fixed on hers, and there passed through her the thought: 'It's going to torture him. He looks too nice for that. I don't believe we ought to see each other.'

"Look!" she said, gently, "you want to help me, don't you? There's lots of time, you know. Some day—perhaps."

Young Croom grasped the arms of his chair. His eyes had a look of pain.

"Very well," he said, slowly, "anything so long as I can see you. I'll wait till it means something more than physiology to you."

Clare sat examining the glacé toe of her slowly wiggling shoe; suddenly she looked straight into his brooding eyes.

"If," she said, "I had not been married, you would wait cheerfully and it wouldn't hurt you. Think of me like that."

"Unfortunately I can't. Who could?"

"I see. I am fruit, not blossom—tainted by physiology."

"Don't! Oh! Clare, I will be anything you want to you. And if I'm not always as cheery as a bird, forgive me."

She looked at him through her eyelashes and said: "Good!"

Then came silence, during which she was conscious that he was fixing her in his mind from her shingled dark head to her glacé kid toe. She had not lived with Jerry Corven without having been made conscious of every detail of her body. She could not help its grace or its provocation. She did not want to torture him, but she could not find it unpleasant that she did. Queer how one could be sorry and yet pleased, and withal, sceptical and a little bitter. Give yourself, and after a few months how much would he want you! She said abruptly:

"Well, I've found rooms—a quaint little hole—used to be an antique shop, in a disused mews."

He said eagerly: "Sounds jolly. When are you going in?"

"Next week."

"Can I help?"

"If you can distemper walls."

"Rather! I did all my bungalow in Ceylon, two or three times over."

"We should have to work in the evenings, because of my job."

"What about your boss? Is he decent?"

"Very, and in love with my sister. At least, I think so."

"Oh!" said young Croom, dubiously.

Clare smiled. He was so obviously thinking: 'Could a man be that when he sees *you* every day?'

"When can I come first?"

"To-morrow evening, if you like. It's 2, Melton Mews, off Malmesbury Square. I'll get the stuff in the morning and we'll begin upstairs. Say six-thirty."

"Splendid!"

"Only, Tony—no importunities: 'Life is real, life is earnest.'"

Grinning ruefully, he put his hand on his heart.

"And you must go now. I'll take you down and see if my uncle's come in."

Young Croom stood up.

"What is happening about Ceylon?" he said, abruptly: "Are you being worried?"

Clare shrugged. "Nothing is happening so far."

"That can't possibly last. Have you thought things out?"

"Thinking won't help me. It's quite likely he'll do nothing."

"I can't bear your being—" he stopped.

"Come along," said Clare, and led the way downstairs.

"I don't think I'll try to see your uncle," said young Croom. "To-morrow at half-past six, then." He raised her hand to his lips, and marched to the door. There he turned. She was standing with her head a little on one side, smiling. He went out, distracted.

A young man, suddenly awakened amid the doves of Cytherea, conscious for the first time of the mysterious magnetism which radiates from what the vulgar call 'a grass widow,' and withheld from her by scruples or convention, is to be pitied. He has not sought his fate. It comes on him by stealth, bereaving him ruthlessly of all other interest in life. It is an obsession replacing normal tastes with a rapturous aching. Maxims such as 'Thou shalt not commit adultery,' 'Thou shalt not covet thy neighbour's wife,' 'Blessed are the pure in heart,' become singularly academic. Young Croom had been brought up to the tinkling of the school bell: 'Play the game!' He now perceived its strange inadequacy. What *was* the game? Here was she, young and lovely, fleeing from a partner seventeen years older than herself, because he was a brute; she hadn't said so, but of course he must be! Here was himself, desperately in love with her, and liked by her—not in the same way, but still as much as could be expected! And nothing to come of it but tea together! There was a kind of sacrilege in such waste.

Thus preoccupied he passed a man of middle height and alert bearing, whose rather cat-like eyes and thin lips were set into a brown face with the claws of many little wrinkles, and who turned to look after him with a slight contraction of the mouth which might have been a smile.

CHAPTER 7

AFTER YOUNG CROOM had gone Clare stood for a moment in the hall recollecting the last time she had gone out of that front door, in a fawn-coloured suit and a little brown hat, between rows of people saying: "Good luck!" and "Good-bye, darling!" and "Give my love to Paris!" Eighteen months ago, and so much in between! Her lips curled, and she went into her uncle's study.

"Oh! Uncle Lawrence, you *are* in! Tony Croom's been here to see you."

"That rather pleasant young man without occupation?"

"Yes. He wanted to thank you."

"For nothing, I'm afraid." And Sir Lawrence's quick dark eyes, like a snipe's or woodcock's roved sceptically over his pretty niece. She was not, like Dinny, a special favourite, but she was undoubtedly attractive. It was early days to have messed up her marriage; Em had told him and said that it wasn't to be mentioned. Well, Jerry Corven! People had always shrugged and hinted. Too bad. But no real business of his.

A subdued voice from the door said:

"Sir Gerald Corven has called, Sir Lawrence."

Involuntarily Sir Lawrence put his finger to his lips. The butler subdued his voice still further.

"I put him in the little room and said I would see if Lady Corven was in."

Sir Lawrence noted Clare's hands hard pressed down on the back of the chair behind which she was standing.

"*Are* you in, Clare?"

She did not answer, but her face was hard and pale as stone.

"A minute, Blore. Come back when I ring."

The butler withdrew.

"Now, my dear?"

"He must have taken the next boat. Uncle, I don't want to see him."

"If we only say you're out, he'll probably come again."

Clare threw back her head: "Well, I'll see him."

Sir Lawrence felt a little thrill.

"If you'd tell me what to say, I'd see him for you."

"Thank you, Uncle, but I don't see why you should do my dirty work."

Sir Lawrence thought: 'Thank God!'

467

"I'll be handy in case you want me. Good luck, my dear!" And he went out.

Clare moved over to the fire; she wanted the bell within reach. She had the feeling, well known to her, of settling herself in the saddle for a formidable jump. 'He shan't touch me, anyway,' she thought. She heard Blore's voice say:

"Sir Gerald Corven, my Lady." Quaint! Announcing a husband to his wife! But staff knew everything!

Without looking she saw perfectly well where he was standing. A surge of shamed anger stained her cheeks. He had fascinated her; he had used her as every kind of plaything. He had——!

His voice, cuttingly controlled, said:

"Well, my dear, you were very sudden." Neat and trim, as ever, and like a cat, with that thin-lipped smile and those daring despoiling eyes!

"What do you want?"

"Only yourself!"

"You can't have me."

"Absurd!"

He made the quickest kind of movement and seized her in his arms. Clare bent her head back and put her finger on the bell.

"Move back, or I ring!" and she put her other hand between his face and hers. "Stand over there and I'll talk to you, otherwise you must go."

"Very well! But it's ridiculous."

"Oh! Do you think I should have gone if I hadn't been in earnest?"

"I thought you were just riled, and I don't wonder. I'm sorry."

"It's no good discussing what happened. I know you, and I'm not coming back to you."

"My dear, you have my apology, and I give you my word against anything of the sort again."

"How good of you!"

"It was only an experiment. Some women adore it, if not at the time."

"You are a beast."

"And beauty married me. Come, Clare, don't be silly and make us a laughing stock! You can fix your own conditions."

"And trust you to keep them! Besides, that's not my idea of a life. I'm only twenty-four."

The smile left his lips.

"I see. I noticed a young man come out of this house. Name and estate?"

"Tony Croom. Well?"

He walked over to the window, and after a moment's contemplation of the street, turned and said:

"You have the misfortune to be my wife."

"So I was thinking."

"Quite seriously, Clare, come back to me."

"Quite seriously, no."

"I have an official position, and I can't play about with it. Look at me!"

He came closer. "I may be all you think me, but I'm neither a humbug, nor old-fashioned. I don't trade on my position, or on the sanctity of marriage, or any of that stuff. But they still pay attention to that sort of thing in the Service, and I can't afford to let you divorce me."

"I didn't expect it."

"What then?"

"I know nothing except that I'm not coming back."

"Just because of——?"

"And a great deal else." The cat-like smile had come back and prevented her from reading what he was thinking.

"Do you want me to divorce you?"

Clare shrugged. "You have no reason."

"So you would naturally say."

"And mean."

"Now look here, Clare, this is all absurd, and quite unworthy of any one with your sense and knowledge of things. You can't be a perpetual grass widow. You didn't dislike the life out there."

"There are some things that can't be done to me and you have done them."

"I've said that they shan't be done again."

"And I've said that I can't trust you."

"This is going round the mulberry bush. Are you going to live on your people?"

"No. I've got a job."

"Oh! What?"

"Secretary to our new Member."

"You'll be sick of that in no time."

"I don't think so."

He stood staring at her without his smile. For a moment she could read his thoughts, for his face had the expression which preludes sex. Suddenly he said: "I won't stand for another man having you."

It was a comfort to have seen for once the bottom of his mind. She did not answer.

"Did you hear me?"

"Yes."

"I meant it."

"I could see that."

"You're a stony little devil."

"I wish I had been."

He took a turn up and down the room, and came to a stand dead in front of her.

"Look at me! I'm not going back without you. I'm staying at the Bristol. Be sensible, there's a darling, and come to me there. We'll start again. I'll be ever so nice to you."

Her control gave way, and she cried out: "Oh, for God's sake, understand! You killed all the feeling I had for you."

His eyes dilated and then narrowed, his lips became a line. He looked like a horse-breaker.

"And understand *me*," he said, very low, "you either come back to me or I divorce you. I won't leave you here, to kick your heels."

"I'm sure you'll have the approval of every judicious husband."

The smile reappeared on his lips.

"For that," he said, "I'm going to have a kiss." And before she could stop him he had fastened his lips on hers. She tore herself away and pressed the bell. He went quickly to the door.

"*Au revoir!*" he said, and went out.

Clare wiped her lips. She felt bewildered and exhausted, and quite ignorant whether to him or to her the day had gone.

She stood leaning her forehead on her hands over the fire, and became aware that Sir Lawrence had come back and was considerately saying nothing.

"Awfully sorry, Uncle; I shall be in my digs next week."

"Have a cigarette, my dear."

Clare took the cigarette, and inhaled its comfort. Her uncle had seated himself and she was conscious of the quizzical expression of his eyebrows.

"Conference had its usual success?"

Clare nodded.

"The elusive formula. The fact is, human beings are never satisfied with what they don't want, however cleverly it's put. Is it to be continued in our next?"

"Not so far as I'm concerned."

"Pity there are always two parties to a conference."

"Uncle Lawrence," she said suddenly, "what is the law of divorce now?"

The baronet uncrossed his long thin legs.

"I've never had any particular truck with it. I believe it's less old-fashioned than it was, but see Whitaker." He reached for the red-backed volume. "Page 258—here you are, my dear."

Clare read in silence while he gazed at her ruefully. She looked up and said:

"Then, if I want him to divorce me, I've got to commit adultery."

"That is, I believe, the elegant way they put it. In the best circles, however, the man does the dirty work."

"Yes, but he won't. He wants me back. Besides he's got his position to consider."

"There is that, of course," said Sir Lawrence, thoughtfully; "a career in this country is a tender plant."

Clare closed the "Whitaker."

"If it weren't for my people," she said, "I'd give him cause to-morrow and have done with it."

"You don't think a better way would be to give partnership another trial?"

Clare shook her head.

"I simply couldn't."

"That's that, then," said Sir Lawrence, "and it's an awkward that. What does Dinny say?"

"I haven't discussed it with her. She doesn't know he's here."

"At present, then, you've no one to advise you?"

"No. Dinny knows why I left, that's all."

"I should doubt if Jerry Corven is a very patient man."

Clare laughed.

"We're neither of us longsuffering."

"Do you know where he is staying?"

"At the Bristol."

"It might," said Sir Lawrence slowly, "be worth while to keep an eye on him."

Clare shivered. "It's rather degrading; besides, Uncle, I don't want to hurt his career. He's very able, you know."

Sir Lawrence shrugged. "To me," he said, "and to all your kin, his career is nothing to your good name. How long has he got over here?"

"Not long, I should think."

"Would you like me to see him, and try to arrange that you go your own ways?"

Clare was silent, and Sir Lawrence, watching her, thought: 'Attractive, but a lot of naughty temper. Any amount of spirit, and no patience at all.' Then she said:

"It was all my fault, nobody wanted me to marry him. I hate to bother you. Besides, he wouldn't consent."

"You never know," murmured Sir Lawrence. "If I get a natural chance, shall I?"

"It would be lovely of you, only——"

"All right, then. In the meantime young men without jobs—are they wise?"

Clare laughed. "Oh, I've 'larned' him. Well, thank you frightfully, Uncle Lawrence. You're a great comfort. I was an awful fool; but Jerry has a sort of power, you know; and I've always liked taking risks. I don't see how I can be my mother's daughter; she hates them; and Dinny only takes them on principle." She sighed. "I won't bore you any more, now." And, blowing a kiss, she went out.

Sir Lawrence stayed in his armchair thinking: 'Putting my oar in! A nasty mess, and going to be nastier! Still at her age something's got to be done. I must talk to Dinny.'

CHAPTER 8

FROM CONDAFORD the hot airs of election time had cleared away, and the succeeding atmosphere was crystallised in the General's saying:

"Well, those fellows got their deserts."

"Doesn't it make you tremble, Dad, to think what *these* fellows' deserts will be if they don't succeed in putting it over now?"

The General smiled.

" 'Sufficient unto the day,' Dinny. Has Clare settled down?"

"She's in her diggings. Her work so far seems to have been writing letters of thanks to people who did the dirty work at the cross-roads."

"Cars? Does she like Dornford?"

"She says he's quite amazingly considerate."

"His father was a good soldier. I was in his brigade in the Boer War for a bit." He looked at his daughter keenly, and added: "Any news of Corven?"

"Yes, he's over here."

"Oh! I wish I wasn't kept so in the dark. Parents have to stand on the mat nowadays, and trust to what they can hear through the keyhole."

Dinny drew his arm within hers.

"One has to be so careful of their feelings. Sensitive plants, aren't you, Dad?"

"Well, it seems to your mother and me an extraordinarily bad lookout. We wish to goodness the thing could be patched up."

"Not at the expense of Clare's happiness, surely?"

"No," said the General, dubiously, "no; but there you are at once in all these matrimonial things. What is and will be her happiness? She doesn't know, and you don't, and I don't. As a rule in trying to get out of a hole you promptly step into another."

"Therefore don't try? Stay in your hole? That's rather what Labour wanted to do, isn't it?"

"I ought to see him," said the General, passing over the simile, "but I can't go blundering in the dark. What do you advise, Dinny?"

"Let the sleeping dog lie until it gets up to bite you."

"You think it will?"

"I do."

"Bad!" muttered the General. "Clare's too young."

That was Dinny's own perpetual thought. What at the first blush she had said to her sister: "You must get free," remained her conviction. But how was she to get free? Knowledge of divorce had been no part of Dinny's education. She knew that the process was by no means uncommon, and she had as little feeling against it as most of her generation. To her father and mother it would probably seem lamentable, doubly so if Clare were divorced instead of divorcing—that would be a stigma on her to be avoided at almost all cost. Since her soul-racking experience with Wilfrid, Dinny had been very little in London. Every street, and above all, the park, seemed to remind her of him and the desolation he had left in her. It was now, however, obvious to her that Clare could not be left unsupported in whatever crisis was befalling.

"I think I ought to go up, Dad, and find out what's happening."

"I wish to God you would. If it's at all possible to patch things up, they ought to be."

Dinny shook her head.

"I don't believe it is, and I don't believe you'd wish it, if Clare had told you what she told me."

The General stared. "There it is, you see. In the dark."

"Yes, dear, but till she tells you herself I can't say more."

"Then the sooner you go up the better."

Free from the scent of horse, Melton Mews was somewhat strikingly impregnated with the odour of petrol. This bricked alley had become, indeed, the haunt of cars. To right and to left of her, entering late that afternoon, the doors of garages gaped or confronted her with more or less new paint. A cat or two stole by, and the hinder parts of an overalled chauffeur bending over a carburettor could be seen in one opening; otherwise life was at a discount, and the word 'mews' no longer justified by manure.

No. 2 had the peacock-green door of its former proprietress whom, with so many other luxury traders, the slump had squeezed out of business. Dinny pulled a chased bell handle, and a faint tinkle sounded, as from some errant sheep. There was a pause, then a spot of light showed for a moment on a level with her face, was obscured, and the door was opened. Clare, in a jade-green overall, said:

"Come in, my dear. This is the lioness in her den, 'the Douglas in her hall'!"

Dinny entered a small, almost empty, room hung with the green Japanese silk of the antique dealer and carpeted with matting. A narrow, spiral staircase wormed into it at the far corner, and subdued light radiated from a single green-paper-shaded bulb hanging in the centre. A brass electric heater diffused no heat.

"Nothing doing here so far," said Clare. "Come upstairs."

Dinny made the tortuous ascent, and stepped into a rather smaller sitting-room. It had two curtained windows looking over the mews, a couch with cushions, a little old bureau, three chairs, six Japanese prints which Clare had evidently just been hanging, an old Persian rug over the matted floor, an almost empty bookcase and some photographs of the family standing on it. The walls were distempered a pale grey, and a gas fire was burning.

"Fleur gave me the prints and the rug, and Aunt Em stumped up the bureau. I took the other things over."

"Where do you sleep?"

"On that couch—quite comfy. I've got a little bath-dressing-room next door, with a geyser, and a what-d'ye-call-it, and a cupboard for clothes."

"Mother told me to ask what you wanted."

"I could do with our old Primus stove, some blankets and a few knives and forks and spoons, and a small tea set, if there's one to spare, and any spare books."

"Right!" said Dinny. "Now, darling, how are you?"

"Bodily fine, mentally rather worried. I told you he was over."

"Does he know of this place?"

"Not so far. You and Fleur and Aunt Em—oh! and Tony Croom—are the only people who know of it. My official address is Mount Street. But he's bound to find out if he wants to."

"You saw him?"

"Yes, and told him I wasn't coming back; and I'm not, Dinny, that's flat to save breath. Have some tea? I can make it in a brown pot."

"No, thank you, I had it on the train." She was sitting on one of the taken-over chairs, in a bottle-green suit that went beautifully with her beech-leaf coloured hair.

"How jolly you look, sitting there!" said Clare, curling up on the sofa. "Gasper?"

Dinny was thinking the same about her sister. Graceful creature, one of those people who couldn't look ungraceful; with her dark short hair, and dark, alive eyes, and ivory pale face, and not too brightened lips holding the cigarette, she looked—well, 'desirable.' And, under all the circumstances, the word appeared to Dinny an awkward one. Clare had always been vivid and attractive, but without question marriage had subtly rounded, deepened and in some sort bedevilled that attraction. She said, suddenly:

"Tony Croom, you said?"

"He helped me distemper these walls; in fact, he practically did them, while I did the bathroom—these are better."

Dinny's eyes took in the walls with apparent interest.

"Quite neat. Mother and Father are nervous, darling."

"They would be."

"Naturally, don't you think?"

Clare's brows drew down. Dinny suddenly remembered how strenuously they had once debated the question of whether eyebrows should be plucked. Thank heaven! Clare never had yet!

"I can't help it, Dinny. I don't know what Jerry's going to do."

"I suppose he can't stay long, without giving up his job?"

"Probably not. But I'm not going to bother. What will be will."

"How quickly could a divorce be got? I mean against him?"

Clare shook her head, and a dark curl fell over her forehead, reminding Dinny of her as a child.

"To have him watched would be pretty revolting. And I'm not going into Court to describe being brutalised. It's only my word against his. Men are safe enough."

Dinny got up and sat down beside her on the couch.

"I could kill him!" she said.

Clare laughed.

"He wasn't so bad in many ways. Only I simply won't go back. If you've once been skinned, you can't."

Dinny sat, silent, with closed eyes.

"Tell me," she said, at last, "how you stand with Tony Croom."

"He's on probation. So long as he behaves I like to see him."

"If," said Dinny, slowly, "he were known to come here, it would be all that would be wanted, wouldn't it?"

Clare laughed again.

"Quite enough for men of the world, I should think. I believe juries can never withstand being called that. But you see, Dinny, if I begin to look at things from a jury's point of view, I might as well be dead. And as a matter of fact, I feel very much alive. So I'm going straight ahead. Tony knows I've had enough physiology to last me a long time."

"Is he in love with you?"

Their eyes, brown and blue, met.

"Yes."

"Are you in love with him?"

"I like him—quite a lot. Beyond that I've no feeling at present."

"Don't you think that while Jerry is here——?"

"No. I think I'm safer while he's here than when he goes. If I don't go back with him he'll probably have me watched. That's one thing about him—he does what he says he'll do."

"I wonder if that's an advantage. Come out and have some dinner."

Clare stretched herself.

"Can't, darling. I'm dining with Tony in a little grubby restaurant suited to our joint means. This living on next to nothing is rather fun."

Dinny got up and began to straighten the Japanese prints. Clare's recklessness was nothing new. To come the elder sister! To be a wet blanket! Impossible! She said:

"These are good, my dear. Fleur has very jolly things."

"D'you mind if I change?" said Clare, and vanished into the bathroom.

Left alone with her sister's problem, Dinny had the feeling of helplessness which comes to all but such as constitutionally 'know better.' She went dejectedly to the window and drew aside the curtain. All was darkish and dingy. A car had drawn out of a neighbouring garage and stood waiting for its driver.

'Imagine trying to sell antiques here!' she thought. She saw a man come round the corner close by and stop, looking at the numbers. He moved along the opposite side, then came back and stood still just in front of No. 2. She noted the assurance and strength in that trim overcoated figure.

'Good heavens!' she thought: 'Jerry!' She dropped the curtain and crossed quickly to the bathroom door. As she opened it she heard the desolate tinkling of the sheep-bell installed by the antique dealer.

Clare was standing in her underthings under the single bulb, examining her lips with a hand-glass. Dinny filled the remains of the four feet by two of standing room.

"Clare," she said, "it's *him!*"

Clare turned. The gleam of her pale arms, the shimmer of her silk garments, the startled light in her dark eyes, made her even to her sister something of a vision.

"Jerry?"

Dinny nodded.

"Well, I won't see him." She looked at the watch on her wrist. "And I'm due at seven. Damn!"

Dinny, who had not the faintest desire that she should keep her rash appointment, said, to her own surprise:

"Shall I go? He must have seen the light."

"Could you take him away with you, Dinny?"

"I can try."

"Then do, darling. It'd be ever so sweet of you. I wonder how he's found out. Hell! It's going to be a persecution."

Dinny stepped back into the sitting room, turned out the light there and went down the twisting stair. The sheep-bell tinkled again above her as she went. Crossing that little empty room to the door, she thought: 'It opens inwards, I must pull it to behind me.' Her heart beat fast, she took a deep breath, opened the door swiftly, stepped out and pulled it to with a slam. She was chest to chest with her brother-in-law, and she started back with an admirably impromptu: "Who is it?"

He raised his hat, and they stood looking at each other.

"Dinny! Is Clare in?"

"Yes; but she can't see anyone."

"You mean she *won't* see *me?*"

"If you like to put it that way."

He stood looking intently at her with his daring eyes.

"Another day will do. Which way are you going?"

"To Mount Street."

"I'll come with you, if I may."

"Do."

She moved along at his side, thinking: 'Be careful!' For in his company she did not feel towards him quite as in his absence. As everybody said, Jerry Corven had charm!

"Clare's been giving me bad marks, I suppose?"

"We won't discuss it, please; whatever she feels, I do too."

"Naturally. Your loyalty's proverbial. But consider, Dinny, how provocative she is." His eyes smiled round at her. That vision—of neck, and curve, and shimmer, dark hair and eyes! Sex appeal—horrible expression! "You've no idea how tantalising. Besides I was always an experimentalist."

Dinny stood still suddenly: "This is my sister, you know."

"You're sure, I suppose? It seems queer when one looks at you both."

Dinny walked on, and did not answer.

"Now listen, Dinny," began that pleasant voice. "I'm a sensualist, if you like, but what does it matter? Sex is naturally aberrational. If anyone tells you it isn't, don't believe them. These things work themselves out, and anyway they're not important. If Clare comes back to me, in two years' time she won't even remember. She likes the sort of life, and I'm not fussy. Marriage is very much a go-as-you-please affair."

"You mean that by that time you'll be experimenting with some one else?"

"Almost embarrassing this conversation, isn't it? What I want you to grasp is that I'm two men. One, and it's the one that matters, has his work to do and means to do it. Clare should stick to that man because he'll give her a life in which she won't rust; she'll be in the thick of affairs and people who matter; she'll have stir and movement—and she loves both. She'll have a certain power, and she's not averse from that. The other man—well, he wants his fling, he takes it, if you like; but the worst is over so far as she's concerned—at least, it will be when we've settled down again. You see, I'm honest, or shameless if you like it better."

"I don't see, in all this," said Dinny drily, "where love comes in."

"Perhaps it doesn't. Marriage is composed of mutual interest and desire. The first increases with the years, the latter fades. That ought to be exactly what she wants."

"I can't speak for Clare, but I don't see it that way."

"You haven't tried yourself out, my dear."

"No," said Dinny, "and on those lines I trust I never may. I should dislike alternation between commerce and vice."

He laughed.

"I like your bluntness. But seriously, Dinny, you ought to influence her. She's making a great mistake."

A sudden fury seized on Dinny.

"I think," she said, between her teeth, "it was you who made the great mistake. If you do certain things to certain horses you're never on terms with them again."

He was silent at that.

"You don't want a divorce in the family," he said at last, and looked round at her steadily. "I've told Clare that I can't let her divorce me. I'm sorry, but I mean that. Further, if she won't come back to me, she can't go as she pleases."

"You mean," said Dinny, between her teeth, "that if she does come back to you she can."

"That's what it would come to, I dare say."

"I see. I think I'll say good-night."

"As you please. You think me cynical. That's as may be. I shall do my best to get Clare back. If she won't come she must watch out."

They had stopped under a lamp-post and with an effort Dinny forced her eyes to his. He was as formidable, shameless and mesmerically implacable as a cat, with that thin smile and unflinching stare. She said, quietly: "I quite understand. Good-night!"

"Good-night, Dinny! I'm sorry, but it's best to know where we stand. Shake hands?"

Rather to her surprise she let him take her hand, then turned the corner into Mount Street.

CHAPTER 9

SHE ENTERED her aunt's house with all her passionate loyalty to her own breed roused, yet understanding better what had made Clare take Jerry Corven for husband. There *was* mesmerism about him, and a clear shameless daring which had its fascination. One could see what a power he might be among native peoples, how ruthlessly, yet smoothly, he would have his way with them; and how he might lay a spell over his associates. She could see, too, how difficult he might be to refuse physically, until he had outraged all personal pride.

Her aunt's voice broke her painful absorption with the words: "Here she is, Adrian."

At the top of the stairs her Uncle Adrian's goatee-bearded face was looking over his sister's shoulder.

"Your things have come, my dear. Where have you been?"

"With Clare, Auntie."

"Dinny," said Adrian, "I haven't seen you for nearly a year."

"This is where we kiss, Uncle. Is all well in Bloomsbury, or has the slump affected bones?"

"Bones *in esse* are all right; *in posse* they look dicky—no money for expeditions. The origin of *Homo Sapiens* is more abstruse than ever."

"Dinny, we needn't dress. Adrian's stoppin' for dinner. Lawrence will be so relieved. You can pow-wow while I loosen my belt, or do you want to tighten yours?"

"No, thank you, Auntie."

"Then go in there."

Dinny entered the drawing room and sat down beside her uncle. Grave and thin and bearded, wrinkled, and brown even in November, with long legs crossed and a look of interest in her, he seemed as ever the ideal pillarbox for confidences.

"Heard about Clare, Uncle?"

"The bare facts, no whys or wherefores."

"They're not 'nice.' Did you ever know a sadist?"

"Once—at Margate. My private school. I didn't know at the time, of course, but I've gathered it since. Do you mean that Corven is one?"

"So Clare says. I walked here with him from her rooms. He's a very queer person."

"Not mentally abnormal?" said Adrian, with a shudder.

"Saner than you or I, dear; he wants his own way regardless of other people; and when he can't get it, he bites. Could Clare get a divorce from him without publicly going into their life together?"

"Only by getting evidence of a definite act of misconduct."

"Would that have to be over here?"

"Well, to get it over there would be very expensive, and doubtful at that."

"Clare doesn't want to have him watched at present."

"It's certainly an unclean process," said Adrian.

"I know, Uncle; but if she won't, what chance is there?"

"None."

"At present she's in the mood that they should leave each other severely alone; but if she won't go back with him, he says she must 'look out for herself.'"

"Is there anybody else involved, then, Dinny?"

"There's a young man in love with her, but she says it's quite all right."

"H'm! 'Youth's a stuff—' as Shakespeare said. Nice young man?"

"I've only seen him for a few minutes; he looked quite nice, I thought."

"That cuts both ways."

"I trust Clare completely."

"You know her better than I do, my dear; but I should say she might get very impatient. How long can Corven stay over here?"

"Not more than a month, at most, she thinks; he's been here a week already."

"He's seen her?"

"Once. He tried to again to-day. I drew him off. She dreads seeing him, I know."

"As things are he has every right to see her, you know."

"Yes," said Dinny, and sighed.

"Can't your Member that she's with suggest a way out? He's a lawyer."

"I wouldn't like to tell him. It's so private. Besides, people don't like being involved in matrimonial squabbles."

"Is he married?"

"No."

She saw him look at her intently, and remembered Clare's laugh and words: "Dinny, he's in love with you."

"You'll see him here to-morrow night," Adrian went on. "Em's asked him to dinner, I gather; Clare too, I believe. Quite candidly, Dinny, I don't see anything to be done. Clare may change her mind and go back, or Corven may change his and let her stay without bothering about her."

Dinny shook her head. "They're neither of them like that. I must go and wash, Uncle."

Adrian reflected upon the undeniable proposition that every one had his troubles. His own at the moment were confined to the fact that his step-children, Sheila and Ronald Ferse, had measles, so that he was something of a pariah in his own house, the sanctity attaching to an infectious disease having cast his wife into purdah. He was not vastly interested in Clare. She had always been to him one of those young women who took the bit between their teeth and were bound to fetch up now and again with broken knees. Dinny, to him, was worth three of her. But if Dinny were going to be worried out of her life by her sister's troubles, then, indeed, they became important to Adrian. She seemed to have the knack of bearing vicarious burdens: Hubert's, his own, Wilfrid Desert's, and now Clare's.

And he said to his sister's parakeet: "Not fair, Polly, is it?"

The parakeet, who was used to him, came out of its open cage on to his shoulder and tweaked his ear.

"You don't approve, do you?"

The green bird emitted a faint chattering sound and clutched its way on to his waistcoat. Adrian scratched its poll.

"Who's going to scratch her poll? Poor Dinny!"

His sister's voice startled him:

"I can't have Dinny scratched again."

"Em," said Adrian, "did any of *us* worry about the others?"

"In large families you don't. I was the nearest—gettin' Lionel married, and now he's a judge—depressin'. Dornford—have you seen him?"

"Never."

"He's got a face like a portrait. They say he won the long jump at Oxford. Is that any good?"

"It's what you call desirable."

"Very well made," said Lady Mont. "I looked him over at Condaford."

"My dear Em!"

"For Dinny, of course. What do you do with a gardener who *will* roll the stone terrace?"

"Tell him not to."

"Whenever I look out at Lippin'hall, he's at it, takin' the roller somewhere else. There's the gong; and here's Dinny; we'll go in."

Sir Lawrence was at the sideboard in the dining room, extracting a crumbled cork.

"Lafite '65. Goodness knows what it'll be like. Decant it very gently, Blore. What do you say, Adrian, warm it a little or no?"

"I should say no, if it's that age."

"I agree."

Dinner began in silence. Adrian was thinking of Dinny, Dinny of Clare, and Sir Lawrence of the claret.

"French art," said Lady Mont.

"Ah!" said Sir Lawrence: "that reminds me, Em; some of old Forsyte's pictures are going to be lent. Considering he died saving them, they owe it to him."

Dinny looked up.

"Fleur's father? Was he a nice man, Uncle?"

"Nice?" repeated Sir Lawrence: "It's not the word. Straight, yes: careful, yes—too careful for these times. He got a picture on his head, you know, in the fire—poor old chap. He knew something about French art, though. This exhibition that's coming would have pleased him."

"There'll be nothing in it to touch 'The Birth of Venus,'" said Adrian. Dinny gave him a pleased look.

"That was divine," she said.

Sir Lawrence cocked his eyebrow.

"I've often thought of going into the question: Why a nation ceases to be poetic. The old Italians—and look at them now!"

"Isn't poetry an effervescence, Uncle? Doesn't it mean youth, or at least enthusiasm?"

"The Italians were never young, and they're enthusiastic enough, now. When we were in Italy last May you should have seen the trouble they took over our passports."

"Touchin'!" agreed Lady Mont.

"It's only a question," said Adrian, "of the means of expression. In the fourteenth century the Italians were expressing themselves in daggers and verse, in the fifteenth and sixteenth in poison, sculpture and painting, in the seventeenth in music, in the eighteenth in intrigue, in the nineteenth in rebellion, and in the twentieth their poetry is spelled in wireless and rules."

"I did get so tired," murmured Lady Mont, "of seein' rules I couldn't read."

"You were fortunate, my dear; I could."

"There's one thing about the Italians," continued Adrian; "century by century they throw up really great men of one sort or another. Is that climate, blood, or scenery, Lawrence?"

Sir Lawrence shrugged. "What do you think of the claret? Put your nose to it, Dinny. Sixty years ago, you two young women wouldn't be here, and Adrian and I would be soppy about it. It's as near perfect as makes no matter."

Adrian sipped and nodded.

"Absolutely prime!"

"Well, Dinny?"

"I'm sure it's perfect, dear—wasted on me."

"Old Forsyte would have appreciated this; he had wonderful sherry. Do you get the bouquet, Em?"

Lady Mont, who was holding her glass with her elbow on the table, moved her nostrils delicately.

"Such nonsense," she murmured, "almost any flower beats it."

The remark caused complete silence.

Dinny's eyes were the first to come to the level.

"How are Boswell and Johnson, Auntie?"

"I was tellin' Adrian: Boswell's taken to rollin' the stone terrace, and

Johnson's lost his wife—poor thing. He's a different man. Whistles all the time. His tunes ought to be collected."

"Survivals of old England?"

"No, modern—he just wanders."

"Talking of survivals," said Sir Lawrence, "did you ever read 'Ask Mamma,' Dinny?"

"No; who wrote it?"

"Surtees. You should. It's a corrective."

"Of what, Uncle?"

"Modernity."

Lady Mont lowered her glass; it was empty.

"So wise of them to be stoppin' this picture exhibition at 1900. D'you remember, Lawrence—in Paris, all those wiggly things we saw, and so much yellow and light blue—scrolls and blobs and faces upside-down? Dinny, we'd better go up."

And when presently Blore brought the message—Would Miss Dinny go down to the study, she murmured:

"It's about Jerry Corven. Don't encourage your uncle—he thinks he can do good, but he can't." . . .

"Well, Dinny?" said Sir Lawrence: "I always like talking to Adrian; he's a well-tempered fellow with a mind of his own. I told Clare I would see Corven, but it's no good seeing him without knowing what one wants to say. And not much then, I'm afraid. What do *you* think?"

Dinny, who had seated herself on the edge of her chair, set her elbows on her knees. It was an attitude from which Sir Lawrence augured ill.

"Judging from what he said to me to-day, Uncle Lawrence, his mind's made up. Either Clare must go back to him or he'll try to divorce her."

"How will your people feel about that?"

"Very badly."

"You know there's a young man hanging round?"

"Yes."

"He hasn't a bean."

Dinny smiled. "We're used to that."

"I know, but no beans when you're out of bounds is serious. Corven might claim damages, he looks a vindictive sort of chap."

"D'you really think he would? It's very bad form, nowadays, isn't it?"

"Form matters very little when a man's monkey is up. I suppose you couldn't get Clare to apply the closure to young Croom?"

"I'm afraid Clare will refuse to be dictated to about whom she sees. She thinks the break-up is entirely Jerry's fault."

"I," said Sir Lawrence, emitting a slow puff, "am in favour of having Corven watched while he's over here, and collecting a shot, if possible, to fire across his bows, but she doesn't like the idea of that."

"She believes in his career, and doesn't want to spoil it. Besides, it's so revolting."

Sir Lawrence shrugged.

"What would you? The law's the law. He belongs to Burton's. Shall I waylay him there and appeal to him to leave her here quietly, and see if absence will make her heart grow fond again?"

Dinny wrinkled her brows.

"It might be worth trying, but I don't believe he'll budge."

"What line are you going to take yourself?"

"Back Clare in whatever she does or doesn't do."

Sir Lawrence nodded, having received the answer he expected.

CHAPTER 10

THE QUALITY which from time immemorial has made the public men of England what they are, tempted so many lawyers into Parliament, caused so many divines to put up with being bishops, floated so many financiers, saved so many politicians from taking thought for the morrow and so many judges from the pangs of remorse, was present in Eustace Dornford to no small degree. Put more shortly, he had an excellent digestion; could eat and drink at all times without knowing anything about it afterwards. He was an indefatigably hard worker even at play; and there was in him just that added fund of nervous energy which differentiates the man who wins the long jump from the man who loses it. And now, though his practice was going up by leaps and bounds, since, two years ago, he had taken silk, he had stood for Parliament. And yet he was the last sort of man to incur the epithet 'go-getter.' His pale-brown, hazel-eyed, well-featured face had a considerate, even a sensitive look, and a pleasant smile. He had kept a little fine dark moustache, and his wig had not yet depleted his natural hair, which was dark and of rather curly texture. After Oxford he had eaten dinners and gone into the Chambers of a well-known Common Law Junior. Being a subaltern in the Shropshire Yeomanry when the war broke out, he had passed into the Cavalry, and not long after into the trenches, where he had known better luck than most people. His rise at the Bar after the war had been rapid. Solicitors liked him. He never fell foul of judges, and as a cross-examiner stood out, because he almost seemed to regret the points he scored. He was a Roman Catholic from breeding rather than observance. Finally he was fastidious in matters of sex, and his presence at a dinner table on circuit had, if not a silencing, at least a moderating effect on tongues.

He occupied in Harcourt Buildings a commodious set of chambers designed for life as well as learning. Early every morning, wet or fine, he went for a ride in the Row, having already done at least two hours' work on his cases. By ten o'clock, bathed, breakfasted, and acquainted with the morning's news, he was ready for the Courts: When at four those Courts rose, he was busy again till half-past six on his cases. The evenings, hitherto free, would now be spent at the House; and since it would be seldom that he could go to bed without working an hour or so on some case or other, his sleep was likely to be curtailed from six hours to five, or even four.

The arrangement come to with Clare was simple. She arrived at a quarter to ten, opened his correspondence and took his instructions from ten to a quarter past. She remained to do what was necessary, and came again at six o'clock ready for anything fresh or left over.

On the evening after that last described, at the hour of eight-fifteen, he entered the drawing room in Mount Street, was greeted and introduced to Adrian, who had again been bidden. Discussing the state of the pound and other grave matters, they waited, till Lady Mont said suddenly: "Soup. What have you done with Clare, Mr. Dornford?"

His eyes, which had hitherto taken in little but Dinny, regarded his hostess with a faint surprise.

"She left the Temple at half-past six, saying we should meet again."

"Then," said Lady Mont, "we'll go down."

There followed one of those discomfortable hours well known to well-bred people, when four of them are anxious upon a subject which they must not broach to the fifth, and the fifth becomes aware of this anxiety.

They were, indeed, too few for the occasion, for all that each one of them said could be heard by the others. It was impossible for Eustace Dornford to be confidential with either of his neighbours; and since he instinctively felt that without preliminary confidence he would only put his foot into it, he was careful to be public-minded and keep to such topics as the Premier, the undiscovered identity of certain poisoners, the ventilation of the House of Commons, the difficulty of knowing exactly what to do with one's hat there, and other subjects of general interest. But by the end of dinner he was so acutely aware that they were burning to say things he mustn't hear, that he invented a professional telephone call, and was taken out of the room by Blore.

The moment he had gone Dinny said:

"She must have been waylaid, Auntie. Could I be excused and go and see?"

Sir Lawrence answered:

"Better wait till we break, Dinny; a few minutes can't matter now."

"Don't you think," said Adrian, "that Dornford ought to know how things stand? She goes to him every day."

"I'll tell him," said Sir Lawrence.

"No," said Lady Mont. "Dinny must tell him. Wait for him here, Dinny. We'll go up."

Thus it was that, returning to the dining room after his trunk-call to someone whom he knew to be away from home, Dornford found Dinny waiting. She handed him the cigars and said:

"Forgive us, Mr. Dornford. It's about my sister. Please light up, and here's coffee. Blore, would you mind getting me a taxi?"

When they had drunk their coffee and were standing together by the fire, she turned her face to it and went on hurriedly:

"You see, Clare has split from her husband, and he's just come over to take her back. She won't go, and it's rather a difficult time for her."

Dornford made a considerate sound.

"I'm very glad you told me. I've been feeling unhappy all dinner."

"I must go now, I'm afraid, and find out what's happened."

"Could I come with you?"

"Oh! thank you, but——"

"It would be a real pleasure."

Dinny stood hesitating. He looked like a present help in trouble; but she said: "Thank you, but perhaps my sister wouldn't like it."

"I see. Any time I can help, please let me know."

"Your taxi's at the door, Miss."

"Some day," she said, "I'd like to ask you about divorce."

In the taxi she wondered what she would do if she could not get in; and then what she would do if she could get in and Corven were there. She stopped the cab at the corner of the Mews.

"Stay here, please, I'll let you know in a minute if I want you again."

Dark and private loomed that little backwater.

'Like one's life,' thought Dinny, and pulled at the ornamental bell. It tinkled all forlorn, and nothing happened. Again and again she rang, then moved backward to look up at the windows. The curtains—she remembered they were heavy—had been drawn close; she could not decide whether or not there was light behind them. Once more she rang and used the knocker, holding her breath to listen. No sound at all! At last, baffled and disquiet, she went back to the cab. Clare had said Corven was staying at the Bristol, and she gave that address. There might be a dozen explanations; only why, in a town of telephones, had Clare not let them know? Half-past ten! Perhaps she had by now!

The cab drew up at the hotel. "Wait, please!" Entering its discreetly gilded hall, she stood for a moment at a loss. The setting seemed unsuitable for private trouble.

"Yes, Madam?" said a page-boy's voice.

"Could you find out for me, please, if my brother-in-law, Sir Gerald Corven, is in the hotel?"

What should she say if they brought him to her? Her figure in its evening cloak was reflected in a mirror, and that it was straight filled her with a sort of surprise—she felt so as if she were curling and creeping this way and that. But they did not bring him to her. He was not in his room, nor in any of the public rooms. She went out again to her cab.

"Back to Mount Street, please."

Dornford and Adrian were gone, her aunt and uncle playing piquet.

"Well, Dinny?"

"I couldn't get into her rooms, and he was not in his hotel."

"You went there?"

"It was all I could think of to do."

Sir Lawrence rose. "I'll telephone to Burton's." Dinny sat down beside her aunt.

"I feel she's in trouble, Auntie. Clare's never rude."

"Kidnapped or locked up," said Lady Mont. "There was a case when I was young. Thompson, or Watson—a great fuss. Habeas Corpus, or something—husbands can't now. Well, Lawrence?"

"He hasn't been in the Club since five o'clock. We must just wait till the morning. She may have forgotten, you know; or got the evening mixed."

"But she told Mr. Dornford that they would meet again."

"So they will, to-morrow morning. No good worrying, Dinny."

Dinny went up, but did not undress. Had she done all she could? The night was clear and fine, and warm for November. Only a quarter of a mile or so away was that backwater of Mews— Should she slip out and go over there again?

She threw off her evening frock, put on a day dress, hat and fur coat, and stole downstairs. It was dark in the hall. Quietly drawing back the bolts, she let herself out, and took to the streets. When she entered the Mews—where a couple of cars were being put away for the night—she saw light coming from the upper windows of No. 2. They had been opened and the curtains drawn aside. She rang the bell.

After a moment Clare, in her dressing-gown, opened the door.

"Was it you who came before, Dinny?"

"Yes."

"Sorry I couldn't let you in. Come in!"

She led the way up the spiral stairs, and Dinny followed.

Upstairs it was warm and light, the door into the tiny bathroom open, and the couch in disorder. Clare looked at her sister with a sort of unhappy defiance.

"Yes, I've had Jerry here; he's not been gone ten minutes."

A horrified shiver went down Dinny's spine.

"After all, he's come a long way," said Clare. "Good of you to worry, Dinny."

"Oh! darling!"

"He was outside here when I got back from the Temple. I was an idiot to let him in. After that—oh! well, it doesn't matter. I'll take care it doesn't happen again."

"Would you like me to stay?"

"Oh! no. But have some tea. I've just made it. I don't want any one to know of this."

"Of course not. I'll say you had a bad headache and couldn't get out to telephone."

When they were drinking the tea Dinny said:

"This hasn't altered your plans?"

"God! no!"

"Dornford was here to-night. We thought it best to tell him you were having a difficult time."

Clare nodded.

"It must all seem very funny to you."

"It seems to me tragic."

Clare shrugged, then stood up and threw her arms round her sister. After that silent embrace, Dinny went out into the Mews, now dark and deserted. At the corner leading into the Square she almost walked into a young man.

"Mr. Croom, isn't it?"

"Miss Cherrell? Have you been at Lady Corven's?"

"Yes."

"Is she all right?"

His face was worried, and his voice anxious. Dinny took a deep breath before answering!

"Oh! yes. Why not?"

"She was saying last night that man was over here. It worries me terribly."

Through Dinny shot the thought: 'If he'd met "that man"!' But she said, quietly:

"Walk with me as far as Mount Street."

"I don't mind your knowing," he said, "I'm over head and ears in love with her. Who wouldn't be? Miss Cherrell, I don't think she ought to be in that place alone. She told me he came yesterday while you were there."

"Yes. I took him away with me, as I'm taking you. I think my sister should be left to herself."

He seemed to hunch himself together.

"Have *you* ever been in love?"

"Yes."

"Well, then you know."

Yes, she knew!

"It's absolute torture not to be with her, able to see that she's all right. She takes it all lightly, but I can't."

Takes it all lightly! Clare's face looking at her! She did not answer.

"The fact is," said young Croom, with incoherence, "people can say and think what they like, but if they felt as I feel, they simply couldn't. I won't bother her, I really won't; but I can't stand her being in danger from that man."

Dinny controlled herself to say quietly: "I don't think Clare's in any danger. But she might be if it were known that you—" He met her eyes squarely.

"I'm glad she's got you. For God's sake look after her, Miss Cherrell."

They had reached the corner of Mount Street, and she held out her hand.

"You may be certain that whatever Clare does I shall stick by her. Good-night! And cheer up!"

He wrung her hand, and went off as if the devil were after him. Dinny went in, and slid the bolts quietly.

On what thin ice! She could hardly drag one foot before the other, as she went upstairs, and sank down on her bed exhausted.

CHAPTER 11

WHEN SIR LAWRENCE MONT reached Burton's Club the following after-noon he was feeling, in common with many who undertake to interfere in the affairs of others, an uneasy self-importance coupled with a desire to be somewhere else. He did not know what the deuce he was going to say to Corven, or why the deuce he should say it, since, in his opinion, by far the best solution would be for Clare to give her marriage another trial. Having discovered from the porter that Sir Gerald was in the Club, he poked his nose gingerly into three rooms before locating the back of his quarry seated in the corner of an apartment too small to be devoted to anything but writing. He sat down at a table close to the door, so that he could simulate surprise when Corven came up to leave the room. The fellow was an unconscionable time. Noting a copy of the British States-man's *vade mecum* beside him, he began idly looking up the figures of British imports. He found potatoes: consumption sixty-six million five hundred thousand tons, production eight million eight hundred and seventy-four thousand tons! Somebody the other day had written to say that we imported forty million pounds' worth of bacon every year. Taking a sheet of paper he wrote: "Prohibition and protection, in regard to food that we *can* produce here. Annual Imports: Pigs, £40,000,000; Poultry, say £12,000,000; Potatoes—God knows how much! All this bacon, all these eggs, and half these potatoes could be produced here. Why not a five-year plan? By prohibition lessen the import of bacon and eggs one-fifth every year, and the import of potatoes by one-tenth every year, increasing home production gradually to replace them. At the end of five years our bacon and eggs and half our potatoes would be all-British. We should save eighty millions on our Imports Bill and our trade would practically be balanced."

Taking another sheet of paper, he wrote:

"To the Editor of *The Times*.
                    "THE THREE P. PLAN."
"SIR,

A simple plan for the balancing of our trade would seem to merit the attention of all those not wedded to the longest way round. There are three articles of food on importing which we expend annually some

—— pounds, but which could be produced in our own country without, I venture to think, causing the price of living to rise to any material extent if we took the simple precaution of hanging a profiteer at the beginning. These articles are Pigs, Poultry, Potatoes. There would be no need to put on duties, for all that is required is——"

But at this moment becoming aware that Corven was passing from the room he said:

"Hallo!"

Corven turned and came towards him.

Hoping that he showed as little sign of embarrassment as his nephew twice removed by marriage, Sir Lawrence rose.

"Sorry I didn't see you when you called the other day. Have you got long leave?"

"Another week only, and then I shall have to fly the Mediterranean probably."

"Not a good month for flying. What do you think of this adverse balance of trade?"

Jerry Corven shrugged.

"Something to keep them busy for a bit. They never see two inches before their noses."

"'Tiens! Une montagne!' Remember the Caran d'Ache cartoon of Buller in front of Ladysmith? No, you wouldn't. It's thirty-two years ago. National character doesn't change much, does it? How's Ceylon? Not in love with India, I hope?"

"Nor with us particularly, but we jog on."

"The climate doesn't suit Clare, apparently."

Corven's expression remained watchful and slightly smiling.

"The hot weather didn't, but that's over."

"Are you taking her back with you?"

"Yes."

"I wonder if that's wise."

"To leave her would be less so. One's either married or not."

Sir Lawrence, watching his eyes, thought: 'Shan't go further. It's hopeless. Besides, he's probably right. Only I would bet——'

"Forgive me," said Corven. "I must get these letters off." He turned and moved away, trim and assured.

'H'm!' thought Sir Lawrence, 'not exactly what you'd call fruitful.' And he sat down again to his letter to *The Times*.

"I must get precise figures," he muttered. "I'll turn Michael on to it." . . . And his thoughts went back to Corven. Impossible, in such cases, to know where the blame really lay. After all, a misfit was a misfit, no amount of pious endeavour, or even worldly wisdom, would cure it. 'I ought to have been a judge,' he thought, 'then I could have expressed my views. Mr. Justice Mont in the course of his judgment said: "It is time to warn the people of this country against marriage. That tie, which was all very well under Victoria, should now only be contracted in cases where there is full evidence to show that neither party has any individuality to speak of." . . . I think I'll go home to Em.' He blotted the perfectly dry letter to *The Times,* put it into his pocket, and sought the darkening placidity of Pall Mall. He had stopped to look in the window of his wine merchant's in St. James' Street, and consider once more where the extra ten per cent on his surtax was to come from, when a voice said:

"Good-evening, Sir Lawrence!" It was the young man called Croom. They crossed the street together.

"I wanted to thank you, Sir, for speaking to Mr. Muskham. I've seen him to-day."

"How did you find him?"

"Oh! very affable. Of course I agree it *is* a bee in his bonnet about introducing that cross of Arab blood into our race-horses."

"Did you show him you thought so?"

Young Croom smiled: "Hardly! But the Arab horse is so much smaller."

"There's something in it, all the same. Jack's only wrong in expecting quick results. It's like politics; people won't lay down for the future. If a thing doesn't work within five years, we think it's no good. Did Jack say he'd take you on?"

"He'll give me a trial. I'm to go down for a week, so that he can see me with horses. But the mares are not going to Royston. He's got a place for them above Oxford near Bablock Hythe. I should be there if I pass muster. It's not till the spring, though."

"Jack's a formalist," said Sir Lawrence, as they entered The Coffee House; "you'll have to mind your p's and q's."

Young Croom smiled.

"You bet. Everything's simply perfect at his stud farm. Luckily I really am frightfully keen about horses. I didn't feel at sea with Mr. Muskham. It's an immense relief to have a chance again; and there's nothing I'd like better."

Sir Lawrence smiled—enthusiasm was always pleasant.

"You must know my son," he said; "he's an enthusiast, too, though he must be thirty-seven by now. You'll be in his constituency—no, just out of it. You'll be in Dornford's, I expect. By the way, you know my niece is acting secretary for him?"

Young Croom nodded.

"I don't know," murmured Sir Lawrence, "whether that'll go on now Corven's over." And he watched the young man's expression.

It had perceptibly darkened. "Oh! it will. She won't go back to Ceylon."

It was said with frowning suddenness, and Sir Lawrence thought: 'This is where I weigh myself.' Young Croom followed him to the weighing machine, as if he did not know how not to. He was very red.

"What makes you sure of that?" said Sir Lawrence, looking up from the historic chair. Young Croom went even redder.

"One doesn't come away just to go back."

"Or one does. If Life were a race-horse it'd be always up before the stewards for running in and out."

"I happen to know Lady Corven won't, Sir."

It was clear to Sir Lawrence that he had lighted on a moment when feeling gets the better of discretion. So the young man *was* in love with her. Was this a chance to warn him off the course? Or was it more graceful to take no notice?

"Just eleven stone," he said; "do you go up or down, Mr. Croom?"

"I keep about ten twelve."

Sir Lawrence scrutinised his lean figure.

"Well, you look very fit. Extraordinary what a shadow can be cast on life by the abdomen. However, you won't have to worry till you're fifty."

"Surely, Sir, you've never had any bother there?"

"Not to speak of; but I've watched it darken so many doors. And now I must be getting on. Good-night to you!"

"Good-night, Sir. I really am awfully grateful."

"Not at all. My cousin Jack doesn't bet, and if you take my advice, you won't either."

Young Croom said heartily: "I certainly shan't, Sir."

They shook hands and Sir Lawrence resumed his progress up St. James' Street.

'That young man,' he was thinking, 'impresses me favourably, and I can't think why—he appears to be going to be a nuisance. What I ought to have said to him was "Thou shalt not covet thy neighbour's wife." But God so made the world that one doesn't say what one ought!' The young were very interesting; one heard of them being disrespectful to Age and all that, but really he couldn't see it. They seemed to him fully as well-mannered as he himself had been at their age, and easier to talk to. One never knew what they were thinking, of course; but that might be as well. After all, one used to think that the old—and Sir Lawrence winced on the curbstone of Piccadilly—were only fit to be measured for their coffins. *Tempora mutantur et nos mutamur in illis'*; but was that true? No more really than the difference in the pronunciation of Latin since one's youth. Youth would always be Youth and Age would be Age, with the same real divergence and distrust between them, and the same queer hankering by Age to feel as Youth was feeling and think as Youth was thinking; the same pretence that it wouldn't so feel and think for the world, and, at the back of all, the instinct that, really given the chance, Age wouldn't have its life over again. Merciful—that! With stealthy quietude Life, as it wore one out, supplied the adjustment of a suitable lethargy. At each stage of existence the zest for living was tailored to what man had before him and no more. That fellow Goethe had attained immortality to the tunes of Gounod by fanning a dying spark into a full-blown flame. 'Rats!' thought Sir Lawrence: 'and very German rats! Would I choose the sighing and the sobbing, the fugitive raptures and the lingering starvations in front of that young man, if I could? I would not! Sufficient unto the old buffer

494

is the bufferism thereof. Is that policeman never going to stop this blamed traffic?' No, there was no real change! Men drove cars now to the same tick as the old horse-'bus and hansom-cab drivers had driven their slipping, sliding, clattering gees. Young men and women experienced the same legal or illegal urge towards each other. The pavements were different, and the lingo in which those youthful hankerings were expressed. But— Lord Almighty!—the rules of the road, the collisions and slips and general miraculous avoidances, the triumphs, mortifications, and fulfilments for better for worse, were all the same as ever. 'No,' he thought; 'the Police may make rules, Divines write to the papers, Judges express themselves as they like, but human nature will find its own way about as it did when I was cutting my wisdom teeth.'

The policeman reversed his sleeves and Sir Lawrence crossed, pursuing his way to Berkeley Square. Here was change enough! The houses of the great were going fast. Piecemeal, without expressed aim, almost shamefacedly, in true English fashion, London was being rebuilt. The dynastic age was gone, with its appendages, feudalism and the Church. Even wars would now be fought for peoples and their markets. No more dynastic or religious wars. Well, that was something! 'We're getting more like insects daily,' thought Sir Lawrence. And how interesting! Religion was nearly dead because there was no longer real belief in future life; but something was struggling to take its place—service—social service— the ants' creed, the bees' creed! Communism had formulated it and was whipping it into the people from the top. So characteristic! They were always whipping something into somebody in Russia. The quick way, no doubt, but the sure way? No! The voluntary system remained the best, because when once it got hold it lasted—only it was so darned slow! Yes, and darned ironical! So far the sense of social service was almost the per- quisite of the older families, who had somehow got hold of the notion that they must do something useful to pay for their position. Now that they were dying out would the sense of service persist? How were the 'people' to pick it up? 'Well,' thought Sir Lawrence, 'after all, there's the 'bus conductor; and the fellow in the shop, who'll take infinite trouble to match the colour of your socks; and the woman who'll look after her neighbour's baby, or collect for the waifs and strays; and the motorist who'll stop and watch you tinkering at your car; and the postman who's grateful for a tip; and the almost anybody who'll try and pull you out of a pond if he can really see you're in it. What's wanted is the slogan: "Fresh air and exercise for good instincts." One might have it on all the 'buses, instead of: "Canon's Colossal Crime," or "Strange Sweepstake Swindle." And that reminds me to ask Dinny what she knows about Clare and that young man.'

So thinking he paused before his house door and inserted his key in its latch.

CHAPTER 12

IN SPITE OF Sir Gerald Corven's assurance, the course before a husband wishing to resume the society of his wife is not noticeably simple, especially if he has but a week wherein to encompass his desire. The experience of that evening had made Clare wary. On leaving the Temple at lunch time the day after, a Saturday, she took train for Condaford, where she carefully refrained from saying that she had sought asylum. On Sunday morning she lay long in bed, with the windows wide open, watching the sky beyond the tall denuded elms. The sun shone in upon her, the air was mild and alive with sounds surprised into life, the twittering once more of birds, the lowing of a cow, the occasional caw of a rook, the continual crooning of the fantails. There was but little poetry in Clare, but for a moment to her easeful stretched-out being came a certain perception of the symphony which is this world. The lacing of the naked boughs and those few leaves against the soft, gold-bright, moving sky; that rook balancing there; the green and fallow upland, the far line of trees; and all those sounds, and the pure unscented air on her face; the twittering quietude and perfect freedom of each separate thing, and yet the long composure of design—all this for a moment drew her out of herself into a glimpse of the universal.

The vision passed; she thought instead of Thursday night, and Tony Croom, and the dirty little boy outside the restaurant in Soho, who had said in such endearing tones: "Remember the poor old guy, Lady; remember the poor old guy." If Tony had seen her the next night! How irrelevant was event to feeling, how ignorant were even the closest of each other. She uttered a little discomfited laugh. Where ignorance was bliss, indeed!

The village church bell began ringing now. Marvellous how her father and mother continued to go every Sunday, hoping—she supposed—for the best; or was it because if they didn't the village wouldn't, and the church would fall into disuse, or at least behind the chapel? It was nice to lie here in one's own old room, feel safe, and warm, and idle, with a dog on one's feet! Till next Saturday she was at bay, like a chased vixen taking advantage of every cover; and Clare drew taut her lips, as a vixen does at sight of hounds. Go back he must—he had said—with her or without. Well, it would be without!

Her sense of asylum was rudely shaken about four o'clock, when, re-

496

turning from a walk with the dogs, she saw a car outside and was met by her mother in the hall.

"Jerry's with your father."

"Oh!"

"Come up to my room, dear."

In that first-floor room adjoining her bedroom Lady Charwell's personality had always more scope than in the rest of the old, tortuous, worn-down house, so full of relics and the past tense. This room's verbena-scented, powder-blue scheme had a distinct if faded elegance. It had been designed; the rest of the house had grown, emerging here and there into small oases of modernity, but for the most part a wilderness strewn with the débris of Time.

Clare turned and turned a china figure, in front of the wood fire. She had not foreseen this visit. Now were conjoined the forces of creed, convention and comfort, and against them was only a defence that it was hateful to lay bare. She waited for her mother to speak.

"You see, darling, you haven't told us anything."

But how tell one who looked and spoke like that? She flushed, went pale, and said: "I can only say there's a beast in him. I know it doesn't show; but there is, Mother; there is!"

Lady Charwell, too, had flushed. It did not suit her, being over fifty.

"Your father and I will help you all we can, dear; only, of course, it is so important to take a right decision now."

"And I having made a wrong one already, can only be trusted to make another? You've got to take my word, Mother, I simply can't talk about it, and I simply won't go back with him."

Lady Charwell had sat down, a furrow between her grey-blue eyes which seemed fixed on nothing. She turned them on her daughter, and said, hesitating:

"You're sure it's not just the beast that is in nearly all men."

Clare laughed.

"Oh! no. I'm not easily upset."

Lady Charwell sighed.

"Don't worry, Mother dear; it'll be all right once we've got this over. Nothing really matters nowadays."

"So they say, but one has the bad habit still of believing that it does."

At this near approach to irony Clare said quickly:

"It matters that one should keep one's self-respect. Really, with him I couldn't."

"We'll say no more then. Your father will want to see you. You'd better take your things off."

Clare kissed her and went out. There was no sound from below, and she went on up to her room. She felt her will-power stiffening. The days when men disposed of their women folk were long over, and—whatever Jerry and her father were concocting—she would not budge! When the summons came, she went to the encounter, blade-sharp, and hard as stone.

They were standing in the General's office-like study, and she felt at once that they were in agreement. Nodding to her husband, she went over to her father.

"Well?"

But Corven spoke first.

"I leave it to you, Sir."

The General's lined face looked mournful and irritated. He braced himself. "We've been going into this, Clare. Jerry admits that you've got much on your side, but he's given me his word that he won't offend you again. I want to appeal to you to try and see his point of view. He says, I think rightly, that it's more to your interest even than to his. The old ideas about marriage may have gone, but, after all, you both took certain vows—but leaving that aside——"

"Yes," said Clare.

The General twirled his little moustache, and thrust the other hand deep into his pocket.

"Well, what on earth is going to happen to you both? You can't have a divorce—there's your name, and his position, and—after only eighteen months. What are you going to do? Live apart? That's not fair to you, or to him."

"Fairer to both of us than living together will be."

The General glanced at her hardened face. "So you say now; but we've both of us had more experience than you."

"That was bound to be said sooner or later. You want me to go back with him?"

The General looked acutely unhappy.

"You know, my dear, that I only want what's best for you."

"And Jerry has convinced you that is the best. Well, it's the worst. I'm not going, Dad, and there's an end of it."

The General looked at her face, looked at the face of his son-in-law, shrugged his shoulders, and began filling his pipe.

Jerry Corven's eyes, which had been passing from face to face, narrowed and came to rest on Clare's. That look lasted a long time, and neither flinched.

"Very well," he said, at last, "I will make other arrangements. Good-bye, Sir; good-bye, Clare!" And turning on his heel, he went out.

In the silence that followed the sound of his car crunching away on the drive could be heard distinctly. The General, smoking glumly, kept his glance averted. Clare went to the window. It was growing dark outside and now that the crisis was over she felt unstrung.

"I wish to God," said her father's voice, "that I could understand this business."

Clare did not move from the window. "Did he tell you he'd used my riding whip on me?"

"What!" said the General.

Clare turned round.

"Yes."

"On *you?*"

"Yes. That was not my real reason, but it put the finishing touch. Sorry to hurt you, Dad!"

"By God!"

Clare had a moment of illumination. Concrete facts! Give a man a fact!

"The ruffian!" said the General. "The ruffian! . . . He told me he spent the evening with you the other day; is that true?"

A slow flush had burned up in her cheeks.

"He practically forced himself in."

"The ruffian!" said the General once more.

When she was alone again she meditated wryly on the sudden difference that little fact about the whip had made in her father's feelings. He had taken it as a personal affront, an insult to his own flesh and blood. She felt that he could have stood it with equanimity of some one else's daughter; she remembered that he had even sympathised with her brother's flogging of the muleteer which had brought such a peck of trouble on them all. How little detached, how delightfully personal, people were! Feeling and criticising in terms of their own prejudices! Well! She was over the worst now, for her people were on her side, and she would make certain of not seeing Jerry alone again. She thought of the long look he had given her. He was a good loser because for him the game was never at an end. Life itself—not each item of life—absorbed him. He rode Life, took a toss, got up, rode on; met an obstacle, rode over it, rode through it, took the scratches as all in the day's work. He had fascinated her, ridden through and over her; the fascination was gone, and she wondered that it had ever been. What was he going to do now? Well! One thing was certain: somehow he would cut his losses!

CHAPTER 13

ONE WHO GAZES at the Temple's smooth green turf, fine trees, stone-silled buildings and pouter pigeons, feels dithyrambic, till on him intrudes the vision of countless bundles of papers tied round with pink tape, unending clerks in little outer chambers sucking thumbs and waiting for solicitors, calf-bound tomes stored with reports of innumerable cases so closely argued that the light-minded sigh at sight of them and think of the Café Royal. Who shall deny that the Temple harbours the human mind *in excelsis*, the human body in chairs; who shall gainsay that the human spirit is taken off at its entrances and left outside like the shoes of those who enter a mosque? Not even to its Grand Nights is the human spirit admitted, for the legal mind must not 'slop over,' and warning is given by the word 'Decorations' on the invitation cards. On those few autumn mornings when the sun shines, the inhabitant of the Temple who faces East may possibly feel in his midriff as a man feels on a hilltop, or after hearing a Brahms symphony, or even when seeing first daffodils in spring; if so, he will hastily remember where he is, and turn to: Collister *v.* Daverday: Popdick intervening.

And yet, strangely, Eustace Dornford, verging on middle age, was continually being visited, whether the sun shone or not, by the feeling of one who sits on a low wall in the first spring warmth, seeing life as a Botticellian figure advancing towards him through an orchard of orange trees and spring flowers. At less expenditure of words, he was 'in love' with Dinny. Each morning when he saw Clare he was visited by a longing not to dictate on parliamentary subjects, but rather to lead her to talk about her sister. Self-controlled, however, and with a sense of humour, he bowed to his professional inhibitions, merely asking Clare whether she and her sister would dine with him, "on Saturday—here, or at the Café Royal?"

"Here would be more original."

"Would you care to ask a man to make a fourth?"

"But won't you, Mr. Dornford?"

"You might like some one special."

"Well, there's young Tony Croom, who was on the boat with me. He's a nice boy."

"Good! Saturday, then. And you'll ask your sister?"

500

Clare did not say: "She's probably on the doorstep," for, as a fact, she was. Every evening that week she was coming at half-past six to accompany Clare back to Melton Mews. There were still chances, and the sisters were not taking them.

On hearing of the invitation Dinny said: "When I left you late that night I ran into Tony Croom, and we walked back to Mount Street together."

"You didn't tell him about Jerry's visit to me?"

"Of course not!"

"It's hard on him, as it is. He really is a nice boy, Dinny."

"So I saw. And I wish he weren't in London."

Clare smiled. "Well, he won't be for long; he's to take charge of some Arab mares for Mr. Muskham down at Bablock Hythe."

"Jack Muskham lives at Royston."

"The mares are to have a separate establishment in a milder climate."

Dinny roused herself from memories with an effort.

"Well, darling, shall we strap-hang on the Tube, or go a bust in a taxi?"

"I want air. Are you up to walking?"

"Rather! We'll go by the Embankment and the Parks."

They walked quickly for it was cold. Lamplit and star-covered, that broad free segment of the Town had a memorable dark beauty; even on the buildings, their daylight features abolished, was stamped a certain grandeur.

Dinny murmured: "London at night *is* beautiful."

"Yes, you go to bed with a beauty and wake up with a barmaid. And, what's it all for? A clotted mass of energy like an ant-heap."

" 'So fatiguin',' as Aunt Em would say."

"But what *is* it all for, Dinny?"

"A workshop trying to turn out perfect specimens; a million failures to each success."

"Is that worth while?"

"Why not?"

"Well, what is there to *believe* in?"

"Character."

"How do you mean?"

"Character's our way of showing the desire for perfection. Nursing the best that's in one."

"Hum!" said Clare: "Who's to decide what's best within one?"

"You have me, my dear."

"Well, I'm too young for it, anyway."

Dinny hooked her arm within her sister's.

"You're older than I am, Clare."

"No, I've had more experience perhaps, but I haven't communed with my own spirit and been still. I feel in my bones that Jerry's hanging around the Mews."

"Come into Mount Street, and we'll go to a film."

In the hall Blore handed Dinny a note.

"Sir Gerald Corven called, Miss, and left this for you."

Dinny opened it.

"DEAR DINNY,

"I'm leaving England to-morrow instead of Saturday. If Clare will change her mind I shall be very happy to take her. If not, she must not expect me to be long-suffering. I have left a note to this effect at her lodgings, but as I do not know where she is, I wrote to you also, so as to be sure that she knows. She or a message from her will find me at the Bristol up to three o'clock to-morrow, Thursday. After that '*à la guerre comme à la guerre.*'

"With many regrets that things are so criss-cross and good wishes to yourself,

I am,

Very sincerely yours,
GERALD CORVEN."

Dinny bit her lip.

"Read this!"

Clare read the note.

"I shan't go, and he can do what he likes."

While they were titivating themselves in Dinny's room, Lady Mont came in.

"Ah!" she said: "Now I can say my piece. Your uncle has seen Jerry Corven again. What are you goin' to do about him, Clare?"

As Clare swivelled round from the mirror, the light fell full on cheeks and lips whose toilet she had not quite completed.

"I'm never going back to him, Aunt Em."

"May I sit on your bed, Dinny? Never is a long time, and—er—that Mr. Craven. I'm sure you have principles, Clare, but you're too pretty."

Clare put down her lipstick.

"Sweet of you, Aunt Em; but really I know what I'm about."

"So comfortin'! When I say that myself, I'm sure to make a gaff."

"If Clare promises, she'll perform, Auntie."

Lady Mont sighed. "I promised my father not to marry for a year. Seven months—and then your uncle. It's always somebody."

Clare raised her hands to the little curls on her neck.

"I'll promise not to 'kick over' for a year. I ought to know my own mind by then; if I don't, I can't have got one."

Lady Mont smoothed the eiderdown.

"Cross your heart."

"I don't think you should," said Dinny, quickly.

Clare crossed her fingers on her breast.

"I'll cross where it ought to be."

Lady Mont rose.

502

"She ought to stay here to-night, don't you think, Dinny?"

"Yes."

"I'll tell them, then. Sea-green *is* your colour, Dinny. Lawrence says I haven't one."

"Black and white, dear."

"Magpies and the Duke of Portland. I haven't been to Ascot since Michael went to Winchester—savin' our pennies. Hilary and May are comin' to dinner. They won't be dressed."

"Oh!" said Clare, suddenly: "Does Uncle Hilary know about me?"

"Broad-minded," murmured Lady Mont. "I can't help bein' sorry, you know."

Clare stood up.

"Believe me, Aunt Em, Jerry's not the sort of man who'll let it hurt him long."

"Stand back to back, you two; I thought so—Dinny by an inch."

"I'm five foot five," said Clare, "without shoes."

"Very well. When you're tidy, come down."

So saying, Lady Mont swayed to the door, said to herself: "Solomon's seal—remind Boswell," and went out.

Dinny returned to the fire, and resumed her stare at the flames.

Clare's voice, close behind her, said: "I feel inclined to sing, Dinny. A whole year's holiday from everything. I'm glad Aunt Em made me promise. But isn't she a scream?"

"Emphatically not. She's the wisest member of our family. Take life seriously and you're nowhere. She doesn't. She may want to, but she can't."

"But she hasn't any real worries."

"Only a husband, three children, several grandchildren, two households, three dogs, some congenital gardeners, not enough money, and two passions—one for getting other people married, and one for French tapestry; besides trying hard not to get fat on it all."

"Oh! she's a duck all right. What d'you advise about these 'tendrils,' Dinny? They're an awful plague. Shall I shingle again?"

"Let them grow at present, we don't know what's coming; it might be ringlets."

"Do you believe that women get themselves up to please men?"

"Certainly not."

"To excite and annoy each other, then?"

"Fashion mostly, women are sheep about appearance."

"And morals?"

"Have we any? Man-made anyway. By nature we've only got feelings."

"I've none now."

"Sure?"

Clare laughed. "Oh! well, in hand, anyhow." She put on her dress, and Dinny took her place at the mirror. . . .

* * *

The slum parson does not dine out to observe human nature. He eats. Hilary Charwell, having spent the best part of his day, including meal times, listening to the difficulties of parishioners who had laid up no store for the morrow because they had never had store enough for to-day, absorbed the good food set before him with perceptible enjoyment. If he was aware that the young woman whom he had married to Jerry Corven had burst her bonds, he gave no sign of it. Though seated next to her, he never once alluded to her domestic existence, conversing freely on the election, French art, the timber wolves at Whipsnade Zoo, and a new system of building schools with roofs that could be used or not as the weather dictated. Over his face, long, wrinkled, purposeful and shrewdly kind, flitted an occasional smile, as if he were summing something up; but he gave no indication of what that something was, except that he looked across at Dinny, as though saying: "You and I are going to have a talk presently."

No such talk occurred, for he was summoned by telephone to a death-bed before he had finished his glass of port. Mrs. Hilary went with him.

The two sisters settled down to bridge with their uncle and aunt, and at eleven o'clock went up to bed.

"Armistice Day," said Clare, turning into her bedroom. "Did you realise?"

"Yes."

"I was in a 'bus at eleven o'clock. I noticed two or three people looking funny. How can one be expected to feel anything? I was only ten when the war stopped."

"I remember the Armistice," said Dinny, "because Mother cried. Uncle Hilary was with us at Condaford. He preached on: 'They also serve who only stand and wait.'"

"Who serves except for what he can get from it?"

"Lots of people do hard jobs all their lives for mighty little return."

"Well, yes."

"Why do they?"

"Dinny, I sometimes feel as if you might end up religious. Unless you marry, you will."

"'Get thee to a nunnery, go!'"

"Seriously, ducky, I wish I could see more of 'the old Eve' in you. In my opinion you ought to be a mother."

"When doctors find a way without preliminaries."

"You're wasting yourself, my dear. At any moment that you liked to crook your little finger, old man Dornford would fall on his knees to you. Don't you like him?"

"As nice a man as I've seen for a long time."

"'Murmured she, coldly, turning towards the door.' Give me a kiss."

"Darling," said Dinny, "I do hope things are going to be all right. I shan't pray for you, in spite of my look of decline; but I'll dream that your ship comes home."

CHAPTER 14

Young croom's second visit to England's Past at Drury Lane was the first visit of the other three members of Dornford's little dinner party, and by some fatality, not unconnected with him who took the tickets, they were seated two by two; young Croom with Clare in the middle of the tenth row, Dornford and Dinny in returned stalls at the end of the third. . . .

"Penny for your thoughts, Miss Cherrell?"

"I was thinking how the English face has changed since 1900."

"It's the hair. Faces in pictures a hundred to a hundred and fifty years ago are much more like ours."

"Drooping moustaches and chignons do hide expression, but was there the expression?"

"You don't think the Victorians had as much character?"

"Probably more, but surely they suppressed it; even in their dresses, always more stuff than was needed; frock coats, high collars, cravats, bustles, button boots."

"The leg *was* on their nerves, but the neck wasn't."

"I give you the women's necks. But look at their furniture: tassels, fringes, antimacassars, chandeliers, enormous sideboards. They *did* play hide-and-seek with the soul, Mr. Dornford."

"And every now and then it popped out, like little Edward after unclothing himself under his mother's dining table at Windsor."

"He never did anything quite so perfect again."

"I don't know. He was another Restoration in a mild way. Big opening of floodgates under him." . . .

"He *has* sailed, hasn't he, Clare?"

"Yes, he's sailed, all right. Look at Dornford! He's fallen for Dinny completely. I wish she'd take to him."

"Why shouldn't she?"

"My dear young man, Dinny's been in very deep waters. She's in them even now."

"I don't know anyone I'd like better for a sister-in-law."

"Don't you wish you may get her."

"God! Yes! Don't I!"

"What do *you* think of Dornford, Tony?"

"Awfully decent, not a bit dry."

"If he were a doctor he'd have a wonderful bedside manner. He's a Catholic."

"Wasn't that against him in the election?"

"It would have been, but his opponent was an atheist, so they cried quits."

"Terrible humbug, politics."

"But rather fun."

"Still Dornford won that Bar point-to-point—he must have guts."

"Lots. I should say he'd face anything in his quiet way. I'm quite fond of him."

"Oh!"

"No intention to incite you, Tony."

"This is like being on board ship, sitting side by side, and—stymied. Come out for a cigarette."

"People are coming back. Prepare yourself to point me the moral of the next act. At present I don't see any."

"Wait!" . . .

Dinny drew in her breath.

"That's terrible. I can just remember the *Titanic*. Awful, the waste in the world!"

"You're right."

"Waste of life, and waste of love."

"Have *you* come up against much waste?"

"Yes."

"You don't care to talk about it?"

"No."

"I don't believe that your sister's going to be wasted. She's too vivid."

"Yes, but her head's in Chancery."

"She'll duck from under."

"I can't bear to think of her life being spoiled. Isn't there some legal dodge, Mr. Dornford; without publicity, I mean?"

"If he would give cause, there need be very little of that."

"He won't. He's feeling vindictive."

"I see. Then I'm afraid there's nothing for it but to wait. These things generally disentangle themselves. Catholics are not supposed to believe in divorce. But if *you* feel this is a case for one——"

"Clare's only twenty-four. She can't live alone the rest of her life."

"Were *you* thinking of doing that?"

"I! That's different."

"Yes, you're very unlike, but to have you wasted would be far worse. Just as much worse as wasting a lovely day in winter is than wasting one in summer."

"The curtain's going up." . . .

* * *

"I wonder," muttered Clare: "It didn't look to me as if their love would have lasted long. They were eating each other like sugar."

"My God, if you and I on that boat had been—"

"You're very young, Tony."

"Two years older than you."

"And about ten years younger."

"Don't you really believe in love lasting, Clare?"

"Not passion. And after that generally the deluge. Only with those two on the *Titanic* it came too soon. A *cold* sea! Ugh!"

"Let me pull your cloak up."

"I don't believe I like this show too frightfully, Tony. It digs into you, and I don't want to be dug into."

"I liked it better the first time, certainly."

"Thank you!"

"It's being close to you, and not close enough. But the war part of the play's the best."

"The whole thing makes me feel I don't want to be alive."

"That's 'the satire.'"

"One half of him is mocking the other. It give me the fidgets. Too like oneself."

"I wish we'd gone to a movie, I could have held your hand."

"Dornford's looking at Dinny as if she were the Madonna of the future that he wanted to make a Madonna of the past."

"So he does, you say."

"He really has a nice face. I wonder what he'll think of the war part. 'Weigh-hey! Up she rises!'" . . .

Dinny sat with closed eyes, acutely feeling the remains of moisture on her cheeks.

"But she never would have done that," she said, huskily, "not waved a flag and cheered. Never! She might have mixed in the crowd, but never that!"

"No, that's a stage touch. Pity! But a jolly good act. Really good!"

"Those poor gay raddled singing girls, getting more and more wretched and raddled, and that 'Tipperary' whistling! The war must have been *awful!*"

"One got sort of exalted."

"Did that feeling last?"

"In a way. Does that seem rather horrible to you?"

"I never can judge what people ought to feel. I've heard my brother say something of the kind."

"It wasn't the 'Into Battle' feeling either—I'm not the fighting man. It's a cliché to say it was the biggest thing that will ever be in one's life."

"You still feel that?"

"It has been up to now. But—! I must tell you while I've a chance—I'm in love with you, Dinny. I know nothing about you, you know nothing about me. That doesn't make any difference. I fell in love with you at once; it's been getting deeper ever since. I don't expect you to say anything, but you might think about it now and then. . . ."

Clare shrugged her shoulders.

"Did people really go on like that at the Armistice? Tony! Did people——?"

"What?"

"Really go on like that?"

"I don't know."

"Where were you?"

"At Wellington, my first term. My father was killed in the war."

"Oh! I suppose mine might have been, and my brother. But even then! Dinny says my mother cried when the Armistice came."

"So did mine, I believe."

"The bit I liked best was that between the son and the girl. But the whole thing makes you feel too much. Take me out, I want a cigarette. No, we'd better not. One always meets people."

"Damn!"

"Coming here with you was the limit. I've promised solemnly not to give offence for a whole year. Oh! cheer up! You'll see lots of me. . . ."

"'Greatness, and dignity, and peace,'" murmured Dinny, standing up, "and the greatest of these is 'dignity.'"

"The hardest to come by, anyway."

"That girl singing in the night club, and the jazzed sky! Thank you awfully, Mr. Dornford. I shan't forget this play easily."

"Nor what I said to you?"

"It was very sweet of you, but the aloe only blooms once in a hundred years."

"I can wait. It's been a wonderful evening for me."

"Those two!"

"We'll pick them up in the hall."

"Do you think England ever had greatness, and dignity and peace?"

"No."

"But 'There's a green hill far away, without a city wall.' Thank you— I've had this cloak three years."

"Charming it is!"

"I suppose most of these people will go on to night clubs now."

"Not five per cent."

"I should like a sniff of home air to-night, and a long look at the stars. . . ."

Clare turned her head.

"Don't, Tony!"

"How then?"

"You've been with me all the evening."

"If only I could take you home!"

"You can't, my dear. Squeeze my little finger, and pull yourself together."

"Clare!"

"Look! They're just in front—now vanish! Get a good long drink at the Club and dream of horses. There! Was that close enough? Good-night, dear Tony!"

"God! Good-night!"

CHAPTER 15

TIME HAS BEEN compared with a stream, but it differs—you cannot cross it, grey and even-flowing, wide as the world itself, having neither ford nor bridge; and though, according to philosophers, it may flow both up and down, the calendar as yet follows it but one way.

November, then, became December, but December did not become November. Except for a cold snap or two the weather remained mild. Unemployment decreased; the adverse balance of trade increased; seven foxes escaped for every one killed; the papers fluttered from the storms in their tea-cups; a great deal of income tax was paid; still more was not; the question: "Why has prosperity gone to pot?" continued to bewilder every mind; the pound went up, the pound went down. In short, time flowed, but the conundrum of existence remained unsolved.

At Condaford the bakery scheme was dropped. Every penny that could be raised was to be put into pigs, poultry and potatoes. Sir Lawrence and Michael were now deep in the 'Three P. Plan,' and Dinny had become infected. She and the General spent all their days preparing for the millennium which would follow its adoption. Eustace Dornford had expressed his adherence to the proposition. Figures had been prepared to show that in ten years one hundred millions a year could be knocked off Britain's purchasing bill by graduated prohibition of the import of these three articles of food, without increasing the cost of living. With a little organisation, a fractional change in the nature of the Briton, and the increase of wheat offals, the thing was as good as done. In the meantime, the General borrowed slightly on his life assurance policy and paid his taxes.

The new Member, visiting his constituency, spent Christmas at Condaford, talking almost exclusively of pigs, instinct telling him that they were just then the surest line of approach to Dinny's heart. Clare, too, spent Christmas at home. How, apart from secretarial duties, she had spent the intervening time, was tacitly assumed. No letter had come from Jerry Corven, but it was known from the papers that he was back in Ceylon. During the days between Christmas and the New Year the inhabitable part of the old house was full: Hilary, his wife, and their daughter Monica; Adrian and Diana, with Sheila and Ronald now recovered from the measles—no such family gathering had been held for years. Even Sir

Lionel and Lady Alison drove down for lunch on New Year's Eve. With such an overwhelming Conservative majority it was felt that 1932 would be important. Dinny was run off her legs. She gave no sign of it, but had less an air of living in the past. So much was she the party's life and soul that no one could have told she had any of her own. Dornford gazed at her in speculation. What was behind that untiring cheerful selflessness? He went so far as to ask of Adrian, who seemed to be her favourite.

"This house wouldn't work without your niece, Mr. Cherrell."

"It wouldn't. Dinny's a wonder."

"Doesn't she ever think of herself?"

Adrian looked at him sideways. The pale-brown, rather hollow-cheeked face, with its dark hair, and hazel eyes, was sympathetic; for a lawyer and a politician, he looked sensitive. Inclined, however, to a sheep-dog attitude where Dinny was concerned, he answered with caution:

"Why no, no more than reason; indeed, not so much."

"She looks to me sometimes as if she'd been through something pretty bad."

Adrian shrugged. "She's twenty-seven."

"Would you mind awfully telling me what it was? This isn't curiosity. I'm—well, I'm in love with her, and terrified of butting in and hurting her through ignorance."

Adrian took a long gurgling pull at his pipe.

"If you're in dead earnest——"

"Absolutely dead earnest."

"It might save her a pang or two. She was terribly in love, the year before last, and it came to a tragic end."

"Death?"

"No. I can't tell you the exact story, but the man had done something that placed him, in a sense—or at all events he thought so—outside the pale; and he put an end to their engagement rather than involve Dinny, and went off to the far East. It was a complete cut. Dinny has never spoken of it since, but I'm afraid she'll never forget."

"I see. Thank you very much. You've done me a great service."

"Sorry if it's hurt," murmured Adrian; "but better, perhaps, to have one's eyes open."

"Much."

Resuming the tune on his pipe, Adrian stole several glances at his silent neighbour. That averted face wore an expression not exactly dashed or sad, but as if contending deeply with the future. 'He's the nearest approach,' he thought, 'to what I should like for her—sensitive, quiet and plucky. But things are always so damnably perverse!'

"She's very different from her sister," he said at last.

Dornford smiled.

"Ancient and modern."

"Clare's a pretty creature, though."

"Oh, yes, and lots of qualities."

"They've both got grit. How does she do her work?"

"Very well; quick in the uptak', good memory, heaps of *savoir faire*."

"Pity she's in such a position. I don't know why things went wrong, and I don't see how they can come right."

"I've never met Corven."

"Quite nice to meet; but, by the look of him, a streak of cruelty."

"Dinny says he's vindictive."

Adrian nodded. "I should think so. And that's bad when it comes to divorce. But I hope it won't—always a dirty business, and probably the wrong person tarred. I don't remember a divorce in our family."

"Nor in mine, but we're Catholics."

"Judging by your experience in the Courts, should you say English morality is going downhill?"

"No. On the upgrade, if anything."

"But surely the standard is slacker?"

"People are franker, not quite the same thing."

"You lawyers and judges, at all events," said Adrian, "are exceptionally moral men."

"Oh! Where did you get that from?"

"The papers."

Dornford laughed.

"Well!" said Adrian, rising. "Let's have a game of billiards. . . ."

On the Monday after New Year's Day the party broke up. In the afternoon Dinny lay down on her bed and went to sleep. The grey light failed and darkness filled her room. She dreamed she was on the bank of a river. Wilfrid was holding her hand, pointing to the far side, and saying: " 'One more river, one more river to cross!' " Hand in hand they went down the bank. In the water all became dark! She lost touch of his hand and cried out in terror. Losing her foothold, she drifted, reaching her hands this way and that, and his voice further and further away, " 'One more river—one more river,' " died to a sigh. She awoke agonised. Through the window opposite was the dark sky, the elm tree brushing at the stars—no sound, no scent, no colour. And she lay quite still, drawing deep breaths to get the better of her anguish. It was long since she had felt Wilfrid so close to her, or been so poignantly bereaved once more.

She got up, and, having bathed her face in cold water, stood at her window looking into the starry dark, still shuddering a little from the vivid misery of her dream. 'One more river!'

Some one tapped on the door.

"Yes?"

"It's old Mrs. Purdy, Miss Dinny. They say she's going fast. The doctor's there, but——"

"Betty! Does Mother know?"

"Yes, miss, she's going over."

"No! I'll go. Stop her, Annie!"

"Yes, miss. It's a seizure—nurse sent over to say they can't do nothing. Will you have the light on, miss?"

"Yes, turn it up."

Thank God they had managed to put the electric light in, at last!

"Get me this little flask filled with brandy, and put my rubber boots in the hall. I shan't be two minutes coming down."

"Yes, miss."

Slipping on a jersey and cap, and catching up her moleskin fur coat, she ran downstairs, stopping for a second at her mother's door to say she was going. Putting on her rubber boots in the hall, and taking the filled flask, she went out. It was groping dark, but not cold for January. The lane was slithery under foot, and, since she had no torch, the half mile took her nearly a quarter of an hour. The doctor's car, with its lights on, stood outside the cottage. Unlatching the door, Dinny went into the ground floor room. There was a fire burning, and one candle alight, but the crowded homely space was deserted by all but the goldfinch in its large cage. She opened the thin door that shut the stairs off, and went up. Pushing the feeble top door gently, she stood looking. A lamp was burning on the window-sill opposite, and the low, sagging-ceilinged room had a shadowy radiance. At the foot of the double bed were the doctor and village nurse, talking in low tones. In the window corner Dinny could see the little old husband crouched on a chair, with his hands on his knees and his crumpled, cherry-cheeked face trembling and jerking slightly. The old cottage woman lay humped in the old bed; her face was waxen, and seemed to Dinny to have lost already all its wrinkles. A faint stertorous breathing came from her lips. The eyes were not quite closed, but surely were not seeing.

The doctor crossed to the door.

"Opiate," he said. "I don't think she'll recover consciousness. Just as well for the poor old soul! If she does, nurse has another to give her at once. There's nothing to be done but ease the end."

"I shall stay," said Dinny.

The doctor took her hand.

"Happy release. Don't fret, my dear."

"Poor old Benjy!" whispered Dinny, pointing.

The doctor pressed her hand, and went down the stairs.

Dinny entered the room; the air was close and she left the door ajar.

"I'll watch, nurse, if you want to get anything."

The nurse nodded. In her neat dark blue dress and bonnet she looked, but for a little frown, almost inhumanly impassive. They stood side by side gazing at the old woman's waxen face.

"Not many like her," whispered the nurse suddenly. "I'm going to get some things I'll want—back under the half hour. Sit down, Miss Cherrell, don't tire yourself."

When she had gone Dinny turned and went up to the old husband in the corner.

"Benjy."

He wobbled his pippin head, rubbing his hands on his knees. Words of comfort refused to come to Dinny. Just touching his shoulder, she went back to the bed and drew up the one hard wooden chair. She sat, silently watching old Betty's lips, whence issued that faintly stertorous breathing. It seemed to her as if the spirit of a far-off age were dying. There might be other people as old still alive in the village, but they weren't like old Betty, with her simple sense and thrifty order, her Bible reading and love of gentry, her pride in her eighty-three years, in the teeth that she ought long since to have parted from, and in her record; with her shrewdness and her way of treating her old husband as if he were her rather difficult son. Poor old Benjy—he was not her equal by any manner of means, but what he would do alone one couldn't think. Perhaps one of his granddaughters would find room for him. Those two had brought up seven children in the old days when a shilling fortunately went as far as three now, and the village was full of their progeny; but how would they like little old Benjy, still argumentative and fond of a grumble and a glass, ensconced by their more modern hearths? Well, a nook would turn up for him somewhere. He could never live on here, alone. Two old-age pensions for two old people made just the difference as against one for one.

'How I wish I had money!' she thought. He would not want the goldfinch, anyway. She would take that and free and feed it in the old greenhouse till it got used to its wings, and then let it go.

The old man cleared his throat in his dim corner. Dinny started and leaned forward. Absorbed in her thoughts, she had not noticed how faint the breathing had become. The pale lips of the old woman were nearly closed now, the wrinkled lids almost fast over the unseeing eyes. No noise was coming from the bed. For a few minutes she sat looking, listening, then passed round to the side and leaned over.

Gone? As if in answer the eyelids flickered; the faintest imaginable smile appeared on the lips, and then, suddenly as a blown-out flame is dark, all was lifeless. Dinny held her breath. It was the first human death she had seen. Her eyes, glued to the old waxen face, saw it settle into its mask of release, watched it being embalmed in that still dignity which marks death off from life. With her finger she smoothed the eyelids.

Death! At its quietest and least harrowing, but yet—death! The old, the universal anodyne; the common lot! In this bed where she had lain nightly for over fifty years under the low sagged ceiling, a great little old lady had passed. Of what was called 'birth,' of position, wealth and power, she had none. No plumbing had come her way, no learning and no fashion. She had borne children, nursed, fed and washed them, sewn, cooked and swept, eaten little, travelled not at all in all her years, suffered much pain, never known the ease of superfluity; but her back had been straight, her ways straight, her eyes quiet and her manners gentle. If she were not the 'great lady,' who was? Dinny stood, with her head bowed, feeling this to the very marrow of her soul. Old Benjy in that dim corner cleared his throat again. She started, and, trembling a little, went over to him.

"Go and look at her, Benjy; she's asleep."

She put her hand under his elbow to help the action of his stiffened knees. At his full height he was only up to her shoulder, a little dried-up pippin of a man. She kept at his side, moving across the room.

Together they looked down at the forehead and cheeks, slowly un-creasing in the queer beauty of death. The little old husband's face went crimson and puffy, like that of a child who has lost its doll; he said in a sort of angered squeak:

"Eh! She'm not asleep. She'm gone. She won't never speak agen. Look! She an't Mother no more! Where's that nurse? She didn' ought to 'ave left 'er——"

"H'ssh! Benjy!"

"But she'm dead. What'll I do?"

He turned his withered apple face up to Dinny, and there came from him an unwashed odour, as of grief and snuff and old potatoes.

"Can't stop 'ere," he said, "with Mother like that. 'Tain't nateral."

"No; go downstairs and smoke your pipe, and tell nurse when she comes."

"Tell 'er; I'll tell 'er—shouden never 'ave left 'er. Oh, dear! Oh, dear! Oh, dear!"

Putting her hand on his shoulders, Dinny guided him to the stairway, and watched him stumbling and groping and grieving his way down. Then she went back to the bed. The smoothed-out face had an uncanny attraction for her. With every minute that passed it seemed the more to proclaim superiority. Almost triumphant it was, as she gazed, in its slow, sweet relaxation after age and pain; character revealed in the mould of that brief interval between torturing life and corrupting death. 'Good as gold!' Those were the words they should grave on the humble stone they would put over her. Wherever she was now, or whether, indeed, she was anywhere, did not matter. She had done her bit. Betty!

She was still standing there gazing when the nurse came back.

CHAPTER 16

SINCE HER HUSBAND's departure Clare had met young Croom constantly, but always at the stipulated arm's-length. Love had made him unsociable, and to be conspicuously in his company was unwise, so she did not make him known to her friends; they met where they could eat cheaply, see films, or simply walk. To her rooms she had not invited him again, nor had he asked to come. His behaviour, indeed, was exemplary, except when he fell into tense and painful silences, or gazed at her till her hands itched to shake him. He seemed to have paid several visits to Jack Muskham's stud farm, and to be spending hours over books which debated whether the excellence of 'Eclipse' was due to the Lister Turk, rather than to the Darley Arabian, and whether it were preferable to breed-in to Blacklock with St. Simon on Speculum or with Speculum on St. Simon.

When she returned from Condaford after the New Year, she had not heard from him for five consecutive days, so that he was bulking more largely in her thoughts.

"DEAR TONY," she wrote him at The Coffee House:
"Where and how are you? I am back. Very happy New Year!
                                        "Yours always,
                                                    "CLARE."

The answer did not come for three days, during which she felt at first huffy, then anxious, and finally a little scared. It was indited from the inn at Bablock Hythe:

"DARLING CLARE,
"I was ever so relieved to get your note, because I'd determined not to write until I heard from you. Nothing's further from my thoughts than to bore you with myself, and sometimes I don't know whether I am or not. So far as a person can be who is not seeing you, I'm all right; I'm over-looking the fitting up of the boxes for those mares. They (the boxes) will be prime. The difficulty is going to be acclimatisation; it's supposed to be mild here, and the pasture looks as if it would be tip-top. This part of the world is quite pretty, especially the river. Thank God the inn's cheap, and I can live indefinitely on eggs and bacon. Jack Muskham has been brick

enough to start my salary from the New Year, so I'm thinking of laying out my remaining sixty odd pounds on Stapylton's old two-seater. He's just off back to India. Once I'm down here it'll be vital to have a car if I'm to see anything of you, without which life won't be worth living. I hope you had a splendid time at Condaford. Do you know I haven't seen you for sixteen days, and am absolutely starving. I'll be up on Saturday afternoon. Where can I meet you?

> "Your ever devoted
>
> "TONY."

Clare read this letter on the sofa in her room, frowning a little as she opened, smiling a little as she finished it.

Poor dear Tony! Grabbing a telegraph form, she wrote:

> "Come to tea Melton Mews.—C."

and despatched it on her way to the Temple.

The importance attaching to the meeting of two young people depends on the importance which others attach to their not meeting. Tony Croom approached Melton Mews without thinking of any one but Clare, and failed to observe a shortish man in horn-rimmed spectacles, black boots and a claret-coloured tie, who looked like the secretary of a learned society. Unobtrusive and unobserved this individual had already travelled with him from Bablock Hythe to Paddington, from Paddington, to The Coffee House, from The Coffee House to the corner of Melton Mews; had watched him enter No. 2, made an entry in a pocket-book, and with an evening paper in his hand was now waiting for him to come out again. With touching fidelity he read no news, keeping his prominent glance on the peacock blue door, prepared at any moment to close himself like an umbrella and vanish into the street-scape. And while he waited (which was his normal occupation) he thought, like other citizens, of the price of living, of the cup of tea which he would like, of his small daughter and her collection of foreign stamps, and of whether he would now have to pay income tax. His imagination dwelled, also, on the curves of a young woman at the tobacconist's where he obtained his 'gaspers.' His name was Chayne, and he made his living out of a remarkable memory for faces, inexhaustible patience, careful entries in his pocket-book, the faculty of self-obliteration, and that fortunate resemblance to the secretaries of learned societies. He was, indeed, employed by the Polteed Agency, who made their living by knowing more than was good for those about whom they knew it. Having received his instruction on the day Clare returned to London, he had already been five days 'on the job,' and no one knew it except his employer and himself. Spying on other people being, according to the books he read, the chief occupation of the people of these islands, it had never occurred to him to look down on a profession conscientiously pursued for seventeen years. He took a pride in his work, and knew himself for a capable 'sleuth.' Though somewhat increasingly troubled in the bronchial regions owing to the draughts he had so often to stand in, he could not by now imagine any other way of passing his time, or any, on the whole, more knowing method of gaining a livelihood. Young Croom's address he had obtained by the simple expedient of waiting behind Clare while she sent her telegram; but having just failed to read the message itself, he had started at once for Bablock Hythe, since when until now he had experienced no difficulty. Shifting his position from time to time at the end of the street, he entered the Mews itself when it became dark. At half past five the peacock door was opened and the two young people emerged. They walked, and Mr. Chayne walked behind them. They walked fast, and Mr. Chayne, with an acquired sense of rhythm, at exactly the same pace. He soon perceived that they were merely going to where he had twice followed Lady Corven already—the Temple. And this gave him a sense of comfort, because of the cup of tea he pined for. Picking his way in and out among the backs of people large enough to screen him, he watched them enter Middle Temple Lane, and part at Harcourt Buildings. Having noted that Lady Corven went in, and that the young man began parading slowly between the entrance and the Embankment, he looked at his watch, doubled back into the Strand, and bolted into an A.B.C. with the words "Cup of tea and Bath bun, miss, please." While waiting for these he made a prolonged entry in his pocket-book. Then, blowing on his tea, he drank it from the saucer, ate half the bun, concealed the other half in his hand, paid, and re-entered the Strand. He had just finished the bun when he regained the entrance to the Lane. The young man was still parading slowly. Mr. Chayne waited for his back view and assuming the air of a belated solicitor's clerk, bolted down past the entrance to Harcourt Buildings into the Inner Temple. There, in a doorway, he scrutinised names until Clare came out. Rejoined by young Croom, she walked up towards the Strand, and Mr. Chayne walked too. When, shortly, they took tickets for a cinema, he also took a ticket and entered the row behind. Accustomed to the shadowing of people on their guard, the open innocence they were displaying excited in him a slightly amused if not contemptuous compassion. 'Regular babes in the wood'—they seemed to him. He could not tell whether their feet were touching, and passed behind to note the position of their hands. It seemed satisfactory, and he took an empty seat nearer to the gangway. Sure of them now for a couple of hours, he settled down to smoke, feel warm, and enjoy the film. It was one of sport and travel in Africa, where the two principals were always in positions of danger, recorded by the camera of some one who must surely have been in a position of still greater danger. Mr. Chayne listened to their manly American voices saying to each other: "Gee! He's on us!" with an interest which never prevented his knowing that his two young people were listening too. When the lights went up he could see their profiles. 'We're all young at times,' he thought, and his imagination dwelled more intensively on the young lady at his tobacconist's. They looked so settled-in that he took the opportunity to slip out for a moment. It might not occur again for a long time. In his opinion one of the chief defects in detective stories—for he was given to busmen's holidays—was the authors made their 'sleuths' like unto the angels, watching for days without, so to speak, taking their eye off the ball. It was not so in real life.

He returned to a seat almost behind his young couple on the other side just before the lights went down. One of his favourite stars was now to be featured, and, sure that she would be placed in situations which would enable him to enjoy her to the full, he put a peppermint lozenge in his mouth and leaned back with a sigh. He had not had an evening watch so pleasant for a long time. It was not always 'beer and skittles' at this season of the year; a 'proper chilly job sometimes—no error.'

After ten minutes, during which his star had barely got into her evening clothes, his couple rose.

"Can't stand any more of her voice," he heard Lady Corven say; and the young man answering: "Ghastly!"

Wounded and surprised, Mr. Chayne waited for them to pass through the curtains before, with a profound sigh, he followed. In the Strand they stood debating, then walked again, but only into a restaurant across the street. Here, buying himself another paper at the door, he saw them going up the stairs. Would it be a private room? He ascended the stairs cautiously. No, it was the gallery! There they were, nicely screened by the pillars, four tables in!

Descending to the lavatory, Mr. Chayne changed his horn spectacles to pince-nez and his claret-coloured tie to a rather floppy bow of black and white. This was a device which had often served him in good stead. You put on a tie of a conspicuous colour, then changed it to a quieter one of a different shape. A conspicuous tie had the special faculty of distracting attention from a face. You became 'that man with the awful tie!' and when you no longer wore the tie, you were to all intents some one else. Going up again to a table which commanded a view, he ordered himself a mixed grill and pint of stout. They were likely to be some two hours over their meal, so he assumed a literary air, taking out a pouch to roll himself a cigarette and inviting the waiter to give him a light for it. Having in this way established a claim to a life of his own, he read his paper like any gentleman at large and examined the mural paintings. They were warm and glowing; large landscapes with blue skies, seas, palms, and villas, suggestive of pleasure in a way that appealed to him strongly. He had never been further than Boulogne and, so far as he could see, never would. Five hundred pounds, a lady, a suite in the sun, and gaming tables handy was not unnaturally his idea of heaven; but, alas, as unattainable. He made no song about it, but, when confronted with allurements like these on the wall, he could not help hankering. It had often struck him as ironical that the people he watched into the Divorce Court so often went to Paradise and stayed there until their cases had blown over and they could marry and come to earth again. Living in Finchley, with the sun once a fortnight and an income averaging perhaps five hundred a year, the vein of poetry in him was dammed almost at source; and it was in some sort a relief to let his imagination play around the lives of those whom he watched. That young couple over there, 'good-lookers' both of them, would go back together in a taxi and as likely as not he'd have to wait hours for the young man to come away. The mixed grill was put before him, and he added a little red pepper in view of his probable future. This bit of watching, however, and perhaps another one or two, ought to do the trick; and on the whole 'easy money.' Slowly savouring each mouthful so that it might nourish him, and blowing the froth off his stout with the skill of a connoisseur, he watched them bending forward to talk across the table. What they were eating he could not see. To have followed their meal in detail would have given him some indication of their states of mind. Food and love! After this grill he would have cheese and coffee, and put them down to 'expenses.'

He had eaten every crumb, extracted all the information from his paper, exhausted his imagination on the mural paintings, 'placed' the scattered diners, paid his bill, and smoked three 'gaspers' before his quarry rose. He was into his overcoat and outside the entrance before they had even reached the stairs. Noting three taxis within hail, he bent his attention on the hoardings of an adjoining theatre; till he saw the porter beckon one of them, then, walking into the middle of the Strand, he took the one behind it.

"Wait till that cab starts and follow it," he said to the driver; "not too close when it stops."

Taking his seat, he looked at his watch and made an entry in his pocket-book. Having before now followed a wrong cab at some expense, he kept his eyes glued on the taxi's number, which he had noted in his book. The traffic was but thin at this hour before the theatres rose, and the procession simplicity itself. The followed cab stopped at the corner of the Mews. Mr. Chayne tapped the glass and fell back on the seat. Through the window he saw them get out and the young man paying. They walked down the Mews. Mr. Chayne also paid and followed to the corner. They had reached the peacock door and stood there, talking. Then Lady Corven put her key into the lock and opened the door, the young man, glancing this way and that, followed her in. Mr. Chayne experienced a sensation as mixed as his grill. It was, of course, exactly what he had hoped for and expected. At the same time it meant loitering about in the cold for goodness knew how long. He turned up his coat collar and looked for a convenient doorway. A thousand pities that he could not wait, say half an hour, and just walk in. The Courts were very particular nowadays about conclusive evidence. He had something of the feeling that a 'sportsman' has seeing a fox go to ground and not a spade within five miles. He stood for a few minutes, reading over the entries in his pocket-book under the lamp, and making a final note; then walked to the doorway he had selected and stood there. In half an hour or so the cars would be coming back from the theatre, and he would have to be on the move to escape attention. There was a light in the upstairs window, but in itself, of course, that was not evidence. Too bad! Twelve shillings the return ticket, ten and six the night down there, cabs seven and six; Cinema three and six, dinner six bob—he wouldn't charge the tea—thirty-nine and six—say two pounds! Mr. Chayne shook his head, put a peppermint lozenge in his mouth, and changed his feet. That corn of his was beginning to shoot a bit! He thought of pleasant things: Broadstairs, his small daughter's black hair, oyster patties, his favourite 'star' in little but a corset belt, and his own nightcap of hot whisky and lemon. All to small purpose; for he was waiting and waiting on feet that ached, and without any confidence that he was collecting anything of real value. The Courts, indeed, had got into such a habit of expecting the parties to be 'called with a cup of tea' that anything short of it was looked upon as suspect. He took out his watch again. He had been here over half an hour. And here came the first car! He must get out of the Mews! He withdrew to its far end. And then, almost before he had time to turn his back, there came the young man with his hands thrust deep into his pockets, and his shoulders, hunched, hurrying away. Heaving a sigh of relief, Mr. Chayne noted in his pocket-book: "Mr. C. left at 11:40 p.m."; and walked towards his Finchley bus!

CHAPTER 17

THOUGH DINNY had no expert knowledge of pictures, she had, with Wilfrid, made an intensive examination of such as were on permanent show in London. She had also enjoyed extremely the Italian Exhibition of 1930. It was, therefore, natural to accept her Uncle Adrian's invitation to accompany him to the French Exhibition of 1932. After a syncopated lunch in Piccadilly they passed through the turnstile at one o'clock on January the 22nd, and took stand before the Primitives. Quite a number of people were emulating their attempt to avoid the crowd, so that their progress was slow, and it was an hour before they had reached the Watteaus.

"'Gilles,'" said Adrian, resting one leg, "that strikes me as about the best picture yet, Dinny. It's queer—when a genre painter of the decorative school gets hold of a subject or a type that grips him, how thoroughly he'll stir you up. Look at the Pierrot's face—what a brooding, fateful, hiding-up expression! There's the public performer, with the private life, incarnate!"

Dinny remained silent.

"Well, young woman?"

"I was wondering whether art was so conscious. Don't you think he just wanted to paint that white dress, and his model did the rest? It's a marvellous expression, but perhaps he had it. People do."

Adrian noted her face with the tail of his eye. Yes! People did. Paint her in repose, render her when she wasn't aware of how she was looking, of keeping her end up, or whatever you might call it, and wouldn't you have a face that stirred you with all that lay behind it? Art was unsatisfactory. When it gave you the spirit, distilled the essence, it didn't seem real; and when it gave you the gross, cross-currented, contradictory surface, it didn't seem worth while. Attitudes, fleeting expressions, tricks of light—all by way of being 'real,' and nothing revealed! He said suddenly:

"Great books and portraits are so dashed rare, because artists won't high-light the essential, or if they do, they overdo it."

"I don't see how that applies to this picture, Uncle. It's not a portrait, it's a dramatic moment, and a white dress."

"Perhaps! All the same, if I could paint you, Dinny, as you truly are, people would say you weren't real."

"How fortunate!"

"Most people can't even imagine you."

"Forgive impertinence, Uncle, but—can *you?*"

Adrian wrinkled up his goatee.

"I like to think so."

"Oh! Look! There's the Boucher Pompadour!"

After two minutes in front of its expanse Adrian continued:

"Well, for a man who preferred it nude, he could paint what covers the female body pretty well, couldn't he?"

"Maintenon and Pompadour. I always get them mixed."

"The Maintenon wore blue stockings, and ministered to Louis the XIVth."

"Oh, yes! Let's go straight from here to the Manets, Uncle."

"Why?"

"I don't think I shall last much longer."

Adrian, glancing round, suddenly saw why. In front of the Gilles were standing Clare and a young man whom he did not know. He put his arm through Dinny's and they passed into the next room but one.

"I noticed your discretion," he murmured, in front of the 'Boy Blowing Bubbles.' "Is that young man a snake in the grass, or a worm in the bud, or——?"

"A very nice boy."

"What's his name?"

"Tony Croom."

"Oh! the young man on the ship? Does Clare see much of him?"

"I don't ask her, Uncle. She is guaranteed to behave for a year;" and, at the cock of Adrian's eyebrow, added: "She promised Aunt Em."

"And after the year?"

"I don't know, nor does she. Aren't these Manets good."

They passed slowly through the room and came to the last.

"To think that Gauguin struck me as the cream of eccentricity in 1910," murmured Adrian; "it shows how things move. I went to that post-impressionist exhibition straight from looking at the Chinese pictures in the B. M. Cézanne, Matisse, Gauguin, Van Gogh—the last word then, hoary now. Gauguin certainly *is* a colourist. But give me the Chinese still. I fear I'm fundamentally of the old order, Dinny."

"I can see these are good—most of them, but I couldn't live with them."

"The French have their uses; no other country can show you the transitions of art so clearly. From the Primitives to Clouet, from Clouet to Poussin and Claude, from them to Watteau and his school, thence to Boucher and Greuze, on to Ingres and Delacroix, to the Barbizon lot, to the Impressionists, to the Post-Impressionists; and always some bloke—Chardin, Lépicié, Fragonard, Manet, Degas, Monet, Cézanne—breaking away or breaking through towards the next."

"Has there ever before been such a violent break as just lately?"

"There's never before been such a violent break in the way people look at life; nor such complete confusion in the minds of artists as to what they exist for."

"And what *do* they exist for, Uncle?"

"To give pleasure or reveal truth, or both."

"I can't imagine myself enjoying what they enjoy, and—what is truth?" Adrian turned up his thumbs.

"Dinny, I'm tired as a dog. Let's slip out."

Dinny saw her sister and young Croom passing through the archway. She was not sure whether Clare had noticed them, and young Croom was clearly noticing nothing but Clare. She followed Adrian out, in her turn admiring his discretion. But neither of them would admit uneasiness. With whom one went about was now so entirely one's own business.

They had walked up the Burlington Arcade, when Adrian was suddenly startled by the pallor of her face.

"What's the matter, Dinny? You look like a ghost!"

"If you don't mind, Uncle, I'd like a cup of coffee."

"There's a place in Bond Street." Scared by the bloodlessness of her smiling lips, he held her arm firmly till they were seated at a little table round the corner.

"Two coffees—extra strong," said Adrian, and with that instinctive consideration which caused women and children to confide in him, he made no attempt to gain her confidence.

"Nothing so tiring as picture-gazing. I'm sorry to emulate Em, and suspect you of not eating enough, my dear. That sort of sparrow-pecking we did before going in doesn't really count." But colour had come back to her lips.

"I'm very tough, Uncle; but food *is* rather a bore."

"You and I must go a little tour in France. Their grub can move one's senses if their pictures can't move one's spirit."

"Did you feel *that?*"

"Compared with the Italian—emphatically. It's all so beautifully thought out. They make their pictures like watches. Unreasonable to ask for more, and yet—perhaps, fundamentally unpoetic. And that reminds me, Dinny, I do hope Clare can be kept out of the Divorce Court, for of all unpoetic places that is IT."

Dinny shook her head.

"I'd rather she got it over. I even think she was wrong to promise. She's not going to change her mind about Jerry. She'll be like a bird with one leg. Besides, who thinks the worse of you nowadays!"

Adrian moved uncomfortably.

"I dislike the thought of those hard-boiled fellows playing battle-dore with my kith and kin. If they were like Dornford—but they aren't. Seen anything more of him?"

"He was down with us for one night when he had to speak."

He noticed that she spoke without 'batting an eyelid,' as the young men called it nowadays. And, soon after, they parted, Dinny assuring him that she had "come over quite well again."

He had said that she looked like a ghost; he might better have said she looked as if she had seen one. For, coming out of that Arcade, all her past in Cork Street had come fluttering like some lonely magpie towards her, beaten wings in her face and swerved away. And now, alone, she turned and walked back there. Resolutely she went to the door, climbed the stairs to Wilfrid's rooms, and rang the bell. Leaning against the window-sill on the landing, she waited with closed hands, thinking: 'I wish I had a muff!' Her hands felt so cold. In old pictures they stood with veils down and their hands in muffs, but 'the old order changeth' and she had none. She was just going away when the door was opened. Stack! In slippers! His glance, dark and prominent as ever, fell to those slippers and his demeanour seemed to stammer.

"Pardon me, miss, I was just going to change 'em."

Dinny held out her hand, and he took it with his old air, as if about to 'confess' her.

"I was passing, and thought I'd like to ask how you were."

"Fine, thank you, miss! Hope you've been keeping well, and the dog?"

"Quite well, both of us. Foch likes the country."

"Ah! Mr. Desert always thought he was a country dog."

"Have you any news?"

"Not to say news, miss. I understand from his bank that he's still in Siam. They forward his letters to their branch in Bangkok. His lordship was here not long ago, and I understood him to say that Mr. Desert was up a river somewhere."

"A river!"

"The name escapes me, something with a 'Yi' in it, and a 'sang'—was it? I believe it's very 'ot there. If I may say so, miss, you haven't much colour considering the country. I was down home in Barnstaple at Christmas, and it did me a power of good."

Dinny took his hand again.

"I'm very glad to have seen you, Stack."

"Come in, miss. You'll see I keep the room just as it was."

Dinny followed to the doorway of the sitting room.

"Exactly the same, Stack; he might almost be there."

"I like to think so, miss."

"Perhaps he is," said Dinny. "They say we have astral bodies. Thank you." She touched his arm, passed him, and went down the stairs. Her face quivered and was still, and she walked rapidly away.

A river! Her dream! 'One more river!'

In Bond Street a voice said: "Dinny!" and she turned to see Fleur.

"Whither away, my dear? Haven't seen you for an age. I've just been to the French pictures. Aren't they divine? I saw Clare there with a young man in tow. Who is he?"

"A shipmate—Tony Croom."

"More to come?"

Dinny shrugged, and, looking at her trim companion, thought: 'I wish Fleur didn't always go so straight to the point.'

"Any money?"

"No. He's got a job, but it's very slender—Mr. Muskham's Arab mares."

"Oh! Three hundred a year—five at the outside. That's no good at all. You know, really, she's making a great mistake. Jerry Corven will go far."

Dinny said drily: "Further than Clare, anyway."

"You mean it's a complete breach?"

Dinny nodded. She had never been so near disliking Fleur.

"Well, Clare's not like you. She belongs to the new order, or disorder. That's why it's a mistake. She'd have a much better time if she stuck to Jerry, nominally at least. I can't see her poor."

"She doesn't care about money," said Dinny coldly.

"Oh, nonsense! Money's only being able to do what you want to do. Clare certainly cares about that."

Dinny, who knew that this was true, said, still more coldly:

"It's no good to try and explain."

"My dear, there's nothing to explain. He's hurt her in some way, as, of course, he would. That's no reason in the long run. That perfectly lovely Renoir—the man and woman in the box. Those people lived lives of their own—together. Why shouldn't Clare?"

"Would you?"

Fleur gave a little shrug of her beautifully fitted shoulders.

"If Michael weren't such a dear. Besides—children." Again she gave that little shrug.

Dinny thawed. "You're a fraud, Fleur. You don't practise what you preach."

"My dear, my case is exceptional."

"So is everybody's."

"Well, don't let's squabble. Michael says your new Member, Dornford, is after his own heart. They're working together on pigs, poultry and potatoes. A great stunt, and the right end of the stick, for once."

"Yes, we're going all out for pigs at Condaford. Is Uncle Lawrence doing anything at Lippinghall?"

"No. He invented the plan, so he thinks he's done his bit. Michael will make him do more when he's got time. Em is screamingly funny about it. How do you like Dornford?"

Asked this question twice in one morning, Dinny looked her cousin by marriage full in the face.

"He seems to me almost a paragon."

She felt Fleur's hand slip suddenly under her arm.

"I wish you'd marry him, Dinny dear. One doesn't marry paragons, but I fancy one could 'fault' him if one tried."

It was Dinny's turn to give a little shrug, looking straight before her.

CHAPTER 18

THE THIRD of February was a day so bland and of such spring-like texture that the quickened blood demanded adventure.

This was why Tony Croom sent an early wire and set out at noon from Bablock Hythe in his old but newly-acquired two-seater. The car was not his 'dream,' but it could do fifty at the pinch he liked to give it. He took the nearest bridge, ran for Abingdon, and on past Benson to Henley. There he stopped to snatch a sandwich and 'fill up,' and again on the bridge for a glimpse at the sunlit river softly naked below the bare woods. From there on he travelled by the clock, timing himself to reach Melton Mews at two o'clock.

Clare was not ready, having only just come in. He sat in the downstairs room, now furnished with three chairs, a small table, of quaint design, cheap owing to the slump in antiques, and an amethyst-coloured chased decanter containing sloe gin. Nearly half an hour he sat there before she came down the spiral stairs in fawn-coloured tweeds and hat, with a calf-skin fur coat over her arm.

"Well, my dear! Sorry to have kept you. Where are we going?"

"I thought you might care to have a look at Bablock Hythe. Then we might come back through Oxford, have high tea there, wander about a bit among the colleges, and be back here before eleven. That do?"

"Perfect. And where will you sleep?"

"I? Oh! tool along home again. I'd be there by one."

"Poor Tony! A hard day!"

"Oh! Not two hundred and fifty miles. You won't want your fur on yet, the car doesn't open—worse luck."

They passed out at the westward mouth of the mews, narrowly missing a motorcyclist, and slid on towards the Park.

"She goes well, Tony."

"Yes, she's an easy old thing, but I always feel she might bust at any moment. Stapylton gave her a terrible doing. And I don't like a light-coloured car."

Clare leaned back, by the smile on her lips she was enjoying herself.

There was little conversation on that, the first long drive they had taken together. Both had the youthful love of speed, and young Croom got every ounce out of the car that the traffic would permit. They reached the last crossing of the river under two hours.

"Here's the inn where I dig," he said presently. "Would you like tea?"

"Not wise, my dear. When I've seen the boxes and paddocks, we'll get out of here to where you're not known."

"I must just show you the river."

Through its poplars and willow trees the white way of the river gleamed, faintly goldened by the sunken sun. They got out to look. The lamb's-tails on the hazels were very forward.

Clare twisted off a spray.

"False spring. There's a lot to come before the real spring yet."

A current of chilly air came stealing down the river, and mist could be seen rising on the meadows beyond.

"Only a ferry here, then, Tony?"

"Yes, and a short cut into Oxford the other side, about five miles. I've walked it once or twice: rather nice."

"When the blossom and meadow flowers come, it'll be jolly. Come along! Just show me where the paddocks lie, and we'll get on to Oxford."

They got back into the car.

"Won't you see the boxes?"

She shook her head.

"I'll wait till the mares are here. There's a subtle distinction between your bringing me to look at boxes, and my coming to look at mares. Are they really from Nejd?"

"So Muskham swears. I shall believe or not when I've seen the syces in charge of them."

"What colour?"

"Two bays and a chestnut."

The three paddocks sloped slightly towards the river and were sheltered by a long spinney.

"Ideal drainage and all the sun there is. The boxes are round that corner under the spinney. There's a good deal to do still; we're putting in a heater."

"It's very quiet here."

"Practically no cars on this road; motorcycles now and then—there's one now."

A cycle came sputtering towards them, stopped, wrenched round and went sputtering back.

"Noisy brutes!" murmured young Croom. "However, the mares will have had their baptism by the time they get here."

"What a change for them, poor dears!"

"They're all to be golden something: Golden Sand, Golden Houri, and Golden Hind, these three."

"I didn't know Jack Muskham was a poet."

"It stops at horses, I think."

"Really marvellous, the stillness, Tony!"

"Past five. The men have stopped work on my cottages—they're converting."

"How many rooms?"

"Four. Bedroom, sitting-room, kitchen, bathroom. But one could build on."

He looked at her intently. But her face was averted.

"Well," he said abruptly, "all aboard. We'll get to Oxford before dark."

Oxford—between lights, like all towns, at its worst—seemed to say: "Doomed to villadom, cars and modernity, I am beyond your aid."

To those two, hungry and connected with Cambridge, it offered little attraction till they were seated in the Mitre before anchovy sandwiches, boiled eggs, toast, muffins, scones, jam, and a large pot of tea. With every mouthful the romance of Oxford became apparent. This old inn, where they alone were eating, the shining fire, red curtains being drawn, the unexpected cosy solitude, prepared them to find it 'marvellous' when they should set forth. A motorcyclist in leather overalls looked in and went away. Three undergraduates chirped in the doorway, selected a table for dinner, and passed on. Now and again a waitress renewed their toast or fiddled at some table. They were deliciously alone. Not till past seven did they rise.

"Let's scout," said Clare. "We've lots of time."

The Oxford world was dining, and the streets were almost empty. They wandered at random, choosing the narrower ways and coming suddenly on colleges and long old walls. Nothing seemed modern now. The Past had them by the throat. Dark towers and old half-lit stonework; winding, built in, glimpsy passages; the sudden spacious half-lighted gloom of a chanced-on quadrangle; chiming of clocks, and the feeling of a dark and old and empty town that was yet brimming with hidden modern life and light, kept them almost speechless; and, since they had never known their way, they were at once lost.

Young Croom had entwined her arm in his, and kept his step in time to hers. Neither of them was romantic, but both just then had a feeling as if they had wandered into the maze of history.

"I rather wish," said Clare, "that I'd been up here or at Cambridge."

"One never got a nooky feeling like this at Cambridge. In the dark this is much more mediæval. There the colleges are together in a line. The 'backs' lay over anything they've got here, but the old atmosphere here is far stronger."

"I believe I could have enjoyed the past. Palfreys and buff jerkins. You'd have looked divine, Tony, in a buff jerkin, and one of those caps with a long green feather."

"The present with you is good enough for me. This is the longest time we've spent together without a break."

"Don't get soppy. We're here to look at Oxford. Which way shall we go now?"

"All the same to me," said his remote voice.

"Hurt? That's a big college! Let's go in."

"They'll be coming out of hall. Past eight; we'd better stick to the streets."

They wandered up the Cornmarket to the Broad, stood before the statues on the right, then turned into a dim square with a circular building in the centre, a church at the end and colleges for its side walls.

"This must be the heart," said Clare. "Oxford certainly has its points. Whatever they do to the outside, I don't see how they can spoil all this."

With mysterious suddenness the town had come to life; youths were passing with short gowns over their arms, flapping free, or wound round their necks. Of one of them young Croom asked where they were.

"That's the Radcliffe. This is Brasenose, and the High's down there."

"And the Mitre?"

"To your right."

"Thanks."

"Not at all."

He bent his uncapped head towards Clare and flapped on.

"Well, Tony?"

"Let's go in and have cocktails."

A motorist, well capped and leathered, standing by his cycle, looked after them intently as they went into the hotel.

After cocktails and biscuits, they came out feeling, as young Croom said: "Bright and early. We'll go back over Magdalen Bridge, through Benson, Dorchester and Henley."

"Stop on the bridge, Tony. I want to see my namesake."

The bridge lights threw splashes on the Charwell's inky stream, the loom of Magdalen lay solid on the dark, and away towards the Christchurch meadows a few lamps shone. Whence they had come the broad half-lighted strip of street ran between glimpsed grey frontages and doorways. And the little river over which they were at standstill seemed to flow with secrecy.

"The Char' they call it, don't they?"

"In the summer I shall have a punt, Clare. The upper river's even better than this."

"Will you teach me to punt?"

"Won't I!"

"Nearly ten! Well, I've enjoyed that, Tony."

He gave her a long side-glance and started the engine. It seemed as if he must always be 'moving on' with her. Would there never be a long and perfect stop?

"Sleepy, Clare?"

"Not really. That was a mighty strong cocktail. If you're tired I could drive."

"Tired? Gracious, no! I was only thinking that every mile takes me that much away from you."

In the dark a road seems longer than by day, and so different. A hundred unremembered things appear—hedges, stacks, trees, houses, turnings. Even the villages seem different. In Dorchester they stopped to make sure of the right turning; a motorcyclist passed them, and young Croom called out: "To Henley?"

"Straight on!"

They came to another village.

"This," said young Croom, "must be Nettlebed. Nothing till Henley now, and then it's thirty-five miles. We shall be up by twelve."

"Poor dear, and you've got to do all this back again."

"I shall drive like Jehu. It's a good anodyne."

Clare touched his coat cuff, and there was another silence.

They had reached a wood when he slackened suddenly. "My lights have gone!"

A motorcyclist skidded past, calling: "Your lights are out, sir!"

Young Croom stopped the engine.

"That's torn it. The battery must be used up."

Clare laughed. He got out and moved round, examining the car. "I remember this wood. It's a good five miles to Henley. We must creep on and trust to luck."

"Shall I get out and walk ahead?"

"No, it's so pitch dark. I might run over you."

After a hundred yards or so he stopped again.

"I'm off the road. I've never driven in darkness like this."

Clare laughed again.

"An adventure, my dear."

"I've got no torch. This wood goes on for a mile or two, if I remember."

"Let's try again."

A car whizzed past, and the driver shouted at them.

"Follow his lights, Tony!" But before he could start the engine the car had dipped or turned and was gone. They crept on slowly.

"Damn!" said young Croom, suddenly, "off the road again!"

"Pull her right in off the road then, and let's think. Isn't there anything at all before Henley?"

"Not a thing. Besides, recharging a battery can't be done just anywhere; but I expect it's a wire gone."

"Shall we leave the car and walk in? She'll be all right here in the wood."

"And then?" muttered young Croom. "I must be back with her by daylight. I'll tell you what; I'll walk you in to the hotel, borrow a torch and come back to her. With a torch I could get her down, or stay with her till daylight, and then come down and pick you up at the Bridge."

"Ten miles walking for you! Why not both stay with her and see the sun rise? I've always wanted to spend a night in a car."

In young Croom a struggle took place. A whole night with her—alone!

"D'you mean you'd trust me?"

"Don't be old-fashioned, Tony. It's much the best thing to do, and rather a lark. If a car came into us, or we were run in for driving without lights, that would be awkward if you like."

"There's never a moon when you want one," muttered young Croom. "You really mean it?"

Clare touched his arm.

"Pull her further in, among the trees. Very slow. Look out! Stop!"

There was a slight bump. Clare said:

"We're up against a tree, and our tail's to the road. I'll get out and see if any one can see us."

Young Croom waited, arranging the cushions and rug for her. He was thinking: 'She can't really love me, or she'd never take it so coolly!' Quivering at the thought of this long dark night with her, he yet knew it was going to be torture. Her voice said:

"All right. I should say no one could see the car. You go and have a look. I'll get in."

He had to feel his way with his feet. The quality of the ground showed him when he had reached the road. It was less densely dark, but he could see no stars. The car was completely invisible. He waited, then turned to feel his way back. So lost was the car that he had to whistle and wait for her answering whistle to find it. Dark, indeed! He got in.

"Half way down, I should say. I'm very comfy, Tony."

"Window down or up?"

"Thank God for that! D'you mind my pipe?"

"Of course not. Give me a cigarette. This is almost perfect."

"Almost," he said in a small voice.

"I should like to see Aunt Em's face. Are you warm?"

"Nothing goes through leather. Are you?"

"Lovely!" There was a silence; then she said: "Tony! Forgive me, won't you? I did promise."

"It's quite all right," said young Croom.

"I can just see your nose by your pipe's glow."

By the light of her cigarette he, in turn, could see her teeth, her smiling lips, her face lasting just to the eyes, and fading out.

"Take off your hat, Clare. And any time you like, here's my shoulder."

"Don't let me snore."

"*You* snore!"

"Every one snores on occasion. This will be it."

They talked for a little. But all seemed unreal, except just being beside her in the dark. He could hear now and again a car passing; other noises of the night there were none; too dark even for the owls. His pipe went out, and he put it away. She lay back beside him so close that he could feel her arm against his. He held his breath. Had she dropped off? Oh! He was in for a sleepless night, with this faint perfume from her egging on his senses and the warmth of her arm tingling into his. Even if this were all, it would be sheer waste to sleep. Drowsily she said:

"If you really don't mind, I *will* put my head on your shoulder, Tony."

"Mind!"

Her head snuggled down on to his scarf; and the faint perfume, which carried with it reminder of a sunny pine wood, increased. Was it credible that she was there against his shoulder, and would be for another six or seven hours? And he shuddered. So still and matter-of-fact! No sign in her of passion or disturbance; he might have been her brother. With the force of revelation he perceived that this night would be a test that he must pass; for if he did not she would recoil, and drop away from him. She *was* asleep. Oh! yes. You couldn't counterfeit that little regular cluck, as of the tiniest chicken—a perfect little sound, faintly comic, infinitely precious! Whatever happened to him now, he would have passed a night with her! He sat—still as a mouse, if mice are still. Her head grew heavier and more confiding with the deepening of her slumber. And, while he sat and listened, his feeling for her deepened too, became almost a passion of protection and of service. And the night, cold, dark, still—no cars were passing now—kept him company; like some huge, dark, enveloping, just breathing creature, it was awake. The night did not sleep! For the first time in his life he realised that. Night was wakeful as the day. Unlighted and withdrawn, it had its sentience; neither spoke nor moved, just watched, and breathed. With stars and moon, or, as to-night, lampless and shuttered, it was a great companion.

His arm grew stiff, and, as if that reached her consciousness, she withdrew her head but did not wake. He rubbed his shoulder just in time, for almost at once her head rolled back again. Screwing round till his lips just touched her hair, he heard again chicklike and bland, that faint rhythmic cluck. It ceased and became the deeper breathing of far-down slumber. Then drowsiness crept on him too; he slept.

CHAPTER 19

Young croom awoke, stiff and unconscious of where he was. A voice said:

"It's just getting light, Tony, but I can't see to read the hymn."

He sat up. "Heavens! Have I been asleep?"

"Yes, poor dear. I've had a perfect night, just a little achey in the legs. What's the time?"

Young Croom looked at his watch's illumined hands.

"Nearly half past six. Pins and needles. Wow!"

"Let's get out and stretch."

His voice, far away, even from himself, answered: "And so it's over."

"Was it so terrible?"

He put his hands to his head, and did not answer. The thought that next night and all the nights to come he would be apart from her again, was like a blow over the heart. She opened the door.

"I'm going to stamp my feet a bit. Then we might have a stroll to warm ourselves. We shan't get breakfast anywhere till eight."

He started the engine to warm the car. Light was creeping into the wood; he could see the beech tree against whose trunk they had passed the night. Then he, too, got out and walked towards the road. Still grey-dark and misty, the wood on either side of its dim open streak looked mournful and mysterious. No wind, no sound? He felt as Adam might have felt dragging towards the Park Gates of Eden without having earned the right to be expelled. Adam! That quaint, amiable, white, bearded creature. Man before he 'fell', a nonconformist preacher in a state of nature, with a pet snake, a prize apple, and a female secretary coy and unshingled as Lady Godiva! His blood began to flow again, and he returned to the car.

Clare was kneeling and attending to her hair with a pocket comb and mirror.

"How are you feeling, Tony?"

"Pretty rotten. I think we'll shove along, and have breakfast at Maidenhead or Slough."

"Why not at home? We could be there by eight. I make very good coffee."

"Fine!" said young Croom: "I'll do fifty all the way."

On that very fast drive they spoke little. Both were too hungry.

"While I'm getting breakfast, Tony, you can shave and have a bath. You'll save time and feel comfy driving back. I'll have mine later."

"I think," said young Croom, at the Marble Arch, "I'd better park the car. You go on in alone; it's too conspicuous driving up at this time in the morning; the chauffeurs are sure to be working. I'll slip along in ten minutes."

When, at eight o'clock he reached the Mews, she was in a blue wrapper, the little table in the downstairs room was set for breakfast, and there was already a scent of coffee.

"I've turned the bath on, Tony, and you'll find a razor."

"Darling!" said young Croom. "Shan't be ten minutes."

He was back again in twelve, and sat down opposite to her. There were boiled eggs, toast, quince jam from Condaford, and real coffee. It was the most delicious meal he had ever eaten, because it was so exactly as if they were married.

"Aren't you tired, darling?"

"Not a bit. I feel thoroughly chirped up. All the same, I don't think we must do it again—too near the hambone altogether."

"Well, we didn't mean to."

"No, and you were an angel. Still, it's not exactly what I promised Aunt Em. To the pure all things are not pure."

"No—blast them! God! How shall I live till I see you again!"

Clare stretched her hand across the little table and gave his a squeeze.

"Now I think you'd better slip off. Just let me look out and see that the coast's clear."

When she had done this he kissed her hand, got back to his car, and by eleven o'clock was standing alongside a plumber in a horse box at Bablock Hythe. . . .

Clare lay in a very hot bath. It was of the geyser type and not long enough, but it provided a good soak. She felt as when, a little girl, she had done something unpleasing to her governess, without discovery. But poor dear Tony! A pity men were so impatient. They had as little liking for cool philandering as for shopping. They rushed into shops, said: 'Have you such and such? No?' and rushed out again. They hated trying on, being patted here and there, turning their heads to look at their back views. To savour what was fitting was to them anathema. Tony was a child! She felt herself much older by nature and experience. Though much in request before her marriage, Clare had never come into close contact with those who, centered in London and themselves, were devoid of belief in anything but mockery, motion and enough money to have from day to day a 'good' time. At country houses she had met them, of course, but withdrawn from their proper atmosphere into the air of sport. Essentially an open-air person, of the quick and wiry, rather than the hefty, type, she observed unconsciously the shibboleths of sport. Transplanted to Ceylon, she had kept her tastes, and spent her time in the saddle or on the tennis ground. Reading many novels, she professed, indeed, to keep abreast of the current, with all its impatience of restraint; but lying in her bath, she was uneasy. It had not been fair to put Tony to such strain as that of last night. The closer she allowed him to come to her, short of the contacts of love, the more she would be torturing him. Drying herself, she made good resolutions, and only with a rush did she reach the Temple by ten o'clock. She might just as well have stayed on soaking in her bath, for Dornford was busy on an important case. She finished what jobs there were, looking idly out over the Temple lawn, whence fine weather mist was vanishing, and sunlight, brightening to winter brilliance, slanted on to her cheek. And she thought of Ceylon, where the sun was never coolly comforting. Jerry! How, in that horrible, common phrase, was he 'keeping'? And what doing about her? All very well to determine that she would not torture Tony, would keep away from him and spare his senses, but without him—she would be dull and lonely. He had become a habit. A bad habit perhaps—but bad habits were the only ones it was painful to do without.

'I'm naturally a light weight,' she thought. 'So is Tony; all the same he would never let one down!'

And the grass of the Temple lawn seemed suddenly the sea, and this window-sill the ship's bulwark, and he and she leaned there watching the flying fish spring up from the foam and flitter away above the green-blue water. Warmth and colour. Airy shining grace! And she felt melancholy.

'A good long ride is what I want,' she thought. 'I'll go down to Condaford to-morrow, and on Saturday be out all day. I'll make Dinny come out with me, she ought to ride more.'

The clerk entered and said: "Mr. Dornford's going straight from the Courts to the 'House,' this afternoon."

"Ah! Do you ever feel hipped, George?"

The clerk, whose face always amused her because it so clearly should have had mutton-chop whiskers on its rosy roundness, replied in his cushiony voice:

"What I miss here is a dog. With my old Toby I never feel lonely."

"What is he, George?"

"Bull terrier. But I can't bring him here, Mrs. Calder'd miss him; besides if he bit a solicitor——"

"But, how perfect!"

George wheezed.

"Ah! you can't have high spirits in the Temple."

"I should have liked a dog, George, but when I'm out there's no one in."

"I don't fancy Mr. Dornford'll be residential here much longer."

"Why?"

"He's looking for a house. I've an idea he'd like to marry."

"Oh! Who?"

George closed an eye.

"You mean my sister?"

"Ah!"

"Yes. But I don't see how you know."

George closed the other eye.

"A little bird, Lady Corven."

"He might do worse, certainly. Not that I'm a great believer in marriage."

"We don't see the right side of marriage in the Law. But Mr. Dornford would make a woman happy—in my opinion."

"In mine, too, George."

"He's a very quiet man, but a fund of energy and considerate. Solicitors like him; judges like him."

"And wives will like him."

"Of course he's a Catholic."

"We all have to be something."

"Mrs. Calder and I've been Anglicans ever since my old dad died. He was a Plymouth Brother—very stiff. Express an opinion of your own, and he'd jump down your throat. Many's the time I've had him threaten me with fire and slaughter. All for my good, you understand. A fine religious old feller. And couldn't bear others not to be. Good red Zummerzet blood, and never forgot it, though he did live in Peckham."

"Well, George, if Mr. Dornford wants me again after all, would you telephone me at five o'clock? I'll look in at my rooms in case."

Clare walked. The day was even more springlike than yesterday. She went by the Embankment and St. James's Park. Alongside the water, clusters of daffodil spikes were pushing up, and tree shoots swelling into bud. The gentle, warming sunlight fell on her back. It couldn't last. There would be a throw-back to winter, for sure! She walked fast out under the chariot, whose horses, not too natural, worried but exhilarated her, passed the Artillery Memorial without a glance, and entered Hyde Park. Warmed up now, she swung out along the Row. Riding was something of a passion with her, so that it always made her restive to see someone else riding a good horse. Queer animals, horses, so fiery and alive at one moment, so dull and ruminative the next!

Two or three hats were raised to her. A long man on a good-looking mare reined up after he had passed and came back.

"I thought it was you. Lawrence told me you were over. Remember me —Jack Muskham?"

Clare—thinking: 'Lovely seat for a tall man!'—murmured: "Of course!" and was suddenly on her guard.

"An acquaintance of yours is going to look after my Arab mares."

"Oh! yes, Tony Croom."

"Nice young chap, but I don't know if he knows enough. Still, he's keen as mustard. How's your sister?"

"Very well."

"You ought to bring her racing, Lady Corven."

"I don't think Dinny cares much for horses."

"I could soon make her. I remember—" he broke off, frowning. In spite of his languid pose, his face seemed to Clare purposeful, brown, lined, ironic about the lips. She wondered how he would take the news that she had spent last night with Tony in a car.

"When do the mares come, Mr. Muskham?"

"They're in Egypt now. We'll ship them in April. I might go over for it; possibly take young Croom."

"I'd love to see them," said Clare; "I rode an Arab in Ceylon."

"We must get you down."

"Somewhere near Oxford, isn't it?"

"About six miles, nice country. I'll remember. Good-bye!" He raised his hat, touched the mare with his heel, and cantered off.

'My perfect innocence!' she thought. 'Hope I didn't over-do it. I wouldn't like to "get-wrong" with him. He looks as if he knew his mind terribly well. Lovely boots! He didn't ask after Jerry!'

Her nerves felt a little shaken; and she struck away from the Row towards the Serpentine.

The sunlit water had no boats on it, but a few ducks on the far side. Did she mind what people thought? Miller of Dee! Only did he really care for nobody? Or was he just a philosopher? She sat down on a bench in the full sunlight, and suddenly felt sleepy. A night in a car, after all, was not the same as a night out of a car. Crossing her arms on her breast, she closed her eyes. Almost at once she was asleep.

Quite a number of people straggled past between her and the bright water, surprised to see one in such clothes asleep before lunch. Two little boys carrying toy aeroplanes stopped dead, examining her dark eyelashes resting on her cream-coloured cheeks, and the little twitchings of her just touched-up lips. Having a French governess, they were 'well-bred' little boys without prospect of sticking pins into her or uttering a sudden whoop. But she seemed to have no hands, her feet were crossed and tucked under her chair, and her attitude was such that she had abnormally long thighs. It was interesting; and after they had passed one of them kept turning his head to see more of her.

Thus, for a full hour of elusive spring, Clare slept the sleep of one who has spent a night in a car.

CHAPTER 20

AND THREE WEEKS passed during which Clare saw young Croom but four times in all. She was packing for the evening train to Condaford, when the sheep bell summoned her down the spiral stairway.

Outside was a shortish man in horn spectacles, who gave her a vague impression of being connected with learning. He raised his hat.

"Lady Corven?"

"Yes."

"Pardon me, I have this for you." Producing from his blue overcoat a longish document, he put it into her hand.

Clare read the words:

> "In the High Court of Justice
>   Probate Divorce and Admiralty Division.
>   The Twenty-sixth day of February, 1932.
>
> "In the Matter of the Petition of Sir Gerald Corven."

A weak feeling ran down the back of her legs, and she raised her eyes to the level of those behind the horn-rimmed spectacles.

"Oh!" she said.

The shortish man made her a little bow. She had a feeling that he was sorry for her, and promptly closed the door in his face. She went up the spiral stairs, sat down on the sofa, and lit a cigarette. Then she spread the document on her lap. Her first thought was 'But it's monstrous—I've done nothing!' Her second: 'I suppose I must read the foul thing!'

She had not read more than: 'The humble petition of Gerald Corven, K.C.B.' when she had her third thought: 'But this is exactly what I want. I shall be free!'

More calmly she read on till she came to the words: 'That your Petitioner claims from the said James Bernard Croom as damages in respect of his said adultery so committed the sum of two thousand pounds.'

Tony! If he had two thousand shillings, it was all! Beast! Revengeful brute! This sudden reduction of the issue to terms of hard cash not only rasped her feelings, but brought her a sort of panic. Tony must not, should not be ruined through her. She must see him! Had they—but of course they had served it on him too.

She finished reading the petition, took a long draw at her cigarette and got up.

She went to the telephone, asked for a trunk call and gave the number of his inn.

"Can I speak to Mr. Croom?—Gone up to London?—In his car?—When?"

An hour ago! That could only mean that he was coming to see her!

A little soothed, she made a rapid calculation. She could not now catch the train to Condaford; and she got another trunk call through to the Grange.

"Dinny? This is Clare. I can't possibly get down to-night—to-morrow morning instead. . . . No! I'm all right; a little worried. Good-bye!"

A little worried! She sat down again, and once more read the 'foul thing' through. They seemed to know everything except the truth. And neither she nor Tony had ever seen a sign that they were being watched. That man with the horn 'specs,' for instance, evidently knew her, but she'd never seen him before! She went into the bathroom and washed her face in cold water. Miller of Dee! The part had become extremely difficult.

'He'll have had nothing to eat,' she thought.

She set the table downstairs with what she had, made some coffee, and sat down to smoke and wait. Condaford, and the faces of her people came before her; the face, too, of Aunt Em; and of Jack Muskham; above all the face of her husband, with its faint, hard-bitten, cat-like smile. Was she to take this lying down? Apart from the damages, was she to let him triumph without a fight? She wished now she had taken her father's and Sir Lawrence's advice and 'clapped a detective on to him.' Too late now—he would be taking no risks till the case was over.

She was still brooding by the electric fire when she heard a car stop outside, and the bell rang.

Young Croom looked chilled and pale. He stood as if so doubtful of his welcome that she seized both his hands.

"Well, Tony, this is pleasant!"

"Oh! darling!"

"You look frozen. Have some brandy!"

While he was drinking, she said:

"Don't let's talk of what we ought to have done; only of what we're going to do."

He groaned.

"They must have thought us terribly green. I never dreamed——"

"Nor I. But why shouldn't we have done exactly what we have done? There's no law against innocence."

He sat down and leaned his forehead on his hands. "God knows this is just what I want; to get you free of him; but I had no business to let you run the risk. It would be all different if you felt for me what I feel for you."

Clare looked down at him with a little smile.

"Now, Tony, be grown-up! It's no good talking about our feelings. And I won't have any nonsense about its being your fault. The point is we're innocent. What are we going to do about it?"

"Of course I shall do whatever you want."

"I have a feeling," said Clare, slowly, "that I shall have to do what my people want me to."

"God!" said young Croom, getting up: "To think that if we defend and win, you'll still be tied to him!"

"And to think," murmured Clare, "that if we don't defend and win, you'll be ruined."

"Oh! Damn that—they can only make me bankrupt."

"And your job?"

"I don't see—I don't know why——"

"I saw Jack Muskham the other day. He looks to me as if he wouldn't like a co-respondent who hadn't given notice of his intentions to the petitioner. You see I've got the jargon."

"If we *had* been lovers, I would have, at once."

"Would you?"

"Of course!"

"Even if I'd said 'Don't'?"

"You wouldn't have."

"I don't know that."

"Well, anyway, it doesn't arise."

"Except that if we don't defend, you'll feel a cad."

"God! What a coil!"

"Sit down and let's eat. There's only this ham, but there's nothing like ham when you feel sick."

They sat down and made motions with their forks.

"Your people don't know, Clare?"

"I only knew myself an hour ago. Did they bring you this same lovely document?"

"Yes."

"Another slice?"

They ate in silence for a minute or two. Then young Croom got up.

"I really can't eat any more."

"All right. Smoke!"

She took a cigarette from him, and said:

"Listen. I'm going down to Condaford to-morrow, and I think you'd better come over. They must see you, because whatever's done must be done with open eyes. Have you a solicitor?"

"No."

"Nor I. I suppose we shall have to have one."

"I'll see to all that. If only I had money!"

Clare winced.

"I apologise for a husband capable of asking for damages."

Young Croom seized her hand. "Darling, I was only thinking of so-licitors."

"Do you remember my answering you on the boat: 'Often more dam-nable, things beginning.'"

"I'll never admit that."

"I was thinking of my marriage, not of you."

"Clare, wouldn't it be far better really not to defend—just let it go? Then you'd be free. And after—if you wanted me, I'd be there, and if you didn't, I wouldn't."

"Sweet of you, Tony; but I must tell my people. Besides—oh! a lot of things."

He began walking up and down.

"D'you suppose they'll believe us if we do defend? *I* don't."

"We shall be telling the exact truth."

"People never believe the exact truth. What train are you going down by?"

"Ten-fifty."

"Shall I come too, or in the afternoon from Bablock Hythe?"

"That's best. I'll have broken it to them."

"Will they mind frightfully?"

"They won't like it."

"Is your sister there?"

"Yes."

"That's something."

"My people are not exactly old-fashioned, Tony, but they're not mod-ern. Very few people are when they're personally involved. The lawyers and the judge and jury won't be, anyway. You'd better go now; and prom-ise me not to drive like Jehu."

"May I kiss you?"

"It'll mean one more piece of exact truth, and there've been three al-ready. Kiss my hand—that doesn't count."

He kissed it, muttered: "God bless you!" and, grabbing his hat, went out.

Clare turned a chair to the unwinking warmth of the electric fire, and sat brooding. The dry heat burned her eyes till they felt as if they had no lids and no capacity for moisture; slowly and definitely she grew an-grier. All the feelings she had experienced, before she made up her mind that morning in Ceylon to cut adrift, came back to her with redoubled fury. How dared he treat her as if he had been a 'light of love'?—worse than if she had been one—a light of love would never have stood it! How dared he touch her with that whip? And now how dared he have her watched, and bring this case? She would not lie down under this!

She began methodically to wash up and put the things away. She opened the door wide and let the wind come in. A nasty night, little whirl-winds travelling up and down the narrow Mews!

'Inside me, too,' she thought. Slamming-to the door, she took out her little mirror. Her face seemed so natural and undefended that it gave her a shock. She powdered it and touched her lips with salve. Then, drawing deep breaths, she shrugged her shoulders, lit a cigarette, and went upstairs. A hot bath!

CHAPTER 21

THE ATMOSPHERE at Condaford into which she stepped next day was guarded. Her words, or the tone of her voice on the telephone, seemed to have seeped into the family consciousness, and she was aware at once that sprightliness would deceive no one. It was a horrible day, too, dank and cold, and she had to hold on to her courage with both hands.

She chose the drawing-room after lunch for disclosure. Taking the document from her bag, she handed it to her father with the words:

"I've had this, Dad."

She heard his startled exclamation, and was conscious of Dinny and her mother going over to him.

At last he said: "Well? Tell us the truth."

She took her foot off the fender and faced them.

"*That* isn't the truth. We've done nothing."

"Who is this man?"

"Tony Croom? I met him on the boat coming home. He's twenty-six, was on a tea plantation out there, and is taking charge of Jack Muskham's Arab mares at Bablock Hythe. He has no money. I told him to come here this afternoon."

"Are you in love with him?"

"No. I like him."

"Is he in love with you?"

"Yes."

"You say there's been nothing?"

"He's kissed my cheek twice, I think—that's all."

"Then what do they mean by this—that you spent the night of the third with him?"

"I went down in his car to see his place, and coming back the lights failed in a wood about five miles from Henley, pitch dark. I suggested we should stay where we were till it was light. We just slept and went on up when it was light."

She heard her mother give a faint gasp, and a queer noise from her father's throat.

"And on the boat? And in your rooms? You say there was nothing, though he's in love with you?"

"Nothing."

"Is that absolutely the truth?"

"Yes."

"Of course," said Dinny, "it's the truth."

"Of course," said the General. "And who's going to believe it?"

"We didn't know we were being watched."

"What time will he be here?"

"Any time, now."

"You've seen him since you had this?"

"Yesterday evening."

"What does he say?"

"He says he'll do whatever I wish."

"That, of course. Does *he* think you'll be believed?"

"No."

The General took the document over to the window, as if the better to see into it. Lady Charwell sat down, her face very white. Dinny came over to Clare, and took her arm.

"When he comes," said the General, suddenly, returning from the window, "I'll see him alone. Nobody before me, please."

"Witnesses out of court," murmured Clare.

The General handed her the document. His face looked drawn and tired.

"I'm terribly sorry, Dad. I suppose we were fools. Virtue is *not* its own reward."

"Wisdom is," said the General. He touched her shoulder and marched off to the door, followed by Dinny.

"Does he believe me, Mother?"

"Yes, but only because you're his daughter. He feels he oughtn't to."

"Do you feel like that, Mother?"

"I believe you because I know you."

Clare bent over and kissed her cheek.

"Very pretty, Mother dear; but not cheering."

"You say you like this young man. Did you know him out there?"

"I never saw him till the boat. And, Mother, I may as well tell you that I've not been in the mood for passion. I don't know when I shall be again. Perhaps never!"

"Why not?"

Clare shook her head. "I won't go into my life with Jerry, not even now, when he's been such a cad as to ask for damages. I'm really much more upset about that than I am about myself."

"I suppose this young man would have gone away with you, at any moment?"

"Yes; but I haven't wanted to. Besides, I gave Aunt Em a promise. I sort of swore to behave for a year. And I have—so far. It's terribly tempting not to defend and be free."

Lady Charwell was silent.

"Well, Mother?"

"Your father is bound to think of this as it affects your name and the family's."

"Six of one and half-a-dozen of the other, so far as that goes. If we don't defend, it will just go through and hardly be noticed. If we do, it will make a sensation. 'Night in a car,' and all that, even if we're believed. Can't you see the papers, Mummy? They'll be all over it."

"I think," said Lady Charwell, slowly, "it will come back in the end to the feeling your father has about that whip. I've never known him so angry as he was over that. I think he will feel you must defend."

"I should never mention the whip in court. It's too easily denied, for one thing; and I have some pride, Mother . . ."

Dinny had followed to the study, or barrack-room, as it was sometimes called.

"You know this young man, Dinny?" burst out the General.

"Yes, and I like him. He *is* deeply in love with Clare."

"What business has he to be?"

"Be human, dear!"

"You believe her about the car?"

"Yes. I heard her solemnly promise Aunt Em to behave for a year."

"Queer sort of thing to have to promise!"

"A mistake, if you ask me."

"What!"

"The only thing that really matters is that Clare should get free."

The General stood with head bent, as if he had found food for thought; a slow flush had coloured his cheekbones.

"She told you," he said, suddenly, "what she told me, about that fellow having used a whip on her?"

Dinny nodded.

"In the old days I could and would have called him out for that. I agree that she must get free, but—not this way."

"Then you *do* believe her?"

"She wouldn't tell a lie to us all like that."

"Good, Dad! But who else will believe them? Would you, on a jury?"

"I don't know," said the General, glumly.

Dinny shook her head. "You wouldn't."

"Lawyers are damned clever. I suppose Dornford wouldn't take up a case like this?"

"He doesn't practise in the Divorce Court. Besides, she's his secretary."

"I must get to hear what Kingsons say. Lawrence believes in them. Fleur's father was a member there."

"Then—" Dinny had begun, when the door was opened.

"Mr. Croom, sir."

"You needn't go, Dinny."

Young Croom came in. After a glance at Dinny, he moved towards the General.

"Clare told me to come over, sir."

The General nodded. His narrowed eyes were fixed steadily on his daughter's would-be lover. The young man faced that scrutiny as if on parade, his eyes replying to the General's without defiance.

"I won't beat about the bush," said the General, suddenly. "You seem to have got my daughter into a mess."

"Yes, sir."

"Kindly give me your account of it."

Young Croom put his hat down on the table, and, squaring his shoulders, said:

"Whatever she has told you is true, sir."

Dinny saw with relief her father's lips twitching as if with a smile.

"Very correct, Mr. Croom; but not what I want. She has told me her version; I should be glad to hear yours."

She saw the young man moisten his lips, making a curious jerking motion of his head.

"I'm in love with her, sir: have been ever since I first saw her on the boat. We've been going about rather in London—cinemas, theatres, picture galleries, and that; and I've been to her rooms three—no, five times altogether. On February the third I drove her down to Bablock Hythe for her to see where I'm going to have my job; and coming back—I expect she told you—my lights failed and we were hung up in a pitch dark wood some miles short of Henley. Well—we—we thought we'd better just stay there until it was light again, instead of risking things. I'd got off the road twice. It really was pitch black and I had no torch. And so—well, we waited in the car till about half past six, and then came up, and got to her place about eight." He paused and moistened his lips, then straightened himself again and said with a rush: "Whether you believe me or not, sir, I swear there was nothing whatever between us in the car, and —there never has been, except—except that she's let me kiss her cheek two or three times."

The General, who had never dropped his eyes, said: "That's substantially what she told us. Anything else?"

"After I had that paper, sir, I motored up to see her at once—that was yesterday. Of course I'll do anything she wants."

"You didn't put your heads together as to what you would say to us?"

Dinny saw the young man stiffen.

"Of course not, sir!"

"Then I may take it that you're ready to swear there's been nothing, and defend the action?"

"Certainly, if you think there's any chance of our being believed."

The General shrugged. "What's your financial position?"

"Four hundred a year from my job." A faint smile curled his lips: "Otherwise none, sir."

"Do you know my daughter's husband?"

"No."

"Never met him?"

"No, sir."

"When did you first meet Clare?"

"On the second day of the voyage home."

"What were you doing out there?"

"Tea planting; but they amalgamated my plantation with some others, for economy."

"I see. Where were you at school?"

"Wellington, and then at Cambridge."

"You've got a job with Jack Muskham?"

"Yes sir, his Arab mares. They're due in the spring."

"You know about horses, then?"

"Yes. I'm terribly fond of them."

Dinny saw the narrowed gaze withdraw from the young man's face and come to rest on hers.

"You know my daughter Dinny, I think?"

"Yes."

"I'll leave you to her now. I want to think this over."

The young man bowed slightly, turned to Dinny, and then, turning back, said with a certain dignity:

"I'm awfully sorry, sir, about this; but I can't say I'm sorry that I'm in love with Clare. It wouldn't be true. I love her terribly."

He was moving towards the door, when the General said:

"One moment. What do you mean by love?"

Involuntarily Dinny clasped her hands. An appalling question! Young Croom turned round. His face was motionless.

"I know what you mean, sir," he said, huskily. "Desire and that, or more? Well! More, or I couldn't have stood that night in the car." He turned again to the door.

Dinny moved and held it open for him. She followed him into the hall, where he was frowning and taking deep breaths. She slipped her hand through his arm and moved him across to the wood fire. They stood, looking down into the flames, till she said:

"I'm afraid that was rather dreadful. But soldiers like to have things straight out, you know. Anyway—I know my father—you made what's called a good impression."

"I felt a ghastly kind of wooden idiot. Where is Clare? Here?"

"Yes."

"Can I see her, Miss Cherrell?"

"Try calling me Dinny. You can see her; but I think you'd better see my mother too. Let's go to the drawing-room."

He gave her hand a squeeze.

"I've always felt you were a brick."

Dinny grimaced. "Even bricks yield to certain pressure."

"Oh! sorry! I'm always forgetting my ghastly grip. Clare dreads it. How is she?"

With a faint shrug and smile, Dinny said:

"Doing as well as can be expected."

Tony Croom clutched his head.

"Yes, feel exactly like that, only worse; in those cases there's something to look forward to and—here? D'you think she'll ever really love me?"

"I hope so."

"Your people don't think that I pursued her—I mean, you know what I mean, just to have a good time?"

"They won't after to-day. You are what I was once called—transparent."

"You? I never quite know what you're thinking."

"That was a long time ago. Come!"

CHAPTER 22

WHEN YOUNG Croom had withdrawn into the sleet and wind of that discomforting day, he left behind him a marked gloom. Clare went to her room saying her head was bad and she was going to lie down. The other three sat among the tea things, speaking only to the dogs, sure sign of mental disturbance.

At last Dinny got up: "Well, my dears, gloom doesn't help. Let's look on the bright side. They might have been scarlet instead of white as snow."

The General said, more to himself than in reply:

"They must defend. That fellow can't have it all his own way."

"But, Dad, to have Clare free, with a perfectly clear conscience, would be nice and ironic, and ever so much less fuss!"

"Lie down under an accusation of that sort?"

"Her name will go even if she wins. No one can spend a night in a car with a young man with impunity. Can they, Mother?"

Lady Charwell smiled faintly.

"I agree with your father, Dinny. It seems to me revolting that Clare should be divorced when she's done nothing except been a little foolish. Besides, it would be cheating the law, wouldn't it?"

"I shouldn't think the law would care, dear. However—!" And Dinny was silent, scrutinising their rueful faces, aware that they set some mysterious store by marriage and divorce which she did not, and that nothing she could say would alter it.

"The young man," said the General, "seemed a decent fellow, I thought. He'll have to come up and see the lawyers when we do."

"I'd better go up with Clare to-morrow evening, Dad, and get Uncle Lawrence to arrange you a meeting with the lawyers for after lunch on Monday. I'll telephone you and Tony Croom from Mount Street in the morning."

The General nodded and got up. "Beast of a day!" he said; and put his hand on his wife's shoulder: "Don't let this worry you, Liz. They can but tell the truth. I'll go to the study and have another shot at that new pigsty. You might look in later, Dinny . . ."

At all critical times Dinny felt more at home in Mount Street than she did at Condaford. Sir Lawrence's mind was so much more lively than her father's; Aunt Em's inconsequence at once more bracing and more soothing than her mother's quiet and sensible sympathy. When a crisis was over, or if it had not begun, Condaford was perfect, but it was too quiet for nerve storms or crucial action. As country houses went, it was, indeed, old-fashioned, inhabited by the only county family who had been in the district for more than three or four generations. The Grange had an almost institutional repute. "Condaford Grange" and "the Cherrells of Condaford" were spoken of as curiosities. The week-ending or purely sporting existence of the big 'places' was felt to be alien to them. The many families in the smaller 'places' round seemed to make country life into a sort of cult, organising tennis and bridge parties, village entertainments, and the looking of each other up; getting their day's shooting here and there, supporting the nearest golf course, attending meets, hunting a bit, and so forth. The Charwells, with their much deeper roots, yet seemed to be less in evidence than almost anyone. They would have been curiously missed, but, except to the villagers, they hardly seemed real.

In spite of her always active life at Condaford Dinny often felt there, as one does waking in the still hours of the night, nervous from the very quietude; and in such troubles as Hubert's, three years before, her own crisis of two years ago, or this of Clare's, she craved at once to be more in the swim of life.

Having dropped Clare at her Mews, she went on in the taxi, and arrived at Mount Street before dinner.

Michael and Fleur were there, and the conversation turned and turned from literature to politics. Michael was of opinion that the papers were beginning to pat the country's back too soon, and that the Government might go to sleep. Sir Lawrence was glad to hear that they were still awake.

Lady Mont said suddenly: "The baby, Dinny?"

"Frightfully well, thank you, Aunt Em. He walks."

"I was countin' up the pedigree, and he makes the twenty-fourth Cherrell of Condaford; and before that they were French. Is Jean havin' any more?"

"You bet," said Fleur. "I never saw a young woman more like it."

"There'll be nothin' for them."

"Oh, she'll wangle their futures all right."

"Such a singular word," said Lady Mont.

"Dinny, how's Clare?"

"All right."

"Any developments?" And Fleur's clear eyes seemed to slide into her brain.

"Yes, but——"

Michael's voice broke the silence.

"Dornford has a very neat idea, Dad; he thinks——"

The neat idea of Dornford was lost on Dinny, wondering whether or not to take Fleur into confidence. She knew no one of quicker brain, or of a judgment on social matters more cynically sound. Further, she could keep a secret. But it was Clare's secret, and she decided to speak to Sir Lawrence first.

Late that night she did so. He received the news with his eyebrows.

"All night in a car, Dinny? That's a bit steep. I'll get on to the lawyers at ten o'clock to-morrow. 'Very young' Roger Forsyte, Fleur's cousin, is there now; I'll get hold of him, he's likely to have more credulity than the hoarier members. You and I will go along, too, to prove our faith."

"I've never been in the City."

"Curious place; built upon the ends of the earth. Romance and the Bank rate. Prepare for a mild shock."

"Do you think they ought to defend?"

Sir Lawrence's lively eyes came to rest on her face.

"If you ask me whether I think they'll be believed—no. But at least we can divide opinion on the question."

"You *do* believe them yourself, don't you?"

"I plank on you there, Dinny. Clare wouldn't try to take *you* in."

Thinking back to her sister's face and to young Croom's, Dinny had a revulsion of feeling. "They *are* telling the truth, and they look like it. It would be wicked not to believe them."

"No end to that sort of wickedness in this wicked world. You look tired, my dear; better go to bed."

In that bedroom, where she had spent so many nights at the time of her own trouble, Dinny had again that half-waking nightmare, the sense of being close to Wilfrid and unable to reach him, and the refrain: 'One more river, one more river to cross,' kept running in her tired head. . . .

In that quiet and yellow backwater, the Old Jewry, the offices of Kingson Cuthcott and Forsyte were tribally invaded at four o'clock next day.

"What's become of old Gradman, Mr. Forsyte?" Dinny heard her uncle say. "Still here?"

'Very young' Roger Forsyte, who was forty-two, answered, in a voice which seemed to contradict his jaw: "I believe he's still living at Pinner, or Highgate, or whatever it was."

"I should be glad to think so," murmured Sir Lawrence. "Old For—er, your cousin thought a lot of him. A regular Victorian piece."

'Very young' Roger smiled. "Won't you all sit down?"

Dinny, who had never yet been in a lawyer's office, looked at the law books along the walls, the bundles of papers, the yellowish blind, the repellent black fireplace with its little coal fire that seemed to warm nothing, the map of an estate hanging unrolled behind the door, the low wicker basket on the table, the pens and sealing-wax and 'very young' Roger, and thought of an album of seaweed, compiled by her first governess. She saw her father rise and place a document in the solicitor's hands.

"We've come about this."

'Very young' Roger glanced at the heading of the paper and over it at Clare.

'How does he know which of us it is?' thought Dinny.

"There's no truth in the allegations," said the General.

'Very young' Roger caressed his jaw, and began reading.

Dinny, from the side, could see that a sharp and rather bird-like look had come on his face.

Noticing that Dinny could see him, he lowered the paper and said: "They seem in a hurry. The petitioner signed the affidavit in Egypt, I see. He must have come over there to save time. Mr. Croom?"

"Yes."

"You wish us to represent you as well?"

"Yes."

"Then Lady Corven and you. Later, perhaps, Sir Conway, you'd come in again."

"Do you mind if my sister stays?" said Clare.

Dinny met the solicitor's eyes. "Not at all." She did not know if he meant it.

The General and Sir Lawrence went out, and there was silence. 'Very young' Roger leaned against the fireplace, and most unexpectedly took a pinch of snuff. Dinny saw that he was lean and rather tall, and that his jaw jutted. There was a faintly sandy tinge in his hair, and in the ruddiness of his hollowed cheeks.

"Your father, Lady Corven, said there was no truth in these—er—allegations."

"The facts are as stated; the inferences are wrong. There's been nothing between Mr. Croom and myself, except three kisses on my cheek."

"I see. About this night in the car, now?"

"Nothing," said Clare: "Not even one of those kisses."

"Nothing," repeated young Croom; "absolutely nothing."

'Very young' Roger passed his tongue over his lips.

"If you don't mind, I think I should like to understand your feelings for each other—if any."

"We are speaking," said Clare, in a clear voice, "the absolute truth, as we've told it to my people; that's why I asked my sister to stay. Tony?"

'Very young' Roger's mouth twitched. To Dinny he did not seem to be taking it quite as a lawyer should; something in his dress, indeed, was a little unexpected—his waistcoat was it, or his tie? That snuff, too—as if a dash of the artist had been suppressed in him. He said:

"Yes, Mr. Croom?"

Young Croom, who had gone very red, looked at Clare almost angrily.

"I'm in love with her."

"Quite!" said 'very young' Roger, reopening the snuff-box. "And you, Lady Corven, regard him as a friend?"

Clare nodded—a faint surprise on her face.

Dinny felt a sudden gratitude towards the questioner, who was applying a bandana to his nose.

"The car was an accident," added Clare, quickly; "it was pitch dark in the wood, our lights had failed, and we didn't want to run any risk of people seeing us together so late at night."

"Exactly! Excuse my asking, but you're both prepared to go into Court and swear there was absolutely nothing that night or on the other occasions, except—did you say—three kisses?"

"On my cheek," said Clare; "one out of doors, when I was in a car and he wasn't, and the others—when were the others, Tony?"

Young Croom said between his clenched teeth: "In your rooms when I hadn't seen you for over a fortnight."

"You neither of you knew you were being—er—shadowed?"

"I knew my husband had threatened it, but we'd neither of us noticed anything."

"About leaving your husband, Lady Corven; any reason you'd care to give me?"

Clare shook her head.

"I'm not going into my life with him, either here or anywhere. And I'm not going back to him."

"Incompatibility, or worse?"

"I think worse."

"But no definite charge. You realise the importance?"

"Yes. But I'm not going into it, even privately."

Young Croom burst out: "He was a brute to her, of course."

"You knew him, Mr. Croom?"

"Never seen him in my life."

"Then——"

"He just thinks it because I left Jerry suddenly. He knows nothing."

Dinny saw 'very young' Roger's eyes rest on herself. "But you do," they seemed to say; and she thought: 'He's no fool!'

He had returned from the fireplace, walking with a slight limp; sitting down again, he took up the document, narrowed his eyes, and said:

"This isn't the sort of evidence the Court likes; in fact I'm not sure it's evidence at all. All the same it's not a very bright prospect. If you could show strong cause for leaving your husband, and we could get over that night in the car—" He looked, bird-like, first at Clare and then at young Croom. "Still, you can't let damages and costs like that go by default, when—er—you've done nothing." His eyes fell; and Dinny thought:

'Not conspicuous—his credulity!'

'Very young' Roger lifted a paper-knife.

"We might possibly get the damages agreed at a comparatively nominal sum, if you put in a defence and then didn't appear. May I ask your monetary position, Mr. Croom?"

"I haven't a bean, but that doesn't matter."

"What exactly will defending mean?" asked Clare.

"You'd both go into the box and deny the charges. You'd be cross-examined, and we should cross-examine the petitioner and the enquiry agents. Candidly, unless you can give good reasons for having left your husband, you're almost bound to have the judge against you. And," he added, in a somewhat human manner, "a night is a night, especially to the divorce court, even in a car, though, as I say, it's not the sort of evidence generally required."

"My Uncle thinks," said Dinny, quietly, "that some of the jury, at all events, might believe them, and that the damages, in any case, would be reduced."

'Very young' Roger nodded.

"We'll see what Mr. Kingson says. I should like to see your father and Sir Lawrence again."

Dinny went to the door and held it open for her sister and young Croom. Glancing back she saw 'very young' Roger's face. It was as if someone had asked him not to be a realist. He caught her eye, gave a funny little cock of his head, and took out his snuff-box. She shut the door and went up to him.

"You'll make a mistake if you don't believe them. They're speaking the absolute truth."

"Why did she leave her husband, Miss Cherrell?"

"If she won't tell you, I can't. But I'm sure she was right."

He considered her for a moment with that sharp glance.

"Somehow," he said, suddenly, "I wish it were you." And taking snuff he turned to the General and Sir Lawrence.

"Well?" said the General.

'Very young' Roger looked suddenly more sandy.

"If she had good reason for leaving her husband——"

"She had."

"Father!"

"It appears she isn't prepared to speak of it."

"Nor should I be," said Dinny quietly.

'Very young' Roger murmured: "It might make all the difference, though."

"Serious thing for young Croom, Mr. Forsyte," put in Sir Lawrence.

"Serious, whether they defend or not, Sir Lawrence. I'd better see them both separately. Then I'll get Mr. Kingson's view, and let you know to-morrow. Will that do, General?"

"It revolts me," said the General, "to think of that fellow Corven!"

"Quite!" said 'very young' Roger, and Dinny thought she had never heard a more doubtful sound.

CHAPTER 23

Dinny sat in the little bare waiting-room turning over *The Times*. Young Croom stood at the window.

"Dinny," he said, turning, "can you think of any way in which I can make this less beastly for her? It's all my fault in a sense, but I have tried to keep myself in hand."

Dinny looked at his troubled face. "I can't; except by sticking to the exact truth."

"Do you believe in that chap in there?"

"I rather do. I like his taking snuff."

"I don't believe in defending. Why should she be ragged in the witness box for nothing? Why does it matter if they bankrupt me?"

"We must prevent that somehow."

"D'you think I'd let——"

"We won't discuss it, Tony. Sufficient unto the day! Isn't this a dingy place? Dentists try much harder—Marcus Stone on the walls, all the old *Bystanders*, and you can bring a dog."

"Could we smoke?"

"Surely."

"These are only stinkers."

Dinny took one, and they puffed for a minute in silence.

"It's too foul!" he said, suddenly. "That fellow will have to come over, won't he? He never can really have cared a scrap for her."

"Oh! yes, he did. '*Souvent homme varie, folle est qui s'y fie!*'"

"Well," said young Croom, grimly, "I'd better be kept from him." He went back to the window and stood looking out. Dinny sat thinking of that scene, when two men had not been kept apart, so pitifully like a dog fight and rending to her in its sequel.

Then Clare came in. There were spots of red in her pale cheeks. "Your turn, Tony."

Young Croom came from the window, looked hard into her face, and passed into the lawyer's room. Dinny felt very sorry for him.

"Ugh!" said Clare: "Let's get out of this!"

On the pavement, she went on:

"I wish now we had been lovers, Dinny, instead of in this mock-pretty state that no one believes in."

556

"We *do* believe."

"Oh! you and Dad. But that snuffy rabbit doesn't, and no one else will. Still, I shall go through with it. I won't let Tony down, and I won't give Jerry an inch that I can help giving."

"Let's have tea," said Dinny. "There must be tea somewhere in the City."

In a crowded thoroughfare they soon saw an A.B.C.

"Then you didn't like 'very young' Roger?" asked Dinny from across the small round table.

"Oh! he's all right—rather decent, really. I suppose lawyers simply can't believe. But nothing will shake me, Dinny, about not going into my married life. I will not, and that's flat."

"I see his point. You start with the battle half won against you."

"I won't allow the lawyers to work it in. We employ them and they must do what we want. I'm going straight from here to the Temple, by the bye, and perhaps on to the House."

"Excuse my reverting for a moment; but what are you going to do about Tony Croom till this comes on?"

"Go on just as we were, except for nights in cars. Though what the difference between day and night—in a car, or anywhere else—is, I don't know."

"I suppose they go by human nature as a whole." And Dinny leaned back. So many girls, so many young men, snatching their teas and rolls and buns and cocoa; chatter and silence and a stale effluvium, little tables, and the attendant spirits. What *was* human nature as a whole? Didn't they say that it had to be changed? The stuffy past wiped out! And yet this A.B.C. was just like the A.B.C. she went into with her mother before the war, and thought so thrilling because the bread was aerated. And the Divorce Court—into which she had never been yet—was that any different?

"Have you finished, old thing?" said Clare.

"Yes. I'll come with you as far as the Temple."

As they paused to part at Middle Temple Lane, a rather high and pleasant voice said:

"What luck!" and a light momentary grip was laid on her arm.

"If you're going straight to the House," said Clare, "I'll run on and get my things and join you here."

"Tactful," said Dornford. "Let's stand against this 'portal.' When I don't see you for so long, Dinny, I feel lost. Jacob served for Rachel fourteen years—longevity is not what it was, so every month I serve is equal to one of his years."

"Rachel and he were walking out."

"I know. Well, I must just wait and hope. I just *have* to wait."

Leaning against the yellow 'portal' she looked at him. His face was quivering. Suddenly sorry, she said:

"Some day, perhaps I shall come to life again. I won't wait any more now. Good-bye, and thank you! . . ."

This sudden intrusion of herself was no comfort to her in her homing bus. The sight of his quivering face made her restless and uneasy. She did not want to cause him unhappiness—a nice man, considerate to Clare, a pleasant voice, an attractive face; and in range of interest nearer to her than Wilfrid had ever been. Only where was that wild, sweet yearning, transmuting every value, turning the world into a single being, the one longed-for, dreamed-of mate? She sat very still in the bus, looking over the head of the woman on the opposite side, who, with fingers crisped on the satchel in her lap, wore the expression of a sportsman about to try a new field or spinney. The lights were coming up in Regent Street of a cold, just not snowy evening. There used to be the low curving roof line, the rather nice, bilious yellow of the Quadrant. She remembered how on the top of a bus she had differed from the girl Millicent Pole about old Regent Street. Changing, changing, everything changing! And before her suddenly closed eyes came Wilfrid's face, with its lips drawn back, as she had seen it last passing her in the Green Park.

Some one trod on her toe. She opened her eyes, and said: "I beg your pardon."

"Granted, I'm sure."

Very polite! People were more polite every year!

The bus had stopped. Dinny hurried from it. She went down Conduit Street, passing her father's tailors. Poor darling, he never went there now. Clothes were so dear, and, of course, he loathed new clothes! She came to Bond Street.

The traffic staggered to a standstill, the whole street seemed one long line of held-up cars. And England ruined! She crossed into Burton Street. And then, in front of her she saw a familiar figure, walking slowly with his head down! She came up with him.

"Stack!"

He raised his head; tears were trickling down his cheeks. He blinked his large dark prominent eyes, and passed his hand over his face.

"You, miss? I was just coming to you." And he held out a telegram.

Holding it up in the dim light, she read:

"Henry Stack, 50a, Cork Street, London. Very sorry to inform you Honourable Wilfrid Desert drowned on expedition up country some weeks ago. Body recovered and buried on spot. Report only just come in. No possible doubt. Condolences. British Consulate Bangkok."

Stonily she stood, seeing nothing. Stack's fingers came up and detached the telegram.

"Yes," she said. "Thank you. Show it to Mr. Mont, Stack. Don't grieve."

"Oh, miss!"

Dinny laid her fingers on his sleeve, gave it a little pull, and walked swiftly on.

Don't grieve! Sleet was falling now. She raised her face to feel the tingling touch of those small flakes. No more dead to her than he had already been. But—*dead!* Away over there—utterly far! Lying in the earth by the river that had drowned him, in forest silence, where no one would ever see his grave. Every memory she had of him came to life with an intensity that seemed to take all strength from her limbs, so that she nearly collapsed in the snowy street. She stood for a minute with her gloved hand on the railing of a house. An evening postman stopped and looked round at her. Perhaps some tiny flame of hope—that some day he would come back—had flickered deep down within her; perhaps only the snowy cold was creeping into her bones; but she felt deadly cold and numb.

She reached Mount Street at last and let herself in. And there a sudden horror of betraying that anything had happened to awaken pity for her, interest in her, any sort of feeling, beset her, and she fled to her room. What was it to anyone but her? And pride so moved within her that even her heart felt cold as stone.

A hot bath revived her a little. She dressed for dinner early and went down.

The evening was one of silences more tolerable than the spasmodic spurts of conversation. Dinny felt ill. When she went up to bed her Aunt came to her room.

"Dinny, you look like a ghost."

"I got chilled, Auntie."

"Lawyers!—they do. I've brought you a posset."

"Ah! I've always longed to know what a posset is."

"Well, drink it."

Dinny drank, and gasped.

"Frightfully strong."

"Yes. Your Uncle made it. Michael rang up." And taking the glass, Lady Mont bent forward and kissed her cheek. "That's all," she said. "Now go to bed, or you'll be ill."

Dinny smiled. "I'm not going to be ill, Aunt Em."

In pursuance of that resolve she went down to breakfast next morning.

The oracle, it seemed, had spoken in a typewritten letter signed Kingson, Cuthcott and Forsyte. It recommended putting in a defence, and had so advised Lady Corven and Mr. Croom. When it had taken the necessary proceedings it would advise further.

And that coldness in the pit of the stomach which follows the receipt of lawyers' letters was felt even by Dinny, the pit of whose stomach was already deadly cold.

She went back to Condaford with her father by the morning train, repeating to her Aunt the formula: "I'm not going to be ill."

CHAPTER 24

BUT SHE *was* ill, and for a month in her conventual room at Condaford often wished she were dead and done with. She might, indeed, quite easily have died if such belief as she had in a future life had grown instead of declining as her strength ebbed. To rejoin Wilfrid, where this world's pain and judgments were not, had a fatal attraction. To fade out into the sleep of nothingness was not hard, but had no active enticement; and, as the tide of health turned back within her, seemed less and less natural. The solicitude of people had a subtle, pervasive healing influence. The village required a daily bulletin, her mother had been writing or 'phoning almost daily to a dozen people. Clare had been down every week-end, bringing flowers from Dornford. Aunt Em had been sending twice a week the products of Boswell and Johnson; Fleur bombarding her with the products of Piccadilly. Adrian had come down three times without warning. Hilary began sending funny little notes the moment she had turned the corner.

On March the thirtieth, spring visited her room with south-west airs, a small bowl of the first spring flowers, some pussy willow, and a sprig of gorse. She was picking up rapidly now, and three days later was out of doors. For everything in nature she felt a zest such as she had not known for a long time. Crocuses, daffodil clumps, swelling buds, sun on the fantails' wings, shapes and colour of the clouds, scent of the wind, all affected her with an almost painful emotion. Yet she had no desire to do anything or see anybody. In this queer apathy she accepted an invitation from Adrian to go abroad with him on his short holiday.

The memorable things about their fortnight's stay at Argelès in the Pyrenees, were the walks they took, the flowers they picked, the Pyrenean sheep-dogs, the almond blossom they saw, the conversations they held. They were out all day, taking lunch with them, and the opportunities for talk were unlimited. Adrian became eloquent on mountains. He had never got over his climbing days. Dinny suspected him of trying to rouse her from the lethargy in which she was sunk.

"When I went up 'the little Sinner' in the Dolomites with Hilary before the war," he said one day, "I got as near to God as I ever shall. Nineteen years ago—dash it! What's the nearest to God you ever got, Dinny?"

She did not answer.

"Look here, my dear, what are you now—twenty-seven?"

"Nearly twenty-eight."

"On the threshold still. I suppose talking it out wouldn't help?"

"You ought to know, Uncle, that talking one's heart out is not in the family."

"True! The more we're hurt the silenter we get. But one mustn't inbreed to sorrow, Dinny."

Dinny said suddenly: "I understand perfectly how women go into convents, or give themselves up to good works. I always used to think it showed a lack of humour."

"It can show a lack of courage, or too much courage, of the sort fanatical."

"Or broken springs."

Adrian looked at her.

"Yours are not broken, Dinny; badly bent, not broken."

"Let's hope so, Uncle; but they ought to be straightening by now."

"You're beginning to look fine."

"Yes, I'm eating enough even for Aunt Em. It's taking interest in oneself that's the trouble."

"I agree. I wonder if——"

"Not iron, darling. It sews me up inside."

Adrian smiled. "I was thinking more of children."

"They're not synthetic, yet. I'm all right, and very lucky, as things go. Did I tell you old Betty died?"

"Good old soul! She used to give me bull's-eyes."

"*She* was the real thing. We read too many books, Uncle."

"Indubitably. Walk more, read less! Let's have our lunch."

On the way back to England they stayed two nights in Paris at a little hotel over a restaurant near the Gare St. Lazare. They had wood fires and their beds were comfortable.

"Only the French know what a bed should be," said Adrian.

The cooking down below was intended for racing men and such as go where they can appreciate food. The waiters, who wore aprons, looked, as Adrian expressed it, "like monks doing a spot of work," pouring the wine and mixing the salads with reverence. He and Dinny were the only foreigners in either hotel or restaurant, not far from being the only foreigners in Paris.

"Marvellous town, Dinny. Except for cars in place of *fiacres* and the Eiffel Tower, I don't see any real change by daylight since I was first here in '88, when your grandfather was Minister at Copenhagen. There's the same tang of coffee and wood smoke in the air, people have the same breadth of back, the same red buttons in their coats; there are the same tables outside the same cafés, the same *affiches*, the same funny little stalls for selling books, the same violently miraculous driving, the same pervading French grey, even in the sky; and the same rather ill-tempered look of not giving a damn for anything outside Paris. Paris leads fashion, and yet it's the most conservative place in the world. They say the advanced literary crowd here regard the world as having begun in 1914 at earliest, have scrapped everything that came before the war, despise anything that lasts, are mostly Jews, Poles and Irishmen, and yet have chosen this changeless town to function in. The same with the painters and musicians, and every other extremist. Here they gather and chatter and experiment themselves to death. And good old Paris laughs and carries on, as concerned with reality and flavours and the past as it ever was. Paris produces anarchy exactly as stout produces froth."

Dinny pressed his arm.

"That was a good effort, Uncle. I must say I feel more alive here than I have for ages."

"Ah! Paris pets the senses. Let's go in here—too cold to sit out. What'll you have, tea or—absinthe?"

"Absinthe."

"You won't like it."

"All right—tea with lemon."

Waiting for her tea, in the quiet hurly-burly of the Café de la Paix, Dinny watched her uncle's thin bearded form, and thought that he looked quite 'in his plate,' but with a queer, interested contentment that identified him with the life around.

To be interested in life and not pet oneself! And she looked about her. Her neighbours were neither remarkable nor demonstrative, but they gave an impression of doing what they liked, not of being on the way to somewhere else.

"They dig into the moment, don't they?" said Adrian, suddenly.

"Yes, I was thinking that."

"The French make an art of living. We hope for the future or regret the past. Precious little 'present' about the English!"

"Why are these so different?"

"Less northern blood, more wine and oil; their heads are rounder than ours, their bodies more stocky, and their eyes are mainly brown."

"Those are things we can't alter anyway."

"The French are essentially the medium people. They've brought equilibrium to a high point. Their senses and intellects balance."

"But they get fat, Uncle."

"Yes, but all over; they don't jut, and they hold themselves up. I'd rather be English, of course; but if I weren't, I'd rather be French."

"Isn't there anything in having an itch for something better than you've got?"

"Ah! Ever noticed, Dinny, that when we say 'Be good!' they say, 'Soyez sage!'? There's a lot in that. I've heard Frenchmen put our unease down to the Puritan tradition. But that's to mistake effect for cause, symptoms for roots. I admit we've got an urge towards the promised land, but Puritanism was part of that urge, so's our wanderlust and colonising quality; so's our Protestantism, Scandinavian blood, the sea and the climate. None of that helps us in the art of living. Look at our industrialism, our old maids, cranks, humanitarianisms, poetry! We jut in every direction. We've got one or two highly mediumising institutions—the public schools, 'cricket' in its various forms—but as a people we're chock full of extremism. The average Briton is naturally exceptional, and underneath his dread of being conspicuous, he's really proud of it. Where, on earth, will you see more diverse bone formation than in England, and all of it peculiar? We do our level best to be average, but, by George, we jut!"

"You're inspired, Uncle."

"Well, you look about you when you get home."

"I will," said Dinny.

They had a good crossing the next day, and Adrian dropped her at Mount Street.

In kissing him good-bye, she squeezed his little finger.

"You've done me a tremendous lot of good, Uncle."

During those six weeks she had scarcely thought at all about Clare's troubles, and she asked at once for the latest news. A defence had been delivered and issue joined, the case would probably be on in a few weeks.

"I've not seen either Clare or young Croom," said Sir Lawrence, "but I gathered from Dornford that they go about as before. 'Very young' Roger still harps on the need for getting her to speak about her life out there. Lawyers seem to regard the Courts as confessional boxes, in which to confess the sins of your opponent."

"Well, aren't they?"

"Judging by the papers, yes."

"Well, Clare can't and won't. They'll make a great mistake if they try to force her. Has anything been heard of Jerry?"

"He must have started, if he's to be here in time."

"Suppose they lose, what is to be done about Tony Croom?"

"Put yourself in his place, Dinny. Whatever happens, he'll probably come in for a salting from the judge. He won't be in a mood to accept favours. If he can't pay up I don't quite know what they can do to him; something unpleasant, no doubt. And there's the question of Jack Muskham's attitude—he's queer."

"Yes," said Dinny, under her breath.

Sir Lawrence dropped his monocle.

"Your aunt suggests that young Croom should go gold-digging, come back rich and marry Clare."

"But Clare?"

"Isn't she in love with him?"

Dinny shook her head. "She might be if he's ruined."

"H'm! And how are *you*, my dear? Really yourself again?"

"Oh, yes!"

"Michael would like to see you some time."

"I'll go round to-morrow."

And that, meaning much, was all that was said about the news that had caused her illness.

CHAPTER 25

Dinny made the effort needed to go round to South Square next morning. Except with Clare on her arrival from Ceylon, she had not been there since the day of Wilfrid's departure to Siam.

"Up in his workroom, Miss."

"Thank you, Coaker, I'll go up."

Michael did not hear her come in, and she stood for a moment looking at the caricature-covered walls. It always seemed to her so odd that Michael, inclined to over-estimate human virtues, should surround himself with the efforts of those who live by exaggerating human defects.

"Am I interrupting, Michael?"

"Dinny! You're looking a treat! You gave us a bad turn, old thing. Sit down! I was only looking into potatoes—their figures are so puzzling."

They talked for some time, and, then, the knowledge of what she had come for invading both, fell silent.

"You've something to give or tell me, Michael."

He went to a drawer, and took out a little packet. Dinny unwrapped it in her lap. There was a letter, a little photograph, a badge.

"It's his passport photo, and D.S.O. ribbon. In the letter there's something for you; in fact, the whole letter is really for you. They're all for you. Excuse me, I have to see Fleur before she goes out."

Dinny sat motionless looking at the photograph. Yellow with damp and heat, it had the uncompromising reality that characterises passport photographs. "Wilfrid Desert" was written across it, and he looked straight at her out of the pasteboard. She turned it face down on her lap, and smoothed the ribbon, which was stained and crushed. Then, nerving herself, she opened the letter. From it dropped a folded sheet, which she set apart. The letter was to Michael.

"New Year's Day.

"Dear old M.M.,—

"Greetings to you and Fleur, and many good years! I'm far up north in a very wild part of this country with an objective that I may reach or not—the habitation of a tribe quite definitely pre-Siamese, and non-Mongolian. Adrian Charwell would be interested. I've often meant to let you know my news, but when it came to writing, didn't—partly be-

565

cause if you don't know this part of the world, description's no use, and partly because it's difficult for me to believe that anybody can be interested. I'm writing now really to ask you to tell Dinny that I am at peace with myself at last. I don't know whether it's the strength and remoteness of the atmosphere out here, or whether I've gained some of the Eastern conviction that the world of other men does not matter; one's alone from birth to death, except for the fine old companion the Universe—of which one is the microcosm. It's a kind of queer peace, and I often wonder how I could have been so torn and tortured. Dinny, I think, will be glad to know this; just as I would be truly glad to know that she, too, is at peace.

"I've written a little, and if I come back from this business, shall try and produce some account of it. In three days from now we reach the river, cross it and follow up a western tributary towards the Himalayas.

"Faint echoes of the crises you've been having trickle out here. Poor old England! I don't suppose I shall ever see her again; but she's a game old bird when put to it, and I can't see her being beaten; in fact, properly moulted, I expect her to fly better than ever.

"Good-bye, old man, my love to you both; and to Dinny my special love.
"WILFRID."

Peace! And she? She rewrapped the ribbon, photograph and letter and thrust them into her bag. Making no noise, she opened the door, went down the stairs, and out into the sunshine. Alone by the river, she unfolded the sheet she had taken from the letter, and under a plane tree as yet bare of leaves, read these verses:

"Lie Still!

"The sun, who brings all earth to bloom,
Corrupts and makes corruption flower,
Is just a flame that thro' the gloom
Of heaven burns a little hour;

And, figured on the chart of night—
A somewhat negligible star—
Is but a pinpricked point of light
As million-million others are;

And though it be the all in all
Of my existence and decay,
It has as simple rise and fall
As I have, and as short a day.

But that no unction to my heart
Will lay; the smallest germ in me
Plays just as passionate a part
As I do, in eternity.

566

The germ and I and sun, we rise,
Fulfil our little lives, and die;
And to all question God replies:
'Lie still! I cannot tell you why!' "

Lie still! The Embankment was nearly empty of people and of traffic.
She walked on, crossing the main lines of the traffic, and came to Kensington Gardens. There on the Round Pond were many small boats, and
many children interested in their vagaries. A bright-haired little boy, something like Kit Mont, was guiding his boat with a stick to a fresh attempt to
cross the pond. What blissful unconsciousness of all else! Was that the
secret of happiness? To be lost in the moment—to be out of oneself, like a
child! He said suddenly:

"It's going! Look!"

The sails filled, the little boat floated away. The small boy stood with
arms akimbo; and, quickly looking up at her, said:

"Ha! I must run!"

Dinny watched him stop now and again with a jerk to calculate the
landing of his boat.

So one ran through life, watching each venture coming to shore, and
at the end lay still! Like birds who uttered their songs, hunted for worms,
preened their feathers, flew without seeming cause, unless for joy; mated,
built nests and fed their young, and when all was over became little stiffened bundles of feathers, and passed into corruption, and dust.

She followed slowly round the pond, saw him again guiding the boat
with his stick, and said: "What do you call your boat?"

"A cutter. I had a schooner, but our dog ate the rigging."

"Yes," said Dinny, "dogs like rigging—very succulent."

"Very what?"

"Like asparagus."

"I'm not allowed asparagus, it's too expensive."

"But you've tasted it?"

"Yes. See, the wind's catching it again!"

Off went the boat, and off went the small bright-haired boy.

Adrian's words came into her head. "I was thinking more of children."

She walked into what in old days would have been called a glade. The
ground was covered with crocuses, yellow, violet, white, and with daffodils; the trees had eagerness in every twig, stretching their buds upward
to the sun's warmth; the blackbirds were in song. And as she walked she
thought: 'Peace! There is no peace. There is life, and there is death!'

And those who saw her thought: 'Nice-looking girl!' 'Those little hats!'
'Where's she goin', I wonder, with her head in the air?' or, again, just:
'Cool!' She crossed the road and came to the Hudson Memorial. It was
supposed to be a home for birds; but beyond a sparrow or two and a fat
pigeon, there were none; nor were more than three people looking at it.

She, who had seen it with Wilfrid, glanced at it for a moment and walked on.

"Poor Hudson! Poor Rima!" he had said.

She went down to the Serpentine and walked along it; the sun was bright on the water; and beyond it the grass was springy and dry. The papers were already talking of drought! The sound currents from north and south and west joined in a mild continuous roaring. Where he was lying it would be silent; strange birds and little creatures would be the only visitors, and odd-shaped leaves would drop on his grave. There came into her mind the pastoral scenes in some film pictures of the Normandy home of Briand, that she had seen at Argelès. "A pity we have to leave all this!" she had said.

An aeroplane droned its way over to the north, a high, silvery, small, noisy shape. *He* had hated them ever since the war. "Disturbers of whatever Gods there be!"

Brave new world! God no longer in His heaven!

She turned a little north to avoid the place where she used to meet him. The roofless tabernacle of oratory close to the Marble Arch was deserted. She left the Park and went towards Melton Mews. It was over! With a queer little smile on her lips she turned into the Mews and stopped at her sister's door.

CHAPTER 26

SHE FOUND Clare in. For the first few minutes they avoided each other's troubles, then Dinny said: "Well?"

"Not at all well. I've split with Tony—my nerves are in rags and his in tatters."

"But do you mean that he——?"

"No. Only I've told him I can't go on seeing him till this is over. We meet meaning not to talk about the thing, then it crops up, and we get all anyhow."

"He must be awfully unhappy."

"He is. But it's only for another three or four weeks."

"And then?"

Clare laughed—no joyful sound.

"But seriously, Clare?"

"We shan't win, and then nothing will matter. If Tony wants me I suppose I shall let him. He'll be ruined, so I shall owe him that."

"I think," said Dinny, slowly, "that I wouldn't let the result affect me."

"That sounds almost too sensible."

"It wasn't worth while to plead innocence unless you meant to carry it through, however the case goes. If you win, wait till you can divorce Jerry. If you don't win, wait till you're divorced. It won't do Tony any real harm to wait; and it'll certainly do you no harm to know for certain how you feel."

"Jerry is quite clever enough to prevent my ever getting evidence against him, if he sets his mind to it."

"Then we must hope you'll lose. Your friends will still believe in you." Clare shrugged. "Will they?"

"I'll see to that," said Dinny.

"Dornford has advised telling Jack Muskham before the case comes on. What do you say?"

"I should like to see Tony Croom first."

"Well, if you come round again this evening, you'll see him. He comes and stares up at me at seven o'clock on Saturday and Sunday evenings. Quaint!"

"No. Very natural. What are you doing this afternoon?"

569

"Riding with Dornford in Richmond Park. I ride with him in the Row early every morning now. I wish you'd come, Dinny."

"No things, and no muscles."

"Darling," said Clare, springing up, "it really was awful while you were ill. We felt ever so bad. Dornford was quite potty. You look better now than you did before."

"Yes, I'm more pneumatic."

"Oh! you've read the book?"

Dinny nodded. "I'll come round this evening. Good-bye; bless you!" . . .

It was almost seven when she slipped out of Mount Street and walked rapidly towards the Mews. A full moon was up with the evening star in a not yet darkened sky. Coming to the west corner of the deserted Mews, she at once saw young Croom standing below No. 2. Waiting till he began to move away, she ran down the Mews and round the far corner to catch him.

"Dinny! How wonderful!"

"I was told I should catch you looking at the Queen."

"Yes, that's what the cat has come to."

"It might be worse."

"Are you all right again? You must have got a chill in the City that foul day."

"Let's walk as far as the Park. I wanted to ask you about Jack Muskham."

"I funk telling him."

"Shall I do it for you?"

"But why?"

Dinny took his arm:

"He's a connection, through Uncle Lawrence. Besides, I've had occasion to know him. Mr. Dornford is perfectly right; it will depend very much on when and what he's told. Let me!"

"I don't know really—I really don't know."

"I want to see him again, anyway."

Young Croom looked at her.

"Somehow I don't believe that."

"Honest Injun."

"It's terribly sweet of you; of course you can do it much better than I, but——"

"That's enough then."

They had reached the Park, and were walking along the rails toward Mount Street.

"Have you been seeing the lawyers much?"

"Yes, our evidence is all taped out. It's the cross-examination."

"I think I might enjoy that, if I were going to tell the truth."

"They twist and turn what you say so, and their tones of voice! I went into that court and listened one day. Dornford told Clare he wouldn't practise in that court for all the gold in France. He's a sound fellow, Dinny."

"Yes," said Dinny, looking round at his ingenuous face.

"I don't think our lawyers care about the job either. It's not in their line. 'Very young' Roger is a bit of a sportsman. He believes we're telling the truth, because he realises I'm sorry we are. That's your turning. I shall go and bat round the Park, or I shan't sleep. Wonderful moon!"

Dinny pressed his hand.

When she reached her door, he was still standing there, and raised his hat to her—or to the moon, she could not be quite sure which . . .

According to Sir Lawrence, Jack Muskham would be up in Town over the week-end; he now had rooms in Ryder Street. She had not thought twice about going all the way to Royston to see him concerning Wilfrid; but he might well think twice about her going to see him in Ryder Street concerning young Croom. She telephoned, therefore, to Burton's Club at lunch time the next day.

His voice brought back the shock of the last time she had heard it, close to the York Column.

"Dinny Cherrell. Could I see you some time to-day?"

The answer came slowly.

"Er—of course. When?"

"Any time that suits you."

"Are you at Mount Street?"

"Yes, but I would rather come to you."

"Well—er—would—? How about tea at my rooms in Ryder Street? You know the number?"

"Yes, thank you. Five o'clock?"

Approaching those rooms she needed all her pluck. She had last seen him reeling in the thick of that fight with Wilfrid. Besides, he symbolised to her the rock on which her love for Wilfrid had gone aground. She only did not hate him, because she could not help remembering that his bitterness towards Wilfrid had been due to his queer appreciation of herself. Only by fast walking, and slow thinking, did she arrive.

The door was opened to her by one who obviously bettered his declining days by letting rooms to such as he had valeted in the past. He took her up to the second floor.

"Miss—er—Cherwell, Sir."

Tall, lean, languid, neatly dressed as ever, Jack Muskham was standing by the open window of a not unpleasant room. "Tea, please, Rodney." He came towards her, holding out his hand.

'Like a slow-motion picture,' thought Dinny. However surprised at her wanting to see him, he was showing no sign of it.

"Been racing at all since I saw you at Blenheim's Derby?"

"No."

"You backed him, I remember. Clearest case of beginner's luck I ever knew." His smile brought out all the wrinkles on his brown face, and Dinny perceived that there were plenty of them.

"Do sit down. Here's tea. Will you make it?"

She gave him his cup, took her own and said:

"Are the Arab mares over yet, Mr. Muskham?"

"I expect them the end of next month."

"You have young Tony Croom to look after them."

"Oh! Do you know him?"

"Through my sister."

"Nice boy."

"He is," said Dinny. "It's about him I've come."

"Oh!"

The thought 'He owes me too much,' darted through her. He could not refuse her this! Leaning back and crossing her knees, she looked him full in the face.

"I wanted to tell you, in confidence, that Jerry Corven is bringing a divorce suit against my sister, and Tony Croom is cited as the co-respondent."

Jack Muskham moved the hand that held his cup.

"He *is* in love with her and they *have* been going about together, but there is no truth in the charges."

"I see," said Muskham.

"The case is coming on quite soon. I persuaded Tony Croom to let me tell you of it; it would be so awkward for him to talk about himself."

Muskham was looking at her with unmoved face.

"But," he said, "I know Jerry Corven. I didn't realise your sister had left him."

"We keep it to ourselves."

"Was her leaving him young Croom's doing?"

"No. They only met on the boat coming over. Clare left Jerry for quite another reason. She and Tony Croom have been indiscreet, of course; they've been watched and seen together in what are known, I believe, as 'compromising circumstances.'"

"How do you mean exactly?"

"Driving back from Oxford late one evening their lights failed and they spent the rest of the night in the car together."

Jack Muskham raised his shoulders slightly. Dinny leaned forward with her eyes on his.

"I told you there was no truth in the charges; there is *none*."

"But, my dear Miss Cherrell, a man never admits——"

"That is why *I* came to you instead of Tony. My sister would not tell me a lie."

Again Muskham made the slight movement of his shoulders.

"I don't quite see—" he began.

"What it has to do with you? This: I don't suppose they'll be believed."

"You mean if I just read the case it would put me off young Croom?"

"Yes, I think you would feel he had not 'played the game.'" She could not quite keep irony out of her voice.

"Well," he said, "has he?"

"I think so. He's deeply in love with my sister, and yet he's kept himself in hand. One can't help falling in love, you know." With those words all the feelings of the past rose up within her, and she looked down so as not to see that impassive face and the provocative set of its lips. Suddenly, by a sort of inspiration, she said:

"My brother-in-law has asked for damages."

"Oh!" said Jack Muskham, "I didn't know that was done now."

"Two thousand, and Tony Croom has nothing. He professes not to care, but if they lose of course it's ruin."

After that there was silence. Jack Muskham went back to the window. He sat on the sill and said:

"Well, I don't know what I can do?"

"You needn't take his job from him—that's all."

"The man was in Ceylon and his wife here. It's not——"

Dinny rose, took two steps towards him and stood very still.

"Has it ever struck you, Mr. Muskham, that you owe me anything? Do you ever remember that you took my lover from me? Do you know that he is dead out there, where he went because of you?"

"Of me?"

"You and what you stand for made him give me up. I ask you now, however this case goes, not to sack Tony Croom! Good-bye!" And before he could answer she was gone.

She almost ran towards the Green Park. How far from what she had intended! How fatal—perhaps! But her feelings had been too strong—the old revolt against the dead wall of 'form' and those impalpable inexorable forces of tradition which had wrecked her love life! It could not have been otherwise. The sight of his long, dandified figure, the sound of his voice, had brought it all back too strongly. Ah, well! It was a relief; an escape of old bitterness pent within her spirit!

The next morning she received this note:

> "Ryder Street.
> "Sunday.
>
> "Dear Miss Charwell,—
> "You may rely on me in that matter. With sincere regard,
> "Yours very faithfully,
> "John Muskham."

CHAPTER 27

WITH THAT PROMISE to her credit she went back to Condaford the following day and gave herself to mitigation of the atmosphere she found there.
Her father and mother, living their ordinary lives, were obviously
haunted and harassed. Her mother, sensitive and secluded, was just
shrinking from publicity discreditable to Clare. Her father seemed to feel
that, however the case went, most people would think his daughter a light
woman and a liar; young Croom would be excused more or less, but a
woman who allowed circumstance to take such turns would find no one to
excuse her. He was clearly feeling, too, a vindictive anger against Jerry
Corven, and a determination that the fellow should not be successful if
he could help it. Faintly amused at an attitude so male, Dinny felt a sort
of admiration at the painful integrity with which he was grasping the
shadow and letting the substance go. To her father's generation divorce
still seemed the outward and visible sign of inner and spiritual disgrace.
To herself love was love and, when it became aversion, ceased to justify
sexual relationship. She had, in fact, been more shocked by Clare's yielding to Jerry Corven in her rooms, than by her leaving him in Ceylon. The
divorce suits she had occasionally followed in the papers had done nothing
to help her believe that marriages were made in heaven. But she recognised
the feelings of those brought up in an older atmosphere, and avoided adding to the confusion and trouble in her people's minds. The line she took
was more practical: The thing would soon be over one way or the other,
and probably the other! People paid very little attention to other people's
affairs nowadays!

"What!" said the General, sardonically. "'Night in a car'—it's the perfect headline. Sets everybody thinking at once how they themselves would
have behaved."

She had no answer, but: "They'll make a symposium of it, darling:
The Home Secretary, the Dean of St. Paul's, the Princess Elizabeth."

She was disturbed when told that Dornford had been asked to Condaford for Easter.

"I hope you don't mind, Dinny; we didn't know whether you'd be here
or not."

"I can't use the expression, 'I'm agreeable' even to you, Mother."

"Well, darling, one of these days you must go down into the battle again."

Dinny bit her lip, and did not answer. It was true, and the more disquieting. Coming from her gentle and unmanaging mother, the words stung.

Battle! Life, then, was like the war. It struck you down into hospital, turned you out therefrom into the ranks again. Her mother and father would hate 'to lose her,' but they clearly wanted her 'to go.' And this with Clare's failure written on the wall!

Easter came with a wind 'fresh to strong.' Clare arrived by train on the Saturday morning, Dornford by car in the afternoon. He greeted Dinny as if doubtful of his welcome.

He had found himself a house. It was on Campden Hill. He had been terribly anxious to know Clare's opinion of it, and she had spent a Sunday afternoon going over it with him.

" 'Eminently desirable,' Dinny. 'South aspect; garage and stabling for two horses; good garden; all the usual offices, centrally heated,' and otherwise well-bred. He thinks of going in towards the end of May. It has an old tiled roof, so I put him on to French grey for shutters. Really, it's rather nice and roomy."

"It sounds 'marvellous.' I suppose you'll be going there instead of to the Temple?"

"Yes, he's moving into Pump Court, or Brick Buildings—I can't remember. When you think of it, Dinny, why shouldn't he have been made co-respondent instead of Tony? I see much more of him."

Otherwise allusion to 'the case' was foregone. It would be one of the first after the undefended suits were disposed of, and calm before the storm was reigning.

Dornford, indeed, referred to it after lunch on Sunday.

"Shall you be in court during your sister's case, Dinny?"

"I must."

"I'm afraid it may make you very wild. They've briefed Brough, and he's particularly exasperating when he likes with a simple denial like this; that's what they'll rely on. Clare must try and keep cool."

Dinny remembered 'very young' Roger's wishing it had been herself and not Clare.

"I hope you'll tell her that."

"I'll take her through her evidence, and cross-examine her on it. But one can't tell the line Brough will take."

"Shall you be in court yourself?"

"If I can, but the odds are I shan't be free."

"How long will it last?"

"More than a day, I'm afraid."

Dinny sighed.

"Poor Dad! Has Clare got a good man?"

"Yes—Instone, very much hampered by her refusal to talk about Ceylon."

"That's definite, you know. She won't."

"I like her for it, but I'm afraid it's fatal."

"So be it!" said Dinny: "I want her free. The person most to be pitied is Tony Croom."

"Why?"

"He's the only one of the three in love."

"I see," said Dornford, and was silent. Dinny felt sorry.

"Would you care for a walk?"

"Simply love it!"

"We'll go up through the woods, and I'll show you where the Cherrell killed the boar and won the de Campfort—our heraldic myth. Had you any family legend in Shropshire?"

"Yes, but the place has gone, sold when my father died; six of us and no money."

"Oh!" said Dinny, "horrible when families are uprooted."

Dornford smiled.

"Live donkeys are better than dead lions."

While they were going up through the coverts he talked about his new house, subtly 'pumping' her for expression of her taste.

They came out into a sunken roadway leading on to a thorn-bush covered down.

"Here's the place. Virgin forest then, no doubt. We used to picnic here as children."

Dornford took a deep breath. "Real English view—nothing spectacular, but no end good."

"Lovable."

"That's the word."

He spread his raincoat on the bank. "Sit down and let's have a smoke."

Dinny sat down.

"Come on part of it yourself, the ground's not too dry."

While he sat there, with his hands hugging his knees and his pipe fuming gently, she thought: 'The most self-controlled man I ever came across, and the gentlest, except Uncle Adrian.'

"If only a boar would come along," he said, "it would be prime!"

"Member of Parliament kills boar on spur of Chilterns," murmured Dinny, but did not add: "Wins lady."

"Wind's off the gorse. Another three weeks and it'll be green down there. Pick of the year—this, or the Indian summer, I never know. And yours, Dinny?"

"Blossom time."

"Um; and harvest: This ought to be glorious then, quite a lot of corn-land."

"It was just ripe when the war broke out. We came up picnicking two days before, and stayed till the moon rose. How much do you think people really fought for England, Mr. Dornford?"

"Practically all—for some nook or other of it; many just for the streets, and buses, and smell of fried fish. I fought mainly, I think, for Shrewsbury and Oxford. But Eustace is my name."

"I'll remember. We'd better go down now, or we shall be late for tea."

And, all the way home, they contended with birds' songs and the names of plants.

"Thanks for my treat," he said.

"I've enjoyed it, too."

That walk had, indeed, a curiously soothing effect on Dinny. So, she could talk with him without question of love-making.

Bank holiday was sou'-westerly. Dornford spent a quiet hour with Clare over her evidence, and then went riding with her in the rain. Dinny's morning went in arranging for spring cleaning and the chintzing of the furniture while the family were up in town. Her mother and father were to stay at Mount Street, she and Clare with Fleur. In the afternoon she pottered with the General round the new pigsties, progressing as slowly as a local builder, anxious to keep his men in work, could make them. She was not alone again with Dornford until after tea.

"Well," he said, "I think your sister will do, if she keeps her temper."

"Clare can be very cutting."

"Yes, and there's an underlying sentiment among lawyers against being cut up by outsiders in each other's presence; even judges have it."

"They won't find her a 'butterfly on the wheel.'"

"It's no good getting up against institutions, you know; they carry too many guns."

"Oh! well," said Dinny, with a sigh, "it's on the knees of the gods."

"Which are deuced slippery. Could I have a photograph of you, preferably as a little girl?"

"I'll see what we've got—I'm afraid only snaps; but I think there's one where my nose doesn't turn up too much."

She went to a cabinet, took a drawer out bodily, and put it on the covered billiard table.

"The family snap-hoard—choose!"

He stood at her side and they turned them over.

"I took most of them, so there aren't many of me."

"Is that your brother?"

"Yes, and this—just before he went to the war. This is Clare the week before she was married. Here's one of me, with some hair. Dad took that when he came home, the spring after the war."

"When you were thirteen?"

"Fourteen nearly. It's supposed to be like Joan of Arc being taken in by voices."

"It's lovely. I shall get it enlarged."

He held it to the light. The figure was turned three quarters, and the face lifted to the branches of a fruit tree in blossom. The whole of the little picture was very much alive; the sun having fallen on the blossom and on Dinny's hair, which hung to her waist.

"Mark the rapt look," she said; "there must have been a cat up the tree."

"And this?" he said: "Could I have this too?"

The snap was one of her a little older, but still with her hair uncut, full face, hands clasped in front, head a little down and eyes looking up.

"No, I'm sorry. I didn't know it was there." It was the counterpart of one she had sent to Wilfrid.

Dornford nodded; and she realised that in some uncanny way he knew why. Seized with compunction, she said:

"Oh! yes, you can. It doesn't matter, now." And she put it into his hand. . . .

After Dornford and Clare had left on Tuesday morning, Dinny studied a map, took the car and set out for Bablock Hythe. She did not care for driving, but she was moved by the thought of Tony Croom deprived of his week-end glimpse of Clare. The twenty-five miles took her well over an hour. At the inn she was told that he would be at his cottage, and, leaving the car, she walked over. He was in shirt-sleeves distempering the walls of the low, timbered sitting-room. From the doorway she could see the pipe wobble in his mouth.

"Anything wrong with Clare?" he said at once.

"Nothing whatever. I just thought I'd like to have a look at your habitat."

"How terribly nice of you! I'm doing a job of work."

"Clearly."

"Clare likes duck's-egg green; this is the nearest I can get to it."

"It goes splendidly with the beams."

Young Croom said, looking straight before him, "I can't believe I'll ever get her here, but I can't help pretending; otherwise the sand would be clean out of my dolly."

Dinny put her hand on his sleeve.

"You're not going to lose your job. I've seen Jack Muskham."

"Already? You're marvellous. I'll just wash-off and get my coat on, and show you round."

Dinny waited in the doorway where a streak of sunlight fell. The two cottages, knocked into one, still had their ramblers, wistaria, and thatched roof. It would be very pretty.

"Now," said young Croom. "The boxes are all finished, and the paddocks have got their water. In fact, we only want the animals; but they're not to be here till May. Taking no risks. Well, I'd rather have this case over first. You've come from Condaford?"

"Yes. Clare went back this morning. She would have sent her love, but she didn't know I was coming."

"Why did you come?" said young Croom bluntly.

"Fellow feeling."

He thrust his arm within hers.

"Yes. So sorry! Do you find," he added suddenly, "that thinking of other people suffering helps?"

"Not much."

"No. Wanting someone is like tooth or earache. You can't get away from it."

Dinny nodded.

"This time of year, too," said young Croom, with a laugh. "The difference between being 'fond of' and 'loving'! I'm getting desperate, Dinny. I don't see how Clare can ever change. If she were ever going to love me, she would by now. If she's not going to love me, I couldn't stick it here. I'd have to get away to Kenya or somewhere."

Looking at his eyes, ingenuously hanging on her answer, her nerve went. It was her own sister; but what did she know of her, when it came to the depths?

"You never know. I wouldn't give up."

Young Croom pressed her arm.

"Sorry to be talking of my mania. Only, when one longs day and night——"

"I know."

"I must buy a goat or two. Horses don't like donkeys; and as a rule they shy at goats; but I want to make these paddocks feel homey. I've got two cats for the boxes. What do you think?"

"I only know about dogs, and—pigs theoretically."

"Come and have lunch. They've got a rather good ham."

He did not again speak of Clare; and, after partaking together of the rather good ham, he put Dinny into her car and drove her the first five miles of the way home, saying that he wanted a walk.

"I think no end of you coming," he said, squeezing her hand hard: "It was most frightfully sporting. Give my love to Clare," and he went off, waving his hand, as he turned into a field-path.

She was absent-minded during the rest of the drive. The day, though still south-westerly, had gleams of sunlight, and sharp showers of hail. Putting the car away she got the spaniel Foch and went out to the new pigsties. Her father was there, brooding over their construction like the Lieutenant-General he was, very neat, resourceful, faddy. Doubtful whether they would ever contain pigs, Dinny slipped her arm through his.

"How's the battle of Pigsville?"

"One of the bricklayers was run down yesterday; and that carpenter there has cut his thumb. I've been talking to old Bellows, but—dash it!— you can't blame him for wanting to keep his men in work. I sympathise with a chap who sticks by his own men, and won't have union labour. He says he'll be finished by the end of next month, but he won't."

"No," said Dinny, "he's already said that twice."

"Where have you been?"

"Over to see Tony Croom."

"Any development?"

"No. I just wanted to tell him that I've seen Mr. Muskham, and he won't lose his job."

"Glad of that. He's got grit, that boy. Pity he didn't go into the army."

"I'm very sorry for him, Dad; he really is in love."

"Still a common complaint," said the General, drily: "Did you see they've more than balanced the Budget! It's an hysterical age, with these European crises for breakfast every other morning."

"That's the papers. The French papers where the print is so much smaller don't excite one half so much. I couldn't get the wind up at all when I was reading them."

"Papers, and wireless; everything known before it happens; and head-lines twice the size of the events. You'd think, to judge from the speeches, and the 'leaders,' that the world had never been in a hole before. The world's always in a hole, only in old days people didn't make a song about it."

"But without the song would they have balanced the Budget, dear?"

"No, it's the way we do things nowadays. But it's not English."

"Do we know what's English and what isn't, Dad?"

The General wrinkled up his weathered face, and a smile crept about the wrinkles. He pointed at the pigsties.

"Those are. Done in the end, but not before they must be."

"Do you like that?"

"No; but I like this hysterical way of trying to cure it even less. You'd think we'd never been short of money before. Why, Edward the Third owed money all over Europe. The Stuarts were always bankrupt. And after Napoleon we had years to which these last years have been nothing, but they didn't have it for breakfast every morning."

"When ignorance was bliss!"

"Well, I dislike the mixture of hysteria and bluff we've got now."

"Would you suppress the voice that breathes o'er Eden?"

"Wireless? 'The old order changeth, yielding place to new. And God fulfils himself in many ways,'" quoted the General, "'lest one good custom should corrupt the world.' I remember a sermon of old Butler's at Harrow on that text, one of his best, too. I'm not hidebound, Dinny, at least I hope not. Only I think everything's talked out too much. It's talked out so much that it's not felt."

"I believe in the Age, Dad. It's dropped its superfluous clothes. Look at those old pictures in *The Times* lately. You smelt dogma and flannel petticoat."

"Not flannel," said the General, "in my day."

"You should know, dear."

"As a matter of fact, Dinny, I believe *mine* was the really revolutionary generation. You saw that play about Browning? There you had it; but that was all gone before I went to Sandhurst. We thought as we liked, and we acted as we thought, but we still didn't talk. Now they talk before they think, and when it comes to action, they act much as we did, if they act at all. In fact, the chief difference between now and fifty years ago is the freedom of expression; it's so free now, that it takes the salt out of things."

"That's profound, Dad."

"But not new; I've read it a dozen times."

" 'You don't think the war had any great influence, then, sir'? They always ask that in interviews."

"The war? Its influence is pretty well over by now. Besides, the people of my generation were already too set. The next generation was wiped or knocked out——"

"Not the females."

"No, they ran riot a bit, but they weren't really in the thing. As for your generation, the war's a word."

"Well, thank you, dear," said Dinny: "It's been very instructive, but it's going to hail. Come along, Foch!"

The General turned up the collar of his coat and crossed over to the carpenter, who had cut his thumb. Dinny saw him examining the bandage. She saw the carpenter smile, and her father pat him on the shoulder.

'His men must have liked him,' she thought. 'He may be an old buffer, but he's a nice one.'

CHAPTER 28

IF ART IS LONG, Law is longer. The words Corven *v.* Corven and Croom
rewarded no eye scanning the Cause List in *The Times* newspaper. Undefended suits in vast numbers occupied the attention of Mr. Justice
Covell. At Dornford's invitation Dinny and Clare came to the entrance
of his court, and stood for five minutes just inside, as members of a cricket
team will go and inspect a pitch before playing in a match. The judge
sat so low that little but his face could be seen; but Dinny noticed that
above Clare's head in the witness box would be a sort of canopy, or protection from rain.

"If," said Dornford, as they came out, "you stand well back, Clare, your
face will be hardly visible. But your voice you should pitch so that it always carries to the judge. He gets grumpy if he can't hear."

It was on the day after this that Dinny received a note delivered by
hand at South Square.

"Burton's Club: 13.iv.32.

"DEAR DINNY—

"I should be very glad if I could see you for a few minutes. Name your
own time and place and I will be there. Needless to say it concerns Clare.
"Sincerely yours,

"GERALD CORVEN."

Michael was out, but she consulted Fleur.

"I should certainly see him, Dinny. It may be a deathbed repentance.
Let him come here when you know Clare will be out."

"I don't think I'll risk his seeing her. I'd rather meet him somewhere in
the open."

"Well, there's the Achilles, or the Rima."

"The Rima," said Dinny. "We can walk away from it."

She appointed the following afternoon at three o'clock, and continued
to wonder what he wanted.

The day was an oasis of warmth in that bleak April. Arriving at the
Rima, she saw him at once, leaning against the railing with his back to
that work of art. He was smoking a cigarette through a short well-

coloured holder in meerschaum, and looked so exactly as when she had seen him last that, for no reason, she received a sort of shock.

He did not offer to take her hand.

"Very good of you to come, Dinny. Shall we stroll and talk as we go?"

They walked towards the Serpentine.

"About this case," said Corven, suddenly, "I don't want to bring it a bit, you know."

She stole a look at him.

"Why *do* you, then? The charges are not true."

"I'm advised that they are."

"The premises may be; the conclusions, no."

"If I withdraw the thing, will Clare come back to me, on her own terms?"

"I can ask her, but I don't think so. I shouldn't myself."

"What an implacable family!"

Dinny did not answer.

"Is she in love with this young Croom?"

"I can't discuss their feelings, if they have any."

"Can't we speak frankly, Dinny? There's no one to hear us except those ducks."

"Claiming damages has not improved our feelings towards you."

"Oh! that! I'm willing to withdraw everything, and risk her having kicked over, if she'll come back."

"In other words," said Dinny, gazing straight before her, "the case you have framed—I believe that is the word—is a sort of blackmailing device."

He looked at her through narrowed eyes.

"Ingenious notion. It didn't occur to me. No, the fact is, knowing Clare better than my solicitors and the enquiry agents, I'm not too convinced that the evidence means what it seems to."

"Thank you."

"Yes, but I told you before, or Clare anyway, that I can't and won't go on with nothing settled, one way or the other. If she'll come back I'll wipe the whole thing out. If she won't, it must take its chances. That's not wholly unreasonable, and it's not blackmail."

"And suppose she wins, will you be any further on?"

"No."

"You can free yourself and her at any time, if you liked."

"At a price I don't choose to pay. Besides that sounds extremely like collusion—another awkward word, Dinny."

Dinny stood still.

"Well, I know what you want, and I'll ask Clare. And now I'll say good-bye. I don't see that talking further will do any good."

He stood looking at her, and she was moved by the expression on his face. Pain and puzzlement were peering through its hardwood browned mask.

"I'm sorry things are as they are," she said, impulsively.

"One's nature is a hell of a thing, Dinny, and one's never free from it. Well, good-bye and good luck!"

She put out her hand. He gave it a squeeze, turned and walked off.

Dinny stood for some unhappy moments beside a little birch tree whose budding leaves seemed to tremble up towards the sunshine. Queer! To be sorry for him, for Clare, for young Croom, and be able to do nothing to help!

She walked back to South Square as fast as she could.

Fleur met her with: "Well?"

"I'm afraid I can only talk to Clare about it."

"I suppose it's an offer to drop it, if Clare will go back. If she's wise she will."

Dinny closed her lips resolutely.

She waited till bed-time, and then went to Clare's room. Her sister had just got into bed, on the foot of which Dinny sat down, and began at once:

"Jerry asked me to see him. We met in Hyde Park. He says he'll drop the case if you'll go back—on your own terms."

Clare raised her knees and clasped them with her hands.

"Oh! And what did you say?"

"That I'd ask you."

"Did you gather why?"

"Partly, I think he really wants you; partly, he doesn't much believe in the evidence."

"Ah!" said Clare, drily: "Nor do I. But I'm not going back."

"I told him I didn't think you would. He said we were 'implacable.'"

Clare uttered a little laugh.

"No, Dinny. I've been through all the horrors of this case. I feel quite stony, don't care whether we lose or win. In fact, I believe I'd rather we lost."

Dinny grasped one of her sister's feet through the bedclothes. She was in two minds whether to speak of the feeling Corven's face had roused in her.

Clare said uncannily:

"I'm always amused when people think they know how husbands and wives ought to behave towards each other. Fleur was telling me about her father and his first wife; she seemed to think the woman made a great fuss for nothing much. All I can say is that to think you can judge anybody else's case is just self-righteous idiocy. There's never any evidence to judge from, and until cine-cameras are installed in bedrooms," she added, "there never will be. You might let him know, Dinny, that there's nothing doing."

Dinny got up.

"I will. If only the thing were over!"

"Yes," said Clare, tossing back her hair, "if only—! But whether we shall be any further on, when it is, I don't know. God bless the Courts of Law."

That bitter invocation went up daily from Dinny, too, during the next fortnight while the undefended causes, of which her sister's might have been one, were softly and almost silently vanishing away. Her note to Corven said simply that her sister had answered: 'No.' No reply came to it.

At Dornford's request she went with Clare to see his new house on Campden Hill. To know that he had taken it with the view of having a home for her, if she would consent to share it, kept her expressionless, except to say that it was all very nice, and to recommend a bird shelter in the garden. It was roomy, secluded, airy, and the garden sloped towards the south. Distressed at being so colourless, she was glad to come away; but the dashed and baffled look on his face when she said: 'Good-bye' hurt her. In their bus, going home, Clare said:

"The more I see of Dornford, Dinny, the more I believe you could put up with him. He's got very light hands; he lets your mouth alone. He really is a bit of an angel."

"I'm sure he is." And through Dinny's mind, in the jaunting bus, passed and passed four lines of verse:

> 'The bank is steep and wide the river flows—
> Are there fair pastures on the farther shore?
> And shall the halting kine adventure those
> Or wander barren pastures evermore?'

But on her face was that withdrawn expression which Clare knew better than to try and penetrate.

Waiting for an event, even when it primarily concerns others, is a process little desirable. For Dinny it had the advantage of taking her thoughts off her own existence and concentrating them on her people's. The family name, for the first time in her experience, was confronted with a really besmirching publicity, and she the chief recipient of her clan's reaction. She felt thankful that Hubert was not in England. He would have been so impatient and upset. In the publicity attendant on his own trouble, four years ago, there had been much more danger of disaster, but much less danger of disgrace. For, however one might say that divorce was nothing in these days, a traditional stigma still clung to it in a country far from being as modern as it supposed itself to be. The Charwells of Condaford, at all events, had their pride and their prejudices; above all they loathed publicity.

When Dinny, for instance, went to lunch at St. Augustine's-in-the-Meads, she found a very peculiar atmosphere. It was as if her Uncle and Aunt had said to each other: 'This thing has to be, we suppose, but we can't pretend either to understand or to approve of it.' With no bluff matter-of-fact condemnation, nor anything churchy or shocked about their attitude, they conveyed to Dinny the thought that Clare might have been better occupied than in getting into such a position.

Walking away with Hilary to see a party of youths off to Canada from Euston Station, Dinny was ill at ease, for she had a true affection and regard for her overworked unparsonical Uncle. Of all the members of her duty-bound family, he most embodied the principle of uncomplaining service, and however she might doubt whether the people he worked for were not happier than he was himself, she instinctively believed that he lived a real life in a world where not very much was 'real.' Alone with her he voiced his feelings more precisely.

"What I don't like, Dinny, about this business of Clare's is the way it will reduce her in the public eye to the level of the idle young woman who has nothing better to do than to get into matrimonial scrapes. Honestly, I'd prefer her passionately in love and flinging her cap over the windmill."

"Cheer up, Uncle," murmured Dinny, "and give her time. That may yet come."

Hilary smiled.

"Well! Well! But you see what I mean. The public eye is a mean, cold, parroty thing; it loves to see the worst of everything. Where there's real love I can accept most things; but I don't like messing about with sex. It's unpleasant."

"I don't think you're being just to Clare," said Dinny with a sigh; "she cut loose for real reasons; and *you* ought to know, Uncle, that attractive young women can't remain entirely unfollowed."

"Well," said Hilary, shrewdly, "I perceive that you're sitting on a tale you could unfold. Here we are. If you knew the bother I've had to get these youths to consent to go, and the authorities to consent to take them, you'd realise why I wish I were a mushroom springing up overnight, and being eaten fresh for breakfast."

Whereupon, they entered the station, and proceeded towards the Liverpool train. A little party of seven youths in cloth caps, half in and half out of a third-class carriage, were keeping up their spirits in truly English fashion, by passing remarks on each other's appearance, and saying at intervals: "Are we daown-'earted? Naoo!"

They greeted Hilary with the words:

"'Ello, Padre! . . . Zero hour! Over the top! . . . 'Ave a fag, sir?"

Hilary took the 'fag.' And Dinny, who stood a little apart, admired the way in which he became at once an integral part of the group.

"Wish you was comin' too, sir!"

"Wish I were, Jack."

"Leavin' old England for ever!"

"Good old England!"

"Sir?"

"Yes, Tommy?"

She lost the next remarks, slightly embarrassed by the obvious interest she was arousing.

"Dinny!"

She moved up to the carriage.

"Shake hands with these young men. My niece."

In the midst of a queer hush she shook the seven hands of the seven capless youths, and seven times said: "Good luck."

There was a rush to get into the carriage, a burst of noise from uncouth mouths, a ragged cheer, and the train moved. She stood by Hilary's side, with a slight choke in her throat, waving her hand to the caps and faces stretched through the window.

"They'll all be seasick to-night," muttered Hilary, "that's one comfort. Nothing like it to prevent you from thinking of the future or the past."

She went into Adrian's after leaving him, and was rather disconcerted to find her Uncle Lionel there. They stopped dead in their discussion. Then the Judge said:

"Perhaps you can tell us, Dinny: Is there any chance at all of mediating between those two before this unpleasant business comes on?"

"None, Uncle."

"Oh! Then seeing as I do rather much of the law, I should suggest Clare's not appearing and letting the thing go undefended. If there's no chance of their coming together again, what is the use of prolonging a state of stalemate?"

"That's what I think, Uncle Lionel; but, of course, you know the charges aren't true."

The Judge grimaced.

"I'm speaking as a man, Dinny. The publicity will be lamentable for Clare, win or lose; whereas, if she and this young man didn't defend, there'd be very little. Adrian says she would refuse any support from Corven, so that element doesn't come in. What *is* all the trouble about? You know, of course."

"Very vaguely, and in confidence."

"Great pity!" said the Judge: "If they knew as much as I do, people would never fight these things."

"There *is* that claim for damages."

"Yes, Adrian was telling me—pretty medieval, that."

"Is revenge medieval, Uncle Lionel?"

"Not altogether," said the Judge, with his wry smile; "but I shouldn't have thought a man in Corven's position could afford such luxuries. To put his wife into the scales! Thoroughly unpleasant."

Adrian put his arm round Dinny's shoulders.

"Nobody feels that more than Dinny."

"I suppose," murmured the Judge, "Corven will at least have them settled on her."

"Clare wouldn't take them. But, why shouldn't they win? I thought the law existed to administer justice, Uncle Lionel."

"I don't like juries," said the Judge abruptly.

Dinny looked at him with curiosity—surprisingly frank! He added:

"Tell Clare to keep her voice up and her answers short. And don't let her try to be clever. Any laughter in court should be raised by the judge."

So saying, he again smiled wryly, shook her hand, and took himself away.

"Is Uncle Lionel a good judge?"

"Impartial and polite, they say. I've never seen him in court, but from what I know of him as a brother, he'd be conscientious and thorough; a bit sarcastic at times. He's quite right about this case, Dinny."

"I've felt that all along. It's Father, and that claim for damages."

"I expect they regret that claim now. His lawyers must be bunglers. Angling for position!"

"Isn't that what lawyers are for?"

Adrian laughed.

"Here's tea! Let's drown our sorrows, and go and see a film. There's a German thing they say is really magnanimous. *Real* magnanimity on the screen, Dinny, think of it!"

CHAPTER 29

OVER WAS THE SHUFFLING of seats and papers, which marks the succession of one human drama by another, and 'very young' Roger said:

"We'll go into the well of the court."

There, with her sister and her father, Dinny sat down, bastioned from Jerry Corven by 'very young' Roger and his rival in the law.

"Is this," she whispered, "the well at the bottom of which truth lies, or *lies?*"

Unable to see the rising 'body' of the court behind her, she knew by instinct and the sense of hearing that it was filling up. The public's unerring sense of value had scented out a fight, if not a title. The judge, too, seemed to have smelt something, for he was shrouded in a large bandana handkerchief. Dinny gazed upward. Impressively high, and vaguely Gothic, the court seemed. Above where the judge sat red curtains were drawn across, surprisingly beyond the reach of man. Her eyes fell to the jury filing into their two-ranked 'box.' The foreman fascinated her at once by his egg-shaped face and head, little hair of any sort, red cheeks, light eyes, and an expression so subtly blended between that of a cod-fish and a sheep that it reminded her of neither. His face recalled rather one of the two gentlemen of South Molton Street, and she felt almost sure that he was a jeweller. Three women sat at the end of the front row, no one of whom, surely, could ever have spent a night in a car. The first was stout and had the pleasant flattish face of a superior housekeeper. The second, thin, dark, and rather gaunt, was perhaps a writer. The third's bird-like look was disguised in an obvious cold. The other eight male members of the jury tired her eyes, so diverse and difficult to place. A voice said:

"Corven versus Corven and Croom—husband's petition," and she gave Clare's arm a convulsive squeeze.

"If your Lordship pleases——"

Out of the tail of her eyes she could see a handsome, small-whiskered visage, winey under its wig.

The Judge's face, folded and far away, as of a priest or of a tortoise, was poked forward suddenly. His gaze, knowing and impersonal, seemed taking her in and she felt curiously small. He drew his head back, as suddenly.

The slow rich voice behind her began retailing the names and positions of the 'parties,' the places of their marriage and co-habitation; it paused a moment and then went on:

"In the middle of September of last year, while the petitioner was up-country in discharge of official duty, the respondent, without a word of warning, left her home and sailed for England. On board the ship was the co-respondent. It is said by the defence, I believe, that these two had not met before. I shall suggest that they had met, or at all events had had every opportunity of so meeting."

Dinny saw her sister's little disdainful shrug.

"However that may be," proceeded the slow voice, "there is no question that they were always together on the ship, and I shall show that towards the end of the voyage the co-respondent was seen coming out of the respondent's stateroom." On and on the voice drooled till it reached the words: "I will not dwell, members of the jury, on the details of the watch kept on the respondent's and co-respondent's movements; you will have these from the mouths of expert and reputable witnesses. Sir Gerald Corven."

When Dinny raised her eyes he was already in the box, his face carved out of an even harder wood than she had thought. She was conscious of the resentment on her father's face, of the Judge taking up his pen, of Clare clenching her hands on her lap; of 'very young' Roger's narrowed eyes; of the foreman's slightly opening mouth, and the third jurywoman's smothered sneeze; conscious of the brownness in this place; it oozed brownness as if designed to dinge all that was rose, blue, silver, gold, or even green in human life.

The slow voice began its questioning, ceased its questioning; the personable owner of it closed, as it were, black wings; and a different voice behind her said:

"You thought it your duty, sir, to institute these proceedings?"

"Yes."

"No animus?"

"None."

"This claim for damages—not very usual, is it, nowadays among men of honour?"

"They will be settled on my wife."

"Has your wife indicated in any way that she wishes you to support her?"

"No."

"Would it surprise you to hear that she would not take a penny from you, whether it came from the co-respondent or not?"

Dinny saw the cat-like smile beneath the cut moustache.

"Nothing would surprise me."

"It did not even surprise you that she left you?"

She looked round at the questioner. So this was Instone, who Dornford had said was "very handicapped"! He seemed to her to have one of those faces, with dominant noses, that nothing could handicap.

"Yes, that did surprise me."

"Now, why? . . . Perhaps you would translate that movement into words, sir?"

"Do wives generally leave their husbands without reason given?"

"Not unless the reason is too obvious to require statement. Was that the case?"

"No."

"What should you say, then, was the reason? You are the person best able to form an opinion."

"I don't think so."

"Who then?"

"My wife herself."

"Still you must have some suspicion. Would you mind saying what it was?"

"I should."

"Now, sir, you are on your oath. Did you or did you not ill-treat your wife in any way?"

"I admit one incident which I regret and for which I have apologised."

"What was that incident?"

Dinny, sitting taut between her father and her sister, feeling in her whole being the vibration of their pride and her own, heard the slow rich voice strike in behind her.

"My Lord, I submit that my friend is not entitled to ask that question."

"My Lord——"

"I must stop you, Mr. Instone."

"I bow to your Lordship's ruling. . . . Are you a hot-tempered man, sir?"

"No."

"There would be a certain deliberation about your actions, at all times?"

"I hope so."

"Even when those actions were not—shall we say—benevolent?"

"Yes."

"I see; and I am sure the jury also does. Now, sir, let me take you to another point. You suggest that your wife and Mr. Croom had met in Ceylon?"

"I have no idea whether they had or not."

"Have you any personal knowledge that they did?"

"No."

"We have been told by my friend that he will bring evidence to show that they had met——"

The slow rich voice interposed:

"That they had had opportunity of meeting."

"We will take it at that. Were you aware, sir, that they had enjoyed such opportunity?"

"I was not."

"Had you ever seen or heard of Mr. Croom in Ceylon?"

"No."

"When did you first know of the existence of this gentleman?"

"I saw him in London in November last, coming out of a house where my wife was staying, and I asked her his name."

"Did she make any concealment of it?"

"None."

"Is that the only time you have seen this gentleman?"

"Yes."

"What made you pitch on him as a possible means of securing a divorce from your wife?"

"I object to that way of putting it."

"Very well. What drew your attention to this gentleman as a possible co-respondent?"

"What I heard on the ship by which I returned from Port Said to Ceylon in November. It was the same ship as that in which my wife and the co-respondent came to England."

"And what *did* you hear?"

"That they were always together."

"Not unusual on board ship, is it?"

"In reason—no."

"Even in your own experience?"

"Perhaps not."

"What else, if anything, did you hear to make you so suspicious?"

"A stewardess told me that she had seen him coming out of my wife's stateroom."

"At what time of day or night was that?"

"Shortly before dinner."

"You have travelled by sea a good deal, I suppose, in the course of your professional duties?"

"A great deal."

"And have you noticed that people frequently go to each other's staterooms?"

"Yes, quite a lot."

"Does it always arouse your suspicions?"

"No."

"May I go further and suggest that it never did before?"

"You may not."

"Are you naturally a suspicious man?"

"I don't think so."

"Not what would be called jealous?"

"I should say not."

"Your wife is a good deal younger than yourself?"

"Seventeen years."

"Still, you are not so old as to be unable to appreciate the fact that young men and women in these days treat each other with very little ceremony and consciousness of sex?"

"If you want my age, I am forty-one."

"Practically post-war."

"I was through the war."

"Then you know that much which before the war might have been regarded as suspicious has long lost that character?"

"I know that things are all very free and easy."

"Thank you. Had you ever, before she left you, had occasion to be suspicious of your wife?"

Dinny looked up.

"Never."

"But this little incident of his coming out of her cabin was enough to cause you to have her watched?"

"That, and the fact that they were always together on the ship, and my having seen him coming out of the house in London."

"When you were in London you told her that she must come back to you, or take the consequences?"

"I don't think I used those words."

"What words did you use?"

"I think I said she had the misfortune to be my wife, and that she couldn't be a perpetual grass widow."

"Not a very elegant expression, was it?"

"Perhaps not."

"You were, in fact, eager to seize on anybody or anything to free yourself?"

"No, I was eager for her to come back."

"In spite of your suspicions?"

"I had no suspicions in London."

"I suggest that you had ill-treated her, and wished to be free of an association that hurt your pride."

The slow rich voice said:

"My Lord, I object."

"My Lord, the petitioner having admitted——"

"Yes, but most husbands, Mr. Instone, have done something for which they have been glad to apologise."

"As your Lordship pleases. . . . In any case, you gave instructions to have your wife watched. When exactly did you do that?"

"When I got back to Ceylon."

"Immediately?"

"Almost."

"That did not show great eagerness to have her back, did it?"

"My view was entirely changed by what I was told on the ship."

"On the ship. Not very nice, was it, listening to gossip about your wife?"

"No, but she had refused to come back, and I had to make up my mind."

"Within two months of her leaving your house?"

"More than two months."

"Well, not three. I suggest, you know, that you practically forced her to leave you; and then took the earliest opportunity open to you to ensure that she shouldn't come back?"

"No."

"So you say. Very well! These enquiry agents you employed—had you seen them before you left England to return to Ceylon?"

"No."

"Will you swear that?"

"Yes."

"How did you come to hit upon them?"

"I left it to my solicitors."

"Oh! then you had seen your solicitors before you left?"

"Yes."

"In spite of your having no suspicions?"

"A man going so far away, naturally sees his solicitors before he starts."

"You saw them in relation to your wife?"

"And other matters."

"What did you say to them about your wife?"

Again Dinny looked up. In her was growing the distaste of one seeing even an opponent badgered.

"I think I simply said that she was staying behind with her people."

"Only that?"

"I probably said that things were difficult."

"Only that?"

"I remember saying: 'I don't quite know what's going to happen.'"

"Will you swear you did not say: 'I may be wanting you to have her watched'?"

"I will."

"Will you swear that you said nothing which conveyed to them the idea that you had a divorce in your mind?"

"I can't tell you what was conveyed to them by what I said."

"Don't quibble, sir. Was the word divorce mentioned?"

"I don't remember it."

"You don't remember it? Did you or did you not leave them with the impression that you might be wanting to take proceedings?"

"I don't know. I told them that things were difficult."

"So you have said before. That is not an answer to my question."

Dinny saw the judge's head poked forward.

"The petitioner has said, Mr. Instone, that he does not know the impression left on his lawyers' minds. What are you driving at?"

"My Lord, the essence of my case—and I am glad to have this opportunity of stating it succinctly—is that from the moment the petitioner had acted in such a way—whatever it was—as caused his wife to leave him, he was determined to divorce her, and ready to snatch at anything that came along to secure that divorce."

"Well, you can call his solicitor."

"My Lord!"

Those simple words were like a shrug of the shoulders put into sound.

"Well, go on!"

With a sigh of relief Dinny caught the sound of finality in the voice of the 'handicapped' Instone.

"You wish to suggest to the jury that although you instituted these proceedings on the first and only gossip you heard, and although you added a claim for damages against a man you have never spoken to—that in spite of all this you are a forbearing and judicious husband, whose only desire was that his wife should come back to him?"

Her eyes went for the last time to the face up there, more hidden by its mask than ever.

"I wish to suggest nothing to the jury."

"Very well!"

There was a rustling of silk behind her.

"My Lord," the slow, rich voice intoned, "since my friend has made so much of the point, I will call the petitioner's solicitor."

'Very young' Roger, leaning across, said:

"Dornford wants you all to lunch with him . . ."

Dinny could eat practically nothing, afflicted by a sort of nausea. Though more alarmed and distraught during Hubert's case, and at the inquest on Ferse, she had not felt like this. It was her first experience of the virulence inherent in the conduct of actions between private individuals. The continual suggestion that the opponent was mean, malicious and untruthful, which underlay every cross-examining question, had affected her nerves.

On their way back to the court, Dornford said:

"I know what you're feeling. But remember, it's a sort of game; both sides play according to the same rules, and the Judge is there to discount exaggeration. When I try to see how it could be worked otherwise, I can't."

"It makes one feel nothing's ever quite clean."

"I wonder if anything ever is."

"The Cheshire cat's grin did fade at last," she murmured.

"It never does in the Law Courts, Dinny. They should have it graven over the doors."

Whether owing to that short conversation, or because she was getting used to it, she did not feel so sick during the afternoon session, devoted to examination and cross-examination of the stewardess and enquiry agents. At four o'clock the petitioner's case was closed, and 'very young' Roger cocked his eye at her, as who should say: "The Court will now rise, and I shall be able to take snuff."

CHAPTER 30

In THE TAXI on the way back to South Square, Clare was silent, till, opposite Big Ben, she said suddenly:

"Imagine his peering in at us in the car when we were asleep! Or, did he just invent that, Dinny?"

"If he'd invented it, he would surely have made it more convincing still."

"Of course, my head *was* on Tony's shoulder. And why not? You try sleeping in a two-seater."

"I wonder the man's torch didn't wake you."

"I daresay it did; I woke a lot of times with cramp. No; the stupidest thing I did, Dinny, was asking Tony in for a drink that night after we went to the film and dined. We were extraordinarily green not to realise we were being shadowed. Were there a frightful lot of people in Court?"

"Yes, and there'll be more to-morrow."

"Did you see Tony?"

"Just a glimpse."

"I wish I'd taken your advice and let it go. If only I were really in love with him!"

Dinny did not answer.

Aunt Em was in Fleur's 'parlour.' She came towards Clare, opened her mouth, seemed to remember that she shouldn't, scrutinised her niece, and said, suddenly:

"Not so good! I do dislike that expression; who taught it me? Tell me about the Judge, Dinny; was his nose long?"

"No; but he sits very low and shoots his neck out."

"Why?"

"I didn't ask him, dear."

Lady Mont turned to Fleur.

"Can Clare have her dinner in bed? Go and have a long bath, my dear, and don't get up till to-morrow. Then you'll be fresh for that Judge. Fleur, you go with her, I want to talk to Dinny."

When they had gone, she moved across to where the wood fire burned.

"Dinny, comfort me. Why do we have these things in our family? So unlike—except your great-grandfather; and he was older than Queen Victoria when he was born."

596

"You mean he was naturally rakish?"

"Yes, gamblin', and enjoyin' himself and others. His wife was long-sufferin'. Scottish. So odd!"

"That, I suppose," murmured Dinny, "is why we've all been so good ever since."

"What is why?"

"The combination."

"It's more the money," said Lady Mont; "he spent it all."

"Was there much?"

"Yes. The price of corn."

"Ill-gotten."

"His father couldn't help Napoleon. There were six thousand acres then, and your great-grandfather only left eleven hundred."

"Mostly woods."

"That was the woodcock shootin'. Will the case be in the evenin' papers?"

"Certain to be. Jerry's a public man."

"Not her dress, I hope. Did you like the Jury?"

Dinny shrugged. "I can't ever tell what people are really thinking."

"Like dogs' noses, when they feel hot and aren't. What about that young man?"

"He's the one I'm truly sorry for."

"Yes," said Lady Mont. "Every man commits adultery in his heart, but not in cars."

"It's not truth but appearances that matter, Aunt Em."

"Circumstantial, Lawrence says—provin' they did when they didn't. More reliable that way, he thinks; otherwise, he says, when they didn't you could prove they did. Is that right, Dinny?"

"No, dear."

"Well, I must go home to your mother. She doesn't eat a thing—sits and reads and looks pale. And Con won't go near his Club. Fleur wants us and them to go to Monte Carlo in her car when it's over. She says we shall be in our element, and that Riggs *can* drive on the right-hand side of the road when he remembers."

Dinny shook her head.

"Nothing like one's own hole, Auntie."

"I don't like creepin'," said Lady Mont. "Kiss me. And get married, soon."

When she had swayed out of the room, Dinny stood looking out into the Square.

How incorrigible was the prepossession! Aunt Em and Uncle Adrian, her father and her mother, Fleur, yes and even Clare herself—all anxious that she should marry Dornford and be done with it!

And what good would it do any of them? Whence came this instinct for pressing people into each other's arms? If she had any use in the world, would that increase it? 'For the procreation of children,' went the words of the old order. The world had to be carried on! Why had the world to be carried on? Everybody used the word 'hell' in connection with it nowadays. Nothing to look forward to but brave new world!

'Or the Catholic church,' she thought, 'and I don't believe in either.'

She opened the window, and leaned against its frame. A fly buzzed at her, she blew it away, and it instantly came back. Flies! They fulfilled a purpose. What purpose? While they were alive they were alive; when they were dead they were dead. 'But not half-alive,' she thought. She blew again, and this time the fly did not come back.

Fleur's voice behind her said:

"Isn't it cold enough for you in here, my dear? Did you ever know such a year? I say that every May. Come and have tea. Clare's in her bath, and very nice she looks, with a cup of tea in one hand and a cigarette in the other. I suppose they'll get to the end to-morrow?"

"Your cousin says so."

"He's coming to dinner. Luckily his wife's at Droitwich."

"Why luckily?"

"Oh! well, she's a wife. If there's anything he wants to say to Clare, I shall send him up to her; she'll be out of her bath by then. But he can say it to you just as well. How do you think Clare will do in the box?"

"Can anyone do well in the box?"

"My father said I did, but he was partial; and the Coroner complimented you, didn't he, at the Ferse inquest?"

"There was no cross-examination. Clare's not patient, Fleur."

"Tell her to count five before she answers, and lift her eyebrows. The thing is to get Brough rattled."

"His voice would madden me," said Dinny, "and he has a way of pausing as if he had all day before him."

"Yes, quite a common trick. The whole thing's extraordinarily like the Inquisition. What do you think of Clare's Counsel?"

"I should hate him if I were on the other side."

"Then he's good. Well, Dinny, what's the moral of all this?"

"Don't marry."

"Bit sweeping, till we can grow babies in bottles. Hasn't it ever struck you that civilisation's built on the maternal instinct?"

"I thought it was built on agriculture."

"By civilisation I meant everything that isn't just force."

Dinny looked at her cynical and often flippant cousin, who stood so poised and trim and well-manicured before her, and she felt ashamed. Fleur said, unexpectedly:

"You're rather a darling."

Dinner, Clare having it in bed and the only guest being 'very young' Roger, was decidedly vocal. Starting with an account of how his family felt about taxation, 'very young' Roger waxed amusing. His Uncle Thomas Forsyte, it appeared, had gone to live in Jersey, and returned indignantly when Jersey began to talk about taxation of its own. He had then written to *The Times* under the *nom de guerre* of 'Individualist,' sold all his investments, and reinvested them in tax-free securities, which brought him in slightly less revenue than he had been receiving net from his taxed securities. He had voted for the Nationalists at the last election, and, since this new budget, was looking out for a party that he could conscientiously vote for at the next election. He was living at Bournemouth.

"Extremely well-preserved," concluded 'very young' Roger. "Do you know anything about bees, Fleur?"

"I once sat on one."

"Do you, Miss Cherrell?"

"We keep them."

"If you were me, would you go in for them?"

"Where do you live?"

"A little beyond Hatfield. There are some quite nice clover crops round. Bees appeal to me in theory. They feed on other people's flowers and clover; and if you find a swarm you can stick to it. What are the drawbacks?"

"Well, if they swarm on other people's grounds, ten to one you lose them; and you have to feed them all the winter. Otherwise it's only a question of the time, trouble, and stings."

"I don't know that I should mind that," murmured 'very young' Roger; "my wife would take them on." He cocked his eye slightly: "She has rheumatism. Apic acid, they say, is the best cure."

"Better make sure first," murmured Dinny, "that they'll sting her. You can't get bees to sting people they like."

"You can always sit on them," murmured Fleur.

"Seriously," said 'very young' Roger, "half-a-dozen stings would be well worth it, poor thing."

"What made you take up law, Forsyte?" struck in Michael.

"Well, I got a 'blighty' one in the war, and had to get something sedentary. I rather like it, you know, in a way, and in a way I think it's——"

"Quite!" said Michael: "Hadn't you an Uncle George?"

"Old George! Rather! Always gave me ten bob at school, and tipped me the name of a horse to put it on."

"Did it ever win?"

"No."

"Well, tell us, frankly: What's going to win to-morrow?"

"Frankly," said the solicitor, looking at Dinny, "it depends on your sister, Miss Cherrell. Corven's witnesses have done well. They didn't claim too much, and they weren't shaken; but if Lady Corven keeps her head and her temper, we may pull through. If her veracity is whittled away at any point, then—!" he shrugged, and looked—Dinny thought—older. "There are one or two birds on the jury I don't like the look of. The foreman's one. The average man, you know, is dead against wives leaving without notice. I'd feel much happier if your sister would open up on her married life. It's not too late."

Dinny shook her head.

"Well, then, it's very much a case of the personal appeal. But there's prejudice against mice playing when the cat's away."

Dinny went to bed with the sick feeling of one who knows she has again to watch some form of torture.

CHAPTER 31

DAY BY DAY the Courts of Law are stony and unchanged. The same gestures are made, the same seats taken; the same effluvium prevails, not too strong, but just strong enough.

Clare was in black on this second day, with a slim green feather in a close-fitting black hat. Pale, her lips barely touched with salve, she sat so still that one could not speak to her. The words "Society Divorce Suit," and the 'perfect' headline, "Night in a Car," had produced their effect; there was hardly standing room. Dinny noticed young Croom seated just behind his counsel. She noticed, too, that the birdlike jurywoman's cold was better, and the foreman's parroty eyes fixed on Clare. The judge seemed to be sitting lower than ever. He raised himself slightly at the sound of Instone's voice.

"If it pleases your Lordship, and members of the jury—the answer to the allegation of misconduct between the respondent and co-respondent will be a simple and complete denial. I call the respondent."

With a sensation of seeing her sister for the first time, Dinny looked up. Clare, as Dornford had recommended, stood rather far back in the box, and the shade from the canopy gave her a withdrawn and mysterious air. Her voice, however, was clear, and perhaps only Dinny could have told that it was more clipped than usual.

"Is it true, Lady Corven, that you have been unfaithful to your husband?"

"It is not."

"You swear that?"

"I do."

"There have been no love passages between you and Mr. Croom?"

"None."

"You swear that?"

"I do."

"Now it is said——"

To question on question on question Dinny sat listening, her eyes not moving from her sister, marvelling at the even distinctness of her speech, and the motionless calm of her face and figure. Instone's voice to-day was so different that she hardly recognised it.

"Now, Lady Corven, I have one more question to ask, and, before you answer it, I beg you to consider that very much depends on that answer. Why did you leave your husband?"

Dinny saw her sister's head tilt slightly backwards.

"I left because I did not feel I could remain and keep my self-respect."

"Quite! But can you not tell us why that was? You had done nothing that you were ashamed of?"

"No."

"Your husband has admitted that he had, and that he had apologised?"

"Yes."

"What had he done?"

"Forgive me. It's instinct with me not to talk about my married life."

Dinny caught her father's whisper: "By Gad! she's right!" She saw the judge's neck poked forward, his face turned towards the box, his lips open.

"I understood you to say you felt you could not remain with your husband and keep your self-respect?"

"Yes, my Lord."

"Did you feel you could leave him like that and keep your self-respect?"

"Yes, my Lord."

Dinny saw the judge's body raise itself slightly, and his face moving from side to side, as if carefully avoiding any recipient of his words: "Well, there it is, Mr. Instone. I don't think you can usefully pursue the point. The respondent has evidently made up her mind on it." His eyes under drooped lids continued to survey what was unseen.

"If your Lordship pleases. Once more, Lady Corven, there is no truth in these allegations of misconduct with Mr. Croom?"

"No truth whatever."

"Thank you."

Dinny drew a long breath and braced herself against the pause and the slow rich voice to the right behind her.

"You, a married woman, would not call inviting a young man to your cabin, entertaining him alone in your room at half-past eleven at night, spending a night with him in a car, and going about with him continually in the absence of your husband, misconduct?"

"Not in itself."

"Very well. You have said that until you saw him on the ship you had never seen the co-respondent. Could you explain how it was from, I think, the second day at sea you were so thick with him?"

"I was not thick with him, at first."

"Oh, come! Always together, weren't you?"

"Often, not always."

"Often, not always—from the second day?"

"Yes, a ship is a ship."

"Quite true, Lady Corven. And you had never seen him before?"

"Not to my knowledge."

"Ceylon is not a large place, is it, from a society point of view?"

"It is not."

"Lots of polo matches, cricket matches, other functions where you are constantly meeting the same people."

"Yes."

"And yet you never met Mr. Croom? Odd, wasn't it?"

"Not at all. Mr. Croom was on a plantation."

"But he played polo, I think?"

"Yes."

"And you are a horsewoman, very interested in all that sort of thing?"

"Yes."

"And yet you never met Mr. Croom?"

"I have said I never did. If you ask me till to-morrow I shall say the same."

Dinny drew in her breath. Before her sprang up a mental snapshot of Clare as a little girl being questioned about Oliver Cromwell.

The slow rich voice went on:

"You never missed a polo match at Kandy, did you?"

"Never, if I could help it."

"And on one occasion you entertained the players?"

Dinny could see a frown on her sister's brow.

"Yes."

"When was that?"

"I believe it was last June."

"Mr. Croom was one of the players, wasn't he?"

"If he was, I didn't see him."

"You entertained him but you did not see him?"

"I did not."

"Is that usual with hostesses in Kandy?"

"There were quite a lot of people, if I remember."

"Come now, Lady Corven, here is the programme of the match—just take a look at it to refresh your memory."

"I remember the match perfectly."

"But you don't remember Mr. Croom, either on the ground, or afterwards at your house?"

"I don't. I was interested in the play of the Kandy team, and afterwards there were too many people. If I remembered him I should say so at once."

It seemed to Dinny an immense time before the next question came.

"I am suggesting, you know, that you did not meet as strangers on the boat?"

"You may suggest what you like, but we did."

"So you say."

Catching her father's muttered: "Damn the fellow!" Dinny touched his arm with her own.

"You heard the stewardess give her evidence? Was that the only time the co-respondent came to your stateroom?"

"The only time he came for more than a minute."

"Oh! He did come at other times?"

"Once or twice to borrow or return a book."

"On the occasion when he came and spent—what was it?—half an hour there——"

"Twenty minutes, I should say."

"Twenty minutes—what were you doing?"

"Showing him photographs."

"Oh! Why not on deck?"

"I don't know."

"Didn't it occur to you that it was indiscreet?"

"I didn't think about it. There were a lot of photos—snapshots and photos of my family."

"But nothing that you couldn't have shown him perfectly in the saloon or on deck?"

"I suppose not."

"I take it you imagined he wouldn't be seen?"

"I tell you I didn't think about it."

"Who proposed that he should come?"

"I did."

"You knew you were in a very dubious position?"

"Yes, but other people didn't."

"You could have shown him those photographs anywhere? Looking back on it, don't you think it was singular of you to do such a compromising thing for no reason at all?"

"It was less trouble to show them to him in the cabin; besides, they were private photos."

"Now, Lady Corven, do you mean to say that nothing whatever took place between you during those twenty minutes?"

"He kissed my hand before he went out."

"That is something, but not quite an answer to my question."

"Nothing else that could give you satisfaction."

"How were you dressed?"

"I regret to have to inform you that I was fully dressed."

"My Lord, may I ask to be protected from these sarcasms?"

Dinny admired the stilly way in which the judge said:

"Answer the questions simply, please."

"Yes, my Lord."

Clare had moved out from under the shadow of the canopy and was standing with her hands on the rail of the box; spots of red had come into her cheeks.

"I suggest that you were lovers before you left the ship?"

"We were not, and we never have been."

"When did you first see the co-respondent again after you left him on the dock?"

"I think about a week later."

"Where?"

"Down near my people's at Condaford."

"What were you doing?"

"I was in a car."

"Alone?"

"Yes, I had been canvassing and was going home to tea."

"And the co-respondent?"

"He was in a car too."

"Sprang up in it, I suppose, quite naturally?"

"My Lord, I ask to be protected from these sarcasms."

Dinny heard a tittering, and heard the judge's voice addressing nobody: "What is sauce for the goose is sauce for the gander, Mr. Brough."

The tittering deepened. Dinny could not resist stealing a glance. The handsome face was inimitably wine-coloured. Beside her 'very young' Roger wore an expression of enjoyment tinctured by anxiety.

"How came the co-respondent to be on this country road fifty miles from London?"

"He had come to see me."

"You admit that?"

"He said so."

"Perhaps you could tell us the exact words he used."

"I could not, but I remember that he asked if he might kiss me."

"And you let him?"

"Yes. I put my cheek out of the car, and he kissed it, and went back to his car and drove away."

"And yet you say you were not lovers before you left the ship?"

"Not in your sense. I did not say that he was not in love with me. He was; at least he told me so."

"Do you suggest that you were not in love with him?"

"I'm afraid I do."

"But you let him kiss you?"

"I was sorry for him."

"You think that is proper conduct for a married woman?"

"Perhaps not. But after I left my husband I did not regard myself as a married woman."

"Oh!"

Dinny had a feeling as if the whole Court had said that word. 'Very young' Roger's hand emerged from his side pocket; he looked at what it contained intently, and put it back. A rueful frown had come on the pleasant broad face of the jurywoman who resembled a housekeeper.

"And what did you do after you had been kissed?"

"Went home to tea."

"Feeling none the worse?"

"No; better if anything."

Again the titter rose. The judge's face went round towards the box. "Are you speaking seriously?"

"Yes, my Lord. I wish to be absolutely truthful. Even when they are not in love, women are grateful for being loved."

The judge's face came round again to gaze at the unseen above Dinny's head.

"Go on, Mr. Brough."

"When was the next occasion on which you saw the co-respondent?"

"At my aunt's house in London where I was staying."

"Did he come to see your aunt?"

"No, to see my uncle."

"Did he kiss you on that occasion?"

"No. I told him that if we were to meet, it must be platonically."

"A very convenient word."

"What other should I have used?"

"You are not standing there to ask me questions, madam. What did he say to that?"

"That he would do anything I wished."

"Did he see your uncle?"

"No."

"Was that the occasion on which your husband said he saw him leaving the house?"

"I imagine so."

"Your husband came directly he had gone?"

"Yes."

"He saw you, and asked who that young man was?"

"Yes."

"Did you tell him?"

"Yes."

"I think you called the co-respondent Tony?"

"Yes."

"Was that his name?"

"No."

"It was your pet name for him?"

"Not at all. Everybody calls him that."

"And he called you Clare, or darling, I suppose?"

"One or the other."

Dinny saw the judge's eyes lifted to the unseen.

"Young people nowadays call each other darling on very little provocation, Mr. Brough."

"I am aware of that, my Lord. . . . Did you call *him* darling?"

"I may have, but I don't think so."

"You saw your husband alone on that occasion?"

"Yes."

"How did you receive him?"

"Coldly."

"Having just parted from the co-respondent?"

"That had nothing to do with it."

"Did your husband ask you to go back to him?"

"Yes."

606

"And you refused?"

"Yes."

"And that had nothing to do with the co-respondent?"

"No."

"Do you seriously tell the jury, Lady Corven, that your relations with the co-respondent, or if you like it better, your feelings for the co-respondent, played no part in your refusal to go back to your husband?"

"None."

"I'll put it at your own valuation: You had spent three weeks in the close company of this young man. You had allowed him to kiss you, and felt better for it. You had just parted from him. You knew of his feelings for you. And you tell the jury that he counted for nothing in the equation?"

Clare bowed her head.

"Answer, please."

"I don't think he did."

"Not very human, was it?"

"I don't know what you mean by that."

"I mean, Lady Corven, that it's going to be a little difficult for the jury to believe you."

"I can't help what they believe, I can only speak the truth."

"Very well! When did you next see the co-respondent?"

"On the following evening, and the evening after that he came to the unfurnished rooms I was going into and helped me to distemper the walls."

"Oh! A little unusual, wasn't it?"

"Perhaps. I had no money to spare, and he had done his own bungalow in Ceylon."

"I see. Just a friendly office on his part. And during the hours he spent with you there no passages took place between you?"

"No passages have ever taken place between us."

"At what time did he leave?"

"We left together both evenings about nine o'clock, and went and had some food."

"And after that?"

"I went back to my aunt's house."

"Nowhere in between?"

"Nowhere."

"Very well! You saw your husband again before he was compelled to go back to Ceylon?"

"Yes, twice."

"Where was the first time?"

"At my rooms. I had got into them by then."

"Did you tell him that the co-respondent had helped you distemper the walls?"

"No."

"Why not?"

"Why should I? I told my husband nothing, except that I wasn't going back to him. I regarded my life with him as finished."

"Did he on that occasion again ask you to go back to him?"

"Yes."

"And you refused?"

"Yes."

"With contumely?"

"I beg your pardon."

"Insultingly?"

"No. Simply."

"Had your husband given you any reason to suppose that he wished to divorce you?"

"No. But I don't know what was in his mind."

"And, apparently, you gave him no chance to know what was in yours?"

"As little as possible."

"A stormy meeting?"

Dinny held her breath. The flush had died out of Clare's cheeks; her face looked pale and peaked.

"No; disturbed and unhappy. I did not want to see him."

"You heard your counsel say that from the time of your leaving him in Ceylon, your husband in his wounded pride had conceived the idea of divorcing you the moment he got the chance? Was that your impression?"

"I had and have no impression. It is possible. I don't pretend to know the workings of his mind."

"Though you lived with him for nearly eighteen months?"

"Yes."

"But, anyway, you again refused definitely to go back to him?"

"I have said so."

"Did you believe he meant it when he asked you to go back?"

"At the moment, yes."

"Did you see him again before he went?"

"Yes, for a minute or two, but not alone."

"Who was present?"

"My father."

"Did he ask you again to go back to him on that occasion?"

"Yes."

"And you refused?"

"Yes."

"And after that you had a message from your husband before he left London, asking you once more to change your mind and accompany him?"

"Yes."

"And you did not?"

"No."

"Now let me take you to the date of January the—er—third"—Dinny breathed again—"that is the day which you spent, from five in the afternoon till nearly midnight, with the co-respondent. You admit doing that?"

"Yes."

"No passages between you?"

"Only one. He hadn't seen me for nearly three weeks, and he kissed my cheek when he first came in to have tea."

"Oh! the cheek again? Only the cheek?"

"Yes. I am sorry."

"So I am sure was he."

"Possibly."

"You first spent half an hour alone, after this separation, having—tea?"

"Yes."

"Your rooms, I think, are in an old mews—a room below a staircase, a room above—where you sleep?"

"Yes."

"And a bathroom? Besides the tea I suppose you had a chat?"

"Yes."

"Where?"

"In the ground-floor room."

"And then did you walk together, chatting, to the Temple, and afterwards to a film and to dinner at a restaurant, during which you chatted, I suppose, and then took a cab back to your rooms, chatting?"

"Quite correct."

"And then you thought that having been with him nearly six hours, you had still a good deal to say and it was necessary that he should come in, and he came?"

"Yes."

"That would be past eleven, wouldn't it?"

"Just past, I think."

"How long did he stay on that occasion?"

"About half an hour."

"No passages?"

"None."

"Just a drink and a cigarette or two, and a little more chat?"

"Precisely."

"What had you to talk about for so many hours with this young man who was privileged to kiss your cheek?"

"What has anyone to talk about at any time?"

"I am asking you that question."

"We talked about everything and nothing."

"A little more explicit, please."

"Horses, films, my people, his people, theatres—I really don't remember."

"Carefully barring the subject of love?"

"Yes."

"Strictly platonic from beginning to end?"

"I should say so."

"Come, Lady Corven, do you mean to tell us that this young man, who on your own admission was in love with you, and who hadn't seen you for three weeks, never once during all those hours yielded to his feelings?"

"I think he told me he loved me once or twice; but he always stuck splendidly to his promise."

"What promise?"

"Not to make love to me. To love a person is not a crime, it is only a misfortune."

"You speak feelingly—from your own experience?"

Clare did not answer.

"Do you seriously tell us that you have not been and are not in love with this young man?"

"I am very fond of him, but not in your sense."

In Dinny flamed up compassion for young Croom listening to all this. Her cheeks went hot, and she fixed her blue eyes on the judge. He had just finished taking down Clare's answer; and suddenly she saw him yawn. It was an old man's yawn, and lasted so long that it seemed never going to end. It changed her mood, and filled her with a sort of pity. He, too, had to listen day after day to long-drawn-out attempts to hurt people, and make them stultify themselves.

"You have heard the enquiry agent's evidence that there was a light in the upstairs room after you returned with the co-respondent from the restaurant. What do you say to that?"

"There would be. We sat there."

"Why there, and not downstairs?"

"Because it's much warmer and more comfortable."

"That is your bedroom?"

"No, it's a sitting-room. I have no bedroom. I just sleep on the sofa."

"I see. And there you spent the time from soon after eleven to nearly midnight with the co-respondent?"

"Yes."

"And you think there was no harm in that?"

"No harm, but I think it was extremely foolish."

"You mean that you would not have done so if you had known you were being watched?"

"We certainly shouldn't."

"What made you take these particular rooms?"

"Their cheapness."

"Very inconvenient, wasn't it, having no bedroom, and nowhere for a servant, and no porter?"

"Those are luxuries for which one has to pay."

"Do you say that you did not take these particular rooms because there was no one of any kind on the premises?"

"I do. I have only just enough money to live on."

"No thought of the co-respondent, when you took them?"

"None."

"Not even just a sidelong thought of him?"

"My Lord, I have answered."

"I think she has, Mr. Brough."

"After this you saw the co-respondent constantly?"

"No. Occasionally. He was living in the country."

"I see, and came up to see you?"

"He always saw me when he did come up, perhaps twice a week."

"And when you saw him what did you do?"

"Went to a picture gallery or a film; once to a theatre, I think. We used to dine together."

"Did you know you were being watched?"

"No."

"Did he come to your rooms?"

"Not again till February the third."

"Yes, that is the day I am coming to."

"I thought so."

"You thought so. It is a day and night indelibly fixed in your mind?"

"I remember it very well."

"My friend has taken you at length through the events of that day, and except for the hours at Oxford, it seems to have been spent almost entirely in the car. Is that so?"

"Yes."

"And this car was a two-seater, with what, my Lord, is called a 'dicky.'"

The judge stirred.

"I have never been in a 'dicky,' Mr. Brough, but I know what they are."

"Was it a roomy, comfortable little car?"

"Quite."

"Closed, I think?"

"Yes. It didn't open."

"Mr. Croom drove and you were seated beside him?"

"Yes."

"Now when you were driving back from Oxford you have said that this car's lights went out about half past ten, four miles or so short of Henley, in a wood?"

"Yes."

"Was that an accident?"

"Of course."

"Did you examine the battery?"

"No."

"Did you know when or how it was last charged?"

"No."

"Did you see it when it was recharged?"

"No."

"Then why—of course?"

"If you are suggesting that Mr. Croom tampered with the battery——"

"Just answer my question, please."

"I *am* answering. Mr. Croom is incapable of any such dirty trick."

"It was a dark night?"

"Very."

"And a large wood?"

"Yes."

"Just the spot one would choose on the whole of that journey from Oxford to London?"

"Choose?"

"If one had designed to spend the night in the car."

"Yes, but the suggestion is monstrous."

"Never mind that, Lady Corven. You regarded it as a pure coincidence?"

"Of course."

"Just tell us what Mr. Croom said when the lights went out."

"I think he said: 'Hallo! My lights are gone!' And he got out and examined the battery."

"Had he a torch?"

"No."

"And it was pitch dark. I wonder how he did it. Didn't you wonder too?"

"No. He used a match."

"And what *was* wrong?"

"I think he said a wire must have gone."

"Then—you have told us that he tried to drive on, and twice got off the road. It must have been *very* dark?"

"It was, fearfully."

"I think you said it was *your* suggestion that you should spend the night in the car?"

"I did."

"After Mr. Croom had proposed one or two alternatives?"

"Yes; he proposed that we should walk into Henley, and that he should come back to the car with a torch."

"Did he seem keen on that?"

"Keen? Not particularly."

"Didn't press it?"

"N—no."

"Do you think he ever meant it?"

"Of course I do."

"In fact, you have the utmost confidence in Mr. Croom?"

"The utmost."

"Quite! You have heard of the expression 'palming the cards'?"

"Yes."

"You know what it means?"

"It means forcing a person to take a card that you wish him to take."

"Precisely."

"If you are suggesting that Mr. Croom was trying to force me to propose that we should spend the night in the car, you are wholly wrong; and it's a base suggestion."

"What made you think I was going to make that suggestion, Lady Corven? Had the idea been present to your mind?"

"No. When I suggested that we should spend the night in the car, Mr. Croom was taken aback."

"Oh! How did he show that?"

"He asked me if I could trust him. I had to tell him not to be old-fashioned. Of course, I could trust him."

"Trust him to act exactly as you wished?"

"Trust him not to make love to me. I was trusting him every time I saw him."

"You had not spent a night with him before?"

"Of course I had not."

"You use the expression 'of course' rather freely, and it seems to me with very little reason. You had plenty of opportunities of passing a night with him, hadn't you—on the ship, and in your rooms where there was nobody but yourself?"

"Plenty, and I did not avail myself of them."

"So you say; and if you did not, doesn't it seem to you rather singular that you suggested it on this occasion?"

"No. I thought it would be rather fun."

"Rather fun? Yet you knew this young man was passionately in love with you?"

"I regretted it afterwards. It wasn't fair to him."

"Really, Lady Corven, do you ask us to believe that you, a married woman of experience, didn't realise the ordeal by fire through which you were putting him?"

"I did afterwards, and I was extremely sorry."

"Oh, afterwards! I am speaking of before."

"I'm afraid I didn't before."

"You are on your oath. Do you persist in swearing that nothing took place between you in or out of the car on the night of February the third in that dark wood?"

"I do."

"You heard the enquiry agent's evidence that, when about two in the morning he stole up to the car and looked into it, he saw by the light of his torch that you were both asleep and that your head was on the co-respondent's shoulder?"

"Yes, I heard that."

"Is it true?"

"If I was asleep how can I say, but I think it's quite likely. I had put my head there early on."

"Oh! You admit that?"

"Certainly. It was more comfortable. I had asked him if he minded."

"And, of course, he didn't?"

"I thought you didn't like the expression 'of course,' but anyway he said he didn't."

"He had marvellous control, hadn't he, this young man, who was in love with you?"

"Yes, I've thought since that he had."

"You knew then that he must have, if your story is true. But is it true, Lady Corven; isn't it entirely fantastic?"

Dinny saw her sister's hands clenching on the rail, and a flood of crimson coming up into her cheeks and ebbing again before she answered:

"It may be fantastic, but it's entirely true. Everything I've said in this box is true."

"And then in the morning you woke up as if nothing had happened, and said: 'Now we can go home and have breakfast!' And you went? To your rooms?"

"Yes."

"How long did he stay on that occasion?"

"About half an hour or a little more."

"The same perfect innocence in your relations?"

"The same."

"And the day after that you were served with this petition?"

"Yes."

"Did it surprise you?"

"Yes."

"Conscious of perfect innocence, you were quite hurt in your feelings?"

"Not when I thought about things."

"Oh, not when you thought about things? What exactly do you mean by that?"

"I remembered that my husband had said I must look out for myself; and I realised how silly I was not to know that I was being watched."

"Tell me, Lady Corven, why did you defend this action?"

"Because I knew that, however appearances were against us, we had done nothing."

Dinny saw the judge look towards Clare, take down her answer, hold up his pen, and speak.

"On that night in the car you were on a main road. What was to prevent your stopping another car and asking them to give you a lead into Henley?"

"I don't think we thought of it, my Lord; I did ask Mr. Croom to try and follow one, but they went by too quickly."

"In any case, what was there to prevent your walking into Henley and leaving the car in the wood?"

"I suppose nothing really, only it would have been midnight before we got to Henley; and I thought it would be more awkward than just staying in the car; and I always had wanted to try sleeping in a car."

"And do you still want to?"

"No, my Lord, it's overrated."

"Mr. Brough, I'll break for luncheon."

CHAPTER 32

DINNY REFUSED all solicitations to lunch, and taking her sister's arm, walked her out into Carey Street. They circled Lincoln's Inn Fields in silence.

"Nearly over, darling," she said at last. "You've done wonderfully. He hasn't shaken you at all, and I believe the judge feels that. I like the judge much better than the jury."

"Oh! Dinny, I'm so tired. That perpetual suggestion that one's lying screws me up till I could scream."

"That's what he does it for. Don't gratify him!"

"And poor Tony. I do feel a beast."

"What about a 'nice hot' cup of tea? We've just time."

They walked down Chancery Lane into the Strand.

"Nothing with it, dearest. I couldn't eat."

Neither of them could eat. They stirred the pot, drank their tea as strong as they could get it, and made their way silently back to the Court. Clare, not acknowledging ever her father's anxious glance, resumed her old position on the front bench, her hands in her lap and her eyes cast down.

Dinny was conscious of Jerry Corven sitting deep in confabulation with his solicitor and counsel. 'Very young' Roger, passing to his seat, said:

"They're going to recall Corven."

"Why?"

"I don't know."

As if walking in his sleep, the judge came in, bowed slightly to the Court's presence and sat down. 'Lower than ever,' thought Dinny.

"My Lord, before resuming my cross-examination of the respondent, I should be glad with your permission to recall the petitioner in connection with the point of which my friend made so much. Your Lordship will recollect that in his cross-examination of the petitioner he imputed to him the intention of securing a divorce from the moment of his wife's departure. The petitioner has some additional evidence to give in regard to that point, and it will be more convenient for me to recall him now. I shall be very short, my Lord."

Dinny saw Clare's face raised suddenly to the judge, and the expression on it made her heart beat furiously.

"Very well, Mr. Brough."

"Sir Gerald Corven."

Watching that contained figure step again into the box, Dinny saw that Clare too was watching, almost as if she wished to catch his eye.

"You have told us, Sir Gerald, that on the last occasion but one on which you saw your wife before you returned to Ceylon—the first of November, that is—you saw her at her rooms in Melton Mews?"

"Yes."

Dinny gasped. It had come!

"Now on that occasion, besides any conversation that took place between you, what else occurred?"

"We were husband and wife."

"You mean that the marital relationship between you was re-established?"

"Yes, my Lord."

"Thank you, Sir Gerald; I think that disposes finally of my friend's point; and it is all I wanted to ask."

Instone was speaking.

"Why did you not say that when you were first examined?"

"I did not see its relevance until after your cross-examination."

"Do you swear that you have not invented it?"

"Most certainly I do."

And still Dinny sat braced against the woodwork with her eyes shut, thinking of the young man three rows behind her. Atrocious! But who would see it here? People's innermost nerves were torn out of them, examined coldly, almost with enjoyment, and put back lacerated.

"Now, Lady Corven, will you go back to the box?"

When Dinny opened her eyes Clare was standing close up to the rail with her head held high and her gaze fixed on her questioner.

"Now, Lady Corven," said the slow rich voice, "you heard that piece of evidence."

"Yes."

"Is it true?"

"I do not wish to answer."

"Why?"

Dinny saw that she had turned to the judge.

"My Lord, when my counsel asked me about my married life, I refused to go into it, and I do not wish to go into it now."

For a moment the judge's eyes were turned towards the box; then strayed from it to stare at the unseen.

"This question arises out of evidence given in rebuttal of a suggestion made by your own counsel. You must answer it."

No answer came.

"Ask the question again, Mr. Brough."

"Is it true that on the occasion of which your husband spoke the marital relationship was re-established between you?"

"No. It is not true."

Dinny, who knew that it was, looked up. The judge's eyes were still fixed above her head, but she saw the slight pouting of his lips. He did not believe the answer.

The slow rich voice was speaking, and she caught in it a peculiar veiled triumph.

"You swear that?"

"Yes."

"So your husband has gone out of his way to commit perjury in making that statement?"

"It is his word against mine."

"And I think I know which will be taken. Is it not true that you have made the answer you have in order to save the feelings of the co-respondent?"

"It is not."

"From first to last, can we attach any more importance to the truth in any of your answers than to the truth in that last?"

"I don't think that is a fair question, Mr. Brough. The witness does not know what importance we attach."

"Very good, my Lord. I'll put it another way. *Throughout* have you told the truth, Lady Corven, and nothing but the truth?"

"I have."

"*Very* well. I have no more to ask you."

During the few questions put to her sister, in a re-examination which carefully avoided the last point, Dinny could think only of young Croom. At heart she felt the case was lost, and longed to take Clare and creep away. If only that man behind with the hooked nose had not tried to blacken Corven and prove too much, this last mine would not have been sprung! And yet—to blacken the other side—what was it but essence of procedure!

When Clare was back in her seat, white and exhausted, she whispered:

"Would you like to come away, darling?"

Clare shook her head.

"James Bernard Croom."

For the first time since the case began Dinny had a full view, and hardly knew him. His tanned face was parched and drawn; he looked excessively thin. His grey eyes seemed hiding under their brows, and his lips were bitter and compressed. He looked at least five years older, and she knew at once that Clare's denial had not deceived him.

"Your name is James Bernard Croom—you live at Bablock Hythe—and are in charge of a horse-breeding establishment there? Have you any private means?"

"None whatever."

It was not Instone who was examining, but a younger man with a sharper nose, seated just behind him.

"Up to September last year you were superintending a tea plantation in Ceylon? Did you ever meet the respondent in Ceylon?"

"Never."

"You were never at her house?"

"No."

"You have heard of a certain polo match in which you played, and after which she entertained the players?"

"Yes, but I didn't go. I had to get back."

"Was it on the boat, then, that you first met her?"

"Yes."

"You make no secret of the fact that you fell in love with her?"

"None."

"In spite of that, is there any truth in these allegations of misconduct between you?"

"None whatever."

And as the evidence he gave to the Court went on and on Dinny's eyes never left his face, as if fascinated by its constrained but bitter unhappiness.

"Now, Mr. Croom, this is my last question: You are aware that if these allegations of misconduct were true, you would be in the position of a man who has seduced a wife in her husband's absence. What have you to say to that?"

"I have to say that if Lady Corven had felt for me what I feel for her, I should have written to her husband at once to tell him the state of things."

"You mean that you would have given him warning before anything took place between you?"

"I don't say that, but as soon as possible."

"But she did *not* feel for you what you felt for her?"

"I am sorry to say, no."

"So that in fact no occasion to inform the husband ever arose?"

"No."

"Thank you."

A slight stiffening of young Croom's figure heralded Brough's rich slow voice, saying with peculiar deliberation:

"In your experience, sir, are the feelings of lovers towards each other ever the same?"

"I have no experience."

"No experience? You know the French proverb as to there being always one who kisses and the other who offers the cheek to the kiss?"

"I've heard it."

"Don't you think it's true?"

"About as true as any proverb."

"According to the stories you both tell, you were pursuing in her husband's absence a married woman who didn't want you to pursue her? Not a very honourable position—yours—was it? Not exactly what is called 'playing the game'?"

"I suppose not."

"But I suggest, Mr. Croom, that your position was not as dishonourable as all that, and that in spite of the French proverb she *did* want you to pursue her?"

"She did not."

"You say that in face of the cabin incident; in face of her getting you in to distemper her walls; in face of the invitation to tea and to spend over half an hour with her at nearly midnight in those convenient rooms of hers; in face of the suggestion that you should spend the night with her in a car, and come to breakfast the morning after? Come, Mr. Croom, isn't that carrying your chivalry rather far? What you say has to convince men and women of the world, you know."

"I can only say that, if her feelings for me had been what mine were for her, we should have gone away together at once. The blame is entirely mine, and she has only treated me kindly because she was sorry for me."

"If what you both say is true, she gave you hell—I beg your pardon, my Lord—in the car, didn't she? Was that kind?"

"When a person is not in love I don't think they realise the feelings of one who is."

"Are you a cold-blooded person?"

"No."

"But she is?"

"How is the witness to know that, Mr. Brough?"

"My Lord, I should have put it: But you think she is?"

"I do not think so."

"And yet you would have us think that she was kind in letting you pass the night with her head on your shoulder? Well, well! You say if her feelings had been yours, you would have gone away at once. What would you have gone away on? Had you any money?"

"Two hundred pounds."

"And she?"

"Two hundred a year, apart from her job."

"Flown away and lived on air, eh?"

"I should have got some job."

"Not your present one?"

"Probably not."

"I suggest that both of you felt it would be mad to fling your caps over the windmill like that?"

"I never felt so."

"What made you defend this action?"

"I wish we hadn't."

"Then why did you?"

"She thought, and her people thought, that as we had done nothing, we ought to defend."

"But *you* didn't think so?"

"I didn't think we should be believed, and I wanted her free."

"Her honour didn't occur to you?"

"Of course it did; but I thought for her to stay tied was too heavy a price to pay for it."

"You say you didn't think you'd be believed? Altogether too improbable a story?"

"No; but the more one speaks the truth, the less one expects to be believed."

Dinny saw the judge turn and look at him.

"Are you speaking generally?"

"No, my Lord, I meant here."

The judge's face came round again and his eyes studied the unseen above Dinny's head.

"I am considering, you know, whether I should commit you for contempt of Court."

"I am sorry, my Lord; what I meant was that anything one says is turned against one."

"You speak out of inexperience. I will let it pass this time, but you mustn't say things of that sort again. Go on, Mr. Brough."

"The question of damages, of course, didn't affect you in making up your mind to defend this action?"

"No."

"You have said that you have no private means. Is that true?"

"Certainly."

"Then how do you mean that it didn't affect you?"

"I was thinking so much of other things that bankruptcy didn't seem to matter."

"Now you have said in examination that you were not aware of Lady Corven's existence until you were on this ship coming home. Do you know a place in Ceylon called Neuralya?"

"No."

"What?"

Dinny saw a faint smile creep out among the Judge's folds and wrinkles.

"Put the question another way, Mr. Brough; we generally call it Neuralya."

"I know Neuralya, my Lord."

"Were you there in June last?"

"Yes."

"Was Lady Corven there?"

"She may have been."

"Wasn't she in the same hotel as you?"

"No. I wasn't in an hotel. I was staying with a friend."

"And you did not meet her playing golf or tennis, or out riding?"

"I did not."

"Or anywhere?"

"No."

"Not a large place, is it?"

"Not very."

"And she's a conspicuous person, isn't she?"

"I think so."

"So you never met her till you were both on this ship?"

"No."

"When did you first become conscious that you were in love with her?"

"About the second or third day out."

"Love almost at first sight, in fact?"

"Yes."

"And it didn't occur to you, knowing that she was a married woman, to avoid her?"

"I knew I ought to, but I wasn't able."

"You would have been able to if she had discouraged you?"

"I don't know."

"Did she in fact discourage you?"

"N-no. I don't think she was aware of my feelings for some time."

"Women are very quick in such matters, Mr. Croom. Do you seriously suggest that she was unaware?"

"I don't know."

"Did you trouble to conceal your feelings?"

"If you mean did I make love to her on the ship—I did not."

"When did you first make love to her?"

"I told her my feelings just before we left the ship."

"Was there any real reason why you should have gone to her stateroom to see those photographs?"

"I suppose not."

"Did you look at any photographs at all?"

"Certainly."

"What else did you do?"

"I think we talked."

"Don't you know? This was an occasion for you, wasn't it? Or was it only one of several occasions of which we have not been told?"

"It was the only time I was inside her stateroom."

"In that case surely you remember?"

"We just sat and talked."

"Beginning to remember, eh? Where did you sit?"

"In the chair."

"And where did she sit?"

"On her bed. It was a small cabin—there was no other chair."

"An outside cabin?"

"Yes."

"No chance of being overlooked?"

"No, but there was nothing to overlook."

"So you both say. I suppose it gave you something of a thrill, didn't it?"

Dinny saw the judge's face poked forward.

"I don't want to interrupt you, Mr. Brough, but the witness has made no secret of his feelings."

"Very well, my Lord. I will put it to him bluntly. I suggest, sir, that on that occasion there was misconduct between you?"

"There was none."

"H'm! Tell the jury why it was that when Sir Gerald Corven came to London you did not go to him and frankly avow your relations with his wife."

"What relations?"

"Come, sir! The fact, on your own showing, that you were seeing all you could of his wife; the fact that you were in love with her, and wanted her to go away with you."

"She did not want to go away with me. I would willingly have gone to her husband, but I had no right to without her permission."

"Did you ask for that permission?"

"No."

"Why not?"

"Because she had told me; we could only meet as friends."

"I suggest she told you nothing of the sort?"

"My Lord, that is asking me if I am a liar."

"Answer the question."

"I am not a liar."

"That is the answer, I think, Mr. Brough."

"Tell me, sir: you heard the respondent's evidence, did it strike you as entirely truthful?"

Dinny saw, and hoped that no one else saw, the quivering of his face.

"Yes, so far as I could judge."

"It was perhaps not quite a fair question. But I may put it this way: If the respondent were to say that she had done, or not done, this or that, you would feel bound in honour to corroborate her statement, where you could, and to believe it where you could not?"

"I am not sure that is quite fair, Mr. Brough."

"My Lord, I submit that it is vital to my case to establish to the jury what the state of the co-respondent's mind has been throughout this business."

"Well, I won't stop the question, but there is a limit, you know, to these generalities."

Dinny saw the first flicker of a smile on young Croom's face.

"My Lord, I don't at all mind answering the question. I do not know what I should feel bound in honour to do, generally speaking."

"Well, let us come to the particular. Lady Corven has said that she could trust you not to make love to her. Would you say that was true?"

Dinny saw his face darken.

"Not quite true. But she knew I did my best not to."

"But now and then you couldn't help it?"

"I don't know what you mean by the expression 'making love'; but now and then I know I showed my feelings."

"Now and then? Mr. Croom, didn't you always show your feelings?"

"If you mean did I always show that I was in love with her—of course I did, you can't hide a thing like that."

"That is a fair admission. I don't want to catch you. I mean more than just showing by your face and eyes that you were in love. I mean downright physical expression."

"Then no, except——"

"Yes?"

"Kissing her cheek three times altogether, and holding her hand sometimes."

"So much she has admitted, and it is all you are prepared to swear to?"

"I will swear there was no more."

"Tell me, did you sleep at all during that night in the car, when her head was on your shoulder?"

"Yes."

"Considering the state of your feelings, wasn't that singular?"

"Yes. But I was up at five that morning and I'd driven a hundred and fifty miles."

"You seriously expect us to believe that after nearly five months of longing you took no advantage of that marvellous opportunity, but just went to sleep?"

"I took no advantage. But I have told you that I do not expect to be believed."

"I don't wonder."

For a long time the slow rich voice went on asking questions, and for a long time Dinny's eyes remained fixed on that bitterly unhappy face, till a sort of numbness came over her. She was roused by:

"I suggest to you, sir, that from the beginning to end of your evidence you have been actuated by the feeling that you must do everything you can for this lady without regard to your own consciousness of what is true? That your attitude, in fact, has been one of distorted chivalry?"

"No."

"Very well. That is all."

Then came the re-examination, and the judge's releasing remark.

Dinny and Clare arose and, followed by their father, walked out into the corridor, and, as quickly as might be, to open air.

The General said:

"Instone's made a mess of it, with that quite unnecessary point of his."

Clare did not answer.

"I am glad," said Dinny. "You'll get your divorce."

CHAPTER 33

THE SPEECHES were over and the judge was summing up. From beside her father, on one of the back benches now, Dinny could see Jerry Corven still sitting in front beside his solicitors, and 'very young' Roger sitting alone. Clare was not in Court. Neither was young Croom.

The judge's voice came slowly, as if struggling past his teeth. It seemed to Dinny marvellous how he remembered everything, for he looked but little at his notes; nor could she detect anything that was not fair in his review of the evidence. Now and again his eyes, turned towards the jury, seemed to close, but his voice never stopped. Now and again he poked his neck forward, priest and tortoise for a moment coalescing; then he would draw it back and speak as it were to himself.

"The evidence not being of the conclusive nature which we expect of evidence tendered to this Court"—(No 'calling with a cup of tea,' she thought), "counsel for the petitioner in his able speech laid great stress, and rightly, upon credibility. He directed your attention especially to the respondent's denial that there was any renewal of the marital relationship between the petitioner and herself on the occasion when he went to her rooms. He suggested that there was reason for her denial in her desire to spare the feelings of the co-respondent. But you must consider whether a woman who, as she says, was not in love with the co-respondent, had not encouraged him, or been intimate with him in any way, would go so far as to perjure herself to save his feelings. According to her account, he was from the beginning of their acquaintanceship in the nature of a friend to her and nothing more. On the other hand, if you believe the petitioner on that point—and there seems no sufficient reason for his volunteering perjury—it follows that you disbelieve the respondent, and she has deliberately denied evidence which was in her favour rather than against her. It seems difficult to believe that she would do that unless she had feelings for the co-respondent warmer than those of mere friendship. This is, in fact, a very crucial point, and the decision you come to as to which is true—the husband's statement or the wife's denial of it—seems to me a cardinal factor in your consideration of whether or not to accept the respondent's evidence in the rest of the case. You have only what is called circumstantial evidence to go upon; and in such cases the credibility of the parties is a very important factor. If on one point you are satisfied that one of the parties is not speaking the truth, then the whole of his or her evidence is tinged with doubt. In regard to the co-respondent, though he conveyed an impression of candour, you must remember that there is a traditional belief in this country, regrettable or not, that a man, whose attentions have involved a married woman in a situation of this kind, must not, in vulgar parlance, 'give her away.' You must ask yourselves how far can you treat this young man, who is quite obviously, and by his own admission, deeply in love, as a free, independent, truthful witness.

"On the other hand, and apart from this question of general credibility, you must not let appearances run away with your judgment. In these days young people are free and easy in their association with each other. What might have seemed conclusive indication in the days of my youth, is now by no means conclusive. In regard to the night, however, that was spent in the car, you may think it well to pay particular attention to the answer the respondent gave to my question: Why, when the lights went out, they did not simply stop a passing car, tell the occupants what had happened and request to be given a lead into Henley. Her answer was: 'I don't think we thought of it, my Lord. I did ask Mr. Croom to follow a car, but it was going too fast.' It is for you to consider, in the light of that answer, whether the respondent really wanted that simple solution of the difficulty they were in, namely, a lead into Henley, where no doubt the damage could have been repaired; or whence at least she could have returned to London by train. It is said by her counsel that to have gone into Henley at that time with a damaged car would have made them too conspicuous. But you will remember that she has said she was not aware that she was being watched. If that was so, you will consider whether the question of conspicuosity would have been present to her mind?"

Dinny's gaze by now had left the judge's face and was fixed upon the jury. And, while she searched the lack of expression on those twelve faces, a 'cardinal factor' was uppermost in her mind: It was easier to disbelieve than to believe. Remove whatever tempering influence there might be from a witness's voice and face, and would not the spicier version of events prevail? The word 'damages' took her eyes back to the judge's face.

"Because," he was saying, "if you should come to a decision in favour of the petitioner, the question of the damages he claims will arise. And in regard to that I must draw your attention to one or two salient considerations. It cannot be said that claims for damages in divorce suits are common in these days, or indeed looked on with any great favour in this Court. It has become disagreeable to think of women in terms of money. Not much more than a hundred years ago it was actually not unknown —though illegal even then—for a man to offer his wife for sale. Such days —thank God—are long past. Though damages can still be asked for in this Court, they must not be what is called 'vindictive,' and they must bear reasonable relation to the co-respondent's means. In this case the petitioner has stated that if any damages are awarded him, they will be settled on the respondent. That is, one may say, the usual practice nowadays where damages are claimed. In regard to the co-respondent's means, if it should become necessary for you to consider the question of damages, I would remind you that his counsel stated that he has no private means, and offered to provide evidence of the fact. One has never known counsel to make a statement of that sort without being sure of his ground, and I think you may take the co-respondent's word for it that his only means of subsistence are derived from his—er—'job,' which appears to carry a salary of four hundred pounds a year. Those, then, are the considerations which should guide you if you should have to consider the amount, if any, of damages to be awarded. Now, members of the jury, I send you to your task. The issues are grave for the future of these people, and I am sure that I can trust you to give them your best attention. You may retire if you wish to do so."

Dinny was startled by the way he withdrew almost at once into contemplation of a document which he raised from the desk in front.

'He really is an old ducky,' she thought, and her gaze went back to the jury rising from their seats. Now that the ordeals of her sister and Tony Croom were over, she felt very little interested. Even the Court to-day was but sparsely filled.

'They only came to enjoy the suffering,' was her bitter thought.

A voice said:

"Clare is still in the Admiralty Court when you want her." Dornford in wig and gown was sitting down beside her: "How did the judge sum up?"

"Very fairly."

"He *is* fair."

"But barristers, I think, might wear: 'Fairness is a virtue, a little more won't hurt you,' nicely printed on their collars."

"You might as well print it round the necks of hounds on a scent. Still, even this Court isn't as bad in that way as it used to be."

"I'm so glad."

He sat quite still, looking at her. And she thought:

'His wig suits the colour of his face.'

Her father leaned across her.

"How long do they give you to pay costs in, Dornford?"

"A fortnight is the usual order, but you can get it extended."

"It's a foregone conclusion," said the General glumly. "Well, she'll be free of him."

"Where is Tony Croom?" asked Dinny.

"I saw him as I came in. At the corridor window—quite close. You can't miss him. Shall I go and tell him to wait?"

"If you would."

"Then will you all come to my chambers when it's over?" Receiving their nods, he went out and did not come back.

Dinny and her father sat on. An usher brought the judge a written communication; he wrote upon it, and the usher took it back to the jury. Almost immediately they came in.

The broad and pleasant face of her who looked like a housekeeper had a mortified expression as if she had been over-ridden; and, instantly, Dinny knew what was coming.

"Members of the jury, are you agreed on your verdict?"

The foreman rose.

"We are."

"Do you find the respondent guilty of adultery with the co-respondent?"

"Yes."

"Do you find the co-respondent guilty of adultery with the respondent?"

'Isn't that the same?' thought Dinny.

"Yes."

"And what damages do you say the co-respondent should be ordered to pay?"

"We think that he should pay the costs of all the parties to the action."

Through Dinny passed the thought: 'The more one loves the more one pays.' Barely listening to the judge's words, she whispered to her father, and slipped away.

Young Croom was leaning against the stone that framed the window, and she thought she had never seen so desolate a figure.

"Well, Dinny?"

"Lost. No damages, just all the costs. Come out, I want to talk to you."

They went in silence.

"Let's go and sit on the Embankment."

Young Croom laughed. "The Embankment! Marvellous!"

No other word passed between them till they were seated under a plane tree whose leaves were not yet fully unfurled in that cold spring.

"Rotten!" said Dinny.

"I've been a complete fool all through, and there's an end of it."

"Have you had anything to eat these last two days?"

"I suppose so. I've drunk quite a lot, anyway."

"What are you going to do now, dear boy?"

"See Jack Muskham, and try and get another job somewhere out of England."

Dinny felt as if she had grasped a stick by the wrong end. She could only be helpful if she knew Clare's feelings.

"No one takes advice," she said, "but couldn't you manage to do nothing at all for a month or so?"

"I don't know, Dinny."

"Have those mares come?"

"Not yet."

"Surely you won't give that job up, before it's even begun?"

"It seems to me I've only got one job at the moment—to keep going somehow, somewhere."

"Don't I know that feeling? But don't do anything desperate! Promise! Good-bye my dear, I must hurry back."

She stood up and pressed his hand hard.

When she reached Dornford's chambers, her father and Clare were already there, and 'very young' Roger with them.

Clare's face looked as though the whole thing had happened to someone else.

The General was saying:

"What will the total costs come to, Mr. Forsyte?"

"Not far short of a thousand, I should say."

"A thousand pounds for speaking the truth! We can't possibly let young Croom pay more than his own share. He hasn't a bob."

'Very young' Roger took snuff.

"Well," said the General, "I must go and put my wife out of her misery. We're going back to Condaford this afternoon, Dinny. Coming?"

Dinny nodded.

"Good! Many thanks, Mr. Forsyte. Early in November, then—the decree? Good-bye!"

When he had gone Dinny said in a low voice:

"Now that it's over, what do you really think?"

"As I did at first: If you'd been your sister we should have won."

"I want," said Dinny, coldly, "to know whether you believe them or not?"

"On the whole—yes."

"Is it impossible for a lawyer to go further than that?"

'Very young' Roger smiled.

"No one tells the truth without mental reservations of some kind."

'Perfectly true,' thought Dinny. "Could we have a taxi?"

In the cab Clare said: "Do something for me, Dinny. Bring me my things to the Mews."

"Of course."

"I don't feel like Condaford. Did you see Tony?"

"Yes."

"How is he?"

"Rotten."

"Rotten?" repeated Clare, bitterly. "How could I help what they sprung on me? I lied for him anyway."

Dinny, looking straight before her, said:

"When you can, tell me exactly what your feeling towards him is."

"When I know myself, I will."

"You'll want something to eat, darling."

"Yes, I'm hungry. I'll stop here in Oxford Street, I shall be cleaning up when you come with my things. I feel as if I could sleep the clock round, and probably I shan't sleep a wink. When you're divorced, Dinny, don't defend—you keep on thinking of better answers."

Dinny squeezed her arm and took the taxi on to South Square.

CHAPTER 34

MORE DEADLY than the atmosphere during a fight is that when it is over. You 'keep on thinking of better answers,' and you feel that life is not worth living. The primary law of existence having been followed to its logical and—win or lose—unsatisfying conclusion, the sand is out of your dolly, you loll and droop. Such were the sensations of Dinny, who had but understudied. Unable to feel that she could be of any real help, she fell back on pigs and had been for a good week in this posture when she received a letter headed:

> "Kingson Cuthcott & Forsyte,
> "Old Jewry.
> "May 17th, 1932.

"MY DEAR MISS CHARWELL,—

"I write to tell you that we have succeeded in coming to an arrangement by which the costs of the action will be met without making any call upon either Mr. Croom or your sister. I shall be grateful if you could take an opportunity of relieving their minds and also your father's mind in the matter.

> "Believe me, my dear Miss Charwell,
> "Very faithfully yours,
> "ROGER FORSYTE."

Reaching her on a really warm morning, to sound of mowing machine and to scent of grass, it would have "intrigued" her if she had not detested the word. She turned from the window and said:

"The lawyers say we need none of us worry any more about those costs, Dad, they've come to an arrangement."

"How?"

"They don't say, but they want your mind relieved."

"I don't understand lawyers," muttered the General, "but if they say it's all right, I'm very glad. I've been worrying."

"Yes, dear. Coffee?"

But she resumed her meditations on that cryptic letter. Did something in Jerry Corven's conduct force him to agree to this 'arrangement'? Was there not someone called 'The King's Proctor' who could stop decrees being granted? Or—what?

Abandoning her first idea of driving over to Tony Croom because of the questions he might ask, she wrote to him and to Clare instead. The more, however, she pondered over the wording of the solicitor's letter, the more convinced she became that she must see 'very young' Roger. There was that at the back of her mind which refused quietus. She, therefore, arranged to see him at a teashop near the British Museum on his way homeward from the City, and went there direct from her train. The place was an 'artifact,' designed, so far as a Regency edifice could be, to reproduce such a 'coffee house' as Boswell and Johnson might have frequented. Its floor was not sanded, but looked as if it should be. There were no long clay pipes, but there were long cardboard cigarette holders. The furniture was wooden, the light dim. No record having been discovered of what the 'staff' should look like, they looked sea-green. Prints of old coaching inns were hung on walls panelled by the Tottenham Court Road. Quite a few patrons were drinking tea and smoking cigarettes. None of them used the long cardboard holders. 'Very young' Roger, limping slightly, and with his customary air of not being quite what he ought to be, uncovered his sandyish head and smiled above his chin.

"China or Indian?" said Dinny.

"Whatever you're having."

"Then two coffees, please, and muffins."

"Muffins! This *is* a treat, dear papa. Those are quite good old copper bed-warmers, Miss Cherrell. I wonder if they'd sell them."

"Do you collect?"

"Pick things up. No use having a Queen Anne house unless you can do something for it."

"Does your wife sympathise?"

"No, she's all for the T.C.R., bridge, golf and the modernities: *I* never can keep my hands off old silver."

"I *have* to," murmured Dinny. "Your letter was a very pleasant relief. Did you really mean that we should none of us have to pay?"

"I did."

She considered her next question, scrutinising him through her lashes. With all his æsthetic leanings, he looked uncommonly spry.

"In confidence, Mr. Forsyte, how did you manage to make that arrangement? Had it to do with my brother-in-law?"

'Very young' Roger laid his hand on his heart.

"'The tongue of Forsyte is his own,' cf. Marmion. But, you needn't worry."

"I need, or shall, unless I know it wasn't that."

"Make your mind easy, then; it had nothing to do with Corven."

Dinny ate a muffin in complete silence, then spoke of period silver. 'Very young' Roger gave an erudite dissertation on its marks—if she would come down for a week-end, he would turn her into a connoisseur.

They parted cordially, and Dinny went towards her Uncle Adrian's. That uneasiness was still at the back of her mind. The trees had leaved enticingly these last warm days, the Square wherein he dwelled had an air quiet and green, as if inhabited by minds. Nobody was at home. "But," said the maid, "Mr. Cherrell is sure to be in about six, miss."

Dinny waited in a small panelled room full of books and pipes, and photographs of Diana and the two Ferse children. An old collie kept her company, and through the opened window seeped the sounds of London streets. She was crumpling the dog's ears when Adrian came in.

"Well, Dinny, so it's over. I hope you feel better."

Dinny handed him the letter.

"I know it's nothing to do with Jerry Corven. You know Eustace Dornford, Uncle. I want you to find out from him quietly whether it's he who is paying these costs."

Adrian pulled at his beard.

"I don't suppose he'd tell me."

"Somebody must have paid them and I can only think of him. I don't want to go to him myself."

Adrian looked at her intently. Her face was concerned and brooding.

"Not easy, Dinny; but I'll try. What's going to happen to those two?"

"I don't know, they don't know; nobody knows."

"How are your people taking it?"

"Terribly glad it's over, and don't care much now it is. You'll let me know soon, won't you, Uncle dear?"

"I will, my dear; but I shall probably draw blank."

Dinny made for Melton Mews, and met her sister on the doorstep. Clare's cheeks were flushed; there was febrility in her whole manner and appearance.

"I've asked Tony Croom here this evening," she said when Dinny was leaving to catch her train. "One must pay one's debts."

"Oh!" murmured Dinny, and for the life of her could say no more.

The words haunted her in the bus to Paddington, in the refreshment room while she ate a sandwich, in the railway carriage going home. Pay one's debts! The first canon of self-respect! Suppose Dornford had paid those costs! Was she as precious as all that? Wilfrid had had all of her according to her heart and her hope and her desire. If Dornford wanted what was left over—why not? She dropped thinking of herself and went back to thought of Clare. Had she paid her debt by now? Transgressors by law—ought to transgress! And yet—so much future could be compromised in so few minutes!

She sat very still. And the train rattled on in the dying twilight.

CHAPTER 35

TONY CROOM had spent a miserable week in his converted cottages at Bablock Hythe. The evidence given by Corven on his recall to the box had seared him, nor had Clare's denial anointed the burn. In this young man was an old-fashioned capacity for jealousy. That a wife should accept her husband's embrace was not, of course, unknown; but, in the special circumstances and states of feeling, it had seemed to him improper, if not monstrous, and the giving of his own evidence, directly after such a thrust at his vitals, had but inflamed the wound. A sad unreason governs sex; to be aware that he had no right to be suffering, brought no relief. And now, a week after trial, receiving her note of invitation, he had the impulse not to answer, to answer and upbraid, to answer 'like a gentleman'—and, all the time, he knew he would just go up.

With nothing clear in his mind and that bruise still in his heart, he reached the Mews an hour after Dinny had gone. Clare let him in, and they stood looking at each other for a minute without speaking. At last she said with a laugh:

"Well, Tony! Funny business—the whole thing, wasn't it?"

"Exquisitely humorous."

"You look ill."

"You look fine."

And she did, in a red frock open at the neck, and without sleeves.

"Sorry I'm not dressed, Clare. I didn't know you'd want to go out."

"I don't. We're going to dine in. You can leave the car out there, and stay as long as you like, and nobody the worse. Isn't it nice?"

"Clare!"

"Put your hat down and come upstairs. I've made a new cocktail."

"I take this chance to say I'm bitterly sorry."

"Don't be an idiot, Tony." She began to mount the spiral stairway, turning at the top. "Come!"

Dropping his hat and driving gloves, he followed her.

To the eyes of one throbbing and distraught, the room above had an air of preparation, as if for ceremony, or—was it sacrifice? The little table was set out daintily with flowers, a narrow-necked bottle, green glasses—the couch covered with some jade-green stuff and heaped with bright cushions. The windows were open, for it was hot, but the curtains were nearly drawn across and the light turned on. He went straight to the window, stifled by the violent confusion within him.

"In spite of the Law's blessing, better close the curtains," said Clare. "Would you like a wash?"

He shook his head, drew the curtains close and sat on the sill. Clare had dropped on to the sofa.

"I couldn't bear to see you in 'the box,' Tony. I owe you a lot."

"Owe! You owe me nothing. It's I——!"

"No! I am the debtor."

With her arms crossed behind her neck, her body so graceful, her face a little tilted up—there was all he had dreamed about and longed for all these months! There she was, infinitely desirable, seeming to say: 'Here I am! Take me!' and he sat staring at her. The moment he had yearned and yearned for, and he could not seize it!

"Why so far off, Tony?"

He got up, his lips trembling, every limb trembling, came as far as the table, and stood gripping the back of a chair. His eyes fixed on her eyes, searched and searched. What was behind those dark eyes looking up at him? Not—love! The welcome of duty? The payment of a debt? The toleration of a pal? The invitation of one who would have it over and done with? But not love, with its soft gleam. And suddenly, there came before his eyes the image of her and Corven—*there!* He covered his face with his arm, rushed headlong down those twisting iron stairs, seized hat and gloves, and dashed out into his car. His mind did not really work again till he was far along the Uxbridge Road; and how he had got there without disaster he could not conceive. He had behaved like a perfect fool! He had behaved exactly as he had to! The startled look on her face. To be treated as a creditor! To be paid! *There!* On that sofa! No! He drove again with a sort of frenzy, and was brought up sharply by a lorry lumbering along in front. The night was just beginning, moonlit and warm. He turned the car into a gateway and got out. Leaning against the gate, he filled and lit his pipe. Where was he going? Home? What use? What use going anywhere? His brain cleared suddenly. Drive to Jack Muskham's, release himself, and—Kenya! He had money enough for that. A job would turn up. But stay here? No! Lucky those mares hadn't come! He got over the gate and sat down on the grass. Relaxed against the bank he looked up. Lot of stars! What had he—fifty pounds—sixty—nothing owing. An East African boat—go steerage! Anything—anywhere away! Close to him on the bank were ox-eyed daisies slowly brightening in the moonlight; the air was scented by ripening grass. If in her eyes there had been one look of love. He let his head fall back on the grass. Not her fault she didn't love him! His misfortune! Home—get his kit together, lock up, straight to Muskham's! It would take all the night! See those lawyers—Dinny, too, if possible! But Clare? No! His pipe ceased to draw; the moon and stars, the ox-eyed daisies, the grassy scent, the shadows creeping out, the feel of the bank, lost all power to soothe. Get on, do something, go on doing something, till he was again on shipboard and away. He got up, climbed back over the gate and started his engine. He kept straight on, instinctively, avoiding the route through Maidenhead and Henley. He passed through High Wycombe and approached Oxford from the north. The old town was lit up and in evening feather when he dropped down on it from Headington and threaded into the quiet Cumnor road. On the little old New Bridge over the Upper Thames he stopped. Something special about this upper river, quiet and winding, and withdrawn from human blatancy! In full moonlight now the reeds glistened and the willows seemed to drip silver into the water, dark below their branches. Some windows in the inn beyond were lamp-lit, but no sound of gramophone came forth. With the moon riding so high, the stars now were but a pricking of the grape-coloured sky; the scent from the reedy banks and the river fields, after a whole week of warmth, mounted to his nostrils, sweet and a little rank. It brought a sudden wave of sheer sex longing—so often and so long had he dreamed of Clare and himself in love on this winding field-scented stream. He started the car with a jerk and turned past the inn down the narrowed road. In twenty minutes he stood in the doorway of his cottage, looking into the moonlit room he had left sunlit seven hours before. There was the novel he had been trying to read, tipped on to the floor; the remains of his cheese and fruit lunch not cleared away; a pair of brown shoes which he had been going to shine up. The big black beams across the low ceiling, and around the big old fireplace, rescued from Victorian enclosure and brown varnish, the copper fire-dogs, and pewter plates and jugs and bowls he had hardily collected, hoping they would appeal to Clare, all his *res angusta domi*, welcomed him dimly. He felt suddenly exhausted, drank half a tumbler of whisky and water, ate some biscuits, and sank into his long wicker armchair. Almost at once he fell asleep, and awoke in daylight. He woke remembering that he had meant to spend the night in action. Level sunlight was slanting in at the window. He finished the water in the jug, and looked at his watch. Five o'clock. He threw open the door. Early haze was bright over the fields. He went out past the mares' boxes and their meadows. A track, sloping down towards the river, led over grass broken by bushy scoops and green banks covered with hazel and alders. No dew had fallen, but the grass and every shrub smelled new.

About fifty yards from the river he threw himself down in a little hollow. Rabbits and bees and birds—nothing else as yet awake. He lay on his back staring at the grass and the bushes and the early sky, blue and lightly fleeced. Perhaps because he could see so little from that hollow all England seemed to be with him. A wild bee close to his hand was digging into a flower, there was a faint scent, as of daisy-chains; but chiefly it was the quality of the grass—its close freshness, its true greenness. 'Greatness and dignity and peace!' That play! Those words had given him a choke. Other people had laughed, Clare had laughed. "Sentimental!" she had said. "No country ever had, or will have 'Greatness and dignity and peace.'" Probably not, certainly not—a country, even one's own, was a mish-mash of beauties and monstrosities, a vague generalisation that betrayed dramatists into over-writing, journalists into blurb. All the same, you couldn't anywhere else in the world get just such a spot, or just such grass to feel and see, a scent that was wellnigh none, a tender fleecy sky, tiny flowers, birds' songs, age and youth at once! Let people laugh—you couldn't! Leave grass like this! He remembered the thrill he had felt six months ago, seeing again English grass! Leave his job before it had begun; chuck it back at Muskham, who had been so really decent to him! He turned over on to his face and laid his cheek to that grass. There he got the scent better—not sweet, not bitter, but fresh, intimate and delighting, a scent apprehended from his earliest childhood—the scent of England. If only those mares would come, and he could get at it! He sat up again, and listened. No sound of train or car or aeroplane, no human sound, no sound of any four-footed thing; just birds' songs, and those indistinguishable and a little far—a long meandering tune wide above the grass. Well! No use making a song! If one couldn't have a thing, one couldn't!

CHAPTER 36

THE MOMENT Dinny had left, Adrian made the not uncommon discovery that he had promised what would need performance. To get one of His Majesty's Counsel to commit himself—how? Too pointed to go to him! Impossible to pump a guest! Em, if he prompted her, would ask them both to dinner, especially if made to understand that the matter concerned Dinny; but even then—? He waited to consult Diana, and, after dining, went round to Mount Street. He found them playing piquet.

"Four kings," said Lady Mont. "So old-fashioned—Lawrence and I and Mussolini. Have you come for something, Adrian?"

"Naturally, Em. I want you to ask Eustace Dornford to dinner, and me to meet him."

"That'll be Dinny. I can't get Lawrence to be chivalrous; when I have four kings he always has four aces. When?"

"The sooner the better."

"Ring, dear."

Adrian rang.

"Blore, call up Mr. Dornford and ask him to dinner—black tie."

"When, my lady?"

"The first evenin' not in my book. Like dentists," she added, as Blore withdrew. "Tell me about Dinny. She hasn't been near us since the case."

"The case," repeated Sir Lawrence, "went much as one expected, didn't you think, Adrian? Any repercussions?"

"Someone has settled the costs, and Dinny suspects Dornford."

Sir Lawrence laid down his cards. "Bit too like a bid for her, that!"

"Oh, he won't admit it, but she wants me to find out."

"If he won't admit it, why should he do it?"

"Knights," murmured Lady Mont, "wearin' a glove, and gettin' killed, and nobody knowin' whose glove. Yes, Blore?"

"Mr. Dornford will be happy to dine on Monday, my lady."

"Put him in my book, then, and Mr. Adrian."

"Go away with him after dinner, Adrian," said Sir Lawrence, "and do it then—not so pointed; and, Em, not a hint, not even a sigh or a groan."

"He's a nice creature," said Lady Mont, "so pale-brown . . ."

With the 'nice creature so pale-brown' Adrian walked away the following Monday night. Their directions were more or less the same, since

638

Dornford was not yet in his new house. To Adrian's relief, his companion seemed as glad of the opportunity as himself, for he began at once to talk of Dinny.

"Am I right in thinking something's happened to Dinny lately—I don't mean that case—but when she was ill and you went abroad together?"

"Yes. The man I told you of that she was in love with two years ago was drowned out in Siam."

"Oh!"

Adrian stole a look. What should Dornford's face express—concern, relief, hope, sympathy? It only wore a little frown.

"There was a question I wanted to ask you, Dornford. Someone has settled the costs granted against young Croom in that case." The eyebrows were raised now, but the face said nothing. "I thought you might have known who. The lawyers will only say that it wasn't the other side."

"I've no idea."

'So!' thought Adrian. 'No nearer, except that, if a liar, he's a good one!'

"I like young Croom," said Dornford; "he's behaved decently, and had hard luck. That'll save him from bankruptcy."

"Bit mysterious, though," murmured Adrian.

"It is."

'On the whole,' Adrian thought, 'I believe he did. But what a poker face!' He said, however:

"How do you find Clare since the case?"

"A little more cynical. She expressed her views on my profession rather freely when we were riding this morning."

"Do you think she'll marry young Croom?"

Dornford shook his head.

"I doubt it, especially if what you say about those costs is true. She might have out of a sense of obligation, but otherwise I think the case has worked against his chance. She's no real feeling for him—at least that's my view."

"Corven disillusioned her thoroughly."

"I've certainly seldom seen a more disillusioning face than his," murmured Dornford. "But she seems to me headed for quite an amusing life on her own. She's got pluck and, like all these young women now, she's essentially independent."

"Yes, I can't see Clare being domestic."

Dornford was silent. "Would you say that of Dinny, too?" he asked suddenly.

"Well, I can't see Clare as a mother; Dinny I can. I can't see Dinny here, there and everywhere; Clare I can. All the same—'domestic' of Dinny! It's not the word."

"No!" said Dornford fervently. "I don't know what is. You believe very much in her, don't you?"

Adrian nodded.

"Enormously."

"It's been tremendous for me," said Dornford, very low, "to have come across her; but I'm afraid so far it's been nothing to her."

"Much to allow for," suggested Adrian. " 'Patience is a virtue,' or so it used to be before the world went up in that blue flame and never came down again."

"But I'm rising forty."

"Well, Dinny's rising twenty-nine."

"What you told me just now makes a difference, or—doesn't it?"

"About Siam? I think it does—a great difference."

"Well, thank you."

They parted with a firm clasp, and Adrian branched off northwards. He walked slowly, thinking of the balance-sheet that confronts each lover's unlimited liability. No waterings of capital nor any insurance could square or guarantee that shifting lifelong document. By love was man flung into the world; with love was he in business nearly all his days making debts or profit; and when he died was by the results of love, if not by the parish, buried and forgotten. In this swarming London not a creature but was deeply in account with a Force so whimsical, inexorable, and strong, that none, man or woman, in their proper senses, would choose to do business with it. 'Good match,' 'happy marriage,' 'ideal partnership,' 'lifelong union,' ledgered against 'don't get on,' 'just a flare up,' 'tragic state of things,' 'misfit'! All his other activities man could insure, modify, foresee, provide against (save the inconvenient activity of death); love he could not. It stepped to him out of the night, into the night returned. It stayed, it fled. On one side or the other of the balance-sheet it scored an entry, leaving him to cast up and wait for the next entry. It mocked dictators, parliaments, judges, bishops, police, and even good intentions; it maddened with joy and grief; wantoned, procreated, thieved and murdered; was devoted, faithful, fickle. It had no shame, and owned no master; built homes and gutted them; passed by on the other side; and now and again made of two hearts one heart till death. To think of London, Manchester, Glasgow, without love appeared to Adrian, walking up the Charing Cross Road, to be easy; and yet without love not one of these passing citizens would be sniffing the petrol of this night air, not one grimy brick would have been laid upon brick, not one bus be droning past, no street musician would wail, nor lamp light up the firmament. A somewhat primary concern! And he, whose primary concern was with the bones of ancient men, who but for love would have had no bones to be dug up, classified and kept under glass, thought of Dornford and Dinny, and whether they would 'click' . . .

And Dornford, on his way to Harcourt Buildings, thought even more intensively of himself and her. Rising forty! This overmastering wish of his—for its fulfilment it was now or never with him! If he were not to become set in the groove of a 'getter-on,' he must marry and have children. Life had become a half-baked thing without Dinny to give it meaning and savour. She had become—what had she not become? And, passing through the narrow portals of Middle Temple Lane, he said to a learned brother, also moving towards his bed:

"What's going to win the Derby, Stubbs?"

"God knows!" said his learned brother, wondering why he had played that last trump when he did, instead of when he didn't . . .

And in Mount Street Sir Lawrence, coming into her room to say 'Good-night,' found his wife sitting up in bed in the lace cap which always made her look so young, and, on the edge of the bed, in his black silk dressing-gown, sat down.

"Well, Em?"

"Dinny will have two boys and a girl."

"Deuce she will! That's counting her chickens rather fast."

"Somebody must. Give me a nice kiss."

Sir Lawrence stooped over and complied.

"When she marries," said Lady Mont, shutting her eyes, "she'll only be half there for a long time."

"Better half there at the beginning than not at all at the end. But what makes you think she'll take him?"

"My bones. We don't like being left out when it comes to the point, Lawrence."

"Continuation of the species. H'm!"

"If he'd get into a scrape, or break his leg."

"Better give him a hint."

"His liver's sound."

"How do you know that?"

"The whites of his eyes are blue. Those browny men often have livers."

Sir Lawrence stood up.

"My trouble," he said, "is to see Dinny sufficiently interested in herself again to get married. After all, it *is* a personal activity."

"Harridge's for beds," murmured Lady Mont.

Sir Lawrence's eyebrow rose. Em was inexhaustible!

CHAPTER 37

SHE WHOSE ABSTINENCE from interest in herself was interesting so many people, received three letters on Wednesday morning. That which she opened first said:

"DINNY DARLING,—

"I tried to pay, but Tony would have none of it, and went off like a rocket; so I'm a wholly unattached female again. If you hear any news of him, let me have it.

"Dornford gets more 'interesting-looking' every day. We only talk of you, and he's raising my salary to three hundred, as compensation.

"Love to you and all,
"CLARE."

That which she opened second said:

"MY DEAR DINNY,—

"I'm going to stick it here. The mares arrive on Monday. I had Muskham down yesterday, and he was jolly decent, didn't say a word about the case. I'm trying to take up birds. There is one thing you could do for me if you would—find out who paid those costs. It's badly on my mind.

"Ever so many thanks for always being so nice to me.

"Yours ever,
"TONY CROOM."

That which she read last said:

"DINNY, MY DEAR,—

"Nothing doing. He either didn't, or else played 'possum,' but if so it was very good 'possum.' All the same, I wouldn't put it past him that it was 'possum.' If you really set store by knowing, I think I should ask him point-blank. I don't believe he would tell you a lie, even 'a little one.' As you know, I like him. In my avuncular opinion he is still on the gold standard.

"Your ever devoted
"ADRIAN."

So! She felt a vague irritation. And this feeling which she had thought momentary, she found to be recurrent. Her state of mind, indeed, like the weather, turned cold again and torpid. She wrote to Clare what Tony Croom had written of himself, and that he had not mentioned her. She wrote to Tony Croom, and neither mentioned Clare nor answered his question about the costs; she concentrated on birds—they seemed safe, and to lead nowhere. She wrote to Adrian: "I'm feeling I ought to be wound-up, only there'd be no dividend for the shareholders. It's very cold and dull, my consolation is that little 'Cuffs' is beginning to 'sit up and take real notice' of me."

And then, as if by arrangement with the clerk of the course at Ascot, the weather changed to 'set warm'; and, suddenly, she wrote to Dornford. She wrote on pigs, their breeds and sties, the Government and the farmers. She ended with these words:

"We are all very worried by not knowing who has settled the costs in my sister's case. It is so disquieting to be under an obligation to an unknown person. Could you by any means find out for us?" She debated some time how to sign herself in this her first letter to him, and finally wrote "Yours always, Dinny Charwell."

His answer came very quickly:

"MY DEAR DINNY,—

"I was delighted to get a letter from you. To answer your last question first. I will do my best to get the lawyers to 'come clean,' but if they won't tell *you*, I can't imagine their telling me. Still, I can try. Though I fancy that if your sister or young Croom insisted they'd have to tell. Now about pigs"—there followed certain information, and a lamentation that agriculture was still not being properly tackled. "If only they would realise that all the needed pigs, poultry and potatoes, nearly all the vegetables, much of the fruits, and much more than the present dairy produce, can really be produced at home, and by a graduated prohibition of foreign produce encourage, and indeed force, our home growers to supply the home market, we should, within ten years, have a living and profitable native agriculture once more, no rise to speak of in the cost of living, and a huge saving in our imports bill. You see how new I am to politics! Wheat and meat are the red herrings across the trail. Wheat and meat from the Dominions, and the rest (bar hot climate fruits and vegetables) home-grown, is my motto. I hope your father agrees. Clare is becoming restive, and I'm wondering if she wouldn't be happier in a more active job than this. If I can come across a good one, I shall advise her to take it. Would you ask your mother whether I should be in the way if I came down for the last week-end this month? She was good enough to tell me to let her know any time I was coming to the constituency. I was again at *Cavalcade* the other night. It wears well, but I missed you. I can't even begin to tell you how I missed you.

"Your ever faithful
"EUSTACE DORNFORD."

Missed her! After the faint warmth those wistful words aroused, she thought almost at once of Clare. Restive! Who would be otherwise in her anomalous position? She had not been down at Condaford since the case. And that seemed to Dinny very natural. However one might say it didn't matter what people thought, it did, especially in a place where one had grown up, and belonged, as it were, to the blood royal of the neighbourhood. And Dinny thought, unhappily: 'I don't know what I want for her —and that's lucky, because one day she'll see exactly what she wants for herself.' How nice to see exactly what one wanted for oneself! She read Dornford's letter again, and suddenly faced her own feelings for the first time. Was she or was she not ever going to marry? If so, she would as soon marry Eustace Dornford as anyone—she liked, admired, could talk to him. But her—past! How funny it sounded! Her 'past,' strangled almost from birth, yet the deepest thing she would ever know! "One of these days you'll have to go down into the battle again." Unpleasant to be thought a shirker by one's own mother! But it wasn't shirking! Spots of colour rose in her cheeks. It was something no one would understand—a horror of being unfaithful to him to whom she had belonged in soul if not in body. Of being unfaithful to that utter surrender, which she knew could never be repeated.

'I am not in love with Eustace,' she thought; 'he knows it, he knows I can't pretend it. If he wants me on those terms, what is it fair for me— what is it possible for me to do?' She went out into the old yew-hedged rose garden where the first burst of roses had begun, and wandered round, smelling at this and that, followed half-heartedly by the spaniel Foch, who had no feelings for flowers.

'Whatever I do,' she thought, 'I ought to do now. I can't keep him on tenterhooks.'

She stood by the sundial where the shadow was an hour behind its time, and looked into the eye of the sun over the fruit trees beyond the yew hedges. If she married him, there would be children—without them it would not be possible. She saw frankly—or thought she did—where she stood in the matter of sex. What she could not see was how it would all turn for herself and for him in the recesses of the spirit. Restless, she wandered from rose-bush to rose-bush, extinguishing the few greenfly between her gloved fingers. And, in a corner, with a sort of despair the spaniel Foch sat down unnoticed, and ate a quantity of coarse grass.

She wrote to Dornford the same evening. Her mother would be delighted if he would come for that week-end. Her father quite agreed with his views on agriculture, but was not sure that anyone else did, except Michael, who, after listening to him carefully one evening in London, had said: "Yes. What's wanted is a lead, and where's it coming from?" She hoped that when he came down he would be able to tell her about those costs. It must have been thrilling to see *Cavalcade* again. Did he know a flower called meconopsis, if that was the way to spell it, a sort of poppy of a most lovely colour? It came from the Himalayas, and so would be suitable for Campden Hill, which she believed had much the same climate. If he could induce Clare to come down it would rejoice the hearts of the aborigines. This time she signed herself 'always yours,' a distinction too subtle to explain even to herself.

Telling her mother that he was coming, she added:

"I'll try and get Clare; and don't you think, Mother, that we ought to ask Michael and Fleur? They were very sweet to put us up so long."

Lady Charwell sighed.

"One gets into a way of just going on. But do, dear."

"They'll talk tennis, and that'll be so nice and useful."

Lady Charwell looked at her daughter, in whose voice something recalled the Dinny of two years back.

When Dinny knew that Clare was coming, as well as Michael and Fleur, she debated whether to tell Tony Croom. In the end she decided not to, sorrowfully, for she had for him the fellow feeling of one who had been through the same mill.

The camouflage above her father's and mother's feelings touched her. Dornford—high time, of course, he was down in the constituency again! Pity he hadn't a place of his own—didn't do to get out of touch with the electors! Presumably he'd come by car, and bring Clare; or Michael and Fleur could call for her! By such remarks they hid their nervousness about Clare and about herself.

She had just put the last flower in the last bedroom when the first car slid up the driveway; and she came down the stairs to see Dornford standing in the hall.

"This place has a soul, Dinny. It may be the fantails on the stone roof, or perhaps the deep way it's settled in, but you catch it at once."

She left her hand in his longer than she had meant to.

"It's being so overgrown. There's the smell, too—old hay and flowering verbena, and perhaps the mullions being crumbled."

"You look well, Dinny."

"I am, thank you. You haven't had time for Wimbledon, I suppose?"

"No. But Clare's been going—she's coming straight from it with the young Monts."

"What did you mean in your letter by 'restive'?"

"Well, as I see Clare, she must be in the picture, and just now she isn't."

Dinny nodded.

"Has she said anything to you about Tony Croom?"

"Yes. She laughed and said he'd dropped her like a hot potato."

Dinny took his hat and hung it up.

"About those costs?" she said, without turning.

"Well, I went to see Forsyte specially, but I got nothing out of him."

"Oh! Would you like a wash, or would you rather go straight up? Dinner's at quarter-past-eight. It's half-past seven now."

"Straight up, if I may."

"You're in a different room; I'll show you."

She preceded him to the foot of the little stairway leading to the priest's room.

"That's your bathroom. Up here, now."

"The priest's room?"

"Yes. There's no ghost." She crossed to the window. "See! He was fed here at night from the roof. Do you like the view? Better in the spring when the blossom's out, of course."

"Lovely!" He stood beside her at the window, and she could see his hands clenched so hard on the stone sill that the knuckles showed white. A bitter wind swept through her being. Here she had dreamed of standing with Wilfrid beside her. She leaned against the side of the embrasured window and closed her eyes. When she opened them he was facing her, she could see his lips trembling, his hands clasped behind him, his eyes fixed on her face. She moved across to the door.

"I'll have your things brought up and unpacked at once. Would you answer me one question: Did you pay those costs yourself?"

He gave a start, and a little laugh, as if he had been suddenly switched from tragedy to comedy.

"I? No. Never even thought of it."

"Oh!" said Dinny again. "You've lots of time." And she went down the little stairway.

Did she believe him? Whether she believed him or not, did it make any difference? The question would be asked and must be answered. 'One more river—one more river to cross!' And at the sound of the second car, she went hurrying down the stairs.

CHAPTER 38

DURING THAT STRANGE WEEK-END, with only Michael and Fleur at ease, Dinny received one piece of enlightenment as she strolled in the garden.

"Em tells me," said Fleur, "you're all worked up about those costs—she says *you* think Dornford paid them, and that it's giving you a feeling of obligation?"

"Oh? Well, it *is* worrying, like finding you owe nothing to your dressmaker."

"My dear," said Fleur, "for your strictly private ear, I paid them. Roger came to dinner and made a song about hating to send in such a bill to people who had no money to spare, so I talked it over with Michael and sent Roger a cheque. My Dad made his money out of the Law, so it seemed appropriate."

Dinny stared.

"You see," continued Fleur, taking her arm, "thanks to the Government converting that loan, all my beautiful gilt-edgeds have gone up about ten points, so that, even after paying that nine hundred odd, I'm still about fifteen thousand richer than I was, and they're still going up. I've only told *you*, in confidence, because I was afraid it would weigh with you in making up your mind about Dornford. Tell me: Would it?"

"I don't know," said Dinny, dully; and she didn't.

"Michael says Dornford's the freshest egg he's come across for a long time; and Michael is very sensitive to freshness in eggs. You know," said Fleur, stopping suddenly, and letting go her arm, "you puzzle me, Dinny. Everybody can see what you're cut out for—wife and mother. Of course, I know what you've been through, but the past buries its dead. It is so, I've been through it, too. It's the present and the future that matter, and we're the present, and our children are the future. And you specially—because you're so stuck on tradition and continuity and that—ought to carry on. Anybody who lets a memory spoil her life—forgive me, old thing, but it's rather obviously now or never with you. And to think of you with 'never' chalked against you is too bleak. I've precious little *moral* sense," continued Fleur, sniffing at a rose, "but I've a lot of the commoner article, and I simply hate to see waste."

Dinny, touched by the look in those hazel eyes with the extraordinarily clear whites, stood very still, and said quietly:

"If I were Catholic, like him, I shouldn't have any doubt."

"The cloister?" said Fleur, sharply: "No! My mother's a Catholic, but—No! Anyway, you're not a Catholic. No, my dear—the hearth. That title was wrong, you know. It can't be both."

Dinny smiled. "I do apologise for worrying people so. Do you like these *Angèle Pernets?*"

She had no talk with Dornford all that Saturday, preoccupied as he was with the convictions of the neighbouring farmers. But after dinner, when she was scoring for the four who were playing Russian pool, he came and stood beside her.

"Hilarity in the home," she said, adding nine presented by Fleur to the side on which she was not playing: "How did you find the farmers?"

"Confident."

"Con——?"

"That whatever's done will make things worse."

"Oh! Ah! They're so used to that, you see."

"And what have *you* been doing all day, Dinny?"

"Picked flowers, walked with Fleur, played with 'Cuffs,' and dallied with the pigs. . . . Five on to your side, Michael, and seven on to the other. This is a very Christian game—doing unto others as you would they should do unto you."

"Russian pool!" murmured Dornford: "Curious name nowadays for anything so infected with religion."

"*Apropos,* if you want to go to Mass to-morrow, there's Oxford."

"You wouldn't come with me?"

"Oh! Yes. I love Oxford, and I've only once heard a Mass. It takes about three-quarters of an hour to drive over."

His look at her was much as the spaniel Foch gave when she returned to him after absence.

"Quarter past nine, then, in my car . . ."

When next day they were seated side by side, he said:

"Shall we slide the roof back?"

"Please."

"Dinny, this is like a dream."

"I wish my dreams had such a smooth action."

"Do you dream much?"

"Yes."

"Nice or nasty?"

"Oh! like all dreams, a little of both."

"Any recurrent ones?"

"One. A river I can't cross."

"Ah! like an examination one can't pass. Dreams are ruthlessly revealing. If you could cross that river in your dream, would you be happier?"

"I don't know."

There was a silence, till he said:

648

"This car is a new make. You don't have to change gears in the old way. But you don't care for driving, do you?"

"I'm an idiot at it."

"You're not modern, you see, Dinny."

"No. I'm much less efficient than most people."

"In your own way I don't know anybody so efficient."

"You mean I can arrange flowers."

"And see a joke; and be—a darling."

It seemed to Dinny the last thing she had been able to be for nearly two years, so she merely replied:

"What was your college at Oxford?"

"Oriel."

And the conversation lapsed.

Some hay was stacked and some still lying out, and the midsummer air was full of its scent.

"I'm afraid," said Dornford suddenly, "I don't want to go to Mass. I don't get so many chances to be with you, Dinny. Let's make for Clifton and sit in a boat."

"Well, it is rather lovely for indoors."

They turned off to the left, and, passing through Dorchester, came to the river by the bends and bluffs at Clifton. Leaving the car, they procured a punt and after drifting a little, moved it to the bank.

"This," said Dinny, "is a nice exhibition of high purpose, I don't think. 'Something done' isn't always what was attempted, is it?"

"No, but it's often better."

"I wish we'd brought Foch; he likes any kind of vehicle where he can sit on one's feet and get a nice sick feeling."

But in that hour and more on the river they hardly talked at all. It was as if he understood—which, as a fact, he did not—how, in that drowsing summer silence, on water half in sunlight, half in shade, she was coming closer to him than ever before. There was, indeed, to Dinny something really restful and reassuring in those long lazing minutes, when she need not talk, but just take summer in at every pore—its scent, and hum, and quiet movement, the careless and untroubled hovering of its green spirit, the vague sway of the bulrushes, and the clucking of the water, and always that distant calling of the wood pigeons from far trees. She was finding, indeed, the truth of Clare's words, that he could 'let one's mouth alone.'

By the time they were back at the Grange, it had been one of the most silent and satisfactory mornings she had ever known. But between his: "Thank you, Dinny, a heavenly time," and his real feelings, she could tell from his eyes there was a great gap fixed. It was unnatural the way he kept his feelings in check! And, as became a woman, compassion soon changed in her to irritation. Anything better than this eternal repression, perfect consideration, patience and long waiting! And all that afternoon she saw as little of him as she had seen much all the morning. His eyes, fixed on her with longing and a sort of reproach, became an added source of vexation, and she carefully refrained from seeming to notice them. "Verra pavairse," her old Scottish nurse would have said.

Bidding him 'Good-night' at the foot of the stairs, she felt a keen pleasure at the dashed look on his face, and an equally keen sense that she was 'a beast.' She entered her bedroom in a curious turmoil, at odds with herself, and him, and all the world.

"Damn!" she muttered, feeling for the switch.

A low laugh startled her. Clare, in her pyjamas, was perched on the window-seat, smoking a cigarette.

"Don't turn up, Dinny, come and sit here with me, and let's puff out of the window together."

Three wide-opened casements laid bare the night under a teazle-blue heaven trembling with stars. Dinny, looking out at it, said:

"Where have you been ever since lunch? I didn't even know you were back."

"Have a gasper? You seem to want soothing."

Dinny expelled a puff of smoke.

"I do. I'm sick of myself."

"So was I," murmured Clare, "but I feel better."

"What have you been doing, then?"

Again Clare laughed, and in the sound was something that made Dinny say:

"Seeing Tony Croom?"

Clare leaned back and her throat showed pale.

"Yes, my dear. The Ford and I went over. Dinny, we've justified the law. Tony no longer looks like a bereaved orphan."

"Oh!" said Dinny, and again: "Oh!"

Her sister's voice, warm and languid, and satisfied, made her cheeks go hot and her breath come quickly.

"Yes, I prefer him as a lover to a friend. How sane is the law, it knew what we ought to have been! And I like his converted cottages. Only there's a fireplace upstairs that still wants opening up."

"Are you going to get married, then?"

"My dear, how can we? No, we shall live in sin. Later, I suppose, we shall see. I think this 'nisi' period is very thoughtful. Tony will come up in the middle of the week, and I shall go down at the week-end. And all so legal."

Dinny laughed. Clare sat up, suddenly, clasping her knees.

"I'm happier than I've been for ever so long. It doesn't do to make other people wretched. Also, women ought to be loved, it suits them somehow. Men, too."

Dinny leaned out of the window, and the night slowly cooled her cheeks. Beautiful and deep it was, out there, the shapes unstirring, dark and as if brooding. Through the tense stillness came a far drone, swelling to the rightful sound of a passing car, and, between the trees, she could see its travelling light burnish up the hedgerows for flying moments, and die beyond the angle of vision. Then the drone grew faint and fainter, and stillness recommenced. A moth flew by, and a little white feather from a fantail on the roof floated down, turning over in the quiet air. She felt Clare's arm come round her waist.

"Good-night, old thing! Rub noses."

Withdrawing from the night, Dinny clasped that slim pyjamaed body. Their cheeks touched, and to each the warmth of the other's skin was moving—to Clare a blessing, to Dinny an infection, as though the lingered glow from many kisses was passing into her.

When her sister had gone, she moved restlessly up and down her dark room.

"It doesn't do to make people wretched! . . . Women ought to be loved. . . . Men, too." Quite a minor prophet! Converted by lightning, like Paul on his way to wherever it was. Up and down, up and down, till at last, quite tired, she turned on the light, threw off her clothes and sat down in a wrapper to brush her hair. Brushing away at it, she stared at her image in the glass with fascination, as if she had not seen herself for a long time. The fever with which she had been infected seemed still in her cheeks and eyes and hair, she looked unnaturally vivid to herself; or was it that the sun, while she and Dornford were sitting in that punt, had left her with this hot feeling in the veins? She finished brushing, shook back her hair, and got into bed. She had left the casements open, the curtains undrawn, and the starry night confronted her lying on her back in the darkness of her narrow room. The hall clock struck midnight faintly—only three hours or so before it would be light! She thought of Clare sunk in beauty sleep close by. She thought of Tony Croom, deep-drugged with happiness, in his converted cottages, and the old tag from *The Beggars' Opera* ran in her mind: 'With blisses her kisses dissolve us in pleasure and soft repose.' But she! She could not sleep! She felt as sometimes when a little girl, that she must roam about, explore the strangeness of the dead of night, sit on the stairs, peep into rooms, curl up in some armchair. And, getting up, she put on her dressing-gown and slippers and stole out. She sat on the top stair, clasping her knees and listening. Not a sound in the old dark house, except a little scraping noise, where some mouse was at work. She rose, clutched the banister, and crept downstairs. The hall smelled musty already, too much old wood and furniture to stand enclosure by the night. She groped across to the drawing-room door and opened it. Here flowers and last year's potpourri and stale cigarette smoke scented the air with a heavy reek. She made her way to one of the French windows, drew the curtains back and opened it. She stood there a minute taking deep breaths. Very dark, very still, very warm. By starlight she could just see the sheen on the magnolia leaves. Leaving the window open, she sought her favourite old armchair, and curled up in it with her feet tucked under her. There, hugging herself, she tried to recapture the feeling that she was a child again. The night air came in, the clock ticked, and the hot feeling in her veins seemed to cool away in measure with its rhythm. She shut her eyes fast, and the sort of cosiness she used to feel in that old chair, as if she were all clasped and protected, stole upon her; but still she did not sleep. Behind her from the window with the rising of the moon a presence had stolen in, a sort of fingering uncanny light, slowly lifting each familiar object into ghostly semblance of itself. It was as if the room had come awake to keep her company; and the feeling she had sometimes had, that the old house had a life of its own, felt, saw, knew its spells of wakefulness and of slumber, tingled once more within her. Suddenly, she heard footsteps on the terrace and sat up startled.

Someone said: "Who is that? Is anyone there?"

A figure stood in the open window; by the voice she knew that it was Dornford, and said:

"Only me."

"*Only* you!"

She saw him come in and stand beside the chair, looking down. He was still in his evening clothes, and, with his back to the faint light, she could hardly see his face at all.

"Anything the matter, Dinny?"

"Just couldn't sleep. And you?"

"I've been finishing a bit of work in the library. I went out on the terrace for a breath, and saw this window open."

"Which of us is going to say: 'How marvellous'?"

Neither of them said anything. But Dinny unclasped herself and let her feet seek the ground.

Suddenly, Dornford put his hands to his head and turned his back on her.

"Forgive my being like this," she murmured, "I naturally didn't expect——"

He turned round again, and dropped on his knees beside her. "Dinny, it's the end of the world, unless——"

She put her hands on his hair and said quietly "——it's the beginning."

CHAPTER 39

ADRIAN SAT writing to his wife.

"Condaford: August 10.

"MY VERY DEAR,—

"I promised to give you a true and particular account of how Dinny went off. Look in *The Lantern* for their conception of 'the bride and bridegroom leaving the church.' Fortunately, the lens of that enquiring organ caught them just before they pushed off—except in movies the camera simply cannot record movement; it always gets the sole of one foot cocked towards the eye, flannelises the knee of the other leg, and upsets the set of the trousers. Dornford looked quite good value—in this style, fourteen-and-six; and Dinny—bless her!—without the 'bride's smile,' almost as if she saw the joke. Ever since the engagement, I've wondered what she's really feeling. Love such as she gave Desert it certainly is not, but I don't believe there's any physical reluctance. When yesterday, I said to her: 'In good heart?' her answer was: 'No half heart, anyway.' We both of us have reason to know that she can go all out in what she does for other people. But she's really doing this for herself. She'll be carrying on—she'll have children—and she'll count. That's as it should be, and so I believe she feels. If she hasn't what hopeful youth calls 'a crush on' Dornford, she admires and respects him, and I think quite rightly. Besides, he knows from me, if not from her, what she's capable of, and won't expect more until he gets it. The weather held up all right, and the church —wherein, by the way your special correspondent was baptised—in the word of Verdant Green never looked 'berrer.' The congregation was perhaps a trifle Early English, though it seemed to me you could have got most of the faces at Woolworth's.

"At the top of the nave, in the more holy positions, came our own gang, County and would-be County. The more I looked at County the more I thought how merciful that the states of life into which it has pleased God to call us has prevented the Charwells of our generation from looking County. Even Con and Liz, who have to stick down here all the time, haven't got quite the hang of it. Remarkable, if you think, that there is such a thing as 'County' left; but I suppose it'll last while there's 'huntin' and shootin'.' I remember, as a boy, out hunting (when I could screw a mount out of our stables or somebody else's), I used to lurk out of reach of people for fear of having to talk to them, their words and music were so trying. Better to be human than County or even would-be County. I must say, that Clare, after all her jollification in the courts, carried it off amazingly, and so far as I could see, nobody had the nerve to show any of the feelings which, as a fact, at this time of day, they probably hadn't got. Then, a little less holy, came the village in force—Dinny's a great favourite with them—quite a show of oldest inhabitants. Some real faces; an old chap called Downer, in a Bath chair, all 'Whitechapel' whiskers and beard, and shrewd remaining brown spaces. He perfectly remembered Hilary and me falling off a hay-cart we oughtn't to have been on. And old Mrs. Tibwhite—a sweet old witch of a thing, who always let me eat her raspberries. The schoolchildren had a special holiday. Liz tells me not one in twenty of them has ever seen London, or indeed been ten miles out of the village, even now. But there's a real difference in the young men and maidens. The girls have most excellent legs and stockings and quite tasteful dresses; and the youths good flannel suits and collars and ties—all done by the motor bike and the film. Lots of flowers in the church, and a good deal of bell-ringing and blowy organ-playing. Hilary did the swearing-in with his usual rapidity, and the old rector, who held the sponge, looked blue at the pace he went and the things he left out. Well, you want, of course, to hear about those dresses. The general effect, as they stood in the aisle, was what you might call delphinian. Dinny, even in white, has that look, and, consciously or not, the bridesmaids were togged up according; and what with Monica and Joan and two young Dornford nieces being slim and tall, they really looked like a planting of blue delphiniums, preceded by four blue tots, sweet, but none as pretty as Sheila. Really, that chickenpox was very perverse; you and your two were terribly missed, and Ronald as a page would just have topped everything up. I walked back to the Grange with Lawrence and Em, an imposing steel-grey presence slightly marred where 'tears had got mixed with her powder sometimes.' In fact, I had to stop her under a stricken tree and do some good work with one of those silk handkerchiefs you gave me. Lawrence was in feather—thought the whole show the least gimcrack thing he had seen for a long time, and had now more hope of the pound going still lower. Em had been to see the house on Campden Hill; she predicted that Dinny would be in love with Dornford within a year, which started another tear, so I called her attention to the tree which had in fact been struck by lightning while she and I and Hilary were standing under it. 'Yes,' she said, 'you were squits—so providential; and the butler made a penholder out of the wood; it wouldn't hold nibs, so I gave it to Con for school, and he cursed me. Lawrence, I'm old.' Whereon Lawrence took her hand, and they walked hand in hand the rest of the way.

"The reception was held on the terrace and lawn; everybody came, schoolchildren and all, a quaint mix-up but jolly, it seemed to me. I didn't know I was so fond of the old place. However much one may believe in levelling-up chances, there's something about old places. They can't be re-created if they're once let slip, and they focus landscape in a queer kind of way. Some villages and landscapes seem to have no core—you can't explain why, but they feel hollow, and shallow and flat. A real old place puts heart into a neighbourhood. If the people who live in it are not just selfish pigs, it means a lot in a quiet way to people who have no actual ownership in it. The Grange is a sort of anchor to this neighbourhood. I doubt if you'd find a single villager, however poor, who grudged its existence, or wouldn't feel the worse for its ruination. Generations of love and trouble, and goodness knows not too much money, have been spent on it, and the result is something very hand-made and special. Everything's changing, and has got to change, no doubt, and how to have the old that's worth saving, whether in landscape, houses, manners, institutions, or human types, is one of our greatest problems, and the one that we bother least about. We save our works of art, our old furniture, we have our cult—and a strong one—of 'antiques,' and not even the most go ahead modern thought objects to that. Why not the same throughout our social life? 'The old order changeth'—yes, but we ought to be able to preserve beauty and dignity, and the sense of service, and manners—things that have come very slowly, and can be made to vanish very fast if we aren't set on preserving them somehow. Human nature being what it is, nothing seems to me more futile than to level to the ground and start again. The old order had many excrescences, and was by no means 'all werry capital,' but now that the housebreakers are in, one does see that you can smash in an hour what has taken centuries to produce; and that unless you can see your way pretty clearly to replace what admittedly wasn't perfect with something more perfect, you're throwing human life back instead of advancing it. The thing is to pick on what's worth preserving, though I don't say there's very much that is. Well, that's all very portentous! To come back to Dinny—they're going to spend their honeymoon in Shropshire, round about where Dornford comes from. Then they come back here for a bit, then settle in on Campden Hill. I hope this weather will last them. Honeymooning in wet weather, especially when one is keener on the other than the other is on the one, should be very trying. Dinny's 'going away' frock, you may like to know, was blue, and suited her not quite down to the ground. We had a minute together. I gave her your love, and she sent you hers, and said: 'Well, I'm very nearly over, Uncle dear. Wish me luck!' I felt like piping my eye. Over what? Well, anyway, if wishes for luck will help, she goes wreathed with them; but all that kissing business is hard to get through. Con and Liz took theirs down at the car. I felt rather a brute looking at their faces when she'd gone. They went away in Dornford's car, with himself driving. After that I confess that I slunk off. They're all right, I know, but it didn't feel like it. There's such cursed finality about a wedding, however easy divorce is or may become; besides, Dinny is not the sort who would take someone who loved her and then let him down; it's the old-fashioned 'for better for worse' there, but I think it'll be 'for better'—in the long run, anyway. I sneaked out of sight into the orchard and then up through the fields to the woods. I hope it was as gorgeous a day with you as it was here. These beechwoods on the slopes are more beautiful than the careful beech-clumps they plant on downs, though even those have a sort of temple-like effect, in spite of being meant as landmarks or to give shade to sheep. I can assure you that wood about half-past five was enchanted. I went up the slope and sat down and just enjoyed it. Great shifting shafts of sunlight coming in below, and splashing the trunks; and ever-so-green cool spaces between—only one word for it, holy. The trees, many of them, go up branchless for a long way, and some of the trunks looked almost white. Not much undergrowth and very little 'life' except jays and a brown squirrel. When you're in a wood as lovely as that, and think of death duties and timber, your heart turns over and over as if you'd supped entirely off Spanish onions. Two hundred years in His sight may be as yesterday, but in mine I confess they're like eternity. These woods are no longer 'shot,' and anybody can come into them. I suppose the young folk do—what a place to wander about in, lovering! I lay down in a patch of sunlight and thought of you; and two small grey wood-doves perched about fifty yards off and talked cosily to each other, so that I could have done with my fieldglasses. Willow-herbs and tansy were out where trees have come down and been cleared away—foxgloves don't seem to flourish round here. It was very restful, except that one ached a bit because it was green and beautiful. Queer, that 'beauty' ache! Lurking consciousness of mortality, perhaps knowledge that all things must slip away from one in time, and the greater their beauty the greater the loss in store! Mistake in our make-up, that. We ought to feel: The greater the earth's beauty, the more marvellous the screen of light and wind and foliage, the lovelier nature, in fact—the deeper and sweeter our rest in her will be. All very puzzling! I know the sight of a dead rabbit out in a wood like that affects me more than it does in a poulterer's shop. I passed one as I was going back—killed by a weasel; its soft limpness seemed saying: 'Pity I'm dead!' Death may be a good thing, but life's a better. A dead shape that's still a shape moves one horribly. Shape *is* life, and when life's gone one can't see why shape should remain even for the little time it does. I'd have liked to stay and see the moon come up and peer about in there, and slowly fill it all up with ghostly glistening; then I might have caught the feeling that shape lives on in rarefied form, and all of us, even the dead rabbits and birds and moths, still move and have their being—which may be the truth, for all I know or ever shall. But dinner was at eight, so I had to come away with the light still green and golden—there flows alliteration again like a twopenny brook! Outside, on the terrace, I met Dinny's spaniel, Foch. Knowing his history, it was like meeting a banshee—not that he was howling; but it reminded me sharply of what Dinny has been through. He was sitting on his haunches, and looking down at nothing, as dogs—especially spaniels—will when things are beyond them, and the one and only scent is no more, for the time being. He'll go with them, of course, to Campden Hill when they come back. I went up and had a bath and dressed, and stood at my window, listening to the drone of a tractor still cutting corn, and getting a little drunk on whiffs from the honeysuckle that climbs and flowers round my window. I see now what Dinny meant by: 'Over.' Over the river that she used to dream she couldn't cross. Well, all life is crossing rivers, or getting drowned on the way. I hope—I believe —she's touching shore. Dinner was just like dinner always is—we didn't talk of her, or mention our feelings in any way. I played Clare a game of billiards—she struck me as softer and more attractive than I've ever seen her. And then I sat up till past midnight with Con, in order, apparently, that we might say nothing. They'll miss her a lot, I'm afraid.

"The silence in my room, when I got up here at last, was stunning, and the moonlight almost yellow. The moon's hiding, now, behind one of the elms, and the evening star shining above a dead branch. A few other stars are out, but very dim. It's a night far from our time, far even from our world. Not an owl hooting, but the honeysuckle still sweet. And so, my most dear, here endeth the tale! Good-night!

"Your ever loving

"ADRIAN."

FORSYTE FAMILY TREE.

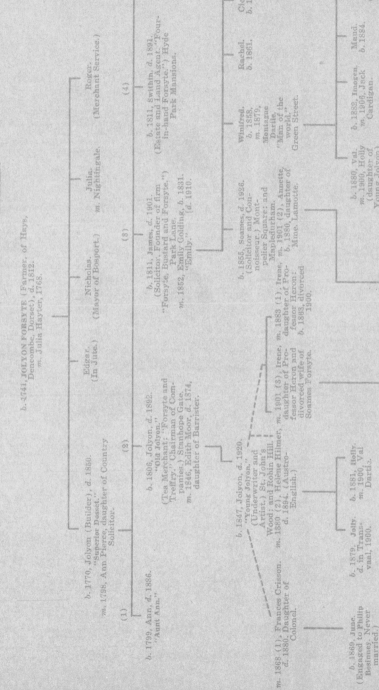

b. 1741, JOLYON FORSYTE (Farmer, of Hays, Dencombe, Dorset), d. 1812.
m. Julia Hayter, 1768.

Edgar.
(In Jute.)

Nicholas.
(Mayor of Bosport.)

Julia.
m. Nightingale.

Roger.
(Merchant Service.)

(1)

b. 1770, Jolyon (Builder), d. 1850.
"Superior Dosset."
m. 1798, Ann Pierce, daughter of Country Solicitor.

(2)

(8)

(4)

b. 1799, Ann, d. 1886.
"Aunt Ann."

b. 1806, Jolyon, d. 1892.
"Old Jolyon."
(Tea Merchant; "Forsyte and Treffry." Chairman of Companies.) Stanhope Gate.
m. 1846, Edith Moor, d. 1874, daughter of Barrister.

b. 1811, James, d. 1901.
(Solicitor. Founder of firm "Forsyte, Bustard and Forsyte," Park Lane.)
m. 1852, Emily Golding, b. 1831. "Emily." [d. 1910.]

b. 1811, Swithin, d. 1891.
(Estate and Land Agent. "Four-in-hand Forsyte.") Hyde Park Mansions.

b. 1847, Jolyon, d. 1920.
"Young Jolyon."
(Under writer and Artist.) St. John's Wood) and Robin Hill.
m. 1868 (1), Frances Crisson, d. 1880, Daughter of Colonel.
m. 1880 (2), Helene Hilmer, d. 1894. (Austro-English.)
m. 1901 (3), Irene, daughter of Professor Heron and divorced wife of Soames Forsyte.

b. 1855, Soames, d. 1926.
(Solicitor and Connoisseur.) Montpelier Square; and Mapledurham.
m. 1883 (1), Irene, daughter of Professor Heron; b. 1883, divorced 1900.
m. 1901 (2), Annette, b. 1880, daughter of Mme. Lamotte.

Winifred,
b. 1858,
m. 1879,
Montague
Dartie,
"Man of the
world."
Green Street.

Rachel,
b. 1861.

Cicely,
b. 1865.

b. 1869, June.
(Engaged to Philip Bosinney. Never married.)

b. 1879, Jolly,
d. in Trans-
vaal, 1900.

b. 1881, Holly,
m. 1900, Val
Dartie.

b. 1880, Val,
m. 1900, Holly
(daughter of
Young Jolyon).

b. 1882, Imogen,
m. 1906, Jack
Cardigan.

Maud,
b. 1884.

Benedict,
b. 1886.
(Almost a
Colonel.)